AN ENCYCLOPEDIA OF CONTINENTAL WOMEN WRITERS

Garland Reference Library of the Humanities, Vol. 698

AN ENCYCLOPEDIA OF CONTINENTAL WOMEN WRITERS

edited by
KATHARINA M. WILSON

VOLUME ONE · A - K

Garland Publishing, Inc.
New York and London, 1991

Library of Congress Cataloging-in-Publication Data

An Encyclopedia of continental women writers /
    edited by Katharina M. Wilson.
        p.   cm.—(Garland reference library of the
    humanities ; vol. 698)
        ISBN 0-8240-8547-7 (acid-free paper)
        1. Women authors—Biography—Dictionaries.
    2. Women in literature—Biography—Dictionaries.
    3. Literature, Modern—Women authors—History
    and criticism—Dictionaries. I. Wilson, Katharina M.
    II. Series.
    PN481.E5   1991
    809'.89287'03—dc20   [B]   91-6930

Printed on acid-free, 250-year-life paper

Manufactured in the United States of America

CONTENTS

How to Use This Book

Writers are listed under their most commonly used names. Library of Congress spelling is used for each individual. Writers are cross-referenced by pseudonym.

INTRODUCTION

This encyclopedia presents basic essays and bibliographies needed for researching continental women as authors of literature and related fields. While it would be preposterous, if not impossible, to make sweeping generalizations about as large and diversified a body of literature as the works of continental women writers from antiquity to the present, a few observations regarding periodic particulars might be justified.

It is generally known that during antiquity and the Middle Ages few women were literate and that the bulk of medieval literature was written by men and for men. Yet, however much outnumbered by men and however much excluded from the literary canon, women did write and did enjoy literary success before the Renaissance. Admittedly, literary activity was restricted to women of the upper classes and/or those professed in monastic orders, but the gamut of their text ranges from lyric poetry and mystical vision to Breton lai and drama, with religious texts predominating.

Among the most fascinating question about women writers of the past is how they differed from their female successors and from their male contemporaries. In contrast with women writers of the more recent past, early women writers did not use male pseudonyms but identified themselves by name and by sex. In addition, unlike the works of women writers of the seventeenth, eighteenth, and even nineteenth centuries, those of medieval women provide little evidence that they were ridiculed for or prevented from accomplishing their literary endeavors (when there is criticism, it usually concerns the authenticity of their mystical experiences, not their right,

willingness, or ability to record them). Imputations that their works were the clever forgeries of men usually stem from subsequent centuries. Indeed, most of them enjoyed literary patronage and literary success. Furthermore, unlike the history of women painters and women composers before the nineteenth century, the literary landscape of women authors in antiquity and the Middle Ages is not peopled with female relatives of male artists; only a few seem to have been related to literary men.

Literary endeavors of men and women alike are not the result of poetic genius alone: education, some financial independence—either in the form of personal wealth, individual or institutional patronage—a modicum of leisure, access to source materials and books, some form of encouragement, and/or religious, political, or emotional zeal are also of significant import. Perhaps the most seminally important contribution of Renaissance humanism to the burgeoning of female literary activity was the availability, on a large scale, of diversified education to laywomen fortunate enough to have had access to books and teachers. Indeed, the education of women was one of the most persuasively argued topoi in the famous Renaissance debate on woman's worth, the *querelle des femmes*. The growing emphasis on the education of women was reflected in the foundation in the early sixteenth century of a new order, the Ursulines, which was exclusively devoted to teaching girls. Many women rose to prominence as poets, humanists, novelists, and translators during the Renaissance, and the rise of the literary vernaculars (particularly in central and eastern Europe) was largely due to the copying and translation work pursued by women. Renaissance women writers can conveniently be categorized in six groups: the *grande dame* (writing predominantly secular works: lyric poetry, letters, translations, orations, novelistic texts); the woman scholar (devoting herself to philological pursuits); the nun (writing biographies, visions, and translations in Latin or the vernacular); the *cortigiama ohesta*, the Italian Renaissance brand of the Greek *Hetaira,* exemplifying the single woman's other alternative (writing mostly vernacular lyric poetry). The fifth and sixth groups were essentially urban and wrote in the vernacular: one the religious activist, usually a member of the urban poor and seldom rewarded for her pamphleteering efforts, and the other the genteel woman, a member of the rural urban patriciate who composed in a variety of devotional or fictional genres.

The seventeenth century witnessed a great surge of literary activity by women. It has been estimated that one percent of the texts published at that time were written by women. A large portion of the works penned by women in the Early Modern era, as in the Middle Ages and the Renaissance, was still devotional or religio-political in nature; but the ratio of religious to secular text became a great deal more balanced as time progressed. Analogously, women scholars, while still considered oddities, did increase in number in the 1600s; the mid- and late seventeenth century therefore witnessed an unprecedented number of women who decided to write polemically and with a collective awareness of their gender in order to address the subject of women's condition and potential, thus partaking in the philosophic/theological debate concerning spiritual equality of the sexes.

In the realm of belles lettres, the seventeenth and eighteenth centuries also saw a great flowering of women's art, giving us several women who—either by necessity or by choice—lived by their pen. Whether conforming to Baroque sensibilities or deliberately avoiding them, seventeenth-century women writers left us both with a legacy of feminist aesthetics (marginal in some cases, but surprisingly pronounced in others) and with a complex picture of female experience in the wide range of intellectual perspectives that they chose to provide. Perhaps the most important aspect of this legacy was the growing collective awareness of gender not only as a determining factor of individual identity but also as the parameter of most tenets of social, political, and intellectual endeavor. During the Middle Ages and the Renaissance women by and large succeeded in intellectual pursuits when they simultaneously rejected the world of women. Several Early Modern women writers gave public expression to the recognition that women as a group suffered discrimination and should be given rights and privileges because of—not despite—their femaleness. The rights and privileges that Early Modern women sought involved remedying the long tradition of patriarchal suppression; their goal was a degree of sexual egalitarianism.

In the nineteenth century the number of women writers increased again. The new group of women writers entering the literary scene were middle class women who found writing (predominantly novels) not only a forum for self-expression but also a means of financial support. It has been estimated that texts by women novelists make up about twenty percent of the books published. Unlike their predecessors, nineteenth century women writers often used male pseudonyms to ensure that their work would be treated with the same critical objectivity as that of men.

Finally, it is in the post-World War II era that women have become (almost) full participants in literary endeavors. Indeed, women are responsible for much of the experimentation that has invigorated European poetry, bringing political, aesthetic, and feminist issues to the forefront.

LIST OF CONTRIBUTORS

Tova Aanderaa
Centerport, New York

Kristiaan Aercke
University of Wisconsin
Madison, Wisconsin

Concha Alborg
Saint Joseph's University
Philadelphia, Pennsylvania

Madeleine Alcover
Rice University
Houston, Texas

J. T. Alexander
University of Kansas
Lawrence, Kansas

W. Brian Altano
Bergen Community College
Paramus, New Jersey

Christine Anderson
West Lafayette, Indiana

Kristine Anderson
New York, New York

Kathy Saranpa Anstine
Sandy Hook, Connecticut

Claudio Antoni
Smith College
Northampton, Massachusetts

Raquel Aquilu de Murphy
Marquette University
Milwaukee, Wisconsin

Brigitte Archibald
North Carolina A & T
    University
Greensboro, North Carolina

Francis Assaf
Moore College
University of Georgia
Athens, Georgia

M. Astman
Barnard College
Columbia University
New York, New York

Jeanette Atkinson
Athens, Georgia

Denise N. Baker
University of North
    Carolina at Greensboro
Greensboro, North Carolina

Charlene Ball
Georgia State University
Atlanta, Georgia

Angelica Bammer
Emory University
Atlanta, Georgia

Marianne Bargum
Suomalaisen Kirjallisuuden
    Seura
Helsinki, Finland

Peter I. Barta
Texas Tech University
Lubbock, Texas

Eniko Molnár Basa
Library of Congress
Silver Spring, Maryland

Fiora Bassanese
University of
    Massachusetts, Boston
Boston, Massachusetts

Michael Bassman
East Carolina University
Greenville, North Carolina

Susan Bassnett
University of Warwick
Coventry, England

Hortense Bates
University of Georgia
Athens, Georgia

Jeanette Beer
Purdue University
West Lafayette, Indiana

Olga Markoff-Belaeff
Oberlin College
Oberlin, Ohio

Catherine Bellver
University of Nevada
Las Vegas, Nevada

Edith Joyce Benkov
San Diego State University
San Diego, California

Joseph Berrigan
University of Georgia
Athens, Georgia

Alda Bianco
University of Wisconsin
Madison, Wisconsin

Maya Bijvoet
San Jose State University
San Jose, California

Randi Birn
University of Oregon
Eugene, Oregon

Michael Bishop
Dalhousie University
Halifax, Nova Scotia, Canada

Paal Bjórby
University of California, Los
    Angeles
Los Angeles, California

Robert E. Bjork
Arizona State University
Tempe, Arizona

Beth Bjorklund
University of Virginia
Charlottesville, Virginia

Merritt Blakeslee
Moore College
University of Georgia
Athens, Georgia

Ronald Bogue
University of Georgia
Athens, Georgia

Susan Brantly
New Haven, Connecticut

Sigrid Brauner
Oakland, California

Mary Lee Bretz
Princeton, New Jersey

Mitzi M. Brunsdale
Mayville State College
Mayville, North Dakota

John Bugge
Emory University
Atlanta, Georgia

John Byrnes
Wabash College
Crawfordsville, Indiana

Joan Cammarata
Manhattan College
Riverdale, New York

Karen Hardy Cárdenas
University of South Dakota
Vermillion, South Dakota

Carlotta Caulfield
Tulane University
New Orleans, Louisiana

Gertrud G. Champa
University of Iowa
Iowa City, Iowa

Balance Chow
University of Georgia
Athens, Georgia

Joseph F. Chorpenning
Allertown College
Center Valley, California

Birute Ciplijauskite
University of Wisconsin
Madison, Wisconsin

Susan Clark
Rice University
Houston, Texas

Albrecht Classen
University of Arizona
Tucson, Arizona

Gunnel Cleve
University of Helsinki
Helsinki, Finland

Lina L. Cofresi
North Carolina State
University
Raleigh, North Carolina

Barbara Cooper
University of Georgia
Athens, Georgia

Nancy Cooper
Modern Language
Association
New York, New York

Robert D. Cottrell
Ohio State University
Columbus, Ohio

Kathryn Crecelius
Massachusetts Institute of
Technology
Cambridge, Massachusetts

Ruth P. Dawson
University of Hawaii at Manoa
Honolulu, Hawaii

Terence Dawson
Marsham, Norwich, England

Christy Desmet
University of Georgia
Athens, Georgia

John Dowling
University of Georgia
Athens, Georgia

Aliki Dragona
State University of New
York at Binghamton
Binghamton, New York

Carolyn A. Durham
The College of Wooster
Wooster, Ohio

Friederike Edmonds
University of California at
Davis
Davis, California

Margaret Eifler
Rice University
Houston, Texas

Dyan Elliott
Indiana University
Bloomington, Indiana

Deborah S. Ellis
Case Western Reserve
University
Cleveland, Ohio

Ana Paula Ferreira
Rutgers University
New Brunswick, New Jersey

Katherina Filips-Jusswig
University of Wisconsin
Madison, Wisconsin

Valeria Finucci
Duke University
Durham, North Carolina

Gabriela Fiori
Florence, Italy

Thomas C. Fox
Washington University
St. Louis, Missouri

Pietro Frassica
Princeton University
Princeton, New Jersey

Elke Frederiksen
University of Maryland
College Park, Maryland

Donald Friedman
Winthrop College
Rock Hill, South Carolina

Marilyn Gaddis-Rose
State University of New
York at Binghamton
Binghamton, New York

Jennifer C. Gage
Brown University
Providence, Rhode Island

†Carolyn Galerstein
University of Texas at Dallas
Richardson, Texas

Lee Gallo
Emory University
Atlanta, Georgia

A. Georgiadou
University of Illinois
Urbana, Illinois

Daniel Gerould
The Graduate School and
University Center
New York, New York

Mary E. Giles
California State University,
Sacramento
Sacramento, California

Ljiljana Ina Gjurgjan
University of Zagreb
Zagreb, Yugoslavia

Jerry Glen
University of Cincinnati
Cincinnati, Ohio

Ruth-Ellen Glümer
University of Minnesota
Minneapolis, Minnesota

Darra Goldstein
Williams College
Williamstown, Massachusetts

Sanda Golopentia
Brown University
Providence, Rhode Island

Cristina González
University of Massachusetts
Amherst, Massachusetts

Kay Goodman
Brown University
Providence, Rhode Island

Marjanne E. Goozé
University of Georgia
Athens, Georgia

Helena Goscilo
University of Pittsburgh
Pittsburgh, Pennsylvania

Diana Greene
University of New Hampshire
Keene, New Hampshire

Regina Grol-Prokopcyk
Buffalo, New York

Maria Luísa Guardiola-Ellis
Bryn Mawr College
Bryn Mawr, Pennsylvania

Jutta Hagedorn
Bielefeld, Germany

Peggy Hager
Eau Claire, Wisconsin

Steven Hale
Mount Berry College
Mount Berry, Georgia

Katharine Hanson
Seattle, Washington

Mary Hatch
Columbia, South Carolina

Thomas Head
Yale University
New Haven, Connecticut

Frode Hermundsgard
St. Olaf College
Northfield, Minnesota

Kittye Delle Robins Herring
Mississippi State University
Mississippi State, Mississippi

Ian Hersey
Berkeley, California

Marie-France Hilgar
University of Nevada
Las Vegas, Nevada

Torild Homstad
Northfield, Minnesota

Bruce Hozeski
Ball State University
Muncie, Indiana

Shaun F. D. Hughes
Purdue University
West Lafayette, Indiana

Linda Hunt
Ohio University
Athens, Ohio

Gabriella Ibieta
Saint Joseph's University
Philadelphia, Pennsylvania

Paula T. Irvin
Newberg, Oregon

Lanae Isaacson
San Jose, California

Nanette Jaynes
University of Georgia
Athens, Georgia

Neda Jeni
University of Illinois
Urbana, Illinois

Jorun B. Johns
California State University
San Bernardino, California

Lathrop P. Johnson
Ball State University
Muncie, Indiana

Mary Greenwood Johnson
University of Kansas
Lawrence, Kansas

Sheila Johnson
Austin, Texas

James Jones
Central Michigan
    University
Mount Pleasant, Michigan

Margaret E. W. Jones
University of Kentucky
Lexington, Kentucky

Frank Joostens
Tilburg University
Le Tilburg, Netherlands

Jean Jost
Bradley University
Peoria, Illinois

JoAnna Juet
University of Georgia
Athens, Georgia

Clara Juncker
Handelshøjskolen i
    København
Frederiksberg, Denmark

Ranee Kaur
University of Georgia
Athens, Georgia

Catriona H. M. Kelly
University of Oxford
Oxford, England

Christine Kiebuzinska
Virginia Polytechnic Institute
    and State University
Blacksburg, Virginia

Rosemarie Kieffer
Féderátion
    Luxembourgeoisie
Luxembourg

Blossom S. Kirschenbaum
Brown University
Providence, Rhode Island

Ann Hibner Koblitz
Wellesley College
Wellesley, Massachusetts

Ruth Goldfarb Koizim
New Haven, Connecticut

Helen Dendririon Kolias
Cornell University
Ithaca, New York

Jurgen Koppensteiner
University of Northern
    Iowa
Cedar Falls, Iowa

Ruth Kreuzer
Canton, New York

An Lammens
Brussels, Belgium

David Larmour
Texas Tech University
Lubbock, Texas

Valerie Lastruyer
West Virginia University
Morgantown, West Virginia

Dorothy L. Latz
New Rochelle, New York

Gertrud Jaron Lewis
Sudbury, Ontario, Canada

Phyllida Link
New York, New York

Maria Nina Lombardo
Chicago, Illinois

Stanley Longman
University of Georgia
Athens, Georgia

Ignacio-Javier Lopez
University of Virginia
Charlottesville, Virginia

Ruth Lundelius
University of Georgia
Athens, Georgia

Clinton Machann
Texas A & M University
College Station, Texas

Kathleen Madigan
Chapel Hill, North Carolina

Michèle M. Magill
North Carolina State
    University
Raleigh, North Carolina

Ursula Mahlendorf
University of California,
    Santa Barbara
Santa Barbara, California

Ronald Maisonneuve
Oyonnax, France

Coro Malaxecheverria
Chapel Hill, North Carolina

Rosalita Marcello
Manhattan College
Riverdale, New York

Harriet E. Margolis
Bloomington, Indiana

Barbara Dale May
University of Oregon
Eugene, Oregon

Laura Jo Turner
    McCullough
Santa Barbara, California

Galina K. McGuire
Milwaukee, Wisconsin

Glenda McLeod
Gainesville College
Gainesville, Georgia

Miriella Melara
University of Nevada, Reno
Reno, Nevada

Judy Mendels
Luzern, Switzerland

Petra Menzel
Paris, France

Guy Mermier
The University of Michigan
Ann Arbor, Michigan

Judith Messick
University of California,
    Santa Barbara
Santa Barbara, California

Colette V. Michael
Northern Illinois University
DeKalb, Illinois

Stephen Mitchell
Harvard University
Cambridge, Massachusetts

Liz Mittman
University of Minnesota
Minneapolis, Minnesota

Cornelia Niekus Moore
University of Hawaii at Manoa
Honolulu, Hawaii

Muriel Morge
University of Georgia
Athens, Georgia

Edward Mornin
The University of British
    Columbia
Vancouver, British
    Columbia, Canada

Maureen E. Mulvihill
Brooklyn, New York

Marie Murphy
Loyola College
Baltimore, Maryland

Eunice D. Myers
Wichita State University
Wichita, Kansas

José Maria Naharro
Greenbelt, Maryland

Irmeli Niemi
Helsinki, Finland

Laura Niesen de Abuña
Ithaca College
Ithaca, New York

Roger C. Norton
State University of New
    York at Binghamton
Binghamton, New York

Patricia W. O'Connor
University of Cincinnati
Cincinnati, Ohio

Margaret Hayford O'Leary
St. Olaf College
Northfield, Minnesota

Ingeborg Majer O'Sickey
Austin, Texas

Karen Offen
Stanford University
Stanford, California

Lisa Goldschen Ohm
Joleta, California

Jeanne A. Ojala
University of Utah
Salt Lake City, Utah

William T. Ojala
University of Utah
Salt Lake City, Utah

Judith Oliver
Colgate University
Hamilton, New York

Alexandra H. Olsen
University of Denver
Denver, Colorado

Lydia A. Panaro
Manhattan College
Riverdale, New York

Paul Pascal
University of Washington
Seattle, Washington

James Patty
Vanderbilt University
Nashville, Tennessee

Zoja Pavlovskis
State University of New
    York at Binghamton
Binghamton, New York

Mickey Pearlman
Cliffside Park, New Jersey

Jean E. Pearson
Bethlehem, Pennsylvania

Janet Perez
Lubbock, Texas

Maya Peretz
Binghamton, New York

Cornelia Peterman
Richmond Heights, Missouri

Richard Pioli
University of Georgia
Athens, Georgia

Brent A. Pitts
Meredith College
Raleigh, North Carolina

Norma Pratt
Altadena, California

Peter R. Prifti
San Diego, California

Douglas Radcliff-Umstead
Kent State University
Kent, Ohio

Rosetta Radtke
Youngsville, North Carolina

Ann Marie Rasmussen
Durham, North Carolina

Mary Ann Reiss
King of Prussia, Pennsylvania

Earl Jeffrey Richards
Toulouse University
New Orleans, Louisiana

Helene M. Kastinger Riley
Clemson University
Clemson, South Carolina

Warwick J. Rodden
Translation Services
St. Paul, Australia

Pat Rogers
University of South Florida
Tampa, Florida

Charlotte Rosenthal
University of Southern Maine
Portland, Maine

Judith Rothchild
Appalachian State
University
Boone, North Carolina

Norma Rudinsky
Oregon State University
Corvallis, Oregon

Rinaldina Russell
New York, New York

Ute M. Saine
Northern Arizona University
Flagstaff, Arizona

Valeria Sajez
Brown University
Providence, Rhode Island

Harold Segel
Columbia University
New York, New York

Susan Sellers
London, England

Monica Shafi
University of Delaware
Newark, Delaware

Sylvia R. Sherno
University of California, Los
Angeles
Los Angeles, California

Sandra Sider
The Hispanic Society
New York, New York

Rimvydas Silbajoris
Columbus, Ohio

Marilyn B. Skinner
Northern Illinois University
DeKalb, Illinois

Christopher Smith
University of East Anglia
Norwich, England

Marilyn Smith
Athens, Georgia

Michael B. Smith
Berry College
Berry, Georgia

Antonio Sobejano
State University of New
York at Binghamton
Binghamton, New York

Paula Sommers
University of Missouri-
Columbia
Columbia, Missouri

Sarah Spence
University of Georgia
Athens, Georgia

Sandro Sticca
State University of New
York at Binghamton
Binghamton, New York

Carol Stos
University of Ontario
Ontario, Canada

Sandra Straubhaar
East Lansing, Michigan

Gabriele L. Strauch
University of Maryland
College Park, Maryland

Giaccomo Striuli
Providence College
Providence, Rhode Island

Irene Suboczewski
Bethesda, Maryland

Judy Tarr
New Haven, Connecticut

Jill G. Timbers
Mt. Pleasant, Michigan

Chris Tomei
Allegheny College
Meadville, Pennsylvania

Suzanne Toliver
University of Cincinnati
Cincinnati, Ohio

Gwen Trottein
Bishop's University
Lennoxville, Quebec, Canada

Laura Jo Turner
Santa Barbara, California

Noël Valis
University of Michigan
Ann Arbor, Michigan

Diane Van Hoof
Baltimore, Maryland

Ria Vanderauwera
Austin, Texas

Eleni Varikas
Paris, France

Irene Varvayanis
Norwegian Information
Service in the U.S.
New York, New York

Gyorgyi Voros
Virginia Polytechnic
Institute and State
University
Blacksburg, Virginia

Henk Vynckier
University of Illinois
Urbana, Illinois

Carla Waal
University of Missouri-
Columbia
Columbia, Missouri

Cory L. Wade
University of Santa Clara
Santa Clara, California

Elissa B. Weaver
Chicago, Illinois

Ann Weiss
East Norriton, Pennsylvania

Rebecca West
Chicago, Illinois

Duey J. White
Gretna, Louisiana

Charity Cannon Willard
Cornwall-on-Hudson, New
York

Androne Willeke
Oxford, Ohio

Charles G. S. Williams
Ohio State University
Columbus, Ohio

Ann Willison
Indiana University
Bloomington, Indiana

Susan Wilson
University of Georgia
Athens, Georgia

Mary E. Wolf
Evanston, Illinois

Steven Wood
Blue Ridge, Georgia

Reiko Yonogi
University of Georgia
Athens, Georgia

Karl A. Zaenker
University of British
Columbia
Vancouver, British
Columbia, Canada

Phyllis Zatlin
East Brunswick, New Jersey

Ingeborg Zeiträg
Hamburg, Germany

Mary F. Zirin
University of California
Altadena, California

AN ENCYCLOPEDIA OF CONTINENTAL WOMEN WRITERS

VOLUME ONE

A

"-a-g"

(see: Fredrika Charlotta [Tengström] Runeberg)

A.P.

(see: Alexandra Papadopoulou)

A.Z.I.N.S.O.

(see: Antonina Niemiryczowa)

Justine Abbing

(see: Carolina Lea de Haan)

Laure Saint-Martin Perman Junot d'Abrantes

*Born November 6, 1784, Montpellier, France;
   died June 7, 1838, Paris*
Genre(s): novel, memoirs
Language(s): French

Descendant of the family Des Commene, Laure Saint-Martin was also distantly related to Napoléon Bonaparte, who, as a general, was a frequent visitor to her mother's fashionable salon. At age sixteen, Laure married General Junot, an aide to Napoléon who made him duc d'Abrantes in 1808. During the consulate and the Empire, she was well-known in court circles. Imperial society met in her salon. Her husband encountered some disfavor and eventually committed suicide in 1813. After the fall of Napoléon, she had to deal with penury and decided to provide for her needs with her writings. Her novels are all but forgotten but her *Mémoires du Souvenir Historiques sur Napoléon, la Révolution, le Directoire, le Consulat, l'Empire et la Restauration (1831–1935)*, in eighteen volumes, show insight into the mores of the time and a first-rate, if somewhat biased, documentary on the life of the Emperor. She painted a vivid—and rather valuable—picture of the period. Part of these memoirs are in fact a biography of the Des Commene, an ancient Greek imperial family who emigrated to Corsica when the Byzantine empire was invaded by the Turks. Her fate was closely linked to that of Napoléon. She was bitterly disappointed when his friends abandoned him, and she lived in retirement. Encouraged by the success of her first *Mémoires*, she wrote a sequel covering the Restoration, the July Revolution, and the first year of the reign of Louis-Philippe, but this fell short of the mark.

Works

Mémoires de Mme la Duchesse d'Abrantes, ou Souvenirs Historiques sur Napoléon, la Révolution, le Directoire, le Consulat, l'Empire et la Restauration, 18 vols. (1831–1835). *Catherine II* (1834). [With Joseph Saraszewiez], *Les Femmes Célèbres de tous les Pays* (1834). *Histoires Contemporaines* (1835). *Mémoires sur la Réstauration ou Souvenirs Historiques sur Cette Epoque, la Revolution de Juillet et les Premières Années du Règne de Louis-Philippe*, 6 vols. (1835–1836). *Scènes de la Vie Espagnole* (1836). *Souvenirs d'une Ambassade et d'un Séjour en Espagne et au Portugal de 1808 à*

1811, 2 vols. (1837). *La Duchesse de Vallombray* (1838). *Etienne Saulnier* (1838). *Hedwidge, Reine de Pologne* (1838). *Louise*, 2 vols. (1839). *Les Deux Soeurs, Scènes de la Vie d'Intérieur* (1840). *Choix de Mémoires et Ecrits des Femmes Françaises aux XVII*, *XVIII*, *XIX* (1892).

Bibliography

Malo, Henri, *Les Années de Bohème de la Duchesse d'Abrantes* (1927). Malo, Henri, *La Duchesse d'Abrantes au Temps des Amours* (1927).

Colette Michael

Louise Ackermann

(a.k.a. Victorine Choquet)

Born November 30, 1813, Paris, France; died August 3, 1890
Genre(s): poetry
Language(s): French

Educated by her father, an erudite man notable for his friendship with the French Encyclopedists, Louise was sent to Berlin to complete her studies. While there she married in 1844 Paul Ackermann, a Protestant minister. After her husband's death, she returned to France and established herself in the country near Nice where, living as a recluse, she began to write poems that were first published in the *Revue des Deux Mondes*. Her first collection of short stories, entitled *Contes*, was published in 1855 by Garnier frères. Her best-known work is the *Poésies Philosophiques*, where one notes the influence of the German philosophers—which she denied—in particular, Schopenhauer and Kant. Imbued with stark pessimism, Louise Ackermann saw very little meaning in the world of *homo sapiens* who, she felt, had no opportunities of acquiring real knowledge. However, she seems to have defended art for art's sake. The *Pensées d'une Solitaire* (1883) were preceded by her autobiography. She had her complete works published in 1885 under the title *Oeuvres. Ma Vie. Première Poésies. Poésies Philosophiques* by A. Lemerre.

Works

Contes et Poésies (1862). *Le Deluge* (1876). *Pensées d'une Solitaire, Precédées d'une Autobiographie* (1882). *Oeuvres. Ma Vie. Première Poésies. Poésies Philosophiques* (1885). *Contes* (1955). *Poésies Philosophiques* (1971).

Bibliography

Citaleux, Marc, *La Poésie Philosophique au XIX Siècle, Mme. Ackermann* (1906). Comte d'Haussonville, "Madame Ackermann, d'après des lettres et des papiers inedits." *Femmes d'Autrefois* (1912). de Pontmartin, Armand, "Madame Ackermann, la Poésie athée...." *Nouveaux Samedis* XI (1875).

Colette Michael

Rosario de Acuña y Villanueva de la Iglesia

(a.k.a. Remigio Andrés Delafón)

Born 1851, Madrid, Spain; died 1923, Madrid
Genre(s): drama, essay, short story, poetry
Language(s): Spanish

Acuña was a sincere proponent of education for women, and wrote often and tenaciously on the questions of equality and freedom for women. This stance, combined with her work in the theater, provoked virulent attacks from conservative critics during her lifetime. Yet Acuña was far from radical or even militant by today's standards, although she was considered a "freethinker" in her time because of her support for civil marriage (a controversial idea that would have made marriage a legal matter rather than a sacramental one and thus would have permitted divorce). Her studies on rural Spanish life and her pedagogical articles were significant contributions to the cause of reform and liberalization, and in the more progressive atmosphere of the Second Republic (1931–1936), she was the object of a commemorative session by the Madrid Atheneum on the occasion of the tenth anniversary of her death.

Perhaps because of the paucity of women who have managed to succeed as dramatists in Spain, Acuña is remembered primarily for her works for the theater. She began in a somewhat post-Romantic vein with tragic historical dramas, including *Rienzi el tribuno* (1876; Rienzi, the Tribune) and *Amor a la patria* (1877; Patriotism), works in verse that deal with conflicts between honor and desire. *Rienzi* is Acuña's best-known work, set in fourteenth-century Italy and focusing on the efforts of di Rienzo to end the nobles' blood feud and unify Rome. The story comes to a bloody end with a treacherous rebellion. *Amor a la patria* recreates the heroic resistance of Spanish peasants to the Napoleonic invasion in the 1808 War of Independence, foregrounding the role of women and their loyalty by contrast with more venal motivations in the male characters. *Tribunales de venganza* (1880; Courts of Revenge) also belongs to the set of versified historical tragedies. Other plays include *El padre Juan* (1891; Father John), an anticlerical prose melodrama whose premiere provoked an uproar because of its attacks on religious fanaticism. In somewhat dualistic, oversimplified fashion, the free-thinking (and non-religious) characters are identified with goodness and enlightenment, while the sinister, hypocritical priest and his minions precipitate a murder. *La voz de la patria* (1893; Voice of the Fatherland) returns to verse to depict the dilemma of an Aragonese youth caught between answering his country's call and saving the honor of his pregnant fiancée.

Acuña's success in the difficult medium of verse theater owes much to her facility as a poet. Non-dramatic poetry works include *Ecos del alma* (1876; Echoes from the Soul); *Morirse a tiempo* (1880; To Die on Time), written in imitation of the then-popular poet, Campoamor, and *Sentir y pensar* (1884), whose intent is more comic than the title may indicate. The writer's interest in the lot of country people appears in *La herencia de las furias o misterios de un granero* (1883 [?]; Legacy of the Furies, or Mysteries of a Granary), *El hijo de los pueblos rurales* (1882; The Child of Rural Villages), and *Influencia de la vida del campo en la familia* (1882; The Influence of Rural Life upon the Family). Additional social concerns, very forward-looking for their day, appear in *El crimen de la calle de Fuencarral* (1880 [?]; The Crime of Fuencarral Street), based on a sensational murder and advocating understanding and regeneration for the delinquent based on society's pro-rata of responsibility; and *Consecuencias de la degeneración femenina* (1888; Consequences of Feminine Degeneracy). *Tiempo perdido* (1881; Time Lost) is a collection of short stories and sketches, *La siesta* (1882), articles and miscellany, while *Cosas mías* (1917; My Things) reprints three feminist essays.

Works

Ecos del alma (1876). *Rienzi el tribuno* (1876). *Amor a la patria* (1877). *El crimen de la calle de Fuencarral* (1880). *Morirse a tiempo* (1880). *Tribunales de venganza* (1880). *Tiempo perdido* (1881). *El hijo de los pueblos rurales* (1882). *Influencia de la vida del campo en la familia* (1882). *La siesta* (1882). *La herencia de las furias o misterios de un granero* (1883 [?]). *Sentir y pensar* (1884). *La casa de las muñecas* (1888). *Consecuencias de la degeneración femenina* (1888). *El padre Juan* (1891). *La voz de la patria* (1893). *Cosas mías* (1917).

Janet Perez

Christen Ada

(see: Christiane Frederick von Breden)

Juliette Adam

(a.k.a. Juliette La Messine, Juliette Lamber, Paul Vasili)

Born October 4, 1836, Verberie, France; died August 25, 1936, Callian
Genre(s): novel, drama, autobiography, journalism, essay, review editor
Language(s): French

Juliette Adam, sometimes known as "La Grande Française," wrote widely and moved in the most important literary and political circles during her long life span. Three salient facets of her life and work can be distinguished: her creative writings (novels, plays, autobiography), her journalism, and her political activism.

Born in the Northern French province of Picardy into a bourgeois family with strong and often contradictory opinions, Juliette Lamber's talents were recognized and cultivated early. She was married at fifteen to Alexis La Messine and had a daughter. The family moved to Paris, where Juliette established herself and made connections with a literary circle including former Saint-Simonians.

Incensed by Proudhon's harsh judgments on women, especially his denigration of women's intelligence, and by his attacks on her literary idols, George Sand and Daniel Stern, she launched a counteroffensive, *Idées antiproudhoniennes* (Antiproudhonien Ideas), which she published at her own expense in 1858. Her entire career from this point on can be interpreted as a refutation of Proudhon's charges. Beginning with *Mon Village* (1860; My Village), and including the second edition of *Idées antiproudhoniennes* (1861), she used the name Juliette Lamber, an altered version of her maiden name, in order to prevent her estranged husband from confiscating her royalties, his property according to the laws of the time.

Nonetheless, her husband demanded to be paid the royalties from this first work, and republished her biography of Garibaldi under his own name. They separated in 1866 (divorce was not then legal in France), and he died the following year. In 1868, she married Edmond Adam, a journalist and political figure. Both were active participants in the establishment of the Third Republic, and Juliette in part is remembered for her tenacious fight to regain Alsace-Lorraine, lost in the Franco-Prussian war; she saw her dream accomplished as a result of the first World War. She founded *La Nouvelle Revue* (The New Review) in 1879, an influential publication with which such authors as Maupassant, Pierre Loti, Flaubert, George Sand, and Frédéric Mistral were associated. The journal was intended to rival and even to displace the distinguished *Revue des Deux Mondes* (The Review of Two Worlds), by promoting a liberal republican perspective and the literary work of talented younger writers such as Paul Bourget. She reserved for herself the reportage on foreign affairs, where she displayed a passionate commitment to revenge by France against Germany for the defeat in 1871. In the 1890s, she opened the review to articles on the woman question, including many of Jeanne E. Schmahl, founder of *L'Avant-Courrière* (The Forerunner). By 1899, however, a series of crises led her to abandon definitively the direction of the *Nouvelle Revue*.

During the last four decades of the nineteenth century, Juliette Adam's salon attracted the cream of literary and political society and even included women, a novelty. Her long life allowed her to see the realization of many of the feminist and political ideals she had held since her first years as a writer, but not the one she had sought vigorously after World War I: the right of French women to vote.

Juliette Adam, like her friends and mentors George Sand and Marie d'Agoult (Daniel Stern), deployed her talents in many genres. She wrote novels, a multi-volume autobiography, travel literature, literary criticism and plays which were performed in her salon. *Le Mandarian* (1860; The Mandarin) is a nineteenth-century version of Montesquieu's *Lettres persanes*, in which among other things she criticizes Michelet's view of woman as sickly in her essence. *Mon Village* (1860; My Village), strongly influenced by Sand's pastoral novels, suggests that perhaps a woman mayor would govern even better than a man. *Voyage autour du Grand-Pin* (1863; The Trip around Grand-Pin) and *Récits du Golfe Juan* (1875; Stories from the Gulf Juan) succeed in evoking the Mediterranean coast that she helped establish as a popular wintering place. Of her "Greek Trilogy," *Païenne* (1883; Pagan) is the best and of most interest today. Her autobiography is designed to present both her life and her times and is notable for her description of her childhood and literary debuts. For the *Nouvelle Revue*, she wrote a wide variety of articles; during that period she also published under the name Paul Vasili, a collective pseudonym that others used as well. She wrote innumerable articles for a great many French and foreign publications.

Juliette Adam was a dominant political and literary presence from the Second Empire through World War I. Her great gifts were often stretched thin as she sought to publish in quantity rather than insisting upon quality. She was a friend and mentor to the most important writers and activists of the Third Republic and supported their work morally and materially; her *Nouvelle Revue* was extremely influential; during World War I, she became celebrated as "la grande

Française" for her unequivocal opposition to German aggression, and she was the only woman invited to attend the signing ceremonies of the Treaty of Versailles. Today, readers are still awed by the arguments the twenty-two year old made against Proudhon's misogyny, and her autobiography is important for those who are interested in the way a woman told her own story.

Works

Blanche de Coucy (1858). Idées anti-proudhoniennes sur l'amour, la femme, et le mariage (1858). Garibaldi, sa vie d'après des documents inédits (1859). Un mot sur l'affaire Mortara (1859). Le Mandarin (1860). Mon Village (1860). La Papauté (1860). Récits d'une paysanne (1862). Voyage autour du Grand-Pin (1863). L'arrière-saison (1865). Dans les Alpes. Nouveaux récits (1867). L'éducation de Laure (1868). Saine et Sauve (1870). Le siège de Paris (1873). Récits du Golfe Juan (1875). Jean et Pascal (1876). Laide (1878). Grecque (1879). Poètes grecs contemporains (1881). La Chanson des nouveaux époux (1882). Païenne (1883). La patrie hongroise. Souvenirs personnels (1884). Le Général Skobeleff (1886). Un rêve sur le divin (1888). Jalousie de jeune fille (1889). Types et paysages de Hongrie (1893). Mon petit Théâtre (1896). La Patrie portugaise. Souvenirs personnels (1896). Non! l'Alsace-Lorraine n'est ni germaine ni germanisée (1902). Le Roman de mon enfance et de ma jeunesse (1902). Mes Premières Armes littéraires et politiques (1904). Mes Sentiments et nos idées avant 1870 (1905). Mes Illusions et nos souffrances pendant le siège de Paris (1906; reissue of the Journal d'une parisienne, with a new preface). Mes angoisses et nos luttes, 1871–1873 (1907). Nos amitiés politiques avant l'abandon de la Revanche (1908). Après l'abandon de la Revanche (1910). Impressions françaises en Russie (1912). Chrétienne (1913). L'heure vengeresse des crimes bismarckiens (1915). Guillaume II (1890–1899) (1917). La Vie des âmes (1919). L'Angleterre en Egypte (1922). Le capitaine Georges Gilbert (1924). L'Egypte-Une leçon diplomatique (1924). Rome au jubilé (1925). Notre Alsace française (1927). Les Arbres (1930).

Translations: A Fascinating Woman [Laide], tr. John Sterling (Mary Neal Sherwood). My Literary Life [Mes Premières Armes littéraires et politiques]. The Romance of My Childhood and Youth [Le Roman de mon enfance et de ma jeunesse]. The Schemes of the Kaiser [Guillaume II], tr. J.O.P. Bland. For a more complete bibliography, including works by Paul Vasili and manuscripts, see Morcos, below, pp. 633–655.

Bibliography

Cormier, Manon, Madame Juliette Adam, ou l'aurore de la IIIe République (Bordeaux, 1934).
Morcos, Saad, Juliette Adam (Cairo, 1961).
Stephens, Winifred, Madame Adam (Juliette Lamber), "La Grande Française" from Louis-Philippe until 1917 (London and New York, 1917).

Kathryn J. Crecelius and Karen Offen

Věra Adlová

Born 1919, Prague, Czechoslovakia
Genre(s): prose, children's literature
Language(s): Czech

Věra Adlová graduated from the faculty of philosophy of Charles University, then worked for many years as an editor for magazines and radio. For several years she was editor-in-chief of the Albatross children's publishing house. Adlová made her literary début in 1946; she has been awarded literary prizes for her writing, some of which has been translated into German, Polish, and Russian. She is now a full-time author.

Works

Vestonie, novel (1946). ivot, Kter. . . Jsme Milovali [The Life We Loved], novel (1948). Na Shledanou, MoŘsk . . . Vlku [See You, Old Sailor], novel for young people (1960). Honička Nad Prahou [Chase over Prague], fairy tale (1962). O Zmrzlé Elektřině [About Frozen Electricity], fairy tale (1963). Mirka To Ví Nejlíp [Mirka Knows Best], novel for young people (1964). Blues Pro Alexandru [Blues for Alexandra], novel for young people (1966). V. . . prodej Spravedliv. . . ch [The Just for Sale], novel (1966). Jarní Symfonie [Spring Symphony], novel for young people (1973). Pohádky Pro Kačenku [Fairy Tales for Kachenka] (1975). Ru'e z Flander [A Rose from Flanders], novel (1976). Říkáte, Abych Věřil? [You Ask Me to Believe?], novel (1979).

Warwick J. Rodden

Etta Palm d'Aelders

*Born 1743, Groningue, Holland; died after
    1795*
Genre(s): pamphlets and feminist tracts
Language(s): French

Revolutionary writer who called herself Baroness Palm d'Aelders, Etta-Lubina Johanna Derista Alders married in 1762 Ferdinand Palm about whom little is known. It seems that soon after his marriage he left for India and never returned. Etta traveled extensively throughout Europe. In 1768, she settled in Paris. Not much has surfaced about her activities until November 26, 1790 when, according to Paule-Marie Duhet, she publicly embraced the feminist cause. This was reported in the *Orateur du Peuple* and in *La Bouche de Fer*. Soon after December 30, 1790, she read in front of the Assemblée Fédérative des Amis de la Vérité a famous speech entitled "Sur l'injustice des loix en faveur des hommes au dépend des femmes" ("On the Injustice of the Laws in Favor of Men at the Expense of Women"). In that speech she asks men to be fair toward the physically weaker but intellectually equal sex. She laments that laws favor men at the expense of women and asks for changes. On February 14, 1791, at the request of the municipality of Creil, she was awarded the French cockade and national medals. On this occasion, she made another speech deploring the state of education for women in the French capital.

The same year, she created the Société Patriotique des Amies de la Vérité, a feminist organization that was intended to be the female version of the Confédération des Amis de la Vérité.

Inveterate defender of equal liberties for men and women, she greatly admired the French revolutionary ideals and wrote a fiery pamphlet (March 23, 1791) attacking the enemies inside and outside of France.

She probably was one of the first women to propose public nurseries and centers where women could ask for help. Following a denunciation by a woman named Louise Robert, Etta made another speech on June 12, 1791 to justify herself. She is also credited with an extollment in 1791 to better morality in France with the help of women in government. The speech was entitled "Appel aux Françaises sur la régénération des moeurs et nécéssité de l'influence des femmes dans un gouvernement" ("Call to the French People on the Regeneration of Morality and the Necessity of Woman's Influence in a Government").

In September 1792, Etta Palm d'Aelders was charged with a diplomatic mission to the United States where the French government wanted to send an ambassador. That attempt ended in failure. She returned to Paris and not much is heard about her until her arrest in January 1793. She was accused of Orangiste affiliation. There exists to date no record of what happened to Etta Palm d'Aelders after that fateful date. It can be presumed without any proof that she might have paid in an unexpected fashion for her fictitious title of baroness.

Works

[Selected essays]. In *Les Tracts Féministes au XVIIe Siècle*, ed. Colette Michael (1986).

Bibliography

Cerati, M., *Le Club des Citoyennes Républicaines Révolutionnaires* (Paris, 1966). Duhet, Paule-Marie, *Les Femmes et la Révolution, 1789–1794* (Paris, 1971). Levy, D.G., H.B. Applewhite, and M.D. Johnson, *Women in Révolutionary Paris, 1789–1795* (Chicago, 1979).

Colette Michael

Marianna Aenou-Koutouzi

(see: Marianna Koutouzi)

Vittoria Aganoor Pompilj

*Born May 16, 1855, Padua, Italy; died May 8,
    1910, Rome*
Genre(s): poetry
Language(s): Italian

A gifted poet, Aganoor wrote in the somewhat romantic and lyrical style popular at the turn of the century in Italy but without any of the morbidity and sexual eroticism associated with Decadent writers like D'Annunzio. Her verse is passionate but controlled; its themes include love, abandonment, bitterness, solitude, and death—motifs often associated with women writers.

Born into a noble family of Armenian extraction, Aganoor's gifts were quickly noted by her parents, and she received special tutoring by poet Giacomo Zanella and Enrico Nencioni. Her private life was family oriented and dignified. A series of unhappy love experiences were recorded poetically in her first collection, *Leggenda eterna* (1900; Eternal Legend) whereas her *Nuove liriche* (1908; New Lyrics) salute her husband, Guido Pompilj, and her new environment, the Umbrian hills.

Having been involved in intellectual pursuits from an early age, Aganoor had created a network of literary friendships, including a lengthy relationship with an important man of letters, Domenico Gnoli. Their friendship blossomed into a romantic rapport that was sung by both parties in verse. However, Gnoli did not wish to remarry, and Aganoor needed emotional support, finding it in Pompilj. Their marriage ended tragically, creating a literary legend: the poet died unexpectedly after surgery, followed a few hours later by her husband, who committed suicide next to her corpse.

Aganoor's verse is somewhat structured and consistently controlled in its language, contents, and show of emotion. The main themes include the female experience of love—shared, unrequited, and conjugal—often viewed through natural analogies. Her work echoes with the voices of other nineteenth-century poets, from the Romantics to her contemporaries. There is often an existential *angst* in her words, an awareness of the impossibility of truly communicating one's thoughts and emotions, aggravated by the shadows of loss and death. During her lifetime, Aganoor was greatly respected and achieved unusual popularity for a woman poet: the first edition of *Leggenda eterna* was so popular that a second was issued within three years. Little known outside of Italy, Vittoria Aganoor is considered a minor but important figure in nineteenth-century poetry.

Works

Leggenda eterna, lyric (1900). *Nuove liriche* (1908). *Poesie complete* (1912).

Bibliography

Costa-Zalessow, Natalia, "Vittoria Aganoor Pompilj." *Scrittrici italiane dal XIII al XX secolo* (Ravenna, 1982), pp. 248–253. *Dizionario biografico degli italiani*, vol. I (Rome, 1960), pp. 360–362. *Dizionario enciclopedico della letteratura italiana*, vol. I (Bari, 1966), p. 29.

Fiora A. Bassanese

Countess d'Agoult

(see: Marie [-Catherine-Sophie de Flavigny], countess d'Agoult)

Marie (-Catherine-Sophie de Flavigny), countess d'Agoult

(a.k.a. Daniel Stern, Countess d'Agoult)

Born December 31, 1805, Franckfort-sur-le Mein, Germany; died March 5, 1876, Paris, France
Genre(s): novel, essay, history
Language(s): French

The Countess d'Agoult is perhaps better known for her romantic life than for her writing. Indeed, some think that her life is more artistic than the novels that were inspired by her life. Her beauty and romantic spirit made her a model for several works during her time. Nevertheless, as Daniel Stern, Agoult was both French and German, living in both countries as political exigencies dictated. After her marriage to Count Charles d'Agoult in 1827, Agoult stayed in France most of her life. She was well known in aristocratic society and was a popular hostess of her own salon. Romantic French artists and writers frequented her place in Paris.

The years following the Revolution of 1830 were so unhappy for her that she left her husband and child in 1835 to live openly with the musician Franz Liszt in Geneva. There, she soon gave birth to their first child. Two more children followed. They lived in Geneva and Italy until 1839 and returned to France, staying together until their relationship disintegrated in 1844.

During the years with Liszt, Agoult came tc be intimate friends with the well-known French woman writer George Sand. Agoult and Liszt introduced Sand to composer Chopin in 1836, and the four traveled and visited together frequently. Sand's five act play *Cosima* (1840) was named after Agoult's second daughter by Liszt, and her *Simon* (1836) is said to have been inspired by the Agoult-Liszt affair. Critics suggest that Agoult is the model for the unpleasant Vicomtesse de Chailly of *Horace* (1841) and the rival of *Consuelo* (1842). It is clear that the former positive images of Agoult turned negative by 1841 as Agoult became progressively jealous and bitter towards her former close friend.

Many of Agoult's contemporaries saw her as beautiful, vain, and socially ambitious. Sand had introduced Agoult to Balzac, who is said to have based his novel *Beatrix* (1839) on Liszt's lover.

After the break from Liszt and Sand, Agoult began to write novels, political commentaries, and literary essays. She described her relationship with Liszt in the roman-à-clef *Nélida* (1846), in which she portrayed herself as Beatrice to Liszt's Dante (in the novel an artist named Guermann). Other short novels appeared in journals: *Valentine* (1838), and *La Boite aux lettres* (1839). Writing under the pseudonym of Daniel Stern after 1841, however, Agoult's literary output was primarily social and historical. She began writing art reviews for *La Presse* but eventually became known as a historian of her times, especially of the Revolution of 1848 (1850–1853), and as a philosopher of republican equality. These latter titles include *Esquisses morales et politiques* (1849), *Essai sur la liberté* (1847), several works on Holland and Florence, and a series of essays on Dante and Goethe, which appeared in the *Revue germanique et française* (1864–1865).

Most comments about Agoult by her contemporaries call the writer a vain, shallow bluestocking. Even Sand came to suspect that Agoult had been jealous of her genius. Recent criticism has ignored her philosophical works and has focused instead on the feminist themes of her fiction. Certainly, a product of a social regime that had disappeared by the time she came of age, she must have felt the effects of the polarities between a liberal and exciting literary world and the repressive controls of her Paris salons.

Works

"Emerson." *La Revue Indépendante* (1846). *Nélida* (1846). *Essai sur la liberté considérée comme principe et fin de l'activité humaine* (1847). *Etats généreux de Prusse* (1847). *Lettres républicaines* (1848). *Esquisses morales et politiques* (1849). *Histoire de la Révolution de 1848*, 3 vols. (1850–1853). *Jeanne D'arc, drame historique en 5 actes et en prose* (1857). *Florence et Turin, études d'art et de politique 1857–1861* (1862). *La Hollande, son passé, sa liberté* (1864). "Le Cap Plouha. Dialogues sur Dante et Goethe, par Daniel Stern." *Revue germanique et française* (1864–1865). *Ponsard: esquisse de sa vie et de son oeuvre* (1865). *Histoires des commencements de la République aux Pay-Bas, 1581–1625* (1872). *Mes souvenirs, 1806–1833* (1877). *Oeuvres de Daniel Stern* (1880). *Sainte Catherine de Sienne par la Comtesse de Flavigny* (1880). *Valentia, Hervé, Julien, La Boite aux lettres* (1883). *Mémoires, 1833–1854* (1927).

Bibliography

Aragonnes, C., *La Comtesse d'Agoult* (Paris, 1935). Barbey D'Aurevilly, *Les Bas-Bleus* (Paris, 1878; rpt. Geneva, 1968). Blanch, L., *Pavilions of the Heart* (New York, 1974). Cate, C., *George Sand, a Biography* (Boston, 1975). Cronin, V., *Romantic Way* (New York, 1966). Crosland, M., *Women of Iron and Velvet* (London, 1976). Desanti, D., *Daniel ou le Visage secret d'une comtesse romantique* (Paris, 1980). Dorland, W., *The Sum of Feminine Achievement* (Stratford, 1967). Fostini, J., ed., *Love Letters* (New York, 1958). Gaulmier, J., *Missions et démarches de la critique* (Rennes, 1973). Haldane, C., *Galley Slaves of Love, the Story of Mme d'Agoult and Franz Liszt* (Harville, 1957). Liszt, F., *Correspondance de Liszt et de la Comtesse d'Agoult 1833–1840* (Paris, 1933). Monod, M., *Daniel Stern, la Comtesse d'Agoult* (Paris, 1937). Ollivier, D., *Autour de Mme d'Agoult et de Liszt* (Paris, 1941). Seché, L., *Muses romantiques* (Paris, 1908). Vier, J., *La Comtesse d'Agoult et son temps*, 6 vols. (Paris, 1955–1963). Watson, P., *Some Women of France* (London, 1936). Winwar, F., *The Life of the Heart: George Sand and Her Times* (New York, 1945).

General references: *Concise Universal Biography,* *Dictionnaire Biographique,* vol. 1 (1933). *Dictionnaire des lettres françaises, le dix-neuvième siècle* (1971). *Dictionnaire des littératures de langue française,* 3 vols. (1984). *Histoire de la littérature française,* vol. 8 (1957). *Oxford Companion to French Literature.*

Marilynn J. Smith

Alfhild Agrell

(a.k.a. Thyra, Lovisa Petterkvist, Stig Stigson)

Born January 13, 1849, Härnüsand, Sweden; died November 8, 1923, Flen
Genre(s): drama, novellas, novels
Language(s): Swedish

Alfhild Agrell is best known for having contributed to the wave of "indignation literature" that arose in the wake of Ibsen's *Et dukkehjem* (A Doll's House). Her efforts in this arena, although historically interesting, do not represent her best literary efforts. Perhaps for this reason, Alfhild Agrell's work was, as one critic has expressed it, "dömd och glömd" ("judged and forgotten") by literary historians.

Alfhild Teresia Martin was the daughter of a confectioner from northern Sweden. In 1868, she married Per Albert Agrell, a businessman and resident of Stockholm. She made her literary debut in 1883 with *Bilder från Italien* (1883; Pictures from Italy), a collection of travel sketches. This first prose attempt was not critically well received, but her next work, a play entitled *Räddad* (1883; Saved) garnered her a great deal of attention. Initially, she was often paired with Anne Charlotte Edgren-Leffler, whose "indignation drama," *Sanna kvinnor* (1883; True Women) appeared that same year.

Almost all of Agrell's plays deal with themes of women's rights. In *Ensam,* (1886; Alone), for example, Thora, after heroically struggling for 18 years to raise her illegitimate child alone, refuses an offer of respectability, that is to say a marriage proposal from the dissolute father of her child, because to accept would be a betrayal of her own humanity. Agrell's plays were popular because of the controversial issues they brought to light, but artistically they are flawed. Her characterizations appear one-dimensional and her plots occasionally rely too heavily on coincidence.

Despite her false start in the genre, short prose sketches proved to be Agrell's element. Agrell's dramas are by and large humorless, but her short stories possess irony and humor; yet she maintains her keen eye for social injustice. In "Ett bröllopsdag" ("A Wedding Day") from *Från Land och Stad* (1884; From Town and Country), Agrell presents a detailed depiction of a Swedish country wedding. There is sad but poignant irony in the fact that the bride's mother is more concerned about how the groom will treat the cow he received as his bride's dowry than she is about how he will treat her daughter. Agrell often makes use of dialect in her rural sketches. Agrell's later prose collections, *I Stockholm* (1895; In Stockholm) and *Hemma i Jockmock* (1898; At Home in Jockmock) became popular successes.

Alfhild Agrell's work constitutes a significant part of the social debates of the 1880s. Until recently, however, her work has received little or no critical attention.

Works

Bilder från Italien (1883). *Dramatiska arbeten 1–2* (1883–1884). *Från land och stad* (1884). *Hvad ingen ser* (1885). *Ensam. En lektion* (1886). *På landsbygden* (1887). *Vår!* (1889). *Under tallar och pinier* (1890). *I Stockholm* (1895). *Hemma i Jockmock* (1896). *Nordanifrån* (1898). *Norrlandsgubbar och norrlandsgummor samt andra gamlingar och ungdomar* (1899). *Ingrid. En döds kärlekssaga* (1900). *Prins Pompom* (1901). *Guds drömmare* (1904). *Norrlandshumör* (1910). *En lappbok* (1919).

Bibliography

Hennel, Ingeborg Nordin, "Två dockhem. Jämförande synpunkter på Agrells Räddad och Ibsens Et Dukkehjem," in *Text, tolkning, värdering,* eds. Karin Westman Berg and Birgitta Onsell (Uppsala, 1981), pp. 39–56. Hennel, Ingeborg Nordin, *Dömd och glömd. En studie i Alfhild Agrells liv och dikt* (Umeå & Stockholm, 1981).

Susan Brantley

Francisca Aguirre

Born 1930
Genre(s): poetry
Language(s): Spanish

Aguirre began her career within the Existentialist current, sharing denunciatory themes with other poets of the 1950s and 1960s. Her poetry, however, is more intimate but does not confine itself exclusively to the perspective of personal testimony. Mainly self-educated and widely read, Aguirre makes use of myth to illuminate her own historical era, a time of defeat and frustration. The pain suffered by all Spaniards during the Civil War is apparent in her poetry. There is a lucidity within the desolation, a keen insight within the pathos that transforms her verse into a living document controlled by a high degree of intellectual rigor. This poet is alert to the danger of excessive sentimentality, and her voice is characterized by its clarity and maturity. Her style is a unique blend of several poetic traditions, and she acknowledges the influence of Luis Rosales.

Works

Itaca [Ithaca] (1972). *La otra música* [The Other Music] (1977). *Los trescientos escalones* [The Three Hundred Steps] (1977).

Prizes: "Leopoldo Panero" poetry prize conferred by the Institute of Hispanic Culture, for *Itaca* (1971).

Bibliography

Miró, Emilio, "Poetisas españolas contemporáneas." *Revista de la Universidad Complutense* XXIV, 95 (Jan.–Feb 1975): 271–310. *Women Writers of Spain*, ed. C. Galerstein (1986).

Paula T. Irvin

Gunnel Maria Ahlin

Born 1918, Orsa, Sweden
Genre(s): novel
Language(s): Swedish

The daughter of school principal Johannes Hellman and his wife Aina, Gunnel completed her high school education, then followed in her father's footsteps and became a teacher. In 1946 she married writer Lars Ahlin with whom she lives a rather retiring life in the Stockholm suburb of Bromma.

A writer in her own right, Gunnel Ahlin has published several novels. In her two first novels *Röster en sommar* (Voices One Summer) and *Här dansar* (Here Dances), published in 1960 and 1962 respectively, she describes the short, beautiful summer landscape of Sweden in poetically lyrical terms. The characters in all of her novels are drawn with great analytical, psychological insight. Her style is lucid, terse and to the point.

Works

Röster en sommar (1960). *Här dansar* (1962). *Puls* (1964). *Refuge* (1967). *Hannibal sonen* (1974). [With Lars Ahlin], *Hannibal segraren* (1982).

Hanna Kalter Weiss

Ilse Aichinger

Born November 1, 1921, Vienna, Austria
Genre(s): novel, short story, radio play
Language(s): German

Austrian novelist, poet, short story writer, and radio playwright. Born in Vienna, she spent her childhood in Linz and completed Gymnasium in Vienna in 1939. Aichinger was of partly Jewish decent, and after the "anschluss" with Germany, she and her family were persecuted and forced to do compulsory service during World War II. She began medical studies after 1945, discontinuing them in the fifth semester in order to complete her first novel, *Die Grössere Hoffnung* (1948; translated in English as Herod's Children, 1963). From 1949 to 1950, in Vienna and later in Frankfurt, she was employed as a reader with S. Filcher Verlag, which later became her own publisher. In Ulm, she worked together with Inge Scholl for the founding of Hochschule für Gestaltung. In 1953, she married the German poet Günter Eich (1907–1972), whom she had met as a fellow member of the post-World War II writers' association "Gruppe 47" which had its first meeting in 1947. At each meeting a prize was offered for the best work, and Aichinger received this prize in 1952 for "Rede unter dem Galgen" ("Speech under the Gallows"), published in Germany in the collection *Der Gefesselte* (1953;

translated in English as *The Bound Man and Other Stories*, 1955).

Ilse Aichinger is said to be a master of "unpretended language." Other characteristics of her works are their unobtrusiveness and clarity, but her works are not simple or easy to understand. Her only novel, *Die grössere Hoffnung*, introduced many of the themes that have preoccupied Aichinger and established what may be called her style. Set against the background of World War II in a country dominated by the Nazis, the novel tells the story of a group of children who try through emigration to escape their threatened fate. The central figure, Ellen, is a half-Jewish girl who is precocious and perceptive. Although Ellen is killed in the end, the novel ultimately offers a "greater hope" suggested by its title, even in the midst of suffering: "all things work together for good in them that love God." When the novel was published in English as *Herod's Children*, people noticed its resemblance to the works of Kafka. In fact, many critics also associate the two. Like Kafka, she uses the convergence of dream and reality; similarly, the simplicity of her style heightens its overall effect. She used the language and vocabulary of everyday experience, but captivating metaphors and unusual characters produce a feeling of alienation from the world.

In the title story of *Der Gefesselte*, her debt to Kafka is very evident. In this story, a man wakes up one morning and finds out that he has been bound with ropes that allow him very limited freedom of movement; he learns to live with his fetters. Sartre's idea of man being constantly bound to the human condition finds expression in this story. The topic of the acceptance of human bondage recurs in several other stories.

In 1953 Aichinger presented her first radio play, "Knöpfe" ("Buttons"), the story of a group of workers in a button factory who spend their working lives in monotonous, repetitive routines. In doing so, these workers begin to lose their individuality, and they gradually turn into buttons. Aichinger also wrote some dialogues and a number of poems.

Speaking about the nature of her work, the literary critic J.C. Alldridge says that the reading public is startled by the unobtrusiveness of her work: "One has often had the impression, when reading one of her works for the first time, of a silent figure, by whom one has been observed and of whose existence one has been unaware."

Works

Die grössere Hoffnung, novel (1948). *Rede unter dem Galgen,* short stories (1952; published in Germany as Der Gefesselte, 1953). "Knöpfe," radio play (1953). *Zu keiner Stunde,* dialogues (1957). *Besuch im Pfarrhause,* radio play (1961). *Wo ich wohne,* stories, dialogues, poems (1963). *Eliza, Eliza,* stories (1965). *Nachmittag in Ostende* (1968). *Auckland,* radio plays (1969). *Nachricht von Tag,* stories (1970). *Dialoge, Erzählungen, Gedichte,* dialogues, stories, poems (1971). *Schlechte Wörter,* stories and radio plays (1976). *Meine Sprache und ich. Erzählungen,* all prose pieces written by the late 1970s (1978). *Verschenkter Rat. Gedichte,* thematically arranged poems written between 1955 and 1978 (1978). *Zu keiner Stunde. Szenen und Dialoge,* extended edition of Zu keiner Stunde, 1957 (1980).

Translations: *The Bound Man and Other Stories* [*Rede unter dem Galgen*], tr. Eric Mosbacher (1955; American ed. 1956). *Herod's Children* [*Die grössere Hoffnung*], tr. Cornelia Schaeffer (1963). *Selected Short Stories and Dialogues,* tr. James C. Alldridge (1968). *Selected Poetry and Prose of Ilse Aichinger,* tr. Allen H. Chappel (1983).

Prizes: Förderungspreis des Oesterreichischen Staatspreises (1952). Preis der Gruppe 47 (1952). Literaturpreis der Freien und Hansestadt Bremen (1954). Immermannpreis der Stadt Duesseldorf (1955). Literaturpreis der Bayerischen Akademie (1961). Ny-ell Sachs-Preis, Dortmund (1971). City of Vienna Literature Prize (1974). Georg Tracke Prize (1979). Petrarca Prize (1982).

Bibliography

Alldridge, J.C., *Ilse Aichinger* (London, 1969). Kleiber, Carine, *Ilse Aichinger: Leben und Werk* (Bern, Frankfurt/Main and New York, 1984). Lindemann, Gisela, *Ilse Aichinger* (München, 1988). Lorenz, Dagmar C.G., *Ilse Aichinger* (New York, 1981). Opel, A., ed., *Anthology of Modern Austrian Literature* (London, 1981). Ungar, Frederick, ed., *Handbook of Austrian Literature* (New York, 1973).

General references: *Cassell's Encyclopedia of World Literature* (New York, 1973). *Columbia Dictio-*

nary of Modern European Literature (New York, 1980). Contemporary Authors, vols. 85–88 (New York, 1980). Encyclopedia of World Literature in the 20th Century, rev. ed. (New York, 1981). The International Who's Who, 1988–1989, 52nd ed. (London, 1988). The Oxford Companion to German Literature, 2nd ed. (New York, 1986). World Authors, 1975–1980, a volume in the Wilson Author Series (New York, 1985).

Reiko Yonogi

Airut

(see: Wilhelmina "Minna" Ulrika [Johnson] Canth)

Aïssé

Born in the Caucasian Mountains; died March 13, 1733, Paris, France
Genre(s): letters
Language(s): French

Born in the Caucasian Mountains, captured by Turkish soldiers as a child, and sold as a slave to the French Marquis de Ferriol, Aïssé found her way to France as a companion to the Marquis. When he was recalled to the East, Ferriol left her with his brother, in whose household she was raised. She received the standard education for a French lady of her day—geography, history, French, and etiquette lessons as well as instruction in the Christian faith. More importantly, however, she was exposed to the company of a number of important figures, including Montesquieu, Lord Bolingbroke, Voltaire, Fontenelle, the Marquise de Villette, and Madame de Duras. The French salon tradition of pure language and subtle analyses was hers from an early age.

Despite her exotic beauty, which Voltaire much admired and which attracted the unwanted attention of the Regent of France, her fame today rests upon her correspondence with Madame Calandrini, a series first published by Voltaire. In many ways, these letters are unique. They are neither the detailed and worldly missives of a Madame de Sévigné, nor are they the love cries of a Madame de Lespinassis. Instead, they are dis-

creet confidences to an old and intimate friend detailing the story of Aïssé's love for the Chevalier d'Aydie, a love both eternal and eternally tormented, a love that produced agonies of religious scruples for the young woman. Unable for some mysterious reason to wed Aydie, despite his urgent requests, Aïssé nevertheless conducted an affair with him for several years. The result of this union was their daughter Célinie, born in 1721.

The couple seems to have been happy, and Célinie, discreetly placed in a convent as Lord Bolingbroke's niece, was often visited by her mother. A crisis of conscience was precipitated by Aïssé's visit to Madame de Calandrini in 1731, when her religious friend repeatedly urged her to repent of her sin and return to God. The letters recording Aïssé's struggles to forsake the chevalier culminate in her early death from respiratory disorders on March 13, 1733. Her chevalier never married. He raised their daughter as his own.

The letters, first published in 1787 with Voltaire's notes, offer a valuable series of genre pictures from the early years of Louis XV's reign. They include character sketches and vivid glimpses of famous salonnières. Historical asides, such as a reference to the Indians' massacre of the French colony in Louisiana, are other sources of interest. In addition, the correspondence delicately unfolds the story of Aïssé's maturation. Written with perfect limpidity and a pliant facility with language, they are the very essence of the epistolary form, achieving a distinctive style by abandoning all pretense to it. The motif of regret, the repeated use of understatement in highly emotional circumstances, and the pervasive sadness of the collection not only justify Voltaire's initially warm reception but also prefigure in many ways the "roman epistolaire de confidence," a form practiced with great success some forty years after Aïssé's death.

Works
Lettres de Mlle Aïssé à Madame Calandrini [The Letters of Mademoiselle Aïssé to Madame Calandrini] (1787).

Bibliography
Arland, Marcel, "Préface," in Lettres de Mlle Aïssé (Paris, 1948). Ferval, Claude, Mademoiselle Aïssé

et son Tendre Chevalier (Paris, 1930). Ravenel, Jules, "Notes," in Lettres de Mlle Aïssé à Madame Calandrini (Paris, 1943). Reid, Joyce, The Concise Oxford Dictionary of French Literature (Oxford, 1986). St. Beuve, Revue des Deux Mondes (January 15, 1846): 1, 191. Wilson, Evangeline, "Aïssé," in Portraits and Backgrounds (New York, 1917), pp. 285–373.

Glenda Wall

Bélla Akhátovna Akhmadúlina

Born 1937, Moscow, the Soviet Union
Genre(s): poetry, translation, prose
Language(s): Russian

One of Soviet Russia's most powerful voices, Akhmadúlina writes poems centered on the chills caused by non-conformity and the fever wrought by an acute awareness of the difficulty of being different in a highly structured society. While sharing much with other contemporary poets such as Voznesenskii, her accent on almost brazen individuality and the inability to fit in is strongly reminiscent of the early Mayakovsky.

Born in 1937, in Moscow, Akhmadúlina began to publish quite early, at the age of eighteen. She then began to attend the Gorki Institute for writers, but was expelled in 1960. Her first book, a collection of poems called Struna (1962; The String) was published during the period of expanded freedom of expression called the "thaw" and was a resounding success. Her next collection of poems, Oznob (1968; The Chill) was published abroad in Frankfurt. One more collection would see publication during the sixties, Uroki muzyki (1969; Music Lessons).

Then in 1977, as though long pent-up, three volumes appeared: Svecha (The Candle), Metel' (The Snowstorm) and Sny o Gruzii (Dreams of Georgia), the last including translations and prose writings. Since then, three more volumes have appeared, Taina (1983; The Secret), Sad (1987; The Garden), and Bella Akhmadúlina (1988) which includes poems from many earlier collections.

While criticized in the official circles for being overly personal and not sufficiently so-

cially instructive, Akhmadúlina actually is quite critical herself—of her surroundings and the people who conform rigidly and unthinkingly to the established behavior. She often describes herself as ill and in need of a sedative to calm the force inside her, as in "The Chill": "Explained the doctor:/—Your illness is simple./ It would be completely harmless,/ except that the frequency of your oscillations/ interferes with the examination—you're invisible." Her substance and condition elude traditional scrutiny so the doctor administers a shock to her system. Then he pronounces her normal at which she is saddened: "I alone knew/ my access to a higher normalcy." Often she is childishly boisterous and disorderly as in "The Boat": "And somewhere, whistling on a pipe/not observing the flowers or their beds/ a strange child runs wild/ and devastates their order."

Akhmadúlina's power resides in her almost unnerving ability to weave between the intensely personal and the clearly drawn constraints of social life. Vivid images erupt from the subliminal threshold only to smash flatly against the staircases, walls and various edifices of the society which surrounds her. The joy of the force of life is what she most highly prizes and is precisely the cause of suspicion and discomfort in those who find themselves near her. She herself is like a flower without a garden to surround her.

As of this writing, Akhmadúlina reads her poetry to large, closely-packed audiences filled with admirers. Acknowledging this, the most recent Soviet collection calls her a famous Russian poetess, but Bélla Akhmadúlina remains a member of the Writers Union only as a translator.

Works

Struna, poetry (1962). Oznob, poetry (1968). Uroki muzyki (1969). Struna (1975). Metel' (1977). Sny o Gruzii, poetry, translations, prose (1977). Svecha (1977). Taina (1983). Sad (1987). Bella Akhmadúlina, poetry (1988).

Translations: Sloneczna dolina, ed. I. Piotrowska, et al. (1964). Struna, tr. V. Daněk (1966). Fever and Other New Poems, tr. G. Dutton and I. Mezhakoff-Koriakin (1968). The New Russian Poets (bilingual), ed. and tr. G. Reavey (1968). Russian Poetry: The

Modern Period, ed. J. Glad and D. Weissbort (1978). *Three Russian Poets*, ed. and tr. E. Feinstein (1979).

Bibliography

Brown, D., *Soviet Russian Literature Since Stalin* (Cambridge: Cambridge University Press, 1978), pp. 116–120. Condee, N., "Akhmadúlina's Poèmy: Poems of Transformation and Origins." *Slavic and East European Journal* 29, 2 (Summer 1985): 176–187. Ketchian, S., "Poetic Creation in Bella Akhmadúlina." *Slavic and East European Journal* 28, 1 (Spring 1984): 42–57. Mustafin, R., "Poisk algoritma: Zametki o poèzii Belly Akhmadulinoi." *Druzhba narodov* (June 6, 1985): 245–252. Novikov, V., "Bol' obnovleniia." *Literaturnoe obozrenie* (Jan. 1, 1985): 50–52. Papernyi, Z., "Pod nazorom prirody." *Oktiabr'* (Oct. 10, 1984): 204–206. Rydel, C., "The Metapoetical World of Bella Akhmadúlina." *Russian Language Triquarterly* (1971): 326–341.

Other references: *O vremia, pogodi...; literaturno-muzykal'naia kompozitsiia*, sound recording, Akhmadúlina reads Tiutchev (Melodiia, 1977).

Chris Tomei

Anna Akhmatova

(a.k.a. Anna Gorenko)

Born June 11, 1889, Odessa, Russia; died March 5, 1966, Domedovo (near Moscow)
Genre(s): poetry
Language(s): Russian

Anna Akhmatova, along with Boris Pasternak, Osip Mandel'shtam, and Marina Tsvetaeva, is widely regarded as one of the leading Russian poets of the twentieth century. Akhmatova, her first husband Nikolai Gumilev, and Mandel'shtam were the major proponents of Acmeism, a reaction in the 1910s and 1920s against the vague mysticism and ethereality of the Symbolist movement. The Acmeists preferred to use simple, classical diction and concrete imagery and to emphasize the immediateness of human situations. Although Akhmatova's later poetry moves away from the emotional restraint of her earlier poems, her writing is always characterized by its economy and control. In addition to poetry, Akhmatova wrote a number of biographical and critical essays on writers and artists, including Modigliani, Blok, Mandel'shtam, and Pushkin.

Akhmatova grew up in a well-to-do family in Tsarskoe Selo, near St. Petersburg. There she met the young poet Nikolai Gumilev, whom she was later to marry. She attended the university at Kiev to study law, but a year later she left to study literature in St. Petersburg. Her marriage to Gumilev in 1910 was a difficult one, in spite of their intellectual kinship; in 1914 Gumilev enlisted in the cavalry, and in 1918 they were divorced. Akhmatova's love poetry from this period often reflects the turbulence of their relationship. Her association with Gumilev, executed as a counterrevolutionary in 1921, and the relatively apolitical nature of her poetry drew the suspicion of the government in the 1920s. Her son Lev Gumilev was arrested several times in the 1930s and 1940s, mainly as a means of censoring Akhmatova; her hardships and suffering during this experience are recounted in the poem *Requiem*. Akhmatova wrote and published patriotic poetry in the 1940s, but her two major late works, *Requiem* (finished in 1940) and *Poem Without a Hero* (begun in the forties and finished in 1962), were not published in the Soviet Union. In 1964 she travelled to Italy to accept the Taormina Prize for Poetry and the following year to Oxford for an honorary D. Litt. The Soviet government had slowly begun to rehabilitate her work during the thaw of the post-Stalin era. The first significant collection of her work without major censorship, *Beg Vremini* (The Course of Time), was published in 1964, and in the following year A. I. Pavlovsky's book-length study appeared. Akhmatova was given the funeral obsequies of the Orthodox church at Komarovo near Leningrad.

Akhmatova's early poems—particularly those in the collections *Evening*, *Rosary*, and *White Flock*—are brief lyrics dealing mainly with the theme of love, usually unrequited or tragic, and use clear, precise images, and a restrained tone. Often a personal object, an architectural detail, or a natural phenomenon will connote the emotional state of the speaker, as in "The Song of the Last Meeting," in which the distraught persona puts her left glove on her right hand. In the longer poem *By the Sea Shore*, published in the magazine *Apollon* in 1915, Akhmatova develops the concept of the double, a theme to which she would return often, most notably in *Poem Without a Hero*. With *Plantain* and *Anno Domini*, Akhmatova begins to deal with broader, more political issues in reaction to the worsening political climate. The persona often laments a lost order and an indefinite future: "All has been plundered, betrayed, sold out,/ The wing of black death has flashed by,/ All has been gnawed away by hungry anxiety." The poet's concern with the public sphere and with her responsibility as poet is further marked by the greater use of allusion. The speaker of "Lot's Wife," for example, describes how the wife turns back to look once more at the familiar sights of home; this desire reflects not only the post-revolutionary nostalgia for the past society but also the artist's fear of having to relinquish the poetry of her beloved concrete images in favor of a more dogmatic, politically "correct" way of writing, and the speaker vows that she will remember and grieve for this tragic act of looking backward. Akhmatova's two masterpieces, *Requiem* and *Poem Without a Hero*, seek to resolve the dilemma of choosing between the public and the private. *Requiem*, first published in Munich in 1963, describes the poet's own grief at the imprisonment of her son. The speaker, in a series of increasingly emotional sections, confronts despair, death, and finally madness, but in the tenth section, "Crucifixion," the subjective perspective gives way to calm, objective description of the solitary grief of the Virgin Mary, who is forbidden to weep. The epilogue returns to the perspective of the grieving mother, but this persona now feels the suffering of all the other women beside her; she vows to commemorate their suffering, asking that if she should be remembered, it should be with a statue outside the unopened prison doors, so that the snow might melt on her bronze eyelids, as the pigeons coo and the ships sail down the Neva. *Poem Without a Hero*, first published in New York in 1960, is a cryptically allusive retrospective of the poet's life and career. Friends and acquaintances from the pre-revolutionary past appear to the speaker/poet, disguised as literary figures. Roles and identities blur, and the experiences of characters in the poem double with those of the poet. Though rich with cultural allusions, the poem nevertheless depicts the inability of the past alone—exemplied in the tragic, self-destructive romanticism of 1913 St. Petersburg—to redeem the present. The poem ends without a definite conclusion, and its final images depict the devastated city of Leningrad in 1943—the embodiment of a Russia which continues to survive, just as the poet survives, by maintaining her sense of suffering and loss.

With the growing number of translations and studies of her works, Akhmatova's importance as a modern writer is becoming increasingly apparent. The disciplined refinement of her earlier lyrics, combined with a probing analysis of the self, place Akhmatova among the best of traditional modern poets; the bolder formal experiments of the middle and late poems, with their synthesis of personal and cultural history, clearly establish her as one of the most original and innovative of all twentieth-century writers.

Works

Vecher [Evening] (1912). *Chyotki* [Rosary] (1914). *Belaya staya* [White Flock] (1917). *Podorozhnik* [Plantain] (1921). *Anno Domini MCMXXI* (1921, 1923). *Iz shesti knig* [From Six Books] (1940). *Izbrannoe* [Selected Poems] (1943). *Stikhotvoreniya 1909–1945* [Poems 1909–1945] (1945). *Izbrannye stikhi* [Selected Poems] (1946). *Stikhotvoreniya* [Poems] (1958). *Stikhotvoreniya 1909–1960* [Poems 1909–1960] (1961). *Requiem* (1963). *Beg vremini* [The Flight of Time] (1965). *Sochineniya* [Works], 2 vols. (1967, 1968). *Tale Without a Hero and Twenty-two Poems by Anna Akhmatova* (1973). *Izbrannoe* [Selected Works] (1974). *Stikhi i Proza* [Poems and Prose] (1976). *Stikhotvoreniia i poemy* [Selected Works] (1976). *Zapiski ob Anne Akhmatovoi* [Letters of Anna Akhmatova], vol. I, 1930–1941 (1976); vol. II, 1952–1962 (1980). *Anna Akhmatova: Stikhi/ Perepiska/Vospominaniia/Ikonografiia* [Anna Akhmatova: Poems/Correspondence/Reminiscences/Iconography] (1977). *Anna Akhmatova o Pushkine* [Anna Akhmatova on Pushkin] (1977). *Stikhvoreniia* [Selected Works] (1977).

Selected translations: *Selected Poems of Anna Akhmatova*, tr. Richard McKane (1969). *Poems of Akhmatova*, tr. Stanley Kunitz with Max Hayward (1974). *Selected Poems*, tr. Walter Arndt, with

Requiem, tr. Robin Kemball, and *Poem Without a Hero*, tr. Carl R. Proffer (1976). *White Flock*, tr. Geoffrey Thurley (1978). *You Will Hear Thunder*, tr. D.M. Thomas (1985).

Bibliography

Dobin, E., *Poeziia Anny Akhmatovoi* [The Poetry of Anna Akhmatova] (1968). Driver, Sam, *Anna Akhmatova* (1972). Eikhenbaum, Boris, *Anna Akhmatova* (1923). Haight, Amanda, *Anna Akhmatova. A Poetic Pilgrimage* (1976). Leiter, Sharon, *Akhmatova's Petersburg* (1983). Mandelstam, Nadezhda, *Hope Against Hope* (1970). Toporov, V.N., *Akhmatova i Blok* [Akhmatova and Blok] (1981). Verheul, Kees, *The Theme of Time in the Poetry of Anna Akhmatova* (1971). Vinogradov, V.V., *Anna Akhmatova. O simbolike—O poezii* (1922).

Stephen Hale

Virgili Alacseal

(see: Caterina Albert i Paradis)

P. Albane

(see: Pauline Caro [Mme. Elme])

Caterina Albert i Paradis

(a.k.a. Virgili Alacseal, Víctor Català)

Born September 11, 1869, L'Escala, Cataluña, Spain; died January 27, 1966, L'Escala, Cataluña, Spain
Genre(s): poetry, drama, novel, short story
Language(s): Spanish, Catalan

A reserved and timid child, greatly influenced by her maternal grandmother's folkstories, Caterina Albert i Paradis was an indifferent student but later mastered French and Italian on her own. Her earliest ambition was to be a doctor, and she also demonstrated great talent in sketching, painting, and sculpting.

Poetry and theatre were her first literary pursuits, and like so many of her generation, she was influenced by Guimerà, Oller, and Maragall, carrying on a life-long correspondence with the latter. Most of her work for theatre was in the minor genre of monologues, and almost all were written around 1897–1899, enjoying a limited success. It was with the publication of "Els cants dels mesos" (a collection of 12 poems) by the revue *Joventut* that Caterina—as Víctor Català—seized the public interest. She borrowed as her pseudonym the name of the protagonist of a novel she was writing but never completed.

Her popularity grew with the publication of her prose works: *Drames rurals* (1902), a collection of short stories, and *Solitud* (1902), her first novel, are two of her most notable works. She continued to write for most of her life but rather sporadically after 1907, producing a second, not very successful novel in 1918, a collection of short stories in 1930 and several works between 1949 and 1951 which revived an enduring interest in her work and its contribution to Catalan.

Admired for her lyricism and irreproachable correctness of form as a poet, she is best known for her short stories and novel about country life. Her version of realism revealed a brooding bitterness and unrelenting despair within the repugnant and even monstrous circumstances that defined the wretched existence of her struggling protagonists. Her prose is remarkable for the strength, expressiveness, and richness of her language and her mastery of style and expression.

Works

Las virgenes, drama (tr. in Castillian of the Italian work *Le vergini*). *Le set princeses*, drama (tr. in Catalan of the Belgian work *Les sept princesses*). *La roja*, drama in Castillian. *L'infanticida*, monologue (1897). *El sete, sant matrimoni* (1897). *El cant dels mesos*, poetry (1898). *Lo llibre nou*, poetry (1898). *La tieta*, monologue (1898). *Verbaglia*, monologue (1898). *Les cartes*, monologue (1899). *Germana pau*, monologue (1899). *Pere Martir*, monologue (1899). *La Vepa*, monologue (1899). "L'anell d'Horub," "Agonia," "Crisantemes," short stories (1901). "La vella," short story (1901). "Idilli eixorc." In *Drames rurals*, short story (1902). *L'alcavota*, "quadro dramatic" (1902–1904). *Marines*, short stories (1903). *Ombrivoles*, short stories (1904). *Solitud*, novel (1904). *Llibre blanc*, poetry (1905). *Caires vius*, short stories (1907). **** (3,000 metres)*, novel (1918; title later changed to *Un film*, 1926). *La Mare Balena*, short stories (1920). *Contrallums*, short stories (1930). *Retablo*, Castillian translations of her own works (1939?). *Mosaic*, collection of autobiographical and literary briefs (1946?). *Eucunys*, literary portraits of illustrious Catalans and others, unpublished (1946). *Vida molta*, short stories (1949). *Jubileu*, short stories (1951).

Bibliography
Lacalle, Angel, *Historia de la literatura española* (Barcelona, 1951). Miracle, Josep, *Caterina Albert i Paradis* (Barcelona, 1978). Terry, Arthur, *A Literary History of Spain. Catalan Literature* (London, 1972).

Carol Stos

Baronesa Alberta

(see: Mercedes Ballesteros)

Anne-Marie Albiach

Born August 9, 1937, Saint-Nazaire, France
Genre(s): poetry, translation
Language(s): French

Albiach began publishing her poetry in London in the late sixties. Along with Michel Coutourier and Claude Royet-Journoud, she founded *Siecle à mains*, a small journal devoted to the presentation of a "poésie critique" or self-reflexive poetry. In addition to her participation in several well-known reviews (including *Change*, *Action Poétique*, *Digraphe*, and *Argile*), Albiach has emerged as a gifted translator of important contemporary poets like Louis Zukofsky and Frank O'Hara.

In her first major collection (*Etat*, 1971) Albiach outlines a "poetics of desire." Insisting that writing is essentially a "physical engagement," she superimposes the language of the body upon the body of language. The body's struggle to liberate itself from the repressive categories of social discourse is dramatized on the irregular surface of Albiach's page. By manipulating typeface, white space, punctuation, and caesura, Albiach forces a relentless confrontation between the abstract and material aspects of language.

Albiach's writing is neither fragmentary nor isolated. One might compare the force of the white spaces which structure "*H II*" *linéaires* (1974) to the integrity of negative shape in drawing. In other words, the dissection of space has a compositional role. The calculated insertion of the blanks allows the poet to maintain several discourses in counterpoint. "*H II*" *linéaires* and Albiach's latest volume *Mezza Voce* (1984) are conceived as referential texts that juxtapose discordant elements of myth, history, and current poetics. Questioning the traditional oppositions that define subject/object, masculine/feminine and prose/poetry, Albiach's texts transport the reader towards the "edges of logic."

All of Anne-Marie Albiach's work is animated by a collective spirit. Drawing on contemporary writers like Jabès, Giroux, Royet-Journoud, and Zukofsky, Albiach emphasizes the irresolvable enigmas of modern consciousness. In this way, she aligns herself with a new generation of poets whose primary concern is not representation but a total reevaluation of the texture of language.

Works
Collections of Poetry: *Flammigère*, poetry (1967). *Etat*, poetry (1971). "*H II*" *linéaires*, poetry (1974). *Césure: le corps* (1975). *Le Double* (1975). *Objet* (1976). *Mezza Voce* (1984).

Translations: *Modern Poetry in Translation* 16 (1963). *TriQuarterly* 35 (1976). *Substance* 23–24 (1979). *The Random House Book of Twentieth-Century French Poetry* (1982).

Bibliography
Action Poétique 74 (Special Albiach Issue) (June, 1978). Astelos, Georges, "Anne-Marie Albiach." *Nouvelle Europe* 11 (1975). Buck, Paul, "New French Writing." *Poetry Information* 15 (Summer, 1976): 50–70. Dobzynski, Charles, "Abstraction, réalisme, baroque." *Europe* 664–664 (1985): 176–182. Hons, Gaspard, "En italique dans le texte: ou le théâtre de l'absence d'Anne-Marie Albiach." *Courrier du centre international d'études poétiques* (Brussels) 165 (1985): 43–45. Sojcher, Jacques, "Anne-Marie Albiach: acte d'engendrement de la parole." *La démarche poétique: Lieux et sens de la poésie contemporaine* (1976). Velay, Serge, "Anne-Marie Albiach: éblouissement alternatif." *Critique* 35, 385–386 (1979): 501–504.

Mary E. Wolf

E.D. Albon

(see: Constanţa Dunca-Şchiau)

Aurora de Albornoz

Born 1926, Asturias, Spain
Genre(s): poetry, Hispanic and Latin American criticism
Language(s): Spanish

Aurora de Albornoz moved with her parents to Puerto Rico at the beginning of the 1940s. She received her bachelor's degree from the University of Puerto Rico and continued her studies at the Sorbonne in Paris and at the University of Salamanca, where she was granted her doctorate. She has been a professor of Spanish and Spanish-American Literature at the University of Puerto Rico and has also taught at the Autonomous University in Madrid. She now lives in Madrid. She has been editor of one journal, *Puerto* (Puerto Rico) and has worked on many others including: *Insula, Revista de Occidente, Sur, Triunfo, El Urogallo,* and *La Torre.* She has taught many series of short courses and lectures dealing with poetry. Her two major fields of work are literary criticism and poetry.

Albornoz has specialized in the study of the poetry of the Generation of '98, especially the work of Antonio Machado. She has dedicated a great part of her critical studies to contemporary poetry, including studies of both Spanish and Spanish-American poetry. She has also published some volumes of her own poetry.

The poetry of Aurora de Albornoz shows the influence of writers such as Juan Ramón Jiménez (of whom she was a student), Marcel Proust, Antonio Machado, Pablo Neruda, and others. Her first collection of poems is *Brazo de Niebla* (1955). The following collection, *Prosas de París,* shows the influence of Proust on Albornoz. In this book, she searches for times past, as did Proust. The collection ends with a reencounter and resurrection of this Proustian time. In 1961 Albornoz published her third collection of poems, *Poemas para alcanzar un segundo.* In this book strong influence of Proust is also noted. Her next collection of poems is *En busca de esos niños en hilera* (1967), which is a series in which the present is intertwined with the past. The predominant theme of this collection, childhood, has been utilized previously. One of her best collections is *Palabras Reunidas (1967–1977).* Here Albornoz leaves behind personal and individual themes to write about universal and collective ones, even though the personal is not totally neglected. The personal "self" and the collective "self" become more intertwined throughout the book. The individual style alternates with the collective style. Her last collection of poems, *Espacio,* was published in 1982.

Aurora de Albornoz not only writes poetry but also studies, analyzes, and writes criticism of twentieth-century Spanish and Spanish-American poetry. Her first critical study deals with the poetry of Antonio Machado. In the book *La presencia de Miguel de Unamuno en Antonio Machado* (1968) Albornoz studies the influence on and relations between the work of Miguel de Unamuno and the poetry of Antonio Machado. Her study is divided into four parts. The first part establishes the personal similarities between Machado and Unamuno. In the second and third parts, Albornoz analyzes the fundamental themes common to both authors. In the fourth part, Albornoz summarizes other points common to the two: similarities in their poetic theory and expression. Albornoz continued to study and analyze the poetry of Machado and others. Her book *Antolojía,* an anthology of the works of José Hierro, includes a detailed critical study of his works. By combining her critical studies of various authors, Albornoz published *Hacia una realidad creada* (n.d.), an interesting collection of critical essays that had previously appeared in literary journals and dealt with the works of Spanish poets from the Generation of '98 to the post-war period. Aurora de Albornoz, in two creative capacities, that of critic and that of poet, presents work filled with life and art. Her poetry is at the same time argumentative and exquisitely written. She reaffirms with her work the obligation on the part of the writer to search for beauty, all the while actively participating to try to solve current social problems. Albornoz tries to achieve, as much in her poetry as in her critical studies, "un lenguaje para crear algo que se aproximase a la obra perfecta, piensa. A esa obra casi perfecta, piensa. A eso que el artista tiene el deber de entregar a los hombres, piensa" ("a language to create something that approximates the perfect work—that almost perfect work—that which the artist has responsibility for delivering to mankind").

Works

Brazo de niebla (1955). Prosas de París (1959). Poemas para alcanzar un segundo (1961). La prehistoria de Antonio Machado (1961). Por la primavera blanca (1962). La obra completa de Antonio Machado (1964). En busca de esos niños en hilera (1967). En el otro costado (1974). Palabras reunidas (1967–1973). Espacio (1982). La presencia de Miguel de Unamuno en Antonio Machado (1968). Nueva antología (Juan Ramón Jiménez)(1972). Antolojía de la obra de José Hierro (1981).

Bibliography

Cano, José Luis, "Aurora de Albornoz: La poesía de José Hierro." Insula 427 (June 1984). Miró, Emilio, "Arte y vida en la poesía de Aurora de Albornoz." Insula 463 (June 1985).

Raquel Aquilu de Murphy

Johanne Sophie Dorothea Albrecht

Born December 1757, Erfurt, Germany; died
    November 16, 1840, Hamburg
Genre(s): poetry, novels, prose
Language(s): German

Sophie Albrecht's most important work was the lyric poetry of her youth and the gothic novels of her later years.

She came from a respectable middle-class family named Baumer; her father was a professor of medicine at the University of Erfurt. He died, however, when his daughter was about fourteen. The next year, at an early age for a girl of her social class, she married Dr. Johann Friedrich Ernst Albrecht, who had been one of her father's students and a boarder in their house since Sophie was ten. Part of Sophie Albrecht's sparsely documented biography has to be pieced together from information about her husband. Young and adventurous, he accepted in 1776 an appointment as personal physician to Count Manteuffel, in distant Reval (now Tallinn, Estonia, USSR). There, Dr. Albrecht, who had already written a small treatise about reproduction in bees, edited a literary anthology that included his wife's first published poems. In 1781 the Albrechts were back in Erfurt, perhaps because of the poor health of Sophie's mother, who died the next year.

During this brief return to her home town, the 25-year-old Sophie Albrecht undertook two projects that were crucial for her future: she published her first book of poetry and plays and had her first experience as an actress, performing successfully in an amateur production of Weisse's Romeo and Juliet. Most actresses of the time, if they had the opportunity to marry someone who was not in the theater, left the stage in an attempt to cast off their outsider status. Sophie Albrecht, already married and middle class, did the opposite. She became a professional actress, joining the important Grossmann troupe in Frankfurt. There she met the rising young poet and playwright Friedrich Schiller and played the role of Luise Miller in the first performance of his Kabale und Liebe. Her background and talent brought increased esteem for her profession.

For a while Albrecht was a member of the prestigious court theater in Dresden. Then, in 1788, she went to a much smaller stage, as a favorite of a Count Bassewitz, at the court of Schwerin. Meanwhile she published another book of poetry and an updated version of a seventeenth-century novel, Aramena. Her collected works appeared, without this novel, in 1791.

Her husband during this time wrote many plays and later several manuals about sexuality that were reprinted well into the nineteenth century. In 1796 he became the director of a new "national theater" in Altona, now a suburb of Hamburg. Although the marriage floundered (the couple divorced in 1796 or 1798) the two Albrechts apparently continued to work together. In September 1796 Sophie Albrecht wrote and delivered the opening address for the new theater, but by 1798 they had both left it.

From then on less and less is known about Albrecht's life. It appears that after her divorce she remarried, though her second husband has not been clearly identified. Some sources claim that after his death she again married J.F.E.

Albrecht. What is certain is that she stopped publishing poetry after the 1791 volumes and wrote prose instead, concentrating on gothic novels, rudimentary mystery stories, and tales set vaguely in the past. But even this writing stopped in 1808. In 1814 Dr. Albrecht died in a typhus epidemic. As the years went on, the once-famous actress was forced to depend increasingly on charity. When she was in her eighties, according to the usually authoritative published catalogue of the Berlin Staatsbibliothek, Sophie Albrecht began publishing cookbooks. In 1840 she died, almost 83 years old. The next year a friend published a small selection of her poems in order to raise money for a gravestone.

Sophie Albrecht wrote exquisite lyric poetry, with love as her most effective theme. She conveyed clear hints of female sexual experience in language that is fresh and simple. Her poetry is never didactic and rarely defensive but often contains a dark note, with contemplation of suicide a recurring motif. Her novels and tales stress darkness and mystery, and she is excellent at evoking atmosphere.

Works

Gedichte und Schauspiele [Poems and Plays] (1781). *Aramena; eine syrische Geschichte, ganz für unsre Zeiten umbearbeitet*, after a novel by Anton Ulrich Duke of Braunschweig, 3 parts (1783–1787). *Gedichte und prosaische Aufsätze*, 2. Th. [Poems and Prose Essays, Part Two] (1785). *Gedichte und prosaische Aufsätze*, 3. Th. [Poems and Prose Essays, Part Three] (1791). *Zwölf Lieder für das Fortepiano* [Twelve Songs for the Piano] (1792; music by Friedrich Strohbach). *Antrittsrede bei Eröffnung des Nationaltheaters in Altona am 1. Sept. 1796* [Welcoming Address at the Opening of the National Theater in Altona on 1 Sept. 1796] (1796). *Legenden* [Legends] (1797; also under the title *Das höfliche Gespenst* [The Polite Ghost] and later, see below, *Ida von Duba*). *Graumännchen, oder die Burg Rabenbuhl; eine Geistergeschichte* [Graumännchen, or Castle Rabenbuhl; a Ghost Story] (1799). *Legenden aus den Zeiten der Wunder und Erscheinungen* [Legends from the Times of Miracles and Apparitions] (1800). [With J.F.E. Albrecht], *Erzählungen* [Tales] (1801). *Der Kummer verschmähter Liebe; als Declamationsstück m. musikalischer Begleitung des Claviers oder Fortepianos bearbeitet* [The Pain of Rejected Love; for Declamation with Musical Accompaniment on the Piano or Fortepiano] (1801). *Ida von Duba, das Mädchen im Walde; eine romantische Geschichte aus den grauenvollen Tagen der Vorwelt* [Ida von Duba, the Girl in the Forest; a Romantic Story from the Dreadful Days of the Past] (1805). *Romantische Dichtungen aus der ältern christlichen Kirche* [Romantic Literature from the Early Christian Church] (1808). *Erfurter Kochbuch für die bürgerliche Küche* [Erfurt Cookbook for the Bourgeois Kitchen] (1839). *Thüringisches Kochbuch für die bürgerliche Küche* [Thuringian Cookbook for the Bourgeois Kitchen] (1839). *Anthologie aus den Poesien von Sophie Albrecht, erwählt und herausgegeben von Fr. Clemens* (1841).

Bibliography

Brinker-Gabler, Gisela, ed., *Deutsche Dichterinnen vom 16. Jahrhundert bis zur Gegenwart. Gedichte und Lebensläufe* (Frankfurt, 1978), pp. 143–148. Eisenberg, Ludwig, *Großes biographisches Lexikon der deutschen Bühne im XIX Jahrhundert* (Leipzig, 1903). Friedrichs, Elisabeth, *Die deutschsprachigen Schriftstellerinnen des 18. und 19. Jahrhunderts. Ein Lexikon* (Stuttgart, 1981), pp. 3–4. Frederiksen, Elke, ed., *Women Writers of Germany, Austria, and Switzerland. An Annotated Bio-Bibliographical Guide* (New York, 1989), pp. 3–4. Pies, Eike, *Prinzipale. Zur Genealogie des deutschsprachigen Berufstheaters vom 17. bis 19. Jahrhundert* (Düsseldorf, 1973), pp. 28–29. Schindel, Carl Wilhelm Otto August von, *Die deutschen Schriftstellerinnen des neunzehnten Jahrhunderts*, vol. 1, pp. 8–9.

Ruth P. Dawson

Jeanne d'Albret

Born 1528, Saint-Germain-en-Laye; died 1572, Paris
Genre(s): poetry, memoirs
Language(s): French

Jeanne d'Albret, daughter of Marguerite de Navarre, received an excellent education. She studied Greek, Latin, Spanish, literature, and the many sciences called "philosophy" in the sixteenth century.

Queen of Navarre and mother of Henri IV, future king of France, she succeeded her father Henri d'Albret and converted to Protestantism in 1555. She was a wise ruler and arranged the marriage of her son to Marguerite of France. She died quite suddenly in Paris, and it was believed she may have been poisoned.

Her poems are often ruined by an excessive amount of affectation and subtleties, as is her *Response de la Royne aux louanges de Du Bellay* (Answer from the Queen to Du Bellay's Praises). Her satirical poems make for easier reading, for instance, the *Chanson sur les amours de Condé et de Mademoiselle de Limeuil* (Song on the Love Affair of Condé and Miss de Limeuil) which gave Jeanne d'Albret the opportunity of criticizing the immorality of the Catholic court of Catherine de Medicis.

Bibliography

Mémoires et poésies de Jeanne d'Albret, ed. Baron de Ruble (Paris, 1893).

Marie-France Hilgar

Isabella Teotochi Albrizzi

Born 1763, Corfu, Greece; died September 27, 1836, Venice
Genre(s): biography, criticism
Language(s): Italian

Isabella Teotochi, best known for her famous literary salon in Venice, was the daughter of count Antonio Teotochi. She first got married to the historian Carlo Antonio Marin, active in the field of Venetian politics and member of the committee of Quarantia but, when their unhappy marriage was annulled, she secretly became the spouse of the inquisitor Giuseppe Albrizzi in 1796.

Her intelligence, affability, and beauty, coupled with a profound knowledge of literature and the arts, contributed to making her one of the most captivating figures of the Venetian intellectual community. Her friends included major authors and artists, such as Antonio Canova, Ugo Foscolo, Lord Byron, who called her "the Venetian Mme. de Staël," Vittorio Alfieri, Ippolito Pindemonte, who celebrated her in his poetry

with the classical name of Temira, and many others.

Legendary were her amorous passions (with Foscolo in particular), but she was also detached enough to describe her admirers in her volume of *Ritratti* (Portraits), which gives us a vivid description of the cultural atmosphere of the time and first-hand impressions of several Italian authors of the eighteenth century. She defended one of Alfieri's tragedies, *Mirra*, against the negative remarks of the abbé Arteaga (*Riposta . . .*), and contributed a painstaking description of Canova's masterpieces in four volumes, blending impressionistic judgments and a solid knowledge of classical art and culture, of which Canova's style intended to be a revival.

Works

Opere di scultura e di plastica di Antonio Canova descritte da Isabella Albrizzi, nata Teotochi [Sculptures and Plastic Works by A.C. Described by I.A. née T.] (1821–1824). *Ritratti scritti da Isabella Teotochi Albrizzi* [Portraits Written by I.T.A.] (1826). *Riposta della Signora Isabella Teotochi Albrizzi all' abate Stefano Areteaga* [Reply of Mrs. I.T.A. to the abbé S.A.] (1826). Vita di Vittoria Colonna [Life of V.C.] (1826).

Bibliography

Malamani, V., *Isabella Teotochi Albrizzi, i suoi amici, il suo tempo* (Torino, 1883). Masi, E., "Il salotto d'Isabella Albrizzi," in *Parrucche e sanculotti nel sec. XVII* (Milano, 1886), pp. 209 ff. Pedrina, M., *Ignoti Amori della "saggia" Isabella* (Ivrea, 1925).

C. G. Antoni

Florenţa Albu

Born 1934, Floroaica-Ialomiţa, Romania
Genre(s): poetry, essay
Language(s): Romanian

A regular contributor to the literary reviews *Viaţa românească* (where she is also editor of the poetry section) and *Scrisul bănăţean*, Florenţa Albu is well known for over ten solid volumes of poetry as well as for her vivid essays and travel notes gathered in *Cîmpia soarelui* (1962; The Plain of the Sun) and *Arborele vieţii* (1971; The Tree of Life).

Albu's first poems speak about Romanian places and people. Her debut volume *Fără popas* (1961; No Rest) is dedicated to the wide plains of the Bărăgan and to the fishermen of the Danube Delta. More abstractly, the hesitation and oscillation between land and sea is at the core of *Fata Morgana* (1966) while the severe and sober rememoration of an irreversible peasant childhood deeply immersed in ritual and war feeds the poet's successive *Măşti de priveghi* (1968; Masks for Death Watch), *Austru* (1971; Auster) and *Elegii* (1973; Elegies).

Serene spiritual meditations on time and love characterize an intermediate creative period manifested in volumes such as *Intrarea în anotimp* (1964; Entrance to Season) and *Himera nisipurilor* (1969; Chimera of the Sands).

Beginning with the volumes *Petrecere cu iarbă* (1973; Party with Grass) humorous accents mingle with the sober tone used in previous work. Fantasy and irony in *Ave, noiemvrie* (1975; Ave, November) as well as the dark tones in *Epitaf* (1973; Epitaph) and *Terase* (1983; Terraces) mark a new, still developing stage in Florenţa Albu's poetic creation.

Works

Fără popas [No Rest] (1961). Cîmpia soarelui [The Plain of the Sun] (1962). Intrarea în anotimp [Entrance to Season] (1964). Constanţa [Constana], children's literature (1964). Fata morgana [Fata Morgana] (1966). Măşti de priveghi [Masks for Death Watch] (1968). Himera nisipurilor [Chimera of the Sands] (1969). Poeme [Poems] (1969). Austru [Auster] (1971). Arborele vieţii [The Tree of Life] (1971). Petrecere cu iarbă [Party with Grass] (1973). Elegii [Elegies] (1973). Ave, noiemvrie [Ave, November] (1975). Umbră arsă [Burned Shadow] (1980). Epitaf [Epitaph] (1983). Terase [Terraces] (1983).

Translations: *Modern Romanian Poetry*, ed. Nicholas Catanoy, tr. A. Bantaş and George Bowering (Oakville, Ottawa, 1977), p. 68. Poems from *Epitaf* (1983) and *Terace* (1983), in *Silent Voices. An Anthology of Contemporary Romanian Women Poets*, tr. Andrea Deletant and Brenda Walker (London; Boston, 1986), pp. 1–8.

Bibliography

Catanoy, Nicholas, "Florenţa Albu." *Umbră arsă* (Bucharest, 1980). Popa, Marian, *Dicţionar de literatură romănă contemporană* (Bucharest, 1977), p. 15. *World Literature Today* 56, 1 (Winter 1982): 99.

Sanda Golopentia

Alcipe

(see: Leonor de Almeida de Portugal)

Josefina Rodríguez Aldecoa

Born 1926, León, Spain
Genre(s): essay, short story, novel
Language(s): Spanish

In her native León, Josefina Aldecoa was one of the founders of the literary magazine *Espadaña*. In 1944 she moved to Madrid where she received her Ph.D. She was married in 1952 to the well-known novelist Ignacio Aldecoa who died prematurely in 1969. She had edited *Revista Española* with him along with other literary figures such as Rafael Sánchez Ferlosio and Alfonso Sastre. She has taught in Spain and the United States.

She has published the essays *El arte del niño* (1960; Children's Art), her doctoral thesis, and *Los niños de la guerra* (1983; The Children of War), a fascinating personal anthology where she reminisces about the writers of the generation of 1950 who, like herself, were children during the Spanish Civil War. Some of those discussed are: Jesús Fernández Santos, Carmen Martín Gaite, Rafael Sánchez Ferlosio, Juan Benet, Ana María Matute, and Josefina's late husband, Ignacio Aldecoa.

Besides a book of short stories, *A ninguna parte* (1961; Towards Nowhere), her first published work of fiction is her novel, *La enredadera* (1984; The Climbing Vine), which was well received by the critics. The novel is divided into four parts, each corresponding to a different season of the year. Time, nevertheless, is not clearly defined; there is approximately one hundred years between the lives of the two protagonists, Clara and Julia. Their characterization works as a counterpoint due to the obvious similarities in their stories. The theme of independence is of feminist interest.

Aldecoa had written two previous novels which were never published: *La casa gris* (The Grey House) and *La casa roja* (The Red House), both about women's issues. Her latest novel, *Porque éramos jóvenes* (1986; Because We Were Young), deals with the "posguerra" generation to which the author herself and her husband belonged. The protagonist, Annick, is a French woman who corresponds with David (a young Spanish man with whom she had had an affair) while she is studying in New York. Each chapter alternates with three different narratives: Annick's letters, Julián's (a friend of David's) point of view in the present, and a series of flashbacks from David's life. The novel lends itself to a feminist interpretation, while it makes a sociopolitical statement about the long years of Franco's regime as well.

In a recent interview, Aldecoa stated that she was encouraged to continue writing novels after the publication success of *La enredadera*; her second novel indicates a promising future for her in this genre.

Works

El arte del niño (1960). A ninguna parte (1961). Los niños de la guerra (1983). La enredadera (1984). Porque éramos jóvenes (1986).

Bibliography

Alborg, Concha, "Porque éramos españoles y Josefina Aldecoa." *Insula*, forthcoming. Sánchez Arnosi, Milagros, "La enredadera, de Josefina R. Aldecoa, más allá maniqueísmo." *Insula* (April 1986): 5, 7.

Concha Alborg

A. Aleksandrov

(see: Nadezhda Durova)

Lidiia Alekseeva

Born 1909, Dvinsk, Russia
Genre(s): poetry
Language(s): Russian

A descendant of a Russian military family originating from French émigrés, Alekseeva followed the path of Russian fugitives from the 1917 revolutionary terror. She left Russia with her family in 1920, eventually settling in Belgrade, Yugoslavia, where she graduated from the Faculty of Philosophy of Belgrade University after specializing in Slavistics. The turmoil of World War II brought her to the United States in 1949, where she generously gave her time to the Slavonic Division of the New York Public Library until her retirement in 1978.

Alekseeva started to write poetry at the age of seven; her publications began to appear since the 1930s in such prestigious émigré literary journals as, among others, *Grani* (Facets), *Vozrozhdenie* (Renaissance), *Novyi Zhurnal* (New Review), *Mosty* (Bridges), *Sovremennik* (The Contemporary). Several volumes of her poetry were published between 1954 and 1980.

A refined master of traditional forms, Alekseeva writes concise, highly original verses. Her lyric landscapes, imbued with pantheistic reverence, include childhood memories of the Crimea—her lost native country—and of those parts of the world where the pilgrimage of an exile has led her. Her poetry, for the most part elegiac and metaphysically conscious of man's permanently vagrant existence, conveys resigned serenity in the face of the divine scope of nature's designs.

Alekseeva has also produced several short stories which appeared in various periodicals and were included in the anthology *Humor and Satire of Post-Revolutionary Russia* (London, 1983).

Alekseeva's idiosyncratic verses, highly valued by her elder fellow-master and relative Anna Akhmatova, represent a lasting contribution to the treasury of Russian poetry.

Works

Lesnoe solntse [Forest Sun], collection of verse (1954). V. puti [On the Road], collection of verse (1959). Prozrachnyi sled [The Transparent Trace], collection of verse (1964). Vremia razluk [Time of Parting], collection of verse (1971). Stikhi [Poems], selected poetry (1980). Slezy bludnogo syna [Tears of the Prodigal Son], translation of the famous epic in verse by Dubrovnik's great seventeenth-century poet, Ivan Gundulich. Humor and Satire of Post-Revolutionary Russia, short stories (1983).

Bibliography

Anstei, Olga, "Prozrachnyi sled" [The Transparent Trace]. *Novyi Zhurnal* 81 (1965). Fessenko, Tatiana, "Dve svetlykh knigi" [Two Lucid Books]. *Russkaia Zhizn'* (Russian Life) (San Francisco, 1973). Fessenko, Tatiana, "Tikhaia muza" [The Quiet Muse]. *Novoe Russkoe Slovo* [New Russian Word], September 14, 1980. Filippov, Boris, "Rossyp' malykh chudes" [Scattering of Small Miracles]. *Mysli na raspashku* [Open Thoughts], Book 2 (Washington, 1982). Nartsissov, Boris, "Dve poetessy zarubezh'a" [Two Poets in Exile]. *Novyi Zhurnal* 150 (1983). Poltoratzky, Nikolai P., ed., *Russian Émigré Literature, A Collection of Articles in Russian with English Résumés* (Pittsburgh, 1972). Anstei, Olga, "Sama po sebe" [On Her Own]. *Novyi Zhurnal* 141 (1980).

Marina Astman

Sibilla Aleramo

(a.k.a. Rina Faccio)

Born 1876, Alessandria, Italy; died 1960, Rome
Genre(s): poetry, novel, diary
Language(s): Italian

Sibilla Aleramo's life and works are inextricably related. Her prose and poetry are autobiographical and confessional attempts at self-affirmation that reflect her always tempestuous existence. Born into a middle-class family, she adored her liberal-minded businessman father for whom she worked as a young girl in the glassworks he managed, first in the progressive atmosphere of Milanese culture, then in the more primitive and backward world of the Italian Marches, where he had moved the family for work-related reasons in 1887. In 1892, young Rina was raped by one of her father's employees and the following year was constrained to marry him. The horror of that loveless marriage and her subsequent escape from it into a life in letters are vividly described in her first, and most successful, novel entitled *Una donna* (A Woman), published in 1906 and greeted with resounding praise in Italy, France, and Germany. Even before the publication of this book, she had begun what was to prove to be a long and complex involvement with the literary and political worlds of male-dominated Italian culture. She wrote for several early feminist journals, including *L'Italia Femminile*, and became involved in socialism. In 1902 she left her husband and young son and moved to Rome where she lived with Giovanni Cena, a well-known poet who encouraged her to write *Una donna* and gave her the pen name she used throughout her career. She would remain with him until 1910; during their eight-year relationship she came to know many important cultural, political, and literary figures including Pirandello, Maria Montessori, and Gorky. Cena was the first of a great number of famous men with whom Aleramo had affairs and to whom she looked for personal and professional fulfillment. From 1910 until 1920, Aleramo was intensely involved in the Florentine literary scene, and had passionate affairs with the poet Vincenzo Cardarelli, the Futurist painter Umberto Boccioni, the writers Giovanni Papini and Giovanni Boine, and, most notably, the poet Dino Campana. Their letters were published by Vallecchi in 1958 and reveal the fevered and highly literary nature of Aleramo's attachments.

Aleramo's second novel, *Il passaggio* (The Passage), was published in 1919; a lyrical autobiography, it met with a generally negative critical response. Her poetry, much of which had already appeared in diverse journals, was collected under the title *Momenti* (Moments) and published in 1921. Having traveled extensively throughout Italy and Europe, in 1925 Aleramo settled in Rome. By then, she had come under the powerful sway of D'Annunzianism and her future works would reflect her unfortunate desire to become the female D'Annunzio. Aleramo did not possess the authentic lyrical talent of her model, and her confessional expressions of thwarted passions and troubled affairs did not reach the level of true art. Several such works were published in the mid- and late twenties, but none attained the success of her first novel. Among them are the failed play *Endimione* (1924); the epistolary novel *Amo, dunque sono* (I Love, Therefore I Am), published in 1927 and recounting her recent affair with Giulio Parise; and *Il frustino* (The Riding Whip), published in 1932 and telling the story of yet another affair with Giovanni Boine. By the advent of Fascism, Aleramo had abandoned her political and social conscience almost entirely in favor of the intimistic art she was practicing. Although she signed Benedetto Croce's antifascist manifesto, for example, she accepted state support from Mussolini's government for many years before his fall in 1943, a decision she would later openly regret. In 1936 she met and became involved with the very young poet Franco Matacotta (1916–1978); he was to be her last great love. Under his influence she became a member of the Communist Party in 1946, and wrote a great deal of ideological verse for various Party publications. She won the Versilia Prize for poetry in 1948 for her collection of verse, *Selva d'amore* (Forest of Love), in which she brought together her poetry written between 1922 and 1942. In the last decade of her life many of her early works were republished; she traveled twice to Russia, and enjoyed the friendship of other Party members. She died in relative poverty in 1960.

Una donna remains Aleramo's masterpiece. Hailed at its appearance as equal in feminist power to Ibsen's *A Doll's House*, it is still a book that speaks eloquently in moving and yet controlled prose to the problem of women's self-definition and fulfillment. Next to it, Aleramo's most important work is her diary, kept over a period of twenty years from 1940 to 1960. It is not great literature, but it is an invaluable source of information on the cultural, political, and literary scenes of modern Italy, and it reveals Aleramo's intelligence and passion. She was a vital presence within Italian letters for most of her long life; her overall worth as a writer is more difficult to assess. By her own admission, she never fully recovered from the traumatic rape and subsequent abandonment of her son, events that shaped her sensibility much more than literary or political influences. Aleramo cannot simply be called an early feminist, nor can she be dismissed as a minor imitator of decadent models such as D'Annunzio. Her work is, instead, an excellent example of the "life as art" and "art as life" mode, an aesthetic attitude that determined much of twentieth-century art, and whose intricacies are still open to exploration.

Works

Una donna [A Woman], prose (1906). *Il passaggio* [The Passage] (1919). *Andando e stando*, prose (1921). *Momenti* [Moments], poetry (1921). *Transfigurazione*, prose (1922). *Endimione*, drama (1924). *Amo, dunque sono* [I Love, Therefore I Am], prose (1927). *Poesie*, poetry (1929). *Gioie d'occasione*, prose (1930). *Il frustino* [The Riding Whip], prose (1932). *Sì alla terra*, poetry (1934). *Orsa minore*, prose (1938). *Dal mio diario*, prose (1945). *Selva d'amore* [Forest of Love], poetry (1947). *Aiutatemi a dire*, poetry (1951). *Gioie d'occasione e altre ancora*, prose (1954). *Luci della mia sera*, poetry (1956). *Lettere: Sibilla Aleramo-Dino Campana*, letters (1958). *Diario di una donna: Inediti 1945/1960*, prose (1978). *Un amore insolito: Diario 1940–1944*, prose (1979).
Translations: *A Woman*, tr. Rosalind Delmar, introd. Richard Drake (1980).

Bibliography

Contorbia, Franco, Lea Melandri, and Alba Morino, eds., *Sibilla Aleramo: Coscienza e scrittura* (Milan, 1986). Falqui, Enrico, *Novecento letterario*, series III (Florence, 1961). Gargiulo, Alfredo, *Letteratura italiana del Novecento* (Florence, 1958). Guerricchio, Rita, *Storia di Sibilla* (Pisa, 1974). Jeffries Miceli, Giovanna, "*Una donna*: Singolare e radicale esperienza di ricerca e liberazione di una coscienza." *Forum Italicum* (Spring 1981): 31–51. Jewell, Keala Jane, "*Un furore d'autocreazione*: Women and Writing in Sibilla Aleramo." *Canadian Journal of Italian Studies* 7 (1984): 148–162. Viano, Maurizio, "Ecce foemina." *Annali d'Italianistica* 4 (1986): 223–241.
General references: *Dizionario degli autori italiani* (Messina-Florence, 1973). *Dizionario della letteratura italiana contemporanea* (Florence, 1973). *I contemporanei* (Milan, 1963). Luti, Giorgio, ed., *Narratori italiani del primo Novecento: La vita, le opere, la critica* (Rome, 1985).

Rebecca West

Alexandra

(see: Alexandra Papadopoulou)

Ellē Alexiou

(a.k.a. Elli Alexiou)

Born 1898 (1893?), Hērakleio, Greece
Genre(s): novel
Language(s): Greek

Ellē (or Elli) Alexiou, the sister of Nikos Kazantzakis' first wife, Galatea, was born in Hērakleio, Crete, just before the turn of the century. She studied French and was employed as a high school French teacher. Because of her political activism, she was forced to leave Greece for Paris in 1945 and later lived in Romania and other East European countries. She was allowed to return to Greece in 1962 after the death of her sister Galatea.

She has written numerous works of fiction as well as criticism, books for children, an anthology of Greek literature of the resistance, and a biography of Nikos Kazantzakis. Many of her books have been translated into Bulgarian, Russian, Romanian, Hungarian, German, and French. She herself has translated works from various European languages into Greek.

Ū' Christianikon Parthenagōgeion (1934; Third Christian Girls School) deals with the life of a young, dedicated, idealistic, and somewhat naively innocent teacher and has a great deal of appeal for all who have attempted to teach.

Louben (1940) takes on the issue of male supremacy by depicting the life of a tyrannical husband and his submissive wife. Alexiou's aim is to arouse her readers (both female and male) against accepting this state of affairs.

Despozousa (1972; Reigning) takes place during the years of the military dictatorship and focuses on social problems of that period. The main characters are young men and women who have left their native Crete (and their traditions and social taboos) and have come to Athens to study. As in her other works, Alexiou's main characters are often spokespersons for her progressive and socialist ideas.

Katereipōmena archontika (1977; Demolished Mansions), written in the twilight of Alexiou's literary career, is comprised of six individual stories, each dealing with an aged female character looking back over her life,

reminiscing and trying to cope with feelings of loneliness, abandonment, and regret.

Works

Sklēroi agōnes gia mikrē zoē [Hard Battles for Short Life], short stories (1931). *Ū' Christianikon Parthenagōgeion* [Third Christian School for Girls], novel (1934). *Louben*, novel (1940). *Anachōrēseis kai metallages* [Departures and Changes], short stories (1962). *Spondē* [Libation], short stories (1964). *Despozousa* [Reigning], novel (1972). *Kai yper tōn zōntōn* [And for the Living], short stories (1972). *Katereipōmena archontika* [Demolished Mansions], short stories (1977). *Anthropoi* [People], short stories.

Bibliography

Langē, Ersē, *Hellēnides pezographoi* (Athens, 1975). Mirasgezē, Maria, *Neoellēnikē Logotechnia*, vol. 2 (Athens, 1982). Savvas, Minas, Review. *World Literature Today* 52, 3 (1978): 502–503.

Helen Dendrinou Kolias

Elli Alexiou

(see: Ellē Alexiou)

Margarita Aliger

Born October 7, 1915, Odessa, Russia
Genre(s): poetry, journalism, translation,
*   reminiscence*
Language(s): Russian

In his 1974 poem, "A Poet at the Market" (Poet na rynke), Evgeny Evtushenko describes meeting Margarita Aliger as she was buying honey for her dangerously ill daughter: "Nobody knew, among the cabbages and salt pork/ that, nearing sixty, forgotten by all,/ the poet was writing as never before." Aliger's has been a life dedicated to poetry and her fellow poets. She adds a distinct female voice to Soviet literature.

Born into a poor Jewish family in Odessa, Aliger grew up with the revolution. At sixteen, already determined to be a poet, she came to Moscow, where she worked as a librarian, published a few verses and eventually was accepted into a night program for writers (the present

Gorky Institute). In the late 1930s Aliger reported on life in Soviet Central Asia in a combination of prose travel sketches and verse diaries.

In a brief autobiography dated from the 1960s-1970s, Aliger speaks of the number of women she knew whose talent had run aground on the rocks of domestic obligation: "I am speaking of everyday life (*byt*), whose power over a woman's fate can be underestimated only by people who are far detached from life and its daily essence" (*Sovietskie pisateli*, p. 22). She lost her only son from meningitis at eighteen months and was left a widow in World War II with two daughters to raise. Aliger found this harsh school of life more effective than all the Writers' Union initiatives "to help authors study life" (p. 23) by sending them on journalistic trips around the USSR and abroad. She remembered World War II as a time "when all our people were together, and knew they were fighting an enemy *outside* that was evil" (Feinstein, p. 142). Working as a correspondent and propagandist throughout the war, Aliger found the subject that enabled her to address her country's wartime experience in the history of the partisan Zoia Kosmode-mianskaia. "Zoia," her narrative poem about the girl's martyrdom, won a national prize in 1943.

After World War II, Aliger travelled and reported (again in both prose and poetry) on her impressions of life abroad, mainly in South American countries; she wrote extensively about Chile before and during the Allende regime. In the 1960s she produced a number of sharp, humorous and yet respectful reminiscences of some of the literary elders who had influenced her life: Maria Chekhova, Samuil Marshak, Kornei Chukovsky, Mikhail Svetlov, and Anna Akhmatova [q.v.], who lived with her off and on in the postwar years.

Aliger once wrote that "Lyrics are my soul, myself as I am." Her poetic voice is modest and kind. Technically much of her verse is marked by prosaic diction, deliberate use of Soviet jargon, stepped lines, and other mildly modernistic devices. The late poems of which Evtushenko spoke so highly were published in *A Quarter of a Century (Chetvert' veka)*, 1981. Along with its companion volume of prose reminiscences and reflections, *A Path Through the Rye (Tropinka po rzhi)*, the collection unites some of Aliger's earlier poems and a new cycle in which she writes "with tenderness and sorrow about the 1930s, the lost [*ushedshikh*] friends" (Khelemsky, p. 22).

Works

Sovetskie pisateli: Avtobiografii, B. Ia. Brainina and A. N. Dmitrieva, comp., vol. 4 (Moscow, 1972), pp. 17–28. Stikhi i proza, 2 vols. (1975). Tropinka vo rzhi, O poezii i poetakh (1980). Chetvert' veka. Kniga liriki (1981).

Bibliography

Feinstein, Elaine, "Poetry and Conscience: Russian Women Poets of the Twentieth Century." *Women Writing and Writing about Women*, ed. Mary Jacobus (New York, 1979), pp. 141–143. Khelemsky, Iakov, "Prodolzhenie monologa." *Znamia* 9 (1982): 227–229. *Kratkaia literaturnaia entsiklopediia*, vol. 1 (Moscow, 1962), cols. 154–155 (D. Bregova). *Modern Encyclopedia of Russian and Soviet Literature*, ed. Harry B. Weber, vol. 1 (Gulf Breeze, Florida, 1977), pp. 118–119. Tarasenkov, A., *Russkie poety XX veka: 1900–1955*, bibliography (Moscow, 1966), pp. 13–14. Turkov, A., "Pered litsom okeana." *Oktiabr'* 2 (1975): 2209–2213.

Mary F. Zirin

Allegro

(see: Poliksena Sergeevna Solovïëva)

Leonor de Almeida de Portugal

(a.k.a. Alcipe, Marquesa de Alorna)

Born 1750, Lisbon, Portugal; died 1839
Genre(s): poetry, translation, paraphrase, letters
Language(s): Portuguese

Following the political execution of her grandmother, the Marquesa de Távora, in 1758, Alcipe, her sister Maria, and her mother, D. Leonor de Almeida, were detained in the convent of Chelas by the Marquês de Pombal. Alcipe spent her youth there, amusing herself in the pursuits of poetry, music, and reading. She was tutored by Filinto, P. Francisco Manuel do Nascimento (b. 1734), until King Jose's death in 1777. It was Filinto who gave her the Arcadian name of "Alcipe." In 1779, she married a German officer and Portuguese citizen, the Count of Oeynhausen, who became Portuguese Ambassador to Vienna in 1780. Alcipe was widowed in 1793, with six children to educate. In response to the Napoleonic invasion, she founded the Society of the Rose and was exiled, nearly destitute, to London in 1804. Returning to Portugal in 1814, she inherited the Marquisate of Alorna and spent her last twenty-five years in the environs of Lisbon, where she founded a literary salon that became the focus for new aesthetic ideas.

Alcipe influenced Portuguese literature to the extent that the contemporary poet Herculano called her "Staël portuguesa." Her philosophical background of Locke, Voltaire, and the Encyclopedia formed the basis for her attack on tyranny and fanaticism as well as her enthusiasm for progress and scientific reason. A pervasive sense of high ideals and love of liberty were constants in her work. With Macedo, Alcipe formed a link between poets of the *Arcadia* and the nineteenth century.

Often inspired by political events, her works contain over 2,000 pages of verse. Her style is an excellent example of the new sensibility, the pre-Romantic mode. Romantic fatalism, exclamation, and violent adjectives tint her vision; she likes solitude and melancholy and has a tendency toward the nocturnal, the funereal, and the pathetic fallacy. However, she still retains and celebrates neo-classical forms, such as epithets and odes and uses a good deal of mythological references and classical allusion. A prime example is her use of Cocytus in a sonnet on the death of her infant son.

Alcipe's range of works is most comprehensive. She wrote sonnets, eclogues, elegies, epithets, and odes, as well as translations or paraphrases of the following: Homer, Horace, Claudian (*De raptu Proserpinae*), Pope (*Essay on Criticism*), Wieland, Thomson (*Seasons*), Goldsmith, Lamartine, and the Psalms. Her letters are expressive and graceful, showing acute social and political understanding at the same time they convey the spontaneity of life. No subject was not fit or interesting material for Alcipe. A long poem of hers on botany described over 100 kinds of scented geraniums. Fireflies, the climate of England, Leibniz, and Robertson's flight in a balloon all fascinated her. Her six-volume masterwork, *Obras Poéticas*, touched on all themes, genres, and structures of literature.

Works

Obras Poéticas (Lisbon, 1844).

Bibliography

Bell, Aubrey F.G., *Portuguese Literature* (1922; rpt. Oxford, 1970). Souto, José Correia Do, *Dicionário Da Literatura Portuguesa* (Porto, 1984).

Rosetta Radtke

María Rosa Alonso

Born 1910, Tacoronte, Canary Islands
Genre(s): essay, novel
Language(s): Spanish

Devoted not only to the literature but also to the art and history of her native Tenerife, María Rosa Alonso is an essayist, a philologist, and a scholar as well as a novelist. Her literary investigations have included the *Poema de Viana*, Manuel Verdugo, Viera y Clavijo, the "endechas" of Guillén Peraza, and other themes of Canarian literature. She was professor of literature at the University of La Laguna from 1942 until her self-exile, for political reasons, in 1954. While in exile in Mérida, Venezuela, she taught Spanish philology at the University of Los Andes. Since her return to Spain in 1968, she has published articles and essays in the important Spanish newspapers as well as works on Spanish linguistics.

Works

En Tenerife, una poetisa. Victorina Bridoux y Mazzini (1835–1862) (1940). San Borondón, signo de Tenerife, essays (1940). Papeles tinerfeños (n.d.?). Comedia de Nuestra Señora de la Candelaria (1943; 2nd ed. 1979). Con la voz del silencio (1945). Otra vez. . . . (1951). El poema de Viana (1952). Pulso del tiempo, essays (1955). Manuel Verdugo y su obra poética (1955). Colón en Canarias y el rigor histórico (1960). Residente en Venezuela (1960).

Bibliography

Artiles, Joaquin, *La Literatura Canaria* (Las Palmas de Gran Canaria, 1979). Galerstein, Carolyn L., ed., *Women Writers of Spain* (New York, 1986).

Rosetta Radtke

Marianne Alopaeus

Born October 9, 1918, Ekenäs, Finland
Genre(s): novel, essay
Language(s): Swedish

Marianne Alopaeus (née Rosenbröijer, 1918) is an author who consistently strives to balance rationality with emotion. The women in her novels are reasoning onlookers; they observe variations of middle-class family life in Finland, and they themselves break out of it or stand aside from it. What drives them to this, or what complicates their relations with society is their need for emotional ties, their love for men, parents, or family. Since her first novel with its symbolical title *Break-up*, Alopaeus has taken up what has since become a standard theme of feminist fiction. She is no typical or ideological feminist, but she gives priority to the need for independence, solitude and an unallied inner life in the women characters in her novels. Conflicts arise when erotic feelings or the straitjacket situations of marriage tie them to a life in which their totality is not accepted.

During her writing life, Marianne Alopaeus has moved from prose fiction to "discussion" novels and autobiographical reflection. Thus it has become more evident that her ideal starting point is closest to liberal bourgeois humanism, inclined to the left, which has its roots in the Scandinavian 1880s. Her liberalism is socially conscious, anti-racist, humanitarian, and includes a strong element of individualism and opposition to both private and public authoritarianism. A glimpse of a Gallic intellect can be seen throughout her work.

The novels *Break-up* (1945), *Dream Without End* (1950), *Outside* (1953), and *Dismissal in August* (1959) are to a great extent about the processes of liberation. *Core of Darkness* (1965), which like *Outside* is set in Paris, takes up contemporary ethical and political questions, woven into two love affairs. *Reflections Round a Boundary* (1971) and *Afflicted by Sweden* (1983) are freely composed extended essays on outlooks on life, containing autobiographical material.

Works

Uppbrott [Break-up] (1945). *Dröm utan slut* [Dream Without End] (1950). *Utanför* [Outside] (1953). *Avsked i augusti* [Farewell in August] (1959). *Mörkrets kärna* [Core of Darkness] (1965). *Betraktelser kring en gräns* [Reflexions on a Boundary] (1971). *Drabbad av Sverige* [Afflicted by Sweden] (1983).

Bibliography

Viljanen, Aulimaija, "Marianne Alopaeus—An Indomitable Searcher." *Books from Finland* 2 (1972).

Thomas Warburton

Marquesa de Alorna

(see: Leonor de Almeida de Portugal)

Concha Alós

Born May 24, 1922, Valencia, Spain
Genre(s): novel, short story
Language(s): Spanish

Concha Alós's father was a waiter. Her grandfather was a shepherd. This working-class background, which is not usually found in writers from Spain, provided Concha Alós with a great deal of thematic and descriptive material for her early novels in particular. Her mother had hopes she would become a dressmaker, but the future novelist's interests and talents took another turn. In 1936 the Spanish Civil War erupted, forcing the family, then located in Castellón, to flee from Franco's troops to a small town in the province of Murcia. Meanwhile, her father had been called to serve in the Republican forces. After the war, he was imprisoned and her mother died. The family, like many others in Spain, suffered humiliating and wrenching hardships during this period. Alós would eventually marry and move to Palma de Mallorca, where she taught school for two years and started writing. All this experience, too, would be incorporated into her fiction. In 1957 she won a prize from the Mallorcan magazine *Lealtad* for her short story "El cerro del telégrafo" (Telegraph Hill). In 1959, her marriage over, she left for Barcelona, where she resides today.

Alós's work needs to be situated within the dual context of women's writing and post-Civil War literature in Spain. The appearance of *Nada* (Nothing) by Carmen Laforet in 1944 seemed to signal a resurgence of fiction by women, among them, Ana María Matute, Carmen Martín Gaite, Dolores Medio, and Elena Quiroga. At the same time the dominant aesthetic during much of the Franco period was social realism. Alós's early novels are good examples, rooted as they are in the miseries and deprivations of the lower classes and of women in particular. Her first novel, *Los enanos* (1962; The Dwarfs), is set in a modest boarding house, filled with desperate characters living on the margins of life and surrounded by hostile, impersonal forces over which they have no control. The "Ship of Fools" framework highlights the importance of circumstance and destiny, while the setting itself, redolent of Balzac's Pension Vauquer and Cela's *colmena* or beehive, suggests a gritty and despairing microcosm of the human condition. Alós's second novel, *Los cien pájaros* (1963; The Hundred Birds), continues in the same vein of social realism, this time focusing on the coming of age of a young, working-class girl. The theme of female liberation from male domination and an oppressive family structure is stated quietly and simply through first-person narration.

The Civil War and its aftermath provided the story line for *El caballo rojo* (1966; The Red Horse) and *La madama* (1969; The Madam). The fear of Franquist reprisals after the war, which is hinted at in the first-named novel, is fully realized in the second. *La madama* is structured round the implicit notion of two interconnecting circles of hell: the literal prison of Clemente, a former Republican soldier, and the dismal domestic struggle for survival of his family. Clemente's hopeless situation and his family's ultimate prostitution point, once again in Alós's fiction, alludes to a bitterly deterministic, even defeatist, perspective of human existence.

In *Las hogueras* (1964; Bonfires), the absence of love provides a dense smoke screen for characters suffocating in their personally created vacuum of boredom, loneliness and incommunication. In this, the novel, though no less representative of social realism than Alós's earlier efforts, does anticipate a new line of development in her work: the exploration of the individual psyche as a bizarre dream world secretly inhabiting ordinary reality. Her first significant step away from the limitations of social realism came in *Rey de gatos* (1972; King of the Cats), a series of nine "narraciones antropófagas," or "cannibal stories," narrated mostly in first person. Here, she deals with such themes as the war between the sexes (also found in *Las hogueras*), jealousy, alienation, and crises of identity but places them within a surreal and hallucinatory cannibalistic universe in which the loss of the human is paramount.

Readers were jolted, however, by the radical departure from conventional linear narration and character construction which her 1975 novel, *Os habla Electra* (Electra Speaks to You), represented. Concentrating on the thematic dichotomy between fertility and the threat of universal destruction, Alós outlined a story of mythic and archetypal proportions, in particular, the struggle between patriarchal and matriarchal modes of being, in which the female—Electra, all Electras—strove to regain a sense of wholeness and personal identity. Weaving deftly between the real and the imaginary, with a series of oneiric images and a fragmented, often deliberately confusing narrative structure, Alós moved fully into experimental fiction with this novel. Unfortunately, she has not been able to sustain the effort. Her next two novels, *Argeo ha muerto, supongo* (1982; Argeo's Died, I Guess), and *El asesino de los sueños* (1986; The Dream Murderer), are an uneasy and sometimes awkward blend of reality and dream, in which she continues to deal with the themes of identity confusion, self-alienation, and the loss of illusion and first love, this time in a more conventional format. The use of a more straightforward casting of fictional events may also reflect a general trend in recent Spanish fiction of the 1980s: the return of storytelling itself. Where this will take Concha Alós is difficult to say. While her work from the 1960s represents a worthy contribution to Spanish neorealism, it is the innovative "deconstructed reality" of *Os habla Electra* that signals a more radical breakthrough in Concha Alós's development as a novelist.

Works

Cuando la luna cambia de color, unpublished ms. (1958). Los enanos (1962). Los cien pájaros (1963). Las hogueras (1964). El caballo rojo (1966). La madama (1969). Rey de gatos (Narraciones antropófagas) (1972). Os habla Electra (1975). Argeo ha muerto, supongo (1982). El asesino de los sueños (1986).

Bibliography

Anales de la Literatura Contemporánea 10 (1985). Arce, C. de, "1964. Concha Alós." Grandeza y servidumbre de 20 Premios Planeta (1972). Ordóñez, E.J., "The Barcelona Group: The Fiction of Alós, Moix and Tusquets." Letras Femeninas 6 (Spring 1980). Ordóñez, E.J., "The Female Quest Pattern in Concha Alós' Os habla Electra." Revista de Estudios Hispánicos 14 (Jan. 1980). Rodríguez, F., Mujer y sociedad: La novelística de Concha Alós (1985). Women Writers of Spain, ed. C.L. Galerstein (1986).

Noël M. Valis

Luisa Isabel Álvarez de Toledo

Born 1936, Estoril, Portugal
Genre(s): novel
Language(s): Spanish

The post-Spanish Civil War novel presents a critical view of contemporary social, economic, and political reality. Luisa Isabel Álvarez de Toledo writes about social injustice and inequality in the rural society of southern Spain.

Luisa Isabel Álvarez de Toledo, the Duchess of Medina Sidonia and three times Grandee of Spain, fully comprehends the profound immorality of Spanish ultraconservatism and the sovereignty of Andalusian landowners. Her narrative has the air of an intense testimonial to circumstances that she had experienced. Because her work is cruelly accusatory, she was condemned by the Supreme Court of Spain for having insulted the Justice Administration in her novel La huelga.

The author's major work, La huelga (1967; The Strike), relates the incidents which take place in Sanlúcar de Barrameda when the peasant farmers strike for higher wages. The events reveal the corruption and villainy of the Andalusian upper class and the misery and hopelessness of the lower class. The exploitation of the workers by the landowners and the inequalities between the rich and the poor are graphically represented in this regional novel of class conflict.

The work of Luisa Isabel Álvarez de Toledo shows traces of a new romanticism in the subject matter of the peasant who awakens to revolution. Álvarez de Toledo presents social criticism in a way that is both artistic and convincing. In her terse prose and fluid dialogues, her characters achieve a depth and dimension uncommon in social novels where the personages generally conform to predictable conduct.

Works

La huelga (1967). La base (1971).

Bibliography

Gil Casado, Pablo, La novela social española (1920–1971) (Barcelona, 1973), pp. 296–298. Jones, Margaret E.W., The Contemporary Spanish Novel, 1939–1975 (Boston, 1985), p. 52.

Joan Cammarata

Verfasserin der Amalia

(see: Marianne Ehrmann)

Núria Amat

Born January 14, 1950, Barcelona, Spain
Genre(s): novel
Language(s): Spanish

Although she has published only two novels to date, Amat is recognized among Spanish feminists as a writer of promise.

Holder of university degrees in Romance philology and library science, Amat is a professor of library science in Barcelona. She also publishes articles in literary journals such as Papeles de Son Armadans and Camp de l'Arpa.

Amat's first book of fiction, Pan de boda (Wedding Bread), is a bride's poetic prophecy of the stifling impact on her of the wedding that is about to take place. It may be viewed as an intensive demythification of the fairy-tale view of marriage. Amat's second novel, longer and more complex, is a playful creation and debunking of a series of myths. *Narciso y Armonía* (Narcissus and Harmony) is the story of a dancer with a mermaid complex who falls in love with a gay male. It initially appears to idealize the concept of androgyny but ultimately subverts the Franco-era integration myth that held that homosexual males could be "cured" by meeting the "right girl." Harmony herself is ultimately integrated into patriarchal society by settling down into a routine marriage and giving up her artistic pretensions.

Although Amat's creative work is still quite limited, it is noteworthy for her mastery of style, her incorporation of feminist concerns, and, particularly in the second novel, her humor.

Works
Pan de boda (1979). Narciso y Armonía (1982).

Bibliography
Zatlin, Phyllis, "Women Novelists in Democratic Spain: Freedom to Express the Female Perspective." *Anales de la Literatura Española Contemporánea* 12 (1987): 29–44.

Phyllis Zatlin

Amparo Amorós

Born c. late 1940s, Valencia, Spain
Genre(s): poetry
Language(s): Spanish

Amparo Amorós received her degree in Hispanic Philology from the Universidad Complutense of Madrid. Currently she is a professor of language and literature at the Instituto Calderón de la Barca of Madrid. She contributes regularly to a variety of Spanish publications, among them *Cuadernos Hispanoamericanos*, *Insula*, *Los Cuadernos del Norte*, *Nueva Estafeta* and *El País*. She has lectured and given poetry readings in Spain, France, Latin America, and the United States.

Amorós' collection of poems, *Ludia*, received an Honorable Mention in the Premio Adonais in 1982. The title of this book is an invented woman's name, which personifies the poetic word. *Ludia* is divided into four parts, titled *Gestos* (Gestures), *Visiones* (Visions), *Exilios* (Exiles) and *Juegos* (Games), which together give Amorós' lyric expression a touch of sensuality. The theme of this book is the game of contemplation, and Amorós makes the reader participate in it. Amorós herself has said that she attempts to create in the reader (who would like an accomplice) a profound and intimate emotion that has nothing to do with superficial sentiment.

On the whole, the poetry of Amparo Amorós is distinguished by a great intimist equilibrium. The poem is intuited; it is an intellectual adventure, experience, and biography. Amorós creates a poetic language that joins the existential with the imagined and thereby attains the essence of the word that for the poet is revelation and destiny.

Works
Ludia (1983). Al rumor de la luz [Murmurs of the Light] (1985). La honda travesía del águila [The Deep Journey of the Eagle] (1986).

Bibliography
Cuadernos para investigación de la Literatura Hispánica, no. 7 (Madrid, 1986), pp. 271–276. Las diosas blancas. Antología de la joven poesía española escrita por mujeres (Madrid, 1985), pp. 27–38. Panorama antológico de poetisas españolas, siglos XV al XX (Madrid, 1987), pp. 309–314.

Carlota Caulfield

Loula Anagnostakē

(see: Loula Anagnostaki)

Loula Anagnostaki

(a.k.a. Loula Anagnostakē)

Born c. 1935–1940, Thessalonikē, Greece
Genre(s): drama
Language(s): Greek

Loula Anagnostaki (or Anagnostakē) belongs to the new generation of modern Greek playwrights who made a break with the past and present characters and situations that are not particularly Greek. In fact, her characters have no country, for they dwell in an *absurd* world in which they are not at home. Anagnostaki is not concerned about theatrical conventions of the past, such as logical development of the plot with a beginning, a middle, and an end, defined setting, interaction between the characters on stage, or clearly stated relationships. Her plays move in unexpected ways toward unexpected finishes, and the audience is put in the position of having to make sense of what is presented. In Anagnostaki's post-modern world, nothing is logical, and time is irrelevant; characters take on "European" dimensions (the influences of Beckett, Sartre, Pinter, and Brecht are obvious); and the play, rather than moving toward a resolution, is a depiction of irresolution, for nothing is resolved, and individuals are not closer to any type of recognition at the end than they were at the beginning. But all is not for nought, for Anagnostaki puts on stage our individual alienation, confusion, and lack of control over our lives, as well as our selfishness and outright meanness, expressed in petty ways that are nevertheless universal. The characters on stage may not relate to each other, but they depict the need to relate, to encounter "the other" in order to reduce the oppressive isolation that envelops them. Thus they are Anagnostaki's version of today's Everyman (and Everywoman).

Her first play, *Dianyktereusē* (Overnight Stop), deals with the different fears of two people of different generations (and thus their lack of understanding of each other). In *Polē* (The City) Elizabeth and Kimon entice an older man, a photographer, to break out of his isolation, but he is left more lonely at the end than he was at the beginning, for they were only playing with his emotions. In *Parelasē* (Parade) two children, Aris and Zoē, act as reflections of what is happening outside their drab room where "leaders" are savagely manipulating gullible crowds.

All of the above are one-act plays, first performed in 1965 and published in 1974 under the general title *Polē* (The City). The *polē* is a modern version of the classical word *polis*, but in Anagnostaki's plays this is what her characters lack, a place they can call their own, a home. This theme is elaborated further in her subsequent works. In *Ē Synanastrophē* (Social Encounter—

first performed in 1967), the setting is a place where people gather to make each other miserable. In *Antonio ē to mēnyma* (Antonio or the Message—first performed in 1972), the setting is misty, like the characters, a house that does not appear to belong to anyone in particular, an undefined place where people encounter each other in ways that bespeak lack of communication, despite the long speeches, and lack of relationships, despite the attempts to establish connections. In fact, in this play that takes place in a house, and during which we see a total of twenty-four people come on stage, there are no blood relationships. The place is just a temporary abode or meeting room for people on their way to another temporary abode or meeting room, people forever on the go, not knowing where they belong or where they want to be.

In Anagnostaki's *Nikē* (Victory—first performed in 1978), one place is replaced by another as members of a family, having left their village in northern Greece and later their home in Piraeus, attempt to improve their situation in a city somewhere in Germany. The mother does not feel at home in her new surroundings and wants to go back. Her daughter, however, tries to relate to the world around her and encourages her brother to marry a German girl, but, before the play is over, he is killed by a "friend." The search for a new home makes people aware of their lack of home and of the fact that they are aliens in more ways than one.

Anagnostaki's works have been performed by Karolos Koun's Art Theater and by the National Theater of Greece. They have also been performed in France, England, Italy, Poland, and Cyprus and have been presented on the BBC, RAI, and Cypriot television.

Works

"Dianyktereusē" [Overnight Stop], "Ē Polē" [The City], and "Parelasē" [Parade], published under the general title *Ē Polē* (1974; "Parelasē" [Parade] also published in *Theatro* [1965], pp. 225–232). *Ē Synanastrophē* [Social Encounter]. *Antonio ē to menyma* [Antonio or the Message] (1971, 1980). *Ē Nikē* [The Victory]. *Ē Kassetta* [The Cassette].
Translations: "The Town," tr. Aliki Halls. *The Chicago Review* 21, 2 (1969).

Bibliography

Bulletin analytique de bibliographie hellènique XXXII (Athens, 1971). Doulis, Thomas, "Loula Anagnostaki and the New Theater of Greece." *The Chicago Review* 21, 2 (1969): 83–87. Halls, Aliki, *Greek Modern Theater: Roots and Blossoms*. Ph.D. diss., Binghamton, N.Y., 1978. Mirasgezē, Maria, *Neoellēnikē Logotechnia*, vol. 2 (Athens, 1982).

Helen Dendrinou Kolias

Anatolitissa (Woman from the Orient)

(see: Alexandra Papadopoulou)

Vita Andersen

Born October 29, 1944, Copenhagen, Denmark
Genre(s): poetry, short story, drama
Language(s): Danish

Whether in prose, poetry, or drama, Andersen's genre is "women's literature" insofar as she expresses the perspectives of women. However, since her protagonists are all downtrodden and depressed, unable to break out of their victimization, it is debatable whether her work can be called "feminist."

Before Andersen's breakthrough poetry collection *Tryghedsnarkomaner* (1977; Security Addicts) was published, she was a contributor to several Danish periodicals, including *Fælleden*, *Hvedekorn* and *Gyldendals Lyrikårbog*. *Tryghedsnarkomaner* became a bestseller in Denmark, and was followed by a short-story collection, *Hold kæft og vær smuk* (1978; Shut Up and Be Pretty). She debuted as a playwright with *Elsk mig* (1980; Love Me) at the Bristol Theater in Copenhagen and then became playwright-in-residence for two years at the Århus Theater, Århus, Denmark (1980–1982). Designated "writer of the year" in 1978 by the Swedish newspaper *Expressen*, Andersen has also been the recipient of the Danish book trade's Golden Laurel (1979) and the Danish Critics' Prize (1987).

Whether written in blank verse, as in *Tryghedsnarkomaner*, or prose, as in *Hold Kæft og vær smuk*, Andersen's monologues express her female characters' misery in flat, seemingly affectless masterpieces of understatement. Security addicts that these women are, totally dependent on men for any scrap of self-worth they can get, they feel they have no choice but to "shut up and be pretty." Their striving toward some abstract ideal of physical perfection and their consequent anxiety about failing to achieve it prevents them from expressing their true selves to their lovers, paradoxically making love impossible. The men in Andersen's works are cold and sometimes brutal, but they are tolerated for lack of any other perceived choice.

In *Elsk mig*, her first play, Andersen brings two monologues into a dialogue through five brief "images" or acts. May and Tom Frank are observed in the first "image" as immature adolescents. In the succeeding scenes, they meet, fall in love, move in together, learn to hate each other, and finally regress back to the emotional states of the first image.

Andersen has also produced two more poetry collections, *Næste kærlighed, eller Laila og de andre* (1978; Next Love, or Laila and the Others) and *Det er bare ærgerligt* (1981; That is Just Annoying); another play, *Kannibalerne* (1982; The Cannibals) and, most recently, a novel, *Hva'for en hand vil du ha* (1987; Which Hand Will You Have?). She is among the youngest of a long line of Danish feminist naturalists going back to the nineteenth century who have employed the sensitivity assigned to the women's role by the patriarchy to expose and criticize the brutality of that same patriarchy. Her works have struck a responsive chord with her sister Danes, as is attested by her popularity in Denmark. Very little of her output is available to the English-speaking world, however, and her fame remains confined to Scandinavia, where she is widely translated.

Works

Tryghedsnarkomaner [Security Addicts] (1977). *Hold kæft og vær smuk* [Shut Up and Be Pretty] (1978). *Næste kærlighed eller Laila og de andre* [Next Love, or Laila and the Others] (1978). *Elsk mig* [Love Me] (1980). *Det er bare ærgerligt* [That Is Just Annoying] (1981). *Kannibalerne* [The Cannibals] (1982). *Hva'for en hand vil du ha* [Which Hand Will You Have?] (1987).

Translations: "To You Gudrun Brun," "Good Breasts are Necessary," "The Wound Eater," "The Beautiful Room," tr. Jannick Storm and Linda Lappin. *Modern Poetry in Translation* 33 (Spring, 1978): 7–9.

Bibliography

Schack, May, "Kvinderollens manglede psykiske rummelighed—om rolle, identitet og narcissisme i Vita Andersens forfatterskab." *Kritik* 60 (1982): 24–39.

Kristine Anderson

André Léo

(a.k.a. Victoire-Léodile Béra, Mme Grégoire de Champseix)

Born August 18, 1824, Lusignan (Vienne), France; died 1900, Paris
Genre(s): essay, novel, polemic
Language(s): French

Born to a retired landowning French naval officer and his third wife, Léodile Béra grew up in the Orleanais countryside. In late 1851 or early 1852 she married Grégoire Champseix, a disciple and lieutenant of Pierre Leroux who had relocated in Lausanne, Switzerland, in the wake of the repression following the revolution of 1848. In 1853 twin sons, André and Léo, were born; according to one account, the couple also had a daughter. The family returned to Paris from Switzerland following the amnesty of 1860 and quickly became active in political causes. Champseix died in late 1863 and his widow began to publish under a pseudonym composed of the names of her twin sons. A number of her novels concerning the problem of marriage for French women appeared in *Le Siècle* in serial form. In 1867 she became very active in debating the problem of women's employment, and in 1868 she founded the *Société pour la Revendication du Droit de la Femme* (Society for the Pursuit of Woman's Right[s]), which merged in 1881 with a second group established in 1870 by Maria Deraismes. Throughout the late 1860s her Parisian residence served as a gathering point for radicals and women's movement figures from Europe and North America.

During the Prussian siege of Paris and the Commune of 1871, André Léo became active as a public speaker and political journalist of repute. In the newspaper *La Sociale*, she repeatedly called the Communards to account for overlooking women's potential contributions to the revolutionary effort. In hiding for two months following the defeat of the Commune, she finally escaped to Switzerland. There she became the associate and companion of Benoît Malon, who subsequently became a major leader of non-Marxian socialism in France. Their union in exile (Switzerland and Italy) lasted six years, but was marred by repeated infidelities on his part. Little is currently known of André Léo's later life, following her return to France in 1880, though she did continue to publish fiction and tracts until the end of the century. The only scholarly study to date is that of Fernanda Gastaldello, which contains many authenticated biographical details, as well as a very extensive bibliography of André Léo's works and a lengthy study of her journalistic and literary contributions.

Works

Un Mariage scandaleux (1862; new ed. 1883). *Une vieille fille; articles de divers journaux sur un mariage scandaleux* (1864). *Observations d'une mère de famille à M. Duruy* (1865). *Les Deux filles de M. Plichon* (1865). *Un Divorce* (1866). *La Femme et les moeurs. Liberté ou monarchie* (1869). *Aline-Ali* (1869). *Légendes corréziennes* (1870). *La Guerre sociale; discours prononcé au Congrès de la Paix à Lausanne, 1871* (1871). *Marianne* (1877). *L'Epousée du bandit* (1880). *L'Enfant des Rudière* (1881). *La Justice des choses* (1891). *La Famille Audroit et l'éducation nouvelle* (1899). Unpublished manuscript memoirs. Descaves collection, International Institute for Social History, Amsterdam. Dossier, Archives de la Prefecture de Police B/A 1008.
Translations: "Woman and morals," partially tr. in *The Agitator* (Chicago) by Kate Newell Doggett (1869). *De Vrouw en de zeden. I. Vrijheid of overheersching? II. De fysieke minderheid der vrouw. III. Verstandelijke minderheid.*

Bibliography

André Léo, une journaliste de la Commune, *Le Lerot reveur* 44 (March 1987). Arnaud, Angélique, "Madame André Léo." *L'Avenir des femmes* (Oct. 15, 1871). *Dictionnaire biographique du Mouvement ouvrier français*, ed. J. Maitron, vol. 2, pt. 5, p. 52. *Dictionnaire de la Commune*, ed. B. Noel (1971), p. 235. Gastaldello, F., "André Léo: Quel Socialisme?" Laureate Thesis, Modern Foreign Language and Literature, University of Padua, Italy, 1978–1979. Lejeune, P., "Une grande journaliste communarde: Léodile Champseix, dite André Léo." *Des Femmes en mouvements* 2 (Feb. 1978): 58–59. Perrier, A., "Grégoire Champseix et André Léo." *Actualité de l'histoire* 30 (1960): 38–39. Schulkind, E., "Socialist Women in the 1871 Paris Commune." *Past and Present* 106 (Feb. 1985): 124–163. Thomas, E., *Les Pétroleuses* (1963; tr. as *The Woman Incendiaries*, 1966).

Karen Offen

Elisabeth Aloysia Andreae

(a.k.a. Illa Andreae)

Born August 8, 1902, Wolbeck/Münsterland, Germany
Genre(s): short story, novel, drama, nonfiction, children's literature
Language(s): German

Andreae was the daughter of a medical doctor and studied history at the universities in Münster and Munich. In 1928 she married a professor of history, Wilhelm Andreae, in Graz, Austria. Today she lives in Gießen north of Frankfurt.

Works

"Der sterbende Kurfürst" [The Dying Duke Electorate], short story (1942; rpt. 1952 as "Das versunkene Reich" [The Lost Empire]). *Helleninkloh*, novel (1942; rpt. 1943 as *Der Griechische Traum* [The Greek Dream]). *Die Väter* [The Fathers], novel (1944). *Elisabeth Telgenbrook*, novel (1947). *Das Geheimnis der Unruh*, *Geschichte eines westfälischen Geschlechts* [The Secret of the Unruh, History of a Westphalian Family] (1947). "Das Friedensmahl" [The Peace Dinner], short story (1948). *Die Hamerincks* [The Hamerinck Family], novel (1950; rpt. 1959 as *Glück und Verhängnis der Hamerincks* [Fortune and Fate of the Hamerinck Family]). *Hille von Hamerinck*, novel (1951). *Das goldene Haus* [The Golden House], short story (1951). *Wo aber Gefahr ist* [Where There is Danger], novel (1951). *Mein ist die Rache* [Revenge Is Mine], novel (1953). *Unstetig und flüchtig* [Always on the Run], novel (1954).

Eva und Elisabeth [Eva and Elisabeth], novel (1955). *Nelly*, children's book (1961; rpt. 1969). *Die Kunst der guten Lebensart, Spielregeln im Umgang mit Menschen* [The Art of Good Manners, Rules in the Daily Contact with People], nonfiction (1961). *Alle Schnäpse der Welt* [All Hard Liquors of the World], nonfiction (1975). *Tüsken Angel un Deergaoren*, novel in low German dialect (1979; 2nd ed. 1980).

Bibliography

Horn, A., "Illa Andreae, eine westfälische Dichterin." *Neues Abendland* 5 (1950). Schreckenberg, W., "Illa Andreae." *Stimmen der Zeit* 150 (1952): 186–194. Review. *Der Romanführer*, vol. III (Stuttgart, 1952), pp. 3–5.

Albrecht Classen

Illa Andreae

(see: Elisabeth Aloysia Andreae)

Lou Andreas-Salomé

Born February 12, 1861, St. Petersburg, Russia; died February 5, 1937, Göttingen, Germany
Genre(s): novel, story, drama, memoirs, essay, criticism
Language(s): German

Lou Salomé was born in St. Petersburg, Russia, but spent most of her adult life in Germany. She is best remembered for her friendships with the great men of her day. Friedrich Nietzsche proposed marriage to her in 1882, which she rejected. Lou later married an Orientalist, F.C. Andreas. In 1897 she met the great poet Rainer Maria Rilke, for whom she was to become a major formative influence and with whom she had an enduring love affair. In 1911 she became associated with the Vienna circle of psychoanalysts and was a friend and disciple of Sigmund Freud. During her life Andreas-Salomé produced a number of fictional works and scholarly essays.

She was born Louise von Salomé in a distinguished German-speaking family that moved in the highest St. Petersburg society. The youngest of six children and the only girl, "Lyolya" had a studious and introspective adolescence. At the age of seventeen she began confirmation studies with a liberal Protestant pastor, H. Gillot, which marked the first in a series of attachments to advanced male thinkers. An emotional crisis in her relationship with Gillot precipitated her departure to Zurich, accompanied by her mother, in 1880. An illness incurred there required a further change of climate, which brought her to Rome in 1882. It was in Rome that, through acquaintances, she met Friedrich Nietzsche. This relationship lasted only eight months; it was complicated by Lou's rejection of his marriage proposal and by the hatred exhibited towards her by Nietzsche's sister Elizabeth.

One of the most inexplicable events in Lou Salomé's life is her startling marriage to the scholar F.C. Andreas in 1887. He seemed to have virtually dropped out of the sky into her life. A few years prior to the marriage to Andreas, Lou Salomé had written her first work of fiction, *Struggling for God* (1885), which featured a Faustian hero in search of faith after losing his belief in God. Her scholarly book entitled *Henrik Ibsen's Female Characters* (1892) was well received critically. Her book on Nietzsche appeared in 1894, and provoked mixed reactions among friends and critics. Her next two novels, *Ruth* (1895) and *From Alien Soul* (1896), are stylistically and thematically similar to her first novel, evoking a "torrid dream world of dire sexuality" (Angela Livingstone).

In 1897 Lou Andreas-Salomé was introduced to Rainer Maria Rilke. Around or after this period she published two more novels, *Fenitschka* (1896), *An Aberration* (1898), and a collection of stories, *Children of Man* (1899). Between this time and her meeting with Freud she published another novel, *Ma* (1901), and a collection of stories, *The Land Between* (1902).

After meeting Freud in September 1911, in Weimar, Lou Andreas-Salomé devoted the rest of her life to the study and practice of psychoanalysis. Up to 1920 she wrote numerous articles on psychoanalytical subjects. She also continued to publish fiction, including *The House* (1919), *The Hour Without God* (1922), a play entitled *The Devil and His Grandmother* (1922), and the novel *Rodinka* (1923). During the last six years of her life she wrote her three final works: *Rainer Maria Rilke* (1928), a long rambling letter entitled *My Thanks to Freud* (1931), and her autobiography *Looking Back*, which was published posthumously.

Unfortunately, Lou Andreas-Salomé's literary gift was not great. She herself did not attribute much importance to her works of fiction. Her novels and stories are characterized by a diffuseness, or, as Angela Livingstone puts it, "an excess of the heavily decorative, a certain amount of rather humorless idiosyncracy . . . and a habit of hinting at things of indescribable mystery and unfathomable significance." Most characteristic is her strict concentration upon inner psychological events at the expense of dialogue, action, and description. One of her most interesting works is the play *The Devil and his Grandmother*, in which are grotesquely juxtaposed psychoanalytical and religious elements.

Noteworthy are some of her products of sustained scholarship—Andreas-Salomé's work of 1894 was the first serious book on Nietzsche ever published. Freud also had a great deal of praise for her psychoanalytical articles and for her skills as a practicing psychoanalyst. She was for him a "synthesizer" of his theories, albeit in an intuitive and not a scientific way.

Works

[Henri Lou, pseud.], *Im Kampf um Gott* (1885). *Henrik Ibsens Frau-Gestalten* (1892). *Friedrich Nietzsche in seinen Werken* Wien (1894). *Ruth* (1895, 1897). *Fenitshcka. Eine Ausschweifung* (1898, 1983). *Menschenkinder* (1899). *Aus fremder Seele* (1901). *Ma* (1901). *Im Zwischenland* (1902). *Die Erotik* (1910). *Drei Briefe an einen Knaben* (1917). *Das Haus* (1919, 1927). *Die Stunde ohne Gott und andere Kindergeschichten* (1921). *Der Teufel und seine Grossmutter* (1922). *Rodinka* (1923). *Rainer Maria Rilke* (1928). *Mein Dank an Freud: Offener Brief an Professor Freud zu seinem 75 Geburtstag* (1931). *Lebensruckblick. Grundriss einiger Lebenserinnerungen*, ed. E. Pfeiffer (1951, 1968). *Rainer Maria Rilke—Lou Andreas-Salomé. Briefwechsel*, ed. E. Pfeiffer (1952). *In der Schule bei Freud*, ed. E. Pfeiffer (1958). *Sigmund Freud—Lou Andreas-Salomé. Briefwechsel*, ed. E. Pfeiffer (1966). *Friedrich Nietzsche, Paul Rée, Lou von Salomé: Die Dokumente ihrer Begegnung*, ed. E. Pfeiffer (1970). For a list of articles by Lou Andreas-

Salomé see Angela Livingstone, *Salomé: Her Life and Work*, 1984, pp. 246–248.

Translations: *The Freud Journal of Lou Andreas-Salomé*, tr. Stanley Leavy (1964). *Sigmund Freud and Lou Andreas-Salomé, Letters*, tr. by W. and E. Robson Scott (1972). *Ibsen's Heroines*, ed., tr., and introd. by Siegfried Mandel (1985).

Bibliography

Bab, Hans Jürgen, *Lou Andreas-Salomé, Dichtung und Persönlichkeit* (unpublished doctoral diss.). Binion, Rudolph, *Frau Lou, Nietzsche's Wayward Disciple* (Princeton, 1968). Koepcke, Cordula, *Lou Andreas-Salomé, Ein Eigenwilliger Lebensweg.* "Ihre Begegnung mit Nietzsche, Rilke, und Freud." (Freiburg i. Br., 1982). Livingstone, Angela, *Salomé: Her Life and Work* (Mount Kisco, New York, 1984). Mackey, Ilona Schmidt, *Lou Salomé, Inspiratrice at interprète de Nietzsche, Rilke, et Freud* (Paris, 1968). Muller-Loreck, Leonie, *Die erzahlende Dichtung Lou Andreas-Salomés: Ihr Zusammenhang mit der Literatur um 1900*. Doctoral diss., 1972. Peters, H.F., *My Sister, My Spouse* (London, 1963). Podach, Erich F., *Friedrich Nietzsche und Lou Salomé: Ihre Begegnung 1882* (Zurich and Leipzig, 1938). Schmidt-Bergmann, Hansgeorg, ed., *Lou Andreas-Salomé* (Karlsruhe, 1986).

Laura Jo Turner

Isabella Andreini

Born 1562, Padua, Italy; died June 10, 1604, Lyons, France
Genre(s): poetry, drama, essay
Language(s): Italian

Born into a rich and prestigious Venetian family, Isabella Canali left home to take up the itinerant life of an actress in a commedia dell'arte company, the "Gelosi." At the age of sixteen, upon the triumphant return of the Gelosi from a tour of France, she married the company's actor-manager, Francesco Andreini. She rapidly became one of Italy's most admired women, not only for her beauty and dramatic talent but also for her intellect, erudition, and writings. Her fame as an actress was almost legendary, her praises sung by poets, fellow actors, noblemen, and royalty. The Gelosi company derived its strength from the talent and dedication of Francesco and Isabella Andreini. Her death in 1604 marked the beginning of the company's steady decline. Under the name of Accesa, she was initiated into the Accademia degli Intenti in Pavia, and given the symbol of the torch and the motto "elevat ardor."

Throughout her acting career, she played the role of the "innamorata," the beloved. Among the stock characters of the commedia, the lovers never had standard names as did Arlecchino, Brighella, or Pantalone. Nevertheless, her use of her own name in most plays made it one of the favorite names for the role. Many of the plays introduced into the repertory of the Gelosi featured her name in the title because of her power to draw an audience: *La Fortunata Isabella* (Lucky Isabella), *Le Burle di Isabella* (Isabella's Pranks), *La Gelosa Isabella* (Jealous Isabella), and *Isabella astrologa* (Isabella the Astrologer). The company performed the piece *La Pazia di Isabella* (Isabella's Madness) for the elaborate marriage festivities of Ferdinando de' Medici and Christine of Lorraine in Florence, May 13, 1589.

Andreini figured prominently in the verses of contemporary poets, often with the theme that the beauty of her spirit makes her virtually immortal. In her husband's *Bravure del Capitan Spavento* (The Exploits of Capitan Spavento), he declared to himself: "Padrone, la vostra amata donna si può dir viva è non morta se viva e colei che gloriosa rimane al mondo per mezzo della virtù." (Master, one may call your beloved alive and not dead if she is alive who remains glorious in the world through her virtue.) Torquato Tasso, G. Chiabrera, and G.B. Marino all sang her praises in their poetry. In France, Isaac du Ryer declared in his collection of poems *Temps perdu* (Times Gone By): "Je ne crois point qu'Isabelle / soit une femme mortelle:/ c'est plutôt quelqu'un des Dieux/ qui s'est déguise en femme, / a fin de nous ravir l'âme / par l'oreille et par les yeux." (I simply do not believe that Isabella is a mortal woman. She is rather one of the gods disguised as a woman in order to enrapture our soul through our ears and eyes.) Sovereigns were also among her admirers: Vincenzo I Gonzaga, Carlo Emanuele I di Savoia, Francesco I, Ferdinando and Maria de' Medici, and Henri IV of France.

Andreini's writings seem to have attracted considerable interest and were reissued in numerous editions. Her pastoral fable *Mirtilla* was first published in Verona in 1588, and was frequently reissued well into the next century. It is a pastoral play featuring the pranks played by Cupid on a shepherd and two shepherdesses in retribution for their lack of obeisance to the god's power. Her collected poetry, published in Milan in 1601 under the title *Rime*, also aroused great interest and was reissued in many editions. The collection includes a great variety of poems: love poems, eulogies, religious poems, sonnets, madrigals, and even jokes. Her other works were published posthumously. Her letters (*Lettere*) were collected and published by Francesco Andreini in 1607 and reprinted several times thereafter. There are 148 letters in the volume, treating a variety of subjects such as the honor of women, the evils of prostitution, and complaints against the power of love. Francesco Andreini also collected many of her theatrical writings and had them published in 1620 with the help of actor-writer Flaminio Scala under the title *Fragmenti di alcune scritture della Signora Isabella Andreini comica Gelosa et accademica Intenta* (Fragments of some writings by Isabella Andreini, Gelosa actress and Intenta academician). The volume contains thirty-one dialogues she called "contrasti amorosi" or "contrasti scenici" (love quarrels or staged quarrels). They all involve one man and one woman and most probably served as extended *lazzi*, prepared and rehearsed sequences of action and dialogue that improvising players might use in their performances whenever they thought it appropriate.

Her husband died in 1624, surviving her by twenty years. Her eldest son, Giovan Battista Andreini (born in Florence in ca. 1579), also became a famous actor and writer.

Works

Mirtilla (1588). *Rime* (1601). *Lettere* (1607). *Fragmenti di alcune scritture* (1620).

Bibliography

Clubb, Louise George, "The State of the Arts in the Andreinis' Time," in *Studies in the Italian Renaissance: Essays in Memory of Arnolfo B. Ferruolo*, ed. Gian Paolo Biasin, Albert N. Mancini, and Nicolas J. Perella (Naples, 1985), pp. 263–281. Costa-Zalessow, Natalia, *Scrittrici italiane dal XIII al XX secolo* (Ravenna, 1982), pp. 117–123. Croce, Benedetto, *Nuovi saggi sulla letteratura italiana del seicento* (Bari, 1949), pp. 165, 308–309. Croce, Bendetto, *Poeti e scrittori del pieno e tardo rinascimento*, vol. III (Bari, 1952), pp. 273–278. Del Cerro, E., "Un'attrice di tre secoli fa: Isabella Andreini." *Natura ed Arte* (1908). Falena, U., "Isabella Andreini." *Rassegna nazionale* (May 15, 1905). Fiocco, Achille, "Isabella Andreini." *Enciclopedia dello spettacolo*, vol. I (Rome, 1954), pp. 555–558. Giacosa, G., *L'Art drammatique el les comediens italiens* (Paris, 1899). Moland, L., *Moliere et la Comedie Italienne* (Paris, 1867). Raya, G., *Lirici del cinquecento* (Milan-Naples, 1933), p. 173. Ruelens, C., *Erycius Puteanus et Isabella Andreini* (1899).

Stanley Longman

Elena Andrés

Born Madrid, Spain
Genre(s): poetry
Language(s): Spanish

Elena Andrés was born in Madrid, Spain. She received her *licenciatura* in Philosophy and Letters and has been a Professor in Language and Literature. Since 1959, her poems have appeared in literary journals and in books. Her work now fills more than five volumes. Her works include *El buscador, Eterna vela, Dos caminos* (winner of the Adonais Prize of 1963), *Desde aquí mis señales*, and *Trance de la vigilia colmada* (second prize, Ambito Literario, 1980).

The poetry of Elena Andrés reflects some aspects of her intimate thoughts. These intimate thoughts are often filled with bitter confessions which denounce the anguish of the human condition. Her first collection of poems, *El buscador* (1959) develops two fundamental themes: nature and humanity. She elaborates these two themes by giving us a profile of man and his surroundings, trying to harmonize the contradictory elements that she perceives in both. She achieves this harmony of man and nature by humanizing nature and naturalizing the human being. In *Eterna vela* (1961), her second book of poems, she investigates more deeply the spiritual intimacy of contemporary man. In this book, Andrés presents her thoughts drawn from her contemplation of what she considers necessary to an essential life, which includes for her not only emotions but also the fundamental and ordinary elements of daily existence. In this collection of poems the human being is trapped between his ancestral past and a future that is as mysterious as that past. The themes that she begins to write about in *El buscador* show a greater development in her technique (especially in the freshness of her images) and in her much more complex nuances and levels of interpretation. *Dos caminos* (1964), which won for her the accéssit of the Adonais prize for the year 1964, shows an advance with respect to her two previous collections of poems, as much in the thematical depth as in the freshness of expression within the confines of a surrealism controlled by reason. In *Dos caminos*, she portrays a "self" which is filled with emotions but also has full consciousness of past life experiences. Andrés feels the need to relive these past personal experiences but at the same time to eliminate those memories that are too painful to her. In order to forget these memories, she takes refuge in a world of reverie and fantasy. *Desde aquí mis señales* (1971) shows a step forward in her constant search for the essence of the human being and the mystery of human existence. In this book, Andrés expresses a more metaphysical thought without concern for the reader's understanding. In fifty-five poems the poet combines the personal and the collective, the intimate and the exterior, the existential and the ethical. Here Andrés proclaims her oneness with the reality that surrounds her, with the reality of life. Andrés affirms her solidarity with other human beings, solidarity filled with pain, anguish over the injustice which all human beings undergo. *Desde aquí mis señales* is considered by the critics to be one of her best collections of poems because in it, according to Teresa Valdivieso, Andrés "achieves a maturity of thought and of expression that is not common among poets—men or women—of her youth." *Trance de la vigilia colmada* (1980) is Elena Andrés' fifth collection of poems. Here she reveals an ideological rhythm that explodes her "self" into an existential anguish. She feels this Pirandellian anguish because she is her personal "self," but at other times she is the "self" that others perceive her to be, and sometimes she feels that she must be both "selves" at the same time.

The poetry of Andrés shows the social consciousness that awakened in her at a certain point in her life. Her poetic work reflects the labor of a writer dedicated to the study of the human being in his temporal dimension and in his eternal projection. Without a doubt, the social consciousness of her poetry is not the essential element to understanding it. Her work constitutes a discourse of multiple and diverse elements taken from different points of view integrated into a clear and unified expression of her thought.

Works

El buscador (1959). Eterna vela (1961). Dos caminos (1964). Desde aquí mis señales (1971). Trance de la vigilia colmada (1980). Paisajes conjurados (unpublished).

Bibliography

Fagundo, Ana María, "Realidad e irrealidad en la poesía de Elena Andrés." *Cuadernos hispanoamericanos* 351 (1979): 641–651. Fernández Almagro, M., "Dos caminos." *ABC* (Madrid) (June 21, 1964), s.p. Fernández Francisco, "El buscador." *Cuadernos* (Paris) 43 (1960): 117. Lacasa, Cristina, "Realidad y alucinación." *Nueva estafeta* 27 (1981): 101. Miró, Emilio, "Ildefonso—Manuel G.1. Elena Andrés." *Insula* 300–301 (1971): 24. Mostaza, B., "Crónica de poesía." *Ya* (Madrid) (October 3, 1962): 17. Rodríquez Santerbas, Santiago, "Las señales de Elena Andrés." *Triunfo* 481 (1971): s.p. Valdivieso, L. Teresa, "La poesía de Elena Andrés como una pluralidad de discursos." *Alauz* 16–17 (Autumn/Spring 1985): 3–11.

Raquel Aquilu de Murphy

Angela da Foligno

Born c. 1248, Foligno, Italy; died January 4, 1309, Foligno
Genre(s): mysticism, autobiography
Language(s): Italian, Latin

For the first forty or so years of her life Angela da Foligno lived the usual life of an Italian wife and mother of her age. Then in 1285 she underwent a religious conversion that led to her to a complete change of life. She became a

Franciscan tertiary and soon gathered around herself a group of disciples, the most famous of whom was Ubertino da Casale.

Her spirituality is thoroughly Franciscan, with an emphasis upon the Passion of Christ, poverty, self-denial and the Way of the Cross. But like the mysticism of St. Catherine of Genoa, two centuries later, Angela da Foligno's leads to disappearance of the self in the all-encompassing love of God. Her mysticism is Christocentric, with Christ playing the role of both goal and means. Our union is to be with Christ in God and our way is through Christ Himself.

Our principal source for Angela da Foligno's doctrine and life is the work of her relative-confessor, Fra Arnaldo, translated into English as *The Book of Divine Consolation*. There also exists a short vernacular compendium of her teaching, translated as "A Lovely and Useful Instruction."

Works

The Book of Divine Consolation, tr. Mary G. Steegmann (New York, 1966). "A Lovely and Useful Instruction," tr. J.R. Berrigan. *Vox Benedictina* 2 (1985): 24–41.

Bibliography

Lachance, Paul, O.F.M., "The Spiritual Journey of the Blessed Angela of Foligno according to the Memorial of Frater A." *Studia Antoniana* 29 (Rome, 1984). *DBI* 3, 186–187.

Joseph Berrigan

Katerina Angelakē-Rooke

(see: Katerina Anghelaki-Rooke)

Katerina Angelaki-Rooke

(see: Katerina Anghelaki-Rooke)

Halma Angélico

(a.k.a. María Francisca Clar Margarit)

Born 1880, Spain; died 1952
Genre(s): drama
Language(s): Spanish

Little is known about the life of this writer important in the early decades of the twentieth century. At least two of her plays were performed commercially in Madrid at a time when women playwrights were almost totally unknown. *Al Margen de la ciudad* (On the Edge of the City) shows a woman surrounded by men who love her. Her gender and the attitude of the men, however, make her feel that she lives only on the periphery or "edge" of life, as the title suggests. Her theatrical version of the story by the Russian Jefrim Sosulia, *AK y la humanidad* (AK and Humanity), was successful in its 1939 premiere, but censors suppressed it almost immediately. Another performed play, *Entre la cruz y el diablo* (Between the Cross and the Devil), takes place in a convent and is reminiscent of Martínez Sierra's *Canción de cuna* (Cradle Song). A fourth play, *La nieta de Fedra* (Fedra's Granddaughter), is published in a volume entitled *Teatro irrepresentable* (Unperformable Theater).

Works

La nieta de Fedra [Fedra's Granddaughter] (1929). *Entre la cruz y el diablo* [Between the Cross and the Devil] (1932). *Al Margen de la ciudad* [On the Edge of the City] (1936). *AK y la humanidad* [AK and Humanity] (1938).

Patricia W. O'Connor

Katerina Anghelaki-Rooke

(a.k.a. Katerina Angelaki-Rooke, Katerina Angelakē-Rooke)

Born 1939, Athens, Greece
Genre(s): poetry, translation
Language(s): Greek

Katerina Anghelaki (or *Angelaki*, or *Anghelakē*) Rooke was born and grew up in Athens. She studied the classics as well as foreign languages and literature in Athens, Nice (France) and Geneva (Switzerland). She graduated from the University of Geneva with the First Prize for Poetry. In 1975–1976 she participated in the

International Writing Program at the University of Iowa. She has also visited and taught in the United States on a Ford Foundation grant and a Fulbright fellowship. She lives part of the year in Athens and the remaining part on the nearby island of Aegina.

In 1986 Anghelaki-Rooke was awarded the second state prize for poetry for her 1984 poetry collection *Oi mnēstēres* (The Suitors). She has written many critical essays and has translated French, Russian, English, and American writers into modern Greek (including Dylan Thomas' *Under Milk Wood* and Edward Albee's *A Delicate Balance*) and some Greek writers into English. Her own poems have been translated into English, French, Russian, Bulgarian, and Italian and have been included in many anthologies of Greek poetry.

In her 1974 poetry collection, Anghelaki-Rooke includes a quotation from George Seferis, which, roughly translated, says: "In essence the poet has one subject: his living body." We cannot help but notice a preoccupation with the body in all of her poetry but not for its own sake but as a way of arriving at truth and authenticity. Anghelaki-Rooke's poetry, although gloomy at times, does not communicate *angst* and despondence. Working within a broad literary and historical tradition, she often resorts to myths and legends which she weaves with Penelopean skill within the textures of her own creations. Many of the female personae she creates (or, more accurately, *recreates*) speak in refreshingly "feminine" voices and thus present a heretofore absent point of view. In so doing, they put into question long-established assumptions and force us to look at familiar characters (such as Odysseus and Penelope, for example) in new ways. But these new ways are not so much destructive as creative, for the reader is made aware not only of the sadness and ugliness of life but also of its possibilities and of the potentialities of the living body.

Works

Lykoi kai synnepha [Wolves and Clouds] (1963). *Poiēmata 63–69* [Poems 63–69] (1971). *Magdalēnē, to megalo thēlastiko* [Magdalene, the Great Mammal] (1974). *Ta skorpia chartia tēs Pēnelopēs* The Scattered Papers of Penelope (1977).

O thriambos tēs statherēs apōleias [The Triumph of a Steady Loss] (1978). *Enantios Erōtas* [Contrary Love] (1982). *Oi mnēstēres* [The Suitors] (1984). **Translations:** *The Body Is the Victory and the Defeat of Dreams*, tr. Philip Ramp (1975). *Contemporary Greek Women Poets*, tr. Eleni Fourtouni (1978). *Modern Poetry in Translation* 34 (Summer 1978). *The Penguin Book of Women Poets*, ed. Carol Cosman, Joan Keefe, and Kathleen Weaver (1978). *Skylark, number 25.* Special Greek Poetry Number, ed. Baldev Mirza. *Twenty Contemporary Greek Poets*, ed. Dinos Siotis and John Chioles (1979). *News of the Universe: Poems of Twofold Consciousness*, comp. Robert Bly (1980). *Four Greek Women: Love Poems*, tr. Eleni Fourtouni (1982). *Women Poets of the World*, ed. Joanna Bankier and Deirdre Lashgari (1983). *Contemporary Greek Poetry*, tr. Kimon Friar (1985). [With Jackie Willcox], *Beings and Things on Their Own* (1986). *Paintbrush: A Journal of Poetry, Translations, and Letters* XIV, 27 (Spring 1987).

Bibliography

Baloumēs, Epam G., "E B' metapolemikē poiētikē genia." *Nees Tomes* (Spring 1985): 9–16. *Bulletin analytique de bibliographie hellènique* xxxii (1971) (Athènes, 1976). Decavalles, Andonis, "Modernity: The Third Stage, the New Poets." *The Charioteer* 20 (1978). Friar, Kimon, ed., *Exē Poiētes* (Athens, 1971). Kolias, Helen Dendrinou, "Greek Women Poets and the Language of Silence." *Translation Perspectives* IV (Binghamton, N.Y., 1988).

Helen Dendrinou Kolias

Maria Angels Anglada

Born 1930, Vich, Spain
Genre(s): poetry, novel, short story
Language(s): Catalan

Following her youth in Vich, Anglada specialized in classical philology (often evident in her creative writing), and won the Josep Pla Prize—Catalan prose's most important award—with her first novel, *Les closes* (1979; The Enclosed). As part of her professional specialization, she has written critical essays on Italian poetry and themes from Greek mythology. In 1972, she collaborated with Nùria Albó in producing a poetry collection, *Díptic*, and in 1978 she published *Memories d'un pages del segle XVIII* (Memoirs of a Peasant of the Eighteenth Century).

The Enclosed is a historical novel set against a nineteenth-century background. Along with its reconstruction of the past century's Catalan society, it recreates the personal history of Dolors Canals in the difficult period preceding the 1868 Revolution and Spain's First Republic. Conflicts between liberal and conservative political factions are relegated to the background of the narrative, presented by Dolors' great-granddaughter. Anglada experiments both with nonlinear narrative and multiple perspectives. In 1980, Anglada returned to poetry, producing a collection characterized by constant references to the Mediterranean and world of classical antiquity, as evoked by its title *Kyaparíssia*.

No em dic Laura (1981; My Name Isn't Laura), a collection of short stories, is likewise characterized by emphasis upon things Greek. Its three subdivisions may be considered either long short stories or novelettes, and each is further subdivided into two, three, or four titled parts. The first, set in Greece under the current military dictatorship, switches to the fifteenth century, providing a poetic recreation of the landscape, as well as various archaeological incidents. The second returns to the period of the Napoleonic wars, treating the same family as in Anglada's first novel, and reiterating similar themes. The third and last tale is set in Vich during the postwar epoch (the writer's childhood), but it is not a simple recreation of times past; rather, it is imaginative fiction combining lyricism and intrigue.

Viola d'amore (1983; Viola of Love) differs from much of Anglada's earlier fiction in no longer depending upon history or archaeological reconstruction. The writer turns to the world of music as her fiction's intertextual referent, preserving the tripartite structures seen in much of her previous writing. The Trio Izvorul features two members (Gerda and Virgili) who recall Thomas Mann, while the third member, of an opposing ideology, constitutes a more direct link with Anglada's earlier fiction. As a whole, the group functions to intensify the lyric climate of the work and to provide counterpoint as well as internal rhythm.

Another of the contemporary group of women narrators in Catalan, Anglada is less concerned than many with feminist issues, preferring to express her love for her land, the theme of hope which comes out of struggle, and an overview of the past in those aspects perceived as most meaningful for the present. She experiments with temporal planes and nonlinear chronology, to emphasize those things that remain although time may pass. A thoughtful and sensitive narrator, Anglada is not prolific but polishes and refines her works.

Works

Díptic (1972). *Les closes* (1979; Spanish tr., *Los cercados*, 1986). *Kyaparíssia* (1980). *No em dic Laura* (1981). *Viola d'amore* (1983).

Bibliography

Women Writers of Spain, ed. C. L. Galerstein (Westport, Conn., 1986).

Janet Perez

Nini Roll Anker

(a.k.a. Jo Nein, Kåre P.)

Born 1873, Molde, Norway; died 1942, Norway
Genre(s): novel, short story, drama
Language(s): Norwegian (bokmål)

Nini Roll Anker wrote novels, short stories, and one play. Her work focused on social problems, the clash of values between people of different backgrounds and traditions, and particularly on the situation of working-class women.

Nini Roll was the daughter of a distinguished judge, and grew up in a highly cultured and aristocratic milieu. When she was nineteen she married Peter Anker, a wealthy estate owner. They were divorced in 1907, and in 1910 she married Johan Anker, an engineer who was a cousin of her first husband.

Writing under the pseudonym Jo Nein, Anker made her literary debut in 1898. *I blinde* describes the situation of an overprotected young woman who comes of age and must make a life for herself. Anker takes up what is to become one of her major themes, the plight of working-class women, in the short-story collection *Lill-Anna og andre* (1906), and again in one of her most well-known works, the novel *Den some henger i en tråd* (1935).

Det svake kjønn, first published in 1915 and revised and shortened for a new edition nine years later, is critical of the Church for encouraging in women a blind submission to authority. *Enken* (1932) is also concerned with women's issues, showing the economic hardship faced by a woman who has sole responsibility for both children and grandchildren.

While she could be highly critical of unjust social institutions, Anker also recognized positive traditional values. Between 1923 and 1927, she produced a trilogy, *Huset i Søgaten, I Amtmandsgården*, and *Under skraataket*, covering three generations in a civil servant's family. In these novels, Anker finds much to admire in traditional values and is critical of the materialism shown by contemporary society.

Kvinnen og den svarte fuglen, written during the German occupation and published posthumously in 1945, is a pacifistic novel. It presents a strong indictment against the power of the military-industrial complex and a call to women around the world to put an end to war.

Nini Roll Anker's works are realistic, with great psychological insight, and ensure her a place among the front rank of Norwegian novelists.

Works

I blinde [Blindly] (1898). *Lill-Anna og andre* [Little Anne and Others] (1906). *Benedicte Stendal* [Benedicte Stendal] (1909). *Per Haukeberg* [Per Haukeberg] (1910). *De vaabenløse* [The Defenseless] (1912). *Det svake kjønn* [The Weaker Sex] (1915). *Fru Castrups datter* [Mrs. Castrup's Daughter] (1918). *Kirken* [The Church] (1921). *Huset i Søgaten* [The House on Shore Road] (1923). *Kvindesind* [Feminine Nature] (1924). *Piken* [The Girl] (1924). *I amtmandsgaarden* [At the Governor's House] (1925). *Under skraataket* [Under the Sloping Roof] (1927). *Liv, livet og jeg* [Liv, Life and Me] (1927). *Prisopgaven* [The Prize Question] (1928). *Vi skriver en roman* [We Write a Novel] (1929). *To ungsdomsår* [Two Years of Youth] (1930). *Enken* [The Widow] (1932). *Elling Torsens hjem* [Elling Torsen's Home] (1934). *På ærens mark* [On the Field of Honor] (1934). *Den*

som henger i en tråd [Hanging by a Thread] (1935). *På egen grunn* [On One's Own Ground] (1936). *Små avsløringer* [Small Disclosures] (1937). *Bak Munkeruds fasade* [Behind Munkerud's Facade] (1938). *Kvinnen og den svarte fuglen* [The Woman and the Black Bird] (1945). *Min venn Sigrid Undset* [My Friend Sigrid Undset] (1946).

Translations: "A Crime," tr. Torild Homstad, in *An Everyday Story*, ed. Katherine Hanson (Seattle: 1984), pp. 69–75.

Bibliography

Björkmann, I.M., "Nini Roll Ankers Stampetrilogi: tillkomst, bakgrund, budskap." With English summary. *Dissertation Abstracts International* (1981). Kielland, Eugenia, *Nini Roll Anker i liv og arbeid* (1948). Knudsen, Marianne Koch, "Utilfredse skal vi være for å kunne kjempe: Kvinneskikkelse i Nini Roll Ankers forfatterskap," in *Et annet språk*, ed. Janneken Øverland (Oslo, 1977), pp. 116–135.

Torild Homstad

Anne de Beaujeu

(see: Anne de France)

Anne de France

(a.k.a. Anne de Beaujeu, Duchesse de Bourbonnais et d'Auvergne)

Born 1461, Belgium; died November 14, 1522, Moulins, France
Genre(s): didactic treatise
Language(s): French

Anne set a precedent for the powerful role played by noblewomen at the French court throughout the Renaissance. Daughter of Louis XI, married in 1474 to Pierre de Beaujeu, younger brother of the duc de Bourbon, Anne and her husband ruled France as regents from 1483 to 1491 during the minority of her brother, Charles VIII. Although her husband was titular head, historians refer to her as the real "king" of France. She successfully pursued her father's dual aims of consolidating royal authority and weakening the power of the war lords. In 1491, she negotiated her brother's marriage to Anne de Bretagne, thus fulfilling her father's hopes of curbing Brittany's independence. She then retired to her Bourbonnais, whose interests she fought to maintain. She also devoted herself to the education of her only child, Susanne, born in 1491, and married thirteen years later to Charles de Bourbon. To Susanne she dedicated her only unpublished work. The latter's premature death in 1521 as well as the disgrace at court of her son-in-law were blows to her health and ended her familial ambitions. She died in 1522 at the age of sixty-one.

Her *Enseignements* belongs to an ancient tradition of didactic treatises that, directed to the young, sum up conventional wisdom. Among her sources were Louis IX's epistle to his daughter entitled *Les Enseignements de Saint Louis à sa fille Isabelle* (c.1267) and Christine de Pizan's *Le Livre des Trois Vertus* (1405), both written for court ladies. While Anne amplifies much of Louis's advice, especially on issues of chastity, reputation, speech, and dress, her work is less a prescription for the cultivation of the spiritual life than a practical conduct-book for a young girl about to be married and to assume an important position at court. Her injunctions on how to avoid the wiles of male seducers, and, if widowed, on how to live, are strongly reminiscent of Pizan's work.

Works

Les Enseignements d'Anne de France, Duchesse de Bourbonnais et d'Auvergne à sa fille Susanne de Bourbon, ed. A.-M. Chazaud (1878; rpt. 1978).

Bibliography

de Chabannes, H., and I. Linares, *Anne de Beaujeu* (1955). de Maulde de La Clavière, R., *Les Femmes de la Renaissance* (1898). Kelso, Ruth, *Doctrine for the Lady of the Renaissance* (1956). Provence, F., *Anne de Beaujeu* (1961).

Anne Larsen

Olga Nikolaevna Anstei

Born March 1, 1912, Kiev, Russia; died May 30, 1985, New York
Genre(s): lyric poetry, prose, essay, literary criticism
Language(s): Russian

Olga Anstei, an extraordinarily gifted master of language, began to write poetry in early childhood in her native Kiev, but none of it could be published under the rigid rules of Lenin and Stalin. A graduate of the Kiev Foreign Language Institute in 1931, she used her talent as a literary critic, bibliographer-librarian until the tumultuous years of World War II forced her in 1943 into permanent exile, first in Western Europe and from 1950 on, in the United States.

Following her settlement in the West, she published her poetry, short stories, sketches, and literary criticism prolifically in the best Russian émigré "thick" journals, almanacs and anthologies. In 1949, her first book of verse, *Dver' v stene* (Door in the Wall), appeared in Munich; in 1976, another book of poetry followed, *Na yuru* (In the Way). Anstei's poetry reflects her profoundly religious world view. Her delicate verses deal with the eternal themes of love, loneliness, emptiness, and the specific motif, shared with most writers in exile, of loss of the homeland illuminated by a radiant consciousness of God's omnipresent grace. Anstei was a skillful translator from English, German, and French. Rilke, Oscar Wilde, Tennyson, and Chesterton acquired new freshness under her pen. In 1960, her translation of Stephen Vincent Benét's "The Devil and Daniel Webster" was published in New York.

The common tragedy of émigré writers compelled Olga Anstei to fight for existence more than for prominence. It remains for her admirers to collect and republish her works scattered all over Russian émigré literary magazines and almanacs.

Works

Poetry: *Dver' v stene* [Door in the Wall], poetry (1949). *Na Zapade* [In the West], ed. Iurii Ivask, poetry in anthology (1953). *Literaturnoe Zarubezh'e* [Literature in Exile], poetry in anthology (1958). *Muza Diaspory* [Muse of the Diaspora], poetry in anthology (1960). *Sodruzhestvo, Iz sovremennoi poezii Russkogo Zarubezh'a* [Cooperation in Friendship, Contemporary Poetry of the Russian Exile], poetry in anthology (1966). *Na yuru* [In the Way], poetry (1976). *Russkii Almanakh* [Russian Almanac], poetry in anthology (1981).

Prose—Short Stories: "Karnaval" [Carnival]. *Vozrozhdenie* 17 (September–October 1951). "Fonarik" [The Flashlight]. *Delo* (1951).

Literary Criticism—Articles, Reviews: "Sled Edgara Po v tvorchestve Bloka i Grina" [Traces of Edgar Poe in the Work of Blok and Grin], *Delo* (1951). "Pushkin i obshchemirovaia kul'tura" [Pushkin and World Culture]. *Literaturnyi Sovremennik* (1954). "Novyi Pasternak" [The New Pasternak]. *Grani* (1960). "Prozrachnyi sled" [The Transparent Trace]. *Novyi Zhurnal* 81 (1965). "Boris Zaitsev, Izbrannoe" (Boris Zaitsev, Selected Works). *Novyi Zhurnal* (1973). "Zlatoustaia Anna vseia Rusi" (Goldenmouthed Anna of all Russia). *Novyi Zhurnal* (1977). "Sama po sebe" [On her Own]. *Novyi Zhurnal* (1980).

Translations: "D'iavol i Daniel Vebster" [The Devil and Daniel Webster], tr. of Stephen Vincent Benét's story in *D'iavol i Daniel' Vebster i drugie rasskazy* [The Devil and Daniel Webster and Other Stories] (New York, 1959). *America's Russian Poets*, ed. and tr. R.H. Morrison (1975).

Bibliography

Struve, Gleb, *Russkaia Literatura v izgnanie* [Russian Literature in Exile] (New York, 1956). Zverev, Fabii, "Poety novoi' emigratsii" [Poets of the "New" Emigration]. In *Russian Émigré Literature, A Collection of Articles in Russian With Résumés in English*, ed. N.P. Poltoratzky (Pittsburgh, 1972). Fessenko, Tatiana, "Ol'ga Nikolaevna Anstei-Liusha." *Novyi Zhurnal* 161 (New York, 1985).

Marina Astman

Anyte

Born Tegea, Arcadia (Greece); exact birth and death dates unknown; fl. approximately 300 B.C.
Genre(s): epigrams
Language(s): Greek

We know nothing of the personal life of Anyte, but an anecdote told by Pausanias (10.38.13) connects her with a miracle performed by the healing god Asclepius and the subsequent construction of his shrine at Naupactus. Her interest in the woodland god Pan is appropriate for a native of Arcadia.

The most important and influential of the Hellenistic women epigrammatists, Anyte is usually credited with twenty-one extant poems, all but one preserved in the *Greek Anthology*. Three other pieces once ascribed to her are not now considered her genuine work. Ancient sources inform us that she also wrote lyric poetry and perhaps epic (Antipater of Thessalonica, *AP* 9.26, terms her "the female Homer"), but only her epigrams have survived.

Thematically, Anyte's epigrams may be grouped into four categories: commemorations of objects dedicated to divinities, epitaphs for human beings, epitaphs on animals, and landscape poems. The first two are standard types of epigram found in the earliest verse inscriptions, but the latter two are apparently Anyte's own invention, and her introduction of bucolic motifs into Greek epigram is crucial for the later development of the European pastoral.

Even in her highly conventional dedicatory and sepulchral quatrains, Anyte displays elegance, exceptional learning, and marked originality. Poem 2 (*AP* 6.153), for example, is a bold artistic experiment in which the dedication-formula is reduced to its starkest elements (object, dedicator, divine recipient, maker of object) and the reader is forced to infer the rationale for the gift from slight textual hints. The funerary epigrams for human beings are devoted exclusively to the pathetic fate of the young—soldiers fallen in war, girls perishing before their nuptial day. The attitudes expressed are orthodox, even androcentric: marriage is viewed as the natural and desirable lot of women without any trace of that anxiety over sexual initiation pervading Erinna's *Distaff* (q.v.). In contrast to most male epigrammatists, however, Anyte does stress the emotional impact of death upon the survivors. In poem 4 (*AP* 7.724) she apparently compares young soldiers who have lost their captain to children mourning a mother—a gender reversal so unusual that most editors obelize the text.

By anthropomorphizing their subjects and, thereby, blurring the distinction between the human and animal realms, Anyte's five epitaphs for beasts and insects affirm the essential importance of such "lesser" lives. Thus poem 9 (*AP* 7.208) recounts the fate of a slain war horse in epic language and invests him with the grandeur of a fallen Homeric hero. In her longest piece, poem 12 (*AP* 7.215), a dolphin cast ashore laments his end, recalling his former pride in seeing his own image serving as the figurehead of a ship. A quatrain (*AP* 7.190) consoling a young girl, Myro, on the loss of her two insect pets displays remarkable tact in its ability to dignify a child's simple grief without becoming precious or falsely sentimental. Anyte's interest in children and capacity to participate imaginatively in their world are also evident in the dedicatory poem 13 (*AP* 6.312), in which a description of a picture of boys riding a goat carries witty undertones of equestrian events at the great Pan-Hellenic athletic contests and so conveys the children's conception of themselves as potential Olympic contenders.

While Anyte's animal poems were much imitated in antiquity, her bucolic landscape pieces had a far greater impact upon subsequent literature. In each of these works, she creates the sensuous picture of an idyllic resting place, the domain of Hermes or his son Pan, offering the tired wayfarer shade, a fresh breeze, and a drink of cold spring water in the parching heat. This vision of the sweet and welcoming but finally temporary "green haven" is taken up by her imitator Nicias and, after him, by Theocritus, the recognized founder of the European pastoral tradition. Noting that Vergil's *Eclogues* are set in an artificial "Arcadia" bearing no resemblance to geographical reality, Reitzenstein suggested that the Roman artist's mythic pastoral homeland is a literary tribute to Anyte and her role in shaping the bucolic genre.

Highly popular in antiquity, Anyte was imitated not only by later generations of Greek epigrammatists but by Roman authors such as Catullus and Ovid. In her hands the epigram, though remaining a minimalist poetic form, becomes capable of evocative and emotionally convincing representation of children, animals, and wild nature.

Works

English tr. in *The Greek Anthology*, tr. W.R. Paton. Loeb Classical Library, 5 vols. (Cambridge, Mass., 1916). Commentary in *The Greek Anthology: Hellenistic Epigrams*, eds. A.S.F. Gow and D.L. Page, 2 vols. (Cambridge, 1965). Greek texts and German tr. in Homeyer, H., *Dichterinnen des Altertums und des frühen Mittelalters* (Paderborn, 1979).

Bibliography

Baale, M.J., *Studia in Anytes poetriae vitam et carminum reliquias* (Haarlem, 1903). Barnard, S., *Classical Journal* 73 (1978): 204–213. Geoghegan, D., *Anyte: The Epigrams* (Rome, 1979). Herrlinger, G., *Totenklage um Tiere in der antiken Dichtung* (Stuttgart, 1930). Luck, G., *Museum Helveticum* 11 (1954): 170–187. Reitzenstein, R., *Epigramm und Skolion* (Gissen, 1893). Snyder, J.M., *The Woman and the Lyre* (Carbondale, Ill., 1989). Trypanis, C.A., *Greek Poetry from Homer to Seferis* (Chicago, 1981). Webster, T.B.L., *Hellenistic Poetry and Art* (New York, 1964). Wilamowitz-Moellendorff, U. von, *Hellenistische Dichtung in der Zeit des Kallimachos*, I (Berlin, 1924).
General references: *Oxford Classical Dictionary*. 2nd ed. (Oxford, 1970), p. 78. Pauly-Wissowa, *Real-Encyclopädie der klassischen Altertumswissenschaft* I.2 (Stuttgart, 1894), pp. 2654–2655.

Marilyn B. Skinner

Renate Apitz

Born twentieth century
Genre(s): novel
Language(s): German

The chief protagonist of the novel *die Hexenzeit* is a woman named Mathilda, who at an early age was raped. Because of this early trauma, she engages in sexual promiscuity and serial marriages and never finds true love. Apitz seems to tell us that marital bliss is just a dream and not a reality. Man in Apitz' novel is seen as the fate and destiny of woman. The critics of *die Hexenzeit* feel that her style is excessively disconnected and erratic.

Works

Die Hexenzeit [The Time of the Witches] (1984).

Bibliography

Kritik 84: Rezensionen zur DDR-Literatur. Herausgegeben von Eberhard Günther, Werner Liersch und Klaus Walter (Halle, Leipzig, 1984).

Brigitte Edith Archibald

Elena Apreleva

(a.k.a. E. Ardov)

Born February 24, 1846, Orenburg, Russia;
died December 4, 1923
Genre(s): fiction, children's literature
Language(s): Russian

Elena Apreleva (née Blaramberg, "E. Ardov") brought an agreeable, light talent to Russian literature of the 1880s. Her father was a French-speaking Belgian general serving in the Russian army, and her mother was Greek. She was educated by tutors in St. Petersburg and passed the government examination for domestic teachers. In 1871 she became a founding editor of the children's magazine *Sem'ia i shkola* (Family and School). The next year Apreleva followed the example of many ambitious Russian women of the time who went to Western Europe for the higher education denied them at home, but frail health prevented her from completing a degree at the University of Geneva.

Apreleva began to write fiction in the mid-1870s under the enthusiastic sponsorship of Ivan Turgenev, who introduced her into Moscow literary circles. Her two novels, *Bez viny vinovatye* (1877; Guilty but Guiltless) and *Rufina Kazdoeva*, display an equal disdain for social lions and disaffected radicals. The *genre* she made her own was the short story or, as she called it, the "quick sketch" (*eskiz*) about a wide range of contemporary characters from the foolishly self-sacrificing to the blindly selfish. "How Aunty Loved" ("Kak Tetushka Liubila") is an exception, a charming flashback to the romantic *mores* of earlier times.

Apreleva lived in Central Asia from 1889 to 1906, but her literary activity never ceased. Between 1888 and 1913 she contributed some sixty sketches and articles to the important Moscow newspaper *Russkie vedomosti* (Russian Gazette). Many of them are ethnographic, describing sympathetically the lives of Crimean and Central Asian peoples. Others include Christmas stories, travel sketches, and autobiographical accounts of her friendships with Turgenev and A.F. Pisemsky.

The last years of Apreleva's life are undocumented. This unpretentious writer, whose career and themes overlap Chekhov's in prose fiction, deserves to be better remembered.

Works

Rufina Kazdoeva (1892). *Eskizy,* (1893).(Aftobiografiia), *Russkie vedomosti 1863–1913,* vol. 2 (Moscow, 1913), pp. 12–15 [bibliography]. *Dva mira: Rasskazy dlia detei* (1909). *Sredneaziatskie ocherki* (1935).

Bibliography

Istoriia russkoi literatury XIX v.: Bibliograficheskii ukazatel', K.D. Muratova, ed. (Moscow-Leningrad, 1962), pp. 133–134. Turgenev, Ivan S., *Polnoe sobranie sochinenii i pisem. Pis'ma,* vols. 11, 12, 12.2 (Moscow-Leningrad, 1966–1967). Vengerov, S.A., *Kritiko-biograficheskii slovar' russkikh pisatelei i uchenykh,* vol. 3 (St. Petersburg, 1892), pp. 370–375.

Mary F. Zirin

Tullia d'Aragona

Born c. 1510, Rome, Italy; died c. 1570, Rome
Genre(s): poetry and prose dialogues
Language(s): Italian

Tullia d'Aragona was born in Rome probably in 1510, illegitimate daughter of Giulia Campana, a celebrated beauty from Ferrara, and Archbishop Pietro Tagliavia d'Aragona, grandson of the king of Naples. She was highly educated and as a child was reputed to have been able to carry on disputations in excellent Latin.

Biographical accounts vary, and the more romantic versions claim that Tullia was forced to become a courtesan on the death of her father. This appears to be total fiction since his death is not recorded until 1558. What is known for certain is that by 1531 she was involved in a relationship with Filippo Strozzi, the Florentine banker who conspired against Cosimo de Medici, ruler of the city, who had him killed in 1538. Letters written by Strozzi confirm his relationship with Tullia though she seems to have continued to live in Rome until at least 1541. In that year some sonnets written by her were received and included in the collected papers of the Roman Academia degli Umidi. One of these sonnets, "Almo pastor," is addressed to Cosimo. She eventually moved to Florence under the patronage of Duchess Elenora of Toledo.

Tullia d'Aragona's biography is full of contradictions and problems. Some biographers have mentioned a husband, but she appears to have been known by the same name throughout her life. Her degree of education is unquestionable, and she ran a literary salon first in Rome and later in Florence after 1555, though the years between 1541 and 1555 are poorly documented. She may have lived for a time in Venice and in Ferrara, her mother's native city. There is also an anecdote that appears in various forms, relating how Tullia d'Aragona transgressed laws concerning the proper dress to be worn by a courtesan. One version of the story has Tullia in Florence, wearing clothes to which, as a courtesan, she was not entitled, and other versions set the story in Venice or Florence, with Tullia refusing to wear the yellow cloak that would mark her out as a courtesan. All versions of the story attest to Tullia's strong-mindedness on this issue and the general belief that she was indeed a courtesan first and a writer second.

Her two best known works were *Guerrino Il Meschino*, a poem of approximately 30,000 lines in 36 cantos of ottava rima and her *Dialogue on the Infinity of Love* published in Venice in 1547. In her preface to *Guerrino*, she defends the rights of women to education and attacks those writers who include indecent material in their books, even including Ariosto in her criticisms. Her *Dialogue on the Infinity of Love* is an account of the conversations between herself and Benedetto Varchi, the Florentine philosopher and historian. Tullia d'Aragona appears to have returned to Rome and to have died in 1569–1570. A portrait supposedly of her, by Alessandro Bonvicino, known as Il Moretto, is in the Martinengo Gallery at Brescia.

The absence of concrete information about Tullia d'Aragona means that romanticized accounts of her life have flourished unhindered. What all have in common is a constant denigration of her abilities as writer and intellectual. She has been criticized for her immoral behavior, for her lovers and reputation as a great beauty, and for the fact that she wrote poetry to the ruler who had her lover Filippo Strozzi murdered. Later on she was accused of hypocrisy when she criticized the immorality of other writers. It appears to have been impossible for Victorian critics especially to reconcile the fact that a courtesan might also have been an intellectual and a writer. This, however, is the only sensible conclusion that a contemporary reader can reach. Tullia d'Aragona was her own woman, taking wealthy and powerful lovers as a means of financial support, a practice that was by no means uncommon for a single woman at the time. She seems to have consistently moved in high social circles, to have been well thought of by some of the leading Humanist intellectuals of her time and has left a very large body of work as evidence of her talent as a writer.

Works

Dialogo della Signora Tullia d'Aragona della infinità di amore, G. Gioliti de Ferrari (Venice, 1547; 2nd ed., 1552). *Rime della Signora Tullia d'Aragona; et di diversi a lei*, G. Gioliti de Ferrari (1547; rev. and rpt. 1549, 1560). *Il Meschino, altramente detto il Guerrino. Fatto in ottava rima dalla signora Tullia d'Aragona. Opera nella quale si veggono e intendono le parti principali di tutto il mondo, e molte altre dilettevolissime cose, da essere sommamente care ad ogni sorte di persona di bellow ingegno*, G.B. e M. Sessa (Venice, 1560).

Bibliography

Axon, W., *Tullia d'Aragona, a poetess of the later Renaissance* (London, 1899). Cosenza, M.E., *Dictionary of the Italian Humanists and of the World of Classical Scholarship in Italy, 1300–1800*, vol. I (Boston, 1962), p. 248. de la Sizeranne, R., *Celebrities of the Italian Renaissance in Florence and in the Louvre* (London and New York, 1926), pp. 81–103. Masson, Georgina, *Courtesans of the Italian Renaissance* (London: Secker and Warburg, 1975). Trollope, T. Adolphus, "Tullia D'Aragona." *A Decade of Italian Women*, Vol. II (London, 1859), pp. 1–29.

Susan Bassnett

Charlotte Arbaleste de la Borde

Born March, 1548, Melun, France; died May
    15, 1606, Saumur, France
Genre(s): memoirs
Language(s): French

The wife of Philippe du Plessis-Mornay, one
of the most influential French Protestant leaders
of the late sixteenth century, Charlotte Arbaleste
composed a series of memoirs that provides a
vivid picture of Huguenot culture and politics
during the troubled period of the Wars of Religion.

Arbaleste was born to a family of the minor
nobility, that of the viscounts of Melun, which,
although Catholic in name, inclined toward the
Huguenot cause. She seems to have been fully
converted to Protestantism by age seventeen,
when she married Jean de Pas, a committed
Huguenot nobleman and soldier. He died just
two years later, while on military service, when a
horse kicked him in the head. After the Saint
Bartholomew's Day massacre, Arbaleste abandoned Paris for the relative safety of Sedan. There
she met Mornay, who was already an important
leader in the Huguenot cause. Despite the social
barriers between them, for he was of higher
noble rank, they were soon married, and Arbaleste
found herself a witness of many of the most
important political developments of her time.
She died, grief stricken, shortly after the death of
her only son.

Arbaleste's memoirs cover most of her life,
from the death of her first husband to her own
last days. They are written in a very simple,
unadorned style, but they also display a wide-
ranging education as evidenced by her use of
classical allusion. They provide a lively account
of personal reactions to such events as the Saint
Bartholomew's Day massacre. Arbaleste consistently portrayed herself in humble terms as the
servant of her husband, but she clearly had great
impact on him. These memoirs were not intended
for publication. Although fragments were published as early as 1624, they were not printed in
full until the nineteenth century.

Works

Mémoires de Charlotte Arbaleste sur la vie de
    Duplessis-Mornay, son mari, ed. A.-D. de la Fontelle
    de Vaudu and P. R. Auguis (1824). "Deux lettres
inédites de Mme. Duplessis-Mornay (1600–1603),"
    ed. C. Rea. Bulletin de la Société de l'histoire du
    Protestantisme 12 (1865): 248–250. Mémoires de
    Madame de Mornay, ed. Henriette de Witt, 2 vols.
    (1868–1869).

Bibliography

de Boislisle, A., "Lettre de la duchesse de La Trémoile
    sur la mort de Mme. Du Plessis-Mornay (mai
    1606)." Notices et documents publiés pour la
    Société de l'histoire de France (1884), pp. 345–
    348. Guizot, F., Notice sur Mme. de Mornay et sur
    ses Mémoires (1869). Schaeffer, A., "Mme.
    Duplessis-Mornay, née Charlotte Arbaleste (1572–
    1606)." Bulletin de la Société de l'histoire du
    Protestantisme 2 (1854): 649–666.
General references: Cioranesco, A., Bibliographie
    de la littérature française du seizième siècle (1959),
    p. 519. Haag, La France Protestante. 2nd ed., I, pp.
    301–304.

Thomas Head

Ticu Sevastia Archip

Born 1891, Tîrgovişte, Romania; died 1965,
    Bucharest
Genre(s): short story, drama
Language(s): Romanian

A mathematician, member of the literary
circle Sburătorul and regular contributor to
Adela Xenopol's Jurnalul scriitoarei (Journal of
the Woman Writer), Ticu Archip is best known
for the first two volumes—Oameni (1946;
People) and Zeul (1949; The God)—of a trilogy
entitled Soarele negru (Black Sun) to which she
devoted ten years of mature writing and which
she never completed (or at least never saw
published in its entirety). The volumes compose
a chronicle of the life of Romanian intellectuals
between 1914 and 1939 with its rivalries, scandals, quests, and tribulations. The first, which is
set in a provincial town situated in the oil-
bearing Prahova Valley, advances a rich and
diverse typology of strong competitive female
characters—the philanthropist Profira Murgeanu,
the authoritative and sensual physician Cora, the
ambitious and picaresquely adventurous Olga
(for whom it has been stated that writer Igena
Floru served as a model)—fighting for the appro-
priation or redistribution of weak males—the

mediocre and seductive lawyer Mihail Drăgescu, the sentimental engineer Ion Dragomir, etc. In the second volume the horizon extends to incorporate intellectuals' life in Bucharest with their escapes to Paris while the god-like historian Dinu Haralamb (in which critics recognized with equal conviction the contemporary mathematician D. Pompei and archaeologist Vasile Pârvan) restores the balance between female and male desire. What is characteristic to Archip, whose penetrating psychological analysis reminds the reader of Hortensia Papadat-Bengescu, is a spectacular de-narrativization of the novelistic structure.

Archip's volumes of short stories— *Colecţionarul de pietre preţioase* (1926; The Precious Stone Collector), *Aventura* (1929; Adventure), and *Patul fraţilor* (1949; Brothers' Bed)—revolve allegorically around mystery, obsession, hallucination, and brutal sexuality. Expressionist plays like *Inelul* (1921; The Ring), *Luminiţa* (which was presented successfully at the Bucharest National Theater in 1927–1928), *Gură de leu* (1935; A Lion's Mouth) add a somber dimension to the author's literary universe.

After the Second World War, Ticu Archip limited her writing activity to the translation into Romanian of works by Dumas-père, J. Verne, J. Conrad, O. Wilde, and M. Gorki.

Works

Inelul [The Ring] (1921). *Colecţionarul de pietre preţioase* [The Precious Stone Collector] (1926). *Luminiţa* (1927). *Aventura* [Adventure] (1929). *Gură de leu* [A Lion's Mouth] (1935). *Soarele negru* [Black Sun], vol. 1; *Oameni*, roman [People, a novel], vol. 2 (1946). *Zeul* [The God] (1949). *Patul fraţilor* [Brothers' Bed] (1949).

Bibliography

Piru, Al, "Ticu Archip." In *Panorama deceniului literar românesc 1940–1950* (Bucharest, 1968), pp. 278–281. Popa, Marian, "Archip, Ticu Sevastia." In *Dicţionar de literatură română contemporană*, 2nd ed. (Bucharest, 1977), p. 28.

Sanda Golopentia

E. Ardov

(see: Elena Apreleva)

Concepción Arenal

Born January 30, 1820, El Ferrol, Spain; died February 4, 1893, Vigo, Spain
Genre(s): novel, drama, poetry, essay
Language(s): Spanish

As a child, Arenal read voraciously but without any particular direction. She taught herself English, French, and Italian. In 1847 she married D. Fernando Carrasco, a contributor to *La Iberia*, who introduced her to the intellectual society of the day. After his death in 1855, Arenal lived quietly with her children, dedicating herself to charitable works, visiting hospitals and prisons, organizing benevolent societies, and writing her most significant works. During the Carlist War she worked for some months in a field hospital and in 1864 was named Visitor General of Women's Prisons. She spent the last years of her life in quiet retirement on an estate near Vigo, Galicia.

Her first works were purely literary—a novel, poetry, and plays—but her true *métier* lay in sociological, educational, and penal studies. She was ahead of her time in proposing legal, educational, and political changes as answers to the wretched social problems plaguing Spain in that era. She believed that better education—particularly for women—and a sincerely Christian and charitable attitude should play an important role in redressing society's ills.

Concepción Arenal's preoccupation with society, her faith in science, education, and progress reflected eighteenth-century notions, but her enthusiasm and optimism were in marked contrast to Romantic lyricism and social rebellion. Her ideas and works caused repercussions beyond Spain's borders and influenced European thought on economics, the judiciary, and education. The inspiration for her essays and her desire to educate her readers combined with a fortuitous variety and sense of style to make her works appealing as well as edifying. She was one of the foremost essayists of her time.

Works

Historia de un corazón, novel. *Fábulas en verso* (1851). *Plegaria a la Virgen*, poetry. *Oda a la abolición de la esclavitud*, poetry. *La beneficencia, la filantropía y la caridad* (1861). *La igualdad social y política* (1862). *Cartas a los delincuentes* (1865).

Cartas a un obrero. La insrucción del pueblo (1878). *El pauperismo*, 2 vols. *Cartas a un señor* (1880). *El visitador del preso. Estudios penitenciarios. La mujer del porvenir. La mujer de su casa* (1883). *Informe sobre la condición social de la mujer española. El reo, el pueblo y el verdugo. Ensay sobre el derecho de gracia. Ensayo sobre el derecho de gentes. Cuadros de la guerra. La educación de la mujer*(1892). *Obras completas*, 22 vols. (1894–1902).

Bibliography

Díaz-Plaja, Guillermo, ed., *Historia general de las literaturas hispánicas* (Barcelona, 1958). Lacalle, Angel, *Historia de la literatura española*(Barcelona, 1951). Mañach, Francisco, *Concepción Arenal* (Buenos Aires, 1907).

Carol Stos

Hannah Arendt

Born October 14, 1906, Hanover, Germany;
died December 1986, New York
Genre(s): scholarly works
Language(s): German, English

Hannah Arendt spent her youth in Königsberg, East Prussia, where her grandfather was a city official. She studied with the important German philosophers of the period, Heidegger and Bultmann (Marburg), Jaspers (Heidelberg), and Husserl (Freiburg). In 1929, her first book on the concept of love in Augustine was published, presumably based on a dissertation. After having been arrested by the Gestapo in 1933, she fled to Paris, where she married the philosophy professor Heinrich Blücher. In 1940, she immigrated to the United States, where she immediately began to contribute to journals such as *Partisan Review, Commentary,* and *Review of Politics.* From 1944 to 1946, she held a leading research position with the *Congress for Jewish Relations.* From 1945 to 1952, she was the secretary of the *Jewish Cultural Reconstruction,* which attempted to find Jewish manuscripts that had been lost during the Nazi regime. Subsequently, she lived as an independent author, occasionally accepting guest professorships at American universities. From 1963 to 1967 and from 1967 to her death, she was professor at the University of Chicago and

the Graduate Faculty of the New School for Social Research in New York, respectively.

A philosopher by training and temperament, Hannah Arendt was thrust by the times into becoming one of the foremost thinkers analyzing European fascism. She became internationally known in that capacity through her *magnum opus, The Origins of Totalitarianism,* in which she presents a brilliant analysis of late nineteenth-century European economic and social conditions as having produced a certain type of personality with an affinity for totalitarianism. First published in English in 1951, it appeared in German in 1955, revised and enlarged as well as translated by Hannah Arendt, a pattern that was to repeat itself with her other main books. In 1958, her biography of Romantic Rahel Varnhagen was published in German, a work that she had nearly finished by 1933. Amplifying her observations on the Hungarian revolution in 1958, entitled *Die ungarische Revolution und der totalitäre Imperialismus,* her second most important book is *On Revolution,* published in English and German in the same year, 1963. Sent by the magazine *The New Yorker,* Hannah Arendt covered the Eichmann trial in Jerusalem, publishing her report in 1963 with a now famous subtitle: *On the Banality of Evil.* Her philosophical legacy is *On Violence* (1970), also published in German in the same year.

Maintaining a high profile in the cultural life of both the United States and Germany, Hannah Arendt has received many distinctions: in 1954, the prize of the American Academy of Arts and Letters; in 1959, the Lessing Prize of Hamburg; the Sigmund Freud Prize of the German Academy for Language and Literature (1967); the Emerson-Thoreau Medal of the American Academy of Arts and Science (1969); and, in 1975, the Danish Sonning Prize.

Works

Der Liebesbegriff bei Augustin(1929). *The Origins of Totalitarianism*(1951). *Elemente und Ursprünge totalitärer Herrschaft* (1955). *Fragwürdige Traditionsbestände im politischen Denken der Gegenwart*(1957). *Die ungarische Revolution und der totalitäre Imperialismus* (1958). *Rahel Varnhagen. Lebensgeschichte einer deutschen Jüdin aus der Romantik* (1959). *Von der*

Menschlichkeit in finsteren Zeiten. Gedanken zu Lessing (1960). *Vita activa oder Vom tätigen Leben* (1960). *Between Past and Future. Six Exercises in Political Thought* (1961). *On Revolution* (1963). *Über die Revolution* (1963). *Eichmann in Jerusalem. A Report on the Banality of Evil* (1963). *Eichmann in Jerusalem. Ein Bericht von der Banalität des Bösen* (1964). *On Violence* (1970). *Macht und Gewalt* (1970). *Crisis of the Republic. Lying in Politics. Civil Disobedience. Thoughts on Politics and Revolution* (1972).

Bibliography

Friedmann, Friedrich Georg, *Hannah Arendt: eine deutsche Jüdin im Zeitalter des Totalitarismus* (Munich, 1985). Young-Bruehl, Elisabeth, *Hannah Arendt: Leben und Werk* (Frankfurt, 1986).

Ingeborg Zeiträg

Chryssoula Argyriadou

(see: Zoe Karelli)

Ariel

(see: Margareta Miller-Verghi)

Camille Armand

(see: Iulia Hasdeu)

Céline Arnauld

Born 1895, Romania; died 1952, Paris, France
Genre(s): poetry, theater, novel
Language(s): French

Born in Romania, Céline Arnauld immigrated to France in the early years of the century and was soon involved with the avant-garde circle that included Apollinaire, Tzara, and Breton, as well as the poet Paul Dermée. It was Dermée whom she would marry, a marriage that would be a major force throughout her life. The couple lived and wrote in Paris, forming one of those ideal literary unions. Dermée's death was a shock from which Arnauld would not recover. It was soon followed by her suicide in 1952.

Arnauld was an early member of the Dadaists and then the Surrealists; indeed, she was the only female poet among them. She collaborated on such journals as *Littérature*, the arm of the modernist movement, *Dada*, and *L'Esprit nouveau*, started by Dermée in 1920. Although her poetry, with its emphasis on dreams and dream-imagery, reflects many of the preoccupations of the Surrealists, its thematic center is rarely that of love. Surrealist poetry conceived of woman as the ideal object; Arnauld as a woman inscribes herself within the universe, with an insistent "I" as subject. She created a distinctive style and syntax as well as a unique vocabulary. *Le Clavier secret* (The Secret Keyboard), with its prose poems, or *La Nuit rêve tout haut* (Night Dreams Aloud), a poem for two voices, both published in 1934, are among the best examples of Arnauld's works, displaying the full range of her virtuosity.

Works

Tournevire (1919). *Poèmes à claires-voies* (1920). *Jeux d'echecs* (1921). *Point de mire* (1921). *Guêpier de diamants* (1923). *L'Apaisement de l'eclipse*, précédé de *Diorama* (1925). *La Nuit rêve tout haut* (1934). *Le Clavier secret* (1934) *Heures intactes* (1936). *Anthologie Céline Arnauld* (1936). *Les Reseaux du réveil* (1937). *Rien qu'une étoile*, suivie de *Plaints-chants sauvages* (1948).

Bibliography

Flouquet, Pierre-Louis, *Un Demi-siècle de poésie*, vol. 5 (Dilbeck-Bruxelles, 1961). Moroy, Elie. *La littérature féminine définie par les femmes écrivains* (Geneva, 1931).

Edith Joyce Benkov

Bettine von Arnim

Born April 4, 1785, Frankfurt-am-Main,
Germany; died January 29, 1859, Berlin
Genre(s): letters, political and social-critical
essays
Language(s): German

Bettine (or Bettina) von Arnim was perhaps the most important woman writer of the German Romantic era; she also had considerable influence on the generation of German writers known as "Jung Deutschland" ("Young Germany"). She was born Elisabeth Catharina Ludovica Magdalena Brentano in 1785, the daughter of Peter Anton Brentano, a merchant of Italian origin who lived in Frankfurt, and Maximiliane Laroche (or La Roche), who had earlier been a friend of the young Goethe. Bettine's grandmother, Sophie von Laroche, had achieved prominence as a novelist, and Bettine's brother Clemens was to become one of the principal lyric poets of the German Romantic movement. In 1801 Bettine became acquainted with the young poetess Karoline von Günderode and was deeply upset when her friend committed suicide in 1806. In 1807 she had her first meeting with Goethe in Weimar and soon began writing enthusiastic and often explicitly amorous letters to the aging poet, whose epistolary replies to her were considerably more reserved. In 1835, after Goethe's death, she would publish a fictionalized adaptation of this correspondence, entitled *Goethes Briefwechsel mit einem Kinde* (Goethe's Correspondence with a Child). In 1811, Bettine married the German Romantic poet and novelist Achim von Arnim, a friend of her brother Clemens, with whom he had published the collection of folk songs known as *Des Knaben Wunderhorn* (The Boy's Magic Horn). The Arnims eventually settled at Achim's family estate at Wiepersdorf, Brandenburg, where they raised a large family. After Achim's death in 1831, Bettine resided frequently in Berlin, where she gradually devoted herself to the cause of political reform and to the plight of the poor and the oppressed in her country. She died in Berlin in 1859 after several years of illness following a stroke.

Her first significant publication was the above-mentioned adaptation of her correspondence with Goethe. This was followed in 1840 by *Die Günderode* (Miss Günderode), an epistolary account of the brief life of the young poetess. In 1843 she published *Dies Buch gehört dem König* (This Book Belongs to the King), which describes and deplores the human suffering brought about by industrialization in Prussian territories. The book appeals directly to the King of Prussia, Friedrich Wilhelm IV, as the one man able to remedy or at least to alleviate some of these problems. In 1844, Bettine published a tribute to her brother's lyric genius, *Clemens Brentanos*

Frühlingskranz (Clemens Brentano's Spring Wreath). Her last major publication, *Gespräche mit Dämonen* (1852; Conversations with Demons) is, like the earlier book addressed to the king, devoted to issues of political and social reform.

Critics have noted that Bettine von Arnim's earlier work, especially the highly popular and influential *Goethes Briefwechsel mit einem Kinde*, expresses what might be regarded as the epitome of a "romantisches Lebensgefühl" ("romantic feeling of life"): an extreme intensity and vivacity of emotion combined with a rare generosity of enthusiasm. It is this same generosity, applied to social and political issues and expressed in some of her later works as well as in her personal, active devotion to the welfare of the poor and the oppressed, that earned her the great respect of the younger generation of German writers and intellectuals in the 1840s and 1850s.

Works

Goethes Briefwechsel mit einem Kinde [Goethe's Correspondence with a Child] (1835). *Die Günderode* [Miss Günderode] (1840). *Dies Buch gehört dem König* [This Book Belongs to the King] (1843). *Clemens Brentanos Frühlingskranz* [Clemens Brentano's Spring Wreath] (1844). *Gespräche mit Dämonen* [Conversations with Demons] (1852). *Sämtliche Werke*, ed. W. Oehlke, 7 vols. (1920–1922). *Werke und Briefe*, vol. 1–4, ed. G. Konrad (1959); vol. 5, *Briefe*, ed. J. Müller (1961).

Bibliography

Arnim, H. von, *Bettina Arnim* (Berlin, 1963). Dischner, G., *Bettina. Bettina von Arnim. Eine weibliche Sozialbiographie aus dem 19. Jahrhundert* (Berlin, 1977). Drewitz, I., *Bettina von Arnim, Romantik-Revolution-Utopie* (Munich, 1969). Mander, G., *Bettina von Arnim* (Berlin, 1982). Milch, W., *Die junge Bettine*, ed. P. Küpper (Heidelberg, 1968). Susman, M., *Frauen der Romantik* (Jena, 1929). Wyss, H., *Bettina von Arnims Stellung zwischen der Romantik und dem Jungen Deutschland* (Bern/Leipzig, 1935).

Richard Unger

Rosa María Arquimbau

(a.k.a. Rosa de Sant Jordi)

Born 1910, Barcelona, Spain
Genre(s): novel, essay, drama
Language(s): Catalan

Born in Barcelona, Rosa María Arquimbau had her first stories published at age fourteen, under the pseudonym of Rosa de Sant Jordi. Her first collection of short stories, written under her own name, was published when she was sixteen and her success as a storyteller earned her invitations to write for many Catalan newspapers and journals. As the number of newspapers decreased in Barcelona, Arquimbau concentrated on writing for journals and magazines, meanwhile publishing a collection of short stories and three novels. She also wrote several plays that enjoyed both critical and popular success. After several years of literary inactivity, she returned to writing with a play that won the Premio Joan de Santa María of 1957 and two novels published in 1970 and 1971, respectively.

In her narratives and plays, Arquimbau follows the tendency of most contemporary Catalan writers to escape from reality and to analyze characters in situations isolated from any specific time. The comedy *L'inconvenient de derse Martines* (The Problem with Calling Martines), for example, is set in the present time—that is, 1957—in the city of Barcelona, but could be set in any city or almost any time. The two-act play examines two families, living on separate floors of an apartment building, that coincidentally share the surname of Martines. When the wife in the Martines family on the main floor learns that the train on which her husband was supposed to be traveling has crashed, she fears the worst, only to learn at the end of the first act that her husband was not on the wrecked train. Her relief is tempered by puzzlement as to where a telegram, sent by her husband to tell her that he was not on that train, has been sent. As it turns out, the telegram went to the Martines family on the lower floor of the building, where the wife's unhappiness over her husband's infidelity is complicated by the cryptic—at least to her—message in the telegram, which leads her to believe that he was on the ill-fated train. When

her husband—who also was not on the train—returns, his wife's obvious concern for his well-being makes him repent his past actions. While the motif of mistaken identity is by no means novel with Arquimbau, her comedy relies on irony and situational humor.

Works

Tres contes breus, story collection (1926). *Historia d'una novia i vint braçalets*, novel (1934). *Es rifa un hombre*, play (1935). *Home i dona*, novel (1936). *L'inconvenient de dir-se Martines* in *Premio Joan de Santa Maria 1957*, play (1958). *La pau es un interval*, novel (1970). *40 anys perduts*, novel (1971). *Almarge*, novel.

Bibliography

"Introduction" to Arquimbau, Rosa María. *L'inconvenient de dir-se Martines* in *Premio Joan de Santa Maria 1957* (Barcelona, 1958). Rosa María, *Quien es quien en las letras españolas*, 2nd edition (1979). Galerstein, Carolyn L., ed., *Women Writers of Spain: an Annotated Bio-bibliographical Guide* (New York, 1986).

Susan Wilson

Marta Pessarrodona Artigues

Born 1941, Terrasa, Spain
Genre(s): poetry
Language(s): Catalan, English, German

Marta Pessarrodona is one of the few poetesses of a group of Catalan writers who were born in the 1940s, the postwar years in Spain. These young poets follow Gabriel Ferrater's poetic form that evolves around personal experiences. There are other poetic influences in this group, and there are some other Catalan poets such as Slavat-Papasseit, Foix and Carner to mention a few. There is also a strong influence of such Anglo-Saxon writers as Eliot, Lowell, and Graves.

Pessarrodona was born in 1941, two years after the Franquist government took over the country. Those were very difficult times for the Catalan arts because any publication in this language was forbidden. Pessarrodona adopted Catalan as her literary language in 1964.

The poetess is the only child of a middle-class family. She attended the Universidad de Barcelona where she specialized in history and

Romance languages. She started to write poems when she was twelve and entered the literary world in 1965 with a limited edition of eight poems. The edition was prepared by a group of friends and included some illustrations.

She met the poet Gabriel Ferrater in 1968, a decisive year in her poetic and personal life. Ferrater wrote the prologue to her first serious publication.

She spent two years in England, from 1972 to 1974, as a Spanish lecturer at the University of Nottingham. England made a strong impression upon Pessarrodona, and London became one of her favorite cities. Her English experiences have been reflected in her work as have many of her personal life events. She has worked in a publishing house and contributed to many periodicals and newspapers as a literary critic. Her interest in other European countries and their literature causes her to travel a lot. In 1984 she received a grant to study German in Berlin. This trip provided material for her recent publication, *Berlin Suite.*

A concern that is repeated in most of her poems is the feminist approach and the topic of friendship. Pessarrodona's poetry is universal. Some of her works have been translated into English and published in the American periodical *The Humanist.*

Most of her poems have been collected in a publication named *Poesia 1969–1981.* All her works end with an epilogue in which Pessarrodona concentrates on the historical surroundings of the work. Her poems depict this reality in a very colloquial language that has a high lyricism. *Setembre 30* (1969) is her first book. It includes twenty-seven poems, divided into six sections. The themes we find in this book center around science, history, creation, and the correlated topics of life and death, love, and faith. We also find the ever-present theme of friendship in Pessarrodona's production.

Vida privada (1973) is another collection of eighteen dramatic poems. Pessarrodona says: "Poetry for me is some kind of strip-tease." In autobiographical form she depicts her world and makes the reader live her world in a very vivid way.

The intellectual interests of Marta Pessarrodona are shown in her work *Memòria I* (1979). The first group of poems express the nostalgia of an exile. In the background we see the English winter with such characteristic details as the snow and squirrels. We find the myth of Nessa in the following poems. The poetess' feelings come to the surface in a very real way.

One of the most personal productions of Pessarrodona is *A favor meu, nostre* from a series dedicated to women. This feminist poetry reaches us through a very intelligent approach. The poems follow a process of individualization. From a collective "nostre" the author transports us to a personalization in "tu" and an intimate revelation in "jo." This work is written in honor of other women writers who encountered many problems writing and publishing.

Berlin Suite (1985), her most recent book, concerns the experiences of Pessarrodona in Berlin. This visit made a deep impression on the writer, who recognizes that her understanding of Europe deepened after her stay in this German city. There are numerous geographical and historical references, concluding with the sad words "the war has not ended" as the writer stands beside the Berlin wall.

Pessarrodona expresses herself in a moral and realistic tone. She is always searching for the values that she considers important for humanity. Her message of sincerity and intimate warmth moves her readers and brings them to experience her vital poetry.

Works

Setembre 30 (1969). *Vida privada* (1973). *Memòria I* (1979). *A favor meu, nostre* (1982). *Poemes 1969–1981* (1985). *Berlin Suite* (1985).

Bibliography

Marco, J., "Memoria i Marta Pessarrodona." *Destino* (July 11, 1969). Miquel, L., "Striptease poética de Marta Pessarrodona." *Diario de Lérida* (May 10, 1973). Parcerisas, F., "In the Way of Mrs. Hughes y la moral de Marta Pessarrodona." *Camp de l'arpa* 6 (March–April 1973). Pi de Cabanyes, O., "Marta Pessarrodona, entrevista." *La generació literaria dels 70* (Barcelona, 1971), pp. 101–112.

Maria Luisa Guardiola-Ellis

"Árva" (Orphan)

(see: Kata Bethlen)

Aspazija

Born March 16, 1865, on a farm in Zemgale,
    Latvia; died November 5, 1943, Dubulti,
    Latvia
Genre(s): drama, lyric poetry, memoirs,
    journalism
Language(s): Latvian

Aspazija, whose real name was Elza Rozenberga, can be numbered among the four or five most distinguished lyric poets in Latvian literature and is one of the most outstanding playwrights in its exceptionally rich tradition of national drama. She was born into a well-to-do farmer's family; her early education was good for her time, but mainly because of parental resistance, she was unable to complete secondary school. After a disastrous early marriage that ended in divorce and after the financial ruin of her parents, she went to Riga to support herself, mainly as a writer. This she was able to do with brilliant success; by the turn of the century she was famous and greatly admired as a dramatist. Her play *Sidraba šķkidrauts* (1905; The Silver Veil) created a furor, for it was understood to symbolize a call for revolution and Latvian national independence from Russia. A mark of her extraordinary popularity was the appearance in 1904 of her collected works in a volume of 700 pages.

In 1897 she married Jānis Pliekšāns, who soon became famous under his pseudonym of Rainis and is considered Latvia's greatest writer. Aspazija shared her husband's political exile in Switzerland (1906–1920). Their interdependence and mutual influence is very complex matter and has not yet been sufficiently studied. It is certain that she greatly furthered his development as a poet, she was his main critic and (to an unverifiable degree) his collaborator. From 1906 on, her reputation was to some extent eclipsed by that of her husband, but she continued producing work of very high caliber until her death.

After Latvia gained independence, Aspazija and Rainis returned from exile. An ardent feminist, for several years she was politically active in the women's rights movement. Since her political views changed throughout her life, she managed to antagonize in turn almost all Latvian political parties and factions, and this factor has to some extent harmed her reputation. Her reputation rests assured, however, on the basis of the colorful, bold, and passionate language of her poetry, both lyric and dramatic, with its virtuosic rhythms and extraordinary gift for metaphor. She is also celebrated for the rich mythical and folkloric content of her plays, such as *Zalša līgava* (The Sea Serpent's Bride). Although the folklore on which she most immediately draws is Latvian, the mythical themes and archetypes involved are universal. Her plays are complex, revealing multiple levels of meaning. Her work succeeds in synthesizing Christian and pagan, romantic, and classical assumptions.

Works

(In the following list an attempt is made to indicate the date of first publication of each work; since first performance sometimes predates publication, and since Russian censorship delayed the printing of some of the early works, the dates are not always clear.) *Atriebēja* (1888). *Prologs* (1894). *Vaidelote* (1894). *Zaudētas tiesības* (1894). *Ragana* (1894). *Saules Meita* (1894). *Naizsniegtais mērķis* (1895). *Sarkanās puķes* (1897). *Zeltīte* (1900). *Dvēseles krēsla* (1904). *Sidraba šķidrauts* (1905). *Saulainais stūrītis* (1910). *Ziedu klēpis* (1912). *Laime* (1913). *Izplesti spārni* (1918). *Raganu nakts* (1923). *Aspāzija* (1923). *Zila debess* (1924). *Boass un Rute* (1925). *Trejkrāsaina saule* (1926). *Torņa cēlējs* (1927). *Asteru laikā* (1928). *Zalša līgava* (1928). *Zelta mākoņi* (1938). *Pūcesspiegelis* (1932). *Velna nauda* (1933). *Dvēseles ceļojums* (1933). *Rudens lakstīgala* (1933). *Kaisītas rozes* (1936). *Zem vakara zvaiganes* (1942).

Translations: *The Silver Veil* and *The Sea Serpent's Bride*, tr. A.B. Stahnke. [Selected poems], *A Century of Latvian Poetry*, ed. and tr. W.K. Matthews (1957).

Bibliography

Stahnke, A.B., *Aspazija: Her Life and Her Drama* (1984). Straumanis, Alfreds, ed., *Baltic Drama: A Handbook and Bibliography* (Prospect Heights, Illinois, (1981).

Other references: A yearbook dedicated to research dealing with Rainis and Aspazija began to appear in Sweden in 1967; for particulars on this *Rainņa un Aspāzijas gadagrāmata*, see Benjamiņs Jēgers, *Latviešu trimdas izdevumu bibliografija—Bibliography of Latvian Publications Published Outside*

Latvia, 1961–1970(Sundbyberg, 1977), item 5769; *1971–1980* (Stockholm, 1988), item 7974.

Zoja Pavlovskis

María Victoria Atencia

Born 1931, Málaga, Spain
Genre(s): poetry
Language(s): Spanish

Atencia started writing poetry in the early fifties after studying music and painting. (She still devotes time to etchings.) Between 1953 and 1961 she published four books of poetry and then remained silent until 1976. In the meantime, she became a professional pilot. Married to the poet and printer Rafael León, mother of four children, happily ensconced in her native Málaga, publishing her work in exquisite limited editions, she actually started reaching a wider circle of readers only in what she herself calls her third period: since 1984. She has been translated to Catalan, Czech, English, French, Italian, Lithuanian, Portuguese, Romanian, Swedish. She herself has translated Rilke, Yevtushenko, Rosalía de Castro, García Lorca's Galician poems, Margherita Guidacci, Josep Janés i Olivá, Claude Esteban.

Her early books, which she later rejected, grope for a personal voice. It is with *Marta & María* that she finds it and from there on continues to add new notes without deviating from the essence. In *Los sueños* (Dreams), impalpable settings predominate. Each poem oscillates between the unreal and the possible, producing the impression of extraordinary lightness. Her poetic world and *credo* are most clearly formulated in *El mundo de M.V.* (World of M.V.): an interplay of everyday reality and abstract tangents. From the tension between the two surges a dynamic affirmation of beauty. Faith in it, quest for essence, sculptured yet almost unnoticeable form, self-assurance which does not prevent marvel and reverence, intense luminosity are the most outstanding characteristics of this poetry, which shows some affinities with that of Jorge Guillén. Consciousness of time is one of her great themes, prompting her to use the present tense in order to capture the fleeting moment. The universe presented is unified, plenary, well integrated; yet she often juxtaposes two different facets, several points of view, two emotive reactions. There is almost continuous use of dialogue: with things, with other beings, with mute witnesses of past times, with her own self.

Ex libris, which gathers four previous books in one volume, reaffirms the constants: ascending movement; majestic serenity; steady and poised tone; preference for blank alexandrine; short, very dense units; artful use of alliterations; frequent play and counterplay with words; great plastic quality. Lucidity goes hand in hand with intuitive spirituality. Doves and sea-gulls crisscross the pages, uniting the two worlds in tension. Infinite tenderness pervades some of her verse, yet it is controlled, terse, full of strength.

In *Compás binario* (Binary Measure) and *Paulina* the ekphrastic element increases; there are more cultural allusions; the condensation is such that some poems become almost hermetic. *Trances de Nuestra Señora* (Trances of Our Lady) presents, in 14 short poems, the life and passion of Our Lady. The voice of the Virgin creates an almost supernatural ambience. Yet, in it, next to the tradition of the mystics and the Psalms, the quandaries of a very earthly woman can be recognized.

Atencia integrates reason with emotion, gracefulness and charm with precision. An accomplished master in the use of all stylistic devices, she does not believe in making a show of them: her terse lines integrate all elements inconspicuously. Affirmation of the mysterious essences is her winged commitment to poetry. Commitment to and celebration of womanhood are present from her very first poems on, where delicate sensitivity melds with barely noticeable eroticism, and where she proclaims her determination to find plenitude and fulfillment through femininity.

Works

Tierra mojada [Wet Earth] (n.d. [1953]). *Los doce cuentos maravaillosos* (1955). *Cuatro sonetos* [Four Sonnets] (1955; modified version, 1956). *Arte y parte* [Art and Part] (1961). *Cañada de los ingleses* [The Path of the English] (1973). *Marta & María* (1976). *Los sueños* (1976). *El mundo de M.V.* (1978). *Venezia Serenissima* (1978). *Paseo de la Farola* [Farola Avenue] (1978). *Himnario* [Hymn

Book] (1978). *El coleccionista* [The Collector] (1979). *Debida proporción* [The Right Proportion] (1981). *Adviento* [Advent] (1983). *Porcia* (1983). *Caprichos* [Whims] (1983). *Ex libris* (1984). *Compás binario* (1984). *Paulina o el libro de las aguas* [Pauline, or the Book of Water] (1984). *Glorieta de Guillén* [Guillén Circle] (1986). *Trances de Nuestra Señora* (1986). *L'Occhio di Mercurio* [Mercury's Eye], bilingual (1988; Italian tr. E. Coco). *De la llama en que arde* [The Flame that Burns Inside] (1988). *La pared contigua* [Contiguous Wall] (1989).

Translations: "Village," "Christina's World," tr. Louis Bourne. *Spain, The Transition Years, 1975–1985* (Frankfurt/Main, Autumn 1985). *Selected Poems*, tr. Louis Bourne (Fredericksburg, Va., 1987).

Bibliography

Carnero, Guillermo, Prologue. *Ex libris* (Madrid, 1984), pp. 9–13. Duque, Aquilino, "Las alas de María Victoria," *Metapoesía* (Sevilla, 1984), pp. 125–127. Janés, Clara, "MVA o el triunfo de la belleza." *Los Cuadernos del Norte* III–16 (Nov.–Dec. 1982): 38–39. Ortiz, Fernando, "La difícil serenidad de María Victoria Atencia." *La estirpé de Bécquer* (Seville, 1985), pp. 253–58. Ugalde, Sharon Keefe, "Time and Ekphrasis in the Poetry of María Victoria Atencia." *Confluencia. Revista hispánica de cultura y literatura* 3, 1 (Fall 1987): 7–12.

Kristiaan P. Aercke

Julie-Marie Aubert

(see: Marie Dauguet)

Marie-Anne-Hubertine Auclert

Born February 10, 1848, Saint-Priest-en-Murat, France; died April 4, 1914, Paris
Genre(s): essay, journalism
Language(s): French

Considered one of the foremost advocates of women's voting rights in France, Hubertine Auclert produced an important body of works touching on women's political equality. She came to Paris in 1872 and was affiliated with Léon Richer and Maria Desraismes, prominent French feminists in republican circles and editors of the journal *Le Droit des femmes* (The Rights of Women). Auclert's concentration on political equality rather than on guarantees of civil and economic equality led her in 1876 to found her own journal *Le Droit de la femme*. Richer and Desraismes considered her planned address to the 1878 International Congress of Women too radical to be delivered; it was published that same year as *Le Droit politique des femmes, question qui n'est pas traitée au Congrès international des femmes* (The Political Rights of Women, an Issue not Raised at the International Congress of Women). In 1880 she attempted to register for the vote and, upon being turned away, refused to pay her taxes, arguing that she had not voted for their expenditure. This affair attracted considerable publicity. The decade of the 1880s witnessed a growing rift between republican (or liberal) feminists, such as Richer and Desraismes, and socialist (or radical) feminists, such as Auclert, on a number of questions, specifically that of civil vs. political rights. At this time liberals favored a gradualist or piecemeal approach (the so-called *politique des brèches*), whereas the socialists championed immediate electoral reform. In 1881, together with Léon Giraud and Antonin Lévrier (whom she married in 1888), she founded the weekly (later monthly) journal *La Citoyenne* (The Female Citizen), which ceased publication in 1891.

Auclert moved to Algeria with her husband in 1888, and, following his death four years later, returned to Paris where she resumed her political activities, publishing articles in various socialist journals which were republished posthumously in book form. She argued for the legal separation of wealth in marriage and for the right of women to retain their maiden names after marriage.

Works

Le Droit politique de la femme [Political Rights of Woman] (1878; rpt. Marseilles, 1879). *Les Femmes arabes en Algérie* [Arab Women in Algeria] (1900). *L'Argent de la femme* [Woman's Money] (1904). *Le Nom de la femme* [Woman's Name] (1905). *Le Vote des femmes* [Women's Vote] (1908). *Les Femmes au gouvernail* [Women at the Helm] (1926; contains a biography by Auclert's sister Marie

Chaumont). *La Citoyenne, Articles de 1881 à 1891* [The Female Citizen, Articles 1881–1891], ed. with commentary by Edith Taieb (1982).

Bibliography
Hause, Steven C., *Hubertine Auclert, The French Suffragette* (New Haven, 1987). Lazare, G., "Marie-Anne-Hubertine Auclert." *Dictionnaire de biographie française*, 4 (Paris, 1948), col. 327–328. Moses, Claire Goldberg, *French Feminism in the Nineteenth Century* (Albany, 1984), pp. 213–218.

Earl Jeffrey Richards

Marguerite Audoux

Born 1863, Sancoins, France; died 1937,
    Saint-Raphael, France
Genre(s): novel, short story
Language(s): French

The story of Marguerite Audoux' success could well be the subject of a novel. A country girl comes to the big city (in this case, Paris) and earns her living as a seamstress. Her eyesight, which has always been weak, grows worse from the strain of the work. A doctor gives her an ultimatum: change careers or go blind. As luck would have it, she has fallen in with a group of young men who themselves form a literary circle. One evening in the course of a discussion, she admits that she too has tried her hand at writing and soon she shares with them a few unfinished chapters from an incomplete novel. Their astonishment is matched only by their enthusiasm; she is encouraged to continue and the result is *Marie-Claire* (1911), a runaway bestseller, which recounts the story of a young country girl who decides to leave for Paris to make her fortune. After its publication, Audoux continued to write until her death in 1937.

Although Audoux achieved instant fame, *Marie-Claire* did not spring overnight from her imagination. Early in her life, Audoux became a voracious reader and would read anything she could find, from novels to almanacs. It was only when reading became too difficult for her that writing replaced it as a source of pleasure. Her fortuitous association with a number of young writers launched her into the literary world. Short stories and sketches began to appear in *Matin* and *Paris Journal*, and soon a collection was published although it attracted little attention. Not so for *Marie-Claire*, which sold over 30,000 copies in its early printings. The novel is an almost perfect blending of style and story. Audoux tells a simple tale in deceptively simple language. *L'Atelier de Marie-Claire* (1920; Marie-Claire's Workshop) was less well received; it suffered by comparison, as do most sequels. In her other works, especially the collection of short stories, *La Fiancée* (1930; Valserine and Other Stories), the subject matter is again well-served by her style. Hers are the works of a self-taught person who had a keen eye for detail and filtered realism through her own brand of subjectivity. Audoux is fairly light reading but nonetheless quite enjoyable.

Works
    Le Chaland de la reine (1910). Marie-Claire (1911). L'Atelier de Marie-Claire (1920). De la Ville au moulin (1926). Douce lumière (1937). La Fiancée (1930).
    Translations: Marie-Claire. Marie-Claire's Workshop. Valserine and Other Stories.

Bibliography
Lanoizélée, Louis, *Marie Audoux* (Paris, 1954). Reyer, Georges, *Un Coeur pur* (Paris, 1947).

Edith Joyce Benkov

August

(see: Kathinka [Katharina] Rosa
    Pauline Modesta Zitz-Halein)

Marie-Catherine le Jumel de Barneville, Baronne d'Aulnoy

Born 1650 or 1651, Barneville-la-Bertrand,
France; died January 13, 1705, Paris
Genre(s): novel, fairy tale, travel literature,
memoirs, short story, devotional
literature, correspondence
Language(s): French

Possibly one of the most enigmatic figures of her age, Marie-Catherine le Jumel de Barneville, Madame d'Aulnoy, was born at Barneville-la-Bertrand in 1650 or 1651, the daughter of Nicholas-Claude le Jumel and Judith-Angelique Coustelier. Little or nothing is known about the circumstances of her childhood, but from latter descriptions, she must have received the usual training given daughters of a minor aristocratic family—lessons in painting, music, and several foreign languages, including Spanish and English. She was also considered a witty, elegant, and easy conversationalist, and in her own works she uses her French to remarkably good effect. Additionally, references to other literary works in her texts reflect a wide acquaintance with popular literature, including Ovid, parodic Renaissance poetry, the Spanish drama, and the French medieval *fabliaux*.

In 1666, when not yet seventeen, she was married to a man three times her own age, François de la Motte, baron d'Aulnoy and one of the household officers of César de Vendôme. It is more than likely that the marriage was arranged and less than welcome to the young bride. The baron, who had purchased his title, possibly with money given by Vendôme for sexual favors, was a handsome, wealthy, but also irritable and high tempered man. Shrewd, ambitious, avaricious, he drank to excess, chased women, and was a noted supporter of the Parisian brothels. Three years after it began, the marriage ended in scandal and execution, with Marie-Catherine fading from public view for nearly twenty years to come.

Although our understanding of those events is less than complete, it appears likely that Marie-Catherine's mother, possibly with her daughter's consent, persuaded two Norman friends to accuse the baron of lèse majesté. Although immediately arrested and, by the order of Colbert, taken to the Bastille, he convinced the authorities of his innocence. His denouncers were then arrested and sent to join d'Aulnoy in prison where, after numerous trials, they confessed under torture that the affair had been carefully planned by d'Aulnoy's mother-in-law. Her objective was to obtain the baron's money while disencumbering both herself and her daughter of his person. The two Normans were beheaded at the Place de Grève, the baron was released after paying the crown a rather hefty fine, and Madame d'Aulnoy and her mother disappeared.

The degree of Madame d'Aulnoy's complicity in the crime, as well as her whereabouts after the executions is unknown. A forced sojourn in a Parisian convent is likely. Certainly she was in Paris in October of 1676 for the birth of her fifth child. In the years to come, she may have travelled extensively—to Flanders, to England, and to Spain, where her mother had fled and where she served as a double agent for both the French and Spanish governments. At any rate, when Marie-Catherine next appears in public records, it is 1685, and she is installed in a convent outside Paris.

By now middle-aged, the baronne turned her hand to writing, most probably as a means of financial support. In 1690, she made her literary debut with her first, and arguably her best, novel, *Histoire d'Hypolite, Comte de Douglas* (The Story of Hypolite, the Count of Douglas). This was a rousing tale of love, adventure, and narrowly averted incest that also included France's first published fairy tale, the "Ile de la Félicité" (The Isle of Happiness), which predates Perrault's more famous collection by a good seven years. The book was an immense success, and within a year had been reprinted by one of France's most prestigious booksellers and publishers, Claude Barbin.

Success brought prosperity and respectability. Madame d'Aulnoy moved to the quartier Saint-Sulpice soon afterwards, delaying little in establishing a salon frequented by such luminaries as the Princess de Conti, the Comtesse de Murat, and Madame and Mademoiselle Desholières. She set to work at a feverish rate, trying her hand at a number of genres. Her *Mémoires de la cour d'Espagne* (1680; The Memoirs of the Spanish

61

Court), also a huge success, was followed in 1691–1692 by another travelogue, *Relation du voyage d'Espagne* (The Story of A Voyage to Spain), another historical novel, *Jean de Bourbon, prince de Carency* (Jean de Bourbon, Prince of Carency), an interesting experiment with the *novella* form, *Nouvelles espagnols* (1692; Spanish Short Stories), and her only two devotional works—*Sentiments d'une âme penitente* (1691; The Sentiments of a Penitent Soul) and *Le retour d'une âme à dieu* (1692; The Return of a Soul to God). In 1693, she turned to historiography for her seventh book, *Nouvelles ou mémoires Historiques* (Stories or Historical Memoirs), a history of Louis XIV's war against Holland. Her last two novels, *Mémoires de la cour d'Angleterre* (1695; Memoir of the English Court) and *Le Compte de Warwick* (1703; The Count of Warwick), returned to an English locale for their exotic setting, and continued to explore her favorite theme, the connections between love and power. Though little read today, these, too, were best-sellers of their day. Her most lasting successes, however, were her two collections of fairy tales—the *Contes de fées* (Fairy Tales), published in 1697 and *Les contes nouveaux ou les fées à la mode* (New Fairy Tales, or Fairies in Fashion), which appeared the following year. Countless re-editions of both works have been printed, fourteen in the eighteenth century alone, and they are still being read and enjoyed today.

By the close of the 1600s, Madame d'Aulnoy stood at the height of her literary fame. A respectable and best-selling author, she was one of nine French women holding membership in the venerable Accademia del Ricovvati of Padua. In just thirteen years, she had produced twenty-eight volumes, including novels, novellas, fairy tales, a history, edifying verse, travel books, memoirs, and letters. It was at this moment, when she seemed at her most secure from social reprobation, that scandal once again erupted in a curious replay from the events of her youth. Her close friend Madame Ticquet was accused of attempting to have her husband, a counselor at the Parlement de Paris, murdered at his own front door. Madame Ticquet, who was reported to have been at Madame d'Aulnoy's on the day of the crime, was arrested, brought to trial, put to torture, and executed at the Place de Grèves.

D'Aulnoy, tainted by the haunting similarity to the trial of her youth, shared in the reprobation and once more retired from public life. Six years later, on January 13, 1705, she died. She was survived by four of her six children.

While Madame d'Aulnoy was not the leading literary figure of her day, neither is she interesting solely for her unusual life. Her works display linguistic talent, an unsettling sense of humor, a gift for rapid narration and parody, an ability to analyze emotions with finesse and delicacy, and a quick ear for coining arresting new words. In her novels, her thematic emphasis upon constancy, faithful love, and "la delicatess des sentiments" leads her to adopt a critical attitude towards a code of morality that often denied freedom of action to women. This stream of social critique, hidden at times, more open at others, is the underground stream feeding much of Madame d'Aulnoy's literary production. Unlike so many of their predecessors, her heroines are not martyrs for love. They are victims of society—of unfeeling parents, of cruel husbands, of constricted opportunity, of isolation, of malevolent circumstances, but most of all of role definitions that force women to live for, in, and through their marriages. Marriage is rarely a happy state in Madame d'Aulnoy's work, and though the ceremony itself often provides the traditional comic ending of her tales, she usually mitigates its appeal with curiously disturbing overtones, most often the death or the bereavement of a woman protagonist. Interestingly, while the heroines of her novels are distinguished principally by their passive suffering, the heroines of the fairy tales are capable of action and function as figures of power. Soldiers, lovers, courtiers, and rulers, they change the worlds of Madame d'Aulnoy's imagination, reminding us that the original audience was not children but adults, the elegant women of salon society during the reign of Louis XIV.

Madame d'Aulnoy has often been undervalued, particularly in reference to her fairy tales, but the complexity of her seemingly conventional stories and the ambiguous moral stances they imply are now attracting the attention that they deserve. In addition to her considerable skills as a storyteller, she has claims on our interest as a covert, but pointed moralist. New editions of many of her works are now needed to enable us to reassess her achievement and her position in French literature.

Works

Histoire d'Hypolite, comte de Duglas [The Story of Hypolite, the Count of Douglas] (1690). *Mémoires de la cour d'Espagne* [Memoires of the Spanish Court] (1690). *Relation du voyage d'Espagne* [The Story of a Visit to Spain] (1691). *Jean de Bourbon, prince de Carency* [Jean of Bourbon, Prince of Carency] (1692). *Sentiments d'une âme penitente* [Sentiments of a Penitent Soul] (1691). *Le retour d'une âme à dieu* [The Return of a Soul to God] (1691). *Nouvelles espagnoles* [Spanish Novellas] (1692). *Nouvelles ou mémoires historiques* [Historical Memoirs] (1693). *Mémoires de la cour d'Angleterre* [Memoirs of the English Court] (1695). *Les contes de fées* [Fairy Tales] (1697). *Les contes nouveaux ou les fées à la mode* [New Tales, or Fairies in Fashion] (1698). *Le Comte de Warwick* [The Count of Warwick] (1692).

Translations: *The Earl of Douglas, An English Story, from the French* [Histoire d'Hypolite] (1774). *The History of John of Bourbon, Prince of Carency. Containing a Variety of Entertaining Novels, . . . Written in French, . . . translated into English* [Jean de Bourbon] (1723). *The Diverting Works of the Countess d'Anois . . . Containing: I. Memoirs of Her Own Life. II. All Her Spanish Novels and Histories. III. Her Letters. IV. Tales of the Fairies . . . Newly done into English* [Nouvelles espagnoles, among others] (1707). *Memoirs of the Court of England in 1675* [Mémoires de la cour d'Angleterre, Mrs. William Henry Arthur, tr.] (1913). *The History of the Earl of Warwick* [Le Compte de Warwick] (1708).

Bibliography

Barchilon, Jacques, *Le conte merveilleux français de 1690–1790* (Paris, 1975). Beeler, James R., "Madame d'Aulnoy, Historical Novelist of the Late Seventeenth Century." Unpublished diss., Chapel Hill, N.C., 1964. de Graff, Amy, *The Tower and the Well* (Birmingham, Ala., 1984. Detering, Elizabeth, "The Fairy Tales of Madame d'Aulnoy." Unpublished diss., Houston, Tex., 1982. Foulché-Delbosc, R., "Madame d'Aulnoy et l'Espagne." *Revue Hispanique* LXVII (June 1926): 1–151. Georges, Cardinal Grentes, ed., *Dictionnaire des lettres françaises*, vol. III (Paris, 1954). Hubert, R., "Poetic Humor in Madame d'Aulnoy's Fairy Tales." *L'Esprit Créateur* III, no. 3 (1963): 123–149. Hubert, R., "L'Amour et la féerie chez Madame d'Aulnoy." *Romanische Forschungen* 75 (1963): 1–10. Hubert, R., "Le sens du voyage dans quelques contes de Madame d'Aulnoy." *French Review* XLVI, no. 5 (April 1973). Jal, Auguste, *Dictionnaire critique de biographie et d'histoire* (Paris, 1872). Mitchell, Jane, *A Thematic Analysis of Madame d'Aulnoy's Contes de Fées* (University of Mississippi Press, 1978). Roche-Mazon, Jeanne, "En marge de 'L'Oiseau Bleu.'" *Cahiers de la Quinzaine* (Paris, 1930). Slater, Maya, "Madame d'Aulnoy and the Adult Fairy Tale." *Newsletter for Seventeenth Century Studies* (1982): 69–75. Storer, Mary E., *Un episode littéraire de la fin du XVIIe siècle: la mode des contes de fées* (Paris, 1928; rpt. 1972). Welch, Marcelle, "La Femme, le mariage, et l'amour dans les contes de fées mondains du XVIIe siècle français." *Papers on French Seventeenth Century Literature* 18 (1983): 47–58.

Glenda Wall

Louise de Boissigny, Comtesse d'Auneuil

Born 17th century, France; died 18th century, France
Genre(s): fairy tale, romance
Language(s): French

Louise de Boissigny, Comtesse d'Auneuil, a fashionable woman of Parisian society, was a *précieuse* who authored several collections of fairy tales in the first years of the eighteenth century. She was allied to Madame de la Force by her marriage to the Comte d'Auneuil, and she presided, in her own right, over a fashionable salon in Paris. Most of her collections were written for women who frequented these gatherings and whose concern with elegant manners are abundantly reflected in her tales. While these clear appeals to a special coterie provide fascinating evidence of its internal daily life, the tales as a whole also betray unmistakable signs of an exhausted literary style.

Possibly this exhaustion was recognized by the author herself. Louise's attempts to accommodate her productions to a declining public taste can be seen in the title of her very first collection, *Tiranee des fées détruite* (1702; The Tyranny of the Fairies Destroyed), which she dedicated to the Duchess of Burgundy. Her preface seems to promise a fresh departure in its depiction of the fairies as "nos ennemies" and in its avowed intention to destroy their tyrannical power, which extends "jusque sur les coeurs." Unfortunately, however, the plan extends no further than the first story. Although the fairies are indeed destroyed, they are resurrected for the remaining tales. In such stories as "Agathe," "La Princesse Léonice," and "Le Prince Curieux," they once again figure as beneficial entities, the essential catalysts in procuring the obligatory ending of a happy marriage.

Their role remains much the same throughout the other fairy tale collections produced by the countess. These collections, published throughout the early eighteenth century in the form of pamphlets, consist of letters whose style mingles the *précieuse* spirit with the conventions of fairy lore. Three such collections are known: *Nouvelles diverses du temps, la Princess des Prentintailles* (1702; Different Stories of the Times, the Princess of Prentintailles), *L'Inconstance Punie* (1702; Inconstance Punished), and *Les Colinettes* (1703; The Small Hills). In their obvious recording of the events of Madame d'Auneuil's circle of friends and in their discussion of contemporary manners, *La Princesse* and *Les Colinettes* in particular can be regarded as early prototypes of the fashion journal.

In her latter works, such as *Les Chevaliers errans* (1705; The Errant Knights) and *Le Génie familier* (The Familiar Genie), the Comtesse d'Auneuil bowed to the growing public boredom with fairy tales. These two novels reduce fairy lore to a minimum while pushing romantic strains to an extreme. The latter story, which falsely purports to be a translation of an Arabian tale, is actually a retelling of the patient Griselda story.

Madame d'Auneuil is not the most talented member of that group of women writers who composed so many collections of fairy tales in Paris during the last years of the seventeenth century. She wrote in obvious haste, without rewrite, and without much attention to anything more than reproducing the traditional story lines that she relied upon for her plots. But she had a happy gift for vivid description and for recording the fashions and concerns of the salon society. Her detailed observations of this world of galanterie, for whose members she penned her tales, is exactly and fascinatingly translated into the conventions of the fairy tale, demonstrating clearly the links between this world and the "féerie" with which it entertained itself. A clear picture of an almost totally feminine society thus emerges. Her tales may be, as Mary Storer has described them, "une féerie des ruelles des dames, de l'époque de décadence" (157), but they have much to tell us about the popularity of this strange fashion, its relationship to a specific social situation, and its possible use by other women writers to express ideas inexpressible in more direct fashions.

Works

La Tyrannie des fées détruite [The Tyranny of the Fairies Destroyed] (1702). *La Princesse de Prentintailles* [The Princess de Prentintailles] (1702). *L'Inconstance punie* [Inconstance Punished] (1702). *Les Chevaliers errants* [The Wandering Knights] (1705). *Le Génie familier* [The Familiar Genie] (1705).

Bibliography

Barchilon, Jacques, *Le Cabinet des Fées (1785–1789)*, vol. xxvii (Geneva, 1978), p. 42. Georges, Cardinal Grente, *Dictionnaire des lettres françaises*, vol. III. (Paris, 1954). Storer, Mary, *La Mode des contes de fées* (Paris, 1928; rpt. 1972, Slatkine).

Glenda Wall

Rose Ausländer

(a.k.a. Rosalie Scherzer)

Born 1901, Czernowitz, Poland
Genre(s): poetry
Language(s): German

Born into a middle-income Jewish family in the capital of Bukowina province, at age five the girl was run over by a coal truck and miraculously survived. At the university, she studied literature and philosophy, becoming particularly interested in Spinoza and publishing her poetry locally. At age twenty-one, she married her fellow student Ignaz Ausländer, from whom she separated three years later, although keeping his name, which was to become strangely significant considering her fate and her poetry: *Ausländer* means foreigner in German. Rose Ausländer's first volume of poetry, *Der Regenbogen*, was published in 1939; the entire edition was destroyed in the war. During the German occupation of Czernowitz from 1941–1945, she hid in a basement of the ghetto, always in danger of being discovered and sent to a concentration camp. She has said of those days that "to write was to live, to survive" and about the German language, her only home: "we understand each other's every word/ we love one another." During those times, she and Paul Celan, whom she had met earlier, would regularly read poetry to each other. Liberated by the Russians, she spent from 1945 to 1963 in New York, working as a secretary and translator of German, translating in her spare time Else Lasker-Schüler and Polish author Adam Mickiewicz into English. Of this period, few of her poems survive, in English or German.

In 1963, Rose Ausländer returned to Europe, first to Vienna and in 1965, to Düsseldorf, where she now lives in a nursing home. Twenty-six years after her first book, she published the second, *Blinder Sommer* (1965), after which some twelve volumes were to follow. Ausländer has received several prizes: the honorary prize of Meersbury in 1965; the silver Heine Taler of the publisher Hoffmann & Campe in 1966; the Droste Prize for women poets in 1977; and the Ida Dehmel Prize. Especially since the publication of her *Gesammelte Gedichte* in 1976, she has become recognized widely.

In her "bold and sad voice" (Marie Luise Kaschnitz), using rhythmic repetitions to give the verse an incantatory lightness, using everyday sayings that reveal peculiarities of everyday Jewish life and of German folklore and language, Rose Ausländer's poetry is a telling witness not only of human, and divine, cruelty but also of the will to survive and the need for forgiveness.

Works

Der Regenbogen (1939). *Blinder Sommer* (1965). *36 Gerechte* (1967). *Inventar* (1972). *Ohne Visum* (1974). *Andere Zeichen* (1975). *Gesammelte Gedichte* (1976). *Noch ist Raum* (1976). *Doppelspiel* (1977). *Es ist alles anders* (1978).

Aschensommer, selected poems (1978). *Mutterland* (1978). *Einverständnis* (1980). *Im Atemhaus wohnen*, selected poems (1981). *Mein Atem heisst jetzt* (1981). *Mein Venedig versinkt nicht* (1982).

Bibliography

Brinker-Gabler, Gisela, *Deutsche Dichterinnen* (Frankfurt, 1978). Glenn, Jerry, "Blumenworte/ Kriegsgestammel: The Poetry of Rose Ausländer." *Modern Austrian Literature* 12, 3/4 (1979). Lindemann, Gisela, "Das Werk der Rose Ausländer." *Die Zeit* (April 7, 1978). Puknus, Heinz, ed., *Neue Literatur der Frauen* (Munich, 1980). Serke, Jurgen, *Frauen schreiben* (Frankfurt, 1982).

Ute Marie Saine

Author of "An Everyday Tale"

(see: Thomasine Gyllembourg)

Dominique Avry

(see: Pauline Réage)

Ángela Figuera Aymerich

Born October 30, 1902, Bilbao, Spain
Genre(s): poetry
Language(s): Spanish

Ángela Figuera Aymerich belongs to a wide-ranging group of post-war Spanish writers concerned with social issues, including Blas de Otero and Gabriel Celaya. Her poetry, like that of another socially committed poet, Gloria Fuertes, dramatizes the problem of women in the Spanish post-war society, but Figuera's lyrics often display a greater self-consciousness in their artifice and their concern with the role of the poet than do those of Fuertes.

Ángela Figuera received her degree in Philosophy and Letters from the Universidad Central and from 1933 to 1936 taught at the Instituto de Huelva and later in Alcoy and Murcia. She has also worked at the Biblioteca Nacional of Madrid. She began publishing fairly late; her first volume, *Mujer de barro* (Woman of Clay), appeared in

1948. Her poems have won several prizes, including the Premio Verbo in 1940 for *Vencida por el Ángel* (Conquered by the Angel), the Premio Ifach in 1952 for *El grito inútil* (The Useless Cry), and the Premio Nueva Espana for *Belleza Cruel*.

Figuera's first two books, *Mujer de barro* and *Soria pura* contain her most direct writing, the former a collection of simple, often earthy love poems, the latter a nostalgic look at her Basque homeland. Figuera's late works are more rhetorical and emotional; she often uses repetition to build a sense of outrage. Other poems rely on a more conversational form and tone to characterize a working class persona, as does the "Carta abierta," an open letter from a frustrated laborer to Jesus, complaining that now it is more of a miracle to feed all of his family than it was for Christ to feed the masses with the fish and the loaves. Other poems, no less urgent, express the despair of a literate poet/speaker at being unable to live spontaneously: "I want to live and love without the weight/ of this knowing and hearing and realizing" ("Belleza cruel"). But despite the problems of its self-consciousness, the vision of the social poet is central, particularly in challenging a society that would repress the truth of poetry:

> If you observe the proper etiquette,
> you can say permitted words:
> summer, light, Spanishness, hat.
> (If your tongue falls silent from shame,
> they'll hang a card on you that says
> "mute,"
> and you can hold out your hand for
> pennies.)

In her later work, *Toco la tierra: Letanias* (I Touch the Earth: Litanies), the poet frequently uses incremental repetition, not for evoking the solemn tone of ritual but for conveying a sense of urgency and frustration over social injustices.

Perhaps Ángela Figuera's chief importance as a socially concerned poet results from what some critics have labelled a weakness—the inability to reconcile the self-consciousness of the poet with the unmediated response necessary for action. But by refusing to effect a simple solution between these two poles, Figuera infuses her poetry with a tension and a personal anguish that result in a richness and complexity absent from a more tendentious art.

Works

Mujer de barro [Woman of Clay] (1948). *Soria pura* [Pure Soria] (1949). *Vencida por el Ángel* [Conquered by the Angel] (1950). *El grito inútil* [The Useless Cry] (1952). *Víspera de la vida* [Eve of Life] (1953). *Belleza cruel* [Cruel Beauty] (1958). *Toco la tierra: Letanías* [I Touch the Earth: Litanies] (1962). *Antología total (1949–1969)* [Complete Anthology], selected poems and recording by Figuera (1973). *Cuentos tontos para niños listos: compuestos in verso llaño* [Silly Stories for Ready Children: Composed in Plain Verse] (1979). *Canciones para todo el año* [Songs for All Year Long] (1984).

Bibliography

Daydí-Tolson, Santiago, *The Post-Civil War Spanish Social Poets* (1983). Mandlove, Nancy, "*Historia* and *Intra-historia*: Two Spanish Women Poets in Dialogue with History." *Third Woman 2* (1984): 84–93. Villa-Fernández, Pedro, "La denuncia social en *Belleza Cruel* de Ángela Figuera Aymerich." *Revista de Estudios Hispanicos 7* (1973): 127–138.

Reference Works: *Espasa-Calpe Enciclopedia Universal*, supp. 1961–1962.

Stephen Hale

Azalais d'Altier

Flourished first half XIII century
Genre(s): poetry
Language(s): Provençal

Azalais d'Altier is known only through a verse letter contained in one manuscript (V149r), "Tanz salutz e tantas amors," (P-C 42a,1) in which she identifies herself in line 6 ("vos tramet N'Azalais d'Altier"). Her dating is based on the fact that line 98 of this piece refers to the addressee as Clara, and editors have surmised that this may have been the *trobairitz* Clara d'Anduza. The letter is a skillful defense of Clara's lover, who has turned to N'Azalais for help. It begins by introducing N'Azalais to Clara, as the two have never met, and employs standard *canso* topoi in a new way: to cement the bond between these two women. The letter consists largely of woman-to-woman advice about the proper treatment of men and the reputation Clara will gain if she acts unwisely. N'Azalais plays throughout on inherent similarities between *amor de lonh* and the friendship of women, given that both are extraphysical: at the end she suggests that Clara do as she advises "tot per amor de me;" and the assumption throughout is that the truer of the two loves is the bond between women.

Works

"Tanz salutz e tantas amors."

Bibliography

Bec, P., "*Trobairitz* et chansons de femme: Contribution à la connaissance du lyrisme féminin au moyen âge." *CCM* 22 (1979): 235–262. Bergert, F., *Die von den robadors genannten oder gefeierten Damen.* (Halle: Niemeyer, 1913), p. 48. Bogin, M., *The Women Troubadours* (New York, 1980). Boutiére, J., and A.-H. Schutz, *Biographies des troubadours*, 2d ed. (Paris, 1964). Branciforti, F., *Il canzoniere di Lanfrancesco Cigala* (Florence, 1954). Bruckner, M., "Na Castelloza, *Trobairitz*, and Troubadour Lyric." *Romance Notes* 25 (1985): 1–15. Chabaneau, C., "Les biographies des troubadours en langue provençale." In *Histoire générale de Languedoc*, X (Toulouse, 1885). Crescini, V., "Axalais d'Altiers." *Zeitschrift fur romanische Philologie* 14 (1890): 128–132. Crescini, V., *Per gli studi romanzi*. Padua: Draghi (1892), p. 76. Dronke, P., *Women Writers of the Middle Ages* (Cambridge, 1984). Mahn, C.A.F., *Die Werke der Troubadours in provenzalischer Sprache* (Berlin, 1846). Perkal-Balinsky, D., *The Minor Trobairitz*. Ph.D. diss., Northwestern University, 1986. Portal, E., *Memoires et comptes-rendus de la Societe scientifique et litteraire d'Alais*, 27, p. 271. Raynouard, M., *Choix des poésies originales des troubadours*, 6 vols. (Osnabruck, 1966). Riquer, M. de, *Los trovadores*, 3 vols. (Barcelona, 1975). Schultz, O., *Die Provenzalischen Dichterinnen* (Leipzig, 1888). Shapiro, M., "The Provençal *Trobairitz* and the Limits of Courtly Love." *Signs* 3 (1978): 560–571. Tavera, A., "A la recherche des troubadours maudits." *Sénéfiance* 5 (1978): 135–161. Véran, J., *Les poétesses provençales* (Paris, 1946).

Sarah Spence

Azalais de Porcairages

Born ca. 1140
Genre(s): poetry
Language(s): Provençal

For N'Azalais we have both a wonderful *canso* and a *vida* (Boutiere, p. 341). The *vida* informs us that the trobairitz was from the Montpellier region, a town now called Portiragnes, and we can date N'Azalais fairly securely by three references—two in the *vida*, one in the *canso*. In the *vida* a countess Ermengarda of Narbonne is mentioned who reigned from 1143–1192. Also, there is a reference to Gui Guerrejat, who can be positively identified as the fifth son of Guillaume VI de Montpellier and brother of Guillaume VII who died in 1177 and was buried in Valmagne, near Portiragnes. In the *canso* Orange is alluded to in such a way as to suggest a personification and to conjecture Raimbaut d'Aurenga; there is, however, no mention of N'Azalais in Raimbaut's work.

N'Azalais' *canso*, "Ar em al fregs temps vengut" (P-C 43, 1), consists of four *coblas doblas* of eight lines each, followed by two *coblas singulars* of eight lines each, and a *tornada* of four lines. The rhyme scheme is *ababccdd*. The relatively complicated rhyme scheme reflects an equally sophisticated lyric. Beginning with a classic reverse *Natureingang* that sings of the beginning of autumn, the *canso* moves into a display of despondency over the distance between herself and someone from Orange. The *canso* continues to develop the image of distance as it makes clear the disparity of rank between herself and her desired one, and her fear over having alienated someone loftier than herself.

Works

Schultz, ed., p. 16. Raynouard, III, 39. Mahn, III, 176. Véran, pp. 116–118. Sakari, p. 184. Riquer, I, 460. Bogin, pp. 94–97. Azais, pp. 146–149.

Bibliography

Azais, G., *Les Troubadours de Béziers* (Geneva: 1973; orig. Béziers, 1869), pp. 2, 3, 138–149. Bec, P., "*Trobairitz* et chansons de femme: Contribution à la connaissance du lyrisme féminin au moyen âge." *CCM* 22 (1979): 235–262. Bogin, M., *The Women Troubadours* (New York, 1980). Boutiére, J., and A.-H. Schutz, *Biographies des troubadours*,

2d ed. (Paris, 1964). Branciforti, F., *Il canzoniere di Lanfrancesco Cigala* (Florence, 1954). Bruckner, M., "Na Castelloza, *Trobairitz*, and Troubadour Lyric." *Romance Notes* 25 (1985): 1–15. Chabaneau, C., "Les biographies des troubadours en langue provençale," in *Histoire générale de Languedoc*, X (Toulouse, 1885). Dronke, P., *Women Writers of the Middle Ages* (Cambridge, 1984). Jeanroy, A., *La Poésie lyrique des troubadours*, vol. 1 (Paris, 1934), pp. 342, 312, 314s, 90n. Mahn, C.A.F., *Die Werke der Troubadours in provenzalischer Sprache* (Berlin, 1846). Perkal-Balinsky, D., *The Minor Trobairitz*. Ph.D. diss., Northwestern University, 1986. Raynouard, M., *Choix des poésies originales des troubadours*, 6 vols (Osnabruck, 1966). Riquer, M. de, *Los trovadores*, 3 vols. (Barcelona, 1975). Sakari, A., "Azalais de Porcairagues, le Joglar de Raimbaut d'Orange." *Neuphilologische Mitteilungen*, 50 (1949): 23–43; 56–87; 174–198. Schultz, O., *Die Provenzalischen Dichterinnen* (Leipzig, 1888). Shapiro, M., "The Provençal *Trobairitz* and the Limits of Courtly Love." *Signs* 3 (1978): 560–571. Tavera, A., "A la recherche des troubadours maudits." *Sénéfiance* 5 (1978): 135–161. Véran, J., *Les poétesses provençales* (Paris, 1946).

Sarah Spence

B

Madame de BAAAs (posthumous)

(see: Marie-Françoise Catherine de Beauvau[-Craon], marquise de)

Ingrid Bachér

Born September 24, 1930, Rostock, East Germany
Genre(s): prose narrative, novel, drama
Language(s): German

Ingrid Bachér is another example of the post-World War II generation of West German writers whose major concern was to reform German literature, to move away from the corrupted language and themes of the Third Reich. These authors of the *Nachkriegsliteratur* generation (post-war generation), have dedicated their work to an at times desperate attempt to cope with the war and with the German past, asking for the reasons and looking behind the facades, an attempt usually referred to as *Vergangenheitsbewältigung*.

In the center of their novels and novellas the reader is confronted with an adult who tries to find his childhood and to evaluate his position in regard to that of his parents and thus of the entire Third Reich and WWII-generation. These characters often seem to be lost or alienated within their own environment, as they have lost a very valuable thing: their past and all that is connected with their childhood. They have to cope with a present life they are not allowed to recall and to identify with, that does not seem to have

any background, as every influence that generally forms the perspective of adult life.

Ingrid Bachér, born in Rostock, now in the DDR, spent her youth in Berlin. A great-granddaughter of the German nineteenth century novella writer Theodor Storm, she studied at the *Hochschule für Musik und Theater* in Hamburg (Institute for Music and Theater). She moved to the Ruhr-region and in 1960 received a stipend from the *Villa Massimo* in Rome, where she stayed for the next six years. Extensive travels led her through much of Central America, impressions of which found their way into her work. Married to the painter Ulrich Erben, she moved to Goch, Lower Rhine.

Ingrid Bachér belonged to the *Gruppe 47* (Group 47), a more or less loose organization of young writers at the time (1947), whose intention it was to help overcome the obstacles for German writers in the confusion of the post-war years, to help find a style and direction through mutual criticism, and to support them in their attempt to communicate with each other (Günter Grass). Bachér admitted that she owed this group much of her success and that she hoped a similar group would form again.

Similar to Luise Rinser, another of the post-war writers and representative of *Neue Sachlichkeit*, Ingrid Bachér mixes dream and reality, which might be a result of the desperate attempt to find reasons for the past events, to find "something" in this vacuum. One example is the story *Lasse Lars oder Die Kinderinsel* (1959; Lasse Lars or: the Island of the Children), a narrative of clear and dreamlike quality. The novel *Schöner Vogel Quetzal* (1959; Beautiful Bird Quetzal) incorporates Central American impressions. The motivation for this novel sprang from a feeling of uneasiness concerning the conformity of the parent generation, of those who had been adults during the war. The central figure tries to compensate for this feeling of dissatisfaction by finding an alternative life in Central America. *Die Tochter* (1965; The Daughter) provides psychological insights into the same situation, and is, again, a story about *Vergangenheitsbewältigung*, an attempt to shed some light on the past. Not much different is the novel *Ich und Ich* (I and I), published a year earlier in 1964.

The story deals with the lives of two women: Ruth, born in 1930, and Lena, who had to flee from Germany in 1930, at the age of fourteen. Lena has returned to her home town from America to take part in a dedication ceremony honoring her grandfather. Even though the town is hers and the people are as familiar to her as much as the streets and houses, she feels alienated. Ruth, who has spent all her life in this town, feels as much a stranger, not knowing why, and thus feels drawn to this woman, so much her senior. Ruth describes Lena's feelings and impressions in such a way that the reader is confused at times not knowing whether it is her own or Lena's uneasiness that is expressed. Lena is desperately trying to find her roots, a link to the past, but she is unsuccessful. Ruth, being able to or at least assuming that she is able to understand Lena, starts identifying with her; thus the title "I and I." Lena dies in a car accident, and unanswerable questions of guilt are put forth, questions that do not only inquire into the whys of the accident but are supposed to lead the attention of the reader to the German past, implying that at times it is impossible to ask such questions. Bachér seems to say that sometimes it is not enough to ask for the simple "why," but issues are too complicated and much more is at stake. Ruth finally discovers that she did not have anything in common with Lena after all; however, she keeps wearing Lena's coat and realizes that she has adopted some of Lena's mannerisms.

Language and style, as can be found in much of the post-war literature of West Germany, again similar to Luise Rinser, are often almost unemotional. Sentences are short and abrupt, stating only what is absolutely necessary without indulging in long relative clauses and ellipses.

Works

Novels, novellas: *Lasse Lars oder Die Kinderinsel* (1958). *Schöner Vogel Quetzal* (1959). *Karibische Fahrt* (1961). *Ich und Ich* (1964). *Die Tochter* (1965). *Das Kinderhaus* (1965).

Drama: *Kasperle sucht die Sonne*, radio play (1951). *Der gestiefelte Kater* (1956). *Ein Weihnachtsabend* (1957, based on Dickens). *Verletzung*, television play (1970).

Bibliography

Lexikon deutscher Schriftsteller, Bd I, A-K (Leipzig). Durzac, Manfred, ed., *Deutsche Gegenwartsliteratur* (Stuttgart, 1981).

Jutta Hagedorn

Ingeborg Bachmann

Born June 25, 1926, Klagenfurt, Austria; died October 17, 1973
Genre(s): lyric poetry, short story, novel
Language(s): German

Ingeborg Bachmann grew up in Kärnten, Austria, spending her formative years from twelve to eighteen under fascist war conditions, imprinting upon her psyche the ravages of violence, brutality, rape, and injustice. After the war she studied philosophy at the universities of Graz, Innsbruck, and Vienna, finishing with a doctoral dissertation on the reception of Martin Heidegger, whose existential philosophy influenced her ideas about the ethics of personal truth and the rigors of language. Working first as a correspondent, she soon came to public notice through reading her poems at a meeting of the *Gruppe 47* in 1952 and began her publishing career. Two volumes of poetry appeared, *Die gestundete Zeit* (1953) and *Aufrufung des Großen Bären* (1956); these collections are important for the bleak but new and evocative language and a radical demand for reevaluation of life. Her subsequent prose is similar in its attempt to break with norms, privileges, habits, and traditions. In contemporary European writing she was the first to focus on feminist problems, mainly on the schism between male and female relationships. Her prose writings set up metaphoric situations that expose insensitive male behavior and a desensitized social and political phallocracy, leaving the woman as a sad and lonely victim in its path. Bachmann's heroine, however, despite her demise, is always portrayed as a determined woman, who no longer is willing to participate in subjugation and will rather die than compromise her belief in reciprocal respect. Bachmann's work is thus always melancholic in tone but stringent in analysis. Her radioplay *Der gute Gott in Manhattan* (1958) and her short story collections *Das dreißigste Jahr* (1961) and *Simultan* (1972) attest to this. Most of all, however, her novel *Malina* (1971), the only completed part of an unfinished trilogy, which was to be entitled *Todesarten*, describes the figurative murders of women by men's self-centricity, men's general inability and unwillingness to love others equally.

Bachmann was also known for her collaboration with the composer H.W. Henze, writing the libretti for the operas *Der Prinz von Homburg* (1960) and *Der junge Lord* (1965). The former is based on a play by H. von Kleist, the latter on a story by W. Hauff. She also was one of the first women writers invited to lecture on poetic theory at Frankfurt University in 1959–1960.

She died an untimely, tragic death, ironically of burns sustained in her apartment, having lived the famous line: "Avec ma main brulée, j'écris sur la nature du feu."

Works

Die kritische Aufnahme der Existenzialphilosophy Martin Heideggers. Dissertation, 1950. *Ein Geschäft mit Träumen*, radio play (1952). *Das Herrschaftshaus*, radio play (1952). *Die gestundete Zeit*, poems (1953). *Die Zikaden*, radio play (1955). *Aufrufung des großen Bären*, poems (1956). *Der gute Gott von Manhattan*, radio play (1958). *Das dreißigste Jahr*, short stories (1961). *Malina*, novel with the fragments *Der Fall Franza* and *Requiem for Fanny Goldmann* (1971). *Simultan*, short stories (1972).

Bibliography

Summerfield, Ellen, *Ingeborg Bachmann. Die Auflösung der Figur in ihrem Roman Malina* (Bonn, 1976). *Text und Kritik.* Heft 6, 4. Aufl. (1980).

Margaret Eifler

Luise Bachmann

Born August 20, 1903, Vienna
Genre(s): novel, fairy tale, short story, radio
drama
Language(s): German

Luise Bachmann was the daughter of a civil servant with deep roots in the peasantry. She was employed as an organist and vocalist, but from 1932 she devoted herself totally to writing, and in 1938 she became a professor at the Viennese Teacher Academy. From 1938–1945 she lived in Salzburg and later in Linz/Donau and lastly again in Vienna.

Her novels, fairy tales, stories, and short stories deal with historical fiction, and quite often the main character is a musician or an actual well-known historical artist.

Works

Der Thomas-Kantor [The Thomas Choirmaster], novel about Johann S. Bach (1936). *Meister, Burger und Rebell* [Master, Citizen and Rebel], novel About Tillman Riemenschneider (1937). *Bruckner*, novel about Bruckner (1938). *Musikantengeschichten* [Stories of Musicians] (1939). *Die andere Schöpfung* [The Other Creation], novel about an architect (1940). *Wirrwarr in Weimar* [Chaos in Weimar] (1941). *Die Entführung aus dem Auge Gottes* [The Abduction from God's Eye], comedy (1941). *Der beste, liebste Papa* [The Best, Dearest Papa], story about Leopold Mozart (1946). *Das Wasser rauscht* [The Water Roars:], story about Franz Schubert (1946). *Bruckners Schweizerreise* [Bruckner's Trip to Switzerland], short story (1947). *Drei Kronen eines Lebens* [Three Crowns of One Life], the fate of Clara Schumann (1947). *Wilbirg*, novel (1948). *Singen und Sagen* [Singing and Narrating], novel about the *Minnesong* (1949). *Goldsucher* [Gold Searcher], novel (1951). *Der Sechsfarbige Strahl* [The Six Colored Ray], novel about Altdorfer (1953). *Historie einer schönen Frau* [History of a Beautiful Woman], novel about Morike (1954). *Das Experiment* [The Experiment], novel about youth (1957). *Die Siegerin* [The Victor], biography of Victoria Rasoamananvo from Madagascar (1958). *Das reiche Fräulein Jaricot* [The Rich Miss Jaricot], biography of a woman socialist/activist (1961). *Das Hahnengiggerl* [The Cock Fop], fairy tale (1961). *Die Schlangenjungfrau* [The Serpent Virgin], fairy tale (1961). *Die Bremerstadtmusikanten* [The Bremen City Musicians] (1961). *Die Stolze Föhre* [The Proud Scots Pine Tree] (1961). *Die gute und bose Tochter* [The Good and Bad Daughter] (1961). *Der wieße Hirsch* [The White Stag] (1961). *Der Schuster von Grein* [The Shoemaker from Grein], radio drama (1961). *Die Speckseite* [The Fat Side], radio drama (1961). *Das Fräulein von Orth* [The Young Lady from Orth], radio drama (1961).

Bibliography

Kosch, Wilhelm, *Deutsches Literatur Lexikon*, vol. I (Bern, 1968). *Kurschners Deutscher Literatur-kalender* (Berlin, 1963).

Brigitte Edith Zapp Archibald

Sophie Louise Charlotte (von Klenow) Baden

Born November 21, 1740, Copenhagen,
    Denmark; died June 6, 1824, Copenhagen
Genre(s): novel, essay, journalism
Language(s): Danish

Sophie Louise Charlotte Baden attained a prominent place in Danish letters as a novelist, correspondent, and a frequent contributor to *Bibliotek for det smukke Kiøn* (Library for the Fair Sex), a journal especially for aristocratic literary and literate women in Copenhagen. Baden's work as a novelist first took the form of a story in letters, *Den fortsatte Grandison* (1784; The Grandison Continuation); together with a series of letters and another shorter story, *Den fortsatte Grandison* was first published as a complete novel in 1792, upon the recommendation of enthusiastic readers and the editors of the *Bibliotek*. Charlotte Baden became a prominent spokeswoman for such cardinal personal virtues as "true sensitivity, authenticity, and rural simplicity" (Dalager, p. 118). Baden also contributed anonymous sketches and letters to *Morgenposten* (The Morning Post) and *Birchs Billedgallerie* (Birch's Picture Gallery); one of her sketches in the latter journal, "Billeder af en Københavnsk Dukke" (Pictures of a Copenhagen Doll), depicts (through letters) the shallowness, superficiality, and coquetterie of the Copenhagen writer, Dorette, in contrast to the wholesomeness of the

unaffected rural girl, Lovise (Dalager, pp. 117–118). Charlotte Baden built her major work, *Den fortsatte Grandison*, upon the precursor novel of Samuel Richardson, the very popular English novelist; Richardson's novel, *The History of Sir Charles Grandison* (1753–1754) served as the form and contextual precedent for Baden's own sequel in letter form. Baden also adapted Richardson's view of women as the true enno-bling moral force, "holding socially destructive tendencies (and male passions) at bay" (*Dansk Litteraturhistorie*, 4, 556).

Sophie Louise von Klenow was the daughter of First Lieutenant, later Major, Gustav Ludvig von Klenow (1703–1772) and Bolette Catharine From (1696–1788). She was born in Copenhagen on November 21, 1740, and died on June 6, 1824; she was buried at Our Lady Church in Copenhagen. Baden became the wife of the pre-eminent university professor, lecturer, and scholarly critic, Jacob Baden, who fulfilled an illustrious academic career at the University of Copenhagen (*Dansk biografisk Leksikon*, "Jacob Baden").

In 1784, Charlotte Baden began writing a continuation in letter form of the life of Clementine, one of the secondary characters of Richardson's novel of manners and mores, *Sir Charles Grandison* (*DLH*, 4, 557). The conflict in Richardson's novel had centered on the opposition between love and religion; in *Den fortsatte Grandison*, Charlotte Baden changed the conflict to one of love and duty, focusing on Clementine's "love for the married Grandison and her duty toward her 'proper' suitor, the nobleman Belvedere" (Dalager, p. 117). Of her own choosing, and to avoid her duty, Clementine retreats to a cloister; instead of serving as a place of respite, escape, and solace, Clementine's cloister be-comes a symbol of the family's and society's (united) efforts to discipline and prepare Clementine for marriage (Dalager, p. 117). Clementine marries her intended Belvedere; the wedding, "depicted nearly symbolically as Clementine's deathday" (Dalager, p. 117), rep-resents Clementine's martyrdom and ultimate acquiescence to her family.

Not only did Charlotte Baden continue Richardson's highly popular novel in letter form; she also adopted Richardson's worldview: women were the primary force for morals, for integrity and sincerity, and for ethical values; "while the character of the man was determined to be passionate (erotic), the woman was depicted as the virtuous being (*par excellence*)" (*DLH*, 4, 556). Richardson, aristocratic Danish women literatæ, and Charlotte Baden considered women the essence of honor and virtue against more primitive male passions and instincts; as such, women were expected to improve family morals, to hone their natural virtues, and to serve as positive social (and socializing) influences over and against more base, always threatening, male passions. The exemplary, didactic novels of Richardson led the way to a reevaluation of women's roles; Richardson's works gained enthusiastic, eager response among the female reading public in Denmark, leading to letters and correspondence among literate women, to discussion and debate "in the reform aristocratic circles," and to "a totally new self-awareness of significance for women's (growing) literary engagement" (*DLH*, 4, 556–557). The new engagement and interest in Richardson's intentionally didactic novels gave initial impetus to the extensive prose works of Charlotte Dorothea Biehl and to the direct dramatization of Richardson's novels by Frederikke (Münster) Brun; both of Baden's immediate Danish predecessors considered Richardson's works "a model for life" (*DLH*, 4, 557). Baden followed on Biehl's and Brun's heels, publishing *Den fortsatte Grandison*, a great many letters defending "women's keen sensitivity in reading and reading choices" (*DLH*, 4, 557), and sketches such as "Billeder af en Københavnsk Dukke" for prominent literary journals. Charlotte Baden added "new psychological dimension (and insights) to Richardson's earlier novel" (*DLH*, 4, 557) while building the essential conflict between love, the heart's domain, and duty to family, to peers, and to society.

With Charlotte Baden, a voice speaks out for a new reform: an aristocratic moral based on sincerity, sensitivity, integrity, and duty. Following Richardson's lead, Charlotte Baden didactically depicts women as the essential force for virtue, ethics, and engagement in the immediate family and the Danish aristocratic society.

Works

Den fortsatte Grandison, novel (1784). "En Fortælling i et Brev" [A Story in a Letter]. [Articles, letters], in *Morgenposten* and *Birchs Billedgallerie*, "Billeder af en Københavnsk Dukke," *Birchs Billedgallerie*. [Letters, articles, sketches], in *Bibliotek for det smukke Kiøn* (*Den fortsatte Grandison*).

Bibliography

Dalager, Stig, and Anne-Marie Mai, *Danske kvindelige forfattere*, vol. 1 *Sophie Brahe-Mathilde Fibiger. Udvikling og perspektiv* (København, 1982). *Dansk biografisk Leksikon*. "Jacob Baden" (København, 1981). *Dansk Litteraturhistorie*, vol. 4 (København, 1983), pp. 556–558.

Lanae Hjortsvang Isaacson

Yelisaveta Bagryána

(see: Belcheva)

Dschu Bai-Lan

(see: Klara Blum)

Balbilla

(a.k.a. Julia Balbilla or Julia)

Flourished c. A.D. 130
Genre(s): epigram
Language(s): Greek

Balbilla was a prominent member of the entourage that accompanied the emperor Hadrian and his wife Sabina on their trip to Egypt in November, A.D. 130. She was apparently high born: her paternal grandfather, she tells us, was king Antiochus IV of Commagene, while her maternal grandfather may have been the famous astrologer Tiberius Claudius Balbillus, who served as Prefect of Egypt from A.D. 55 to 59.

Of her works, only five epigrams, which were carved on one side of Colossus of Memnon in Egypt, are extant. Each is prefaced by an explanatory line of prose. The poems are essentially laudatory and, as such, take their place in the long and rather undistinguished tradition of encomiastic writing. Nevertheless, in Balbilla's pieces, the praise of Hadrian and Sabina is conveyed by means of an interesting conceit: the statue of Memnon, unable to contain its excitement at the sight of the illustrious visitors, actually speaks. In one poem, the statue, although it cannot normally make an utterance until the sun shines upon it, does its best to offer a greeting to Hadrian before sunrise and repeats it more loudly later. The Emperor is pleased and greets the statue in return. In another poem, the statue cleverly remains silent because it wishes to detain the enchanting and expectant Sabina, but eventually speaks to avoid incurring Hadrian's displeasure.

Despite the fragmentary condition of several lines, some general points can be observed. The language imitates the Aeolian dialect of Sappho—no doubt because Balbilla, as a woman poet, thought this appropriate. She fully adheres to metrical rules. The flattery of the imperial couple is relatively restrained and is spiced with personal details about Balbilla and the date of the trip, some Egyptian proper names, and a reference to Cambyses. The poems gain in artistry by eschewing details of what the statue says; the picture of Memnon and Hadrian exchanging greetings in a blaze of Egyptian sunlight remains curiously vivid.

Bibliography

Cougny, E., ed., *Epigrammatum Anthologia Palatina* (with Latin translation), vol. 3.1 (Paris, 1890), nos. 177–181. Kaibel, G., ed., *Epigrammata Graeca Ex Lapidibus Conlecta* (Berlin, 1878), nos. 988–992. West, M.L., "Die griechischen Dichterinnen der Kaiserzeit." *Kyklos: Festschrift R. Keydell* (Berlin, 1978), pp. 106–108.

David H.J. Larmour

Julia Balbilla

(see: Balbilla)

Mercedes Ballesteros

(a.k.a. Baronesa Alberta)

Born 1913, Madrid
Genre(s): novel, journalism, drama
Language(s): Spanish

Mercedes Ballesteros was born into a comfortably-situated family of intellectuals. Her father, Antonio Ballesteros, was a distinguished historian as was her mother, Mercedes Gaibrois, the first woman elected to the Academy of History in Spain. Her childhood was happy and advantaged; she traveled extensively with her family and began writing her observations while on these trips. She collaborated for years on the highly-respected humor magazine, *La Codorniz* (The Partridge), writing under the name of the Baronesa Alberta. One of her novels, *Taller* (The Shop), won the Alverez Quintero Prize of the Royal Spanish Academy and was later adapted for the stage by Ballesteros and Juan Ignacio Luca de Tena as *Las chicas del taller* (The Shopgirls). *El chico* (The Little Boy), *Mi hermano y yo por esos mundos* (My Brother and I Abroad), autobiographical stories, and *La sed* (The Thirst), a novel, are also important among her many narrative publications. After marriage to theater director Claudio de la Torre, Ballesteros wrote several successful plays which, like her other writings, show excellent characterizations and sophisticated wit. *Las mariposas cantan* (Song of the Butterflies), her most successful play about a young widow who finds her Prince Charming, won the Tina Gascó Prize in 1952. Another very successful play, *Lejano pariente sin sombrero* (Distant Relative Without a Hat), has been performed in Spain and Spanish America.

Works

Este mundo [This World] (1950). *Así es la vida* [That's Life] (1953). *El perro del extraño rabo* [The Dog with the Strange Tail] (1953). *Quiero ver al doctor* [I Want to See the Doctor] (1953). *Eclipse de tierra* [Eclipse of the Earth] (1954). *Las mariposas cantan* [Song of the Butterflies] (1955). *La cometa y el eco* [The Comet and the Echo] (1956). *Invierno* [Winter] (1959). *Verano* [Summer] (1959). *Taller* [The Shop] (1960). *La sed* [The Thirst] (1965). *Mi hermano y yo por esos mundos* [My Brother and I Out There in the World] (1962). *Lejano pariente sin sombrero* [Distant Relative Without a Hat] (1966). *El chico* [The Little Boy] (1967).

Bibliography

O'Connor, Patricia W., *Dramaturgas españolas de hoy* (Madrid, 1989). O'Connor, Patricia W., "Mercedes Ballesteros' Unsung Poetic Comedy: *Las mariposas cantan.*" *Crítica Hispánica* 7.1 (1985): 57–63.

Patricia W. O'Connor

Marie-Claire Bancquart

Born 1932, Paris, France
Genre(s): poetry, novel, essay, biography
Language(s): French

Marie-Claire Bancquart has been a prolific writer since the publication in 1972 of *Projets alternés* (Alternate Plans). She lives in Paris, where she teaches literature at the Sorbonne and is president of the arts council of La Maison de la Poésie. She is married to the musician-composer Alain Bancquart. Apart from her some ten volumes of poetry, she has also published critical books and essays on *fin de siècle* France, surrealism, Anatole France, and others.

Projets alternés aptly established at the outset of her literary career the dualistic, divided state both of the world at large and her own innermost sense of being-in-the-world. The collection thus evokes intensely the problems of meaning, belonging, non-absolution, ruination, writing as distortion, the "absence" of God, "scented massacre," and so on. Notions of "return," renewal, and waiting may, however, compensate for this bleakness though the overall tone is tense and disquieted.

In 1978, a more fully articulated collection, her fifth, appeared: *Mémoire d'abolie* (Memory of an Abolished Woman). Although once more needs and desires surface—for warmth, caresses, greater "centering," dehiscence—the book as a whole continues to stress the difficulties of being and saying. Marie-Claire Bancquart's place of habitation is thus shifting and unstable though it thus retains greater universality. *Malaise*, rancor, a sense of marginality, and self-deconstruction continue to weigh heavily. And whilst there is a desire to "find language of grass and radiolarian,"

and "self-pronouncement [remains] /between two oblivions," language impales us upon its pre-existence, its fixity, its self-imposition, its bloodless pallor. Despite, however, this insistence upon dreams of self-annihilation and end-time of humanity, Marie-Claire Bancquart is alert to the facileness of "entering negation" even if quite unsure of achieving her desire for some perhaps salutary "after-consciousness."

Partition (The Score) appeared three years later, after *Voix* (Voice), in 1981. A crucial shift in tone, even in effort, may be clearly detected, even though the volume does not yield any of the poet's earlier dismay and anguish. If, then, the disarray of love and body, minimality and failure, exile and incomprehension, persists at once globally and personally, other factors emerge and demonstrate beyond any doubt the combative, yet delicately resilient character of Marie-Claire Bancquart's work.

Votre visage jusqu'à l'os (Your Face to the Bone, 1983) shows how the poet is forced into "close navigation," tense articulation of the intense, a difficult insertion of love into the "terrible nudity of all things."

Marie-Claire Bancquart's collection *Opportunité des oiseaux* (Opportunity of Birds) was published in 1986. Marie-Claire Bancquart offers a sense of the growing nearness of the "ungraspable." The volume articulates greater affirmation and speaks of alliance, allegiance, potential universal meaning, a language "covering all of existence."

Works

Projets alternés, poetry (1972). *Proche*, poetry (1972). *Paris des surréalistes*, essays (1973). *Mains dissoutes*, poetry (1975). *Cherche-terre*, poetry (1975). *Mémoire d'abolie*, poetry (1978). *Images littéraire du Paris fin de siècle*, essays (1978). *Voix* (1979). *L'Inquisiteur*, novel (1980). *Partition*, poetry (1981). *Votre visage jusqu'à l'os*, poetry (1983). *Anatole France, tome I*, essays (1984). *Anatole France, un sceptique passionné*, biography (1984). *Les Tarots d'Ulysse*, novel (1984). *Opportunité des oiseaux*, poetry (1986).

Bibliography

Astier, Pierre, "Poésie contre le langage mou." *Paris-Journal* (Dec. 1986). Ayguesparse, Albert, "Marie-Claire Bancquart: *Mémoire d'abolie*:

Cherche-terre." *Marginales* 1984–1985 (Nov.–Dec. 1978): 82–83. B., A., "Marie-Claire Bancquart et les malaises de l'âme." *Monde des livres* 11407 (Oct. 1981): 19. Bishop, Michael, "Contemporary Women Poets," in *Contemporary French Poetry*, *Studies in Twentieth-Century Literature* (Fall 1988). Bishop, Michael, "Marie-Claire Bancquart: *Opportunité des oiseaux.*" *World Literature Today* (Autumn 1987). Blot, Jacques, "Quatre chants de la féminité." *Monde des livres* 10101 (July 1977): 14. Bosquet, Alain, "Un mois de poèmes." *NRF* 249 (Sept. 1973): 70–77. Brindeau, Serge, *La Poésie contemporaine de langue française depuis 1945* (1973), p. 128. Juin, Hubert, "Marie-Claire Bancquart ou la mémoire immédiate." *Monde des livres* 10417 (July 1978). "Marie-Claire Bancquart." *Journal des poètes* 4–5 (1982): 2.-3. P., M., "Les Ténèbres et les couleurs de Marie-Claire Bancquart." *Monde des livres* 11317 (June 1981): 23.

Michael Bishop

Teresa Landucci Bandettini

(a.k.a. Amarelli Etrusca)

Born 1763, Lucca, Italy; died 1836, Lucca
Genre(s): poetry
Language(s): Italian

Teresa Bandettini was born in Lucca of Benedetto and Maria Alba Micheli. At age seven she was orphaned, and with her family in difficult financial condition, she was not able to follow a regular course of study. Instead, she studied the classics, and at age fifteen she became a professional dancer. Between 1779 and 1789 she traveled across Northern Italy, earning fame as a literary ballerina. While in the theater, she would read Dante during the intervals. One day in Verona she demonstrated her great talent for poetic improvisation by chance. Attending a session given by an improviser, she answered him in rhyme; he was so pleased with her skill that he gave her lessons, which were enough to allow her to tour the principal towns of Italy, achieving great success wherever she went.

She traveled to Imola in 1789, where she contracted a marriage with Peter Landucci, by whom she had three sons and a daughter. He recognized her marvelous inspiration, freshness, and elevated poetic sentiments and helped her gain public recognition. Shortly thereafter, she met the Count L. Savioli, who introduced her to the literary society of Bologna and helped in the composition of the poem "La morte di Adone," in octaves, which she published in Parma in 1790. She soon abandoned dance to dedicate herself to poetry. She held first place in numerous academies of improvisation, elaborating in rhyme whatever arguments were presented on the spot. Her great successes in Ferrara, Padua, and Verona brought her in contact with the famous improvisor G. Mollo, also traveling at the time. When in Mantua, she and her husband entertained G. Murari dalla Corte, who introduced her to A. Bozzoli and S. Bettinelli, with whom she was friends until the latter's death. In 1793, Bandettini performed for the public in Parma and Pavia. After that time she was introduced to A. Mazza, F. Arrivabene, and Bodoni. She was a great success, and on this occasion L. Mascheroni dedicated the sonnet "Deh, come dietro al buon cantor di Enea" to her.

In March 1794, she was honored with the name "Amarilli Etrusca," and her work was preserved in the appendix along with that of A. Kauffman. When she returned to Lucca, she was admitted to a women's literary circle held by Marchese E. Bernardini; she also joined the Academia deglio Osruri and other prestigious groups.

Despite her noteworthy success, Bandettini was constantly preoccupied with financial problems. The situation worsened with the fall of the government. Although she remained apolitical, she left Lucca because of the subject of Jacobinism. In 1800, she went first to Venice, meeting several dignitaries, and then to Parma and Vienna, where she was disappointed in being denied a stipend by the Austrian Court, despite her popularity. In 1805, she was awarded an annual pension from the Duke of Modena following the publication of the poem *La Teseide* in twenty cantos, and the translation of Q. Smirneo Calabro's *Paralipomeni* of (1815, 1818). Desiring to return to the town of her birth, Bandettini sought a pension from the Court of Modena with permission to continue receiving compensation from Lucca. In 1819 she returned to that city with her husband, who was gravely ill and who died soon after.

Despite illness, Bandettini continued to write throughout her life, publishing *Discorso sulla poesia* in 1831. Her poetry affected many, and she was honored as the greatest poet of her time, recalling the great masters such as Pareni, Mascheroni, Monti, and Alfieri, among whom Bandettini will be remembered.

Works

La Teseide (1805). *Discorso Sulla Poesia* (1831). A collection of Bandettini's improvised poems can be found in B. Croce, "Gli Improvvisatori," in *La Letteratura italiana del Settecento* (Bari, 1949), pp. 299–311.

Bibliography

Del Chiappa, G., *Biografia di Teresa Bandettini* (Pavia, 1847). Ferri, P. L., *Bibliografia femminile italiani* (Roma, 1842), pp. 33–37. Franceschi, F., "Elogio di Amarilli Etrusca," in *Saggio di prose diverse* (Lucca, 1806), pp. 41–56. Paganini, P., "Notizie biografiche inedite di Amarilli Etrusca" (Lucca, 1904), p. 32. Sforza, G., "Amarilli Etrusca e il romantiscismo," *Giorn. ligustico di archeol, storia e letterat.* 19 (1892): pp. 393–398.

Jean Jost

Anna Banti

(a.k.a. Lucia Lopresti Longhi)

Born 1895, Florence, Italy; died 1985, Ronchi
Genre(s): novel, drama, essay, biography,
  translation
Language(s): Italian

Anna Banti took a degree in art history before realizing that her true vocation was in literature. Her work has been multifaceted, to say the least. An accomplished critic, Banti directed for years one of the most prestigious Italian literary journals, *Paragone*. She also translated French and English novels (her favorite writers were Colette and Virginia Woolf), wrote biographies of female colleagues (for example, one on Matilde Serao), became a successful dramatist, and cultivated a life-long interest in Caravaggio and his followers. Her most productive years were devoted to writing novels.

Banti's production is substantial; she wrote tirelessly up to her death at the age of ninety. As critics noted from the very beginning, Banti enjoyed recasting the lives of assertive women of the past. Her technique was one combining fictional confession and historical reconstruction. Published in 1947, *Artemisia* still remains her best novel. Its writing must have been a true act of love since the finished manuscript, lost during the upheaval of World War II, had to be totally rewritten. The novel is based on the life of the Caravaggesque painter Artemisia Gentileschi, whose talent is still recognized today in artistic circles and whose work is displayed, for example, at the Uffizi Gallery in Florence. Banti's heroine, Artemisia, is a powerful woman who is able to turn what promises to be a destiny of loss into one of unabashed victory and outstanding recognition. For a woman raped and rejected at age fifteen and later made (in)famous by an ill-conceived trial, the only choice other than permanent seclusion would have been to be unconventional. This is what Artemisia decides to be in the conservative, papist society of seventeenth century Rome. She then works with a vengeance to make herself a recognized artist despite her position and the sex-related gossip of patrons and jealous colleagues. Artemisia's story is thus one of self-assertion, her paintings powerful statements of an "I" that chooses to dramatize itself even when working on religious subjects.

Lavinia, the protagonist of the short and acclaimed story "Lavinia fuggita" in *Le donne muoiono*, is also an artist, but in another medium. Lavinia's interest in musical composition is as unconventional as Artemisia's pursuit of a pictorial career. Like her, Lavinia ends confronted with a world that cannot comprehend a female vocation in a male-dominated field.

La camicia bruciata is a historical novel. Once again a woman fights, in the name of freedom of choice, the limitations imposed on her sex. Although Marguerite Louise is presented throughout as a negative heroine, it is her transgressive behavior and her refusal to accept a life of imprisonment and silence that make her fight of universal importance.

Banti's style is a perfect medium for her historical renderings; it is precise and yet flowing, immediate and yet lyrical. During her long career she won all the most prestigious Italian literary prizes.

Works

Il coraggio delle donne (1940). *Sette lune* (1941).
Le monache cantano (1943). *Artemisia* (1947). *Le
donne muoiono* (1951). *Il bastardo* (1953). *Allarme
sul lago* (1954). *La monaca di Sciangai e altri racconti*
(1957). *Corte Savella* (1960). *Opinioni* (1961). *Le
mosche d'oro* (1962). *Campi elisi* (1963). *Matilde
Serao* (1965). *Noi credevamo* (1967). *Je vous ecris
d'un pays lointain* (1971). *La camicia bruciata*
(1973). *Da un paese vicino* (1975).

Bibliography

Barberi-Squarotti, Giorgio, "Appunti intorno alla
narrativa di Anna Banti." *Letteratura* 7 (1959): 114–
122. Biagini, Enza, *Anna Banti* (Milano, 1978).
Contini, Gianfranco, "Parere ritardato su *Artemisia.*" *Altri esercizi (1942–1971)* (Torino, 1972), pp.
173–178. Dazzi, Manlio, "I racconti di Anna Banti."
Nuova Antologia 498 (1966): 336–347. Del
Beccaro, Felice, "Anna Banti." *Letteratura italiana
contemporanea*, ed. G. Mariani and M. Petrucciani,
vol. 2 (Roma, 1980), pp. 511–518. Falqui, Enrico,
"Anna Banti." *Prosatori e narratori del Novecento
italiano* (Torino, 1950), pp. 229–233. Finucci,
Valeria, "A Portrait of the Artist as a Female Painter:
The Kunstlerroman Tradition in Anna Banti's *Artemisia.*" *Quaderni d'italianistica* 8 (1987): 157–
193. Nozzoli, Anna, *Tabu' e coscienza. La
condizione femminile nella letteratura italiana del
Novecento* (Firenze, 1978). Peritore, G.A., "Stile e
tecnica narrativa di Anna Banti," in *Novecento*, ed.
Gianni Grana (Milano, 1980), pp. 7526–7531.

Valeria Finucci

Maria Banuş

Born 1914, Bucharest, Romania
Genre(s): poetry, drama, memoirs, journalism,
    children's literature, translation
Language(s): Romanian

Maria Banuş made her debut at age fourteen
with a poem published in Arghezi's well-known
literary journal *Bilete de papagal*. A graduate in
law and philology at the Bucharest University,
she became a regular contributor to *Azi, Caiet de
poezie* (a poetry supplement of *Revista Fundaţiilor
Regale*) and, later on, to *Contemporanul, Flacăra,
Iaşul literar*, and *Secolul 20*.

Her first volume of poetry—*Ţara fetelor*
(1937; The Land of Young Girls)—was both
strong and precise in its unprecedented depiction of the female adolescent self torn between
urgent physical premonitions of triumphant vitality or aggressive sexuality and ready-made
sacrificial schemes or humbling scenarios. Hesitant healthy violence is at the core of the poet's
creativity. Banuş speaks of thoughts that are
"meaty like water lilies," of buffalo-bellied springs,
and whip-like lips. With knees trembling like
jugs too full of milk and mouths ripening like
pale strawberries, with the tops of their fingers
like the flesh of white cherries, eighteen-year
young women longing for the "pollen of caresses" rock themselves into tamed encounters:
"I lead you (Ć the woman's knees) toward him (Ć
the beloved) as if you were two lambs" ("Song for
Rocking My Knees").

During the war Banuş wrote memorable
poems of pain and anxiety about Jewish suffering
and became engaged in the political left. What
happened after the war though, and throughout
the fifties is still a sad enigma. From an intense
and innovative poet with a clear-cut lyrical profile, Banuş unexpectedly moved into a
nomenklatura proclaimer of "revolutionary
transformations" and totalitarian happiness. Most
of the new poems she included in the volumes
Bucurie (1949; Joy), *Fiilor mei* (1949; To My
Sons), *Versuri alese* (1953; Selected Poetry),
Bucureşti oraş iubit (1954; Bucharest, Beloved
City), *Despre pămînt* (1954; Speaking of the
Earth), *Ţie-ţi vorbesc, America* (1955; I Speak to
You, America!), and *Se arată lumea* (1956; The
World Reveals Itself) either glorify the "struggle
between classes," the "liquidation of people's
enemies," agricultural collectivization, the elec-
trification, the competent leadership of the
communist party, or demask greedy capitalists
inside and outside the country. Even the poetic
form is affected. Banuş writes now huge epic
poems, fables, political pamphlets, conventional
anti-war agitatoric verse. While her war memories have started to fade and she has—to say the
least—lost any contact with the reality around
her, the poet received in one and the same year
(1949) the Academy Prize "G. Coşbuc" for Poetry
and the State Prize for Drama, Second Class; her
volumes are translated into Russian, Chinese,
Vietnamese, Hungarian, Bulgarian, Czechoslovakian, and published in Cuba and Mexico; her

circumstantial poems become part of the obligatory and unique curriculum in all the schools of Romania.

Twenty years after *Ţara fetelor*, in 1957 Banuş started a slow operation of poetic recovery. With *Torentul* (1959; The Torrent) and *Magnet* (1962; Magnet) the poet abandoned epic verse. Her melancholic meditation on irrepetability, vulnerability, and love as a privileged means of cosmic integration mark the beginning of a late and tenacious struggle to erase the immediate past and connect the quest for totality and spiritual revival that will from now on be central to her poems with the erotic hunger of her 1937 debut volume. Volumes like *Metamorfoze* (1963; Metamorphoses), *Diamantul* (1965; The Diamond), or *Tocmai ieşeam în arenă* (1967; I Was Just Stepping in the Arena) continue and expand at another age the poetic monograph of female time, and of physical and affective erosion. Pungent images speak of old age (with its "empty gums and avaricious jaws," with its onion-like innumerable peels behind which there seems to be no bulb), of its biological and spiritual mysteries, and of modest though ecstatic survival. More pessimistic, *Portretul din Fayom* (1970; The Portrait of Fayum) and *Oricine şi ceva* (1972; Anybody and Something) contain somber and sarcastic images of degradation—physical, moral, or volitional.

In 1945, Banuş has made her debut as a playwright with *Petrecere în familie* (Family Party). It was followed by *Ziua cea mare* (1949, 1951; The Great Day), a play of jubilant triumph over "anticommunist sabotage." Other plays, such as *Îndrăgostiţii* (1954; The Lovers), or the comedy *Magie interzisă* (1970; Forbidden Magic), all of them published in the retrospective volume *Scrieri III. Teatru* (1978; Writings III. Theatre) are of rather documentary relevance.

Banuş was a prolific journalist. The volume *Din cronica acelor ani. Articole* (1955; From Those Years' Chronicle. Articles) brings together articles about tractors, about Romanian writers like Neculuţă, Vlahuţă, Eminescu, or Caragiale, or about Soviet and Russian literature.

In 1978 Banuş published an important volume of memoirs entitled *Sub camuflaj. Jurnal 1943–1944* (Blackout. Journal 1943–1944). In it, she found strong accents to evoke the aspirations and tension that define her inner life as an assimilated Jew.

Maria Banuş is the editor and translator of an impressive anthology of love poems from around the world (1965; *Din poezia de dragoste a lumii*). She translated into Romanian works by Shakespeare, Goethe, Rilke, Pushkin, Browning, Neruda, Maiakovski, Hikmet, Vaptzarov, Frénaud, Strindberg, Lars Gustafson, and others. An almost finished translation of Lewis Carroll's *Alice in Wonderland* in which Banuş had invested a considerable amount of effort got lost during World War II.

Works

Ţara fetelor [The Land of Young Girls] (1937). *Petrecere în familie* [Family Party], play (1945). *Bucurie. Poeme* [Joy. Poems] (1949, 1st edition; 1949, 2nd edition, enlarged). *Fiilor mei. Poem* [To My Sons. A Poem] (1949). *Ziua cea mare* [The Great Day], play (1949, 1951). *Versuri alese* [Selected Poetry] (1953). *Bucureşti oraş iubit* [Bucharest, Beloved City] (1954). *Despre pămînt. Poem* [To Speak of the Earth. A Poem] (1954). *Îndrăgostiţii* [The Lovers. A Play] (1954). *Din cronica acelor ani. Articole* [From Those Years' Chronicle. Articles] (1955). *Ţie-ţi vorbesc, Americă!* [I Speak to You, America! A Poem], poem (1955). *Se arată lumea. Versuri* [The World Reveals Itself], poetry (1956). *La porţile raiului. Poem* [At the Gates of Heaven. A Poem] (1957). *Poezii* [Poems] (1958). *Poezii* [Poems], .in the collection "Cele mai frumoase poezii" (1959). *Torentul. Versuri* [The Torrent. Poetry] (1959). *Poezii* [Poems], with a foreword by Tudor Vianu (1961). *Prin oraşul cu minuni* [Through the City of Miracles] (1961). *Magnet* [Magnet] (1962). *Metamorfoze* [Metamorphoses] (1963). *Diamantul* [The Diamond] (1965). *Din poezia de dragoste a lumii* [Love Poetry from Around the World], translations of poetry (1965). *Tocmai ieşeam în arenă* [I Was Just Stepping in the Arena] (1967). *Portretul din Fayum* [The Portrait of Fayum] (1970). *Magie interzisă* [Forbidden Magic], comedy (1970). *Scrieri I–II. Poezii* [Writings I–II. Poems] (1971). *Noru visătoru şi amicii săi* [Cloud the Dreamer and His Friends] (1971). *Oricine şi ceva* [Anybody and Something] (1972). *Hai copii prin Bucureşti* [Kids, Let's Go Through Bucharest] (1973). *Scrieri III. Teatru* [Writings III. Theatre] (1978). *Sub camuflaj. Jurnal 1943–1944* [Blackout.

Journal, 1943–1944] (1978). *Noiembrie inocentul* [Innocent November] (1981). *Orologiu cu figuri* [Horologe with Figures] (1984).

Translations: Volumes: *A nagy nap/ Ziua cea mare* (1951). *Der Grosse Tag*. Theaterstück in 3 Aufzugen/ *Ziua cea mare* (1952). *Radost/ Bucurie*, tr. Jan Vladislav and Marie Kavkova (1952). *Velikij den'*. P'esa v treh dejstvijah, pjati kartinah/ *Ziua cea mare*, tr. Kul'manova (1954). *To You, America, I Speak/ Ţie-ţi vorbesc Americă.*, tr. Alfred Margul Sperber (1956). *Válogatott versek/ Versuri alese* (1956). *Stihi/ Poezii* (1958). *Stihi/ Poezii* (1960). *Novi Spazi/ Spaţii noi*, ed. and tr. Dragoş Vranceanu and Andrea Zanzotto (1964). *Joie/ Bucurie*. Preface by Guillevic (1966). *Éclats des glaces foraines*. Traduction revue par Alain Bosquet (1979). *Der grosse Tag*. Schauspiel in 3 Akten/ *Ziua cea mare*, tr. by Josef Dollinger (n.d., before 1960). Poems: *Antologia della poesia romena*, ed. by Salvatore Quasimodo, tr. Mario De Micheli and Dragoş Vrănceanu. (1961; "Lettera"/ "Scrisoare"; "Ninna-nanna per i bambini di guerra"/ "Cîntec de leagăn [pentru copiii războiului]"; "Pogrom"; "Maternità"/ "Maternitate"; "Nascita"/ "Naştere"; "Il passato"/ "Trecutul"). Bosquet, Alain, ed. *Anthologie de la poésie roumaine* (1968; "Une autre cité"/ "Altă cetate"; "Lettre"/"Scrisoare"; "Solstices"/"Solstiţiu"; "L'avalanche"/ "Cutremur," tr. Claude Sernet; "Poésie"/ "Poezie," tr. Alain Bosquet). Hubert, Juin, ed. and tr. *Poèmes roumains. Des origines à nos jours* (1958; "Aux portes du Paradis,"—fragment/ "La porţile raiului"—fragment; "Pogrom"). *Le Journal des Poètes* 34 (1964), 4. Special issue devoted to Romanian poetry. ("Naissance"/"Naştere," tr. Guillevic). *Lírai világtájak*, ed. and tr. Franyó Zoltan and Endre Károly. (1967; "Szeretem est a földgolyót"/ "Iubesc această lume"). *Literatura rumana contemporánea*. Special issue, *Unión*, 1968 ("Sueño con angel"/ "Vis cu înger'"' "El pasado"/ "Trecutul," tr. Belkis Cuza Male). Maurer, Georg, ed. and tr. *Rumänien erzählt* (1955; "Frieden für immer"/ "Pace pentru totdeauna"). Micheli, Mario De, ed. and tr. *Poeti romeni del dopoguerra* (1967; "Pogrom"; "Richiamo"/ "Chemare"; "Felice contradizzione"/"Fericita contradicţie"; "Il passato"/ "Tre două ruine"; "Destino"/ "Destin"; "Poesia"/ "Poezie"; "Lucifero"/ "Lucifer"; "Alchimia"/ "Alchimie"; "I mostri"/ "Monştrii"; "Nel microcosmo"/ "În microcosm"). Neruda, Pablo, ed. and tr. *44 poetas rumanos* (1967; "La carta"/

"Scrisoare"' "Viento de marzo"/ "Vînt de martie"; "Maternidad"/"Maternitate"; "Nunca"/"Niciodată"; "La canción de los cabellos blancos"/ "Cîntecul părului alb"; "El pasado"/"Trecutul"; "Trasponiendo cielos"/ "Cu ceruri strămutate"; "Breve encuentro"/ "Scurtă întîlnire"). *Poètes et prosateurs roumains d'aujourd'hui*. Special issue, *Marginales*. Ruvue bimestrielle des Idées, des Arts et des Lettres, 23 (1968), *119-120* ("Noces"/ "Nuntă"; "Un ange en rêve"/ "Vis cu înger"). *Román költök antológiája* (1951; "Dnyeszteren-túli álom"/ "Vis cu Transnistria"; "Induló"/ "Marş"; "Nálunk, egy üzemben"/ "La noi într-o uzină"; "Fehlivás"/ "Chemare," tr. Nemes Nagy Ágnes; "Márciusi szél"/ "Vînt de martie"/ "Húzd fel a horgo nyt"/ "Ancora sus," tr. Hegedüs Géza; "Fiaimnak"/"Fiilor mei," tr. Fodor József). *Román költök antológiája* (1961; Bölcsödal a háború gyermekeinek"/ "Cîntec de leagăn [pentru copiii războiului]"; "Most döntjük"/ "Dărîmăm"; "Amerika, hozzád szólok!"/ "Ţie-ţi vorbesc, Americă"—fragment tr. Majtényi Erik). Sadeckij, A., ed. *Antologija rumynskoj poezii*(1959; "Vesna v roce"/ "Primăvara-n crîng"; "Razruşaem"/ "Dărîmăm"; "U zelenogo stola"/ "La masa verde"; "V gorah Gruzii"/ "În munţii Georgiei," tr. T. Spendiarova; "Materinstovo"/ "Maternitate"; "O zemle"/ "Despre pămînt," tr. I. Gurova; "Velikaja nade'da"/ "Marea speranţă," tr. E. Aksel'rod; "Otdyh"/ "Vacanţă"; "S toboj, govorju, Amerika"/ "Ţie-ţi vorbesc, Americă," tr. S. Servinskoj). Sarov, Taško, ed. and tr. *Antologija na romanskata poezija* (1972; "Retrospektiva"/ "Retrospectivă"; "Ednaš angelot na smrtta"/"Odată, îngerul morţii"; "Pesna za lulanje na kolenata"/ "Cîntec de legănat genunchii"). Stančev, L., A. Muratov, and J. Stratiev, eds. *Rum"nski poeti* (1956; "V Maramureš"/ "Din Maramureş," tr. Mladen Isaev; "Geroite na Doftana"/ "Slavă eroilor Doftanei," tr. Angel Todorov; "Fabrikant"t"/ "Patronul," tr. Jordan Stratiev; "V gruzinskite planini"/"În munţii Georgiei," tr. Cvetan Angelov. Szemlér Ferenc, ed. and tr. *Változott egekben*(1969; "Múlt"/"Trecutul"; "Tüzhely elött"/ "La foc"; "Változott egekben"/ "Cu ceruri strămutate"). Vainer, Nelson, ed. and tr. *Antologia da poesia romena* ("Maternidade"/ "Maternitate"). *Werk uit Roemenië. Poëzie* (1966; "De vreugde"/ "Bucuria"; "Hetverleden"/ "Trecutul"; "Brief"/ "Scrisoare"; "Verzoek aan het leven"/ "Vieţii, o rugă," tr. Stefan Mesker).

English Translations: Catanoy, Nicholas, *Modern Romanian Poetry* (1977; "Nocturne"/ "Nocturnă," tr. A. Margul-Sperber and Nelson Ball; "A Letter"/ "Scrisoare," tr. E. Roditi). Deletant, Andrea and Brenda Walker, eds. and tr. *Silent Voices. An Anthology of Romanian Women Poets* (1986; "Separation"; "Natural"; "Us, Yorick"; "Amazing"; "The Lost Child"; "Migration"; "The Tree"; "Time"; "The Wedding"; "Eighteen"). MacGregor-Hastie, Roy, ed. and tr. *Anthology of Contemporary Romanian Poetry* (1969; "Dream with an Angel"/ "Vis cu înger"; "Solstice"/ "Solstițiu"). *The Literary Review*. Special issue, "An Anthology of Romanian Feminine Lyricism," 1964.

Bibliography

Călinescu. G., "Ceva despre poezia Mariei Banuș," in *Literatura nouă* (Craiova, 1972), pp. 148–155. Călinescu, Matei, "Maria Banuș" *Steaua* X 7 (1959): 56–62. Crohmălniceanu, Ovid S., "Poezie politică." *Gazeta literară* II (1955), 41, 1, 5. Fischer, Liliana, "Maria Banuș." *Studii și cercetări de istorie literară și folclor* IV (1955): 213–221. Micu, Dumitru, *Poezia Mariei Banuș* (Bucharest, 1956). Mirodan, Al, *Dicționar neconvențional al scriitorilor evrei de limbă română* (Tel Aviv, 1986), pp. 99–112. Piru, Al, *Panorama deceniului literar românesc 1940–1950* (Bucharest, 1968), pp. 109–112. Popa, Marian, *Dicționar de literatură română contemporană*, 2nd ed. (Bucharest, 1977), pp. 54–55. Sorescu, Roxana, "Maria Banuș," in Bucur, Marin, ed., *Literatură română contemporană I. Poezia* (Bucharest, 1980), pp. 163–169. Stancu, Zaharia, *Antologia poeților tineri* (Bucharest,)1934, pp. 5–9. Vitner, Ion, "Ură și iubire." *Contemporanul* (1956), 30, 3; 31, 3.

Sanda Golopentia

Catherine de Bar (Soeur Mechtilde du Saint Sacrement)

Born December 31, 1614, Saint-Die (Lorraine), France; died April 6, 1698, Paris
Genre(s): spiritual writings
Language(s): French

Born into a family ennobled because of public service, she was intended by her father for a well-chosen marriage. She, however, was early aware of a religious vocation and entered a religious order in 1631. Her convent life was interrupted by the Thirty Years War which forced members of the community to flee for their lives. They had barely reestablished themselves when they were devastated by the Plague. Taking refuge in a Benedictine convent, Catherine was attracted to life there and in July 1634 became a Benedictine novice, taking her final vows in 1640 as Catherine de Sainte-Mechtilde.

The same year Lorraine suffered from a terrible famine which forced this community of sisters to disperse. Sister Catherine then found refuge at St. Mihiel, where she became Mechtilde du Saint Sacrement. At about that time, St. Vincent de Paul persuaded a reforming abbess of Montmartre to interest herself in the fate of these unfortunate sisters, and so Sister Mechtilde was received into the reforming convent there. The following year, however, she left Paris for Normandy where a new community, allied to Port Royal, was founded at Burbery. There she experienced the influence of mystics.

In 1643, Parisian friends offered her a large establishment at St. Maur-des Fossés, where she opened a boarding school for students of social standing, an undertaking that attracted the interest of the Queen Mother, Anne of Austria. She later returned to Normandy as Prioress of Bon-Secours at Cannes, and later, she was at Rambervilliers. By then the War of the Fronde was devastating France, causing her to return to St. Maur, where she became the spiritual advisor to Marie de la Guesle, Countess of Châteauvieux. It was for her that Sister Mechtilde wrote a Breviary centering on devotion to the Holy Sacrament, leading eventually to the foundation of a new community of Benedictines on the Rue du Bac in Paris, devoted to Perpetual Adoration, of which Madame de Châteauvieux was a sponsor. This foundation was Sister Mechtilde's inspiration for such works as the *Véritable Esprit* (1682; The True Spirit), which made her one of the great spiritual writers of the seventeenth century.

The community experienced various difficulties, first of all from the Jansenists, who had hoped to attract Sister Mechtilde to their doctrines, but the group flourished and eventually established ten similar communities, one as far away as Poland.

This period of prosperity was marked by an extended correspondence between Sister Mechtilde and the elderly Duchess of Orleans, sister-in-law of Louis XIII. On the other hand, her mystical spirituality attracted the antipathy of Bossuet. The end of her long life was also beset by various other troubles. She had lived eighty-four years when she died on 6 April 1698.

Works

Ecrits Spirituels à la Comtesse de Châteauvieux [Spiritual Writings to the Countess of Châteauvieux], ed. Abbot Louis Cognet (Paris, 1965). *Le Véritable Esprit des Religieuses Adoratrices Perpetuelles du Très-Saint Sacrement de l'Autel* [The True Spirit of the Perpetually Worshiping Sisters of the Very Holy Sacrament of the Altar] (1803).

Bibliography

Cognet, Abbot Louis, Introduction to *Ecrits Spirituels* (Paris, 1965).

Charity C. Willard

Galerana Baratotti

(see: Arcangela Tarabotti)

Carmen Barberá

Born 1927, Cuevas de Vinromá (Castellón de la Plana), Spain
Genre(s): novels, poetry
Language(s): Spanish

Also a poet, the novelist Barberá is notable for her sensitivity to the complexities of human relationships. Five of her novels have received literary prizes. *Adolescente* (1957; Adolescent) reveals the problems of a marriage between a sensitive young woman and an older husband who ignores her. The mother lives only for her child, who expresses the difficulties of having an older father. Her parents are so different from each other, and both are so different from her, that the adolescent's family life is full of tension. *Tierras de luto* (1976; Lands of Mourning) delineates the human ability to survive despite tragedy, depression, and loneliness.

Works

Tiempo interior, poetry. *Despedida al recuerdo*, poetry (1955). *Adolescente*, novel (1957). *Al final de la ría*, novel (1958). *Debajo de la piel*, novel (1959). *Las esquinas del alba*, novel (1960). *La colina perdida*, novel (1964). *Cartas a un amigo*, poetry (1965). *Tierras de luto*, novel (1976). *Rapto de locura*, novel (1982).

Carolyn Galerstein

Teresa Barbero

(see: Teresa Barbero Sanchez)

Natalie Clifford Barney

Born October 31, 1876, Dayton, Ohio; died February 2, 1972, Paris, France
Genre(s): autobiography, epigram, essay, dialogue
Language(s): French

Natalie Clifford Barney was born into a wealthy family in Dayton, Ohio, in 1876. From her mother, a portrait painter who studied with Whistler, she inherited her interest in the arts; from her father, she inherited two million dollars. When at the age of 21 she became independently wealthy, she settled in Paris, where she became a central figure in artistic and literary circles, and where her salon at 20 Rue Jacob became a gathering place for artists and intellectuals for over fifty years.

Although Barney's works include epigrams, sketches, plays, essays, and a novel, she is better known for her life than for her works. She lived openly as a lesbian in a time when such a life was completely unacceptable to conventional society although both psychoanalysis and homosexual rights movements in Germany and England were drawing attention to homosexuals and lesbians and were helping to create a climate in which such "deviance" could be acknowledged.

Barney had many love affairs and many more lasting friendships. The most famous of her lovers were the poet Renée Vivien (Pauline Tarn) and the painter Romaine Brooks (the latter relationship lasted over fifty years). Her literary and artistic friends included the writer Remy de

Gourmont, who made her famous as the "Amazone" in his *Lettres à l'Amazone* (Letters to the Amazon), Gertrude Stein, Colette, and Ezra Pound.

Her influence on the artistic and intellectual life of Paris was greatest during the 1920s and 1930s. Her salon at 20 Rue Jacob was a gathering place for artists and writers, who congregated there at 4:00 p.m. each Friday to consume tea and cucumber sandwiches and to read and perform their works. Gertrude Stein, Colette, Mata Hari, Virgil Thomson, Georges Antheil, Ezra Pound, Ernest Hemingway—all were guests at Natalie Barney's salon.

Barney appears as a character in several fictional works. Remy de Gourmont first made her famous as the "Amazone," and Barney then took the name of "The Amazon" in two of her own works, *Pensées d'une Amazone* (Reflections of an Amazon) and *Nouvelles Pensées de l'Amazone* (New Reflections of the Amazon). She appears as a character in an autobiographical novel by Liane de Pougy, which tells the story of Pougy's affair with Barney. Renée Vivien portrays her as "Vally" in her novel *Une femme m'apparut* (A Woman Appeared to Me); a figure resembling Barney also appears in much of Vivien's melancholy love poetry. Djuna Barnes satirized her and her circle in *The Ladies' Almanack*. And Radclyffe Hall, in *The Well of Loneliness*, gives the most memorable portrait of Barney in her character of "Valerie Seymour," a symbolically named tower of strength who looks out over the turbulent world and serves as a beacon that guides and inspires less courageous souls.

Prior to the 1970s, Barney's unconventional life had seemed more interesting to biographers than her literary work. Her accomplishments are now being re-evaluated, and she is now seen as a precursor of the "second wave" of the women's movement. Along with Renée Vivien, she sought to create poetry in which women and women's experience were central. Barney and Vivien were influenced by French Symbolist poetry, the courtly love tradition, and the poetry of the Greek poet Sappho, as Karla Jay has shown in *The Disciples of the Tenth Muse: Natalie Clifford Barney and Renée Vivien*.

Barney's works include epigrams, biographical studies, and meditations on love and friendship. Like the epigrams of La Rochefoucauld and Oscar Wilde, hers are trenchant critiques on manners and society. Her essays reveal a vision of a future world without sex roles or guilt over sexual relations, yet they never lose their elegant lightness of tone nor their irony. Radclyffe Hall's "pale yet ardent light of the fanatic" (Hall, *The Well of Loneliness*) may show through in such essays as "L'Amour défendu" ("Love Defended"), "Des amours à l'Amour" ("From Loves to Love"), and "Aspects d'un ange" ("Aspects of an Angel"); but it is always veiled in humor, charm, and a manner that manages to be both self-deprecating and egotistical.

Barney indeed remains a paradox: an eighteenth-century wit, sedate and old-fashioned in appearance and manner, she lived in quiet defiance of her age. She hated its egalitarianism, its introspection and self-absorption, its preoccupation with psycho-analysis and with the self. She was anti-fascist yet elitist, pacifist yet apolitical; mystical yet anti-religious; self-absorbed yet generous. She sought total freedom to control her own life. Thanks to her great wealth, she achieved that freedom. Natalie Clifford Barney belongs to those nineteenth and twentieth century pioneers who sought to define and justify homosexuality not only as a sexual choice but as a way of life. She also stands among women's rights advocates—though she never spoke for rights nor engaged in political action. Her whole life, however, was a political act, for she openly chose her own sex as lovers and companions with pride and without repentance. As an original if minor voice in French literature, as a patron (matron?) of the arts, and as an outspoken and fearless model of women's independence as well as for freedom for gays and lesbians, Natalie Barney remains one of the most original and provocative literary figures of the early twentieth century.

Works

Quelques portraits-sonnets de femmes (1900). *Cinq petits dialogues grecs* (Antithèses et parallèles) (1902). *Actes et entr'actes* (1910). *Je me souviens* (1910). *Pensées d'une amazone* (1920). *Poems et poèmes: autres alliances* (1920). *Aventures de l'Esprit* (1975). *The One Who Is Legion, or A.D.'s After-Life* (1930). *Nouvelles Pensées de l'Amazone*

(1939). *Souvenirs indiscrets* (1960). *Traits et portraits* (1975). "The Woman Who Lives with Me" (n.d.)

Unpublished papers: [With Natalie Clifford Barney], "The Color of His Soul." MS. (Paris, Bibliothèque Doucet). Letters to Alice Pike Barney. MS. (Paris, Bibliothèque Doucet). "Les Amants de la poule." MS. (Paris, Bibliothèque Doucet). "Amazon's Notebook." MS. (Paris, Bibliothèque Doucet). "Autur d'une Victoire." MS. (Paris, Bibliothèque Doucet). "Brothers in Arms." MS. (Paris, Bibliothèque Doucet). "Faune et phono." MS. (Paris, Bibliothèque Doucet). "Les Jours inutilisables." MS. (Paris, Bibliothèque Doucet). "Her Legitimate Lover." MS. (Paris, Bibliothèque Doucet). "Le Mystère de Psyché." MS. (Paris, Bibliothèque Doucet). "Salle des pas perdus." MS. (Paris, Bibliothèque Doucet). "Nos secrètes amours." MS. (Paris, Bibliothèque Doucet). Letters (Beinecke Rare Book and Manuscript Library, Yale University).

Translations: *Selected Writings of Natalie Clifford Barney*, ed. and introd. Miron Grindea (London, 1963).

Bibliography

Chalon, Jean, *Portrait d'une séductrice* (Paris, 1976). Translated into English as *Portrait of a Seductress: The World of Natalie Barney*, tr. Carol Barko (New York: Crown, 1979). Jay, Karla, *The Amazon and the Page: Natalie Clifford Barney and Renée Vivien* (Bloomington and Indianapolis, 1988). Jay, Karla, *The Disciples of the Tenth Muse: Natalie Clifford Barney and Renée Vivien*. Diss., New York University, 1984. Wickes, George, *The Amazon of Letters: The Life and Loves of Natalie Barney* (New York, 1976).

Charlene Ball

Deborah Baron

Born 1887, Uzda, White Russia; died 1956, Israel
Genre(s): novel, short story
Language(s): Hebrew

Deborah Baron was born in Uzda, White Russia, in 1887, the daughter of the local rabbi. Little is known about her life in Uzda, but she must have developed a great love for her small town, because the town and its everyday life became the major theme of her writings. When Baron left Russia in 1911 she took all of the sketches she had written and collected about small-town life and expanded them into stories for a weekly newspaper, *Ha-Po'el ha-Za'ir* (The Young Worker) in Turkish Palestine. Her husband, Joseph Aharonovitz, edited this Labor weekly, and soon Baron became editor of its literary supplement, a position she held for many years.

Most of Baron's stories are set in Eastern Europe, in the *shtetls* (small Jewish villages) she knew and loved best. Some stories are situated in Palestine, and one, *Ha-Golim* (Exiles), in Egypt, where she was involuntarily exiled for four years during and following World War I. The heart and soul of Baron's work was, however, in the burdened existence of those in the European *shtetls*. Even though she was writing of a beloved time past, she was able to free herself from a complete idealization in her characters and in their actions, although her compassion for them is quite transparent. She cannot be deemed guilty of sentimentality, but rather praised for her realistic portrayals of the difficult life of the poor and often oppressed Jewish people. She was able to exalt traditional culture, where people accepted fate with a quiet sorrow, but yet they seemed to possess a love and a courage that endured beyond the tragedies of life.

Characters in Baron's stories are simple people, struggling to cope with everyday life and its infinite variety of experiences. They are true artistic creations, however, for these characters are exposed at a level beyond their reactions, at a level where they hide their deepest thoughts and feelings. Not only is Baron capable of describing a baker realistically as a baker, but she goes beyond this to portray him as an artist who lovingly creates, watches, and gingerly handles his work, which seems to contain a part of himself. The miller is a typical father-in-law, uncomfortable in his new position; however, he is able to care for his cow in the most affectionate of manners. Although these characters may border on the sentimental, Baron's artistry has enough edge, perhaps taken from her own experiences with like people, to create realistic characters, ones with whom we can all identify and understand in some way. It may even be argued that Baron's twinge of sentimentality draws the reader even closer to each of her characters.

Baron's compassion for her characters is nowhere more evident than in her portrayals of Jewish women. Each woman, whether girl or grandmother, has special qualities that make her representative of all women in this Jewish culture. They each lead a quiet, often suffering existence, bearing the weight of traditionalism and its burdensome expectations. The best example of such womanhood is Fradel, a brave Jewish woman who somehow manages to hold to ancestral traditions, yet remain an individual, one who alone faces the many tragedies which fill her life. Fradel's strength does not diminish but rather seems to increase as she faces at a young age the death of her parents, bears the burden of a failed marriage that ends in divorce, tragically faces the death of her only child, and resigns herself to remaining distant from a lover who never married because of his love for her. In all of this adversity, tragedy, and pain Fradel remains true to her tradition, never failing to follow all the prescribed laws for women. She is the ultimate symbol of the orthodox Jewish woman; her tragedies represent the endless tragedies and oppressions of all Jewish women, as they struggle to cope and even survive (especially in the ghettos of Eastern Europe), quietly resigning themselves to their fate and living life with pride and dignity in their character.

Deborah Baron spent the last twenty years of her life as a bedridden invalid. She continued to write her masterful stories of the *shtetl* throughout this time. Undoubtedly, this experience strengthened her love and compassion for humans and their often tragic existence. She was able to capture these feelings and place them at the heart of all of her moving accounts of the lives of poor, small-town people, whose inner experiences and personalities she compassionately and sympathetically revealed. The actual *shtetls* in Eastern Europe ceased to exist not more than a decade after Baron came to Palestine, but her accounts of them and their people remained relevant long after her death in 1956.

Works

Sippurim [Stories] (1926–1927). *Ketanot* [Trifles] (1933). *Mah she-hayah* [That Which Was] (1939).

[Editor], *Kethuvi Josef Ahronovitz* (1940–1941). *Le 'eth 'atah* [For the Time Being] (1942–1942). *Mi-sham* [From There] (1945–1946). *Ha-Laban* [The Soul] (1946–1947). *Shavririm* [Splinters] (1948–1949). *Parshiyot* [Chapters] (1951). *Hulyot* [Links] (1952–1953). *Me-emesh* [Of Last Night] (1954–1955). *Agav-urba* [By the Way] (1960). *Ha-Golim* [Exiles] (1970).

Bibliography

Halkin, Simon, *Modern Hebrew Literature* (New York, 1950). Hanoch, Itzhak, ed., Joseph Schachter, tr., *The Thorny Path* (Jerusalem, 1969). Penueli, S.Y., and A. Ukhmani, eds., *Hebrew Short Stories, Vol. 1* (Tel Aviv, 1965). Silberschlag, Eisig, *From Renaissance to Renaissance II: Hebrew Literature in the Land of Israel: 1870–1970* (New York, 1977).

JoAnne C. Juett

Maria Isabel Barreno de Farias Martin

Born July 10, 1939, Lisbon, Portugal
Genre(s): essay, journalism, novel, short story
Language(s): Portuguese

Maria Isabel Barreno is part of a very active group of Portuguese women writing today. Born and educated in Lisbon, she studied social sciences at the university and worked at the National Institute for Industrial Research. In 1961 Barreno started to publish short stories in the newspapers, but her first major works were sociological articles in the journal *Analise Social* (Social Analysis) and two books on the rural and urban worker. The novel *De Noite as Árvores sao Negra* (1968) brought her critical and public acclaim and established her as an important literary figure. In the same year Barreno co-authored *A Condiçao da Mulher Portuguesa*, beginning an era of open feminist activism. Her next novel, *Ous Outros Legítimos Superiores*, subtitled "Chapters of Philosophic Fiction," addresses social problems and the eternal quandaries of human values. In 1972 Barreno collaborated with the novelist Maria Velho de Costa, and the poet Maria Teresa Horta in the composition of perhaps the most internationally well-known contemporary Portuguese work, the *Novas Cartas Portuguesas*. Inspired by a seventeenth-century book by a cloistered nun, the "Three Marias," as they became known, wrote about women in Portuguese society, their reactions to war and social problems, and the search of women for insight into their nature. Accused by the government of "offending the public morals," the three writers were arrested and tried for this work but were finally absolved in 1974 after the fall of the dictatorship of Marcello Caetano. A lull followed in Barreno's literary production, but in 1976 she came back with *A Imagen da Mulher na Imprensa*, an analysis of the presentation of women in literature and the press. The novel *A Morte da Mae*, published in 1979 and translated into French, resumes Barreno's fictional work. In 1982 another novel, *Inventário de Ana* marks the interest of the writer in exploring different time sequences and lives in the existence of her characters. *Contos Analógicos*, published in 1984, follows this tendency towards a production that is a mix of science fiction and psychological narrative. Barreno utilizes experimental techniques and suppresses any linear narrative in her most recent works. Her latest collection of short stories, *O Mundo Sobre U Otro Desbotado* (1986), explores the limits of the human mind and questions the conventional ideas about reality and the linearity of time. Maria Isabel Barreno is also a gifted painter and textile artist.

Works

[With with C. A. Fernandes de Almeida and F. Henriques Vara], *Adaptaçao do Trabalhador de Origem Rural ao Meio Industrial e Urbano* [The Adaptation of the Rural Worker to the Urban-Industrial Environment] (1966). [With with C. A. Fernandes de Almeida and Leonel Costa], *Os Trabalhadores e o Progresso Técnico* [Workers and Technical Progress] (1967). [With others], *A Condiçao da Mulher Portuguesa* [The Situation of the Portuguese Women] (1969). *Da Noite as Árbores sao Negras* [At Night the Trees Are Black] (1968). *Os Outros Legítimos Superiores* [The Other Legitimate Superiors] (1970). [With Maria Teresa Horta and Maria Velho da Costa], *Novas Cartas Portuguesas* [New Portuguese Letters] (1972). *A Imagen da Mulher na Imprensa* [The Image of Women in Print] (1976). *A Morte da Mae* [The Mother's Death] (1979). *Inventario de Ana* [Ana's Inventory] (1982). *A Dama Verde* [The Green

Woman] (1983). *Contos Analogicos* [Analogic Stories] (1983). [With Joaquin Moura Ramos], *Sinos do Universo* [Bells of the Universe] (1984). *O Falso Neuro* [The False Neuter] (1985). *O Mundo Sobre o Outro Desbotado* [One World Discolored over Another] (1986).

Bibliography

Coelho, Nelly Novaes, "*Novas Cartas Portuguesas* e o Processo de Conscientizaçao da Mulher: Seculo XX" [*New Portuguese Letters* and the Process of Consciousness Raising in Women: 20th Century] *Letras* (Curitiba) 23 (1975): 165–171.

Lina L. Cofresí

Hanna Barvinok

(see: Oleksandra Myxajlivna Kuliseva)

Rutger Bas

(see: An Rutgers van der Loeff-Basenau)

Maria Constantinova (Marie) Bashkirtseff

Born November 24, 1858, Gavrontsi (Poltava, Ukraine), Russia; died October 31, 1884, Paris, France
Genre(s): diary, letter
Language(s): French, Russian

A promising painter from a landed Russian family, Marie Bashkirtseff gained considerable literary fame during the decade after her early death in 1884 because of the posthumous publication of a diary written in French. Her mother arranged for its partial publication, an action typical of the family's indulgence of her daughter's desires. After several years of marriage, her mother had returned to her parents' estate with Marie and a son, and in 1870 she began extended travels in Europe with her children, other relatives, and a physician.

Marie Bashkirtseff started her diary at age fourteen in Nice. She wrote that she would be absolutely honest when recording her thoughts and feelings, and some critics have compared this outpouring to contemporary literary realism and naturalism. However, she or an early editor of her diary actually altered her birthdate from November 1858 to November 1860 and attributed more social prestige to her family than was warranted (Cosnier, Moore). As an adolescent, Bashkirtseff already believed that her diaries would merit publication; hence, the reader is often aware of her trying to create certain impressions for posterity. The personality that emerges is highly intelligent, sensitive, strong-willed, intense, contradictory, sometimes romantic, and very egotistical. When she recognized that her education was deficient, she insisted on being tutored in classical and modern languages. She mastered Latin, French, English, Italian, and German and delved into history and sciences. In her diary she confided in 1875, "I elevate myself intellectually for the present; my soul is great, I am capable of great things." Not surprisingly, readers often have strong reactions to the diary's author. Some note the remarkable independence displayed at a time when young women of all social classes were typically taught modesty and restraint. Others dismiss the diaries as the boring record of a self-absorbed individual.

Determined to gain public recognition of her talent, Bashkirtseff at first hoped to become a singer. When her voice gave out, she persuaded her family to move to Paris in 1877 so that she could study painting at the *atelier Julian*, one of the few studios admitting women when the prestigious *Ecole des Beaux Arts* was closed to them. Bashkirtseff understood the differences in the social roles typically assigned to men and women, but she did not wish to devote herself to domesticity, and she envied men's liberty to move about freely in public. The realization that her ambitions challenged social conventions led her to a meeting of feminist Hubertine Auclert's *Société le droit des femmes* in the early 1880s. However, the attractive and fashion-conscious Bashkirtseff also enjoyed her family's access to certain Parisian social circles and so went incognito to the meeting and wrote under an assumed name in Auclert's newspaper. Later she commented on the unattractiveness of Auclert's following and realized that embracing feminism led to ridicule in Parisian drawing rooms.

Bashkirtseff's devotion to art after 1877 resulted in encouragement from her teacher Julian and the artist Tony Robert-Fleury, who often visited the studio. In 1880, 1881, 1882, and 1884 she exhibited paintings at the official Salon, obtained two honorable mentions, and in 1884 received national and international recognition. However, she had contracted tuberculosis, which eroded her health and eventually, despite a determination to work until the end, left her bedridden. During the last year of her life she continued to seek communication with those whom she regarded as great intellects and so wrote letters under assumed names to Emile Zola, Edmond de Goncourt, and Guy de Maupassant. She also had a close friendship with the cancer-stricken painter Jules Bastien-Lepage, whose artistic style she sometimes emulated.

The publication of part of Bashkirtseff's diaries in 1887 created, by 1890, a "cult" of admirers (D., "Two Views")—such as British prime minister William Gladstone, who judged her "a true genius"—and so gave her "the fame which had eluded her in life" (Collister). More recently, questions about the authenticity of various published versions of the diary have been raised, and literary and feminist scholars continue to study it and to recommend publication of the unabridged manuscripts of the diary.

Works

Journal de Marie Bashkirtseff [Journal of Marie Bashkirtseff] (1887; tr. A.D. Hall, 1890). *Journal de Marie Bashkirtseff* (1890). Manuscript of *Journal*, Bibliothèque Nationale, Nouvelles Acquisitions Françaises 12305–12389. *Lettres de Marie Bashkirtseff* [The Letters of Marie Bashkirtseff] (1891; tr. Mary J. Serrano, 1891).

Bibliography

Breakell, Mary, "Marie Bashkirtseff: The Reminiscences of a Fellow Student." *Nineteenth Century* 62 (1907): 110–125. Cahuet, Albéric, *Moussia, ou la vie et la mort de Marie Bashkirtseff* (Paris, 1926). Cahuet, Albéric, *Moussia et ses amis* (Paris, 1930). Collister, Peter, "Marie Bashkirtseff in Fiction: Edmond de Goncourt and Mrs. Humphrey Ward." *Modern Philology* 82 (August 1984): 53–69. Cosnier, Colette, *Marie Bashkirtseff, un portrait sans retouches* (Paris, 1985). Creston, Dormer (Dorothy Julia Baynes), *The Life of Marie*

Bashkirtseff (New York, 1937). D., "Two Views of Marie Bashkirtseff." *The Century* 18 (May 1890): 28–32. Gladstone, W.E., "Journal de Bashkirtseff." *Nineteenth Century* 26 (1889): 602–607. Jaccard, Annie-Claire, "La Recherche ontologique de Marie Bashkirtseff," in *Intime, intimité, intimisme*, ed. Raphael Molho and Pierre Reboul (Lille, 1976), pp. 199–217. Moore, Doris Langley, *Marie and the Duke of H.: The Daydream Love Affair of Marie Bashkirtseff* (Philadelphia, New York, 1966). Overton, Gwendolen. "Marie Bashkirtseff." *Forum* 48 (1912): 492–504. Theuriet, André, and George Clausen, Walter Sickert, and Mathilde Blind, *Julien Bastien-Lepage and His Art* (London, 1892), pp. 148–190. Union des femmes peintres et sculpteurs, *Catalogue des oeuvres de Mlle Bashkirtseff* (Paris, 1885). Wagenknecht, E., "Marie Bashkirtseff in Retrospect." *South Atlantic Quarterly* 43 (January 1944): 63–75.

Linda L. Clark

Laura Maria Caterina Bassi Verati

Born 1711, Bologna, Italy; died 1778, Bologna
Genre(s): scientific treatise, belles lettres
Language(s): Latin, French, Italian

Laura Bassi was an academic celebrated in her time for her vast cultural knowledge and proficiency in letters, philosophy, and science. Bassi was born in Bologna to Giovanni Bassi, an advocate, and Rosa Maria Cesari. Her first grammar teacher was Lorenzo Stegani, followed by Gaetano Tacconi, instructor of medicine, who taught logic, metaphysics, and natural philosophy. Her academic accomplishment was so great that by age twenty she was able to achieve a rank surprising to the public. The disputation "Concerning Universal Philosophical Things," which she presented on April 17, 1732 to the Cardinal Legate Girolamo Grimaldi, Archbishop Prospero Lambertini, and a multitude of literati, religious affiliates of every order, and members of the nobility, constituted an event of general interest and of great importance in her life.

Such was the impression aroused that in May of the same year she was awarded the Laureate in Philosophy with a solemn ceremony held in the hall of Hercules in the public Palazzo. The college of Philosophy admitted her by acclamation, and the Senate Academy conferred upon her a professorial chair at the university. This encouraged Bassi to continue her thesis on natural bodies of water, elements of other bodies, and universal parts, following an *ex officio* readership in universal philosophy that she continued until her death.

Bassi was elected to many literary societies and carried on extensive correspondence with the most eminent European men of letters. She was well acquainted with classical literature as well as that of France and Italy. In 1738, she married the physician and medical lecturer Giuseppe Verati, with whom she had several children. She diligently provided for their education and care. Her most illustrious pupil, Lazzaro Spallanzani (1729–1799), was first educated by his father, who was an advocate, then sent to the Jesuit College at Reggio di Modena when fifteen, and finally attended the University of Bologna, where he studied with Laura Bassi. His scientific interests have been attributed to her. Under her guidance, he studied natural philosophy and mathematics, as well as ancient and modern languages. After taking Orders, he became professor of logic, metaphysics, and Greek at the Universities of Reggio, Modena, and Pavia.

Throughout her life, Bassi continued to deliver public lectures on experimental philosophy and physics. In 1776, she was given a professorial chair in physics from the University of Bologna. Her remarkable achievements as well as great scientific accomplishments mark her as one of the most outstanding and influential women of the time.

Works

"De problemate quodam hydrometrico," in *De Bononiensi scientarium et artium Instituo atque Academia Commentarii* (Academicorum quorundam opuscola varia) IV, Bononiae (1757), pp. 61–73. "De Problemate quodam mechanico," ibid., pp. 74–79. *Philosophica studia* (1732).

Bibliography

Borsi, A., *Una gloria bolognese del sec.* XVIII (Laura Bassi) (Bologna, 1915). Cazzani, P., "I cento anni dell'Instituo magistrale 'Laura Bassi,'" in *Studi e inediti per il primo centinario dell'Instituo magistrale Laura Bassi* (Bologna, 1960), pp. 9–15, 43–52. Comelli, G.B., "Laura Bassi e il suo primo trionfo," in *Studi e Memorie per la storia dell'Università di Bologna* (Bologna, 1912). De Tipaldo, E., *Biografia degli italiani illustri*, VII (Venice, 1840), p. 190 ff. Fantuzzi, G., *Elogio della dottoressa Laura Maria Caterina Bassi Verati* (Bologna, 1778). Ferrucci, C. Franceschi, "Vita di Laura Bassi Verati," in *Prose e versi* (Florence, 1873), pp. 750–788. Garelli, A., *Lettere inedite alla celebre Laura Bassi scritte da illustri italiani e straniere* (Bologna, 1883). Masi, E., "Laura Bassi e il Voltaire," in *Studi e ritratti* (Bologna, 1881). Simeoni, L., *Storia dell'Università di Bologna*, II, pp. 95, 114, 120. Tomassi, R., "Documenti reguardanti Laura Bassi conservati presso l'Archiginnasio." In *L'Archignnasio* LVII (1962), pp. 319–324.

Jean E. Jost

Yocheved Bat-Miriam

Born 1901, Keplits, White Russia; died 1980, Israel
Genre(s): poetry
Language(s): Hebrew

Very little is known about the personal life of Yocheved Bat-Miriam. She was born in Keplits (White Russia) in 1901, and there she received a traditional Hasidic upbringing. Her education began in the Jewish tradition, but later she received a modern education as she studied at the Universities of Odessa and Moscow. She was schooled in both Russian and Hebrew.

By 1922 Bat-Miriam was prepared to attempt publishing her poetry. She soon discovered, however, that as a Jew, her works were not welcome in publications coming out under the new Soviet communist regime. Therefore, in 1923 Bat-Miriam's first poems appeared in Hebrew journals. Publishing abroad, however, was not preferable to Bat-Miriam, so in 1929 she moved to Palestine.

The early poetry of Bat-Miriam was published in the collection *Me-Rahok* (From Afar) in 1932. These are personal poems, lyrically romantic, that reach into a vision of her past of an unrequited, yet inspiring love. These poems lack the emotion one expects to experience, yet this is not to be criticized, but rather seen as Bat-

Miriam's ability to portray the place of the traditional Jewish woman. This woman seeks to know love, but instead of experiencing the rapturous pleasure of a man's nearness, she must savor the inspiration of his voice which she hears at a distance. However, she manages to depict the uniqueness of each Jewish woman's response in her poem *'Anayyim* (Eyes), as she speaks of a variety of reflections, such as sorrow, desire, first love, and pride of conquest. This cycle of poetry demonstrates Bat-Miriam's longing for life as it used to be, which is no longer possible in such a rapidly changing world.

In a posthumously published volume of poetry, *Shirim* (Verses), Bat-Miriam displays her delight in the sacredness of Jewish traditionalism. Romanticism is no longer found in this cycle, but there is a deep spiritual reverence for the Jewish life which has not been replaced by any corresponding level of spirituality. Various items stand as symbols of the intense religiosity of the Jewish family, such as the prayer shawl and the prayerbook. While some may interpret her descriptions of a Jewish home as metaphoric, others may see the literalism in her phrases. The shoulders which are "a book of prayer and praise to the Lord," and the door to her father's house which is "an illuminated title page of the hymnal" parallel the *Shema* from Deuteronomy 6, where the word of the Lord was commanded to be worn and posted on the doorposts of every Jewish home. Bat-Miriam dreams not only of the Jewish home of her childhood but also of the Jewish home God intended for each traditional Jewish family.

Not only does Bat-Miriam demonstrate a devout traditionalism in her depiction of the Jewish woman and the Jewish home, she also applies this thought to her national poems, *Erez Israel* (The Land of Israel). Bat-Miriam yearns to identify with her new land, but she cannot lose the romantic images of her past. The vision of her life as she would have it in her beloved Israel is but a distant vision for her. Memories of a distant world and vain longings for their revival in her present existence also characterize her collection *Demuyot Me-Ofek* (Images from the Horizon).

The tragedy of the Jewish people was not lost upon Bat-Miriam. She writes her *Mi-Shirey Russia* (Songs of Russia), longing for a Jewish existence there that is no longer possible. She sings of the tragic existence of Jewish ghettos in *Shiram La-Ghetto* (Ghetto Verse), and how this is the existence furthest imaginable from what God intended for the chosen ones.

Through all of her writing Bat-Miriam stands for traditionalism, life as it once was. Most of all, she portrays the traditional Jewish woman as the true heroine of life, who strives to soothe and please, to make all others happy, although she bears the burden of work, worry and solitude. Bat-Miriam depicts the Jewish past with which she urges all Jews to reconcile. This ability to seek understanding of their true identity is what Bat-Miriam sees as the only shining ray of hope in an otherwise disrupting future.

Works

Me-Rahok [From Afar] (1932). *Erez Israel* [Land of Israel] (1937). *Reayon* [Interview] (1940). *Demuyot me-Ofek* [Images from the Horizon] (1941). *Mi-Shirey Russia* [Songs of Russia] (1942). *Shirim La-Ghetto* [Ghetto Verse] (1946). *Shirim* [Verse] (1963).

Bibliography

Borash, A., ed., *Mivhar Hashirah Haivriz Hahadasha* (Jerusalem, 1948). Burnshaw, Stanley, T. Carmi, and Ezra Spicehandler, eds., *The Modern Hebrew Poem Itself* (New York, 1965). Carmi, T., ed., *The Penguin Book of Hebrew Verse* (New York, 1981). Frank, Bernard, tr., *Modern Hebrew Poetry* (Iowa City, 1980). Halkin, Simon, *Modern Hebrew Literature* (New York, 1950). Mintz, Ruth F., ed., *Modern Hebrew Poetry* (Berkeley, 1966). Penueli, S.Y., and A. Ukhmani, eds., *Anthology of Modern Hebrew Poetry, Vol. 2* (Jerusalem, 1966). Silberschlag, Eisig, *From Renaissance to Renaissance II: Hebrew Literature in the Land of Israel: 1870–1970* (New York, 1977). Waxman, Meyer, *A History of Jewish Literature, Vol. 4* (Cranbury, N.J., 1960).

JoAnne C. Juett

Battista da Montefeltro

Born 1383, Urbino, Italy; died 1450, Urbino
Genre(s): oratory
Language(s): Latin

Daughter of Antonio, Count of Urbino, Battista was married on June 14, 1405, to Galeazzo Malatesta, heir of Pesaro. Battista was one of the most famous women of the Quattrocento. A daughter of the da Montefeltro and hence an aunt of the illustrious Federigo, she was herself a renowned scholar. One of her pupils was her own granddaughter, Costanza da Varano. Battista was the woman to whom Leonardo Bruni dedicated his *De studiis et litteris*. . . . An oration by her to the Emperor Sigismund is available in *Her Immaculate Hand*.

Bibliography

Cosenza, 3, 2087–2088. King, Margaret L., and Albert Rabil, *Her Immaculate Hand* (Binghamton, 1983), pp. 35 ff.

Joseph Berrigan

Battista da Varano

Born April 9, 1458, Camerino, Italy; died May 31, 1524, Camerino
Genre(s): mysticism, autobiography
Language(s): Italian

The natural daughter of Giulio Cesare da Varano, Lord of Camerino, Battista da Varano was influenced by Franciscan preaching to meditate upon Christ's Passion. This led in turn to her rejection of the world and her entrance into a convent of Poor Clares, first in Urbino and later in Camerino.

The recipient of many spiritual graces, Battista da Varano has left us a spiritual autobiography and a record of her conversations with Christ on His Passion.

Works

Le opere spirituali, ed. Giacomo Boccanere (Iesi, 1958). *My Spiritual Life*, tr. J.R. Berrigan (Draft Translation Series, Matrologia Latina, 1986). *The Mental Sorrows of Christ in His Passion*, tr. J.R. Berrigan (Draft Translation Series, Matrologia Latina, 1986).

Joseph Berrigan

Baudonivia

Born first half of the seventh century
Genre(s): hagiography
Language(s): Latin

Baudonivia composed a *Life of Saint Radegund*, the wife of King Chlotar. The king released Radegund from their marriage vow in order that she might become abbess of the monastery of the Holy Cross, which he had earlier founded for her in Poitiers. This royal abbess became one of the great models of female spirituality in Merovingian culture.

The famed Venantius Fortunatus composed the first version of Radegund's life, but the community of the Holy Cross felt that it omitted far too much detail. Between 609 and 614, Baudonivia, a member of the community, wrote a new life at the request of her abbess, explicitly to supplement Fortunatus' account. Baudonivia had herself known the saint and used her own recollections and those of her fellow nuns to compose a portrait of the saint that is much richer in personal detail than that of Fortunatus. The additions concern such topics as the married life of the saint, her collection of relics, and brief examples of the spiritual advice that she gave to her community. Such detail has insured that the portrait of Radegund is one of the clearest of any we possess from the Merovingian age.

Baudonivia wrote in a style of Latin typical of Merovingian chancery circles, that is, filled with "barbarisms" and conventional phrases, many borrowed from Fortunatus himself. While she was well educated for her cultural milieu, her work has suffered among modern scholars in comparison to that of Fortunatus. The nuns of the Holy Cross themselves clearly felt the need for the detailed depiction of their abbess that Baudonivia provided for their liturgical commemoration of the saint, a purpose that the account of Fortunatus did not fulfill.

Works

Vita s. Radegundis, in B. Krusch, ed., *Monumenta Germaniae historica, Scriptores rerum merovingicarum*, II, pp. 377–395; for a full list of editions, see pp. 360–364. A partial French translation is provided in Aigrain, R., *Vie de sainte Radegonde, reine de France, par s. Fortunat* (1910), pp. 48–59.

Bibliography

Coudanne, L., "Baudonivie, moniale de Sainte-Croix et biographe de sainte Radegonde," in *Etudes mérovingiennes* (1953), pp. 45–51. Delaruelle, E., "Sainte Radegonde, son type de sainteté et la chrétienité de son temps," in *Etudes mérovingiennes* (1953): 65–74. Fontaine, J., "Hagiographie et politique de Sulpice Sévère à Venance Fortunat." *Revue d'histoire d'église de France* 62 (1976): 113–140. Graus, F., *Volk, Herrscher und Heileger im Reich der Merowinger* (1965), pp. 409–412. Krusch, B., *op. cit.*, pp. 359–362.

General references: Chevalier, *Répetoire bio-bibliographique*, p. 470. *Dictionnaire d'histoire et geographie ecclésiastique*, VI, pp. 1357–1360. *Histoire littéraire de la France*, III, pp. 491–493. Manitius, *Geschichte der lateinischen Literatur des Mittelalters*, I, p. 173. Molinier, *Les sources de l'histoire de France*, II, nn. 96 and 121.

Thomas Head

Vicki Baum

Born January 24, 1888, Vienna, Austria; died
August 29, 1960, Hollywood, California
Genre(s): novel, tale, novelette, drama,
screenplay
Language(s): German, English (after 1941)

Although she grew up in the latter days of the Emperor Franz Josef in *fin-de-siècle* Vienna, Vicki Baum's childhood was anything but romantic. In an early autobiographical sketch she offhandedly describes herself as "the single child of a good family in very bourgeois surroundings," but her memoirs, written late in life, reveal that behind the closed doors of the Baum residence lived a sadistic nurse, a manic-depressive mother, and a temperamental father, who, when confronted with domestic problems, went home to his mother. In order to escape this Strindbergian ménage, she turned early to music and writing. Music paid off first: by the age of eleven she was performing publicly on the harp and not long thereafter became first a concert harpist, then a music teacher. A youthful marriage to an ineffectual *Kaffeehaus* poet soon ended in an amicable divorce, and she went to Germany where she married a childhood friend, Richard Lert, who was at the time conducting the orchestra in which she was playing.

Her writing meanwhile had continued privately by fits and starts. Interrupted by her musical career, a brief stint as a nurse during WW I, two marriages and the birth of two sons, it bore fruit quite by accident when one day a friend came upon her desk filled with stories and novels and sent one of the latter off to the publishing house of Ullstein. To her surprise it was accepted, and in 1926 she moved to Berlin and took a job as an editor for one of her publisher's magazines.

Even so, her literary career progressed rather slowly at first. The turn came with *Menschen im Hotel* and the subsequent dramatization of its English version, *Grand Hotel*. In 1931 she was invited to come to New York to see the play, and what had been planned as a two-week visit became a permanent change of residence. She brought her family to America, found work in California as a screenwriter, became an American citizen in 1938, and, as a gesture of repudiation of Hitler's Austria, began soon thereafter to write in English.

Grand Hotel established the formula for most of her subsequent works. It is an early example of the "group novel," constructed along the lines of Thornton Wilder's *Bridge of St. Luis Rey*, in which several strangers are brought together in a single place—here a luxury hotel in 1929 Berlin—to experience a sort of mass peripeteia. The technique lent itself well to melodramatic plots and adaptation for the stage and cinema. Baum is a superb storyteller, and her books are filled with romance, adventure, love at first sight—everything, in fact, but real people. Her characters all fulfill their obligations to the plot with relentless efficiency, providing pathos, eccentricity, tenderness, romance, and depravity as required, and on the rare occasions when they briefly come alive—on a clothes-shopping spree, a ride in a fast open car or a slow open airplane—one gets the feeling they are much like their creator. As one critic observed, Vicki Baum has "everything which makes for a wide audience: the pipe-dreams of little people come true, a self-assured keyhole familiarity with what passes for the *grand monde*, a marshmallow softness."

All of this detracted not in the least from her popularity. Though she never again reached the heights of *Grand Hotel*, her subsequent books attracted a large and loyal following as she globe-trotted her way through a couple of dozen variants of the G.H. theme. *Hell in Frauensee* assembles its cast about a swimming pool; *Hotel Shanghai* brings together nine persons destined to be killed in a Japanese air raid; *Hotel Berlin '43* returns to the scene of her first triumph for a routine anti-Nazi melodrama; the more ambitious *Weeping Wood* traces the people involved in the production of rubber through a series of predictable confrontations tailored to scratch the itches of the day, from the exploitation of Brazilian plantation workers by Big Business to the employment of the finished product—here a rubber hose—by a Nazi on a Jew.

It is all too easy to be patronizing toward Vicki Baum. Her books may be *kitsch*, but they are *kitsch* of the highest quality. What she did she did exceptionally well, and perhaps the most accurate assessment of her talents was her own, when she once described herself as "a first-class second-rate author."

Works

Novels: *Frühe Schatten* (1919). *Eingang zur Bühne* (1920). *Der Tanz der Ina Raffay* (1921). *Die Welt ohne Sünde* (1922). *Ulle, der Zwerg* (1924). *Feme* (1926). *Hell in Frauensee* (1927). *Stud. Chem. Helene Willfüer* (1928). *Menschen im Hotel* (1929). *Zwischenfall in Lohwinckel* (1930). *Leben ohne Geheimnis* (1932). *Der grosse Einmaliens* (1935). *Die Karriere der Doris Hart* (1936). *Der grosse Ausverkauf* (1937). *Liebe und Tod auf Bali* (1937). *Das Ende der Geburt* (1937). *Die grosse Pause* (c. 1939). *The Ship and the Shore* (1941). *The Christmas Carp* (1941). *Marion Alive* (1942). *Hotel Berlin '43* (1944). *Mortgage on Life* (1946). *Headless Angel* (1948). *Danger from Deer* (1951). *The Mustard Seed* (1953). *Tiburon* (1956). *Written on Water* (1956). *Theme for Ballet* (1958). *Rendezvous in Paris* (n.d.).

Plays: *Grand Hotel* (1930). [With John Golden], *Divine Drudge* (based on *Zwischenfall in Lohwinckel*, 1933). *Pariser Platz* (1931).

Screenplays: *Dance, Girl, Dance* (RKO, 1940). Contributor to *Unfinished Business* (Universal, 1941). Contributor of story ideas to *Honeymoon* (RKO, 1946) and to *Powder Town* (RKO, 1962). Other: *The Weeping Wood*, tales (1943). *It Was All Quite Different*, memoirs (1964). *Die andern Tage*, novelettes (1922). *Der Weg*, novelette (1925). *Tanzpause*, novelette (1926). *Schlosstheater*, novelettes (1921).

Robert Harrison

Gertrud Bäumer

Born November 12, 1873, Hohenlimburg, Germany; died March 25, 1954, Bethel/ Bielefeld
Genre(s): novel, essay, autobiography, nonfiction, letters
Language(s): German

Gertrud Bäumer, the daughter of a theologian, was a leading German feminist in her days. After having taught at a primary school for several years, she studied in Berlin and received her Ph.D. in 1905 with a dissertation on Goethe's *Satyron*. Together with Helene Lange and Friedrich Naumann, she was an active member in the women's movement and founded the National Women's Service during WW I. She edited, first together with Helene Lange, then later by herself, the journal *Die Frau* (The Woman), 1893–1944; the *Handbuch der Frauenbewegung* (Handbook of the Women's Liberation Movement), 1901–1906; and, together with Naumann and Theodor Heuss, the first president of the Federal Republic of Germany, the journal *Hilfe* (Help), 1915–1940. From 1916–1920 she ran the Social Pedagogical Institute (together with Marie Braun) and the Social Women's School in Hamburg. She was a delegate from 1920–1933 for the Democratic Party in the National Assembly and then in the Imperial Diet. From 1920–1933 she headed the sections "school" and "youth welfare" in the Department of the Interior, and for some time she was a delegate for youth politics at the League of Nations in Geneva. Because of her political views she lost her public positions with the rise to power of the Nazis in 1933. Since then she dedicated all her energy to literature and histori-cal, cultural and social studies. In her novels she focuses on medieval women and their role in society. Her most successful novel was *Adelheid, Mutter der Königreiche* (1936; Adelheid, Mother of Kingdoms). Her literary style and motives are closely related to those of Ricarda Huch.

Works

Novels and short stories: *Sonntag mit Silvia Monika* [A Sunday with Silvia Monika] (1933). *Adelheid, Mutter der Königreiche* [Adelheid, Mother of Kingdoms] (1936). *Der Park* [The Park] 1937). *Der Berg des Königs* [The Royal Mountain] (1938). *Das königliche Haupt* [The Royal Head] (1951).

Autobiography: *Lebensweg durch eine Zeitenwende* [A Life's Path Crossing The Threshold to a New Age] (1933; reprinted under the title *Im Licht der Erinnerungen* [In the Light of Memories] in 1953).

Essays, studies and letters: *Die Frau in der Kulturbewegung der Gegenwart* [The Woman in the Cultural Movement of the Present Times] (1904). *Goethes Satyron* [Goethe's Satyron] (1905). *Die Frauenbewegung und die Zukunft unserer Kultur* [The Women's Movement and the Future of our Culture] (1909). *Die soziale Idee in den Weltanschauungen des 19. Jahrhunderts* [The Social Idea in the Ideologies of the 19th Century] (1910). *Die Frau und das geistige Leben* [Woman and the Intellectual Life] (1911). *Der Wandel des Frauenideals in der modernen Kultur* [The Change of the Ideal of Women in Our Modern Culture] (1911). [With L. Droescher], *Von der Kinderseele* [On the Souls of Children] (1912). *Ida Freudenberg* (1912). *Was sind Wir unserem geistigen Ich schuldig?* [What Do We Owe Our Intellectual Self?] (1912). *Entwicklung und Stand des Frauenstudiums und der höheren Frauenberufe* [Development and Present Situation of Studies for Women and of Advanced Jobs for Women] (1912). *Die Frau in Volkswirtschaft und Staatsleben der Gegenwart* [The Woman in Economy and Public Life in the Present Time] (1914). *Der Krieg und die Frau* [War and Women] (1914). *Die Lehren des Weltkriegs für die deutsche Pädagogik* [Consequences of WW I for German Pedagogy] (1915). *Weit hinter den Schützengräben* [Far Behind the Trenches] (1916). *Zwischen Gräbern und Sternen* [Between Tombs and Stars] (1919). *Helene Lange* (1918). *Studien über Frauen* [Studies on Women]

(1920). *Fichte und sein Werk* [Fichte and His Work] (1921). [With others], *Das Reichsgesetz für Jugendwohlfahrt* [The Imperial Law for Youth Welfare] (1923). *Die seelische Krisis* [The Crisis of the Soul] (1924). *Die Frau in der Krisis der Kultur* [The Woman in the Crisis of Our Culture] (1926). *Europäische Kulturpolitik* [European Cultural Politics] (1926). *Deutsche Schulpolitik* [German School Politics] (1928). *Grundlagen demokratischer Politik* [Foundation of Democratic Politics] (1928). *Grundsätzliches und Tatsächliches zur Bevölkerungsentwicklung* [Fundamental Aspects and Facts of the Development of the Population] (1929). *Nationale und internationale Erziehung in der Schule* [National and International Education in School] (1929). *Die Frauengestalten der deutschen Frühe* [Women Figures in the German Past] (1929). *Neuer Humanismus* [New Humanism] (1930). *Schulaufbau, Berufsauslese, Berechtigungswesen* [Reconstruction of the School, Selection of Jobs, Justification] (1930). *Heimatchronik während des Weltkriegs* [Home Chronicle During the Time of WW I] (1930). *Sinn und Formen geistiger Führung* [Meaning and Forms of Intellectual Leadership] (1930). *Die Frau im neuen Lebensraum* [The Woman in New Living Space] (1931). *Goethe— überzeitlich* [Goethe—From a Transcendental Viewpoint] (1932). *Krisis des Frauenstudiums* [Crisis of Women Studies] (1932). *Die Frau im deutschen Staat* [The Woman in the German Nation] (1932). *Familienpolitik* [Family Politics] (1933). *Der freiwillige Arbeitsdienst der Frau* [The Voluntary Work Service of the Woman] (1933). *Männer und Frauen im geistigen Werden des deutschen Volkes* [Men and Women in the Intellectual Development of the German People] (1934). *Ich kreise um Gott* [I Am Circling Around God] (1935). *Wolfram von Eschenbach* (1938). *Krone und Kreuz* [Crown and Cross] (1938). *Gestalt und Wandel* [Form and Change] (1939; published in a new form in two volumes under the title *Bildnis der Liebenden* [Picture of the Lovers], 1958, and *Frauen der Tat* [Women in Action], 1959). *Das Antlitz der Mutter* [My Mother's Face] (1941). *Der ritterliche Mensch* [The Chivalric Person] (1941). *Die Macht der Liebe* [Love's Power] (1942). *Der neue Weg der deutschen Frau* [The New Way for the German Woman] (1946). *Die Reichsidee bei den Ottonen* [The Imperial Idea under the Ottonians] (1946).

Das hohe Mittelalter als christliche Schöpfung [The High Middle Ages as a Christian Creation] (1946). *Eine Woche im Mai* [A Week in May] (1947). *Der Jüngling im Sternenmantel* [The Youth in the Coat of Stars] (1947). *Der Dichter Fritz Usinger* [The Poet Fritz Usinger] (1947). *Die christliche Barmherzigkeit als geschichtliche Macht* [Christian Mercy as Historical Power] (1948). *Ricarda Huch* (1949). *Die drei göttlichen Komödien des Abendlandes* [The Three European Divine Comedies, a study on Dante's *Divina Commedia*, Wolfram von Eschenbach's *Parzival* and Goethe's *Faust*] (1949). *Frau Rath Goethe* (1949); *Das geistige Bild Goethes im Licht seiner Werke* [Goethe's Spiritual Perspective in the Light of His Work] (1950). *Otto I. und Adelheid* [Otto I and Adelheid] (1951). *Eleonora Duse* (1958). *Wahrzeichen deutscher Geschichte* [Prophetic Symbols of German History] (1958). *Des Lebens wie der Liebe Bande* [Bonds of Life and Love]; letters 1903–1950, ed. E. Beckmann (1956).

Editions: *Der Traum vom Reich* [The Dream about the Empire] (1955). *Goethe's Freundinnnen* [Goethe's Girl Friends] (1909). *Die Religion und die Frau* [Religion and the Woman] (1911). *Der deutsche Frauenkongreß Berlin* [The German Women Congress in Berlin] (1912). *Die Deutsche Frau in der sozialen Kriegsfürsorge* [The German Woman in the Veterans' Welfare System] (1916). *Eine Hand voll Jubel* [A Handful of Jubilation] (1934). *Der Denker* [The Thinker] (1950).

Periodicals edited: *Die Frau* [The Woman] (1893–1944). *Hilfe* [Help] (1915–1940). *Handbuch der Frauenbewegung* [Handbook of the Women's Movement] (1901–1906).

Bibliography

Fassbinder, K.M., "Zu den letzten Werken G.B.'s." *Hochland* 34 (1936–1937). Goetz, W., et al., *Gabe für G.B* (1931). Greven-Aschendorff, B., *Westfälische Lebensbilder* 12 (München, 1969), pp. 162–196. Roesch, Hans, "G.B.," *Handbuch der deutschen Gegenwartsliteratur*, 2nd ed., vol. 1 (1969). Weitzel, Karl, "G.B.: *Adelheid, Der Jüngling im Sternenmantel, Der Park*." *Der Romanführer* III, 1 (Stuttgart, 1952), pp. 13–16.

Albrecht Classen

Emilia Pardo Bazán

Born 1851, La Coruña, Spain; died 1921,
Madrid, Spain
Genre(s): novel, short story, literary criticism,
history
Language(s): Spanish

Emilia Pardo Bazán stands out in the history of Spanish literature as one of Spain's few recognized women writers before the twentieth century. She was famous in her own time not only as a novelist, short story writer, and literary critic and historian of the first order but also as a woman of amazing versatility and independence. In an age when women were advised to remain in the roles assigned by convention—wife, mother, nun—Pardo Bazán audaciously wrote feminist essays and introduced into Spain the shocking theories of French naturalism propounded by Émile Zola. Although she never subscribed to the determinist theories of Zola's naturalism, she did employ its techniques and themes. Pardo Bazán's literary interests, however, exceeded any one literary school or method, and during her long career she wrote in the traditional style of Spanish realism and the spiritual-mystical mode in fashion during the turn of the century. She also incorporated the dictates of naturalism, modifying them to suit the temper of her talent and times. Eclectic is the word that best applies to Pardo Bazán.

Emilia Pardo Bazán's intellectual curiosity and determination were manifested early; she virtually educated herself, reading avidly and widely in classical and modern literature, learning English so that she could read that literature, reading French and Italian literature in the original languages, and delving into philosophical and aesthetic problems. She wrote essays and books on subjects as varied as St. Francis and Christian mysticism, modern French and Russian literature, and the Russian revolution. No subject seemed inappropriate to this energetic woman who even founded a literary magazine for which she herself wrote all the material for several years.

Although married and the mother of three children, she spent most of her time apart from her husband, maintaining a home in Madrid where she reigned over a literary salon. In recognition of her intellectual abilities and acute knowledge of modern literature, she was honored as the first woman to occupy a professorship at the University in Madrid.

Pardo Bazán was a controversial figure, inspiring both acclaim and disdain, but she was nonetheless accepted, even by those less than enthusiastic about her insistence on proving herself as a writer and an intellectual, and becoming one of the most significant writers of her time. Her reputation has grown in the years since her death. Today Pardo Bazán is seen as a major writer and critic and as a pioneer in women's issues. She wrote twenty novels, several volumes of literary criticism and history, hundreds of short stories, and hundreds of essays.

Works

Obras completas., 44 vols. (1886–1926). *Obras completas*, ed. Federico Carlos Sainz de Robles, 2 vols. (1947).

Translations: *Short Stories by Emilia Pardo Bazán*, ed. Albert Shapiro and F.J. Hurley (1933). *The Son of the Bondwoman*, tr. Ethel Harriet Hearn (1976).

Bibliography

Baquero Goyannes, Mariano, "Emilia Pardo Bazán." *Temas Españoles*, Num. 526 (Madrid, 1971). Barroso, Fernando José, *El Naturalismo en la Pardo Bazán* (Madrid, 1973). Bravo-Villasante, Carmen, *Vida y obra de Emilia Pardo Bazan* (Madrid, 1962). Bretz, Mary Lee, "Naturalismo y feminismo en Emilia Pardo Bazán." *Papeles de Son Armadans* 87 (Dec. 1977): 195–219. Brown, Donald Fowler, *The Catholic Naturalism of Pardo Bazán*. University of North Carolina Studies in the Romance Languages and Literatures 28 (Chapel Hill, N.C., 1957). Clémessy, Nelly, *Emilia Pardo Bazán romancière. La critique, la théorie, la pratique. Thèses, Mémoires et Travaux*, 2 vols. (Paris, 1973). Davis, Gifford, "The Critical Reception of Naturalism in Spain before *La cuestion palpitante*." *Hispanic Review* XXII, 2 (April 1954): 97–108. Eoff, Sherman H., *The Modern Spanish Novel. Comparative Essays Examining the Philosophical Impact of Science on Fiction* (New York, 1961). Giles, Mary E., "Impressionist Techniques in Descriptions by Emilia Pardo Bazan." *Hispanic Review* XXX, 4 (Oct. 1962): 304–316. Giles, Mary E., "Symbolic Imagery in *La sirena negra*," *Papers on Language and Literature* 4 (1968): 182–191. Giles, Mary E., "Feminism and the Feminine in Emilia

Pardo Bazan's Novels." *Hispania*63, 2 (May 1980), 356–357. Glascock, Clyde C., "Two Modern Spanish Novelists: Emilia Pardo Bazán and Armando Palacio Valdés." *University of Texas Bulletin*, 2625 (1926). González Lopez, Emilio, *Emilia Pardo Bazán, novelista de Galicia* (New York, 1944). Hilton, Ronald, "Doña Emilia Pardo Bazán and the Europeanization of Spain." *Symposium* 6–7 (1952–1953): 298–307. Hilton, Ronald, "Emilia Pardo Bazán et le mouvement féministe en Espagne." *Bulletin Hispanique* LIV (1952): 153–164. Lopez-Sanz, Mariano, *Naturalismo y espiritualismo en la novelística de Galdós y Pardo Bazán* (Madrid, 1985). Martín, Elvira, *Tres mujeres gallegas del siglo XIX: Concepción Arenal, Rosalía de Castro, Emilia Pardo Bazán* (Barcelona, 1962). Nelken, Margarita, *Las escritoras espanolas* (Barcelona-Buenos Aires, 1930). Osborne, Robert E., *Emilia Pardo Bazán, su vida y sus obras* (Mexico, 1964). Pattison, Walter T., *Emilia Pardo Bazán* (New York, 1971). Pattison, Walter T., *El naturalismo español. Historia externa de un movimiento literario* (Madrid, 1965). Scari, Robert M., "Aspectos distinctivos del lenguaje de Morrina." *Cuadernos hispanoamericanos* CV, 313 (July 1976): 191–199. Varela Jácome, Benito, *Estructuras novelísticas de Emilia Pardo Bazán* (Santiago de Compostela: Anejo XXII, 1973).

Mary E. Giles

Salomėja Bčinskaitė-Bučienė

(a.k.a. Salomėja Nėris)

Born 1904, Kiršai, Lithuania; died 1945, Moscow
Genre(s): poetry
Language(s): Lithuanian

Salomėja Nėris was designated Lithuanian SSR People's Poet in 1954. She studied Lithuanian literature, German, and pedagogics at the University of Kaunas, Lithuania, and taught high school from 1928 to 1941. She published her first collection of poems, *Anksti rytą* (Early in the Morning), in 1927. Youthful romantic and religious leanings led Nėris to a conservative Roman Catholic world view. Later, extensive travels in Western Europe brought Nėris closer to a leftist political stance, leaning toward a certain romantic idealism reminiscent of Louis Aragon, Berthold

Brecht or, even more, Federico Garcia Lorca. In 1931 Nėris demonstratively, with a public announcement, joined the left-wing Lithuanian artists' group "The Third Front," declaring that henceforth her poetry was to become political and serve the working class. In 1937, while in Paris, Nėris joined the sculptor Bernardas Bučas in a common-law marriage and returned to live in Kaunas. In 1938 Nėris received the Lithuanian republic State Prize for Literature for her collection *Diemed'iu 'ydėsiu* (I'll Bloom Like Wormwood). In 1940, as Soviet tanks were rolling across Lithuania, Nėris wrote an adulatory "Poem to Stalin" and read it at a Plenary Session of the USSR Supreme Soviet to welcome Lithuania's inclusion into the Soviet Union. In 1941 Nėris became a deputy to the Lithuanian SSR Supreme Soviet. In the same year she withdrew to Russian under the German attack and lived in Moscow, Penza, and Ufa, writing strident anti-fascist poetry in praise of the Soviet country and regime. She returned to Lithuania in 1944, became seriously ill, and was taken to Moscow for special care, where she soon died.

Nėris was well-read in several languages. Tolstoy, Dostoevsky, Romain Roland, and Stefan Zweig were among her favorites in prose, and Friedrich Schiller, Johann Wolfgang Goethe, Heinrich Heine, and Alexander Pushkin, as well as Anna Akhmatova, Alexander Blok, Paul Verlain, Rainer Maria Rilke, and Charles Baudelaire among her favorite poets. Nėris has also translated a number of works from these authors.

Her poetry might best be characterized by its melodious passion. There is a vibrant intensity in the experience of life that reaches, and swells, at the point of pain as it transforms itself into deceptively simple, yet extremely subtle, poetic language. In it, sound recurrences combine with grammatical, intonational, and emotional points of stress to produce a haunting, persistent feeling of rhythm, simultaneously enchanting and relentless, driving readers to draw their breath in pain to hear her story.

In her early period, until about 1940, that story is predominantly personal. The poet tells us with poignant openness how wonderful and how painful it is to experience the process of living as a continuous becoming of poetry. There is defiance in her verse, particularly toward the bourgeois values that, she felt, made her an outcast at home because of her unconventional marriage; her work takes a challenging stance against the norms and mores of her society and time. There is also contemplation, where the poet's word reaches out gently, precariously, to touch the highly sensitive, indeed, agonizing, issue of one's own mortality that confronts the surging passion to live, to drink deeply of beauty, freedom, and love. In this thematic frame, a number of poems subtly utilize associations with the imagery and diction of Lithuanian folk songs without, however, any direct imitation of their style or prevalent themes.

While it is quite likely that Nėris turned to the left at least partially out of contempt for what she thought was the Philistine, mindless life of the bourgeoisie, it could also be that the horrors of Stalin's regime did reach her attention to some extent, but it was too late; she had allowed herself to be trapped in an ideological dead-end, with capitalist greed, fascist insanity, and Russia's monumental inhumanity blocking every exit. All she had left was the Soviet war machine—she was now part of it, was functioning as one of its cogs, in effect independently, of her own will. Only the searing yearning for her homeland, boundless love, and desperate burden of dispossession shines through her later, politically committed poetry to sustain in her readers that strange enchantment they had always felt toward her verse. Even stylistically, the harsh and often wooden verbal structures of bolshevik rhetoric seems mixed in a peculiar, elusive way with passages of the previous graceful, luminous beauty, so full of love for the native land.

Placed in a historical framework, Nėris fills a transitional stage between the rhetorical patriotic romanticism of such poets as the "bard of national awakening" Jonas Mačiulis-Maironis (1862–1932) and the intimate, experimental modernistic or expressionistic verse of such major Lithuanian poets of the twenties, thirties, and forties as Bernardas Brazd'ionis (b. 1907), a poet of great lyrical pathos whose passion for the ideal has similarities with the works of Nėris or Jonas Aistis (1904–1973), a soulful lover of the spare

and sometimes harsh Lithuanian landscape who nevertheless liked to experiment with modernistic turns of style and vocabulary, and perhaps especially Antanas Miškinis (1905–1983) whose bucolic, folkloric, passionate verse was enchanted, enthralled, with song. At the other end of the spectrum, her poetry has given a personal tinge and some human feeling to the Socialist Realist doggerel pursued by an entire host of Soviet Lithuanian poets that did not end their song until approximately the sixties. A number of women poets, Judita Vaičiūnaitė (b. 1937), Janina Degutytė (b. 1928), Violeta Palčinskaitė (b. 1943) and others, have acknowledged their thematic and emotional, if not necessarily stylistic, indebtedness to Nėris, by all means one of the major leading Lithuanian poets of any time.

Works

Anksti rytą, poems (1927). Pėdos smėly, poems (1931). Diemed'iu 'ydėsiu, poems (1938). Eglė 'alčiu karalienė, poem/tale (1940). Poema apie Stalina (1940). Dainuok, širdie, gyvenimą, poems and tales in verse (1943). Lakštingala negali nečiulbėti, poems (1945). Bolševiko kelias, narrative poem (1960). Marija Melninkaitė, narrative poem (1963). širdis mana–audrų daina, collected poems (1974). Kaip 'ydėjimas vyšnios, collected poems (1978). Salomėja Nėris. Poezija, collected poems (1979).

Bibliography

Alekna, V., "S. Nėris da'numų 'odynas," in Poetika ir metodologija (1980). Areška, V., Salomėja Nėris. Gyvenimo ir kūrybos ap'valga (Vilnius, 1974). Girdzijauskas, J., "Nėries ir Putino metrikos dominantės.–Nėries eilėdara ir stilius," in J. Girdzijauskas, Lietuvių eilėdara. XX am'ius (Vilnius, 1979). Korsakas, K., "Kovos ir pergalės poetė." Pergalė (1964). Kubilius, V., Salomėjos Nėries lyrika. Studija (Vilnius, 1968). Skirmantas, P., "Priegaid'ių pasiskirstymas izometriškuose S. Nėries ir V. Mykoloačio-Putino tekstuose." Literatūra (1976).

R. Šilbajoris

Marie Beauharnais (Anne F. Mouchard, Comtesse de)

(a.k.a. Fanny)

Born October 4, 1737, Paris, France; died July
2, 1813, Paris
Genre(s): poetry, novel, short story, letters
Language(s): French

"Fanny," the daughter of a "recevoir général des finances," started writing poetry at age ten. However, she never rose up to her own expectations and ambitions, and her career as author and patron of litterateurs and philosophers was fraught with scandal and controversy. On the one hand, she was praised by people of the stature of Dorat and Cubières, was received with pleasure by the Academie des Arcades in Rome and was a member of the Academie at Lyons. And on the other hand, wagging tongues doubted the integrity and authorship of her poems and tales while journals like La Harpe (The Harp) wrote that her work was so uniformly bad it did not even merit dispute.

Fanny married Comte Claude de Beauharnais, a man about twenty years her senior, on March 1, 1753. They separated amicably in 1762, after which Fanny returned to her father's house in Montmartre and opened a salon. Though a great many of Paris' fashionable intelligencia including Dorat and his followers frequented Fanny's salon, her "Fridays" were never as successful as her rival, Mme Geoffrin's "Wednesdays." However, Dorat remained her most faithful admirer, and their liaison continued until Dorat's death in 1780. Dorat's place in her affections was later taken by Cubières who even started calling himself "Dorat-Cubière" to please her. Mme de Beauharnais' career was interrupted by the Revolution and later by the Reign of Terror. She was taken prisoner by the "Terreur" and tortured. But after the short interval, she reopened her salon and lived the rest of her life promoting literature. She died on July 2, 1813.

Her literary career started in 1772 with the publication of a collection of poems and prose. Her authorship of that collection was questioned by her peers, who avowed that Dorat had more than a hand in it. Fanny went on to write several novels, short stories, poems and letters that afford a peculiar view of the values and fashions of her age.

Works

Melanges des Poesies Fugitives et de Prose sans Consequence (1772). Lettres de Stéphanie (1778). L'Abaillard Suppose ou Le Sentiment a L'Epreuve (1780). Par Amour (1781).

Bibliography

Pellisson, M., Les Hommes de Lettres au XVIIIe Siecle (1911). Marnet, D., La Vie Parisienne au XVIIIe Siecle (1914).

Ranee Kaur

Germaine Beaumont

Born 1890, Petit-Couronne (Normandy),
France; died 1983, Montfort-l'Amaury
Genre(s): poetry, novel
Language(s): French

A poet and novelist, Colette's secretary and for a number of years an influential member of the jury to select the winner of the Prix Femina, Germaine Beaumont's work deserves to be remembered more than it has been. It was esteemed during her lifetime, her novel Piège having been awarded the Prix Théophraste-Renaudot in 1930, and in 1949, her work as a whole was selected for the important prize of the Société des Gens de Lettres. For many years she contributed a weekly Chronicle in verse to Les Nouvelles Littéraires. She also translated Virginia Woolf's Journal d'un Ecrivain.

Her novels, said to be influenced by the English novel, usually center on mysterious lives led in old country houses and behind garden walls, where solitary and frequently eccentric men and women live out their lives. Agnès de Rien (Agnes of Nothing), made into a movie, is considered a particularly outstanding example of her work, although somewhat different is her interesting evocation of the streets of Rouen in Silsauve, which with Les Légataires (The Heirs) and Le Temps deshilas (Lilac Time) form a trilogy. Her last work, Une Odeur de trètle blanc (A Scent of White Clover), was published when she was ninety years old.

Works

Disques [Recordings] (1930). Pièges [Traps] (1935). La Longue Nuit [The Long Night] (1936). Les Clefs

[The Keys] (1939). *Agnès de Rien* [Agnes of Nothing] (1943). *La Roue de l'Infortune* [The Wheel of Adversity] (1946). *Silsauve* (1952). *Les Légataires* [The Heirs] (1966). *Colette. Le Chien claus l'Arbone* [The Dog in the Tree] (1975). *Une Odeur de Tretle Blanc* [A Scent of White Clover] (1981).

Charity C. Willard

Madame Jeanne-Marie Le Prince de Beaumont

*Born April 26, 1711, Rouen, France; died
    1780, Chavanod, Haute-Savoie, France*
Genre(s): novel, didactic work
Language(s): French

Madame Le Prince de Beaumont was a popular novelist and a prolific writer of educational works for women and children, Christian apologetics, and moral tales which were widely read throughout Europe and America between 1750 and ca. 1830.

Coming from a large artistic family—the painter Jean-Baptiste Le Prince was her younger brother—Marie Le Prince taught at a convent school for teachers in Rouen. When her unhappy marriage was annulled in 1745, she turned to writing to supplement a meager income. Her first novel, *Le Triomphe de la Vérité*, was published in 1748, the same year as two works in which she argues that women's natural qualities are superior to those of men. Shortly after, she settled in London, where she quickly established a reputation as a governess and started a monthly magazine, the *Nouveau Magasin français*, aimed primarily at women. She also wrote full-length didactic works such as the *Éducation complète* (1753), which was used by the Princess of Wales; *Civan, roi de Bungo* (1754), which was set in Japan; and the *Anecdotes du XIVe siècle* (1759); as well as the highly popular epistolary novels, *Lettres de Madame Du Montier* (1756) and *La nouvelle Clarisse* (1767). Many of her books ran to several editions and were translated into every major European language. In 1758 she bought a house near Annecy, France, to which she retired with her second husband and where she continued writing until her death.

The most important of her works, the *Magasin des Enfants* (1756), is divided into journées in which a governess called Mlle Bonne converses with seven pupils (Ladies Sensée, Spirituelle, Tempête, etc.) who are aged between five and thirteen. Each day, the lessons on history, geography, and science are alternated with Bible stories and fairy tales, including the classic version of "La Belle et la Bête" (adapted from a rambling 362–page story by Mme de Villeneuve, q.v.). Though always present, the morality is never saccharine, and many of the tales (e.g. "Le Prince au long nez") reveal considerable humor. It is the first work written not for a specific child, but for children in general; the first to address children as children and not as mini-adults, and to do so without being condescending. She continued her success with the *Magasin des Adolescentes* (1760), which introduces the same girls and others in their teens (Miss Frivole, Lady Sincère, etc.) to philosophy, and with *Instructions pour les jeunes Dames* (1764), which outlines the duties of a wife. One of her themes throughout is that women should rely not on men but on their own inner resources and to do this they must understand religion. In *Les Américaines* (1770), Mme Bonne asks the same young women, now her friends, to imagine how they would react in a European city if they had been transported there suddenly from the forests of America. The ensuing dialogue introduces the women to theology. In spite of her generally conservative views, Mme Bonne is constantly respectful of her pupils' individuality: "Each Lady is made to speak according to her particular Genius, Temper and Inclination." The question and answer technique is designed to stimulate their independent thought, greater self-awareness, and ability to conduct a reasoned debate: "Oui Messrs. les tirans, j'ai dessein de les tirer de cette ignorance crasse, à la quelle vous les avez condamnées. . . . Je veux leur apprendre à penser, à penser juste, pour parvenir à bien vivre" (1756, I, p. xi). At a time when women received virtually no formal education, this intention was revolutionary.

Mme Le Prince de Beaumont's achievement can be measured by the success which her works enjoyed and the rapid improvement in women's education between 1760 and 1785. The *Magasin des Enfants* was frequently reprinted; in the nineteenth century, its format was much copied but never equalled. When her books fell out of fashion, except for two or three of her fairy tales—notably "La Belle et la Bête"—none was ever republished. They were the first victims of a movement that she did much to create. She was the first editor of a woman's monthly magazine, the founder of children's literature in France, and an indefatigable promoter of women's equal right to learning.

Works

Le Triomphe de la Vérité, ou, Mémoires de M. de la Villette (1748; tr. The Triumph of Truth, or, Memoirs of Mr. de la Villette, 1755). Lettre en réponse à "L'Année merveilleuse" (1748). Arrêt solennel de la nature (1748). Lettres diverses et critiques (1750). Le Nouveau Magasin français, ou, Bibliothèque instructive (1750–1752, 1755). Éducation complète, ou, Abrégé de l'histoire universelle, mêlée de géographie, de chronologie . . . à l'usage de la famille royale de la princesse de Galles (1753). Civan, roi de Bungo, histoire japonnoise, ou, Tableau de l'éducation d'un prince (1754; tr. Civan, King of Bungo, 1800). Lettres de Mme. Du Montier à la marquise de ΔΔΔ, sa fille, avec les réponses (1756; tr. The History of a Young Lady of Distinction. In a Series of Letters Which Passed Between Madame Du Montier, and the Marchioness De ΔΔΔ, Her Daughter, 1758). Magasin des Enfants, ou, Dialogues entre une sage gouvernante et plusieurs de ses élèves (1756; tr. The Young Misses Magazine, or, Dialogues Between a Discreet Governess and Several Young Ladies of the First Rank Under Her Education, 1757?). Anecdotes du XIVe siècle, pour servir à l'histoire des femmes illustres de ce temps (1758). Lettres curieuses, instructives et amusanntes, ou, Correspondance historique, galante, etc. entre une dame de Paris et une dame de province (1759). Magasin des Adolescentes . . . Pour servir de suite au "Magasin des Enfants" (1760; tr. The Young Ladies Magazine . . ., 1760). Principes de l'Histoire-Sainte (1761). Instructions pour les jeunes Dames qui entrent dans le monde et qui se marient . . . Pour faire suite au "Magasin des Adolescentes" (1764; tr. Instructions for Young Ladies on Their Entering into Life, Their Duties in the Married State, and Towards Their Children, 1764). Lettres d'Émérance à Lucie (1765; tr. Letters from Émérance

to Lucy, 1766). Mémoires de Madame la Baronne de Batteville, ou, La Veuve parfaite (1766; tr. The Virtuous Widow: or, Memoirs of the Baroness de Batteville, 1768). La nouvelle Clarisse, histoire véritable (1767; tr. The New Clarissa: a True History, 1768). Magasin des Pauvres, des Artisans, des Domestiques et des Gens de la campagne (1768; tr. Dialogues for Sunday Evenings; Translated from a Work of Madame Le Prince de Beaumont Called "Magasin des Pauvres," 1797?). Les Américaines, ou, La Preuve de la Religion Chrétienne, par les lumières naturelles (1770). La Double Alliance, ou, Les heureux naturels, histoire du marquis DΔΔΔ (1772/73). Le Mentor moderne, ou, Instructions pour les garçons et pour ceux qui les élèvent (1772). Manuel de la Jeunnesse, ou, Instructions familières, en dialogues (ca. 1773). Contes moraux (1774; tr. Moral Tales, 1775). Oeuvres mêlées de Mme. Le Prince de Beaumont: Extraites des Journaux & Feuilles périodiques qui ont paru en Angleterre pendant le séjour qu'elle y a fait (1775: reprint of Le Nouveau Magasin français). Nouveaux Contes moraux (1776). La Dévotion éclairée, ou, Magasin des Dévotes (1779).

Bibliography

Barchilon, Jacques, "'Beauty and the Beast': From Myth to Fairy Tale," Psychoanalytic Review 46 (1959): 19–29. Bettelheim, Bruno, "Beauty and the Beast," in The Uses of Enchantment (1976): 303–310. Clancy, Patricia A., "Mme. Leprince de Beaumont: Founder of Children's Literature." Australian Journal of French Studies 16 (1979): 281–287. Clancy, Patricia A., "A French Writer and Educator in England: Mme. Le Prince de Beaumont," Studies on Voltaire and the Eighteenth Century 201 (1982): 195–208. Stewart, Joan Hinde, "Allegories of Difference: An Eighteenth-Century Polemic," Romantic Review 75 (1984): 283–293. Wilkins, Kay S., "Children's Literature in Eighteenth-century France," Studies on Voltaire and the Eighteenth Century 176 (1979): 429–449.

Terence Dawson

Marie-Françoise Catherine de Beauvau(-Craon), marquise de

(a.k.a. Madame de BĄĄĄs
[posthumous])

*Born December 8, 1711, Lunéville, France;
died July 3, 1786, Scey-sur-Saône
Genre(s): poetry, epigram, correspondence
Language(s): French*

The Marquise de Boufflers played a significant role at the court set up in Lunéville by the Polish king Stanislas, who assumed the Duchy of Lorraine following his exile from Poland in 1735. She married the captain of Stanislas' guards, the Marquis de Boufflers-Remiencourt, and had two sons. She became a lady-in-waiting at the ducal court. At one time she was simultaneously the mistress of Stanislas, of his Minister of Finances Devaux, and of his Minister of State, earning the title "Dame de Volupté" (Lady of Pleasure). She herself proudly flaunted the title in an epitaph she composed for herself:

> Ci-gît, dans une paix profonde,
> Cette Dame de Volupté
> Qui, pour plus grande sûreté,
> Fit son paradis de ce monde.

("Here lies, in a deep peace, that lady of pleasure who, to be even safer, made her paradise of this world.") Voltaire and Mme du Châtelet spent most of 1749 at the court of Lunéville and became close friends with the Marquise de Boufflers. Years later the Marquise wrote a sharp protest against the Archbishop of Paris' refusal to sanction Voltaire's burial in Paris.

Her occasional verses exhibit a polished Epicurean and exquisitely mundane sophistication. The following quatrain should suffice as a demonstration:

> Nous ne sommes heureux qu'en espérant de l'être;
> Le moment de jouir échappe à nos désirs;
> Nous perdons le bonheur faute de le connaître,
> Nous sentons son absence au milieu des plaisirs.

("We are happy only in hoping to be happy; the moment of enjoyment escapes our desires; we lose happiness for want of knowing it, we feel its absence in the midst of pleasures.") Her occasional pieces were published in an appendix to the works of her younger son, Stanislas-Jean Boufflers. Her correspondence with him and with Devaux survives but has not been edited.

Works

"Pièces fugitives." *Oeuvres du chevalier de Boufflers* II (1828): 263–274 (some of the verses printed here were also composed by other family members).

Bibliography

Maugras, Gaston, *La Cour de Lunéville au 18ᵉ siècle* (Paris, 1904). *La Marquise de Boufflers* (Paris, 1907).

Earl Jeffrey Richards

Simone de Beauvoir

*Born January 9, 1908, Paris, France; died April 14, 1986, Paris
Genre(s): novel, essay, travel books, short story, drama, autobiography
Language(s): French*

Simone de Beauvoir was one of the most important literary figures in France after the Second World War. Her name is permanently linked to Existentialism and Jean-Paul Sartre, her companion for 51 years.

Born into an upper middle-class family, she enjoyed a secure and happy childhood, accepting her privileged position in society and the Catholic beliefs and bourgeois values of her parents without question. Educated in a strict girls' school in Paris, Simone soon rebelled against her bourgeois world which she found shallow and insincere. By age fourteen, she had lost faith in God and was determined to become a writer and teacher, rejecting marriage and children. Her growing alienation from family and friends of her class brought her to an early awareness of solitude and death which were later common themes in her writing. Realizing that men held a favored position in society, she began to consider her own role as woman, the importance of love, and an ideal relationship with a man.

Simone wanted to pursue higher education, but her parents objected to her studying philosophy, which she preferred, so she studied literature and the classics. Her first attempts at writing (a novel and short stories) were disappointing, and her education was unsatisfying. She completed her undergraduate work in 1928 and planned a higher degree thesis on Liebniz. While preparing for the *agrégation*, she met Sartre. She placed second on the national list for the exam; Sartre was first. Simone had finally met someone she considered intellectually superior to her, and she no longer felt alone. "It was the major event of my life," she said. Sartre's ideas conflicted with her staid, puritan, bourgeois world, but in Sartre she had found her ideal man. "I trusted him so completely that he guaranteed me the sort of absolute security formerly provided by my parents and by God."

The first phase of her life had ended. She began teaching part-time and tried to write, at times only because Sartre insisted that she persevere. Her dependence on him was obvious, a situation that often concerned her. They had agreed not to marry, not to lie to one another, and to be free to have love affairs without recrimination. For several years they taught in different towns, but their relationship was never interrupted. Simone had no success in writing, abandoning one project after another because she was not able to incorporate her experiences into her works. She and Sartre were not yet involved in politics though they associated with many leftist intellectuals who sympathized with the working classes. They travelled extensively, first in Europe, and eventually all over the world. They had failed to recognize the Nazi threat to peace in the 1930s until they were shocked into action with the German occupation of France in 1940. Only then did they discard their self-centered, self-satisfied existence and become involved in the world around them.

When the war began Simone and Sartre were both teaching in Paris. His literary career was launched in 1936, but Simone could not get any of her stories or novels published. Sartre was mobilized in 1939 and taken prisoner in June 1940. Simone fled Paris when the Germans entered the city but returned shortly thereafter and led a constrained, austere, though not uncomfortable lifestyle during the war years. After Sartre returned to Paris (1941), they finally be-

came involved in affairs outside of themselves. They collected and distributed information for the French Resistance, which was their way of dealing with a situation beyond their control. De Beauvoir was dismissed from her teaching post for vague "moral" reasons in 1943. There was great literary activity in Paris during the Occupation, and she finally had two works published, *L'Invitée* (She Came to Stay) and *Pyrrhus et Cinéas*. Along with Albert Camus, she and Sartre began devising a new philosophy for the postwar world. Her only play, *Les Bouches inutiles* (1945), was not well-received and closed after 50 performances. But her novel, *Le Sang des Autres* (The Blood of Others) won great acclaim. It is one of the few good novels about the Occupation and has been underrated by many critics.

In 1945 Sartre and de Beauvoir started a new literary and political journal, *Les Temps modernes*, a vehicle for the dissemination of existentialism, which was now in favor among French intellectuals. In her writing de Beauvoir concerned herself with moral and ethical issues, including feminism. She toured America (1947), and began a love affair with Nelson Algren. *L'Amérique au jour le jour* (America Day by Day) reveals her anti-American attitude; she and Sartre were pro-Soviet at this time, and strongly anti-Gaullist which cost them popularity in France. When her controversial two-volume *Le Deuxième Sexe* (The Second Sex) was published, de Beauvoir was harshly attacked for her frank discussion of sex, motherhood, and women's inferior status. As in much of her work, the influence of Sartre's ideas, even his terminology, is obvious. Woman as "other," as an appendage of man, is not complete in herself. Undoubtedly, this reflected her own situation, her dependence on Sartre and Algren. She admitted that she was depressed when she and Algren broke up after four and a half years; it signalled sexual decline and advancing age. These dreaded feelings diminished when, in 1952, she began living with Claude Lanzmann, a 27-year-old writer; the affair lasted six years. Her spirit was rejuvenated, but her relations with Sartre did not change. Sartre and Lanzmann had embraced Marxism, and de Beauvoir followed, as usual.

In 1954 de Beauvoir won the prestigious prix Goncourt for her novel, *Les Mandarins* (The

Mandarins), about a small circle of leftist intellectuals whose hopes for a better society were shattered after the Liberation. Following a trip to China and Russia the next year, she wrote *La longue Marche* (The Long March), a rather tedious, pedantic study of China, which she felt embodied the hope for the future. But political activism could not eradicate her fear of growing old. She had begun writing the autobiography in four volumes that was to be a tremendous success: *Mémoires d'une jeune fille rangée* (1958; Memoirs of a Dutiful Daughter); *La Force de l'âge* (1960; The Prime of Life); *La Force des choses* (1963; Force of Circumstances); *Tout compte fait* (1972; All Said and Done). Writing kept her fears at bay: "Creation is adventure; it is youth and freedom." Her book on old age, *La Vieillesse* (The Coming of Age), examines the biological aspects of aging and the situation of the elderly from antiquity to the present. Like women, the elderly are passive, inert; they are also defined as "Other."

By 1970 de Beauvoir was active in the *Mouvement de libération des femmes*; she later became president of the feminist group *Choisir* and the *Ligue du droit des femmes*. Refusing to be labelled a feminist, she advocated women's rights, contraception, and abortion. She signed the "Manifesto" along with several hundred women who said they had had illegal abortions.

Sartre lost the sight of his one good eye in 1973, and until his death in 1980, de Beauvoir devoted herself to helping him with his work. She published an account of his last ten years, based on interviews, in 1981, *La Cérémonie des Adieux* (Adieux: A Farewell to Sartre); it was her last published work. Much of her literary work was based on Sartre's philosophical ideas: man is "essential," the subject; woman is "inessential," the object. Men must have "projects" which define and give meaning to life; lacking "projects," women do not achieve a full identity but remain passive, not active. All de Beauvoir's works revolve around her own feelings and experiences; at times her views are "too personal to be completely valid.... Too often she looks in her mirror and thinks she sees humanity." But she also spoke forcefully for the disinherited, the oppressed, the "other."

Works

L'Invitée (1943). *Pyrrhus et Cinéas* (1944). *Le Sang des autres* (1945). *Les Bouches inutiles; pièce en deux actes et huit tableaux* (1945). *Tous les hommes sont mortels* (1946). *Pour une morale de l'ambiguité* (1947). *L'Amérique au jour le jour* (1948). *L'Existentialisme et la sagesse des nations* (1948). *Le Deuxième Sexe*, 2 vols. (1949). *Les Mandarins* (1954). *Privilèges* (1955; includes "Faut-il brûler Sade?" "La Pensée de droit, aujourd'hui." "Merleau-Ponty et le pseudo-Sartrisme."). *Mémoires d'une jeune fille rangée* (1958). *Brigitte Bardot et le mythe de Lolita* (1960). *La Force de l'âge* (1960). *Djamila Boupacha*, with Gisèle Halimi, (1962) [1962; Djamila Boupacha; The Story of the Torture of a Young Algerian Girl Which Shocked Liberal French Opinion]. *The Marquis de Sade; An Essay*, ed. Paul Dinnage (1962). *La Force des choses* (1963). *Une Mort très douce* (1964]. *Les Belles Images* (1966). *La Femme rompue* (1967). *La Vieillesse* (1970). *Tout compte fait* (1972). *Quand prime le spirituel* (1979). *La Cérémonie des Adieux, suivi de Entretiens avec Jean-Paul Sartre* (1981).

Translations: *The Blood of Others* [*Le Sang des autres*] (1948). *The Ethics of Ambiguity* [*Pour une morale de l'ambiguité*] (1949). *She Came to Stay* [*L'Invitée*] (1949). *America Day by Day* [*L'Amérique au jour le jour*] (1952). *The Second Sex* [*Le Deuxième Sexe*] (1952). *All Men Are Mortal* [*Tous les hommes sont mortels*] (1955). *The Mandarins* [*Les Mandarins*] (1956). *Brigitte Bardot and the Lolita Syndrome* [*Brigitte Bardot et le mythe de Lolita*] (1960). *The Prime of Life* [*La Force de l'âge*] (1962). *Force of Circumstances* [*La Force des choses*] (1964). *A Very Easy Death* [*Une Mort très douce*] (1966). *Les Belles Images* (1968). *The Woman Destroyed* [*La Femme rompue*] (1969). *The Coming of Age* [*La Vieillesse*] (1972). *All Said and Done* [*Tout compte fait*] (1974). *Memoirs of a Dutiful Daughter* [*Mémoires d'une jeune fille rangée*] (1974). *Old Age* [*La Vieillesse*] (1977). *Adieux: a Farewell to Sartre* [*La Cérémonie des Adieux, suivi de Entretiens avec Jean-Paul Sartre*] (1981). *When Things of the Spirit Come First: Five Early Tales* [*Quand prime le spirituel*] (1982).

Bibliography

Armogathe, D., *Le Deuxieme Sexe. Simone de Beauvoir* (1977). Ascher, C., *Simone de Beauvoir.*

A Life of Freedom (1981). Bieber, K., *Simone de Beauvoir*(1979). Cayron, C., *La Nature chez Simone de Beauvoir* (1973). Cottrell, R. D., *Simone de Beauvoir*(1975). Descubes, M., *Connaître Simone de Beauvoir* (1974). Evans, Mary, *Simone de Beauvoir, a Feminist Mandarin* (1985). Francis, Claude, *Les écrits de Simone de Beauvoir: la vie, l'écriture* (1979). Gagnebin, L., *Simone de Beauvoir ou le refus de l'indifférence* (1968). Gennari, G., *Simone de Beauvoir*(1958). Henry, A. M., *Simone de Beauvoir: ou l'échec d'une chrétienté* (1961). Jaccard, A.-C., *Simone de Beauvoir* (1968). Julienne-Caffie, S., *Simone de Beauvoir* (1966). Keefe, T., *Simone de Beauvoir: A Study of Her Writings* (1983). Lasocki, A.-M., *Simone de Beauvoir ou l'entreprise d'écrire* (1971). Leighton, J., *Simone de Beauvoir on Women* (1975). Madsen, A., *Hearts and Minds: The Common Journey of Simone de Beauvoir and Jean-Paul Sartre* (1977). Marks, E., *Simone de Beauvoir: Encounters with Death* (1973). Moubachir, C., *Simone de Beauvoir ou le souci de différence* (1972). Romero, C. Z., *Simone de Beauvoir* (1978). Schwarzer, A., *After the Second Sex: Conversations with Simone de Beauvoir*(1984). Spronk, J. M., *An Analytical Study of Simone de Beauvoir*(1961). Van der Berghe, C. L., *Dictionnaire des Idées dans l'oeuvre de Simone de Beauvoir* (1967). Wasmund, Dagny, *Der "Skandal" der Simone de Beauvoir: Probleme der Selbstverwirklichung im Existentialismus, dargelegt an den Romangestalten Simone de Beauvoirs* (1963). Zephir, J. J., *Le Neo-feminisme de Simone de Beauvoir* (1982).

Jeanne A. Ojala

William T. Ojala

Beatrix Beck

Born July 30, 1914, in the Canton of Vaud, Switzerland
Genre(s): novel
Language(s): French

Although born in Switzerland, she was the daughter of the Belgian novelist Christian Beck and of an Irish mother. She lost her father when she was two years old.

Married in 1936 to Naum Szapiro, she was, like her mother, left a widow with a small child in the course of a war. After a variety of occupa-

tions undertaken to earn her living, she became André Gide's secretary in 1950.

Her novels have, in large measure, been inspired by her own life. Her first three tell the story of Barny, in effect her own story, with considerable verve and wit. The most successful of these was *Léon Morin, Prêtre,* which won the Prix Goncourt in 1952, in part, no doubt, because it centered on the popular idea of the worker-priest.

Children's language and experiences with the adult world provide themes for her later novels: *Noli* (1978) and *La Décharge* (1979), the latter awarded the Prix du Livre Inter '79.

Works

Barny (1948). *Une Mort Irrégulière* [An Irregular Death] (1951; Prix des Neuf). *Léon Morin, Prêtre* (1952; Prix Goncourt; Am. tr. *The Passionate Heart,*1953; Eng. tr. *The Priest,* 1953; film, 1961). *Contes à l'Enfant Né Coiffé* [Tales of a Child Born with Combed Hair] (1953). *Des Accommodements avec le Ciel* [Working Things Out with Heaven] (1953). *Le Muet* [The Muet] (1963). *Cou Coupé Court Toujours* [A Neck Always Cut Short] (1967).

Bibliography

de Boisdeffre, Pierre. *Une Histoire Vivante de la Littérature d'Aujourd'hui,* 6th ed. (Paris, 1966). Godin, H.J.G., *The Creative Process in French Literature* (New York, 1974).

Charity Cannon Willard

Catherine Bedacier-Durand

Born ca. 1650; died 1714, Paris, France
Genre(s): novel, poetry, fairy tale
Language(s): French

Very little is known about the life of Catherine Bédacier-Durand. Her first novel, *La Contesse de Mortane,* was published anonymously in 1699. The heroine is so rigorously virtuous that she allows the man who loves her to speak to her only twice during two years. The novel comprises two fairy tales, a genre most popular at the end of the seventeenth century in France.

Works

Her *Memoires Secrets de la Cour de Charles VII* (1700) narrates a succession of short-lived love affairs in which the romanesque overpowers actual history. This scenario is similar to her other novels: *L'Histoire des amours de Grégoire VII, du Cardinal de Richelieu, de la Princesse de Condé, et de la Marquise d'Urfé* (1700), *Le Comte de Cardonne ou La Constance victorieuse* (1702), *Les Belles Grecques ou l'Histoire des plus fameuses courtisanes de la Grèce* (1712), *Henry Duc des Vandales* (1714). Her other works include: *Ode qui a remporté le prix de poésie en l'année 1701* [The Ode that Won the Poetry Prize for the Year 1701], *Les petits soupers de l'été de l'année 1699, ou aventures galantes, avec l'origine des fées* [Light Suppers of the Summer of 1699 or Gallant Adventures with the Origin of Fairies] (1702), *Les avantures galantes du chevalier de Thémicourt* (1706), *La vengeance contre soy-même et le chat amoureux. Contes en vers* [Vengeance Against Oneself and the Cat in Love. Tales in Verse] (1712).

Bibliography

Oeuvres de Mme D., 12 vols. (Paris, 1737)

Marie-France Hilgar

Anne Beffort

Born 1880, Luxembourg; died 1966, Davos, Switzerland
Genre(s): essay, tale
Language(s): French

At a time when academic studies were hardly accessible to young Luxembourg women, Anne Beffort, daughter of a gardener's family, herself a schoolmistress, proved her undaunted courage by her personal efforts to rise above the condition of a school mistress and find access to higher studies. The money saved from her income enabled her to go to Paris to the Sorbonne where she became docteur de l'université with a thesis on the dramatist Alexandre Soumet. When she came back to Luxembourg, Anne Beffort became one of the first women teachers of the first Lycée de jeunes filles founded in 1909 in the capital. From that moment on her name found a place in the cultural life of Luxembourg—a cultural life oriented towards French civilization.

In 1937 Anne Beffort founded the Society of the Friends of Victor Hugo's House in Vianden, and she was the first president of the society. In 1961 she collected her most important writings in two volumes. She wrote tales whose seeming simplicity somewhat conceals her lively intelligence and reveals a critical mind embedded in innate kindness. Her themes relate to everyday life and to the two world wars of which she was a witness.

Many of her essays are devoted to the problems of teaching, the history of the Lycée de jeunes filles of Luxembourg, and to French letters, in particular to Victor Hugo. The language of her essays is striking in its lucidity and ease of expression. She is one of the first Luxembourg women writers, a pioneer in literature and a very important personality as such.

Works

Souvenirs [Recollections] (1961). *Victor Hugo et nous* [Victor Hugo and the Luxembourgers] (1961).

Bibliography

Gilson, Willy, "Anne Beffort," in *Une Pure Parisienne* (Luxembourg, 1938), and *Les Pages de la Self* 14 (1968): 18–22. Kieffer, Rosemarie, "L'édifice immense du souvenir" [The Boundless Fabric of Recollection], *Arts et Lettres* 4 (1966): 375–378. Oster, Auguste, "Anne Beffort," *Les Pages de la Self* 14 (1968): 13–16. Frieden, Madeleine, "Anne Beffort et la Société des Amis de Victor Hugo" [Anne Beffort and the Society of the Friends of Victor Hugo], *Les Pages de la Self* 14 (1968): 23–26. Kieffer, Rosemarie, "Vianden rend hommage à Anne Beffort" [Vianden Pays a Tribute to Anne Beffort], *Les Pages de la Self* 14 (1966): 27–30.

Rosemarie Kieffer and Liliane Stomp-Erpelding

Dorothea Beier

Flourished second half of fifteenth century, Zagan, Poland
Genre(s): mystical writings
Language(s): Latin

Dorothea Beier (Behir, Beyerinne) lived in Zagan, lower Silesia. After her husband's death, she became a noted contemplative (*vidua . . . excellentis contemplacionis et seraphici fervoris*). Between 1457 and 1464, she felt compelled by divine admonition to confide to her confessor, the abbot Simon Arnoldi, all the visionary gifts she had received (*gracias et revelaciones*). Arnoldi recorded Dorothea's revelations in Latin with the intention of inciting similar fervor in his readers. Dorothea spent most of her widowed life as an anchorite at the Augustinian monastery in Zagan. She died a pauper in a hostel nearby.

Dorothea Beier's revelations were apparently added to a manuscript containing the *Liber specialis gracie* by Mechthild of Hackeborn. While this MS. does not seem to be extant, Kurt Ruh (following J. Klapper) implies that a copy of the MS. may exist in the University Library at Wroclaw (Poland) even now. From an example of the manuscript's content given in the account of Silesian writers, it may be assumed that Dorothea stands in the tradition of women mystics attempting to use their spiritual insights to lead licentious clergy back to the strict morals of the church. The writer compares Dorothea to Saint Brigit of Sweden, a comparison which—while its validity remains impossible for us to judge—speaks of the high esteem Dorothea Beier received from her contemporaries.

Bibliography

Klapper, J., "Die Mystikerin Dorothea Beier," in J.K., *Die Schlesier des Mittelalters nach schlesischen Klosterhandschriften* (Breslau, 1937), p. 30f.
Stenzel, Gustav Adolf, ed. "De quodam devotaria," in *Scriptores rerum Silesiacarum* (Breslau, 1835), vol. 1, p. 325f.
General references: *NDB* (*Neue deutsche Biographie*), vol. II (1955), p. 19 (Robert Samulski); *Verfasserlexikon*, 2nd ed., vol. I (1978), pp. 684f. (Kurt Ruh).

Gertrud Jaron Lewis

Beitlerin

(see: Magdalena von Freiburg)

Mar Ivanova Belčeva

Born September 8, 1868, Sevlievo, Bulgaria; died March 16, 1937, Sofia
Genre(s): poetry, memoirs, translation
Language(s): Bulgarian

Belčeva, one of the most literate Bulgarian women of her time, is best remembered for her liaison and friendship with the great poet Penco P. Slaveikov. Belčeva was born in a patriotic family, her father being the leader of the local revolutionary committee during the April Uprising of 1876 against the Turks. She graduated from the secondary school in Veliko Tŭrnovo and continued her education at a school for women in Vienna, where she studied foreign languages and music. Back in Bulgaria, she was a teacher in Ruse and Sofia. In 1886 she married Hristo Belčev, a poet, economist, and minister of finance in the Stefan Stambolov cabinet. In 1891 Belčev was assassinated while walking with Stambolov, who was the real target of the assassin. The death of her husband had a profound effect on her life. To overcome her grief and to enhance her knowledge, Belčeva went to Geneva, where she continued her studies in philology.

Her encounter in 1903 with Slaveikov, whom she knew from childhood, was a momentous event in her life. Her friendship with the poet was vital to him during his most critical and difficult years of exile. However, his untimely death in 1912 was another tragedy that Belčeva never forgot.

Under the influence and inspiration of Slaveikov she published her first verses in 1907 and collaborated regularly in the prestigious journal *Misŭl*. Her first collection of poetry, *Na praga stŭpki* (1918; Footsteps on the Threshold), included one hundred and twenty poems. It was followed by *Soneti* (1926; Sonnets) and *Izbrani pesni* (1931; Selected Songs).

Belčeva was a lyric poet. Her poetry reflects her life's experiences, especially the loss of her beloved husband and friend. Although her writing was influenced by Slaveikov, she developed her own poetic style and form of writing. Her love songs from *Na praga stŭpki* reflect the sincerity of love and friendship gone but, notwithstanding the death of the loved one, still pure and strong in her memory. In *Soneti* the religious-mystical elements predominate, and the theme of resurrection occurs frequently in her verse. Her best verses are those that describe her intimate, feminine, spiritual feelings and thoughts. Belčeva had a longing for an eternal God and truth. Her *Soneti* shows a melancholic, tormented poet who finds her only hope in the Divine.

Belčeva was well versed in French, German, Italian, Polish, and other literatures. She translated into Bulgarian Nietzsche's *Also sprach Zarathustra* and Hauptmann's *Die versunkene Glocke*. She popularized Slaveikov's works by giving frequent public lectures, editing an anthology of his works, and writing her reminiscences of the poet. Interest in Belčeva has recently increased, and the critic Ivan Spasov regards her as a poetess with distinctive originality and individuality.

Works

Na praga stŭpki (1918). Penco Slaveikov: Begli spomeni (1925). Soneti (1926). Izbrani pesni (1931).

Bibliography

"Belčeva, Mara Ivanova," in *Rečnik na Bŭlgarskata Literature*, ed. Georgi Canev et al. (Sofia, 1976). Konstantinov, G., "Pesnite na Mara Belčeva." *Zlatorog*, XII, 1 (1931): 38–42. Moser, Charles A., *A History of Bulgarian Literature, 865–1944* (The Hague and Paris, 1972), pp. 130–134. Spasov, Ivan, *I Slŭnceto vŭrni* (Sofia, 1987), pp. 7–87.

Philip Shashko

Belcheva

(a.k.a. Yelisaveta Bagryána)

Born April 29, 1893, Sofia, Bulgaria
Genre(s): poetry
Language(s): Bulgarian

Bagryána began writing while symbolism was still dominant in Bulgarian literature. Nonetheless, she belongs to the realist tradition following P.K. Yavorov and D. Debelyanov. Her early poetry does not reflect revolutionary ardor either; rather, she remains a vivid interpreter of life and a resounding voice of the human spirit.

Born in 1893, she attended school in Turnovo. She then taught for two years in the village of Avtanè then later returned to Sofia where she finished the historical-sociological program at the University of Sofia. Her first poem was published in 1915, but, being a perfectionist, she did not publish anymore until 1921. Her first collection, *Vechnata i sviatata* (1927; The Eternal and the Sacred) was immediately recog-

nized as a great work and enjoyed immense success. She published two more collections, *Zvezda na moriaka* (1932; The Mariner's Star) and *Sŭrtso choveshko* (1936; The Human Heart) before World War II. During this war she published some patriotic poems such as "My Son Is at the Front" (1944). She embraced the new Bulgaria, but did not lose her characteristic, intimate voice. Her post-war collections *Pet zvezdi* (1953; Five Stars), *Liubliu tebia, Rodina* (1956; I Love You, Motherland) and *Ot briag do briag* (1963; From Shore to Shore) reverberate with flights of the soul, sometimes outward in exuberance, sometimes inward in contemplation.

While the folk styles of verse have exerted their influence on Bagryána's poems, the epic tone and motifs are transformed into songs of life and love in the modern world. Thus in a poem called "Penelope of the Twentieth Century" (1936), folk motifs like negative construction (It is not . . ., nor is it . . .) interlard her images of herself as the eternal feminine light, healing her returning lover: "And your torn, disheveled life/ my tears will lighten." Her thirst for freedom and desire for joy are not echoes of youthfulness; they are the enduring base of consciousness throughout her oeuvre. Her inner experience reveals a depth of perception without psychologization and a wellspring of poetic feeling undominated by time.

Works

Sviatata i vechnata (1927). Zvezda na moriaka (1932). Syrtso choveshko (1936). Pet zvezdi (1953). Liubliu tebia (1956). Ot briag do briag (1963). Izbrani stikhotvoreniia (1964). Izbrana lirika v dva toma (1973).
Translations: *Elissaveta Bagryana* (English) (1970).

Bibliography

Brainina, B., "Samodiva: Elisaveta Bagrjana i ee stikhi." *Novyi mir* 47.7 (Moscow, 1971), pp. 245–257. Knudsen, E. "The Counter-points of Elisaveta Bagrjana." *Canadian Slavonic Papers* 16 (Toronto, 1976), pp. 353–370.

Chris Tomei

Marthe Bellefroid

(a.k.a. Rose Gronon)

Born April 4, 1901, Antwerp, Belgium; died
*   September 16, 1979, Antwerp*
Genre(s): novella, novel, dramatic script
Language(s): Dutch, French

Marthe Bellefroid was a teacher in Antwerp before she began writing fiction under the pseudonym Rose Gronon. Her first works were in French: *Chandeleur* (1936, a collection of novellas) and *Le Livre d'Arnd* (1949, a novel). From the early 1950s onward, however, she wrote only in Dutch. Gronon's creative talent found expression in a series of novels, which, though sometimes labelled historical because of historical-mythological settings and characters, are of psychological and literary-technical interest.

Her best novel and the one most currently read is *De Ramkoning* (1962; The Ram King). The return of Agamemnon after the victory at Troy and the subsequent tragic events in the palace and the family of the Atreids are told from the point of view of Clytaemnestra, Agamemnon's wife, who is traditionally decried as *the* example of the unfaithful wife. Gronon invites us forcibly to a different interpretation of the mythic material. *De Ramkoning* is also correctly praised for the very skillful manipulation of the flashback technique. Because of the "difficult" character of the novel, the reader is forced to pay very close attention to the text. Not only the intricate interplay of present tense and flashback narration, but also the abundant use of delicate hints that are picked up again at some later point in the narrative and that acquire full meaning only in retrospect, are techniques that Gronon uses masterfully in order to "put the reader to work."

In later novels such as *De ballade van Doña Maria de Alava* (1963)—also "historical fiction," set in a sinister Spanish court atmosphere during the era of the Inquisition—Gronon attempted the same *tour de force*, but with less success. She never quite again achieved the tense structure, the bewildering blend of direct diction and indirect presentation, and the powerful emotion of *De Ramkoning*. But her later novels excel in at least one other point: the dreaminess and blurred reality that often felicitously result in the typical "Grononesque" fictional-historical atmosphere that is, together with psychology, Gronon's strongest quality.

Works

Chandeleur (1936). Le Livre d'Arnd (1949; reworked in Dutch in 1956 as De Gyldenlöve Saga). Orso (1953). De late oogst (1954). De Groene Dijk (1955). Sarabande (1957). Het huis aan de Sint-Aldegondiskaai (1958). Ik zal leven (1959). De Ramkoning (1962). De Ballade van Doña Maria de Alava (1963). De Man die Miguel heette (1963). De roodbaard (1965). De Reis (1966). Ik, Hasso van Bodman (1966). Persephone (1967). Pentheus (1969). Iokaste (1970). Herfst (1971). Anders (1972). Venetiaanse Het Land Mordor (1973). Ishtar (1974). Dag, kind (1978). De Heks (1978).

Bibliography

de Ceulaer, J., *Te Gast Bij Vlaamse Auteurs 4* (Antwerpen, 1964). Kemp, B., "Twee Romancières: Rose Gronon en Maria Rosseels." *Dietsche Warande en Belfort* (1968).

Kristiaan P. Aercke

Louise Bellocq

(see: Marie-Louise Boudat)

Maria Bellonci

Born 1902, Rome, Italy
Genre(s): novel, journalism
Language(s): Italian

Born in Rome, the daughter of a well-known chemist, Maria Bellonci has passed most of her life in her native city. A very sensitive child, she showed a great interest for the humanities at an early age. At nineteen she had already written her first novel, *Clio e le amazzoni* (Cleo and the Amazons), still unpublished. She is the widow of the writer Goffredo Bellonci. In 1944, she organized in collaboration with her husband "Amici della domenca," very successful Sunday gatherings which, attended by the foremost intellectuals of the time, became the center of Italian cultural life. The prestigious Strega prize was conceived during one of these gatherings. Maria Bellonci became deeply interested in history of the Italian Renaissance, which determined the course of her literary career. *Lucrezia Borgia*, which many believe is her best work, has been translated into twelve languages and is considered a classic of its kind. It received the Viareggio prize in 1939. The novel, the result of eight years of research, is an excellent portrayal, offering probing analyses of a legendary figure that had become a stereotype of evil and deceit. Bellonci's capacity to depict the inner motivations, the conflicts, and the peculiarities of her historical characters has been confirmed in other works, such as *Segreti dei Gonzaga* (1947; The Gonzaga's Sectets), *Pubblici Segreti* (1965; Public Secrets), *Tu vipera gentile* (1972; You Gentle Viper). This last work is a collection of three long essays dealing with the intrigues and struggle for power of the Gonzaga and Visconti's families in the mid-1300s. She collaborates with the RAI (the national broadcasting network), and numerous national and foreign magazines. Bellonci also wrote a history of the Strega Prize, *Come un racconto qli anni del Premio Strega*. In 1982, her novel *Delitto di Stato* (Crime of State) was made into a TV film under the direction of Giuseppe De Bosio.

Works

Lucrezia Borgia, la sua vita e suoi temi (1939). I segreti dei Gonzaga (1947). Milano Viscontea (1956). Pubblici segreti (1965). Come un racconto gli anni del premio "Strega" (1970). Tu vipera gentile (1972).

Bibliography

Barberi-Squarotti, Giorgio, *Poesia e narrativa del secondo novecento* (Milano, 1978). Ceratto, Marino, *Il "Chi è" delle donne italiane, 1945–1982* (Milano, 1982). Grillandi, Massimo, *Invito alla lettura di Maria Bellonci* (Milano, 1983). Manacorda, Giuliano, *Vent'anni di pazienza* (Firenze, 1972). Pacifici, Sergio, *The Modern Italian Novel*, 3 vols., 1967–1979 (Carbondale, 1979). Pampaloni, Geno, "Introduzione." *Tu vipera gentile* (Milano, 1973). Petrignani, Sandra, *Le signore della scrittura* (Milano, 1984). Pullini, Giorgio, *Il romanzo del dopoguerra italiano* (Milano, 1961).

Giacomo Striuli

Maria Elisa Belpaire

Born January 31, 1853, Antwerp, Belgium;
died June 9, 1948, Antwerp
Genre(s): essay, memoirs, biography
Language(s): Dutch

Surnamed "The Wise Woman of Flanders" and "the Mother of the Flemish Movement," Maria Elisa Belpaire played a central role in the artistic and social emancipation of a region that, having lost its medieval splendor, had become a cultural backwater from the seventeenth century onward. French had gradually become the only language for administration and education, and the native tongue, Flemish (a term denoting the variety of Dutch spoken in Flanders), had been more or less actively suppressed, especially since the foundation of the Belgian state in 1830.

Born into the French-speaking upper class in Flanders, Maria Elisa Belpaire nevertheless decided to use Flemish in her writings. She first tried her hand at poetry and, true to her ideal of edifying the Flemish people, collected and translated a large number of fairy tales in collaboration with two other women writers. She soon settled for the genre that suited her best: the essay.

Brought up in a highly cultured milieu and personally acquainted with many artists and intellectuals, it seemed natural that she would write about art, music, and literature. Throughout her many essays, among them studies on Beethoven and Dickens and the varied collection *Kunst-en Levensbeelden* (1913, 1919; Images of Art and Life), her style and tone remained those of a nineteenth-century Romantic: impassioned and lyrical. So did her value judgments: the literature and art she appreciated had to deal with love, genius, spiritual passion, ecstasy, and the religious drive for infinity. She joined the Christian thinkers of her time in defending a Christian-humanistic ideal of art: art is not value free but the expression of "moral grandeur," "higher life," or an "ideal image," and a union of "truth" and "beauty." In her programmatic essay *Christen ideaal* (1899; Christian Ideal), she argued that the Christian ideal of art, like that of holiness, could be found in the eight Beatitudes of the Sermon on the Mount.

Though she lived well into the twentieth century, Belpaire never warmed to the new artistic and literary movements emerging at the turn of the century. She denounced the moderns for showing the seamy side of life, and she deplored the secularization of art and literature for there could be no artistic inspiration without a sense of God.

While in many ways a woman belonging to the "old" order, Belpaire was in the vanguard of nascent Christian democratic movements, shifting emphasis from traditional Christian charity (many of her relatives were involved in philanthropy) to organized social action. She set up women's organizations, and was very active at the Yser Front in World War I, where she took up the cause of Flemish soldiers commanded by French-speaking officers they could not understand. She cofounded *De Belgische Standaard*, a front newspaper, in which she promoted Catholic ethics and wrote many contributions on the rights of Flemings. Her work at the front—when she was already in her sixties—earned her the epithet "mamieke," little mother. *De vier wondere jaren* (1920, 1938; The Four Wondrous Years) is an interesting account of her experiences at the front.

An advocate of women's education, Belpaire not only founded and financially supported a number of Catholic schools for girls, which she wanted to be run by lay personnel, not nuns, and open to non-Catholics who subscribed to broad humanistic ideals, but also a prestigious women's college. Her reasons were typical of her bourgeois background, and indeed of many nineteenth-century feminists who paved the way for more radical changes later. In "Vrouweninvloed" (Woman's Influence), published in *Kunst- en levensbeelden*), Belpaire advanced the thesis that, though men are intellectually superior to women, women outdo their partners in the moral field and are generally "wiser." Furthermore, since woman's realm is the intimacy of the home, her influence is not always visible, yet it is much more effective than man's, whose realm is the outside world. Obviously a good education could only enhance the quality of woman's impact. It seems a curious reasoning for a woman who herself never nurtured a family and whose impact on public life was, without any doubt, direct and immense.

Yet Belpaire only commented at rare moments on her "peculiar" position as a woman in a male-dominated cultural and social environment. On co-signing a letter of protest addressed to the Belgian Archbishop, Cardinal Mercier, who had proclaimed that Flemish was not a language fit for science and scholarship in the context of a heated debate on reforming education in Flanders and ending French supremacy, she wrote: "He (the cardinal) will always keep looking for the priest who put me up to this, since it has not entered his mind that a woman can have a conviction of her own, and act according to it."

Throughout her life Belpaire remained a patron of the arts and a promoter and initiator of many cultural initiatives. She brought about and financed the fusion of two Catholic journals into *Dietsche Warande en Belfort*, which became the authoritative voice of broad-minded Catholic Flemish intellectuals.

She also translated work by Björn Björnson and Johannes Jörgensen, a young Catholic convert, from Danish. She received the Literary Prize of the Province of Antwerp in 1933 and became Doctor Honoris Causa of the University of Louvain in 1937. Her most valuable writings are probably the vast volumes on the life and history of her relatives, *De families Teichmann en Belpaire* (1925–1934), and her own memoirs, *Gestalten in 't verleden* (1947; Figures in the Past), which all offer a fascinating insight into the life of a socially committed bourgeois milieu and the cultural history of a period that witnessed many crucial changes.

Though Maria Elisa Belpaire was duly honored during her long life, a full study on the work and significance of this extraordinary and perseverant woman who firmly believed in the edification of a suppressed people and, to a lesser extent, of a suppressed sex, has yet to be written.

Works

Uit het leven (1887). [With H. Ram and L. Duykers], *Wonderland* (7 vols., 1894–1924). *Herfstrozen* (1897). *Christen ideaal* (1899, 1921). *Het landleven in de letterkunde der XIXde eeuw* (1902, 1923). *Kunst-en levensbeelden* (1906, 1913; Vol. 2, 1919). *Constance Teichmann* (1908, 1926). *Beethoven* (1911, 1947). *Na veertig jaar* (1912). *Antwerpen vóór honderd jaar, 1814* (1919). *De vier wondere jaren* (1920, 1938). *Alphonse Belpaire* (1922). *Na vijftig jaar* (2 vols., 1924). *August Cuppens*(1925). *De families Teichmann en Belpaire* (3 vols., 1925–1934). *Charles Dickens* (1929). *Reukwerk* (1932). *Gestalten in 't verleden* (1947).

Bibliography

Dietsche Warande en Belfort (supplement to March/April issue, 1948). Eeckhout, J., *Litteraire profielen* 2 (1927). Persyn, J., *De wording van het tijdschrift Dietsche Warande en Belfort en zijn ontwikkeling onder de redactie van Em. Vliebergh en Jul. Persyn (1900–1924)* (1963). Persyn, Jul, *Gedenkdagen*, 2 (n.d.). Roose, B.A., *De wijze vrouw van Vlaanderen* (1948). Schrooten, H., *De sociale en politieke actie van mej. M. Belpaire tijdens de Eerste Wereldoorlog. 1914–1918* (1978). Westerlinck, A., "Afscheid van een Onwaerdeerlijke Vrouw," *Dietsche Warande en Belfort* (1948).

General references: *Nationaal Biografisch Woordenboek* 2 (1966; article on Belpaire by J. Persyn). *De Nederlandse en Vlaamse auteurs van middeleeuwen tot heden* (1985). *Moderne encyclopedie van de wereldliteratuur* (1980–1984). *Winkler Prins Lexicon der Nederlandse letterkunde* (1986).

Ria Vanderauwera

Vizma Belševica

Born 1931
Genre(s): poetry, prose, film script, translation
Language(s): Latvian

Vizma Belševica is considered among the leading poets in Soviet Latvia. She studied at the Latvian State University in Riga, and when attending the Gorki Institute of Literature in Moscow, she came to know Bella Akhmadulina, Yuri Kazakov, and Andrei Voznesenski, who esteemed her highly as a Soviet poet. Despite having been excommunicated and banned from publication and also having seen her books denounced and recalled, during which time she eked out a living from her skill as a translator, Belševica continued to enjoy recognition as a writer of note beyond her own shores. All this in the face of seriously fluctuating health.

Three of her five published volumes of poetry have been translated into Russian and many of her works have appeared in poetry anthologies abroad. To her credit she also has two volumes of short stories that explore the vagaries of human relations. Belševica is also known as a writer of film scripts and a translator of Russian, English, and American writers, including Kipling, Hemingway, and Axel Munthe.

Works

Jūra Deg [The Ocean Burns] (1966). *Gadu Gredzeni* [The Rings of Years] (1969). *Madarās* [Madders] (1976). *Kamola Tinēja* [The Winder of Yarn] (1981).

Warwick J. Rodden

Illuminata Bembo

Born c. 1410, Venice, Italy; died May 18, 1496, Bologna
Genre(s): hagiography
Language(s): Italian

Illuminata, the daughter of a prominent Venetian noble family, was a nun of the Franciscan order (Poor Clares) and author of the *Mirror of Illumination*, a life of the noted visionary and spiritual writer St. Catherine of Bologna.

Illuminata entered the monastery of Corpus Domini in Ferrara in 1430. Catherine of Bologna, who entered the same monastery the following year, soon gained renown for her piety and visions. In 1456, she became the abbess of a new monastery in her native Bologna and died there in 1463. Some of the nuns of Corpus Domini, including Illuminata, followed her to Bologna. By 1472, Illuminata had become abbess of the community. She composed the *Mirror of Illumination* in Italian at some unknown time after Catherine's death. This very personal portrait of Catherine differs significantly in tone from her "official" life, written in Latin by Catherine's confessor for use in the canonization procedures. Although Illuminata does recount such events as the beginnings of the new community in Bologna, the *Mirror* is less a biography than a meditation on the spiritual life of the saint intended for the continuing instruction of the community's members. It tells not only of Catherine's visions and devotional practices but describes how she acted as a spiritual director for the nuns of her community. Illuminata includes reminiscences about conversations between the saint and Illuminata herself, who had lived in an adjoining cell. The manuscript of the work was kept and used at the monastery, where it remains today, but the work was not printed until over three centuries later. A shorter version of Catherine's life, edited by van Ortroy, is also probably the work of Illuminata.

The *Mirror of Perfection* reflects the memory of a great teacher composed by a student trying to continue her work. It provides a remarkable portrait of life in a vigorously reformed convent of the fifteenth century.

Works

Specchio d'illuminazione sulla vita di s. Caterina da Bologna (1787; reprinted in Melloni, G., *Atti o memorie degle uomini illustri in santita nati o morti in Bologna*, vol. IV ([ost. ed. A. Benati and M. Fanti; 1971], pp. 289–300). Nuñez, L.M., *La santa nella storia, nelle lettere, e nell'arte* (1912), pp. 158–160.

Thomas Head

Bo'ena Benešová

Born November 30, 1873, Nový Jičín,
  Czechoslovakia; died April 8, 1936,
  Prague
Genre(s): short story, novel
Language(s): Czech

Benešová began to publish stories only after moving from her home in Nový Jičín to Prague when she was in her mid-thirties, and another ten years passed before she published her first novel. Although she became a protégée of Rů'ena Svobodová, Benešová developed an independent style that set her apart from Svobodová and other prose writers of the time.

In her stories, she most often depicts what she called "cruel youth," the fate of young people from the Moravian bourgeoisie, usually girls, who enter life with high ideals and faith in truth and justice, only to be wounded by "harsh reality." Typical examples are found in the collection *Kruté mládí* (1917; Cruel Youth).

Beginning with her first novel, *Člověk* (1920; Man), Benešová searched for a more positive vision—of the rebirth of the human spirit and moral regeneration. In the trilogy *Úder* (1926; The Blow), *Podzemní plameny* (1929; Underground Flames), and *Tragická duha* (1926–33; The

Tragic Rainbow), Benešová dealt with Czech participation in World War I and the Revolution of 1918 by describing the inner experiences of typical characters.

Her last major work was a novella entitled *Don Pablo, Don Pedro, and Věra Lukášová*, which centers on the moral crisis of a girl's puberty and develops Benešová's favorite theme of the contrast between the purity of youth and the distorted world of adults.

In her straightforward prose, Benešová showed a consistently tragic and intense interest in moral values.

Works

Verše věrné i proradné (1909). *Nedobyta vítězství* (1910). *Tři povídky* (1914). *Myšky* (1916). *Kruté mládí* (1917). *Člověk* (1919–1920). *Tiché dívky* (1922). *Oblouzení* (1923). *Úder* (1926). *Podzemní plameny* (1929). *Není člověku dovoleno* (1931). *Tragická duha* (1933). *Don Pablo, Don Pedro, a Věra Lukašová* (1936).

Bibliography

Götz, F., *Básnický dnešek* (1931). Pujmanová, M., *Bo'ena Benešová* (1935). Salda, F.X. *Kritické projevy 10* (1957).

General references: *Čeští spisovatelé deseti století*, ed. R. Šťastný (1974); and *Čeští spisovatelé 19. a počátku 20. století*, eds. K. Homolová, M. Otruba, and Z. Pešat (1982).

Clinton Machann

Maria Beneyto Cunyat

Born 1925, Valencia, Spain
Genre(s): poetry, novel, short story, literary
  criticism
Language(s): Spanish (Castilian), Catalan

Only very schematic information is available on this writer, despite her relatively recent date of birth. Her family, belonging to the moderately liberal, small Valencian middle class, moved from the Catalan-speaking area of Valencia to Madrid while she was still an infant. Although surrounded by Castilian (the official language of Spain) in Madrid, the influence of Catalan within her family was sufficiently strong that the future writer grew up essentially bilingual, publishing in both languages. The Spanish Civil War (1936–

39) scarred her childhood, as it did nearly all of her generation. It appears that she subsequently may have lived for a time in Venezuela, presumably as a result of the exile of her parents; the date of return to Spain is likewise unavailable. Beneyto began writing in the periodical press, publishing both short stories and literary criticism in newspapers both in Venezuela and in Spain, but these have not been gathered for publication as collected volumes.

Notwithstanding the systematic discrimination against the vernacular languages under the Franco regime (including the temporary outlawing of Catalan and others), Beneyto's allegiance to Catalan was strong, and she began publishing her poems in Valencian (a Catalan dialect) during the 1950s, at a time when very little literature was published in the minority tongues, especially by women. She is thus a pioneer in the literary renaissance of Catalan, which becomes visible in the 1970s as the final years of the Franco regime witnessed a resurgence of cultural nationalism after the vernacular languages were officially legitimized. *Altre veu* (1952; Another Voice) was followed by another poetry collection, *Ratlles a l'aire* (1956; Lines in the Air), which was awarded the City of Barcelona Prize. From the late 1960s onward, she turned increasingly to prose. Her novel, *La dona forta* (1967; The Strong Woman), depicts the psychological effects of a strong, domineering, emotionless mother upon a weak and timid son. It was awarded the Senent Prize while still in manuscript (1965). At more or less the same time, Beneyto wrote *La gent que viu al mòn* (1966; People Who Saw the World), and in 1976, she published *Vidre ferit de sang* (Blood-Wounded Glass), a slim collection of poetry awarded the Ausiàs March Prize.

Works

Altre veu (1952). *La dona forta* (1967). *La gent que viu al mòn* (1966). *Ratlles a l'aire* (1956). *Vidre ferit de sang* (1976).

Janet Perez

Konstancja Benislawska

Born 1747, Poland; died 1806
Genre(s): hymns
Language(s): Polish

Benislawska is the author of religious hymns, *Piesni sobie spiewane* (1776; Songs Sung to Oneself), a collection of beautiful and intensely emotional hymns that are, unfortunately, now largely forgotten. Of noble origin, she lived in Livonia, away from the cultural centers of the Polish Kingdom. She started writing poetry at the age of twenty-eight, after having given birth to a number of children.

Bibliography

Borowy, Waclaw, *Od Kochanowskiego do Staffa. Antologia liryki polskiej* (London, 1954). Milosz, Czeslaw, *The History of Polish Literature* (Berkeley, 1969).

Maya Peretz

Julija Beniuševičiūtė-ymantienė

(see: emaitė)

Thérèse Bentzon

(see: Marie-Thérèse de Solms Blanc)

Beobachterin (Observing Woman)

(see: Marianne Ehrmann)

Victoire-Léodile Béra

(see: André Léo)

Nina Berberova

Born 1901, St. Petersburg, Russia
Genre(s): poetry, prose, criticism
Language(s): Russian

Nina Berberova was born and educated in St. Petersburg. Before leaving Russia in June 1922, she participated in a book of essays, *Ushkuiniki* (River Pirates), in February 1922. After her emigration she first lived in Berlin and Prague, and from 1925–1950, in Paris. In 1950, Berberova moved to the United States, where she taught Russian literature at Yale (1958–63) and Princeton (since 1963).

In Paris Berberova contributed regularly to the Russian émigré press, the journal *Sovremennye Zapiski* (Contemporary Notes), the newspaper *Poslednie Novosti* (Latest News) and others. In 1926 she was co-editor of the young émigrés' literary journal *Novyi Dom* (New House) and in 1948–50 the editor of the literary section of the Parisian Russian newspaper *Russkaia Mysl'* (Russian Thought). During her stay in Paris Berberova published three novels, biographies of Tschaikovsky, Borodin, and Aleksandr Blok, and a collection of short stories. Her play *Madame* was staged in the Parisian Russian theater in 1938. In the United States Berberova continued her active literary participation in major émigré publications as *Novyi Zhurnal* (New Review) and the almanac *Mosty* (Bridges); she also published important literary-historical materials, especially noteworthy are those on her close companion, the eminent poet Vladislav Khodasevich. Her autobiography *Kursiv moi* (The Italics are Mine) appeared in English and Russian (1969, 1972); in addition, Berberova published her novel *Zheleznaia Zhenshchina* (The Iron Woman) in 1980, a collection of verses *Stikhi: 1921–1983* (Verses: 1921–1983) in 1984, and a groundbreaking study on Russian Freemasonry in 1986.

A prolific and successful author of fiction and poetry as well as on matters of Russian literary and cultural history with emphasis on émigré problems, Berberova has established herself as one of the most important figures among Russian writers in exile.

Works

Poslednie i pervye [The Last and the First] (1930). *Povelitel'nitsa* [Lady Sovereign] (1932). *Bez zakata* [Without Decline] (1938). *Chaikovskii: istoriia odinokoi zhizni* [Tschaikovsky: The Story of a Lonely Life] (1936). *Borodin* (1938). *Alexandre Blok et son temps* [Aleksandr Blok and His Time] (1948). *Oblegchenie uchasti. Shest' povestei* [Relieved Fate. Six Short Stories] (1949). *Kursiv moi* [The Italics are Mine] (1972), *Zheleznaia zhenshchina* [The Iron Woman], autobiography (1980; 2nd ed., 1982). *Stikhi: 1921–1983* [Verses: 1921–1983] (1984). *Liudi i lozhi: Russkie masony 20–go stoletia* [Men and Lodges: Russian Freemasons of the 20th Century] (1986). Vladislav Khodasevich, *Literaturnye stat'i i vospominania* [Literary Articles and Reminiscences], ed. Nina Berberova (1954).

Translation: *The Italics are Mine* [*Zheleznaia zhenshchina*], tr. Philippe Radley (New York, 1969).

Bibliography

Pachmus, Temira, "Berberova, Nina Nikolaevna," in *Handbook of Russian Literature*, ed. Victor Terras (New Haven, 1985). Poltoratzky, Nikolai P., ed., *Russian Émigré Literature, A Collection of Articles in Russian with English Résumés* (Pittsburgh, 1972). Struve, Gleb, *Russkaia literatura v izgnanie* [Russian Literature in Exile] (New York, 1956).

Marina Astman

Ol'ga Berggol'ts

Born May 3, 1910, St. Petersburg, Russia; died November 13, 1975, Leningrad, Soviet Union
Genre(s): poetry, drama, prose
Language(s): Russian

Ol'ga Berggol'ts is one of the most well-known Soviet Russian authors to write about her country's struggle with Nazi Germany.

The daughter of a St. Petersburg doctor, she became famous as a poet although she received recognition for her other publications, which included newspaper reports, dramas, and fiction. At the time of the Russian revolution in October 1917, she was still a child. She belongs to the first generation raised and trained in the spirit of the Soviet Union. She received a degree in philology from the Leningrad State University in 1930. Her first publications were children's stories. In the 1930s she worked as a correspondent for a newspaper in Kazakhstan. She launched herself as a lyricist with three anthologies of verse: *Poems* (1934), *The Book of Songs* (1935) and *Fall* (1938). Some of her poems and many of her short stories in the collection *Night in the New World* (1935) are hackneyed celebrations of the first five-year-plan and other programs of the Soviet state.

Berggol'ts had a tragic life. In the 1930s, both of her daughters died; her husband was executed in the Stalinist purges, and she too was imprisoned. Shortly after her release from captivity, Hitler attacked the Soviet Union, and soon she found herself in besieged Leningrad, where her second husband died of starvation.

At this time, her favorite genre was the diary. From a personal angle she recreates the experiences of the siege in her famous *Leningrad Notebooks* (1942), which contains such poems as the "February Diary" and the "Poem of Leningrad." The theme of the blockade of the city, the suffering and the resistance of the inhabitants informed the best of her tragic poetic works like "Leningrad" (1944) and "Your Road" (1945) and the plays *They Lived in Leningrad* (1944) and *In Our Land* (1947). In the war, she worked as a commentator for Leningrad Radio; her broadcasts were later published in a separate volume entitled *Leningrad Speaking* (1946).

Even well after 1945, the theme of the war preoccupies her writing. The defense of Sevastopol in 1941–42 is the major concern of her tragedy in verse, *Loyalty* (1954). Her *Diurnal Stars* (1959), which she referred to as her "main book," is a fictional account of her life with major emphasis on the years of the war. Individual and social relations expressed in a highly lyrical idiom characterize her later writings. Before her death, she compiled several collections of poems: *Poems-Prose* (1961), *Poems* (1966), *Faith* (1970), *Memory* (1972).

Her poems are unadorned and lack a variety of prosodic forms; in all her writings, she regards her own soul as the central focus. Yet the individual is of interest only inasmuch as he or she is a manifestation of the universal. She is sometimes tendentious, but her writing is powerful in her best works. The city plays a major part in her creative life; she is a Leningrad writer, and as such, she adds a well-articulated Soviet voice to the literary heritage of that historical place.

Works

Sobrannye socheneniia, three vols., collected works (1972–1973). *Poemy*, poems (1974).

Translations: "Return" and "Promise," in *Modern Russian Poetry*, ed. and tr. V. Markov and M. Sparks (1967), pp. 756–759.

Bibliography

Fiedler-Stolz, Eva-Marie, *Ol'ga Berggol'c* (Munich: Verlag-Otto-Sagner in Kommission, 1977). Khrenkov, Dm., *Ot serdtsa k serdtsu* (Leningrad: Sovetskii pisatel', 1979). Siniavskii, Andrei, "The Poetry and Prose of Ol'ga Berggolts," in *For Freedom of Imagination.*, tr. Laszlo Tikos and Murray Peppard (1971), pp. 37–62.

Peter I. Barta

Clara Bergsøe

Born 1837, Copenhagen, Denmark; died 1905, Copenhagen
Genre(s): biography
Language(s): Danish

Clara Bergsøe helped to bridge a generation gap between the founding figures of the women's movement in Scandinavia and the new generation of women that arose in 1880. Her brother Vilhelm Bergsøe was a popular author of fiction and travelogues; however, both he and Clara Bergsøe's other brother suffered poor health due to congenital syphilis. She never married and dedicated her life to taking care of her brothers, who travelled widely despite their infirmities. At an early stage, Clara Bergsøe became interested in the women's movement and was a good friend of Camilla Collett. During the morality debates in Scandinavia of the 1880s, visitors to the Bergsøe home left with a sense of history of the issues that were being discussed. Toward the turn of the century, Clara Bergsøe published biographies of Johanne Luise Heiberg, Camilla Collett, and Magdalene Thoresen based on her personal acquaintance with these women, thereby helping to recover their achievements for a new generation. Clara Bergsøe also became the model for novellas written by Ola Hansson and Laura Marholm.

Works

Johanne Luise Heibert, et billede fra romantikens tid (1896). *Camilla Collett, et livsbillede* (1902). *Magdalene Thorensen, portrætstudie* (1904).

Bibliography

Bergsøe, Vilhelm, *Henrik Ibsen paa Ischia og "Fra Piazza del Popolo"* (Copenhagen, 1907). Widell, Arne, *Ola Hansson i Tyskland* (Uppsala, 1979), pp. 67–68.

Susan Brantly

Emilie Berlepsch

Baptized November 25, 1755, Gotha, Gemany; died July 27, 1830, Lauenberg
Genre(s): poetry, essay, travel literature
Language(s): German

Emilie Berlepsch was most accomplished as a writer of prose (she is especially well known for an admirable travel book), and is also important for her pioneering prefeminist views.

Nothing is known of the childhood of Emilie Berlepsch *nee* von Oppel, except that she was the daughter of an aristocratic high official at the court of Altenburg and Sachsen-Gotha. At age seventeen she married a court chief justice in Hannover. While living variously in Ratzeburg, in Hannover, and at her husband's isolated castle south of Göttingen, she had at least four children, two of whom died in early childhood. The marriage went through a series of crises, ending about 1787 in divorce. Now began a period of over a decade when Emilie Berlepsch was unmarried. She used the time to do a number of things that were unusual for a woman—traveling, for example, and giving dramatic readings. In 1787 she began her publishing career with a collection of poems, essayistic letters, idylls, and one dramatic sketch. Another volume, mostly of poetry, followed in 1794. Meanwhile her unpolished but important essay containing the germs of a feminist analysis of marriage was published in *Der teutsche Merkur* in 1791.

There were many rumors about the men in whom Berlepsch was supposed to be interested. One was the novelist Jean Paul, who always made good use of his bachelorhood in his relations with women. More important for Berlepsch's writing was the Reverend James MacDonald. Inspired by him, she visited Scotland and on her return wrote her most successful work, *Caledonia*, a four-volume account of her travels. While she was finishing this composition, she married an otherwise unknown estate owner named Harms. For the last 25 years of her life, living in Switzerland, Hannover, and Schwerin, Emilie von Harms was largely silent as a writer.

It is her prose and especially her discussions of women's issues that make Berlepsch noteworthy. Although many of her writings contain a personal element, she also dealt with political issues, often speaking out in vehement opposition to the French Revolution. Her language is refined, her sentences long and complex. She strove to meet the classicist literary standards of her day. In *Caledonia* she effectively combines strong emotional elements with extensive informational passages, on history, for example, literature, and agriculture. Her prefeminist thought, advocating that women learn self-reliance because of the misogynist society in which they live, was the product of her experience and not of her ideals, which remained confusedly patriarchal.

Works

Sammlung kleiner Schriften und Poesien Erster Theil [Collection of Short Prose and Poems, pt. 1] (1787). "Einige zum Glück der Ehe nothwendige Eigenschaften und Grundsätze" [Some Characteristics and Principles Necessary for Happiness in Marriage] (1791). *Sommerstunden* [Summer Hours] (1794). *Einige Bemerkungen zur richtigen Beurtheilung der erzwungenen Schweitzer-Revolution und Mallet du Pans Geschichte derselben* [Some Remarks About the Correct Evaluation of the Forced Swiss Revolution and of Mallet du Pan's History of It] (1799). *Caledonia*, 4 vols. (1802–1804).

Bibliography

Dawson, Ruth, "'And this shield is called—self-reliance.' Emerging Feminist Consciousness in the Late Eighteenth Century," in *German Women in the Eighteenth and Nineteenth Centuries. A Social and Literary History*, ed. Ruth-Ellen B. Joeres and Mary Jo Maynes (Bloomington, 1986), pp. 157–

174. Friedrichs, Elisabeth, *Die deutschsprachigen Schriftstellerinnen des 18. und 19. Jahrhunderts. Ein Lexikon* (Stuttgart, 1981), pp. 22–23. Frederiksen, Elke, ed., *Women Writers of Germany, Austria, and Switzerland. An Annotated Bio-bibliographical Guide* (New York, 1989), pp. 29–30. Gillies, Alexander, "Emilie von Berlepsch and her *Caledonia*," *German Life and Letters* 29 (1975): 75–90. Schindel, Carl Wilhelm Otto August von, "Harms, Emilie." *Die deutschen Schriftstellerinnen des neunzehnten Jahrhunderts*, vol. 1 (Leipzig, 1823), pp. 189–90.

Ruth P. Dawson

Catherine Bernard

Born 1662, Rouen, France; died September 16, 1712, Paris
Genre(s): lyric poetry, narrative fiction, tragedy
Language(s): French

When at 23 Catherine Bernard abjured the reformed religion of her family, she was well enough known to be given a special notice in the *Mercure galant* praising her "ouvrages galants." She had begun precociously to write verse and had received compliments from her cousin Fontenelle while still very young. She was also complimented by the attribution of a romance, *Frédéric de Sicile* (by Pradon?), as well as her cousin's *Relation de l'île de Bornéo*. At eighteen she had left her native Rouen to make her fortune as an author in Paris. She remained poor but in the fullest sense became a professional woman of letters.

Her first novel, *Eléonore d'Yvrée* (1687), inaugurated a series exemplifying "Les malheurs de l'amour." Published with a dedication to the Dauphin and a moralizing preface, the novel in its use of history, narrative structure, and theme of the dutiful sacrifice of passion followed self-consciously in the tradition of Mme de Lafayette's *La Princesse de Clèves*. Praising its economy of plot and dialogue, concision of style, and portrayal of psychological nuance in the *Mercure* (September 1687), Fontenelle underscores this renewal of the novel whose innovations he himself had lauded. *Le Comte d'Amboise* (1689) at greater length continues to explore the noble

refusal of passion and reaffirms the heritage of the novelist's first model. Seeking variation as Mme de Lafayette herself had in *Zaïde*, Bernard complicates her plot in the more adventure-laden *Inès de Cordoue* (1696). The drama of its heroine's sacrifice has brought less attention to this last novel than has one of its two preliminary *contes de fées*, "Riquet à la Houppe." Probably with her blessing, Charles Perrault retold the tale in his *Contes* (1697). Bernard's novels were republished in the widely circulated "Bibliothèque de campagne" (1739, 1785).

Bernard was the most successful woman tragedian in seventeenth-century France. *Laodamie* (1689), the last new tragedy staged at the Guénégaud theatre, had the long, profitable first run of 23 performances (with three more in 1690–91). *Brutus*, dedicated to the Duchesse d'Orléans, ran for 27, December 18, 1690 to the following August and was restaged eight times before 1700. It was revived with the collaboration of the Comédie-Française in 1973. Effectively unified, both plays show the mixture of Cornelian and Racinian models common in tragedies of the 1690s. *Laodamie*, a reversal of Racine's *Bérénice*, dramatizes (as does *Eléonore d'Yvrée*) the rivalry of two women whose characters remain noble despite differing responses to love. An already considerable dramatic interest given to "the people" is amplified in the more Cornelian *Brutus*, a dramatization of the problematics of love versus patriotism that pits Brutus' sons against their father. Bernard humanizes Brutus but by shifting heroic focus to Titus creates a political study of tyranny. Ample and unacknowledged borrowing by Voltaire for his *Brutus* (1730) was denounced in the *Mercure* (March 1731).

Having reached the summit of a poet's career that successful tragedy represented, Bernard renounced the theatre and the more showy and fashionable early verse, with the support of the patronage of the Chancelière de Pontchartrain, whose austerity seconded her own tendency to moral severity. Some dozen poems continued, however, to appear in worthy collections (notably Bouhours' of 1693, 1701), including an epigram playing on Pontchartrain's capitation tax reform and a bantering petition to the king for payment of a pension of 200 francs that had rewarded her encomiastic verse, for which she three times won the coveted poetry prize of the Académie française (1691, 1693, 1697). Decorated also in the *Jeux floraux*, Bernard was given her place in the Parnassus of women writers by the Paduan Ricovrati. These honors and patronage were continuously sought by dedications and verse, but they only just rescued Bernard during the last decades of her life from an abject poverty that she never sought to relieve by lesser means than those she conceived to be part of the noble profession of letters.

Works

Les Malheurs de l'amour. Première nouvelle: Eléonore d'Yvrée (1687). Le Comte d'Amboise, nouvelle galante (1689). Laodamie, reine d'Epire, tragédie (1689). Brutus, tragédie (1690). Inès de Cordoue, suivi de l'histoire d'Abenamar et de Fatime (1696). Recueil des plus beaux vers . . . Bouhours (1701). Pièces de poésies qui ont remporté le prix de l'Académie française (1763; for 1691, 1693, 1697).

Bibliography

Asse, Eugène, *Une nièce du grand Corneille: Mlle Bernard* (1900). Gevrey, Françoise, "Eléonore d'Yvrée ou la vie abstraite." *Cahiers de littérature du XVIIe siècle* 2 (1980): 159–178. Hipp, Marie-Thérèse, "Quelques formes du discours romanesque chez Mme de Lafayette et chez Mlle Bernard." *Revue d'Histoire Littéraire de la France* 77 (1977): 507–522. Kinsey, Susan R., *Mlle Bernard. A Study in Fiction and Fantasy* (1979; see *DAI* 40, 295A). Lachèvre, Frédéric, *Bibliographie des recueils collectifs de poésie publiés de 1597 à 1700*, vol. 3 (1904). Lancaster, H.C., *A History of French Dramatic Literature in the Seventeenth Century*, vol. 4 (1940). Mazour, Charles, "Le *Brutus* de Catherine Bernard et Fontenelle. La Tradition de l'héroïsme." *Etudes Normandes* 3 (1987): 49–61. Niderst, Alain, *Fontenelle à la recherche de lui-même, 1657–1702* (1972). Roche-Mazon, Jeanne, "De qui est Riquet à la Houppe?" *Revue des Deux Mondes* 4 (1928): 404–36. Rpt. *Autour des contes des fées* (1968).

Charles G.S. Williams

Laure de Berny

Born May 24, 1777, Livry, France; died July 27, 1836
Genre(s): letters
Language(s): French

Mme de Berny was born at the château of Livry on May 24, 1777. She was the daughter of Louise-Marguerite-Emilie Quelpée de Laborde, one of Queen Marie-Antoinette's "femmes de chambre." Her father was Philipp Joseph Hinner, a German musician born in Weltzlar in 1754, who served as harpist to the royal court. Her godparents were Louis XVI and Marie-Antoinette, and she was given the names Louise-Antoinette-Laure, being generally known as Laure. It may have been to ensure her some protection during the difficult days of the French Revolution that she was married in 1793, at the age of sixteen, to Charles-Gabriel de Berny, a magistrate who was to occupy high administrative office. Before then, however, he suffered a period of imprisonment during the Terror. The marriage was unhappy, though six children had already been born by 1801 when the couple separated. Mme de Berny formed a liaison with a Corsican by the name of Campi, by whom she had a daughter. After a while there was a reconciliation; Charles and Laure de Berny took a house in Villeparisis, then a quiet small town a dozen miles east of Paris. It was to Villeparisis, too, that Honoré de Balzac's parents moved when they found life in the capital too expensive, and the young writer joined them there in 1821, having failed ignominiously in his first attempt to fend for himself in Paris.

Honoré de Balzac gained an entry in the de Berny household as tutor to the children of the family. But soon he fell under the spell of Laure. He was twenty-three and gauche; she was forty-five and elegant. In her he found the maternal encouragement that he never received from his mother, and to some extent she also filled the gap that had been left in his emotional life when his sister Laure got married. But above all Laure de Berny—"la Dilecta" as Balzac was to think of her—represented high social and cultural standards that were immensely attractive to a young man painfully aware that he was uncouth and provincial in his attitudes. She was a link with the more gracious days of the Ancien Régime, and the impact on Balzac's outlook and self-esteem was immense. She became his mistress in March 1822.

Balzac was to trace an affectionate portrait of Laure de Berny in his novel *Le Lys dans la vallée* (published in 1835), and she contributed to his life-long interest in the question of the older woman. As well as developing his artistic talents by her encouragement and advice, she gave him financial backing in his disastrous attempt to make his fortune in the world of printing. When Balzac went bankrupt, Laure de Berny's son, Alexandre, took the firm over and brought it to profitability. The liaison between Mme de Berny and Balzac lasted for almost a decade, though he more than once gave her reason for jealousy. They parted company in 1832, but Balzac never forgot what he owed her. After legally separating from her husband in 1834, she died after two years of ill health at La Bouleaunière on July 27, 1836.

Bibliography

Hanotaux, Gabriel, and Georges Vicaire, *La Jeunesse de Balzac*, 2nd ed., with *Correspondance de Balzac et de Madame de Berny* (Paris, 1921). Ruxton, Geneviève, *La Dilecta de Balzac: Balzac et Mme de Berny, 1820–1836* (Paris, 1909).

Christopher Smith

Bertha of Willich

Flourished in the first half of the eleventh century
Genre(s): hagiography
Language(s): Latin

A nun of the Benedictine convent of Willich (near Bonn) and sister of St. Wulphemus, Bertha composed the life of St. Adalaide (d. 1015), daughter of Count Magingoz of Guelder, Willich's founder. Adalaide was the first abbess of Willich and later became abbess of St. Mary's of Cologne.

Bertha began her work shortly before 1056, dedicating it to Archbishop Anno of Cologne, a benefactor of the community. Her brother's biographer, Conrad, remarked that Bertha "shone in the knowledge of literature." She had not personally known her subject and obtained much of her information from the saint's former ser-

vant, Egilrad. The work betrays many of the concerns of the nascent Gregorian reform movement. It focuses on Adalaide's contact with and influence on the nobility, particularly the imperial family, and her advocacy of the Benedictine rule as an instrument of reform. Bertha was probably influenced not only by the atmosphere of Willich but also by her brother and his circle.

Works

Vita s. Adalheidis, in O. Holder Egger, ed., *Monumenta Germaniae historica, Scriptores in folio*, XV, 755–763. For a full list of editions, see *Bibliotheca hagiographica latina*, no. 67.

Bibliography

General references: Manitius, *Geschichte der lateinischen Literatur des Mittelalters*, II, 469–470.

Thomas Head

Sister Bertken (Berta Jacobs)

Born 1427, Utrecht, The Netherlands; died 1514, Utrecht
Genre(s): poetry, religious prose
Language(s): Dutch

At the age of twenty-four, Sister Bertken (Dutch: Suster Bertken), in all likelihood a daughter of a well-to-do Utrecht middle-class family, became a canoness in the monastery of Jerusalem near Utrecht, a monastery of Augustinian regulars where she remained for six years. In 1457, at the symbolically significant age of 30, Bertken was granted permission by Bishop David of Burgundy to be enclosed as a recluse in a cell built into the wall of the "Buurkerk" in Utrecht. There she lived for the next 57 years. Only on June 25, 1514, after this 57–year-long period of steadfast endurance, did she die. She was buried, in accordance with her own wishes and in the presence of the church and city authorities of Utrecht as well as a numerous public of citizens, in her cell in the Buurkerk. A Latin *vita* of this local *mulier sancta* was enclosed in a bottle and placed in Bertken's coffin by the authorities and the prior of the monastery of regular Augustinian canons in Utrecht, who supervised the Jerusalem-monastery and guarded the keys of Bertken's cell during her life, inscribed a Dutch translation of the *vita* on the title page of the *Legenda Aurea* of his monastery.

Two small volumes of prose and poetry are all that remain of Bertken's *oeuvre*: *Een boecxken gemaket ende bescreven van Suster Bertken die lvii iaren besloten heeft gheseten tot Utrecht in dye buerkercke* (A Little Book Composed and Written by Sister Bertken Who Was a Recluse at the Buurkerk in Utrecht for 57 Years) and *Suster Bertken's boeck dat sy selver gemaect ende becreven heeft* (The Book of Sister Bertken Which She Composed and Wrote Herself)—both published posthumously in 1516 by the Utrecht printer Jan Berntsz. The first is a series of meditations on the passion of Christ and the second a miscellaneous collection of prayers, "A Pious Colloquy Between the Loving Soul and Her Beloved Bridegroom Jesus," "A Vision of the Birth of Christ," and eight poems.

Bertken's *oeuvre* or, rather, whatever Jan Berntsz decided to publish from the manuscripts found in Bertken's cell following her death, has received little scholarly attention and less true understanding in Dutch literary scholarship as its study has suffered from the imprudent application of the stereotype of the charming, simple, and pious Middle Ages. Reinder P. Meijer's assertions, in his *The Literature of the Low Countries*, that "Her religious world was simple and so was her representation of it" and that "the cliché of 'charming medieval simplicity' might have been coined to describe her work" (69) are typical of this approach. Yet, increasingly, Bertken has been shown to be a significant medieval woman writer who drew from a long literary, didactic, theological, and mystical tradition—a tradition going back to *Canticles* and the Church Fathers and continuing into her own age and culture, especially in the remarkable works of Hadewych of Antwerp, Jan Ruusbroec, Beatrice of Nazareth and the spirituality associated with the beguine movement and the *devotio moderna*. Viewed in the light of this tradition and the special thematic concerns which her 57–year-long existence as *reclusa* imposed on Bertken, her writings reveal a consistent and original literary and mystical program—a program which revolves around the expression, in an often oblique and demanding language and rhetoric, of a number of related voices inside Bertken, those of the woman, the *mystica* and the recluse.

Works

Johanna Snellen, ed., *Een boecxken gemaket van suster Bertken die lvii jaren besloten heeft gheseten tot Utrecht in dye buerkercke. Naar den Leidschen druk van Jan Seversen* (1924). van de Graft, C. Catharina, ed., *Een boecxken . . .* (1955). The Snellen-text is based on the edition of Bertken by the Leiden printer Jan Seversen, whereas de Graft reproduces the text of the earliest published version by the Utrecht printer Jan Berntsz. See also Henk Vynckier, "Poetry from Behind Bars: Some Translations from the Dutch Recluse Sister Bertken (1430–1517)." *Mystics Quarterly* (Fall 1988).

Bibliography

Dezaire, P.N., "Suster Bertken. Een mystieke dichteres." *De nieuwe taalgids* 36 (1942): 208–217. Enklaar, Th., "Zuster Bertken en de Noordnederlandse renaissance." *Lezende in buurmans hof* (1956). Heeroma, K., "Het ingekluisde lied." *Maatstaf* 16 (1968): 433–454. Meeuwisse, Karel, "Zuster Bertkens Passieboekje." *Dancwerc. Opstellen aangeboden aan Prof. Dr. D. Th. Enklaar ter gelegenheid van zijn vijfenzestigste verjaardag* (1959): 208–221. J.G. de Jong, Martien, *Het Kerstvisioen van Berta Jacobs* (1961). Vynckier, Henk, "The Nativity in the Cell: The Intellectual and Mystical Background of Sister Bertken's *A Vision of the Birth of Christ.*" *Mystics Quarterly* (Fall 1988).

General references: Knuvelder, G.P.M., *Handboek tot de geschiedenis van de Nederlandse letterkunde*, vol. 1 (1970), pp. 408–409. Meijer, Reinder P., *The Literature of the Low Countries* (1971), pp. 68–70. van Mierlo, Jozef, *Geschiedenis van de letterkunde der Nederlanden*, vol. 2 (1940), pp. 203–204.

Henk Vynckier

Aurora Bertrana

Born 1899, Gerona, Spain; died 1974, Barcelona, Spain
Genre(s): novel, short story
Language(s): Catalan

The daughter of Prudenci Bertrana, a well-known Catalan writer of the turn of the century, Aurora was able to become a world traveler, visiting not only Europe and North Africa but also South America and Oceania. Her cosmopolitan upbringing is reflected in her fiction, which not only utilizes exotic settings but displays an unusual depth of understanding of other countries. Bertrana experienced personally the hardship and tragedy of war during Spain's civil conflict and the Second World War, and two of her early novels bear witness to this experience: *Tres presoners* (1957; Three Prisoners), a simple, yet intensely emotional narrative set during the Spanish Civil War, and *Entre dos silencis* (1958; Between Two Silences), based on the writer's volunteer work in a village that had been totally destroyed. *La nimfa d'argila* (1959; The Clay Nymph) presents a study in infantile psychology, the portrait of a girl whose childhood is abruptly ended. *Fracàs* (1966; Failure) comes much closer to the narrative of sociopolitical criticism popular in Spain during the late 1950s and 1960s with its denunciation of the upper classes for their selfishness and ambition and, more particularly, for the hypocrisy that cloaks such motives beneath the mask of religiosity and respectability. Still very contemporary in its focus but less *engagé* is *Vent de grop* (1967; Tailwind), a love story set against the background of the developing tourist industry in a small fishing village on the Costa Brava. Although some writers of the period began to display environmental concerns, Bertrana limits her focus to evocation of the emotional disappointment and frustration between two young lovers when one tires of the relationship and decides to end it.

Most of Bertrana's collections of short fictions are thematically unified: *El Marroc sensual i fanàtic* (1936; Sensual and Fanatic Morroco) is a recreation of travel impressions, including the writer's intellectual and emotional responses, as is also the case to some extent with *Peikea, princesa caníbal i altres contes oceànics* (1980; Peikea, the Cannibal Princess and Other Oceanic Stories), which reflects time spent in an area perceived as a Utopian society, an idealized landscape suffused with tenderness. *Oviri i sis narraciones més* (1965; Oviri and Six Other Stories) proceeds from close observation of a cat named Oviri to half a dozen other tales with animal protagonists that probe human/animal relationships.

Bertrana's well-defined individuality as a writer is due in part to her thematics, her inclusion of settings and characters seldom found in the works of most women writing during the early postwar decades in Spain. Her cosmopolitan focus, the depth of emotion in her novels, and occasional lyric fantasy in the shorter fiction combine with a finely-crafted style to create an unmistakable fictional voice.

Works

Paradisos Oceanics (1930). El Marroc sensual i fanàtic (1936). Camins de somni (1955). Tres presoners (1957). Entre dos silencis (1958). La nimfa d'argila (1959). Ariatea (1960). Oviri i sis narracions més (1965). Fracàs (1966). Vent de grop (1967). La ciutat dels joves (1971). Peikea, princesa caníbal i altres contes oceànics (1980).

Bibliography

General references: *Women Writers of Spain*, ed. C.L. Galerstein (Westport, CT, 1986).

Janet Perez

Augustina Bessa-Luís

Born 1922 (1923?), Vila Mea, Amarante, Portugal
Genre(s): novel, short story, theater, travel literature
Language(s): Portuguese

Bessa-Luís is a very imaginative writer whose works evoke Proust's fascination with time, Kafka's attraction to the absurd, and Balzac's inventiveness. The influence of Camilo Castelo Branco is also apparent. Her early narrative works went unnoticed, but her third novel, *A sibila* (The Sybil), was awarded two consecutive prizes (the "Delfim Guimaraes" in 1953 and the "Eça de Queirós" in 1954) and established her reputation as a talented writer with a very original style.

Works

Novels: *Mundo Fechado* [Closed World] (1948). *Os Super-Homens* [The Supermen] (1950). *A Sibila* [The Sybil] (1953). *Os Incuráveis* [The Incurable] (1955). *A Muralha* [The Wall] (1957). *O Susto* [The Fright] (1958). *Ternos Guerreiros* [Tender Warriors] (1960). *O Manto* [The Cloak] (1961). *O Sermao do Fogo* [The Sermon of the Fire] (1963).

Os quatro rios [The Four Rivers] (1964). *A dança das espadas* [Sword Dance] (1965). *Canção diante de uma porta fechada* [Song in Front of a Closed Door] (1966). These three novels comprise the trilogy *As relações humanas* [Human Relationships]. *Homens e mulheres* [Men and Women] (1967). *As categorias* [The Categories] (1970). Series entitled *A bíblia dos pobres* [The Bible of the Poor].

Short Story: *Contos Impopulares* [Unpopular Stories] (1951–1953).

Theater: *O inseparável, ou o amigo por testamento* [Inseparable, or, The Bequeathed Friend] (1958).

Travel: *Embaixada a Caligula* [On a Mission to Caligula] (1960).

Literary Criticism: *Florbela Espanca, a vida e a obra* [Florbela Espanca, The Life and the Work] (1979).

Bibliography

Antunes, M., "Os Incuráveis, um grande romance." *Brotéria* 63, 2 (1956). Carvalho, J., "A. Bess-Luís e o romance moderno." *Segundo Congresso Brasileiro de Língua e Literatura* (1971). *Columbia Dictionary of Modern European Literature*, ed. J.-A. Bédé and W.B. Edgerton (1980). *Literatura Portuguesa Moderna*, ed. M. Moisés (1973). Quadros, A., "Os Romances de Agustina Bessa-Luís." *Crítica e Verdade* (1964). de Vasconcelos, T., "Bessa-Luís: o romance e a arte de escrever." *Cidade Nova* 3, 6 (1954).

Paula T. Irvin

Kata Bethlen

(a.k.a. "Árva" [Orphan])

Born November 25, 1700, Bonyha, Hungary;
died July 29, 1759, Fogaras, Hungary
(now Romania)
Genre(s): memoirs
Language(s): Hungarian

Bethlen is one of the earliest writers of memoirs in Hungary. She was led to writing by her unhappy first marriage and subsequent religious conflicts with the children of that first marriage. She was throughout her life active in the cultural and intellectual life of her country as a member of the important Bethlen family, the niece of the Chancellor of Transylvania Miklos Bethlen, as well as, in her second marriage, the

wife of the son of a later Chancellor, Mihály Teleki. Her first marriage was politically motivated, and the antagonism between her strong Protestant views and the Catholicism of her husband's family wounded her deeply. The Heller family denied her access to her children, and her daughter's malicious teasing seems to have touched her most deeply, for it is mentioned in her writings. After the death of her first husband, she remarried and, as the mistress of her husband's large estates, was active in fostering education in Transylvania. This marriage was happier, but her husband and the children of this marriage died early, therefore the epithet "orphan."

Her diary was written primarily as a personal response to the pressures her first husband's family put on her to convert. She published her writings under the titles: *Védelmező erős pajs* (1759; Protecting, Strong Shield) and *Bujdosásának emlékezetkönyve* (1733, 1735; The Memoirs of Her Exile) and the collected work, which includes her letters: *Életének maga által valo rövid leírasa Széki gróf Teleki József özvegye, Bethleni Bethlen Kata grófnő írasai és levelezése* (1759; Her Life, Written by Herself, the Writings and Correspondence of . . .). Her writings, however, mirror more than her personal troubles, for they also reflect the political struggles of the day and the duties and tasks of the leading families in this conflict.

Her correspondence shows a clever, skillful woman who encouraged industrial development on her estates. She established gardens and nurseries to propagate better stock, had a paper-mill and glass works, and employed numerous artisans, including embroiderers, a major cottage industry of the time. She studied natural science to counteract the effects of natural disasters and sought to aid her tenants in adopting progressive farming practices. She learned medicine and pharmacology to better minister to the needs of her community and contributed generously to the advance of learning by establishing schools and scholarships. She also contributed to the education of girls, which she felt was sadly neglected. As a patron of Péter Bód, the Protestant scholar and publisher, she fostered printing and scholastic reform. The library he assembled for her was one of the most important of the age. While he was her chaplain (1743–1749) he collected over 500 manuscripts in addition to numerous books. Unfortunately, an 1847 fire destroyed the library.

It was her memoirs, however, that assured Bethlen a place in Hungarian literature. Her life's story (*Életenek maga altal . . .*) is a personal history shot through with the concerns of the day. She is not merely a religious writer, though her pietistic leanings would suggest that she sees the religious struggle in national terms, within the context of the forcible re-conversion efforts of the Hapsburg family in the eighteenth century; her pietistic comments are eclipsed by her determined political views. In this, she is a good representative of the Hungarian Baroque and unites the literature of her day with that of the Reform period of the nineteenth century.

Her memoirs, in succinct, almost colloquial, language, are surprisingly open in spite of their melancholy nature. They give details and personal reactions that are lacking in the works of her male contemporaries such as Francis Rákoczi II. Perhaps her goal of justifying God's ways to man, rather than of accounting for her own actions, accounts for this openness.

Also important are her letters, which are remarkable even when compared with the correspondence of predecessors such as Zsuzsanna Lorántffy, Anna Bornemissza, or Ilona Zrinyi. Especially after the death of her second husband, she wrote extensively and brought a new, intimate style to this genre. While not free of Baroque ornament and formality, they nevertheless exhibit a simplicity and elegance of language that make them akin to the letters of Mme de Sevigné and others at the Court of Louis XIV.

Between 1742 and 1751 she wrote a collection of poetic prayers, which she published under the title *Védelmező erős pais.* These show an interesting blend of traditional meditative lyrics and the popular genres of the day and her strongly Puritanical views. The style of the letters is also reflected in her major work, the memoirs, on which she worked from 1740 on. We do not have a complete manuscript, and the printed version stops in mid-sentence at June 20, 1751. She followed, in style, the memoirs of János Kemény and Miklos Bethlen, which she knew, but her work is also closely related to the *Confessions* of Francis Rákoczi. In the preface she endeavors to give a moral and didactic framework to her autobiography; in reality, it is her personal life and her commentary that provide interest. The compactness and economy of earlier parts is diluted later, but here the details of everyday life are more numerous. The interspersed prayers give it both a more personal and a more lyrical flavor.

Works

Védelmező erős pais (1759). *Bujdosásának emlekezetkönyve* (1733; 7 editions in her lifetime). *Élétenek maga által való leírása*, ed. Miklós K. Pap (1881). *Teleki Józsefné széki grof B.K. írásai és levelezése, 1700–1759*, ed. Lajos Szadeczky-Kardoss (1922–1923). *B.K. Önéletleírasa*, intro. Mihaly Súkösd (1963).

Bibliography

Gróf Bethlen Kata, ed. K. Papp, Miklos (Kolozsvár, 1881–1882). Hegyaljai, Géza Kiss, *Árva Bethlen Kata* (Budapest, 1922). Kiss, Tamas, "Árva Bethlen Kata." *Protestáns Szemle* (1939), pp. 451–461. Németh, László, "Bethlen Kata." *Kelet népe* (1940). Németh, S. Katalin, "A levélíró B.K." *Irodalomtörténet* 1 (1979): 3–17. Robotos, Imre, "A héterkőlcs drámája." *Uj Tükör* 28 (1979) :22–23. Szadeczky, Lajos, "Gr. Bethlen Kata végrendelete és alapítólevelei." *Történelmi Tár* (1859), pp. 531–549, 737–749.

Enikő Molnár Basa

Betitia

(see: Proba)

Margarete Beutler

(a.k.a. Margarete Friedrich-Freksa, Margit Friedrich)

Born January 13, 1876, Gollnow (Pommern), Germany (now Poland); died June 3, 1949, Gammertingen bei Tübingen
Genre(s): lyric, short prose, drama, novel, autobiography
Language(s): German

Born in the provincial town of Gollnow (Pommern, now in Poland), where her father was mayor, Margarete Beutler grew up in Berlin, where she attended a teachers' college for women (*Lehrerinnenseminar*; women in Germany, it might be recalled, were not admitted to university studies on a regular basis until the beginning of this century and even then could not take qualifying examinations). Her first published works—verse and short prose—appeared in the famous journal *Simplicissimus* in 1897. Her first volume of poetry was published in 1902 and was well received. Her verse is highly sensual and celebrates the instincts. The following excerpt provides a good example of these qualities:

> Nun badet sich in Mittagglut die Heide
> und atmet kaum
> Ich lieg im Kraut, die Augen fest
> geschlossen,
> am grauen Weidenbaum—es hat ein
> Traum,
> ein weißer Traum, sich mir ins Herz
> ergossen.
> [Now the heath bathes in midday glow
> and barely breathes
> I lie in the grass, with my eyes tightly
> closed,
> at the foot of a grey willow—a dream,
> a white dream has poured itself into my
> heart.]

She had one son out of wedlock before moving to Munich in 1903, where she joined the staff of the journal *Jugend*. Her verse glorifies, among other things, unwed motherhood. In Munich she became friends with such famous writers as Christian Morgenstern and Frank Wedekind. Morgenstern introduced her to another writer, Kurt Friedrich-Freksa, whom she later married, and with whom she had a son. Besides her own compositions, she edited a long work by Grimmelshausen and translated the works of Clément Marot, Molière, and Beaumarchais into German. After the Nazi seizure of power, she declined joining the *Reichsschriftumskammer*—a kind of Nazi writers' union—and published nothing else for the rest of her lifetime. Several unpublished works survive in manuscript, including two plays, *Die Kätterle von Leonburg* and *Das Lächeln von Frau Li*; a novel, *An der Ehe Narrenseil*; and an autobiographical fragment, *Kindheit*.

Works

Gedichte (1902, 1903). *Neue Gedichte* (1908). *Leb wohl, Bohème! Ein Gedichtsbuch* (1911).

Bibliography

Brinker-Gabler, Gisela, Karola Ludwig, and Angela Wöffen, "Beutler, Margarete." *Lexikon deutschsprachiger Schrift-stellerinnen, 1800–1945* (Munich, 1986), p. 32. As noted there, the entry in Kosch, *Deutsches Literatur-Lexikon*, 3 ed. (1966), vol. 9, p. 726, is highly flawed. Soergel, Albert, and Curt Hohoff, *Dichtung und Dichter der Zeit, Vom Naturalismus bis zur Gegenwart* I (Düsseldorf, 1964), pp. 300–301.

Earl Jeffrey Richards

Magdalena Beutlerin

(see: Magdalena von Freiburg)

Baiba Bičole

Born 1931, Riga, Latvia, Soviet Union
Genre(s): poetry
Language(s): Latvian

Born into a distinguished literary family (her mother a poet and critic, her father a renowned literary historian and critic), Baiba Bičole fled from the Soviet occupation of Latvia in 1944 and eventually immigrated to the United States. She wrote her verse in free rhyme, intermingling the erotic and the sacred, the body and the primary elements. With her first volume of poetry published in 1966, Bičole won the coveted Zinaida Lazda Prize and has since put out three other volumes of her work.

Works

Burot [To Cast Spells] (1976). *Grie'os* [I Turn] (1981).

Warwick J. Rodden

Charlotte Dorothea Biehl

Born June 2, 1731, Copenhagen, Denmark;
died May 15, 1788, Copenhagen
Genre(s): drama, short story, novel,
autobiography, translation, historical letter
Language(s): Danish

The literary production of Charlotte Dorothea Biehl positions itself in the struggle between the feudal aristocracy and the emerging bourgeoisie that characterized Danish society and its theater in the mid-eighteenth century. Inspired by French and English moral-sentimental drama, Biehl was the major Danish dramatist in the 1764–1772 period. With a series of sentimental comedies and singspiels, as well as later fiction and prose, she represents a new bourgeois morality, which internalized aristocratic hierarchies and ceremonies as "inner nobility."

Born into a family of Castellans, Biehl spent her childhood years at Copenhagen Castle and her mature life at Charlottenborg Castle. She was consistently subjected to the whims of an authoritarian father, who prevented his intelligent daughter from reading and, ultimately, from marrying. As a member of the bourgeoisie, yet living among the aristocracy and as a victim of the patriarchal family yet seemingly supporting the institution, Biehl expressed in her writings the contradictions of her life.

Biehl's first and most successful play, *Den Kierlige Mand* (1764; The Loving Husband), sets the high moral tone that characterized her theatrical productions. By appealing to her maternal feelings, a husband rescues his normally dutiful wife from the temptations of festivity and flirtation. *Den Forelskede Ven* (1765; The Friend in Love) and *Den Ædelmodige* (1767; The Noble One) establish a morality of love, while the subtly subversive *Den Listige Optraekkerske* (1765; The Shrewd Fraud) depicts a fraudulent, seductive exploiter of men, duly punished in the end. Seven of Biehl's plays were collected in *Comedier* (1773; Comedies), published at the end of her most productive years in the theater. Her successful translation of Cervantes' *Don Quixote* appeared in 1776–77.

Moralske Fortaellinger I-IV (1781–82; Moral Tales) opened the second phase of Biehl's career with a series of tales advocating control, self-repression, and rationality in response to the German sentimental-rebellious novel epitomized by Goethe's *Leiden des Jungen Werthers* (1774).

The third phase of Biehl's production began with her monumental epistolary novel, *Brevvexling Imellem Fortroelige Venner* (1783; Correspondence Between Intimate Friends), with Richardson's *Pamela* (1740) as her model. In 1784, she furthermore recorded in letter form her memories of Danish royalty. In 1787, she offered her autobiography, entitled *Mit Ubetydelige Levnetsløb* (My Insignificant Life), as a birthday present to a friend.

While often heavy-handedly moralistic, Biehl's literary works, written under absolute monarchy and patriarchy, represent a new bourgeois consciousness as well as a new feminine voice.

Works

Comedier (1773). *Betragtning over Jesu Lidelse og Død* (1773). *Silphen* (1773). *Kierligheds-Brevene* (1774). *Den Prøvede Troskab* (1774). *Euphemia* (1775). *Den Sindrige Herremands Don Quixote af Mancha Levnet og Bedrifter* (1776–77). "Søster B.: En Tale Holden i Kiede-Forsamlingen d. 13de Martii 1778" (1778). *Et Oratorium af Gio. Batta Pergolesi. Poesien af C.D. Biehl* (1780). *Moralske Fortaellinger I-IV* (1781–1782). *Brevvexling Imellem Fortroelige Venner I-III* (1783). *Den Tavse Pige eller De Ved Tavshed Avlede Mistanker* (1783). "C.D. Biehls Anekdoter om Christian VI i 2 Breve til Joh. v. Bulow" (1784). "Upartiske Anmaerkninger til en Falsk og Ondskabsfuld Historie" (1784). *Interiører fra Kong Frederik den Femtes Hof: C.D. Biehls Breve og Selvbiografi* (1784). *Interiører fra Kong Christian den Syvendes Hof: Efter Charlotte Dorothea Biehls Breve* (1784). *Orpheus og Eurydice* (1786). "Hovmesterinden" (1786). *Den Uforsigtige Forsigtighed* (1787). "Til Hs. Kgl. H. Cronprindsen d. 4. April 1784" (1794). "Regeringsforandringen den 14de April 1784" (n.d.).

Bibliography

Bech, Svend Cedergreen, [Introduction], *Brev fra Dorothea: Af Charlotta Dorothea Biehls Historiske Breve* (Copenhagen, 1975). Dahlerup, Pil, [Introduction], *Pigeopdragelse* (Copenhagen, 1969). Dalager, Stig, and Anne-Marie Mai, *Danske Kvindelige Forfattere I* (Copenhagen, 1982), pp. 97–116. Jensen, Johan Fjord, et al., *Dansk*

Litteraturhistorie IV (Copenhagen, 1983), pp. 128–141, 444–448. Plesner, K.F., "En Dansk Forfatterinde fra Det Attende Århundrede: Charlotte Dorothea Biehl." *Edda* 27 (1927).

Clara Juncker

Bieiris de Romans

Flourished first half of the thirteenth century [?], Romans (Drôme), Southern France
Genre(s): canso
Language(s): Occitan

The Occitan *canso* (or love song) "Na Maria, pretz e fina valors" (PC 93, 1) is ascribed by a rubric in the single fourteenth- or fifteenth-century manuscript that preserves it (MS. *T*, Paris, B.N. fr. 15211, fo. 208b) to the otherwise unknown *trobairitz* (or woman troubadour) Na (or Lady) Bieiris de Romans, who is presumed to have flourished in the first half of the thirteenth century. It is probable that *Romans* refers to the cantonal seat of that name in the *arrondissement* of Valence (Drôme) in the Rhône valley of the Dauphiné. The *canso*, a hymn of erotic love addressed to a "Lady Maria," raises difficult questions of attribution and intention. The poem is composed of two *coblas* (or strophes) and two *tornados* (or envoys). It opens with an apostrophe to the Lady Maria and a list of the qualities possessed by her: worth, wit, beauty, cultivated speech, charm, lack of guile, etc. The speaker then begs for her love, asserting that in her lies all hope for joy and urging her not to give her love to a false (male) lover.

In the medieval Occitan *canso*, where scholars conventionally have identified the author with the speaking voice of his text, an erotic apostrophe by the author's persona to a member of the same sex would imply a homosexual relationship. If its author is a woman, "Na Maria" is "the sole extant example of medieval love poetry written in a vernacular language by one woman to another" (Boswell 265). Critical opinion is divided on the questions of the gender of Bieiris and the proper context in which to read "Na Maria." Factors favorable to the view that its author is not a woman include the rarity of celebrations of homosexual, and particularly of lesbian, love in the medieval lyric, their virtual non-existence in Occitan poetry, and the improbability that a male troubadour should have chosen to adopt a feminine persona. It has been asserted that the rubric is a mistranscription of *N'Alberis de Roman* or Alberico da Romano, a thirteenth-century Italian nobleman, patron, and occasional troubadour (Schultz, "Nabieiris"); for *En* ("Lord"), the masculine counterpart of *Na*, contracts to *N'* before a vowel. The possibility that the rubric contains a copyist's error is strengthened by the fact that the song contains no internal markers identifying the speaking voice as that of a woman. On the contrary, it conforms in every respect to the conventions of the troubadour song with a masculine poetic voice.

In favor of the opposing view, it has been proposed that the song is a devotional work, a literary exercise, a piece of innocent flattery, a joke, or half of a *tenso atypique* (or dialogue poem alternating not by strophes, as is normal, but by halves) between a male and a female voice, only the first half of which has survived (Huchet 64). This latter suggestion does not resolve the problem of the name given by the rubric, for even if, as often happens with *tensos*, the name of only one interlocutor is given, Bieiris would have to refer to the male, the female necessarily being named Maria. While the hypothesis that it is a paean to the Virgin is rendered implausible by its erotic character (esp. v. 16), the suggestions that it is facetious (Bec 198), ironic, or fragmentary are not so easily dismissed.

Bibliography

Bec, Pierre, *Burlesque et obscénité chez les troubadours. Pour une approche du contre-texte médiéval* (Paris, 1984), pp. 197–200. Bogin, Meg, *The Women Troubadours* (New York and London, 1976), pp. 176–177. Boswell, John, *Christianity, Social Tolerance, and Homosexuality. Gay People in Western Europe from the Beginning of the Christian Era to the Fourteenth Century* (Chicago and London, 1980). Dronke, Peter, *Women Writers of the Middle Ages. A Critical Study of Texts from Perpetua (d. 203) to Marguerite Porete *(d. 1310)* (Cambridge, 1984), p. 98. Huchet, Jean-Charles, "Les Femmes troubadours ou la voix critique." *Littérature* 51 (October 1983), pp. 59–90. Schultz, Oscar. *Die Provenzalischen*

Dichterinnen. Biographien und Texte nebst Anmerkungen und einer Einleitung (Leipzig, 1988; Geneva, 1975), pp. 16, 28. Schultz, Oscar, "Nabieiris de roman." *Zeitschrift für romanische Philologie* 15 (1891): 234–235.

Anna Bijns

Born 1493, Antwerp, Belgium; died 1575, Antwerp
Genre(s): poetry
Language(s): Dutch

Born in the almost superstitiously pious Catholic lower middle class of Antwerp, Anna Bijns became a private school teacher in that city upon the death of her father in 1516. Franciscan Minorites had tutored her and had probably stimulated her early talent for verse-making in the flourishing style of the Chambers of Rhetoric though it is not certain whether she actually ever belonged to such a Chamber. Bijns remained closely connected with Minorites throughout her sad and rather isolated life as a poor schoolmistress and spinster. The Franciscans were the most militant and the most intellectual among the local clergymen to resist the swiftly rising fortunes of, first, the Lutherans (from 1515 until 1526), and then the Anabaptists (1534–1539) and the Calvinists (after 1526) in Antwerp. Despite ever harsher countermeasures imposed by the Spanish government of the Low Countries, these three reformational movements (and Calvinism foremost) succeeded in weaning ever larger segments of the cosmopolitan and well-to-do Antwerp bourgeoisie and aristocrats away from Catholicism.

Bijns had been writing light "foolish" and "amorous" refrains in the rhetorical style of *nugae difficiles* in the early decades of the sixteenth century, but the adverse fortunes of orthodox Catholicism changed her inclination. Bijns blamed the progress of "heresy" (all the phenomena of which she conveniently but rather inaccurately designated as "Lutherie") partly on the ineffective preaching of the well-intending but hopelessly unprepared parish clergy. The Reformation was effected in the Southern Netherlands to a great extent by means of polemical pamphlets. It was in this often vile and vulgar logomachy that Bijns engaged as *miles christi*—though not without fear that her "frail womanhood" might make her fail in this self-ordained task as "the "avenging angel of the insulted faith." It is not unlikely that Bijns undertook this task after some prodding by Minorite acquaintances who knew her talent and temperament.

Whether Bijns really understood all the delicate nuances of the reformational arguments or the intricacies of Catholic orthodoxy at that very complex time hardly matters. Hers was the only strong Catholic voice in print against a whole army of anonymous Protestant poets. She saw the poet's—any poet's—mission as dual but indivisible: as an artist (s)he must draw beauty from pure devotion, and as *miles christi* (s)he must make use of this talent in defense of the beleaguered Church.

As a sensitive woman from the ranks of the people, Bijns recognized that the excesses of both Reformation and Counter-Reformation were entangling ever more ordinary people, and she felt that the parish clergy were failing in their task as shepherds of the common flock. This attitude would explain the tone and lay-out of the polemical Counter-Reformational refrains that make up her first collection in print.

A thicker, more aggressive volume was published in 1548, this time openly under Franciscan aegis and perhaps not entirely under the author's control. Generally, Bijn's Counter-Reformational poems are specifically anti-Lutheran. She presents Luther as her personal enemy, his life as odious, his doctrines as the devil's own. There is obviously no sophistication in her argument that murder, theft, sacrilege, countless orphans, and runaway monks are all evils directly traceable to Luther's greed and pride. Bijns' metaphorical arsenal and vituperative tone clearly suggest that it was her purpose to protect the ordinary, simple flock of well-meaning souls against Luther's temptations by means of a presentation of "Lutherie" as an utterly nauseating and blinded life-style. Images of light versus dark, health versus corruption, underlie her black-and-white ideas. She extracted hyperbolic images from execution scenes, daily life, and official revocations of former heretics, and her inductive and apostrophic arguments were designed to appeal to her audiences' emotions.

A third volume (over 250 pages) was published in 1567 as a fund-raiser for the restoration of the Franciscan monastery which had fallen victim to a reformed arsonist's anger. This collection contains a variety of themes, and some refrains were already decades old. The general tone of the volume matched very well the rather defeatist *mea culpa* attitude which had by then settled in the Catholic camp, following the apparent success of the Reformation in Antwerp. The selection includes refrains very different from those previously published, such as tender expressions of self-accusation, contemplative meditation, Bonaventuran praises of Nature, *ars moriendi* poems, and refrains expressing pity for the damned.

At least until 1533, Bijns had been accumulating a body of "amorous" and "foolish" refrains twice the size of that of her contrareformational and spiritual work. Published only in the late nineteenth century, these sometimes scatological, sometimes folksy-witty refrains reveal quite another Anna Bijns. Eros is treated whimsically. There are some sensitive anatomy refrains, for instance those with the "Bonaventura" acrostic—probably a reference to the Franciscan Bonaventura, a staunch advocate of celibacy and asceticism—but mostly the poems are bellicose and suggest amorous frustration. Bijns attacks male hypocrisy in many misandric refrains, and (typically) associates the unfaithful lover with Luther. "Man" is, like Luther, a faithless hypocrite. "Woman" is an innocent, trusting, easily ensnared believer. Some refrains express a rather grotesque view of marriage.

It is obvious that for Bijns as a woman independence comes first and that she sees Man, that wolf in sheep's clothing, as rather an inferior creature. Yet she is a poet full of surprises and contradictions, and so there are some genuinely tender love lyrics in the oeuvre of this versatile writer. Though her contrareformational collections were published several times and earned her during her lifetime the epithet "Brabantian Sappho," and in spite of a highly unusual early translation into Latin of some of her work, Anna Bijns was buried with a pauper's service in the Cathedral of Antwerp. Her burial confirmed her life's motto: "Sour rather than sweet." By the time of her death in 1575, "Lutherie" was on the wane

again, crushed under ever heavier Spanish pressure.

Katharina Boudewijns is generally considered the foremost of Bijns' successors, but this Brussels aristocrat had little, indeed, of the raciness of her Antwerp predecessor. Anna Bijns achieved mastery of the difficult rhetorical refrains to a greater degree than any other poet using that poetic form in the Dutch language. Bijns was also the first in her literature to deny the all importance of the rhyme scheme. No rigid syllable count clogs her refrains; rather, a rhythmical qualitative verse not earlier achieved in the language proved the perfect vehicle for her warm-blooded concerns.

Works

Konstighe Refereyne vol schoone Schrifturen ende Leeringhen (1646). *Den Gheestelijcken Nachtegael* (1623). *Anna Bijns, Refreinen* (1949). *Anna Bijns. Meer zuurs dan zoets* (1975).

Translations: "Anna Bijns, Lesbia Teutonica," in *Renaissance Women Writers* (1986), tr. Kristiaan Aercke with critical introduction. "Antwerp's Sharpest Tongue Against Luther," tr. Kristiaan Aercke, in *Vox Benedictina* II, 3 (1985): 224–238.

Bibliography

Roose, Lode, *Anna Bijns, een rederijkster uit de hervormingstijd* (Gent, 1963). Basse, Maurits, *Het Aandeel der Vrouw in de Nederlandsche Letterkunde* I (Gent, 1920).

Kristiaan P. Aercke

S. Corinna Bille

Born August 29, 1912, Lausanne, Switzerland; died October 24, 1979, Veyras (Valais), Switzerland
Genre(s): novel, short story, poetry
Language(s): French

The daughter of the painter Edmond Bille, S. Corinna Bille spent a happy childhood in Siders, Valais, the Swiss Alpine canton in which her mother was born. At the age of twenty-two she went to Paris, came under the influence of the Surrealists, and made an unhappy marriage that was later annulled. Her return to Switzerland in 1937 plunged her into a crisis aggravated by serious illness. After her recovery she married the writer Maurice Chappaz, with whom she had three children. In later years Corinna Bille traveled widely, among other places to Africa, Lebanon, and Russia, but she always returned to her beloved Valais, where she died in 1979.

There are two main influences on the work of Corinna Bille: painting and nature. The peaks and valleys of the Alps are an integral part of her work, and her characters embody the powerful, amoral, calamitous, and pitiless forces at work in nature. In the novel *Théoda*, for instance, set in a nineteenth-century peasant milieu and based on a true incident, an adulterous love affair ends in murder and public execution. It is a melodramatic subject, but Bille tells the story without sentimentality. Since her protagonists are not individualists, her tales often depict the conflict between traditional values and customs on the one hand and modern development on the other. Transitions and transformations, at times supernatural, are also favorite subjects. Bille's reputation as a master of the short story is based on her fluid and elegant style, which evokes much in a few, precise words. In addition to her poetry and fiction, Corinna Bille edited her father's memoirs and wrote non-fiction essays on the Alps and a number of children's books.

Works

Printemps [Spring], poetry (1939). *Théoda*, novel (1944; 1978). *Le Grand Tourment* [The Great Anguish], novellas, ill. Edmond Bille (1951). *Le Sabot de Vénus* [Venus's Wooden Shoe], novel (1952, 1970, 1982). *Florilège alpestre* [Alpine Album], essay (1953). *Douleurs paysannes* [Rural Sorrows], novellas (1954, 1978). *L'Enfant aveugle* [The Sightless Child], stories (1955, 1980). *A pied du Rhône à la Maggia* [On Foot from the Rhone to the Maggia] (1957). *Le Pays secret*, poetry [The Secret Land], ill. Edmond Bille (1961). [Editor], *Jeunesse d'un peintre* [A Painter's Youth] by Edmond Bille (1962). *L'Inconnue du Haut-Rhône* [The Stranger from the Upper Rhone], plays (1963). *Entre hiver et printemps* [Between Winter and Spring], novellas (1967, 1980). *La Fraise noire* [Black Strawberries], novellas (1968, 1976). *Le Mystère du monstre* [The Mystery of the Monster], children's stories (1968). *Suite d'Anniviers*, poetry, in *Le Sabot de Vénus* (1970). *Juliette éternelle* [Eternal Juliet], novellas (1971). *La Perle rose du lac noir* [The Pink Pearl from the Black Lake], children's book (1972). *Cent petites histoires cruelles* [One Hundred Cruel Little Tales] (1973, 1985). *La Demoiselle sauvage* [The Savage Maiden], novellas (1974). *Finges. Forêt du Rhône* [Finges. The Forest of the Rhone], poetry, novella; photographs by Suzi Pilet (1975). *Le Salon ovale* [The Oval Parlor], novellas, baroque tales (1976, 1987). *La Maison musique* [The Music House], children's stories (1977). *Les invités de Moscou* [The Guests from Moscow] (1977). *Cent petites histoires d'amour* [One Hundred Little Love Tales] (1978). *La Montagne déserte* [The Uninhabited Mountain], poetry (1978). *Deux passions* [Two Passions], novellas (1979). *Le Sourire de l'araignée et autres contes* [The Spider's Smile and Other Stories], children's stories (1979). *Soleil de la nuit* and *Un goût de rocher* [Night Sun; A Taste of Flint, poetry (1980). *Le Bal double* [The Double Ball], novellas (1980). *Le Patin noir* [The Black Skate], novel (1982). [With others], *L'Aventure de Chandolin* [The Adventure of Chandolin], essay (1983). [With Maurice Chappaz], *Le Partage de minuit* [Midnight Sharing], novella (1984). *Abîme des fleurs, trésor des pierres: récits du Rhône et de la Maggia* [The Abyss of Flowers, the Treasure of Stones: Tales from the Rhone and the Maggia] (1985; contains *A pied du Rhône . . .* [1957], *Florilège alpestre* [1953] and two previously uncollected pieces). *Trente-six petites histories curieuses* [Thirty-six Strange Little Stories] (1985; volume also contains *Cent petites histoires cruelles*). German translations: *Theoda*, tr. Marcel Pobé (1964), tr. Elisabeth Dütsch (1985). *Schwarze Erdbeeren* [*La Fraise noir*], tr. Marcel Schwander (1975). *Zwei Mädchenleben* [*Deux passions*], tr. Erika Tophoven-Schöningh (1980). *Ländlicher Schmerz* [*Douleurs paysannes*], tr. Elisabeth Dütsch (1989).

Bibliography

Favre, Gilberte, *Corinna Bille: Le vrai conte de sa vie*, photo-biography (Lausanne, 1981). Ghirelli, Marianne, "Ueber Corinna Bille." *Neue Zürcher Zeitung* 14./15 (March 1981): 67–68. Huber, Margrit, "Schreiben, um leben zu können—S. Corinna Bille." *Schritte ins Offene* 14.1 (1984): 19–20. *L'Arrache-plume. Chroniques de littérature romande 1965–1980*, reviews of C.B.'s work (Lausanne, 1980; Genève, 1980). Makward,

Christiane, "Trois heures d'un après-midi en Valais: S. Corinna Bille." *Swiss-French Studies/Etudes Romandes* 1.1 (1980): 7–15. Moser, Monique, "De Cézanne à Redon: l'exemple des peintres dans l'écriture de Corinna Bille." *Etudes Francaises* (21.1) (1985): 45–57. Moser-Verrey, Monique, "Les fôrets de Corinna." *Swiss-French Studies/Etudes Romandes* 1.1 (1980): 16–33. Quindoz, Isabelle, "Notes bibliographiques sur S. Corinna Bille." *Swiss-French Studies/Etudes Romandes* 1.1 (1980): 34–42. Schneider, Judith Morganroth, "S. Corinna Bille. Exploring the Feminine Labyrinth." *Folio: Papers on Foreign Languages and Literatures* 11 (1978): 136–48. Schwendimann, Max A., "S. Corinna Bille." *Gegenwartsdichtung der Westschweiz: Zwölf Autorenportraits mit Textproben*, ed. Max A. Schwendimann (Bern, 1972), pp. 53–66.

Ann Marie Rasmussen

Raphaële Billetdoux

Born 1951, Paris, France
Genre(s): novel, film
Language(s): French

Raphaële Billetdoux made her literary debut when she was barely twenty with *Jeune fille en silence* (1971; A Quiet Young Girl), written with a fellowship from the Del Duca Foundation. This first novel recounts, in a semi-autobiographical fashion, episodes in the life of a young girl. The novel is uneven, with occasional awkwardness, the result of trying to achieve certain stylistic effects. Her second novel, *L'Ouverture des bras de l'homme* (1973; The Opening of a Man's Arms), was awarded the Prix Louis Vilmorin. *Prends garde à la douceur des choses* (Look Out for the Sweet Things), which won the Prix Interallie in 1976, treats the coming of age of a young girl and is more successful. In 1980, Billetdoux left literature for a time to experiment with other media. Her training in the cinema lead to the production of *La Femme-enfant* (Woman-child), which again takes up the story of a girl's entrance into the adult world. The film was among the winners at the Cannes Festival in 1980 and was distributed in the United States as well as Europe.

Billetdoux's more recent work reflects a surer mastery of style and a broadening in thematics. *Lettre d'excuse* (1981; Letter of Apology) is an epistolary novel tracing the disintegration of a marriage. Love, art, and friendship are all called into question as the wife slowly decides upon suicide. In *Mes Nuits sont plus belles que vos jours* (Night without Day), which won the Prix Renaudot in 1985, the male narrator picks up a woman at a cafe; their chance encounter engenders a brief liaison as well as the conversations which make up a novel in which violence and sensuality of the style reflect its theme.

Works

Jeune fille en silence (1971). *L'Ouverture des bras de l'homme* (1973). *Prends garde à la douceur des choses* (1976). *Lettre d'excuse* (1981). *Mes Nuits sont plus belles que vos jours* (1985).

Translations: *Night without Day* [Mes Nuits sont plus belles que vos jours], tr. Derek Mahon (1987).

Edith J. Benkov

Charlotte Johanna Birch-Pfeiffer

Born June 23, 1799, Stuttgart, Germany; died
August 25, 1868, Berlin
Genre(s): drama, novella, correspondence
Language(s): German

Charlotte Birch-Pfeiffer, author of seventy-four dramas, many of them highly sentimental or based on successful novels, exercised a major shaping influence upon the German-language theater of the mid-nineteenth century. She was born in 1799 in Stuttgart. When her literarily inclined father (a schoolmate of Schiller's, he supposedly is responsible for saving the manuscript of *Die Räuber* by hiding it in his mattress) went blind in 1809, the young girl read to him from the classics and in this manner obtained a solid literary education. Sharing her father's love of the theater, she made her stage debut at the Munich Isarthortheater in 1813, in part with the support of the Bavarian King Max Joseph. From 1818 to 1826 she was a member of the Munich Hoftheater, with guest appearances in Prague, Stuttgart, Kassel, Hannover, Berlin, Dresden, and Hamburg. In 1825 she married the Danish writer Christian Andreas Birch, with whom she had two children. From 1827 to 1830 she was a member of the Theater an der Wien (she did not succeed in joining the celebrated Viennese Burgtheater), from 1837 to 1842 the director of the Stadttheater in Zurich, and from 1844 until her death a member of the Berlin Hoftheater. Her activities as an actress take second place to her influence as a dramatist. Critics generally found her too pathetic and sentimental, but her plays were enormously successful with the theater-going public of her day, and she wrote highly effective dramatizations of the novels of Sir Walter Scott, Victor Hugo, George Sand, and Charlotte Brontë (her version of *Jane Eyre* won critical praise and was translated into English), among others. She wrote many popular family melodramas (the so-called *Rührstück*), such as *Mutter und Sohn* and *Eine Familie*. While some critics preferred to dismiss her work as "homemade herring salad on the stage menu" (*häuslicher Heringsalat an der Wirtstafel der Bühne*), none could deny the powerful influence she exerted on the theatrical practices of her time. Other, more sympathetic critics noted, "Let us learn from this woman instead of grumbling about her" ("Lassen Sie uns von dieser Frau lernen, statt über sie zu schimpfen"). The writings of Heinrich Laube, the renowned nineteenth-century German drama critic, director of the Viennese Burgtheater from 1849 to 1867 and playwright, make frequent mention of her and her works, attesting to the fact that Birch-Pfeiffer was an important figure in the history of the German-language theater during the nineteenth century.

Works

Gesammelte Dramatische Werke, 23 vols. (1863–1880). Of the seventy-four plays collected in these volumes, only two have been translated into English: *Twixt Axe and Crown* [Elizabeth, Prinzessin von England] (1870), and *Jane Eyre, or the Orphan of Lowo* [sic] (1870). *Gesammelte Novellen und Erzählungen*, 3 vols. (1863–65). *Charlotte von Birch-Pfeiffer und Heinrich Laube im Briefwechsel*, ed. Alexander von Weilen (1917).

Bibliography

Goedeke, Karl, *Grundriß der Geschichte der deutschen Dichtung*, ed. Carl Diesch, vol. 11, pt. 1 (Düsseldorf, 1951), pp. 96, 464–65. Hes, Else, *Charlotte Birch-Pfeiffer als Dramatikerin, Ein Beitrag zur Theatergeschichte des 19.Jh.s.* (Stuttgart, 1914.; diss., University of Breslau, 1913). Laube, Heinrich, "Charlotte Birch-Pfeiffer," in *Theaterkritiken und dramaturgische Aufsätze*, vol. 2 (Berlin, 1906), pp. 357–84. Laube, Heinrich, *Schriften über Theater*, ed. Deutsche Akademie der Künste zu Berlin., selected and intro. Eva Stahl-Wissen (Berlin, 1959), pp. 166, 168, 172, 201, 236–8, 265, 280. Richter, Karl, "Birch-Pfeiffer, Charlotte Johanna," in *Neue Deutsche Biographie*, vol. 2 (Berlin, 1955), pp. 252–253. Schauer, H., "Rührstück." *Reallexikon der deutschen Literaturgeschichte*, vol. 3 (1929), pp. 127–130. von Weilen, Alexander, "Karl Gutzow und Charlotte Birch-Pfeiffer, Eine Abrechnung," in *Beiträge zur Literatur- und Theatergeschichte (Festschrift Ludwig Geiger)* (Berlin, 1918), pp. 311–323. Ziersch, Roland, *Charlotte Birch-Pfeiffer als Darstellerin*. Diss., University of Munich, 1930.

Earl Jeffrey Richards

Georgette Bisdorff

Born 1944, Luxembourg
Genre(s): literary criticism, children's literature
Language(s): French

After completing her secondary school studies at the Lycée Robert-Schuman in Luxembourg, Georgette Bisdorff took up philosophy and literature, which she eventually gave up to become a schoolmistress; from 1970 to 1973 she was a free student at the University of Aix-en-Provence (France); she was also trained in France as a librarian.

At present she works as a schoolmistress in Luxembourg, does literary and art criticism, and writes tales for children. Georgette Bisdorff reviews with great subtlety those books on which she comments in the press; she stresses the variegated hues, the lights and shades of paintings whose particularities she studies. She is especially interested in collections of Luxembourg painters, and she is also an expert in the history of the *santons* (clay figures in the Christmas crib) of Provence (France).

For children she writes tales imbued with charming fantasy, blended, however, with touches of topical problems. She handles the

French language with remarkable mastery due to both long experience and deep love.

Works

Flocon de Neige et Autres Contes [Snowflake and Other Tales] (1983).

Translation: The Resistance of the Luxembourg People from 1940 to 1944, tr. Gino Candidi (1977).

Bibliography

Kieffer, Rosemarie, "La littérature féminine" [Women Writers], in Littérature luxembourgeoise de langue française [Luxembourg Literature in the French Language] (Sherbrooke; Quebec, 1980).
Kieffer, Rosemarie, "La langue et la littérature luxembourgeoises" [The Luxembourg Language and Literature], in Nouvelle Europe (1985), pp. 36, 48.

Rosemarie Kieffer and Liliane Stomp-Erpelding

Louise Cathrine Elisabeth Bjørnsen

(a.k.a. Elisabeth Martens)

Born April 9, 1824, Roholte, Denmark; died December 27, 1899, Copenhagen
Genre(s): novel
Language(s): Danish

With her novels depicting the promise, hopes, and resignation of talented, intelligent women, Louise Cathrine Elisabeth Bjørnsen earned contemporary recognition and a "faithful following of readers" (Dansk biografisk Leksikon, 2, 204). Bjørnsen chose to depict the intellectual woman who often lives on the fringe of society, working for others economically better situated in life and resigning herself to a cordial "understanding," a less-than-passionate married life. Bjørnsen's works deal with idealistic, hopeful young women who ultimately (and necessarily) settle for less than they envision and deserve and then pay an additional price in bitterness, lost illusions, and regret.

Louise Cathrine Elisabeth Bjørnsen was born in Roholte, Denmark, on April 9, 1824; she was the daughter of the parish priest in Kongsted, Frederik Cornelius Eberhard Bjørnsen (1781–1831), and Rebekka Adolphine Rabeholm (1786–1858). Bjørnsen's father died when she was still

very young, and her education, in housekeeping and literature, fell completely to her mother, Rebekka Rabeholm. Bjørnsen lived as a novelist until her death in Copenhagen on December 27, 1899; she never married (DbL2, 204). In 1855, Louise Bjørnsen made her literary début with Hvad er Livet? (What Is Life?) (Dansk Litteraturhistorie, 6, p. 137). Written under the pseudonym Elisabeth Martens, Hvad er Livet depicted "the position of the governess in society, familiar and intimate, but based on deprivation and insufficient employment opportunity for unmarried women" (Stig Dalager and Anne-Marie Mai, Danske kvindelige forfattere 1, 1983, p. 173). Hvad er Livet was an immediate success, followed by a second printing in 1857 and a third in 1881 (DLH, 6, p. 137). Hvad er Livet traces the lives of Anna, "clever and industrious, the very best student in school" (Dalager, 1, p. 178), and Mathilde who "lacks ability and industry but (uses) her social status (to avoid) the teacher's reprimands" (Dalager, 1, p. 178). Bjørnsen employs her characters Anna and Mathilde in order to sketch two types of education for young women: the "social" education of Mathilde and Anna's practical "knowledge and experience with the demands of living" (Dalager, 1, p. 177). Anna lives as a governess in the house of an affluent, influential family; she serves "partially as society dame, partially as servant, (always) condescendingly treated by the household" (DbL2, 204). Anna falls head over heels in love with a young painter, only to lose him to the favored, fortunate daughter of her "family"; Anna eventually marries "into the civil service class" (Dalager, 1, p. 175), resigning "the grand (romantic) love . . . to a secure marriage" (DLH, 6, p. 137). Hvad er Livet is a poignant account of a fate all too common for the daughters of the middle and poor classes. Reality for many such young women meant a large measure of resignation, bitterness, and disappointment.

Louise Bjørnsen's second novel, En Qvinde (1860; A Woman), also struck a responsive chord with the reading public (DbL, 2, 204); the work deals with the same theme as Hvad er Livet: resignation of hopes, dreams, and expectations. In En Qvinde, the protagonist, Thora, possesses "both the material and intellectual gifts for emancipation; she writes, performs, composes, reads scholarly journals" (*DLH*, 6, p. 137). Yet Thora's dreams and expectations come to naught; the narrator reveals and "corrects Thora's faulty vision of the future," and the central character "ends in complete resignation, with religious and social engagement as a replacement for the illusions of her youth" (*DLH*, 6, p. 137). Both *Hvad er Livet* and *En Qvinde* reflect the moral tone, the bitterness, and the resignation of the first novels of Danish women writers (*DbL2*, 204). Bjørnsen continued her literary career with *Fortællinger* (1866; Stories); *Hvad behøvedes der for at leve?* (1869; What Was Necessary to Live?); *Fra Fortid og Nutid* (1878; From the Past and Present); and, *Til Høstaftenerne* (1893; For Autumn Evenings). Such works did not win as much acclaim as her two earlier novels, but they did attract the attention of a firmly loyal circle of Bjørnsen readers (*DbL2*, 204). Two additional novels, *Sangerinder* (1876; Songstresses) and *To Søstre* (1890; Two Sisters), are important because of Bjørnsen's stylistic *rapprochement* to the social drama of the 1870s (*Sangerinder*) and because of the author's skillful, accurate portrayal of a young woman in love (*To Søstre*).

Louise Bjørnsen's novels won both contemporary audience and, later on, many steady, loyal readers. Her works, *Hvad er Livet* and *En Qvinde* among them, describe the hopes, dreams, and disappointments of many talented women bravely but idealistically facing life, work, and love on their own.

Works

Hvad er Livet (1855; 1857; 1881). *En Qvinde* (1860). *Fortællinger* (1866). *Hvad behøvedes der for at leve?* (1869). *Sangerinder* (1876). *Fra Fortid og Nutid* (1878). *To Søstre* (1890). *Til Høstaftenerne* (1893).

Bibliography

Dalager, Stig, and Anne-Marie Mai, *Danske kvindelige forfattere 1: Fra Sophie Brahe til Mathilde Fibiger. Udvikling og perspektiv.* 2 vols (Copenhagen, 1983). *Dansk biografisk Leksikon*, 2, 3 ed. (1979). *Dansk Litteraturhistorie*, 6, *Dannelse, folkelighed, individualisme 1848–1901* (Copenhagen, 1985).

Lanae Hjortsvang Isaacson

Marion Blaise

Born 1955, Luxembourg
Genre(s): poetry, essay
Language(s): French

After completing her secondary-school education in Luxembourg, Marion Blaise pursued her studies of modern languages and literature at the Universities of Strasbourg, Metz, and Paris as well as at the Miami University of Oxford (Ohio) in the United States of America. At present she is a grammar school teacher in Luxembourg and an assistant professor of French linguistics at the university level.

Marion Blaise carried out deep research into linguistics, and this special schooling has marked her lyrical poetry. She has a very strong sense of the denotation of words and of the structure of language. Her own experience—her discoveries all along her travels, the human encounters that she was lucky to make—finds expression in a lyrical language that she puts into a poetry of striking plasticity and as pure as a precious stone. Marion Blaise contributes to a certain number of literary reviews. As an essayist she wrote an excellent study on "the fantastic elements in the prose of the Luxembourg poet Paul Palgen."

Works

Le fantastique dans la prose de Paul Palgen [The Fantastic Elements in the Prose of Paul Palgen] (1980). "Literature luxembourgeoise de langue française" [Luxembourgish Literature in the French Language], collective work pub. by Rosemarie Kieffer. *Soleils mouvants* [Moving Suns] (1984).

Rosemarie Kieffer and Liliane Stomp-Erpelding

Anna Blaman

(see: Johanna Petronella Vrugt)

Marie-Thérèse de Solms Blanc

(a.k.a. Thérèse Bentzon)

Born September 21, 1840, Seine-Port (Seine-et-Oise), France; died February 1907, Paris
Genre(s): criticism, novel, short story,
*   textbook, translations, travel observations*
Language(s): French

Marie-Thérèse de Solms Blanc, who used her mother's maiden name, Bentzon, as a pen name, was a novelist and "grande dame" well known in bourgeois and aristocratic circles during the late nineteenth century. Three of her novels (*Un Remords*, 1878; *Tony*, 1884; *Constance*, 1891) received recognition from France's literary "immortals" of the Académie Française, but she did not gain great critical acclaim or enjoy an enduring literary reputation.

Bentzon's family background was aristocratic: her maternal grandparents were the Marquis and Marquise de Vitry, although her mother was the child of the marquise's first marriage to a Danish army officer; her mother married the Count de Solms. Thérèse de Solms grew up in the chateau of the Marquis de Vitry, who was not rich but was nonetheless regarded as the protector of a nearby village. She and her brother were educated by their mother and an English governess. Her command of English later enabled her to interpret American society and literature to a French audience. Married at age sixteen to Alexandre Blanc, a friend of her father, she became a mother at seventeen and separated from her husband at nineteen. Nearly impoverished and obliged to earn a living, she became a writer. Her stepfather, the Count d'Aure, an equerry to Napoleon III, introduced her to George Sand, who, in turn, recommended her to the editor of the *Revue des Deux Mondes*, the prestigious literary review favored by polite society and those aspiring to be recognized by it. Having gained experience by writing for newspapers and minor journals, she began in 1871 to publish translations, articles about foreign authors, many of her own novels, and travel observations in the *Revue des Deux Mondes*.

Typically, Bentzon wrote one novel a year. *Constance*, one of her few novels issued in several editions, was about the dilemma of a heroine caught up in the contemporary religious and political controversy over divorce. Divorce and remarriage after divorce had been legalized by the French Revolution, outlawed by the Bourbon Restoration in 1816, and relegalized in 1884. Constance's moral objections to divorce made her consider becoming the mistress of a man divorced through no fault of his own; she was saved from disgrace by her suitor's scruples and a Protestant pastor's advice. Bentzon herself was a devout Catholic and shared the conservative political leanings of Ferdinand Brunetière, chief editor of the *Revue des Deux Mondes* as of 1893. Her novels chronicled French mores but not in the fashion of literary realists. Contemporaries described her work as "moral idealism," a term also appropriate for her textbook, *Causeries de morale pratique* (1899). Intended for girls' secondary schools, the book gave advice to pupils whose origins were rarely humble. Thus Bentzon and her coauthor, Mlle Chevalier, counseled bourgeois girls to learn to manage a household and servants, to perfect conversational skills and musical talents so as to preside successfully over social occasions, and to regard intellectual pursuits undertaken for the sheer joy of learning as vastly superior to those chosen only to make money. They did warn, however, that young women should consider preparing for work in case financial disaster struck. Discussing the religious duties of women, the authors also tried to accommodate the anticlericalism of many middle-class husbands by stating that men could be moral without actually practicing a religion; they did not indicate that the same was possible for women.

In 1893 Bentzon made her first visit to the United States and Canada, and in 1897, a second. From these travels emerged books about American mores. Especially successful was a volume on American women, *Les Américaines chez elles* (1895). Admiring the independence of many American women and aware of her own distress as a teenaged wife, she suggested that French girls could profit from more contact with the world and men before marriage. Among the American and English authors whom Bentzon tried to make familiar to the French through translations and critical essays were Mark Twain, Hamlin Garland, Henry James, Walt Whitman, Robert Louis Stevenson, Rider Haggard, Sarah

Orne Jewett, Bret Harte, Sidney Lanier, Edward Bellamy, Rudyard Kipling, and the antifeminist Mrs. Humphrey Ward. Visits to England, Russia, and Germany also provided material for her writing. Shortly before her death, Bentzon received the Legion of Honor.

Works

Criticism: *Littérature et moeurs étrangères* [Foreign Literature and Customs] (1882). *Les Nouveaux Romanciers américains* [New American Novelists] (1885).

Novels and Stories: *Le Roman d'un muet* [The Novel of a Mute] (1868). *Un Divorce* [A Divorce] 1872). *Armelle* (1872). *La Vocation de Louise Madelette* [The Vocation of Louise Madelette] (1873). *Une Vie manquée* [A Life Lacking] (1874). *Le Violon de Job; Sous le masque; Sang-Mêlé; Armelle* [The Violin of Job; Under the Mask; Blood Mingled; Armelle] (1875). *Un Châtiment* [A Punishment] (1876). *La Grande Saulière; Ma tante Hermine* (1877). *La Petite Perle; Désirée Turpin* [The Little Pearl; Désirée Turpin] (1878). *Un Remords* [Remorse] (1878). *L'Obstacle* [The Obstacle] (1879). *Georgette* (1880). *Yette, histoire d'une jeune créole* [Yette, Story of a Young Creole] (1880). *Amour perdu: Galatée, Jacinte, Yvonne* [Lost Love] (1881). *La Veuvage d'Aline* [Aline's Widowhood] (1881). *Miss Jane; Pierre Cervin* (1882). *Le Retour* [The Return] (1882). *Le Meurtre de Bruno Galli; Eva Brown* [The Murder of Bruno Galli; Eva Brown] (1883). *Tony* (1885). *Pierre Casse-Cou* [Pierre Dare-Devil] (1886). *Figure étrange; Un Gascon* [Strange Appearance; A Gascon] (1886). *Une Conversion; Exotique; La Dot de Katel* [A Conversion; Exotic; The Dowry of Katel] (1886). *Emancipée* [Emancipated Woman] (1887). *Le Mariage de Jacques; Un Accident; Le Plat de Taillac* [The Marriage of Jacques; An Accident; The Dish of Taillac] (1888). *Tentée* [Tempted] (1889). *Constance* (1891). *Le Parrain d'Annette* [The Godfather of Annette] (1893). *Geneviève Delmas* (1893). *Jacqueline* (1893, 1895). *Une double Epreuve* [A Double Test] (1896). *Malentendus* [Misunderstandings] (1900). *Tchevolek* (1900). *Au-dessus de l'abîme; Jalouse; A Trianon* [Above the Abyss; Jealous; At Trianon] (1902).

Textbook: *Causeries de morale pratique* [Talks on Practical Behavior] (1899).

Travel Observations: *Notes de voyage: Les Américaines chez elles* [The Condition of Women in the United States: A Traveler's Notes] (1895). *Choses et gens d'Amérique* [Things and People in America] (1898). *Notes de voyage: Nouvelle France et Nouvelle Angleterre* [A Traveler's Notes: New France and New England] (1899). *Femmes d'Amérique* [Women of America] (1900). *Questions américaines* [American Questions] (1901). *Promenades en Russie* [Promenades in Russia] (1903).

Bibliography

Bertaux, Mario, "Biographical Sketch of Madame Blanc," in Bentzon [Blanc], *The Condition of Women in the United States, A Traveler's Notes,* tr. Abby Langdon Alger (Boston, 1895; rpt., New York, 1972), pp. 7–18. Betham-Edwards, Matilda, *Friendly Faces of Three Nationalities* (Freeport, N.Y., 1969; 1st ed., 1911), pp. 215–229. Fields, Mrs. James T., "Notable Women: Mme. Blanc ('Th. Bentzon')." *The Century Magazine* 66 (1903): 134–39. Leguay, P., *Dictionnaire de biographie française,* vol. 5 (Paris, 1951). West, Joan M., "America and American Literature in the Essays of Th. Bentzon: Creating the Image of an Independent Cultural Identity." *History of European Ideas* 8 (1987): 521–35.

Linda L. Clark

Ana Blandiana

Born 1942, Timiş Dara, Romania
Genre(s): Poetry, short story, essay, journalism, children's literature, translation
Language(s): Romanian

Ana Blandiana is the most important representative of a generation which is referred to in Romanian literary criticism under the name of "the generation of the struggle against inertia."

She studied in Oradea and Cluj graduating in Philology in 1967, worked as an editor with *Viaţa studenţească* and *Amfiteatru* and, since 1975, as a librarian at the Institute of Fine Arts in Bucharest. She has been for a long time a regular columnist in the Writers' Union weekly magazine *România literară* and made her poetic debut in 1964 with the jubilant, intensely vital volume *Persoana întîi plural* (First Person Plural). This was followed by, at a regular pace, the volumes *Călcîiul vulnerabil* (1966; The Vulnerable Heel), and *A treia taină* (1969; The Third Sacrament), in which the voice of the poet is energetic and severe, proclaiming the Midas-like destiny of the writer ("All that I touch transforms into words") and acknowledging with lucid fervor and pain the "great law of maculation," which informs life, love, and reflection as well. In 1970 Blandiana was awarded the Poetry prize of the Writers' Union for *A treia taină* and published the first retrospective selection of poems—*Cincizeci de poeme* (Fifty Poems) which brought her the Mihai Eminescu Academy prize for Poetry. The themes of sensual love, mature poetic consciousness, sin and purification, sarcasm and suffering combine in the strong volumes *Octombrie, noiembrie, decembrie* (1972; October, November, December), *Poezii* (1974; Poems), *Somnul din somn* (1977; The Sleep in Sleep), *Poeme* (1978; Poems, a retrospective selection published in the prestigious collection "Cele mai frumoase poezii" [The most beautiful poems] and prefaced by Al. Philippide), and *Ora de nisip* (1983; The Hour of Sand).

Blandiana is a unique singer of the couple, with its agonizing affective and cognitive complementations, blind spots, and atrophies ("You see only the moon,/ I see only the sun,/ You yearn for the sun,/ I yearn for the moon,/ But we stay back to back,/ Bones united long ago,/ Our blood carries rumours/ From one heart to the other/ . . ./ How equal are we?/ Are we to die together or will one of us carry,/ For a time/ The corpse of the other stuck to our side/ Infecting with death, slowly, too slowly,/ Or perhaps never to die completely/ But carry for an eternity/ The sweet burden of the other,/ Atrophied forever,/ The size of a hunch,/ The size of a wart . . ./ Oh, only we know the longing/ To look into each other's eyes/ And so at last understand,/ But we stay back to back,/ Grown like two branches / . . .")

At the same time, the poet put into words Romania's unnoticed "transhumance" (or "emigration") to sleep, dream, and *încânemoarte* (stillnotdeath), its gradual exit from human communication, its systematic destruction by "venomous winters," under moons "as precise as the handcuff(s)," its "almost happy despair." Blandiana's verse is, by now, one of the best introductions to a contemporary perception of existence in Romania ("It's snowing with malice,/ The snow falls with hate/ Above waters icy with loathing,/ Above orchards blossomed by evil,/ Above embittered birds who suffer,/ . . ./ Only I know/ That once a flurry of snow/ Was love at the beginning.—/ It's so late/ And hideously it's snowing,/ And my mind's stopped working/ So I wait/ To be of use/ To this wolf that's starving.")

In December 1984, Blandiana published in the students' magazine *Amfiteatru* a group of poems which were widely circulated and intensely commented on throughout Romania. The authorities reacted by retrograding the poetry editor of the magazine and depriving the free-lance author of the right to publish for several months. The best known among the incriminated poems came to be the poignant "Children's Crusade" in which the poet rose her voice against the official natalist policy forced upon Romanian women at times of economic and political disaster ("An entire people not yet born, but doomed for birth,/ already in columns before being born, fetus next to fetus . . ./ An entire nation which cannot see, cannot hear,/ cannot understand, but which advances through/ the cramps of woman's body by the blood and/ womb of mothers which have not been asked.") Less explicit in its exasperated invocation of the common places of daily misery, the companion poem "Totul" (Everything) remains an expression of the Eastern European ghetto in which the political connotations of each of the members of the enumeration are hard to understand for the Western readers who will perceive the hiatus between two different worlds rather than the blunt Romanian context to which Blandiana refers (". . . leaves, words, tears,/ cans, cats,/ streetcars from time to time, queueing for flour/ (with) ladybugs, empty bottles, speeches,/ eternal T.V. images,/ Colorado bugs, gas,/ little flags, the European championship (soccer) cup,/ buses running with propane cylinders,/ same old portraits,/ apples not accepted abroad,/ newspapers, rolls,/ fake oil, carnations,/ airport welcomes, *cico* lemonade, (chocolate) sticks,/ Bucharest salami, diet yogurt,/ Gypsy women selling Kent cigarettes, Crevedia eggs,/ rumours,/ the Saturday T.V. serial,/ surrogate coffee,/ the peoples' struggle for peace, the choirs,/ the yield crop, Gerovital; the cops on Calea Victoriei,/ the

"Singing of Romania," adidas,/ the Bulgarian compote, political jokes, Ocean fish,/ everything.")

A recent poem continues this political pamphlet trend in Blandiana's poetry. It speaks about President Ceausescu in the frame of the ancient (and itself problematic) Romanian myth of "Master builder Manole." Like Manole, who walled his wife and child in the church he was erecting in order to make sure the construction endures through time, Ceausescu the church-destroyer is paradoxically viewed as a ". . . builder of our private inferno . . ./ Grand master surpassing all the others/ Not through his knowledge,/ but through the exasperation to build" who has managed to wall in a whole nation.

A volume regrouping the articles Blandiana had published under the rubric "Antijurnal" (Anti-journal) in the literary magazine *Contemporanul* appeared in 1970 under the title *Calitatea de martor* (The Quality of Witness). It marked the beginning of a sustained essayistic and short-story writing activity, followed by the volumes *Eu scriu, tu scrii, el ea scrie* (1976; I Write, You Write, He, She Writes), *Cele patru aotimpuri* (1977; The Four Seasons), *Cea mai frumoasă dintre lumile posibile* (1982; The Most Beautiful of All Possible Worlds), and *Coridoare de oglinzi* (1984; Corridors of Mirrors); for this volume Blandiana was granted the 1984 Journalism prize of the Writers Union.

Blandiana's prose, centered upon moral meditation and the quest for superior transparence, raises many of the acute ethical questions facing Romanian intellectuals today. It speaks in terms which deserve future analyses about the strength to persist in not winning (*Calitatea de martor*) and exposes the reader to contrastive perceptions of Europe, Romania, and the United States by a traveller whose soul stays poetic (*Cea mai frumoasă dintre lumile posibile*) or to the eternal dilemmas of choosing between speech and silence, acting and bearing, winning and losing which ground not only Blandiana's art but also her generation's basic encounter with life.

Ana Blandiana translated into Romanian works by Michel de Ghelderode.

Works

Persoana întîi plural [First Person Plural] (1964). *Călcîiul vulnerabil* [The Vulnerable Heel] (1966). *A treia taină* [The Third Sacrament] (1969). *Cincizeci de poeme* [Fifty Poems] (1970). *Calitatea de martor* [The Quality of Witness] (1970; 2nd ed., 1972). *Octombrie, noiembrie, decembrie* [October, November, December] (1972). *Poezii* [Poems] (1974). *Eu scriu, tu scrii, el, ea scrie* [I Write, You Write, He, She Writes] (1976). *Somnul din somn* [The Sleep in Sleep] (1977). *Cele patru anotimpuri* [The Four Seasons] (1977). *Poeme* [Poems], preface by Al. Philippide (1978). *Cea mai frumoasă dintre lumile posible* [The Most Beautiful of All Possible Worlds] (1978). *Ora de nisip* [Hour of Sand] (1983). [With Romulus Rusan], *Coridoare de oglinzi* [Corridors of Mirrors] (1984). *Convorbiri subiective* [Subjective Conversations] 1975).

Translations: Bosquet, Alain, ed., *Anthologie de la poésie roumaine.* (1968; "Elegie de dimineaţă"/ "Pastel de matin"; "Fii înţelept"/"Sois sage"; and "Din clipa . . ."/"C'est à partir . . ." tr. Claude Sernet; "Ar trebui"/"il faudrait" tr. Alain Bosquet). De Micheli, Mario, ed. and tr., *Poeti romeni del dopoguerra* (1967; "Triptic"/"Trittico"). *Literatura rumana contemporánea*, in *Union*, special issue dedicated to contemporary Romanian literature (1968; "Ochii statuilor"/"Los ojos de las estatuas," "Calmă"/"Cálma" tr. Belkis Cuza Malé). Mesker, Stefan, ed., *Werk uit Roemenie. Poëzie* (1966; "Elegie de dimineaţă"/"Ochtendpastel"). *Poesía rumana actual*, special issue, *Cuadernos Hispanoamericanos* 221 (1968) ("Ochii statuilor"/ "Los ojos de las estatuas"; "Iarba"/"La hierba"). *Poètes et prosateurs roumains d'aujourd'hui*, special issue, *Marginales*. Revue bimestrielle des Idées, des Arts et des Lettres 23 (1968): 119–120 ("Elegie de dimineaţă"/"Pastel du matin"; "Din clipa . . ."/ "Dès l'instant . . ."). Sarov, Taško, ed. and tr., *Antologija na romanskata poezija* (1972; "Pieta"; "Goană"/"Gonenje"). *Signos* 1, issue dedicated to Romania (1970) ("Iarba"/"La hierba"; "Ora spitalelor"/"Hora de los hospitales"). Špoljanskaja, D., ed., *Šal'noe leto—Molodye pisateli Rumynii. Stihi i proza.* (1968; "Restul pe masă"/"Sdača na stole"; "Fii înţelept"/"Bud' mudrym"; "În liniştea mare"/"Spokojstvie"; "Ştiu, puritatea . . ."/"Kto zaet . . ."; "Ora spitalelor"/"Čas bol'nic"; "Pînă la stele"/ "Do zvezd" tr. V. Kornilova). *30 poeţi români/ 30 poètes roumains* (1978; "Genealogie"/"Généalogie" and "Din auster şi din naivitate"/"L'austère et la naïveté" tr. Irina Radu).

English Translations: Deletant, Andrea, and Brenda Walker, tr., *Silent Voices. An Anthology of Contemporary Romanian Women Poets* (1986), pp. 21–36 (poems from *Octombrie, noiembrie, decembrie*, 1972; *Somnul din somn*, 1977, and *Ora de nisip*, 1983). Duţescu, Dan, ed. and tr., *Romanian Poems* (1982), pp. 231–233 ("Fall," "Herder of Snowflakes," and "Which One of Us"). Emery, George, ed., *Contemporary East European Poetry* (1983), pp. 344–347 ("From a Village," "Song," and "Dance in the Rain" tr. Irina Livezeanu; "Links" tr. Michael Impey). Impey, Michael H., tr., "Three Romanian Poems—Ana Blandiana; Constanţa Buzea; Gabriela Melinescu. Translated from the Romanian by M.H.I.," *Books Abroad* 50, 1 (1976): 34–35. MacGregor-Hastie, Roy, ed. and tr., *Anthology of Contemporary Romanian Poetry* (1969) ("Din clipa . . ."/"From That Moment . . .").

Bibliography

Dimisianu, Gabriel, "Calitatea de martor," in *Valori actuale* (Bucharest, 1974), pp. 90–92. Dorian, Marguerite, "Ana Blandiana. *Cea mai frumoasă dintre lumile posibile*," *World Literature Today* (Fall 1972). Golopentia, Sanda, "Încânemoartea." *Lupta* 91 (December 15, 1987): 14. Iorgulescu, Mircea, *Al doilea rond* (Bucharest, 1976), pp. 285–289. Pop, Ion, *Poezia unei generaţii* (Bucharest, 1973). Popa, Marian, *Dicţionar de literatură română contemporană*, 2nd ed. (Bucharest, 1977), pp. 98–99. Raicu, Lucian, "Ana Blandiana—Spiritual şi terestru;—*Calitatea de martor*," in *Critica—formă de viaţă* (Bucharest, 1976), pp. 297–305.

Sanda Golopentia

Agnes Blannbekin

Born Plambach, Austria; died March 10, 1315, Vienna, Austria
Genre(s): revelations
Language(s): German, Latin

According to an early note in the Neresheim manuscript, Agnes Blannbekin was the daughter of a peasant in Plambach in the diocese of St. Pölten in Lower Austria. The name of this location probably was the source of her second name.

Very early, at the age of seven, she began strict fasting and secretly gave her own food away to the poor. As soon as possible she joined the Beguines and became a nun of the Franciscan Tertiary Order in Vienna. During the church services and periods of silent prayer she began to experience revelations, but not as a union with God in love, which would have been the typical mystical experience. Instead she heard heavenly voices, which conveyed to her insight and understanding of spiritual things, which is strikingly paralleled by Robert of Boron's *Estoire dou Graal*. Probably she was not a mystic in the proper sense of the word and did not follow the typical meditations, but she had a life full of heavenly grace and favor. Repeatedly she expressed the feeling of sweetness through eating the Eucharist and kissing the altar. She also claimed to feel the presence of Christ's foreskin in her mouth. Special favors by God were the *imber lacrimarum*, a rain of tears onto her at all times of the day, sudden appearances of light at times of need, and the appearance of Christ with a lamb during mass who kisses her on her cheeks. At Christmas night she could hold the Christ child next to her heart, and often she obtained special grace for other people. Her revelations were probably written down by her confessor, who might be identical with the person Ermenricus, who signed his name at the end of the manuscript containing her revelations. These revelations only demonstrate a chronological order according to the liturgical year. The theological knowledge derives, in all likelihood, not from Agnes herself but from the confessor, even though she claims to have been literate. Some of the almost scandalous aspects of her revelations, such as the reference to Christ's foreskin, his nude appearance and that of monks, or the transformation of bad priests into horrible animals, caused an immediate protest by the Jesuits when the manuscript was published in 1731. Subsequently, it was quickly confiscated; some copies, however, have survived. The only extant manuscript, Codex 384, is kept in the Cistercian convent at Zwettle. It breaks off at chapter 189. Another manuscript, which could have contained her revelations, was lost in a fire at the Strasburg library in 1870.

Works

Ven. Agnetis Blannbekin, que sub Rudolpho Habspurgico & I. Austriacis Impp. Wiennae floruit, Vita et Revelationes Anonymo Ordd. F.F. min. e Celebri Conv. S. Crucis Wiennensis, ejusdem Virg. Confess . . . , ed. Bernardus Pez (1731). A new edition is being prepared by Peter Dinzelsbacher: Leben und Offenbarung der Wiener Begine Agnes Blannbekin (a1315), Göppingen (1989–1890), GAG 419. A selection of excerpts from Pez can be found in J. Chmel, Kleinere historische Mitteilungen III (1849), pp. 46–100.

Bibliography

Dinzelbacher, Peter, Vision und Visionsliteratur im Mittelalter (Stuttgart, 1981). Dinzelbacher, Peter, "Die Vita et Revelationes der Wiener Begine Agnes Blannbekin (a1315) im Rahmen der Viten- und Offenbarungsliteratur ihrer Zeit." Frauenmystik im Mittelalter, ed. P. Dinzelbacher and D.R. Bauer (Ostfildern, Stuttgart, 1985), pp. 152–177. Planizza, O., Agnes Blannbekin, eine österreichische Schwärmerin aus dem 13. Jahrhundert, nach den Quellen (Zurich, 1898). Ruh, Kurt, "Agnes Blannbekin," in Die deutsche Literatur des Mittelalters, Verfasserlexikon, 2nd rev., ed. Kurt Ruh et al., vol. 1 (Berlin–New York, 1978), cols. 887–890. Rupprich, H., Das Wiener Schrifttum des ausgehenden Mittelalters, Sitzungsberichte der Österreichischen Akademie der Wissenschaften, Philosophisch-historische Klasse 228/5 (Vienna, 1954), pp. 40–45. Strauss, R., Studien zur Mystik in Oesterreich, mit besonderer Berücksichtigung von Agnes Blannbekin. Ph.D. diss., Vienna, 1948. Tschulik, W., Wilbirg und Agnes Blannbekin. Ph.D. diss., Vienna, 1925. von Görres, Johann Joseph, Die christliche Mystik, vol. II (Munich-Regensburg, 1836; 2nd ed., 1879), pp. 242–245.

Albrecht Classen

Karen (Tanne) Christence Dinesen Blixen-Finecke

(see: Isak Dinesen)

Marion Bloem

Born August 24, 1952, Arnhem, The
   Netherlands
Genre(s): novel
Language(s): Dutch

Marion Bloem was born of an Indonesian mother and a Dutch father. In 1983 she published a very remarkable autobiographical novel that has since become a pocket best-seller: Geen gewoon Indisch meisje (Not a Common Indonesian Girl). It was followed in 1987 by Lange reizen, korte liefdes (Long Journeys, Short Loves), in which the female main character is torn between a volatile surrender to amorous looks and a longing for emotional autarchy. During her studies—she started working as a clinical psychologist in 1976—Bloem staged a play for Amnesty International on political prisoners in Indonesia. She was first known as a writer of children's books (for the 11-plus age group), dealing mainly with the bodily and cultural awareness of adolescent girls: e.g., De Geheime Plek (1980; The Secret Spot) and Brieven van Souad (1986; Letters from Souad). Women at that age of life is one of the subjects of her scientific publications—some of them written with her husband Ivan Wolffers, a physician. She also shot a few television documentaries and short movies that underline her major concerns—the ambivalence of social, sexual, and ethnical identity and the problems of racism and discrimination linked in a pluricultural society. Bloem's nervous style is based on alert associations of an often lyrical shortness.

Works

De Geheime Plek [The Secret Spot] (1980). Geen gewoon Indisch meisje [Not a Common Indonesian Girl] (1983). Brieven van Souad [Letters from Souad] (1986). Lange reizen, korte liefdes [Long Journeys, Short Loves] (1987).

Bibliography

Dornseiffer, S., Lexicon van de jeugdliteratuur (1986). Meulenbelt, A., Wie weegt de woorden, interviews (1985), pp. 57–73.

Frank Joostens

Klara Blum

(a.k.a. Dschu Bai-Lan)

Born 1904, Czernowitz, Russia
Genre(s): poetry, novel
Language(s): German

Klara Blum studied psychology and literature in Vienna and immigrated to Moscow, where she lived as teacher, translator, and journalist from 1934 to 1945. In 1938, she married a Chinese communist there and later left with him to China, where she became a citizen in 1952. Since 1947, she has been teaching at universities in Canton and Nanking. Klara Blum's poetry and prose is didactic and historical. Some of her works are adaptations of Chinese epics and folk culture.

Works

Die Antwort (1939). Erst recht (1939). Wir entscheiden alles (1940). Donauballaden (1942). Schlachtfeld und Erdball (1944). Der Hirte und die Weberin (1951). Li Dji, Wang Gue und Li Hsiang Hsiang (1954). Das Lied von Hong Kong (1959). Der weite Weg (1960).

Bibliography

Brinker-Gabler, Gisela, *Deutsche Dichterinnen* (Frankfurt, 1986). *Deutsches Literatur-Lexikon* (1968 edition).

Ute Marie Saine

Ilse Blumenthal-Weiss

Born October 14, 1899, Berlin-Schöneberg,
Germany; died August 10, 1987,
Greenwich, Connecticut
Genre(s): poetry
Language(s): German

Ilse Blumenthal-Weiss has only very recently begun to receive recognition as a poet, although her first postwar collection appeared in 1954. Since she failed to leave Europe and spent the war years in a concentration camp, she did not fit the standard definition of an "exile poet" and, accordingly, was not included in the numerous scholarly studies of exile literature. Now, however, her poetry is coming to be acknowl-

edged as one of the most poignant memorials to the victims of the Holocaust.

Blumenthal-Weiss, the daughter of Gottlieb Weiss, the owner of a large clothing store, and Hedwig Weiss-Brock, led an active and eventful life in pre-Hitler Germany. She earned a diploma as a physical education teacher, traveled extensively, corresponded with Rilke, and published a volume of poetry, *Gesicht und Maske* (1929; Face and Mask). She married the dentist Herbert Blumenthal in 1920. In 1937 she fled to Holland, where she remained until being deported to Theresienstadt in 1944. Her husband and son Peter died in concentration camps. After the war Blumenthal-Weiss and her daughter Miriam immigrated to the United States. For many years she lived in New York, where she worked as a librarian at the Leo Baeck Institute.

In the verse of *Das Schlüßelwunder* (1954; The Key Miracle) and *Mahnmal* (1957; Memorial), traditional forms predominate, and the content is with few exceptions based on the Holocaust. In spite of the general similarities, there is a wide variety of form (blank verse and numerous stanzaic and rhyme patterns), tone (from satiric to elegiac), and perspective (personal and universal, religious, humanistic, and, in a broad sense, political). *Ohnesarg* (1984; Coffinless) is also dominated by the memory of the Holocaust, but the form and style of the poems are less traditional: most are written in a laconic free verse. This book also contains an interesting factual account of the author's experiences during the war.

Blumenthal-Weiss will be remembered as one of the few survivors of a concentration camp to memorialize the victims of the Holocaust in German verse. Although not a prolific poet, her wide range of thematic variations and poetic forms is reflective of the variety of responses to the Holocaust.

Works

Gesicht und Maske (1929). Das Schlüsselwunder: Gedichte (1954). Mahnmal: Gedichte aus dem KZ (1957). Begegnungen mit Else Lasker-Schueler, Nelly Sachs, Leo Baeck, Martin Buber (1977). Ohnesarg: Gedichte und ein dokumentarischer Bericht (1984).

Jerry Glenn

Anne-Marie Fiquet du Bocage née La Page

Born October 22, 1710, Rouen, France; died
August 8, 1802, Paris
Genre(s): poetry, drama, letters, travel writing
Language(s): French

The life and professional literary career of the celebrated Mme Bocage records one of the most privileged examples of female achievement and notoriety in the eighteenth century.

Unlike so many literary women of the early-modern era, Bocage enjoyed the distinct advantages of a comfortable and enlightened family background, formal education in the liberal arts, a supportive and literary spouse, and opportunities to benefit from the work of her contemporaries through extensive travel and the cultural exposure of the salon world. She reportedly was also a great beauty and gifted conversationalist. The motto of her admirers was "*Forma Venus, arte Minerva*" ("A Venus in form, a Minerva in art"). Voltaire, an ally, called her "La Sappho de Normandie." Fontenelle and Clairaut were also enthusiastic promoters of her work.

Bocage was born into a well-established, bourgeois family of Rouen, the La Pages. Her father, a successful official with the Department of Commerce, encouraged the precocious Bocage from an early age to develop her obvious aptitude for writing, especially poetry. After formal training at an exclusive Parisian convent, Bocage married, at the age of seventeen, Pierre-Joseph Fiquet du Bocage, an established poet-translator with special interests in English literature (see his *Melanges*, 3 vols., 1751; and his *Lettres*, 2 vols., 1752). These two devotees of the contemporary cultural scene became well known throughout the Rouen arts community. Around 1734, they began to spend about eight months of each year in Paris, where their custom was to open up their house one night each week to the literati of the city. The Bocage salon in Paris attracted French, British, American, Italian, and German writers and intellectuals. Jean-François Marmontel, a chronicler of eighteenth-century salon life, complained, however, that the Bocage salon lacked the color and verve of other contemporary salons.

In addition to their salon activities, the Bocages traveled throughout England, Holland, and Italy. Mme Bocage, in her diverting letters to her sister, provides a good account of their travels, and she also documents the international recognition given her and her husband. This particular body of literature shows Mme Bocage to be a skilled and entertaining epistolarist and valuable travel-writer, whose eye for foreign manners and morals compares most favorably with that of her celebrated English contemporaries in the genre—Mrs. Thrale, Lady Mary Wortley Montagu, and Celia Fiennes.

Mme Bocage did not rush into the public light of professional authorship, but rather launched her career in her mid-thirties, after first having benefited from the guidance of parents, educators, spouse, and distinguished friends, and from extensive travel and cultural exposure. It was not until 1746, at the age of thirty-six, that Mme Bocage distinguished herself as a literary professional. In that year, she won the First Prize for Poetry from The Academy of Rouen for her verse "De influence mutuel des beaux-arts et des sciences" ("On the Mutual Influence of the Fine Arts & the Sciences"). Bocage's maiden success was followed by her *Le paradis terrestre* (1748), a poem inspired by John Milton's great epic *Paradise Lost*. Her *Paradis*, cast as an epilogue to Milton's poem, was harshly criticized by the German writer Friedrich Melchior Grimm as a cold, servile imitation of its English master. Johann Christoph Gottsched was more supportive. In his *Anmuthige Celehrsamketi* (1754), he instances Bocage's poem as an example of the equality of the female mind. Other contemporary supporters of Bocage's work, outside of France, included the Spanish writer Ignacio de Luzan (*Memorias literarias de Paris*, 1750) and Josefa Amar y Borbon ("Discuso," *Mem. Lit.*, 32, 1786). Bocage's Miltonic imitation was followed by another work, also inspired by a great English poet, Alexander Pope, whose *Temple of Fame* (1715) Bocage adapted in her *Temple de la Renommee* (1749).

One of Bocage's principal longer works, and the one most known today, especially by feminists, is her play *Les Amazones* (1749), performed by the Comediens Ordinaire du Roi eleven times in July and August of 1749. Al-

141

though it was widely translated (into Italian, 1756; into German, 1762), Bocage's *Amazones* was only a middling success. Precedents for the play's theme, gynecocracy (the rule of woman), existed in the writings of the late medieval French feminist Christine de Pisan, as well as in the plays of several seventeenth-century English male playwrights—Fletcher (*Sea Voyage*, 1622), Howard (*Woman's Conquest*, 1670 and *Six Days Adventure*, 1671), D'Urfey (*Commonwealth of Women*, 1685), et al. Assuming the existence of an Amazon state as historical fact, Bocage represents her heroines as feminist paradigms of capable governance and high civic principles, even if their ideology is tested by Queen Orinthe's fatal love for Theseus, King of Athens. Although a tragedy, Bocage's play does not conclude with the dissolution of the matriarchal community. The dialogues in the play between the amazon Menalippe and Theseus lay out the principles of the Amazon "counterculture" (quite literally) and reflect to some degree the more extreme features of radical seventeenth- and eighteenth-century feminist thought, which surely attracted the conservative but intellectually alert Bocage and her sororal circle. Regrettably, she was embarrassed during the run of *Les Amazones* by charges of plagiarism. It was thought that the play's authentic author was either her friend Abbe de Resnel or Monsieur Linaut. Perhaps because of this episode, which slightly blemished her early reputation, Bocage never again wrote for the stage. (French women, it might be noted, would not begin to make significant advances in the theatre until the work of Mme de Graffigny, in the 1750s.)

Bocage's *Amazones* was followed in 1756 with an original epic poem that suggested an apparent change in her literary repertoire, *La Columbiadne* (1756). This long poem of ten cantos celebrated the discovery of America and the heroism of Columbus. It also revealed Bocage's continuing interest in historical models of individuality and accomplishment. Bocage's feminist attraction to the Amazon prototype is still apparent, several years later, in *Columbiadne*, when Columbus falls in love with a powerful Indian queen, described by Bocage as a "mighty Amazon," more ferocious than Penthesilea.

During the 1760s, Bocage returned to her fondness for imitation and produced *La Mort d'Abel*, a paraphrase in verse of *Tod Abels* (1758), a species of idyllic heroic prose-poems by Salomon Gessner, a Swiss pastoral poet. Bocage's choice of subject-matter again demonstrates her preoccupation with heroic figures of the past. With the death of her devoted husband in August 1767, she was left a relatively wealthy widow, free to pursue her literary interests with minimal domestic and social obligations.

Overall, Bocage's oeuvre shows a broad range of genres: verse-drama, light social verse, verse-epic, pastoral verse, travel literature, and letter-writing. She was most successful as a writer of society-verse, then so much in vogue. But Bocage also distinguished herself as a student of feminism, even if her writings are not stridently polemical (cf. Marie du Gournay, Jacquette Guillaume). Bocage was a delightful, fresh presence on the eighteenth-century literary scene, and she attracted wide attention on the Continent and in England. Present-day French scholars would do well to give her work more serious contextual analysis.

Works

De influence mutuel des beaux-arts et des sciences (1746). *Lettre de Madam ΔΔΔ . . . sur l'Opera comique* (1746). *Le Paradis Terrestre, poem imite de Milton* (1746; sometimes recorded "1748"). *Temple de la Renommee*, translation of Pope's *Temple of Fame*, 1715 (1749). *Les Amazones, tragedie en cinq actes* (1749). *Lettres de Madame Du Bocage* (1750, 1757, 1758). *La Columbiadne, ou la Foi portee au Nouveau Monde* (1756). *La Mort d'Abel* (1760). *Le Recueil des Oeuvres de Mme Du Bocage*. 3 vols. (1762, 1764, 1770). *Lettres Concerning England, Holland, and Italy, By the celebrated Madame Du Bocage . . . written during her Travels. Translated from the French*, 2 vols. (1770). *Oeuvres poetiques editees de Madame Du Bocage*, 2 vols. (1788).

Bibliography

Biographical Dictionary & Synopsis of Books Ancient & Modern, ed. C.D. Warner (Detroit, 1965). Gill-Mark, Grace, *Anne-Marie du Bocage: Une Femme de Lettres au XVIII⁺ Siecle*. In *Biblio. de la Reveue de Litterature Comparee*, 41 (Paris, 1927). Hale, Sarah Josepha, in *The Woman's Record*

(New York, 1855). Kleinbaum, A.W., *The War Against the Amazons* (New York, 1983). Martal, L., "Du Bocage," in *Dictionnaire de Biographie Française* (Paris, 1967). Prather, C.C., "The View from Germany," in *French Women & The Age of Enlightenment*, ed. S.I. Spencer (Bloomington, 1984). Rudat, E.M.G., "The View from Spain.," in Spencer, *op. cit.* Turgeon, F.K., "Unpublished Letters of Mme du Bocage." *MP* (1929–1930), pp. 321–338. Virolle, Roland, "*Types sociaux en Normandie au XVIIIe siecle: Anne-Marie du Bocage, la dixieme muse.*" *Etudes Normandes* (1979), pp. 66–80.

Maureen E. Mulvihill

Cecil Bødker

Born March 27, 1927, Fredericia, Denmark
Genre(s): poetry, drama, children's fiction
Language(s): Danish

Although Bødker's visionary poetry and experimental fiction has been lauded by Danish critics, her international reputation seems destined to rest upon her juvenile fiction, for which she has won many awards and much praise.

Cecil Bødker grew up in the Jutland countryside with five brothers, studied for a silversmith's certificate, and then when she was twenty-one, went to work at the Georg Jensen silversmith shop in Copenhagen. She remained there for four years, then spent a year at Markström's silversmith in Stockholm, Sweden before setting up her own shop. In the meantime, she had also been writing poetry since she was ten. In 1955 a selection of her best poems was published as *Luseblomster* (Lice-flowers), promptly winning her the first of a series of cash prizes that enabled her to exchange her career as a silversmith for one as a writer. Originally classified as modernist, Bødker's writing has gone through several stages, developing from highly abstract poetry into experimental prose, eventually acquiring a deceptive simplicity. In addition to numerous Danish literary prizes, including the first ever granted by the Danish Academy for a children's book, Bødker has won the prestigious Hans Christian Andersen Medal awarded by the International Board on Books for Young People, the Silver Pencil from the Nether-

lands (1972), and the 1975 Mildred Batchelder Award from the American Library Association. She currently lives in Fredericia, Denmark.

Bødker has applied the careful craftsmanship she learned as a silversmith to her writing. The short, unrhymed verses of her first poetry collections, *Luseblomster* (1955; Lice-flowers) and *Fygende Heste* (1956; Drifting Horses) weave concrete details into vivid but abstract metaphors, creating a highly original vision of reality. Her third, *Anadyomene* (1959; Aphrodite), was the first entire collection to be composed according to a plan—all of the poems in it are based on the title poem. In addition to displaying her skill in a longer form, *Anadyomene* also reveals another aspect of the poet: her sense of humor. After this, Bødker turned the bulk of her energies to prose, publishing *Øjet* (1961; The Eye), a collection of short stories about modern anxieties that won her the Critics Prize for that year. In 1965 she published *Tilstanden Harley* (The Harley Condition), a rather experimental prose work that employs some of the lyrical qualities of her poetry in what one of her critics has termed an "abstract tale," featuring a Harley-Davidson motorcycle as its central symbol of escape. In 1968 her last poetry collection, *I vædderens tegn* (In the Sign of the Ram) appeared. Since then she has published fiction and drama exclusively. Since one of Bødker's persistent themes has always been the passage from childhood to maturity seen as a fall from grace, and her insight into the psychology of small boys is evident in such works as *Fortællinger omkring Tavs* (1971; Tales about Tavs), her subsequent involvement in juvenile fiction is a natural development. Her series of books about Silas, a boy who is raised in a travelling circus troupe and who runs away because he doesn't want to learn sword-swallowing, are set in an unspecified time and place and combine the picaresque with the mythic. The same qualities are found in *Leoparden* (1970; The Leopard), which portrays the adventures of an Ethiopian boy that leaves home to get advice on how to catch the leopard that has been stealing cattle, only to discover that it is really a human thief who suddenly wants him dead because he knows too much. In the 1980s, Bødker returned to adult fiction and produced two novels, *Evas Ekko* (1980; Eva's Echo), and

Tænk pa Jolande (1981; Think about Jolande), for the first time featuring female protagonists and dealing with women's concerns. Her most recent work is *Marias barn* (1983; Mary's Child), a two-part retelling of the life of Jesus.

It is appropriate that one of Bødker's many awards should bear the name of her countryman, Hans Christian Andersen, who also became renowned for his tales for children, while his works written for mature audiences are now forgotten by everyone except specialists. Like Andersen's tales, Bødker's juvenile fiction has a mythic quality which can appeal to everyone, largely derived in her case from both the strong role played by coincidence in her plots, making the adventures seem fated, and the larger-than-life characters like the horse-crone in the Silas books, who is a superhumanly strong, unscrupulous, and cruel female personification of the human will to survive.

Works

Luseblomster [Lice-flowers] (1955). *Fygende Heste* [Drifting Horses] (1956). *Anadyomene* [Aphrodite] (1959). *Øjet* [The Eye] (1961). *Latter: radiospil* [Laughter: A Radio Play] (1964). *Samlede digter* [Collected Poems] (1964). *Badekarret* [The Bathtub] (1965). *Tilstanden Harley* [The Harley Condition] (1965). *Pap* [Cardboard] (1967). *Silas og den sorte hoppe* [Silas and the Black Mare] (1967). *Dukke min* [My Doll] (1968). *I vædderens tegn* [In the Sign of the Ram] (1968). *Silas og Ben-Godik* [Silas and Ben-Godik] (1969). *Timmerlis* (1969). *Leoparden* [The Leopard] (1970). *Dimma Gole: Fortælling om en ethioperdreng* [Dimma Gole: Tale about an Ethiopian Boy] (1971). *Fortællinger omkring Tavs* [Tales About Tavs] (1971). *Kvinden som gik bort over vandet* [The Woman Who Walked Away over the Water] (1971). *Salthandlerskens hus* [The Salt-Dealer's House] (1972). *Skyld*. Stage play [Guilt] (1972). *En vrangmaske i Vorherres strikketøj* [A Wrong Stitch in Our Lord's Knitting] (1974). *Barnet i sivkurven* [The Child in the Basket of Rushes] (1975). *Da jorden forsvandt* [When the Earth Disappeared] (1975). *Jerutte fra Ræverød* [Jerutte from Fox Clearing] (1975). *Jerutte redder Tom og Tinne* [Jerutte Saves Tom and Tinne] (1975). *Far, mor og barn* [Father, Mother and Child] (1976). *Jerutte og bjørnen på Ræverød* [Jerutte and the Bear at Fox Clearing] (1976). *Silas fanger et firspand* (1976). *Silas stifter familie* [Silas Starts a Family] (1976). *Jerutte besøger Hundejens* [Jerutte Visits Dog-Jens] (1977). *Robinson* (1977). *Silas pa Sebastiansbjerget* [Silas on Sebastian's Mountain] (1977). *Den udvalgte* [The Chosen One] (1977). *Silas og Hestekragen mødes igen* [Silas and the Horse-Crone Meet Again] (1978). *Silas møder Matti* [Silas meets Matti] (1979). *Evas ekko* [Eva's Echo] (1980). *Tænk på Jolande* [Think About Jolande] (1981). *Den lange vandring* [The Long Wandering] (1982). *Syv år for Rakel* [Seven Years for Rachel] (1982). *Marias barn: drengen* [Mary's Child: The Boy] (1983). *Marias barn: Manden* [Mary's Child: The Man] (1984). *Silas. Livet i bjergbyen* [Silas. Life in the Mountain Village] (1984). *Silas. De blå heste* [Silas. The Blue Horses] (1985). *Silas. Sebastians aru* [Silas. Sebastian's Inheritance] (1986). *Ægget der voksede* [The Egg that Grew] (1987). *Maria fra Nazaret* [Mary of Nazareth] (1988). *Silas. Ulverejsen* [Silas. Wolf-journey] (1988).

Translations: *The Leopard* [*Leoparden*], tr. Gunnar Poulsen (1975). *Silas and Ben Godik* [*Silas og Ben-Godik*], tr. Sheila LaFarge (1978). *Silas and the Black Mare* [*Silas o den sorte hoppe*], tr. Sheila LaFarge (1978). *Silas and the Runaway Coach* [*Silas fanger et firspand*], tr. Sheila LaFarge (1978). For a list of English translations of individual poems and short stories, see Carol L. Schroeder, *A Bibliography of Danish Literature in English Translation, 1950–1980* (Copenhagen, 1982).

Bibliography

Bredsdorff, Thomas, *Sære fortællere. Hovedtræk af den ny danske prosakunst i tiåret omkring 1960* (Copenhagen: Gyldendal, 1967), pp. 186–195. Clausen, Claus, *Digtere i forhør: Samtaler med tolv danske forfattere* (Copenhagen: Gyldendal, 1966), pp. 121–140. Pinborg, Jan, "Om nogle digter af Cecil Bødker." *Catholica* (Copenhagen) 21 (1964): 157–167. Vinterberg, Søren, "Cecil Bødker," *Danske digtere i det 20. århundrede*, vol. 4, ed. Torben Brostrom and Mette Winge (Copenhagen: Gad, 1980–1982) pp. 219–228.

Kristine Anderson

Imma von Bodmershof

*Born August 10, 1895, Graz, Austria; died
1982, Glöhl, Germany*
Genre(s): novel, short story, poetry
Language(s): German

Her father, Carl von Ehrenfels, was a famous
professor for philosophy at the University of
Prague (CSSR). Imma studied art history, philosophy, and graphology at the Universities of
Prague and Munich. Through her studies of
graphology she was in contact with Ludwig
Klages. Norbert von Hellingrath, a well-known
Hölderlin scholar, was her first fiancé, but he
died in 1916 in World War I. Imma established
literary links with Rainer Maria Rilke and the
circle around Stefan George. In 1925 she married
Dr. W. von Bodmershof and lived with him on
the estate Rastbach in Lower Austria since then.
She was a member of PEN since 1950 and
received the Major Austrian State Award. Her
main literary motifs and themes circle around
man's quest for his own true self.

Works

Der zweite Sommer [The Second Summer], novel
1937. *Die Stadt in Flandern* [City in Flanders],
novel (1939; rpt. 1952 as *Das verlorene Meer* [The
Lost Sea]). *Therese Pirnagel*, short story (1941).
Begegnungen im Frühling [Encounters in Spring]
(1942; rpt. 1985). *Die Rosse des Urban Roithner*
[Urban Roithner's Horses], novel (1950; rpt. 1982).
Solange es Tag ist [As Long as the Day Lasts], with
the short stories "Milch auf Gestein" [Milk on
Rock], and "Der Tanz" [The Dance] (1953). *Sieben
Handvoll Salz* [Seven Handfuls of Salt], novel (1958;
rpt. 1984). *Haiku*, poems (1962). *Unter acht
Winden* [Under Eight Winds], short stories se-
lected by H. Jappe (1962). *Die Bartabnahme* [The
Removal of the Beard], 2nd ed. (1986). *Sonnenuhr*
[Sundial] (1970), poems. *Im fremden Garten Blüht
Jasmin, Haiku* [In the Foreign Garden Jasmine Is
Blooming, Haiku], poems (1979).

Bibliography

Aichinger, Ingrid, "Der Zwang zur Entscheidung
vor dem Chaos. Untersuchungen zu Imma
Bodmershofs Roman *Sieben Handvoll Salz*."
Modern Austrian Literature 12, 3/4 (1979): 97–
111. "Bodmershof, Imma," *Deutsches Literatur-
Lexikon*, 3rd rev. ed., vol. II (Bern-Munich, 1968),
cols. 655f. Fiechtner, H.A., "Imma von
Bodmershof," *Wort in der Zeit* 3 (1957). O.
Heuschele, "Imma von Bodmershof." *Handbuch der
deutschen Gegenwartsliteratur*, 3rd rev. ed., vol. I
(Munich, 1969), p. 127f. Langer, N., "Imma von
Bodmershof," in N. Langer, *Dichter aus Österreich*,
vol. I (Vienna, 1956). Lennartz, Franz, *Deutsche
Schriftsteller der Gegenwart*, 11th ed. (Stuttgart,
1978), pp. 86–88. Schmidt, Adalbert, *Dichtung und
Dichter Österreichs im 19. und 20. Jahrhundert*, vol.
2 (Salzburg, 1964), pp. 136–138.

Albrecht Classen

Kari Bøge

Born August 19, 1950, Stockholm, Sweden
Genre(s): novel, poetry
Language(s): Swedish

Kari Bøge has embarked on a highly successful dual career as author and artist. In both
aspects of her promising career, she has stressed
independence, freedom from dogma and rigid
conformity, and creativity in describing many
levels of experience. Kari Bøge has sought to
depict differing points of view (*Contemporary
Norwegian Prose Writers*, p. 37). Bøge has used
her artistic gifts for writing and painting to the
full, in new and liberating ways for her audience
and herself.

As a very young child, Kari Bøge lived with
her parents in many parts of Europe until her
family finally settled permanently in Norway.
Not agreeing with the approaches of various
"schools," Bøge followed her own course in writing and painting, teaching herself, revising her
technique, and developing her own styles from
the beginning (*Contemporary Norwegian Prose
Writers*, p. 37). Bøge's career as a painter led to
an invitation to join the Young Artists' Society in
1968 when she was but 18 years old. She has also
illustrated a series of children's books and works
for young adults.

Bøge's literary career began with *Asmerelda*,
her lyric début of 1971. In 1974, Bøge's first
novel, *Viviann hvit* (Viviann, White), was published. The protagonist of *Viviann hvit* is a
woman with a masculine outlook on life. She
becomes pregnant and then participates in and
experiences to the full a dialogue between femi-

nine reality and masculine theory. *Viviann hvit* is the first in a series of four connected novels; the other works are *Lyset er så hvitt om sommeren* (1975; The Light is so White in Summer); *Sommerregn om natten* (1976; Summer Rain at Night); and *Viviann og Lin* (1980; Viviann and Lin). Kari Bøge has enthusiastically depicted her first experience with the novel and the work *Viviann hvit* as "particularly exciting [especially] when one discovers the right way of writing a book" (*Contemporary Norwegian Prose Writers*, p. 37). Bøge discovered her own forte and strength as a writer in the *Viviann* novels. She has also collaborated with Arild Stubhaug in writing the New Norwegian (dialect) work, *Til avtalt Tid* (1979; At the Appointed Time). Bøge's latest work is *Irrganger* (Labyrinths), published in 1984.

With her emphasis on individuality, artistic freedom and creativity, and on the description, study, and portrayal of many different facets of experience, Kari Bøge has a very promising, rewarding career in sight. Bøge's interest in portraying experience graphically, through illustrations and painting, and through writing, is notable. Her initial novel, *Viviann hvit*, has already received critical attention and merited acclaim in Norway. Kari Bøge has taken her well-earned place among a new, innovative, spirited generation of Norwegian artists and literati.

Works

Asmerelda (1971). *Viviann hvit* [Viviann, White] (1974). *Lyset er så hvitt om sommeren* [The Light is so White in Summer] (1975). *Sommerregn om natten* [Summer Rain at Night] (1976). *Til avtalt Tid* [At the Appointed Time, with Arild Stubhaug] (1979). *Viviann og Lin* [Viviann and Lin] (1980). *Irrganger* [Labyrinths] (1984).

Bibliography

Et annet Språk. Analyser av norske Kvinnelitteratur (Oslo, 1977). *Aschehoug og Gyldendals Store Norske Leksikon, Bind 2, Ben-Ch* (1983), p. 566. *Contemporary Norwegian Prose Writers.* The Norwegian Authors' Association, tr. David McDuff (Oslo, 1985). Engstrøm, Claus og Marianne Koch Knudsen, "Viviann hvit." *Kjerringråd* 2 (1975). Økland, Einar, "Samtale med Kari Bøge, Cecilie Løveid, Marie Takvam." *Basar* 1 (1975).

Lanae Hjortsvang Isaacson

Helena Boguszewska

Born October 18, 1883, Warsaw, Poland; died November 11, 1978, Warsaw, Poland
Genre(s): novel, short story, essay, children's literature
Language(s): Polish

Boguszewska's philosophy was influenced by psychology but even more by sociology. She wrote in the tradition of the Polish "positivists," who looked to science for progress and improvement of life and society. She was acutely interested in the plight of the underclass, especially as it affected children. Her style is realistic, almost documentary, in depicting living conditions among the unfortunate and underprivileged. Although she did not overlook the psychology of her characters, she basically saw individuals as social creatures and products of their environment (as did the naturalists) but without making them pathetic. At the same time, she recognized that suffering by innocents was often caused by life's inherent unfairness and by circumstances beyond human control, such as physical deformity or other handicaps. Though her writings should be viewed as inspirational, they are not didactic or moralizing. They make their point by illustration, for example by introducing a crippled child as a character in children's books. Her very first novel, *Świat po niewidomemu* (1932; The Invisible World), was dedicated to an institution for blind children.

In her writings for adults, Boguszewska also concentrated her attention on workers and the poor, who had rarely appeared in literature until then. Together with her husband Jerzy Kornacki, she wrote *Jadą wozy z cegłą* (1935; Wagons with Bricks Are Rolling By) and *Wisła* (1935; The Vistula River) describing the lot of folk who dwell on the banks of the river, working as diggers and boatmen. On the other hand, *Całe życie Sabiny* (1934; Sabina's Entire Life) is a psychological novel. After World War II, Boguszewska wrote *Czekamy na życie* (1947; We Are Waiting for Life), a fictionalized memoir of childhood depicting intellectual life of Warsaw, and in 1955 appeared *Las* (The Forest), coauthored with her husband, a novel about partisan activities. In *Czarna kura* (1952; The Black Hen) she returns to a societal theme in examining the new postwar awareness of their role by village people.

For her work on behalf of children's welfare and other achievements, Boguszewska was decorated with three orders, and her works have been translated into several languages but not, so far, into English.

Works

Novels: *Świat po niewidomemu* [The Invisible World] (1932). *Ci ludzie* [These People] (1933). *Całe żcie Sabiny* [Sabina's Entire Life] (1934). *Jadą wozy z cegłą* [Wagons with Bricks Are Rolling by, co-authored] (1935). *Wisła* [The Vistula River, co-authored] (1935). *Polonez* [Polonaise], 4 vols., co-authored (1936–1939). *Czekamy na życie* [We Are Waiting for Life] (1947). *Żelazna kurtyna* [The Iron Curtain] (1949). *Czarna kura* [The Black Hen] (1952). *Las* [The Forest], co-authored (1955). Short stories and essays: *Przedmieście* [City Outskirts], co-authored (1934). *Adolf i Marian* [Adolf and Marian] (1934). *Nigdy nie zapomnę* [I Shall Never Forget] (1946). *Pozbierane dzieci* [Collected Children] (1955). *Poprzez ulice* [Across the Street] (1961). Articles, children's books and textbooks.

Bibliography

Dąbrowski, Mieczysław, "Boguszewska—jej życie." *Literatura* (Warsaw) (February 24, 1972): 1, 9. Knysz-Rudzka, Danuta, "Boguszewska Helena." *Literatura polska: Przewodnik encyklopedyczny*, ed. Julian Krzyżanowski, vol. 1 (Warsaw, 1984). Korzeniewska, Ewa, ed., *Słownik współczesnych pisarzy polskich*, vol. 1 (Warsaw, 1963). Matgowska, Hanna Maria, "Wśród ludzi Przedmieścia." *Literatura* (Warsaw) (November 11, 1976): 3.

Irene Suboczewski

Cecilia Böhl de Faber y Larrea

(see: Fernán Caballero)

María Dolores Boixadós

Born 192?, Lérida, Spain
Genre(s): novel
Language(s): Spanish

María Dolores Boixadós worked in a bank in Barcelona as she started to publish. Her novel *Aquas muertas* (Stagnant Waters) was a finalist for the first Nadal Prize in 1945. Boixadós married in 1946 and moved to Venezuela, where she started her studies in medicine and worked with her husband in cancer research. She has taught in the universities of Los Andes, Mérida, and Caracas. In 1966 she won the "Premio Don Quijote" in México for her novel *Retorno* (Return). Since 1959, she has lived in the United States with her family and seems to have relinquished her literary career. A book announced as forthcoming, *Niños abandonados en el mundo* (The Abandoned Children of the World) does not show up in any sources. Chronologically, she belongs to the "posguerra" generation.

Aquas muertas remained unpublished until 1970 despite the fact that it was a finalist for the first Nadal Prize of 1945 awarded to Carmen Laforet's *Nada* (Nothing), a novel with which it has much in common. Narrated in third person, it is the story of a young woman from Alicante, Elena Just, who goes to Madrid to study. The novel takes place in the years after the Civil War in a residence for women. The protagonist is a shy, withdrawn person who becomes obsessed with some letters written by a former student. Its style is somewhat dated and unoriginal with an excessive use of adjectives.

Boixadós' musical interest is reflected in her best novel *Balada de un músico* (1968; A Musician's Ballad), which is the story of a pianist, Señor Mases, who plays at a café in Barcelona in the years before the Civil War. The descriptions of the political times and the characters—the old monarchist, his granddaughter, and the protagonist's dutiful wife—are engaging. There is a symbolic relationship between the bloody events which are taking place and the symphony that Señor Mases is writing.

The winner of the "Premio Don Quijote" of 1960, *Retorno* (1967) is a traditional novel in that it is divided into chapters, but it contains two different narrative lines. One takes place in Pueblo, a fictitious town in Catalonia, after the Civil War; the other, narrated in the first person and printed in cursive, is the story of a woman from Spain who lives in the South of the United States. An unrealistic element is present in this narrative that contrasts with the sordid life in Spain. The novel presents an interesting view of life in the United States as seen by an immigrant.

María Dolores Boixadós' literary career is a mystery of sorts; like Eulalia Galvarriato, another finalist of the Nadal Prize, and Luisa Forrellad, an actual winner (in 1953) for *Siempre en capilla* (Always Under Siege), she seems to have ceased publishing despite a fair amount of early recognition.

Works

Retorno (1967). *Balada de un músico* (1968). *Aquas muertas* (1970).

Bibliography

Cachero, José Mariz Martinez, *Historia de la novela española entre 1936 y 1975* (Madrid, 1979), p. 86.

Concha Alborg

Laudamia Bonanni

Born 1909, Acquila, Abruzzi, Italy
Genre(s): novel, journalism, short story
Language(s): Italian

Laudamia Bonanni was born in southern Italy, in the city of Acquila, in 1909. A schoolteacher like her mother, she was already teaching at seventeen in a small mountain town of Abruzzi. Later she became a social worker, working for some twenty years to rehabilitate minors. She was also a journalist.

Her literary debut came about clamorously and unexpectedly with the publication in 1948 of a volume including four short stories, *Il fosso* (The Ditch), which was awarded the "Gli amici della domenica" (The Sunday Friends) prize and was lauded by Eugenio Montale. Childhood and war are dominant themes in her works. These stories already contain the major concerns and contrasts found in her later works. The locale is a mountainous region of southern Italy. The protagonists are young and older women who must endure the immobility and harshness of the

rural life in wartime, the brutality of men, the burden of poverty and ignorance. It is easy to see in the detailed depiction of social reality and the exactness of the style the influence of Giovanni Verga's "verismo." A larger edition of this work came out in 1954 with the title *Palma e sorelle* (Palm and Sisters). In 1963 her publisher, Bompiani, combined these two works in a single edition. The locale is still the hostile and desolate world of Abruzzi, and women are the protagonists. In the story "Palma," a woman's desire to see her son become a better person than the husband she has come to loathe is not fulfilled. Another, "Monaca di casa," tells of a girl who as the result of a grotesque ritual is proclaimed a "monaca di casa," "a nun of the household," by fanatically religious aunts. She will then transform herself from "Clementina" to "Donna Clemenza," a strict and respected religious person who will turn her house into a convent. Other works follow: *L'imputata* (1960; The She-Defendant) and *L'adultera* (1964; The Unfaithful Wife), considered her major work. The author's preference though is for *L'imputata*, recipient of the 1960 Viareggio prize. This work reveals a greater stylistic maturity. No longer is the flow impaired by excessive search for the most appropriate word and phrase. The novel underscores once again Bonanni's pessimistic view of society and its capacity to deal with evil and injustice. As the novel opens a dead infant is found in the trash of a tenement house. This macabre episode is a grim warning of the story's tragic events: a teenager commits suicide and another kills his mother's lover unaware that he is about to become his stepfather. The focus of the novel is on Gianni, a child who is loved and respected by the other children but who gradually withdraws into an angry private world. Despite the author's stated preference for *L'imputata*, critics admire more the *L'adultera*'s narrative and stylistic strategies. It is also a tale of death and moral degradation that begins when the woman-protagonist (a travelling saleswoman) is accompanied by her husband to the rail station. Her husband has just returned from six years of confinement in a war camp. During her trip she has time to rethink about her frustration and loneliness: she married the wrong man; she never loved her daughter; she had squalid extramarital affairs. The novel ends tragically with the scene in which she is found dead in the bathtub inside the apartment of a stranger. She probably committed suicide by turning on the gas. Her husband is then called to identify her body. After the publication of this work, Laudamia Bonanni entered a long interval of depression which was interrupted with the publication in 1974 of a new work, a long and serious study of violence and juvenile delinquency, *Vietato ai minori* (1974, Forbidden to Minors). In 1977 appeared *Città del tabacco* (Tobacco City) and, in 1979, the novel, *Il bambino di pietra* (The Child of Stone), an attack on traditional family values. Another work also published by Bompiani in 1982 is *Le droqhe* (Drugs). She contributed to the leading newspapers and literary journals: *Il Resto del Carlino, Il Tempo, Il Corriere d'informazioni, Il Giornale d'Italia, La Gazzetta del popolo; Il Gazzettino.* Laudomia Bonanni has been living alone in Rome for the last nineteen years.

Works

Storie tragiche della montagna (1927). *Noterelle di cronaca scolastica* (1932). *Avventura di nuovo fiore* (1939). *Le due penne del papagallino Verzé* (1948). *Il fosso* (1949). *Palma e sorelle* (1954; 1960). *L'imputata* (1960). *L'adultera* (1964). *Vietato ai minori* (1974). *Città del tabacco* (1979). *Il bambino di pietra* (1979). *Le droghe* (1982).

Bibliography

Baldacci, Luigi, *Epoca* (August 9, 1964). Barberi-Squarotti, Giorgio, *Poesia e narrativa del secondo novecento* (Milano, 1978). Ceratto, Marino, *Il "Chi è" delle donne italiane, 1945–1982* (Milano, 1982). De Robertis, Giuseppe, *La Nazione* (September 1, 1960). Lombardi, Olga, "Laudamia Bonanni." *I contemporanei* (Milano, 1973); *Belfagor* (July 31, 1985). Manacorda, Giuliano, *Vent'anni di pazienza* (Firenze, 1972). Pacifici, Sergio, *The Modern Italian Novel*, 3 vols., 1967–1979 (Southern Illinois University Press: 1979). Pampaloni, Geno, *Belfagor* (January 1960). Petrignani, Sandra, *Le signore della scrittura* (Milano, 1984). Pullini, Giorgio, *Il romanzo del dopoguerra italiano* (Milano, 1961).

Giacomo Striuli

Jytte Borberg

Born July 16, 1917, Romanshorn, Switzerland
Genre(s): novel, drama
Language(s): Danish

Borberg's writing is not easily placed into any category. By virtue of her age she belongs to the same generation as Tove Ditlevson; however, the year of her late debut and the abstract style of her first two novels led critics to classify her with the small group of female modernists. In the seventies, however, she began to write in a somewhat more realistic style and to reveal a distinct feminist consciousness. These have been her characteristic traits ever since.

Although Borberg was born in Switzerland, she has lived in Denmark since she was four years old. Her career began late, after 29 years of marriage to Allan Borberg, a prominent Danish psychiatrist in Viborg, and after her three children had grown to adulthood. Her first published work was *Vindebroen* (1968; The Drawbrige), a collection of short stories. She has been the recipient of several Danish awards, including a State's Lifelong Grant to Authors (1984) and the Adam Oehlenschlager award (1984). Since her husband's death in 1979, she has lived in Copenhagen.

Borberg's first two "modernist" books, *Vindebroen* and *Næeldefeber* (1970; Nettle Rash), have an abstract quality due to a neglect of naturalistic details such as time, place, and the characters' biographies in order to concentrate on situation and its place in a social design. *Næeldefeber*, for example, takes place in a society vaguely reminiscent of South Africa, where a white elite rules a vast black underclass, but the novel concentrates on the narrow existence of Joe and Alice Barker, a white man and his wife who live in a luxurious villa. The title refers to the allergic reactions Joe experiences every day when he comes home. Unbeknownst to him, he is allergic to Alice's pet cat, which she hides every night in the black servant's house. This modernist approach was modified in the seventies by the growing feminist consciousness of the times, resulting in *Orange* in 1972. *Orange* is told in the first person from the title character's point of view. Orange breaks away from her marriage to a banker and goes wild in her quest for self-fulfillment, love, and freedom. She is completely amoral, and when published, the novel was read as an inside portrait of femininity at its worst. Today it is possible to discern its criticism of the social roles women must play and its portrayal of the difficulty of breaking out of them. Borberg's next novel, *Turné* (1974; Tour), has two parallel plots. In one, men in a mime troupe go on tour in an attempt to revitalize their group, but after numerous fiascos, they break up. In the other plot, the men's wives, who initially had nothing in common but the careers of their husbands, come together, begin to socialize, and form their own support group. The novel contrasts the men's hierarchized role-playing, both on and off stage, with the spontaneity of the women. Although the novel examines several important contemporary feminist issues, it has not been considered entirely successful artistically. The works that have won Borberg the most acclaim, both popular and critical, are her two novels about Eline Besser, *Eline Besser's læretid* (1976; Eline Besser's Apprenticeship); and *Det bedste og det værste, Eline Besser til den sidste* (1977; The Best and the Worst, Eline Besser to the Last). They tell the life story of the title character from the time she enters the service of a bourgeois family in the year 1900 when she is fifteen until her death at age seventy-two. In the first volume, Eline is an innocent young servant-girl fascinated by upper-class life who ends up pregnant by the end of the book. By this time her social consciousness has also been somewhat raised through her association with Hilda, the cook, who is a political activist and serves as her mother-figure. In the sequel, *Det bedste og det værste*, Eline's pregnancy ends in the birth of her daughter Laura at the poultry farm where Eline is now an apprentice. In the first five chapters, Laura grows up and goes to school while Eline supports them with her poultry raising. These chapters continue to be written in the third person omniscient like the first book; in subsequent chapters, however, Eline takes the pen in her own hand to tell her own story, revealing that up to now it has been written by one of Laura's school-chums. Eline now proceeds to relate her inner life and the profound significance of her erotic experiences, to which outside observers

and third person narrators have not, of course, had access.

The power of sex to energize and liberate the personality is a frequent theme in Borberg's works although she is not optimistic about marriage or any kind of long-term pair-bonding. Her next two novels, *Rapport fra havbunden* (1979; Report from the Bottom of the Sea) and *Nu og aldrig* (1979; Now and Never), repeat the same theme in stories of women who break out of their identities, which have been defined by their husband's jobs, by having affairs with other men. *Sjælen er gul* (1981; The Soul Is Yellow) continues the tradition of *Orange* and the Eline Besser books of featuring a woman who achieves personal and artistic liberation through a catalyzing experience. It happens to the main character, Lotte, former painter and psychiatric patient, while she is attending an adult education course on the painter Olivia Holm-Mueller, who becomes a liberating influence for her. One of Borberg's techniques is to refrain from drawing clear distinctions between what really "happens" and what Lotte imagines, implying that Lotte's "reality" is more real than the "normal" one surrounding her.

Borberg's originality may well derive from the fact that she is "out of step," so to speak, with her generation, whether figured from the date of her birth or the year of her literary debut. She writes realistically about common female experience in the seventies and eighties but as seen through a defamiliarizing eye and employing some of the distancing techniques she learned from the modernists.

Works

Vindebroen [The Drawbridge] (1968). *Nældefeber* [Nettle Rash] (1970). *Orange* (1972). *Portræt af et år* [Portrait of a Year] (1973). *Turné* [Tour] (1974). *Eline Bessers læretid* [Eline Besser's Apprenticeship] (1976). *Rundfart* [Sightseeing Excursion], radio play (1976). *Sluk ilden!* Street play [Put Out the Fire!] (1976). *Døren er åben.* [The Door is Open], television play (1976–1977). *Det bedste og det værste: Eline Besser til det sidste* [The Best and the Worst: Eline Besser to the Last] (1977). *En god kone* [A Good Wife], stage play (1978). *Rapport fra havbunden* [Report from the Bottom of the Sea] (1979). *Nu og aldrig* [Now and Never] (1979).

Sjælen er gul [The Soul is Yellow] (1981). *Kul og gronne skove* [A Good Wife], stage play (1981–1982). *Alice og mig* [Alice and I] (1982). *Slaraffenland* [Fool's Paradise] (1982). *Skyggernes Bog* [Book of the Shadows] (1983). *Stella Urania* (1985). *Nat og dag* [Night and Day] (1987). *Vejmandens datter* [Roadmender's Daughter] (1987). *Maskerade* [Masquerade] (1988). Translations: *Orange*, German tr. Ursula Gunsilius (1975). *Det bästa och det värsta: Eline Besser til slutet* [*Det bedste og det vaerste*] Swedish tr. Ann-Mari Seeberg (1979).

Bibliography

Gaul, Bente, *Undertrykkelse, Oplevelse og modstand i den nye kvinderoman* (Copenhagen, 1978).

Kristine Anderson

Elisabeth Borchers

Born February 27, 1926, Homberg/ Niederrhein, Germany
Genre(s): poetry, short story, radio drama, children's literature, essay, translation
Language(s): German

Elisabeth Borchers grew up in Alsace and worked, after studies in France and the United States in 1959, at the University for Designing in Ulm. She lived in Neuwied and Berlin from 1960 to 1971. Since 1971 she has been working as a lector for a publishing house. Her poems excel in mystic metaphors and a different kind of reality. In her short stories she reveals the ordinary life of the common man in modern society. *Eine glückliche Familie* (A Happy Family) talks about the triviality of the German and American affluent society. Borchers' radio plays became very popular in Germany and abroad. She also demonstrated her skills in numerous translations. She received the Radio Prize and the Writer's Prize of the South German Radio Station in 1967 for her radio play *Rue des Pompiers* from her collection *Nacht aus Eis* (Night Full of Ice). In 1967 she received the Cultural Prize of the German Industry and in 1976 the Roswitha-Medal from the City of Gandersheim.

Works

Poems: *Gedichte* [Poems] (1961). *Der Tisch, an dem wir sitzen* [The Table, at Which We are Sitting] (1967). *Gedichte* [Poems] (1976). *Wer lebt* [He Who Is Living] (1986).

Radio plays: *Nacht aus Eis. Szenen und Spiele* [Night Full of Ice. Scenes and Games] (1965). *Feierabend* [After Work] (1965). *Rue des Pompiers* (1965). *Anton S. oder die Möglichkeiten* [Anton S. or the Possibilities] (1967). *Ist die Stadt denn verschlossen* [Is the City Locked?] (1967).

Children books and short stories: [With D. Blech], *Erzählungen: Bi, Be, Bo, Ba, Bu—die Igelkinder* [Short Stories: Bi, Be, Bo, Ba, Bu—The Hedge Hog Children] (1962). [With D. Blech], *Und oben schwimmt die Sonne davon* [And Above Us the Sun Is Swimming Away] (1965). *Das alte Auto* [The Old Car] (1965). *Das rote Haus in einer kleinen Stadt* [The Red House in a Small Town] (1970). *Eine glückliche Familie* [A Happy Family, short stories] (1970). *Das große Lalula* [The Big Lalula] (1971). *Papperlapapp sagt Herr Franz der Rennfahrer* [Papperlapapp says Mr. Franz the Car Racer] (1971). *Schöner Schnee* [Beautiful Snow] (1972). *Das sehr nützliche Merk-Buch für Geburtstage* [The Very Useful Memory Book for Birthdays] (1975). *Briefe an Sarah* [Letters To Sarah] (1977). *Die Zeichenstunde* [The Drawing Hour] (1977). *Das Insel-Buch für Kinder* [The Insel Book For Children] (1979). *Das Adventbuch* [The Advent Book] (1979). [With W. Schlote], *Paul und Sarah oder wenn zwei sich was wünschen* [Paul and Sarah, or When Two Are Wishing Something] (1979). [With W. Schlote], *Heut wünsch ich mir ein Nilpferd* [Today I am Wishing a Hippopotamus,] (1981). [With L. Brierly], *Der König der Tiere und seine Freunde* [The King of the Animals and His Friends].

Essays: *Lektori salutem* (1978).

Editions: *Lesebuch* vol. 1: *Der Einbruch eines Holzfällers in eine friedliche Familie* [Textbook vol. 1: A Woodcutter's Attack on a Peaceful Family] (1971). *Märchen deutscher Dichter* [Fairy Tales of German Poets] (1973). *Ein Fisch mit dem Namen Fasch* [A Fish Named Fasch] (1972). *Das Weihnachtsbuch* [A Christmas Book] (1973). *Das Buch der Liebe* [The Book of Love] (1975). *Das Insel-Buch der Träume* [The Insel-Book of Dreams] (1975). *Das sehr nützliche Merkbuch für Geburtstage* [The Very Useful Notebook For Birthdays] (1975). *Seht, der Träumer kommt daher* [See, The Dreamer is Coming Along] (1975). *Liebe Mutter* [Dear Mother] (1976). *Das Poesiealbum* [The Poetry Album] (1980). *Lektüre zwischen den Jahren* [Reading Material for the Time Between Two Years] (1980). *Im Jahrhundert der Frau* [In the Century of Woman] (1986).

Translation: *Poems*, tr. Ruth and Matthew Mead (1969).

Bibliography

Baier, L., "Versuch zu Gedichten von Elisabeth Borchers," in *Text und Kritik* 9 (1965): 3–6. Hinck, W., on *Die große Chance* in *Frankfurter Anthologie* 5 (1980): 235–238. Wapnewski, Peter, on *Chagall*, in W. Hinck, ed., *Gedichte und Interpretationen*, vol. 6 (Stuttgart, 1982), pp. 242–256.

Albrecht Classen

Isabel de Borja

Born January 15, 1498, Gandía, Spain; died October 28, 1557, Madrid
Genre(s): devotional works
Language(s): Spanish

Isabel was born into the highly distinguished Borja or Borgia family. She was the daughter of Juan de Borja, assassinated in Rome, perhaps by his brother, the infamous Caesar Borgia (and thus granddaughter of the Borgia Pope Alexander VI), and María Enriquez de Luna, first cousin of King Ferdinand II of Aragón. In early childhood she showed an inclination for study and religion and took vows in the Discalced Clarisse Order in Gandía. The Order of Clarisse Nuns (Clarisas), founded by Santa Clara of Asis and dedicated to the most absolute poverty and penance, was the equivalent for women of the Franciscan Order. Isabel, called Sor Francisca de Jesús in the convent, lived an exemplary life of religious virtue. She was named abbess of the Order and founded several convents in La Rioja, Valladolid, and Madrid. She is remembered as the founder of the Royal Discalced Clarisse Order (Descalzas Reales) in Madrid, although she never lived in this convent since she died in the year of its establishment.

Works

"Carta" ["Letter"] to her nephew San Francisco de Borja, manuscript in the Royal Discalced Convent in Madrid. Various other "Letters." Many "Exercicios santos" ["Spiritual Exercises"] and "Exhortaciones espirituales" ["Spiritual Exhortations"] directed to her nuns, manuscripts in the Convent of the Royal Discalced Clarisse Nuns (Descalzas Reales) in Madrid. Both are mentioned in the *Relación histórica de la Real fundación del monasterio de las Descalzas de S. Clara de la villa de Madrid . . .* , by Father Juan Carrillo of the Order of Saint Francis (1616).

Bibliography

Amorós, L., "El monasterio de Santa Clara de Gandía y la familia ducal de los Borjas." *Archivo Iberoamericano* 20 (1960): 441–486; 21 (1961): 227–282, 339–458. Nonell, Jaime, *Vida y virtudes de la venerable señora doña Luisa de Borja y Aragón* (Madrid, 1892). Serrano y Sanz, Manuel, *Apuntes para una biblioteca de escritoras españolas*, 2 vols. (Madrid, 1903; rpt. *Biblioteca de Autores Españoles*, vols. 268–271). Simón Díaz, Jorge, *Bibliografía de la literatura hispánica*, vol. VI (Madrid, 1973), p. 619.

Ruth Lundelius

Adelheid (Heidi) von Born-Hansson

Born 1936, Stockholm, Sweden
Genre(s): novel, poetry
Language(s): Swedish

Heidi von Born's parents, Eric von Born and Birgit Möller, were both writers, so writing came to Heidi naturally. The fact that her Finnish parents took her back to Finland for seven years at the age of nine, during which she longed desperately to be back in Stockholm, the poverty she experienced as a child, the early death of her mother, and her relationship to her four successive stepmothers play a decisive role in von Born's writing. She made her debut with a collection of poems, *Det förtrollade huset* (The Enchanted House), at the age of eighteen while working for her Ph.D. candidacy. In retrospect, von Born calls this work "a battering ram out of self-hatred and guilt feelings" from which she felt a need to free herself. Since then she has published continuously both poetry and novels.

Von Born has been described as a "social writer" concerned with the fate of the most vulnerable, oppressed and degraded in her society. But her writing is, at the same time, autobiographical. In her novels, the protagonists are mostly young people in conflict with themselves and others. Bringing her own experience to her craft, von Born is able to give these characters the necessary lifelike dimensions. While she keeps herself at a safe yet compassionate distance, she portrays her protagonists with obvious diagnostic, psycho-analytical insight. Clear and concise, von Born maintains a high literary standard in her work.

Works

Det förtrollade huset (1956). *Leken är förbi* (1957). *Molnen kommer med morgonen* (1958). *Pavane* (1959). *Tre* (1960). *Martinas dagar* (1962). *Frigångare* (1964). *Insida* (1966). *Spårhunden* (1968; Vår bok). *Handen full* (1969). *Dagar som de faller* (1972). *Den tredje handen* (1974). *Aldrig mer tillbaka* (1975). *Simulantens liv* (1977). *Det japanska skriket* (1979). *Hungerbarnen* (1981). *Förväxling* (1983). *Hummerkriget* (1983). *Kungariket Atlas* (1984). *Den vita öknen* (1986). "Huset som sjönk-ett återbesök," autobiographical essay, *Svenska Dagbladet* (January 5, 1987), p. 8.

Bibliography

Algulin, Ingemar, *Contemporary Swedish Prose* (Stockholm, 1983), pp. 53, 81. Lindmarker, Ulrika, "Det stinkande 50-talet: Jag och min syster var ofta svultna." *Svenska Dagbladet-Weekend* (October 17, 1986): 7. Rosengren, Bernt, "Om det viktiga, omöjliga." *Aftonbladet* (October 6, 1986): 4.

Hanna Kalter Weiss

Anna Louisa Geertruida Bosboom-Toussaint

Born September 16, 1812, Alkmaar, The
    Netherlands; died April 13, 1886, 's-
    Gravenhage
Genre(s): novella, historical novel
Language(s): Dutch

The daughter of descendants of Huguenot refugees, Geertruida (Truitje) Bosboom-Toussaint became Holland's most prolific and popular nineteenth-century historical novelist.

After her broken engagement to the critic and historian R.C. Bakhuizen van den Brink, she moved into lodgings, unmarried, at age 36—a thing unheard of among the respectable Dutch bourgeoisie of the period. (It is no coincidence that independent and headstrong women occasionally occur in her work.) In 1851, she married the painter Jan Bosboom, five years her junior. By that time, she had already established herself as a major writer.

Her debut, the novella *Almagro* (1937), was based on an episode of Schiller's *Die Räuber*. *De graaf van Devonshire* (1838; The Count of Devonshire), Bosboom-Toussaint's first historical novel, was inevitably inspired by Sir Walter Scott and the French Romantics, but it also announced her own specific use of the genre. The historical facts, though meticulously documented and researched, serve mainly as a background for the psychological conflicts of the protagonists.

Bosboom-Toussaint chose the seventeenth century—Holland's most glorious period—as the setting of her next major novel, *Het Huis Lauernesse* (1840; The House of Lauernesse). This was in line with the leading critical journal *De Gids*, which wanted Holland to produce a proud nationalistic literature of its own. The treatment of the material, however, clearly bore the author's own stamp. Using a complex plot involving the story of a young noblewoman who angers and alienates her Roman Catholic fiancé by adopting the reformed religion, Bosboom-Toussaint depicted the sometimes drastic effect of the Reformation on social and domestic life. It became her most popular work.

Her most ambitious piece of work is certainly the Leicester series (1846–1855), which some critics regard as her absolute masterpiece. In an attempt to "interpret" history, Bosboom-Toussaint pictured Leicester very favorably. He may have failed as a statesman (his abortive mission in Holland, e.g.), but he was saved as a Christian because he preserved his spiritual integrity. Other important historical novels are *Graaf Pepoli* (1860; Count Pepoli) and the three-volume *De Delftsche wonderdokter* (1870–1871; The Delft Quack).

Though Bosboom-Toussaint also wrote some minor novels—an apparent effort to alleviate her family's constant money problems—she undoubtedly stood out among contemporary historical novelists, such as Oltmans and Van Lennep, not in the least because she was able to combine romantic sentimentality and imagination (adventures, escapes, disguises, etc.) with skillful characterization and a "modern" psychological approach. She was a master at writing dialogues and devising complex, dramatic plots. Her style occasionally suffered from ornamentality and digressions slowing down the plot line. Curious is the deliberate use of archaizing language (on the instigation of *De Gids*), which sometimes led to unwanted anachronistic effects.

Her religious views, present throughout her work, are akin to those of the Réveil, a conservative evangelical movement of the period. In *Het Huis Lauernesse*, which was basically meant as a tribute to Holland's reformist fervor, Bosboom-Toussaint did not refrain from referring to the pain and destruction caused by the religious schism. Her sympathy clearly lies with figures who embody Christian humanistic ideals rather than fanatic militancy, such as the kindhearted preacher in *Het Huis Lauernesse* or Gideon Florensz, Leicester's religious counselor in the book of the same name.

Two works are of special interest to modern feminist criticism: *Mejonkvrouwe de Mauléon* (1848; Mademoiselle de Mauléon), a historical novel about Bossuet's alleged mistress, and *Majoor Frans* (1874; Major Francis), a contemporary novel of manners made up of letters and journal fragments. In Bosboom-Toussaint's interpretation, Mademoiselle de Mauléon sacrificed her love for Bossuet to the higher ideals of the Church and, as the author suggests with characteristic insight, to his career as a prominent churchman. Yolande de Mauléon, like the woman hiding behind the nickname Major Francis, is the victim of malicious gossipers for whom young unattached women are naturally suspect. The clearly emancipationist note in *Majoor Frans*—the protagonist wants to be financially independent and has but little respect for received values—is toned down at the end when she fulfills her greatest wish, subjecting herself to the man she loves (a rich heir into the bargain) and serving him.

Truitje Bosboom-Toussaint was not only immensely popular with the general public, she was also on equal footing with the major men of letters of the period. She seemed to have emancipated herself successfully, though not without difficulty, from the condescending tone with which women writers were usually approached. When, at the peak of her career, she was criticized by the religious authorities for the lack of an edifying message in *Majoor Frans*, Bosboom-Toussaint, a devout Christian herself, typically replied that she did not consider it necessary to "constantly psalmodize in order to fight for the true religion."

Works

Almagro (1837). *De graaf van Devonshire* (1838). *Het Huis Lauernesse* (1840). *Eene kroon voor Karel den Stouten* (1842). *De graaf van Leycester in Nederland. De vrouwen uit het Leycestersche tijdvak. Gideon Florensz* (1846–1855). *Mejonkvrouwe de Mauléon* (1848). *Het huis Honselaarsdijk in 1638* (1849). *Media-Noche* (1852). *Graaf Pepoli* (1860). *De Delftsche wonderdokter* (1870–1871). *Majoor Frans* (1874; film version, 1915). *Langs een omweg* (1878). *Raymond de schrijnwerker* (1880). *Het kasteel Westhoven op Walcheren in Zeeland* (1882). *Volledige romantische werken* (25 vols., 1885–1888; rpt. 1898–1901). Tazelaar, C. *Onuitgegeven brieven van mevrouw Bosboom-Toussaint* (1934). **Translations:** *Major Francis* [*Majoor Frans*], tr. J. Ackroyd (1885).

Bibliography

Anbeek van der Meyden, A.G.H., *De schrijver tussen de coulissen* (1978). Bosboom, J., *Brieven van A.L.G. Bosboom-Toussaint aan E.J. Potgieter* (1913). Bouvy, J.M.C., *Idee en werkwijze van Mevrouw Bosboom-Toussaint* (1935). Busken Huet, C., *Litterarische Fantasiën en kritieken* 2, 11 and 16 (1865–1885). Drop, W., *Verbeelding en historie. Verschijningsvormen van de Nederlandse historische roman in de negentiende eeuw* (1958). Dyserinck, J., *A.L.G. Bosboom-Toussaint. Levens— en karakterschets* (1911). Goote, M., "Mevrouw A.L.G. Bosboom-Toussaint en haar romans," *Nederlandse Historiën* 11 (1977). Potgieter, E.J., *Kritische Studiën* 1 (1875). Reeser, H., *De jeugdjaren van A.L.G. Bosboom-Toussaint, 1812–1851* (1962). Reeser, H., *De huwelijksjaren van A.L.G. Bosboom-Toussaint 1851–1886* (1985). Stamperius, H., introduction to *Mejonkvrouwe de Mauléon* (1981). Stapert-Eggen, M., introduction to *Mejonkvrouwe de Mauléon* (1977). Ten Brink, J., *Mevrouw A.L.G. Bosboom-Toussaint* (1886). Uyterlinde-Maris, W., introduction to *Mejonkvrouwe de Mauléon* (1982). Zilverberg, S.B.J., introduction to *Het Huis Lauernesse* (1980). **General references:** *Cassell's Encyclopaedia of World Literature. De Nederlandse en Vlaamse auteurs van middeleeuwen tot heden* (1985). Knuvelder, G.P. *Handboek tot de geschiedenis der Nederlandse letterkunde 3* (1971). *Moderne encyclopedie van de wereldliteratuur* (1980–1984). *Winkler Prins Lexicon der Nederlandse letterkunde* (1986).

Ria Vanderauwera

Marie-Louise Boudat

(a.k.a. Louise Bellocq)

Born January 20, 1909, Charleville, Ardennes, France
Genre(s): novel, short story
Language(s): French

Boudat's *quart d'heure* in the limelight came in 1960, when her novel *La Porte retombée* was awarded the Prix Femina. The jury's decision prompted one of its members to quit in a fit of pique, pronouncing the work to be anti-Semitic.

Works

Le Passager de la belle aventure, novel (1952). *La Ferme de l'ermitage*, novel (1955; tr. Anne Carter as *Fled Is That Music*, 1962). *La Porte retombée*, novel (1960). *Mesdames Minnigan*, novel (1963). *Contes de mes bêtes au vent*, stories (1963). *Contes de mes bêtes sous la lune*, stories (1964). *Contes de mes bêtes à l'aventure*, stories (1968).

Robert Harrison

Katharina Boudewijns

Born ca. 1520, Brussels, Belgium; died after 1603, Brussels
Genre(s): contrareformational and dramatic poetry, translation
Language(s): Dutch

The daughter of the Clerk to the mighty Council of Brabant, Katharina married another aristocrat, Nicholas de Zoette, lawyer and secretary to the same Council. When Nicholas died, his well-educated wife was left with five children. She then acquired the protection of the Countess d'Arenberg, as appears from the dedication of Boudewijns' collection of spiritual poetry, *Het Prieelken der Gheestelijker Wellusten* (1587, 1603; The Bower of Spiritual Voluptuousness).

In this volume Boudewijns used rhetoricians' poetical forms to express her disappointment with the Calvinist domination of Brussels (1581–1586). Calvinist rule resulted, for example, in the temporary closing of churches. Genuine fear arose among Catholics concerning the future of their creed in Brussels and the Southern Netherlands. Boudewijns' sensitive poems do not seem to have been intended as a bulwark for Catholic orthodoxy to check Calvinist (and democratic) progress. Very much unlike the polemical rhetoric and the virulent scorn heaped upon the followers of the Reformation some decades earlier by the Antwerp teacher Anna Bijns, Boudewijns' resigned and rather nostalgic lyric poetry expresses consolatory concerns in a quite impersonal style. Her longing for mystical (re)union with the Lost Husband is almost purely medieval. More refined than Anna Bijns, more medieval in inspiration, Boudewijns is also a far more discreet poet. Invectives are scarce in her poetry, and the conventional catalogue of the opponents' vices and sins in contrareformational poetry is reduced to the charge of rebellion, of tyranny. The lack of humility and obedience of the Calvinists must surely lead to spiritual and economic decline, according to Boudewijns. A despairing tone of "fin du siècle" awareness can thus be detected in her poetry, which emphasizes the return to God and Christ as the only alternative to the evil of the times.

In the 1580s, Boudewijns also wrote a brief morality play. Very likely this *Schoon Spel van*

Sinnen van Twee Personen, te weten Liefde ende Eendrachtigheyt (A Beautiful Morality for Two Persons, to Wit Love and Concord), was never performed. The allegorical voices of Love and Concord debate the issues of contemporary vice; Concord has to concede that embracing a pure and blessed poverty is the only way towards a better life for "radix malorum est cupiditas."

Boudewijns also responded to the contemporary interest in systems of meditation and the improvement of one's personal spiritual life. In 1567, she translated into Dutch a Spanish tract on discretion, "very necessary and profitable for all those aspiring to Christian perfection," by Seraphin de Fermo (Brussels, 1568).

Works

Het Prieelken der Gheestelijker Wellusten (1927). "Het Prieelken der Gheestelijker Wellusten," "Een Schoon Spel van Sinnen van Twee Personen . . . ," and various other poems, in *Het Prieelken der Gheestijker Wellusten* (1872). *Een schoon tractaet, sprekende van der excellenter Deucht des Discretiens* (1568).

Bibliography

Buitendijk, W.J.C., *Het Calvinisme in de Spiegel van de Zuidnederlandse Literatuur der Contrareformatie* (Groningen, 1942), pp. 116–120. Rombauts, Edw., *Geschiedenis van de Letterkunde der Nederlanden*, III (Den Bosch, n.d.), pp. 139–145.

Kristiaan P. Aercke

Ina Boudier-Bakker

Born April 15, 1875, Amsterdam, The
  Netherlands; died December 26, 1966,
  Utrecht
Genre(s): novel, novella, drama
Language(s): Dutch

Boudier-Bakker's main concern in constructing a novel or story was to make her characters act according to a limited set of characteristics throughout and to create entire families along these fixed and parallel lines. Her attempts at psychological realism are limited to outward manifestations of the behavior of the Dutch bourgeoisie in the first half of the twentieth century.

The early short-story collection *Kinderen* (1905; Children) consists of a series of impressions of unappreciated or misunderstood children observed with much love and warmth yet little genuine knowledge of child psychology. In her first novels and longer narratives, on the other hand, some tragic fate takes its course through events that are narrated with great skill and intelligence, be it without any sense of inner necessity. *Armoede* (Poverty), her "great" novel, of 1909, is a "familieroman" depicting on a large canvas the life and spiritual poverty of the better circles in Holland in the years preceding the second World War. In comparison with her previous work, this novel marks a step forward, even though the author's limited perspective on class and class distinctions prevents her from raising serious social questions and from fathoming the characters' deeper motivation. Ina Boudier-Bakker concentrated on what she knew best, the domestic life and interpersonal relations of prominent citizens of Amsterdam. Characters not belonging to that class remain unreal, lifeless shades.

Her essentially conservative and anti-feminist stance is especially clear in *Spiegeltje* (1917; Little Mirror). The singing career of Marianne Roske, who is unmarried and secretly in love with her brother-in-law, is presented as a mere surrogate source of fulfillment. When Marianne temporarily takes over her sick sister's household, she suddenly loses interest in her art and experiences the simple pleasures of family life with "triumphant joy."

In the novella *De Straat* (1924; The Street), which is better in style, technique, and vision, Ina Boudier-Bakker describes the closed community of a village and the villagers' reactions to a request that they adopt Hungarian orphan children, thus allowing their individual as well as collective characteristics to emerge from within the group. This concentration on an almost self-contained group is very successful. In her later works, however, she went back to the epic mode and the wide canvas.

De klop op de deur (The Knock on the Door), by far her best-known and most popular work, went through twelve editions in three years following its publication in 1930. It was made into a television series in 1970. In it Ina Boudier-

Bakker intended to show, through the life of three generations of wealthy Amsterdammers, the penetration of modern ideas into the Netherlands of the preceding fifty years. At the center of her attention is the women's movement with its limited gains and many deficiencies. In the world of her narrative the *natural* woman is by nature a *married* woman, the incarnation of what the solemn Dutch bourgeoisie wanted their women to be, beings always safe but never free or responsible. Rather than an accurate portrayal of the influence of modern thought on the Dutch bourgeoisie from 1880 to 1930, *De klop op de deur* is an important historical document concerning Dutch upper-middle class mentality in the last decade before the second World War.

Ina Boudier-Bakker's works are narrow in scope both from a social and from a psychological point of view; they promote the traditional values of the class to which she herself belonged. Nevertheless, as a female novelist, treading almost virgin territory in Dutch literature, her achievements are considerable, and her books are still read.

Works

Machten (1902). Kinderen (1905). Armoede (1909). Bloesem (1912). Het spiegeltje (1917). De straat (1924). Tooverlantaarn (1929). De klop op de deur (1930). Vrouw Jacob (1935). Dierentuin (1941). De kleine kruisvaart (1955). Finale (1957). Momenten (1961).

Bibliography

Campen, M.H., *Nederlandse romancières van onze tijd* (1917), pp. 74–103. Ritter, P.H., Jr., *De vertelster weerspiegeld. Leven en werken van Ina Boudier-Bakker* (1931). Romein-Verschoor, Annie, *Vrouwenspiegel. De Nederlandse romanschrijfster na 1880* (1935), pp. 87–97; 123–125. Rössing, J.H., *Ina Boudier-Bakker* (1931). Stuiveling, Garmt, "In Memoriam Ina Boudier-Bakker." *De Gids* 130–i/ii (1967): 105–107.

Maya Bijvoet

Marie-Françoise Catherine de Beauvau(-Craon), marquise de Boufflers

(a.k.a. Madame de BĄĄĄs)

Born December 8, 1711, Lunéville, France;
  died July 3, 1786, Scey-sur-Saône
Genre(s): poetry, epigram, correspondence
Language(s): French

The Marquise de Boufflers played a significant role at the court set up in Lunéville by the Polish king Stanislas, who assumed the Duchy of Lorraine following his exile from Poland in 1735. She married the captain of Stanislas' guards, the Marquis de Boufflers-Remiencourt, and had two sons. She became a lady-in-waiting at the ducal court. At one time she was simultaneously the mistress of Stanislas, of his Minister of Finances Devaux and of his Minister of State, earning the title "Dame de Volupté" (Lady of Pleasure). She herself proudly flaunted the title in an epitaph she composed for herself:

Ci-gît, dans une paix profonde,
Cette Dame de Volupté
Qui, pour plus grande sûreté,
Fit son paradis de ce monde.

("Here lies, in a deep peace, that lady of pleasure who, to be even safer, made her paradise of this world.") Voltaire and Mme du Châtelet spent most of 1749 at the court of Lunéville and became close friends with the Marquise de Boufflers. Years later the Marquise wrote a sharp protest against the Archbishop of Paris' refusal to sanction Voltaire's burial in Paris.

Her occasional verses exhibit a polished Epicurean and exquisitely mundane sophistication. The following quatrain should suffice as a demonstration:

Nous ne sommes heureux qu'en
espérant de l'être;
Le moment de jouir échappe à nos
désirs;
Nous perdons le bonheur faute de le
connaître,
Nous sentons son absence au milieu
des plaisirs.

("We are happy only in hoping to be happy; the moment of enjoyment escapes our desires; we lose happiness for want of knowing it, we feel its absence in the midst of pleasures.") Her occasional pieces were published in an appendix to the works of her younger son, Stanislas-Jean Boufflers. Her correspondence with him and with Devaux survives but has not been edited.

Works

"Pièces fugitives." *Oeuvres du chevalier de Boufflers*, II (1828), pp. 263–274 (some verses also composed by other family members).

Bibliography

Maugras, Gaston, *La Cour de Lunéville au 18ᵉ siècle* (Paris, 1904). *La Marquise de Boufflers* (Paris, 1907).

Earl Jeffrey Richards

Rita Boumē Papa

(see: Rita Boumi Papa)

Rita Boumi Papa

(a.k.a. Rita Boumē Papa)

Born 1906, Syros, Greece; died 1986, Athens
Genre(s): poetry, prose, translation
Language(s): Greek

Rita (Margarita) Boumi (or *Mpoumē*, or *Boumē*) Papa (or *Pappa*) grew up on the Aegean island of Syros. She was educated in Greek public schools and spent one year in a French boarding school. At the age of fifteen she went to live with a wealthy older brother and his Italian wife in Syracuse, Sicily. While in Syracuse she studied early childhood education. She left Sicily in 1929 and returned to Syros where from 1930 to 1936 she reorganized and directed the Institute for the Protection of Babes and Infants. In 1936 she married Nikos Papas and lived with him in Trikala, Thessaly, until 1939, at which time they moved to Athens. She has written and spoken on many social and political issues and has participated in international conferences on children and on women. She has also edited several periodicals: *Ionios Anthology* in 1929–1930, *Cyclades* in 1930–1932, and *The Poets' Newspaper* during 1956–1958.

In her literary work, she has had the support of her husband, Nikos Papas, also a poet. Together they published a two-volume international anthology of poetry in 1952. She has translated many Eastern European poets and Italian playwrights into modern Greek. In 1973, she published *O mavros adelphos* (The Black Brother), an anthology of black American and African poetry translated into modern Greek. She has been widely translated in other European languages and, along with Jenny Mastorakē, is widely admired outside Greece. Translations of whole books or selected poems have been published in French, Polish, Russian, Bulgarian, Hungarian, Romanian, Dutch, and Italian.

Her poetic achievement includes sixteen volumes of poetry, one of which was written in Italian. She received the First Prize for Poetry from the Academy of Athens for her 1935 collection entitled *Oi sphygmoi tēs sigēs mou* (The Pulse of My Silence). She also received the First Prize of the National Resistance for her 1945 publication, *Athēna—Dekemvrēs 1944* (Athens—December 1944). Her Italian collection of poems (*Ritorno in Optitzia*) was awarded the International Prize of Syracuse, and her book of poems for children, *Ē magikē phlogera* (The Magic Flute), also received an award.

In her later years she turned to prose. In 1975 she published a collection of stories, *Otan peinousame kai polemousame* (When We Hungered and Fought), dealing with the period of the Nazi occupation of Greece (1941–1945) and, in 1976, *Morgan-John, o gyalinos pringipas kai oi metamorphoseis tou* (Morgan-John, the Glass Prince and His Transformations).

With the publication of Rita Boumi Papa's first book, *Tragoudia stēn agapē* (1930; Songs to Love), a collection of traditional love sonnets, she was immediately recognized for her lyricism and sensitivity and was compared to Sappho. However, her stay in Sicily and her training had made her profoundly aware of the plight of the underdog and the oppressed and her sympathies surfaced slowly at first but much more definitely as she grew older. Eventually she renounced formalism and became a poet of protest against suffering and human injustice. This development was paralleled by her evolving awareness of her function as a poet, as a spokesman for the common man and woman who may not be able to express what they feel.

Her convictions led to such collections as *Chilia skotōmena koritsia* (A Thousand Slain Girls), a poetic documentation of the fate of so many girls who were cruelly killed during the Greek Civil War for being "on the wrong side." The poet enters into the individual lives of the girls and speaks of their suffering with convincing accuracy and emotional appeal. The implication is that these girls were unique and yet representative of the needless and senseless killing of "the enemy" during any war.

One of her last poetic works, *Phōs ilaron* (Light Serene), a highly personal meditative poem published in 1966, seems to be both an appreciation of her past and a justification or apology for the way she had led her life. The fighting spirit of her social poetry is replaced here by the mellowness and serenity of age reflecting back on youth and life.

Works

Tragoudia stēn agapē [Songs to Love] (1930). *Oi sphygmoi tēs sigēs mou* [The Pulse of My Silence] (1935). *To pathos ton seirēnon* [The Passion of the Sirens] (1938). *Athēna—Dekemvrēs 1944* [Athens—December 1944] (1945). *Kainourgia chloē* [New Grass] (1949). *Ritorno in Optitzia*, in Italian [Return to Optitzia] (1949). *O paranomos lychnos* [The Unlawful Lamp] (1952). *To rodo tēs Ypapantēs* [The Rose of Ypapantē] (1960). *Lampro Phthinoporo* [Splendid Autumn] (1961). *Anthophoria stēn erēmo* [Flower Procession in the Desert] (1962). *Chilia skotōmena koritsia* [A Thousand Slain Girls] (1963, 1974). *Den yparchei allē doxa* [There Is No Other Glory] (1964). *Eskērē amazona* [The Tough Amazon] (1964). *E magikē phlogera* [The Magic Flute] (1965). *Skiouma* (1965). *Phos ilaron* [Light Serene] (1966). *Otan peinousame kai polemousame* [When We Hungered and Fought]. *Diegēmata 1941–1945* [Stories 1941–1945] (1975). *Morgan-John, o gyalinos pringipas kai oi metamorphoseis tou* [Morgan-John, the Glass Prince and His Transformations] (1976). **Anthologized Translations:** *Modern Poetry in Translation* 34 (Summer, 1978). Dalven, Rae, *Modern Greek Poetry* (New York, 1949; rpt. Miami, 1976.) *The Singing Cells: Modern Greek Poems*, tr. John Richmond and Bryan McCarthy (Montreal, 1970). *Modern Greek Poetry: From Cavafis to Elytis.*, tr. Kimon Friar (New York: 1973). *Contemporary Greek Women Poets*, tr. Eleni Fourtouni (New Haven, 1978). *Modern Greek Poetry*, tr. Kimon Friar (Athens, 1982).

Bibliography

Decavalles, Andonis, "Modernity: The Third Stage, The New Poets." *The Charioteer*, v. 20 (New York, 1978). Friar, Kimon, *Modern Greek Poetry* (New York, 1973). Mirasgezē, Maria, *Neollenikē Logotechnia*, vol. 2 (Athens, 1982). Politēs, Linos, *Historia tēs Neoellenikēs Logotechnias*, 3rd ed. (Athens:, 1980). Demetrius, K.K., [review], *World Literature Today* 72, 1 (Winter, 1978): 157.

Helen Dendrinou Kolias

Catherine de Bourbon

Born 1558, Paris, France; died 1604, Nancy
Genre(s): poetry, letters
Language(s): French

The daughter of Jeanne d'Albret and of Antoine de Bourbon, Catherine was born five years after her illustrious brother, Henri IV, who became one of the most popular kings of France. Catherine's life was not happy. She had many suitors because it was believed that Henri IV and his wife would never have any children, and a son of Catherine would likely become the king of France. Henri used his sister for his own political ends, promising to allow her to marry, but not actually allowing her to until she was in her forties. Her husband, the Duke of Lorraine, had been told by Henri that she would convert to Catholicism, but she had no intention to do so. She died at the age of forty-six without having realized her most fervent wish, that of becoming a mother.

The sonnets and stanzas Catherine de Bourbon wrote were all inspired by her religious beliefs.

Bibliography

Lettres et poésies de Catherine de Bourbon, ed. Raymond Ritter (Paris, 1927.)

Marie-France Hilgar

Duchesse de Bourbonnais et d'Auvergne

(see: Anne de France)

Ida Boy-Ed

(a.k.a. Ida Cornelia Ernestine, née Ed)

Born April 17, 1852, Bergedorf, Germany;
died June 13, 1928, Travemünde
Genre(s): novel, short story
Language(s): German

Born the daughter of a self-made newspaper publisher, Ida Boy-Ed grew up in a literary and political family in Lübeck. With the encouragement of her father, she began very early to write novellas and sketches.

This changed with her early marriage to the businessman Carl Johann Boy, whose family disapproved of her writing. In 1878, Ida Boy-Ed tried to escape the stifling atmosphere of her home (which she shared with her in-laws), and moved to Berlin to support herself and her oldest son through her writing. She had already achieved some minor success with newspaper pieces and serial novels.

However, she did not find the opportunities she had hoped for in Berlin, and under increasing family pressure returned to Lübeck a year and a half later. There she kept house, raised her four children, and spent every spare minute writing.

Success finally came to her. Her first book, a collection of novellas, was published in 1882; many more followed over the years. Most of her novels use her own background, the Hanseatic bourgeoisie. Critical acclaim for her novels was high, and financial success followed. Although she wrote constantly and mainly for financial reasons, her work was considerably better than that of some of her contemporaries (e.g., Courths-Mahler, Eschstruth). Her concern for the problems of women is expressed throughout her work, which led her to write detailed studies of Charlotte von Stein, Germaine de Staël, and Charlotte von Kalb.

Her success also brought her public recognition in her home town. Her home became a cultural center in Lübeck: artists, musicians, and writers met there, among them the young Thomas Mann, whom she encouraged.

In addition to over 70 novels and collections of stories, she also published innumerable articles and essays in newspapers and magazines.

Works

Ein Tropfen (1882). *Getrübtes Glück* (1884). *Seine Schuld* (1885). *Männer der Zeit* (1885). *Dornenkrone* (1886). *Masken* (1887). *Die Unversuchten* (1887). *Abgründe des Lebens* (1887). *Ich!* (1888). *Eine Lüge?* (1888). *Fanny Förster* (1889). *Nicht im Geleise* (1890). *Aus Tantalus Geschlecht* (1891). *Malergeschichten: Psychologische Studien* (1892). *Lea und Rahel* (1892). *Empor!* (1892). *Ein Kind* (1892). *Zuletzt gelacht* (1893). *Sieben Schwerter* (1894). *Sturm* (1894). *Die Schwestern* (1894). *Werde zum Weib* (1894). *Hermine von Preuschen; Konrad Telman; Ninfa* (1895). *X* (1896). *Die Lampe der Psyche* (1896). *Nichts* (1897). *Eine reine Seele* (1897). *Ein kritischer Moment; Kreuzträgerin* (1897). *Zwei Novellen* (1898). *Erdrückt; Eine Malergeschichte* (1898). *Die Flucht* (1898). *Die Schuldnerin* (1899). *Zwei Männer* (1900). *Nur ein Mensch* (1900). *Um Helena* (1901). *Aus einer Wiege* (1901). *Die säende Hand* (1902). *ABC des Lebens* (1903). *Die große Stimme* (1903). *Gesina* (1903). *Die Ketten* (1904). *Heimkehrfieber* (1905). *Der Festungsgarten* (1905). *Eine Wohltat* (1906). *Um ein Weib* (1906). *Die holde Törin* (1907). *Fast ein Adler* (1907). *Ein Echo* (1908). *Die Kadettenmutter und andere Marineerzählungen* (1909). *Geschichten aus der Hansastadt* (1909). *Nichts über mich* (1909). *Ein königlicher Kaufmann* (1910). *Nur wer die Sehnsucht kennt* (1911). *Charlotte von Kalb. Eine psychologische Studie* (1912). *Ein Augenblick im Paradies* (1912). *Eine Frau wie du!* (1913). *Stille Helden* (1914). *Des Vaterlandes Kochtopf: Allerlei Rezepte für Küche und Herz in Kriegestagen* (1915). *Die Opferschale* (1916). *Das Martyrium der Charlotte von Stein. Versuch ihrer Rechtfertigung* (1916). *Erschlossene Pforten* (1917). *Die Stimme der Heimat* (1918). *Der Theoretiker und andere Novellen* (1920). *Glanz* (1920). *Brosamen* (1922). *Germaine von Staël* (1922). *Harte Probe* (1923). *Annas Ehe* (1923). *Das spärliche Brünnlein* (1924). *Das Eine* (1925). *Gestern und Morgen* (1926). *Aus alten und neuen Tagen* (1926). *Mit tausend Masten* (1931).

Bibliography

de Mendelssohn, Peter, "Vorbemerkungen des Herausgebers." *Thomas Mann, Briefe an Otto Grautoff und Ida Boy-Ed* (Frankfurt/Main, 1975). *Ida Boy-Ed. Eine Auswahl von Peter de Mendelssohn* (Lübeck, 1975). *Kürschner's Deutscher Literatur-Kalendar, Nekrolog 1902–1935*(Rpt. Berlin, 1973), pp. 81–82. *Neue Deutsche Biographie*, vol. 2 (Berlin, 1955), p. 495.

Hortense Bates

Birgitte Cathrine Boye

Born March 7, 1742, Gentofte, Denmark; died October 17, 1824, Copenhagen
Genre(s): poetry, drama, psalms, songs
Language(s): Danish

Although esteemed and honored by her contemporaries as "a genuinely poetic spirit and a fine, noble woman [of] character" (*Dansk biografisk Leksikon*, 2, 406), Birgitte Cathrine Boye now holds a more modest place in Danish literary history. Boye initially contributed 20 psalms, based on David's Psalm 104, to *Harboes og Guldbergs Salmebog*(Harboe's and Guldberg's Book of Psalms); 18 of her psalms won a place in the first collection of didactic, purposefully ennobling poems. In all, Birgitte Boye eventually composed 125 psalms, contributing these and 24 translations to *Den Guldbergske Salmebog* (1778; Guldberg's Book of Psalms); her achievement was notable and impressive in her day. Boye's psalms vary "from psalms for the Church Calendar, evensongs, and psalms to biblical texts, to songs for Church meetings and the Passion" (Stig Dalager og Anne-Marie Mai, *Danske kvindelige forfattere*, 1, p. 118). All the psalms praise God's omnipresence and didactically "unite godly benevolence with praise of the monarchy and of the Danish State" (Dalager, 1, p. 118), under the monarch's protective, fatherly guidance. Boye's psalms, even those praising nature, are "a point of departure for a tribute to God's wisdom and omnipotence" (*DbL2*, 405). Birgitte Boye also wrote dramatic poetry (1780; the pastorale, *Melicerte*), two heroic plays, *Gorm den Gamle* (1781; Gorm the Old) and *Sigrid eller Regnalds Død* (1795; Sigrid or Regnald's Death), songs, such as the National Song for Crown Prince Frederik's Return from Norway (H.J. Birch, *Billedgallerie for Fruentimmer* I, 1793, pp. 219–220), and romances in folk ballad style. Her contemporaries in the Danish Church and Literary Societies were quick to praise her poetry, but only one of her many psalms still retains a place in the current book of psalms for the Danish Church.

Birgitte Cathrine Boye was the eldest of a loving, godly family of seven children; her parents were the sheriff, later royal hunting *aide de camp*, of Jægersborg Forest, Jens Johanissen (1711–1172), and Dorthea Henriksdatter (1712–1772). Birgitte Boye was born on March 7, 1742, in Gentofte; at thirteen years of age, she was betrothed to a young nobleman, Herman Michelsen Hertz. She married Hertz when she was twenty-one and raised four children, the youngest of whom, Jens Michael, became the bishop of Ribe Cathedral. Not only did Hertz manage a household, raise four children, and write poetry, songs, and plays; she also read extensively, becoming well-acquainted with the major contemporary authors and works of English, French, and German literature. In 1773, Hertz answered an appeal from *De skønne Videnskabers Selskab* (The Society for Belles Lettres and Fine Arts) to write "holy poetry" for a new collection of psalms, eventually the Guldberg Collection. She won wide recognition for her poems praising God, king, and country. Hertz' husband died in 1775, and she was left in difficult straits until Guldberg, publisher of the book of psalms, came to her aid and that of her sons, who were seeking entrance into Helsingør (Elsinore) Academy. In 1778, Hertz married a customs inspector and judicial adviser and official, Hans Boye. After her second marriage, Boye directed her literary talents to dramatic poetry, and she also won recognition and acclaim for her dramatic compositions. In honor of Queen Juliane Marie's birthday in 1780, Boye wrote a pastorale, *Melicerte*, for performance at the Court Theatre of Fredensborg; the play is now considered "pure convention . . . [in which Boye] outdid her own literary colleagues in trivializing the female protagonist, Melicerte" (Dalager, 1, p. 119). Boye's heroic play, *Gorm den Gamle*, written in 1781 for Christian VII and performed finally in 1783 at the Royal Theatre, depicted the title character as "a warrior and bloodthirsty avenger who, without 'female tenderness,' protects the land's gentle, good women" (Dalager, 1, p. 119). For her later, simpler but more skillful heroic play, *Sigrid eller Regnalds Død*, Boye drew on Saxo's writings. Birgitte Boye died on October 17, 1824, in Copenhagen. Among her contemporaries, Birgitte Boye earned the highest praise for her psalms, dramatic praise poems, and songs of God's presence and love, for her heroic plays, and for her extensive, impressive knowledge of the literary currents of her day.

Works

Salmer i Den Guldbergske Salmebog (1778). *Melicerte* (1780). *Gorm den Gamle* (1781). "Frederiks Hjemkomst fra Norge; Tanker ved Kiøbenhavns Ruiner" (1795). *Sigrid eller Regnalds Død* (1795).

Bibliography

Birch, H.J., *Billedgallerie for Fruentimmer I* (1793), pp. 202–224. Dalager, Stig, and Anne-Marie Mai, *Danske kvindelige forgattere 1. Fra Sophie Brahe til Mathilde Fibiger. Udvikling og perspektiv.* 2 vols. (Copenhagen, 1983). *Dansk biografisk Leksikon*, 2, 3 ed. (1979).

Lanae Hjortsvang Isaacson

Karin Boye

Born 1900, Gothenburg; died 1941, Alingsås
Genre(s): lyric poetry, essay, prose fiction
Language(s): Swedish

Karin Boye has been recognized as one of the major modern writers in Swedish literature. Born into an upper middle class milieu, she completed high school in 1920 and went on to a teacher's seminary where she took her exam as public school teacher in 1921. She continued her studies at Uppsala University from 1921–1926 and two more years at Stockholm's "högskola," from where she received her master's degree in 1928. After graduation she taught at various schools at different times in her short life. But already during her high school years Boye was profoundly interested in political issues, and soon she became a member of the left radical *Clarté*. Another major interest was Freud's psychoanalytical theories, which just then were

becoming more generally known. Together with Erik Mesterton and Josef Riwkin she co-founded the journal *Spektrum* in 1931. During the same year she was elected into the distinguished Swedish literary society *Samfundet de Nio*. In 1929 Boye married her Clarté colleague Leif Björk, but this marriage soon ended with a divorce in 1931. More openly yielding to her homosexual leanings after that, she lived with her German girlfriend in her home in Stockholm. Boye's split between the social bourgeois mores of her upbringing and her strong innate desire to be free of them became early the major theme in Boye's literary work. Her erotic split showed itself in periodically severe depressions for which she sought psychoanalytical help, especially during the years 1932–1933 while she was in Berlin. The treatment did not alleviate her deep inner anguish, later compounded by the fact that her girlfriend was dying of cancer. In April of 1941 she walked out into her beloved Swedish woods outside of Alingsås and committed suicide.

Already in her earliest poetry Boye gave expression to her inner battle between moral commitment and spontaneous abandonment to life's vital forces. Her first poetry collection, *Moln* (Clouds), came out in 1922 and became an immediate success. Its lyric quality deepened in *Gömda land* (Hidden Countries), and with her third collection *Härdarna* (The Hearths), in which a courageous trust in providence fights victoriously the forces of social estrangement, she completes the poetry of her youth. Eight years later she published the deeply psychological *För trädets skull* (1935; For the Sake of the Tree), a collection which is unique not only in Swedish, but world literature. The symbolic language in these poems both conceals and concedes her tragic personal problem. Thematically intertwined with the political developments on the European scene, which just then began to threaten the personal freedom of each individual, the "tree," whose roots are threatened below the earth's surface, stands as the symbol of the individual. *De sju dödssynderna* (1941; The Seven Deadly Sins) came out posthumously, edited by her friends Victor Svanberg and Hjalmar Gullberg, who also wrote an introduction to the selection. Pitting love and death against each other, Boye had tried for a last time to solve her problem—without success.

Boye began her prose publications with her novel *Astarte* (1931), which won her the prize in the Nordic Novel Competition. Here, too, she discusses the confrontation between the will to live free versus the demands of cultural traditions. In her next novel, *Merit vaknar* (1933; Merit Awakens), she takes a stand for reality against an exaggerated idealism. The same theme is variously repeated in her collection of short stories, *Uppgörelser* (1934; Settlements) and the novel *Kris* (1934; Crisis). Though she takes a stand for life and gratification in *Kris*, the conflict between free abandonment to life's forces and duty ends in a sad defeat in her next novel *För lite* (1936; Too Little). The next collection of short stories, *Ur funktion* (1940; Out of Function), is again concerned with moral problems. Boye's last, completed, and possibly greatest work was the novel *Kallokain* (1941). Again inspired by the political developments on the European continent, Boye shows the psychological danger to the individual in a futuristic "police state" of the 21st century. *Bebådelse* (Annunciation), a novel fragment, short stories, and sketches, came out posthumously in 1941. Boye even tried her hand at playwriting. Her play *Hon som bär templet* appeared in *Bonniers Litterära Magasin* in 1941, and was put on stage by an ensemble in Stockholm that same year. Four of her essays, "Dagdrömmeriet som livsåskådning," "Om litteraturkritiken," "Språket bortom logiken," and above all "Rädslan och livet," (Daydreaming as Philosophy of Life, About Critic of Literature, The Language Beyond Logic, Fear and Life), which she published in *Spektrum* during the years 1931-1932, are important for any study of Karin Boye and her work.

Karin Boye's work, especially her novel *Kallokain*, has been translated into numerous languages, such as English, German, Danish, Norwegian, Hungarian, and Portuguese.

Boye's opus is collected in *Samlade Skrifter*, 1-11 (Stockholm, 1947-1949), with introductions by her friend and biographer Margit Abenius. Her poetry is brought together in *Dikter* (Stockholm: 1942). S. Linder edited a reprint of selected poems under the title *Till dig* (Stockholm: 1963).

Over the years, Boye's poetry and prose have been republished in editions and selections too numerous to list here, and interest in her work is increasing as time goes by.

Works
Translations: *Kallokain*, tr. Gustaf Lannestock, intro. Richard B. Vowles (Madison, Wis., 1966; New York, 1985).

Bibliography
Abenius, Margit, *Drabbad av renhet: En bok om Karin Boyes liv och diktning* (Stockholm, 1950; 2nd ed. 1965). Abenius, Margit, *Kontakter* (Stockholm, 1944). Abenius, Margit, and Olof Lagerkrantz, eds., *Karin Boye: Minnen och studier* (Stockholm, 1942). Ekelöf, G., "Kallokain." *Blandade kort.* (Stockholm, 1957). Fjeldstad, Anton, "Allusjon og myte i Karin Boyes Kallokain." *Tidskrift för Litteraturvetenskap.* Lund (1972-1973): 240-248. Fjeldstad, Anton, "Stilen i Karin Boyes roman 'Kallokain.'" *Edda* (1972): 101-116. Gustafsson, Barbro, "Ett ögonblicks hängivelse." *Edda* (1975): 157-160. Gustafsson, Barbro, "Framtidens öde land: Oswald Spengler, T.S. Eliot och Karin boye." *Svensk Litteraturtidskrift* 3 (1975): n.p. Janzon, Å, "Bilden av Boye." *Bonniers Litterära Magasin* (1941): 64-66. Kjellén, A., "Havssymbolik hos Karin Boye: En utvecklingslinje i hennes 20-talsdiktning." *Diktaren och havet* (Stockholm, 1957), pp. 297-313. Lagerkrantz, Olof, "Min stackars unge, min mörkrädda." *Svenska lyriker* (Stockholm, 1961; rev. ed. *Tretton lyriker*, Stockholm, 1973). Ljungdell, Ragna, "Trädet som blev ett berg." *Det oförstörbara* (Stockholm, 1945), pp. 132-149. Mjöberg, J., "Der förnekade mörkret." *Samlaren* (1954): n.p. Petherick, Karin, "Karin Boye (1900-1941)." *Essays on Swedish Literature: From 1880 to the Present Day*, ed. Irene Scobbie (Aberdeen, 1978), pp. 141-144. Stolpe, S., *Kämpande dikt* (Stockholm, 1938). Svanberg, Birgitta, "Längtan efter moderliga män." *Könsroller i litteraturen från antiken till 1960-talet* (Stockholm, 1968). Svanberg, V., "Karin Boye." *Ord och Bild* (1941), pp. 510-515. Svanfeldt, G., "Död amazon av Hjalmar Gullberg." *Lyrisk tidsspegel* (1947), pp. 230-238. Tideström, G., "Min hud är full av fjärilar av Karin Boye." *Lyrisk tidsspegel* (1947), pp. 218-223. Tideström, G., "Bön till solen." *Lyrisk tidsspegel* (1947), pp. 224-229. Tideström, G.,

"Dödsrunor." *Bonniers Litterära Magasin* (1941), pp. 341–342.

For further editions of Karin Boye's work, secondary literature, book reviews, and newspaper articles on Karin Boye see *Svenskt Författar-lexikon: Bibliografisk handbok till Sveriges moderna litteratur*, containing compilations of everything published concerning Swedish authors and published every five years by Svenskt Författarlexikons Förlag, Rabén och Sjögren, Stockholm. See also the Swedish Catalogue of Publications.

Hanna Kalter Weiss

Louise Brachmann

Born February 2, 1777, Rochlitz, Germany;
died September 17, 1822, Halle, Germany
Genre(s): poetry, short fiction, novel
Language(s): German

Louise Brachmann was educated by her mother. Through her friendship with Sidonie von Hardenberg she came in contact with Sidonie's brother, the poet Novalis, who recognized her talent and recommended her to Friedrich von Schiller. Brachmann contributed to Schiller's journals *Die Horen* and *Musenalmanach*.

Within four years after her first suicide attempt in 1800, her parents, a sister, and three of her closest friends died. Being financially destitute, Brachmann embarked on a literary career. Like Sophie Mereau, whom she met in Jena, Brachmann published her poems and short fiction in contemporary journals. However, despite several attempts, she failed to attract a reputable publisher to sponsor her work during her lifetime. Continuing personal and financial problems led to a second suicide attempt that was thwarted. Only a few days after this incident she wrapped her shawl around a rock and successfully drowned herself in the river Saale.

Works

Lyrische Gedichte (1800). *Gedichte* (1808). "Einige Züge aus meinem Leben in Beziehung auf Novalis." *Kinds Harfe* 2 (1815). *Romantische Blüten* (1817). *Das Gottesurteil. Rittergedicht in fünf Gesängen* (1818). *Novellen und kleine Romane* (1819). *Schilderungen aus der Wirklichkeit* (1820). *Novellen* (1822). *Romantische Blätter* (1823). *Verirrungen oder Die Macht der Verhältnisse*, novel (1823). *Auserlesene Dichtungen von L.B.*, F.K.J. Schütz, ed., 2 vols. (1824). *Erzählungen und Novellen*, F.K.J. Schütz, ed., 4 vols. (1825). *Auserlesene Erzählungen und Novellen*, K.L.M. Müller, ed., 4 vols. (1825–1826). **Translation:** *The Three Sons* [*Die drei Söhne*] (1827).

Bibliography

Brinker-Gabler, G., *Deutsche Dichterinnen vom 16. Jahrhundert bis zur Gegenwart* (Frankfurt am Main, 1978), pp. 153–157 (contains work selections, pp. 154–157). Brümmer, F., "L.B.," in *Allgemeine Deutsche Biographie* 47 (1903). *Erinnerungen an L.B. und den Schiller-Körner-Kreis* (1937). Franzen, M., *Landschaft und Menschen in den Novellen L.Bs.* Diss., Halle, 1947. Müllner, A., "Sappho," in *Morgenblatt für gebildete Stände* (Oct. 1822), pp. 343–344. Schütz, ed., [biographical sketch], *Erzählungen und Novellen*. Wernicke, M., *L.B.*, play (1896 and 1911).

Helene M. Kastinger Riley

Sophie Brahe

Born ca. 1556, Knudstrup (Knutstorp), Scania, (now) Sweden; died 1643, Helsingør, Denmark
Genre(s): poetry, correspondence, scientific writing
Language(s): Danish, Latin

Together with her famous brother, Tycho Brahe (1546–1601), Sophie Brahe represents the flowering of letters and sciences during the Danish Renaissance. As the daughter of a prominent family, Sophie Brahe exhibited keen insights into human nature and fine talents for poetry, for letters and humanities, and for scientific studies. Making the most of her innate gifts, Brahe collaborated with her brother Tycho at the latter's observatory, Uranienborg, on Hven Island. The association of the two Brahes was so close and constant that the nineteenth-century poet Johan L. Heiberg cautioned that "Denmark must never forget the noble woman who, in spirit much more than flesh and blood, was Tycho Brahe's sister; the shining star in our Danish heaven is indeed a double one" (Johan Ludvig Heiberg, "Sophie Brahe," *Prosaiske Skrifter*, p. 364).

Sophie Brahe was born in Knudstrup about 1556; she was the daughter of a renowned Danish family. Her father, Otto Brahe, served as Royal Counsel to King Christian III, and her mother, Beate Bille, was also of a noble family. Sophie Brahe received an exemplary education; "she was a very gifted woman, possessing unique talents and an even more unique refinement of these talents" (Heiberg, p. 277). Upon the untimely death of her first husband, the nobleman Otto Thott of Eriksholm (in 1588), Sophie Brahe dedicated herself to her only son, Tage Thott; to the administration of Eriksholm (until Tage Thott reached maturity); to scientific studies with her brother; and to independent studies of genealogy, astrology, and botany. With her renewed work at Uranienborg, Sophie Brahe's life took a turn to the dramatic—or rather the heroic-tragic. On Hven, Brahe met Erik Lange of Engelsholm-Solvig. Lange was an eager young nobleman, bent on studying astronomy with the great Tycho Brahe. The Lange family was very prominent, but Erik Lange had frittered away much of the family's considerable fortune in vain attempts to find the Stone of Wisdom, make gold, and carry on very dubious experiments. Sophie Brahe fell deeply in love; the couple was formally engaged in 1590, despite strenuous objection from the entire Brahe family, except Tycho, with whom Sophie Brahe "shared a special sympathy" (Heiberg, p. 278). The Brahe family looked with disdain on Lange's declining fortunes and lack of concrete plans and prospects. Lange abruptly left Denmark in 1590 to pursue futile studies in Germany (and to escape creditors), while Brahe remained behind, confronting her own family. Brahe and Lange finally married in 1602, in Eckernförde, Germany; at the time of their marriage, Brahe was 46 years old and Erik Lange was much past his prime, a broken, penniless man who depended on his wife: "the prospects were poor in every way. With sorrow, longing, and waiting, youth had simply wasted away" (Heiberg, p. 323). Brahe's fortunes continued to decline after her marriage, until Lange's death in Prague in 1613; at that time, Brahe disclaimed her husband's debts and any claims on his inheritance. She returned to Denmark (Helsingør) in 1616. Brahe continued her genealogical and astrological writings, living in somewhat more favorable circumstances until her death in 1643 at the advanced age of 87.

Sophie Brahe's long period of waiting, isolation from Erik Lange, and conflict with her family, led to her major work, a long versified letter in Latin, *Urania Titani [Urania til Titan]* (1594; Urania to Titan), addressed to Erik Lange. The letter is characterized by elegant poetic expression, by notable attention to mythological background, and by "such a genuine passion . . . such an intense expression of mutually shared feelings, that it never fails to touch even a later generation" (Lauritz Weibull, "Sophie Brahe. Ett bidrag . . . ," 38). (Sophie Brahe's long song, *Nu vil jeg for eder kvæde* [1590–1592; Now I Will Sing for Thee], also written for Lange, could conceivably be Brahe's own Danish precedent for the Latin poem, *Urania Titani*.) In any case, *Urania Titani* constitutes "a burning hymn to love, containing such a warm, human feeling and such genuine poetry . . . that we very much regret not having . . . the Danish original" (J.A. Fridericia, "Træk af kvindeidealets Omdannelse." *Tilskueren*: 1898, 473).

Brahe's other preserved writings include a long letter from Eckernförde to her sister, Margrethe Brahe, and various genealogical works in addition to "the long, intense love letter to Erik Lange" (Stig Dalager, *Danske kvindelige forfattere*, 1, p. 25). The letter to Margrethe (1602) has been described as "a nonpareil in Danish correspondence of the time" (*Dansk biografisk leksikon*, 428). In her letter to Margrethe, Sophie Brahe "expresses her strong personal feelings, her humanism, and her self-confidence" (Dalager, 1, p. 24). Brahe's considerable genealogical interests led to *Slægtebogen* (1626; The Family History Book), an impressive 900-page study of Danish nobility, "a highpoint of Renaissance Danish work, built on oral tradition and written sources" (DBL, 428). An additional work representing Brahe's extensive genealogical correspondence, study, and including all informative letters on the family, *Kopibogsamlinger* (1624–1640; Copy Book Collections), is now preserved in the collection of *Svenska Riksarkivet* (Swedish Royal Archives, Stockholm).

Sophie Brahe's many interests and her dedication to science were remarkable for her time—and ours. Her poem, *Urania Titani*, offers new insights into her personality, her long-lasting passion for Erik Lange, and the depth of her skill and learning. With her remarkable education and her special "genius for poetry" (Weibull, 38), Sophie Brahe represents a new epoch and force in Danish letters, "one of the very first exponents of Renaissance culture in Denmark" (Dalager, 1, p. 31).

Works

Nu vil jeg for eder kvæde (1590–1591). *Urania Titani: Urania til Titan* [Urania to Titan] (1594), in *Resenii Inscriptiones hafniensis*, Danish tr. Johan Ludvig Heiberg, in "Sophie Brahe. En hverdagshistorie fra det 16de og 17de Aarhundrede" (Urania, 1846). *Prosaiske Skrifter: Niende Bind* (1861), pp. 275–364. *Brev til Margrethe Brahe* [Letter to Margrethe Brahe] (1602). Heiberg, "Sophie Brahe." *Prosaiske, Skrifter: Niende Bind*, pp. 275–364. *Sophie Brahes regnskabsbog* [Sophie Brahe's Records] (1627–1640). *Slægtebogen* [The Family History Book] (1626). *Kopibogsamlinger* [Copy Book Collections] (1624–1640).

Bibliography

Dalager, Stig, and Anne-Marie Mai, *Danske kvindelige forfattere. 1. Sophie Brahe-Mathilde Fibiger. Udvikling og perspektiv* (København, 1982), pp. 24–31. *Danmarks adels aarbog* (1888), V, 112; 1950, LXVII:II, 18. *Dansk biografisk Leksikon: Andet Bind* (København, 1979), pp. 427–428. Fridericia, J.A., "Træk af kvindeidealets Omdannelse." *Tilskueren.* 1898, pp. 465–479. Heiberg, Johan Ludvig, "Sophie Brahe. En hverdagshistorie fra det 16de og 17de Aarhundrede." *Prosaiske Skrifter: Niende Bind* (Kjøbenhavn, 1861), pp. 275–364. Weibull, Lauritz, "Sophia Brahe. Ett bidrag till den genealogiska forskningens historia i Danmark." *Historisk Tidskrift för Skåneland. Andra Bandet* (1904, 1908), pp. 38–76.

Lanae Hjortsvang Isaacson

Gerd Brantenberg

Born October 27, 1941, Fredrikstad, Norway
Genre(s): novel
Language(s): Norwegian

One of the more outspoken feminist writers in Norway today and an active participant in the Norwegian Women's movement since the early 1970s, Gerd Brantenberg has used fiction to attack society's attitudes toward such taboo subjects as homosexuality, with humor as one of her foremost weapons. Her novels have been translated into German, Dutch, Danish, Swedish and English.

Her first novel *Opp alle jordens homofile* (1973; Arise All Gays of the Earth) is an attack on the attitudes toward lesbian women, attitudes found both within and outside of homosexual circles. *Egalias døtre* (1977; Egalia's Daughters), subtitled *A Satire of the Sexes*, is an experimental parody on sex roles, where Brantenberg invents a new language to underscore the inherent inequities between the sexes. In the imaginary land of Egalia, a complete mirror image of contemporary Western society, the "wim" have all the power and the "menwim" stay at home minding the children and making pretty "pehoes" for their sons to wear to the "Maidmen's ball." The menwim begin to organize, however, challenging the existing order and demanding equal rights. This novel has been made into a musical titled *Egalia*.

Sangen om St. Croix (1979; The Song of St. Croix) and its sequel *Ved Fergestedet* (1985; At the Ferry Landing) are set in the 1950s in the town of Fredrikstad, Gerd Brantenberg's childhood home. In the two novels the story of the people is told against the background of the town itself, the fate of the one inextricably intertwined with the fate of the other.

Although not all of Gerd Brantenberg's books have been equally well received, she has been praised for her sharp sense of humor as well as her skillful use of language.

Works

Opp alle jordens homofile [Arise All Gays of the Earth] (1973). *Egalias døtre* [Egalia's Daughters] (1977). *Ja, vi slutter* [Stop Smoking] (1978). *Sangen om St. Croix* [The Song of St. Croix] (1979). *Favntak*

[Embrace] (1983). *Ved Fergestedet* [By the Ferry Landing] (1985).

Translations: *Egalia's Daughters,* tr. Louis Mackay (Seattle, 1985). *Mädchenwelten* [*Sangen om St. Croix*] (Berlin, 1982). *Vom andern Ufer* [*Opp alle jordens homofile*] (Munich, 1983).

Bibliography

Haslund, Ebba, "Egalias døtre!" *Vinduet* 34.4 (1980): 59–60. Nilsen, Tove, "Romanen om femtiåra." *Vinduet* 34.2 (1980): 80. Næss, Atle, "Kvinner som elsker. Gerd Brantenberg: *Favntak*." *Vinduet* 37.4 (1983): 77–78. Næss, Atle, "Språket i tre østfoldromaner" (about *Sangen om St. Croix*). *Syn og Segn* 88 (1982): 423–427. Pettersen, Egil, "Språklig lokalkoloritt i to barndomsskildringer." *Festskrift til Einar Lundeby 3. okt. 1984*, pp. 196–210. Spansdahl, Ulla, "*Favntak.* Bokomtale." *Kjerringråd* 1: 29–30.

Margaret Hayford O'Leary

Käthe Braun-Prager

Born 1888, Vienna, Austria; died 1967, Vienna, Austria
Genre(s): poetry, aphorism, essay
Language(s): German

A painter as well as an author, Käthe Braun-Prager's lyric poetry follows the tradition of C.F. Mayer, Rilke, and Hofmannsthal. She particularly enjoyed writing aphorisms as well as lyric poetry. Braun-Prager, an early feminist, was an admirer and friend of Rosa Mayreder and wrote the Epilogue to Mayreder's *Die Krise der Väterlichkeit.* After the rise of Hitler she moved to London, where she lived from 1938 to 1948. During her literary career, she won several prizes: Marianne Hainisch Preis, the Preis der Theodor Körner Stiftung, and the Preis des Wiener Kunstfonds der Zentralsparkasse.

Works

Bei der Kerze, poetry (1929). *Verfrühter Herbst,* poetry (1932). *Grosse Frauen der Heimat,* essays (1936). *Ahnung und Einblick,* aphorisms (1937). *Stern im Schnee,* poetry (1949). *Liebe,* anthology (1954). *Reise in die Nähe,* prose (1954). *Buch der Mütter,* essay (1954). [With Felix Braun], *Das Buch der Frauen* (1955). *Verwandelte Welt,* poetry (1956). *Heimkehr,* prose (1958). *Mondwolke,* poetry (1963).

Bibliography

Kunst unser Zeit (1964), p. 41. Langer, Norbert, *Dichter aus Österreich,* parts 1–5, 4 vols., II (1957), p. 23. Schmidt, Adalbert, *Dichtung und Dichter Österreichs im 19 und 20 Jahrhundert,* vol. II (Salzburg, 1964), p. 372. Schmidt, Adalbert, *Literaturgeschichte,* 2nd ed. (Salzburg, 1968), p. 681.

M.A. Reiss

Christiane Frederick von Breden

(a.k.a. Christen Ada)

Born 1839, Vienna, Austria; died 1901, Vienna, Austria
Genre(s): poetry, novel
Language(s): German

Breden had very little formal education. Her father was imprisoned during the Revolution of 1848 and died soon thereafter. The family became impoverished, and Breden became an actress at the age of fifteen when she joined a group of wandering actors. After marrying Sigmund von Neupaur she returned to Vienna. Her husband was mentally ill, and when he died soon thereafter, she was again left in great poverty. She then made her living by various means, including prostitution. She had written her first poetry *Lieder einer Verlorenen* (1868; Songs of a Lost One) at the deathbed of her husband. Her friends recognized her talent and encouraged her to continue writing. *Lieder einer Verlorenen* became known for its lyricism, but it also created a sensation because of its eroticism and the readers' curiosity regarding the author who was said to have "destroyed" the ideal of womanhood. In 1870 she published *Aus der Asche* (Out of Ashes) and in 1878, *Aus der Tiefe* (Out of the Depths), both collections of poetry known for their social tone and emphasis. In 1873 Breden married the nobleman Adalmar von Breden, who bought up all editions of *Lieder einer Verlorenen* in order to spare his wife any embarrassment. After her marriage she became a leader in the

Viennese literary circle to which Anzengruber belonged. In 1873 she wrote the novel *Ella*, a prose supplement to *Lieder einer Verlorenen*, where she describes the life of a traveling actress and the hardships encountered by a young woman trying to make a living. She can be considered a pioneer of the women's movement because she created a woman who feared stagnation and longed for self-realization.

The novel *Unsere Nachbarn* (1886; Our Neighbors) takes place in a tenement house in which she had lived in her early youth. In both *Unsere Nachbarn* and *Jungfer Mutter* (1892; Virgin Mother), Breden uses a photographic technique, drawing realistic portraits of her time such as the seamstress, the housewife, the lamplighter, the prostitute, etc. Breden was influenced by Heine in both poetry and prose. Her work is extremely subjective, and she refers to her own youth, graphically describing misery, cold, and hunger. Her early work belongs to the beginning of impressionism, but later she was influenced by naturalism. Although her lack of education is sometimes evident, genuine passionate feeling is always present in her poetry and prose.

Works

Lieder einer Verlorenen, poetry (1868). *Aus der Asche*, poetry (1870). *Faustina*, drama (1871). *Schatten*, poetry (1873). *Vom Wege*, fiction (1874). *Aus der Tiefe*, poetry (1878). *Aus dem Leben*, fiction (1878). *Unsere Nachbarn*, fiction (1884). *Als sie starb*, fiction (1888). *Jungfer Mutter*, fiction (1892). *Wiener Leut'*, drama (1893). *Als er heimkehrte*, fiction (1912). [Editor], *Aus der Tiefe*, novel by Marianne Lukas.

Bibliography

Bohr, E., *Ada Christen*. Diss., Wien, 1924. Gronemann, H., *Ada Christen, Leben und Wirken* (1947). Katann, O., *Erzieher, Seine Briefe and Ada Christen* (Wien, 1948). Lebner, M., *Ada Christen, eine Monographie*. Diss., Wien, 1933. Lukas, M., *Aus der Tiefe, Ada Christens Lebensroman* (1952). Rabitsch, M., *Ada Christen*. Diss., Wien, 1939.

General references: Nagl, Zeidler, Castle, *Deutschösterreichische Literaturgeschichte* (Wien, 1930), 705ff. Schmidt, Adalbert, *Dichtung und Dichter Österreichs im 19 und 20 Jahrhundert*, vol. II (Salzburg, 1964), p. 459.

M.A. Reiss

Marie Bregendahl

Born November 6, 1867, Fly, Denmark; died
    July 22, 1940, Copenhagen
Genre(s): novel, short story
Language(s): Danish

Marie Bregendahl belongs to the school of regional writers who in the early 1900s reacted against the "decadence" and narcissism of *fin de siècle* literature by finding their material in the psychological and rural landscapes of their native regions.

Bregendahl grew up on a prosperous farm near Skive, not far from the modest home of Jeppe Aakjaer, who in 1893 became her husband and later emerged as the leading poet among the regionalists. In *Smaa Kommentarer til Aakjaers Erindringer* (1936; A Short Commentary to Aakjaer's Memoirs), Bregendahl briefly refers to the temperamental differences that led to the couple's divorce in 1900. As a single mother, Bregendahl supported their son by working as a housekeeper and a proofreader, and, from 1912, as a full-time writer.

Hendrik i Bakken (1904; Hendrik of the Hill), Bregendahl's debut novel, portrays an eccentric introvert whose dutiful wife cannot love him and thus rejects his awkward advances. The couple is caught in a no-fault, no-win marital deadlock that results in physical and mental death. Bregendahl based her second novel, *En Dødsnat* (1912; A Night of Death), on the early death of her own mother, which left the twelve-year-old girl with full responsibility for the care of her younger siblings.

Written in a collectivist form and in characteristic matter-of-fact prose, Bregendahl's seven volumes of *Billeder af Sødalsfolkenes Liv* (1914–1923; Pictures of the Sødal People's Lives) portray the daily existence of West Jutland farmers in the second half of the nineteenth century. Centered in the village community and its productive work, Bregendahl's novel cycle also explores the psychological make-up of her representative characters.

After a series of less successful short story collections, Bregendahl produced the acclaimed *Holger Hauge og Hans Hustru* I-II (1934–1935; Holger Hauge and His Wife), seen by modern critics as a rewriting of Danish history between

1877 and 1901 from the peasant perspective and as a study of a relationship between a man and a woman whose conflicting values represent the material and ideological changes in the lives of the period's Danish peasantry.

As the chronicler of vanished rural life-styles and value systems, Bregendahl has traditionally been classified as a regional realist. A new generation of critics, however, is pointing to the tensions between old familial and productive communities and new sexual and emotional economies, which in Bregendahl's novels and short stories create a subtext of femininity and feminism.

Works

"Ved Lars Skraedders Sygeseng" (1902). *Hendrik i Bakken* (1904). *En Dødsnat* (1912). *Billeder af Sødalsfolkenes Liv I-VII* (1914–1923). *I De Lyse Naetter* (1920). *I Haabets Skaer* (1924). *Thora* (1926). *Med Aabne Sind* (1926). *Den Blinde Rytter* (1927). *Naar Julen Er Naer* (1927). *Holger Hauge og Hans Hustru I-II* (1934–1935). *Møllen og Andre Fortaellinger* (1936). *Smaa Kommentarer til Aakjaers Erindringer* (1936). *Filtret Høst* (1937). *Birgitte Borg* (1941).
Translations: "The Boundary," tr. W. Glyn Jones, *Contemporary Danish Prose*, ed. Elias Bredsdorff (1958). *A Night of Death.*, tr. Margery Blanchard (1931). "Hans Goul and His Kin," tr. Lida S. Hanson, *American-Scandinavian Review* 19 (May 1931). "Nils Hofman and Kirsten Hauge," tr. Lida S. Hanson, *American-Scandinavian Review* 21 (January 1933).

Bibliography

Andersen, Peter Martin, *Marie Bregendahl* (Copenhagen, 1946). Falgaard, Jørgen, "Marie Bregendahl og Det Gamle Bondemiljø" (Nogle Aspekter af Hendes Sødalsdigtning)." *Extracta 4* (1972): 86–91. Hesselaa, Birgitte, "Marie Bregendahl." *Danske Digtere i Det* 20, Aarhundrede I, ed. Torben Brostrøm and Mette Winge (Copenhagen, 1980), pp. 182–196. Hjordt-Vetlesen, Inger-Lise, *Forlokkelse og Familie: Om Den Kvindelige Identitetskonflikt i Marie Bregendahls Forfatterskab* (Odense, 1977). Pedersen, Frank Røjkjaer, "Marie Bregendahl: 'Billeder af Sødalsfolkenes Liv.'" *Skrifter fra Institut for Litteraturhistorie* 2.4 (1981): 56–67. Raaschou, Carl, "Bonde-og Almuesindet hos Marie Bregendahl." *Skivebogen: Historisk Aarbog for Skive og Omegn* 58 (1967): 25–57.

Clara Juncker

Catherine Breillat

Born ?
Genre(s): novel, poetry, film
Language(s): French

Breillat's successes are not limited to the novel and poetry. Three of her works, *Police*, *Tapage nocturne* (Disturbing the Peace), and *36 Fillette* have been turned into films for which Breillat wrote the script.

Works

L'Homme facile (1968). *Le Silence* (1971). *Les Vêtements de mer* (1971). *Le Soupirail* (1974). *Tapage nocturne* (1979). *Police* (1985). *36 Fillette* (1987).
Translations: *A Man for the Asking* [*L'Homme facile*].

Edith Joyce Benkov

Toril Brekke

Born June 24, 1949, Oslo, Norway
Genre(s): novel, poetry, journalism, children's literature
Language(s): Norwegian

The contemporary Norwegian writer Toril Brekke is an advocate of political activism, social concern, and personal engagement. Brekke's works deal with the modern scene, with both the personal milieu of her everyday characters and the social, political, and economic problems confronting and molding an increasingly more cosmopolitan and complex Norwegian society. Brekke's work as a journalist and typographer has set its mark on her succinct, abrupt style and on her choice of modern settings, social problems and contemporary characters.

Toril Brekke was born on June 24, 1949, in Oslo, Norway. She completed studies of music with an Artium Degree in 1968, and she then prepared to enter the university for a degree in sociology. In the spring of 1969, Brekke finished her studies as a public music school teacher. She then worked at a bakery, the setting for her early novel, *Jenny har fått sparken!* (1976; Jenny Has Been Fired). In 1970, Brekke began to study typography while working for the advertising department of Oslo's major newspaper, *Aftenposten*; she continued her work with *Aftenposten* on a full-time, permanent basis, from 1973 to 1975. In 1972, Brekke married; divorced in 1981, she is the mother of three sons. In 1975, Brekke moved to Northern Norway (Narvik) where she remained until her divorce. Brekke's literary *début* took place in 1976, with some modest poems in such Norwegian literary journals as *Profil* and *Vinduet*, and with the novel, *Jenny har fått sparken!* Brekke worked as a public school teacher from 1979 to 1980 and as a journalist until 1982. Since 1982, Toril Brekke has devoted herself to her literary career. Her works have been translated into Swedish, Danish, German, Dutch, and English. In addition to her literary, fictional works, Toril Brekke has contributed to a report for the United Nations Conference on Women, Nairobi, 1985: *Kvinner i verden: En rapport.* forord av Åse Kleveland (1986; Women: A World Report).

Toril Brekke has played an active role in social affairs since the early 1960s. Her concerns are wide-ranging; in the early 1960s, Brekke, a self-described "political activist since the age of twelve" (*Oktober Forlag*, 1987), participated in the movement against nuclear weapons. Brekke has also written for children; her works include a novel for younger readers, *Gutten i regnet* (1978; The Boy in the Rain), and *Mikkel og brødrene hans* (1980; Mikkel and His Brothers).

One of Toril Brekke's major works to date is *Den glyne tonen*. In this novel, Brekke sketches the marriage of Marion and Georg, two people who, on the surface, share a conventional, upper-class marriage, three lovely children, and material comfort but who come from and remain "worlds apart."

Brekke's journalistic style is both her *forté* and her failing; *Den glyne tonen* moves quickly, engaging us with its action, its minute, precise reality and detail, its modern tone and description, and its dramatic scenes. *Den glyne tonen* lapses into *cliché* in its limited, tangential attempts to explain Marion's discontent, the source of her *ennui*. Elin, a friend of Marion, attempts to

lay the blame on an oppressive, patriarchal, "owner" society, but, as Åsfrid Svensen notes, this argument no longer works for the modern society in which Elin and Marion live (Svensen, "Der gylne tonen . . .," 40–41). Marion's unhappiness seems to stem from her own lack of "engagement for *medmennesker*" (engagement with her friends and associates, Svensen, 43), from Marion's own inability to share feelings, and from a definite distance between Marion and Georg. As Svensen suggests, "the novel is most interesting when the superficial journalistic report is broken by signals (suggesting) a lack of personal freedom and a terror which lie much deeper (in Marion herself)" (Svensen, 43).

Toril Brekke's other works include *Filmen om Chatilla* (1983; The Film About Chatilla) and *Jakarandablomsten og elleve andre noveller fra Afrika* (1985; The Jacaranda Flower and Eleven Other Short Stories from Africa) and her *début* novel, *Jenny har fått sparken!* Brekke's first novel depicts "a successful strike by women workers at a bakery, where the strikers receive moral support and theoretical help from representatives of the Communist Workers Party" (Øverland, p. 243). Toril Brekke's most recent novel, *Sølvfalken* (1986; The Silver Falcon), has already received much acclaim as "a woman's novel about worldwide patriarchy . . . a long stride forward for Brekke's literary career" (*Nøkkel til Årets Bøker*, 1986).

Although she is still relatively young, Toril Brekke has contributed significantly to modern Norwegian literature. Her concern for social and political causes, her desire to use her writing as a means of addressing (*and* solving) problems, her succinct style, and her personal activism reflect her training as a journalist and her knowledge of milieu and contemporary problems. The 1985 contribution to *Kvinner i Verden* is a definite signal of the author's social concern and engagement. Toril Brekke's recent novel, *Sølvfalken*, suggests that Brekke has come into her own.

Works

Jenny har fått sparken! (1976). *Gutten i regnet* (1978). *Mikkel og brødrene hans* (1980). *Den gylne tonen* (1981). *Filmen om Chatilla* (1983). *Jakarandablomsten og elleve andre noveller fra*

Afrika(1985). *Kvinner i verden*(1986). *Sølvfalken* (1986).

Bibliography

Aschehoug & Co. (W. Nygaard & Søn). Information. Answer to Inquiry, Information on Toril Brekke (Oslo, 1987). *Nøkkel til Årets Bøker: 1986* Oslo. 39 (Årgang, 1986), p. 22. *Norsk bokfortegnelse*(Oslo, 1980–1986). *Oktober Forlag*. Besvarelse på Forespørgsel. Answer to Inquiry, Information on Toril Brekke (Oslo, 1987). Øverland, Janneken, "Når dobbel undertrykking forenkles: Toril Brekkes roman *Jenny har fått sparken!*" Irene Engelstad and Janneken Øverland, *Frihet til å skrive: Artikler om kvinnelitteratur fra Amalie Skram til Cecilie Løveid* (Oslo, 1981), pp. 242–249. Svensen, Åsfrid, "Den gylne tonen som forstummet. Toril Brekkes roman. Situasjons-rapport om familie og parforhold anno 1980." *Vinduet* 2, pp. 39–43.

Lanae Hjortsvang Isaacson

Sophia Elisabet (Weber) Brenner

Born 1659, Stockholm, Sweden; died 1730, Stockholm

Genre(s): poetry

Language(s): Swedish, German, Latin, Italian, French

Sophia Brenner is considered Sweden's first Swedish-language female poet of significance, but modern readers and scholars seem to give her little attention. Most of her efforts were occasional poetry (to a great extent poems for weddings and funerals), where her sure sense of rhyme, meter, and rhetorical flourishes made her extremely popular during her own lifetime.

Brenner's childhood and married life provided fortuitous circumstances for the development of her poetic gifts. Her father, a merchant of German extraction, believed in the education of women, and she received instruction in Latin and other unusual subjects for girls at the time. She married Elias Brenner, a Finnish-Swedish numismatist and miniaturist, in 1680. He, too, encouraged his wife's writing, and they often played host to the outstanding cultural figures of the time, including Urban Hjärne, Haquin Spegel,

and Jacob Frese. These two factors were of great importance in establishing her literary "career" and fame. Their marriage was a long and happy one although 13 of their 15 children died during Sophia Brenner's lifetime, and their financial situation never allowed them to feel secure.

Brenner utilized alexandrines for most of her verse, which showed Carolingian piety, common sense, and occasional irony, expressing the values and outlook of the Swedish bourgeoisie. At their best, her lyrics are charming and gracious, often revealing her (for that time) "feminist" views. She believed in the equality of the sexes and in women's right to an education. However, she expressed contentment with her role as wife and mother. In addition to occasional poems, she composed religious verse which displays pietistic influences.

Although Sophia Brenner is all but forgotten today, her position as the "Honored Lady" of Swedish verse was firmly and unanimously proclaimed by her contemporaries.

Works

Minne öfwer den förundrans-wärde stora americanska aloen [Regarding the Wonderful Large American Aloe Plant . . .] (1708). *Poetiska dikter* [Lyric Poems] (1713). *Vårs Herres och Frälsares Jesu Christi alldra heligaste pijnos historia rijmvijs betrachtad* [The Story of the Most Holy Passion of Our Lord and Savior Jesus Christ in Verse Form] (1727). *Poetiska dikter II* [Lyric Poems II] (1732; published posthumously).

Bibliography

Berg, Karin Westman, "Sophia Elisabeth Brenner: Den kvinnliga skaldekonstens moder i Sverige?" Ardelius, Lars, and Gunnar Rydström, eds., *Författarnas litteraturhistoria* (Stockholm, 1977). Hagberg, Knut, "Fru Brenner." *Bygd och hävd* (Stockholm, 1934). *Svenskt litteraturlexikon* (Lund, Sweden, 1964). Tigerstedt, E.N., ed., *Ny illustrerad svensk litteraturhistoria (II)*(Stockholm, 1967).

Kathy Saranpa Anstine

Bridget of Sweden

Born ca. 1303, Uppland, Sweden; died July
23, 1373, Rome, Italy
Genre(s): divine revelations
Language(s): writings in Latin (dictated in
Swedish)

Bridget is representative of a number of women (such as Hildegard of Bingen or Catherine of Siena) who achieved prominence in the high and late Middle Ages through the reception of visions or revelations that were believed to be of divine origin. This inspiration provided Bridget with an authority and assured her of an audience which would otherwise have been denied a woman of her times. Like other female visionaries, she assumed an active role in public life and used her position to criticize corruption in both Church and State. Bridget's writings also reflect an acute awareness of the problems which were peculiar to the fourteenth century—the devastation of the One Hundred Years War, the bubonic plague, the "Babylon Captivity" of the popes in Avignon, and civil unrest in Rome.

Bridget was the seventh child born to a powerful family of Swedish nobles. Her father, Birger Persson, was lawman (governor) for Uppland. In 1316 at the age of thirteen or fourteen, Bridget was married to Ulf Gudmarsson (later made lawman for Närike in East Gothland). Bridget's married life was a model of conventional piety, but she was nevertheless absorbed by the responsibilities and the distractions of her station: she bore eight children and was required to attend the young king and his wife at court for several years. In 1341, Bridget and Ulf made a pilgrimage to Santiago de Compostella in Spain. On the return trip, Ulf sickened and voluntarily withdrew into the Cistercian monastery of Alvastra.

Ulf's death in 1344 was the turning point in Bridget's life, and the first of her visions date from this time. A celestial voice concealed in a bright cloud greeted Bridget as Christ's spouse and God's mouthpiece, who was especially appointed to convey His will to humanity. In 1345, she was directed to found a religious order, for which Christ dictated the rule (*Regula Sancti Salvatoris*). The order of the Holy Saviour, which became familiarly known as the Brigittines, received papal approval in 1371.

After living in retreat at the monastery of Alvastra for several years (1345–1349), Bridget was commanded to go to Rome for the Jubilee year of 1350, where she was told to remain until the Pope and the Emperor met in that city. (This was an unlikely event in that the papacy had resided at Avignon since 1309 and was estranged from the German Emperors.) Except for the various pilgrimages she undertook (including one to the Holy Land in 1371), Bridget remained in Rome until her death in 1373, constantly urging the return of the pope from Avignon. She was attended by her daughter, Catherine (later canonized), and her two confessors—Peter Olaf, canon of Skenninge, and Peter Olaf, prior of Alvastra. Bridget also acquired a large popular following due to her reputation for piety, her almsgiving, and her prophecies. Her prophecies likewise earned her a considerable number of enemies in that she was an unabashed supporter of papal politics, her visions served to buttress the corrupt system of indulgences for the remission of sins, and she occasionally made prophetic forays into secular politics. This divided reaction to Bridget is reflected by the events surrounding her canonization. After many delays, she was canonized in 1391. Even so, her cult remained a bone of contention, and her canonization required confirmation first at the Council of Constance (1414–1418), later at the request of the Swedish king (1419), while the orthodoxy of the *Revelaciones* had to be defended at the Council of Basle (1431–1443). The validity of her revelations and her claims to sanctity were questioned by churchmen as eminent as Jean Gerson in his work *De probatione spirituum* (1415).

Although Bridget remained awake for her visions she experienced the rapture and ecstasy often associated with mystical transcendence. She received the visions in Swedish but was instructed that they should be translated into Latin. The task of translation fell primarily to her confessors, the two Peters, although it was initially undertaken in Sweden by Master Mathias, canon of Linköping cathedral and an eminent theologian. On her deathbed she appointed Alphonse of Pecha, the retired bishop of Jaen, who had acted as her spiritual director, occasional confessor, and translator, as her literary executor. It was he who edited and divided the

Revelaciones into seven books in time for the opening of the canonization process (1377). Book Eight and a final book of additional revelations (*Extravagentes*) were added to the original seven (these latter books also being augmented) around 1380. Unfortunately, Alphonse of Pecha showed little skill as editor. The work follows no logical or chronological sequence and tends to be repetitious. Considering Bridget's dependence on others in the translation and presentation of her work, it is difficult to ascertain how much control she had over the final product. Bridget herself tells us that she permitted her translators to make minor additions to heighten the effect of her revelations, while she gave her assistants a free hand in changing anything that was not entirely orthodox. Nevertheless, Bridget, following a divine prompting, did begin to learn Latin, which Peter of Skenninge later testified was sufficient for her to oversee the production of her works.

The *Revelaciones* themselves are a series of short, didactic passages which sometimes take the form of a dialogue. The identity of the celestial speaker alternates between Christ, the Virgin Mary, or another saint, while Bridget is invariably referred to as the Bride of Christ. Very often, the vision is presented as a warning to a particular individual who is in need of reform. There are a number of themes that recur throughout the *Revelaciones*: unregenerate society is continuously warned of God's wrath, urged to repent and do penance, bullied by graphic descriptions of souls in Hell or purgatory, and periodically reassured of God's mercy. Church corruption is contrasted with projections of a purified Church, which can only be realized with the Pope's return to the Holy See. On the devotional side, Bridget is particularly concerned with Christ's passion and the veneration of His Virgin Mother. Unlike the writings of many medieval visionaries, the *Revelaciones* tend to be pragmatic and didactic rather than speculative, devotional rather than mystical. Moreover, while many prophets of this period were revolutionaries who were hostile to the Church Militant, and predicted its overthrow, Bridget differed in that her enemies were those who opposed the organized Church. While denouncing outright corruption, not even sparing the Pope himself, she aggressively defended the *status quo*.

The Latin of the *Revelaciones* is poor, the style plain, and the organization scanty; nevertheless, Bridget's stern message of repentance had considerable impact on her age and her prophecies (and some spurious ones attributed to her) were still influential after her death, especially in the fifteenth century. The religious order that she founded is still in existence. Bridget was and still remains a controversial figure in so far as many were repelled by the aggressive and outspoken nature of her revelations and challenged the source of her inspiration. Even so, Bridget's visions were the vehicle by which she transcended the usual barriers of education and gender and played an active role in religion and politics.

Works

Revelaciones and minor works, ed. B. Ghotan (1492); ed. C. Durante (1606). A modern critical edition is in progress in *Samlingar utgivna av Svenska Fornskriftsällskapet*, Latinska Skrifter, Ser. 2 (1956–).

Translations: Fourteenth-century Swedish tr. in *Heliga Birgittas Uppenbarelser*, ed. G.E. Klemming. 5 vols. (1857–1884). Fifteenth-century English extracts in *Revelations*, ed. R. Cummings, EETS, O.S. 178 (1929). *Revelations and Prayers of St. Bridget of Sweden: Being the "Sermo Angelicus" or Angelic Discourse concerning the Excellence of the Virgin Mary* (1928), tr. E. Graf. See extracts in Obrist (bibliography below) and in *Revelations* (1972), tr. Anthony Butkovich.

Bibliography

Bergendoff, Conrad, "A Critic of the Fourteenth Century: St. Birgitta of Sweden," in *Medieval and historiographical essays in honor of James Westfall Thompson*, ed. J. Lea and E. Anderson (Chicago, 1938), pp. 3–18. Bergh, Birger, "A Saint in the Making: St. Bridget's Life in Sweden (1303–1349)," in *Papers of the Liverpool Latin Seminar*, ed. Francis Cairns, vol. 3, ARCA Classical and Medieval Texts, Papers and Monographs 7 (1981), pp. 371–384. Celletti, Maria C., "Brigida di Svezia," *Bibliotheca Sanctorum*, vol. 3, pp. 439–532. Colledge, Eric, "*Epistola solitarii ad reges*: Alphonse of Pecha as Organizer of Birgittine and Urbanist Propaganda," *Mediaeval Studies* 18 (1956): 19–49. Collijn, I., ed. *Acta et processus canonizacionis Beate Birgitte*, Samlingar utgivna av Svenska Fornskriftsällskapet, Latinska Skrifter, ser. 2 (Uppsala, 1924–1931), esp. the *vitae* of her confessors, the two Peters, pp. 73–101 and 614–664 (longer version); *vita* by Birger, archbishop of Uppsala (d. 1383), in *Acta Sanctorum* Oct. IV, pp. 485–493. Also see Master Mathias' prologue to *Rev.*, Bk. 1 and Alphonse of Pecha's Preface to Bk. 8. Debongnie, P., "Brigitte de Suède," *Dictionnaire d'histoire et de Géographie*, vol. 10, pp. 719–728. Jørgensen, Johannes, *Saint Bridget of Sweden*, tr. Ingeborg Lund, 2 vols. (London, 1954). Kilström, B.I., and C.G. Frithz, *Bibliographia Birgittina*, i Urval. Soc. Sanctae Birgittae (1973). Klockars, Birgit, *Birgitta och hennes värld* (Stockholm, 1971). Kraft, Salomon, *Textstudier til Birgittas Revelationer* (Uppsala, 1929). Obrist, Barbara, "The Swedish Visionary Saint Bridget of Sweden," in *Medieval Women Writers*, ed. K.M. Wilson (Athens, Ga., 1984), pp. 227–251. *Theologische Realenzyklopädie*, vol. 6, pp. 651–652. Vernet, F., "Brigitte de Suède," *Dictionnaire de Spiritualité ascétique et mystique*, vol. 1, 1943–1958. Westman, Knut B., *Birgitta-Studier I* (Uppsala, 1911).

Dyan Elliot

Marguerite Briet

(a.k.a. Hélisenne de Crenne)

Born ca. 1510, Abbeville, France; died ? (after August 1552)

Genre(s): novel, letters, allegorical treatise, translation

Language(s): French

One of the first novelists in French literature, Hélisenne de Crenne was born into a Picardian family of minor nobility sometime around 1510. Her real name, recorded in the Latin chronicle *De Abbavilla*, was Marguerite Briet. What little we know about her life comes primarily from her long, semi-autobiographical novel, *Les Angoysses douloureuses qui procedent d'amours* (The Sad Agonies Which Come from Love). Such a source is naturally suspect since it is impossible to determine which of its incidents are fictive and which are not. If we trust Part I (generally considered the most autobiographi-

cal), Marguerite was very young when she wed Philippe Fournel, seigneur de Crasnes. We know from various legal documents that the couple had a son (Pierre Fournel), that their stormy marriage ended in separation before 1552, that a love affair precipitated the divorce and furnished material for Marguerite's novel; that this novel was a great popular success; that it was followed by three other volumes—a collection of letters, an allegorical treatise, and a translation of the first four books of the *Aeneid*. Further details, however, are unavailable. We do not know why Marguerite chose her *nom de plume*, which two years later was also given to a character in *Amadis de Gaul* by another Picardian writer. Nor do we know how Marguerite de Briet met Denis Janot, who published not only her novel but also *Amadis*.

It seems likely that some incidents in the novel—the tragic love, Hélisenne's cruel imprisonment by her husband, her tortured treatment at the hands of other in-laws—had a factual basis. In writing *Les Angoysses* (The Sad Agonies), which appeared in three parts from 1538 to 1560, she avowed two motives: (1) to encourage women to evade the "embrasements" ("hugging and kissing") of love and (2) to relieve her sufferings and anxieties by telling of them. Both aims were traditional to sixteenth-century literature. Both, however, come to perfect fruition in the plot, which records a fascinating exploration of feminine sexuality within Renaissance society.

Since the novel was probably published in installments, its plan is rather confused. Part I is told by Hélisenne herself, who also figures as narrator and heroine. It tells of her early life, the beginning of her tragic affair, and her imprisonment by an angry husband. The narrative voice in Part II is her lover's, Guénélic, who tells of the adventures he and his friend Quezinstra encounter as they seek the missing lady all over Europe. They find her in Part III, which is also narrated by Guénélic but which concentrates on Hélisenne's sufferings. While the two young men rescue the heroine, she immediately succumbs to a fatal disease. Her deathbed/repentance scene is followed by Guénélic's death and by the couple's descent to the Elyssian Fields, guided by Mercury. After the lovers' death, Venus and Athene briefly squabble over who has the rights to Hélisenne's book, but Jupiter has it carried to Paris where it is published to perpetuate the couple's memory.

At least the last event is verifiable. Published in eight editions from 1538 to 1560, this sprawling and operatic story was an immediate success. Kitty Delle Robbins-Herring credits its popularity to the novel's continuation of themes treated in poems, prose romances, and love complaints of the period. Indeed, Hélisenne's plot and characterizations are deeply indebted to Boccaccio's *Fiammetta* and Antoine de la Sale's *Petit Jehan de Saintré*; her style is heavily influenced by Lemaire de Belges. A.M. Schmidt, however, traces the novel's success to Marguerite's bold manipulation of her own story. Readers were enthralled by these confessions of a fallen woman/abused wife. The novel's mixture of fact and fiction is still one of its most attractive features. Marguerite herself seems to have been taken with it. She continued to publish under Hélisenne's name despite Hélisenne's death at the end of the book.

Despite the use of her romantic heroine's name, Marguerite wrote her other works in a heavily didactic strain, continuing the novel's avowed intention of dissuading women from the pursuit of love. A collection of public epistles or essays, *Les epistres familières et invectives* (Informal and Invective Letters), and an allegorical treatise, *Le songe de Madame Hélisenne . . . la considération duquel est apte à instiguer toutes personnes de s'aliéner de vice et s'approcher de vertu* (The dream of Madame Hélisenne . . . the consideration of which is apt to move everyone to leave vice and approach virtue) appeared in 1532. In 1541, she published a translation of the first four books of Virgil's *Aeneid*.

Even though Hélisenne's themes were familiar ones for her time, neither the book nor its author was bereft of originality. She invested her story with a novel intensity; her analysis of her own fall and her subsequent equations between "lovelessness and liberty" were evidence of a distinct voice. Her exploration of feminine sensuality was explicitly, even daringly, specific not only in the details of Hélisenne's violent passion but also in the author's emphasis upon clothing, hair, facial expressions, and body movements. Most critics have noted the novel's voyeuristic appeal. Not only must we consider Hélisenne's scrutiny by her husband (named after the many-eyed Greek giant Argus) but also our own delight as readers in spying upon their affairs. The book offers a complex study of the heroine's impossible situation and of passion's destructive role in our own lives. Its moral—that women should flee love—was amply supported by the details of its narrative.

A word should also be said about Marguerite's language, which has been the subject of much critical debate. The novel is nothing short of extravagant, often excessive in its style. Although representative of her period in general, the frequency with which Marguerite embellishes can be disconcerting to modern readers. Her language abounds in Latinisms, convoluted syntax, repetitions, obsolete French words, and neologisms, either original with the author or borrowed from other writers. It has often been criticized as over-extravagant, verbose, pretentious, and Latinate. The humanist Étienne Pasquier believed that Rabelais had her in mind when he mocked the Latin jargon of the Limousin school. Claude Colet's editing of her collected works in 1550 implicitly asserted that her language needed correcting, as did his preface, which notes that the work was undertaken at the urging of two women who found the book unreadable as written. Such criticism, however, often says more about the critic's assumptions than Marguerite's writing. While her style is difficult—she never uses a common word if she can find a learned and obscure one—so is the language of Rabelais and Maurice Scève. Moreover the prose model which she followed—middle French—sanctioned her extravagance. Middle French prose relished complicated syntax and vocabulary, repetitions, long sentences, and scholastic terminology. When compared with the other writers of her day, she did as well as most and better than some. Her books were read before Colet's editions; some readers who deplored her Latinisms praised them as stylistic features in texts by men. It seems at least probable that the learned style and overtly sensuous subject were disconcerting—both in her day and our own—because they issued from the pen of a woman. It's at least possible such criticism explains Marguerite's relatively short career and her turn to edifying or scholarly genres in her work after *Les Angoysses* (The Agonies).

Many twentieth-century critics, sensing that she has been misjudged, have reassessed her work. Some (Gustave Reynier and Henriette Charasson) credited her novel with breaking new ground for the pastoral (*L'Astrée*), psychological (*La Princesse de Clèves*), and sentimental novel. Others (L.M. Richardson) have taken note of the *Familiar and Invective Letters*, where Hélisenne defends her sex with a vigor unequalled by any other French Renaissance woman. Indeed, a translation of the letters along with two new critical editions of *Les Angoysses doulerouse* Part I have recently been published. This work indicates that we have only begun to evaluate her position.

Marguerite/Hélisenne left readers a fascinating legacy. Her novel is both frank confession and elaborate artifice, moral tract and sensuous narrative, self-assertion and self-doubt. *Les Angoysses* (The Agonies) gives us a powerful experience of the Renaissance woman.

Works

Les Angoysses douloureuses qui procedent d'amours: Contenantz troys parties, Composees par Dame Hélisenne: Laquelle exhorte toutes personnes a ne suyvre folle Amour [The Sad Agonies which come from love: contents in three parts written by Lady Hélisenne, which book exhorts all people not to follow foolish love] (1538). (Part one has been published in a new edition by Paule Demats, *les Angoyssesses douloureuses qui procedent d'amours (1538), Première partie* [Paris, 1968] and by Jérôme Vercruysse, same title [Paris, 1968]). *Familieres et invectives de ma dame Hélisenne, composes par icelle dame, De Crenne* [Intimate and Invective letters of My Lady Hélisenne, composed by this lady of Crennes] (1539). *Les quatre premiers livres des Eneydes du treselegant poete Virgile, traduictz de latin en prose Françoyse par ma dame Helisenne, à l'elucidtation et decoration desdictz libres, diriqez à tresillustre et tresauguste Prince Françoys, premier de ce nom invictissime Roy de France* [The first four books of the Aeneid of the most polished poet Virgil, translated from Latin into French prose by my lady Helisenne, in the translating of which there are many thoughts which by means of phrasing are added here: which serves greatly to the elucidation and decoration of these books, dedicated to the most famous and august Prince Francis, the first of

that name, invincible King of France] (1541). *Le Songe de madame Hélisenne, composé par ladicte Dame, la consideration duquel est apte à instiquer toutes personnes de s'aliener de vice et s'approcher de vertu* [The Dream of Madame Hélisenne, composed by this lady, the consideration of which is apt to instigate all people to avoid vice and approach virtue] (1541). *Les oeuvres de ma dame Hélisenne q'elle a puis naqueres recogneues et mises en leur entier. Cest ascavoir les angoisses douloureuses qui procedent d'amours, Les Epistres familieres et invectives. Le songe de ladicte dame, let tout mieulx que pr cy devant redigees au vray, et imprimees nouvellemet par le commandement de ladicte Dame de Crenne* [The Complete and recognized works of my lady Hélisenne. That is, The Sad Agonies which come from love. Intimate and Invective letters. The Dream of this Lady, all better than before, composed according to the truth and printed anew by the said Lady De Crennes' command] (1543).

Translations: *A Renaissance Woman: Hélisenne's Personal and Invective Letters* [*Les Epistres familieres et invectives*] (1986).

Bibliography

Baker, J.J., "Fiammetta and the *Angoysses douloureuses qui procedent d'amours.*" *Symposium* 27 (Winter 1973): 303–308. Baker, J.J., "France's First Sentimental Novel and Novels of Chivalry." *Bibliothèque d'Humanisme et Renaissance* 36 (1974): 33–45. Bergal, Irene, "Hélisenne de Crenne: A Sixteenth-Century French Novelist." Ph.D. diss., University of Minnesota, 1966. Berrong, Richard, "Hélisenne de Crenne's *Les Angois es Douleureuses Qui Procèdent d'Amours.*" *The USF Language Quarterly* 22 (Fall-Winter 1983): 20–22. Charasson, Henriette, "Les origines de la sentimentalité moderne: d'Hélisenne de Crenne à Jean de Tinan." *Mercur de France* 86 (1910): 193–216. Conley, Tom, "Feminism, *Écriture*, and the Closed Room: The *Angoysses douloureuses qui procedent d'amours.*" *Symposium* 27 (Winter 1973): 322–331. Guichard, J.M., "Hélisenne de Crenne.: *Revue du XIXe siècle* 2d ser., 8 (1840): 276–284. Jordan, Mary Farr, "The *Angoysses Douloureuses* of Hélisenne de Crenne." Ph.D. diss., Harvard University, 1969. Lafranc, Abel, "A propos d'Hélisenne de Crenne." *Revue des Livres Anciens* 2(1917): 376–377. Loriente, Suzanne Marie-Marguerite, "L'Esthétique des *Angoysses Douloureuses*

Qui Procedent d'Amours d'Hélisenne de Crenne."
Ph.D. diss., University of Southern California, 1982.
Loviot, Louis, "Hélisenne de Crenne." *Revue des Livres Anciens* 2 (1917): 137–145. Neubert, Fritz, "Antike und Christentum bei den ersten französischen Epistoliers der Renaissance. Hélisenne de Crenne und Estienne du Tronchet (1539 und 1569)" *Romanische Forschungen* 77 (1965): 1–41. Neubert, Fritz, "Die französischen Briefschreiber der Renaissance und ihre Verleger." *Germanisch-Romanische Monatsschrift* 49, 18 (1968): 349–360. Neubert, Fritz, "Hélisenne de Crenne (ca. 1500–ca. 1560) und ihr Werk. Nach den neuesten Forschungen." *Zeitschrift für Französische Sprache und Literatur* 80 (1970): 291–322. Possenti, Antonio, "Hélisenne de Crenne nel secolo dei romantici e la prima conquista della critica." *Francia* 13 (January-March 1975): 27–40. Robbins-Herring, Kittye Delle, "Hélisenne de Crenne: Champion of Women's Rights." *Women Writers of the Renaissance and Reformation*, ed. K. Wilson (Athens, 1987), pp. 177–218. Richardson, L.M., *The Forerunners of Feminism in French Literature of the Renaissance from Christine de Pisan to Marie de Gournay*m (Baltimore, 1929). Saulnier, V.-L., "Quelques nouveautés sur Hélisenne de Crenne." *Bulletin de l'Association Guillaume Budé*, 4th ser., no. 4 (1964): 459–463. Vercruysse, J., "Hélisenne de Crenne: Notes biographiques." *Studi Francesi* 31 (January-April 1967): 77–81. Waldstein, Helen, "Hélisenne de Crenne: A Woman of the Renaissance." Ph.D. diss., Wayne State University, 1965.

Glenda Wall

Anna Brigadere

Born October 1, 1861, Zemgale, Latvia; died June 25, 1933, Zemgale
Genre(s): drama, novel, short story, lyric poetry
Language(s): Latvian

Of the numerous Latvian women writers, Anna Brigadere and Aspazija (*q.v.*) are the most distinguished, their contribution to the rich national theater unsurpassed (although equalled) by other Latvian dramatists. Brigadere's novels are also outstanding.

Daughter of a farm laborer, Brigadere was able to complete only three years of primary school and subsequently became an autodidact. Her childhood in the country was permeated with the influence of Latvian folklore, which is strongly felt in her work. When her mother died in 1874, the family moved to the town of Jelgava and later to Ventspils. During a succession of jobs as seamstress and shopgirl, and later as teacher, she garnered a store of observations of all walks of life, which she later used in her writing. Between 1882 and 1884 Brigadere found employment as a governess in Russia, largely because of her self-acquired familiarity with German language and literature. In 1885 she succeeded in finishing a teachers' course and continued working as tutor and governess. Influenced by a prolonged stay at a hospital, she wrote her first story, "Slimnīcā" (1896; In the Hospital), which was published in 1896.

Beginning in 1897 she was able to devote herself fully to literature, both as writer and as editor of several magazines. Her popularity was very great: her later years were spent at a country home of her own, Sprīdīši, given to her by the nation in recognition of her achievement. After Brigadere's death Sprīdīši was turned into a museum in her memory.

Along with her contemporaries Jānis Poruks (1871–1911) and Kārlis Skalbe (1879–1945), Brigadere is a quintessentially Latvian writer, occupying a position midway between Western emphasis on reason and Eastern European emphasis on feeling yet with a share in both. Although firmly ensconced in the middle class, she exposes its shallowness in her realistic stories and novels. At the same time she is an idealist, and her writing is frequently symbolic. Her masterpiece, the autobiographic trilogy of novels, *Dievs, daba, darbs* (God, Nature, Work), *Skarbos vējos* (Harsh Wind), and *Akmeņu sprostā* (In a Stone Cage) has always been one of the most widely admired works in Latvian literature, especially the first novel. The whole forms a *Bildungsroman* full of well-drawn characters, particularly women, notable for its profound love of nature, deep religious feeling, and belief in the ennobling power of work—attitudes that are basic to the Latvian national character. Latvian folklore shaped Brigadere's literary style, its often laconic concentration, its precision and clarity, as well as her ethical outlook, which is marked by optimism, insistence on inner clarity, and emphasis upon human dignity and worth. Her folkloric plays, such as *Sprīdītis* (Thumbling) and *Maija un Paija* (Maija and Paija), rival the trilogy in effectiveness and popularity. In these she combines a variety of fairytale motifs and situations to express her views in highly poetic form and language. Of her other plays, the comedies are realistic and distinguished by lively satire. Her psychological plays are less successful, since the resolution of the plots often fail to emerge convincingly from the nature of the characters. Her lyric poetry is limpid and perfect in form. Brigadere's highest achievement, however, is in the autobiographic trilogy and the folkloric plays.

Works

Aiz lidzrietības (1897). Atkalredzēšanās (1901). Izredzētais (1901). Sprīdītis (1903). Ceļa jūtīs (1904). Ausmā (1907). Čaukstenes (1907). Pie latviešu miljonāra (1909). Zvanīgs zvārgulītis (1909). Princese Gundega un karalis Brusubārda (1912). Dzejas (1913). Raudupiete (1914). Spēka dēls (1916). Mazā majā (1918). Ilga (1920). Maija un Paija (1921). Paisums (1921). Hetēras mantojums (1924). Sniegputenī (1924). Lielais loms (1925). Sievu kari ar Belcebulu (1925). Lolitas brīnumputns (1926). Dieviškā seja (1926). Dievs, daba, darbs (1927). Kvēlošā lokā (1928). Kad sievas spēkojas (1929). Šuvējas sapnis (1930). Skarbos vējos (1931). Pastari (1931). Karaliene Jāna (1932). Akmeņu sprostā (1933). Kalngali (1934). Kopoti raksti [Complete Works], 20 vols. (1912–1939). Translations: Maija and Paija, tr. Ilze Raudsepa, in The Golden Steed, ed. Alfreds Straumanis (1979). [Selected poetry], in A Century of Latvian Poetry, ed. and tr. W.K. Matthews (1957).

Bibliography

Straumanis, A., ed., *Baltic Drama: A Handbook and Bibliography* (Prospect Heights, Ill., 1981). Mauriņa, Zenta, *Baltais ceļš* (Riga, 1935).

Zoja Pavlovskis

Ivana Brlić-Ma'uranić

(a.k.a. I.B.M.)

Born 1874, Ogulin, Yugoslavia; died 1938, Zagreb
Genre(s): children's literature
Language(s): Croatian

One of Yugoslavia's outstanding writers of children's literature, Ivana Brlić-Ma'uranić excelled in creating original stories and fables, the characters and motifs of which were drawn extensively from Slavic folklore. In some respects, then, her creative contribution shares the neoromantic orientation of some of her contemporaries, notably Nazor and Vidrić. This establishes her connection with the Croatian Moderna, although she was never a part of the symbolism or impressionism most often associated with that movement. Brlić-Ma'uranić was lovingly called the "Croatian Andersen," a tribute both to her great artistic success and her popularity that still prevails.

Brlić-Ma'uranić was never a stranger to creative literature. Her father was Vladimir Ma'uranić, a writer and historian as well as a member of three Academies of Science, the Yugoslavian, Czech, and Polish. Vladimir was the eldest son of the great poet Ivan Ma'uranić who wrote *Smrt Smail-age Čengić* (The Death of Smail-Aga Čengić).

Her first collection of poems and stories appeared in 1902 in a limited edition (for her friends) under the title *Valjani i nevaljani, zbirka pripovijedaka i pjesmica za dječaka* (The Worthwhile and the Worthless, a Collection of Tales and Poems for Children). Both this book and the following one, *Škole i praznici* (1905; Schools and Holidays), attracted some favorable attention. Her third work, *Slike, I* (1912; Pictures, I) augured the tremendous acclaim her next two works were to have. The most influential literary figure of the time, Antun Gustav Matoš, responded very positively to both *Pictures, I* and her next production, *Čudnovate zgode šegrta Hlapića* (1913; The Strange Fortunes of the Novice Hlapić). In *Priče iz davnine* (1916; Stories from Long Ago), though, he discerned "a classic book."

Stories from Long Ago is considered to be Brlić-Ma'uranić's greatest work. One modern critic calls it "our most beautiful fables." Another points out that *Stories from Long Ago* is not just valuable as a literary work and a part of the cultural heritage, "but they are considered our own story of the past, the story that we always happily remember." *Stories from Long Ago* has gone through twelve editions so far, testifying to the accuracy of the critics' estimation. It has been translated into ten languages, adapted as a play, radio show, television production, and puppet theater performance, to mention some of the stories' popularizations.

Although she wrote two more collections of tales, *Knjiga omladini* (1923; A Book to Young People), *Dječja čitanka o zdravlju* (1927; Children's Reader About Health) and her novel, *Jaša Dalmatin, potkralj Gud'erata* (1937; Jasa Dalmatin, Viceroy of Gud'erat), which were published by some of the most prestigious publishing houses in Yugoslavia, it was for *Stories from Long Ago* that Brlić-Ma'uranić was thrice nominated for the Nobel Prize in Literature. In 1937, a year before her death, Brlić-Ma'uranić became the first female member of the Yugoslavian Academy of Sciences and Arts.

As a writer, Brlić-Ma'uranić is best known for her clarity of images and rhythmic and sonorous prose. She described her style as the process of representing "the heart in pictures" (*srce u sliku*). The musicality of her prose enhances the wealth of magical and mythological beings that people her creations and creates a picturesque impression not unlike certain types of oral literature. The following line from *Stories from Long Ago* illustrates her control over both the euphonic flow of words and the evoked imagery: *Jutro bijelo, kano krilo golubovo, a mekane magle nad ponikvom prohode, rekao bi: bijelorune ovce.* ("The morning is white like a pigeon's wing and the fogs pass by over the hollow as, one might say: white-fleeced sheep.") The first five words sound like a traditional line from the *deseterac*, the decasyllabic folk-line that regularly displays caesura after the fourth syllable. The sentence is saturated with alliteration and assonance producing a musical effect. The image, also, is poetic, the white morning like a pigeon's wing suggesting both the dove-like color and the emotional association of peaceful protection. This example could be multiplied a thousand

times, and more analysis would yield a still clearer understanding of the depth of Brlić-Ma'uranić's art, but this single example may by itself illustrate the power of her creative production. It may be seen why Brlić-Ma'uranić's art transcends its generic design of children's literature and has become a part of the national culture. *Stories from Long Ago* still retains great popularity in Yugoslavia, ensuring Brlić-Ma'uranić a lasting position in Yugoslavian literature.

Works

Valjani i nevaljani (1902). *Škola i praznici* (1905). *Slike* (1912). *Čudnovate zgode šegrta Hlapiča* (1913). *Priče iz dauvnine* (1916). *Knjiga omladini* (1923). *Dječja čitanka o zdravlju* (stihovi) (1927). *Mir u duši, Posebni otisak iz Hrvatske revije* (1930). *Zgode i nezgode šegrta Hlapiča* (no date). *Jaša Dalmatin, Potkralj Gud'erata* (1937). *Srce od licitara* (1938).

Translations: *Croatian Tales of Long Ago*, tr. F.S. Copeland (1924). *La Paix de L'Âme*, tr. Cécile Baron d'Ottenfels (1929). *Leggende Croate, favole antiche*, tr. Umberto Urbani (1957). *Die Verschwundenen Stiefel. Die Wunderbaren Erlebnisse des Schusterjungen Gottschalk*, tr. Else Byhan (1959). *Das Schlangenmädchen aus dem Zauberwald* (1966). *Lavendel og Rosmarin*, tr. Thorkil Barfod (1929).

Bibliography

Ivana Brlić-Ma'uranić. Zbornik radova, ed. D. Jelčić et al., Izdavačko knjiʼarsko poduzeć (Zagreb, 1970); contains complete list of articles and secondary literature, pp. 261–286.

Christine Tomei

Martine Broda

Born 1947, Paris, France
Genre(s): poetry, essay, translation
Language(s): French

Born in 1947, Martine Broda is presently a researcher at the Centre National de Recherche scientifique in Paris, where she is working on poetry. Apart from her own poetry, she has published major translations of Celan, written books on Jouve (1982) and Celan (1986), and collaborated with various literary journals: *Action poétique, Banana Split, Critique, Le Nouveau Commerce, La Quinzaine littéraire, Sud,* etc.

Double (1976; Double), which is the second of the four slim but striking *plaquettes* she has published to date, offers us spare texts, hemmed in by white space, like a voice from a distance, barely real, yet urgent. Its own blatant syntactic ellipses seem to mime that precarious equilibrium of which Broda speaks, between division and fusing, intimacy and unspeakableness, communication and dislocation, fullness and absence. The notion of "double"-ness is, of course, central to all of this, and the text makes at least adequately implicit the questions of (ex)change, of looking and dreaming, the relation between reality and mind and soul, the shimmering effects of love, and so on. Love, indeed, lies tantalizingly at the heart of this text which is near-mystical in its implications.

Five years later appeared *Tout ange est terrible* (1983; Every Angel Is Appalling). A meditation upon a line from Rilke, this volume again articulates itself in splayed, "holed" forms emblematic of that blinking, intermittent exchange/equivalence of presence and absence. The writing retains an enigmatic quality, despite its air of simplicity. Besides, this very "imperfection" and obscurity may be said to pertain closely to the contradictions—of brilliance and beauty, lack and shame, earth's abominable, ambiguous states—that underpin the volume's imaginative "structure." "This world is this world," Martine Broda exclaims, in her somber evocation of the ineffableness (pain, solitude, death) of much that flickers across the half-lit screen of things. Poetry, as for so many women poets, however, lies in deep, painful and even ambivalent connection with love. Death may be the founding experience, yet Martine Broda seeks to move beyond, marrying brevity with deprivation and, yet, possible beauty, too.

Passage (1986; Passage) is the latest collection to appear. Although somewhat reminiscent of a poet such as Anne-Marie Albiach, Martine Broda remains more "centered," despite her poetry's broken, disconnected quality. *Passage* thus recounts the difficulties of "passage," exchange, communion, love, whilst succeeding in rendering us alert to the endless marginal, near-imperceptible ways in which these difficulties

unfold. If the intensity of mourning and speaking are locked together, it should be noted, too, that the voice emerging is purged, stripped of all but the barest traces.

Works

Route à trois voix, poetry, in *Le Nouveau Commerce* 35 (1976). *Double*, poetry (1978). *Jouve, L'Age d'homme*, essays (1982). *Tout ange est terrible*, poetry (1983). *Dans la main de personne*, essays (1986). *Passage*, poetry (1986).
Translations: *La Rose de Personne*, tr. Paul Celan, in *Le Nouveau Commerce* (1979).

Bibliography

Bishop, Michael, "Contemporary Women Poets," in *Contemporary French Poetry, Studies in Twentieth-Century Literature* (Fall 1988).

Michael Bishop

Suzanne Brøgger

Born November 18, 1944, Copenhagen, Denmark
Genre(s): essay, autobiography, novel, poetry, translation, journalism
Language(s): Danish

The perspective of an exile who regards all social verities with a fresh, skeptical eye seems to suit Suzanne Brøgger, who grew used to moving between cultures at an early age. Some of her literary heroes—Karen Blixen, Henry Miller, Anais Nin, and Emmanuelle Arsan—also belonged to an international society and experienced similar uprootings. Her insights, like theirs, confront human sexuality and thus have the power to shock.

Suzanne Brøgger has been a world-traveler since childhood, when her stepfather, Svend Brøgger, was assigned to Ceylon and then Thailand. She therefore received part of her schooling in Denmark (Bernadotteskolen in Hellerup, Th. Langs pigekostskole in Silkeborg, and Copenhagan University) and part in the Middle East. Her consequent facility with Eastern languages gained her freelance employment as a journalist reporting from the Soviet Union and the Middle East. The collection *Brøg* (1980; Brew) includes articles she wrote from abroad between 1965 and 1980. A strikingly beautiful woman who has also had experience as an actress, notably in the role of Helena in the Danish Royal Theater's production of *Troilus and Cressida*, she knows how to present herself in the media with flair and to dramatize her role as author. She has been the recipient of several Danish literary prizes, including the "Golden Laurel" in 1982 and a Danish State's Art Foundation lifelong grant from 1985.

Brøgger stepped into the international limelight with her work *Fri os fra kærligheden* (1973; Deliver Us From Love), a highly polemical and controversial critique of Western mores which was translated into more than seven languages. Mingling essays, short stories and slice-of-life accounts of personal experiences, Brøgger called into question a number of assumptions about western values such as the nuclear family, privacy, and the incest taboo. Although *Fri os fra kærligheden* was subtitled "A radical feminist speaks out" in one of its English editions, Brøgger denies this connection. Indeed, she often takes feminists to task for accepting and working within patriarchal structures instead of trying to break free of them and forge new ways of living. She is particularly contemptuous of the monogamous couple unit that is considered the ideal social arrangement in Western society, finding it too stifling. "What there will be a need for in future is not specialization, but generalization: to be able to love more than one person, more than one race, more than one sex—and not merely a single representative of the opposite sex," she has asserted. She continued to write in the same vein in her next published book, *Kærlighedens veje og vildveje* (1975; The Right and Wrong Ways of Love).

In her autobiographical works, *Crème fraiche* (1978; Fresh Cream) and *Ja* (1979; Yes), Brøgger writes frankly about her own sexual relationships, continuing to protest against exclusive forms of love to promote her own somewhat utopian ideal of universal love. Despite reservations about Brøgger's brand of utopianism, Danish critics consider these two works her best; Jens Kistrup goes so far as to call *Crème Fraiche* one of the major works of contemporary Danish literature.

With *En gris som har været oppe at slås kan man ikke stege* (1979; A Pig That's Been Fighting Can't Be Roasted), Brøgger breaks with the cosmopolitan world of her international travels to concentrate on a lyrical description of life in a rural Danish community and her relationship with her neighbors there. In this work, she eschews linear form for repetition of mythic themes to reflect her beliefs about cyclical nature and a holistic universe.

Tone, an epic commemorative prose poem about Tone Bonnen, a milliner, appeared in 1981. Here, Brøgger draws on Nordic and Greek mythology to recount and celebrate the life of an obscure and now forgotten woman who nevertheless passionately loved life, suffered and eventually died of bone cancer. Although some critics have thought the form of *Tone* gets in the way of readers' ability to relate to the character, nevertheless, the work as a whole reveals Brøgger's ongoing development as an initially popular writer who continues to take her craft more and more seriously.

Brøgger has steadfastly remained loyal to her original point of view and continued to write about her own characteristic themes. Her style, however, has steadily changed in a more literary direction and increasingly involves much experimental play among genres.

Works

Brøg [Brew] 1980). *Crème Fraiche* [Fresh Cream] (1978). *Edvard og Elvira. En ballade* (1988). *En gris som har været oppe at slås kan man ikke stege* [A Pig that's Been Fighting Can't Be Roasted] (1979). *Ja* [Yes] (1984). *Fri os fra kærligheden* [Deliver Us From Love] (1973). *Kærlighedens veje og vildveje* [The Right and Wrong Ways of Love] (1975). *Den pebrede susen. Flydende fragmenter og fixeringer* [The Pepper Whistle. Floating Fragments and Fixations] (1986). *Tone. Epos* (1981).

Translations: *Deliver Us From Love*, tr. Thomas Teal (1976). "No Man's Land" (excerpt from *Kærlighedens veje og vildeveje*), tr. Christine Badcock, in *No Man's Land: An Anthology of Modern Danish Women's Literature* (1987). "A Visit with Henry Miller," tr. Gregory Stephenson, *Seahorse*, 2, 4 (1983): 1–6.

Bibliography

Brøndsted, Mogens, "Brøgger, Suzanne." *Dansk biografisk leksikon*, vol. 16 (Copenhagen, 1984), pp. 265–266. Kistrup, Jens, "You Shouldn't Be

Allowed to Put Up With It!" *Out of Denmark: Isak Dinesen/Karen Blixen 1885–1985 and Danish Women Writers Today*, ed. Bodil Wamberg (Copenhagen, 1985), pp. 77–88. Sandstrom, Bjarne, "Personlighedens råderum: En læsning af Suzanne Brøggers *Tone* some portrætdigt." *Kritik*, 60 (1982): 24–39. Schack, May, "Suzanne Brøgger." *Danske digtere i det 20 århundrede*, ed. Torben Brøstrom, vol. 5, pp. 269–276.

Kristine Anderson

Afke Brouwer-De Beer

Born 1896, Koehoel, The Netherlands
Genre(s): journalism, essay
Language(s): Fries

Was granddaughter of the Fries poet, Waling Dijkstra. Publicist and editor. Published articles in Fries periodicals: *De Tsjerne*; *Fryske en Frij*.

Works

Ljocht en skaed op't skoallepaed [Sketches on the Life and Suffering of Children].

Mary Hatch

Irja Agnes Browallius

Born October 13, 1901, Helsinki, Finland;
died December 9, 1968, Stockholm,
Sweden
Genre(s): novel, short story
Language(s): Swedish

The realistic, almost naturalistic portrayals of peasant life that Browallius has presented to her reading public, primarily in novel form, have painted a society critics have seen as pessimistic and void of redemption. Stylistically compared to her contemporaries Vilhelm Moberg and Ivar Lo-Johansson, she focuses unsentimentally on the psychology of her characters rather than on the potential for social change, the latter subject one dear to many other writers of her time.

Irja Browallius did not grow up in the countryside milieu of her most famous literary creations. Daughter to the actors Carl and Gerda Browallius (Mrs. Browallius was of an Italian family), she spent her childhood in Stockholm

and received a formal education, including studies in medicine (at the Karolinska Institute) and painting. She became an elementary school teacher in 1927, a position which would take her and her mother (now divorced) to the rural province of Närke. Here she was able to study the lives of her pupils and their families, material that she would work into many prose works. Her debut came in 1934 with the short story collection *Vid byvägar och älgstigar* (By Village Roads and Elk Paths). The novels that secured her fame, however, appeared three and four years later: *Synden på Skruke* (Sin at Skruke) in 1937 and *Elida från gårdar* (Elida from the Farms) in 1938. At this time she left her teaching job to become a full-time writer.

Her later novels, with the exception of *Vänd ryggen åt Sivert* (Turn Your Back on Sivert) of 1951, have not received the critical acclaim of the earlier works, but she has been considered a major novelist and insightful depictor of human psychology. Some detractors see an anachronistic quality about her writing: the bleak, fate-dominated view of life as well as her narrative technique are reminiscent of the Iceland sagas; the realism and Darwinistic determinism remind the reader of such Scandinavian authors as J.P. Jacobsen in the 1880s.

But Browallius does display artistic gifts; her psychological insight is keen, and her ability to reproduce the Närke dialect is impressive. She has been labeled "en sagoberättarska," a storyteller, and her narration is sure and compelling, if at times long-winded and stilted.

Works

Novels: *Josef gipsmakare* [Joseph the Plasterer] (1935). *Plats på scenen!* [Ready Onstage!] (1936). *Synden på Skruke* [Sin at Skruke] (1937). *Elida från gårdar* [Elida from the Farms] (1938). *Två slår den tredje* [Two Beat the Third] (1939). *Marméns* (1940). *Någon gång skall det ljusna* [Someday It Will Become Light] (1941). *Ringar på vattnet* [Rings on the Water] (1942). *Mot gryningen* [Toward Dawn] (1943). *Eldvakt* [Tender of the Fire] (1945). *Ljuva barndomstid* [Sweet Childhood] (1946). *Jord och himmel* [Earth and Heaven] (1947). *Karusellen* [The Carousel] (1949). *Vänd ryggen åt Sivert* [Turn Your Back on Sivert] (1951). *En fågel i handen* [A Bird in the Hand] (1952). *Ung* [Young] (1954).

Paradisets dagg [Dew of Paradise] (1957). *Vårbräckning* [As Spring Breaks] (1959). *Om sommaren sköna* [In the Beautiful Summertime] (1961). *Ut ur lustgården* [Out of the Garden of Eden] (1963). *Skur på gröna knoppar* [Rain Shower on Green Buds] (1965). *Instängd* [Shut In] (1967).

Short story collections: *Vid byvägar och älgstigar* [By Village Roads and Elk Paths] (1934). *Torplyckan* [Cottage Joy] (1953).

Drama: *Den stora boten* [The Great Message] (1943).

Bibliography

Claësson, Bissi, "Irja Browallius och hennes släkt." *Svensk litteraturtidskrift* 32 (1969). Engman, Bo, and Månsson, Lilian, eds., *Litteraturlexikon* (Stockholm, 1974). Gustafson, Alrik, *A History of Swedish Literature* (Minneapolis, 1961). Harrie, Ivar, and Browallius, Irja, "Bönder i Skruke." Holm, Ingvar, ed., *Vänkritik* (Stockholm, 1959). Holmberg, Olle, *Skratt och allvar i svensk litteratur* (Stockholm, 1963). Linder, Erik Hjalmar, *Ny illustrerad svensk litteraturhistoria: Fyra decennier av nittonhundratalet* (Stockholm, 1958). Runnquist, Åke, *Moderna svenska författare* [which mistakenly lists Browallius' place of birth as Stockholm] (Stockholm, 1967). Schwanbom, Per, "In memoriam: Irja Browallius 1901–1968." *Bonniers litterära magasin* 38 (March 1969). Sjöström, Gunnar, ed., *Vem är vem i Norden* (Stockholm, 1941).

Kathy Saranpa Anstine

leanness, and violent candor. Humor enlivens these eleven stories of desire, terror, and horror. She describes a time of difficulty and the epoch following across the continent, combining the sanity and wisdom of Hungary and the sorrow of Israel. Her lucid Italian prose is reminiscent of another place and tongue in another mode to exorcise the darkness.

The romance *La sacre nozze* (The Sacred Wedding) appeared in 1969, followed by the collection of stories *Due stanze vuote* (Two Empty Rooms) and the romances *Transit* and *Mio splendido disastro* (My Splendid Calamity). Her poetry is collected in two volumes, entitled *Il tatuaggio* (The Tattoo) and *In difesa del padre* (In Defense of the Father). She is an active broadcast journalist in radio and television. Additionally, Bruck has directed the films *Improvviso* (1979; The Unexpected) and *Quale Sardegna* (1982; Ah, Sardinia!) and recently the romance *Un giorno da Donna* (One Day of the Woman). Her creative contributions have extended beyond the literary domain into other mediums as she continues to experiment in new genres.

Works

Andremo in città (rpt. 1982). *Chi ti ama cosi* [How I Love You So] (1959; rpt. 1974). *Due stanze vuote*. *Il tatuaggio* [The Tattoo]. *In difesa del padre* [In Defense of the Father]. *La sacre nozze* [The Sacred Wedding] (1969). *Mio splendido disastro* [My Splendid Calamity]. *Transit*.

Jean E. Jost

Edith Bruck

Born 1932, Hungary
Genre(s): autobiography, romance, stories,
*   poetry*
Language(s): Italian

Edith Bruck was born in Hungary in 1932 but was deported as a young girl. This provided her with the opportunity to see other countries, such as Israel, and in 1954 she settled in Rome. Four years later she published an autobiography entitled *Chi ti ama cosi* (How I Love You So) and then a book called *Andremo in città* (We Will Go to the City; rpt. 1982), which was made into a film. This book reveals intelligence, energetic

Christine Brückner

Born 1921, Schmillinghausen/Waldeck,
*   Germany*
Genre(s): novel, short story
Language(s): German

Christine Brückner's books have been shaped by her experiences during and after World War II. After "helping in the war effort" for five years as a young woman, she made a living as cook, accountant, and cafeteria director in 1945. Her diploma as librarian in 1946 helped her find a position as research assistant at the Art Department of the University of Marburg, which permitted her to study art history and literature there. Since 1954, she has been a full-time writer. In 1980, she was elected vice president of the German PEN, and in 1982, she received the Goethe Prize of Hesse.

Because Christine Brückner has been considered merely a pop writer by the German literary scene, there is hardly any secondary literature about her writings. The popularity of the televised version of her Poenichen novels has not endeared her to critics and fellow authors. It is true that her books are written simply and sometimes conventionally. Nevertheless, they deal poignantly with two important themes: first of all, the traumas of the war and post-war periods and second, with the problems women have during marriage, separation, and divorce, as well as their attempts to liberate themselves from their traditional roles. It would seem that in the fictitious speeches of eleven indignant women, which she has united in the volume entitled *Wenn du geredet hättest, Desdemona* (If You Had Only Talked, Desdemona), Christine Brückner has overcome some of her problems and reached a wider educated public for the first time. Its publication date of 1983 also includes Brückner among the growing number of contemporary feminist writers. She has also written a number of children's books.

Works

Ehe die Spuren verwehen (1954). *Die Zeit danach* (1961). *Der Kokon* (1966). *Überlebensgeschichten* (1973). *Jai che und Levkojen* (1975). *Nirgendwo ist Poenichen* (1977). [With O.-H. Kühner], *Erfahren und erwandert* (1979). *Wenn du geredet hättest, Desdemona. Ungehaltne Reden ungehaltner Frauen* (1983).

Ingeborg Zeiträg

Carry van Bruggen

(see: Carolina Lea de Haan)

Til Brugman

Born September 16, 1888, Amsterdam, The Netherlands; died July 24, 1958, Gouda
Genre(s): short story, novel, children's literature
Language(s): Dutch, German

Mathilde Maria Petronella Brugman was the daughter of a tyrannical and bigoted mother. Her father, who owned French vineyards, had a knowledge of fifteen different languages and a passion for literature. Til Brugman left home when she was eighteen, after eight years in a Catholic boarding school. It was the start of an adventurous but often poverty-stricken life. She met the constructivist painter Mondrian and other members of *de Stijl* (Rietveld, Van Doesburg) and got also involved in the dadaist movement, writing poems, pamphlets, and grotesque prose and earning her bread with office and teaching jobs. Her stays in Amsterdam and 's-Gravenhage were repeatedly interrupted by long journeys abroad, and she managed to take university courses in London and Paris. Til Brugman acquired a thorough command of French, English, German, Italian, Spanish, Russian, and the three Scandinavian languages. Moreover, she read Latin and even Japanese. She was interested in psychology and was committed to the political left. Between 1930 and 1939 she lived in Berlin, where she published two grotesque stories in German—under the title *Scheingehacktes* (1935; Bogus Meatballs)—and did translation work. Her first Dutch novel, *Bodem* (Soil), appeared in 1946. Its deliberately archaic style contrasts with both the fluency of her children's books and the freakishness of her satirical pieces. Two novels, a few short stories, and several grotesques have still not been published.

Works

De houten Christus [The Wooden Christ] (1949). *Spanningen* [Tensions] (1953). *De zeebruid* [The Sea-Bride] (1957).

Bibliography

Kossmann, A., *Jaarboek van de Maatschappij der Nederlandse Letteren 1958–1959* (1959).

Frank Joostens

Sophie Christiane Friederike (Frederikke) Brun

*Born June 3, 1765, Gräfentonna-Gotha,
Sachsen (Saxony) Germany; died March
25, 1835, Copenhagen, Denmark
Genre(s): poetry, letters, travelogue
Language(s): German*

At her beloved, elegant Sophienholm on Bagsværd Lake, a salon of international and, to a certain degree, aristocratic character, and in Merchant Constantin Brun's (refined) salons in the Palace on Bredgade, Friederike Brun was a catalyst for the refined, cosmopolitan, literary circles of her day. Like her more provincial contemporary, Karen Margrethe (Kamma) Rahbek of Bakkehuset, Brun offered a cultural home, "a literary, sensitive, salon sociability" (*Dansk Litteraturhistorie* 4, p. 580), for intellectuals, artists, and writers. With her great talent as a storyteller and her knowledge and experience in European literary salons, such as that of Madame de Staël in Geneva (*DbL*2, 586), Friederike Brun drew Danish and European literati to a meeting point, to a center of entertainment, sensitive conversation, and social refinement.

Sophie Christiane Friederike (Frederikke) Münter (Brun) was born in Gräfentonna-Gotha, Sachsen (Saxony), on June 3, 1765. She was the daughter of the Presiding Church Superintendent in Gräfentonna, Balthasar Münter (1735–1793), and Magdalena Sophia Ernestine Friederike von Wangenheim (1742–1808), and she was the sister of the writer Friederich Münter. When Friederike Münter was barely a few weeks old, Balthasar Münter accepted an appointment as Parish Priest of Skt. Petri Church in Copenhagen; in the Danish capital, the Münters quickly joined "the influential and culturally prominent German society circles (of) A.P. Bernstorff and Ernst Schimmelmann" (*DbL*2, 585). Friederike Münter was a very precocious child, fond of reading and dramatizing Samuel Richardson's novels and capable of "reading Ossian in English at thirteen and Tasso in the original Italian at fourteen" (*DbL*2, 585). She also made her first attempt at poetry in 1782, with a collection of German poems privately printed by her father. Münter's first trip abroad, to Germany

with her parents, acquainted her with such prominent literary figures as Herder, Klopstock, Bürger, and Wieland and led to her first travel journal, *Tagebuch meiner ersten Reise* (1782; Diary of My First Journey). With her lively wit, spirit, and intelligence, Friederike Münter attracted many suitors; her father's mild insistence and concern for her economic security led Münter to accept the hand of the Copenhagen merchant, Constantin Brun; he and Münter were married shortly after her eighteenth birthday. There were five children from the marriage, among them Ida, the later Comtesse de Bombelles. After the birth of Ida, Friederike Brun developed a severe case of influenza; when the attack subsided, Brun was left deaf. Her severe deafness never impeded Brun's later social prominence or the liveliness of conversation, sociability, and entertainment at Sophienholm (*DbL*2, 585–587). Brun embarked on a series of travels for treatments and recreation, with Constantin Brun or alone. From 1790 to 1791, the Bruns travelled through France and Switzerland, meeting the German poet, Friedrich Matthisson, and the Swiss writer, Charles Victor de Bonstetten. Friederike Brun shared the companionship of both men, first primarily Matthisson's in Lugano and Rome (1795–1796), but Bonstetten eventually "stepped definitively into the foreground . . . becoming the completely dominating (passion) of Brun's life" (*DbL*2, 585). Even managing to win over Constantin Brun with his charm, Bonstetten and his son moved into the Brun home in Copenhagen; the Bonstettens shared the residence with Friederike and Constantin Brun from 1798 to 1801. Brun accompanied Bonstetten on his return to Switzerland, remaining with him there until 1803, when she returned alone—and inconsolable— to Copenhagen (*DbL*2, 585). In 1805, Brun made her final trip south, first to Geneva, where she resided with Madame de Staël and Bonstetten, then to Rome, where she lived in the same congenial company from 1807 to 1810 (*DbL*2, 586). In 1810, Constantin Brun issued an ultimatum to his wife; she was either to forsake her daughter Ida and remain with Bonstetten on a fixed pension or to return to Denmark immediately. Brun chose the latter course, never to see Bonstetten again but to continue writing to him until his death (1832). The relationship between the Bruns, never passionate, was not restored to harmony: "Brun gave up her travels and friend, while (Constantin) had to reconcile himself to foreigners . . . (and) a salon of European format . . . where the most prominent intellectuals and artists met with the aristocrats, foreign diplomats and travellers" (*DbL2*, 586). Sophienholm and the Palace on Bredgade became the centers of cultural life and *belles lettres*, with Friederike Brun at the helm of it all, until her death on March 25, 1835.

Friederike Brun's extensive collections (in 15 volumes) of poetry, letters, artistic and literary articles, personal sketches, and travel descriptions are nearly exclusively written in the German of her literary circle and cultural heritage. In addition to the early editions of her poems (1782) and the poems published by Friedrich Matthisson (*Gedichte*, 1795, Poems), Brun wrote two additional volumes of poetry, *Neue Gedichte* (1812; New Poems) and *Neueste Gedichte* (1820; Newest Poems); her poetry "belongs stylistically to the *Empfindsamkeit* category, but with a certain classical quality" (*DbL2*, 586). More remarkable and noteworthy are Brun's many travel descriptions, characterizations of noted individuals, and depictions of life in Europe: "In many instances genres cross each other in (her) individual works, which often combine travel, personal sketches, and art and cultural descriptions from (Brun's) many European trips" (Dalager, 1, p. 139). Such works as *Prosaische Schriften I-IV* (1799–1801; Prose Writings), which included *Tagebuch über Rom* (1795–1795; Diary of Rome) and *Episoden aus Reisen I-II* (1806–1809; III, 1816; IV, 1818; Episodes from Travels); *Briefe aus Rom* (1808–1810; Letters from Rome); and, her last book, *Römisches Leben I-II* (1833; Life in Rome), reveal Brun's perceptive, precise, artistic sense, her sympathetic feelings for Italian nature, art, and culture, and her ability to sketch the "significant personalities she had met in Rome" (*DbL2*, 586) and elsewhere. Friederike Brun's most important work is certainly her fine autobiography of the first 15 years of her life in the cultured Danish-German Münter milieu in Copenhagen, *Wahrheit aus Morgenträume* (began 1810, published 1824; Truth from Morning Dreams; in Danish, *Ungdomserindringer*, Memories of Youth). The

work includes an addition, *Idas ästhetische Entwicklung* (1824; Ida's Aesthetic Development), in which Brun, as representative of "German-Danish enobling cultural humanism" (Dalager, 1, p. 142), provided an educational program for the development of the feminine *forte*, the exemplary aesthetic and artistic talents inherent in women. *Idas ästhetische Entwicklung* is dedicated to Madame de Staël, the most complete incarnation of Brun's aesthetic humanistic ideal. Brun also carried on an extensive correspondence with her contemporaries, among them the mild governess of Bakkehuset, Karen Margrethe (Kamma) Rahbek, of course Madame de Staël of Geneva and Italy, and Bonstetten, and especially, over 20 years, Caroline von Humboldt, with whom Brun shared her deepest bitterness and "boredom with life . . . (and her disappointing) constant comparison between 'the man God gave me and the man my heart chose'" (Dalager, 1, p. 147, and Louis Bobé, *Friederike* [*Frederikke*] *Brun*, p. 58).

The cultural background, education, and experience, and the various travels of Friederike Brun were those of a European cosmopolitan, of a representative of the refined, artistic-literary salon tradition of European savants and connoisseurs. Yet Brun enjoyed her acquaintance with many Danish artists, poets, and writers, B. Thorvaldsen, Johannes Edwald, Jens Baggesen, Adam Øhlenschläger, J.H. Heiberg, and B.S. Ingemann (*DbL2*, 586). Brun's personality was a unique meld of sentimentality and practicality, of clarity, romance, vision, and a deep understanding of the famous and less notable people she came to know. Friederike Brun's writings and her salons at Sophienholm and Bredgade reflect her "internationally oriented intellect" as well as her sensitivity and knowledge of Danish cultural life *and* her personal *ennui* after a life of extensive travel and one great passion.

Works

Gedichte (1782). *Tagebuch meiner ersten Reise* (1782). *Gedichte* (1795). *Tagebuch über Rom* (1795–1796). *Prosaische Schriften*, I-IV (1799–1801). *Episoden aus Reisen* I-IV (1806–1809; 1816; 1818). *Briefe aus Rom* (1808–1810). *Wahrheit aus Morgenträume* (1810–1824). *Neue Gedichte* (1812). *Neueste Gedichte* (1820). *Idas ästhetische*

Entwicklung (1824). Briefe, Artiklen, Beiträge. *Hören; Musenalmanach; Iris; Nytaarsgave for Damer; Minerva; Tilskueren. Römisches Leben*, I–II (1833).

Bibliography

Bobé, Louis, *Friederike (Frederikke) Brun, født Münter og hendes kreds hjemme og und* (Copenhagen, 1910). Dalager, Stig, and Anne-Marie Mai, *Danske kvindelige forfattere 1. Fra Sophie Brahe til Mathilde Fibiger. Udvikling og perspektiv.* 2 oplag (Copemhagen, 1983). *Dansk Litteraturhistorie, 4, Patriotismens tid, 1746–1807* (Copenhagen, 1983). *Dansk Litteraturhistorie, 5, Borgerlig enhedskultur, 1807–48* (Copenhagen, 1984). Olbrich, Rosa, *Die deutsch-dänische Dichterin Friederike Brun, ein Beitrag zur empfindsam-klassizistische Stilperiode* (Breslau, 1932). Steenstrup, Johannes, *Den danske kvindes historie* (Copenhagen, 1917).

Lanae Hjortsvang Isaacson

Janina Brzostowska

Born July 7, 1907, Wadowice, Poland; died 1986
Genre(s): poetry, novel
Language(s): Polish

Brzostowska was born in Wadowice in the mountain area of Beskidy, in a middle-class family of intelligentsia. Her father, Jan Dorozinski, was a high school principal and teacher, author of poetry published under the pen name of Julian Mrok, and the author of "Zarys psychologii elementarnej" (An Outline of Basic Psychology); her mother, Julia née Berner, was a pianist. Brzostowska started writing poetry at eleven, and several years later her poems "Matka" (Mother) and "Sen w ogrodzie" (A Dream in the Garden) appeared in a school newspaper "Nasz lan" (Our Field). Brzostowska studied Polish and French at the old Jagiellonian University in Cracow, where her family moved, and continued her poetic activity.

In the summer of 1924 she joined the group of poets of the Beskid region called "Czartak," founded by such well known men of letters as Emil Zegadlowicz, Edward Kozikowski and Jan Nepomucen Miller, who organized in order to "pour the light onto the world from the top of this Hilly Republic according to the age-old truth that all joy comes from the mountains," and "prove with a new form of art that Poland has the right to occupy her newly acquired place among the free nations. . . ." Brzostowska's ties with the poets of the "Czartak" were ones of friendship rather than of program; because of a lung disease she developed in her youth, she lived and worked alone.

Her formal debut was made in 1925 with a volume of poems connected with urban rather than country life, and it was very favorably received due to its original language, "organically isolated," as one of the critics put it. The source of her poetry was perceived in a "desire to define that which cannot be expressed and her fear of what is transitory but unfamiliar." The 18-year-old was praised for her wisdom concerning the vanity of things, and her calm meditation on death. The title of the volume of poems called "On Land and My Love" was viewed as a definition of her poetic program: to write about the land, not only that of her region and its people, but to involve herself with human life in a broader sense. Her poetry describing love, nature and the life of common people met with general recognition. The last book she published with the "Czartak" was the volume of subtle and meditative lyrical poems entitled "Erotyki." She formally left the group in 1929, yet she remained close to the friends of her youth and remembered them warmly. In the same year she moved to Warsaw for good but never joined another literary group and was always perceived as an isolated phenomenon in Polish literature. Though relatively little known, she was included among the important women poets next to Kazimiera Illakowiczowna and Maria Pawlikowska-Jasnorzewska by prominent historian of literature and critic Aleksander Brueckner.

Having moved to the capital city, Brzostowska attempted prose and in 1933 published her first novel "The Jobless of Warsaw," in the vein of a series of journalistic reports, dubbed by the critics as "a cry of protest" of the unemployed from the depth of their physical and moral misery. That first novel was soon withdrawn from publication by censorship. Brzostowska's second novel describes the process of a woman's coming of age and, according to the critics, reveals the author's subtle psychological insight in dealing with social questions. From 1938 to 1939, Brzostowska was an editor of the bimonthly *Skawa*, devoted to the problems of her native region of Beskid. One of its collaborators was the famous artist, philosopher and man of letters Stanislaw Ignacy Witkiewicz, known as Witkacy. After almost a decade, Brzostowska returned to poetry with her two volumes of verse published in 1939, which remained basically unknown, for their circulation was interrupted by the outbreak of war. The main subjects of her lyrical poetry are love and the passage of time.

Brzostowska spent the years of the German occupation in Warsaw and engaged in the conspiratorial activity of patriotic resistance; deported from Warsaw with the rest of the inhabitants after the 1944 uprising, she was one of the first who returned to settle among the ruins of the totally razed city. She wrote poetry but published little during the times of relative lack of political oppression of art; translating poetry became her main occupation, her greatest achievement being the 1961 translation into Polish of the complete "Songs" of Sappho. In 1969 in Vienna, those poems were sung in Polish by the Japanese singer Emiko Iiama with music by the Polish composer Andrzej Hundziak.

Works

Poetry: *Szczescie w cudzym miescie* [Happiness in a Strange City] (1925). *O ziemi i mojej milosci* [On Land and My Love] (1925). *Erotyki* [Erotic Poems] (1926). *Najpiekniejsza z przygod* [The Most Beautiful of Adventures] (1929). *Naszyjnik wiecznosci* [A Necklace of Eternity] (1939). *Zywiol i spiew* [The Elements and the Song] (1939). *Plomien w cierniach* [Flame among Thorns] (1947). *Giordano Bruno*, historical poem (1953). *Wiersze* [Poems] (1957). *Zanim noc . . .* [Until the Night] (1961). *Czas nienazwany* [Time without Name] (1964). *Obrona swiatla* [In Defense of Light] (1968). *Pozdrowienie* [Greetings] (1969). *Szczescia szukamy* [In Search of Happiness] (1974). *Poezje wybrane* [Selected Poetry] (1974). *Eros* (1977). *Spiew przedwieczorny* [A Song at Nighttime] (1979). *Poezje zebrane* [Collected Poems] (1981).

Novels: *Bezrobotni Warszawy* (1933; rpt. 1947, 1950). *Kobieta zdobywa swiat* [A Woman Conquers the World] (1937).

Maya Peretz

Lukrecija Bogašinović Budmani

Born October 26, 1710, Dubrovnik,
Yugoslavia; died June 8, 1784, Dubrovnik
Genre(s): poetry
Language(s): Croatian

Although today Lukrecija Bogašinović Budmani is forgotten (none of her works having ever been printed), she was one of the most popular poets of Baroque Dubrovnik. Other than the fact that she was the only child of her parents, and the granddaughter of the poet Petar Toma Bogašinović, who in 1684 published what proved to be a popular epic concerning the recent defeat of the Turks by the King of Poland at Vienna, nothing is known about her childhood and youth. However, they could hardly have been happy because of her father's misfortune. He, employed as a clerk by the government of Dubrovnik, was in 1710 apparently unjustly accused of being chiefly responsible for the great shortage in the state granary and was sentenced to five years of galley labor and banishment from Dubrovnik, with the additional obligation of paying a huge fine to the government in yearly installments, which he did until his death. So Lukrecija did not even live with her father from her birth up to her thirty-third year, when his banishment was revoked and he returned to Dubrovnik. When she first started writing is unknown. On the evidence of her works it is clear that she knew Italian and had a considerable knowledge of the poetry of her time.

Very late, in her forty-third year, Lukrecija married Šimun Budmani, a merchant by profession. Ten years later she was a childless widow. Although her husband left her no property, she was supported in her widowhood by the real estate that she had inherited from her father's brother and her mother's sister. When she died in 1784, she was accorded a solemn funeral in the Dominican church of Dubrovnik and was laid beside her parents, not her husband, who had been buried in another church.

Only four works of Lukrecija have been preserved in manuscript, even though it is likely that she wrote more. All four treat a biblical theme, and all four were written after her fiftieth year, so that it is reasonable to suppose that they were not her first attempts at poetry. The first three are epics: *Posluh Abrama Patrijarke* (1763; The Obedience of Patriarch Abraham) in 760 verses, *Život Tibije i njegova sina* (1763; Life of Tobith and His Son) in 1684 verses, and *Život Jozefa Patrijarke* (1770; Life of Patriarch Joseph) in 1996 verses. The fourth work is a pastoral eclogue, *Razgovor pastirski vrhu porodenja Gospodinova* (1764; The Shepherds' Conversation on the Lord's Nativity), in 1504 verses. All those works are written in stanzas of four verses, each verse consisting of four trochees, with the rhyme scheme *abab*, the usual stanza of the Baroque poetry of Dubrovnik.

The adaptation of biblical tales into vernacular epics, primarily for moralistic and didactic purposes, is almost unknown today, but it was very popular in the Baroque, and Lukrecija had many Italian and Croatian predecessors for her epics. Although she did not have her works printed, so many manuscripts—now in various libraries and archives of Dubrovnik and Zagreb— have been preserved (many of these contain, naturally, faulty and abridged versions), that they must have been popular and admired during her life and well into the nineteenth century. Perhaps the chief merit of Lukrecija's epics is in the psychological truth and realism of her biblical adaptations. Where the Bible gives little more than the facts of the story, she tries to account for the characters' psychology and motivation, in order to make them more familiar to the readers. She was not a great poet, but her epics deserve our interest by their strong dramatic element, shown in the many dialogues in the crucial moments, and in the skill with which the author had given her own contemporary setting to the biblical stories, so that they read as if they took place in eighteenth-century Croatia. The author, with an obvious moralistic purpose, often addressing her young female readers in particular, stresses the importance of the family and analyzes the relations between its various members.

Her heroes—Abraham, the heavily tested father and husband, the saintly Tobith, Joseph, the ideal man in his just and magnanimous treatment of his brothers—are presented as moral examples to the readers by their nobility, generosity, and, above all, unshakable piety.

Works

Posluh Abrama Patrijarke (1763). *Život Tobije i njegova sina* (1763). *Život Josefa Patrijarke* (1770). *Razgovor pastirski vrhu porodenja Gospodinova* (1764).

Bibliography

Markovic, Zdenka, *Pjesnikinje starog Dubrovnika* (1970).

Neda Jeni

Marie-Thérèse-Charlotte Buret

(a.k.a. Marie de Sormiou)

Born ca. 1865; died after 1941
Genre(s): poetry, drama
Language(s): French

The titles of several of Buret's works suggest that she took part in the classicizing Provençal literary revival begun in the mid-nineteenth century; her *Ode à la Provence* (Ode to Provence) was recited at the Théâtre Antique at Orange on August 6, 1906. Her verse play *Hylaeos* was performed in the outdoor theater at Champigny-la Bataille on June 13, 1909.

All that is known of her is that, in 1885, she married a certain Alfred de Ferry (1853–1927). (According to the *Dictionnaire de biographie française*, he was administrator of the hospitals of Marseille during the First World War and a French delegate to the Red Cross from 1917 on.)

Works

Ode à Provence (1906). *Chants de soleil* (1906). *La Vie triomphante* (1908). *Hylaeos*, pièce en vers en un acte et deux tableaux (1909). *Cantique au Cantique des cantiques* (1935). *Calvaire de l'homme, poèmes de guerre* (1941).

James S. Patty

Carmen Burgos Seguí

(a.k.a. Colombine)

*Born 1876, Almería, Spain; died 1933,
    Madrid, Spain*
Genre(s): essay, novel, short story
Language(s): Spanish

Better known by her pseudonym, Colombine was a teacher at the Escuela Normal de Madrid, an active feminist and a regular contributor to the most significant magazines and newspapers in Madrid. She travelled in Europe and America. She was fervently interested in issues dealing with women's rights such as the vote for women and divorce as reflected by her essay "La mujer moderna y sus derechos." She is also credited with valuable literary studies on Renan, Tolstoy, Larra, and Leopardi. In her own works of fiction, her style tends to realism or a kind of mitigated naturalism.

Works

Essays: *Ensayos literarios. Arte de saber vivir. Notas del alma. El veneno del arte. Los inadaptados. Ellas y ellos o ellos y ellas.*

Novels: *Los anticuarios. La malcasada. El último contrabandista. Todos menos ése.*

Short Stories: *Cuentos de Colombine.* "La novela corta española." Promoción de "El Cuento Semenal" (1901–1920). Estudio preliminar, selección y notas de F.C. Sainz de Robles (1952). (Carmen de Burgos included among featured authors.)

Bibliography

Bleiberg, G., and J. Marías, *Diccionario de la literatura española* (Madrid, 1953). *Diccionario de la literatura española*, vol. I, Authors (Barcelona, 1975). Diez-Echarri, E., and J.M. Roca Franquesa, *Historia general de las literaturas españolas e hispánicas* (Madrid, 1968). Valbuena Prat, A., *Historia de la literatura española*, 6th ed., rev. and expanded (Madrid, 1960).

Carol Stos

Claude de Burine

Born 1933, St. Léger des Vignes, France
Genre(s): poetry, prose
Language(s): French

Claude de Burine grew up in rural France but later, from 1949 to 1956, lived in Casablanca, where she also taught. After returning to Paris she was divorced from the engineer Robert Lefèvre, met many poets—Rousselot, Guillevic, Bosquet and others—and also her second husband, the artist Henri Espinouze, with whom she lived until his death in 1982. She lives still in Vichy, and sometimes Paris, "preferring being to seeming."

Claude de Burine's first collection, *Lettres à l'enfance* (Letters to Childhood), appeared in 1957 and like her next two collections, *La Gardienne* (1960; The Guardian) and *L'Allumeur de réverbères* (The Lamplighter), was to reappear in abbreviated form in her substantial volume of 1969, *Hanches* (Hips). These earliest texts date back to 1952, in fact, and reveal a somewhat more reflective tone and a less densely metaphorical and "Rimbaldian" quality than those of later years. They intensely evoke the peace and love available to both body and soul; a willingness even to die within the ecstasy of earthly (but always more than earthly) love; and, in the closing poems, the difficulties and yet an oddly unspoiled and courageous serenity at the time of loss and separation.

Hanches plunges back into these early moments of bliss and disruption and yet goes distinctly beyond them. Prefaced by Alain Bosquet and illustrated by Espinouze, the collection, as Bosquet says, is simply life itself, "with its stridences, its daily scars, its periodic bleeding of ideal served cold, its bedding down with subdued metaphysics like an adolescent learning what pleasure is. Nothing debatable. Nothing to be corrected." The tone of the poetry is one of intimacy, beyond all gratuitousness, centered upon the earthiness and the sacredness of life. The atmosphere is one of expectancy before the endless unfolding of the "snowy, fairy-like quality of existence." Founded upon passion and urgency, Claude de Burine's writing does not exclude prayer and quieter modes. Death, in her poetry, is absorbed within a larger context that does not exclude intense grief any more than an abiding sense of wonder and "glory."

Le Passeur (The Ferryman) appeared in 1976 and in the following year received the Prix Max Jacob. Jean Breton speaks of the poet's "powerful identification with nature," her paradisiacal eroticism—what Senghor called the "magnificent carnal flowers" of her poems—, her ability to create "fabulous allegories" set in the matter of everyday experience. The whole volume offers a welcoming, a caressing, of things and people.

Le Cahier vert (1980; The Green Notebook) is the compelling account, in an elliptical and poetically charged prose, of a passion, indeed a profound love, and its dissolution. Memories, reverie, ecstasy and pain, knowledge and blindness, certainty and precariousness: these are some of the centers around which the book spins the fictional figures of its reality. The language of creation may be anchored in chagrin or soaring in joy, but it is above all a place of passage, exchange, consciousness.

La Servante (The Servant) also was published in 1980. As everywhere in de Burine's work, body and soul unite, absence and vibrant reality melt into something transcending them both, simplicity and complexity exchange their "logics," as do death and "destiny." "The poem," she tells us, "is waiting, whispering of leaves on a pensive shoulder in silhouette as we enter a new district." She is about to publish both a novel and a substantial collection of new poetry.

Works

Lettres à l'enfance, poetry (1957). *La Gardienne, Le Soleil dans la tête*, poetry (1960). *L'allumeur de réverbères*, poetry; pref. Jean Rousselot (1963). *Hanches*, poetry; pref. Alain Bosquet (1969). *Le Passeur*, poetry (1976). *Le Cahier Vert*, prose (1980). *Marcel Arland*, essays (1980). *La Servante*, poetry (1980).

Bibliography

Arland, Marcel, *La Nouvelle Poésie française, Poésie I* (1984), p. 25. Béarn, Pierre, "L'érotisme dans la poésie féminine." *La Passerelle* (Aut. 1985). Boisdeffre, Pierre de, *Histoire de la littérature française* (Paris, 1985), pp. 213, 234–235, 242–243. Bosquet, Alain, preface, *Hanches* (Paris, 1969). Breton, Jean, preface, *La Poésie féminine contemporaine. Poésie I* (1974). Brindeau, Serge, "Claude de Burine." *La Poésie contemporaine de langue Française depuis 1945* (Paris, 1973), pp. 390–391. Moulin, Jeanine, *Huits siècles de poésie féminine* (Paris, 1963). Rousselot, Jean, preface, *L'Allumeur des réverbères* (Mortemart, 1963). Rousselot, Jean, *Poètes français d'aujourd'hui* (Paris, 1965), p. 265. Senghor, Léopold Sédar, *La Nouvelle Poésie française, Poésie I* (1984), p. 25.

Michael Bishop

Marguerite Burnat-Provins

Born 1872, Arras, France; died 1952
Genre(s): poetry, novel
Language(s): French

Marguerite Burnat-Provins was a woman of many talents. Not only did she teach art history, but she was also actively involved in painting, print making, poster design, and in the decorative arts. Her literary endeavors were primarily in the areas of poetry and novels. Indeed, writing had always come easily to her. Even as a child, she enjoyed her composition classes so much so that she would often write her friends' themes as well as her own! She left her native Arras to marry and lived in Vevey, a Swiss village that served as the inspiration for her early works. Her passion for accuracy in the rendering of a scene, for capturing the color of a dialogue, was her undoing when the townspeople realized that she had used them in her poetry, and she was forced to leave. Although Switzerland would remain her principal residence for the rest of her life, her later travels, especially a stay in Brittany, would influence her work. The *Livre du pays d'Armor* (The Book of the Land of Armor) and *Heures d'hiver* (Winter Hours), both published in 1920, are inspired by the Breton people and countryside.

Burnat-Provins wrote constantly for some twenty years and then sporadically as she grew older. Her written production was matched only by her output of watercolors, many of which were destroyed or stolen during World War I along with a number of poems and the original editions of her poems. The visual and the written arts were closely linked for Burnat-Provins. Her first book, *Tableaux valaisans* (Valaisian Scenes), was more than just a collection of poetry. She did the layout, design, and the illustrations, working closely with printers on all aspects of production. This was the first of a total of five collaborations, the Vevey poems of 1903–1907. She strove to create books that were complete artifacts.

The sensuality of her written landscapes and of the book-as-object is transformed into a spiritual and physical eroticism in *Le Livre pour toi* (1908; A Book for You) and *Cantique d'été* (1910; Song of Summer) which can be seen as a diptych of sorts. She celebrates the beauty of the male body as male poets had celebrated women for centuries and thus opens up previously untouched thematics. The love poems of these two collections received as much praise for their innovation as they did condemnation for what some considered their pornographic images. *La Fénêtre ouverte* (The Open Window) and the *Boule de verre* (Glass-Ball) poems form another unit in her love poetry, contrasting stoicism after the departure of the beloved with the high emotions of loss, resignation gives way to tears.

Burnat-Provins produced an enormous oeuvre, not all of which is of equal worth. The rapidity with which she wrote often manifests itself in stylistic weaknesses and a certain impression of carelessness. Such a manner of writing might seem better suited to prose, and although Burnat-Provins was a poet, she had no affinity for verse. It is not surprising then, that in the formal aspects of her poetry, she exhibits the same individualistic approach as she had to theme. Her originality and independence are clear in her choice of the prose-poem at a time when verse was dominant. Her painter's eye could be given free rein in prose and image is not subject to form. Thus the best of her poems are not unlike her watercolors—fluid, evocative, with a feeling of spontaneity and freedom.

Works

Tableaux valaisans (1903). *Heures d'automne* (1904). *Chansons rustiques* (1905). *Le Chant du Verdier* (1906). *Sous les Noyers* (1907). *Le livre pour Toi* (1908). *Le Coeur sauvage* (1909). *Cantique d'Eté* (1910). *La Fénêtre ouverte sur la vallée* (1911); selections in *Revue de Belgique* (1909). *La Servante* (1914). *Poèmes de la Boule de verre* (1917). *Nouveaux Poèmes de la Boule de verre* (1918). *Vous* (1919). *Le Livre du Pays d'Armor*

(1920). *Heures d'hiver* (1920); selections appeared in the *Revue Parisienne* (1918). *Poèmes troubles* (1920). *Poèmes de la Soif; Poèmes du Scorpion* (1921). *Contes en vingt lignes* (1922). *Le Voile* (1929). *Choix de poèmes* (1933). *Près du Rouge-gorge* (1937). *La Cordalca* (1943). Poems were also contributed to *Vers et prose* 13 and 15 (1908) and *La Nouvelle Revue* 8 (1913).

Bibliography

Heritier, Jean, *Essai de critique contemporain, Première série* (Paris, 1920). Malo, Henri, *Marguerite Burnat-Provins* (Paris, 1920). Numerous reviews of her works appear in the *Mercure de France*.

Edith J. Benkov

Andreas Burnier

(see: Catharina Irma Dessaur)

Irina Nikolaevna Bushman

Born 1921, Pushkino (Tsarskoe Selo), the Soviet Union
Genre(s): poetry, essay, literary criticism, translation
Language(s): Russian, German

Irina Bushman (née Sidorova-Evseeva) is one of the most gifted Russian poets of the modern era. Due to the merciless events of World War II she was condemned to the existence of an exiled writer in Germany in the postwar years. She began her career as a student of literature and philology by publishing poetry and short stories in the 1950s and 1960s in the "thick" literary journals *Svoboda* (Liberty), *Sovremennik* (Contemporary), the almanac *Mosty* (Bridges) in Munich, and in *Novyi Zhurnal* (New Review) in New York. Occasionally, her poetry appeared in the New York daily *Novoe Russkoe Slovo* (New Russian Word). Bushman's cycle of short stories, *Krasnoe i seroe* (The Red and the Grey), published serially in *Svoboda*, Munich, 1950–1960, reflect the dark and light sides of Soviet military life during and immediately following World War II. Likewise, Bushman was very successful in the ballad genre on contemporary issues and historical motifs (especially memorable is her treatment of Ophelia, Anne Boleyn, and Van Gogh). As an essayist and literary critic Bushman contributed perceptive articles on Boris Pasternak to a *Collection of Articles on Boris Pasternak* in 1962 and published a book *Poeticheskoe iskusstvo Mandel'shtama* (1964; The Poetic Art of Mandelshtam). She also translated into German Fedor Abramov's novella *Vokrug da okolo* (1964; Beating About the Bush).

A "Petersburgian" by origin, Bushman is faithful to the eminent Petersburg note and carries on the tradition begun by Pushkin. In her verse lines the eternal themes of love, death, separation at times acquire a heavy brazen sound only to alternate with volatile, light-flowing poetical diction; her skillfully used modernistic devices, the pauses, broken lines, new metrical and rhythmical variations as well as innovative rhyme schemes assure Bushman a secure place among the first-rate Russian poets of the twentieth century.

Works

"O rannei lirike Pasternaka" [On the Early Poetry of Boris Pasternak] and "Pasternak i Ril'ke" [Pasternak and Rilke], *Sbornik statei, posviashchennyi tvorchestvu B.L. Pasternak* [Collection of Articles Dedicated to B.L. Pasternak] (1962). *Poeticheskoe Iskusstvo Mandel'shtama* [The Poetic Art of Mandelshtam] (1964). *Ein Tag im "Neuen Leben,"* tr. of Fedor Abramov's novella *Vokrug da okolo* [Beating About the Bush] (1964). *Krasnoe i seroe* [The Red and the Gray], cycle of short stories, published serially in *Svoboda* [Liberty] (1950–1960). Poetry appeared in the literary journals *Svoboda* [Liberty], *Sovremennik* [Contemporary], and *Novyi Zhurnal* [New Review], and the almanacs *Mosty* [Bridges] and *Sodruzhestvo* [Cooperation in Friendship].

Bibliography

Zverev, Fabii, "Poety 'novoi' emigratsii" [Poets of the 'New' Emigration], in *Russian Émigré Literature, A Collection of Articles in Russian with Résumés in English*, ed. N.P. Poltoratzky (Pittsburgh, 1972).

Marina Astman

Christina Busta

Born April 23, 1915, Vienna, Austria
Genre(s): lyric poetry, legends
Language(s): German

The Austrian poet Christina Busta has created a remarkable volume of lyrics with predominantly mythological and Christian themes. She uses the story of the creation as the starting point to criticize her world. She does not resort to traditional values, instead her poems search for peace in nature and a new sense of humanity. In the style of Montaigne, she is exploring the *condition humaine* and new ways of recovering humanity in the Platonic terms of the True, the Good, and the Noble in Man. Busta was born on April 23, 1915 in Vienna as WW I began to tear apart the splendor of the centuries old Hapsburgian empire. Her childhood was fatherless and lonely, since her mother did not want to expose her to other people. Her first poetic efforts bloomed in 1925, but she had to start working very early to support her mother. In 1933 she began with her study of English and *Germanistik*, but she could not finish her courses due to financial problems. She married the musician Maximilian Dimt in 1940, who, however, was conscripted in 1942 and sent to the front. In 1944 he was reported missing in action. After the war, Busta worked as a translator for the British and managed hotels in Vienna. Since 1950 she has been working for the public libraries in Vienna. Various times her poetic qualities were noticed, such as in 1933 by the public radio in Vienna, or in 1943 by the poet Josef Weinheber, but she only came forth with her first poem, "An den Schmerz" ("Ode to Pain") in 1946 in *Die österreichische Furche* Nr. 47, November 23 (under her married name of Dimt). In 1947 she published seven poems in Otto Basil's journal *Plan*. Her first collection of poems appeared in 1950, and she has published regularly to date.

In all her poems she has tried to transform fear, horror and guilt of the post-War years into joy, love, and redemption using images from the Bible, classicism, mythology and nature. Busta perceives the creature in man with its need for love and warmth. She declared her later poems (*Inmitten aller Vergänglichkeit*) to be love letters, since they all talk to another poetic "you."

Many Slavic elements, which she derived from her Bohemian and Moravian forefathers, permeate her poetry (similar to Paul Celan's poetry). They focus on the human aspect and human perspective in our life. Influences both from Paul Lehmann, Karl Heinrich Waggerl, Bertold Brecht, and even Friedrich Hölderlin are detectable. Above all, however, her religious thoughts are the underlying force in her poetry. A number of literary awards were given to her: 1950 Promotion Prize for Lyrics in addition to the Austrian State Award; 1954 Georg-Trakl Award; 1955 Prize for Lyrics by the Süddeutsche Rundfunk, 1956 Prize of the *Neue Deutsche Hefte in Berlin*.

Works

Jahr für Jahr [Year by Year] 1950). *Der Regenbaum* [The Rain Tree] (1951). *Lampe und Delphin* [Lamp and Dolphin] (1955). *Die Scheune der Vögel* [The Barn of Birds] (1968). *Das andere Schaf* [The Other Sheep] (1959). *Die Sternenmühle, Gedichte für Kinder und ihre Freunde* [The Mill of Stars: Poems for Children and Their Friends] (1959). *Unterwegs zu älteren Feuern* [On the Way to Older Fireplaces] (1965). *Salzgärten* [Gardens of Salt] (1975). *Die Zauberin Frau Zappelzeh, Gereimtes und Ungereimtes für Kinder und ihre Freunde* [The Sorceress Ms. Zappelzeh, Rhymed and Not-Rhymed Poems for Children and Their Friends] (1979). *Wenn du das Wappen der Liebe malst* [When You Are Painting the Coat of Arms of Love] (1981). *Inmitten aller Vergänglichkeit* [Amidst All Transition] (1985).

Bibliography

Künzel, F.P., "Nachwort," *Inmitten aller Vergänglichkeit*, pp. 88–93. Miller, J.W., "Christina Busta: Contemporary Austrian Religious Poet," *Studies in Language and Literature*, Proceedings of the 23rd Mountain Interstate Foreign Language Conference (Richmond, 1976), pp. 391–400. Retiz, L., "Faith and Language in a Lyric Cycle by Christina Busta," *Modern Austrian Literature* 12, III/IV (1979): 347–372. Scheichl, S.P., "Stiluntersuchung und sprachliches Verstehen von Texten: Am Beispiel eines Gedichtes von Christina Busta," *Jahrbuch für Internationale Germanistik* 14, 2 (1982): 100–126. Strutz, J., "Krippensermon für unsere Zeit: Über einige Probleme der Lyrik Christina Bustas." *Literatur und Kritik* 165/166 (1982): 3–15. Suchy, V., "Einleitung," *Das andere Schaf* (1959), pp. 5–38. Waldinger, E., "Der Regenbaum," *Books Abroad* (1953), p. 63. Waldinger, E., "Lampe und Delphin," *Books Abroad* (1956). Weilandt, F., "Das lyrische Werk von Christina Busta," *Formen der Lyrik in der Österreichischen Gegenwartslyrik*, ed. W. Schmidt Dengler (Vienna, 1981), pp. 70–94.

Albrecht Classen

Buttelerin, Büttlerin

(see: Magdalena von Freiburg)

Constanţa Buzea

Born 1941, Bucharest, Romania
Genre(s): poetry, children's literature
Language(s): Romanian

Constanţa Buzea graduated in Philology at the Bucharest University in 1967, having made her debut in 1957 in the literary journal *Tînărul scriitor* and published her first volume of verse in 1963. Since 1973 she has functioned as an editor for the journal *Amfiteatru*. Buzea, who is the author of 15 volumes of poetry, is unanimously recognized as one of the greatest contemporary Romanian poets.

Her voice rang deep and true almost from the beginning. The poet abandoned from her second volume the militant accents of *De pe pămînt* (1963; From the Earth). *La ritmul naturii* (1966; In the Rhythm of Nature) and *Norii* (1968; Clouds) are already volumes of fluent abstract meditation upon poetry, love, and spiritual change. In 1970 Constanţa Buzea produced a volume on death, sickness and satiation—*Agonice* (Agonizing [Poems])—and one on maternity and its drive—*Coline* (Hills). Since 1971 she has published, for a while on an yearly basis, mature volumes of essential lyricism such as *Sala nervilor* (1971; Hall of Nerves), *Leac pentru îngeri* (1972; Remedy for Angels), *Răsad de spini* (1973; Thorn Transplant), *Pasteluri* (1974; Pastels), *Ape cu plute* (1975; Rivers with Rafts), *Limanul orei* (1976; Haven of the Hour), *Ploi de piatră* (1979; Stony Rains), *Umbra pentru cer* (1981; Shadow for the Sky), and *Planta memoriei* (1985; Memory Plant).

Buzea's reflexive poetry dwells in "the poor valleys of the mind." The poet practices a kind of superior oblivion, she "thoroughly forgets" whatever might bring her back to the surface and the concrete. In the *camera obscura* of the soul, like Hölderlin, Rilke, or Trakl, the "mild savage" "saddled with words hanging round [her] neck" celebrates the austere genesis of the poem, the privileged moment of inspiration which sets forth the coagulation of poetic feeling into verse and image. Unflinching in this poetic vigil—or, if one looks at it from the outside world, in this poetic somnolence ("Poetry is itself a sleep/ From which you don't wake up")—the "imprudent" poet produces a superlative confession, one might say a meta-confession, in which external biography is rejected in favor of a quintessential exposure of her most hidden lyrical pulsations.

In proclaiming the autonomy of one's poetic destiny, Buzea grants her poems a survival dimension which is far beyond any political or ideological connotations. In her poetic universe, the mind "in which [the poet] still resist[s] as in a kingdom" has as its nearest equivalent the "shell of laughter" which protects the child. Even when speaking of "gifts [changed] into farce" or of "raw bread under a burnt crust," of "death-mill[s]" and "the process of becoming gentle invalids" the poet stays detached, imperative and serene, for degradation, devaluation, and disintegration are always counterbalanced in the long run by the inalterable regenerative power of living poetry.

Buzea's verse is ceremonial, majestic, severely disciplined in its amplitude, one is tempted to say apodictic. The poet masters like few others the choice of "hurtful words/ beautiful and cold," she knows that, in the end, lyricism is coldness rather than warmth ("Accumulating a coldness which is all mine/ Would have been generous"), that one encounters one's soul especially when it snows, that dying is "a beautiful illness," and that the poet true to self never hesitates. At times, the last strophe of a poem would indicate to the reader, in a glimpse, its lyrical etymology. In her lucid invocation of the lyrical forces of the soul Buzea has managed to transform her poems into deeply energizing though still melancholic texts. In this, as well as in the organic musicality of her verse, she reminds the Romanian reader of Mihai Eminescu.

Buzea wrote a number of books for children, among which are *Cărticica de doi ani* (1970; Booklet for the Two-year-old), *Aventurile extraordinare ale lui Hap Pap* (1970; The Extraordinary Adventures of Hap Pap) in collaboration with poet-husband Adrian Păunescu), *Cărticica de trei ani* (1972; Booklet for the Three-year-old), *Cărticica de patru ani* (1974; Booklet for the Four-year-old), *Cărticică pentru fetițe-veverițe și băieți-vevereți* (1979; Booklet for Squirrel-girls and Squirrel-boys).

In 1972 Buzea was awarded the Poetry prize of the Writers Union for her retrospective volume (1963–1971) *Leac pentru îngeri* (Remedy for Angels). In 1974 she received the Academy prize "Mihai Eminescu" for her volume *Pasteluri* (Pastels).

Works

De pe pămînt [From the Earth] (1963). *La ritmul naturii* [In the Rhythm of Nature] (1966). *Norii* [Clouds] (1968). *Agonice* [Agonizing (Poems)] (1970). *Coline* [Hills] (1970). *Cărticica de doi ani* [Booklet for the Two-year-old] (1970). *Sala nervilor* [Hall of Nerves] (1971). *Leac pentru îngeri* [Remedy for Angels] (1972). *Cărticica de trei ani* [Booklet for the Three-year-old] (1972). *Răsad de spini* [Thorn Transplant] (1973). *Pasteluri* [Pastels (Still-Life Poems)] (1974). *Cărticica de patru ani* [Booklet for the Four-year-old] (1974). *Ape cu plute* [Rivers with Rafts] (1975). *Limanul orei* [Haven of the Hour] (1976). *Poeme* [Poems] (1977). *Ploi de piatră* [Stony Rains] (1979). *Cărticică pentru fetițe veverițe și băieți vevereți* [Booklet for Squirrel-girls and Squirrel-boys] (1979). *Umbra pentru cer* [Shadow for the Sky] (1981). *Planta memoriei* [Memory Plant] (1985). [With Adrian Păunescu], *Aventurile extraordinare ale lui Hap Pap* [The Extraordinary Adventures of Hap Pap] (1970).

Translations: *Poeti romeni del dopoguerra* ["L'età"/ "Vîrstă"], ed. and tr. Mario De Micheli (1967). *Antologija na romanskata poezija* ["Sonot na bojata"/ "Cîntec pentru luptător"], ed. and tr. Taško Sarov (1972). *30 poeți români/30 poètes roumains* ["Septembre"/"Septembrie" and "Golgotha"/ "Golgota" tr. Ileana Vulpescu] (1978), pp. 215–223.

English Translations: *Silent Voices. An Anthology of Contemporary Romanian Women Poets*, tr. Andrea Deletant and Brenda Walker (1986), pp. 37–47 (poems from *Poeme*, 1977; *Ploi de piatră*, 1979; *Umbră pentru cer*, 1981 and *Planta memoriei*, 1985). *Romanian Poems*, ed. and tr. Dan Duțescu (1982), pp. 226–228 ("The Dreams of Colour"; "The Wing"; "About the Fall of Leaves"). Impey, Michael, "Three Romanian Poets—Ana Blandiana; Constanța Buzea; Gabriela Melinescu," *Books Abroad* 50, I (Winter 1976): 34–35.

Bibliography

Iorgulescu, Mircea, "Revizuiri lirice." *Al doilea rond* (Bucharest, 1976), pp. 264–268. Pop, Ion, *Poezia unei generații* (Cluj-Napoca, 1973). Raicu, Lucian, "Constanța Buzea: *Norii, Sala nervilor.*" *Structuri literare* (Bucharest, 1973), pp. 333–338. Raicu, Lucian, "O lirică a destinului (Constanța Buzea)." *Practica scrisului și experiența lecturii* (Bucharest, 1978), pp. 339–343.

Sanda Golopentia

C

Fernán Caballero

(a.k.a. Cecilia Böhl de Faber y Larrea)

Born December 25 or 27, 1796, Morges,
Switzerland; died April 7, 1877, Sevilla,
Spain
Genre(s): novel, short story
Language(s): Spanish

Fernán Caballero was the unusual product
of an unlikely alliance between a German
Hispanist and an early Spanish feminist who also
espoused Catholic traditionalist views. This rich
and divergent cultural background would play a
key role in her intellectual and literary development. Another influence came later in the lively
friendship she struck up with Washington Irving
in 1828–1829. Undoubtedly, the experience of
her three marriages would also sift indirectly into
her fiction, most notably in *Clemencia* (1852). Her
first husband, Captain Planels, was, by all accounts, a brute but, mercifully for Cecilia, died in
1817. She then married the Marqués of Arco-
Hermoso in 1822, who unfortunately left her
afterward in much strained economic circumstances. Sometime after his death in 1835, she
met an English aristocrat whom we know from
correspondence only as "Federico Cuthbert." It
was a short, unhappy love affair. This 1836
episode was followed by one last attempt at
matrimony in 1837, when Cecilia, then almost
forty-one, married twenty-three-year-old Antonio Arrom de Ayala. In 1859 Arrom de Ayala
committed suicide after a series of financial and
business debacles. Fernán Caballero's last years
were lonely ones, marked by gradual impover-
ishment and emotional depression over her own

life and the fall of her patroness, Queen Isabel II,
in 1868. By the time she died in 1877, her literary
fortunes and popularity were on the wane, and a
rising young writer, Benito Pérez Galdós, would
soon surpass the tentative and contradictory
strides she had made toward the modern realist
novel.

Fernán Caballero's best-known novel, *La
Gaviota* (The Sea Gull), originally appeared in
1849 as a magazine serial (several of her novels
and stories would first see the light in this form).
She was immediately hailed as the "Spanish Sir
Walter Scott." Given the rather barren literary
period—1850–1870—it is not surprising that
the idealized setting, lachrymose romanticism
and melodramatic touches of *La Gaviota* would
be equally appealing for its fresh realistic sketches
of the Andalusian character and customs. Fernán
Caballero's enthusiasm and love for local folkways
and traditional beliefs spilled over into several
volumes of *costumbrista* sketches and tales
(sometimes also awkwardly inserted in her longer
fiction).

Cecilia's ideological outlook is essentially
one of romantic conservatism, that is, an idealized embellishment of Spain's Catholic and
monarchical institutions, emphasizing submission to authority and the natural adherence to
customs and a living tradition. Her hostility to
modern-day liberalism and foreign influence
surfaced in such ideologically polarized fictions
as *Elia, o la España treinta años ha* (1857; Elia, or
Spain Thirty Years Ago) and *Un servilón y un
liberalito, o tres almas de Dios* (1859; A Loyalist
and a Liberal, or Three Souls of God). On an
individual level, conservatism, when disclosed

in personal and especially marital relationships, meant a strong and sometimes quite inflexible belief in the application of reason to sentiment. Such is the case for *Clemencia*: here, the beneficent and civilized use of reason as opposed to the savagely destructive force of passion (and more explicitly, raw sexuality) is the principal dichotomy exploited imagistically as the tension between civilization-garden and barbarism- (i.e., passion) tree.

Despite her ideological distortions, overtly moralizing stance, and failure to move beyond *costumbrismo*, Fernán Caballero cannot be lightly dismissed in Spanish literary history. As the initiator of both the regional novel and the thesis novel of ideological conflict, she remains a significant figure in the renaissance of nineteenth-century Spanish narrative.

There are six Madrid editions of her Complete Works, none reliable (the first in 1855–1858, and the latest in 1917–1928). Several of her novels—*La Gaviota* (1972), *Clemencia* (1975), *Elia* (1968), *La familia de Alvareda* (1979)—have been reedited in more accessible, modern editions.

Works

Clemencia (1852). *Cuadros de costumbres populares andaluzas* (1852). *Lágrimas* (1853). *La estrella de Vandalia* (1855). *Obras completas*, 19 vols. (1855–1858). *Con mal o con bien a los tuyos te ten* (1856). *La familia de Alvareda* (1856). *La Gaviota* (1856). *Una en otra* (1856). *Cuadros de costumbres* (1857). *Elia, o la España treinta años ha* (1857). *Lady Virginia* (1857). *Relaciones* (1857). *Un verano en Bornos* (1858). *Cuentos y poesías populares andaluces* (1859). *Un servilón y un liberalito, o tres almas de Dios* (1859). *Deudas pagadas* (1860). *Vulgaridad y nobleza* (1860). *San Telmo, recuerdos del 1 de enero de 1861* (1861). *El Alcázar de Sevilla* (1862–1863). *Colección de artículos religiosos y morales* (1862). *La farisea* (1863). *Las dos gracias o la expiación* (1865). *La mitología* (1867). *Cuentos, oraciones, adivinas y refranes populares e infantiles* (1877). *Epistolario* (1912). *El refranero del campo y poesías populares* (1912–1914). *Obras de Fernán Caballero*, 5 vols. (1961).

Translations: *Alvareda Family* [La familia de Alvareda] (1872). *Elia, or Spain Fifty Years Ago* [Elia] (1868). *The Old and the New* [Un servilón y un liberalito] (1882). *The Sea Gull* [La Gaviota] (1965). See also R. S. Rudder, *The Literature of Spain in English Translation* (1975).

Bibliography

Gullón, G., "El costumbrismo moralizante de Fernán Caballero." *El narrador en la novela del siglo XIX* (1976). Heinermann, T., ed., *Cecilia Böhl de Faber (Fernán Caballero) y Juan Eugenio Hartzenbusch. Una correspondencia inédita* (1944). Herrero, J., *Fernán Caballero: Un nuevo planteamiento* (1963). Kirkpatrick, S., "On the Threshold of the Realist Novel. Gender and Genre in *La Gaviota*." *PMLA* 98 (1983). Klibbe, L.H., *Fernán Caballero* (1973). Montesinos, J.F., *Fernán Caballero. Ensayo de justificación* (1961). Valis, N.M., "Eden and the Tree of Knowledge in Fernán Caballero's *Clemencia*." *Kentucky Romance Quarterly* 29 (1982).

General references: *Diccionario de literatura española*, eds. G. Bleiberg and J. Marías (1972). *Dictionary of Literature of the Iberian Peninsula*, eds. G. Bleiberg, M. Ihrie, and J. Pérez (forthcoming). *Ensayo de un diccionario de mujeres célebres*, F.C. Sainz de Robles (1959). *Literatas españolas del siglo XIX*, J.P. Criado y Domínguez (1889). *Women Writers of Spain*, ed. C.L. Galerstein (1986). Other references: *La España* (Aug. 25, 1849). Rpt. in *Obras de Fernán Caballero*, vol. 5 (1961).

Noël M. Valis

Hélène Cadou

Born 1925, Mesquer, France
Genre(s): poetry
Language(s): French

Hélène Cadou was born in Mesquer, on the Atlantic coast of France, and spent a peaceful childhood and youth, which was suddenly shattered by the outbreak of war. In 1943, when she was studying philosophy, she met the poet René Guy Cadou who was then teaching at Clisson. From the outset "recognising" each other, they were not to part until her husband's early death in 1951 in Louisfert, near Châteaubriant, where they lived. Since that time, Hélène Cadou has written a poetry that manifestly transcends the limitations of matter in continuing a "dialogue" that death has not silenced. She has worked for many years as a librarian in Orléans.

Although Hélène Cadou published in the years following her husband's death two short volumes of poetry, *Le Bonheur du jour* (1956; The Happiness of the Day) and *Cantate des nuits intérieures* (1958; Cantata of Inner Nights), it was only in the late 1970s that her work was really discovered and that she began to publish extensively. *En ce visage l'avenir* (In this Face the Future) appeared in 1977, followed by a second edition in 1978. Dedicated to her husband, as are a number of her collections, this elegant volume reveals constantly, though with a discretion and simplicity that are very much Hélène Cadou's, the principles of openness and availability, astonishment and nonpossessiveness that inform her contact with the world. Here is a poet who seeks not shelter, but rather contents herself with freedom, openness, (ex)change and love—that "answer" to all questions.

Miroirs sans mémoire (1979; Mirrors Without Memory) appeared a year later and was to be followed rapidly by *L'Innominée* (1980; The Innominate) and *Une ville pour le vent qui passe* (1981; A City for the Passing Wind). Among the many factors at play one might note the following: the joining of self and other; the primacy of the earth and yet the sense of transcendence; existence as "grace," despite suffering; language as a force at once single, specific, and interactive, infinitely penetrating; the fragility and the promise of (poetic) language; a recurrent questioning that gives to Hélène Cadou's work a mood less of serenity than of quiet urgency.

Longues pluies d'Occident (1983; Long Rains of the West) resumes the quest, for a future rather than a past, of the earlier books. If there is an element of greater uncertainty here, a sensitivity to wound and even vanity, the expression of a need for vigilance, care and healing, all of this is nevertheless recuperated within a larger whole, a greater vision, at once cosmic and simple.

The most recent volume published by Hélène Cadou is a collection of her work (previously not in print) from the period 1960–1980: *Poèmes du temps retrouvé* (1985; Poems of Time Regained). Familiar constants abound: the word of the other, her husband, within her; pure love as all-determining power of illumination; the fusion of past, present, and future in a "seeing" beyond apparent categories, a sense of the merging of being; the consequent interlocking logics of life and death, change and infinity, distance and oneness. In sum, *Poèmes du temps retrouvé* is a poetry of quiet passion, if intuited, unpretentiously visionary knowledge, but a knowledge rooted in almost faceless simplicity and unerring love.

Works

Poetry: *Trois poèmes* (1949). *Le Bonheur du jour* (1956). *Cantate des nuits intérieures* (1958). *Les Pèlerins chercheurs de tréfle* (1977). *En ce visage l'avenir* (1977). *Miroirs sans mémoire* (1980). *L'Innominée* (1980). *Une ville pour le temps qui passe* (1981). *Le Jour donne le signal* (1981). *Longues pluies d'Occident* (1983). *Poèmes, Missives* (1984). *Poèmes du temps retrouvé* (1985).

Bibliography

B., L., "Hélène Cadou." *Figaro Magazine* (Dec. 1978). B., J.-D., "Hélène Cadou: 'La poésie est le langage de l'avenir.'" *République du centre* (maMayi 1985). Baget, Jean-Louis, "Hélène Cadou: 'La page où tu disais ton amour et la vie.'" *Presse Océan* (Nantes) (Sept. 1980). Boisdeffre, Pierre de. Refs, in *Histoire de la littérature française* (Paris, 1985), p. 197. Bosquet, Alain, and Seghers, Pierre, refs. in *Les Poèmes de l'année*. 1959. Brindeau, Serge, "Hélène Cadou." *La Poèsie contemporaine depuis 1945* (Paris, 1973), p. 328. Dauby, Jean, "Hélène Cadou: *Poèmes du temps retrouvé*." *Cahiers Froissart* 34 (July 1985). Dobzynski, Charles, "Hélène Cadou: *Poèmes du temps retrouvé*." *Europe* (Oct. 1985). "Le Goncourt de la poésie décerné aujourd'hui." *Figaro* (May 1978). Hervieu, L.-Françoise, "Dire son amour au-delà de l'invisible." *Ouest France* (Oct. 1985). Hervieu, L.-Françoise, "*Miroirs sans mémoire* d'Hélène Cadou." *Ouest France* (Dec. 1979). L., R., "Hélène Cadou." *Lettres Française* (July 1956). Lheritier, Antony, "Hélène Cadou: *Miroirs sans mémoire*." *La Bretagne à Paris* (Feb. 1980). "*L'Innominée* par Hélène Cadou." *République du centre* (Orléans) (Oct. 1981). P., Y., "*Poèmes du temps retrouvé* par Hélène Cadou." *Le Pèlerin* (Jan. 1985): 23. Poggioli, Yves, "Hélène Cadou." *Nice Matin* (April 1958). Secrétain, Roger, "Hélène Cadou." *République du centre* (April 1977).

Michael Bishop

Rosa María Cajal

Born 1920, Zaragoza, Spain
Genre(s): novel
Language(s): Spanish

The necessity to support herself forced Cajal to take office employment and postpone her literary career, but after moving to Madrid, she began publishing newspaper articles and stories in various magazines. She won third prize in a Zarzuela libretto contest and was also a finalist for the Premio Gijón for short novels in 1951. Her first published novel, *Juan Risco* (1948), an early example of the existentialist novel in Spain, was a finalist for the Premio Nadal. In this novel the protagonist bitterly withdraws from human society after faking suicide and taking on another identity, which has led only to emptiness and self-contempt. *Primera derecha* (1955; First Floor Right) was a finalist for the Premio Ciudad de Barcelona and is typical of the family-oriented novels written by many women after the Spanish Civil War. It details the life of a matriarch who lives only for her children and for her husband, whom she considers merely another child. *Un paso más* (1956; One Step Further) is the only one of Cajal's novels to present an unconventional woman as the protagonist. In a situation rare during the 1950s, the young woman leaves her village to build a career in business in the city. She seeks independence and, despite self-doubts, proves stronger than men and other women.

Works

Juan Risco (1948). Primera derecha (1955). Un paso más (1956). El acecho (1963).

Bibliography

Díaz, Janet W., "Rosa María Cajal." *Hispania* 58, no. 3 (1975): 555–556. *Teatro de agitación política, 1933–1939* (Madrid: Edicusa, 1976). *Aproximación a R. Alberti y María Teresa Leon: La mano en el cajón* (1976). *Cervantes, el soldado que nos enseñó a hablar*, juvenile historical fiction (Madrid: Altalena, 1978). Galerstein, Carolyn, "The Spanish Civil War: The View of Women Novelists." *Letras Femeninas* X, no. 2 (Fall 1984): 12–18.

Carolyn Galerstein

Elisabeth von Calenberg-Göttingen

(a.k.a. Elisabeth von Münden)

Born August 24, 1510, Brandenburg, Germany; died May 25, 1558
Genre(s): works of religious advice
Language(s): German

The works of Elisabeth von Calenberg-Göttingen (1510–1558) give witness to what was then a new movement in Germany: the Lutheran Reformation. Like many other noblewomen, she supported Martin Luther. In her case, this support had personal as well as political consequences. Widowed at age thirty, Elisabeth was entrusted with the sole care of her four young children and the regency of a Duchy. Based on her authority as a mother and a regent, her works were to be tools in introducing the Reformation into her family and her lands, teaching those entrusted to her care the basics of a Christian life and the consolation of a Christian faith.

Born the daughter of Joachim I of Brandenburg (1449–1535) and Elisabeth of Denmark, Elisabeth experienced as a child the dissension the Reformation sowed in many a family. Her mother fled to Saxony after Joachim threatened to jail her for her Reformation leanings. Elisabeth's own circumstances proved to be better. Having become the second wife of Erich I of Calenberg-Göttingen at age fifteen, she found a spouse tolerant of her Lutheran inclination. After his death, as a regent (1540–1545) for her young son Erich II, Elisabeth, with the help of the theologian Antonius Corvinus, set out to introduce the Reformation in her duchy. Her church ordinance (1542) and a judicial ordinance (1544) were to bring order in religious and judicial matters; her "Letter to All Subjects," a collection of thematically arranged biblical proverbs, was designed to give witness to an ethical mode of living based on the Bible. In this way, Elisabeth tried to put her lands in order in anticipation of her son's rule. The same motive guided her in her ruler's manual, written for her son in 1545, an advisory work touching upon all matters of faith and morals that a young ruler should know. In the foreword, she based her authority to teach him on the fact that she was his mother, in this case the only parent, and on her regency. The first part is devoted to showing a young adult, her son, Christian faith and ethics. It contains motherly advice interspersed with biblical quotations. She sometimes refers to particular situations of young noblemen, but, in general, her advice is applicable to all young Christians. Although the language in this part shows the frankness and clarity visible in the ordinances, the frequent quotations make reading difficult. The second part is much easier to read. In it, the regent Elisabeth provides a convenient handbook for young Christian rulers with clear guidelines for all circumstances and situations. This work is not only important because it is the first one of its kind written in German but also because it clarifies the faith and ethics of a new movement.

Elisabeth was not to have much happiness from the rule of her son. The marriage she had arranged for him did not last, and the advice she had so authoritatively given him was not followed. Erich seldom consulted with his mother, returned to Catholicism, and chose the side of the emperor in disputes among the princes of the empire.

Her second piece of motherly advice was written as a wedding gift on the occasion of the marriage of her daughter Anna Maria (1532–1568), who, in 1550, became the second wife of Albrecht von Preussen. It is called "Lessons to My Dearly Beloved Daughter Anna Maria," and in it Elisabeth tells her daughter how to be a good wife and mother. It is the advice of one woman to another, the authority to give such advice based solely upon the authority of motherhood. Although Anna Maria must have had representational duties as the wife of Albrecht, these are not touched upon. Instead, in short lines, Elizabeth refers to the duties of marriage partners to one another, especially the duties of a wife, and then cites appropriate biblical passages. As such her instruction is more an instigation for further reading than actual advice. This marriage did not bring much happiness either. Although she did provide Prussia with the long awaited heir, Anna Maria had a difficult time at the often hostile Prussian court. She died at age thirty-six, leaving her son Albrecht Friedrich a ruler's manual, illustrated with little exemplary tales from the

Old Testament, an immensely readable examplebook for royal children.

In her widowhood, Elisabeth again wrote a booklet with thoughts and prayers for other widows. Like her previous works, it is a combination of prayerlike sayings, biblical quotations and statements based on a deeply felt, biblically based faith. It also gives testimony to Elisabeth's own harsh widowhood, spent as the sole parent of four young children, as a regent of a debt-ridden duchy, and as a not always successful manipulator in German politics.

Works

Kirchenordnung [Church ordinance] (1542). *Ober vnd Hoffgerichts Ordnung in vnser Leibzucht Münden* [Judicial Ordinance] (1544). *Ein christlicher Sendebrieff der... Fürstin Elisabeth... om alle irer . . . Undertanen . . . geschrieben Christliche besserung und ein newes Gottseliges leben so in dieser letzten bösen zeit die hohe nod fordert belangend. Mit einer vorrede Antony Corvini. MDXLV* [Letter to my Subjects] (1545). "Unterrichtung vnd ordnung unser von gots gnaden, Elisabeth ... hertzogin zu Braunschweig und Lüneberg . . . Witwe, so wir aus gantz mutterlicher wolmeinung... vnserm freundlichen hertzlieben son zu kunfftiger . . . regierung . . . gestalt haben" [Lessons to My Dearly Beloved Son] (1545). "Ein freundtlicher vnd mutterlicher vnderricht vnser von gottes gnaden Elisabet... so wir aus ganz mutterliche liebe . . . der frauen . . . Anna Maria, . . . vnser hertzgelibten tochter zu irem angefangenen ehestande zu ehren und besten gestalt haben . . ." [Lessons to My Dearly Beloved Daughter Anna Maria] (1550). *Etliche lieder, so mein gnedige fürstin vnd frawe die von Henneberg ... in Irem elende zu Hannober gemachtt... Anno 1544 u. 1555* (Songs). *Eine Anzeigung und Trost aus göttlicher Schrift gezogen, wo von Witwen gehandelt wird, beide im Alten und Neuen Testament. Anno 1556. Second ed: ca. 1575. Third ed.: Der Widwen Hanbüchlein durch eine Hocherleuchte Fürstliche Widwe vor vielen Jaren selbst beschrieben vnd verfasset . . . In verlegung Bartholomäj Voigts. Other eds.:* Jena 1606 and Dresden 1609 (Handbooklet for Widows).

Bibliography

Moore, Cornelia Niekus. "Die adelige Mutter als Erzieherin, Erbauungsliteratur adeliger Mütter für ihre Kinder." *Europäische Hofkultur im 16. und 17. Jahrhundert* (Hamburg, 1981), pp. 505–510. Strombeck, Friedrich C. von. *Deutscher Fürstenspiegel*(Braunschweig, 1826), pp. 55–131. Traeger, Lotte. "Das Frauenschrifttum in Deutschland von 1500–1650." Diss. (Prague, 1943), pp. 51f. and Anhang p. 3. Tschackert, Paul. *Elisabeth von Münden . . . ihr Lebensgang und ihre Werke* (Berlin and Leipzig, 1899). Zedler, Johann Heinrich. *Grosses Vollständiges Universal-Lexikon* (Leipzig und Halle, 1735; Graz [Austria], 1961), VII, pp. 863–864.

Cornelia Niekus Moore

Isabel Calvo de Aguilar

Born 1916, Caldas de Reyes (Ponte Verde), Spain
Genre(s): novel
Language(s): Spanish

During the 1950s, Isabel Calvo de Aguilar founded and for six years served as president of the Associación de Escritoras Españolas. Also during this time, she edited what is considered her major work, the *Antología bibliográfica de escritoras españolas*, published in 1954 to dispute the assertion that Spain had produced no important contemporary women writers. She has won several awards for her writing, including the Portuguese Premio de Periodismo Costa del Sol.

As a novelist, Calvo de Aguilar has attempted to attract a wide audience. To accomplish this, she writes mysteries that combine love stories with intrigue, adventure and careful psychological studies of her characters and the crimes that they commit. *La danzarina inmóvil* (The Immobile Dancer), for example, opens with the trial of taxidermist Alberto Castillo for the apparently senseless murder of his wife, the world-famous ballerina Niska Poltrova. The crime and the criminal's identity are established facts from the very beginning—admittedly a departure from the structure of most traditional mystery novels—but Calvo de Aguilar's concern is discovering, not the criminal himself, but the reasons for his actions: the other characters involved in, and the circumstances leading up to, the crime. In this, she succeeds. Her simple, yet fluid and eloquent style brings the characters to life, drawing the reader into their minds and hearts until he begins to understand why Castillo, a man more in love with his wife's art than with the woman herself, feels compelled to freeze her—almost literally—in time, preserving forever with his "art" the grace and beauty of her art at its peak. The crime itself is described in a detached, almost clinical fashion that makes it all the more believable and horrifying. With her skillful handling of plot and character and her easy mastery of style, Calvo de Aguilar seems deserving of her designation by critics as the "Agatha Christie of Spain."

Works

Antología de escritoras españolas (1954). *Doce sarcáfogos de oro*(1951). *La isla de los siete pecados* (1952). *El misterio del palacio chino* (1951). *El monje de los Balkanes. El numismático.*
Translations: Portuguese tr. of *La danzarina inmóvil.*

Bibliography

Galerstein, Carolyn L., ed., *Women Writers of Spain: An Annotated Bio-bibliographical Guide* (New York, 1986). "Introduction" to Calvo de Aguilar, Isabel. *La danzarina inmóvil* (Madrid, 1954). *Quién es quién en las letras españolas*, 3rd ed. (1979).

Susan Wilson

Ilie Cambrea

(see: Margareta Miller-Verghi)

Jeanne Louise Henriette Campan

Born October 6, 1752, Paris, France; died May 16, 1822, Nantes
Genre(s): history, educational writing
Language(s): French

Best known for her memoirs on the "private" life of Marie Antoinette, Campan was born the daughter of M. Genet, the first clerk of the Minister of Foreign Affairs. It was his dedication to the education of all his children that resulted in her receiving a thorough education in which she excelled both in the study of music and foreign languages. This aptitude brought her to the attention of the court of Louis XV, where she obtained the position of Reader to the Princess in 1767. Her association with the court continued through the reigns of Louis XV and Louis XVI. Soon after her marriage to M. Campan, the son of the Secretary of the Queen's Closet, Campan obtained the position of *femme de chambre* to Marie Antoinette. Eventually Campan became the First Lady of the Bedchamber of the Queen. She retained this position until the Terror of 1793, almost losing her life as well as her position. For the next decade she was head of a well-known school for ladies in St. Germaine. In 1805, she was named by Napoleon to be the head of the school at Ecouen, an institution established by the Emperor for the orphaned daughters of the Legion of Honor. She retained this position until Napoleon lost power in 1814, after which she was largely neglected until her death in 1822. The following year her *Memoires* appeared, providing a fascinating look inside the doomed court of Louis XVI and Marie Antoinette. Other works appeared after her death, most due to the efforts of M. Barriere and M. Maigne.

Works

Memoires sur la Vie privee de la Reine Marie Antoinette (1823). Also, "The Conversations of a Mother with Her Daughters," which is mentioned by F. Barriere in his "Biographical notice of Madame Campan" in above work. De l'education (1824). Journal anecdotique de Mme. Campan (1824–1825). Conseils aux jeunes filles (1830). Correspondance inedite de Mme. Campan avec la Reine Hortense (1835). Conversation of Madame Campan Comprising Secret Anecdotes of the French Court (n.d.).

Translations: The *Memoires* have been translated into English numerous times beginning in 1848 and continuing into the twentieth century with editions appearing in 1906, 1909, and 1930.

Stephen Wood

Condesa de Campo Alange

(see: María de los Reyes Lafitte y Pérez del Pulgar)

Amélie-Julie Candeille

Born July 30, 1767, Paris, France; died February 3, 1834, Paris
Genre(s): comedy, historical novel, poetry, memoirs
Language(s): French

Julie Candeille combined the professions of singer, musician, actress, dramatist, novelist, and memorialist in a career spanning the *ancien régime*, the Revolution, First Empire, and Restoration. Her father, an actor and musician, taught her to sing and to play the harpsichord at a very young age. She tells the story in her unpublished memoirs that she was asked as an eight-year old to play the harpsichord at the salon of Sophie Arnould the same evening that the child Mozart was asked to play. The story must be apocryphal: she claims that Mozart, born in 1756, was only three—rather than eleven—years older than herself. In a sense, the fiction she concocted about Mozart is exemplary for her career, so deeply marked by her eagerness for recognition. She began to sing when she was still very young, and as her voice had not properly developed, it broke during a performance, ending her career as a singer but launching her into a second career—under royal patronage—as an actress at the Comédie Française when she was eighteen. She remained there from 1786 to 1790, acting only minor roles but cultivating her talents as a dramatist. By 1791 she had moved to the Théâtre de la rue Richelieu, called the Théâtre de la République after 1793. During this time she wrote her first and most successful drama, *Catherine, ou La belle fermière* (Catherine, or the Beautiful Female Farm-bailiff), first performed on November 27, 1792, in which she played the title part. This work enjoyed enormous success, running for over 150 performances, a fact which means quite simply that it was the most popular dramatic work during the Reign of Terror. The play, based on Marmontel's story "La Bergère des Alpes" (The Alpine Shepherdess), is highly sentimental: it unites benevolent nobles and happy peasants. The title-heroine turns out to be the widow of a dissolute nobleman and takes the position of farm-bailiff in order to gain distance from her unhappy first marriage. Her father-in-law appears on the scene—he is the older brother of the marquise whose lands the fair Catherine administers—and recognizes her and brings about her second and much happier marriage. The popularity of such a play during the bloodbath of the Reign of Terror is nothing short of astounding. The play's idyllic, escapist qualities endeared it to audiences throughout the early part of the nineteenth century; it became a standard in the dramatic repertory and was even reprinted in 1823. It also was translated into both Dutch and Italian.

Julie Candeille's other dramatic works were less successful: the public accepted her *Le commissionnaire* (The Commissioner), first performed November 28, 1794, but rejected *La bayadère* (The Hindu Dancing Girl) produced on February 24, 1795, in which she also played the title role. During the Empire she eked out a living by giving music lessons. Her personal life, like her professional one, was extremely turbulent. Her first marriage ended in divorce after a few months. She separated from her second husband Jean Simons, a wealthy carriage maker, when he was ruined financially. Napoleon refused to grant her a pension, noting "one should not authorize wives to do without their husbands" ("il ne fallait pas autoriser les femmes à se passer de leurs maris"). She welcomed the Restoration in print and was obliged to flee to England when Napoleon returned from Elba. Upon her return to Paris in late 1816, Louis XVIII granted her a stipend. In 1822 she married Hilaire-Henri Périé de Senonvert, a former student of the painter David and twelve years her junior. She used her connections to have him named director of the museum at Nîmes. After trying her hand at writing several historical novels, she published *Essai sur les félicités humaines, ou Dictionnaire du bonheur* (1829; An Essay on Human Felicities, or Dictionary of Happiness). She spent considerable effort on denying persistent rumors that she had portrayed the goddess Reason during Republican rites in November 1793. She suffered a stroke in late 1833 and returned to Paris where she died on February 3, 1834. She was buried in Père-Lachaise, selling the part of the plot reserved for her husband who had predeceased her but was still buried in Nîmes so that she could raise the necessary funds for her own funerary monument.

Works

Catherine, ou la belle Fermière (1793, 1798). *Le commissionnaire* (1794). *Agnès de France, ou le XIIᵉ siècle, roman historique* (1821). *Bathilde, reine des Francs, roman historique* (1814). *Blanche d'Évreux* (1824). *Lydie, ou les Mariages manqués* (1824; Lydia, or Missed Marriages). *Geneviève, ou le Hameau* [Geneviève or the Hamlet] (1822). *Essai sur les félicités humaines, ou Dictionnaire du bonheur* (1828). *Souvenirs de Brighton, de Londres et de Paris* [Memories of Brighton, London and Paris] (1818).

Bibliography

Terrin, Charles, "Julie Candeille, Actrice, Musicienne, Femme de lettres." *Revue des Deux-Mondes* 8. pér., vol. 33 (1936): 403–425.

Earl Jeffrey Richards

Pureza Canelo

Born December 9, 1946, Moraleja (Cáceres), Spain
Genre(s): poetry, children's literature
Language(s): Spanish

Pureza Canelo was born in Moraleja, a small town in Cáceres, Extremadura, Spain. The youngest of four children, Canelo says that she was a "mala oveja" (black sheep) during her boarding-school years, spent first in Salamanca and later in Madrid. Stifled and distracted as a young student, her consolation were summers spent in Moraleja, during which she exercised her bent towards poetry. The town itself is important to Canelo for its associations with an idyllic childhood and for the early awareness it inspired in the poet of a sense of freedom, especially in the presence of nature. Moraleja came to acquire further importance during Canelo's adolescence, when her brother Luis, a painter, installed a studio in the family home. This studio was dubbed the "inspiration room," for it was there that Luis Canelo began to evolve as a painter and where Pureza Canelo produced not only her first creative efforts at the age of fourteen but also those which earned her the Adonais Award in 1970, at the age of twenty-four.

Having abandoned first a course of studies in information and tourism and then in teaching, Pureza Canelo settled in Madrid, supporting herself in a variety of jobs, including photocopying, tending children, and interpreting psychometric examinations. During this period she began to frequent the Café Lyon where she met such writers as José Infante, José García Nieto and Carmen Conde. She began to publish in the reviews *Aquelarre*, *Artesa*, *Caracola*, and *Poesía española* and in 1968 received an award for her children's stories.

Canelo's first book, *Celda verde* (1971; Green Cell), compiles poems written during the period 1961–1969. This collection reveals some of the preoccupations of the young poet: an acute sense of time and space, as well as the notion of poetry as a "splendid imprisonment." Canelo perceives poetry as a kind of genesis, and as such she creates a world that is primordial, pristine, and infinite. Trees, vines, insects, birds, and other animals exist in a mysterious, dream-like state where past, present, and future converge. Nature is also the place of life and creativity, equivalent to poetry itself, where the poet pursues herself: "Espérame, / en la palabra" ("Wait for me, / in the word").

In Canelo's second collection, *Lugar común* (1971; Common Place), her verses are more extended than in *Celda verde*, her penchant for what has been called an "alogical syntax" even more apparent. This results in a dense, complex poetry, resembling interior monologue, which Canelo compares to the opening of a tap or to a volcano erupting daily. (Elsewhere she speaks of her need for "poetry that overflows, without a fixed course.") The quotidian quality of reality reinforces the poet's own insistence on "el ahora viviente" ("the living now"). In "Paseo por Moraleja" ("Stroll Through Moraleja") the poet contemplates in wonderment a wall, a blossom, pears fallen from a tree, and values each object for its uniqueness and mystery. So too does she value the word for being both commonplace and eternal. Canelo repeatedly mixes verb tenses and employs the progressive form of verbs as well as "commonplace" colloquialisms—all to underscore the mystery, spontaneity and authenticity of individual experience. Paradox is a constant because "todas las corrientes son verdad" ("all

currents are true"). In *Lugar común* Canelo again asserts her obligation to "arrimar / cada día mi hombro a la palabra, salir, o / hacerme viva" ("put my shoulder each day to the word, leave, or make myself alive"). The word is thus the means by which she daily recreates herself and her world and yet, as in *Celda verde*, she observes that the poem has a will of its own: "Este poema quiere ser lo que él quiera" ("This poem will be what it wants").

Lugar común was granted the prestigious Adonais Award in 1970 although not without heated debate and the resignation of José Luis Cano, one of the founders of the prize. Following this painful experience that nevertheless assured the young poet critical attention, Pureza Canelo came to grips with the fact that her work was now no longer only for herself but for a public. She began to fill in the gaps in her studies of poetry: César Vallejo, Gerardo Diego, Jorge Guillén, Luis Cernuda, Juan Ramón Jiménez.

Pureza Canelo calls *El barco de agua* (1974; The Boat of Water) a "transitional" work. This collection contains reflections on poetry in which poetry and life are often fused. The certainty of her own womanhood, for example, is intimately connected with poetry: "Soy una mujer; / ahora, en confianza, ¿tendrá eso que ver con los poemas?" ("I am a woman; now, confidentially, does that have to do with the poems?"). The mystery of existence mirrors the mystery of poetry. "Palabras con Luis" ("Words with Luis") is like a palindrome: the second section of the poem mirrors the first, but in reverse order. The mirror effect emphasizes Canelo's belief in "el caos de unión del tiempo y la materia" ("the chaotic union of time and matter"), and in the continual process of rebirth which is for her the mystery of life and poetry.

The 1979 collection entitled *Habitable: primera poética* (Inhabitable: First Poetics) is divided into three parts: a statement in verse of Canelo's poetics; poems that each bear the name "poem of . . .," thus testifying to the autonomy of the individual poem; and a kind of "repose" which exhibits the poet's desire to inhabit the poem itself. The language is of a startling originality, the syntax once again a challenge to logic, reflecting the spontaneity and intemporality of the world created by Canelo. Her verses destroy poetic boundaries because she seeks to defy "la broma de la nada" ("the joke of nothingness") by inventing her own order, her own plenitude.

Pureza Canelo's poetry possesses a dreamlike quality, yet she is intensely attuned both to concrete, external reality and to her own highly charged inner reality. That dreamlike quality, resembling a state of unconsciousness, the complexity of her images and metaphors, and her portrayal of a persona overtaken by the poetic state have led some critics to link her with surrealism. Others deny this association with surrealism because of her awareness of the creative act and her stated will to create a poetic order. Canelo acknowledged in *Tendido verso: segunda poética* (1986; Extended Verse: Second Poetics) that she has not yet achieved the plenitude she seeks in her poetry. Still, she asserts her intention—her "voluntad hacia adelante" ("will forward")—to continue striving towards the fullness that is the object of her very private vision.

Works

Celda verda [Green Cell] (1971). *Lugar común* [Common Place] (1971). *El barco de agua* [The Boat of Water] (1974). *Espacio de emoción* [Space of Emotion] (1974). *Vega de la paloma* [The Dove's Plain] (1981). *Habitable: primera poética* [Inhabitable: First Poetics] (1979). *Tendido verso: Segunda poética* [Extended Verse: Second Poetics] (1986).

Translations: Hammer, Louis, and Schyfter, Sara, *Recent Poetry of Spain* (1983).

Bibliography

Pureza Canelo, Clara Janés, ed. (1981).

Other references: *ABC*, Madrid (July 15, 1979). *La estafeta literaria*, Madrid (May 1, 1974). *Nueva estafeta* 12 (Nov. 1979). *Atlántida*, Madrid (March-April 1971). *Pueblo*, Madrid (Jan. 5, 1980). *Hoy*, Badajoz (May 18, 1972). *Anales de la literatura española contemporánea* 6 (1981).

Sylvia R. Sherno

Wilhelmina "Minna" Ulrika (Johnson) Canth

(a.k.a. Wilja, M.C., Teppo, -nn-, Airut, X)

Born March 19, 1844, Tampere, Finland; died May 12, 1897, Kuopio, Finland
Genre(s): drama, journalism, short story, aphorism, translation
Language(s): Finnish (one play in Swedish)

Minna Canth ranks among Finland's best dramatists, working above all with social issues: the plight of the worker, of women, of the poor. Her gift for dialogue and plot have made her plays among Finland's most frequently produced. She remains one of the harshest and most outspoken critics of social injustice in Finland and retains a respected place in the Finnish literary Parnassus.

Canth was the first-born daughter of a working-class family in the industrial town of Tampere. The family's move to Kuopio in 1853 marked an improvement in economic and social status; her father opened a shop there and became a successful merchant. He encouraged the gifted child in her reading and musical pursuits, and she received an education of the quality usually reserved for the (primarily Swedish-speaking) upper class. Throughout her career, Canth was thus able to understand and portray the entire spectrum of Finnish society. In 1863, Minna Johnson left home to attend the newly-established teachers' seminary in Jyväskylä, the first of its kind to offer instruction in Finnish and to accept both male and female students. The atmosphere of burgeoning Finnish nationalism there sealed Minna's fate: she vowed to dedicate herself to the education of the Finnish people. In Jyväskylä she met her future husband, the science teacher Johan Ferdinand Canth. They married in 1865, a union which produced six children. She assisted her husband in editing two newspapers, *Keski-Suomi* and *Päijänne* and contributed articles and short stories that dealt for the most part with social issues, including women's emancipation. She lost her husband in 1879 and, to support her family, took over her father's shop in Kuopio in 1880. By this time she had written her first play, *Murtovarkaus* (published in 1883 but completed in 1879); her second, *Roinilan talossa*, appeared in 1885 (but had been finished in 1883). These "innocent" comedies did little to prepare audiences for her next play, *Työmiehen vaimo* (1884), which attacked working conditions, women's subservient role in the household (even when she clearly could manage better than her husband) and alcoholism. The play *Kovan onnen lapsia* (1888) was even more acerbic in its social criticism, so much so that it nearly put an end to her dramatic career, for even the more "radical" Finnish writers found it too strong, not to mention the conservative owners of the Finnish theater. She then turned to somewhat less controversial matters in *Papin perhe* (1891), a play about the "generation gap," with a runaway daughter who becomes a successful actress; the curtain closes on a proud and reconciled family. With *Sylvi* (1893), Canth turns to more psychological portrayals. This play deals with adultery and the destructive force of erotic feelings. It was written in Swedish for the theater in Stockholm; she had become frustrated with the Finnish theater direction and looked for more appreciation in Sweden. *Anna Liisa* (1895), her last and possibly best play, signals her reconciliation with the Finnish theater. This tragedy presents the fate of a woman who murders her own (illegitimate) baby, a not uncommon crime among young peasant girls at the time. Some critics have seen the influence of Tolstoy in this drama. Though Canth's plays are of greatest importance, her short stories deserve attention as well; they treat for the most part the same issues discussed in the dramas of the mid-1880s, and often satirize the (usually Swedish-speaking) middle class. Canth also created and edited the short-lived journal *Vapaita aatteita* (Free Ideas) from 1889–1890. She continued to contribute articles on social issues to Finnish periodicals throughout her lifetime (most of her short stories were also first published in this format). Canth died of a heart attack, the last of a series which had plagued her for a year and a half, in 1897.

Minna Canth has become a legend in Finland. She was the first Finnish-speaking feminist in her country and is considered a seminal figure there not only in the women's rights movement but for social reform in all other areas as well. She considered herself a socialist but believed in a religion-based socialism although she attacked the church itself. The contribution she made to the then-embryonic Finnish-language literature can hardly be overestimated. Her work is uneven, sometimes more political polemics than inspired literary achievement, but her artistic genius can be witnessed in some of her finer works, in *Anna Liisa* or *Papin perhe*. A champion of women and of the proletariat, she has been honored with a statue in downtown Kuopio, the nurturing mother, tireless reformer, and literary artisan in one woman.

Works

Plays: *Murtovarkaus* (1883). *Roinilan talossa* (1885). *Työmiehen vaimo* (1885). ("From the Drama *The Worker's Wife*." Excerpt translated by Elli Tompuri in *Voices from Finland*, 1947). *Kovan onnen lapsia* (1888). *Papin perhe* (1891). *Sylvi* (1893). *Anna Liisa* (1895).

Short stories: *Novelleja ja kertomuksia* (1878). *Hanna* (1886). *Köyhää kansaa* (1886). *Kansan ääniä* (1889). *Novelleja* (1892).

Other prose: *Hän on Sysmästä* (1893). *Spiritistinen istunto* (1894). *Kotoa pois* (1895). *Arvostelu neiti Ellen Keyn viime lausunnoista naisasiassa* (1896). *Suolavakka*. [Collected aphorisms] (1954).

Bibliography

Ahokas, Jaako, *A History of Finnish Literature* (Bloomington, Indiana, 1973). von Frenckell-Thesleff, Greta, *Minna Canth och "Det unga Finland"* (Helsinki, 1942). Hagman, Lucina, *Minna Canthin elämäkerta* (Helsinki, 1911). Kuusi, Matti, and Simo Konsala, general eds., *Suomen kirjallisuus* (Helsinki-Keuruu, 1963–1970). Laitinen, Kai, *Suomen kirjallisuuden historia* (Helsinki, 1981). Tarkianinen, Viljo. *Minna Canth* (Helsinki, 1921).

Kathy Saranpa Anstine

Čapcová

(see: Rů'ena Svobodová)

Iseut de Capion

*Flourished first quarter of thirteenth century,
Capion or Chapieu (Lozère), southern
France*
*Genre(s): dialogue poem with a frame
narrative*
Language(s): Occitan

Iseut de Capion, whose literary vocation is reflected in her name, that of the celebrated heroine of the Tristan romances, is the author of half of a short debate poem exchanged with another lady, Almois de Castelnou. Both *Capion* (*castrum de Capione*, today Chapieu, a castle whose ruins may still be seen near the hamlet of Lanuéjols) and *Castelnou* (modern Chastel-Nouvel) have been identified with locales lying only a few kilometers apart on either side of the town of Mende (Lozère) at the edge of the Massif Central in Languedoc (Brunel). (The suggestion of Bogin [165–166], repeated by Dronke [100], that the two names refer to locales in the Vaucluse east of Avignon [Caseneuve and Les Chapelins] and the consequent mid-twelfth-century date for Almois and Iseut is not persuasive). Each belonged to a powerful family of the region, Iseut to the du Tournel) family, Almois to the Randon family, and the two were active in the first quarter of the thirteenth century. The only medieval manuscript to preserve the text (MS. *H*, Rome, Biblioteca Vaticana 3207, fols. 45–46) prefaces each speaker's part with a short prose narrative (or *razo*) that furnishes a context for the verse. The text is illustrated with a stylized portrait miniature of each woman declaiming her poetry, as are the poems of five other *trobairitz* (or woman troubadours) in the manuscript (Rieger 391). Iseut pleads with Almois to forgive the latter's knight, Gui de Tournon, who, having committed a great fault toward Almois, continues to refuse to seek her forgiveness. Although well disposed towards the knight, Almois, who exhibits an ironic aloofness with regard to her erstwhile lover (Dronke), replies that she cannot pardon him unless he first repents, and she subtly suggests that Iseut may be able to prevail upon him to do so.

Bibliography

Boutière, Jean and A.-H. Schutz, *Biographies des troubadours. Textes provençaux des XIIIe et XIVe siècles. Edition refondue, augmentée d'une traduction française, d'un appendice, d'un lexique, d'un glossaire et d'un index des termes concernant le "Trobar,"* par Jean Boutière avec la collaboration d'I.-M. Cluzel. Les Classiques d'Oc (Paris, 1964), pp. 244–422. Bogin, Meg, *The Women Troubadours* (New York and London, 1976), pp. 92–93, 165–166. Brunel, Clovis, "Almois de Châteauneuf et Iseut de Chapieu." *Annales du Midi* 28 (1916): 462–471. Dronke, Peter, *Women Writers of the Middle Ages. A Critical Study of Texts from Perpetua (d. 203) to Marguerite Porete (d. 1310)* (Cambridge, 1984), pp. 100–101, 300. Rieger, Angelica, "'Ins e.l cor port, dona, vostra faisso.' Image et imaginaire de la femme à travers l'enluminure dans les chansonniers de troubadours." *Cahiers de Civilisation Médiévale* 28 (1985): 385–415. Schultz, Oscar, *Die Provenzalischen Dichterinnen. Biographien und Texte nebst Anmerkungen und einer Einleitung* (Leipzig, 1888; Geneva, 1975), pp. 12–13, 25. Véran, Jules, *Les Poétesses provençales du Moyen Age et de nos jours* (Paris, 1946), pp. 71–74.

Merrit R. Blakeslee

Enrichetta Caracciolo

(a.k.a. Enrichetta Caracciolo Forino)

*Born February 17, 1821, Naples, Italy; died
March 17, 1901, Naples*
Genre(s): memoirs
Language(s): Italian

During the wane of European Romanticism, Enrichetta Caracciolo—aristocrat, feminist, and former nun—produced a devastating depiction of life in the convents of southern Italy and a searing statement of the inferiority and powerlessness of women in traditional Catholic society. Her memoirs offer an engrossing tale of oppression and rebellion set against the bucolic landscape of Naples and the deceptive serenity of the cloisters. As an example of feminine subjugation, Caracciolo's autobiography is universal and atemporal; as a book emerging from the tumult of revolution and social upheaval, it is clearly the product of a significant historical moment (the Italian Risorgimento), a defined political viewpoint (feminist Republicanism), and a particular sociocultural milieu (the repressive and conservative Bourbon nobility).

Born into the ancient Caracciolo family, granddaughter of the Prince of Forino, Enrichetta Caracciolo was the second of five girls born to a cadet who had gone into government service. Her childhood was somewhat uncertain as the family moved from city to city in the kingdom, following the vagaries of her father's career and popularity at Court. At his death, the family suffered a severe financial setback and returned to Naples. Within the year, Enrichetta was forced by her mother to enter a cloistered Benedictine order (1840).

Having no true vocation, the young woman's religious experience proved tempestuous and debilitating. She abandoned the convent several times after taking final vows, both with and without the approval of her superiors. At one point she was forcibly arrested and returned to the nuns. Her own experiences and those of other women encountered in the twenty years she remained a Benedictine form the basis of her memoirs, titled *Misteri del chiostro napoletano* (1864; Mysteries of a Neapolitan Cloister).

Caracciolo left the convent permanently in 1860 with the fall of the Bourbon monarchy. Professing anticlerical, republican views, she quickly came to the attention of Giuseppe Garibaldi, leader of the new regime, who made her inspector of the city's seminaries for girls. She married a soul-mate, Giovanni Greuther of the princely Sanseverino family—another rebellious aristocrat turned social activist. Widowed in 1885, Caracciolo continued to work as a journalist and feminist propagandist until her death.

Stylistically, the *Misteri* is a nineteenth-century hodgepodge: it blends characteristics of the historical novel, personal reminiscence, adventure tale, Romantic subjectivity, and pulp fiction. The mix is sometimes disconcerting. However, it is known that one Spiridione Zambelli, acting as Caracciolo's agent, altered and edited the text, possibly changing its tone in places. Defects notwithstanding, the book became an immediate best seller in Italy and abroad, due in large measure to its anticlerical stand and

heart-rending tale of persecution and victimization.

As a feminist text, Caracciolo's book speaks against the exploitation and segregation of women. Depersonalized in their habits, cut off from social and sexual intercourse, alienated from their bodies, her nuns represent feminine extremes of self-sacrifice, impotence, and exclusion, leading to madness, suicide, and death.

Works

Memoirs: *Misteri del chiostro napoletano. Memorie di Enrichetta Caracciolo de' prinicipi di Forino ex monaca benedettina* (1864). Reissued as *Le memorie di una monaca napoletana* (1964; The Memoirs of a Neapolitan Nun).

Bibliography

Briganti, A., "Caracciolo, Enrichetta." *Dizionario biografico degli italiani*, vol. 19 (Rome, 1976), pp. 348–349. Morandini, Giuliana, "E[nrich]etta Caracciolo Forino: La religiosa." *La voce che è in lei* (Milan, 1980), pp. 90–105. Sciarelli, F., *Enrichetta Caracciolo dei principi di Forino ex monaca benedettina: ricordi e documenti* (Naples, 1894).

Fiora A. Bassanese

Mariana de Caravajal y Saavedra

Born early 1600s, Jaén, Spain; died 1664?, Granada or Madrid?, Spain
Genre(s): short story
Language(s): Spanish

We know very little about this writer, whose very name is variously spelled as Carabajal, Carvajal, and Caravajal. According to Serrano y Sanz, her most assiduous and reliable biographer, she was born probably around the turn of the century in Jaén, raised in Granada, and married into an upper-class family like her own in the year 1635. When her husband died in 1656, he left Doña Mariana and her nine children in a precarious financial situation, which she remedied with a petition to Philip IV for a widow's pension of two hundred ducats. Since her husband had appointed her his executrix and legal guardian of their children, one suspects she was a strong-willed, very capable woman for her social station and time. The clear-headed and plainspoken narrative voice of her stories may very well be a reflection of Doña Mariana's own temperament and character.

The only surviving works of Caravajal we know are her *novellas*, which appeared in 1663 under the title *Navidades de Madrid, y noches entretenidas, en ocho novelas* (Christmas in Madrid, or Entertaining Nights, in eight tales). No one has been able to find a second edition of 1668, which Serrano y Sanz mentions, but a later one did appear in 1728. More recently, she has been reedited in the form of a dissertation in 1974. Doña Mariana also wrote twelve plays, but these, as well as a promised second part to her stories, are presumably lost or perhaps were never written. The eight stories comprising her *Navidades de Madrid* are: "La Venus de Ferrara" (The Venus of Ferrara), "La dicha de Doristea" (Doristea's Good Fortune), "El amante venturoso" (The Fortunate Lover), "El esclavo de su esclavo" (The Slave Enslaved), "Quien bien obra siempre acierta" (Virtue Is Its Own Reward), "Zelos vengan desprecios" (Love Conquers All), "La industria vence desdenes" (Industry Conquers Disdain), and "Amar sin saber a quién" (The Mysterious Lover).

Caravajal has most often been paired with her better-known predecessor in the *novella* tradition, María de Zayas y Sotomayor, whose feminist voice of dissent is more favorably viewed today than Caravajal's evident compliance with Counter-Reformation conformity. Thus critical opinion of her work tends to regard her as insipid and inferior in imagination and style. On the other hand, her artless spontaneity and coherent narrative structure lend considerable charm to stories that have most often been taken literally as first-hand sources of information about the domestic lifestyles and values of the seventeenth-century Spanish upper classes (see Bourland), rather than as representative examples of escapist literature. Like Zayas' work, Caravajal's stories are codified, artificial constructs and belong more properly to the world of *romance*. They are not realistic fictions. Set in the conventional frame-tale of eight unrelated stories narrated during the Christmas holidays, Caravajal's work also needs to be understood within the context of the aristocratic—and self-justifying—values of legiti-

macy and power. The subtly subversive way in which she deals with their absence and the subsequent crisis of male authority in her fiction is perhaps what most interests us today. For in showing how feminine reliance upon masculine effectiveness and strength, though in the end recompensed and validated, is sorely tested by repeated male betrayal, Caravajal also undermines the very base upon which her fiction rests.

Works

Navidades de Madrid, y noches entretenidas, en ocho novelas (1663). Also 1728 and 1974 eds.

Bibliography

Bourland, C.B., "Aspectos de la vida del hogar en el siglo XVII según las novelas de D.ⁿ Mariana de Carabajal y Saavedra." *Homenaje ofrecido a Menéndez Pidal*, II (1925). Jiménez, J., "Doña Mariana de Carvajal y Saavedra, mujer y escritora en la España de los Felipes." *Explicación de Textos Literarios* (1978). Jiménez, J.A., "Introducción," "Doña Mariana de Caravajal y Saavedra. *Navidades de Madrid y noches entretenidas, en ocho novelas.* Edición crítica y anotada" (1974). Pfandl, L., *Historia de la literatura nacional española en la Edad de Oro* (1952). Valis, N.M., "The Spanish Storyteller: Mariana de Caravajal." *Women Writers of the Seventeenth Century*, ed. K. Wilson and F. Warnke (1989).

Articles in reference works: Sainz de Robles, F.C., *Ensayo de un diccionario de mujeres célebres* (1959). Serrano y Sanz, M., *Apuntes para una biblioteca de escritoras españolas desde el año 1401 al 1833*, I (1903). *Women Writers of Spain*, ed. C.L. Galerstein (1986).

Noël M. Valis

R.I. Carda

(see: Ricarda [Octavia] Huch)

Marie Cardinal

Born March 9, 1929, Algiers, Algeria
Genre(s): novel
Language(s): French

Marie Cardinal's life and writings may be envisaged as an honest and at times uncomfortable endeavor to integrate disparate experiences; her search for happiness always implies the reconciliation of opposing forces. Born in Algeria of a French settler family, she soon became aware both of her European heritage and of the Algerian situation in which she was brought up. A sense of her own privilege and an awareness of the poverty of the local population shaped her early perceptions, and a strait-laced upbringing was contrasted with the easy-going ways she observed all around. She first broke free as she made her way up the educational ladder, opting for taxing courses in philosophy in which she achieved impressive results. After leaving the university and marrying in 1953 she taught in French schools abroad, and a sense of alienation grew in the years of her absence from Algeria during the tumultuous period of decolonization. Just as she was to miss the sunny beaches and warm seas of the Algerian coast when she lived in somewhat harsher environments, so, too, she was to feel a sense of exile from what she not unnaturally regarded as her homeland. Her personal problems were exacerbated and expressed by these powerful external pressures.

Since about 1960 Marie Cardinal has devoted herself to writing. Though *Ecoutez la mer* won a prize as a promising first novel in 1962, it was not really until the publication of *Les Mots pour le dire* that she really came to the fore. Already in *La Souricière* of 1965 she had explored the theme of the young woman who has grown up close to nature and who collapses physically as well as mentally under the strains of a marriage in which repeated pregnancies are but one aspect of a situation that becomes intolerable. Now the theme is explored at greater length and in a more systematic fashion. Beginning at a moment of crisis, the novel presents a course of psychoanalysis, chronicling the heroine's cure as contrasted with a series of backward glances into the various traumatic experiences that, from early childhood on, had produced the mental condition and its distressing physical manifestations. Told in graphic detail and with the passionate vigor of a classic French quest for self-awareness, *Les Mots pour le dire* made a great impact, even if its Freudian aspects might now be regarded as a little too obvious.

After *Les Mots pour le dire* there was something of a resurgence of interest in Marie Cardinal's earlier works, especially in *La Clé sur la porte*, which examines the problems of a mother living with teenage children, and she herself became one of the spokeswomen of feminism in France. In addition to *Autrement dit*, essentially a collection of essays in which she takes up the issues of *Les Mots pour le dire*, she composed the text of *La Cause des femmes*, Gisèle Halimi's outspoken and influential autobiography, which is itself a document in the story of women's demands for fair treatment in the twentieth century. In *Au pays de mes racines*, Marie Cardinal offers a sensitive account of a return visit to post-colonial Algeria with her daughter.

Works

Ecoutez la mer [Listen to the Sea] (1978). *La Mule du corbillard* (1963, 1979). (With Christine Cardinal) *Guide junior de Paris* (1964). *La Souricière* (1965, 1978; The Mousetrap). *Cet été-là (suivi du scénario de Jean-Luc Godard, Deux ou trois choses que je sais d'elle* (1967, 1980). Lucien Bodard (avec la collaboration de Marie Cardinal) *Mao* (1970). *La Clé sur la porte* [The Latchkey's There] (1972, 1975). Gisèle Halimi (propos recueillis par Marie Cardinal) *La Cause des femmes* [The Case for Women] (1973, 1976). *Les Mots pour le dire* (1975, 1977). Film: *Les Mots pour le dire* [The Words to Say It] (1983). Translation: Marie Cardinal, *The Words to Say It*, tr. Pat Goodheart, with preface and afterword by Bruno Bettelheim (1984). *Autrement dit* (1977, 1978). Preface to Sidonie Gabrielle Colette, *Claudine à l'école, L'Ingénue libertine, Chérie* (1977). *Une vie pour deux* (1978, 1980). Preface to Melvin McNair, Joyce Tillerson, George Brown, and Jean McNair, *Nous. Noirs américains évadés du ghetto* (1978). *Au pays de mes racines* (suivi de *Au pays de Moussia* by Bénédicte Cardinal) [To the Land of My Roots] (1980, 1982). Preface to *La Sexualité des femmes*, texte établi à partir d'une enquête de *F magazine*, ed. Suzanne Horer (1980, 1982). *Le Passé empiété* (1983).

Christopher Smith

Carlot

(see: Anne Charlotte Leffler)

Maria del Carmen Rubio y Lopez Guijarro

Born 1915, Ibi, Philippine Islands
Genre(s): poetry, novel
Language(s): Spanish

Born of a Spanish father and an American mother, this author currently resides in Madrid. She has collaborated on several literary magazines, such as *Gemma*, *Clarín*, and *El Ería*. She is an honorary member of the Centro Cultural Literario y Artístico AGA de Aranguren (Vizcaya). When the Civil War began, she was a *maestra nacional*, and the school where she taught was burned to the ground. Her literary concerns are the Civil War and its devastating effects (particularly as seen from the point of view of the victors), conjugal and family life, and the maintenance of existing social structures. She particularly treats the conflict between generations. Favorite themes are the need for resignation in the face of disappointment and pain and acceptance of one's destiny. Her writing is somewhat didactic and has a strong spiritual orientation. Her novels, romantic in theme and plot, are melodramatic and propagandistic at times. She won the "El Ería" prize in 1981 for her novel *La rebeldía de los hijos. Historia de una familia (1936–1966)* (The Rebellion of the Children. Story of a Family 1936–1966).

Works

Hojas sueltas que lleva el viento [Fallen Leaves Carried by the Wind] (n.d.). *Margarita y sus problemas* [Margaret and Her Problems] (n.d.). *Una mujer maltratada por el destino* [A Woman Mistreated by Destiny] (n.d.). *Por los senderos de la vida* [On the Paths of Life] (1977). *El precio del perdón* [The Price of Forgiveness], novel (1981). *La rebeldía de los hijos. Historia de una familia (1936–1966)* [The Rebellion of the Children. Story of a Family 1936–1966] (1982). *Relatos de una prisión* [Tales of a Prison] (1982). *Extraña noche de bodas* [Strange Wedding Night] (1982).

Bibliography

This information was all gathered from primary sources in the Biblioteca Nacional in Madrid. The author has published many of her own works, and they are not widely available in Spain or the United States, nor is there any critical assessment of her work published to my knowledge.

Paula T. Irvin

Pauline Caro (Mme Elme)

(a.k.a. P. Albane, Auteur du Péché de Madeleine)

Born 1835; died 1901, Paris
Genre(s): novel
Language(s): French

Mme Caro published thirteen novels, several of which saw several editions. Her first, *Le Péché de Madeleine*, appeared in 1864 and was well received. Most of Caro's works promote domestic virtuousness.

Very little is known about Caro's personal life. Her husband was a professor of philosophy at the Lycée de Rouen and published numerous studies and translations of German writers, most notably Goethe. There is no indication that Caro's works were significant responses to an unhappy domestic life.

There is little criticism of Caro's work. Although they were well-received publicly, her novels were rather ignored critically. Thematically Caro's novels are in the traditional mode of chaste love stories that are at once virtuous and passionate. In such stories the young woman who keeps striving for goodness will find the ideal love to fill out the rest of her life.

Works

Le péché de Madeleine (1864). *Flamen, par l'auteur du Péché de Madeleine* (1866). *Histoire de Souci* (1868). *Les Nouvelles amours de Hermann et Dorothée, propos d'un franc tireur* (1872). *Amour de jeune fille, par Mme E. Caro* (1892). *La fausse route* (1890). *Fruits amers* (1892). *Complice! par Mme E. Caro* (1893). *L'Idole* (1894). *Les lendemaines* (1895). *Idylle nuptiale* (1896). *Pas à pas* (1898). *Aimer c'est vaincre* (1900).
Works in English: *A Young Girl's Love*, tr. A. Lorangier (1892). *The Idol* (1894).

Bibliography

Pailleron, M.-L. *F. Buloz et ses amis: les Ecrivains du Second Empire* (Paris, 1924).

General references: *Dictionnaire biographique francaise*, vol. 7 (1956).

Marilynn J. Smith

Ana Caro Mallen de Soto

Born ca. 1600, probably in Sevilla, Spain; died ca. 1645–1650
Genre(s): drama, poetry
Language(s): Spanish

Ana Caro enjoyed considerable fame during her lifetime and was praised by numerous contemporary authors, including the dramatist Matos Fragoso as well as Vélez de Buevara, who referred to her as the "tenth muse" of Sevilla and member of a fictitious literary academy in his picaresque novel *El diablo cojuelo* (The Lame Devil). She was also eulogized by the sixteenth-century antiquarian Rodrigo Caro as "a famous poetess who has written many plays and other works of poetry."

However, very little is now known of her life, and some of her literary manuscripts may have perished. She was born into a distinguished Andalusian family and must have received a far more meticulous education than the average girl of her time, for she demonstrates familiarity with the humanistic learning of this age. That she was able to indulge her literary inclinations bespeaks a life of financial ease and social prestige. Most of her life was spent in Seville, and numerous references of civic pride are found in her writings. Many of her works are long poetic narratives of local events, written in the highly embellished, metaphoric style typical of the Baroque, and are of interest today only to scholars. These include the following: "Narration of the Grand Celebrations in the Convent of San Francisco of Sevilla for the Holy Martyrs of Japan" (Sevilla, 1628), "The Grand Victory that Jorge de Mendoza y Piçaña, Governor-general of Ceuta, Won Over the Moors of Tetuán" (Sevilla, 1633), and "The Narration of the Grand Celebration in the Church of San Miguel in Sevilla on the Occasion of the Events in Flanders" (Sevilla, 1635).

In January 1637, Ana Caro went to Madrid, where she was evidently received into the innermost literary and social circles. Here she met and befriended the short story writer and outspoken feminist María de Zayas. During her short stay in the capital she wrote the *Account of the Royal Celebrations in the Palace of the Buen Retiro for the Coronation of the King of the Romans and Entry into Madrid of the Princess of Cariñán* (Madrid: Imprenta del Reino, 1637). This lengthy poetic narrative in three parts describes the lavish festivities of the Court during February 15–25, 1637, in honor of the naming of Ferdinand III as Holy Roman Emperor and the arrival of the Princess of Cariñán, who had some importance for Spanish politics. The work is typical of courtly poetry with its abundance of hyperbole, mythological allusions, inverted syntax, and the extravagant praise of Philip IV as the Sun King and of his minister, the Duke of Olivares.

Early in 1637 she was back in Sevilla. Her works from this period include a short piece in verse, the "Sacramental Loa . . . in four languages," for the Corpus Christi celebrations of 1639. She also wrote several *autos sacramentales* or short verse dramas performed in the streets on movable stages. Her last known work—a prefatory sonnet—appeared in 1645, and she must have died soon afterward. Most of Ana Caro's poetry was closely connected to her native city of Sevilla. She is but little known today, and principally for two extant plays: *El Conde de Partinuplés* (The Count of Partinuples) and *Valor, agravio y mujer* (Valor, Dishonor, and Woman). Both depict popular female stock characters: the woman averse to love and marriage and the woman disguised as a man.

El Conde de Partinuplés, first published in the *Laurel de comedias de diferentes autores. Quarta Parte* (1653), is based on a popular romance of chivalry. The plot always hinges on a beautiful lady—in this play, the Princess Rosaura—who remains invisible to her suitor. However, Rosaura is not actually disdainful of men but rather fearful of an ominous prophecy. The plot develops in an atmosphere of magic and romance and, through the supernatural powers of Aldora, the lovers are brought together in a happy conclusion. *Valor, agravio y mujer* is a delightful comedy of errors that incorporates most of the stock situations of Golden Age drama: disguise and mistaken identity, intrigue, misdirected love, misspoken conversations, *double entendre*, etc., until the heroine, Leonor, ingeniously resolves the complications and gets her man. In this play the author shows a considerable talent for comic dialogue and skillful craftsmanship.

Many of Ana Caro's works were described or published by Serrano y Sanz in the *Apuntes para una biblioteca de escritoras españolas*, and several of the poetic narratives have recently been edited.

Works

El Conde de Partinuplés. In the *Biblioteca de autores españoles*. Vol. 49: *Dramáticos posteriores a Lope de Vega* (Madrid, 1924). *Contexto de las reales fiestas que se hizieron en el Palacio del Buen Retiro a la coronación del Rey de Romanos, y entrada en Madrid de la Señora Princesa de Cariñán*. Facs. ed. Antonio Pérez y Gómez (Valencia, 1951). "Grandiosa vitoria que alcançó de los Moros de Tetuán Iorge de Mendoça y Piçaña, General de Ceuta, quitándoles gran suma de ganados cerca de las mesmas puertas de Tetuán." ed. Francisco López Estrada. In *Homenaje a Blecua* (Madrid, 1983). "Loa sacramental, que se representó en el carro de Antonio de Prado, en las fiestas del Corpus de Sevilla, este año de 1639." ed. F. López Estrada. In *Revista de Dialectología y Tradiciones Populares* (*Homenaje a Vicente García de Diego*), 32 (1976): 263–274. "Relación de la grandiosa fiesta, y octava, sobre los sucesos en Flandes, que en la iglesia parroquial del glorioso San Miguel de la Ciudad de Seuilla, hizo don García Sarmiento de Sotomayor. . . ." (1635). "Relación, en que se da cuenta de las grandiosas fiestas, que en el convento de N.P.S. Francisco de la Ciudad de Sevilla se an hecho a los Santos Mártires del Iapón." ed. F. López Estrada. In *Homenaje a Antonio Pérez y Gómez*. 2 vols. (1978). *Valor, agravio y mujer*. ed. Manuel Serrano y Sanz. In *Apuntes para una biblioteca de escritoras españolas*. 2 vols. (Madrid, 1898; rpt. in *Biblioteca de Autores Españoles*, vol. 268, 1975).

Bibliography

De Armas, Frederick, "Ana Caro de Mallén Soto." *Women Writers of Spain: An Annotated Bio-bibliographical Guide*, ed. Carolyn L. Galerstein (New York, 1986). De Armas, Frederick, *The Invisible Mistress. Aspects of Feminism and Fantasy in the Golden Age* (Charlottesville, 1976). La Barrera y Leirado, Cayetano Alberto de, *Catálogo bibliográfico y biográfico del teatro antiguo español desde sus orígenes hasta mediados del siglo XVIII* (Madrid, 1860; rpt. London, 1968). Lundelius, Ruth, "Ana Caro and the *Comedia*." *Women Writers of the Seventeenth Century*. ed. Katharina Wilson and Frank Warnke (Athens, 1989). Ordóñez, Elizabeth, "Women and Her Text in the Works of María de Zayas and Ana Caro." *Revista de Estudios Hispánicos* 19, 1 (1985): 3–15. Serrano y Sanz, Manuel, *Apuntes para una biblioteca de escritoras españolas*. 2 vols. (Madrid, 1903; rpt. in *Biblioteca de Autores Españoles*, vol. 268, Madrid, 1975). Simón Díaz, José, *Bibliografía de la literatura hispánica*, vol. VII (Madrid, 1967), pp. 494–496.

Ruth Lundelius

Yvonne Caroutch

Born 1937, Paris, France
Genre(s): poetry, novel, short story, essay,
drama, translation
Language(s): French

Yvonne Caroutch's first book appeared in 1954 when she was just seventeen. Since then she has published numerous collections and *plaquettes*, novels and short stories, translations and essays. In addition she has written widely on tantric art and Tibet and has had many exhibitions of her painting. Member of the Prix Apollinaire Committee, she has also been involved in various radio and television broadcasts. Speaking of her poetry, for which she remains perhaps principally known, Luc Bérimont has claimed that "she is quite unskilled in the art of fine needle-point. She lives with astral tides, plants, the voluntary flow of rivers and the cracking of torrid summers." Michel Manoll evokes the "density" and "suaveness" of her work, which is marked with "exceptional gracefulness"; whereas Jean Grosjean is struck by both the tense alertness of her writing and its curious "comas" and "sharp syncopes."

Lieux probables (1968; Probable Places) is somewhat characteristic of Yvonne Caroutch's earlier work. Centered upon desire, corporality, and emotion, it is torn between an apocalyptic sense, a sense of "hellishness," of not knowing the self, and an opposing sense of some "pure instant of pure presence." The tensions of eros and some intuited astral-cosmic beyond are evident and call out for reconciliation. Yvonne Caroutch's search is directed finally much less *to* matter than *through* it, much less to past and nostalgic recovery than to a future, something as yet invisible.

Portiques du sel (Salt Porticoes) appeared in 1978 and may reasonably be said to reflect Yvonne Caroutch's more contemporary preoccupations and that rather gnomic, yet sharply eloquent, metaphoricity so central to her mode of expression. In many respects the constants are more prevalent than the variations, the latter manifesting themselves in endlessly renewed emblems and symbols rather than radical shifts of thought or feeling. Powerfully eloquent, profoundly felt, Yvonne Caroutch's work offers both lucidity and hope, observation and vision.

Works

Poetry: *Soifs* (1954). *Les Veilleurs endormis* (1955). *L'Oiseleur du vide* (1957). *Paysages provisoires* (1965). *Lieux probables* (1968). *Corridors ou Tombeau du Zodiaque* (1971). *La Voie du cœur de verre* (1972). *La Fête hermétique* (1973). *Hordes Virginales du matin* (1975). *La Fête sous la glace* (1977). *Portiques du sel* (1978). *Tente cosmique* (1982). *Bestiaire d'éveil* (1984).
Novels: *Le Gouvernement des eaux. Giordano Bruno, le voyant de Venise. Le Grand Transparent et le grand écorché. Chromatismes.*
Essays: *Panorama de la littérature fantastique en France et à l'étranger* (1978). *La Licorne alchimique. Ungaretti* (1980). *Renaissance tibétaine* (1982). *Un Saturne gai* (1982).

Bibliography

Boisdeffre, Pierre de. *Histoire de la littérature française* (Paris, 1985), p. 213. Brée, Germaine, and Morot-Sir, Edouard, *Du surréalisme à l'empire de la critique* (Paris, 1984), pp. 164, 215. Breton, Jean, Preface to *La Poésie féminine contemporaine, Poésie I* (1974). Brindeau, Serge, "YC." *La Poésie contemporaine de langue française depuis 1945* (Paris, 1973), pp. 107–108. Herney, Carl Williams, "Contemporary French Women Poets: A Bilingual and Critical Anthology." Binghamton, N.Y., *Diss.*

Abstr. Int. 36, 4 (Oct. 1975): 2197–A. Lepage, Jacques, "YC: *Le Gouvernement des eaux.*" *Marginales* 139 (July 1971): 71–72. Moulin, Jeanine, *Huits siècles de poésie féminine* (Paris, 1963). "Poetry Since the Liberation." *Yale French Studies* 21 (1958). Stary, Sonja, "YC: *Le Gouvernement des eaux.*" *French Review* 45, 1 (Oct. 1971): 192.

Michael Bishop

Maria Judite de Carvalho

Born 1921, Lisbon, Portugal
Genre(s): short story
Language(s): Portuguese

After studying German philology at the University of Lisbon, Carvalho lived in France and Belgium for six years. On her return to Portugal, she contributed to several Portuguese publications.

Her stories focus on two main themes: failure of communication and frustration in human relationships, especially within the family. By emphasizing the feminine characters and their point of view, the author presents a photographic image of the modern world. Her detached attitude heightens this effect. Carvalho's style is simple and direct, and, according to the *Columbia Dictionary of Modern European Literature,* "there may be few examples in any language of such poignant accounts of the tragic inability to communicate."

Works

Tanta Gente, Mariana [So Many People, Mariana] (1959). *As Palavras Poupadas* [Words Left Unsaid] (1961)—received Camilo Castelo Branco Prize awarded by fellow writers. *Paisagem sem barcos* [Scene Without Boats] (1963). *O seu amor por Etel* [His Love for Ethel] (1967). *Flores ao telefone* [Flores Is on the Phone] (1968). *Os Idolatras* [The Idolaters] (1969). *Tempo de Merces* [Time of Favors] (1973).

Bibliography

Lepecki, M. L., "Sobre Maria Judite de Carvalho." *Minas Gerais, Suplemento Literario* (Feb. 16, Feb. 23, and Mar. 2, 1974). *Columbia Dictionary of Modern European Literature,* eds. J.-A. Bédé and W.B. Edgerton (1980). *Encyclopedia of World*

Literature in the 20th Century, ed. L. Klein (1981).
Literatura Portuguesa Moderna, ed. M. Moisés (1973).

Paula T. Irvin

Sofia Pérez Casanova de Lutoslawski

Born 1862, Almeiras (Coruña), Spain; died 1958
Genre(s): poetry, short story, novel, essay, travelogue, journalism
Language(s): Spanish, Polish

Sofia Pérez Casanova was born in the village of Almeiras in Spain's northwestern Galician province of La Coruña. At the age of twenty-five, she married a Polish nobleman and sometime philosopher and thereafter lived largely outside Spain, while making regular visits home and continuing to contribute to the Spanish press. She learned Polish well enough to publish in that language and also took an active part in the feminist movement, especially working to improve health care and hygiene for women. A cultivator of many genres, she became well known for her lyrics, characterized by a romantic quest for meaning and the anguished expression of impossible love. However, she also wrote poetry of social consciousness on the problems of miners and sailors, specifically shipwrecks and mine disasters (*Poesías*, 1885). Other poetry collections are *Fugaces* (1898; Fleeting) and *El cancionero de la dicha* (1911; Songbook of Happiness). Official critical recognition in her lifetime included receipt of the Cross of Alfonso XII and admission to the Real Academia Gallega.

Casanova's long-lasting fascination with Russia is visible in her first novel, *El doctor Wolski. Páginas de Polonia y Rusia* (undated, ca. 1905; Dr. Wolski: Pages from Poland and Russia), which traces the relationship between an idealistic Polish doctor and his skeptical, hedonistic Russian friend. The Russian-educated doctor, a scientific researcher, develops a formula for genetic engineering, which leads him to break with his tubercular Russian fiancée and marry a robust Polish woman (who is apparently sterile). The topic of the inapplicability of scientific theory to human realities, especially love and procreation, was a popular one in Spain early in the present century and was treated by such famous novelists as Unamuno, Baroja, and Pérez de Ayala.

In *Lo eterno* (1905; The Eternal), Casanova attempts a psychological study of a priest's conflict between his ecclesiastical vow of chastity and the temptations of the flesh. The possible solution offered by Protestantism complicates the hero's struggle before the conflict is resolved via a somewhat melodramatic martyrdom. *Más que amor: cartas* (1909; More Than Love: Letters), an epistolary novel with some possible autobiographical content, involves an exiled Spanish widow living in Poland who attempts unsuccessfully to regenerate a philandering Madrid politician and infuse idealism and morality into the life of her correspondent. In two collections of brief fiction, *El pecado* (1911; Sin) and *Exóticas* (1912; Exotics), more explicitly feminist concerns are expressed. The eleven short stories of Sin, set largely in Galicia, treat sexual and marital incompatibility and study feminine guilt, while the shorter pieces of *Exóticas* develop social and feminist questions, paint family scenes, and recount the writer's problems with Russian censors.

Princesa rusa (1922; Russian Princess) portrays the "dolce vita" of Russian nobility and diversions of the frivolous international set, and especially the problem of divorce in marriages involving mixed nationalities and religions. Casanova's Russian femme fatale, married to a Spanish Marquis, is cynically oblivious to historical crises even after her jealous husband is killed in battle. The contrasting values of wealthy Eastern European exiles and traditional Spanish expatriates are also treated in *Como en la vida* (1930; As in Life), which juxtaposes existence in a rural Galician *pazo* (country manor) with the erotic frivolity of the turn-of-the-century equivalent of the jet-set. Something of a continuation of the same novelistic world, now more somber and faced with impending doom, appears in *Las catacumbas de Rusia roja* (1933; Red Russian Catacombs), which depicts the conflict between revolutionaries and counter-revolutionaries after the Bolshevik revolution. The hedonistic Russian princess, now widowed, reappears as the lover of an idealistic revolutionary whose first love is his mission.

Casanova also treated Russia in a collection of essays and short stories entitled *De Rusia. Amores y confidencias* (1927; From Russia, Love and Confidences), in *Sobre el Volga helado* (1903; On the Frozen Volga), a travel narrative, and *Viajes y aventuras de una muñeca española en Rusia* (1920; Travels and Adventures of a Spanish Doll in Russia), a lengthy didactic tale for children. Her international residence and first hand experience of the problems posed by the conflict of varying cultures and ethnicities are more lightly treated in *La madeja* (1913; The Skein), a brittle comedy of manners and adultery set in a French spa.

Although largely ignored by Spanish critics (as are the vast majority of women writers), Casanova is of interest because she provides an almost unique perspective, that of the intelligent and literate Spanish woman in the late nineteenth century exposed to international norms and attitudes. Her writings, especially her fiction, faithfully record the clash of values and cultures. Occasionally flawed by contrivance or a hint of melodrama, her narratives nonetheless exercise a powerful attraction with their presentation of a vanished world and way of life, almost forgotten in this century of rapid change.

Works

El cancionero de la dicha (1911, 1912). *Las catacumbas de Rusia roja* (1933). *Como en la vida* (1930, also in *Novelas y cuentos* 1947). *De Rusia. Amores y confidencias* (1927). *El doctor Wolski. Páginas de Polonia y Rusia* (1905?). *Lo eterno* (1907, 1920). *Exóticas* (1912). *Fugaces* (1898). *Idilio epistolar* (1931). *La madeja. Comedia frívola en tres actos y en prosa* (1913). *Más que amor: Cartas* (1909). *Obras completas*, 4 vols. (1925–1927). *El pecado* (1911, 1942). *Poesías* (1885). *Princesa rusa* (1922). *Sobre el Volga helado; narración de viajes* (1903, 1919). *Viajes y aventuras de una muñeca española en Rusia* (1920).

Bibliography

For articles in reference works, see *Women Writers of Spain*, ed. C.L. Galerstein (Westport, Conn., 1986).

Janet Perez

Alexandra Casian

(see: Otilia Cazimir)

Nina Cassian

(a.k.a. Maria Veniamin)

Born 1924, Galaţi, Romania
Genre(s): poetry, prose, children's literature, essay, translation, composition, book illustration
Language(s): Romanian

Nina Cassian was born in Galaţi on the Danube; she moved to Bucharest early in her life to study drama as well as painting. She was acknowledged as a poet, a writer of fiction and of books for children, an active critic, journalist and translator while at the same time maintaining parallel careers as a pianist, composer, and book illustrator. In 1985, at the age of sixty, Nina Cassian immigrated to the United States and settled in New York where she continues to write and teaches creative writing.

Cassian's first volume of poetry—*La scara 1/1* (1948; On the Scale 1/1) was at once tender and caustic, lucid, ironical, playfully surrealist, parodical in its evocation of Freud, Ion Barbu, or Poe. She renounced her work in the same year ("I was a decadent poet") to become a tame citizen writer and produced during the fifties a set of officially militant volumes of poetry about the socialist homeland or the glorious 1917 Russian Revolution, such as *Sufletul nostru* (1949; Our Soul), *An viu, nouă sute şi şaptesprezece* (1949; Living Year, Nine Hundred and Seventeen), *Tinereţe* (1953; Youth), or *Florile patriei* (1954; Flowers of Homeland). The recovery came at the end of the fifties, when Nina Cassian turned again toward real poetry and published one after the other, in hurried recuperation, solid volumes of authentic and original meditation upon the couple, nature (with a marked preference for the sea), and the poet's art, such as *Virstele anului* (1957; The Year's Ages), *Dialogul vîntului cu marea* (1957; Dialogue of Wind and Sea), *Sărbătorile zilnice* (1961; Daily Holidays), *Să ne facem daruri* (1963; Let's Give Gifts to One Another), *Disciplina harfei* (1965; Discipline of the

Harp). With *Sîngele* (1966; Blood), *Destinele paralele* (1967; Parallel Destinies), and *Ambitus* (1969; Ambitus), Cassian's lyricism goes through a new metamorphosis: it integrates violence as a crucial dimension of life, memory, and love, recuperates the experimental risks of the debut, sharpens and matures its characteristic tension between instinct and intellect, its confessive acuity. Subsequent volumes such as *Marea conjugare* (1971; Grand Conjugation) and *Recviem* (1971; Requiem), the last motivated by the death of the poet's mother, open to anxiety, perplexity in front of the human, social, or natural absurd, loneliness of post-love existence, aging with its accompanying deprivation of the candid forms of affectivity, the sad lucidity of indifference, anticipation of death, the loyal acknowledgment of decrease in lyrical combustion. This innovative poetic recuperation of arid inner spaces will be continued in *De îndurare* (1981; Mercy) and *Numărătoarea inversă* (1983; Counting Backwards), which were granted the Bucharest Writers' Association Award in 1982 and the Writers' Union Award in 1983, respectively.

To orient oneself in Cassian's polymorphous lyricism, the reader might keep in mind that the author published with a certain regularity revealing and, with the exception of the first, rigorous anthologies of her work as a poet: *Versuri alese* (1955; Selected Poems), which she later renounced except for one poem; *Cronofagie* (1970; Chronophagy); *Spectacol în aer liber. O altă monografie a dragostei* (1974; Show in the Open. Another Monograph of Love); *O sută de poeme* (1975; Hundred Poems), *Call Yourself Alive? Love Poems* (1988). More subjectively, but most interestingly as well, in her 1988 anthology, she chose to mention as volumes significant for her poetic evolution only *La scara 1/1* (1948; On the Scale 1/1), *Dialogul vîntului cu marea* (1958; Dialogue of Wind and Sea), *Sîngele* (1966; Blood), *Lotopoeme* (1972; Lottery Poems), *De îndurare* (1981; Mercy), and *Numărătoarea inversă* (1983; Counting Backwards).

Speaking of her poems, Cassian situated them at the upper limit of the profane and the lower one of the sacred. Forever in movement and agonic combustion, torn between feeling and cognition, generosity and self-legitimation, integration and struggle, resignation and passionate pleading, the ever-changing poet did not concede to plunging twice in the same self.

In her vast exploration of the seasons of love, Cassian voices adverse love, the bitterness of the encounter between strong, reflexive women and irresponsible lovers, when confronting, like a modern Mariana Alcoforado, disloyal, lukewarm, and episodic male engagement. She found enduring accents to depict female pain in front of male betrayal: "God, how well I remember that pain!/ My soul, taken unawares/ jerked like a decapitated hen./ Blood spattering everywhere, on the street, the table in the café,/ but mostly over your unconscious hands." (1966; The Blood).

Cassian is the only speaker of and poet in an imaginary language (called *limba spargă* and used in *Lotopoeme* (1972; Lottery Poems) that she invented in order to write poetry that Romanian proved unable to nurture. Her organic relationship with language and words is at the core of one of her late American poems: "Letters fall from my words/ like teeth might fall from my mouth./ Lisping? Stammering? Mumbling?/ On the last silence?/ Please God take pity/ on the roof of my mouth./ On my tongue,/ on my glotis,/ on the clitoris in my throat/ vibrating, sensitive, pulsating/ exploding in the orgasm of Romanian." (1987; Licentiousness).

Cassian's fiction—*Confidenţe fictive* (1974; Fictitious Confessions) and *Jocuri de vacanţă* (1984; Vacation Games)—is auto-ironic, often sarcastic, expanding the singular, at times atrocious humor already present in her poetry.

Out of the numerous and widely translated (into French, German, Russian, English, etc.) books for children written by Cassian—*Nică fără frică* (1950; Fearless Niko), *Ce-a văzut Oana* (1952; What Oana Saw), *Prinţul Miorlau* (1957; Prince Miaow), *Bot Gros, căţel fricos* (1957; Big Muzzle, Puppy Fearful), *Chipuri hazlii pentru copii* (1958; Funny Faces for Kids), *Aventurile lui Trompişor* (1959; The Adventures of Trunky, the Elephant), *Încură-lume* (1962; A Fumbler), *Povestea cu doi pui de tigru numiţi Ninigra şi Aligru* (1969; The Story of Two Tiger Cubs Named Ninigra and Aligru; English tr. Tigrino and Tigrene), *Între noi copiii* (1974; Between Us Kids)—the first and the penultimate were granted the State Prize in 1952 and the Writers' Union Award in 1969, respectively.

Nina Cassian is a well-known translator into Romanian of Vladimir Mayakovski, Sergei Mihalkov, Molière, Bertolt Brecht, Jannis Ritsos, Paul Celan, Christian Morgenstern, Shakespeare, Max Jacob, and Apollinaire, among many others.

Works

La scara 1/1 [On the Scale 1/1] (1948). *An viu, nouă sute şi şaptesprezece* [Living Year Nine Hundred and Seventeen] (1949). *Sufletul nostru* [Our Soul] (1949). *Cîntece pentru Republică* [Songs for the Republic] (1950). *Nică fără frică, basm* [Fearless Niko, A Tale] (1950). Successive revised editions in 1953, 1956, and 1959. *Ce-a văzut Oana. Versuri şi cîntece* [What Oana Saw. Poems and Songs] (1952). *Horea nu mai este singur* [Horea Is Alone No More] (1952). *Tinereţe. Versuri* [Youth. Poems] (1953). *Florile patriei. Versuri* [Flowers of the Homeland. Poetry] (1954). *Versuri alese* [Selected Poems] (1955). *Les écrivains de Roumanie dans leurs maisons de creation* [Literary Creation Homes for Writers in Romania] (1955). *Bot Gros, căţel fricos. Versuri* [Big Muzzle, Puppy Fearful. Poetry] (1957). *Vîrstele anului. Versuri* [The Year's Ages. Poetry] (1957). *Dialogul vîntului cu marea. Motive bulgare. Versuri* [Dialogue of Wind and Sea. Bulgarian Motives. Poetry] (1957). *Prinţul Miorlau* [Prince Miaow] (1957). *Chipuri hazlii pentru copii* [Funny Faces for Kids] (1958). *Aventurile lui Trompişor. Versuri* [The Adventures of Trunky, the Elephant. Poetry] (1959). *Sărbătorile zilnice* [Daily Holidays] (1961). *Spectacol în aer liber* [Show in the Open] (1961). *Încurcă-lume* [A Fumbler] (1962). *Curcubeu* [Rainbow] (1962). *Să ne facem daruri* [Let's Give Gifts to One Another] (1963). *Cele mai frumoase poezii* [The Most Beautiful Poems] (1963). *Disciplina harfei* [Discipline of the Harp] (1965). *Sîngele* [Blood] (1966). *Destinele paralele* [Parallel Destinies] (1967). *Ambitus* [Ambitus] (1969). *Povestea cu doi pui de tigru numiţi Ninigra şi Aligru* [The Story with Two Tiger Cubs Named Ninigra and Aligru] (1969). *Cronofagie 1944–1969* [Chronophagy 1944–1969] (1970). *Marea conjugare* [Grand Conjugation] (1971). *Recviem* [Requiem] (1971). *Atît de grozavă şi adio. Confidenţe fictive* [So Wonderful and Adieu. Fictitious Confidences] (1971). Republished in an enlarged version in 1976 under the title *Confidenţe fictive. Proze. O sută de poeme* [Hundred Poems] (1974). Illustrated by the author. *Lotopoeme* [Lottery Poems] (1972). *Spectacol în aer liber. O altă monografie a dragostei* [Show in the Open. Another Monograph of Love] (1974). *Între noi copiii* [Between Us Kids] (1974). *De îndurare* [Mercy] (1981). *Numărătoarea inversă* [Counting Backwards] (1983). *Jocuri de vacanţă* [Vacation Games] (1984).

Translations: *Blue Apple*, tr. Eva Feiler. Crosscultural Review Series, ed. Stanley Barkin (1982). *Lady of Miracles*, tr. Laura Schiff (Berkeley). "Post-Meridian," *The New Yorker* (November 1986). "Four Poems," *The New Yorker* (April 1987). "Tigrino and Tigrene. A Narrative Poem for Children," *The Lion and the Unicorn* (Brooklyn College, 1987). *Call Yourself Alive? The Love Poems of N.C.*, tr. Andrea Deletant and Brenda Walker (London and Boston, 1988). Catanoy, Nicholas, ed., *Modern Romanian Poetry*. Oakville, tr. A. Margul-Sperber and Barbara Caruso (Ottawa, 1977), p. 67. Deletant, Andrea, and Brenda Walker, tr., *Silent Voices. An Anthology of Contemporary Romanian Women Poets* (London and Boston, 1986), pp. 49–66. Duţescu, Dan, ed. and tr., *Romanian Poems* (Bucharest, 1982), pp. 140–142. Emery, George, ed., *Contemporary East European Poetry* (Ann Arbor, 1983), pp. 316–318, tr. Bryan Swann and Michael Impey; Stavros Deligiorgis; Laura Schieff and Virgil Nemoianu; Marguerite Dorian and Elliott Urdang. Feiler, Eva, tr., *Translation* IX (Fall 1982): 245–246. MacGregor-Hastie, Roy, ed. and tr., *Anthology of Contemporary Romanian Poetry* (London, 1969).

Bibliography

Caraion, Ion, "Nina Cassian." *Duelul cu crinii* (Bucharest, 1972), pp. 23–27. Piru, Al, *Panorama deceniului literar romănesc 1940–1950* (Bucharest, 1968), pp. 193–194. Piru, Al, "Nina Cassian." *Poezia romănească contemporană 1950–1975* (Bucharest, 1975), pp. 335–349. Raicu, Lucian, "Nina Cassian: *Ambitus*." In *Structuri literare* (Bucharest, 1973), pp. 236–241. Raicu, Lucian, "*Confidenţe fictive* (Nina Cassian)." *Practica scrisului şi experienţa lecturii* (Bucharest, 1978), pp. 251–254.

Sanda Golopentia

Castelloza

*Flourished late twelfth or early thirteenth
    century, Mayonne (Haute-Loire), southern
    France*
Genre(s): canso
Language(s): Occitan

Castelloza is the author of three *cansos* (or
love songs) that carry her name and a fourth that
can confidently be attributed to her on the basis
of its juxtaposition with her other songs in MS. *N*
and its thematic similarities to them (Paden et al.
163–165). Her songs are preserved in five
manuscripts, in four of which she is the subject
of a short biography or *vida*, while her conventionalized portrait miniature illustrates her songs
in three. According to her biography, she was the
wife of Turc de Mairony and loved Arman de
Breon, who was the subject of her love songs.
Turc de Mairony, whose existence is independently confirmed by a reference to him in 1212,
was presumably the lord of the castle of Mayonne,
situated in the commune of Venteuges (arr. Le
Puy, Haute Loire). A family of Brion held a castle
of that name in the commune of Compains (arr.
Issoire, Puy de Dôme), but there is no record of
an Arman. Castelloza addresses one poem to the
trobairitz (or woman troubadour) Almois de
Castelnou, mentioned in a document dated 1219,
while one song (Song IV) shows marked similarities to a piece by the troubadour Peirol, who
flourished between 1185 and 1221. Hence,
Castelloza's poetic activity may be situated
sometime in the last two decades of the twelfth
and the first two decades of the thirteenth centuries.

It has been persuasively argued that the four
texts of the reconstituted Castelloza canon
compose "a brief lyrical cycle, where an inner
progression can be perceived, and where rever-
berations from one piece to the next heighten
poetic meaning, so that the group as a whole is
imaginatively richer than the four pieces considered separately" (Dronke, "Castelloza," 132).
Song I, "Amics, s'ie.us trobes avinen" (PC 109,1),
propounds a series of antitheses that the next
three poems attempt to resolve. The disdainful
lover is envisaged as both "charming, humble,
open, and compassionate" (I: 1–2) and "wicked,
despicable, and haughty" (I: 4). The poetic voice

admits that it might be said that she is in error in
pleading her own cause with a knight (I: 19), but
she prizes less highly the demands of convention
and social mores than those of her heart. In the
final three stanzas of the song, the antitheses
enunciated in the first three stanzas—the hostile
versus the acquiescent lover, her (feigned) rejection of him versus her fidelity towards him,
her vigorous prosecution of her suit versus her
resigned silence, and her death from unhappy
love versus her healing accomplished through
perseverance in her one-sided affection—are
resolved in favor of fidelity, perseverance, and
joy through or beyond the indignities of her
unfaithful knight. He who would reprove her
choice is, she avers, much of a fool who "doesn't
know how it is with me, nor has seen you with
the eyes I saw you with, when you told me not to
worry, for at any time it could happen that I
would again have joy" (I: 26–31). This hope
appears to buoy her up, leading her to choose to
praise her beloved publicly and privately to
remain faithful to him although it does not
prevent her from addressing to him her pleas and
reproaches, which she declines to entrust to a
messenger. Her course of action is determined:
she will espouse loyalty and will find her joy in
the very act of proclaiming her love. Yet, in a swift
reversal, she concludes that she must die "if you
choose not to permit me any joy" (I: 45–46).

Songs II, III, and IV reiterate the elements of
Song I: hope and despair, acceptance and indifference, salvation and death; but the depiction of
the lady's plight darkens with each successive
text. Song I suggests the first recognition by the
lady of the beloved's indifference, shortly after
she has declared her own passion to him. In Song
II ("Ja de chantar non degr'aver talan," PC 109,2),
the poetic voice admits to knowing that the
knight loves another and recounts an episode in
which she purloined a glove belonging to the
knight only to return it for fear of causing him
harm through the suspicions of his mistress. In
Song III ("Mout avetz faich long estatge," PC
109,3), speaking as though her liaison is at an
end and with it all hope of reciprocation and joy
in love (III: 8–12), she alludes repeatedly and
graphically to her own death (III: 6, 15–16, 39–
40). However, she concludes with the promise of
forgiveness and welcome should her beloved

choose to return after hearing her song. In Song IV ("Per joi que d'amor m'avenga," PC 461,191), which begins "henceforth" (IV: 2), the note of resignation has deepened, for the lady laments that another reigns in her place (IV: 9–10). Conspicuously lacking in the songs of Castelloza is the presence in the abstraction *joi*, so frequently invoked by the poetic voice, of a transcendental power that would permit the elevation of that joy to the status of an ideal. The object, the knight, fails utterly to embody a system of values having the power automatically to ennoble the striving of the subject towards an absolute (Shapiro 564). The pretense of the poetic voice to find wholeness, identity, and fulfillment—*joi*, in a word—in her posture of noble fidelity rings hollow; for in this poetic universe *joi* exists only as its obverse, a shadowy reflection of itself.

Bibliography

Blakeslee, Merritt R., "La Chanson de femme, les Héroïdes, et la *canso* occitane à voix de femme: Considérations sur l'originalité des trobairitz." In *"Farai chansoneta nueva . . ." Essais sur la liberté créatrice (XIIe-XIIIe s.)*. Hommage à Jean Charles Payen, eds. Jean-Louis Backès, et al. Bogin, Meg, *The Women Troubadours* (New York and London, 1976). Bruckner, Matilda Tomaryn, "Na Castelloza, *Trobairitz*, and Troubadour Lyric." *Romance Notes* 25 (1984–1985): 239–253. Dronke, Peter, "The Provençal *Trobairitz*: Castelloza," in *Medieval Women Writers*. ed. Katharina M. Wilson (Athens, 1984).pp. 131–152. Paden, William D., Jr., et al., "The Poems of the *Trobairitz* Na Castelloza." *Romance Philology* 35 (1981–1982): 158–182. Rieger, Angelica, "'Ins e.l cor port, dona, vostra faisso.' Image et imaginaire de la femme à travers l'enluminure dans les chansonniers de troubadours." *Cahiers de Civilisation Médiévale* 28 (1985): 385–415. Shapiro, Marianne, "The Provençal Trobairitz and the Limits of Courtly Love." *Signs: Journal of Women in Culture and Society* 3 (1978): 560–571. Schultz, Oscar, *Die Provenzalischen Dichterinnen. Biographien und Texte nebst Anmerkungen und einer Einleitung* (Leipzig, 1888; Geneva, 1975), pp. 12, 23–24.

Merritt R. Blakeslee

Henriette Julie de Castelnau, Countess of Murat

*Born 1670, Brest, France; died 1716, Château
de la Buzadière in the Province of Maine
Genre(s): novel, memoirs
Language(s): French*

Daughter of a governor of Brest, Henriette de Castelnau was married to Nicolas, Count of Murat, at the age of sixteen. She appeared at the royal court in Breton dress and spoke in the Breton language, although she wrote in French. Her charm and wit gained for her considerable social success, but her conduct met with the disapproval of Madame de Maintenon, who had her exiled to Loches, where she occupied herself with writing. Under the Regency, she was allowed to return to court through the influence of her friend, the Marquise de Parabère.

Works

Le Comte de Dunois [The Count of Dunois] (1671). *Le Voyage de Campagne* [The Country Voyage] (1679). *Histoire Galante des Habitants de Loches* [The Courtly Story of the Inhabitants of Loches] (1696). *Les Mémoires de la Comtesse de Murat ou la Défense des Dames* [The Memoirs of the Countess of Murat or the Defense of Ladies] (1697). *Histoires Sublimes et Allégoriques* [Sublime and Allegorical Stories] (1699).

Bibliography

Rudel, Y.M., "H. de Castelnau, comtesse de Murat, romancière et mémorialiste bretonne," *Nouvelle Revue de Bretagne* (1948): 285–290.

Charity C. Willard

Lalo di Castro

(see: Galatea Kazantzaki)

Rosalía de Castro

*Born 1837, Santiago de Compostela, Spain;
died 1885, Santiago de Compostela
Genre(s): lyric poetry, novel
Language(s): Spanish, Galician*

Rosalía de Castro came from a region of Spain that breeds melancholy and nostalgia. In her case melancholy was intensified by misfortune, beginning with the fact of her illegitimacy that haunted her all her life. She was raised in secrecy by a peasant woman until "adopted" by her mother at the age of nine. At nineteen she moved to Madrid where she came in contact with poets and writers and began a literary career for which she had shown talent since childhood. In Madrid she met and married a young Galician writer, Manuel Martínez Murguía, a dwarf. With marriage, suffering deepened; not only did her husband mistreat her, but she fought against poverty to raise her five children and overcome her own emotional and physical frailties. She died of cancer at a young age, having lived reclusively the last years of her life.

Although she wrote novels, including *La hija del mar* (1859), *Flavio* (1861), *Ruinas* (1864), and *El caballero de las botas azules* (1867), she is remembered almost exclusively as a poet. Her poetry was inspired by her native region, its customs, people, traditions, and folk songs. Her voice is restrained, yet sadly probing, melancholy but not morbid. She is the inheritor of Romanticism, but, like her contemporary, Gustavo Adolfo Bécquer, with whom she often is compared, she trims away the excesses of the earlier convention and reveals a lyrical voice of startling purity.

Perhaps because she wrote more poetry in Galician than Spanish, she was not fully appreciated for many years. In this century, however, she has been recognized by many as Spain's foremost woman poet.

Works

Cantares gallegos (1863). *Follas novas* (1880). *En las orillas del Sar* (1884). *Obras completas*, ed. V. García Marti (1952).

Translations: Balbontín, José Antonio. *Three Spanish Poets: Rosalía de Castro, Federico García Lorca, Antonio Machado*, intro. José Picazo (London, 1961). *Beside the River Sar*. Selected poems from *En las orillas del Sar*, tr. S. Griswold Morley (Berkeley, 1937).

Bibliography

Albert Robaato, Matilde, *Rosalía de Castro y la condición femenina* (Madrid, 1981). Davies, Catherine, "Rosalía de Castro: Criticism 1950–1980: The Need for a New Approach." *Bulletin of Hispanic Studies* 60 (July 1983): 211–220. Havard, Robert G., "'Saudades' as Structure in Rosalía de Castro's *En las orillas del Sar*." *Hispanic Journal* (Fall 1983): 29–34. Kulp, Kathleen K., *Manner and Mood in Rosalía de Castro: A Study of Themes and Style* (Madrid, 1968). *Rosalía de Castro* (Boston, 1977). Lázaro, Angel, *Rosalía de Castro: Estudio y antología* (Madrid, 1967). Mayoral, Marina, *La poesía de Rosalía de Castro* (Madrid, 1974). Miller, Martha La Follette, "Parallels in Rosalía de Castro and Emily Dickinson." *The Comparatist* 5 (May 1981): 3–9. Nogales de Muniz, María Antonia, *Irradación de Rosalía de Castro* (Barcelona, 1966). Odriozola, Antonio, "Rosalía de Castro: Guía bibliográfica." *Nuevo Hispanismo* (Winter 1982): 259–283.

Mary E. Giles

Concha Castroviejo Blanco-Ciceron

Born 1912, Santiago de Compostela, Spain
Genre(s): novel
Language(s): Spanish

Castroviejo studied at the University of her native city and at the University of Bordeaux. From 1939 to 1950 she lived and taught in Mexico. Upon her return to Spain she completed the course at the Official School of Journalism in Madrid and has since maintained an active journalistic career, publishing articles and criticism in both Spanish and foreign periodicals and winning a number of journalism prizes. The primary theme of her novels is the devastating effects of the Spanish Civil War (1936–1939). Her first novel, *Los que se fueron* (1957; Those Who Went Away), follows a group of post-war Spanish exiles to Paris and then to Mexico. The heroine, a widow with a young son, refuses to waste her time with other expatriates who sit around in cafes bemoaning the loss of their homeland. Eschewing marriage to a wealthy Mexican, she develops a successful career and gives up hope of return to Spain, realizing that her son's future lies in Mexico. *Víspera del odio* (1959; Eve of Hate) is a psychological novel that received the Premio Elisenda de Montcada. The novel explores the development of a woman's hatred for her husband, but the Civil War provides the impetus for the narrative structure. The themes are the woman's self-sacrifice and the utilization of the chaos of war as an excuse for the greed of the old order and for personal vindictiveness. Castroviejo has also published short stories and detective novels and is known for her children's books. Her works have been translated into Czech, English and French.

Works

> *Los que se fueron* (1957). *Víspera del odio* (1959). *Los piratas* (1962). *El Zopilote* (1962). *Los días de Lina* (1971).

Bibliography

Rey, Antonio Domínguez, "Concha Castroviejo." *La Estafeta Literaria* 528 (1973): 15–17. Galerstein, Carolyn, "The Spanish Civil War: The View of Women Novelists." *Letras Femeninas* X, No. 2 (fall 1984): 12–18. Valdivieso, Teresa, "El drama de lo tangencial en *Víspera del odio* y *Una mañana cualquiera*." *Letras Femeninas* XII, Nos. 1–2 (primavera-otoño, 1986): pp. 24–33.

Carolyn Galerstein

Víctor Català

(see: Caterina Albert i Paradis)

Caterina da Bologna

Born September 8, 1413, Bologna, Italy; died
*   March 9, 1463, Bologna*
Genre(s): spiritual counsel
Language(s): Italian

The patroness of Bologna, daughter of Giovanni Vigri and Benvenuta Mammolini, St. Catherine was reared in Ferrara, her father's native city, at the court of the d'Este. It was in Ferrara that she became a Poor Clare in 1432. She and some of her associates came to Bologna and entered a monastery built for them on July 22, 1456. She remained there until her death on March 9, 1463. She is the author of a work published after her death, *Le sette armi spirituali*, ed. C. Foletti (Verona, 1983).

Bibliography

"The Weapons of the Spirit," in *Renaissance Women Writers*, ed. K.M. Wilson (Athens, Ga., 1987). Nunez, L-M, O.F.M., *La Santa nella storia, nelle lettere, e nell'arte* (Bologna, 1912).

Joseph Berrigan

Caterina da Genova

Born 1447, Genoa, Italy; died September 14,
*   1510, Genoa*
Genre(s): mysticism
Language(s): Italian

Caterina da Genova was the daughter of Santiago Fieschi. Despite her wishes to enter a convent, Caterina was married at sixteen to Giuliano Adorno. They would remain together until his death in 1497, but from 1473, when she converted him to a more perfect Christian life, they lived contentedly and cared for the ill. She is, then, one of the rarest of types, a married mystic. She never entered any third order but always remained a lay woman.

The best book ever written in English on mysticism is devoted to her: F. von Hugel's two volume *The Mystical Element of Religion as Studied in St. Catherine of Genoa and her Friends* (London, 1908). Her teaching brings the Christian to the very point of self-annihilation in the love of God.

Works

> *The Treatise on Purgatory and the Dialogue*, tr. H.D. Irvine and C. Balfour (1946). Nugent, Donald C., "Saint Catherine of Genoa: Mystic of Pure Love," in *Women Writers of the Renaissance and Reformation*, ed. Katharina M. Wilson (Athens: 1987), pp. 67–80.

Joseph Berrigan

Caterina da Siena

Born 1347 (?), Siena, Italy; died April 29,
*   1380, Rome*
Genre(s): letters, mysticism, autobiography
Language(s): Italian

A Doctor of the Church and patroness of Italy, Caterina da Siena is one of the most influential authors of late-medieval Europe. The daughter of Jacopo Benincasa and Lapa Piagenti, Caterina was the youngest of more than twenty children. She refused to marry and became a Dominican tertiary. Soon enough a group of disciples gathered around her, and she became a powerful force in Italy during the second half of the fourteenth century. Although she never learned to write, she has left a large number of letters dictated to secretaries and a Dialogue of Divine Love. Gifted with a very strong personality, she tended to identify her views with both the Church and God. Her most important role came at the very end of her life when she went to Rome to rally support for Urban VI at the inception of the Great Schism. Her devotion to the papacy guaranteed that she would remain influential even after her death.

Works

Libro della divina dottrina [The Book of Divine Teaching], ed. Matilde Fiorilli (Bari, 1912). Le lettere di S. Caterina da Siena [The Letters of St. Catherine], ed. Piero Misciatelli, 6 vols. (Florence, 1970). Bell, Holy Anorexia, 22–53. DBI 22, 361–379.

Joseph Berrigan

Catherine II (the Great), Empress of Russia

Born April 21/May 2, 1729, Stettin,
    Pomerania; died November 6/17, 1796,
    St. Petersburg, Russia
Genre(s): treatise, law, letters, translation,
    memoirs, history, criticism, comparative
    word list, comedy, comic operas, drama,
    fable, collection of proverbs, satire
Language(s): Russian, French

Varied literary activity and patronage of literature were only two of the many interests pursued by Empress Catherine II, born Sophie Auguste Friedrike, princess of Anhalt-Zerbst. Brought to Russia in 1744 to marry Grand Duke Peter Fedorovich, the Holstein-born crown prince of Russia, her cousin, and the future Peter III, Sophie converted to Russian Orthodoxy with the new name of Ekaterina Alekseevna, Catherine or Catharine in English. Her marriage in 1745 proved to be unhappy and politically perilous,

for the young couple had trouble producing the desired heir for the childless Empress Elizabeth (Grand Duke Peter may well have been sterile and impotent). When after several miscarriages Catherine finally gave birth to Paul in 1754 (probable father: Sergei Saltykov), the baby was taken away to be raised by Empress Elizabeth. Catherine involved herself in other romantic and political intrigues in the next several years as Empress Elizabeth's health deteriorated and her husband's defects became blatant. Her romance with Stanislas Poniatowski produced a daughter who died early, and her romance with Grigory Orlov produced a son, Aleksei Bobrinskoi, born two months before the coup d'etat of June 28/ July 8, 1762 that displaced Peter III, who was killed a week later. Proclaimed Catherine II and officially crowned in Moscow in September 1762, she began an extraordinary reign of more than thirty-four years that left quite a mark on Russian, European, and world history. The hallmarks of her reign were policies of "enlightened absolutism" that aimed at order and stability, economic growth and cultural development, military power, territorial expansion, and international repute.

Literature interested Catherine even before she came to Russia. She learned French well and had at least heard of the works of Voltaire and of Moliere, Racine, and Corneille. In the difficult years before she won the throne she read avidly and widely, learned Russian quite well, and began to write informally, including an early draft of memoirs for her mentor, British envoy Sir Charles Hanbury-Williams, with whom she corresponded frequently in 1756–1757 on mainly political subjects. By then she already sensed a great destiny. Upon gaining the throne she soon established contact with the French philosophers Diderot, D'Alembert, and Voltaire, whom she sought to enroll in her efforts to enlighten Russia. Some of her letters to them were published at the time and served further to advertise her enlightened program. She also encouraged other Russian writers and the translation of foreign works into Russian. The average number of titles published annually in Russian rose from 161 in the early 1760s to 373 in the 1790s.

Her first widely known full-scale treatise was the famous Nakaz (Instructions) of 1767–1768 to the newly convened Legislative Commission, a compendium of some 655 articles borrowed largely from Montesquieu, Beccaria, and the German cameralists that provided guidelines for the work of the commissioners. It came out in many Russian editions and the Academy of Sciences issued a quadrilingual version in Russian, German, French, and Latin. It was quickly translated into all the main European languages and published abroad in English, Dutch, Italian, Swedish, Polish, and modern Greek. Subsequent Russian legislation often cited this work, which announced that Russia was a European state, argued that absolute monarchy was the best government for such a large and diverse empire, and advocated a general program of benevolent-sounding reforms to promote progress in economic, social, and cultural development under firm central guidance. The *Nakaz* was composed in French, then rendered into Russian by assistants, and edited by the empress in consultation with various advisers. Catherine's authorship in this and many other instances involved other people. Especially obscure was her participation in the first Russian satirical journals in 1769. Apparently she supplied some items for the periodical *Vsiakaia vsiachina* (All Sorts and Sundries), but exactly which ones is uncertain. The same is true of her part in *Antidote*, a work that aimed to counteract some negative views about Russia popularized in France by Jean Chappe d'Auteroche.

Catherine's five comedies of the early 1770s all satirized such common foibles as gossiping, hypocrisy, hypochondria, parental tyranny, and religious superstition. All were issued without her name but were performed first at court. At least one, *O Vremia!*, drew upon a foreign model, Gellert's *Betschwester*. She undoubtedly received considerable assistance in writing these plays, especially from her secretary and longtime friend Ivan Elagin. Later Catherine dismissed such writings as "trifles" that she indulged in merely for diversion. Their quality in literary terms was certainly quite low, but they may still be important as facts of Russian intellectual and cultural history, and as examples to others.

In the 1780s Catherine's literary activity revived and broadened to include several works for her grandsons, Alexander and Konstantin. These were the fables about Khlor and Fevee, a Russian ABC, a conversation and stories, and selected Russian proverbs. In 1780 she published her first antimasonic work, which was deliberately misdated 1759. In 1785–1786 her trilogy of antimasonic comedies appeared with *The Deceiver*, *The Deluded*, and *The Siberian Shaman*, all three of which attacked freemasonry as an international conspiracy and ridiculed its devotion to ritual. All three were quickly translated into German and published by C. F. Nicolai. She also indulged in two adaptations of Shakespeare's *The Merry Wives of Windsor* and *Timon of Athens* as *Vot kakavo* (This 'Tis to Have Linen and Buck-Baskets) and *Rastochitel'* (The Spendthrift), both in 1786. Later she offered two "imitations" of Shakespeare. Her comic operas, written with Aleksandr Khrapovitskii, were quite popular mainly because they employed the best composers, musicians, set designers, and elaborate stage machinery and costumes. She professed to see in them a form of therapy (for depression in particular).

In the 1780s Catherine also took an interest in Russian history and supervised the compilation of excerpts from the medieval chronicles, a chronology from 862 to 1462, and a genealogy of the princes of the house of Riurik. The first three parts of these materials had been serialized in the new journal *Sobesednik liubitelei rossiiskogo slova* in 1783–1784. She also sponsored the compilation of a comparative word list of selected terms in all known languages, including those of American Indian tribes.

Catherine wrote some seven different drafts of an autobiography beginning in the mid-1750s and concluding in the 1790s. None was finished, and none was published until long after her death. Indeed, the first printed version appeared outside Russia under the sponsorship of the revolutionary emigré Aleksandr Herzen as an attack on the legitimacy of the Romanov dynasty. Fairly full Russian editions were printed in the early twentieth century. The different versions contradict each other in many details, and none gives much treatment of her life beyond her accession to the throne. They were written mostly in French, with some Russian passages and fragments. She dedicated them to different friends, but she seems to have had no intention of publication. It is slightly ironic, therefore, that her literary reputation abroad should be mainly based upon these memoirs of her life before she became empress. Some editions include a number of her letters, the genre in which she wrote the most words; her known letters number more than 10,000, and the Russian state archives undoubtedly hold even more.

In fiction Catherine certainly displayed little literary talent, yet she did show some audacity and foresight in setting an example of toying with various genres, especially in adapting foreign works to Russian tastes and customs. Certainly she received considerable direct assistance in the composition and editing of her works, some of which may be considered to have been written "by committee," as it were. The same is true of much of her nonfiction, especially of her *Nakaz*, and her authorship of important state documents such as the Charter to the Nobility of 1785. She may have demonstrated greater originality in some of her letters to friends, particularly those to her Parisian agent and confidant, Melchior Grimm.

Works

Nakaz o sochinenii proekta novogo ulozheniia (1767). Anonymous contributions to *Ksiakaia vsiachina* (1769). *Antidote, ou examen du mauvais livre intitulé: Voyage en Sibérie en 1761* (1770). *O vremia!* (c. 1772). *Gospozha Vestnikova s sem'eiu* (1774). *Imianiny gospozha Varchalkinoi* (1774). *Peredniaia znatnogo boiarina* (1772). *Voprositel'* (1772). *Taina protivo-nelepnogo obshchestva (Anti-absurde) otkrytaia ne prichastnym onomu* (1780). *Skazka o tsareviche Khlore* (1781). *Rossiiskaia azbuka dlia obucheniia iunoshestva chteniiu* (1781). *Razgovor i razskazy* (1782). *Vybornyia rossiiskiia poslovitsy* (1783). *Skazka o tsareviche Fevee* (1783). *Komediia "Obmanshchik"* (1785). *Vol'noe, no slaboe perelozhenie iz Shakespira, Komediia "Vot kakovo imet' korzinu i bel'e"* (1786). *Komediia "Obol'shchennyi"* (1786). *Komediia "Shaman Sibirskoi"* (1786). *Rastochitel'* (1786). *Novgorodskii boratyr' Boeslaevich'* (1786). *Opera komicheskaia "Fevei"* (1786). *Podrazhanie Shakespiru. Istoricheskoe predstavlenie bez sokhraneniia featral'nykh obyknovennykh pravil, iz zhizni Riurika* (1786). *Zapiski kasatel'no rossiiskoi istorii*, pt. I-VI (1787–1794). *Nachal'noe upravlenie Olega* (1787). *Opera komicheskaia*

"Khrabroi i smeloi vitias' Akhrideich'" (1787). *Komediia "Razstroennaia sem'ia ostorozhkami i podozreniiami"* (1788). *Skazka o Gore-bogatyre Kosometoviche i opera komicheskaia iz slov skazki sostavlennaia* (1789). *Fedul s det'mi* (1790).

Editions of collection works: *Sochineniia*, 3 vols., ed. A. Smirdin (1849–1850). *Sochineniia*, 3 vols., ed. V.F. Solntsev (1893). *Sochineniia*, ed. A.I. Vvedenskii (1893). *Sochineniia, na osnovanii podlinnykh rukopisei*, vols. I-V, VII-XII, ed. A.N. Pypin (1901–1907).

Translations into English: *Memoirs of the Empress Catherine II, Written by Herself* (1859). *Memoirs of Catherine the Great*, tr. Katharine Anthony (1927). *The Memoirs of Catherine the Great*, ed. Dominique Maroger (1955). *Voltaire and Catherine the Great: Selected Correspondence*, ed. A. Lentin (1974). "Catherine the Great's Instructions (NAKAZ) to the Legislative Commission, 1767," in Paul Dukes, ed., *Russia under Catherine the Great*, vol. II (1977).

Bibliography

Cross, A.G., "A Royal Blue-Stocking: Catherine the Great's Early Reputation in England as an Authoress." *Gorski Vijenats: A Garland of Essays offered to Professor Elizabeth Mary Hill*, eds. R. Auty, L.R. Lewitter, and A.P. Vlasto (Cambridge, 1970), pp. 85–99. Cross, A.G., and G.S. Smith, *Eighteenth Century Russian Literature, Culture and Thought: A Bibliography of English Language Scholarship and Translations* (Newtonville, Mass., 1984). de Madariaga, Isabel, *Russia in the Age of Catherine the Great* (New Haven and London, 1981). Karlinsky, Simon, *Russian Drama from Its Beginnings to the Age of Pushkin* (Berkeley and London, 1985). Marker, Gary, *Publishing, Printing, and the Origins of Intellectual Life in Russia, 1799–1800* (Princeton, 1985). Raeff, Marc, ed., *Catherine the Great: A Profile* (New York, 1972). Stepanov, V.P., and Iu. V. Stennik, *Istoriia russkoi literatury XVIII veka: Bibliograficheskii ukazatel'*, ed. P.N. Berkov (Leningrad, 1968).

J.T. Alexander

Eva Cattermole Mancini

(a.k.a. Contessa Lara)

Born 1849, Florence, Italy; died 1896, Rome
Genre(s): poetry, novel, short story, children's
* literature*
Language(s): Italian

Through her father, who was a private music teacher, Cattermole grew up in contact with the children of powerful and intellectual families, when Florence was the capital of Italy from 1860 to 1870. When she was very young, she married a lieutenant, E.F. Mancini, son of a famous statesman, Stanislao Mancini, and the poet Laura Beatrice Oliva. She separated from her husband after a sensational trial in Milan, whereby he was indicted for killing her lover, a cavalry officer, in a duel. For the rest of her days, she lived in Rome on her modest income from her writing, contributing to several journals and papers, among which were *Il Fieramosca, Nabab, Corriere di Roma, Caffaro, Fracassa, Fanfulla della domenica, Illustrazione italiana, Tribuna illustrata*. She was murdered by a young lover who resented her rejection of him.

The publication of *Canti e ghirlande* (Songs and Garlands) in 1867 had brought young Cattermole to the attention of a literary figure of the time, Francesco Dall'Ongaro. Her career, however, was not launched until 1883, when a book of poetry, *Versi* (Verses), was brought out by Angelo Sommaruga, a publisher who had been scandalizing Italian literary circles with his provocative publicity methods. The recurring themes of that collection are the domestic scene and the dramas of conjugal life: quarrels, reconciliations, suspicions, betrayals. Strains of romantic passion, with the implicit revolt against conventional society, and her talent for photographic descriptions associated Cattermole with the Milanese group of *Scapigliatura*. In a new volume, *Nuovi versi* (1897; New Verses), her constant theme, love, seems to have deepened into an exalted desire for total dedication to a man, thus reflecting her mood in a period of life when she lived with a young, and later celebrated, scholar, Giovanni Alfredo Cesareo. In her later poetry—*Ancora versi* (More Verses), published posthumously in 1897—Cattermole shows her basic psychological conflict, as she alternately expresses a wish for a new life, quiet and sentimentally satisfying, on one side, and sudden longings for reckless self-determination, on the other. Her most successful poems are sketches of interiors, recreated with the simple, but decisive description of a few objects, with a suggestion of a color or an odor, where an erotic feeling is suddenly alluded to with delicate but vivid longing. A pronounced cult of death emerges at the end of her production, together with other decadent themes in the manner of Gabriele D'Annunzio, who then dominated the Roman literary scene. Her beauty and her sensational life in end-of-the-century Rome made Contessa Lara appear as the prototype of D'Annunzian heroines, as they were described in *Il piacere* (1889; The Pleasure) and *L'innocente* (1891; The Innocent). Throughout her career, Cattermole wrote many short stories; she published an autobiographical novel, *L'innamorata* (1892; Woman in Love), and two books for children—*Una famiglia di topi* (1895; A Family of Mice) and *Il romanzo della bambola* (1896; The Doll's Novel).

Works

Canti e ghirlande (1867). *Versi* (1883). *Ancora versi* (1886). *Nuovi versi* (1897). *Così è* (1887). *L'innamorata* (1892). *Storia d'amore e di dolore* (1893). *Il romanzo della bambola* (1896). *Una famiglia di topi* (1895). *Storia di Natale* (1897). *Novelle* (1914). *La Madonna di Pugliano* (1917).

Bibliography

Barbiera, R., *Il salotto della contessa Maffei* (Milan, 1895). Borgese, Maria, *La Contessa Lara, una vita di passione e di poesia nell'Ottocento italiano* (Milan, 1936). Costa-Zalessow, N., *Scrittrici italiane dal XIII al XX secolo* (Ravenna, 1982), pp. 235–239. Croce, B., *Letteratura della nuova Italia*. IV (Bari, 1914), pp. 315–355. Morandini, G., *La voce che è in lei, Antologia della narrativa femminile italiana tra Ottocento e Novecento* (Milan, 1980), pp. 200–216. Squarciapino, G., *Roma bizantina* (Turin, 1950), pp. 172–180, 358–361.

Rinaldina Russell

Charlotte-Rose Caumont de la Force

Born 1650, Château de Caseneuve, France;
    died March 16, 1724, Paris
Genre(s): novel, poetry
Language(s): French

Charlotte-Rose was until 1673 lady-in-waiting of the Queen of France, Marie-Thérèse; she then entered in the service of the Duchesse de Guise. Her love life was far from dull. After seducing the marquis de Nesles, she managed to talk a rich young man into marrying her, but her father-in-law had his son incarcerated and the marriage annulled.

Charlotte-Rose's first novel, *Les Fées, contes des contes* (The Fairies, Tales of Tales), was published anonymously in 1692. Two years later in *L'Histoire secrète de Marie de Bourgogne*, when a letter falls out of the pocket of the Comte d'Angoulême, the reader is reminded of a similar incident happening in *La Princess de Clèves* by Madame de Lafayette. Charlotte-Rose's novels are full of perfectly beautiful princesses and accomplished young men. Such heroes are found also in *L'Histoire de Marguerite de Valois, Reine de Navarre* (1696), *Henri IV Roi de Castille, surnommé l'Impuissant* (1695) and *Gustave Vasa, histoire de Suède* (1697–1698).

In 1697, her libertine poems brought forth from Louis XIV an order to retire to a convent outside Paris. While in the Benedictine Abbey of Gercy-en Brie, she wrote the *Histoire de Catherine de Bourbon, duchesse de Bar* (1703), *Adélaïs de Bourgogne*, and the *Jeux d'esprit de la comtesse de Conti à Eu* (1862; Games of Wit of the Countess of Conti in Eu). Her turbulent life is reflected in the characters of her *Contes*; realism is mingled with the supernatural, and morality has a meager role.

In 1704, Charlotte-Rose came to reside in the Benedictine Abbey of Notre-Dame de la Consolation in Paris, but only in 1713 did she recover her full freedom. During her later years she spent her time writing religious poetry.

Works

Les Fées, contes des contes (1692). L'Histoire secrète de Marie de Bourgogne (1694). L'Histoire de Marguerite de Valois, Reine de Navarre (1696).

Henri IV, Roi de Castille, surnommé l'Impuissant (1695). Gustave Vasa, histoire de Suède (1697–1698). Histoire de Catherine de Bourbon, duchesse de Bar (1703). Adélaïs de Bourgogne (1862). Jeux d'esprit de la comtesse de Conti à Eu (1862).

Bibliography

La Force, Duc de, "Une romancière au XVIIᵉ siècle et ses aventures" [A Novel Writer in the XVIIth Century and Her Adventures]. *Revue des Deux Mondes* (1954).

Marie-France Hilgar

Marthe-Marguerite le Valois de Villette de Mursay, Comtesse de Caylus

(a.k.a. Alice Golay, Alica Rivaz)

Born 1673, Niort, France; died February 15, 1729, Paris
Genre(s): memoirs and letters
Language(s): French

A great-granddaughter of Agrippa d'Aubigné, Caylus seemed destined for a Protestant upbringing and marriage. But in 1680 during an absence of her father the marquis de Villette, later the distinguished naval commander, she was, with her two brothers, surreptitiously "rescued" by their aunt, Mme de Maintenon. The education she personally oversaw with her considerable pedagogical skill began with her niece's unresisting conversion to Catholicism. She was married at thirteen, again by her aunt's arrangement, to Jean-Anne de Tubières, comte de Caylus (d. 1704). For the most part she lived apart from her husband at court in the company of her aunt and friends who she easily won among younger members of the royal family. Racine wrote for her the Prologue to Esther, which she gave at the first Saint-Cyr performance before moving on to play the leading role (better than Champmeslé, Mme de Sévigné reckoned).

Too outspokenly gay, with the duchesse de Condé, too fond of gaming, and especially too familiar with the duc de Villeroy, Caylus fell from royal favor in 1693 and remained at the distance of Paris until 1707. There she sought the spiritual direction of the Oratorian Père de La Tour. Once again amid court diversions, she received tributes (in verse from La Fare and in prose by abbé Choisy) and seemed to the Academician Gédoyn the perfect model of urbanité.

Caylus became a writer through the efforts of her son, Anne-Claude (1692–1765), antiquarian, art historian (and patron of Watteau), novelist, first collaborating with him perhaps on a translation of Pope's *The Rape of the Lock* (1728). At his bidding near the end of her life (perhaps dictated to him), she composed her *Souvenirs*. Neither they nor her letters appeared in print during her son's lifetime.

Caylus's memoirs were first edited for publication by Voltaire in 1770 with a preface in which he praises their value as documents, thanks to Caylus's candor, of the private life of Louis XIV (and the already much falsified life of Mme de Maintenon). No pretensions to writing history are made, however, by the narrator of the memoirs, who initially disavows any authorial claim except naturalness. The casually controlled flow of anecdotes with its crispness of wit and quickly sketched portraits has seemed, to readers from Sainte-Beuve onward, to evoke the court conversation in which Caylus reveled, it may also preserve that between mother and son. Although the memoirs do no overt account-settling, their urbanity occasionally casts a somewhat sinister light on Regency society. Rather than turn inward, the first-person narration is most often directed toward complexly portraying Mme de Maintenon. *Souvenirs* remains first of all a memorial of unforced admiration and filial gratitude to that remarkable woman who had shaped her own life as unrelentlessly as she had her niece's.

Works

Souvenirs (1770). Tr., *La Boucle de cheveux enlevée* (? anon., 1728). *Lettres* (1805), in Anne-Claude de Tubières, comte de Caylus, *Mémoires*.

Bibliography

Clouzot, Hélène, "Le Véritable texte des souvenirs de Mme de Caylus." *Revue des Travaux de l'Académie des Sciences morales et politiques* 98 (1938): 355–373. Cordelier, Jean, *Madame de Maintenon* (1955). Noël, Bernard, ed., *Souvenirs de Madame de Caylus* (1965). Sainte-Beuve, C.-A., "Madame de Caylus et ce qu'on appelle urbanité," *Causeries du lundi* 3 (1850): 56–77.

Charles G. S. Williams

Otilia Cazimir

(a.k.a. Alexandra Casian, Alexandra Gavrilescu, Dona Sol, Magda, Ofelia, G. Topîrceanu—the last an allonym, Topîrceanu being a close poet friend of O.C.)

Born Cotul Vameşului (Neamţ), Romania; died 1967, Iaşi
Genre(s): poetry, short story, novel, memoirs, children's literature, translation
Language(s): Romanian

Born Alexandra Gavrilescu, Otilia Cazimir spent her whole life in the Moldavian city of Iaşi and wrote in close contact with the literary circle around *Viaţa românească*. She made her poetic debut in 1912 with a pen name, Otilia Cazimir, produced in joint cooperation by the famous literary critic Ibrăileanu—who coined the Cazimir part—and the acclaimed novelist Sadoveanu—who matched it with Otilia. (Both of the writers' literary godfathers belonged to the Moldavian connection.) Cazimir was contributor to *Viaţa românească, Însemnări literare, Lumea—bazar săptămînal, Adevărul literar, Bilete de papagal, Însemnări ieşene, Revista Fundaţiilor Regale, Lupta, Cuvântul liber, Adevărul*, etc. Between 1937 and 1947 she functioned as Inspector General of the Theaters in Moldavia. She received the Prize of the Romanian Academy in 1927, the French prize Femina in 1928, the National Prize for Literature in 1937, and was decorated with *Ordinul Muncii* in 1954.

Cazimir's volumes of poetry—*Lumini şi umbre* (1923; Lights and Shadows), *Cîntec de comoară* (1930; Treasure Song), *Poezii* (1939; Poems)—depict forest and field—this last with weeds, crickets, and clover—loading themselves into silent chariots and journeying obediently towards the village yards; the bones of long-forgotten bishop Gherasim mingling with the sinful flesh of a poor wandering girl buried in the same, now anonymous, grave; the ancestors' smile visiting for seconds the young lips of their offspring; quince and tobacco aromas functioning as evanescent alter egos of grandparent couples; sonorous wooden houses vibrating violin-like; in a word, the universe turning domestic. The domestic in turn perpetuates and proclaims its cosmic ties. At the same time, one senses, in volumes such as *Fluturi de noapte* (1926; Night Butterflies), or *Licurici* (1930; Fireflies), a different poetic vein, cerebral, allegorical, fable-oriented, at times reaching the humorous rhymed chronicle, the epigram, and even circumstantial political lyricism such as is to be found in the volume *Partidului de ziua lui* (1961; To the [Communist] Party, on its Anniversary).

Her prose—*Grădina cu amintiri* (1929; Garden with Memories) and *În tîrgușorul dintre vii* (1939; Town Between Vineyards), for example—brought Otilia Cazimir recognition as an unequalled master of the poetic sketch, reminding the reader of Saint-Exupery and at times of Colette in her lyrical exaltation of a miraculous and austere childhood. In a more realistic vein, the volume *Din Întuneric* (Darkness) presents the daily life of a woman physician while *Prietenii mei scriitori* (1960; My Writer Friends) and *Inscripții pe marginea anilor* (1973; Inscriptions on the Years) attest to the author's gift as a memorialist.

Cazimir's books for children—among which one can mention *Jucării* (1938; Toys), the novel *A murit Luchi* (1942; Luchi Died), *Baba Iarna intră-n sat* (1954; 1957; 1959; Old Woman Winter Enters the Village)—became classics of the genre. Many of them were translated into Russian and Hungarian.

Cazimir translated into Romanian works by Chekhov, A.I. Kuprin, V.G. Korolenko, Gorki, A. Tolstoi, C. Fedin, V. Kataev, A. Gaidar, Lev Kassil, Bubennov, Maupassant, Conan Doyle, and Giraudoux among others.

Works

Lumini și umbre [Lights aand Shadows] (1923). *Fluturi de noapte* [Night Butterflies] (1926). *Din intuneric Fapte și întîmplări adevărate. Din carnetul unei doctorese, schițe* [Darkness. Real Facts and Events. From the Notebook of a Woman Physician, Sketches] (1928). *Grădina cu amintiri și alte schițe* [Garden with Memories and Other Sketches] (1929). *Licurici, cronici fanteziste și umoristice* [Fireflies, Fanciful and Humoristic Chronicles] (1930). *Cîntec de comoară, poezii* [Treasure Song, Poems] (1930). *Jucării* [Toys] (1938). *Poezii* [Poems] (1939). *În tîrgușorul dintre vii* [Town Between Vineyards] (1939). *A murit Luchi* [Luchi Died] (1942). *Catinca și Catiușa, două fete din vecini* [Catinca and Catiușa, Two Girls from the Neighborhood] (1948). *Stăpînul lumii* [The Master of the World] (1948). *Alb și Negru* [White and Black] (1949). *Baba Iarna intră-n sat* [Old Woman Winter Enters the Village] (1954; 1957; 1959). *Întuneric. Din carnetul unei doctorese, schițe* [Darkness. From the Notebook of a Woman Physician, Sketches] (1956). *Versuri* [Poetry] (1957; 1965). *Albumul cu pose, povestiri* [The Picture Album, Stories] (1958). *Poezii* [Poems] (1959). *Prietenii mei scriitori . . .* [My Writer Friends] (1960). *Partidului de ziua lui* [To the (Communist) Party on Its Anniversary] (1961). *Poezii* [Poems] (1964). *Inscripții pe marginea anilor* [Inscriptions on the Years] (1973).

Translations: Bosquet, Alain, ed., *Anthologie de la poésie roumaine* (Paris, 1968). ("Pluie printanière"/ "Ploaie de primăvară," tr. Alain Bosquet; "Confession"/"Confesiune," tr. Robert Sabatier). *Le journal des poètes* 34, 4 (1964) ("Pluie printanière"/"Ploaie de primăvară"). Mesker, Stefan, ed., *Werk uit Roemenië. Poëzie* (Brussels: Den Haag, 1966) ("Nieuwe maan"/"Crai-nou" and "Lenteregen"/ "Ploaie de primăvară"). Neruda, Pablo, ed. and tr., *44 poetas romanos* (Buenos Aires, 1967) ("Lluvia primaveral"/"Ploaie de primăvară" and "Naturaleza muerta"/"Natură moartă"). Ritsos, Jannis, *Antologhia rumanikis piiseos* (Athens, 1961) ("Nature morte"/"Natură moartă" and "I thimonies tu sanu"/"Căpițele de fin"). Kopeczi, Bela, ed., *Román költok antologiája* (Budapest, 1961) ("Titok"/"Taina," tr. Rab Zsuzsa; "Bölcsobal"/"Cîntec de leagăn, cîntec de pace," tr. Jékely Zoltán). Vainer, Nelson, ed. and tr., *Antologia da poezia romena* (Rio de Janeiro, 1966) ("Segredo"/"Taina").

English Translations: Catanoy, Nicholas, ed., *Modern Romanian Poetry* (Oakville, Ottawa, 1977), pp. 30, 63 ("Haycarts"/"Căpițele de fin" and "The Mystery"/"Taina," tr. N. Apotheker, L. Lowenfels, and R.G. Everson). Duțescu, Dan, ed. and tr., *Romanian Poems* (Bucharest, 1982), pp. 48–49 ("The Shadow"/"Umbra"). *The Literary Review* (1964).

Bibliography

Arghezi, Tudor, "Otilia Cazimir." In *Tablete de cronicar* (Bucharest, 1960), pp. 78–80. Călinescu, George, *Istoria literaturii romăne. Compendiu* (Bucharest, 1968), 324–326. Ciopraga, C., "Otilia

Cazimir, poetă a sufletelor simple." In Otilia Cazimir, *Poezii* (Bucharest, 1964). Manolescu, Nicolae, *Poezia romănă modernă*, vol. 2 (Bucharest, 1968), pp. 255–256. Perpessicius, "Otilia Cazimir: *Grădina cu amintiri*, schiţe" and "Otilia Cazimir: *Licurici*, cronici fanteziste şi umoristice." *Menţiuni critice*, vol. 3 (Bucharest, 1936), pp. 92–96; 253–257.

Sanda Golopentia

Maria Grazia Centelli

Born 1518 or 1519, Prato (?); died May 7,
1602, Prato, Italy
Genre(s): drama
Language(s): Italian

Maria, the daughter of Lorenzo Centelli, became a Dominican nun in the convent of San Vincenzo in Prato. She took the veil in 1531, at the age of twelve or thirteen, though it is clear neither when she entered the convent nor when she professed. The Chronicle of the convent of San Vincenzo indicates that she held all of the important offices of her house and conducted them with singular intelligence and to the great satisfaction of the community. She was prioress twice from 1578 to 1580 and again from 1584 to 1586, a period of great difficulty for San Vincenzo, which strongly protested the imposition by the Council of Trent of enclosure on the nuns. She was a dramatist who wrote for her convent's theater; she has left at least one work clearly attributable to her, the *Tragedia di Eleazzaro ebreo*, a five-act play in prose. She died at the age of ca. 84 comforted by Caterina de' Ricci, a nun of her convent and future saint, famous for her sanctity and visions.

Maria Centelli wrote the *Tragedia di Eleazzaro ebreo* (The Tragedy of Eleazar the Jew) when she had achieved some seniority in the convent, perhaps when she was novice mistress since novice mistresses often wrote plays for their charges to perform for convent celebrations. Though the *Eleazzaro* is a tragedy, it follows the form of the genre of spiritual comedy, a genre which combines elements of religious theater and classical secular theater. It combines a morally edifying story, whose characters are saintly, noble, and heroic, with a humorous secondary plot of jokes and pranks by servants and peasants. The *Eleazzaro* takes its title and main plot from the second and fourth Maccabees's account of the martyrdom of the old scribe Eleazar under the persecutions of Antiochus IV (ca. 215–165 B.C.). It tells the story of the ninety-year-old Eleazar's refusal to deny his faith to avoid torture and death. He refuses to give up for one day's release from suffering the fruit of his lifetime's devotion to God. The secondary action is a parallel story in which Fenena, a seventy-eight-year-old slave woman, freed by Eleazar as he prepares for death, foolishly demands the dowry her former master has offered the young women of his household. Other servants promise her a husband, trick her, and beat her up (a typical *beffa*, or practical joke story, of the Italian *novella* tradition). Her beating parallels Eleazar's, and her story enacts by negative example the message of his sacrifice. The scribe chooses to deny himself comfort in his old age; Fenena wants just that. He sacrifices himself for what is right; she dramatizes an egotistical desire for what is inappropriate.

Despite the double tragedy of the martyrdom of Eleazar and the disappointment and beating of Fenena, much of the action, and, indeed, its most successful moments are comic. The humor is not limited to the subplot, for even in the biblical story, low characters speak a comic language of malapropisms and vulgarities. The play's humorous moments outweigh the serious ones with which they continuously alternate, never, however, undermining the spiritual message that is stated repeatedly and embodied in the double plot. The comic subplot presents not only the spiritual lesson of renunciation of the world but also directs it specifically to the female audience through its call for the renunciation of marriage when marriage is inappropriate. Indeed, the subject of marriage figures prominently in convent theater and was clearly of much interest to convent women, who were mostly daughters of the upper class destined for the religious life to preserve family patrimony.

Little is known about Sister Maria Grazia, but we can learn something about her education and her mind from the play she wrote. It, above all, reveals an unusual command of the vernacular literary language and a good sense of the comic. Long speeches and the lectures on virtue with which her play abounds were typical of the didactic literature of the time, and she had a good enough sense of her audience to temper the lesson with a large measure of comic relief. Sister Maria Grazia seems to have had some acquaintance with secular literature, judging from the reminiscences in her play of classical theater and of the Italian short story tradition; this may have been indirectly acquired through convent performances of the spiritual comedies written for the nuns by secular playwrights such as Giovan Maria Cecchi. This sort of theater flourished in the convents of Tuscany, and San Vincenzo may have been well known for its productions. The Domenican nuns of Santa Caterina da Siena in Florence in 1594 seem to have commissioned from San Vincenzo a spiritual comedy, the *Comedia di Teodosio imperadore quando che fu ripreso da S. Ambrogio e scomunicato . . .*, for performance in their convent.

Works

Tragedia di Eleazzaro ebreo, ms., Riccardiana Library, Florence, cod. ricc. 2974, n.2.

Bibliography

Anon., *Le nostre sorelle*. Archives of San Vincenzo, 168A, C. 30 (typescript collection of information from various earlier documents, many now lost. Last entry is dated 1943.) Emanuele, Angelo, *Virtù d'amore di Suor Beatrice del Sera* (Catania: F. Tropea, 1903), pp. 43–44. Razzi, Fra Stefano, *Cronache*. Archives of San Vincenzo, Ms. 22 in the necrology (c. 192r). Partial Rpt. in C.M. Di Agresti, O.P., *Santa Caterina de' Ricci cronache—diplomatica—lettere varie*. "Collana Ricciana," fonti V (Florence: Olschki, 1969), pp. 105–106. Weaver, Elissa, "Spiritual Fun: A Study of Sixteenth-Century Tuscan Convent Theater," in Mary Beth Rose, ed. *Women in the Middle Ages and Renaissance: Literary and Historical Perspectives* (Syracuse, N.Y., 1986), pp. 183–185.

Elissa B. Weaver

Laura Cereta

Born 1469, Brescia, Italy; died 1499
Genre(s): letters, oration, invective
Language(s): Latin

Cereta was born to noble parents, Veronica di Leno and Silvestro Cereta, a jurisprudent and humanist, who was often employed in the bureaucracy of Brescia. She was tutored first in a convent, then at home in the humanities by her father. From her writings we learn that she also studied mathematics and astrology and read extensively on religious subjects. At fifteen, she married the merchant Pietro Serina but was widowed after only 18 months. It seems certain that Cereta discussed philosophical questions at meetings of learned people in convents and in private homes. She died suddenly at age thirty and was buried in the church of San Domenico in Brescia.

Most of Cereta's literary output is in the form of Latin epistles, one of the genres more assiduously cultivated by fifteenth-century humanists. Written when she was between sixteen and eighteen years of age, her letters are addressed to members of her family, to prelates, and to professional people of her community. In many of them she expresses her grief for the death of her husband, who shared her interest in learning. What transpires from all of them are the values current among contemporary humanists: a love of truth, a great respect for learning as the only activity that distinguishes humanity, a driving wish to immortalize her name. Cereta does not make much of the often-debated conflict between learning and religious belief; she upholds them equally and quotes instances of people who were religious as well as erudite. Indicative of her mental attitudes is the motivation that she gives of her love for astrology as her desire to read the rational language that God has used in the workings of the spheres. Cereta had a strong sense of her own intellectual value, which she vehemently defended against detractors in a letter conceived as a traditional "invective."

Thirteen of her letters were titled and written as formal orations on a series of topical subjects: avarice, death, fate and chance, war and its causes, the Turkish menace, the advisability of marriage for men and women, the advantages of an active life, self-control and ensuing happiness. One letter gives geographical details upon a request. There is also an amusing funeral oration on the death of an ass, which is to be read as a parody of a much-practiced genre.

For the modern reader what is most striking is Cereta's defense of women and of their right to receive an education on equal footing with men. She touches on the relation between the sexes in several letters and at considerable length in the notes she addressed to Bibulus Sempronius. Very revealing are her complaints about the isolation she faced as a female scholar, about the difficulty in finding time to study, and about the envy driving men and women of her town to detract from her achievements. In the last years of her life, she was subject to considerable pressure to abandon her studies and embrace the religious life.

Works

Laurae Ceretae Brixiensis Feminae Clarissimae Epistolae jam primum e MS in lucem productae a Jacopo Philippo Thomasino, qui eius vitam et notas addidit (1640). Albert Rabil, Jr., ed., *Laura Cereta: Quattrocento Humanist* (1981), pp. 109–175. "Letter to Augustinus Aemilius, Curse Against the Ornamentation of Women." "Letter to Bibulus Sempronius, Defense of the Liberal Instruction of Women." "Letter to Lucilia Vernacula, Against Women Who Disparage Learned Women." *Her Immaculate Hand: Selected Works By and About the Women Humanists of Quattrocento Italy*, eds. Margaret L. King and Albert Rabil, Jr. (1983), pp. 77–86.

Bibliography

"Book-lined Cells. Women and Humanism in the Early Italian Renaissance," in Patricia H. Labalme, ed., *Beyond Their Sex: Learned Women of the European Past* (New York, 1980), pp. 66–90. Caccia, E., "Cultura e letteratura nei secoli XV e XVI." *Ibid.*, pp. 486, 494–496, 517. Capriolus, M. Helius. *Chronica de rebus Brixianorum* (Brescia, 1505), XIII. Cistellini, A. "La vita religiosa nei secoli XV e XVI." *Storia di Brescia* (Brescia, 1963), II, 423. Cremona, V., "L'Umanesimo bresciano." *Ibid.*, pp. 546, 564–566. King, M.L., "Thwarted Ambitions: Six Learned Women of the Italian Renaissance." *Soundings* 59 (1976): 280–304. Lenzi, Maria Ludovica, "Le prime umaniste." *Donne e Madonne: L'educazione femminile nel primo Rinascimento italiano* (Turin, 1982), pp. 189–216. Palma, M., "Laura Cereta." *Dizionario biografico degli Italiani* (Rome, 1960), pp. 729–730. Peroni, V., *Biblioteca bresciana* (Bologna, 1818), I, pp. 251–252. Rabil, A., Jr., *Laura Cereta: Quattrocento Humanist* (Binghamton, New York, 1981). Rossi, O., *Elogi istorici dei Bresciani illustri* (Brescia, 1620), pp. 196–200, 226–228. Treves, Pia Sartori, *Una umanista bresciana del secolo XV: Laura Cereta Serina* (Brescia, 1904). Tiraboschi, G., *Storia della letteratura italiana* (Milan, 1833), III, p. 169. Trochismo, Giordano, "Vita, costumi e scritti di Laura Cereta Serina, nobile Bresciana," in *Le dame bresciane per sapere, per costume e per virtù eccellenti*, Giambattista Rodella, ed., (Brescia, 1789). Zanelli, Agostino, "Laura Cereta al Vescovo Zane." *Brixia sacra*, XIV (1923): 273–278.

Rinaldina Russell

Muriel Cerf

Born 1951, Paris, France
Genre(s): novel
Language(s): French

Cerf's originality, which won her the Valéry Larbaud Prize for young authors in 1975, mainly rests with her innovative style. Cerf spent a bourgeois youth, as the only daughter of an affectionate father, part-time poet and musician, for whom she felt a boundless admiration and whose image is ubiquitous in her novels. Then followed an adolescence in the turbulent Paris of the late 1960s. Cerf received a classically oriented education: *baccalauréat* (section Philosophy) at seventeen, followed by four years of involvement with Oriental art in the Ecole du Louvre. She had been fascinated by Oriental civilizations since a documented "illumination at the Cernush Museum" (*Paris Match*, July 7, 1978), where she learned that there was only one issue: suicide or creation. She chose the latter and departed to Asia. Thus started her career as a professional writer briefly interspersed with some assignments for the French press. A biography of Cerf needs to be approached through her creative oeuvre.

Cerf's first novels, *L'Antivoyage* (1974) and *Le Diable Vert* (1975), narrate her own peregrinations in the Far East. Introducing her broad knowledge of the Oriental world, applying her infinite curiosity to people and environment, she relates her Oriental experiences in a fluid narrative where the cultural essayistic tone alternates smoothly with the personal anecdotes.

The journey continues to Brazil with *Amérindiennes* (1979). As always, the setting is richly and sensuously evoked; Cerf is seen to develop already here a self-reflexive, erudite, and ironic style with great concern for the *mot exact*.

Long journeys are not the only point of interest in Cerf's work. *Les Rois et Les Voleurs* (1975) treats her adolescence in Paris: the novel shows how action, ambition, and knowledge coalesce as Cerf, a brilliant student from a sheltered bourgeois environment, participates in gang activities in order to experience life. Colorful events and characters populate a text in which nothing is a random occurrence. *Le Lignage du Serpent* (1978) takes place in the domestic atmosphere of provincial France. Cerf describes her youth as a "bouquet of scents," naive but already replete with emotions, prim but already thirsting for all experiences.

Une Passion (1981) marks Cerf's professional commitment to the art of writing: her concern with style, erudition, and sensuous experience has never been so high. This thick novel narrates the turbulent love between a young Jewish woman writer and a Lebanese Christian. Their love story is continued in *Maria Tiefenthaler* (1982).

In *Une Pâle Beauté* (1984) the Lolita-type protagonist is in love with an elderly man. Here a doubting Cerf examines her own condition as a young woman writer, as she had done with more self-assurance in *Une Passion*.

Works

L'Antivoyage (1974). Le Diable Vert (1975). Les Rois et les Voleurs (1975). Hiéroglyphes de nos Fins Dernières (1977). Le Lignage du Serpent (1978). Les Seigneurs du Ponant (1979). Amérindiennes (1979). Une Passion (1981). Maria Tiefenthaler (1982). Une Pâle Beauté (1984). Dramma per Musica (1986). Doux Oiseaux de Galilie (1988). Street Girl (1985). La Nativité à l'étoile (1989).

Bibliography

Paris Match (June 28, 1975): 3. Paris Match (July 7, 1978): 24. Beaumarchais, J.P. de, et al., Dictionnaire des Littératures de Langue Française, I (Paris, 1984).

Muriel Aercke

Rosa Chacel

Born June 1898, Valladolid, Spain
Genre(s): novel, short story, essay, poetry, autobiography, memoirs
Language(s): Spanish

Rosa Chacel is an artistic follower of the internationally known critic-philosopher José Ortega y Gasset, and a member of the Generation of 1927. Because the latter considers artistic expression (style) and content to be equally important, psychological perceptions and interior monologue prevail over traditional novelistic plot. While the intellectual style of some writers of the Generation of 1927 lacks genuine feeling, Chacel manages to balance polished writing, an exploration of personality, and emotion.

Rosa's first serious interest was art—painting and sculpture. At the School of Fine Arts in Madrid, she met her future husband, Timoteo Pérez Rubio. When ill health forced her to abandon her artistic studies, she began frequenting the center of Madrid's literary scene, the Ateneo. There she met Ortega and Ramón Gómez de la Serna, who invited her collaboration in the leading intellectual journals of the period.

While in Italy (1921 to 1930), Chacel wrote *Estación, ida y vuelta* (Station, Round Trip), a *Küntslerroman* influenced by Joyce's *Portrait of the Artist As a Young Man* and by Proust's *Remembrance of Things Past*. Rosa's seminal work, published in 1930, later resulted in the more profound novel, *La sinrazón*. In 1936 she also published her first book of poetry, entitled *A la orilla de un pozo*.

During the Spanish Civil War (1936–1939), Chacel and her son Carlos lived in France while Timoteo helped coordinate the Republican government's efforts to protect the Prado Museum's art collection during the bombing of Madrid. After the war, the entire family lived in France and then Greece, before immigrating to Rio de Janeiro in 1940. Chacel and Carlos spent each school year in Buenos Aires and summer vacation in Rio with Timoteo.

Teresa was published in Buenos Aires in 1941 when the political situation in Spain prevented its publication there. The novel, commissioned by Ortega in 1930, explores the themes of political exile and the ostracism and alienation experienced by Teresa Mancha, a woman who dares to defy nineteenth-century mores. This fictional biography of the mistress of Spain's revolutionary Romantic poet, José Espronceda, portrays a bittersweet passion worthy of the Romantic movement. The novel was Chacel's second published in Spain, finally appearing in 1963.

Memorias de Leticia Valle (Memoirs of Leticia Valle), planned in Italy prior to 1930, was finally published in 1945. This diary presents the themes of jealousy, artistic education, and possible child molestation, from the perspective of Leticia (a precocious adolescent, trapped between childhood and adulthood).

One of Chacel's best novels, *La sinrazón* (1960), is also a confessional diary. The protagonist examines the existence and will of God as well as his own reason for being. His quest leads him beyond reason (*razón*) to *la sinrazón*, a term which literally means "without reason," while also connoting injury and injustice. The work, published in Spain in 1970, won the Critics' Prize in 1977.

During the same period, Chacel also published a collection of short stories about life in Spain, Brazil and Argentina, *Sobre el piélago* (On the High Seas). This first volume was greatly expanded, first in *Ofrenda a una virgen loca* (1961; Offering to a Crazy Virgin), and again in *Icada, nevda, diada* (1971). The latter's title is three variations on the word *nada* and the concept of nothingness. Its topics include double suicide, the exercise of one's will to overcome difficulties, self-created realities, a child's view of the world, and the artist's *Weltanschauung*.

With a Guggenheim Fellowship, Chacel spent two years in New York City, writing a book-length study of love, films, and art, *Saturnal* (1972; Saturnalia). Thereafter, Chacel visited Europe in 1961, researching the essay *La confesión* (Confession), a comparative analysis of the confessional essays of Kierkegaard, Rousseau, and St. Augustine.

1976 saw the publication of *Barrio de Maravillas* (The Maravillas Parish), winner of the prestigious Critics' Prize and the first novel in a trilogy that Chacel describes as a history of her generation of writers. *Barrio* covers the period preceding World War I. *Acrópolis* (1984) continues the story of the same female artists from 1914 to 1931, and *Ciencias naturales* (1988) explores the period of exile during and after the Spanish Civil War. Chacel's prose reaches its zenith in these two novels, combining interior monologue, omniscient narrative, Platonic dialogue, brilliant descriptions, and the narrator's philosophical/esthetic discussion.

In 1977 the widowed Chacel returned to Madrid to live. There she published her second poetry collection, two volumes of diaries, and an autobiography. Today she continues writing in several genres. Of special interest is a published collection of unfinished works, *Novelas antes de tiempo* (Novels before Their Time), in which she discusses the ideas and techniques used, presents each incomplete novel, and then explains how she will finish the work, time permitting. Time is a primary concern for this octogenarian who fears that she will not complete her many projects.

This author's basic style has not changed during her more than fifty years of writing, though it has matured and become increasingly concentrated. Rosa Chacel is one of the last surviving novelists of the Generation of 1927 and is indisputably one of its best.

Works

Novels: *Acrópolis* [The Acropolis] (1984). *Barrio de Maravillas* [The Maravillas Parish] (1976). *Estación, ida y vuelta* [Station, Round Trip] (1930). *Memorias de Leticia Valle* [Memoirs of Leticia Valle] (1945). *Novelas antes de tiempo* [Novels before Their Time] (1981). *La sinrazón* [Beyond Reason] (1960). *Teresa* (1941).

Short Story Collections: *Icada, nevda, diada* [Variations on the Theme of Nothingness] (1982). *Ofrenda a una virgen loca* [Offering to a Crazy Virgin] (1961). *Sobre el piélago* [On the High Seas] (1952).

Poetry: *A la orilla de un pozo* [Beside a Well] (1936). *Versos prohibidos* [Forbidden Verses] (1978).

Essays: *La confesión* [Confession] (1971). *Saturnal* [Saturnalia] (1972). *Los títulos* [Titles] (1981).

Autobiography and Memoirs: *Alcancía* [Potpourri] (1982). [2 vols. I: *Ida* (Departure); II: *Vuelta* (Return).] *Desde el amanecer* [Since Dawn] (1972). *Timoteo Pérez Rubio y sus retratos del jardín* [Timoteo Pérez Rubio and His Portraits of a Garden] (1980).

Bibliography

Aguirre, Francisca, "Rosa Chacel, como en su playa propia." *Cuadernos Hispanoamericanos* 296 (1975): 298–315. Albarracín Sarmiento, Carlos, "Lectura de *La sinrazón*." *Sur*, 274 (January–February 1962): 59–64. Crispin, John, "Rosa Chacel y las 'Ideas sobre la novela.'" *Insula* 262 (September 1968): 10. Joly, Monique, J. Tena, and Ignacio Soldevila-Durante, *Panorama du roman espagnol d'après-guerre (1939–1975)* (Montpellier, 1979), pp. 112–117, 175–184, 321–330. Marra-López, José R., "Rosa Chacel: La búsqueda intelectual del mundo." *Narrativa española fuera de España (1939–1961)* (Madrid, 1963). Myers, Eunice D., "*Estación, ida y vuelta*: Rosa Chacel's Apprenticeship Novel." *Hispanic Journal* 4.2 (Spring 1983): 77–84. Myers, Eunice D., "Narcissism and the Quest for Identity in Rosa Chacel's *La sinrazón*." *Perspectives on Contemporary Literature* 8 (1982): 85–90. Porlán, Alberto, *La sinrazón de Rosa Chacel*. De palabra 5 (Madrid, 1984). A collection of in-depth interviews with the author.

Eunice D. Myers

Marie de Champagne

Born 1145, France; died 1198
Literary patron
Language(s): French

Daughter of Louis VII and Aliénor d'Aquitaine, king and queen of France; Marie married Henri I le Libéral, Count of Champagne, 1164. Although she was probably never herself an author, Marie de Champagne is nonetheless a significant literary figure for her patronage of a constellation of poets, her participation in courtly love casuistry, and her role as a transmitter of literary taste.

A number of poets of the first order frequented Marie's court at Troyes and produced works inspired or commissioned by her. Chrétien de Troyes began his romance *Lancelot* at the command of Marie, whom he addresses as "my lady of Champagne" and credits with the plot and inner meaning of the work. The trouvère Gautier d'Arras also mentions Marie in his romance, *Eracle*. Book III of Andreas Capellanus' *De arte honeste amandi* records nine of Marie's celebrated verdicts on issues of love. In addition to her patronage of these authors, Marie sponsored trouvères Conon de Béthune and Gace Brulé, and such lesser-known poets as Guillaume de Garlande and Huon de Valery.

Marie's court also became an important center for the translation of Scripture into the vernacular. Sometime during the last quarter of the twelfth century, Marie commissioned a rhymed translation of Psalm 44, the Eructavit. In 1190 Evratus dedicated to Marie his compendious metrical Genesis.

Twelfth-century Champagne may rightfully be viewed as the meeting ground *par excellence* for the cultures of oc and oil. Under Marie's protection the enlightened court at Troyes rivalled even the royal court in breadth and brilliance of literary activity.

Bibliography

Benton, J.F., "The Court of Champagne as a Literary Center." *Speculum* 36 (1961): 551–591. Dyggve, H.P., *Trouvères et protecteurs de trouvères dans les cours seigneuriales de France* (1942). Lafitte-Houssat, J., *Troubadours et cours d'amour* (1950). Lejeune, R., "Le Rôle littéraire de la famille d'Aliénor d'Aquitaine." *Cahiers de civilisation médiévale* 1 (1958): 319–337. McCash, J.H.M., "Marie de Champagne and Eleanor of Aquitaine: A Relationship Reexamined." *Speculum* 54 (1979): 698–711.

Brent A. Pitts

Ernestina de Champourcín (y Morán de Loredo)

Born 1905, Vitoria, Alava, Spain
Genre(s): poetry, novel, essay
Language(s): Spanish

Chronologically, Champourcín belongs to the "Generation of 1927," which included Lorca,

Aleixandre, Alberti and many other famous poets (her late husband, the poet Juan José Domenchina, may be classed a lesser member of the same group). Champourcín shares with other members of the generation a formation under the aegis of the "Generation of 1898," and especially the poetic hegemony of Juan Ramón Jiménez, with whom she was personally acquainted (publishing her memoirs of him in 1981). In a general way, the group exhibits initial traits of European modernism, subsequently evolving through a modified surrealism, and still later in the direction of neorealism, social engagement, and existentialist concerns. These broad outlines can also be discerned in the evolution of Champourcín's work, although she herself has divided the development of her poetry into three stages: human love, divine love, and retrospection. The first stage lasted from 1926 when her first collection, *En silencio* (In Silence), appeared, until 1936, when the Spanish Civil War (1936–1939) erupted. This was also the year of Champourcín's marriage, and she was soon to accompany her husband into exile in Mexico where he died in 1959 (she remained, working as a translator, until the mid-1970s). Exile produced a rupture in Champourcín's poetic production, as well as in her vital circumstances, resulting in a sixteen-year period in which no poems appeared. When she returned to the publication of poetry, the thematic character of her poems had changed radically, becoming religious and biblical, and her form is more prosaic. The divine love period spanned from 1952 to 1974, as the poet sought inspiration in the Scriptures and characterizes herself as a seeker of light and truth in search of mystical or cosmic union with the deity. In 1974, she published her first collection after return from exile, following some six years of silence, seemingly ending her period of metaphysically inspired poetry. The works composed after return from exile exhibit certain traces of earlier periods, but are on the one hand much more immediate in their concern with such worldly problems as war and human alienation and on the other hand are more personal and biographical as the poet looks backward at life in exile, old friends, travels, loneliness, and longing.

During her first decade of publishing, Champourcín produced four poetry collections and a novel, *La casa de enfrente* (1936; The House Across the Street), which adopts the format of a diary to reconstruct the childhood and adolescence of a girl up to and including her first love affair. Significant poetry collections during this period are *Ahora* (1928; Now), reminiscent of poetic greats of the previous generation such as Antonio Machado and Juan Ramón Jiménez, and exhibiting the cult of metaphor typical of the Generation of 1927; *La voz en el viento* (1931; Voice in the Wind), in which the "human love" themes are especially noteworthy; and *Cántico inútil* (1936; Useless Canticle), her longest and most surrealist collection, although it is varied both metrically and thematically to an extent that makes it difficult to characterize. While displaying the fully developed "human love" themes, it also anticipates the early traits of the "divine love" stage to follow much later.

Presencia a oscuras (1952; Presence in Shadows) is illumined by the poet's belief that "God is in all poetry," initiating a poetry of praise and religious aspiration more fully developed in *El nombre que me diste* (1960; The Name You Gave to Me), *Cárcel de los sentidos* (1964; Prison of the Senses), *Hai-kais espirituales* (1967; Spiritual Hai-kus), *Cartas cerradas* (1968; Closed Letters), and *Poemas del Ser y del Estar* (1974; Poems of Being and Becoming—actually an untranslatable play on the two Spanish verbs "to be"). Religious themes are minimized in the poet's final works, although cosmic gropings are not entirely absent. *Primer exilio* (1978; First Exile) and *La pared transparente* (1984; The Transparent Wall) coincide in being inspired more in memory than in emotions and mystic meditations giving rise to the first and second periods, respectively. Now past eighty, Champourcín is unlikely to modify her poetic trajectory again (indeed, retrospective verse is a frequent characteristic of aged poets). However, she has begun to receive some of the recognition she was denied for decades in Spain because of her exile and may eventually be acclaimed as the most important woman poet of the Generation of 1927.

Works

Ahora (1928). *Cántico inútil* (1936). *Cárcel de los sentidos* (1964). *Cartas cerradas* (1968). *La casa de enfrente* (1936). *En Silencio* (1926). *Hai-Kais espirituales* (1967). *El nombre que me diste* (1960). *La pared transparente* (1984). *Poemas del Ser y del Estar* (1974). *Presencia a oscuras* (1952). *Primer exilio* (1978). *La voz en el viento* (1931).

Janet Perez

Mme Grégoire de Champseix

(see: André Léo)

Madeleine Chapsal

Born September 1, 1925, Paris, France
Genre(s): interview, article, literary criticism,
  filmscript, novel
Language(s): French

Madeleine Chapsal is a contemporary "femme de lettres" whose career has moved her steadily in the direction of literary creativity. Younger than the established literary and philosophical luminaries she interviews, she overcomes her awe with a refreshing irreverence at times. Her degree was in law, but she found, and founded, affinities with many of France's leading intellectuals after World War II. She published interviews with Bachelard, Bataille, de Beauvoir, Borges, Breton, Céline, Chardonne, Giono, Lacan, Leiris, Malraux, Mauriac, Merleau-Ponty, Montherlant, Paulhan, Prévert, Rostand, Sagan, Sartre, Tzara, and Vailland.

Chapsal wrote literary reviews and conducted interviews with literary and intellectual figures for *l'Express* from 1953 to 1979. She also published frequent reports on the literary scene from Paris in *The Reporter* from 1954 through 1966. Some of these articles are highly informative to the non-French reader, for they communicate a sense of the tenor of literary life via literary prizes, summaries of important new works, and echoes of the reaction of the French press to them.

Aside from her work as a literary and philosophical mediator, Madeleine Chapsal has published one volume of poetry (*Divine Passion*) and numerous novels that have been translated into many languages. Her latest at this writing, *La maison de jade*, was on the best-seller list of *l'Express* for several weeks. Both in her poetry and in her novels, her most frequent theme is the striving for recognition of women by men and the troubled dialectic of male-female relations. She is clearly a "feminist" author, but so far her concerns are with the liberation of the female personality more than with social issues. She received considerable attention on the French literary television show "Apostrophes" when she admitted that the jilted lover portrayed in *La maison de jade* was herself. (See "Madeleine Chapsal: 'Il n'y a que l'amour pour consoler l'amour,'" in *Marie-Claire*, Feb. 1987.)

It is too early to assess Madeleine Chapsal's importance as a poet or novelist. She has a wide readership but has received little attention in literary circles. Her reputation and importance are clearly established, however, in her anthologies of key interviews of French writers and philosophers. She has also produced a filmscript: "Mourir à Madrid."

Works

Vérités sur les jeunes filles (1960). *Les écrivains en personne* (1960). *Quinze écrivains: entretiens* (1963). *Mourir à Madrid* (1963). *Révolution d'octobre . . .* (1967). *Les professeurs pour quoi faire?* (1970). *Un anniversaire chez les dragons* (1973). *Un été sans histoire* (1973). *Je m'amuse et je t'aime* (1974). *Une promenade au coeur des choses* (1974). *La fête sauvage* (1976). *Grands cris dans la nuit du couple* (1976). *Le dialogue sexuel* (1976). *Le compte-bêtes* (1977). *La Jalousie: Jeanne Moreau, Nadine Trintignant, Régine Deforges, Sonia Rykiel, Pauline Réage, Michèle Montrelay: Entretiens* (1977). *Une femme en exil* (1978). *La passagère de l'Exodus* (1978). *Un homme infidèle* (1980). *Divine passion* (1981). *Envoyez la petite musique . . .* (1984). *Rykiel* (1985). *Un flingue sous les roses: pièces de théâtre* (1985). *La maison de jade* (1986).

Translations into English: *A Lion in the Garden* (1955). Articles published in *The Reporter:* "French

Writing, 1954: The Tired Young Men" (May 11, 1954). "A Prize-Winning Novel by Simone de Beauvoir" (Jan. 27, 1955). "Paris Report on a Charming Monster" (Feb. 24, 1955). "A Lion in the Garden" (Nov. 3, 1955). "Jean Cocteau Joins the Immortals" (Nov. 15, 1955). "The Goncourt Prize Winner: How People Become French" (Jan. 26, 1956). "Françoise Sagan Wins Her Second Round" (May 17, 1956). "A Statue Come to Life" (June 14, 1956). "Il Reste Toujours La Bicyclette" (Feb. 21, 1957). "Mais Ce N'est Plus La France" (Oct. 17, 1957). "A Communist Writer Indifferent to Politics" (Nov. 13, 1958). "Forgetting and Remembering" (Aug. 20, 1959). "Sins Out of Context" (Nov. 12, 1959). "A Union Without Issue" (Sept. 29, 1960). "Two Flags by the Sea" (Feb. 2, 1961). "The Prison of Jean Giono" (July 4, 1963). "Grieving, Going On" (Oct. 8, 1964). "Who Is Robbe-Grillet?" (July 14, 1966).

Translations into German: *Das Fest der wilden Tiere* [La fête sauvage].

Translations into Japanese: *Shitto* [La Jalousie]. *Fūfu no yoru no ōkina sakebi* [Grands cris dans la nuit du couple].

Michael B. Smith

Julie-Françoise Bouchaud des Hérettes Charles

(a.k.a. Elvire)

Born July 4, 1784, Paris, France; died December 18, 1817, Paris
Genre(s): correspondence
Language(s): French

Julie Charles was born in Paris, her father a merchant from Nantes, her mother a Creole from Santo Domingo. She was taken as an infant to Santo Domingo but was forced to flee the unrest accompanying the slaves' rebellion there, returning to France sometime in late 1792. For the next eight years it appears that the conditions in which she lived were very poor and that she contracted tuberculosis. Her mother's brother, who had some ties to the Revolution, arranged her marriage to Jacques-Alexandre-César Charles, a celebrated physicist, in 1804. She was barely twenty; he was fifty-eight. Her husband's posi-

tion permitted Julie Charles to maintain a salon where she received scholars, writers, and politicians. While taking the waters at Aix-les-Bains during late summer 1816, she met the poet Lamartine, six years her junior. Scholars have speculated intensely on the exact nature of their relationship. Whether they were lovers is, however, trivial. Lamartine transformed the ailing woman into an idol. As P.E. Charvet noted, "Whether Julie Charles was anything like the sentimentalized portrait Lamartine painted of her many years later is irrelevant. By fading early she quickly became the ethereal Elvire, that pathetic phantom hovering over the poems, the ideal image of woman for a whole generation: the pallid, faintly anemic and thereby interesting type who suffered from the vapours, went into a decline and aroused men's protective solicitude." Upon returning to Paris from Aix she maintained an extensive, daily correspondence with Lamartine, who for many years kept her letters bound in a volume before finally destroying them. Four of these letters, however, survive and are of value primarily to students of Lamartine. Anatole France, who himself contributed to the cult around "Elvire," also published a number of her letters to other correspondents. The letters to Lamartine are highly charged and rhetorical. The other letters seem comparatively prosaic.

Works
Doumic, René, "Les lettres d'Elvire à Lamartine." *Revue des Deux-Mondes* 75. année; 5ᵉ période, vol. 25 (1905): 574–602; reprinted as a separate volume (1905, 1906). France, Anatole, "L'Elvire de Lamartine." *Oeuvres complètes* 24 (1934): 247–324.

Bibliography
Charvet, P.E. *The Nineteenth Century, 1789–1870* (A Literary History of France, IV) (London, 1967), p. 93. Leguay, P. "Charles, Julie-Françoise Bouchaud des Hérettes, Mme." *Dictionnaire de biographie française* 8 (Paris, 1959), col. 581–582.

Earl Jeffrey Richards

Belle de Charrière

(a.k.a. Isabella van Tuyll van
  Serooskerken)

*Born 1740, Zuylen, Holland; died 1805,
  Neufchâtel, Switzerland*
Genre(s): novel, essay, comedy
Language(s): Dutch

Born in her family's château near Utrecht, her life was divided almost equally between Holland and Switzerland, the home of her husband, Charles-Emmanuel de Charrière, an estimable but uninteresting aristocrat whom she insisted on marrying in 1771. Too intelligent and lively herself for a conventional life, she directed her energies toward trying to escape its limitations by intellectual means. In her early years this involved travels and friendships, notably with James Boswell, who was for a short period her suitor, and especially a long, clandestine correspondence with the Baron Constant de Rebecque, seigneur d'Hermenches, a Swiss army officer whom she met in 1760. This correspondence, which lasted until 1775, offers important insight to her personality.

To the second part of her life belong most of her writings, especially her novels—*Lettres neuchâteloises* (1784), *Mistress Henley* (1784), *Lettres écrites de Lausanne* (1785), with its sequel *Calistes* (1787), and *Trois femmes* (1797)— some of which are partially autobiographical in their reflections of the boredom of an unsatisfactory marriage. The French Revolution and the influx of French émigrés to Switzerland inspired the *Lettres trouvées dans des portes-feuilles d'émigrés* (1793) and two comedies, *L'Emigré* and *L'Inconsolable* (1794).

Between 1786 and 1794 her life was enlivened by an intimate friendship with the budding writer Benjamin Constant, the nephew of her earlier friend, Constant d'Hermanches. She undoubtedly exercised an important influence on his early literary career, although his devotion was eventually transferred to Madame de Staël. These two women could not have represented more clearly the difference between eighteenth-century rationalism and the onset of nineteenth-century romanticism in their ideas and outlook.

Belle de Charrière's final years were lonely, in spite of contacts with several young friends. The new literature that was now appearing had little to say to her, and her essentially cosmopolitan spirit prevented her from ever feeling entirely at home in the Swiss countryside. It is her reflections on her life, rather than that life itself, which give interest to her writings.

Bibliography

Farnum, Dorothy, *The Dutch Divinity; a Biography of Madame de Charrière, 1740–1805* (London, 1959). Godet, Philippe, *Madame de Charrière et ses amis* (Geneva, 1906). Winiker, Rolf, *Madame de Charrière: Essai d'un itinéraire spirituel* (Lausanne, 1970).

Charity Cannon Willard

Gabrielle-Emilie le Tonnilier de Breteuil Châtelet-Lomont

Born 1706, Paris, France; died 1749, Luneville
*Genre(s): letters, poetry, philosophical and
  scientific treatises*
Language(s): French

This extraordinarily gifted intellectual spanned the disciplines, performing experiments in physics, chemistry, and math; writing poetry; and translating Virgil, Ovid, and Horace into fluid French. In 1735, she wrote an essay on Newton's discoveries on optics and later translated and analyzed his *Principia Mathematica*, thus furthering the revival of French science. Her works reflect the influence of Gottfried Leibniz's epistemology. Regarded as one of the great beauties of the early eighteenth century, she possessed remarkable determination, energy, and influence in the aristocratic and intellectual circles of France.

Madame du Châtelet, the youngest of four children, was her father's indulged favorite, and thus developed exorbitantly expensive tastes. The five-foot-nine-inch beauty towered over most of her lovers, including Richelieu and Voltaire. As an ungainly youth, she desperately sought affection, finding it with hard study from her tutors. Her excellence in gymnastics, fencing, and riding derived from talent and diligence. Luck, a head for mathematics, and an instinct for cards brought her money, which she rapidly spent. But it was the works of Descartes, Newton, Locke, Pope, and Leibniz that excited her fertile intellect.

In 1725, Madame du Châtelet wed the Marquis Florent-Claude du Châtelet-Lomont, a heavyset man with florid face, loud voice, and a love of food and drink. Ten years her senior, he allowed her freedom from interference in her life and demanded the same. Edwards notes that "the story to the effect that the bride halted the ceremony in order to correct the clergyman's pronunciation of a Latin phrase may be apocryphal." She spent three months completely and lavishly refurbishing her groom's town house behind the Louvre. During this period she became pregnant with Gabrielle-Pauline, who inherited both her mother's good looks and her intellect. The following year, son and heir Florent-Louis-Marie was born; the son took after his military father. Seven years later, Victor-Esprit was born but did not survive infancy.

Madame du Châtelet lived the typical aristocratic life, awakening at mid-morning to breakfast in bed, spending several hours preparing for afternoon guests and philosophical conversation (when she was pregnant, she received guests from her bed) but also reading far into the night. Requiring only two to four hours sleep, she absorbed volumes—in the original Greek and Latin, modern French, German, English, and Spanish—during the wee hours. Also, like other aristocrats, she accepted her husband's open affairs and engaged in her own. Du Guebriant and the Comte de Vincennes, the one physically dashing and the other intellectually stimulating, and Duke de Richelieu, a lifelong friend, preceded the love of her life, François Arouet, or Voltaire. This genius was in intellectual matters her equal and her spur. The intensity of their minds matched that of their passion. Together they flouted custom, appearing together at inns and operas and even before King Louis.

The Marquis de Châtelet's chateau at Cirey was a high, rambling structure in the deep woodlands at the eastern edge of Champagne not far from Holland. The building was badly in need of repair. Madame du Châtelet, providing the direction, and Voltaire, providing the funds, lavishly refurnished it as their hideaway. This proved a safe retreat for the provocative Voltaire, whose political writings kept him in permanent danger. Working with the intense fury of the compulsive, Voltaire accomplished miracles in three months. Here the two cultivated all the arts and wrote prodigiously, organizing meals and meetings around their writing schedules. Occasionally Madame du Châtelet's husband Florent-Claude would visit, with or without his current mistress, and all remained extremely civil, if interested in dissimilar matters. Life at Cirey seemed ideal and solved many problems—it offered work space, co-habitation, and safety. Additionally, she was able to keep Voltaire cut off from Paris life and the charms of other attractive women.

Social life continued apace as well, although Madame du Châtelet was not comfortable when Voltaire was invited to the homosexual court of Crown Prince Frederick of Prussia. This storm she weathered, and for a while, that of Voltaire's niece, Madame Denis, who wheedled great sums of money from her devoted uncle. Others attended the couple at Cirey for long or short visits, always keeping the occupants' lives stimulated. Meanwhile, Madame du Châtelet's growing reputation spread across the continent as her brilliant books were reviewed with awe. Voltaire's controversial dramas continued to get him in trouble, sometimes leading to seclusion.

Sometime between 1745 and 1747 Voltaire began an affair with his niece, the widowed Madame Denis, unbeknownst to Madame du Châtelet. The stress of his double life led to irascibility and dyspepsia, and to Madame du Châtelet's further neglect. Voltaire's waning interest brought her sorrow, despite her calm acceptance of the situation. Finally she turned to the handsome and vigorous thirty-two-year-old Saint-Lambert, a passionate man who helped her forget her humiliation. By him, the forty-three-year-old Madame du Châtelet became pregnant, and in 1749, soon after childbirth, she died, presumably of a heart ailment. Voltaire mourned greatly, writing "I have not lost merely a mistress, I have lost the half of myself—a soul for which mine was made, a friend whom I saw born. The most tender father does not love his only daughter more truly" (Edwards, 268).

The contributions left by Madame du Châtelet are so extensive and diverse that they mark her as a greatly influential intellectual, known and respected by the scholars of her day. Her great energy, zeal, and devotion to knowledge are unsurpassed, and her legacy is one to be emulated.

Works

Aeneid, tr. in *Les Lettres de la Marquise du Châtelet*. Theodore Bestermann, ed. (Geneva, 1958). *Dissertation sur la nature et la propagation du feu* (1744). *Doutes sur les religions reculées adresses a Voltaire* (1792). *Institutions de Physique* (1740). *Traduction des principes mathematiques de la philosophie naturelle de Newton* (1759). *Traité Sur le Bonheur* (1744).

Bibliography

Asse, Eugene, *Lettres de la Marquise du Châtelet* (Paris, 1806). Bestermann, Theodore, *Studies on Voltaire and the Eighteenth Century*. 2 vols. (London, 1956). Desnoiresterres, M., *Voltaire et la société française* (Paris, 1867). Fervale, Claude, *Madame du Chatelet: Une Maitresse de Voltaire* (Paris, 1918). Hamel, Frank, *An Eighteenth Century Marquise* (New York, 1911). Longchamp, *Memoires sur Voltaire* (Paris, 1826). Mitford, Nancy. *Voltaire in Love* (New York, 1958). Stern, Jean. *Voltaire et sa nièce Madame Denis* (Paris, 1957). Vaillot, Rene. *Madame du Chatelet* (Paris, 1978). Voltaire. *Correspondence*. 11 vols. (Paris, 1881–1897).

Jean E. Jost

Françoise-Madeleine de Chaugy

Born 1611, Cuzy, France; died September 7, 1680, Turin, Italy
Genre(s): history
Language(s): French

A nun of the Visitation order, Chaugy composed a number of works chronicling the early history of that order, and, most particularly, the lives and spirituality of its two founders, St. Jeanne-Françoise de Chantal and St. François de Sales.

Born with the given name Jacqueline to a family of the minor nobility in the Nivernais, Chaugy was largely raised by her aunt, Françoise de Toulonjon, who was the daughter of Jeanne-Françoise de Chantal. Chaugy received a remarkable education for a woman in early seventeenth-century France. In 1628 she entered the Visitation order at its motherhouse in Annecy, taking the name Françoise-Madeleine in religion. Mother Chantal was still abbess in that convent and soon employed her young grand-niece as private secretary, a role in which Chaugy served until the saint's death in 1641. Afterwards Chaugy took upon herself the role of the order's historian out of her strong personal devotion to the spiritual teachings of both its founders, teachings which she desired to propagate. Her writings brought her increased influence both within and without her cloister and led to confrontations with Bishop d'Arenthon d'Alex of Annecy-Geneva. After exile from her own convent, she became the superior of Visitation houses in Montferrand, Crest, Carpentras, and Turin, where she died.

Chaugy was not an extremely original writer. Her works were largely either compilations of the writings and teachings of her two saintly heroes or simple descriptive annals. She was, however, an eminently successful propagandist for and disseminator of the spiritual teachings of both her subjects, who understood the importance of making such works available for the literate public, both religious and lay. A number of her works were explicitly designed to provide liturgical and contemplative readings for the members of her order, as well as for the interested laity. They are valuable both for the information they contain about the early history of the Visitation order and as a record of how spiritual direction functioned in the early seventeenth century. Chaugy was also unusual as a woman who took responsibility for telling the story of a community of religious women, rather than leaving that task for the community's male confessors.

Works

L'histoire des fondations de l'Ordre de la Visitation Sainte-Marie (1637–1638). *Mémoires sur la vie et les vertus de Jeanne-Françoise Frémyot de Chantal* (1642). *Abrégé de la vie du Bienheureux François de Sales, evesque et prince de Genève* (1645–1646).

Statuts, office et litanie pour la Confrérie de Saint François de Sales (1673). *Méditations tirées des offices de l'Eglise et des écrits de saint François de Sales, evesque et prince de Genève, instituteur des religieuses de la Vistitations Sainte-Marie*, 3 vols. (1676). *L'Année Sainte de la Visitations Sainte-Marie* (1689). *Lettres de la vénérable mère Françoise-Madeleine de Chaugy* (1838).

Bibliography

Lecouturier, E., *Françoise-Madeleine de Chaugy et la tradition salèsienne au XVIIe siècle*, 2 vols. (1933). Sermand, J.-F., *La vie de la Mère Françoise-Madeleine de Chaugy, religieuse de la Visitation Sainte-Marie D'Annecy, secrétaire de sainte Chantal, rédigée d'après les Mémoires manuscrits conservés dans diverses maisons de cet Institut* (1839). General references: *Dictionnaire de Spiritualité*, II, 811–813.

Thomas Head

Charlotte Saumaise de Chazan, Comtesse de Brégy

Born 1619, Paris, France; died April 13, 1693, Paris
Genre(s): letters, portraits, poetry
Language(s): French

Charlotte Saumaise de Chazan was a lady-in-waiting of the Queen of France, Anne d'Autriche, wife of Louis XIII. She married the Comte de Brégy when she was still very young. Because of her influence at the court, her husband obtained several important positions, as ambassador to the courts of Poland, Sweden, and the Netherlands. Many men claimed to be in love with her, but Charlotte seemed to have been a faithful wife. She lamented the fact that her husband gave her four children and asked for a separation. Her fight with her husband, who eventually disowned his legitimate children for the profit of his illegitimate one, exemplifies the *précieuses* protests. Charlotte was against the institution of marriage by principle, and she refused to consider motherhood a duty.

Charlotte was in good terms with Christina of Sweden and wrote a portrait of her in 1658 as well as many poems.

Works

La réflexion de la lune sur les hommes [The Thoughts of the Moon About Men] (1654). *Les lettres et poésies de Mme la comtesse de B.* (1666). "Portraits," in Barthélemy, Edouard de, *La galerie des portraits de Mlle de Montpensier.*

Bibliography

Mongrédien, Georges, "La Comtesse de Brégy." *Revue de France* (1929). Tallémant des Réaux, *Historiettes* (Paris, 1970).

Marie France Hilgar

Andrée Chedid

Born 1920, Cairo, Egypt
Genre(s): novel, poetry, drama, essay, short story
Language(s): French

Andrée Chedid is of Egypto-Lebanese origin and was educated at a number of boarding schools in Cairo and in Paris. She maintained a loving relationship with her parents, who had separated when she was very young. She had very little family life. She received her BA from the American University in Cairo and married Louis Chedid, a medical student, when she was twenty-one. In 1946 they moved to Paris where Louis earned his medical degree.

Chedid's Egyptian childhood, the emotional bond established with the land itself and its many tones, images and faces, played an important role in her formation as a writer. Her writings are most often situated in Egypt but with an exceptional awareness of Europe pulsing through them as well. She lingers over the differences in these cultures and their people, often with a nostalgia and timeless effect. Concerned with the past and with modernity, her writings reflect a personal quest that seeks not only within the self but outside of it as well, peering into the environment and its forces.

Chedid is a prolific writer with a list of works that includes novels, poems, numerous successfully produced plays, essays on Lebanon, war, poetics, and others. In 1976 she received the Louise Labé prize for poetry and in 1979 the Goncourt prize for the short story.

Works

Novels: *Le Sommeil délivré* (1952). *Jonathan* (1955). *Le Sixième jour* (1960). *Le Survivant* (1963). *L'Autre* (1969). *La Cité fertile* (1972). *Nefertiti et le rêve d'Akhnaton* (1974). *Les Marches de sable* (1981).

Poetry: *Textes pour une figure* (1949). *Textes pour un poème* (1950). *Textes pour le vivant* (1953). *Textes pour le terre aimée* (1955). *Terre et poésie* (1956). *Terre regardée* (1960). *Double-pays* (1965). *Contre-chant* (1969). *Visage premier* (1972). *Fêtes et lubies* (1973). *Prendre corps* (1973). *Fraternité de la parole* (1975). *Cérémonial de la violence* (1976). *Le coeur et le temps* (1977). *Cavernes et soleils* (1979).

Short Stories: *Les Corps et le Temps suivi de l'Etroite Peau* (1979).

Plays: *Théâtre I* (1981).

Essays: *Le Liban* (1974). *Guy Levis-Mano* (1974).

Richard J. Pioli

Wilhelmine von Chézy

Born January 26, 1783, Berlin, Germany; died January 28, 1856, Geneva, Switzerland
Genre(s): novel, poetry, essay, drama
Language(s): German

Helmina von Chézy was the granddaughter of the well-known German folk-poetess Anna Luisa Karsch and showed an early talent for writing. At age fourteen she wrote a novel (later destroyed), and after her move to Paris (1801) she wrote numerous poems, essays, and articles of a belletristic, political, and cultural nature for European journals. Both of her marriages were failures. In 1800 she divorced Baron Hastfer, whom she had married the year before. Friedrich Schlegel acquainted her with the French Orientalist A.L. de Chézy, whom she married in 1805 and from whom she took "indeterminate leave" with her two sons in 1810. One of these sons later wrote a harshly critical characterization of his mother in his autobiography (1863).

Helmina von Chézy was an immensely productive writer and was socially and politically active. Her fervor frequently caused her difficulties with authorities, but she usually found friends in high places who assisted her cause. Despite a dedicatory sonnet to him, Napoleon confiscated her book *Life and Art in Paris* (1805–1807); E.T.A. Hoffmann effected her vindication in a libel suit brought against her by the "Invaliden-Prüfungs-Commission" in Berlin—a result of her charitable work in the hospitals of Belgium and the lower Rhine valley that she had carried out on orders of King Frederick William; Archduke Johann settled a similar brush with Austrian authorities for her in the aftermath of her charitable work in Hallstadt (1826).

Among Chézy's work there are some poems of exquisite beauty that deserve inclusion in anthologies and literary histories. Even her dedicatory poems often show a freshness, subtlety, and sensitivity in the choice of metaphor coupled with a purity and simplicity of form that is both startling and moving. Examples are the poems to her grandmother ("Anna Louisa Karschin") and to her friend ("In das Stammbuch der Fräulein Therese von Winkel"). The latter captures in the rose-metaphor a technique that made Rilke famous a century later. Her poem "Snow Flowers" skillfully compares the falling snow crystals with the shower of blossoms in spring time as manifestations of divine and never-ending love. This poem ranks among the best of the Romantic era.

Chézy maintained contact with many contemporaries of note. Among them were Mme de Genlis, Jean Paul, F. Creuzer, Achim von Arnim, the brothers Boisserée and Schlegel, A. v. Chamisso, and E.T.A. Hoffmann. She wrote the libretto to Carl Maria von Weber's opera *Euryanthe*, and her play "Emma and Eginhard" was staged with music by Hettersdorf. Many of her poems, too, were set to music by contemporary composers like Josef Dessauer, and others. Her portrait was painted by well-known artists such as Vogel von Vogelstein, Flor, and Hensel. She traveled widely and lived in Paris (1801 ff.), Heidelberg (1810 ff.), Berlin, Dresden (1817 ff.), Vienna (1823 ff.), Munich (1830 ff.), and Geneva. Numerous essays and poems by her appeared in important contemporary journals, almanacs, and yearbooks such as the *Freimüthige* and Gubitz' *Gesellschafter*. Gravely ill and almost blind she dictated her memoirs (*Unvergessenes*) to her grand-niece who had come to nurse her in Geneva, where Chézy died on January 28, 1856.

Works

Selection: *Geschichte der schönen und tugendsamen Euryanthe* (1804). *Leben und Kunst in Paris*, 2 vols. (1805–1807). *Gedichte der Enkelin der Karschin*, 2 vols. (1812). *Blumen in Lorberen von Deutschlands Rettern gewunden* (1813). *Die Silberlocke im Briefe* (play, 1815). *Gemälde von Heidelberg* (1816). *Taschenbuch für Reisende und Einheimische in Heidelberg* (1816). *Emma. Eine Geschichte* (1817). *Neue Auserlesene Schriften der Enkelin der Karschin* (1817). *Blumen der Liebe* (1818). *Erzählungen und Novellen*, 2 vols. (1822). *Euryanthe von Savoyen* (1823). *Stundenblumen*, 3 vols. (1824 ff.). *Der Wunderquell. Eine dramatische Kleinigkeit* (1824). *Jugendgeschichte, Leben und Ansichten eines papiernen Kragens* (1829). *Herzenstöne auf Pilgerwegen* (1833). *Norika. Neues und ausführliches Handbuch für Alpenwanderer und Reisende durch das Hochland und Österreich* (1833). *Unvergessenes*, 2 vols. (1858).

Editorial work: *Französische Miscellen* (1803–1807). *Leben und romantische Dichtungen der Tochter der Karschin* (1805; works of Chézy's mother, Caroline v. Klencke). *Aurikeln* (1818; with autobiography). *Altschottische Romanzen* (1818). *Iduna. Schriften deutscher Frauen gewidmet den Frauen* (1820).

Bibliography

Chézy, W., *Erinnerungen aus meinem Leben*, 4 vols. (Schaffhausen, 1863 ff.; vols. I and II about his mother). Götze, A., "Frau v. Staël, Chamisso und H.v.C.," *Arch.* 189 (1952–1953). Holland, H., "H.v.C." *Allgemeine Deutsche Biographie* 4 (1876): 119–120. Hosäus, W., "H.v.C." *Mitteilungen des Vereins für anhalt. Geschichte* (1890). Hupfeld, D.R., "Schriftstellernde Frauen vor 150 Jahren." *Roperto-Carola* 15 (1933). Kastinger Riley, H.M., *Achim von Arnim* (Reinbek, 1979) (on Arnim and Chézy, passim.). Martini, F., "H.v.C." *Neue Deutsche Biographie* (1957). Meyer-Lüdtke, I., *H.v.Cs Stellung in der Pseudoromantik*. Diss., Berlin, 1944. Müller, H.v., *E.T.A. Hoffmann und Jean Paul, M. Dörffer und C. Richter, H.v.C. und Adelheid v. Bassewitz. Ihre Beziehungen zueinander und zu gemeinsamen Bekannten* (1927). Petersen, J., and Rogge, H., "A.v. Chamisso und H.v.C. Bruchstücke ihres Briefwechsels." *Mitteilungen aus dem Literatur-Archiv in Berlin* 19 (1923). Reitz, E., *H.v.C.* Diss., Frankfurt, 1923. Riedel, K., *Karl Krauses Spuren im schöngeistigen Schrifttum von F.G. Wetzel, H.v. Kleist, Jean Paul, Goethe, H.v.C., u.a.* (1941).

Helene M. Kastinger Riley

Claudine Chonez

Born 1917, Paris, France
Genre(s): poetry, essay, novel, short story
Language(s): French

Claudine Chonez's first book, *Morsure de l'ange* (Bite of the Angel), appeared in 1935. Since then she has published nine collections of poetry, five translations, four critical essays, and five novels. She studied literature at the Sorbonne and sculpture at the Ecole Nationale Supérieure des Beaux-Arts. She was a foreign news journalist for many years until 1946. Since then she has worked regularly for French Radio and Television, having until 1968 her own radio literary series. She has written for many literary and art publications, has lectured widely, and is a reader with Albin Michel.

Among her earlier collections of poetry, *La Mise au monde* (The Birthing), published in 1969, stands out as a mature exploration of the difficulties and the challenge of reconciliation. It focuses upon the paradoxes of arrival and separation, birth and self-consumption, death and other space, love's problematics and simplicity.

La Mise au monde followed a period of both intensely creative novelistic activity and earlier critical and poetic production (with books on Claudel, Fargue, and Giono) and was followed in the 1970s by *La Mise à nu* (1973; The Laying Bare), *George Sand* (1975), and *Les Yeux d'amandes amères* (1977; Bitter Almond Eyes). Her work intimates a strange ultimate equivalence of all polarities and suggests furthermore that the only real contacts ever made are made by the soul.

Annulation des navires (1984; Annulment of Ships) is Claudine Chonez's latest book and the only one she has published since *Les Yeux d'amandes amères*. Once more the principle of love guides the collection, an embattled, dialectical principle *à la Char* though it be. And, as one might expect, there are no neatly arranged arguments, no elegantly articulated patterns of debate. "I am not," she states, "a structured discourse/ at most speech with hiccupping." Her task, recognizing deep ignorance as to our origins, our ultimate logic, and purpose, is to cultivate a deeper sense of our ephemeralness and essential, joyous "nothingness," whilst avoiding the traps of sterility, (self-)breakage, and gratuitousness. Her task is to open herself to all others, things and persons, avoiding all betrayal of their ceaseless gift to us; to laugh and smile "before the orgiastic thunderbolt."

Works

Poetry: *Morsure de l'ange* (1935). *A force de naître* (1937). *Il est temps* (1938). *Demain la joie* (1947). *Levée d'écrou* (1952). *Les Portes bougent* (1957). *Poèmes choisis* (1959). *La Mise au monde* (1969). *Les Yeux d'amandes amères* (1977). *Annulation des navires* (1984).

Novels: *Les Amants couronnés* (1958). *Les Maillons de la chaîne* (1962). *L'Ascenseur* (1963). *Ils furent rois tout un matin* (1967).

Essays: *La Mise à nu* (1973). *Introduction à Paul Claudel* (1946). *Léon-Paul Fargue* (1948). *Jean Giono* (1954). *George Sand* (1975).

Bibliography

Albérès, R.-M. "Fuir, là-bas fuir. . . ." *Nouvelles littéraires* 2079 (July 1967), 5. Albérès, R.-M. *Le Roman d'aujourd'hui 1960–1970* (Paris, 1970). Boisdeffre, Pierre de, *Histoire de la littérature française* (Paris, 1985), pp. 234–238. Brindeau, Serge, *La Poésie contemporaine de langue française depuis 194* (Paris, 1973), pp. 30, 861. Carité, Maurice, "D'un amour à l'autre." *Annales* 248 (June 1971): 52–56. Chapelan, Maurice, "Une folie préméditée avec sagesse." *Figaro Littéraire* 1306 (May 1971): II. Duranteau, Josane, "Un roman de CC: *Ils furent rois tout un matin.*" *Monde des livres* 7020 (August 1967), II. Gros, Léon-Gabriel, "Deux poètes et leurs critiques." *Cahiers du Sud* 300 (1950): 304–311. Guibert, Armand, "Poètes et poésies." *Two Cities* 6 (été 1961): 81–84. Kanters, Robert, "Schéhérazade et quelques autres." *Figaro Littéraire* 842 (June 1962): 2. Moulin, Jeanine, *Huit siècles de poésie féminine* (Paris, 1963). Ormesson, Jean d', "Travaux de dames." *Nouvelles littéraires* 2284 (July 1971): 6. Rousselot, Jean, *Poètes français d'aujourd'hui* (Paris, 1965), p. 291. Saint-Exupéry, Antoine de, *Carnets* (1972). Thérive, André, "CC: *L'Ascenseur.*" *Revue des Deux Mondes* 3 (February 1964): 443–444. Wurmser, André, "Amours de toutes les couleurs." *Lettres françaises* 1386 (May 1971): 7. Wurmser, André, "De l'amourette au grand amour." *Lettres françaises* 1194 (August 1967): II.

Michael Bishop

Victorine Choquet

(see: Louise Ackermann)

Sofia Chrisoscoleu

(see: Sofia Cocea)

Lena Christ

Born October 30, 1881, near Munich, Germany; died June 30, 1920, Munich
Genre(s): novel, short story
Language(s): German

Lena Christ was born the illegitimate child of a Bavarian sharecropper's daughter. She never knew her father and spent her first seven years with her grandparents in the country. Lena then joined her mother who was managing a restaurant near Munich university, whose owner she had married. After the birth of her stepbrothers, Lena felt seriously estranged from her mother. At age seventeen, she temporarily escaped into a convent and, four years later, into a bad marriage with an accountant. Caring in dire poverty for three children after having been abandoned, Lena Christ contracted a near-fatal illness, and her children were taken away from her. After regaining her health, she began working as a secretary of the writer Peter Jerusalem, who later published under the name Benedix. He motivated her to write the story of her life, which she was to do in *Erinnerungen einer Uberflüssigen*, her magnum opus. Christ married Benedix in 1912.

Lena Christ's entire oeuvre deals in a lively and partly bitter, partly humorous way with the social and economic changes taking place in Bavaria at the turn of the century, and especially with the problems of country people migrating to Munich. Basing herself largely on autobiographical material, Lena Christ avoids both extremes of idealizing and banalizing her characters, in a fashion that, before her, only Ludwig Thoma was able to master. Her success was appreciated by critics such as Werner Mahrholz—who compared her to nineteenth-century Droste—and Josef Hofmiller. Shortly before her collected short stories, *Die Bauern*, appeared in print, she separated from Benedix. Trying to alleviate her economic misfortune, she forged paintings and was caught. Out of shame, she committed suicide when she was barely thirty-nine years old.

Works

Erinnerungen einer Uberflüssigen (1912). Lausdirndlgeschichten (1913). Mathias Bichler (1914). Unsere Bayern anno 14 (1914). Unsere Bayern anno 14/15 (1915). Die Rumpelhanni (1916). Madam Bäurin (1919). Die Bauern (1919). Werke (1970 and 1981) (Contains al, 3, 6, 7, 8 above).

Bibliography

Goepfert, G. *Das Schicksal der Lena Christ* (Munich, 1971).

Ute Marie Saine

Inger Christensen

Born January 6, 1935, Vejle, Denmark
Genre(s): poetry, novel, drama, translation
Language(s): Danish

Christensen is considered by some to be the most important writer of the sixties generation in Denmark. She has been called a modernist although her treatment of such topics as self, language, writing, and the word, plus her use of strictly structured systems to expose the artificiality of all systems, are characteristics of postmodernism.

Christensen was trained as a teacher at the Århus Seminarium, where she took her teacher's examination in 1958. While still a student, she began to publish her first poems in the magazine *Hvedekorn*, and under the influence of Poul Borum, to whom she was married from 1959 to 1976, became interested in modernist philosophies and methods, which she found congenial to her own talent. Her first book was *Lys* (Light),

a collection of poems published in 1962, shortly followed by *Græs* (Grass) the following year. A three-year Arts Foundation Grant gave her the opportunity to finish *Det* (It), her masterwork, in 1969. She has received numerous other Danish prizes, including the Kjeld Abell prize in 1978 and the Søren Gyldendal prize in 1983. In 1978 she became a member of the Danish Academy. She resides in Copenhagen.

Christensen's major theme is the relationship between the self and the world, encompassing nature, other people, and language. A rigorously intellectual writer strongly influenced by contemporary European currents, especially structuralism, she once said in an interview, "The structure of a work of art is not generally seen as a kind of philosophy. But I think about it as such, and have done so since my first poetry collection." This was *Lys* (1962; Light), which is structured around the progression of the seasons as the I-narrator, who is, in the first poem, located in a desolate, snow-driven landscape, and goes from winter to summer and comes out of the darkness into the light. If the title of this collection reflects its visionary, abstract character, the title of the next one, *Græs* (1963; Grass), reflects a concern with more earthly things. The most important section of this book is "Møde" (Meeting), a series of short poems in which the French poet Rimbaud is featured as a main character. "Møde" ends the book on a note stressing the individual's need for a meeting with the rest of the world, especially other people.

These two poetry collections were followed by two novels, *Evighedsmaskinen* (1965; The Perpetual Motion Machine) and *Azorno* (1967). *Evighedsmaskinen* takes place in a small town dominated by a fundamentalist religious sect that believes a new savior will be born to them on Christmas night. The community will ensure that his life imitates Christ's in all its main events. When such a child is born, however, his parents try to protect him from his assigned fate. Despite their best efforts, the inevitable happens: on his thirtieth birthday, he is seized and buried alive. He manages to dig his way out of his burial chamber and goes wandering into the night.

Her next novel, *Azorno*, begins as letters written by several woman characters who are competing with each other to be the one who gets to meet Azorno, the protagonist of a romantic novel the writer Sampel is working on. The epistolary form eventually becomes a dairy. *Azorno* expresses the idea that we are all characters in each other's novels.

As impressive as all her work up to this point may be, it was only an apprenticeship for her masterwork, *Det* (1969; It), which one critic has called a "word-cathedral." It is a book-length poem constructed on a mathematical number system based on linguistic theory. Its three main sections are "Prologos," a long prose poem about the creation of the world; "Logos," further divided into three parts: "The Scene," "The Action," and "The Text"; and "Epilogos." Each of the three chapters of the "Logos" section consists of eight series of eight poems each; each series is named after categories in the Danish linguist Viggo Brøndal's book on prepositions. The source for Christensen's development and variations on sentence structure in *Det* is Noam Chomsky's theory of Transformational Grammar. As for subject matter, *Det* encompasses many of the philosophical and ideological debates taking place during the sixties, such as the influence of the Chinese Cultural Revolution in Denmark, French structuralism, and the anti-psychiatry of R.D. Laing. In spite of its formidable intertextuality and structure, *Det* is a very readable book and was a best-seller as well as a critical success in Denmark.

Christensen's next major work was *Det malede værelse* (1976; The Painted Room), a historical novella about the Renaissance painter Andrea Mantegna, who is best known for his frescoes in the *camera degli sposi* in the royal castle in Mantua. A person entering this room has the illusion of being in the middle of the activity portrayed on the walls and the ceiling. This effect inspired the structure of Christensen's work, which is written in three parts, from three different viewpoints. Her interest in painting also plays a role in some of her dramatic works, for example the television play "Ægteskabet mellem lyst og nød" (1978; The Marriage Between Lust and Need), in which there is a discussion of decorating a young girl's room with Renaissance and Surrealist paintings.

In 1979 Christensen published another book of poetry, *Brev i April* (Letter in April), an auto-biographical narration in short poems of a trip taken by a woman poet with her small son. She ironically contrasts her own intellectualizations with the child's ingenuous response to nature. *Alfabet* (Alphabet) followed in 1981. Like *Det*, this poetry collection is also constructed on a mathematical principle: each section, beginning with a new letter of the alphabet, contains the number of lines equal to the sum of the number of lines in the preceding two sections. The series does not finish the alphabet, however, but breaks off at the letter "n."

Christensen's other writings include essays, a number of translations, mostly of German works into Danish, and original dramatic works. Her drama is influenced by absurdists like Ionesco and Beckett. It includes her radio trilogy composed of *Speljltigeren* (1966; The Mirror-Tiger), *Klædt på til at overleve* (1967; Dressed to Survive), and *Et uhørt Spil* (1969; An Unheard Play) a stage play, *Intriganterne* (1972; The Intriguers), the libretto for Ib Nørholm's opera *Den unge park* (1972; The Young Park), and two television plays.

Christensen's importance to contemporary Danish letters is attested by her election to the Danish Academy and the respectful discussion she receives in histories of contemporary Danish and Scandinavian literature. Poul Borum has said that *Det* belongs to world literature; yet, the translations of it into French and English have not yet been published. In general, she has been translated less than some of her contemporaries with lesser reputations and has thus not yet received the international reputation she seems to deserve.

Works

Ækteskabet mellem lyst og nød [The Marriage Between Lust and Need], television play (1978). *En aften på Kgs. Nytorv* [An Evening in Kongens Nytorv], radio play (1975),. *Alfabet* [Alphabet] (1981). *Azorno* (1967). *Brev i april* [Letter in April] (1979). *Del af labyrinten* [Part of the Labyrinth] (1982). *Det* [It] (1969). *Evighedsmaskinen* [The Perpetual Motion Machine] (1964). *Græs* [Grass] (1963). *Intriganterne* [The Intriguers] (1972). *Klædt på at overleve* [Dressed to Survive], radio play (1967). *Den lange ukendte rejse* [The Long, Unknown Journey] (1982). *Lys* [Light] (1962). *Det* malede værelse: en fortælling fra Mantua [The Painted Room: A Tale from Mantua] (1976). *Masser af sne til de trængede får* [Masses of Snow for the Needy Sheep], radio play (1979). *Ørkenens luftsyn* [The Desert's Air-Scene] television play (1975). *Spejltigeren* [The Mirror-tiger], radio play (1966). *Et uhørt spil* [An Unheard Play], radio play (1969). *Den unge park* [The Young Park], libretto for an opera by Ib Nørholm; television broadcast (1972). *En vinteraften: Ufa og andre spil* [A Winter's Evening in Ufa and Other Plays] (1987). *Æter* [Ether] (1987). Christensen has also contributed numerous short pieces to Danish periodicals and anthologies.

Translations: *Azorno* (German), tr. Hanns Grössel (Frankfurt: S. Fischer, 1972). *Lettre en avril*, tr. Janine and Karl Poulsen. *Arcane* 17 (1985). For English translations of individual poems in periodicals and anthologies, see Carol L. Schroeder, *A Bibliography of Danish Literature in English Translation, 1950–1980.* Susanna Nied writes about her translation of *Det* in the *Danish Literary Journal* (see bibliography) in 1982, and excerpts appeared in *No Man's Land: An Anthology of Modern Danish Women's Literature* (Copenhagen, 1987), but this translation has not yet been published in its entirety.

Bibliography

Borum, Poul, *Danish Literature: A Short Critical Survey* (Copenhagen, 1979). Harder, Uffe, "Inger Christensen and Other Women Poets." *Out of Denmark* (Copenhagen, 1985), pp. 135–153. Nied, Susanna, "Inger Christensen—Language and Beyond." *Danish Literary Journal* (Copenhagen, 1982), p. 9. Paludan, Marie-Louise, "Inger Christensen," in *Dansk biografisk leksikon*, ed. Sv. Cedergreen Bech, 3rd ed. (Copenhagen, 1979). *Tegnverden: En bog om Inger Christensens forfatterskab*, ed. Iben Holk (Århus, 1983). Zeruneith, Keld, "Inger Christensen," in *Danske digtere i det 20 århundrede*, ed., Torben Brostrøm and Mette Winge (Copenhagen, 1980–1982), vol. 4, pp. 228–238.

Kristine Anderson

Queen Christina of Sweden

Born 1626, Stockholm, Sweden; died 1689, Rome
Genre(s): essay, maxim, autobiography, letters, aphorisms
Language(s): primarily French

Queen Christina of Sweden, though a peripheral character in literature, occupied center stage in seventeenth-century politics and intellectual life. She is a baffling, enigmatic figure, and her abdication at age twenty-eight, like her conversion to Roman Catholicism, remains only partially explained. When King Gustav Adolf was killed in the Thirty Years War, the Swedish nation rallied behind six-year old Christina, his only surviving child. The prospective monarch was given an aggressively masculine upbringing in which her neurotic mother was allowed no part. This education suited Christina, who was notoriously unfeminine by the standards of her day in her appearance, demeanor, and interests. Her exaggerated pride in her own considerable accomplishments notwithstanding, she became an unflinching misogynist. Her concomitant aversion to the prospect of marriage and childbirth was certainly a decisive factor in her abdication.

A child prodigy, Christina grew into a restless, driven young woman who ate and slept irregularly and suffered from frequent ill health and nervous exhaustion. She ascended the throne at age eighteen and despite the long period of regency government, forcefully asserted her will over that of the aristocracy. Christina made a lasting contribution to Swedish culture not through her writings, but through her court. During her reign, Stockholm changed from a provincial capital to a center of feverish cultural and intellectual activity along the French model. The young queen was widely praised for her great erudition and fascinated her contemporaries. Her court attracted prominent artists and scholars, including Descartes. Christina also assembled a magnificent library. Particularly through her support of the ballet, she played a significant role in the development of Swedish drama. Georg Stiernhielm, the "father of Swedish literature," was her poet laureate.

Christina's literary efforts have attracted little attention and are generally dismissed as derivative and undistinguished. Her language of choice was French though she conducted a voluminous correspondence in German, Swedish, Latin, and Italian as well. In Rome Christina became a leading cultural force, founding at least two academies and supporting artists, writers, and scholars. Her belletristic efforts probably did not begin until fairly late in her life and may have been suggested as a diversion by the Italian Cardinal Azzolino, her partner in Vatican political intrigues and possibly the object of her unrequited love.

Christina composed well over a thousand maxims, which reflect the influence of La Rochefoucauld. Two biographical sketches of Alexander the Great and Caesar reveal her fixation on notions of *virtú*, heroism and greatness. Around 1687, Christina contributed the theme and some embellishments to the verse drama *Endymion*, composed by her protégé Alessandro Guidi. An autobiographical fragment, begun in 1681, provides remarkably intimate glimpses of the former queen's personality and vulnerabilities. At its worst, Christina's style is repetitive, obscure, and uninspired. At its best, it is vigorous and concrete and has moments of genuine pathos. Yet in its very lack of originality, Christina's *oeuvre* could provide valuable insight into the conventions of courtly literature and international literary currents in the seventeenth century. For this reason, her works have an aesthetic as well as documentary value and are a legitimate topic not only for the historian but also for the literary scholar.

Works

Christina's works are included in Arckenholtz, Johann, *Mémoires concernant Christine, reine de Suède, etc.*, 4 vols. (1751–1760). Microfilm. *History of Women*, 31.1 (New Haven, Conn.: Research Publications Inc., 1975).

Translations: Atkinson, Jeanette Lee, tr., "The Life of Queen Christina by Herself, Dedicated to God" (selections), in *Women Writers of the 17th Century* (1989). Birch, Una., tr., *Maxims of a Queen . . .* (selections) (1907). Taunton, Margaret T., *Christina, Queen of Sweden. A Brief Notice of Her Life, Conversion, and Death, with Her Maxims and*

c (1862). *The Works of Christina of Sweden. Containing Maxims and Sentences, in Twelve Centuries and Reflections on the Life and Actions of Alexander the Great. Now first translated from the original French. To which is prefix'd an Account of her life, character, and writings, by the translator* (1753).

Bibliography

Arckenholtz, Johann, *Mémoires concernant Christina, reine de Suède, etc.*, 4 vols. (Amsterdam and Leipzig, 1751–1760). Atkinson, Jeanette Lee, "Queen Christina of Sweden: Sovereign between Throne and Altar," in *Women Writers of the 17th Century*, eds. Katharina M. Wilson and Frank Warnke (Athens, Ga., 1989), pp. 405–414. Cassirer, Ernst, "Descartes und Königin Christina von Schweden." *Descartes: Lehre, Persönlichkeit, Wirkung* (Stockholm, 1939), pp. 177–301. Masson, Georgina, *Queen Christina* (first American ed., New York, 1969). Mitchell, Stephen A., "The Autobiographies of Agneta Horn and Queen Christina Compared." Chapter IV of his *Job in Female Garb: Studies on the Autobiography of Agneta Horn*. Skrifter utgivna av Litteraturvetenskapliga institutionen vid Göteborgs universitet, 14 (Göteborg, 1985), pp. 72–77. Stolpe, Sven, *Fran Stoicism till mystik: Studier i Drottning Kristinas Maximer*. Diss., Uppsala, 1959 (Stockholm, 1959). Stolpe, Sven, *Drottning Kristina*. 2 vols. *Den svenska tiden*(I), *Efter tronavsägelsen*(II) (Stockholm, 1960, 1961). Weibull, Curt, *Drottning Christina*. 2nd ed. (Stockholm, 1934).

Jeanette L. Atkinson

Theophyle Christlieb

(see: Kathinka [Katharina] Rosa Pauline Modesta Zitz-Halein)

Solveig Christov

Born October 29, 1918, Drammen, Norway
Genre(s): novel, drama, short story
Language(s): Norwegian (bokmål)

Solveig Christov has written in several genres, ranging from novels and short stories to plays, some of which have been produced at the National Theater. It is in the area of the novel, however, that she has contributed most. While she has written a number of allegorical novels, the latter half of Christov's authorship has concentrated on psychological-realistic examination of the problems of love.

Christov made her literary debut in 1949 with *Det blomstrer langs blindveien* (Flowers Along the Cul-de-sac). Her first critical success was *Torso* (1952), a symbolical-allegorical vision of the post-war international political situation. *Demningen* (1957; The Dam) is another allegorical picture of contemporary society, where an obsession with protecting oneself against catastrophe leads to destruction. *Syv dager og netter* (1955; Seven Days and Nights) is about a woman who is torn between her dream of love and the realities of married life. The story of a man who meets a woman he had been close to many years before is told in *Elskerens hjemkomst* (1961; The Lover's Return), while the stories in *Jegeren og viltet* (1962; Hunter and Prey) and the novel *Skyldneren* (1965; The Debtor) emphasize the themes of guilt and responsibility. Both *Under vintermånen* (1954; Beneath the Winter Moon) and *Skyldneren* deal with the occupation during World War II, though several other works have the war as background.

Though Christov's style has been criticized for its chilly control, and some of her novels for lacking substance, there is agreement among literary historians that the artistic effect in the best of her works lies in the tension between the tautly controlled outer form and the inner passion. She has also been praised for her concern with political issues and her bold experimentation with form.

Works

Det blomstrer langs blindveien [Flowers along the Cul-de-sac] (1949). *På veiene til og fra* [On the Roads To and Fro] (1951). *Torso* (1952). *Under vintermånen* [Beneath the Winter Moon] (1954). *Syv dager og netter* [Seven Days and Nights] (1955). *Det hemmelige regnskap* [The Hidden Reckoning] (1956). *Demningen* [The Dam] (1957). *På rødt pass* [With a Red Passport] (1957). *Korsvei i jungelen* [Cross-roads in the Jungle] (1959). *Elskerens hjemkomst* [The Lover's Return] (1961). *Jegeren og viltet* [Hunter and Prey] (1962). *Skyldneren* [The Debtor] (1965). *Tre paradis* [Paradise Three] (1966). *Befrielsen* [The Liberation] (1966). *Tilfellet Martin* [The Martin Case] (1970). *Noveller* [Short Stories] (1974). *Knivsliperens dagbok* [Diary of a Knife-Grinder] (1976). *Reisen for lenge siden* [The Journey Long Ago] (1978).

Translations: "The Paradise Fish," tr. Nadia Christensen, in *An Everyday Story*, ed. Katherine Hanson (Seattle, 1984), pp. 158–165. "A Vacant Bed," tr. C. Gelland. *Scandinavian Review* 52.2 (1964): 310–313.

Bibliography

Beyer, Harald and Edvard, *Norsk litteraturhistorie* (Oslo, 1978), pp. 434–435. Brekke, Paal. "Men mannssamfunnet består." *Samtiden* 70 (1961): 647–655. Dahl, Willy, *Fra 40-tall til 70-tall* (Oslo, 1977), pp. 52–53, 99–100. Dahl, Willy, *Norges litteratur III: Tid og tekst 1935–1972* (Oslo, 1989), pp. 146, 149, 209, 232. Dahl, Willy, *Norges Litteraturhistorie*, vol. 6, ed. Edvard Beyer (Oslo, 1975), pp. 215–217. Houm, Philip, "Katter—og et engasjert engasjement." *Gleder og gremmelser* (Oslo, 1974), pp. 167–168. Høverstad, Helene, "Solveig Christov: Menneskes herlighet." *Nordiske noveller. Teksthefte til programserien i Skolekringkastinga vinteren 1970–71* (Oslo, 1973), pp. 53–54. Jørstad, Ragnhild, "Mennesker underveis. En analyse av flukt/oppbruddsmotivet i tre verker av Solveig Christov." (Hovedoppgave, Oslo, 1972). Longum, Leif, *Et speil for oss selv* (Oslo, 1968), 41–51. Rønneberg, Anton, "Solveig Christov: Veversken." *Ti års fjernsynsteater* (Oslo, 1971), pp. 173–174. Schou-Knudsen, Anne, "Solveig Christovs skuespill (*Det hemmelige redskap*, *På rødt pass*, *Befrielsen*)" (Hovedoppgave, Oslo, 1978).

Margaret Hayford O'Leary

Crystallia Chryssoveryi

Born 1862, Athens, Greece; died 1904, Athens
Genre(s): poetry
Language(s): Greek

Crystallia Chryssoveryi was born in 1862. She graduated from the Arsakeion School for training teachers and became a distinguished teacher and pedagogue. She was married to

Leonidas Dascalopoulos and dedicated all her leisure time to reading and writing. She was one of the main contributors to the first Greek feminist publication *Efimeris ton Kyrion* (The Ladies' Newspaper) and also published her poems in *Imeroloyion tis Efimerithos ton Kyrion* (Almanac of the Ladies' Newspaper).

As most of her contemporaries, Chryssoveryi used the archaic language (*katharévoussa*) which, surprisingly, does not spoil the lyrical quality and harmony of her verse but often adds to it. She was very much influenced by the pessimistic atmosphere of the Greek romantic school. Desire for escape, love of nature, and tormented introspection mainly characterize her poetry in which she explores female subjectivity better than most nineteenth-century women writers. Chryssoveryi is the first who gave a powerful poetic expression to the celebration of female love and sisterhood. In her poems, the nostalgic recollection of the past takes on the idealization of childhood and adolescence as a period of female bonding and equal intersubjective relations that are doomed to emotional disintegration and physical separation by women's obligation to marry.

Crystallia Chryssoveryi died in Athens at the age of forty-two without having the opportunity to have her poems published in an anthology.

Works

"Thiati remvazo" [Why Am I Dreaming?], in *Efimeris ton Kyrion* (March 31, 1891). "O Horismos mas" [Our Separation], in *Efimeris ton Kyrion* (November 10, 1891). "I epithymia tis" [Her Longing], in *Efimeris ton Kyrion* (July 26, 1892). "Ta anthi tiz karthias mou" [The Flowers of My Heart], in *Efimeris ton Kyrion* (September 19, 1893).

Bibliography

Tarsouli, Athina, *Ellinithes Piitries (Greek Women Writers)* (Athens, 1951).

Eleni Varikas

Lidia Korneevna Chukovskaya

Born 1907, St. Petersburg, Russia
Genre(s): novel, memoirs
Language(s): Russian

Lidia Chukovskaya was born between two revolutions in Russia and would live through the terror of Stalin's purges and the following turbulent times. Her father, Korney Chukovsky, was famous as a writer of children's verse and well-known as a literary critic, language critic and editor. Among the regular visitors to the Chukovsky's house were such artistic figures as I. Repin, B. Shaliapin, A. Tolstoy and V. Mayakovsky. Chukovskaya received an enviable education in her home town of Petrograd-Leningrad at the Literature Department of the Institute for the History of the Arts. The list of her professors is again auspicious including Shcherba, Tynianov, Eikhenbaum and Zhirmunsky.

Chukovskaya worked for about ten years in the children's literary section of the Leningrad State Publishing House. The event which had the greatest affect on her life was the arrest and subsequent execution of her husband Lev Bronshtein in 1937. Meanwhile many of her friends were disappearing, and she herself lost her job, barely escaping arrest. Chukovskaya did not know her husband was dead; she was never told. This period of her life is marked by long frustrating waits outside the various offices of Soviet officialdom, hoping, like the hundreds of others in the same plight, for some information about a lost loved one. It was during this time that she became acquainted with Anna Akhmatova, one of her fellow-sufferers. Akhmatova had given up writing down her verse, fearing arrest and the possibility of compromising her son. Chukovskaya realized the importance of saving her verses, though, and at great personal risk kept a journal of her meetings with Akhmatova, saving Akhmatova's poetry by memorizing it and later writing it down.

Chukovskaya's novels, *Sofya Petrovna* (The Deserted House) and *Spusk pod vodu* (Going Under), describe women undergoing extreme anguish during two significant points in the Soviet regime. The former takes place during the purges, the latter before the thaw. Chukovskaya's prose style is clear and fluid, free from superfluous detail and sentimentality. Both these works impress the reader as personal, natural experiences of difficult circumstances.

Chukovskaya was expelled from the Writers' Union in 1974 after having openly criticized M. Sholokhov for his censure of Sinyavsky and Daniel and publishing defenses of A. Solzhenitsyn and B. Pasternak abroad. Surely she believes as she writes in her letters and as her female protagonist in *Going Under*, that one must preserve the awful truth and transmit it faithfully—or maintain silence.

Works

Slovo predostavlaetsya detjam (1942). Opustelyj dom (1965). Otkrytoe slovo (1976). Zapiski ob Anne Axmatove, vol.1 (1976); Zapiski ob Anne Axmatove, vol. 2 (1980). Pamjati detstva (1983). Translations: Going Under, tr. P. Weston (1972). The Deserted House, tr. A. Werth (1967).

Bibliography

Klimoff, A., Introduction to *The Deserted House* (Massachusetts, 1967), pp. i–xiii. Breitbart, E., "Xranitel'nica tradicii." *Grani* 104 (1977): 171–182.

Christine Tome

Fausta Terni-Cialente

Born November 29, 1900, Cagliari, Italy
Genre(s): novel
Language(s): Italian

Throughout her career, Fausta Cialente has remained true to her instinct to fictionalize the autobiographical episodes of her life, making the personal a paradigm of a vaster sociopolitical sphere. Thus, her novels originate in the events of Cialente's long and peripatetic life. Events are transfigured by memory and imagination and framed by a perceptive interpretation of the relationship between the individual and the historical. Her style is grounded in the European tradition of realism but is open to the subjective musings of the narrating persona.

Born into an artistically inclined family that would produce a famous actor (brother Renato) as well as an important novelist, Cialente's growing years were punctuated by constant moves, brought on by the demands of her father's career as an Army officer. After her marriage to composer Enrico Terni (1921), the couple lived in the Western colony in Egypt, which would provide the "exotic" locale for her first novels. Politically engaged, Cialente joined the war effort working at the British General Headquarters in Cairo for several years, where she prepared anti-Fascist radio and print propaganda.

Returning to Italy after her husband's death in 1947, the novelist continued to write, often using her Middle Eastern experience for inspiration. In 1976, Cialente was awarded the prestigious Strega Prize for *Le quattro ragazze Wieselberger* (1976; The Four Wieselberger Girls), a tribute to the enduring quality of her writing.

Fusing memory, historical reality, and autobiographical data with precise descriptions of customs, characters, and locales, Cialente manages to unite the personal aspects of her novels with collective issues. Social concerns surface throughout, for the narration touches on topics such as colonialism, dehumanization in war, and bourgeois obtuseness. In works such as *Cortile a Cleopatra* (1936; Courtyard to Cleopatra) and *Ballata levantina* (1961; Levantine Ballad), the author suggests that "Levantinism" offers a civilized and refined alternative to the disintegration of culture, community, and morals in modern times.

The sense of loss provides a melancholy note often found in Cialente's writing, whether it be in the lyrical remembrance of the past or in the sadness of the uncertain present. This tone is balanced, however, by her sense of concrete reality. This sense of loss is heightened by the realization that the personal is an emblem, as in *Le quattro ragazze Wieselberger*, where the gradual dissolution of the family through time, war, and death closely parallels the fate of Italy in the same fifty-year span.

Significantly, Fausta Cialente's journalistic endeavors echo the novelist's concern with the social and political aspects of individual experience.

Works

Natalia (1930). *Cortile a Cleopatra* (1936/1973). *Pamela o la bella estate* (1936/1962). *Ballata levantina* (1961/1974). *Un inverno freddissimo* (1966/1976). *Il vento sulla sabbia* (1972). *Interno con figure* (1976). *Le quattro ragazze Wieselberger* (1976). *Diario di una donna* (1978). Translations: *The Levantines*, tr. Isabel Quigly (1963).

Bibliography

Cecchi, Emilio. "Prefazione." In *Cortile a Cleopatra* (Milan, 1973). Paolini, Alcide. "Prefazione." In *Le quattro ragazze Wieselberger* (Milan, 1976). Reina, Luigi. *Invito al 900* (Naples, 1986).

Fiora A. Bassanese

Pilar Cibreiro Santalla

Born 1952, Villaboa (El Ferrol), Spain
Genre(s): poetry, novel
Language(s): Spanish, Galician

Pilar Cibreiro was born in Villaboa, a small village in the northwestern region of Spain known as Galicia. In 1971 she travelled to London, where she spent three years. She has written several lyrical works, both in Spanish and in Galician, still unpublished.

Her first appearance in the literary world was through a collection of stories entitled *El cinturón traído de Cuba y otros cuentos de invierno* (1985; The Belt Brought Back from Cuba and Other Winter Stories). This first work was very well received by the critics. In December 1985, Cibreiro published another short story, "Pilar de Campos," in a very well known Spanish literary journal. This story is closely related to her first collection in that it is dedicated to the memory of one of her main sources of inspiration, a recently deceased grandmother.

Pilar Cibreiro is a magnetic storyteller. *El cinturón traído de Cuba* is composed of a series of stories about her home town and its inhabitants through the course of this century as seen through Cibreiro's eyes as well as recalled from childhood stories told to her by elderly relatives. Cibreiro uses this multiple perspective to narrate the same event as a means both to objectivize what is observed and to increase the mystery

surrounding her characters' lives and deaths. Indeed, it is death that prevails as a sustained theme throughout the stories. Death, rain, and fog permeate the lives of these courageous men and women, most of them marked by the fate of emigration and by the brutality of the Spanish Civil War.

Cibreiro creates a precise, suggestive language impregnated with regionalisms that give color to the stories about events and characters belonging to her village, Villaboa. The ever-present rain serves as a backdrop for these stories, creating the perfect mood for readers to immerse themselves in a magical world of ghosts, passionate adventures, and men engulfed by the sea. The author recreates a lost world that can exist only through memory. The mood of these stories is not limited to the gloomy; love and a sensuality that goes to the most primal, essential center of human life also play an important role. With her unencumbered and evocative style, Cibreiro, on the surface, seems to be stressing the descriptive and anecdotal, although what she is really portraying is the deepest sphere of the human soul.

Works

El cinturón traído de Cuba y otros cuentos de invierno [The Belt Brought Back from Cuba and Other Winter Stories] (1985). "Pilar de Campos." *Insula* 469 (dic. 1985): 16.

Bibliography

Sanchez Arnosi, Milagros. "*El cinturón traído de Cuba.*" *Insula* 468 (nov. 1985): 19.

Coro Malaxecheverría

Hélène Cixous

Born 1937, Oran, Algeria
Genre(s): fiction, essay, critical-theoretical text
Language(s): French

Hélène Cixous is one of the most well-known and important French women writers at work today. A professor of literature at the University of Paris VIII—Vincennes at St. Denis, she co-founded the school and initiated its Women's Studies program. Her first published text, *Le Prénom de dieu*, appeared in 1967; her doctoral thesis in 1968 was entitled *L'Exil de James*

Joyce ou l'art du remplacement. Also that year she founded the review *Poetique* with Gérard Genette and Tzvetan Todorov. In 1969 *Dedans* was awarded the Prix Médicis and in 1973 she began to write on questions of sexual difference and on female experience and writing. In the mid-seventies she published exclusively with Editions des femmes in a gesture of political commitment to, and in solidarity with, the women's movement. By 1982 she stopped publishing with des Femmes so that she could continue to experiment with a variety of other writerly means.

Cixous denies that she is a theorist, preferring her writing to be seen as a process of working to recast the mythic past with a newer, more subversive feminism. This project makes it difficult to label her a novelist as well. Rather her texts are combinations of majestic writerly energies that find their sources in poetry, fable and the wonder of "tableaux." The wide array of myth employed in her work undergoes a significant rewriting with the aim of surpassing the traditional phallocentric authority of the present (and past) social order. This reading *otherwise* of myths directs its power to the reinstallation of the female voice that has been silenced by masculine discourse. Such a transformation becomes a new ground upon which Cixous' "methodology" of female self-discovery, recovery and rewriting rests. In reassembling patriarchal myths Cixous employs a more useful and appropriate female mythopoetic creativity to reach a great liberation. Because of this activity, it is perhaps better to understand Cixous as a poet-theoretician of women's approaches to writing with myth or through myth.

This re-employment of myth, past and present, underscores Cixous' belief in the central concern of language as a co-opted entity, co-opted by the idealized version of man. Thus, with the critique of this status of language offered by Lacan and Derrida, both of which have greatly influenced her, Cixous exposes and dismantles the logic of phallocentrism. The book becomes the property of *écriture feminine* or feminine writing, the property of a kingdom of libidinal and maternal affirmation.

In her 1975 manifesto, "The Laugh of the Medusa," Cixous entreats women to write,

without defining the feminine practice of writing in theoretical language. Instead, she shares a vision of writing that would be free of any limitation or boundary, a writing that constantly reinvents new representations of formerly impossible realities. In this manner she opposes the demonstrations and justifications of philosophy for the openness of the poetic thereby privileging the vocal and musical elements of language as well. In the same year, Cixous and Catherine Clément published *La jeune née*, one of the most popular works in feminist studies. Clément and Cixous analyze the nature and operations of representations of women in Western culture. The second half of the book is a dialogue between these two disagreeing writers.

Works

Le Prénom de Dieu (1967). *Dedans* (1969). *L'Exil ou l'art du remplacement* (1969; The Exile of James Joyce). *Le Troisième Corps* (1970). *Les Commencements* (1970). *La Pupille* (1971). *Un Vrai Jardin* (1971). *Neutre* (1972). *Tombe* (1973). *Prénoms de personne* (1974). *Portrait du soleil* (1974). *Révolutions pour plus d'un Faust* (1975). *La Jeune Née* [The Newly Born Woman] (1975). *Un K. incompréhensible: Pierre Goldman* (1975). *Souffles* (1975). *Portrait de Dora* (1976). *La* (1976). *Partie* (1976). *La Venue à l'écriture* (1977). *Angst* (1977). *Préparatifs de noces au delà de l'abîme* (1978). *Chant du corps interdit/Le Nom d'Oedipe* (1978). *Vivre l'orange* (1979). *Anankè* (1979). *Illa* (1980). *Ou l'art de l'innocence* (1981). *Limonade tout était si infini* (1982). *Le Livre de Promethea* (1983). *La Prise de l'école de Madubaï* (1984). *L'Histoire terrible mais inachevée de Norodom Sihanouk roi du Cambodge* (1985). *La Bataille d'Arcachon* (1986). *Entre l'écriture* (1986). *L'Indiade ou l'Inde de leurs rêves* (1988).

Richard J. Pioli

Stephanie Claes-Vetter

Born February 25, 1884, Zutphen, Holland;
*   died October 9, 1974, Elsene, Belgium*
Genre(s): novel
Language(s): Dutch

Introduced to Flemish literature through her husband, popular author Ernest Claes,

Stephanie Claes-Vetter was one of the earliest "Flemish" advocates of the emancipation of women in Flanders.

She was a co-editor of the highly respected literary ladies magazine *De Lelie* (The Lily) from 1909–1914. Her first novel, *Eer de Mail Sluit* (Before the Mail Closes), was published in 1915, and was followed by a beautiful collection of short stories called *Verholen Krachten* (Hidden Forces) in 1927. She was a revelation in Flanders where narrative language, style, and novelistic treatment have often suffered from heavy-handedness, and she introduced a more delicate, imaginative Dutch freshness to Belgian literature.

In her first novels, Claes-Vetter deals with the attitudes and values of the Dutch bourgeoisie but later projected the typically Dutch atmosphere on Brussels upper-class lifestyles and mores. This is the subject of her most important psychological novels that move in the direction of the *tendens romans*, novels that pose social, political questions such as *Als de dagen Lengen* (1940; When the Days Lengthen), *Haar eigen Weg* (1944; Her Own Way), *Martine—Een Ontgoocheling* (1954; Martine—a Disappointment). Implicit in her treatment of sociopolitical themes is the problem of the identity and role of women in marriage.

Works

Eer de Mail Sluit (1915). *Stil Leven* (1926). *Verholen Krachten* (1927). *Miete* (1932). *Als de Dagen Lengen* (1940). *Haar Eigen Weg* (1944). *Vrouwen Zonder Betekenis* (1952). *Martine—Een Ontgoocheling* (1954). *Angst* (1960).

Bibliography

Lissens, R.F., *De Vlaamse Letterkunde van 1780 tot heden* Brussels (1973).

An Lammens

María Francisca Clar Margarit

(see: Halma Angélico)

Clara d'Anduza

Born first half of thirteenth century, Languedoc (?), France
Genre(s): poetry
Language(s): Provençal

The author of one *canso*, "En greu esmai et en greu pessamen" (P-C 115, 1; one manuscript: C359v), Clara d'Anduza was probably wife or daughter of Bernard d'Anduze and thus from Languedoc. While she has no *vida*, she is mentioned in the *razo* to a poem of Uc de Saint Circ. He was reputed to be her lover and apparently wrote songs in her honor. According to the *razo*, jealousy caused by a Na Ponsa broke up their affair. One is tempted to wonder if Na Ponsa might not in fact be Azalais d'Altier: while the names bear no relation, the friendship between N'Azalais and a certain Clara's lover reported in "Tants salutz e tantas amors" could be one to cause this kind of jealousy.

Clara's *canso* consists of three *coblas unissonans* of eight lines each, followed by a *toronada* of four lines. The rhyme scheme is *abbacddc*; all lines are ten syllables long. It tells of a pair of lovers separated by *lauzengiers* and "fals devinador" and of the pain and grief this has caused.

Works

Ed. Raynouard III, 335; Schultz, p. 26; Véran, p. 130; Mahn, III, p. 210; Bogin, 130–13; Perkal-Balinsky, pp. 153–156.

Bibliography

Bec, P., "*Trobairitz* et chansons de femme: Contribution à la connaissance du lyrisme féminin au moyen âge." *CCM* 22 (1979): 235–262. Bogin, M., *The Women Troubadours* (New York, 1980). Boutiére, J., and A.-H. Schutz, *Biographies des troubadours*. 2nd ed. (Paris, 1964). Branciforti, F., *Il canzoniere di Lanfrancesco Cigala* (Florence, 1954). Bruckner, M., "Na Castelloza, *Trobairitz*, and Troubadour Lyric." *Romance Notes* 25 (1985): 1–15. Chabaneau, C., "Les biographies des troubadours en langue provençale." In *Histoire générale de Languedoc* X (Toulouse, 1885). Dronke, P., *Women Writers of the Middle Ages* (Cambridge, 1984). Mahn, C.A.F., *Die Werke der Troubadours in provenzalischer Sprache* (Berlin, 1846). Perkal-Balinsky, D., *The Minor Trobairitz*. Diss. Northwestern Univ., 1986. Raynouard, M., *Choix des poésies originales des troubadours*, 6 vols. (Osnabruck, 1966). Riquer, M. de, *Los trovadores*, 3 vols. (Barcelona, 1975). Schultz, O., *Die Provenzalischen Dichterinnen* (Leipzig, 1888). Shapiro, M., "The Provençal *Trobairitz* and the Limits of Courtly Love." *Signs* 3 (1978): 560–571. Tavera, A., "A la recherche des troubadours maudits." *Sénéfiance* 5 (1978): 135–161. Véran, J., *Les poétesses provençales* (Paris, 1946).

Sarah Spence

Clarac

(see: Annemarie Schwarzenbach)

Clare of Assisi

Born 1193, Assisi, Italy; died 1253, Assisi
Genre(s): works of monastic spirituality
Language(s): Latin

As a young woman of noble standing in Assisi (the daughter of Favarone and Ortolana), Clare was attracted to the ideal of poverty espoused by her contemporary, Francis of Assisi. Following Francis' example, Clare founded an order of religious women known as the Poor Ladies of Assisi (like Francis' Poor Men), and later as the Clarissas or Poor Clares in her honor.

Like Francis, Clare focused her life on the practice of the ideal of poverty and looked suspiciously on the composition of theology. The few writings that survive contain a strong, pragmatic statement of the ideals which inspired her and governed the order: four letters of spiritual advice addressed to Agnes of Prague between 1234 and 1253; the *Rule* for her new order composed in 1254; and an autobiographical reflection, known as the *Testament*, probably written shortly before her death. While the authenticity of these works has been frequently discussed, they are all generally accepted as genuine although the Latinity of both the *Rule* and *Testament* was improved by scribes at the papal chancery. A letter to Ermentrude of Bruges is probably a summary of two authentic letters made in the seventeenth century, and there is no guarantee of the authenticity of a blessing included in the *Legend of St. Clare*.

While Clare's spiritual ideals and life were predicated on the faithful imitation of the genius of Francis, she demonstrated her own genius in translating those ideals into a feminine version.

Works

"Epistolae ad b. Agnetem," in W. Seton, ed., *Archivum franciscanum historicum* 17 (1924): 513–319. "Regula." *Seraphicae Legislationis Textus Originales* (1897), pp. 49–75. "Testamentum." *Ibid.*, pp. 273–280. *Escritos de santa Clara y documentos contemporaneos*, I. Omaechevarria, ed. (1970).
Translation: Vaughn, J., and I. Brady, eds., *Francis and Clare. The Complete Works* (1982).
Concordance: Godet, J-F., and G. Mailleux, eds., *Opuscula Sancti Francisce, Scripta Sanctae Clarae. Corpus des sources franciscaines*, vol. 5 (1976).

Bibliography

Archivum franciscum historicum 46 (1953). Brooke, R., and C. Brooke, "St. Clare," in *Medieval Women*, ed. D. Baker (1978), 275–287. Cicarelli, D., "Contributi alla recensione degli scritti di S. Chiara." *Miscellanca Francescana* 78 (1978): 347–374. De Robeck, N., *Saint Clare of Assisi* (1951). *Franzkanische Studien* 35 (1953). Grau, E., and L. Hardick, eds., *The Legend and Writings of St. Clare* (English tr., 1953). *S. Chiara d'Assisi, 1253–1953. Studi e Cronaca del VII Centenario* (1954). Iriarte, L., *Letra y Espiritu de La Regla de Santa Clara* (1974).
General references: *New Catholic Encyclopedia*, III, 912–913. *Dictionnaire d'histoire et de geographie ecclésiastique*, XII, pp. 1032–1036.

Thomas Head

Clark

(see: Annemarie Schwarzenbach)

Clark-Schwarzenbach

(see: Annemarie Schwarzenbach)

257

Marie de Clèves

(a.k.a. Madame d'Orléans)

Born 1426, France; died 1487, Chaunay, France
Genre(s): poetry
Language(s): French

Marie de Clèves was a princess of the House of Marck. Daughter of Adolf IV, Duke of Clèves, and Marie of Burgundy, she would become the third wife of Charles I, Duke of Orléans in 1440 in a match made solely for political reasons. At their marriage in 1440, Charles was 35 years her senior, yet their union would result in a son, the future Louis XII. Advancing age and military failures contributed to Charles' withdrawal from the center of the political stage and his shift to literary endeavors. Marie, too, would concentrate her energies on the arts. She commissioned many works and had an extensive private library. Her participation in the world of letters was not limited to that of a patron of writers; she was an active poet and produced many short works. After the death of her husband, she continued to be an active figure at the court, known for her piety and her good works, until 1480 when she married an Artesian gentleman some years her junior. This marriage, it appears, was inspired by love and not reasons of state and would end Marie's reign at the court.

As wife of Charles d'Orléans, who was recognized as an accomplished poet, it is not surprising that her work was overshadowed by his, especially since she was neither a stylistic nor a thematic innovator. The bulk of her works are rondeaus and ballads centering on love. Nonetheless, she was not without talent. Her poems are well-wrought and compare favorably to those written by the members of Charles' entourage. Marie's poetry is an excellent example of the tastes and conventions of her period.

Works

Selections in: *Les Poésies de Charles d'Orléans* (1856). *Autour de Charles d'Orléans: Rondeaux et autres poésies du XVe* (1889). *Poètes et romanciers du Moyen-Age* (1943).

Bibliography

Champion, Pierre, *Histoire poétique du XVe siècle* (Paris, 1923).

Edith J. Benkov

Bente Clod

Born 1946, Copenhagen, Denmark
Genre(s): novel, poetry, drama
Language(s): Danish

More than anything Bente Clod is a feminist activist whose debut as a writer was an award-winning article in a major Danish newspaper on women's sexuality, relationships, and sex role stereotypes that expressed such controversial views that she became almost notorious for a time. She has held workshops for aspiring women writers and has founded a school with a permanent writing program. Clod was active in the women's movement right from the start; she has been co-editor of an alternative periodical, *Seksualpolitik*, addressing sexuality from a cultural and political aspect, and has been a member of the Danish lesbian liberation front.

Clod's first book, *Det autoriserede danske samleje og andre naerkampe* (1976), is a collection of her early controversial articles on sexuality, feminism, and sex role stereotypes. Her first novel, *Brud* (1977), falls within the so-called confessional genre, based heavily on Clod's own life and her coming out as bisexual. *Syv sind* (1980), Clod's next novel, is a mixture of a *Bildungsroman* and a realistic novel with elements of utopian visions. *Opbrud* (1978), a collection of poetry, is perhaps a little didactic whereas *Imellem os* (1981), also a collection of poetry, shows that though the struggle for independence has a high price, there is also hope for the future and for love.

Clod is an uncompromising feminist who is always willing to risk her reputation as a writer for her vision. Some of her books may not have come out the way they were intended, but most of them are truly beautiful in their daring execution of what the future might hold, in their descriptions of women's lives and feelings. Her use of a confessional style has given other women the courage to write about their lives, and her help and support as teacher and instigator are invaluable.

Works

Det autoriserede danske samleje og andre naerkampe (1976). Brud (1977). Kvinder må aldrig tabe hinanden af syne (1977). Undervejs. Beretninger fra de seneste års landskaber (1977). Opbrud (1978). Syv sind (1980). Imellem os (1981). Vent til du hører mig le (1983).

Bibliography

Andersen, Bruun Michael, ed., *Dansk litteraturhistorie 8* (1985). Bryld, Mette, *Overgangskvinden* (Odense, 1982). Holst, Lisbeth, *Fri os fra kaerligheden Omkring Bente Clod's "Brud" og Marilyn French's "Kvinder"* (1981). *Kritik* 55. Scott, Sørensen Anne, *Kvindesituation/kvindelighed/kvindekamp* (1978).

Merite von Eyben

Sofia Cocea

(a.k.a. Sofia Chrisoscoleu, Sofia Hrisoscoleu)

Born 1839, Fälticeni, Romania; died 1861, Vaslui
Genre(s): essay, journalism, poetry
Language(s): Romanian

Sofia Cocea's was a short and intense life. At the age of thirteen, she translated from French into Romanian and published the novel *Palmira și Flaminia sau Secretul* (1852; Palmira and Flaminia or The Secret) by Mme de Genlis and the play *Maria sau Mustrările de cuget ale unei mame* (1852; Maria or The Qualms of Conscience of a Mother). The last looked immoral to the censor Gh. Asachi who proposed—but did not get—its interdiction by the Secretary of State. At the age of seventeen, Sofia Cocea applied for an official grant to study education abroad and was rejected. She then became a teacher and joined the group of writers and publicists who, immediately after the 1848 revolution, prepared the unification of Romania.

Her lively political essays, firm, courageous, slightly ironic, were published in the most important Unionist journals of the time: *Tribuna română, Reforma, Gazeta poporului, Zimbrul,*

Foiletonul Zimbrului, Românul, Dacia, as well as in *Steaua Dunării, Gazeta de Moldavia,* etc. She wrote about the economic and social plight of the peasants, women's vs. men's rights, the state of the Romanian culture and public education, the external policy of the Romanian principalities, etc.

Sofia Cocea's occasional poems are by far superseded by her journalism and polemic essays.

She was one of the initiators of the Romanian feminist movement as well as a strong militant for the Union of the Romanian principalities.

Works

Operile doamnei Sofia Chrisoscoleu, născută Coce [The Works of Madam Sofia Chrisoscoleu, born Coce] (1862). Preface by Iulia A[ricescu].

Bibliography

Bassarabescu, I.A., *O scriitoare necunoscută din epoca Unirii Principatelor* (Bucharest, 1940). Byck, J., "O pamfletară acum o sută de ani." *Gazeta literară* V (1958): 10. Cîncea, Paraschiva, *Sofia Cocea (1839–1861)* (Bucharest, 1975). Emilgar [Emil Gîrleanu], "Sofia Hrisoscoleu." *Arhiva* XIII (1902): 1–2. Groholschi, Profira C., *O ziaristă romîncă* (Piatra-Neamț, 1919). Zăstroiu, Romulus, *Dicționarul literaturii romîne de la origini pîna la 1900* (Bucharest, 1979), pp. 196–197.

Sanda Golopentia

Gabrielle de Coignard

Born ?, Toulouse, France; died 1594?, Toulouse
Genre(s): poetry
Language(s): French

We know little about Gabrielle de Coignard aside from her works. She was born in Toulouse of a noble family and married the President of the Parliament of Toulouse, le sieur de Mansencal de Miremont. Her marriage appears to have been a singularly happy one. Upon her husband's death, she retired from society and devoted herself to the education of her two daughters. During this solitude, she wrote poems to amuse herself, poems which usually expressed the religious devotion typical of the late sixteenth century. These works form her entire *corpus*.

The poems are graceful, learned, and religious in inspiration. They are all meditative; most focus on the goodness and wisdom of God. In her text, Gabrielle herself, a self-effacing woman who never sought to publish her work, claims that the one true knowledge is how to achieve salvation. Despite this disclaimer against classical erudition, however, the poet was obviously well-read, even learned. A wide variety of forms appear in the collection, which includes odes, stances, sonnets, and extended poems. As her biographer Colletet notes, the language is often remarkable for its beauty and sweetness. In *Les Femmes Poètes au XVIeme siècle*, Léon Feugère describes it as being reminiscent of Malherbe's.

Gabrielle's gender often influences her pieces. Sometimes she evokes feminine exemplars of piety, as in her poem devoted to Judith; often she reminds her God of her vulnerability as a widowed mother. In these latter pieces, she sometimes recalls the earlier poetry of Christine de Pizan, who was also widowed young and left with the care of young children. We have no proof that she knew Christine's work, but she does appear to have read Louise Labé, with whom she has very little in common as a writer aside from a deep acquaintance with Italian literature.

After her death, Gabrielle de Coignard's works were gathered by her children and published in 1595 as *Oeuvres chrestiennes de feue dame Gabrielle de Coignard* (The Christian Works of the Late Lady, Gabrielle de Coignard). While she was included by P. Hilarion de Coste and P. Jacob in their *Histoires des femmes illustres*, and while Guillaume Colletet included her in his *Histoire des poetes français*, she has been neglected since. Today, her name cannot be found in any of the standard histories of French literature or in any of the usual dictionaries of French writers. Nor has her work been republished since 1595. Especially in light of her thematic links to other French women writers—like Christine de Pizan, she wrote of her widowhood; like Marguerite de Navarre, she concentrated on religious themes; like Louise Labé, she was greatly influenced by Italian literature—she deserves further study.

Works

Oeuvres chrestiennes de feue dame Gabrielle de Coignard [The Christian works of the Late Lady Gabrielle de Coignard] (1595).

Bibliography

Feugère, Léon, *Les Femmes Poètes au XVIeme siècle* (1860; rpt. Paris, 1969), pp. 35–38.

Glenda Wall

Louise Révoli Colet

Born August 15, 1810, Aix en Provence,
France; died March 8 or 9, 1876, Paris
Genre(s): poetry, social history, drama, novel
Language(s): French

A prolific poet, dramatist, and prose writer, Colet's passionate affairs with nineteenth-century French writers Victor Cousin, Gustave Flaubert, and Alfred de Musset gave inspiration to her work and to others'. Her detractors have called Colet a "pushy femme de lettres," and "*le* bas-bleu meme" (*the* blue stocking). Her best-known works were scandal ridden, but her most artistically intentioned works are imitative of better romantic poems. Although her letters to Flaubert were destroyed, the letters Flaubert wrote to Colet while composing *Madame Bovary* are valuable for his statements about art.

Even as a young woman Colet wrote verses. Shortly after her marriage to a composer and flute teacher at the Paris Conservatory, she published her first collection of poems *Fleurs du Midi* (1836). Under the patronage of Victor Cousin, who was a respected philosopher in the French Academy and later a Cabinet minister, Colet won literary awards for her poems and was able to see some verse-dramas produced. When it became known that she was carrying Cousin's baby, Alphonse Karr gossiped about the news in *Les Guêpes* in 1840. Colet responded by stabbing him in the back with a kitchen knife and publishing an angry retort. A few months after she met Flaubert in 1846, Colet separated from her husband, who later died in 1851. She continued to write and win prizes from the French Academy (for *Le Musée de Versailles*, 1839; *Le Monument de Molière*, 1843; and *L'Acropole d'Athenes*, 1853). With the final rupture from Flaubert in

1855, Colet turned to Alfred de Musset, whose poetry Flaubert considered too emotional and sentimental to be good art. Colet added her analysis of the poet's personality by publishing the third novel about Musset upon his death. George Sand had written *Elle et lui* (1859) as a roman à clef about her own affair with the romantic poet, and his brother Paul came to his defense by publishing *Lui et elle*. Colet wrote her account in *Lui* (1860), in which the "him" is Musset, whom the heroine must resist in order to be true to the Flaubert character, Léonce. Flaubert wrote of his liaison with Colet as a "very long irritation" rather than a wound. The novel only served to put the final "bouquet" on their affair (letter to Ameilie Bosquet, 1859).

The final twenty-five years of her life were spent traveling and publishing social commentaries and histories. Colet described life in Holland (1859), Naples under Garibaldi (1860), Italy (1862), and the opening of the Suez Canal in 1869.

It may seem unfair to ignore the volumes of poetry in favor of investigating the one novel that created such a literary furor that whatever aesthetic value it may have is overlooked. In fact, much of Colet's poetry shows a certain strength of rhythm and sound. A few lines, for example, from "Amor nel cor" show the rising vehemence at Flaubert's deriding her inscription on one of her gifts to him in *Madame Bovary*: "C'était pour lui, pour lui qu'elle aimait comme un Dieu!" (It was for him, for him, whom she loved as a god.) And, surely her several awards were to honor more her poetry than her beautiful eyes and clear skin, a subtle inference made by many critics who have never understood Flaubert's nine-year stormy relationship with what they dismiss as a secondary force.

That one controversial novel is *Lui*, recently translated with a subtitle of "A View of Him" (1986). As the novel is clearly based on events well known in 1859 and to all Flaubert specialists, it was traditionally viewed as a noble account of the poet's unswerving allegiance to the unfeeling artist. Specifically, it was Colet's character Stéphanie de Rostan, still in love with a Flaubert-like artist Léonce, who tries to quiet the amorous Musset character of Albert de Lincell. In both art and life the heroine did not get her man, ending out her days alone and shunned. To that end, recent criticism suggests that *Lui* is a study of the difficulties of the professional woman writer in the age of Realism in France.

Works

Fleurs du Midi (1836). *La jeuness de Goethe, comédie en un acte, en vers* (1839). *Les Funérailles de Napoléon* (1840). *Penserosa, poésies nouvelles* (1840). *La Jeunesse de Mirabeau* (1841). *Oeuvres de Mme Louise Colet, née Révoil. Poésies* (1842). *Le Monument de Molière, poème* (1843). *Deux mois d'émotions* (1843). *Les coeurs brisés* (1843). *Folles et Saintes* (1844). *Oeuvres choisies de Tommasso Campanella*, trans. Colet (1844). *Historiettes morales* (1845). *Le Marabout de Sidi-Brahim* (1845). *L'Empéreur de Russie près de sa fille mourante* (1845). *Le Chant des vaincus, poésies nouvelles* (1846). *Réveil de la Pologne* (1846). *Les grands jours de la République* (1848). *La Colonie de Mettray, poème* (1852). *Ce qui est dans le coeur des femmes, poésies nouvelles* (1852). *Le Poème de la Femme. Premier récit. La paysanne* (1853). *Enfances célèbres* (1854). *Ce qu'on réve en aimant, poésies nouvelles* (1854). *Le Poème de la Femme. Deuxième récit. La Servante* (1854). *Madame Duchatelet* (1854). *Madame Hoffman-Tanska. La provinciale à Paris, l'institutrice* (1854). *Quatre poèmes couronnés par l'Académie Française. Le musée de Versailles, Le Monument de Molière, La Colonie de Mettray, l'Acropole d'Athenes* (1855). *Le Poème de la Femme. Troisième récit. La Réligieuse* (1856). *Une Histoire de Soldat* (1856). *Un drame dans la rue de Rivoli* (1857). *Le Comte de Landeves, suivi de la Marquise de Gange* (1858). *Promenade en Hollande* (1859). *Lui, roman contemporain* (1860). *Naples sous Garibaldi, Souvenirs de la guerre de l'indépendance* (1860). *Pélerinage à Versailles et à Trianon* (1861). *L'Italie des Italiens*, 4 vols. (1862–1864). *Richess oblige, Contes et nouvelles pour l'adolescence* (1862). *Les derniers marquis. Deux mois aux Pyrénées* (1866). *Les derniers Abbés, moeurs réligieuses d'Italie* (1868). *La Satire du siècle I. Paris matière* (1868). *Ces petits Messieurs* (1869). *Réponse aux "Guêpes" de M. Alphonse Karr* (1869). *Les Dévotes du grand monde, types du Second Empire* (1873). *La Verité sur l'anarchie des esprite en France* (1873). *Edgar Quinet, l'"Esprit nouveau"* (1876). *Les Pays Lumineux, Voyage en Orient* (1879).

Works in English: *Lui, A View of Him*, tr. M. Rose (1986).

Bibliography

Banville, T., *Camées parisiene* (Paris, 1866). Barbey D'Aurevilly, J. ,*Les Oeuvres et les hommes: Une partie—les bas-bleus* (Paris, 1878; rpt. Geneva, 1968). Dumesnil, R., *Le Grand amour de Flaubert* (Paris, 1945). Gourmont, R., *Promenades littéraires iii* (Paris, 1907). Jackson, J., *Louise Colet et ses amis littéraires* (New Haven, 1937). Lescure, M., *Eux et elles: Histoires d'un scandale* (Paris, 1860; rpt. Geneva, 1973). *Mélanges à la mémoire de Franco Simone* (Geneva, 1984). Sedgwick, H., *Alfred de Musset 1810–1857* (Indianapolis, 1931). Steegmuller, F., *Flaubert and Mme Bovary, a Double Portrait* (New York, 1950). *Translation Perspectives* (1984).

General references: *Dictionnaire de biographie française*, vol. 9. *Dictionnaire de littérature française*. *Encyclopedia Britannica*.

Other references: *A l'Ecart* (1980). *Historia* (Sept. 1980). *Partisan Review* (Jan. 1953). *Revue de Paris* (Nov. 1908). *Le Temps* (3 avr. 1934).

Marilynn J. Smith

Sidonie-Gabrielle Colette

Born January 28, 1873, Saint-Sauveur-en-Puisaye, France; died August 3, 1954, Paris

Genre(s): novel, essay

Language(s): French

Colette spent her first twenty years in her native Burgundy. In 1893 she married Henry Gauthier-Villars (known as Willy), a Parisian publisher and habitué of the demimonde. Fifteen years her senior and always in need of money, Willy urged his young wife to write her girlhood memoirs. "And that" Colette explained later, "is how I became a writer."

Her first novel, *Claudine á l'école* (1900; *Claudine at School*, published under Willy's name) was an immense commercial success. Three more "Claudine" novels followed, taking the heroine from her country school to Paris and marriage. Separated from Willy in 1906 (the divorce became final in 1910), Colette supported herself by working as a mime and dancer in various music-halls. She continued to write, however, and in 1910 published *La Vagabonde* (The Vagabond), a novel about a music-hall dancer who yearns for the comforting presence of a man but who ultimately chooses the lonely life of independence. In 1912, Colette married Henry de Jouvenel. They were divorced in 1925. During World War I, she turned to journalism, but returned to fiction in 1920 with the publication of *Chéri*, the novel that firmly established her reputation in France. In 1925, she began a liaison with Maurice Goudeket, who was seventeen years her junior. They were married in 1935, the year Colette was elected to the Belgian Royal Academy. Other honors followed. In 1945 she was elected to the Goncourt Academy, and in 1953 she was named Grand Officer of the Legion of Honor.

Beginning in the late 1930s, Colette began to suffer from arthritis. During her last years, she was confined to her bed, which she liked to call her "raft." At her death, the French government accorded her a state funeral.

Colette's work can be divided into two broad categories: on the one hand, fiction; on the other hand, chronicles, journals, and reminiscences. The fiction deals with the pangs of love and the ravages of desire. In most of the novels, the protagonist is a woman who longs to "submit" to love even while rebelling against the loss of freedom that inevitably accompanies love. In *Chéri*, Colette depicts an aging demimondaine, Léa, who, when confronted with the shocking fact that she is growing old, renounces love and, accepting her status as "an old woman," gives her young lover in marriage to a woman half her age.

Acceptance of the inevitable is a fundamental principle in the moral code of Colette's heroines, many of whom live on the fringe of society as music-hall dancers or courtesans. Another is the imperative to be happy, which for Colette means controlling the appetites, reducing as much as possible the gap between desire and fulfillment, and finding beauty and joy in ordinary things. These, in fact, are the themes of her books of reminiscences. In *La Maison de Claudine* (1929; *My Mother's House*) and *Sido* (1953), she idealized her mother, Sido, whose love of nature and lucid, unsentimental view of human affairs

Colette describes in prose that is a model of elegance.

Colette may be accused of focusing on a narrow range of human experience. She had no interest in philosophy, religion, or politics. She was concerned, rather, with love (maternal and passionate, heterosexual and homosexual) and with what she called the female's "mission to endure." A first-rate stylist, Colette has now attained the status of a classic French author.

Works

Claudine à l'école [Claudine at School] (1900). *Claudine à Paris* [Claudine in Paris] (1901). *Claudine en ménage* [The Indulgent Husband] (1902). *Claudine s'en va* [The Innocent Wife] (1903). *Minne* [Minnie] (1904). *Dialogue de bêtes* [Creatures Great and Small] (1904). *Les égarements de Minne* [Minnie's Misconduct] (1905). *Sept dialogues de bêtes* [Creatures Great and Small] (1905). *La retraite sentimentale* [The Retreat from Love] (1907). *Les vrilles de la vigne* [The Vine's Tendrils] (1908). *L'ingénue libertine* [The Innocent Libertine] (1909). *La vagabonde* [The Vagabond] (1911). *L'envers du music-hall* [Music-Hall Sidelights] (1913). *L'entrave* [The Shackle] (1913). *Mitsou ou comment l'esprit vient aux filles* [Mitsou] (1919). *Chéri* [Chéri and The Last of Chéri] (1920). *La maison de Claudine* [My Mother's House and Sido] (1922). *Le blé en herbe* [Ripening Seed] (1923). *La femme cachée* [The Hidden Woman] (1924). *L'enfant et les sortilèges. Musique de Maurice Ravel* [The Boy and the Magic] (1925). *La fin de Chéri* [Chéri and The Last of Chéri] (1926). *La naissance du jour* [Break of Day] (1928). *La seconde* [The Other One] (1929). *Sido* [My Mother's House and Sido] (1929). *Ces plaisirs* (1932. Reedited in 1941 as *Le pur et l'impur* [The Pure and the Impure]. *La Chatte* [The Cat] (1933). *Duo* [Duo] (1934). *Mes apprentissages* [My Apprenticeship] (1936). *Bella-Vista* [Bella-Vista] (1937). *Le Toutounier* [Le Toutounier] (1939). *Chambre d'hôtel* [Chance Acquaintances] (1940). *Journal à rebours* [Looking Backwards] (1941). *Julie de Carneilhan* [Julie de Carneilhan] (1941). *De ma fenêtre* (1942). *Gigi et autres nouvelles* (1944). *Trois...six...neuf* [Three...Six...Nine] (1944). *L'étoile vesper* [The Evening Star] (1946). *Le fanal bleu* [The Blue Lantern] (1949). Other works include: books on animals; books of remi-

niscences; collections of short stories; several volumes of correspondence; hundreds of newspaper articles; film scripts; stage adaptations of some of her novels.

Bibliography

Cottrell, Robert D. *Colette* (New York, 1974). Crossland, Margaret. *Colette: The Difficulty of Loving* (London, 1973). Davies, Margaret. *Colette* (Edinburgh, 1961). Goudeket, Maurice, *Près de Colette* (Paris, 1956; English tr., Close to Colette, New York, 1957). Marks, Elaine, *Colette* (New Brunswick, 1960). Sarde, Michèle, *Colette, libre et entravée* (Paris, 1978; English tr., Colette Free and Fettered, New York, 1980). Stewart, Joan Hinde, *Colette* (Boston, 1983).

Robert D. Cottrell

Camilla Collett

Born 1813, Kristiansand, Norway; died 1895, Kristiania (Oslo)
Genre(s): novel, essay
Language(s): Norwegian

Camilla Collett stands out as a true pioneer in the literary and cultural history of her country. She was born just at the time that 400 years of Danish rule over Norway was ending, and during her lifetime she witnessed tremendous changes in Norwegian society, politics, and culture and the flowering of a national literature. Camilla Collett participated in this process by writing Norway's first novel, *Amtmandens Døttre* (The Governor's Daughters), published in 1854–1855. With its realistic and critical depiction of contemporary society, *The Governor's Daughters* anticipated the social realism that characterizes Norwegian novels of the 1870s and 1880s. And in its portrayal of marriage as an often loveless and spiritually void institution, which stifles women in particular, Collett's book represents Norway's first feminist novel. Camilla Collett did not produce much fiction after *The Governor's Daughters*, but she continued to engage herself in improving the situation of women, and she has been credited with laying the foundation for the women's emancipation movement in Norway.

Camilla Collett was born into a prominent Norwegian family. Her father, Nicolai Wergeland, was one of the signers of the Norwegian constitution in 1814, and her brother, Henrik Wergeland, has been hailed as Norway's greatest romantic poet. A child of the Enlightenment, Nicolai Wergeland brought his children up in keeping with the writings of Rousseau. For Henrik this meant an opportunity for almost limitless exploration and development, but for Camilla, Rousseau did not prescribe the same education—a woman's duty was to serve the needs of her husband and this should be instilled in her as a child. Accordingly, Camilla was sent to finishing schools, first a year in Kristiania (present-day Oslo), and then two years in Germany.

Camilla Wergeland is said to have possessed a delicate, even ethereal beauty and, with her charm and many talents, could have attracted any suitor she chose. But when she was seventeen, it was her ill fortune to fall hopelessly in love with J.S. Welhaven, a man who was the bitter opponent of both her father and her brother in a conflict that split the country's authors and cultural leaders into two hostile camps. For a period of several years, Camilla and Welhaven met each other at social events and carried on a correspondence, but social conventions prevented Camilla from expressing her emotions and Welhaven carefully guarded his. Finally, all hope was lost when Welhaven declared that no affair of the heart could take precedence over commitment to his cause. This unhappy love affair had a profound and lasting affect on Camilla. It was obviously an impetus for her novel *The Governor's Daughters*, and she wrote openly about it in her journals and letters (compiled and published between 1926–1934) and in her memoirs *I de lange Nætter* (1862; During the Long Nights).

In 1841, at twenty-seven years of age, Camilla married Peter Jonas Collett. He respected her talent and ambition and gave her the necessary support and encouragement to pursue her writing. His untimely death in 1851 was a great personal loss, and it also left her in the difficult position of being a widow with four sons. With stubborn determination, she completed her novel and for the next thirty years there was a steady stream of stories, articles and essays from her pen.

Camilla Collett was in many ways a citizen of Europe. She lived abroad—in Copenhagen, Rome, Dresden, Paris—for extended periods of time, and through her travels and her reading came in contact with current ideas and trends. She admired the writings of George Sand in particular, but at the time she wrote *The Governor's Daughters*, Collett felt that many of Sand's ideas were too radical. Though she does lament in her novel the fact that young girls were deprived of the education and training that would enable them to develop their talents, Collett does not argue that women should have the opportunity to pursue a life and a career independent of marriage. There is no question but that marriage promised the happiest and most fulfilling future for the Governor's four daughters. But it should be a marriage based on mutual love and respect, not a union forced upon young women by parents whose primary interest was social and financial status. *The Governor's Daughters* is sharply critical of the superficiality and injustice of social conventions, but its underlying message is a plea for love. And woman, Collett contends, with her greater emotional capacity, is better able to recognize love and should therefore be free to declare her love.

On the issues of love in marriage and the importance of women's personal emancipation (a woman's right to assert her personality and to develop her abilities), Collett stood firm throughout her life. But as the years went by, she understood more clearly the need for social and political change as well. Her views became increasingly radical, and her writing took on a polemic tone. Her many articles and essays first appeared in newspapers and magazines, and she periodically compiled and published them in book form.

When these articles were first printed in the press, they were anonymous (*The Governor's Daughters* was also published anonymously, though the author's identity was not kept secret for long). The stigma attached to a woman who made her writing public was keenly felt by Collett, who nonetheless did not hesitate to attack this prejudice in her own writing. She wrote book reviews and essays on literature, some of which were the first examples of feminist literary criticism in Norway. She called for a new image of woman, denouncing the typical role in which women were cast as self-effacing, self-sacrificing saints. There can be little doubt that Collett was heard and heeded by her male contemporaries, most notably Henrik Ibsen.

For most of her life Camilla Collett was a solitary figure with no female colleagues to join her in her struggle. However, she lived to see arise a generation of women writers and activists who, inspired by her example, carried on the work to which she had dedicated her life.

Works

Novels: *Amtmandens Döttre* (1854–1855).

Stories and memoirs: *Fortællinger* (1860). *I de lange Nætter* (1862).

Articles and essays: *Sidste Blade I-V* (1868–1873). *Fra de Stummes Leir* (1877). *Mod Strömmen I-II* (1879–1885).

Letters and journals: *Dagböker og breve I-V*, ed. Leiv Amundsen (1926–1934).

Translations: *An Everyday Story. Norwegian Women's Fiction*, ed. Katherine Hanson (1984).

Bibliography

Aarnes, Sigurd Aa. *Sökelys på Amtmandens Döttre* (Oslo, 1977). Agerholt, Anna Caspari. *Den norske kvinnebevegelses historie.* Oslo. 1937. Benterud, Aagot. *Camilla Collett. En skjebne og et livsverk* (Oslo, 1947). Beyer, Edvard, ed. *Norges Litteratur Historie*, vol. 2 (Oslo, 1974). Bonnevie, Mai Bente, et al. *Et annet språk. Analyser av norsk kvinnelitteratur* (Oslo, 1977). Engelstad, Irene, et al. *Norsk kvinnelitteraturhistorie* (Oslo, 1988). Gravier, Maurice. "Camilla Collett et la France." *Scandinavica*, vol. 4, nr. 1. London. 1965. Hanson, Katherine. "Ibsen's Women Characters and Their Feminist Contemporaries." *Theatre History Studies* (Grand Forks, 1982). Jensen, Elisabeth Møller. *Emancipation som lidenskab: Camilla Collett i liv og værk. En læsning i Amtmandens Døttre* (Charlottenlund, 1987). *Kvinner og böker. Festskrift til Ellisiv Steen* (Oslo, 1978). Rasmussen, Janet E. "Dreams and Discontent: The Female Voice in Norwegian Literature." *Review of National Literatures. Norway*, vol. 12, 1983. Steen, Ellisiv. *Diktning og virkelighet. En studie i Camilla Colletts forfatterskap* (Oslo, 1947). Steen, Ellisiv. *Den lange strid. Camilla Collett og hennes senere forfatterskap* (Oslo, 1954). Steen, Ellisiv. *Camilla Collett om seg selv* (Oslo, 1985).

Katherine Hanson

Colombine

(see: Carmen Burgos Sequí)

Vittoria Colonna, Marchesa di Pescara

Born 1492, Colonna castle at Marino, south of Rome, Italy; died February 25, 1547, Rome
Genre(s): poetry
Language(s): Italian

"The most famous woman in Italy" during the Renaissance, as Burckhardt called her, was born to a noble Roman family whose role in political and military matters was very significant. Her father, Fabrizio Colonna, is memorialized in Machiavelli's *The Art of War.* Her mother, Agnese da Montefeltro, was the younger daughter of Duke Federigo of Urbino and Battista Sforza, and the sister of Guidobaldo, whose famous court provided Castiglione with the setting for his *Book of the Courtier.* The political and intellectual matters of Vittoria's time helped her to acquire not only a humanistic education but also assured that her life and ideas would always remain tied to Italy's struggles.

When Vittoria was three years old, a marriage to Ferrante Francesco d'Avalos, marquis of Pescara, was arranged by Fabrizio to strengthen his alliance with Ferdinand II, king of Naples. The wedding took place on the island of Ischia in 1509. Pescara, himself a man of war, would have little time for his marriage. A year later he joined Fabrizio and the forces of Pope Julius II and Spain against the French in northern Italy. Until his death in 1525, Pescara distinguished himself in battle with a zeal that left very little attention for anything else. Vittoria remained at her home in the south, although she traveled often to Marino and to Rome. She formed great friendships with the prominent intellectuals of the day, including Pietro Bembo, and perhaps also Castiglione and Ariosto. After Pescara's death she resided at the Convent of San Silvestro in Rome, although she did not join the order.

Vittoria's travels were considerable and she made many friends, from her close association with the famous poet Jacopo Sannazaro in Naples to her most important and spiritual friendship with Michelangelo Buonarroti. For over a decade they wrote letters and poems to each other, and the painter lavished her with sketches and other pieces of his work. Both were also deeply interested in religious reform. She was later to become an ardent supporter of the Capuchin Order and her influence helped in procuring privileges for the Capuchins from Paul III.

The poetry (*Rime*) of Vittoria Colonna was praised by her contemporaries, although much of it could only be read in manuscript, due to the reluctance of the poet in publishing them. Her first poem to be printed appeared in a book of Bembo's poetry in 1535. Three years later an entire book of poetry was published in Parma, the first of approximately twenty editions to appear in the sixteenth century. Vittoria's verse, which thematizes love and spirituality, offers an impressive fusion of Petrarchan and Neoplatonic elements. The sonnet form is maintained throughout, from the poems of love begun shortly after the death of her husband, to the spiritual poems she wrote during the 1530s and 1540s and which reflect the extent of her religious conversion. The meditative quality of this work, especially Vittoria's final religious poem, "The Triumph of Christ's Cross," anticipates numerous later writers of the Baroque tradition.

Works

Rime, ed. Alan Bullock (1982). *Carteggio*, ed. Ermanno Ferrero and Giuseppe Müller (1892).

Richard J. Pioli

Denisa Comănescu

Born 1954, Buzău, Romania
Genre(s): poetry
Language(s): Romanian

After studying Romanian and English at the Bucharest University, Denisa Comănescu became an editor for the Univers Publishing House. In 1979 she received the Debut Prize of the Writers' Union. Since then she has published several significant volumes such as *Izgonirea din paradis* (1979; Banishment from Paradise), *Cuţitul de argint* (1983; Silver Knife), and *Urma focului* (1986; Trace of Fire).

Comănescu's is a somber poetry of dismal urban childhood, deserted highways, love and solitude. Discouragement—"There's no seed of victory planted in me" ("To the Friend Who Asked Me to Dedicate This Poem to V")—seems to be the dominant note in Comănescu's late volumes. The poet expresses in an exemplary way the state of mind of a whole generation.

Works

Izgonirea din paradis [Banishment from Paradise] (1979). *Cuţitul de argint* [Silver Knife] (1983). *Urma focului* [Trace of Fire] (1986).

Translations: Deletant, Andrea, and Brenda Walker, trs., *Silent Voices. An Anthology of Contemporary Romanian Women Poets* (London and Boston, 1986), pp. 66–75 (poems from *Izgonirea din paradis*, *Cuţitul de argint*, and *Urma focului*).

Sanda Golopentia

Concepción Espina (de la Maza)

(see: Concha Espina)

Concha Espina

(a.k.a. Concepción Espina [de la Maza])

Born 1869, Santander, Spain; died 1955, Madrid
Genre(s): novel, short story, drama
Language(s): Spanish

Espina has been termed the first Spanish woman writer to earn her living exclusively from her writings, a possibly inaccurate statement but one that reflects her wide popularity. Twice nominated for the Nobel Prize (once lost by a single vote), she won several prizes, including the Royal Academy's prestigious Fastenrath for *La esfinge maragata* (1914; English translation, Mariflor, 1924); the National Prize for Literature for *Altar mayor* (1926; High Altar), and a major theatrical prize for *El jayón* (1918; The Foundling). Espina's prestige sufficed to have her named a cultural representative of King Alfonso XIII to the Antilles (1928), and she later served as a visiting professor at Middlebury College. Although generally conservative and rarely considered a feminist, Espina was among the most successful women writers in the first quarter of the twentieth century.

Raised in a religious home and educated in a convent, Espina hastily married in 1892 following her mother's death and her father's bankruptcy, accompanying her husband to Chile where two of their five children were born. Financial difficulty prompted her to begin writing as a newspaper correspondent, but her journalism compounded incipient marital problems, which ultimately led to separation in 1916.

Espina is associated with the regional variant of realism, with early novels usually set in rural Santander and featuring detailed descriptions of nature and conservative ideology. The author of some fifty books, including novels, plays, and poetry, she is best known for her fiction. While influenced by post-romantic sentimentalism as well as realistic currents, she remained essentially apart from major literary movements. Her importance for feminists is her focus on female protagonists. As a sentimentalist, she often wrote of unrequited or impossible love yet had sufficient vision to portray some women as victims of their own sentimentality, trapped in an intellectual vacuum by the conflict between romantic illusion and the harsher realities of daily life with the then-typical male-female relationships. In later works, Espina moves beyond her native region and one-to-one relationships to study the impact of varied social realities on her characters. Her plays were few, concentrating on internal moral dilemmas of women in their roles as mother, daughter, fiancée, and wife. Two collections of Espina's brief fiction explore critical issues in Spanish history during the early twentieth century: the need for national reform, the conflict between traditional values and progress, materialism versus idealism, and the hostilities of the civil war.

The popular *folletín* (serialized novel of the nineteenth century), with its melodrama, suspense, and dependence on coincidence, provided a model for Espina's first foray into long fiction, *La niña de Luzmela* (1909; The Girl From Luzmela), which also includes the sentimental novel and moralistic fiction among its forebears. Plot takes primacy over characterization, and

style is superior to both the one-dimensional characters and soap-opera plot. The writer's concept of suffering as a fundamental part of human existence and her depiction of virtue in conflict with evil appear here and in *Despertar para morir* (1910; To Awake to Die), although more sophistication is evident in the latter, which analyzes moral decadence in Madrid's turn-of-the-century aristocracy and develops the tragic consequences of marriage as an economic transaction. In *Agua de nieve* (1911; English translation, The Woman and the Sea, 1934), suffering continues as a major avenue for plumbing life's deeper meaning, but simplistic conflicts between good and evil are replaced by analysis of the Spanish woman and the heroine's internal struggles in her quest for happiness.

Among Espina's best and most successful novels is *La esfinge maragata* (1914; English translation, Mariflor, 1924), which refines the best of her regionalistic vision of northern Spain while incorporating some of the fervor for national regeneration of the "Generation of 1898." *La esfinge maragata* is set in the isolated, backward, impoverished, semi-desert Maragatería district of León's border with Galicia. Following classic realistic/naturalistic procedure, Espina spent months there observing details of village life, geography, and social environment, and documenting local dialect and folklore. While provincial and localistic, the novel is also a vigorous denunciation of social and familial situations of women. Florinda, the heroine, raised in Galicia (humid and green), returns to live with her grandmother, Dolores, in a desolate, sterile land, her once wealthy family now impoverished. Modern, independent, frank, cultured, and optimistic, with an urban mentality, Florinda contrasts with her traditional grandmother's feudal outlook; coarse, uneducated ways; lack of independence; and rural mentality. Another contrast is established between the strong, silent, long-suffering women, and the men who are brutal, domineering, and dehumanized, or else weak. Life in Maragatería is an endless cycle of emigration and living at the subsistence level. Harsh economic realities eventually triumph and Mariflor ends by accepting the same economic basis for matrimony as generations of Maragatan women before her.

Unlike its predecessors, *El metal de los muertos* (1920; The Metal of the Dead) is most emphatically social protest fiction. Following World War I, Spain was experiencing unrest prior to the Civil War, and Espina moved closer to the left, although remaining moderate. This social epic, her most ambitious work, has been ranked by most critics among her best achievements, and for it also the diligent author personally researched the area and way of life described (in the Río Tinto copper mines in the Andalusian province of Huelva). Espina depicts a miners' strike between 1910 and 1920, a struggle supported by a group of bourgeois intellectuals inspired by humanitarian socialism (a term avoided by the novelist, whose chief organizer speaks instead of return to early Christian values). Contemporary concern with pollution, industrial wastes, and poisonous by-products lends an up-to-date air to this novel of nearly seven decades ago. Espina introduces a large cast, ranging from brutalized prostitutes to oldtime miners, administrators and labor officials, achieving something approaching the collective protagonist. The main plot is complicated by involved, amorous subplots, but the primary conflict remains the struggle between capitalism and the workers' welfare.

Espina's most nearly feminist novel is *La virgen prudente* (1929; The Wise Virgin), examining societal pressures and cultural prejudices that condition women's attitudes and produce internal contradictions. The symbolically named protagonist, Aurora de España (Dawn of Spain), an idealistic young lawyer, struggles with family, friends, and suitors, intent on independence despite their resistance. The contrast between this work and her novels from the mid-1930s onward is enormous, as wartime experiences rendered Espina extremely pro-Franco, producing highly politicized post-war texts of national exaltation, tending again to the melodrama of her apprenticeship years, with their Manichean duality of good and evil. *Altar mayor* (1954; High Altar), awarded the highest recognition of any of Espina's works, the National Prize for Literature (for more than six decades the most prestigious literary prize won by any woman writer in Spain), is aesthetically inferior to *La esfinge maragata* and lacks the dramatic impact and social significance of *El metal de los muertos*. Conceived as an exaltation of traditional Spanish values and national history, it is set in Covadonga (Asturias) where the Reconquest began in 711.

Blind from 1937 on, Espina continued to write, and two novels of her final years are of interest for the feminist scholar. *El más fuerte* (1947; The Strongest) presents a male protagonist who, after eighteen years of successful marriage, faces (with his wife) the test of parenting three children through adolescence. In the process, he acquires self-knowledge and becomes better acquainted with the younger generation, but his wife founders in a futile effort to recover the past. *Un valle en el mar* (1950; A Valley in the Sea) focuses on the theme of rape and its consequences in a stratified rural Cantabrian village. The delineation of social values is informative and reasonably objective, and the two central characters transcend the unidimensional flatness and melodramatic traits of the minor personages to rank among Espina's more memorable creations.

An independent figure who resists facile categorization, Espina changes repeatedly during her half-century career, with neither her ideology nor her themes remaining constant. Although her aesthetics are not innovative, her frequent changes in setting and subject matter evince a desire for novelistic progress. Espina was especially interested in feminine psychology, although her analyses were less of individuals than of a type: the woman who was forebearing, long-suffering, self-abnegating, chaste, born "to love and suffer." Her poetics are eclectic and results are uneven. From today's perspective, some works seem outmoded because she often drew upon the past's more dated literary manifestations (postromanticism, melodrama, sentimentalism). Her move to the right after the Civil War also hurt her fame and created an "ideology gap" for many readers. Her wartime *Esclavitud y libertad: diario de una prisionera* (1938; Slavery and Liberty: Diary of a Prisoner) recounts her incarceration by radical leftists and helps to explain her changed attitude. Nevertheless, her writing as a whole is representative of a broad social spectrum and interests sociologically because of her middle-class origins and identification. The enhanced respect she won for women writers in official circles through her own popular success continues to benefit her successors.

Works

Agua de nieve (1911). Alas invencibles (1938). Altar mayor (1954). El caliz rojo (1923). Despertar para morir (1910). Dulce nombre (1921). La esfinge maragata (1914). Flor de ayer (1934). El fraile menor (1942). El jayón (1918). Llama de cera (1925). El más fuerte (1947). El metal de los muertos (1920). Moneda blanca (1942). La niña de Luzmela (1909). Una novela de amor (1953). La Otra (1942). Retaguardia (1937). La rosa de los vientos (1916). La tiniebla encendida (1940). Un valle en el mar (1950). Victoria en América (1944).

Translations: Mariflor, tr. Frances Douglas (1924). The Red Beacon, tr. Frances Douglas (1924). The Woman and the Sea, tr. Terrell Tatum (1934).

Bibliography

Bretz, Mary Lee, *Concha Espina* (Boston, 1980). Canales, Alicia, *Concha Espina* (Madrid, 1974). Nicholson, Helen Schenk, *The Novel of Protest and the Spanish Republic* (Tucson: University of Arizona Press, 1939). de Nora, Eugenio, *La novela española contemporánea* (Madrid, 1963), vol. 2.

Janet Perez

Corina

(see: Veronica Micle)

Corinna

Born fifth or third century B.C., Tanagra, Boeotia (Greece), but the date is strongly disputed; the earliest references to her occur in first century B.C. authors
Genre(s): poetry
Language(s): Greek

Corinna, next to Pindar the most renowned Boeotian poet in antiquity, is firmly associated with him in the ancient biographical tradition: various anecdotes represent her as his teacher (Plutarch, *Glor. Athen.* 4.347F) or, alternatively, his poetic rival, victorious over him in singing contests once or several times (Pausanias 9.22.3; Aelian, *VH* 13.25; Suda s.v. "Korinna"). Literary citations preserve only a few lines of her work;

when, at the beginning of this century, substantial passages on papyrus were first brought to light, scholars unhesitatingly deemed Corinna's style and subject matter "primitive." Her interest in retelling obscure local legends in a simple, straightforward manner and in a literary dialect colored by Boeotian vocabulary, pronunciation, and spelling was considered evidence of a limited, parochial talent. Consequently, she was relegated to the category of "minor [and not particularly interesting] voices."

In 1930 Edgar Lobel presented a strong stylistic argument for jettisoning the ancient biographical evidence and moving Corinna's date down to the third century B.C. The subsequent learned controversy, not yet resolved, forced scholars into an attentive rereading of her fragments and ultimately led to a new appreciation of her art. Corinna is now thought to be a subtle, engaging, and occasionally quite witty storyteller. The recent discovery of a new fragment (*PMG* 655), apparently from the prologue to a published verse collection, reveals her as a self-conscious artist: there she titles her poems *Weroia* (the word may mean "narratives"), assigns them to the lyric genre of *partheneia* or compositions to be sung and danced by choruses of young girls, and boasts of the esteem her "clear-teasing voice" has brought her native city. The fragment breaks off as she is summarizing the contents of these choral lyrics, which apparently dealt with the exploits of such mythic figures as Cephisus and Orion.

The "Berlin Papyrus" (*PMG* 654), the longest extant sample of her poetry, contains passages from two tales: first, the account of a musical competition between the eponymous heroes of two Boeotian mountains, Helicon and Cithaeron; second, the prophecy of Acraephen, denizen of Apollo's oracle on Mount Ptoios, regarding the fate of the nine daughters of the river Asopus. The "Contest of Helicon and Cithaeron" is much admired for its economy, verve and humor. In only twenty-three lines (all that is legible of the preserved text), Corinna recapitulates the finale of one competitor's prize song and then briskly informs us that the gods, under the supervision of the Muses, decided the winner by dropping secret ballots into golden urns. When Cithaeron is proclaimed victor and garlanded, Helicon throws a violent tantrum, hurling a boulder on high and smashing it into a thousand pebbles. This personification of a peak with unruly human impulses is a lively and delightful touch. Since tradition from Hesiod onward makes Mount Helicon the principal haunt of the Muses, the poet may have finally described how the goddesses mollified the sore loser by promising to honor him with their abiding presence. In the "Daughters of Asopus," a much lengthier fragment, Acraephen advises Asopus, who is searching for his nine missing daughters, that they were secretly abducted by Zeus, Poseidon, Apollo and Hermes and will eventually become the mothers of a race of demigods. To lend authority to his prediction, the prophet summarizes the history of his oracular seat. At his urging, Asopus apparently submitted to the will of the gods and accepted the loss of his daughters. As these female figures bear the names of nine major Greek settlements, Corinna is clearly providing an aetiological account of how each came to be associated with its particular patron divinity. Her poem, furthermore, had patriotic overtones, for the single bride she bestowed upon Hermes was her own native city Tanagra (Pausanias 9.20.2).

It should be noted that Corinna, though she writes compositions for young girls to sing, is by no means a woman-oriented poet. Her narratives seem to have dealt principally with the feats of male gods and heroes—Hermes and Ares, Orion, Orestes, the "Seven against Thebes." She views her mythic heroines from a traditional, fully patriarchal perspective. Raped by Zeus and his companions, the Asopids may count themselves blessed in their semi-divine offspring; late references mention tales of the daughters of Minyas, who refused to worship Dionysus and were punished with madness, and of Metioche and Menippe, who sacrificed themselves to save their city. Finally, in the most enigmatic of her fragments (*PMG* 664a), she reproaches Myrtis, another Boeotian poet (q.v.), because "being a woman, she entered into contention (*eba . . . pot erin*) with Pindar." The Greek phrase can mean either participation in an actual contest or literary emulation. In either case, it suggests that Myrtis' rivalry with a male poet is unseemly, as she must necessarily fall short of Pindar's greatness due to her sex. Corinna's delicate *Weroia*

therefore serve as an illustration of what the proper woman poet can and should compose.

Works

Greek texts and German translations in Homeyer, H. *Dichterinnen des Altertums und des frühen Mittelalters* (Paderborn, 1979). Greek texts in *Poetae Melici Graeci*, ed. D.L. Page (Oxford, 1962). English translations in *Lyra Graeca* III, tr. J.M. Edmonds. Loeb Classical Library (Cambridge, Mass., 1959).

Bibliography

Cupaiuolo, N., *Poetesse Greche: Corinna* (Naples, 1939). Kirkwood, G.M., *Early Greek Monody: The History of a Poetic Type* (Ithaca, 1974). Page, D.L., *Corinna* (London, 1963). Snyder, J.M., *The Woman and the Lyre* (Carbondale, Ill., 1989). Trypanis, C.A., *Greek Poetry from Homer to Seferis* (Chicago, 1981). Weiler, I., *Der Agon im Mythos* (Darmstadt, 1974).

General references: *Cambridge History of Classical Literature I: Greek Literature*, eds. P.E. Easterling and B.M.W. Knox (Cambridge, 1985), pp. 239–241, 749–750. *Oxford Classical Dictionary*, 2nd ed. (Oxford, 1970), p. 290. Pauly-Wissowa, *Real-Encyclopädie der klassischen Altertumswissenschaft* XI.2 (Stuttgart, 1922), pp. 1393–1397.

Other references: Bowra, C.M., *Problems in Greek Poetry* (Oxford, 1953), pp. 54–65. Clayman, D.L., *Classical Quarterly* 28 (1978): 396–397. Ebert, J., *Zeitschrift für Papyrologie und Epigraphik* 30 (1978): 5–12. Guillon, P., *Bulletin de Correspondence Hellénique* 82 (1958): 47–60. Idem, *Annales de la Faculté des Lettres et Sciences Humaines d' Aix* 33 (1959): 155–168. Latte, K., *Eranos* 54 (1956): 57–67. Lobel, E., *Hermes* 65 (1930): 356–365. Segal, C.P., *Eranos* 73 (1975): 1–8. Skinner, M.B., *Tulsa Studies in Women's Literature* 2 (1983): 9–20. Snyder, J.M., *Eranos* 82 (1984): 125–134. West, M.L. *Classical Quarterly* 20 (1970): 277–287.

Marilyn B. Skinner

Elena Lucrezia Corner

*Born June 5, 1648, Venice, Italy; died July 26,
1684, Padua*
Genre(s): poetry
Language(s): Latin

Daughter of Giovan Battista Corner and
Zanetta Boni, Elena Lucrezia Corner is the first
woman to receive the doctoral degree. Sprung
from the Venetian patriciate, she was able to
complete her work and receive her doctorate in
philosophy at Padua. She had anticipated that
theology would be her field but she encountered
an immovable obstacle in the Bishop of Padua,
Gregorio Cardinal Barbarigo, the chancellor of
the University, and had to settle for a laureate in
philosophy, July 25, 1678.

She was the fifth of seven children and the
object of an intense campaign on the part of her
father; she was to be the rehabilitation of the
family. Corner herself preferred the quiet life; at
eighteen she became an oblate of the Benedictine
order. She was thus able to avoid marriage but
still lived in the world.

She received her education in Venice from
the local clergy and became proficient in both
Latin and Greek. For her doctorate the central
figure is Carlo Rinaldini, a professor of philosophy at Padua from 1667, after he had spent
eighteen years at Pisa. What remains of her
works, mostly poetic, may be found in *Opera quae
quidem haberi potuerunt*, ed. B. Bacchini (Parma,
1688) (The Surviving Works).

Works

Opera quae quidem haberi potuerunt (The Surviving Works), ed. B. Bacchini (Parma, 1688).
General references: *DBI* 29, 174–179.

Joseph Berrigan

Natalia de Oliveira Correia

*Born September 13, 1923, Isle of S. Miguel,
Azores; died ?*
*Genre(s): essay, journalism, literary criticism,
novel, poetry, short story, drama*
Language(s): Portuguese

Natalia Correia is an institution in Portuguese
letters of the twentieth century. Born in the

Azores, she was educated in mainland Portugal
and started early a long and distinguished career
that would touch virtually every field of literature,
from works of children's literature, theater, novel,
essay, literary criticism, and travel books to poetry, the medium in which she has received the
most critical attention. Correia's intellectual life
bears witness to the political and sociological
changes of contemporary Portugal. Correia was
director and editor of several journals and worked
as a consultant to the Department of Culture. She
was elected to the National Congress and was an
important part of the movement of resistance
against the fascist dictatorships of Salazar and
Caetano. Her *Antologia de poesia erotica e satirica*
(1966) was censured by the government of Antonio Salazar, and she was condemned to two
years of house arrest for "abusing the freedom of
the press."

Correia's trajectory as a poet started in 1947
with the publication of *Rios de nuvens*, and from
that book through fourteen more volumes she
has developed the themes of love, nature, and the
telluric forces of women. Her latest collection of
poems, *O Armisticio* (1986), has as its main
theme the need for the current patriarchal system
to give way to a government based on female
wisdom as the only hope for world survival.

In the theater and novel, Correia is equally
important and versatile. Her first novel, *Anoiteceu
no barrio* (1946), deals with the impact of a
changing society on the everyday life of common
people, while her most famous play, *Erros meus,
ma fortuna, amor ardente*, commissioned in 1981
by the National Theater in commemoration of
the four-hundredth anniversary of the death of
the poet Luis de Camoes, deals with the life and
works of this distinguished member of Portuguese
letters. As a literary critic and essayist, Correia is
also important. Her anthologies and critical essays range from the work of the medieval troubadours to the surrealist poets and each one has
expanded the realm of Portuguese literary history.
A perceptive observer, her travel diaries range
from a chronicle of a visit to the United States in
Descobri que era europeia (1951) to a reflection
on contemporary life in *Nao percas a Rosa* (1978).
She has also worked in children's literature and
is an excellent painter. Natalia Correia is truly

one of the most talented members of twentieth century Portuguese intellectual life.

Works

Poetry: *Rios de nuvens* [Rivers of Clouds] (1947). *Poemas* [Poems] (1955). *Dimensao encontrada* [Found Dimension] (1957). *Passaporte* [Passport] (1958). *Comunicacao* [Communication] (1959). *Cantico do pais emerso* [Canticle of the Emersed Country] (1961). *O vinho e a lira* [Wine and Lyre] (1966). *Matria* (1968). *As macas de Oreste* [Orestes' Apples] (1970). *A mosca iluminada* [The Illuminated Fly] (1972). *O anjo de ocidente a entrada do ferro* [The Angel of the West at the Iron Door] (1972). *Poemas a rebate* [Poems to Alarm] (1975). *Epistola aos Iamitas* [Epistle to the Iamitas] (1976). *O diluvio e a pompa* [Deluge and Pomp] (1979). *O armisticio* [The Armistice] (1985).

Novels: *Anoiteceu no barrio* [Dusk in the Neighborhood] (1946). *A madona* [The Madonna] (1968).

Plays: *O progresso de Edipo* [Oedipus' Progress] (1957). *O homunculo* [The Dwarf] (1965). *O Encoberto* [The Concealed] (1969). *Erros Meus, Ma Fortuna, Amor Ardente* [My Mistakes, My Fortune, Impassioned Love] (1981).

Essays: *Poesia de arte e realismo poetico* [Art, Poetry and Poetic Realism] (1958). *Uma estatua para Herodes* [A Statue for Herodes] (1974). *A lingua portuguesa en perigo* [The Portuguese Language in Peril] (1979).

Anthologies and Literary Criticism: *A questao academica de 1907* [The Academic Question of 1907] (1962). *Antologia da poesia erotica e satirica* [Anthology of Erotic and Satirical Poetry] (1966). *Cantares galego-portugueses* [Galician-Portuguese Ballads] (1970). *Trovas de D. Dinis* [The Songs of D. Dinis] (1970). *A mulher* [Women] (1973). *O surrealismo na poesia portuguesa* [Surrealism in Portuguese Poetry] (1973). *Antologia de poesia portuguesa no periodo barroco* [Anthology of Baroque Portuguese Poetry] (1983). *A ilha de Sam Nunca* [Sam Nunca's Island] (1982).

Diaries and Travel Books: *Descobri que era europeia* [I Discovered that I was a European] (1951). *Nao percas a Rosa* [Do Not Miss the Rose] (1978).

Children's Literature: *Grandes aventuras dum Pequeno Heroi* [The Grand Adventures of Little Hero] (1947).

Bibliography

Simoes, Joao G., "Critica Literaria: *A Madona, A Mosca Iluminada*" [Literary Criticism: *The Madonna, The Illuminated Fly*]. *Diario de Noticias* (Lisbon) (April 13, 1972): 18, 19. Souto, Jose Correia de, *Dicionario da Literatura Portuguesa* [Dictionary of Portuguese Literature] (Porto, 1984).

Lina L. Cofresi

Maria Corti

Born 1915, Milan, Italy
Genre(s): journalism, criticism, fiction
Language(s): Italian

Maria Corti is known primarily for her vast and diverse scholarly production. Now retired, she taught at the University of Pavia for many years as an historian of the Italian language and a philologist. She recently established at Pavia a research center in which are gathered the manuscripts and letters of several important contemporary writers; in conjunction with the center, she publishes the review *Autografo* in which the center's materials are described and analyzed. Her own scholarly work has concentrated primarily on medieval and contemporary texts, as well as on critical methodologies and theoretical issues. Corti is active on the editorial boards of several journals, including *Strumenti critici* and *Alfabeta*; she writes regularly for the Roman newspaper *La Repubblica*. Much like Umberto Eco, she is a cultural mentor whose vivacious presence within the Italian intellectual scene is matched by her tireless efforts to bring Italian culture to other countries. She has traveled to and taught in several European countries and in America, where her impeccable scholarship and enthusiastic pedagogical talents are widely known. Her study, *Principi della comunicazione letteraria* (1976), has been translated into English (An Introduction to Literary Semiotics, 1978); her most recent studies include *Il viaggio testuale: le ideologie e le strutture semiotiche* (1978; The Textual Voyage: Ideologies and Semiotic Structures) and *La felicità mentale: nuove prospettive per Cavalcanti e Dante* (1983, Mental Happiness: New Perspectives on Cavalcanti and Dante).

Maria Corti has published four works of fiction. The first, *L'ora di tutti* (The Hour of Everyone), published in 1962, won the Crotone literary prize in 1963. It tells the story of a southern Italian community that is put to the test when invaded by the Turks. The second, *Il ballo dei sapienti* (The Dance of the Wise), is situated in the contemporary academic world of the sixties (the book was published in 1966) and paints a vivid picture of academia's conventions and hypocrisies. In 1986, after a trip to America, Corti published *Voci dal Nord Est* (Voices from the Northeast); a sort of fictionalized travel diary, it contains chapters on several eastern universities where Corti taught during her trip; on a visit to Emily Dickinson's house; on Chicago; on Corti's own terrible experience of being mugged. There are portraits of colleagues and students, and, throughout, a commentary on the American scene as observed and understood by the foreign protagonist Marta. Corti attempts to avoid a merely documentaristic reproduction of places, people, and events by using a subjective and meditative prose whose origins are to be found in the musings of the thinly veiled autobiographical protagonist: a woman, like her creator, of strong personal opinions and ideological convictions. The result is a book that is midway between fiction and social commentary. Her latest work of fiction, *Il canto delle sirene* (The Song of the Sirens), was published in 1989. A meditation on humankind's eternal search for knowledge, it is a moving and fully realized intellectual autobiography as well as a highly original novel that reveals Corti's exceptional talents as a creative writer.

In an interview published on April 26, 1986 in *La Stampa*, Corti states her belief in the synergistic interrelationship of scholarly and creative writing: "The best critics are also writers. I am thinking of Valéry, of Baudelaire. . . . Creative writing gives a certain humility to the critic, who must understand and not judge." Corti's own career reflects her constant search for understanding—of texts, cultures, and language itself—as well as her ability to share that understanding with both academic and general readers.

Works

Selected Scholarly Works: *Studi sulla sintassi della lingua poetica avanti lo Stilnovo* (1953). *Metodi e fantasmi* (1969). *I metodi attuali della critica in Italia* (1970, with co-editor Cesare Segre). *Principi della comunicazione letteraria* (1976). *Il viaggio testuale: le ideologie e le strutture semiotiche* [The Textual Voyage: Ideologies and Semiotic Structures] (1978). *La felicità mentale: nuove prospettive per Cavalcanti e Dante* [Mental Happiness: New Perspectives on Cavalcanti and Dante] (1983).

Fiction: *L'ora di tutti* [The Hour of Everyone] (1962). *Il ballo dei sapienti* [The Dance of the Wise] (1966). *Voci dal Nord Est* [Voices from the Northeast] (1986). *Il canto delle sirene* [The Song of the Sirens] (1989).

Translation: *An Introduction to Literary Semiotics* [Principi della comunicazione letteraria], tr. Margherita Bogat and Allen Mandelbaum, 1978.

Bibliography

Dizionario della letteratura italiana contemporanea (Florence, 1973). Interview (on *Voci dal Nord Est*) in *La Stampa*, 26 April, 1986. West, Rebecca, Review of *Il canto delle sirene* in *Annali D'Italianistica* 7 (1989).

Rebecca West

Marthe Cosnard

Born April 14, 1614, Séez, France; died 1659, Séez
Genre(s): drama
Language(s): French

Little is known about the life of Marthe Cosnard except for the fact that she and her family lived in Normandy. She wrote a religious tragedy, *Les Chastes Martirs* (1650), which she dedicated to Anne d'Autriche, wife of Louis XIII.

The subject is derived from the *Agatonphile* of Jean Pierre Camus, a pious novel published in 1621, which was also dramatized by Françoise Pascal in 1655. The edifying purpose of Camus is retained by Marthe Cosnard who shows she was influenced by Corneille's *Polyeucte*; as Agathon and Tryphine are put to death because they are Christians, three more people become courageous enough to join them. The prefect of Sicily and his wife, impressed, first resolve to persecute Christians no longer, then to become Christians, too. The action takes place in twenty-four hours, the place is reduced to a palace, its grounds and a prison, but the action is not unified as the various love affairs have no effect on the *dénouement*. Marthe Cosnard knew how to link scenes, and she carefully respected the proprieties.

Works

Les Chastes Martirs (1650).

Bibliography

Lachèvre, Fréderic, "Corneille et Mlle Cosnard: la tragédie des *Chastes Martyrs*, 1650." *Glanes bibliographiques* (1929). Lancaster, Henry Carrington, *A History of French Dramatic Literature in the Seventeenth Century* (1966). La Sicotière, L. de, "Une muse normande inconnue—Mlle Cosnard de Sées." *Bulletin de la Société de l'Orne* (1884). Stegmann, André, *L'héroisme cornélien—Genèse et signification* (Paris, 1968).

Marie-France Hilgar

Maria de Fatima Bivar Velho da Costa

Born June 26, 1938, Lisbon, Portugal
Genre(s): essay, journalism, novel, poetry,
*   short story*
Language(s): Portuguese

Maria Velho da Costa is part of the group of contemporary Portuguese women writers whose work strives to expand and change the limits of the traditional literature of that country. Born and educated in Lisbon, Costa studied German philology at the university and taught in private schools for a time. She later worked at the National Institute for Industrial Research with fellow writer Maria Isabel Barreno. In 1966 Costa published her first novel, *O Lugar Comun*, which was well received by the critics. In 1969 her second book, *Maina Mendes*, a collection of three short novels, caused a critical uproar for her approach to the theme of women in Portuguese society. In 1972 she published two books, *Ensino Primario e Ideologia*, a collection of essays on education, and *Novas Cartas Portuguesas*, written in collaboration with Maria Isabel Barreno and Maria Teresa Horta. This last work, perhaps the most famous of the feminist European books of the decade, was hailed internationally as the "coming of consciousness of Portuguese and European women," and brought the three writers into the limelight of Portuguese literature and into the displeasure of the dictatorship of Marcello Caetano. Accused of "offending public morals," the three writers were arrested and taken to court. The political coup of April 1974 changed the intellectual climate of the nation, and *Novas Cartas Portuguesas* was suddenly declared a book of literary merit.

An active intellectual, Costa has served as president of the Portuguese Writers Association and continues to write for newspapers and journals. Some of her articles and essays appeared in three volumes: *Desescrita* (1973), *Cravo* (1975), and *Da Rosa Fixa* (1978). In 1979 her novel, *Casas Pardas*, received the "City of Lisbon" prize for her insight into the lives of women of that city, whom she presents as framed by the architectural forms of the houses they inhabit. In 1979 Costa published *Corpo Verde*, a collection of erotic poems illustrated by artist Julio Pomar, which in many ways coincides with the work and themes of Maria Teresa Horta. The novel *Lucialima* (1983), is perhaps her most mature work, refining and honing her view of women, and using the themes of self-exploration, preoccupation with the self, and at times an almost lyrical approach to reality that have been constants in her work. The book, *O Mapa Cor da Rosa* (1984), written for Lisbon newspapers while she was teaching at King's College in London, is a collection of articles on English life through the eyes of a Portuguese woman. *Missa in Albis* (1988), a love story told from the point of view of a woman, is considered by Costa to be her last work of fiction.

Works

O Lugar Comum [The Common Place] (1966). *Maina Mendes* (1969). *Ensino Primário e Ideologia* [Elementary Education and Ideology] (1972). [With Maria Isabel Barreno and Maria Teresa Horta], *Novas Cartas Portuguesas* [New Portuguese Letters] (1972). (2nd ed. 1980). *Desescrita.* [Unwritten] (1973). *Cravo* [Spike] (1975). *Português, Trabalhador, Doente Mental* [Portuguese, Worker, Mentally Ill] (1977). *Casas Pardas* [Brown Houses] (1977). *Da Rosa Fixa* [The Fixed Rose] (1978). *Corpo Verde* [Green Body] (1979). *Lucialima*

(1983). *O Mapa Cor da Rosa* [The Rose Colored Map] (1984). *Missa in Albis* (1988).

Bibliography

Cabrita, António, "Maria Velho da Costa." *Jornal de Letras, Artes e Ideas* (Lisbon) 8 (314) (July 12–18, 1988): 8–10. Coelho, Nelly Novaes, "*Novas Cartas Portuguesas* e o Processo de Conscientizaçao da Mulher: Seculo XX" [*New Portuguese Letters* and the Process of Consciousness Raising in Women: 20th Century]. *Letras* (Curitiba): 23(1975): 165–171. Passos, Maria Armanda, "Este É o Livro da Reconciliaçao" [This Is the Book of Reconciliation], *Jornal de Letras, Artes & Ideas* (Lisbon) 2(58) (May 7–16, 1983): 6–8.

Lina L. Cofresí

Costanza da Varano

Born 1426, Varano, Italy; died July 13, 1447, Pesaro
Genre(s): letters, oratory
Language(s): Latin

Costanza da Varano was the daughter of Piergentile da Varano and Elizabetta di Galeazzo Malatesta. On September 6, 1433, he father was executed, and she had to flee with her mother and siblings to Pesaro, where she was educated, principally by her grandmother, Battista da Varano. On December 8, 1444, she married Alessandro Sforza, the lord of Pesaro. She gave birth to a son, Costanzo, on July 5, 1447, and died eight days later. Like her grandmother, she was one of the educational ornaments of the Quattrocento. Two of her orations and several of her letters are found in *Her Immaculate Hand*.

Works

Cosenza, 2, 1132. *Her Immaculate Hand*, 39–44; 53–56.

Joseph Berrigan

Marie-Sophie Risteau Cottin

Born March 21,1770, Paris, France; died August 25, 1807, Paris
Genre(s): novel, verse, letters
Language(s): French

The works of Sophie Cottin, who though now forgotten was perhaps one of the best-known and most widely read authors of her time, must be seen in the context of pre-Romanticism in France. Though baptized a Catholic, she was raised as a Protestant, preferring the name "Sophie" to that of "Marie." She was raised by her mother in an extraordinarily cultivated household; her early letters mention her readings in the Latin classics. Despite this classical training and Protestant upbringing, her novels, which have non-classical settings (Spain, England, the Crusades), exhibit the kind of melancholy sentimentality favored by Rousseau and the religiosity promoted by Chateaubriand. Her father was a director of the Compagnie des Indes. In 1789 she married a wealthy banker, Jean-Paul-Marie Cottin, who came from a recently ennobled family and whose own grandfather had also been a director of the Compagnie des Indes. Her husband died, financially ruined, in 1793, after having been denounced as an aristocrat by the Revolutionary authorities. The marriage had been childless, and she never remarried. In the midst of the political turmoil of this time, she chose to retire to a family estate in Champlan. Her circle of friends included the medieval historian Joseph-François Michaud, from whom she apparently took much of the medieval inspiration of her later works.

Her first novels, *Claire d'Albe* (1799) and *Malvina* (1800), were published anonymously. Like her three remaining novels, *Amélie de Mansfield* (1803), *Mathilde, ou, Mémoires tirés de l'histoire des Croisades* (1805; Mathilda, or, Memoirs from the History of the Crusades) and *Elizabeth, or Les exilés de Sibérie* (1806; Elizabeth, or the Exiles of Siberia), these works explore highly sentimental themes, often with great pathos. The opinion of Roman d'Amat, writing in the *Dictionnaire de biographie française*, that Sophie Cottin's works are unreadable nowadays, seems excessively harsh. Earlier, more sympathetic critics saw in her works an accurate depiction of human psychology. Their immense success, evidenced first by the many editions printed during the nineteenth century and second by the numerous translations of her works into the major European languages, suggests that their position in literary history needs to be reevaluated. Her last novel, *Elisabeth*, was widely used as a standard text for French language instruction outside of France, seen in school editions from London (1822), New York (1st ed., 1852, 8th ed. 1867), and Leipzig (8th ed., 1883).

Works

Oeuvres complètes, 11 vols. (Paris, 1811). Another 13 editions of her works in French were published between 1815 and 1838. There are numerous English translations of her individual novels, most published during the first half of the nineteenth century.

Bibliography

d'Amat, Roman, "Marie-Sophie-Risteau Cottin." *Dictionnaire de biographie française* 9. (Paris, 1961), col. 848–849. Arnelle (de Clauzade, Arnelle), *Une oubliée, Mme. Cottin d'après sa correspondance* (Paris, 1914). de Ganniers, A., "Mme. Cottin pendant la Terreur, d'après sa correspondance inédite et publiée ici pur la première fois." *Le Correspondant* n.s. 116 (1888), pp. 443–467, 707–725. Rösler, Georg, *Beiträge zur Kenntnis von Mme Cottin* (Leipzig, 1908).

Earl Jeffrey Richards

Ida Coudenhove

Born December 2, 1901, Ronsperg, Bohemia
Genre(s): novel, essay
Language(s): German

Ida F. Coudenhove can be called a writer by vocation: she saw writing as a form of missionary work and as a service to the Catholic Church and to God. Her work is thus mainly concerned with the analysis of man and Christianity.

Born in 1901, she experienced two world wars and a world full of suffering and insecurity. Her strong religious conviction helped her to handle the uncertainties she was faced with and was, in turn, reinforced by them. Her first years of schooling were spent at the College of the Sacred Heart in Pressbaum, near Vienna, Austria, from where she transferred to the Lyceum of the Loretto Nuns in St. Poelten. She had already decided to live a monastic life, and in 1921 she entered the novitiate of the Convent of St. Poelten.

Ida Coudenhove had started writing when still young, and, convinced of the power of her literary work, a priest friend persuaded her to re-examine her decision. In 1925, she left the convent again and started on a serious literary career. In the same year, Ida became an active member in the German Youth Movement in its Catholic League Neuland in Austria. Later, she moved to Germany where she became responsible for the leadership of girls in this league. The spiritual work she had intended to do in the convent was now taken up again while educating and guiding young girls in the religious environment of the league. Seeing social work as essential for the development of Christian perfection in man, she took up training at the Caritas College for Social Work in Freiburg/Breisgau, between 1925 and 1932. In Vienna and Freiburg she took up sociology and history; shortly afterward she changed her plans again and accepted the post of Secretary for Catholic Girls in the Diaspora-Diocese of MeiBen, now East Germany. In 1935, Ida Coudenhove married Carl Josef Goerres; the marriage was childless.

It can be assumed that Ida Coudenhove was partly supported by her brother Count Richard, as he was the president of the Pan-European Union and expressed in his own work the urge for freedom, peace, justice, and humanity in general. During the time of the Third Reich, Ida shared the fate of many writers whose works were burnt or banned. Her last novel was forbidden to be sold in Germany.

The themes of her work circle around the problems of modern man and religion in modern society. *Das Wesen des Heiligkeit* (1933; The Nature of Sanctity) and *Das Kloster und die Welt* (1935; The Cloister and the World) discuss the justification and definition of a saint and the relationship between the religious and the secular. In her opinion, holiness is a real and common rather than an exceptional occurrence; it is not reserved for people working within a religious organization and vocation but is open to everybody. In *The Nature of Sanctity*, Ida Coudenhove discusses the "humanness" in saints and emphasizes that this trait is too much neglected. Elizabeth of Hungary is for her one example of this issue. In *The Cloister and the World* this idea was taken up again and is continued. Here she discusses Jean d'Arc and examines the vocation to holiness in her example. Jean d'Arc did not become a saint in the first place because of her visions and her supposed mission from God, but because she was capable of restoring peace and order in a country shaken by war and insecurity. She did not work within a religious context but as a warrior in a secular mission.

Maria Ward, eine historische Romanze (1939; Mary Ward, a Historical Romance) deals with the saintly but not canonized foundress of the congregation of St. Poelten. The book is dedicated to the convent and the work its inmates were doing, a thanksgiving for her own education; it was also intended as a memorial for the foundress, who, in the seventeenth century, distinguished herself by her extraordinary efforts to revive religion and religiosity in a century of religious wars.

Zwei deutsche Heilige (n.d.; Two German Saints) was intended as a contribution to debates about the "Nordic spirit and Christianity," which occupied theologians and the laity during the first years of the Third Reich. The book is not a contemporary study but deals with historical figures again; the Blessed Henry Suso, a German mystic of the fourteenth century, and St. Radegund, a German princess and a prisoner of war.

Des Anderen Last, ein Gespräch über die Barmherzigkeit (1940; The Burden of the Other, A Discussion of Charity) is a criticism against totalitarian states that had abolished works of charity and almsgiving as obsolete and had used this Christian idea for their own political purposes. *Das Verborgene Antlitz* (1942; The Hidden Face) discusses another historical figure, St. Therese of Lisieux. The first edition was destroyed during the bombardment of Freiburg, and only after 1945 could the work be republished.

Works

Das Wesen der Heiligkeit (1933). *Das Kloster und die Welt* (1935). *Maria Ward, eine historische Romanze* (1939). *Zwei deutsche Heilige* (n.d.). *Des Anderen Last, ein Gespräch über die Barmherzigkeit* (1940). *Das Verborgene Antlitz* (1942).

Translations: *The Nature of Sanctity* [Das Wesen des Heiligen] (1933). *The Cloister and the World* [Das Kloster und die Welt] (1935). *Mary Ward, a Historical Romance* [Maria Ward, eine historische Romanze] (1939).

Bibliography

Hoehn, Matthew, ed. *Catholic Authors, Contemporary Biographical Sketches, 1930–1947*. Newark: St. Mary's Abbey, 1948.

Jutta Hagedorn

Countess of Septimania
(see: Dhouda)

Madame Sophie-Remi de Courtenai de la Fosse-Ronde

Born ?
Genre(s): polemical essay
Language(s): French

Not much is known about Sophie de Courtenai de la Fosse-Ronde, but she is credited with a pamphlet presented to the Etats Generaux in 1789; in this pamphlet, entitled *L'Argument des Pauvres aux Etats Generaux*, Madame de Courtenai brilliantly defends the cause of the poor. She argues against unjust and burdensome taxes raised only for the enjoyment, but not the need, of the rich. She also suggests an equitable means for levying taxes so that everyone, including the rich, is taxed according to his revenues and not according to whimsical and arbitrary standards. She begins her argument with the words: "Les Pauvres, les Riches, les Princes, les Rois, tous cherchent le bonheur; tous, surs que Dieu en est le centre, ils le désirent tous. Mais, où pourront le trouver les infortunés que le sort paroit condamner à souffrir, sans qu'il leur soit permis de se plaindre?" (The Poor, the Wealthy, Princes and Kings, all seek happiness; all, certain that God is at the center of it, all desire it. But, where can it be found by the hapless ones that fate seems to have condemned to suffering, without allowing them ever to complain?").

Works

Courtenai de la Fosse-Ronde, Madame Sophie-Remi de, *L'Argument des Pauvres aux Etats Generaux* (s.l.: s.n., 1789, In-8, 15p.).

Bibliography

Michael, Colette, ed., *Les Tracts Feministes au XVIII Siecle* (Geneva, 1986), pp. 60–66.

Colette Michael

Hedwig Courths-Mahler

(a.k.a. Ernestine Friederike Elisabeth Mahler)

Born February 18, 1867, Nebra/Unstrut, Germany; died November 26, 1950, Tegernsee
Genre(s): novel
Language(s): German

Hedwig Courths-Mahler was born after her father's death and raised in modest circumstances and without much affection by her stepfather. She worked at a variety of jobs, such as servant, companion, and salesgirl before embarking on her literary career.

It was while she was still employed as a salesgirl that she began to write down her fantasies of what life should be like, as opposed to the way it was. Life should include a benevolent force, which would bestow on those unjustly hurt by life a large fortune (usually through inheritance) and marriage. Marriage would be the way to overcome any existing obstacles between bourgeoisie and aristocracy.

Her novels, of which she produced an average of four per year, were received enthusiastically by her reading public, though condemned severely by the literary and critical establishments. Her "happy end" stories satisfied a huge audience, which wanted its tales unambiguous and dreamed of a world where the good were beautiful and rewarded with financial security and the promise of marital bliss and where the bad were ugly and received their just deserts. A number of the novels were turned into stage plays and movie scripts.

Hedwig Courths-Mahler was so successful (reputedly over 30 million copies of her books have been sold) that her name has practically become a German synonym for this type of romantic novel. Critical acclaim (rightfully) eluded her, but for millions of readers she provided pleasure by articulating their fantasies and dreams.

Her daughters Margarete Elzer and Friede Birkner followed in her footsteps and continued the family tradition of romantic novels.

Works

Scheinehe (1905). *Untreue* (1907). *Welcher unter Euch?* (1907). *Im Waldhof* (1909). *Auf falschem Boden* (1910). *Der Sohn des Tagelöhners. Erzählung aus dem Leben von Relham* (1910). *Der Wildfang. Erzählung aus der Gegenwart* (1910). *Es irrt der Mensch* (1910). *Das Gänsemädchen von Dohrna* (1911). *König Ludwig und sein Schützling. Erinnerungsblätter zur 25. Wiederkehr des Todestages König Ludwigs II. von Bayern* (1911). *Liselottes Heirat* (1911). *Die wilde Ursula* (1912). *Ich lasse dich nicht!* (1912). *Aus erster Ehe* (1913). *Das Halsband* (1913). *Der stille See* (1913). *Des Anderen Ehre* (1913). *Ein Schritt vom Wege* (1913). *Gib mich frei* (1913). *Was Gott zusammengefügt* (1913). *Die Bettelprinzeß* (1914). *Hexengold* (1914). *Käthes Ehe* (1914). *Unser Weg ging hinauf* (1914). *Deines Bruders Weib* (1915). *Die Kriegsbraut* (1915). *Die schöne Lilian* (1915). *Die Testamentsklausel* (1915). *Ich will* (1915). *Mammsell Sonnenschein. Erzählung für junge Mädchen* (1915). *Sanna Rutlands Ehe* (1915). *Arme kleine Anni* (1916). *Der tolle Haßberg* (1916). *Die Aßmanns* (1916). *Die drei Schwestern Randolf* (1916). *Frau Bettina und ihre Söhne* (1916). *Griseldis* (1916). *Lena Warnstetten* (1916). *Prinzeß Lolo* (1916). *Ein deutsches Mädchen und andere Erzählungen* (1917). *Meine Käthe und andere Erzählungen* (1917). *Seine Frau* (1917). *Das Amulett der Rani* (1918). *Die schöne Unbekannte* (1918). *Eine ungeliebte Frau* (1918). *Amtmanns Käthe* (1919). *Armes Schwälbchen. Eine Erzählung für junge Mädchen* (1919). *Das Drama von Glossow* (1919). *Der Scheingemahl* (1919). *Diana* (1919). *Die Adoptivtochter* (1919). *Die Geschwister* (1919). *Die Kraft der Liebe* (1919). *Friede Sörrensen* (1919). *Hans Ritter und seine Frau* (1919). *Liane Reinold* (1919). *Sein Kind* (1919). *Zwei Frauen* (1919). *Annadores Vormund* (1920). *Dein ist mein Herz* (1920). *Die Herrin von Retzbach* (1920). *Die Stellvertreterin* (1920). *Im Buchengrund* (1920).

O du mein Glück (1920). *Ohne dich kein Glück* (1920). *Rote Rosen* (1920). *Vergib, Lori. Eine Erzählung für junge Mädchen* (1920). *Verschmäht* (1920). *Was tat ich dir?* (1920). *Zur linken Hand getraut* (1920). *Arbeit adelt* (1921). *Der Müßigganger—Da zog ein Wanderbursch vorbei* (1921). *Der Mut zum Glück* (1921). *Die Menschen nennen es Liebe* (1921). *Die Stiftssekretärin* (1921). *Glückshunger* (1921). *Ich darf dich nicht lieben* (1921). *Licht und Schatten* (1921). *Sommerfrische und andere Erzählungen* (1921). *Wer wirft den ersten Stein?* (1921). *Das stolze Schweigen* (1922). *Die Pelzkönigin* (1922). *Die schöne Kalifornierin* (1922). *Eine fromme Lüge* (1922). *O du Jungfer Königin* (1922). *Von welcher Art bist du?* (1922). *Wem nie durch Liebe Leid geschah* (1922). *Dora Linds Geheimnis* (1923). *Durch Leid zum Glück* (1923). *O Menschenherz, was ist dein Glück?* (1923). *Wenn zwei sich lieben* (1923). *Betrogene Liebe* (1924). *Das Heiligtum des Herzens* (1924). *Das ist der Liebe Zaubermacht* (1924). *Der Australier* (1924). *Der verhängnisvolle Brief* (1924). *Die schöne Melusine* (1924). *Die Sonne von Lahori* (1924). *Es gibt ein Glück* (1924). *Fräulein Domina* (1924). *Opfer der Liebe* (1924). *Vergangenheit* (1924). *Versöhnt* (1924). *Verstehen heißt verzeihen* (1924). *Britta Riedbergs Fahrt ins Glück* (1925). *Feenhände* (1925). *Herz, nicht verzag! und andere Novellen* (1925). *Mein liebes Mädel* (1925). *Nur ich allein* (1925). *Wenn Wünsche töten könnten!* (1925). *Willst du dein Herz mir schenken?* (1925). *Wo du hingehst . . .* (1925). *Das Geheimnis einer Namenlosen. Roman aus der Vorkriegszeit* (1926). *Das verschwundene Dokument* (1926). *Die Verbannten* (1926). *Frau Majas Glück* (1926). *Hannelores Ideal* (1926). *Ich liebe dich, wer du auch bist* (1926). *Ihr Retter in der Not* (1926). *Im fremden Lande* (1926). *Seine indische Ehe* (1926). *Verschwiegene Liebe—Verschwiegenes Leid und eine andere Erzählung* (1926). *Die Perlenschnur* (1927). *Die verschleierte Frau* (1927). *Fräulein Chef* (1927). *Nun ist alles anders geworden* (1927). *Sein Mündel* (1927). *Sie hatten einander so lieb* (1927). *Aschenbrödel und Dollarprinz* (1928). *Der verlorene Ring* (1928). *Die Erbin* (1928). *Die heimlich Vermählten* (1928). *Die Inselprinzessin* (1928). *Frau Juttas Befreiung* (1928). *Ich hab so viel um dich geweint* (1928). *Du bist meine Heimat* (1929). *Harald Landry, der Filmstar* (1929). *Magdalas Opfer* (1929). *Nach dunklen Schatten*

das Glück (1929). *Verkaufte Seelen* (1929). *Allen Gewalten zum Trotz sich erhalten* (1920). *Der Abschiedsbrief* (1930). *Die Tochter der zweiten Frau* (1930). *Die verstoßene Tochter* (1930). *Liebe ist der Liebe Preis* (1930). *Schweig still, mein Herz* (1930). *Schwester Marlens Geheimnis* (1930). *Trotz allem lieb ich dich!* (1930). *Um Diamanten und Perlen* (1930). *Des Schicksals Wellen* (1931). *Die Flucht vor der Ehe* (1931). *Die Liebe höret nimmer auf* (1931). *Die ungleichen Schwestern* (1931). *Du—meine Welt* (1931). *Mit mir bis in den Tod* (1931). *Unschuldig schuldig* (1931). *Auf der Jungfernburg* (1932). *Da sah er eine blonde Frau* (1932). *Das Erbe der Rodenberg* (1932). *Des Herzens süße Not* (1932). *Die Herrin von Armada* (1932). *Erika und der Einbrecher* (1932). *Helen Jungs Liebe* (1932). *Ihr Reisemarschall* (1932). *Judys Schwur* (1932). *Wie ist mein armes Herz so schwer* (1932). *Wo ist Eva?* (1932). *Das Findelkind von Paradiso* (1933). *Das Rätsel um Valerie!* (1933). *Gerline ist unschuldig* (1933). *Heide Rosenaus Kampf ums Glück* (1933). *Ich glaube an Dich* (1933). *Ich liebe einen Anderen* (1933). *Ihr Geheimnis* (1933). *Was ist denn Liebe, sag?* (1933). *Was ist mit Rosemarie?* (1933). *Heimchen, wie lieb ich Dich* (1934). *Ich heirate Bertie* (1934). *Ich kanns Dir nimmer sagen* (1934). *Ich weiß, was du mir bist* (1934). *Nur wer die Sehnsucht kennt* (1934). *Seine große Liebe* (1934). *Siddys Hochzeitsreise* (1934). *Dorrit in Gefahr* (1935). *Dorrit und ihre Schwester* (1935). *Frauen in Not* (1935). *Heidelerche* (1935). *Ich hab dich lieb!* (1935). *Was tut man nicht für Dorothy?* (1935). *Was wird aus Lori?* (1935). *Will's tief im Herzen tragen* (1935). *Die entflohene Braut* (1936). *Du darfst nicht von mir gehen* (1936). *Lissa geht ins Glück* (1936). *Sag, wo weiltest du so lange?* (1936). *Weit ist der Weg zum Glück* (1936). *Zwischen Stolz und Liebe* (1936). *Daniela, ich suche dich* (1937). *Eine andere wirst du küssen* (1937). *Hilfe für Mona* (1937). *Lady Gwendolins Ebenbild* (1937). *Jolandes Heirat* (1938). *Unser Tag wird kommen* (1938). *Wir sind allzumal Sünder* (1938). *Nur aus Liebe, Marlies* (1939). *Flucht in den Frieden* (1948).

Bibliography

Klein, Albert, *Die Krise des Unterhaltungsromans im 19. Jahrhundert. Ein Beitrag zur Theorie und Geschichte der ästhetisch geringwertigen Literatur* (Bonn, 1969). Krieg, W., *"Unser Weg ging hinauf."*

Hedwig Courths-Mahler und ihre Töchter als literarisches Phänomen. Ein Beitrag zur Theorie über den Erfolgsroman und zur Geschichte und Bibliographie des modernen Volkslesestoffes (Wien, 1954). Reimann, Hans, *Hedwig Courths-Mahler. Schlichte Geschichten fürs traute Heim. Geschmückt mit 30 reizenden Bildern von George Grosz* (Hannover, 1922). Riess, Curt, "Hedwig Courths-Mahler schreibt: Rote Rosen," in Curt Riess, *Bestseller. Bücher, die Millionen lesen* (Hamburg, 1960). Schulz, Hans Ferdinand, "Ein Kapitel Courts-Mahler," in H.F. Schulz, *Das Schicksal der Bücher und der Buchhandel. System einer Vertriebskunde des Buches* (Berlin, 1960). Sichelschmidt, Gustav, *Hedwig Courths-Mahler, Deutschlands erfolgreichste Autorin. Eine literatursoziologische Studie* (Bonn, 1967). Willenborg, G., "Autoritäre Persönlichkeitsstrukturen in Courths-Mahlers Romanen." *Kölner Zeitschrift für Soziologie und Sozialpsychologie* (1962).
General references: *Neue Deutsche Biographie 3.* (Berlin, 1957), 3, p. 383.

Hortense Bates

Johanna Desideria Courtmans-Berchmans

Born September 6, 1811, Oudegem, Belgium; died September 22, 1890, Maldegem, Belgium
Genre(s): novel, poetry, drama
Language(s): Dutch

After the death of her husband in 1856, Courtmans-Berchmans started a secular boarding school which, in Catholic Flanders, was highly criticized and the subject of much controversy. Notwithstanding the opposition, the school continued in existence until 1885. At the age of fifty she started to write a series of novels and short stories dealing with the problems and the resistance she encountered as a result of her lifestyle and school. Her previously published poems and a few plays had not been very popular, but with the advent of her work on the dogmatic attitudes and provincialism of village life, she attracted wide interest and praise. Her major works, for example, *Het Geschenk van de*

Jager (1864; The Hunter's Present) and *De Zwarte Hoeve* (1864; The Black Farm), still contain traces of romanticism, but Courtmans-Berchmans is clearly on the road to the Flemish Realism that reaches its major realization with Virginie Loveling (1836–1923).

Courtman's novels have a certain documentary quality to them, but the occasionally naive social criticism she expresses gives them a somewhat moralizing tone. Courtmans-Berchmans received the State prize for exceptional Flemish literature, awarded once every five years, for her book *Het Geschenk van de Jager.*

Works

De Zwarte Hoeve (1864). *De hut van Tante Klara* (1865). *Het Plan van Heintje Barbier* (1866). *Moeder Daneel* (1868). *De Koewachter* (1873). *Rozeken Pot* (1879).
Collected Works: *Verhalen en Novellen* (22 vols., 1883–1890). *Volledige Prozawerken* (33 vols., 1923).

Bibliography

Degroote, G., *Vrouwe Courtmans Brieven aan haar zoon Emile.* In Handleidingen Kon. Zuidned. Mij. voor Taal- en Letterk. en Gesch (Brussel, XVIII, 1964; XIX, 1965). *Huldeblijken. Mevrouw Courtmans 1811–1890* (Brussel, 1961). Pée, J., *Mevrouw Courtmans. Een Letterkundige Studie* (Antwerpen, 1933). Streuvels, S., *Over Vrouwe Courtmans* (Maldegem, 1911). Van Hoorde, J., *Vrouwe Courtmans-Berchmans* (Antwerpen, 1883).

An Lammens

Ioana Crăciunescu

Born 1950, Bucharest, Romania
Genre(s): poetry
Language(s): Romanian

After studying at the Institute of Dramatic Art in Bucharest, Ioana Crăciunescu became an actress and joined the Nottara Theatre Company in 1973. She has published five volumes of verse and was awarded the Bucharest Writers' Union Prize in 1981.

Crăciunescu's recent poetry—as represented by the volumes *Iarnă clinică* (1983; Clinical Winter) and *Maşinăria cu aburi* (1984; Steam Machinery)—speaks about fear, shame, failure, despair, grief, and suicide. Fear and shame are correlative with female existence: "I'm frightened and ashamed/ of myself, of my bones, of my sex" ("Clinical Winter"). Male verbal aggression deepens the tensionate loneliness confirming the basic lack of solidarity between the sexes: "in a pub some drunkards accost you/ with lewd gestures/ their words piercing right into you fresh/ from the sewers/ they shower you, splash you, and there's no protection" ("Involuntary Memory"). Failure is passed from one generation to the other through dry advice of disenchanted elders: "Eat up everything on your plate, wipe your mouth/ with your ambitions I'm past it/ But you're destined for a great failure" ("Involuntary Memory"). Life, though, and love shrivel into despair. Spring itself can bring happiness only inasmuch as it replaces the monotonous daily annihilation with the hope for violent and, in a sense, more useful extinction: "You stay stretched out in the green meadow,/ a herd of lambs graze madly from your flesh" ("Peacocks in the Old Park"). "It's snowing in your brain" says the poet, and suicide—"quick or slow"—opens the only imaginable door to the future.

Crăciunescu belongs to a generation of young poets (mostly women) whose essential strength comes from articulating with unprecedented directness the real "sentiment de l'existence" in contemporary Romania.

Works

Iarnă clinică [Clinical Winter] (1983). *Maşinăria cu aburi* [Steam Machinery] (1984).
Translations: Deletant, Andrea, and Brenda Walker, trs., *Silent Voices. An Anthology of Contemporary Romanian Women Poets* (London and Boston, 1986), pp. 77–88 (poems from *Iarnă clinică* and *Maşinăria cu aburi*).

Sanda Golopentia

Daniela Crăsnaru

Born 1950, Craiova, Romania
Genre(s): poetry, children's literature
Language(s): Romanian

In 1973, Daniela Crăsnaru graduated with a degree in Romanian and English from Craiova University and published her first volume of poetry. Since then she has worked as an editor at the Eminescu Publishing House and has produced eight volumes of poems as well as several children's books. She has also been awarded the Poetry Prize of the Writers' Union.

Crăsnaru's first volumes—*Lumină cît umbră* (1973; As Much Light as Shadow), *Spaţiul de graţie* (1976; Space of Grace), and *Arcaşii orbi* (1978; Blind Archers)—impress by their lyrical frankness. The poet opposes indifference, moral evasion, derision, irony, cynicism, bravado. She advocates non-naive candor, passion, loyalty, courage: "I refuse to accept that words/ could be the cheapest/ currency."

Although considerably darker, her later volumes—*Cringul hipnotic* (1979; Hypnotic Grove) and *Niagara de plumb* (1984; Niagara of Lead)—continue this trend. Words can still act, declares Crăsnaru: "Words above facts/ words like huge Saint-Bernards/ warming the victims with their own bodies,/ every now and again saving what's left to be saved" ("Onto the Straight"). Poetry is not to be conceived of as a "sad luxury" in this "cynical century," its mission perdures and amplifies. "Look, I still breathe" proclaims the poet, although around, inescapably "Everything is for our own good./ . . ./ The card you clock in with./ The anadin, the valium, the ethic and rhetoric./ The hotel receptionist, who carefully checks/ that we don't have different names (Wink! Wink!)/ that we don't have different addresses (Nudge! Nudge!)/ the laws, decrees/ and their amendments./ Everything is for our own good" ("Everything Is for Our Own Good"). When cathartically detailing the nonstop performance which "prey(s) on the peace of (the) docile retina," the "hurried visit of the leading comedian" ("Suddenly a respectful space is made: arriving, now at the last moment, the car of the leading comedian./ Hurrying, for he must appear on stage./ He can't accept that he of all people,/ can be paid for nothing, he, the one who knows all the parts,/ grocer, porter, nanny, Roman emperor, cobbler,/ first soldier, second soldier, great inquisitor,/ gentle pontiff, people, crowd" ["The Stage Dressing Room"]), when asking again and again the only question that matters—"How much longer?"—Daniela Crăsnaru goes far beyond the limits of what can be safely written and published in contemporary Romania.

Works

Lumină cît umbră [As Much Light as Shadow] (1973). Spaţiul de graţie [Space of Grace] (1976). Arcaşii orbi [Blind Archers] (1978). Cringul hipnotic [Hypnotic Grove] (1979). Niagara de plumb [Niagara of Lead] (1984).
Translations: Deletant, Andrea, and Brenda Walker, trs., Silent Voices. An Anthology of Contemporary Romanian Women Poets (London; Boston: Forest Books, 1986), pp. 89–102 (poems from Crîngul hipnotic and Niagara de plumb).

Bibliography

Caraion, Ion. "Confruntarea cu indiferenţa—Daniela Crăsnaru." Jurnal I. (Bucharest, 1980), pp. 209–214. Popa, Marian, Dicţionar de literatură română contemporană (Bucharest, 1977), p. 170.

Sanda Golopentia

Marguerite de Crayencour

(see: Marguerite Yourcenar)

Hélisenne de Crenne

(see: Marguerite Briet)

Miza (Sarmiza) Cretzianu

Born 1905, Turnu-Serverin, Romania; died 1978, Bucharest
Genre(s): short story, novel
Language(s): Romanian
Miza Cretzianu's first volume—a collection of fifteen short stories entitled De pe Valea Motrului (1946; From the Motru Valley)—is a burlesque and cynical evocation of small boyar families from the southwestern part of Romania that enjoyed an immediate and lasting success

both with literary critics and the general public. She left an unpublished novel—Cucoana de la Steic (The Lady from Steic).

Works

De pe Valea Motrului [From the Motru Valley] (1946). Cucoana de la Steic [The Lady from Steic] (unpublished).

Bibliography

Călinescu, G., "Miza Cretzianu." Literatura nouă (Craiova, 1972), pp. 55–60. Piru, Al, "Miza Cretzianu." Panorama deceniului literar românesc 1940–1950 (Bucharest, 1968), pp. 354–356.

Sanda Golopentia

Claudia Cridim

(see: Claudia Millian)

Jacques Croisé

(see: Zinaïda Schakovskoy)

Teresia Benedicta a Cruce

(see: Edith Stein)

Paulina Crusat

Born 1900, Barcelona, Spain
Genre(s): novel, poetry, criticism
Language(s): Spanish
The daughter of an upper-middle-class family, Crusat was raised in a cultured atmosphere that stimulated her literary inclinations. Although she won her first poetry prize at the age of twelve, Crusat has not been a constant or prolific writer. After her marriage, she moved to Sevilla, where she has written literary criticism and novels. Nora attributes to her an excellent anthology of contemporary Catalan poets, published in 1952. Most of her fiction appeared in the 1950s and early 1960s; she has written nothing since 1965.
Mundo pequeño y fingido (1953; Small, Feigned World) is frankly subjective and non-mimetic, rejecting the documentary, "testimonial"

neo-realism then in vogue. Set in Switzerland around 1820, it presents an excellent psychological exposition and analysis of several first-generation Romantics. Crusat's major work is a two-part novel under the title, *Historia de un viaje* (Story of a Voyage). The first of the two volumes is *Aprendiz de persona* (1956; Apprentice Person). Like its companion piece, this narrative has a probable autobiographical basis. It describes the youthful years of Monsi, the female protagonist, with particular attention to changes undergone during development. The effect of strict societal codes and lack of freedom upon her adolescence is contrasted with a final glimpse of Monsi after marriage, when comparable freedom as an adult has apparently provided some chance for self-discovery. The second of the two linked novels, *Las ocas blancas* (1959; The White Geese) reconstructs the old-fashioned and vaguely unreal world of 1916 in Barcelona, which provides the frame for a poetic evocation of female passage from adolescence to adulthood. Six teenage girls and their activities (attendance at the opera, evening strolls, carnival, dances, New Year's Eve party-going, the first serious boyfriends and long dresses) are the focus of this product of attenuated feminism. The Spanish critic Eugenio de Nora has suggested a possible allusion to Virginia Woolf's *The Voyage Out* in the linked novels and notes affinities between the two writers. *Relaciones solitarias* (1965; Solitary Relations), a full-length novel in the epistolary mode, is constructed in four parts that correspond to the seasons of the year. It, too, concentrates upon psychological and emotional analysis, but like most of Crusat's writing, it is out of print.

Although her production is limited, Crusat's writing is of high quality, constructed with intelligence, art and sincerity, and holds the reader's interest. Her limited appeal for critics and public around the mid-century in Spain is probably due to deliberate self-distancing from the more tendentious "critical" realism then in vogue.

Works

Aprendiz de persona (1956). *Mundo pequeño y fingido* (1953). *Las ocas blancas* (1959). *Relaciones solitarias* (1965).

Bibliography

General references: Nora, Eugenio [García] de, *La novela española contemporánea, III* (2 ed., 1968). *Women Writers of Spain*, ed. C.L. Galerstein (Westport, Conn., 1986).

Janet Perez

Matilda Cugler-Poni

(a.k.a. Matilda Kugler-Poni)

Born 1851, Iaşi, Romania; died 1931, Iaşi
Genre(s): poetry, short story, drama, translation
Language(s): Romanian, German

Born in a family of Austrian descent, Matilda Cugler-Poni made her debut as a poet in 1867 and was the first woman to be actively involved in a literary circle in Romania. The circle was a prestigious one—*Junimea*—and Matilda Cugler-Poni regularly contributed to its outstanding journal, *Convorbiri literare*, between 1867 and 1892.

Her poems, first gathered in a volume in 1874 under the title *Poesii*, are romantic in the manner of Heine and Lenau and speak about longing, abandonment, or betrayal.

In the short stories, Matilda Cugler-Poni portrays the life of suburban vagabonds, handicraftsmen, or small merchants in a naturalist manner and from a moralist perspective.

Her most acclaimed work is the comedy in two acts entitled *Un tutor* (1881; A Tutor).

Works

Poesii [Poems] (1874, 2nd ed., 1885). *Un tutor* [A Tutor] (1881, 2nd ed., 1914). *Fata stolerului* [The Carpenter's Daughter] (1884, 2nd ed. 1886). *Sfîntul Nicolae* [Saint Nicholas] (1885). *Poezii* [Poems] (1885). *Povestiri adevărate* [True Stories] (n.d.). *Poezii* [Poems] (1927). *Scrieri alese* [Selected Writings] (1971). Edited and with an Introduction by Ion Nuţă.

Bibliography

Călinescu, G., *Istoria literaturii române de la origini pînă în prezent* (Bucharest, 1941), pp. 367–368. Cioculescu, Şerban, Vladimir Streinu, and Tudor Vianu, *Istoria literaturii române moderne*, 2nd ed. (Bucharest, 1971), p. 190. Dafin, Ioan, *Figuri ieşene,*

vol. III (Iaşi, 1927), pp. 58–62. Fassel, Horst,
"Zwischen zwei Sprachen. Unferöfentliche Gedichte
von Mathilde Kugler-Poni." *Volk und Kultur* XXVI
(Bucharest, 1974), p. 12. Gerota, C., "O uitată
figură convorbiristă." *Convorbiri literare* LXX
(1937), pp. 1–5. Mănucă, Dan, *Dicţionarul
literaturii romăne de la origini pînă la 1900*
(Bucharest, 1979), p. 251.

Sanda Golopentia

Kate Cukaro

(a.k.a. Kate Xucaro, Kate Zuccaro)

Born 1955, Civita, Cosenza, Italy
Genre(s): poetry, folklore, monographs
Language(s): Albanian

Cukaro began her literary career upon the
completion of studies in medicine in Florence
and Naples.

A volume of her poetry was published under
the title *Gabim* (1982; Mistake). Other poems of
hers have appeared in various Arbëresh periodicals. Her work includes also material on the
folklore of the Arbëresh people.

Elfriede Czurda

Born April 25, 1946, Wels, Austria
Genre(s): prose, poetry, radio drama, essay
Language(s): German

Elfriede Czurda won rapid and wide recognition in the 1980s as a writer of postmodern
sensibility. She is best known for her prose
works, which unite the sophisticated code of
late-century urban life with the imaginative, experimental literary form of her Austrian heritage.
Male-female relations are her central theme; but
avoiding the stereotypes and clichés of the currently popular novel of "relationships," she writes
with insight, intelligence, and critical awareness
on the complexity of interpersonal relations.

Czurda was born in Wels, Upper Austria, in
1946. After receiving her high school diploma in
Linz in 1968 she went to London to learn the
language. Thereafter she studied art history and
archaeology at the University of Salzburg, and
she spent the year 1972–1973 doing research in
Paris and La Rocelle. In 1974 she received her
doctorate from the University of Salzburg with a
dissertation on the works of Eugene Fromentin,
a nineteenth-century French painter, writer, and
art historian. Since 1980 she has lived as a free-
lance writer in West Berlin. She however retains
ties with her Austrian homeland and is a member
of the Graz Authors' Association.

How does one experience happiness? Is it
possible to express it in language? Those are the
questions to which Czurda responded in her first
major work, *Diotima oder Die Differenz des
Glücks* (1982; Diotima or the Difference of
Happiness). Happiness, if only for moments, is
presented as paradigmatically realizable in a love
relationship, and thus the figures of Diotima,
beloved of Hölderlin, and Abelard, the famous
lover of Héloise, are conjured up. The protagonist in the novel is a first-person female narrator
who constructs for herself an image of an ideal
partner. The narration emphasizes the idea of a
construct, as opposed to reality, and the male
antagonist serves mainly as a foil for projection of
the hopes, dreams, and wishes of the narrator.
The work is essentially a monologue, and the
various personae, both historical and contem-
poraneous, function as sounding boards and
echo chambers for the thoughts and feelings of
the protagonist. It is a montage of dream, vision,
and experience, combined with quotations and
associations and shaped by fragmentary analyses
and contradictory emotions. The three parts
represent phases of development—indeed, a
development toward dissolution and destruction
of the ideal. Whereas the first part illustrates the
heights of mystical ecstasy, the final part narrates
almost naturalistically an ordinary day fraught
with anxiety and isolation. That happiness is a
fragile construction has been said before; new,
however, are the contours of emotion that Czurda
captures in refined lyrical prose.

Signora Julia (1985) is also a treatise, rather
an allegory, on the unreality of love. The lovers
are stylized as a literary-historical pair, whereby
Shakespeare's Juliet becomes a "Signora," the
Italian designation for an adult woman, and her
phantom lover, Arkadius, bears the name of a
paradisiacal landscape. The plot is spare: Arkadius
departs on various journeys in an effort to find
his roots, hence himself; as Julia waits for him,
her longing turns to anger until she herself

departs and is thus gone when he finally returns. The figures communicate—or fail to—in a dialogue of letters, which are often reported in indirect speech, with the subjunctive itself pointing up the illusion. Erotic and sensual elements are interspersed with intellectual and masculine megalomania in prototypical form, and the quotations, clichés, and snippets of conversation ring true as an authentic conglomerate culled from advertising, movies, and popular culture. With sarcastic distance the author registers the arrogant efforts to men to define themselves solely in terms of power. The linguistic performance is brilliant, and perhaps such an anti-fascistic, anti-patriarchal novel needed to be written, although one could also say that the effort deserved a better cause.

Czurda's popularity stems in part from the fact that she meets the needs of a particular generation. She speaks for a class of educated and critical young women who have read and thought a great deal and who are eager to use their trained intellect not only for abstract thought but also for expression of emotion. Her language is cool, hence powerful, although at times overwrought. Her characters seem to consist wholly of language, which creates its speakers and also generates itself ad infinitum. Czurda is a writer from whom one is certain to hear more in the coming years.

Works

ein griff = eingriff inbegriffen (1978). *Fast 1 Leben. Ein Fragment* (1981). *Diotima oder Die Differenz des Glücks. Prosa* (1982). *Der Fußball-Fan oder: Da lacht Virginia Woolf. Hörspiel* (1982). *Signora Julia. Prosa* (1985). *Kerner. Ein Abenteuerroman* (1987).

Beth Bjorklund

D

Maria Dąbrowska

Born 1889, Kalisz, Poland; died 1965
Genre(s): short story, novel, drama, translation
Language(s): Polish

Several times proposed as a possible candidate for a Nobel Prize for Literature—an honor she never received—Maria Dąbrowska enjoys a secure place in the history of Polish literature as the outstanding woman prose writer of the twentieth century. Born Maria Szumska near the city of Kalisz, she was educated mostly in private schools in Kalisz and Warsaw and pursued university studies in the natural sciences in Lausanne, Switzerland (1908–1909) and in Brussels, Belgium (1909–1912). While in Brussels she also began studying economics, philosophy, and sociology at the Université Nouvelle. In the years that she was out of Poland, Dąbrowska was actively involved in Polish émigré circles, especially in the Belgian capital. Her keen interest in social and economic issues, particularly the cooperative movement, was strengthened by her marriage in 1911 to Marian Dabrowski (who died in 1925), a Socialist activist who was forced to emigrate from Russian Poland after the revolution of 1905–1907. Following her return to Poland in 1914, Dąbrowska began a career as a journalist writing mainly about economics and politics. From 1918 to 1924 she was also employed in the Ministry of Agriculture in Warsaw.

Dąbrowska's strong sense of social justice and her liberal political views set her on an inevitable collision course with the regime of Marshal Józef Piłsudski in the interwar period. She took up the cause of the political opposition, vigorously opposed the intensifying anti-Semitism of the 1930s, especially in the period from Piłsudski's death in 1935 to the outbreak of war in September 1939, and became a passionate advocate of land reform to improve the lot of the peasants. During the German occupation of Poland from 1939 to 1945, Dąbrowska lived in Warsaw where she played an active role in the underground cultural life of the city. Inactive publicly as a writer during the postwar Stalinist decade, Dąbrowska resumed her prolific literary career in 1955. Her later years brought her well-deserved national acclaim. In 1957 she received an honorary doctorate from the University of Warsaw and in 1962, on the occasion of the fiftieth anniversary of her literary career, the Polish Academy of Sciences organized an international symposium in her honor in Kalisz and Warsaw. The proceedings of the symposium were published in 1963, two years before her death at the age of seventy-five.

Although her earliest work of fiction, the novella *We Francji . . . ziemi cudzej* (In France . . . a Foreign Land) was written in 1912, Dąbrowska's first literary success was the collection of stories about poor rural people entitled *Ludzie stamtąd* (Folk from Over Yonder), which appeared in 1926. This was followed in 1932 by the first two volumes of the four-volume novel *Noce i dnie* (Nights and Days) which was her greatest literary accomplishment and the basis of her fame as a writer. The remaining two volumes of the immense work were published in 1933 and 1934. The great bulk of Dąbrowska's subsequent literary work consists of collections of stories, among them *Znaki życia* (1938; Signs of Life) and *Gwiazda zaranna* (1955; The Morning Star, translated into English under the title *A Village*

Wedding and Other Stories). A second attempt at a large "family saga"—*Przygody człowieka myślącego* (The Adventures of a Thinking Man)—remained unfinished and was published in book form posthumously in 1970. Long interested in the career of Joseph Conrad, Dąbrowska began writing a series of essays about him in the early 1930s; the entire collection was published in book form in 1959 under the title *Szkice o Conradzie* (Essays on Conrad). Dąbrowska's oeuvre also includes two weak historical plays—*Geniusz sierocy* (1939; The Orphan Genius) and *Stanisław i Bogumił* (1948; Stanislaus and Bogumił)—and a translation of the *Diary* of Samuel Pepys which she undertook during the wartime occupation and which was published in 1952.

Nights and Days, the work of fiction for which Dąbrowska is most admired and for which she will be most remembered, is a family chronicle type of novel. In it, the author's principal interest—the impact on a remote provincial farm of the transformations of Polish society from the January insurrection of 1863 down to 1914 and World War I—is traced through the family histories of its two main characters, Bogumil Niechcic and Barbara Ostrzeńska. A sweeping panorama of fifty years of turbulent Polish history, *Nights and Days* compensates for its great length with a number of finely etched character portraits, faithfully and often arrestingly recreated historical episodes, and an unerring sense of social dynamics. Although intended originally as a psychological novel, the immense work grew into a novel of vast social proportions far exceeding the boundaries of its original village setting. Of the many interesting feminine portraits in the novel by far the most commanding is that of the central character, Barbara, a superb study of a highly complex woman set in the frame of great change in Polish society, the Polish family, and the role of women.

Works

Uśmiech dzieciństwa. Wspomnienia (1923). Ludzie stamtąd (1926). Noce i dnie (4 vols., 1932–1934). Znaki życia (1938). Geniusz sierocy (1939). Stanisław i Bogumił (1948). Gwiazda zaranna (1955). Myśli o sprawach i ludziach (1956). Szkice z podróży (1956).

Harold B. Segel

Anne Lefèbvre Dacier

Born 1647 (or 1651), Saumur, France; died August 1720, Paris
Genre(s): scholarship, translation
Language(s): French

The "learnedst woman in Europe" was the description that the English traveler Martin Lister gave of Mme Dacier in 1699, and few would have disagreed. Born in 1647, according to her latest biographer, or a little later, she was the daughter of Tanneguy Lefèbvre, a noted, if somewhat wayward classical scholar who taught at the Protestant Academy of Saumur. Finding her more responsive than his sons, he gave her a grounding in Greek and Latin that was exceptional by any standards and which, in particular, very few women of the time were able to enjoy. On the death of her father in 1672 it seems that financial circumstances obliged her to marry a printer and bookseller by the name of Jean Lesnier. Either he died or he left her before long, and Mme Dacier went to Paris where she began to contribute editions to the famous series of classical works "ad usum Delphini" which appeared between 1674 and 1698 under the general direction of the Count de Montausier ostensibly to serve as textbooks for the Dauphin, the decidedly unintellectual heir to the French throne. She renewed contact with André Dacier, a Protestant scholar who had been a pupil at the Academy of Saumur, and in 1683 they were married.

The couple were converted to Catholicism in 1685, around the time of the Revocation of the Edict of Nantes. Malicious tongues questioned whether there had been a genuine change of heart, but there is evidence that the couple had considered theological issues conscientiously, though it is undeniable that conversion opened the road to acceptance in official circles. André Dacier was elected to both the Académie des Inscriptions et des Médailles and to the Académie Française in 1695. When he was received officially into the latter, the Abbé de Clérambault did not only praise Dacier's work but, in a noteworthy departure from precedent, concluded his speech by paying tribute to the scholarship of Mme Dacier. Yet another honor came Dacier's way: he was appointed Librarian of the King's Library, and he and his wife were given an apartment in the Louvre. Mme Dacier had three children, but they all predeceased her, the death of the last, a gifted daughter, at the age of eighteen casting a dark shadow over her later years when she became too ill to continue her work. She died in 1720, leaving a reputation for erudition and for personal charm, for she knew how to carry her learning lightly.

Mme Dacier had a very considerable role in the diffusion of knowledge about classical works, and here her activity may be regarded as a late phase of the work of the Renaissance humanists, for her aim was always to explicate the texts and facilitate access to them. Modern standards of textual criticism cast doubt on her methods and her emendations, yet at the time her editions of Calimachus and Sappho, of Florus, Dictys and Dares served a real purpose, as did her translations of Greek and Latin comedies. In her day she was renowned above all for her annotated translations of the *Iliad* (1699) and the *Odyssey* (1708). Nowadays, however, she is chiefly remembered for her contribution to a vigorous debate on the nature and status of the Homeric epics. Houdar de la Motte brought out a free version of the *Iliad* that, Mme Dacier felt, offered only a travesty of his achievement and compounded his offense with a preface which treated Homer with scant respect. In her lengthy *Des Causes de la Corruption du goût* (1714) she defended Homer with tenacity and vigor, though la Motte is generally thought to have had the better of the polemic, and she returned to the same cause more than once in her last years.

Works

Des Causes de la corruption du goût [Causes of the Corruption of Taste] (1714). *Homère défendu contre l'apologie du R.P. Hardouin, ou Suite des causes de la corruption du goût* [Homer Defended Against the Apologia by the Reverend Father Hardouin, on the Continuation of the Causes of Corruption of Taste] (1716). Many editions and translations of Greek and Latin texts.

Bibliography

Farnham, Fern, *Madame Dacier: Scholar and Humanist* (Monterey, 1976). Simonsuuri, Kirsti, *Homer's Original Genius: Eighteenth Century Notions of the Early Greek Epic* (Cambridge, 1979).

Christopher Smith

Ulla Dahlerup

Born March 21, 1942, Copenhagen, Denmark
Genre(s): novel, short story
Language(s): Danish

By demanding the right of teenage girls to diaphragms, the young Ulla Dahlerup in 1963 introduced the sexual revolution into all Danish homes. Born in Copenhagen in 1942, she has consistently participated in the public debates of her time, mostly as a free-lance journalist.

Gløder i Asken (1961; Embers in the Ash) and *Jagt Efter Vinden* (1962; Chasing the Wind), Dahlerup's first novels, are studies in adolescent narcissism, loneliness, and frustration in the nuclear age. Her gloomy portrayal of modern alienation continues in *Sankt Jørgens Gaard* (1969; St. George's Court), her only collection of short stories.

Dahlerup's latest novel, *Søstrene* (1979; The Sisters), is an obituary of the women's movement, which, in her representation, began in euphoria and freedom and ended in censorship, discipline, and Marxism. Following a woman's group from its beginning in 1970 until its dissolution and disillusion seven years later, Dahlerup depicts the erotic and political tensions of the seventies in the milieus characteristic of the decade: the political meetings, the consciousness-raising groups, the demonstrations, the communes, and the theaters and bars of Copenhagen.

As the outraged reception of *Søstrene* has most recently demonstrated, Ulla Dahlerup remains the gadfly of rebellion in contemporary Denmark, stinging conformity and uniformity at both ends of the political spectrum with her primarily polemical pen.

Works

Gløder i Asken (1961). *Jagt Efter Vinden* (1962). *Sankt Jørgens Gaard: Noveller* (1969). *Søstrene* (1979).

Clara Juncker

Daniela Dahn

Born 1949, Berlin, East Germany
Genre(s): feuilleton, radio drama
Language(s): German

Daniela Dahn is a representative of the modern East German writer-publicist-generation after World War II. Her work is relatively unknown in the West and concentrates in a feuilletonistic manner on modern questions that do not necessarily reflect the problems of her own country but those of man in modern times in general. Born in 1949 in Berlin, she lived in the little town of Kleinmachow, East Germany, where she went to school and finished her pre-university education in 1968. During 1968/69 she had an internship (*Volontariat*) with the East German TV-corporation (Fernsehen der DDR), and until 1973 Daniela Dahn studied journalism at the Karl Marx University in Leipzig. Until 1982 she was an editor for the East German Television, since then she has worked as a free-lance writer and publicist. With a journalistic background, most of Daniela Dahn's publications involve the discussion of contemporary problems. She made a name in her country by feuilletons and radioplays and several texts for anthologies, one of them *Seitenspruenge* (Sidejumps). In 1980, her first book was published, a collection of feuilletons called *Spitzenzeit. Feuilletons* (Peaktime. Feuilletons). Some of the questions discussed in these articles are more of a metaphysical nature: Are the questions of life more promising than the answers? What will happen in a world without anniversaries? How would Marx judge the modern woman? Daniela Dahn's aim in all her feuilletons and particularly in the collection *Spitzenzeit* is to ask provocative questions, to question established ideas and positions, to ask the "meaning of life."

Daniela Dahn is a juggler with words and meanings, even though the first impression suggests a pleasant "simplicity" and "un-intellectual" usage of language. She seems to be talking to and addressing everybody as she discusses everyday problems of everyday people. Why do we know so few people and why do we have these tremendous problems establishing contact with others, even though we wish the contact? Why do we find it so difficult to consciously select our acquaintances but rather form relations with people who are thrown in our way by circumstances? Provocatively, she calls these thoughts *Wahlbekanntschaften* (Selective Acquaintances). The title essay of the collection discusses another modern problem: our dependence on technology. What happens when we have to spend the evening in darkness because the fuses are blown out? One would assume that a young couple knows what to do, but that is not the case. However, the first impression is misleading, as very soon it becomes apparent that Daniela Dahn is not talking about dark rooms and bored young couples but about the lack of communication in this world, the burned fuses of politics, the general inability to try something different. *Collage*, describing a visit to a garbage dump, tries to re-evaluate recent German history, which is presented through letters written by a young soldier during the war years.

Works

Spitzenheit. Feuilletons (1980). Prenzlauer Berg-Tour (1987).

Jutta Hagedorn

Camille d'Alb

(see: Constanța Dunca-Șchiau)

A. Dan

(see: Mercedes Salisachs)

Daphne

(see: Anna Rupertina Fuchs[in])

Emily Daphne

(see: Emily Kourteli)

La Comtesse Dash

(see: Gabrielle-Anne Du Poilloüe de Saint-Mars)

Ekaterina Romanovna Dashkova (née Vorontsova)

Born March 17, 1743, St. Petersburg, Russia;
died January 4, 1810, Moscow
Genre(s): poetry, memoirs, didactic works
Language(s): Russian and French

A member of a prominent family in eighteenth-century Russia, Princess Dashkova received an excellent education. In her youth she read voraciously the best-known works of Enlightenment thinkers, whose views she would espouse for the rest of her life. A friend of the Grand Duchess Catherine (the future Catherine II), Dashkova later came to be regarded with suspicion by the Empress on account of her own political ambitions. She is the author of several didactic works in various genres, in both poetry and prose. The most interesting of her works are her memoirs, which contain valuable information on the reign of Peter III and accession of Catherine II, descriptions of Moscow life in the mid-eighteenth century, and portraits of famous Russian and European figures.

The daughter of R.I. Vorontsov was brought up in the home of her uncle, state chancellor M.I. Vorontsov. She actively participated in the *coup d'état* of June 1762 that brought Catherine II to power, but her influence in court circles did not last. Beginning in 1769 she spent more than ten years abroad, during which time she met some of the most famous writers and scholars of the day, including Adam Smith, Voltaire, and Denis Diderot. Upon her return to Russia in 1783 she was appointed director of the Petersburg Academy of Sciences, and in the same year she was made head of the Russian Academy. Thus Princess Dashkova became the first woman in the history of Russia to occupy an important government post (two in this case). She founded the periodicals *Conversational Companion of Lovers of the Russian Word* (1783–1784) and *New Monthly Compositions* (1786–1796). She renewed the publications of earlier scientific periodicals and reinstated public readings at the Academy in Russian on math, physics, mineralogy, and natural history. Princess Dashkova also presided over the Academy's publication of a dictionary of the Russian language (6 parts, 1789–1794). Unfortunately, her activities in academy affairs were cut short by Paul I, who sent her into exile in 1796. She spent the last ten years of her life on her estate, Troitskoe, where she wrote her famous memoirs in the years 1804–1805. These memoirs were first translated into Russian by A.I. Herzen in 1859.

An energetic and independent woman, Dashkova emerges as a clear expression of the *Zeitgeist* of the Age of Reason. Her several poems and prose works are didactic in nature. Unfortunately, this early literary output has not been systematized or sufficiently researched. Her most important and best-known work is her *Memoirs*. Although lacking in strict historical accuracy, they provide an interesting account of her relations with the Empress Catherine and descriptions of some of the most famous personalities of the age.

Works

Zapiski: 1743–1810, ed. with article and commentary by G.N. Moiseeva (1985).

Translation: *Memoirs of the Princess Daschkaw, Lady of Honour to Catherine*, 2 vols., ed. by Mrs. W. Bradford (1840).

Bibliography

Krasnobaev, B.I., "Glava dvukh akademii." *Voprosy istorii* 12 (1971): 84–98. Lozinskaya, L. Ya., *Vo glave dvukh akademii* (Moscow, 1983).

Laura Jo Turner McCullough

Marie Dauguet

(a.k.a. Julie-Marie Aubert)

Born 1860, La Chaudeau, France; died 1942,
La Chaudeau
Genre(s): poetry, novel
Language(s): French

Marie Dauguet's youth was spent in the village in Haute-Saone where she was born. She was educated by her parents who encouraged her love for nature and the countryside. At the age of fifteen, she went with her father to Beuchot, an industrial town in the Vosges where he was starting up a factory. Her marriage in 1880 to Henri Dauguet, a childhood friend, was happy and is reflected in *Clartés* (Bright Spots), a travel journal with interspersed poems that recounts their voyage through Italy in spring and summer of 1905 and unites observations of nature with observations of Italians and their culture. Although she lived far from the Paris literary salons, she would leave her mountain retreat annually for a visit to Paris. Dauguet was well known to contemporary critics who judged her to be one of the best female poets of the period.

Before coming to writing, Dauguet tried her hand at both painting and musical composition. Neither proved as satisfactory to her as did writing. She had a keen sense of artistic merit and was highly self-critical. Indeed, she threw out much more than she ever published. Nature, both as subject and as imagery, dominates her work. The musicality of her verse reflects her concern with words and sounds. In all her works, she employs a rich and varied vocabulary and incorporates dialectical forms, rare words as well as neologisms. Her poetry reflects a learned simplicity and charm that seems ingenuous.

Although she writes with an apparent lack of artifice, her work is a perfect example of studied spontaneity. She is erudite and her familiarity with Classic as well as French bucolic poetry, e.g., Vergil's *Georgics* or Du Bellay's *Jeux Rustiques* (Rustic Games), permeates her early collections, *Par l'amour* (1908; Through Love) and *Les Pastorales* (1908; Pastoral). *L'Essor victorieux* (1911; Flight Triumphant) represents a radical shift in style. She breaks with her earlier influences as well as with conventional imagery while sacrificing none of the poetic virtues of her work. *Ce n'est rien, c'est la vie* (1924; It's Nothing, It's Life) belongs to the genre of philosophical poetry. It recounts life felt, weighed, and recreated through reflection, revealing the greatness and profundity of woman's soul. The collection received great critical acclaim at its publication and is still considered her best work.

Works

La Naissance du poète (1897). *A Travers le Voile* (1902). *Par l'amour* (1904). *Paroles du vent* (1904). *Clartés, notes et pochades* (1907). *Les Pastorales* (1908). *L'Essor victorieux* (1911). *Ce n'est rien, c'est la vie* (1924). *Passions* (1938). *Au fond des bois, au bord de l'eau* (n.d.). *Enlisée* (novel, n.d.). In addition, Dauguet contributed numerous poems and articles to the *Mercure de France* and *La Grande Revue*, among others, especially during the years from 1902–1910.

Bibliography

Heritier, Jean, *Essai de critique contemporain, Première série* (Paris, 1920). Numerous reviews of works in the *Mercure de France*.

Edith J. Benkov

Ingeborg Day

Born 1940, Graz, Austria
Genre(s): memoir, short story
Language(s): English, German

Ingeborg Day is an Austro-American writer. Born in Graz in 1940, she came to the United States in 1957 as an exchange student. Upon her graduation from the *gymnasium* in Graz, she married an American and lived in the Midwest as a homemaker, student, and German teacher for many years. After her divorce and the death of one of her children she moved to New York where she became an editor for *Ms.* magazine. Now a freelance writer, Day is one of those rare cases of authors who are brought up in one language and write in another. After writing under a pseudonym for some time (a fact Day does not wish to discuss), her American publisher allowed her to write a book about her native Austria, something she had always wanted to do as she explained in an interview. The book, *Ghost Waltz*, did not sell well in the United States and is out of print. In Austria, however, Day was encouraged to publish a German version. *Geisterwalzer* came out in 1983 and has since appeared in book club and paperback editions.

The subject of *Geisterwalzer* couldn't be more Austrian. Day attempts to uncover the truth about her father's activities as an Austrian Nazi. In America, ironically, on television and in her high-school history class, Day first learns about Nazi atrocities. Back home in Graz, knowing that her father was a Nazi, she starts asking questions, but she never receives an answer. Her parents react with hostility, but she persists.

Day's book, which is in part memoir, part fiction, also recaptures Austria's painful history after World War I. Moving in flashbacks between present-day New York and Austria, Day tries to purge herself of anti-Jewish tendencies that torment her. She does not know their origin and becomes obsessed by the thought that her beloved parents might be responsible for her latent anti-Semitism. Her story has a somewhat happy ending although doubts linger on whether she will ever reach the peace of mind she yearns for.

Geisterwalzer has another dimension. The author tries to come to grips with the eternal problem of emigrants. Day's gallant efforts to become a true American, constantly alluded to in the book, obviously have not succeeded. While she is totally at home in the English language, her attempts to repress her Austrian past have failed. The book shows that she is torn between nostalgic yearning for her homeland and stubborn refusal to admit it.

In her thematic preoccupation with her native country's Nazi past, Day shows affinities with contemporary Austrian writers such as Peter Henisch, Brigitte Schwaiger, and Jutta Schutting. *Geisterwalzer* is an important literary contribution to Austria's coming to terms with the darker chapters of its history.

Works

Ghost Waltz (1980). Geisterwalzer (1983).

Bibliography

Bartsch, Kurt, "Jüngste Bestrebungen: Dominanten der siebziger Jahre," in *Geschichte der deutschen Literatur vom 18. Jahrhundert bis zur Gegenwart*, ed. Viktor Žmegač, Vol. III/2 (Königstein, 1984), p. 822. Koppensteiner, Jürgen, "Das Erbe des Holocaust: Zu Ingeborg Days Autobiographie *Geisterwalzer.*" *Literatur und Kritik* 229/230 (1988): 467–472.

Jürgen Koppensteiner

Teresa de Cartagena

Born fifteenth century, Spain
Genre(s): treatise
Language(s): Spanish

Teresa de Cartagena belonged to an illustrious Christian family of Jewish origin, which achieved great prominence in Castile due to the literary accomplishments of its members. Teresa was the granddaughter of Pablo de Santa María, who was first chief rabbi and later bishop of Burgos. Among other writers, Álvar García de Santa María and Alonso de Cartagena were her relatives. Given her unusual background, it is not surprising that Teresa de Cartagena studied in Salamanca, became a nun, and wrote a couple of treatises.

Having lost her hearing in her youth, Teresa composed a book entitled *Arboleda de los Enfermos* (The Grove of the Sick), mostly to console herself by studying in great detail the many positive aspects of illness, which in her opinion leads to God. To demonstrate this, she quoted not only the Bible, but also authors such as Saint Augustine and Saint Bernard. The knowledge and skill that Teresa displayed in this work, and even the fact that she had written it, caused bewilderment in Castile, where there were practically no women authors at the time. She was accused of having plagiarized the works of others and even of not having composed the work herself.

To answer these accusations, Teresa composed a book entitled *Admiraçión Operum Dey* (Wonder at the Works of God), which some critics consider the first example of feminist writing in the Iberian Peninsula. She defends the idea that women are not inferior to men in the eyes of God. In her opinion, both sexes complement each other, and if God made men stronger physically and to some extent mentally than women, it was so that they would be able to deal with the outside world. Women stay inside and therefore do not need to be as strong as men. Having made this concession, Teresa stresses that although there are important natural differences between men and women, many differences are cultural, and the attitude with respect to literature is one of them. She explains that women do not write because they are not trained or encouraged to do it. Teresa attributes the bewilderment her literary activities had caused to the fact that people believed women did not write because they were not capable of doing it. She states that the ability to write is a gift from God to the individual, man or woman, and people should wonder at this gift and not at the identity of the receiver. She concludes that to deny that both men and women can receive this gift is to deny the power of God.

As can be seen, Teresa de Cartagena was capable not only of expressing herself in writing but also of reflecting about the writing process. These were very unusual accomplishments for a woman in medieval Castile. Some critics think she became a writer because she was marginalized by her Jewish origin and acute deafness. No doubt these circumstances had something to do with her desire to express herself in writing. However, she could do it because, having come from a literary family, she had the necessary training and encouragement. The same thing can be said of Florencia Pinar, a poet who also came from a literary family. As for the historian Leonor López de Córdoba, although she did not come from a literary family, she was familiar enough with the writing process to dictate her work to a notary. The only three significant women authors of medieval Castile wrote because, apart from the desire to do so, they had direct or indirect access to the pen. Teresa de Cartagena's analysis of the situation was indeed accurate.

Works

Arboleda de los Enfermos (mid-fifteenth century).
Admiración Operum Dey (second half of the fifteenth century).

Bibliography

Deyermond, Alan D., "Spain's First Women Writers." In Women in Hispanic Literature. Icons and Fallen Idols, ed. Beth Miller (Berkeley, Calif., 1983). Hutton, Lewis J., ed., Teresa de Cartagena, "Arboleda de los Enfermos" y "Admiración Operum Dey" (Madrid, 1967). Serrano y Sanz, Manuel, Apuntes para una biblioteca de autoras españolas. I. Biblioteca de Autores Españoles, 268 (Madrid, 1903).

Cristina González

Alba de Céspedes

Born 1911, Rome, Italy
Genre(s): novels, short stories, poetry, drama
Language(s): Italian and French

Alba de Céspedes was born of a prominent Cuban family; her paternal grandfather had served as the first president of Cuba. Her father followed a diplomatic career that included the ambassadorship to Italy, where he married an Italian citizen who became de Céspedes' mother. Years later de Céspedes herself married the Italian diplomat Franco Bounous. This foreign service background has taken her to France, the United States, Cuba, and Pakistan.

As a child, Alba de Céspedes began writing poetry and plays. The period of her literary apprenticeship occurred during the Fascist era (1922–1955), when no official literary critics took women authors seriously. She began publishing some short stories in 1935, and in 1938 attracted international attention with her novel Nessuno torna indietro, a probing study of eight women. Although Nessuno torna indietro eventually was translated in twenty-four languages, the spirit of mediocrity and deliberate avoidance of truthfulness about everyday Italian life led the censors to ban that book and also de Céspedes' following narrative work, Fuga (1940). A period of internal warfare in Italy followed the establishment of the Nazi-directed puppet state of the Italian Social Republic from the autumn of 1943 to the war's end. During this period, Alba de Céspedes joined the Partisan cause to broadcast from Radio Partigiana in Bari under the code name of Clorinda.

From 1944 to 1948, de Céspedes directed the review Mercurio. Her journalistic articles appear frequently in Epoca and La Stampa. With the novel Dalla parte di lei, the writer begins to investigate the societal and domestic circumstances that undermine marriage: after a single year of marriage the young wife Alessandra kills her husband. Significantly, the author does not shift responsibility to the difficult conditions of life in Rome under Nazi occupation but reveals the disastrous collapse of intimate communication that leads to the murder. Similarly, in the novel Quaderno proibito (1952), the protagonist comes to acknowledge the absolute failure of her aspirations and the emptiness of her relationship with her husband and children. That intense examination of a strong-willed female protagonist seeking a freedom of self-expression in a society that relegates women to the decorative roles of wife—mother, mistress, and nun—continues in the novels Prima e dopo (1955) and Il rimorso (1963). With the novel La bambolona (1967) the writer presents a male protagonist whose comically obsessive preoccupation with a younger woman from a class below his eventually results in disaster for him.

Spending her time between Paris and Rome, de Céspedes pursued her literary concern with the problems of freedom. The May 1968 university student revolts in France inspired her volume of verse *Chansons des filles de mai*. Her narrative focus on modern woman's struggle to achieve emancipation and then retain her integrity reappears in the novel *Nel buio della notte* (1976). Ironically, although the novels of Alba de Céspedes are among the most widely translated of any Italian novelist, including Moravia and Calvino, her feminism has attracted the coldness or indifference of Italy's literary critics.

Works

L'anima degli altri (1935). Io, suo padre (1936). Concerto (1937). Nessuno torna indietro (1938). Fuga (1940). Dalla parte di lei (1949). Quaderno proibito (1952). Prima e dopo (1955). Invito a pranzo (1955). Il rimorso (1963). La Bambolana (1967). Chansons des filles de mai (1969). Nel buio della notte (1976).

Translations: There's No Turning Back [Nessuno torna indietro] (1941). The Best of Husbands [Dalla parte di lei] (1952). The Secret [Quaderno proibito] (1957). Between then and now [Prima e dopo] (1959). Remorse [Il rimorso] (1967). La Bambolana [La Bambolana] (1969).

Bibliography

Bellario P., in *Tempo* (February 2, 1950). Bellonci, G., in *Giornale d'Italia* (December 14, 1949). Cecchi, E., *Libri nuovi e usati* (Naples, 1958). Pancrazi, P., *Italiani e stranieri* (Milan, 1957). Pullini, G., *Il romanzo italiano del dopoguerra* (Padua, 1972).

Douglas Radcliff-Umstead

M. Francisco de Cuevas

(see: Luisa Sigea de Velasco)

Janina Degutytė

Born 1928, Kaunas, Lithuania
Genre(s): poetry, children's literature
Language(s): Lithuanian

In 1955 Degutytė graduated from the University of Vilnius, majoring in Lithuanian language and literature. She taught high school from 1955 to 1957 and was editor of the Lithuanian Belles Lettres Publishing House from 1958 to 1961. Since then, Degutytė has been a free artist by profession. She was awarded the honorary title of Meritorious Worker in the Arts of the Soviet Lithuanian Republic in 1978.

The larger half of Degutytė's creative output consists of poems and tales for children, thirteen volumes out of twenty-three published by 1983. She has also translated poetry, notably E. Verhaeren and Rainer Maria Rilke. In 1968 Degutytė received a state prize for her collection *Pilnatis* (1967; Full Moon) and a Young Communist League prize for *Saulėtos dainelės* (1972; Little Sunny Songs, poems for children) in 1974.

Degutytė is a contemplative poet, focused upon her own self-perceptions at the very edge of encounter with nature, people, and history. Hers is not an inward-directed thought; rather, it is more of a process of transferring the gift of oneself to the surrounding world, an outreach, often in sorrow and even anger, mostly in love, during which the poetic word is born. Degutytė is an intensely national poet, for her mind's greatest jewel is her native land in its ephemeral Arcadian beauty and, most particularly, in the heart-wrenching, bloody, tenebrous history of its people through the ages, under constant attack by greedy neighboring empires. Her feeling for her own people does not make her insensitive to others; on the contrary, it causes her to be even more responsive to the outrages humanity perpetrates upon itself throughout the ages. In this spirit Degutytė writes of fourteenth-century Flanders, torn by internal strife, quoting Til Eulenspiegel, "the ashes clamor at my heart":

Your nights, o Flanders, are so bright
   from burning pyres
Your winters, Flanders, are so warm
   from burning pyres
Your earth is gray from ashes.
And every midnight
Sings my anxious bird
and ashes clamor at my heart,
and ashes clamor at my heart . . .

In effect, Flanders becomes for Degutytė a generic name to include all humanity, and particularly her own much-tortured country. In her deep feelings for all the world's unfortunates,

Degutytė reaches the point of defying the "king's law," like Antigone of old, to mourn the freedom fighters against the Soviet occupation in Lithuania as well as those who died in battle with them, while the regime was leaving the dead guerrillas in city squares to be despised and spat upon. In her mourning, Degutytė weaves in motifs from Lithuanian mythological songs, thus reaching out in her cry of sorrow to the deepest recesses of the nation's racial memory. In one of these songs, for instance, the Morning Star, sun's daughter, was going to have a wedding, but the god Perkūnas, in a jealous rage, struck her lover to death; the Morning Star could not wash clean her lover's bloody shirt, except in some mythical time when nine suns would rise. Degutytė translates the meaning of this cruel myth into the context of the bloody conflicts in Lithuania after the Second World War:

> My limbs are aching from the cold lake's
> water,
> My mouth is dry in blowing wind, my
> eyes are full of tears
> And yet my hands cannot wash out these
> shirts,
> Cannot wash out my brothers' dried-up
> blood.
> What will I tell my mother back at
> home? . . .
> The shirts are blooming, blooming tulips
> red . . .
> And how am I to wash these set-in
> stains,
> With my own life made barren by the
> northern wind?
> —So, in this lake, with the nine rivers
> flowing,
> So, in the morning, when nine red
> dawns are rising . . .

Thus in Degutytė's poem do myth and history meet to unite the poem's persona with the ancient daughter of the sun, and her fate with the present destiny of the nation. We may add that here Degutytė extends her references to folk art as well, for the tulips that provide a counterpoint to the roses in the song are actually one of the most common motifs in the woven patterns of women's national costumes. In this way the women, sun's daughters all, have always worn their destiny.

Degutytė's appeal to her readers rests mostly on this sort of sacrificial nobility of soul combined with her talent for strongly affective poetic language. She is not, however, at one with the latest generation of Lithuanian poets, for whom similar sentiments must seek expression in complex, modernistic, indeed post-modern stylistic structures that strain the traditional capabilities of the Lithuanian language toward new boundaries.

Works

Ugnies lašai, poems (1959). *Dienos—dovanos*, poems (1969). *Saulė ir dainelė*, poems for children (1961). *Ant 'emės delno*, poems (1963). *Rugelis dainuoja*, poems for children (1963). *Sniego lelija*, poems for children (1964). *Mano diena*, poems for children (1965). *Šiaurės vasaros*, poems (1967). *Mėlynos deltos*, collected poems (1968). *Pelėd'iuko sapnas*, tales for children (1969). *Debesų pilis*, poems for children (1970). *Šviečia sniegas* (1970, poems). *Saulėtos dainelės*, poems for children (1972). *Prieblandų sodai*, poems (1974). *Kregždės lopšinė*, poems for children (1976). *Tylos valandos*, collected poems (1978). *Saulės pėdom*, poems for children (1979). *Tarp saulės ir netekties*, poems (1980). *Juokias duonelė*, poems for children (1982). *Piemenaitė karalaitė*, poems for children (1982). *Klevų viršūnės*, poems for young people (1983).

Bibliography

Bra'ėnas, P., "Paslaptis, kurią reikia įveikti," in P. Bra'ėnas, *Žmogus ir 'odis prozoje* (1978). Dirgėla, Petras and Povilas, "Sakmės būtinybė," in A. Bučys, ed. *Literatūros atvaizdai*, Vol. V (1979). Šilbajoris, R., "Tėvynė ir asmuo Janinos Degutytės poezijoje." *Metmenys* (1969). Sprindytė, J., "Filosofuojantys lyrikai," in J. Sprindytė, *Kritikos akvarelės* (1980).

R. Šilbajoris

Agatha Deken

Born December 10, 1741, Amstelveen, The
    Netherlands; died November 14, 1804,
    The Hague
Genre(s): poetry, novel, essay
Language(s): Dutch

Orphaned at an early age, Agatha Deken was raised in an orphanage at Amsterdam in a pietistic environment that held for the young Agatha no other promises than a life-long existence as a servant. However, when in 1770 she became employed by the family Bosch, she entered an upper middle class milieu that permitted her to develop her literary talents. She published the poems that she wrote during this period in collaboration with Maria Bosch, the infirm daughter of her employers, two years after the death of Maria in 1773, in a volume entitled *Stichtelijke gedichten* (Edifying Poems). However, Aagje Deken would not be remembered today in Dutch literary history were it not for her collaboration with another Dutch woman writer, Elizabeth Wolff. In 1776, Agatha sent the controversial Elizabeth Wolff a critical letter reprimanding her for her unconventional beliefs concerning society, religion, education, and the role of women and her satirical attacks on established religion. This letter, which testified to Deken's sensitivity and her clear understanding of Wolff's mind and writings, led to a life-long friendship between the two authors. After the death of Betje's husband in 1777, Betje invited Aagje to live with her and they remained together the rest of their lives—even sharing a ten-year exile in France following the Prussian invasion of Holland in 1787. When Betje Wolff died on November 5, 1804, Aagje only survived her companion by nine days. Both are buried at the cemetery of Scheveningen.

Works and Bibliography

For more information and bibliography concerning Aagje Deken's oeuvre, please refer to the essay on Elizabeth Wolff-Bekker. However, the following publications, authored by Aagje Deken without the cooperation of Betje Wolff, should be mentioned: *Mijn offerande aan het vaderland* [My Offerings To The Fatherland] (1799); *Liederen voor den boerenstand* [Songs for the Peasant Class] (1804) and the posthumous *Liederen voor ouderen en kinderen* [Songs for the Old and the Young] (1805).

Henk Vynckier

Carmen de Rafael Marés de Kurz

(a.k.a. Carmen Kurtz)

Born September 18, 1911, Barcelona, Spain
Genre(s): novel, short story, children's
literature
Language(s): Spanish

Though from Catalan-speaking Barcelona, Carmen Kurtz writes exclusively in Spanish. She is an award-winning writer of prose fiction for adults and children. At least six movies have been based on her juvenile novels, all in collaboration with Arturo Kaps and Herta Frankel.

Her life and works have an international perspective: two of her ancestors, Catalan emigrants, married women from the United States, her father was born in Cuba and her mother in Baltimore, Maryland. After completing her studies in Barcelona, Kurtz, like her protagonist in her first novel, *Duermen bajo las aguas* (1955; They Sleep Underwater), went to England in 1929, where she studied English for a year. She also speaks Catalan and French. She was married to a Frenchman, Pierre Kurz Klein, from 1935 until his death in 1962. Their daughter Odile (now a frequent illustrator of her mother's stories for children) was born during their sojourn in France in 1935–1943.

Perhaps because she belongs chronologically to the generation of 1910–1920, her novels are more personal than those of her literary contemporaries of the Generation of 1954, which is noted for its more generalized social commentary. She explores interpersonal relationships, the effects of war on individuals, and the importance of family heritage.

Kurtz's first novel (winner of the 1954 Ciudad de Barcelona Prize) is largely autobiographical. The prestigious Planeta Prize followed in 1956 for her *El desconocido* [The Stranger], which examines the psychosocial crises of a couple reunited after the husband's twelve-year captivity in Russia. In *La vieja ley* (1956; The Old Law), a woman searches for happiness and love within the context of stifling provincial life in the 1920s to 1940s. *Detrás de la piedra* (1958; Behind the Rock), based on a true story, chronicles small-town hypocrisy and ideological repression during the Franco era. *El becerro de oro* (1964; The Golden Calf) illustrates bourgeois obsession with money; *Las algas* (1966; Seaweed) contrasts country/city and authenticity/artificiality; *En la punta de los dedos* (1968; At Your Fingertips) repeats the themes of hypocrisy and old age. In *Entre dos oscuridades* (1969; Between Two Kinds of Darkness) a dying executioner remembers those criminals he considered "innocent" victims despite their crimes. The lighter novel *Cándidas palomas* (1975; Innocent Doves) depicts prepubescent girls in the 1970s. Perhaps Kurtz's best work, and certainly her most ambitious, is the trilogy *Sic transit* (So It Goes), the history of three generations of Catalan immigrants and the eventual return of their descendants to Spain: *Al otro lado del mar* (1973; To the Other Side of the Sea), *El viaje* (1975; The Voyage), and *El regreso* (1976; The Return). The title of the trilogy is a clever reference to the Latin phrase *sic transit gloria*, so goes glory.

Kurtz's shorter works include *En la oscuridad* (1963; In the Dark), a finalist for the Café Gijón Prize; two collections of short stories, and at least twenty-seven books for young readers. Most popular of the latter are fifteen novels about the adventures of a twelve-year-old boy named Oscar and his pet goose Kina. All the books in the series inform while they entertain, and most have either won or been finalists for juvenile fiction awards.

In recent years Kurtz has concentrated her creative efforts on works for children. Nonetheless, she is also an important, prize-winning author of adult fiction, who accomplishes her stated purpose of criticizing the hypocrisy and self-righteousness of the Spanish middle class, thus awakening their sense of responsibility to the poor and to their country.

Works

Adult Fiction: *Duermen bajo las aguas* [They Sleep Underwater] (1954). *El desconocido* (The Stranger) in *Premios Planeta* (1955–1958). *La vieja ley* [The Old Law] (1956). *Detrás de la piedra* [Behind the Rock] (1958). *Al lado del hombre* [Beside the Man] (1961). *El último camino* [The Last Road] (1961). *En la oscuridad* [In the Dark] (1963). *Siete tiempos* [Seven Epochs] (1964). *El becerro de oro* [The Golden Calf] (1964). *Las algas* [Sea-weed] (1966). *En la punta de los dedos* [At Your Fingertips] (1968). *Entre dos oscuridades* [Between Two Kinds of Darkness] (1969). The trilogy *Sic transit* [So It Goes] (1973, 1975, 1976). *Al otro lado del mar* [To the Other Side of the Sea] (1973). *El viaje* [The Voyage] (1975), and *El regreso* [The Return] (1976). *Cándidas palomas* [Innocent Doves] (1975).

Children's Fiction: *Oscar Cosmonauta* [Oscar the Cosmonaut] (1962). *Oscar espía atómico* [Oscar, Atomic Spy] (1963). *Oscar y el Yeti* [Oscar and the Abominable Snowman] (1964). *Color de fuego* [The Color of Fire] (1964). *Oscar y Corazón de Púrpura* [Oscar and the Purple Heart] (1965). *Oscar espeleólogo* [Oscar the Spelunker] (1966). *Oscar y los OVNI* [Oscar and the UFO's] (1967). *Oscar y los hombres-rana* [Oscar and the Frogmen] (1967). *Oscar agente secreto* [Oscar, Secret Agent] (1968). *Oscar en el Polo Sur* [Oscar at the South Pole] (1969). *Oscar en el laboratorio* [Oscar in the Laboratory] (1970). *Oscar en los juegos olímpicos* [Oscar at the Olympics] (1971). *Oscar en África* [Oscar in Africa] (1974). *Chipita* (1975). *Oscar en las Islas* [Oscar in the Islands] (1977). *Oscar, Kina y el laser* [Oscar, Kina and the Laser] (1979). *Oscar, Buna y el Rajá* [Oscar, Buna and the Rajah] (1980). *Veva* (1980). *Veva y el mar* [Veva and the Sea] (1981). *Piedras y trompetas* [Rocks and Trumpets] (1981). *La paloma y el cuervo* [The Dove and the Crow] (1981). *La ballena y el cordero* [The Whale and the Lamb] (1981). *Fanfamús* (1982). *Querido Tim* [Dear Tim] (1983). *Pepe y Dudú* [Pepe and Dudú] (1983). *Pitos y flautas* [Whistles and Flutes] (1983).

Bibliography

Díaz-Plaja, Guillermo, "Entre dos oscuridades de Carmen Kurtz." *Cien libros españoles* (Salamanca, 1971), pp. 317–320. Kurtz, Carmen, *El autor enjuicia su obra* (Madrid, 1966), pp. 111–122. Moix, Ana María, "Carmen Kurtz y la literatura infantil." *Insula* 260–261 (1968): 25. Myers, Eunice D., "Autotextuality and Intertextuality in *El desconocido* by Carmen Kurtz." *Hispania* 71 (March 1988): 43–49. Myers, Eunice D. "Four Female Novelists and Spanish Children's Fiction." *Letras Femeninas* 10, No. 2 (Fall 1984): 40–49.

Eunice D. Myers

Remigio Andrés Delafón

(see: Rosario de Acuña y Villanueva de
la Iglesia)

Grazia Deledda

(a.k.a. Ilia di Sant'Ismael)

*Born September 27, 1871, Nuoro, Sardinia;
died August 15, 1936, Rome
Genre(s): novel, drama, poetry
Language(s): Italian*

One of Italy's most important modern novelists, Grazia Deledda is often seen as a transitional figure, combining the form of the nineteenth-century novel with the existential outlook
of twentieth-century fiction. Critics have linked
her with several nineteenth-century movements—romanticism, *verismo* (the late nineteenth century naturalistic movement that dealt
realistically with common problems faced by the
lower classes), and decadence (with its emphasis
on the complex psychological portrayal of unusual states of mind)—but her work is much too
varied (over forty novels and short story collections published between 1890 and 1937) and
too complex to be categorized so easily.

Deledda was born into a middle-class family
in Nuoro, Sardinia. Educated only through elementary school, Deledda read passionately a
variety of popular and serious nineteenth-century writers, including Scott, Byron, Heine, Hugo,
Chateaubriand, Sue, Balzac, Carducci,
D'Annunzio, Verga, De Amicis, Tolstoy,
Turgenev, and Dostoevsky. These two influences—her birthplace and her reading—were to
shape practically all of her own work. Except for
her last novels, all of Deledda's work centers on
the people of Sardinia and their ancient customs
and beliefs and describes in detail the harsh,
desolate landscape that surrounds them. Deledda
once stated that she wished to do for Sardinia
what Tolstoy had done for Russia, and her emphasis on individuals caught up in tragic circumstances often beyond their control is reminiscent
of the Russian novelists. Deledda married in
1900 and moved to Rome with her husband,
Palmiro Madesani; although she remained in
Rome for the rest of her life, she continued to
write about her native island, recalling and dis-
tilling people, places, and customs. In 1926
Deledda won the Nobel Prize for literature. She
died in Rome in 1936, and her last novel, the
autobiographical *Cosima*, was published the following year.

Deledda's earliest works, such as *Nell'azurro*
(1890) and *Stella d'oriente* (1891), show most
clearly the influence of the romantic novel, with
its emphasis on adventure and exaggerated plot
devices. But in the 1890s her novels and stories
begin to concentrate more on the Sardinian land
and people, particularly such works as *Anime
oneste* (1895) and *La via del male* (1896), and in
1895 Deledda published a study of Sardinian
culture, *Tradizioni populari di Nuoro in Sardegna*.
The Sardinian setting was to furnish her with
characters and themes for almost all of her novels
even after she moved to Rome. Often the poetic
descriptions of the wild countryside and fierce
climate serve to characterize the harshness of the
characters' lives or the inner conflict of the protagonist. The customs of her Sardinian characters reflect the survival of an ancient, even pre-
Christian way of life; these old beliefs inevitably
come into conflict with the demands of the
modern world, a conflict which dominates
Deledda's work. In *Dopo il divorzio* (1902, revised as *Naufraghi in porto* in 1928), the protagonist Constantino Ledda is sent to prison for
27 years for killing his uncle; a new divorce law
allows his wife Giovanna, who is living in poverty, to remarry a landowner, but her new life
proves worse than her poverty and she is scorned
by the villagers. After the real murderer of
Constantino's uncle confesses, the innocent man,
shattered by what he considers to be his wife's
betrayal, returns to his village and eventually
begins a passionate but loveless affair with
Giovanna. Unable to find happiness, he eventually kills Giovanna's cruel mother-in-law and is
sentenced to hard labor in prison; Giovanna's life
deteriorates still further. Deledda shows how on
the one hand the traditional prohibition of divorce, which had provided security and stability,
also proved inflexible and repressive, while on
the other hand the new order fails to support
those whom it purports to liberate. In many
novels the decay of the old order is typified by the

dissolution of the patriarchal family unit; often the patriarch is harsh and unyielding, or he is absent and the remaining male protagonists are weak or isolated from the real world. The almost certain failure of the protagonist to resolve the conflict between the old and the new gives Deledda's novels a sense of fatalism and even futility; but the public failure does not eliminate the obligation to act ethically, and this defeat often leads a character to seek a private expiation, often through self-renunciation. In *Elias Portolu* (1903), a young man (Elias) falls in love and has an affair with his brother's fiancee; Elias plans to become a priest, but then his brother dies. Elias' own son by the affair dies, and he decides not to marry his brother's widow, as custom demands, but to become a priest. The title character of *La Madre* (1919; The Mother) threatens to expose her son, a priest, for his love for a parishioner. He gives up his lover, but his mother plans to denounce him in church. Unable to do so, she dies at Mass in front of her son. After 1921, Deledda began to concentrate on the psychological states of her characters, as in *Il segreto dell' uomo solitario* (1921; The Secret of the Solitary Man) and less on Sardinia as a setting. Her last novels have thinner, more allegorical plots and are often situated in undefined, atemporal settings, for example *Il paese del vento* (1931; The Country of the Wind).

While Deledda is certainly significant as a historical figure, linking nineteenth-century forms and techniques with a modern skepticism, her work is also important as a document of a particular place and time and as a treatment of the universal problems of guilt and moral responsibility in a world of contradictory values.

Works

Nell'azurro [In the Blue] (1890). *Stella d'oriente* [Star of the East] (1891) pseud. Ilia di Saint'Ismail. *Amore regale* [Royal Love] (1892). *Fior di Sardegna* [Flower of Sardinia] (1892). *Racconti sardi* [Sardinian Tales] (1894). *Anime oneste* [Honest Souls] (1895). *Tradizioni popolari di Nuoro in Sardegna* [Popular Traditions of Nuoro in Sardinia] (1895). *La via del male* [The Way of Evil] (1896). *Il tesoro* [The Treasure] (1897). *L'ospite* [The Guest] (1897). *Giffah, Nostra Signora del Buon Consiglio, Le disgrazie che puo causare il denaro, I tre talismani*

[Giffa, Our Lady of Good Counsel, The Disgraces That May Produce Money, The Three Talismans] (1899), four fables published as separate volumes. *Le tentazioni* [The Temptations] (1899). *La giustizia* [Justice] (1899). *Il vecchio della montagna* [The Old Man of the Mountain] (1900). *La regina delle tenebre* [The Queen of the Shadows] (1901). *Dopo il divorzio* [After the Divorce] (1902); revised as *Naufraghi in porto* [Shipwreck in Port] (1920). *Elias Portolu* (1903). *Cenere* [Ashes] (1904). *Nostalgie* [Nostalgias] (1905). *I giuochi della vita* [The Games of Life] (1905). *Amori moderni* [Modern Loves] (1907). *L'ombra del passato* [The Shadow of the Past] (1907). *Il nonno* [The Grandfather] (1908). *Il nostro padrone* [Our Master] (1910). *Sino al confine* [To the Boundary] (1910). *Nel deserto* [In the Desert] (1911). *Chiaroscuro* (1912). *Colombi e sparvieri* [Doves and Hawks] (1912). *Canne al vento* [Reeds in the Wind] (1913). *Le colpe altrui* [The Guilt of Others] (1914). *Marianna Sirca* (1915). *Il fanciullo nascosto* [The Hidden Boy] (1915). *L'incendio nell'oliveto* [The Fire in the Olive Grove] (1918). *Il ritorno del figlio* [The Return of the Son]. *La bambina rubata* [The Stolen Baby] (1919). *La madre* [The Mother] (1919). *Cattive compagnie* [Bad Company] (1921). *Il segreto dell'uomo solitario* [The Secret of the Solitary Man] (1921). *Il Dio dei viventi* [The God of the Living] (1922). *Il flauto nel bosco* [The Flute in the Forest] (1923). *La danza della collana* (The Dance of the Necklace). *A sinistra* [On the Left] (1924). *La fuga in Egitto* [The Flight to Egypt] (1925). *Il sigillo d'amore* [The Seal of Love] (1926). *Annalena Bilsini* (1927). *Il vecchio e i fanciulli* [The Old Man and the Children] (1928). *Il dono di Natale* [The Christmas Gift] (1930). *La casa del poeta* [The House of the Poet] (1930). *Il paese del vento* [The Country of the Wind] (1931). *La vigna sul mare* [The Vineyard on the Sea] (1932). *Sole d'estate* [Summer Sunlight] (1933). *L'argine* [The Embankment] (1934). *La chiesa della solitudine* [The Church of Solitude] (1936). *Cosima* (1937). *Il cedro del Libano* [The Cedar of Lebanon] (1939).

Selections of works: *Versi e prosi giovanili* [Early Prose and Poetry] (1938), ed. A. Scano. *Romanzi e novelle* [Romances and Novels] (1941–1955), ed. E. Cecchi, 4 vols.

Theatre: With C. Antona Traversi, *L'edera* [Ivy] (1912). With C. Guastalla and V. Michetti, *La grazia* [Grace] (1921).

Poetry: *Paesaggi sardi* [Sardinian Landscape] (1896). "Lauda di Sant'Antonio" [Laud of Saint Anthony] (1893).

Translation: *Eugenia Grandet* by Balzac (1930).

Translations: *After the Divorce*, tr. Maria Lansdale (1905). *After the Divorce*, tr. Susan Ashe (1985). *Ashes*, tr. Helen Colvill (1908). *The Mother*, tr. Mary Steegman (1923) (preface by D.H. Lawrence).

Bibliography

Balducci, Carolyn, *A Self-Made Woman* (1975). Capanua, L., *Gli "ismi" contemporanei* (1898). *Convegno nazionale di studi Deledianni* (1974). De Michelis, Euralio, *Grazia Deledda e il Decadentismo*, with bibliography (1938). Petronio, Giorgio, "Grazia Deledda." *Letteratura italiana, I Contemporanei* (1963). Piromalli, Antonio, *Grazia Deledda* (1968). Piromalli, Antonio, "Grazia Deledda. La crisi della societa pastorale sarda e la struttura narrativa ottocentesca: l'insidia 'decadente' nell'intensità lirica dell'epos popolare." *Novecento*, ed. Gianni Grana, with bibliography (1982).

General references: Bondanella, Peter, and Julia Conaway Bondanella, eds., *Dictionary of Italian Literature* (1979). Caccia, Ettore, "Grazia Deledda." *Dizionario critico della letteratura italiana* (1974). *Dizionario enciclopedico della letteratura italiana* (1966).

Stephen Hale

Yanette Deletang-Tardif

Born 1902, Roubaix, France; died 1976, Paris, France
Genre(s): poetry, novel, criticism
Language(s): French

Writing did not become a part of Deletang-Tardif's life until after her marriage. Her first two works, *Eclats* (1929; Flashes), dedicated to her mother and *Générer* (1930; Engendering), dedicated to her newborn son, reveal the transition from daughter to mother and poet. She was one of the founding members of the "Ecole de Rochefort," the only woman among a group of poets who banded together during World War II. While they broke to a certain extent with Surrealism, they advocated neither a new poetic radicalism nor a return to the past. Rochefort, a town in Anjou, was the center of their activities, which consisted principally of writing and publishing. Deletang-Tardif collaborated on the "Anatomie poétique de l'Ecole de Rochefort I" (Poetic Anatomy I, the Rochefort School), a theory statement of non-theory stances published in 1941.

There is a happy eclecticism in Deletang-Tardif's works. While she is known principally as a poet, her output was not limited to poetry. She wrote prose fiction in the form of the novel, e.g. *Les Séquestrées* (1945; The Prisoners), a surrealist text in the style of Breton and had projected before her death a collection of short stories and another novel. She published a number of critical works, including her *Edmond Jaloux* (1947), the first major study of that author. Deletang-Tardif's close friendship with Jaloux provided her with insights that became the basis for many other critics' studies. Her taste for German led to translation of the poetry of Nietzsche and Goethe.

Many influences and many styles find their way into a career that spanned nearly four decades. She wrote as comfortably in fixed forms (sonnets, for example) as in free verse; she mixed prose poems with verse. Even when she chose traditional forms, she infused them with a new vocabulary and new themes. In the 1930s and 1940s, Romanticism, especially the German writers and the French poet Nerval, was as strong an influence as Paul Valéry or Paul Eluard, to whom she dedicated *Préssentiment de la rose* (1941; Presentiment of the Rose). In the 1950s there was a marked return to more formal strictness in her poems. The *Chants royaux* (1956; Royal Songs) inspired by the works of Guillaume de Machaut, a late medieval poet, and *Les Emblèmes* (1957; Emblems) inspired by Renaissance poetry, and in particular the sonnets of Louise Labé, are generally considered her masterpieces.

Works

Eclats (1929). *Générer* (1930). *Vol des oiseaux* (1931). *Confidences des îles* (1934). *Briser n'est rien* (1934). *L'Année poétique* (1934). *La Colline* (1935). *Morte en songe* (1938). *Préssentiment de la rose* (1941). *Poèmes du vitrier* (1941). *Tenter de vivre* (1943). *Edellina, ou Les Pouvoirs de la musique* (1943). *Sept chants royaux* (1945). *Les Séquestrées* (1945). *Poésies de Goethe* (tr., 1946).

EdmondJaloux(1947). *L'Eclair et le temps*(1951). *La Nuit des temps* (1951). *Chants royaux* (1956). *Les Emblèmes* (1957). *Almanach* (1958). *Les Eléments perdus* (1963). *De la Transparence en poésie* (1964). *Poésies complètes de Nietzsche* (tr., n.d.).

Translations: Selections in Domna Stanton, ed., *The Defiant Muse* (New York, 1986).

Bibliography

Bouhier, Jean, *Les Poètes de l'Ecole de Rochefort* (Paris, 1983). Delbreuille, Jean-Yves, *L'Ecole de Rochefort* (Lyon, 1987).

Edith J. Benkov

Claire Demar

Born 1799/1800; died August 3, 1833
Genre(s): tracts
Language(s): French

Little is known of her. She was married and worked together with the socialist group of Saint-Simon in Paris. In her work she vocally expressed her attitude against marriage and her fervent support of the fight against capitalism, the family as such, and even maternity. In many ways she can be called an early communist. Together with her lover Perret Desessarts she committed suicide on August 3, 1833.

Works

Appel d'un femme au peuple sur l'affranchement de la femme [A Woman's Appeal to the People on the Question of Emancipation of Women] (1833). *Textes sur l'affranchisement des femmes,* ed. V. Pelosse (Paris, 1976). *Ma loi d'avenir* [My Law of Future Developments] (1834).

Bibliography

d'Amat, Roman, "Demar." *Dictionnaire de biographie française,* vol. 10 (Paris, 1965), p. 966. Kleinau, Elke, *Die frae Frau. Soziale Utopien des frühen 19. Jahrhunderts.* Geschichtsdidaktik, 46 (Düsseldorf, 1987).

Albrecht Classen

Demo

Born c. second century A.D., Greece
Genre(s): poetry
Language(s): Greek

Demo, a Greek poet, seems to have flourished in the second century of our era, although she has left us very little information about her personal life and her traveling to Egypt to the Colossus of Memnon. What little we know about her derives from two distiches of an epigram scratched on one of the legs of the colossal statue near Egyptian Thebes. In the epigram she proudly claims herself as a poet. Her language appears aeolic in flavor. Bernand acknowledges the Homeric influence (*Iliad* I. 572; *Odyssey* III. 163).

That Demo belongs to the second century depends upon a conjecture based upon some slight similarities in her dedicatory distich and another poet's inscription clearly written in the time of Hadrian.

Works

The text of the epigram accompanied with a German translation appears in Helene Homeyer, *Dichterinen des Altertums und des frühen Mittelalters* (München, 1979), which is derived from the text of A. et E. Bernand, *Les inscriptions Grecques et Latines du Colosse de Memnon* (Paris, 1960). (Institut Français d'Archaeologie Orientale. XXXI). Nr. 83 (S. 179 ff.). Mt Kommentar.

Edward E. Best, Jr.

Kikē Dēmoula

(a.k.a. Kiki Dimoula)

Born 1931, Athens, Greece
Genre(s): poetry
Language(s): Greek

Kikē (or *Kiki*) Dēmoula (or *Dimoula*) is a bank employee in Athens and writes poetry in her spare time. Her first poems appeared in *Nea Estia* in 1949, and, as a consequence, she is sometimes grouped with the older "poets of essence" writing immediately after World War II and the Greek Civil War. The events of these wars left a lasting impression on the young Dēmoula also, but, unlike the poets of essence such as Melissanthē and Elenē Vakalo, who sought refuge from reality in post-symbolism and post-surrealism, Dēmoula expresses her bitterness, frustration, and disillusionment more directly, often resorting to irony, sarcasm, and understatement.

Many of her poems give the impression of being dramatic monologues, but, more often than not, the one addressed by the persona (speaking in the first person) may be the implied reader as well as the implied listener. By her interplay of first and second person Dēmoula succeeds probably more than any other Greek woman poet in bringing the reader into the poem and thus engaging him or her in an apparent "conversation."

More specifically, however, the "I" in Dēmoula's poems is usually a female "I," and the implied listener (the "you") is usually a male. Thus the disillusionment, frustration, and bitterness of her poems are the results of being female in the twentieth century. Much of Dēmoula's writing, therefore, may be termed "feminist." She is probably the most important figure among those of the "older" generation who wrote with a conscious awareness of the problematic situations women have to face.

Dēmoula's best-known collection is *To ligo tou kosmou* (The Smallness of the World), for which she received the National Prize for Poetry. Some of her work has been translated into Italian and English.

Works

Poiēmata [Poems] (1952). *Erevos* [Darkness] (1956). *Erēmēn* [By Default] (1958). *Epi ta ichnē* [On the Traces] (1963). *To ligo tou kosmou* [The Smallness of the World] (1971, 1972, 1983). *To teleutaio sōma mou* [My Last Body] (1981). *Chaire Poté* [Rejoice Never] (1988).
Translations: *Contemporary Greek Poetry*, tr. Kimon Friar (1958). *Contemporary Greek Women Poets*, tr. Eleni Fourtouni (1978).

Bibliography

Anghelaki Rooke, Katerina, "A Note on Greek Poetry in the 1970s." *Modern Poetry in Translation* 34 (Summer, 1978): 3–4. *Bulletin analytique de bibliographie hellènique, 1971* (Athènes, 1976). Decavalles, Andonis, "Modernity: The Third Stage, the New Poets." *The Charioteer* 20 (New York, 1978). Kolias, Helen Dendrinou, "Greek Women Poets and the Language of Silence." *Translation Perspectives IV* (Binghamton, N.Y., 1988). Mirasgezē, Maria, *Neoellēnikē Logotechnia*, vol. 2 (Athens, 1982).

Helen Dendrinou Kolias

Zsófia Dénes

Born 1885, Hungary; died 1988, Budapest, Hungary
Genre(s): biography, memoirs
Language(s): Hungarian

Zsófia Dénes was an active member of Hungary's literary community from the beginning of the century. In the 1910s, she was the Paris-based correspondent of *Pesti napló* and *Világ*. She also lived in Vienna for several years between the two World Wars. For a short period, she was the fiancée of the famous Hungarian Symbolist poet, Endre Ady. This relationship informed her books *Hours Instead of Life* (1935) and *At That Time the Linden-Trees Were Loving* (1957).

Following her stay in Paris in 1964, in several books she summarized her youthful and recent experiences in that city. *A Pedestrian on the Left Bank* (1965), *The Paris Merry-Go-Round* (1966), and *Rainbow* (1970) recount her meetings with some famous writers and artists.

Her writings are colorful and entertaining. The broad chronological spectrum with which Dénes, an intelligent and sophisticated woman, surveys her unusually eventful career in Paris, Vienna, and Budapest, lends a particular appeal to her works.

Works

Élet helyett órák (1935). *Akkor a hársak épp szerettek* (1957). *Gyalog a bal oldalon* (1965). *Párisi körhinta* (1966). *Szivárvány* (1970). *El ne lopd a léniát* (1978). *Szivárvány Pesttől Párisig* (1979).

Bibliography

Magyar Irodalmi Lexikon (Budapest, 1976). Pomogáts, Béla, *Az ujabb magyar irodalom története* (Budapest, 1982).

Peter I. Barta

Marie Dentière

(a.k.a. "Un marchand de Genève," "Un femme chrestienne de Tornay," Marie d'Enntière)

Born c. 1500, Tournai, Belgium; died 1561, Geneva, Switzerland
Genre(s): history, polemic
Language(s): French

A Protestant pamphlet writer and preacher, Dentière was involved in the reform movement in Geneva and was one of the few published female authors of early Protestantism.

Born to a noble family of Tournai, Dentière entered a local Augustinian convent. Joining the reform movement alongside other members of her family, she left her abbey in the 1520s and married Simon Robert, a former priest of that diocese who had become an evangelical pastor. After Robert's death, she married another evangelical preacher, Antoine Fromment, with whom she went to Geneva during the violent controversies of the early 1530s. Dentière became personally active in the reform movement, preaching to female audiences and publishing two works during the turbulent course of that decade.

The War for and Deliverance of the City of Geneva, Faithfully Prepared and Written Down by a Merchant Living in That City provided a lively and partisan interpretation of the long struggle between the Catholic duke of Savoy and the Protestant citizens of Geneva in the years 1524–1536. It was a hard-hitting document intended to influence public opinion during the reorganization of the secular and religious governance of the city immediately after the defeat of the Savoyard regime.

By 1539 a number of Dentière's friends, including the recently-arrived John Calvin, had been exiled from Geneva. In that year she wrote *A Most Beneficial Letter, Prepared and Written Down by a Christian Woman of Tournai, and Sent to the Queen of Navarre, Sister of the King of France, Against the Turks, the Jews, the Infidels, the False Christians, the Anabaptists and the Lutherans.* This work was intended to win support for those exiles, by bringing their plight before Marguerite de Navarre, the sister of the French king, Francis I, and a woman sympathetic to the evangelical cause. The religious rulers of her city were described as schemers and "cockroaches" who spread dissension and looked out for their own economic interests. Dentière defended evangelical theology through attacks on Catholic and even Lutheran opinion, buttressed by a series of sophisticated citations of canon law and other traditional theological sources. She also included an opening "Defense of Women," a consideration of the role of women in theological discourse. For Dentière the priesthood of all believers included women: "For we ought not, any more than men, hide and bury within the earth that which God has . . . revealed to us women. Although we are not permitted to preach in assemblies and public churches, nevertheless we are not prohibited from writing and giving advice in all charity one to the other."

The work was impounded by the city council. Dentière and Fromment fought an ongoing legal battle to gain its release but were unsuccessful even after the return of Calvin. Her radical stance on theological issues was unacceptable to her former allies. The couple became the objects of ridicule among the Genevan pastorate, and Dentière died in 1561 shortly after her husband, who had long since resigned his parish, had been charged with adultery. No printed copies of the *War and Deliverance* and only one of the *Useful Letter* survive today. She was a fine rhetorician, who offered one of the earliest feminist critiques of the role of women in the life of the Christian community.

Works

La guerre et deslivrance de la ville de Genesve, fidèlement faicte et composèe par ung Marchant demourant en icelle (1536). *Epistre très utile, faicte et composèe par une femme chrestienne de Tornay, envoyèe à la Royne de Navarre, seur du Roy de France, contre les Turcz, Juifz, Infideles, Faulx chrestiens, Anabaptistes et Lutheriens* (1539).

The entire text of *La guerre et deliverance* and extracts from the *Epitre très utile* are printed in Albert Rilliet, "Restitution de l'écrit intitulé: *La guerre de deslivrance de la ville de Genesve* (1536)," *Mémoires et documents publiées par la société d'histoire et d'archéologie de Genève* 20 (1881): 309–384. Other extracts from the *Epistre très utile* are printed in Aimé-Louis Herminjard, ed. *Correspondance des réformateurs dans les pays de langue française*, 9 vols. (Geneva: 1866–1897), V, pp. 295–304. The only surviving copy of this work is Geneva, Bibliothèque municipale, D. Den. 1.

Bibliography

Berthoud, G., *Antoine Marcourt, réformateur et pamphlétaire* (1973). Dufour, T., *Notice bibliographique sur le Catéchisme et la Confession de Foi de Calvin (1537) et sur les autres livres imprimés à Genève et à Neuchâtel dans les premiers temps de la réforme (1533–1540)* (1878). Douglass, J., *Calvin, Women, and Freedom* (1986). Head, T., "A Propagandist for the Reform: Marie Dentière," in Katharina Wilson, ed., *Women Writers of the Renaissance and Reformation* (1987). Revilliod, G., "La chronique du Marchand de Genève." *Mémoires et documents publiées par la société d'histoire et d'archéologie de Genève* 13 (1863): 27–39.

General references: Haag, *La France protestante*, 2nd ed., V, pp. 238–249. Hauser, *Sources de l'histoire de France*, II, p. 113.

Thomas Head

Maria Deraismes

Born 1828, Paris, France; died February 6, 1894, Paris
Genre(s): drama, lecture, essay
Language(s): French

Maria Deraismes was Parisian, gifted, single, well-educated, very wealthy, politically a Republican of the radical, anticlerical variety, and a long-time advocate of women's rights. She had become an accomplished artist and a performing musician before turning to letters.

Most of her plays were produced as drawing-room entertainment, but one was reportedly presented at Baden during the social season. In 1867 her interest in the condition of women was piqued by Barbey d'Aurevilley's diatribe against bluestockings in the *Nain Jaune*, and she was recruited by Léon Richer as a public lecturer on behalf of women's rights. Some of her early lectures were published in the *Revue des cours littéraires* and later compiled in *Eve dans l'humanité*; her articles appeared from 1869 on in *Le Droit des femmes, L'Avenir des femmes*, edited by Richer, and several other Parisian newspapers. Her first published volume was her *Eve contre Dumas fils*, a reply to the playwright

in the Affaire Dubourg, concerning a husband's right in France to kill an adulterous wife without being prosecuted for murder.

Well before the Paris Commune Maria Deraismes emerged as an outspoken advocate of major change in the legal and educational status of women, arrived at through step-by-step tactics. Her salon also became a center for anticlerical Republican politics. Many of her male friends and supporters were Freemasons, and in 1882 she was initiated into a dissident mixed-sex lodge. Bouts of ill health periodically curtailed her political activities.

Deraismes was also an organizer. In 1870 she and Léon Richer founded the *Société pour l'Amélioration du sort de la femme*, which functioned with some interruptions until the First World War. In 1878 she co-sponsored with Richer the First International Congress on Women's Rights, held in Paris. She also co-sponsored the second congress in 1889 and was among the first women to adopt the term "féminisme" in the early 1890s. By the time of her death in early 1894, she was eulogized by some as the very personification of the French feminist movement. Her supporters on the Paris Municipal Council named a street in her honor and private subscribers raised a statue in the Square des Epinettes.

Maria Deraismes' contribution was not without its critics. Some found her approach either too hesitant (for placing priority on reform of the Civil Code over political rights), too dogmatic (for insisting squarely on an anticlerical feminism, which alienated would-be supporters among moderate and liberal Catholics), or too bourgeois (for advocating equality of the sexes within the family, a single restrictive standard of moral behavior for women and men, and for not offering more support to the nascent socialist women's movement). Following Maria's death, her widowed elder sister Anna Feresse-Deraismes presided over the publication of her collected works; although the major works are gathered, these "complete works" are far from complete and a critical edition would be welcome.

Maria Deraismes remains a very accessible writer. Her varied publications reveal a masterful prose style, a frank and unabashed discussion of issues, marked by common sense, a gentle yet ironic sense of humor, and a recognition of human weakness. She can be credited with several linguistic innovations, distinguishing the "deux genres" or two genders from the "deux sexes," and secularizing the religious term "consoeurs" to address her female listeners and readers.

Works

Plays: *A bon chat, bon rat, comédie-proverbe en une acte, en prose* (1861). *Un neveu, si'il vous plaît, comédie en 3 actes et en prose* (1862). *Le Père coupable, comédie en 4 actes et en prose* (1862). *Retour à ma femme, comédie en 1 acte et en prose* (1862).

Essays and Speeches: *Aux femmes riches* (1865). *Théresa et son époque; à propos des courtisanes* (1865). *Nos principes et nos moeurs* (1868). *L'Ancien devant le nouveau* (1869). *Eve contre Dumas fils* (1872). *France et progrès* (1873). *Le Théatre de M. Sardou, conférence* (1875). *Lettre au clergé français* (1879). *Ligue populaire contre l'abus de la vivisection, discours . . . 23 Sept. 1883* (1884). *Les Droits de l'enfant* (1887). *Epidémie naturaliste* (1888). *Eve dans l'humanité* (1891).

Collections: *Le Théatre chez soi* (1864). *Oeuvres complètes de Maria Deraismes*, ed. Mme Feresse-Deraismes, 4 vols. (1895–1898). *Maria Deraismes, Ce que veulent les femmes: Articles et discours de 1869 à 1894*, préface, notes et commentaires de O. Krakovitch (1980).

Bibliography

Bidelman, Patrick Kay, "Maria Deraismes, Léon Richer, and the Founding of the French Feminist Movement, 1866–1878." *Third Republic/Troisième République* 3–4 (1977). Bidelman, Patrick Kay, *Pariahs Stand Up! The Founding of the Liberal Feminist Movement in France, 1858–1889* (Westport, Conn., 1982). Brault, Eliane, *La Franc-Maçonnerie et l'emancipation des femmes* (Paris, 1953). Brault, Eliane, *Maria Deraismes. Cahiers laiques* 70 (July–Aug. 1962). Jean-Bernard (pseud. J.-B. Passerieu), "Notice—Maria Deraismes." Deraismes, *Oeuvres complètes*, vol. 1, "France et Progrès"; "Conférence sur la noblesse" (Paris: 1895). Krakovitch, Odile, "Préface." *Maria Deraismes, Ce que veulent les femmes* (Paris, 1980). Moses, Claire G., *French Feminism in the Nineteenth Century* (Albany, N.Y., 1984). Schmahl, Jeanne E., "Maria Deraismes and the Woman's Movement in France." *The Englishwoman's Review* (April 16, 1894).

General references: *Dictionary of Modern Peace Leaders* and *Historical Dictionary of the Third French Republic 1870–1940* (both by Patrick K. Bidelman). The notice on Deraismes in the *Dictionnaire de biographie française*, vol. 10, is not reliable.

Karen Offen

Maria Dermoût

(see: Helena Anthonia Maria Elisabeth Dermoût-Ingerman)

Helena Anthonia Maria Elisabeth Dermoût-Ingerman

(a.k.a. Maria Dermoût)

Born June 15, 1888, near Pekalongan, Java, Dutch East-Indies (now Indonesia); died June 27, 1962, The Hague, The Netherlands
Genre(s): novel, short story, autobiography
Language(s): Dutch

When Indonesia became independent in 1949, Maria Dermoût, like many Dutch, moved to Holland. She had been born on Java, the daughter of a wealthy land-owner, and had grown up surrounded by her family and the large Javanese staff that helped to make up the large household. She had married in the Indies and raised her family there. Her life had been shaped by a unique blend of a Western cultural heritage, reinforced by frequent trips to Holland, and the Eastern culture of the country in which her family had lived for several generations. Then, in 1949, she moved to Holland and only then, at the age of sixty-two, did she begin to publish her literary work. During the last ten years of her life, she finished two novels and several bundles of short stories, all of which are situated in the former colony she had called her home. These works show the influence of Javanese story-telling as well as a thorough understanding and appreciation of the culture of the islands. *Only Yesterday* is the revealing title of one of her novels. Like her other works, it presents an attempt to recreate, illustrate, and ultimately immortalize the lifestyle that she and other Dutchmen had experienced in the archipelago and that now had become irrevocably a thing of the past.

Works

Nog pas Gisteren [Only Yesterday] (1951). De tienduizend dingen [Ten Thousand Things, novel] (1955). Spel van tifa-gong's [The Play of Tifa Gong's] (1954). De juwelen haarkam [The Jewel Comb], short stories (1956). De kist en enige verhalen [The Casket and Other Stories] (1958). De Sirenen [The Sirens], short stories (1963). "Maria Dermoût, Schrijvers over zichzelf," autobiographical article, De Haagse Post (November 26, 1955). Verzameld Werk [Collected Works] (1970).

Translations: The Ten Thousand Things [De tienduizend dingen] tr. Hans Koningsberger (1958, rpt. 1984). The Ten Thousand Things, ed. E.M. Beekman (1983). Yesterday, a novel (Nog pas Gisteren), tr. Hans Koningsberger (1959, rpt. 1960). "The Copper Dancer." The Uncommon Reader (1965). "The Copper Dancer." Harper's Bazaar (April 1961), tr. Etty Kist and James Brockway. "The Sirens." Harper's Bazaar (Feb. 1962). "The Sirens." Insulinde, Selected Translations from Dutch Writers of Three Centuries on the Indonesian Archipelago (1978). "The Bracelet." Harper's Bazaar (Nov. 1962). "The South Sea." Harper's Bazaar (Jan. 1956). "The Shark Fighter." Harper's Bazaar (Jan. 1966). "Kwan Yin's Snake." Harper's Bazaar (April 1966). "Mary." Harper's Bazaar (Feb. 1967). "The Buddha Ring" Harper's Bazaar (Jan. 1968).

Bibliography

Balliett, Whitney, "Himpies and the Turtles," book review of The Ten Thousand Things. The New Yorker (May 3, 1958): 136–138. Hartoko, Dick, "Op zoek naar de tuin van Kleyntjes." Ons Erfdeel 19, 1 (1976): 88–96. Mitgang, Herbert, "Ghosts in a Spice Garden," book review of The Ten Thousand Things. The New York Times Book Review (March 2, 1958): 35. Nieuwenhuys, Rob, Oost-Indische Spiegel (Amsterdam, 1972), pp. 459–473. Nieuwenhuys, Rob, Mirror of the Indies: A History of Dutch Colonial Literature, tr. Frans van Rosevelt, ed. E.M. Beekman (Amherst, 1982), pp. 255–267. Notermans, Jef, "Drie Gratiëen en de 'Gordel van Smaragd.'" Vacature 83 (1971): 5 (Feb. 16), 4–5; 6 (Feb. 25), 9; 12 (April 27), 6–7; 14 (May 18), 8–9. Robinson, Tjalie, "Interview met Maria Dermoût." Haagse Post (July 5, 1958). Woude, Johan van der, Maria Dermoût: de vrouw en de schrijfster (The Hague, 1973).

Cornelia N. Moore

Jeanne Deroin

Born December 31, 1805, Paris, France; died
    April 2, 1894, England
Genre(s): journalism, pamphlets
Language(s): French

From a Parisian working-class background, Jeanne Deroin began her working life as a seamstress. She became committed to improving the condition of women through her involvement with the Saint-Simonians in the early 1830s. Subsequently she explored the teachings of Fourier and Cabet. Through self-education she turned schoolmistress, earning her certificate as a teacher after several failures and founding a school in the 1840s. In the meantime she had married and became the mother of three children, but she always signed her publications and carried on her political activities with her given name.

Deroin reentered public record as a political journalist and activist during the Revolution of 1848. In Eugenie Niboyet's La Voix des femmes, she called for nomination of distinguished women as candidates to the Constituent Assembly. Meanwhile she threw herself into organizing women's clubs, workshops and self-help associations for women workers, campaigning for equal pay for equal work, and other measures that would promote women's economic independence. Following the Legislative Assembly's crackdown on women's clubs in June 1848, she announced women's intention of continuing their participation in political and associational life with the founding of the short-lived La Politique des femmes, which published only two issues. In early 1849 she founded another newspaper, L'Opinion des femmes, to continue her work. In this journal she set down her own vision of "woman's mission," and launched her controversial campaign as a candidate for the Assembly. Her endeavors were brought to a halt in 1851 when she and Pauline Roland were arrested and imprisoned for attempting to found a mixed-sex association of workers. She left France in 1852 for what was to become a lifelong exile in England. Between 1852 and 1854 she published three women's almanacs, one of which appeared in both French and English.

Jeanne Deroin reappears in the French press during the early 1880s, corresponding with Léon Richer on the problems of children born out of wedlock in Richer's periodical, *Le Droit des femmes*.

Works

Contributed articles to *La Femme libre* (1832–1833). *Campagne électorale de la citoyenne Jeanne Deroin, et Pétition des femmes au peuple [16 mars 1848]* (1848). *Lettre d'une femme à M. Athanase Coquerel* (s.d. [1848]). *Cours de droit social pour les femmes, 1re livraison* (1848). Contributed articles to *La Voix des femmes* (1848). Ed., *La Politique des femmes* (1848). Ed., *L'Opinion des femmes* (1849). *Association fraternelle des démocrates socialistes des deux sexes pour l'affranchissement politique et social des femmes* (1849). *Lettre aux associations sur l'organisation du crédit* (1851). *Du Célibat* (1851). Ed., *Almanach des femmes 1852, Almanach des femmes, 2e année/Women's almanack, 1853, Almanach des femmes, 1854.* Contributed articles to *Le Droit des femmes* (1880s). Translations: [With Pauline Roland], "Letter to the Convention of the Women of America" (June 15, 1851). *History of Woman Suffrage*, I. Reprinted in *Women, the Family, and Freedom*, I (1983), doc. 87. "Le Travail des femmes." *Almanach des femmes, 1852*, tr. K. Offen, in *Victorian Women: A Documentary Account of Women's Lives in Nineteenth-Century England, France, and the United States*, eds. E. Hellerstein, L. Hume, and K. Offen (1981), doc. 64.b. "Appel aux femmes." *La Femme libre*, no. 1 (1832), tr. Anna Doyle Wheeler, revised by K. Offen. "Aux Citoyens français!" *La Voix des Femmes* (March 27, 1848), tr. K. Offen. "Mission de la femme dans le present et dans l'avenir." *L'Opinion des femmes* (Jan. 28, March 10, April 10, 1849), tr. K. Offen. "Aux Citoyens membres du Comité électoral démocratique et socialiste." *L'Opinion des femmes* (April 10, 1949), and "Réponse à Proudhon." *La Démocratie Pacifique* (April 13, 1849), tr. S.G. Bell. "A M. Michelet. Droit politique des femmes." *L'Opinion des femmes*, no. 7, tr. K. Offen. All published in *Women, the Family, and*

Freedom: The Debate in Documents, ed. Susan Groag Bell and Karen Offen, vol. I (1983), documents 36, 70, 77, 84, 85, 87.

Bibliography

Adler, Laure, *A l'Aube du féminisme: les premières journalistes (1830–1850)* (Paris, 1979). Albistur, Maïté, and Daniel Armogathe, *Histoire du féminisme français* (Paris, 1978). Fraisse, Geneviève, "Les Femmes libres de 48, moralisme et féminisme." *Les Révoltes logiques* (1975). Moon, S. Joan, "The Utopian Socialist Sources of French Feminism: The Movement for Women's Rights during the Second Republic." Unpublished article (1976). Moses, Claire G., *French Feminism in the Nineteenth Century* (Albany, N.Y., 1984). Offen, K., "The Theory and Practice of Feminism in Nineteenth-Century Europe." *Becoming Visible: Women in European History*, 2nd ed. (Boston, 1987). Ranvier, Adrien, "Une Féministe de 1848, Jeanne Deroin." *La Révolution de 1848* (1908–1909). Riot-Sarcey, Michelle, "La Conscience féministe des femmes de 1848; Jeanne Deroin et Désirée Gay." *Un Fabuleux Destin, Flora Tristan: Actes du Premier Colloque International Flora Tristan, Dijon 3 et 4 Mars 1984* (Dijon, 1985). Thomas, Edith, *Les Femmes de 1848* (Paris, 1948). Wild, H., "Nos Contemporaines: Jeanne Deroin et Julie Daubié." *Congrès international des oeuvres et institutions féminines; Actes* (Paris, 1889).

General references: *Dictionnaire de biographie française*, vol. 10, pp. 1139–1141.

Karen Offen

Marceline Félicité Josèphe Desbordes-Valmore

Born June 20, 1786, Douai, France; died July 23, 1859, Paris, France
Genre(s): letters, novel, drama, poetry, short story, children's literature
Language(s): French

Admired by the contemporary critic Charles-Augustin Sainte-Beuve and the poet Charles Baudelaire for the sincerity and naturalness of her poetry, Marceline Desbordes-Valmore has received varying assessments in French literary histories. In Max Milner's *Romantisme, 1820–1843* (1973), she is rated "one of the greatest poetesses of the French language"; in *Histoire de la littérature française* (1970, edited by Jacques Roger), she is simply grouped with the "minor poets" of romanticism.

What is not in doubt is that Desbordes-Valmore's often sad and difficult life is reflected in her poetry, which frequently deals with unrequited romantic love or concern for children. The daughter of a maker of coats of arms, she and her siblings grew up in poverty, for the French Revolution's attack on aristocratic privilege ruined her father's business. The strain in the parents' relationship prompted Mme Desbordes to depart with Marceline around 1801 for Guadaloupe, where there were relatives. Her mother's death and ruinous conditions in Guadaloupe necessitated her return to France, where she resumed work as a singer and actress. Estrangement from some of her family resulted from an ultimately unhappy liaison and the birth in 1810 of a son, who died in 1816. Recent scholarship (Ambrière, 1987) has identified this child's father as Eugène Debonne and not, as was long thought, Henri de Latouche, a minor writer whom she met later. For a time, Marceline Desbordes earned considerable amounts as an actress, and in 1817 she married actor Prosper Lanchantin, known on stage as Prosper Valmore, seven years her junior. Devoted to her husband, whose talent was mediocre, she accepted an itinerant and often financially precarious existence in provincial cities where he found acting jobs. In 1823 she left the stage for good to devote herself to three children born since 1820.

A writer of verse since at least 1810, Desbordes-Valmore published her first volume of poetry in Paris in late 1818. Other volumes followed in the next decades. Her simple and direct style appealed to such major contemporary literary figures as Alfred de Vigny, Victor Hugo, Alphonse de Lamartine, and Charles-Augustin Sainte-Beuve and also won her patronage from socially prominent women such as Madame Julie Recamier and the minor novelist Sophie Gay. The theme of longing in her poetry for a man named "Olivier" aroused much speculation about the man's identity, now believed to be Latouche. Other poetry, such as "A une mère qui pleure aussi" (To a Mother Who Also Cries), expressed her great love for children.

Indeed, she and Hugo have been called the first significant poets of childhood (Clement). To earn additional money, Desbordes-Valmore also wrote novels, such as the autobiographical *Atelier d'un peintre*, and stories for children. In 1826 she obtained a government pension for needy writers. Her connections with prominent individuals enabled her to obtain employment for her husband, who finally gave up his unsuccessful acting career, at the Bibliothèque Nationale, and for her son, at the education ministry. Additional tragedy occurred with the deaths of her daughters, Inès in 1846 and Ondine, a promising writer, in 1851. Desbordes-Valmore died of cancer in 1859.

Desbordes-Valmore's place in French literature has been assured not only by her poetry but also by the judgments of major poets like Baudelaire, who saw in her work "the delicious accent of the [true] woman," and Paul Verlaine, who celebrated her as a "sublime poet."

Works

Letters: *Correspondance intime de Marceline Desbordes-Valmore* [Private Correspondance of Marceline Desbordes-Valmore], ed. Benjamin Rivière (1896). *Lettres inédites* [Unedited Letters], ed. Hippolyte Valmore (1912). *Lettres de Marceline Desbordes-Valmore à Prosper Valmore* [Letters of Marceline Desbordes-Valmore to Prosper Valmore], ed. Boyer d'Agen (1924).

Novels: *L'Atelier d'un peintre, scènes de la vie privée* [The Studio of a Painter, Scenes of Private Life] (1833). *Une raillerie de l'amour* [A Mockery of Love] (1833). *Le Salon de Lady Betty: moeurs anglaises* [The Salon of Lady Betty: English Customs] (1836). *Huit femmes* [Eight Women] (1845). *Violette* (1859).

Drama: [With Elise Moreau, M. de Jussieu, et al.], *Arlequin, pièce à tiroirs pour desmoiselles* [Harlequin, Play in Episodes for Young Women] (n.d.).

Poetry: *Elégies, Marie et romances* [Elegies, Marie and Romances] (1818). *Poésies de Mme Desbordes-Valmore* [Poetry of Mme Desbordes-Valmore, 3d edition] (1820). *Elégies et poésies nouvelles* [Elegies and New Poetry] (1825). *Poésies de Madame Desbordes-Valmore* [Poetry of Madame Desbordes-Valmore] (1830). *Les Pleurs* [The Tears] (1833). *Pauvres Fleurs* [Poor Flowers] (1839). *Contes en vers pour les enfants* [Stories in Verse for Children]

(1840). *Poèsies* [Poetry] (1842). *Bouquets et prières* [Bouquets and Prayers] (1843). *Les Anges de la famille* [Angels of the Family] (1849). *Poésies de Mme Desbordes-Valmore* [Poetry of Mme Desbordes-Valmore] (1860). *Oeuvres poétiques* [Poetic Works, 3 volumes] (1886–1887; vol. 4, 1922).

Short Stories: *Les Veillées des Antilles* [Evenings of the Antilles] (1821). *Poésies* [Poetry] (1822).

Stories for Children: *Le Livre des petits enfants* [The Book of Little Children] (1834). *Contes en prose pour les enfants* [Stories in Prose for Children] (1840). *Jeunes têtes et jeunes coeurs* [Young Minds and Young Hearts] (1855).

Bibliography

Ambrière, Francis, *Le Siècle des Valmore: Marceline Desbordes-Valmore et les siens* [The Century of the Valmore], 2 vols. (Paris, 1987). Baudelaire, Charles, *Oeuvres complètes* [Complete Works] (Paris, 1968). Boulenger, Jacques, *Mme Desbordes-Valmore, sa vie et son secret* [Mme Desbordes-Valmore, Her Life and Her Secret] (Paris, 1927). Clement, N.H., *Romanticism in France* (New York, 1939). Jasenas, Eliane, *Marceline Desbordes-Valmore devant la critique* [Marceline Desbordes-Valmore and the Critics] (Geneva, 1962). Leguay, P., "Desbordes-Valmore, Marceline-Félicité-Josèphe, dame Lanchantin." *Dictionnaire de biographie française* [Dictionary of French Biography], vol. 10 (Paris, 1964). Milner, Max, *Le Romantisme, 1820–1843*, vol. 12 of *Littérature française*, 16 vols., ed. Claude Pichois (Paris, 1970–1978). Moulin, Jeanine, *Marceline Desbordes-Valmore*, revised ed. (Paris, 1983). Roger, Jacques, ed., *Histoire de la littérature française* [History of French Literature], 2 vols. (Paris, 1970). Sainte-Beuve, C.A., *Madame Desbordes-Valmore* (Paris, 1870). Verlaine, Paul, *Oeuvres poétiques complètes* [Complete Poetic Works], ed. Jacques Borel (Paris, 1962).

Linda L. Clark

Antoinette du Ligier De La Garde Deshoulières (Des Houlières)

Born 1634 (1638?), Paris, France; died 1694, Paris
Genre(s): poetry, drama, maxims
Language(s): French

Antoinette Deshoulières enjoyed the many advantages of being born into a wealthy Parisian family, the La Gardes. She received an excellent education in the liberal arts, and was reportedly talented in geometry, philosophy, Latin, Italian, Spanish, and especially poetry, in which she demonstrated an early aptitude. Henault, a contemporary poet of some reputation and a close friend of the La Gardes, tutored the young Antoinette in versification.

In 1651, she married Seigneur Deshoulières, a lieutenant-colonel of the great Condé, who participated in the civil war of the Fronde. Becoming troublesome to the queen-regent, Mme Deshoulières's husband suffered the confiscation of his property soon after their marriage. Mme Deshoulières accompanied her husband through many perilous times and circumstances and even went to Brussels, where a Spanish court resided, to obtain some claims on her husband's behalf. This gesture resulted in her temporary imprisonment in a state facility for eight months. Because of her husband's strenuous exertions, she was finally released. With the conclusion of the civil war, Monsieur Deshoulières obtained a post in Guinne, where he retired with his wife and family.

The years spent in Guinne, in retirement with her husband, were the most productive of Mme Deshoulières's literary life. During this period, she had the opportunity to visit Vaucluse, the scene of Petrarch's great inspiration, and to produce her most characteristic poetry. Her short, light sentimental lyrics of sensibility (e.g., idylls "*Les Moutons*" and "*Le Ruisseau*") are generally acknowledged to be among the most memorable of her work. She also wrote maxims, influenced by the work of her friend La Rochefoucauld (e.g., "Il n'est pas si facile qu'on pense,/D'etre honnete homme, et de jouer gros jeu," etc.). In addition to an annual pension of 2,000 livre from Louis XIV,

Mme Deshoulières was a member of the Academies of Arles and Ricoverati in Padua. Her colorful circle of distinguished literary and cultural personalities included the Corneilles, Flechier, Quinault, Saint-Aignon, the Duke of Nevers, Tallemont, Voltaire and Rochefoucauld, all particular allies of hers and prominent personalities of the Rambôuillet salon. Mme Deshoulières herself appears in the *Grand dictionnaire des précieuses* as "Dioclee."

Mme Deshoulières and her husband had several children. Of these, a daughter, Antoinette-Thérèse (1662–1718), inherited her mother's literary talent and took a prize for poetry in 1688 at the French Academy for a poem entitled "Eloge de l'establishment de Saint-Cyr." The young Antoinette-Thérèse even outdistanced Fontenelle in this competition.

Mme Deshoulières was neither a feminist intellectual nor an apologist, but a skilled writer of social verse and light, sentimental lyrics of observation and moral reflection. Her poem on the subject of reflection was translated by Yvor Winters. She also wrote for the stage and lived to see her dramatic work produced and well reviewed during her lifetime. She composed an opera—*Zoroastre*; two tragedies—*Genseric*, mounted at the Hôtel de Bourgogne in 1680, and *Jules-Antoine*—as well as a comedy, *Les Eaux de Bourbon*. Mme Deshoulières distinguished herself as one of the earliest French women of letters after Christine de Pisan. Some of her correspondence to Madeleine de Scudery is reproduced in facsimile by Alfred Morrison in his *Catalog of Autograph Letters* (1885).

Her verse was collected and published in Paris in 1688. Her complete works were published in Paris in a two-volume edition in 1797. Some editions are graced with an engraved frontispiece portrait of Mme Deshoulières by LaLuze. She also sat to Mlle Cheron, whose portrait of her was engraved by Van Schupen. As entries for Deshoulières in the NUC amply demonstrate, her writings were reissued throughout the seventeenth and eighteenth centuries.

Works

Poesies (1688). Oeuvres choisies (1768, 1882). Les Oeuvres completes, 2 vols. (1797, 1799).

Bibliography

Cosman, C.C., et al., eds., *Penguin Book of Women Poets* (New York, 1978). Hale, Sarah Josepha, *Woman's Record* (New York, 1855). *Hoefer's Nouvelle Biographie Generall* (Paris, 1885). Prather, C.C., "The View from Germany." *French Women in the Age of Enlightenment*, ed. S.I. Spencer (Indiana, 1984).

General references: Leguay, P., "Deshoulières." *Dictionnaire de biographie française* (Paris, 1965).

Maureen E. Mulvihill

Marie-Catherine Desjardins

(see: Madame de Villedieu)

Catharina Irma Dessaur

(a.k.a. Andreas Burnier)

Born July 3, 1931, 's-Gravenhage, The Netherlands
Genre(s): poetry, novel, essay
Language(s): Dutch

Andreas Burnier recalls that, growing up in hiding during the war years, she soon became aware of the fact that women enjoyed only limited freedom in a masculine society and, much more dramatically, that she felt like a boy trapped in a girl's body. It was almost inevitable that Burnier's first attempts at functioning in an adult masculine world failed: her studies in philosophy were thwarted by a male professor who refused to supervise her and her marriage ended in a divorce after ten painful years. She went back to school and made a career in academe. She has been professor of criminology at the University of Nijmegen since 1973.

Her first novel, *Een tevreden lach* (1965; A Contented Laugh), was an instant success with the critics, to a great extent because of its experimental and clever structure. Burnier shifts from first to third person narrative, mixes various text types and genres, and alternates narrative with lyrical prose, the purpose of which is to convey the main character's search for identity, individual freedom, and full development. Though Simone is a lesbian, and lesbianism is a recurring motif in Burnier's work, she insists that it is not the main theme. Homosexuality mainly serves to emphasize woman's angst and basic loneliness in a man's world. Similar themes are elaborated in *Het Jongensuur* (1969; The Boys' Hour), a novel, and in *De verschrikkingen van het noorden* (1967; The Horrors of the North), a collection of short stories.

From 1970 onwards, Burnier's work became more militant and essayistic. In *De huilende libertijn* (1970; The Crying Libertine), she showed the absurdness of both superfluous feminism and male "sex fascism" by depicting a society that is the grotesque (feminist) reverse of our present male-dominated world. Disappointed, the main character Jean begins to write a scientific essay entitled "Beyond Reductionism." The exposure of the reductionist course (Western) civilization is taking and the possible remedies are the main themes in Burnier's further work—fiction or nonfiction.

Darwin, Marx, and Freud, the "anti-trinity," are at the root of this reductionist tendency, according to Burnier. They stripped man (or woman) of his (or her) spiritual values and reduced them to animal dullness, materialist greed, and sex drive respectively. This theme underlies *De reis naar Kíthira* (1976; The Journey to Kíthira), a novel (though Burnier later said that the form of the essay would have better suited the ideas expressed in it), *De zwembadmentaliteit* (1979; The Swimming Pool Mentality), a collection of essays, and, again, the novels *De litteraire salon* (1983; The Literary Salon) and *De trein naar Tarascon* (1986; The Train to Tarascon) (the latter is Burnier's most traditionally structured work of fiction). Women, suggests the author, can save this sadly dehumanized world.

Feminism is for Burnier more than a fight for concrete women's rights and interests; it involves a total metamorphosis of civilization as we know it. Humanity can be saved and reborn, thanks to the full integration of feminine creativity (spiritual values) with abstract masculine thinking (rationalism, empiricism). Burnier argues her point referring to concepts and symbols from antiquity, eastern philosophy, and lost utopian civilizations. A desire to be assimilated in a big cosmic plan of divine love and the conviction that reincarnation is a step towards the projected better world increasingly prevail. *De droom der rede* (1984; The Dream of Reason), written under her real name, C.I. Dessaur, which she uses for her academic publications, is a philosophical treatment of these ambitious themes.

Andreas Burnier is also the writer of poetry, many lectures, book reviews and articles. She has spoken out for homosexual causes and against abortion and euthanasia, which she persistently associates with Nazist practices. More a "woman of ideas" than a novelist or even an essayist, Andreas Burnier has a special place in present-day Dutch letters.

Works

Een tevreden lach (1965). *De verschrikkingen van het noorden* (1967). *Het jongensuur* (1969). *De huilende libertijn* (1970). *Poëzie, jongens en het gezelschap van geleerde vrouwen* (1974). *De reis naar Kíthira* (1976). *De zwenbadmentaliteit* (1979). *Na de laatste keer* (1981). *De litteraire salon* (1983). *Belletrie 1965–1981* (1985). *Essays 1968–1985* (1985). *De trein naar Tarascon* (1986).
[C.I. Dessaur, pseud.], *Foundations of theory-formation in criminology; a methodological analysis* (1971). *De droom der rede* (1984).

Bibliography

Bibep, *Veertien Vrouwen. Interviews* (1974). De Moor, W., *Wilt u mij maar volgen?* (1980). Roggeman, W.M., *Beroepsgeheim 2* (1977). Schuyt, K. *Jan Campertprijzen 1980* (1980). Van Marissing, L., *28 interviews* (1971). Vos, Th. and S. Bakker, *Andreas Burnier* (1980).
General references: *De Nederlandse en Vlaamse auteurs van de middeleeuwen tot heden* (1985). *Kritisch Lexicon van de Nederlandstalige Literatuur na 1945* (article on Burnier by D. Schouten, 1982). *Moderne encyclopedie van de wereldliteratuur* (1980–1984). *Winkler Prins Lexicon der Nederlandse letterkunde* (1986).

Ria Vanderauwera

Livia De Stefani

Born 1913, Palermo, Italy
Genre(s): novel
Language(s): Italian

Born 1913, Palermo, Italy, Livia De Stefani is the daughter of a noble Sicilian land-owning family. She studied at home with a tutor. A very precocious child, she wrote poetry at an early age; at ten she was asked to contribute to a weekly publication, *Giornalino della domenica*. She married at seventeen and moved to Rome. Sicily though is a constant locale in her writings. It provides all the elements of drama, passion, murder, and revenge that confer an epic dimension to her works. Fifteen years ago her husband passed away, but she still lives in Rome with her sisters. She has a son and two daughters. At thirty-eight, De Stefani published her first novel, *La vigna di uve nere* (The Vineyard of Black Grapes) (1953). Set in the desolate Sicilian countryside, the book tells of the incestuous love of a brother, Nicola, for his sister, Rosaria. Their father is devastated by the discovery that his "primogenito," his firstborn, the one who should carry on the family's honor, may instead bring about its end with shame and dishonor. Tragically, Rosaria's suicide will be the only way to protect Nicola and his family. The events are presented vividly and concretely. The facts unfold in an classical ambience of inevitable doom which, at the conclusion of the story, affords the readers a sense of detachment and conciliation. Two years later three stories collected in the volume *Gli affatturati* (The Bewitched Ones) appeared. The focus is no longer on the victims on poverty but on the aristocrats—victims of their fears and prejudices. The book is a successful attempt to satirize the Italian upper classes. *Passione di Rosa* (1958; Rosa's Passion) is a novel full of action and romance. It deals with the unrequited love of Rosa for Ruggiero who is unfaithful and dislikes her. Set in Sicily and California the story has all the elements of the feuilleton: contrasted love, betrayal, violence, crime, imprisonment, revenge, and a multitude of minor characters. *Viaqqio di una sconosciuta* (Travels of a Stranger) is a collection of seventeen stories. The title story relates the story of a young woman who, having aborted her baby, aimlessly wanders through the streets of Rome. Mood and tone are more important than action in this account of the protagonist's cruel life. The capacity of the author to portray psychotic perception of reality is proof of De Stefani's power of the imagination. *La signora di Cariddi* (1975; The Lady of Cariddi) relates the confession of

Emanuela's murder. The book is another example of character portrayal and of social satire. In the moral degradation of the aristocratic Sicilian woman it is possible to see an emblematic significance. De Stefani's work has been translated in Germany, Austria, Switzerland, France, Argentina, Spain, Sweden, England and the United States.

Works

Fiction: *La vigna di uve nere* (1953). *Gli affatturati* (1955). *Passione di Rosa* (1958). *Viaggio di una sconosciuta e altri racconti* (1963). *La signora di Cariddi* (1971). *La stella di Assenzio* (1985).
Poetry: *Preludio* (1940).
Translations: *Black Grapes* (158). *Rosa* (1963).

Bibliography

Barberi-Squarotti, Giorgio, *Poesia e narrativa del secondo novecento* (Milan, 1978). Ceratto, Marino, *Il "Chi è" delle donne italiane, 1945–1982* (Milan, 1982). Clementelli, Elelena, *I contemporanei* (Milan, 1973). De Tommaso, Pietro, *Belfagor* (March 31, 1959). Manacorda, Giuliano, *Vent'anni di pazienza* (Firenze, 1972). Pacifici, Sergio, *The Modern Italian Novel*. 3 vols. 1967–1979 (Southern Illinois University Press, 1979). Petrignani, Sandra, *Le signore della scrittura* (Milan, 1984). Prisco, Mario, *Idea* (September 6, 1953). Pullini, Giorgio, *Il romanzo del dopoguerra italiano* (Milan, 1961). Raya, Giuseppe, *Fiera Letteraria* (July 21, 1963). Seroni, Alberto, *Vie Nuove* (November 29, 1953).

Giacomo Striuli

Suzon de Terson

Born 1657, Puylaurens, Albigeois, France; died 1685
Genre(s): poetry
Language(s): French, Occitan

The daughter of a Protestant lawyer, Suzon de Terson was considered a child prodigy in the literary circles of her home town, Puylaurens in Albigeois. At the age of seventeen, she married a thirty-four-year-old Protestant minister, Elie Rivals. De Terson often accused herself of spending too much time writing poetry and not enough time helping her husband in his apostolate.

Of her eighty poems extant, fifteen are written in Occitan. Her unique theme is love, which she treats with originality, with a tone of authenticity, and lack of literary ambition.

Tendre délicatesse, an elegy written by de Terson in 1674, shows intense, passionate feelings that remind us of those typical of Racinian heroines. *Fierté en songe* (Proud When Sleeping), also dating from 1674, demonstrates the power of psychological investigation.

If Suzon de Terson's life were better known, we might guess the names of the shepherds populating her poetry. The poetess does not write in the abstract; it is obvious she is very much in touch with her emotions.

Bibliography

Poésies diverses de Demoiselle Suzon de Terson (1657–1685). Lo libre occitan (1968).

Marie France Hilgar

Luisa Sigea de Velasco

(a.k.a. Luisa Sigea Toletana, M.
Francisco de Cuevas)

Born ca. 1530, Tarancón, Spain; died ca. 1560
Genre(s): poetry
Language(s): Spanish, Latin

Having spent the first twelve years of her life in the Toledo area, the Spanish writer Luisa Sigea de Velasco is also known as Luisa Sigea Toletana. Shortly after her family moved to Lisbon in 1542, she entered the service of Doña María, the daughter of King Manuel. In 1555, Luisa moved to Torres Novas and soon married Francisco de Cuevas, a nobleman from Burgos. The couple relocated to the Court at Vallodolid three years later when Francisco was named secretary and Luisa a lady of the Court; but within a few months, at the death of their protectress Doña María, they were both unemployed. Luisa wrote several letters, including one to Philip II, soliciting the reinstatement of their positions, but without success. Her death soon after this prompted heartfelt eulogies by learned men.

Luisa, who even as a child exhibited extraordinary talent, embodied physical beauty and a prodigious erudition. She was very knowledgeable in philosophy, poetry, and history and commanded several languages: Latin, Greek, Hebrew, and Chaldaic. Her literary celebrity during and after the Renaissance, which she shared with Beatriz Galindo (*la Latina*) and Oliva Sabuco de Nantes, extended beyond Spain to Portugal and France. *Cintra*, her Latin poem, influenced poets across the centuries, extending its inspirational message to Byron's era in verses replete with a profound sentiment of nature and elegant bucolic reminiscences.

Works

Cintra, Latin poem published by Juan Nicot, Paris (1566). *Colloquium Habitum apud villam inter Flaminiam Romanam et Blesillam Senensem*. Latin and Spanish poems published by Cerdá y Rico in *Clarorum Hispanorum opuscula selecta et rariora*, II. Latin letters published by A. Bonilla San Martín in *Clarorum Hispaniensium epistolae ineditae*.

Joan Cammarata

Dhouda

(a.k.a. Countess of Septimania)

Flourished A.D. 840, Uzes, southern France
Genre(s): treatise
Language(s): Latin

Dhouda wrote a loving and instructive manual for her older son William. Her husband, Count Bernard of Septimania, the Imperial Chamberlain of Louis the Pious (814–840), took William away to be trained at court and to act as Bernard's pledge of loyalty to the Emperor's fourth son, Charles the Bald (875–877). Dhouda stayed in Uzes in order to manage the family's estates. As the mistress of these estates, Dhouda carried out the financial responsibilities and obligations which made Bernard's royal duties and war services possible. In the *Manual*, Dhouda expressed her hope that her thoughts would inspire William even though she was separated from him.

Dhouda's *Manual* indicates an extraordinary level of learning for a lay woman in Carolingian times. In her writing of Latin, Dhouda's maternal solicitude overcame the difficulties typical of lay use of a chirographic language. Dhouda's *Manual* offered William ethical and moral advice intended to counter some of the worldly influences her son would face during his training with his father at the imperial court.

At court, Bernard's love affair with the Empress Judith, second wife of Louis the Pious, disgraced both families, sent Judith into the nunnery of St. Radegunde in Poitiers, and sparked warfare between the three sons of Louis' first wife Ermengard and Judith's son, Charles the Bald. In spite of the palace intrigues forged against the Empress Judith by Bishop Agobard of Lyons' ecclesiastical faction, Louis forgave Judith. The Empress returned from the St. Croix nunnery and continued to press her claims for Charles' inheritance—an inheritance which included lands that Bishop Agobard claimed for the Church. Rumors that Bernard had fathered Charles were put aside, and Bernard was put in charge of carrying out Louis and Judith's demands that Charles' inheritance portion be carved into the prior, three-way division of the kingdom made in 817. In 840, after Louis' death, Bernard returned to Uzes and fathered his second son by Dhouda.

Dhouda's loyalty and devotion were no better met in her husband with this second son than with her first. Bernard took this infant away before he was baptized, leaving Dhouda without so much as knowledge of the child's name for two years. Although Dhouda's marriage dealt her many harsh circumstances during her lifetime, writing the *Manual* for her son highlights Dhouda's life in history and literature.

Works

Manual, ed. Mabillon. *Patrologia Latina* 106, pp. 109–118.

Bibliography

Agobard of Lyons, *Libri duo pro filis et contra Judith uxorem Ludovici Pii.* McNamara, Jo Ann, and Suzanne Wemple, "The Power of Women through the Family in Medieval Europe, 500–1100," in Mary Hartman and Lois W. Banner, eds., *Clio's Consciousness Raised* (1974), pp. 103–117. Riché, Pierre, *Dhouda: Manuel pour mon fils. Sources Chrétiennes 225* (Paris, 1975). Waitz, G., ed., *MGH Script.* 15, pp. 274–279.

Duey White

The Countess of Dia

Flourished late twelfth century, Dia (Drôme), southern France
Genre(s): canso
Language(s): Occitan

The four *cansos* (or love songs) attributed to the Countess of Dia by the manuscripts in which they figure make her the *trobairitz* (or woman troubadour) with the largest extant corpus, both in terms of securely ascribed works and of the number of copies of those songs. "A chantar m'er" (PC 46,2) figures in no fewer than fifteen manuscripts, one of which also gives its melody. A short *vida* (or biography) of the Countess survives in four manuscripts, and conventionalized portrait miniatures illustrate nine of her songs. While she has traditionally been referred to as "Beatritz de Dia," there is no textual authority for this usage, and it is more accurate to refer to her as the "Contessa de Dia," the only denomination used in the manuscripts that contain her poems.

Her *vida* says that she was the wife of William of Poitiers and later fell in love with Raimbaut d'Aurenga, about whom she composed many good songs. She has been identified with Philippa, wife of Aimar II of Poitiers, Count of Valentinois and Dia (Schultz 9), with Beatrix, wife of William II of Poitiers (Pillet 41), and with Isoarde, daughter of the Count of Dia (Pattison 29). On the evidence of her *vida* and of the geographical proximity of Dia and Orange (*Aurenga* in Occitan), it has traditionally been asserted that she was the co-author, with the celebrated troubadour Raimbaut d'Aurenga, of the *tenso* (or dialogue poem) "Amics, en gran consirier" (PC 46,3Ć389,6). However, the historical accuracy of the *vida* is suspect, and there is no firm evidence to confirm this conjecture. To the contrary, the three manuscripts that contain the *tenso* ascribe it only to Raimbaut. The Raimbaut referred to in the *tenso* is not necessarily the troubadour of that name (d. 1173) but perhaps his grand-nephew Raimbaut IV (d. 1214) (Pattison 27–28). Alternatively, it is not impossible that the author of the *vida*, noting thematic and linguistic similarities between the *tenso* and the Countess' songs, especially "Estat ai en greu consirier" (PC 46,4), simply invented the liaison between the two. Finally, it has been suggested that the *vida* is to be read metaphorically. The names of Raimbaut and William of Poitiers (which would refer to the first troubadour, who flourished in the late eleventh and early twelfth centuries) would represent the two styles of poetry practiced by the Countess (Huchet 62–63).

In only one song, "Ab joi et ab joven m'apais" (PC 46,1), is the joy of love evoked in terms of unalloyed happiness. In this song, which demonstrates considerable technical virtuosity in joining morphological pairs at the rhyme, the Countess celebrates the qualities of her beloved, whom she addresses under the *senhal* (or pseudonym) of Floris, the protagonist of the romance *Flore et Blancheflor*. "Fin joi me don' alegranssa" (PC 46,5) begins as a celebration of the joy of love but degenerates into a denunciation of the slanderers and the envious who place obstacles in the way of love. "A chantar m'er," is a lament of unhappy love by a lady. The poetic voice protests against the indifference and arrogance of her beloved, complaining that her exceptional qualities are of no avail in preserving his affections. "Estat ai" is an erotic reverie. The latter two songs, both separation laments, conform to the paradigm of the Occitan *canso* with a feminine poetic voice as practiced by all of the other *trobairitz* (or woman troubadours) who composed in this genre. On the other hand, the Countess' other two songs ("Ab joi et ab joven" and "Fin joi me don' alegranssa") are unique among the *cansos* of the *trobairitz* in being simple transpositions of the troubadour *canso* with a masculine poetic voice (Blakeslee).

Bibliography

Blakeslee, Merritt R., "La Chanson de femme, les *Héroïdes*, et la *canso* occitane à voix de femme: Considérations sur l'originalité des *trobairitz*," in *"Farai chansoneta nueva . . ." Essais sur la liberté créatrice (XIIe-XIIIe s.). Hommage à . . . Jean Charles Payen*, eds. Jean-Louis Backès, et al. (Caen, 1989). Boutière, Jean, and A.-H. Schutz, *Biographies des troubadours. Textes provençaux des XIIIe et XIVe siècles. Edition refondue, augmentée d'une traduction française, d'un appendice, d'un lexique, d'un glossaire et d'un index des termes concernant le "Trobar," par Jean Boutière avec la collaboration d'I.-M. Cluzel*. Les Classiques d'Oc (Paris, 1964), pp. 445–446. Bogin, Meg, *The Women Troubadours* (New York and London, 1976), pp. 82–91, 163–164. Dronke, Peter, *Women Writers of the Middle Ages. A Critical Study of Texts from Perpetua (d. 203) to Marguerite Porete (d. 1310)* (Cambridge, 1984), pp. 103–105. Faucheux, Christian, "Etude sémantique et syntaxique de l'oeuvre de la Comtesse de Die." *Signum* (Royal Military College of Canada, Kingston, Ontario, Canada) 1.1 (January 1974): 1–17; 1.2 (May 1974): 5–16. Huchet, Jean-Charles, "Les Femmes troubadours ou la voix critique." *Littérature* 51 (October 1983): 59–90. Kussler-Ratyé, Gabrielle, "Les chansons de la comtesse Béatrix de Dia." *Archivum Romanicum* 1 (1917): 161–182 (The only critical edition of the poems). Pattison, Walter T., *The Life and Works of the Troubadour Raimbaut d'Orange* (Minneapolis, 1952). Pillet, Alfred, *Bibliographie der Troubadours, ergänzt, weitergeführt und herausgegeben von Henry Carstens* (Halle, 1933; New York, 1968). Rieger, Angelica, "'Ins e.l cor port, dona, vostra faisso.' Image et imaginaire de la femme à travers l'enluminure dans les chansonniers de troubadours." *Cahiers de Civilisation Médiévale* 28 (1985): 385–415 (contains two reproductions and a discussion of the portrait miniatures of the Countess). Schultz, Oscar, *Die Provenzalischen Dichterinnen. Biographien und Texte nebst Anmerkungen und einer Einleitung* (Leipzig, 1888; Geneva, 1975), pp. 8–9, 17–19. Véran, Jules, *Les Poétesses provençales du moyen âge et de nos jours* (Paris, 1946), pp. 163–181.

Merritt R. Blakeslee

Eugenia Diener

Born January 7, 1925, Kiev, The Soviet Union
Genre(s): short story, memoirs, poetry,
*   travelogue*
Language(s): Russian

Diener's writing was born mainly out of her World War II experiences, best documented in her recent book *Ogliadyvaias' nazad* (1987; Looking Back). American and other autobiographical themes are also found in her work.

At the time of the German invasion of the USSR in 1941, she had just finished high school and had made her first attempts to enroll at a Kiev university. After a happy childhood in an educated family, the war proved to be a terrible turning point. It started a chain of events that in the end led her away from her homeland. In a strange and unforeseeable way it also enabled her to see the rest of the world. Her husband, whom she had married during the war, was killed in an air raid; her father, who served in the Russian army, was declared missing in action at the front. After the war she studied economics at the University of Muenster in West Germany. In 1951, with her little daughter and her mother, she immigrated to the United States. A few years after her arrival she married an American dentist. In the United States she found the time and the urge to write. The overwhelming events of her life continue to dominate her poems and her prose.

Diener is a member of the American PEN Club and the Russian Writers Club in New York, of which she is secretary-treasurer.

Works

Dal'nie Pristani (1967). S deviatogo vala (1977). Molchalivaia liubov' (1979). Ogliadyvaias' nazad (1987). Her poems, short stories, and travelogues have appeared also in various emigre periodicals.

K. Filips-Juswigg

Die Neuberin

(see: Friedericke Caroline Neuber)

Gertrud Dietz

(see: Gertrud Fussenegger)

Laura Di Falco

Born 1910, Canicattini Bagni, Siracuse, Italy
Genre(s): novel
Language(s): Italian

Di Falco, like Livia De Stefani, Sciascia and other southern writers, has undertaken to write about the passions, the conflicts, the myths of her people. Her characters are often victims of loneliness, isolation, and bitterness. After high school, she was able to obtain her father's permission to leave Sicily and her family to study at the University of Pisa where she graduated with honors in

philosophy. Di Falco went to Rome and became a teacher. She began her literary career by contributing articles to newspapers and magazines. The translation of her first novel *Paura del giorno* (1954; Fear of Day) received an enthusiastic critical reception in France. The book vividly describes how Erina, a young woman, endures the hardships of the immediate postwar years. The heroine of *Una donna disponibile* (1959; A Free Woman) shows great affinity to Ibsen's Nora and Flaubert's Emma Bovary. The theme of the story is then a woman's solitude and her desire to evade a suffocating family environment. The book—finalist at the Strega Award—has been praised as an example of Di Falco's portrayal of the fate of modern women. *Tre carte da gioco* is about a triangle between two brothers—Mario, a journalist and Aldo, his indecisive brother—and Giulia, a sensitive woman who helps them mature. Set in Sicily, the story takes place in the climate of disillusionment that followed the Hungarian revolution. In the next novel *Le tre mogli* (1967; Three Wives), Di Falco returns more directly to Sicilian concerns. The book is a remarkable work that has inspired comparison with Giuseppe Tommasi di Lampedusa's *Il Gattopardo* (1958; The Leopard). Di Falco's work is a commentary on Sicilian society. It deals with the life of the protagonist, who, because of a physical deformity, is forced by his parents to enter a seminary. This is an account of his life-long attempt to overcome his humiliation by pursuing wealth and power. Di Falco gives us an accurate and poignant description of the decadence of Sicilian aristocracy as reflected in the lives of three women, Diomira, Giulietta, and Ofelia. The Spanish edition of this novel had great success in Spain and Latin America. *Miracolo d'estate* (Summer Miracle) is a haunting tale of a woman's desperate desire to have a child. It is a science fiction story relating how a lonely woman's love is capable of turning her doll into a living creature. The "child" reveals herself to be a cold, rational, and unloving being who threatens the psychological integrity of the mother-maker. Another novel that became popular in Czechoslovakia is *L'inferriata* (1976; The Iron Grating). This accurate and merciless analysis of Sicilian political life was awarded the

Sybaris-Magna Prize. Di Falco is also an accomplished painter.

Works

Paura del giorno (1954). *Una donna disponibile* (1959). *Tre carte da gioco* (1962). *Le tre mogli* (1967). *Miracolo d'estate* (1971). *L'inferiata* (1976). *Piazza delle quattro vie* (1982).

Bibliography

Barberi-Squarotti, Giorgio, *Poesia e narrativa del secondo novecento* (Milano, 1978). Ceratto, Marino, *Il "Chi è" delle donne italiane, 1945–1982* (Milano, 1982). Manacorda, Giuliano, *Vent'anni di pazienza* (Firenze, 1972). Pacifici, Sergio, *The Modern Italian Novel*. 3 vols., 1967–1979 (Carbondale, 1979). Petrignani, Sandra, *Le signore della scrittura* (Milano, 1984). Pullini, Giorgio, *Il romanzo del dopoguerra italiano* (Milano, 1961).

Giacomo Striuli

Blaga Dimitrova

Born 1922, Byala Slatina, Bulgaria
Genre(s): poetry, prose
Language(s): Bulgarian

Born in northern Bulgaria, Blaga Dimitrova spent her childhood in Turnovo. She is known for her strongly passionate love poems, as well as for poetry that is both meditative and dramatic in mood. She has also received praise for her philosophical prose, which has been published abroad in translation. A two-volume series entitled *Blaga Dimitrova, Selections* was published in Sofia in 1982. A French translation of one of her works *L'Enfant Qui Venait du Vietnam* was produced by Mireille Gansel and the author and depicts children caught up in the Vietnam conflict, 1961–1975.

Works

Time Reversed (1966). *Condemned to Love: Poems About Vietnam* (1967). *Selected Poems* (1968). *Izbrani Tvorbi v Dva Toma* [Selected Works in Two Volumes] (1982). *Pamet: Poeziia* [Memory: Poems] (1982). *Otklonenie; Lavina* [Declination; Lavina] (1982).

Translation: *Journey to Oneself* (1969).

Warwick J. Rodden

Kiki Dimoula

(see: Kikē Dēmoula)

Isak Dinesen

(a.k.a. Karen [Tanne] Christence Dinesen Blixen-Finecke)

Born April 17, 1885, Rungsted, Denmark;
September 7, 1962, Rungstedlund, buried
in the garden at Rungstedlund
Genre(s): novel, poetry, essay, drama
Language(s): Danish, English

With her fantastic tales and her fantastic life of adventure, heart-ache, suffering, and challenge, the Danish writer Karen Blixen has enjoyed international *renommé*. Writing in English and in Danish, Blixen won recognition in the United States, in Great Britain, in her native Denmark, indeed, internationally, for her extraordinary tales. Set in the past, in the aristocratic old order of *noblesse oblige*, Blixen's stories and her accounts of life in Africa attain a timeless quality. Her life as a member of an upper-class Danish family; as an aristocratic adventurer, the Baroness; and, as the story-teller *par excellence*, Isak Dinesen-Karen Blixen, is itself a legendary account of passion, pride and pain, of glory and suffering, of fate, rise and fall for an idea—and an ideal.

Karen Christence Dinesen was born at Rungstedlund in Rungsted, Sjælland, Denmark, on April 17, 1885. The building in which she was born, the former Rungsted Inn, had had an interesting history prior to her birth: the king of Sweden, Karl II, had lodged there in 1700; the poet Johannes Ewald had made the Inn his home (1773 to 1776), indeed Karen Blixen's later study had been *Ewalds Stue*, Ewald's quarters; and Wilhelm Dinesen, Karen's father, had purchased and resided at Rungstedlund from 1879 to 1895, writing *Boganis Jagtbreve* (Boganis' Letters from the Hunt) during the decade 1880–1890 (Lasson-Svendsen, pp. 190–194). At the time of Dinesen's birth, Rungstedlund was still spartan in structure but close to the shore and the charming fishing villages. Dinesen's parents were the author and aristocratic landowner Wilhelm Dinesen (1845–

1895) and Ingeborg Westenholz (1856–1939), the daughter of Regnar Westenholz, a member of the mercantile, financially prominent, and governing classes. Her upbringing, family, and orientation were all patrician, in complete harmony with the upper classes and removed from radical social and feminist movements. Together with her two sisters, Ellen Alvilde and Inger Benedicte, and her younger brothers, Thomas Fasti and Anders Runsti, Dinesen was educated at home, under the supervision of her mother Ingeborg and her maternal aunt, Moster Bess, and a series of select house tutors. Dinesen's typically upper-class education concentrated on the role of woman as wife, mother, and participant in cultured leisure pursuits. From her father, Dinesen inherited an inclination for adventure, self-fulfillment, and freedom. Her mother's ideas of respectability, duty, and responsibility contrasted markedly to the free aristocratic ideals and adventurous spirit of her father, who had lived among the North American Indians (hence the name, Boganis); served in the 1864 Danish war with Prussia; participated in the Franco-Prussian War (1970–1971), the Commune Movement in Paris (*Paris under Communen*, 1889), *and* the Russian-Turkish War of 1877; and had also been a member of the Danish Parliament until his suicide in Copenhagen, on March 28, 1895 (Lasson-Svendsen, pp. 26, 40).

With the unexpected death of Wilhelm Dinesen, Karen Dinesen, her brothers and sisters fell under the even more stringent discipline of Ingeborg Westenholz Dinesen and Moster Bess; as her mother before her, Ingeborg Dinesen was left a widow with five young children to bring up and with the attendant responsibilities at Rungstedlund and her own childhood home, Folehave. Many years later, Karen Dinesen (Blixen) recalled her mother's harsh directive to behave better than other children, as well as her own deep sorrow at her father's death when she was but an impressionable ten-year-old.

As a very young girl, Karen Dinesen found expression for her considerable fantasy in her own plays, poems, and stories for the families at Rungstedlund and Folehave. Her first play, "Hovmod staar for Fald" (Pride Goeth before a Fall), was performed by the eleven-year-old Karen, her family, and friends in May, 1896. The

only revised, published comedy from her childhood was entitled "Sandhedens Hævn" (The Revenge of Truth). Between the ages of fifteen and twenty, Dinesen also published several poems, among them, "Medvind" (Breeze) and "Roersang" (The Rower's Song, Lasson-Svendsen, p. 54). Danish folktales, the Icelandic family sagas, and the Norwegian sagas were all important to Karen Dinesen's writing, even influencing her "saga," "Grojotgard Alveson og Aud" (*DbL*: 2, 233). In this early work, Karen Dinesen first expressed an ideal central to her entire *oeuvre*: "A man achieves the destiny he alone can claim, the fate he alone can bear" (*DbL*: 2, 233). Dinesen's extensive study of Danish classical literature and English prose and poetry encouraged youthful dreams and fantasies.

As a young girl of the upper classes, Karen Dinesen frequented the family estates, Katholm in Jutland (the home of her paternal uncle, Wentzel Laurentzius Dinesen) and, during the continual round of summer parties and balls, Frijsenborg, the home of her half-cousins, Daisy and Inger Frijs. Dinesen also visited her Swedish relatives in Skåne, members of the Blixen-Finecke family, including the brothers, Hans and Bror. The young Karen Dinesen fell head-over-heels in love with her cousin Hans, and she was later to marry (unhappily, as it turned out), Hans' twin, Bror. In 1898–1899, Karen Dinesen studied in Switzerland with a close friend, Else Bardenfleth (*DbL*: 2, 233); Dinesen's early love of Shakespeare was also encouraged and enriched by a stay in Oxford in 1904. From an early age, Karen Dinesen had demonstrated considerable talent for drawing, and she therefore enrolled in Charlotte Sode's Drawing School in Copenhagen. In 1903, Dinesen was accepted as an art student at the Royal Academy, with Professor Viggo Johansen as her principal teacher. In addition to studying art, Karen Dinesen wrote short stories; three of these were accepted for publication under the pseudonym Osceola: "Eneboerne" (The Hermits, *Tilskueren*, August 1907); "Pløjeren" (The Plowman, *Gads danske Magasin*, October 1907); "Familien de Cats" (The de Cats Family, *Tilskueren* January 1909, *DbL*: 2, 234). On reading the first story, the literary historian-critic of the day, Valdemar Vedel, acknowledged the talent of its author. Publication of Dinesen's early stories brought her modest fame and critical encouragement from the publishers. A literary career was a distinct possibility for Dinesen. However, she feared being trapped in a literary career (Donald Hannah, "*Isak Dinesen*" *and Karen Blixen: The Mask and the Reality*, p. 19). In a sense, Dinesen was already trapped by the female role; she yearned to pursue her dreams (and she did so, briefly, by excursions to Paris "to study art" in 1910 and to Rome in 1912), but she "clearly sat between two chairs: she and her clever sisters were perhaps too unique for many (patrician) young men and not unique enough for the artistic life in poetry, song, and music" (*DbL*: 2, 234).

On the twenty-third of December, 1912, Karen Dinesen announced her formal engagement to Bror Blixen-Finecke of Näsbyholm (*DbL*: 2, 234); the couple had no definite plans, only a determination to leave both Denmark and southern Sweden. A relative had recently returned from British East Africa (Kenya) and spoke glowingly of the prospects there. Bror Blixen left early in 1913 for Africa in order to find a suitable property in Kenya for a coffee plantation. With financial help from the Dinesen and Westenholz families, the couple acquired M'Bagathe and M'Bogani Estates with the intention of growing coffee as the Karen Coffee Co., Ltd (*DbL*: 2, 234). The elevation of the property proved far too high for coffee. Karen Dinesen left Denmark in December, 1913, to join her *fiancé*, and the couple was married in a civil ceremony in Mombasa, on January 14, 1914.

For the first time in her life, Karen Blixen felt completely happy at the farm near Nairobi, under the Ngong Hills; she later poignantly expressed her feelings of belonging, of home and the rightness of her life in her work, *Den afrikanske Farm* (Out of Africa). Karen Blixen quickly became involved in the lives of the European, principally English, settlers and in the affairs of the natives, the Kikuyu and the Masai. The farm proved a financial disaster from the very beginning, and Karen Blixen's life in Africa proved one of great economic trials and personal suffering, of great passion, love, *and* the adventure she had longed for. The marriage to Bror Blixen quickly collapsed; Bror Blixen had no real interest in the farm when the prospect of adventure and ready,

more easily won, capital loomed on the horizon in the form of safaris into Kenya's wilderness. In addition, Bror Blixen infected his young wife with syphilis, and in 1915 she had to return to Denmark to undergo secret and belated treatment. Bror and Karen Blixen separated in 1921, finally divorcing in 1925; from 1921 on, Karen Blixen tried single-handedly during her long absences in Denmark, with help from her brother Thomas and her servant Farah Aden, to keep the coffee plantation from failing. At this point, Karen Blixen began to write stories, preparing for an inevitable return to Denmark and a possible literary career. In 1925, Blixen visited the prominent critic Georg Brandes in Copenhagen; with his assistance, her very early marionette comedy, "Sandhedens Hævn" (The Revenge of Truth), was published in *Tilskueren* in May, 1926, under the name of Karen Blixen-Finecke (*Dbl* 2, 235).

Despite her fears and doubts, the failure of her health, her farm, her finances, and her marriage, Karen Blixen retained a belief in her own talent; her brother, Thomas Dinesen, was her loyal companion and support during her early literary comeback years in Kenya, even before she left Africa for good. Not only did she receive encouragement from Thomas, she also received literary and artistic critique from her one love, the English aristocrat and *emigré*, Denys Finch Hatton (1887–1931). Finch Hatton listened to her stories, commenting freely and competently on her efforts; he read the Bible and fine literature with her. Denys Finch Hatton was, quite simply, the decisive catalyst for Karen Blixen. Denys Finch Hatton died in an airplane crash on May 4, 1931, toward the end of Karen Blixen's stay in Kenya. By 1931, even before Finch Hatton's death, it was only too apparent that the farm would fail despite all Karen Blixen's efforts, loans, and struggles, and in August of 1931, accompanied by the ever faithful Farah, Karen Blixen "retraced her route of 18 years before, returning via Mombasa to Europe and an uncertain future" (*DbL*: 2, 124).

Karen Blixen returned to Rungstedlund, her mother and home, with a determination to continue writing in English but with no literary contacts. With the financial help of Thomas Dinesen and a warm welcome from her mother

Ingeborg Dinesen, Karen Blixen worked continually, alone, in two separate rooms of the family home (Lasson-Svendsen, p. 139). All her efforts to create a literary life in place of all she had lost in love, health, finances, and hopes for Africa resulted in her first successful collection of stories in English, *Seven Gothic Tales*, published initially by the American publishers Harrison Smith-Robert Haas, in April, 1934. For this collection, Karen Blixen chose the pseudonym Isak Dinesen as part of a literary stratagem and mask to free herself from literary tastes for realism. The name Isak, which means laughter in Hebrew, was also particularly appropriate for the ironic wit of an author who had already experienced much joy—and sorrow—in life. *Seven Gothic Tales* was an immediate success in the United States, England, and Sweden. Karen Blixen's own translation *Syv fantastiske fortællinger*, was published in September, 1935. *Seven Gothic Tales* depicted individuals invariably driven toward the fulfillment of their destiny. Blixen's use of an archaic narrative style and her inclusion of the irrational link the author to trends in modern European literature (*DbL*: 2, 236).

Karen Blixen's next work, the phenomenally beautiful and poignant account of her African adventure and life, *Den afrikanske Farm* (Out of Africa), was written in Skagen in Jutland (in both Danish and English) and was published in 1937. The work begins on a note of tragedy, with mention of a farm once owned and now lost for good: "I had a farm in Africa at the foot of the Ngong Hills" (*Den afrikanske Farm*, p. 9). In *Den afrikanske Farm*, Karen Blixen combines autobiography and myth and deeper personal insights (*DbL*: 2, 236). In Africa, in a time of joy and tragedy, Karen Blixen's horizons widened far beyond youthful conflicts between bourgeois Christian responsibility and a free life of danger, love, and nature. Blixen came to view the free aristocrat as an ideal, one who fully comprehends destiny, joy, and tragedy. In *Den afrikanske Farm*, Blixen no longer writes of responsibility, of "doing the right thing," but of the duty to live as God planned, to fulfill one's special destiny, however tragic, in a universal design or an even greater mosaic (*DbL*: 2, 236). The writer Karen Blixen gained in stature and nobility by under-

standing God's intention and living according to her own destiny. As she eloquently expressed it, "Yes, certainly, I thought, that was the intention, and now I understand it all" (*Den afrikanske Farm*, p. 205). In her work on the African experience, Karen Blixen's defeat is transformed to victory, her own fate becomes a blessing, for she has lived her part in God's plan; Blixen has realized final triumph in the sheer telling of her tale—and myth—of Kenya before the land was changed by commerce and a new world.

Karen Blixen's ideals of duty, honor, and destiny, of aristocratic *noblesse oblige*, and of the elemental grandeur of tragedy are also important in *Vintereventyr* (1942; Winter's Tales). In *Vintereventyr*, characters either fulfill or betray God's plan . . . and their destiny (*DbL*: 2, 237). The tale "Sorg-Agre" (Sorrow Acre), for example, is a deceptively simple story built on a 1634 legend from southern Jutland. In the legend, a young man has been accused of setting fires on the estate of a country lord. The Blixen story from *Vintereventyr* takes place around 1775 and includes reference to the Danish author, Johannes Ewald, and his "new work" *Balders Død* (Balder's Death, Hannah, p. 83). The youth's mother strikes a bargain with the old lord, agreeing to reap, harvest, and bind an entire field of corn, "sorrow acre," a superhuman feat, in exchange for her son's life. Anne-Marie, a simple farmer's wife, wins her son's freedom by offering her own life. But Blixen's reworking of the legend into her tale is not as simple as it would appear. The old feudal order, represented by the aristocratic lord, apparently triumphs, for the lord stands by his word and by the terrible tragic bargain, come what may, and Anne-Marie pays the supreme price for her son's life. However, a new voice speaking for the individual enters the tale in the person of Adam. The young, aspiring nephew of the old lord, Adam, will inherit the landed estates, the old lord's young wife, and a new era. The old system of feudal lord and subject will end—or has already ended—but, in spite of its demise, the aristocratic order of honor, law, and tragedy still holds a fascination. Despite his enthusiasm for the new time, Adam recognizes a pattern of order and harmony beyond the fate, tragic or fortuitous, of a single individual ("Sorg-Agre," *Fra det gamle Danmark*: 2, 233).

Vintereventyr appeared during the Second World War (1942), a difficult, trying time in Denmark as elsewhere, when Blixen's readers needed fantasy and heroic tales of tragedy. For Karen Blixen, World War II brought another round of financial duress, as she was unable to secure the American and English honoraria for her works, *Seven Gothic Tales*, *Out of Africa*, and *Winter's Tales* (Lasson-Svendsen, p. 166). As financially threatened as ever, Karen Blixen was on the point of selling Rungstedlund (Lasson-Svendsen, 167). In 1944, Blixen published another book, what the Danes call "en gyser" (a thriller), *Gengældelsens Veje* (1946; The Angelic Avengers), under the fantastic pseudonym Pierre Andrézel. The book caused quite a stir, and Blixen later disclaimed, then acknowledged, authorship. Between 1942 and 1956, Blixen worked on a monumental novel of one hundred chapters, *Albondocani*, a religious work or work with a religious theme (*DbL*: 2, 237). Blixen's health continued to deteriorate, particularly after the decisive year 1955–1956. Her life became a round of operations and hospital visits from which she returned all the weaker and more debilitated in body, if not in spirit (Lasson-Svendsen, p. 175). Needless to say, she was unable to realize her plan for *Albondocani*, but her finances, as precarious as her health, pressed her onward, and she did complete a single chapter of the work, *Kardinalens tredje Historie* (The Cardinal's Third Story) in 1952 (*DbL*: 2, 238).

In the late 1940s, Blixen's Rungstedlund—and the mythical Baroness herself—became a drawing card for a group of younger Copenhagen intellectuals. The editors of the new literary periodical *Heretica*, Thorkild Bjørnvig and Bjørn Paulsen; the authors Frank Jæger, Aage Henriksen, and Jørgen Gustava Brandt; the publisher-actor Ole Wivel; and the actor, Erling Schroeder, were all drawn to the aristocratic aura, to the "baroness-myth," which Blixen revelled in and was only too eager to foster (Dalager, 2, p. 101), and to Rungstedlund, which had become a literary salon. In the case of Bjørnvig, the editor of *Heretica*, a close friendship resulted between critic and author (Lasson-Svendsen, p. 169). Bjørnvig has described the nature of Blixen's possessive friendship and eventual domination in his book, *Pagten* (1974; The Pact). Karen Blixen

contributed to the first annual volume of *Heretica* with her *Breve fra et Land i Krig* (Letters from a Land at War) written after a stay in Berlin in 1940.

Karen Blixen also began a series of radio conversations, commentaries, stories, and readings: *Daguerrotypier* (1951; Daguerrotypes). Blixen's own English stories, "Uncle Seneca" (1951; Onkel Seneca), "Babette's Feast" (1950; Babettes Gæstebud), and "The Ghost Horses." (1950; Spøgelseshestene) were also translated into Danish and read on the radio to the enjoyment of many listeners. Blixen also used the radio to speak out on a variety of causes: humane treatment of animals, the dispossessed, and, finally, efforts to preserve and designate Rungstedlund as a national monument. After her near-fatal illnesses of 1955–1956, Blixen's literary career was necessarily curtailed. *Sidste Fortællinger* (Last Stories) appeared in 1957 and *Skæbne-Anekdoter* (Anecdotes of Destiny) in 1958, but both books were reduced in terms of formal plan. "Ringen" (The Ring), the last story of the last collection, is true to Blixen's *oeuvre* in dealing with the mystery that fatefully changes life—for good or ill (*Dbl* 2, 238).

Karen Blixen had first won acclaim in the United States and, at the very end of her life, in early 1959, she accepted an invitation from the Fund for the Advancement of Education, Ford Foundation, to appear in New York, Washington, and Boston. The four-month stay and her reading/lecture tour proved very taxing, and Blixen returned home greatly weakened. She continued writing, producing the Danish version of *Shadows on the Grass* (1960; Skygger paa Græsset) at the Dragør home of her friend and secretary, Clara Svendsen. (Rungstedlund underwent repair and restoration in 1958–1960; the estate grounds and park were set aside as a bird reserve, while the house was deeded to the Danish Literary Academy as the Rungstedlund Foundation [Lasson-Svendsen, p. 195].) At Dragør and Rungstedlund, Blixen continued to receive visitors, writers, family, and friends until her death at age seventy-seven on September 7, 1962 (*DbL*: 2, 238). She died in the home where her fantastic, eventful, and (as she described it) wholly, entirely happy life had begun (Hannah, p. 176).

Karen Blixen has been called both an author of timeless works, of works pitting individuals of any age against fate, universal plan, and destiny, and "a foreign bird in Danish literature" (Dalager 2, p. 101), a writer removed from her land and time and from contemporary modernism and realism. The self-created (and sustained) baron-ess-of-Rungsted-myth; the aristocratic ideal of *Out of Africa*; the fascination with the archaic, feudal aristocracy, all seem to distance her from our century, from our time and culture. However, in creating symbolic characters, Blixen explores inner powers warring within an individual. Shared archetypal myths, symbols, and beliefs live on universally as part of a greater pattern and plane, as Blixen explores the mind of the individual, the self, and the I (Dalager 2, p. 103), as well as the force, direction, and influence of life's pattern on the symbolic characters of her story-myths. Karen Blixen's *oeuvre* shares much with modernism in its presentation through reflections, reversals, and breaks with tradition (*DLH*: 8, 104); her authorship is also distinguished from modernism by its reworking of the historical-social bases for interpretation (*DLH*: 8, 104). With her fantastic stories of the past, of other enchanting, fanciful, and often tragic times, and with her mythically poignant and grand story of Africa, her life and symbolic dream of life in *Den afrikanske Farm*, Karen Blixen has created a symbolic world filled with wonder and a sense of individual destiny within a far greater, more impressive universal scheme.

Works

"Grjotgard Alveson of Aud" (1905). "Eneboerne" [The Hermits] (1907). "Pløjeren" [The Plowman] (1907). "Familien deCats" [The deCats Family] (1909). "Sandhedens Hævn" [The Revenge of Truth] (1926). Seven Gothic Tales [*Syv fantastiske fortællinger*] (1935). *Den afrikanske Farm* [Out of Africa] (1937). "Sorte og hvide i Afrika," Foredrag afholdt i Lund (1938); *Blixeniana* (1979). *Vintereventyr* [Winter's Tales] (1947). *Gengældelsens Veje* [The Angelic Avengers] (1944, 1946). *Breve fra et Land i Krig* [Letters from a Land at War] (1940, 1948). "The Ghost Horses." *Ladies Home Journal* (October 1951). *Daguerrotypier* (1951). *Kardinalens Tredje Historie* [The Cardinal's Third Story] (1952). *Sidste Fortællinger*

[Last Tales] (1957). *Skæbne-Anekdoter* [Anecdotes of Destiny] (1958). "Babettes Gæstebud" [Gabriel Axel, Babettes Gæstebud] (1958; film, 1987). "Rungstedlund: En radio-tale" (1958). "On Mottoes of my Life" (1960). "Introduction," Truman Capote, *Holly* (1960). *Shadows on the Grass* [Skygger paa Græsset] (1960). "Sandhedens Hævn" [The Revenge of Truth: A Marionette Comedy] (1960). "Introduktion," Basil Davidson, *Det genfundne Afrika* (1962). *Osceola: 1962* ("Grojtgard Alvesøn og Aud," "Pløjeren," "Eneboerne," "Familien deCats"; Poems: "Vinger," "Maaneskin," "Medvind," "Vuggesang," "En Stjerne," "Balladen om mit Liv," "Ex Africa.") *Ehrengard* (1963). *Fra det gamle Danmark I-II*, From old Denmark I-II (1963). *Kongesønnerne og andre efterladte fortællinger* [The Princes and other posthumous Tales]. "Karen Blixen fortæller," Louisiana Grammofonplader (1964).

Essays: Essays, 1965: "Mit Livs Mottoer" [My Life's Mottos] (1960). "Daguerrotypier" [Daguerrotypes] (1951). "En Baaltale med 14 Aars forsinkelse" (1953). "Fra Lægmand til Lægmand" [From Layman to Layman] (1954). "Breve fra et Land i Krig" [Reunion with England] (1944). "Om Retskrivning" (1938). "H.D. Branner: Rytteren" (1952). *Samlede Essays* [Collected Essays] (1969, 1977). *Moderne Ægteskab og andre Betragtninger* [Modern Marriage and Other Considerations] (1924; first published 1977).

Bibliography

Andersen, Hans and Frans Lasson, ed., *Blixeniana* (Copenhagen, 1977). Andrup, Birthe, *Kære Baronesse* (Charlottenlund, 1985). Bjørnvig, Thorkild, *Pagten: Mit venskab med Karen Blixen* (Copenhagen, 1974). Blixen, Karen, *Den afrikanske Farm* (Copenhagen, 1963). Blixen, Karen, *Babettes Gæstebud* (Copenhagen, 1987). Blixen, Karen, "Sorg-Agre," *Fra det gamle Danmark: II* (Copenhagen, 1963). Dalager, Stig, and Anne-Marie Mai, *Danske kvindelige forfattere. Bind 2. Fra Adda Ravnkilde til Kirsten Thorup. Udvikling og perspektiv* (Copenhagen, 1982). Dinesen, Thomas, *Tanne* (Copenhagen, 1974). Dinesen, Wilhelm, *Boganis' Jagtbreve* (Copenhagen, 1889). Dinesen, Wilhelm, *Fra Paris under Communen* (Copenhagen, 1899). Dinesen, Wilhelm, *Nye Jagtbreve* (Copenhagen, 1982). Hannah, Donald, "*Isak Dinesen" and Karen Blixen: The Mask and the*

Reality (New York, 1971). Henriksen, Aage, *Karen Blixen og marionetterne* (Copenhagen, 1952). Johannesson, Eric O., *The World of Isak Dinesen* (Seattle, 1961). *Kamantes Tales from Out of Africa* (New York, 1975). Lasson, Frans, and Clara Svendsen, *Karen Blixen: En Digerskæbne i Billeder* (Copenhagen, 1969). Schroeder, Erling, *Pierrot: Erling Schroeder fortæller om Karen Blixen* (Copenhagen, 1984). Thurman, Judith, *Isak Dinesen: The Life of a Story-Teller* (New York, 1982). *Karen Blixen: En fortællers Liv.* (Copenhagen, 1983). *Out of Africa* (film) 1985. Wamberg, Bodil, ed., *Out of Denmark. Isak Dinesen/Karen Blixen 1885–1984 and Danish Women Writers Today* (Copenhagen: The Danish Cultural Institute, 1985).

General references: *Dansk biografisk Leksikon* (1979), 2, pp. 233–239. *Dansk Litteratur Historie 7: Demokrati og Kulturkamp*, 1901–1945; 1984, pp. 390–397; *Dansk Litteratur Historie* 8: *Velfærdsstat og kulturkritik*, 1945–1980, 1985, pp. 96–104.

Lanae Hjortsvang Isaacson

Dionis

(see: Margareta Miller-Verghi)

Ana Diosdado

Born May 21, 1938, Buenos Aires, Argentina
Genre(s): drama, television plays, novel
Language(s): Spanish

The most prominent woman dramatist in contemporary Spain, Diosdado achieved national recognition with her first play, *Olvida los tambores* (1970; Forget the Drums). Two of her five original stage plays of the 1970s numbered among the decade's dozen longest-running Spanish works. An actress as well as a writer, in the 1980s she has authored and starred in two television series while continuing her involvement in the legitimate theatre, including versions of foreign plays and the staging in fall 1986 of her own *Cuple* (Popular Song).

Daughter of Spanish actor-director Enrique Diosdado, she made her acting debut at the age of four in Argentina. In 1950, the family returned to Madrid where Diosdado completed her high school education before pursuing an acting career. She began writing novels in the 1960s and was a finalist for the Planeta prize in 1969, but her real importance is as a dramatist. In addition to her own stage and television plays, she has prepared Spanish adaptions of major foreign works. She is married to the actor Carlos Larrañaga, a well-known leading man of stage and film.

Winner of major theatre prizes, *Olvida los tambores* remains Diosdado's most successful play to date. Carefully structured, on the pattern of the "well-made play," its first act has the rapid pace of comedy but the second takes a more serious tone. The action centers on two sisters and their husbands, all of them in their twenties, and the tension between tradition and nonconformity. Pili and Lorenzo incarnate the materialism and hypocrisy of the provincial middle-class, while Alicia and Tony are exponents of a youth culture and a rebellion against the consumer society. Initially the audience's sympathies lie with Alicia and Tony, but gradually it becomes clear that Tony's surface idealism is marred by his militancy—the drums of the title. Indirectly he causes the death of Lorenzo in the final moments of the play.

Diosdado's other major stage hit, *Usted también podrá disfrutar de ella* (1973; You, Too, Can Enjoy Her), is also a realistic play dealing with a contemporary situation—the exploitation of individuals by capitalist enterprises—but is less traditional in structure and staging. It calls for a nonrepresentational staging to facilitate the free flow among six locations at five moments in time. The "Her" of the title is a perfume whose advertising promotion features a discreetly nude model. When the perfume becomes connected in the media with the deaths of several children, the model becomes the object of widespread animosity. The disillusioned magazine reporter, who writes the story of the model's destroyed life, ultimately commits suicide himself. The more widely-acclaimed of her two television series, *Anillos de oro* (1983; Wedding Rings), featured Diosdado in the role of a divorce lawyer. The series consisted of thirteen one-hour segments: separate dramatic episodes framed by the personal story of the lead character. The stories of the clients as well as the frame story reflect realistically the tension between traditional sex roles and attitudes on marriage and changing lifestyles during a time of great social transition in democratic Spain.

Diosdado has experimented with the history play and allegorical theatre, but her reputation is based on her realistic stage and television plays, works in which she has captured the concerns of contemporary society.

Works

En cualquier lugar, no importa cuándo, novel (1965). *Olvida los tambores*, stage play (1972). *El okapi*, stage play (1972). *Los comuneros*, stage play (1974). *Usted también podrá disfrutar de ella*, stage play (1975). *El teatro por dentro: Ceremonia, representación, fenómeno colectivo*, essay (1981). *Y de Cachemira, chales*, stage play (1983). *Casa de muñecas*, adaptation of a play by Henrik Ibsen (1983). *Anillos de oro*. 2 vols., television plays (1985). *Segunda enseñanza*, television plays (in press).

Bibliography

Anderson, Farris, "From Protest to Resignation." *Estreno* 2.2 (1976): 29–32. Bremón, Anunchi, Interview. *El Pais Semanal* (July 1, 1984): 10–14. Segura, Florencio, "*Olvida los tambores*, un teatro joven?" *Razón y Fe* 879 (1970): 347–350. Zatlin-Boring, Phyllis, "The Theater of Ana Diosdado." *Estreno* 3.1 (1977): 13–17; "Ana Diosdado and the Contemporary Spanish Theater." *Estreno* 10.2 (1984): 37–40.

General references: *Dictionary of Literature of the Iberian Peninsula* (New York; Westport, Connecticut; London, in press). *El espectador y la critica*, ed. Francisco Alvaro (Valladolid, 1959–1970, 1978–; Madrid, 1971–1977). *Women Writers of Spain: An Annotated Bio-Bibliographical Guide*, ed. Carolyn L. Galerstein (New York; Westport, Connecticut; London, 1986).

Phyllis Zatlin

Dora d'Istria

(see: Elena Gjika)

Neel Doff

(a.k.a. Cornelia Hubertina)

Born Buggenum, The Netherlands; died 1942, Brussels, Belgium
Genre(s): autobiographical narrative
Language(s): French

Neel Doff's dispassionate and sober accounts of her experiences as a poor, hungry child in Amsterdam and as a painter's model and prostitute reduced to this trade by her family's poverty was praised by such prominent French literati as Laurent Tailhade and Octave Mirabeau, who nominated her first book *Jours de famine et de détresse* (Days of Hunger and Misery) for the prestigious Prix Goncourt.

Her work was immediately translated into a number of languages, but while the English and Russian translations were successful, the Dutch translation, by Anna van Gogh-Kaulbach, received little attention. Having had very little formal instruction as a child in Amsterdam, Neel Doff preferred to write in French, the language of her later years, because she had never learned to spell correctly in Dutch. Had she been able to write her stories in her mother tongue, however, it is unlikely that she would have found a Dutch publisher willing to put them on the market during her lifetime. Only about thirty years after her death did her countrymen get a chance to read her narratives in their own language. By then, open discussions of social problems and sexual and erotic subjects had become the literary norm, and Neel Doff's books became wildly popular even though her descriptions are almost devoid of sensuality. Prostitution to her was a necessary evil that she practiced as a cruel and repulsive obligation.

Her life is a true Pygmalion story. The third of nine children born to a Frisian father and a Walloon mother, Neel grew up in poverty. Her situation became worse as the number of children in the family increased and her father was out of work for longer periods of time. To supplement the family income, she started doing small jobs when she was eight, and before she was twelve she worked full time running errands and delivering hats for a hatmaker. When she was sixteen, the family moved to Antwerp and later to Brussels. Neel and her older sister Mina worked in a bordello to earn money to feed the family.

This miserable existence of hunger, cold, and ill health came to an end when a wealthy young German fell in love with Neel and took her into his house. The liaison lasted for some time, during which Neel enjoyed the comfort he could offer her and began to read a great deal.

Soon after, she met the love of her life, the French-speaking law student Fernand Brouez, a very wealthy young man with socialist ideals and an interest in literature, the arts, and philosophy. He married the beautiful Neel Doff, made her take private lessons in French grammar and orthography, history and geography, and even sent her to the Brussels conservatory to improve her diction. He also introduced her to world literature. They moved in the artistic circles in Brussels, and Neel became acquainted with many prominent people of the city. This marriage, very happy by all accounts, lasted only a few years; for Ferdinand became seriously ill and died at the age of thirty-five.

The young widow inherited his considerable fortune. During the next ten years, Doff traveled through Europe, sojourning in Switzerland, on the French Rivièra, and often in Paris. A second marriage to a Belgian lawyer, Georges Sérigires, a friend of her late husband, proved less happy. She often lived separately from her husband, with whose friends she did not feel at home and whose city, Antwerp, she never liked. In 1909, when she was already in her fifties, she began writing her childhood memories after witnessing, from the window of her stately Brussels dwelling, how a poorly clad boy was treated with hostility by a group of playing children. This brought back long repressed memories of the humility and misery she and her siblings had suffered as children.

Jours de famine et de détresse (1911; Days of Hunger and of Misery) was written in a few days. Two more volumes of recollections, *Keetje* (1919; Little Kate) and *Keetje Trottin* (1921; Keetje the Errand Girl), followed as well as a number of pseudo-fictional stories. Her directly autobiographical work, however, is considered her best. The recollections are not presented in chronological order, but rather as they occur to the narrator. Each story is organized around one specific incident. *Jours de famine et de détresse* contains episodes from the early years in Amsterdam and ends with her life as a prostitute in Brussels. *Keetje* also contains memories of that difficult period and then recounts her affair with the German and her encounter with and love for Brouez (called André in the book). *Keetje Trottin* again deals with her early years in Amsterdam.

In *Keetje Tippel* (1972; Keetje the Street Walker) her Dutch translator Wim Zaal has selected a number of episodes from the two *Keetje* volumes and arranged them chronologically.

All the stories in these volumes are told by a first-person narrator who calls herself Keetje Oldema, a rather transparent pseudonym, since both Keetje and Neel were common abbreviations of Cornelia and Oldema is a typical Frisian name. Her narrative manner is spontaneous and without any sensationalism. The rape in the story *Het roosje* (The Little Rose), which took place on the day she first menstruated, is described as a painful and wholly incomprehensible operation. Neel Doff's simplicity and directness were very modern in her day. As opposed to the florid language of the impressionistic and naturalistic mode still fashionable then, she wrote very succinctly, went straight to the point, and used terminology and details with which even male authors in Holland might not have gotten away.

Her books are not only interesting from a literary perspective, they are also important social documents on the lifestyle of large segments of the Dutch population in the nineteenth century.

Her diary entries in *Quitter tout cela!* (To Leave All That!) and *Au jour le jour 1932–35* (From Day to Day, 1932–35) celebrate the beauty of the countryside, whose colors and smells she still absorbs with the eagerness of the deprived slum child she used to be. For all her happiness in her first marriage and the wealth and comfort of her later life, Neel Doff reveals repressed hostility toward men in general and their exploitative sexual practices in particular. In this respect, some of her observations approach the ideas of modern feminists.

Though she wrote only in French, the spirit of her work is Dutch. Her works are therefore considered as belonging to Dutch literature rather than to French literature.

Works

Jours de famine et de détresse (1911). Contes farouches (1913). Keetje (1919). Keetje Trottin (1921). Michel (1922). Angélinette (1923). Une fourmi ouvrière (1935). Quitter tout cela! (1937). Au jour le jour 1932–35 (1937).

Translations: Dagen van honger en ellende [Jours de famine et de détresse], tr. Wim Zaal (1970). Keetje Tippel, tr. Wim Zaal (1972). De avond dat Mina mij meenam. Verhalen over Keetje Tippel, tr. Wim Zaal (1974). Afscheid. Van dag tot dag 1932–35 en vier kleine nagelaten verhalen [Quitter tout cela! and Au jour le jour 1932–35], tr. R. de Jong-Belinfante (1975).

Bibliography

Greshof, Jan, Ménagerie. Herinneringen en beschouwingen (1958). Nienaber-Luitingh, M., "Beknopte inleiding tot het leven en werk van de schrijfster Neel Doff." Standpunte 37–35 (October, 1984): 16–27. Pierson-Piérard, Marianne, Neel Doff par elle-même (1964).

Maya Bijvoet

Heather Dohollau

Born 1925, Penarth, Wales
Genre(s): poetry, essay
Language(s): French

Born in Penarth, not far from Cardiff, in South Wales, Heather Dohollau came to France in 1947, upon the death of her mother. After studying in Paris at the Ecole des Beaux-Arts, she lived in London for two years before settling permanently in France in 1951 at the time of her marriage. Living first, for seven years, on the Ile de Bréhat in Brittany, she moved to Saint-Brieuc, where she works as a librarian at the Centre d'Action Culturelle. She has seven children. Her first publication, an essay on Segalen, did not appear until 1974. Due, in part, to the encouragement and friendship of Guilloux, Jouve and Bonnefoy, Heather Dohollau is about to publish the fifth collection (L'Adret du jour, The Adret of Day) of an opus of great and moving profundity.

After her essay on Segalen and a monograph on Rilke (1974–1975), her first collection of poetry appeared: Seule Enfance (1978; Only Childhood). Its preoccupations are numerous, but all are central: reality and time; the visible and the invisible; the "equilibrium" of here and there; love and mortality; the enigma and simplicity of being; angelic presence and the "weight" of nothingness. Poetic voice occurs here "in a place of nothing for the pursuit of everything." Condemned to passing, our passage is fullness: "Finding in the immense void/ The faithful places/ Of a never lost paradise."

La Venelle des portes (1980; The Alley of Doors), beautifully illustrated, like her next two books, by Tanguy Dohollau, plunges us again, with perhaps greater intensity through the same serenity, into an exploration of the infinite depths of our finite being. The writing is spiritually rich, and filled with a sense of simplicity in no way reductive. Although the tone is never didactic, it has constant urgency: "Why do we not do/ the most important?/ To keep the impossible intact." Although we are already in paradise, we have almost everything to remember.

After La Réponse (1982; The Answer), a very finely respectful meditation upon the last hours of Jules Lequier, wherein so many crucial factors of existence are (re)lived and weighed, Heather Dohollau published Matière de lumière (1985; Matter of Light). The volume is the provisional crowning achievement of a brief but brilliantly insightful and serenely intense and original literary career. It treats of the simple mysteries of opaqueness and light, matter and soul, "music" and nothingness, death and birth, decline and freshness, presence and absence. Poetry, for Heather Dohollau, is a place of gathering and retention, close to disappearance and death yet a path of fragile light and flickering shadow (c.f. "Torcello"). The love sought is beyond all appearances, limitations, vagarish impotence; just as reality is a continual "baptism" of what it does not appear to be, of divinity. Heather Dohollau's poetic voice comes from a "listening to the Eternal speak of the trees."

Works

Poetry: Seule Enfance (1978). La Venelle des portes (1980). La Réponse (1982). Matière de lumière (1985).

Bibliography

Bishop, Michael, "Contemporary Women Poets." *Contemporary French Poetry, Studies in Twentieth-Century Literature* (Fall 1988).

Michael Bishop

Jim Dollar

(see: Marietta Shaginian)

Marion Dönhoff

Born 1909, East Prussia
Genre(s): journalism
Language(s): German

Marion Hedda Ilse, countess Dönhoff, was born at Friedrichstein, the estate of her family since 1666, daughter of a member of the House of Lords of the German Reich. After receiving her doctorate in economics (1935), she traveled through Europe, Africa and the United States, before she assumed the administration of the family estate in 1938. When the Soviet army invaded East Prussia in 1945, she fled westward on horseback. In her book *Namen die keiner mehr nennt*, she gives a highly interesting personal social history of her rural province still shaped by remnants of feudalism. This book, which became a best-seller of several editions in the 1960s, is written in a tone appreciably different from that of the *revanchist* refugee organizations of the Adenauer era. In 1946, she became a leading editor of the renowned liberal German weekly *Die Zeit* in Hamburg, where she took over as vice editor in chief of the political section in 1955, becoming general editor-in-chief and co-owner in 1968 and 1972, respectively. Through her political commentaries expressed in innumerable articles, she came to be the first woman in Germany to reach such a wide audience. Since the early 1960s she proposed that West Germany take a more active role in resolving the remaining tensions with the nations of the Eastern Bloc and has summarized the development of German *Ostpolitik* in her essay "Deutsche Aussenpolitik von Adenauer bis Brandt. 25 Jahre miterlebt und kommentier." In 1976, she published the book *Menschen die wissen worum es geht*, which contains seventeen portrait studies of politicians. In 1979, Marion Dönhoff accepted on behalf of *Die Zeit* the highly important European Erasmus Prize for understanding among nations. As an individual, she was awarded many distinctions: 1962, honorary doctorate, Smith College; 1966, Theodor Heuss Preis; 1971, Peace Prize of the Börsenverein des deutschen Buchhandels.

Works

Den Freunden zum Gedächtnis. In memoriam 20 Juli 1944 (1946). *Namen die keiner mehr nennt* (1962). *Die Bundesrepublik in der Ära Adenauer. Kritik und Perspektiven* (1963). *Reise in ein fernes Land.* With R.W. Leonhardt and Theo Sommer (1964). *Welt in Bewegung. Berichte aus 4 Erdteilen* (1965). *Menschen die wissen worum es geht. Politische Schicksale 1916–1976* (1976). *Von gestern nach übermorgen: zur Geschechte der BRD* (1981). *Amerikanische Wechselbäder* (1983).

Ingeborg Zeiträg

La Compiuta Donzella

Born thirteenth century, Florence, Italy
Genre(s): sonnet
Language(s): Italian

La Compiuta Donzella—"the accomplished young lady"—is the only name by which history records one of the first Italian women poets, who lived in Florence in the second half of the thirteenth century. Nothing is known about her, not even her name, and the only poems by her that have been preserved in a Florentine codex are three sonnets. One of them is a courteous answer to a poem by a fellow poet in which he praises her greatly and expresses a wish to visit her. The other two are connected by their theme. In the first, "A la stagion che il mondo foglia e fiora," which has found its place in almost all anthologies of Italian poetry, the poetess laments her unhappy fate, for her father wants her to marry against her will. The second, "Lasciar voría lo mondo e Dio servire," declares her wish to abandon the sinful world and dedicate her life to God. Perhaps those sonnets are autobiographical and tell the reader something about La Compiuta Donzella's life, but that must remain a speculation. Her fame rests primarily on the second sonnet mentioned above, which is unparalleled in its beauty and freshness.

Bibliography

Azzolina, L., "La Compiuta Donzella di Firenze." *Antologia Siciliana* (1902). Chiari, A., "La Compiuta Donzella." *Idagini e letture* (1954). Mazzoni, G., "I fedeli d'amore e la Compiuta Donzella." *Almae luces malae cruces* (1941). Viscardi, A., *Storia della letteratura italiana* (1960).

Neda Jeni

Geneviève Dormann

Born 1933, Paris, France
Genre(s): novel
Language(s): French

Although she has been a journalist and a chronicler, Geneviève Dormann is best known for her novels about women. She received the "Prix des Quatre-Jurys" in 1971, the "Prix des Deux-Magots" in 1974, and the "Grand Prix de la Ville de Paris" in 1980.

Her characters are well defined, strong-willed, flamboyant, modern women dealing with everyday situations such as jobs, finances, children, social pressures, and love's joys and pains. Her last two novels concern, however, the lives of two non-fictional women of the past. *Le roman de Sophie Trébuchet* (The Story of Sophie Trébuchet) tells the story of Victor Hugo's mother, a remarkable woman who grew up during the Révolution of 1789. Colette, a talented writer from the beginning of this century, who provoked many scandals with her independence, originality, and liberated ways, is the subject of Dormann's last book, which reveals a new side to an already well-known writer. Though the feminist interpretation is that Colette was exploited by her first husband Willy, Dormann asserts that Colette was never a victim of the men in her life. She depicts her as a consenting, sensuous, and cheerful fool for love, who always remained strong because of her vigorous appetite for life.

Though some critics might point out that hers are not very accurate biographies, Dormann's characters are very real and lifelike, and she gives them a chance to explain their choices and attitudes. Her style is spontaneous, simple, pleasant, and easy to read, but her dialogues and comments are sometimes too contemporary for the times that are being depicted, therefore weakening the credibility of her stories.

Works

La première pierre (1957). *La Fanfaronne* (1959). *Le Chemin des Dames* (1964). *La Passion selon Saint-Jules* (1967). *Je t'apporterai des orages* (1971). *Le Bateau du Courrier* (1974). *Mickey l'Ange* (1980). *Fleur de Péché* (1980). *Le Roman de Sophie Trébuchet* (1982). *Amoureuse Colette* (1984). Translations: *The Seasons of Love* [*La Fanfaronne*], tr. Elaine Desautels (New York, 1960). *The Way Life Is* [*Le Chemin des Dames*], tr. Merloyd Laawrence (New York, 1966). *Colette: A Passion for Life* [*Amoureuse Colette*], tr. David Macey (London, 1985).

Bibliography

Macey, David, and Jane Brenton, *Colette: A Passion for Life* (New York, 1985). Slawy-Sutton, Catherine, Review in *French Review* (May 1986). General references: De Beaumarchais, M.A., Review in *Dictionnnaire des Littératures de Langues Françaises* (Paris, 1984). Also see articles in *Le Nouvel Observateur* (3/10/1980); *Le Point* (3/10/1980); *Le Point* (7/14/1980).

Michèle M. Magill

Gertrud Dorn

(see: Gertrud Fussenegger)

Marie Dorval

Born January 7, 1798, Lorient, France; died May 20, 1849, Paris
Genre(s): letters
Language(s): French

The life of Marie Dorval was scarcely less tempestuous than the Romantic dramas which she interpreted with a conviction that impressed Parisian audiences for a generation. Marie-Thomase-Amélie Dorval was the illegitimate daughter of a seventeen-year-old actress and of an actor who lost no time in abandoning her mother. Poverty meant that she had to begin her theatrical career early, taking the roles of children and performing sentimental songs. When her mother died, in 1813, she hurriedly married a dancing master who had taken the stage name of "Dorval." Together they lived the precarious lives of touring players for some four years. He left her with the intention of seeking his fortune in St. Petersburg but died before he got there. Meantime, Marie Dorval was beginning to make some impression. Her first major success was as the unfortunate countess in Beaumarchais' *La Mère coupable* (The Guilty Mother) at Strasbourg in 1817. She was persuaded to take some lessons at the Paris Conservatoire though she never completed a full training there, and then she found the ideal place to display her talents and temperaments at the Théâtre de la Porte-Saint-Martin in Paris. One of the major so-called boulevard theatres of the time, it specialized in vivid melodrama, with spectacle reinforcing the impact of the clash of extravagant characters undergoing extraordinary adventures and expressing their responses with unbridled energy. Often she was partnered by the great Frédérick Lemaître (1800–1876); among their triumphs was Ducange's *Trente Ans dans la Vie d'un Joueur* (1827; Thirty Years in a Gambler's Life). Marie Dorval was hailed for her portrayal of the wretched Amélie who is shown first aged sixteen, then thirty-one and finally forty-six as, at each stage, she witnesses and responds to the gradual destruction of her husband because he cannot conquer the desire to gamble. Having established her position as one of the queens of melodrama she married, in 1829, an undistinguished man of letters, Jean-Toussaint Merle, who adopted a complaisant attitude towards her frequent infidelities.

When Alexandre Dumas *père* and Victor Hugo, after some initial success with *Henri III et sa Cour* (Henri III and His Court) and *Hernani*, tired of the endless struggle to have more of their Romantic works put on at the Comédie-Française, it was natural they should look to the boulevard theatres which were, in the view of their critics, the right place for them in any case. This gave Marie Dorval a great opportunity, and she seized it. At the Théâtre de la Porte-Saint-Martin her Adèle created a sensation in Dumas' *Antony* in which Romantic sensibility is given full scope in a contemporary setting. She was no less impressive as the heroine in Hugo's historical drama *Marion Delorme*, also in 1831. The public was, however, hostile, despite the excellence of her performance, when she took the lead in Eugène Scribe's *Dix Ans, ou La Vie d'un Femme* (Ten Years, or a Woman's Life); by all accounts her performance was powerful, but that was not enough to make Parisian audiences respond sympathetically to the presentation of the life of a fallen woman. Though deeply hurt, Marie Dorval had two more great Romantic successes to come. Coming at last to the Comédie-Française, where great efforts had to be made to overcome the prejudices of more conservative actors and actresses, she played Kitty Bell in the première of Alfred de Vigny's *Chatterton*. A mixture of frailty and of passion that bordered on hysteria made her great in the part, and her famous tumble down the stairs to land fainting away was a high point of boulevard physical acting that clashed unforgettably with the more staid traditions of the French grand manner. In Hugo's *Angelo* Marie Dorval took the role of Catarina while the redoubtable Mlle Mars was La Tisbe; the actresses hated one another, but that only put them on their mettle and the performances were much admired. Soon after this, personal animosities forced Marie Dorval to leave the Comédie-Française where she had never felt at home. Touring the provinces she met with a rapturous welcome at first. She returned to the Comédie-Française to star in George Sand's *Cosima*, but the play was a total failure, and she showed all her old skill in the tear-jerking melodrama *Marie-Jeanne, ou la Fille du Peuple*, by A.-P. Dennery and J. de Mallian. By now, however, her health was beginning to give cause for alarm, and the complications of her personal life were getting the better of her. A stormy affair with Alfred de Vigny had concluded bruisingly, with the poet venting his ire in the enraged verses of "La Colère de Samson." Marie Dorval had had two legitimate daughters, but one had run away and the other died of tuberculosis. It was left to the husband of a daughter she had had by the musical director of the Théâtre de la Porte-Saint-Martin to help out his mother-in-law, who was reduced to the exhausting routines of touring minor theatres in the provinces to eke out a living. She died in poverty on May 20, 1849. There was some irony in the fact that it was left to Rachel, the rising star of the new Neo-classical generation, to organize a benefit performance to pay off her debts. Alexandre Dumas wrote a moving account of her last days which was sold to cover the costs of her funeral.

It was as a passionate actress that Marie Dorval made her name. Her letters, to Alfred de Vigny and to George Sand, are interesting documents and possess some literary merit too.

Works

Marie Dorval, *Lettres à Alfred de Vigny*, ed. Charles Gaudier (1942). George Sand-Marie Dorval, *Correspondance inédite*, ed. Simone-André-Maurois, préface de André Maurois (1953).

Bibliography

Charlier, G., *Marie Dorval en Belgique* (Bruxelles, 1955). Dumas, Alexandre, père, *La Dernière Année de Marie Dorval* (Paris, 1855). Hagenauer, Paul, *La Vie douloureuse de Marie Dorval* (Paris, 1972). Moser, F., *Marie Dorval* (Paris, 1947). Nozière, *Madame Dorval*. "Acteurs et actrices d'autrefois: documents et anecdotes" (Paris, 1926). Pollitzer, M., *Trois reines de théâtre* (Paris, 1958). Sand, George, "Mars et Dorval" and "Dorval." *Questions d'art et de littérature* (Paris, 1878).

Christopher Smith

Theone Drakopoulou

(a.k.a. Myrtiotissa)

*Born 1883, Constantinople, Turkey; died
    1968, Athens, Greece*
Genre(s): poetry
Language(s): Greek

She was the daughter of the Greek consul in Constantinople. Her sister, Aura Theodoropoulou, was a well-known music critic. Her family moved to Crete and subsequently to Athens, when she was still very young. She started her career as an amateur theater actress, mainly in Shakespearean roles and later she was a teacher of speech at the Conservatory of Athens. She was married to S. Pappas, whom she divorced a few years later.

Her literary work is mainly poetic. Her first collection of poems, *Tragoudia* (Songs), was published in 1919 though she had been occasionally contributing since 1911 in the periodicals *Noumas* and *Panathenaea*. Her two collections, the *Kitrines Floges* (The Yellow Flames) in 1925 and *Kravges* (Cries) in 1939, are considered her best literary output. In 1953 she made a collective publication of all her work with the title *Poiēmata* (Poems). A romantic and sentimental nature is reflected in all her poems (c.f. "Voluptas," "Ta Oneira mou" [My Dreams], "Makria mou stathikes" [You Stood Away from Me], "Chorismos" [Separation], "Apopse" [Tonight], "Nanai ē zoē yia sena" [May the Life be for You], "Klaiei ē vrochē [The Rain is Crying]). The themes of despair and disappointment, which she experienced frequently in her personal life, interchange with outbursts of love for nature (c.f. "Ēsykia" [The Fig Tree], "O dendra" [Oh Trees], "To dasos" [The Forest], "Sto akrogiali" [At the Seashore]). Her verse is elegant, spontaneous and passionate but is often lacking in perfection of plasticity and musicality as K. Palamas remarks in his introduction to the *Kitrines Floges*; he also criticizes the constant tone of melancholy and unhappiness in her poetry and complains of ". . . a lack of fresh air in the light and joy of life. . . ." Her unfulfilled love for the poet L. Mavilis, killed in the war of 1912, inspired many of her poems, such as "S'agapo" (I Love You), "Thelo na xereis" (I Want You to Know), "Vradiazei" (It's Getting Dark), and "Makria mou stathikes" (You Stood Away from Me) and also inspired K. Palamas' "Oi Vomoi" (The Altars), "Diplomonaxia" (Double Solitude), and "To nyphiko krevati tha sou kamo" (I'll Make the Bridal Bed for You). Her poem collection *Ta dora tēs agapēs* (The Gifts of Love) in 1932 won her the award from the Academy of Athens and *Cries* won her the National Poetry Prize. In 1921, she published *Ellinika poiemata katallila di'apangelian* (Poems for Recitation) prefaced by K. Palamas; in 1930 she published the chronicle *G. Pappas sta paidika tou chronia* (G. Papas in his Childhood), which contains much autobiographical information. She made regular contributions to the periodicals *Noumas*, *Nea Estia*, *Alexandrine Art*, and the *National Herald* of New York. She translated Euripides' *Medea*, also a collection of poems by Comtesse de Noailles in 1928.

Love, melancholy, despair, and nature are not Myrtiotissa's only themes in poetry; she also writes about the years of Greece's civil war ("Tha Xechaso pote" [Shall I Ever Forget]); about the liberation of Greece from Nazi occupation ("Apolytrosi" [Liberation]), also in memorial of her poet friend P. Yannopoulos, who committed suicide ("Sto filo pou mas efyge" [To the Friend Who Left Us]), about her school years, about famous women in Greek history ("Bouboulina," "Souliotisses"). Her poetic talent is best revealed in her erotic poems. Myrtiotissa has also been among the first Greek women to fight for the emancipation of women. Together with M. Polydouri she occupies an outstanding place as a lyric poetess in Greece.

Works

Poetry: *Songs* (1919). *Poems for Recitation* (1921). *The Yellow Flames* (1925). *The Gifts of Love* (1932). *Cries* (1939). *Collected Work* (Apanta), ed. Alvin Redman Hellas (1965).

Prose: *Anthology for Children* (2 vols., 1930). "G. Pappas, his Childhood" (1952).

Translations: A collection of poems by Comtesse de Noailles (1928). Euripides' *Medea* (1932).

Translations of Her Work in English: A limited number of her poems have been translated. These include "I Love You," in *The Penguin Book of Greek Verse*, ed. C.A. Trypanis, New York (1979) and "Women of Souli," in *Modern Greek Poetry*, ed. Rae Dalven, New York (1971).

Bibliography

Athanasiades, T., "Preface to Myrtiotissa's *Collected Work*." (Athens, 1965) p. 497. Augeris, M., M.M. Papaioannou, et al., *The Anthology of Greek Poetry*, v. 4B. (Athens, 1959). Boumi, R., and N. Pappas, *World Anthology*, v. 2 (Athens, 1953), pp. 533–534. Dalven, Rae, *Modern Greek Poetry* (New York, 1971). Deliyanni-Anastassiadi, G., *Anthology from the Greek Poetry*, v. 2. (Athens, 1976), pp. 240–243. Dimaras, C.Th., *A History of Modern Greek Literature* (New York, 1972). Drandakis, P., *Great Greek Encyclopedia*, v. 9 and v. 2 suppl. (Athens, 1957). Karantonis, A., "Introduction to Myrtiotissa's *Collected Work*," (Athens, 1965), pp. 11–32. Kokkinis, S., in *Anthology of Poetry for Schools* (Athens, 1973). Liatsos, D., *Greek Women in our Literature* (Athens, 1966), pp. 23–24. Matsis, D., *Greek Women in our Poetry* (Athens, 1966) p. 23. Mavroeidi-Papadaki, S., "Myrtiotissa." *Gynaika* [Woman], 457 (Athens, 1968). Meraklis, M.G., *The Greek Poetry*, pp. 490–497. "Myrtiotissa," special issue of *Nea Estia* 900, v. 84 (Athens, 1968). Palamas, K., "Introduction to the *Yellow Flames*" (Athens, 1925). Palamas, K., *Apanta* 14 (Athens, 1960), pp. 497–502. Panayiotopoulos, M., *Neohellenic Poetic Anthology*, v. 3 (Athens, 1979), pp. 9–18. Paraschos, Kl., *Greek Lyric Poets* (Athens, 1953), pp. 208–210. Porphyris, K., *Poetic Anthology 1650–1964* (Athens, 1964), pp. 374–377. Tarsouli, A., *Greek Poetesses* (Athens, 1953), pp. 91–107. Trypanis, C.A., *The Penguin Book of Greek Verse* (Athens, 1971).

A. Georgiadou

Ingeborg Drewitz

Born January 10, 1923, Berlin, West Germany; died November 25, 1986
Genre(s): novel, essay
Language(s): German

After having studied literary history and philosophy at the University of Berlin, Ingeborg Drewitz received her doctorate in 1945. Soon after, she became one of the co-founders of the Verband deutscher Schriftsteller, the association of German writers, whose vice president she was from 1969–1980. She became a member of PEN in 1964. In 1981, she was nominated honorary professor of the Berlin Free University where she had also briefly taught in 1973–1974. In 1983, she lectured as guest professor at the University of Texas, Austin. Ingeborg Drewitz' literary *oeuvre* is an attempt to practice and realize the social and pedagogical mission and dimension that literary texts have. They are written to help the average reader and citizen to understand social and political problems of today. Her early works, especially several radio plays, deal with the shock and embarrassment of having lived her youth during national socialism. Her mature works are a coming to terms with contemporary society, political power, and the failure and guilt of individuals and groups when confronted with that society and power. Drewitz has been accused of resignation: to this she has replied that her texts, far from belaboring human failure, are supposed to enable human beings to resist. As critic Klaus

Anthes has put it, Drewitz "takes the world as it has, regrettably, become, but only in order to change it, in the imagination as well as in practice. . . . She communicates to the public her incorruptible sense of justice and her impartial humanity." Through her biography of the German Romantic *Bettine von Arnim*, Drewitz became known in wide circles, which has also enriched the discussion concerning feminism and creativity. In 1980, Drewitz received the Carl von Ossietzky Medal of the International League for Human Rights.

Works

Fiction: *Der Anstoss* (1958). *Im Zeichen der Wölfe* (1963). *Das Hochhaus* (1979). *Octoberlicht* (1981). *Eis auf der Elbe* (1984).

Essays and Criticism: *Bettine von Arnim. Romantik Revolution. Utopie* (1969). *Städte 1945. Berichte und Bekenntnisse* (1970). "Der freie Autor—eine Fiktion?" *Merkur* 2 (1973): 98–105. *Mit Sätzen Mauern eindrücken. Briefwechsel mit einem Strafgefangenen* (1979). *Schrittweise Erkundung der Welt. Reiseessays aus 30 Jahren* (1982). *Die deutsche Frauenbewegung* (1983). *1984—Am Ende der Utopien. Literatur und Politik* (1984).

Editions: *Schatten im Kalk. Lyrik und Prosa aus dem Knast* (1979). *Dichtung im ausgehenden 20. Jahrhundert* (1981).

Bibliography

Anthes, Klaus, "Ingeborg Drewitz." *Deutsche Volkszeitung* (January 15, 1983). Gollwitzer, Helmut, "Die Realität des Strafvollzugs." *Frankfurter Hefte* 8 (1980): 75–77. Langner, Ilse, "Ingeborg Drewitz—Charakter und Image." *Neue Rundschau* (1970). Rudolph, Ekkehart, "Ingeborg Drewitz." *Aussage zur Person: 12 deutsche Schriftsteller im Gespräch* (Tübingen, 1977).

Ingeborg Zeiträg

Jette Drewsen

Born 1943, Vejle, Denmark
Genre(s): novel, drama
Language(s): Danish

Jette Drewsen has studied psychology at the University of Copenhagen but dropped out of school to get married and raise three children. Drewsen was one of the first Danish women writers to write books that were directly influenced by the women's movement and was thus among the pioneers of women's literature in Denmark. Her style has been described by different critics as subjective realism or feminist realism. Drewsen is a so-called "cultural worker," i.e., a writer who is involved in other cultural activities such as producing literary radio programs, reviewing books, editing literary periodicals, etc. Drewsen has been co-editor of a periodical called *Luftskibet*, she has written for the stage *Hva' drømmer du om?* (1981) and a play for television, *Opbrud inden døre* (1982), based on her first novel *Hvad taenkte egentlig Arendse?* (1972).

Drewsen's first book is a classical description of what Betty Friedan called "the problem that has no name." It is the story of a young wife and mother who feels her identity slipping away while performing her endless chores around the house, being solely responsible for her children and financially dependent on her up-and-coming professional husband, who is losing his respect for her because of the role he and society have forced her into. *Fuglen* (1974) shows that being single and able to support oneself is not enough to solve the problem. Here the protagonist is a single mother and an artist in an uncommitted relationship, which means that her lover has the freedom she wants but cannot have because of her child and the expectations society has instilled in her and which she has internalized. But where the protagonist in the first book revolted against her situation, this one quietly commits suicide.

Pause (1976) is a positive version of her second book, describing a woman who can handle her situation as single parent and artist. *Tid og sted* (1978) is a collective novel attempting to tell the story of Drewsen's generation of women, following them from when they were teenagers in the early sixties, through the student revolt in 1968 into the seventies; and their various reactions to the women's movement. Here we see the conditions which shaped the women in Drewsen's earlier books and are thus allowed to understand more fully why their lives turned out that way.

Midtvejsfester (1980) follows these women into the 1980s, now more or less committed to being single but with one or several marriages behind them, children who are now teenagers, and careers which have been possible in spite of the rules of the male-dominated society in which they live and against which they are continually struggling.

In her accurate, realistic depictions of women's lives in the 1970s and 1980s, Drewsen's analyses of the gains and conflicts of the women's movement have proved her solidarity with its hopes and frustrations. Her works are important feminist documents. Drewsen's integration of children into her stories, her ability to observe and describe the anguished, wonderful, draining, never-ending day-to-day process of mothering, of the biological and psychological reality of being a woman, provide valid new insights.

Works

Hvad taenkte egentlig Arendse? (1972). Fuglen (1974). Pause (1976). Tid og sted (1978). Midtvejsfester (1980). Ingen erindring (1983).

Bibliography

Brostrøm, Torben, and Mette Winge, ed., Danske digtere i det 20. århundrede (1982). Clausen, Claus, ed., Lit/80—en al—manak (1980). Dalager, Stig, and Anne-Marie Mai, Danske dvindelige forfattere 2 (1982). Gaul, Bente, Undertrykkelse, oplevelse og modstand i den nye kvinderoman (1978). Holmgaard, Alice, and Anne Aagaard, Kvindebevidsthed omkring den seksuelle frigørelse (1976). Levy, Jette, De knuste spejle (1976). Richard, Anne-Birgitte, Kvindesituation/kvindelighed/kvindekamp (1978).

Merite von Eyben

Paola Drigo

Born 1876, Castelfranco, in the Veneto, Italy;
     died 1938, Padua, Italy
Genre(s): short story, novel, memoirs, poetry
Language(s): Italian, with some Friulan dialect

Paola Drigo was born in the medieval town of Castelfranco in the Veneto, daughter of garibaldino Valerio Bianchetti of Asolo, wife of an engineer from Mussolente (Bassano del Grappa). Born in comfortable circumstances, she wrote of humble characters, the diseredati, revealing the drama of their lives and their profound humanity. Her modest oeuvre consists of

three collections of stories: La Fortuna (1913; As Luck Would Have It), Codino (1918), and La Signorina Anna (1932), a volume of poetry, Col mio infinito, (1921; In Company with my Infinite), a brief memoir, Fin d'anno (1936; Year's End), and one novel, her masterpiece, Maria Zef (published in 1936, two years before the author's death, forgotten during the Second World War and its aftermath, and reissued in 1982). (One source lists a reprinting in 1953.) A final story, "Window on the River," about Padua, where Drigo spent the previous winter, was written in the hospital the summer before she died. A single source lists a work of fiction called La signorina di Friours, 1929. Maria Zef was twice translated into film: the earlier version of 1954 directed by Luigi De Marchi, released under both original title and as Condannata senza colpa; and the 1981 film made for RAI-TV3, produced by the Friuli regional government and directed by Vittorio Cottafava.

Drigo was drawn to write about poverty, hunger, privation, illness—and acceptance of these conditions. In the Veneto, an agricultural economy dominated until well into the twentieth century, resisting industrialization, Drigo wrote of a vitiated aristocracy, of prospering dairy-farmers, of healthy good-hearted enterprising countryfolk constrained by circumstances and forced to make difficult decisions, and of emigrant laborers who sometimes returned. The wind and the mountain are two features that figure importantly in her lucid narrative style, as she renders the drama of daily life with a dry compassionate humor and a strict lyricism. She presents survival through life-threatening crises in harsh landscapes, looking on, as critic Manara Valgimigli wrote, with an unwavering implacable eye. Winter was her favorite season; bare branches, clear outlines, a world reduced to essentials, austere. In Mario Apollonio's view, Maria Zef signals the farthest limit of verismo (realism) narrative of the 1930s and imposes on the post-Second World War verismo a sorrowful intensity. Gualtiero Amici ranks Drigo on the same artistic plane, for Maria Zef, with Matilde Serao and Nobelist Grazia Deledda.

In Maria Zef, fourteen-year-old Mariutine comes down at harvest-time with her mother, baby sister, and dog from their isolated hut high above the Alpine grazing grounds in the Carnia region, to sell wooden housewares to farmers in the valley of the Po. In a season of excessive flooding and rot, sales lag. Desperately and unaccountably sick, the mother collapses and dies. Nuns shelter the orphans until their paternal uncle can claim them. The little girl cannot walk on her hurt foot. She is carried up the mountain at night by Pieri, a youth they have recognized on the train. Only on home ground, alone, does Mariutine recognize the magnitude of her loss. Pieri later visits to say he is emigrating but will return for Mariutine, who agrees to wait. She cleans the hut, tends the sheep, takes charge of provisions, and prepares for winter. When her sister has to be hospitalized, descent to the hospital occasions contrasts between their meager lives and the prosperity of an extended family whom they visit at Carnival time. The master, a smart and successful hunchback, dances with and flatters Mariutine and plots to seduce her. Her uncle, observing, is goaded to jealous anger and rape. Life goes on: the flock must be watered, the dog eats, the chores are waiting. Confined to the hut by rigors of winter, surrounded by inhuman silence, Mariutine's hopes alternate with qualms and defeats, in a relentless process of physical and moral degradation. The uncle schemes to find Mariutine paid work as a domestic. She comes to a new understanding of her mother. There is no villain, for her uncle has been presented as provident, skilled, and ingenious though brutish, taciturn, and given to drinking. Their desperate struggle, waged without hate, ends in bloodshed.

Works

La Fortuna (1913). Codino (1918). Col mio infinito (1921). La Signorina Anna (1932). Fin d'anno (1936). Maria Zef (1936, 1982).

Bibliography

Amici, Gualtiero, *Narratori italiani da Verga alla neo-avanguardia; profili critico-bibliographfici* (Bologna, 1973). Bocelli, A., *Nuova antologia* (Feb. 16, 1938): 350–351. Migliore, Benedetto, Essay on Drigo's "La Fortuna" from *Il Giornale di Sicilia* (Apr. 6–7, 1913). In *Saggi critici: scrittori contemporanei della letteratura italiana fra le due guerre*, ed. Virgilio Caprera (Rome, 1961)—collected by Migliore's sister Anna. Musatti, A., *Ateneo Veneto* (Feb. 1938): 109–111. Pancrazi, P., *Scrittori italiani dal Carducci al D'Annunzio* (Bari, 1943), pp. 195–220. Pancrazi, Pietro, and Giuseppe Zoppi, In Enrico Falqui, *Novecento Letterario, Serie Quinta* (Florence, 1957). Russo, L., *I narratori* (Milano, 1958). Valgimigli, Manara, *Uomini e scrittori del mio tempo* (Florence, 1943), pp. 195–219; and more recent reviews of the reissued book and the film versions of *Maria Zef*.

Blossom S. Kirschenbaum

Annette von Droste-Hülshoff

Born January 10, 1797, Münster, Westphalia; died May 24, 1848, Meeresburg, Lake of Constance
Genre(s): lyric poetry, novella, short story
Language(s): German

Droste-Hülshoff belonged to the group "Junges-Deutschland" (Young Germany) and is considered a great representative of regional art.

Annette von Droste-Hülshoff belonged to an old Westphalian aristocratic family. She was born at Hülshoff, a castle near Münster, and passed an uneventful life, mostly at her mother's home but partly with her married sister in an old castle, Meeresburg, near the Lake of Constance.

Outwardly, there seemed little to ruffle her, but beneath the surface she lived an intense life of spiritual and emotional conflict, learning in suffering "what she taught in song" (Robertson). Her best friend was a young Westphalian author, Levin Schucking (1817–1883), who opened up the world of literature to her and encouraged her in her writing. Eventually their friendship, in spite of the disparity of their years, grew into a deep, suppressed passion, which Annette herself broke off. Retiring and unattractive, she was physically far from robust and died in the revolution year of 1848.

Annette von Droste-Hülshoff is one of the most independent lyric poets of the nineteenth century. Her poetry shows extraordinarily little subservience to tradition; at most, the influence of Byron among the moderns is noticeable in her narrative poems, *Walther* written in 1818, *Das Hospiz auf dem grossen St. Bernhard* (The Great St. Bernard Hostel) written in 1838, and the magnificent *Schlacht im Loener Bruch* (The Battle of Loener Bruch) also written in 1838.

Her verse rarely expresses lyric sweetness or romantic sentiment; indeed it is often repellent in its acerbic realism. But her love for the red soil of the native Westphalia, its forests and its moors, is perhaps deeper than that of any other German poet for her homeland; and for nature's most hidden secrets she has an almost preternatural clearness of vision.

Annette von Droste-Hülshoff's technical mastery and self-abnegating restraint are classic in the pre-romantic sense of the word but her language is full of color. She is a woman of great earnestness, realistic observation, and deep psychological insight, firmly rooted in the land and among the people of her province.

In her religious poems contained in *Das Geistliche Jahr* (The Spiritual Year) she revealed her ardent Catholicism though grievous religious crises and doubts were not alien to her. *Das Geistliche Jahr* consists of 72 songs: one for every Sunday of the year and one for every Church holiday. However, one seldom notices any specific reference to the Catholic Church; they are mostly religious poems praising Jesus and Mary.

Die Judenbuche (The Jew's Beech Tree) is her best novel, one of the finest narratives of the mid-century, a tragic tale of ignorance, crime, and social prejudice in which the sins of the fathers are visited upon their sons. The story was inspired by an actual murder in Droste's Westphalia. An old town drunk, Mergel, neglected and debauched, is found dead one day near an old beech tree. His son, Friedrich, disreputable and unsocial, murders a Jewish merchant to whom he owes money and places him at the same beech tree where his own father died in drunkenness. He flees. All the Jews of the area come with a mysterious inscription in Hebrew and place it on the tree. After many years Friedrich returns; no one recognizes him but the thought of his own act of murder leaves him no peace so that he hangs himself on the beech tree. In this work, Droste introduces new and modern elements: social injustice, environmental influence, the role of the conscience, and the psychology of crime.

In addition to writing prose and poetry, she helped the Brothers Grimm with their collection of fairy tales and Ludwig Uhland with his *Volkslieder* (Folksongs).

Works

Der Spiritus familiaris des Rosstäuschers (1838). *Das Hospiz auf dem grossen St. Bernhard* (1838). *Des Arztes Vermächtnis* (1838). *Das Malerische und Romantische Westfalen* (1839). *Die Judenbuche* (1842). *Gedichte* [Poems] (1844). *Das Geistliche Jahr. Nebst eine Anhang Religiöser Gedichte.* [The Spiritual Year Together With an Appendix of Religious Poems] (1851).

Bibliography

Alker, Ernst, *Die Deutsche Literatur im 19. Jahrhundert* (Stuttgart, 1961). Arens, Eduard and Karl Schulte-Kemminghausen, *Droste-Hülshoff Bibliographie* (Munster, 1932). Badt, B., *Annette von Droste-Hülshoff, ihre Dichterische Entwicklung und ihr Verhältnis zur englischen Literatur* (Breslau, 1909). Hesselhaus, C., *Annette von Droste-Hülshoff Die Entdeckeng des Seins in der Dichtung des 19. Jahrhunderts* (Halle, 1943). Koenig, Robert, *Deutsche Literaturgeschichte.* Vol. 2 (Leipzig, 1910). Kosch, Wilhelm, *Deutsches Literatur-Lexikon. Biographisches und bibliographisches Handbuch* (Bern, 1949). Krell, Leo and Leonhard Fiedler, *Deutsche Literaturgeschichte* (Bamberg, 1960). Martini, Fritz, *Deutsche Literaturgeschichte* (Stuttgart, 1965). Robertson, J.G., *A History of German Literature* (New York, 1931). Staiger, Emil, *Annette von Droste-Hülshoff* (Zurich, 1932).

Brigitte Archibald

Juliette Drouet

Born April 10, 1806, Fougères, France; died
*   May 11, 1883*
Genre(s): letters
Language(s): French

Julienne-Joséphine (known as "Juliette") Gauvin was born of poor parents, who died shortly after her birth. She was brought up by her uncle, a lieutenant in the coastal artillery called René-Henri Drouet, and took his name. At the age of ten she was sent to the Benedictine convent at Picpus for her education, and there was talk of her entering the order. She was, however, a pretty girl and had ideas of her own. What exactly happened after leaving the convent in 1822 is not known, but by 1825 she had become the mistress of Jean-Jacques ("James") Pradier, a distinguished sculptor who was also notorious as a womanizer. She was the model for a number of his statues, including the figure of Strasbourg on the Place de la Concorde in Paris. In 1826 she had a daughter, Claire, by Pradier, but the liaison broke up the year after when she began her career as an actress in Brussels. She returned to Paris to play at the Odéon in 1831, at about which time she had become the mistress of Prince Demidof. Soon after, Victor Hugo met her for the first time, on January 2, 1833, when his *Lucrèce Borgia* was being read through in preparation for a performance, at the Théâtre de la Porte-Saint-Martin in Paris. When the play was produced, Juliette Drouet was given the role of the Princesse Négroni; it gave her every opportunity to impress with her beauty without putting any strain on her limited acting ability. She became Hugo's mistress in February 1833; his marriage to Adèle had broken down, and he was in search of the adoring companionship that he found necessary to maintain his creative energy. Juliette still cherished ambitions as an actress, and Hugo wrote the role of Jane in *Marie Tudor* for her and that of the Queen in *Ruy Blas*. But he was unable to overcome the opposition of the formidable Mlle George who was determined she should not have the first of these two parts, and Madame Hugo intervened powerfully to deny her the second. Perhaps Hugo was not too disappointed, for his policy would be to arrange Juliette's life so that she should be entirely devoted to him and his interests. He cut her off from the frivolous amorality of the life she had led previously, he settled her financial affairs, complaining bitterly of her spendthrift ways, and he settled her in an apartment near his own in the Place Royale. At first Juliette was tempted to kick over the traces, only to return to Hugo more devoted than ever, and after she had run away to her native Brittany, the pair exchanged vows that were only the more solemn because they were pronounced without benefit of clergy in the church at Renan on August 8, 1834. Thereafter Juliette settled into a simple, unruffled, not to say monotonous style of life, providing Hugo with ordinary domestic comforts and dog-like devotion and acting as his

copyist. The couple also took touring holidays together, and it was in the course of one of these trips that on September 9, 1843, Hugo learned, when reading a newspaper in a café, that his beloved daughter Léopoldine had been drowned in a boating accident. The shock, grief, and guilt which Hugo then felt crystallized when Juliette's daughter Claire died after a long illness on June 21, 1846, and the bond between the lovers became stronger than ever. Juliette's devotion survived, though not without some strain, even after such notorious infidelities as Hugo's liaison with Mme Léonie Biard, and Hugo was always to recall with gratitude the efforts she made to protect him when he was convinced his life was threatened during the dangerous days of the *coup d'état* of December 1851.

Juliette followed Hugo into exile, to Brussels, Jersey, and, finally, Guernsey. Once Hugo had bought himself Hauteville House there, he found his mistress comfortable accommodation nearby. There she lived for some eighteen years, supporting Hugo emotionally and maintaining an air of great propriety. The liaison was, of course, no secret to Mme Hugo, and at Christmas 1864 she invited Juliette to her house, and the two women became friends. After Mme Hugo's death, on August 26, 1868, Juliette refused to marry Hugo, but when in 1870 the exile ended and the poet returned to Paris she was at his side to share the triumph for more than a decade. She died after a long illness on May 11, 1883, and Hugo never recovered his composure afterwards. He had, however, succeeded in bringing to reality one of the most potent myths of the nineteenth century: Juliette Drouet was a shining example of the fallen woman redeemed by love.

Juliette Drouet also has a place in literary history for the some 17,000 letters which she wrote to Hugo. Sometimes their sentimentality cloys, and it is almost embarrassing to eavesdrop on lovers' sweet nothings. But there is strength here too, perhaps in part because of the long familiarity with Hugo's own writings which Juliette copied so industriously, and it is the record of a great love which nothing could quench. The letters are a precious document in their own right.

Works

Lettres à Victor Hugo, ed. Jean-Luc Benoziglio (1970). Mille et une lettres d'amour à Victor Hugo, ed. Paul Souchon (1951). Souchon, Paul, Olympio et Juliette: Lettres inédites de Juliette Drouet à Victor Hugo (1940).

Bibliography

Maurois, André, Olympio ou La Vie de Victor Hugo (Paris, 1954). Souchon, Paul, "Juliette Drouet, inspiratrice de Victor Hugo," Amantes et égéries (Paris, 1942).

Christopher Smith

Elzbieta Druzbacka

Born c. 1695, Poland; died c. 1765, Tarnow, Poland
Genre(s): verse romance
Language(s): Polish

Born probably in western Poland (maiden name: Kowalska), Druzbacka was raised and educated at aristocratic courts in southern and eastern parts of the country. About 1725, she married a landed gentleman and provincial official, Kazimierz Druzbacki, and lived in the country. Widowed about 1740, she managed her two villages herself and participated actively in the social life of the aristocracy. Depressed after the death of her daughter and grandchildren, she joined a monastery of Bernardine nuns in Tarnow, in southern Poland, where she died. Known mainly as the author of a fantastic tale about a young prince's life in fairyland and his return to mortal life on earth, Fabula o ksiazeciu Adolfie, dziedzicu Roksolanii (probably an adaptation of Marie d'Aulnoy's L'Histoire d'Hippolyte, comte de Douglas, 1690). Several other lengthy romances in verse with very lengthy titles remained unpublished.

Works

Dusza po wielu grzechach zabierajac sie do poprawy zycia szuka po pustyniach S. Marii Egipcjanki, aby ja nauczyla sposobu pokuty szczerej i droge pokazala do szczesliwej wiecznosci [A Soul Seeking to Atone for Sins . . .] (1746). Opisanie zycia sw. Dawida, krola izraelskiego [Life Story of David, King of Israel] (written before 1750). (Reprinted in fragments by W. Kubacki in "Odrodzenie" 34 [1947]). Swieta Maria Magdalena jak wielka stala sie ohyda plci bialoglowskiej w grzechach swoich, tak wielka ozdoba w pokucie, stateczna w milosci Jezusa az do smierci krzyzowej [On Mary Magdalene's Sins and Redemption] (written before 1750). Do tegoz J.O. Ksiazecia (J.J. Zagulskiego) JMci na Biblioteke Publiczna warszawska [On the Warsaw Public Library] (written before 1750). Opisanie czterech czesci roku [Four Seasons Described] (before 1750). Forteca do Boga wystawiona, piacia bram zamknieta to jest dusza ludzka z piacia zmyslami [A Human Soul, with Its Five Senses, Is Like a Fortress Built for God, Enclosed Within Its Five Gates]. Snopek na polu zycia ludzkiego zwiazany [A Sheaf of Corn Assembled on the Field of Man's Life]. Trzy monarchinie [Three Queens]. Punkta do poprawienia zepsutych obyczajow polskich [Rules for Correcting Corrupted Morals of the Poles]. Pochwala lasow [In Praise of Forests]. Skargi kilku dam w spolnej kompanii bedacych, dla jakich racyi z mezami swojemi zyc nie chca [Several Ladies' Common Complaints Concerning the Reasons for Which They Refuse to Live with Their Husbands]. Zbior rytmow duchownych, panegirycznych, moralnych i swiatowych W. Imci Pani Elzbiety z Kowalskich Druzbackiej, skarbnikowej zydaczewskiej, zebrany i do druku podany . . . [Collected Verse] (1752).

Bibliography

Krzyzanowski, Julian, History of Polish Literature (Warsaw, 1978). Lange, A., Skarbiec poezji polskiej (Warsaw, 1903). Lange, A. "Lamus," vol. 4 (1912).

Maya Peretz

Denise Dubois-Jallais

(a.k.a. Denise D. Jallais, Denise Jallais)

Born 1931, France
Genre(s): poetry, biography, essay
Language(s): French

Denise Dubois-Jallais started to write poems as a teenager. At eighteen, she published her first volume of poems, Matin triste (Sad Morning), which received excellent critical response. She was noticed by Aragon and Elsa Triolet who encouraged her to pursue a literary career. Since then, she has published poetry regularly. In

1955, she won a contest in the prestigious women's magazine *Elle* (She) for having written an essay on her everyday life as a housewife. *Elle* dedicated one of its September 1955 issues entirely to her, and for many French middle-class housewives, she became a symbol of women's success and liberation. The magazine invited her to Paris where she visited the offices of *Elle*. She was won over by the work atmosphere and decided on the spot to become a journalist. The editor in chief hired her the same day and it is through her contributions to this very influential magazine that her name became widely known.

Denise Dubois-Jallais nonetheless continued her work as a poet, publishing several volumes of poetry, one of which, *Exaltation de la vie quotidienne* (Exaltation of Daily Life), received the Prix Louise Labé (Prize Louise Labé). *Exaltation* includes most of her previously published poems. She has another collection of poems in preparation.

Dubois-Jallais also published a biographical document on the attachée de presse Nicole Corbassière, *La Lionne assise* (The Sitting Lioness), another one on Hélène Lazareff, the founder and chief editor of *Elle*, *La Tzarine* (The Tzarine). With Mounia, she co-authored a biography of the famous French-West Indian model who worked for Givenchy and Yves Saint-Laurent.

Although Denise Dubois-Jallais' poetry shows real sensitivity and mastery, her journalistic career overshadows at the present time all of her other works. The publicity which surrounded her debuts and her exceptional ascension to journalism have somewhat made her a stereotype of all housewives' fantasy, without giving her all the recognition she truly deserves.

Works

Collections of Poems: *Matin triste* [Sad Morning] (1952). *L'Arbre et la Terre* [The Tree and the Earth] (1954). *Les Couleurs de la mer* [The Colors of the Sea] (1955). *La Cage* [The Cage] (1958). *Pour mes Chevaux sauvages* [For My Wild Horses] (1966). *Exaltation de la vie quotidienne* [Exaltation of Daily Life] (1976).

Documents: *La Lionne assise* [The Sitting Lioness] (1974). *La Tzarine* [The Tzarine] (1984). *Princesse Mounia* [Princess Mounia, co-authored with Mounia] (1987).

V. Lastinger

Stéphanie Ducrest, Countess of Genlis

Born January 25, 1746, Champercy, near
    Autun, France; died December 31, 1830,
    Paris
Genre(s): poetry, novel, tract, children's
    literature, drama, memoirs
Language(s): French

Mistress to the Duke of Orleans (later Philippe-Egalité), tutor to the future Louis Philippe I and his royal siblings, friend of Talleyrand, and correspondent to Napoleon, Stéphanie de Genlis was involved in political events from before the French Revolution through the Revolution of 1830. She was a prolific and popular writer of novels, educational tracts, children's literature, and personal memoirs. Her works total about 140 volumes.

Caroline-Stéphanie-Félicité Ducrest de Saint Aubin, Countess of Genlis and later Marquise of Sillery, lived a life lifted from romance. After her father's financial disaster, Genlis went to Paris, where at the age of ten she began to develop a lifelong taste for high society, theater, and learning; she also studied music avidly, devoting as many as ten hours a day to practice. Genlis was always a formidable presence; in Paris, her beautiful face and voice, plus her skill at playing the harp, became her ticket to aristocratic society. Genlis's marriage also belongs to the world of romance. Charles-Alexis Bruslart, who had seen a miniature of Genlis when he met her father in an English prison, went to Paris upon his release and fell in love with her; their marriage was secret, and met with strong opposition from his family. Genlis was seventeen.

Genlis became the mother of three children and a social phenomenon; she met the Duke of Chartres (later the Duke of Orleans, and finally Philippe-Egalité) and probably became his mistress. At thirty-one Genlis retired to Bellechasse with the Duke of Chartres' young princesses, her own children, and an "adopted daughter" who may have been Genlis' illegitimate daughter with the Duke; later, Genlis became tutor or "gouvernante" to the young princes, an unprecedented move that raised scandal.

During the tumult of the French Revolution, Genlis took the Princess Adelaide, her most devoted student, to safety in England, then brought her back to France at the Duke's insistence. Labeled as émigrés, Genlis and Adelaide were ordered to leave France and finally took refuge in a Swiss convent; Genlis' husband and the Duke of Orleans were both executed. From 1793 until 1800 she lived as an exile, often unwelcome, sometimes in danger, and always poor. Genlis received help from her son-in-law, from her protector General Dumouriez, and from her friend Talleyrand; she eked out her meager funds by painting, giving harp lessons, and by writing. She produced a great deal of work from 1794 on that sold readily. Finally Genlis was permitted to return to Paris, but had great difficulty adjusting to the now unfamiliar city.

In 1804 she received a pension from the emperor Napoleon and corresponded with him. In 1812 new editions of her works came out; Napoleon gave her the honorary title of Inspector of the schools in her Parisian borough. She lived through the Revolution of 1830; having seen her former student come to the throne as Louis-Philippe I and having expressed the opinion that he lacked the strength necessary to a king, she died.

A large number of Genlis' early writings concern education. Her *Theatre of Education* (1779–1780), the *Theatre of Society* (1781), *The Annals of Virtue* (1782), *Adelaide and Theodore, or Letters on Education* (1782), and *Tales of the Castle* (1784) all reflected her experience at Bellechasse; some characters in *Tales of the Castle* even bear the names of those children who listened to the stories. *Adelaide and Theodore* is a response to Rousseau's *Émile*. Rousseau's Sophie was a secondary character existing primarily as a future wife for Émile, but Genlis focuses on Adelaide's rather than on the boy's education. Genlis believed that since girls were born to a "monotonous and dependent life," they should receive their education at home from their mothers, preparing themselves for future life as wives who counsel their husbands wisely while remaining submissive to them, and as mothers who mold their own children's characters. Genlis believed, in opposition to Rousseau, that "man, if left to himself, would be necessarily vengeful and would consequently be lacking in spiritual nobility and generosity." The *Theatre of Educa-*

tion offers plentiful examples of young boys and girls who, exiled to convents, permitted to travel around Europe following fashion, or left to the care of a lazy governess, risk becoming incorrigible fools, liars, and gossips.

Genlis' *Theatre of Education* puts her principles into practice. Although the moral message of her little plays can be heavy-handed and although the good characters espouse only the most virtuous sentiments, the pleasure of histrionic performance is manifest. The plays are primarily for girls, although there are some parts for brothers and fathers.

While Genlis indulges a taste for melodrama, the importance of social responsibility is also hammered home. Even in "Beauty and the Monster," a reworking of the fairy tale, the heroine can overcome her aversion to the monster (who of course becomes a prince) not only because he loves her but because he charitably provides a haven for the "unhappy." From these plays one also glimpses the wisdom Genlis must have gained from her hard experience with court intrigue; "The Generous Enemies," for instance, shows how two devoted friends can be turned against one another by a scheming sister-in-law and a profligate husband. Most poignant, perhaps, is "The Good Mother" who is willing to separate from her best-loved daughter in order to make her a good match. Considering Genlis' closeness to her charges and their devotion to her, the plays' insistence on the primacy of a mother or governess who acts as mother is both touching and coercive.

Although Genlis' works for children stress the individual's power to save himself from bad habits and influences, her novels, written primarily during her exile and the years of poverty after her return to France, recognize more clearly the pernicious effects of illicit love and intrigue in the adult world. *The Knights of the Swan*, the first novel published during her exile, is different in form and intent from most of Genlis' novels. A highly artificial "troubadour novel" celebrating the old regime symbolically through the court of Charlemagne, the novel contrasts the constitutional monarchy of Charlemagne with the anarchic rebellion of the Saxons, who represent the Jacobins during the Reign of Terror. Genlis apparently hoped to ingratiate herself with the

French émigrés as well as to earn badly-needed money. Her best known historical novels, *La Duchesse de la Vallière* (1804) and *Mademoiselle de Clermont* (1802) (often considered her best novel) are more melodramatic.

In *The Influence of Women on French Literature*, Genlis argues that women are suited not to epic or tragedy, but to "real actions." Genlis takes her own advice in three novels dealing with unmarried mothers: *The Rival Mothers* (1806), *Alphonsine* (1806), and *Alphonse* (1809). Her choice of this topic is especially interesting because Pamela, Genlis' adopted daughter, was rumored to be her illegitimate child, fathered by the Duke of Orleans. The mothers in these novels, having become entangled in illicit affairs, resist attempts to deprive them of their children; eventually they give the children to the care of another family but supervise their education, either at close quarters or from afar.

Genlis' *Memoirs* came out in 1825; and although they contain inaccuracies caused by failure of memory or Genlis' need to justify herself, they contain valuable information about people and events of the eighteenth century. In her last years, Genlis hoped to rewrite Diderot's *Encyclopedia* in order to make it reflect orthodox religious and moral principles. Her reverence for religion and morality remained unshaken.

Genlis' educational works were popular in England during the 1780s and went through multiple editions but were less popular in the nineteenth century. Her novels sold well, but she was treated with contempt by later Victorian critics. The contradiction between Genlis' devotion to religion, morality, and feminine submission and her social and literary career, plus the close relationship between her life and art, make her a fascinating subject for study.

Works

Théâtre à l'usage des jeunes personnes (1779–1780). *Théâtre de Société* (1781). *Les Annales de la Vertu ou cours d'histoire à l'usage des jeunes personnes* (1782). *Adèle et Théodore ou Lettres sur l'éducation* (1782). *Les Veillées du Château ou cours de morale à l'usage des enfants par l'auteur d'Adèle et Théodore* (1784). *Discours sur la suppression des Couvens de religieuses et l'éducation publique des femmes* (1791). *Lecons d'une Gouvernante à ses Elèves* (1791). *Les Chevaliers du Cygne ou la cour de Charlemagne* (1795). *Précis de la conduite de Madame de Genlis depuis la Révolution* (1796). *Les Petits Émigrés ou Correspondence de quelques enfants* (1798). *Les Voeux téméraires ou L'enthousiasme* (1799). *La Petit La Bruyère ou Caractères et moeurs de ce siècle à l'usage des enfants* (1799). *Les Mères Rivales ou la Calomnie* (1800). *Nouvelle heures à l'usage des enfants* (1801). *Nouvelle méthode d'Ensignement pour la première enfance* (1801). *Projet d'une Ecole rurale pour l'éducation des filles* (1801). *Mademoiselle de Clermont, Nouvelle Historique* (1802). *L'Epouse impertinente par air, suivet de Mari corrupteur et de la femme philosophe* (1804). *Souvenirs de Félicie L.* (1804). *La Duchesse de la Vallière* (1804). *Le Comte de Corke ou la séduction sans artifice* (1805). *Madame de Maintenon* (1806). *Alphonsine ou la Tendresse maternelle* (1806). *Suite des Souvenirs de Félicie* (1807). *La Siège de La Rochelle ou le Malheur de la conscience* (1807). *Bélisaire* (1808). *Sainclair ou la victime des Sciences et des Arts* (1808). *Alphonse ou le Fils naturel* (1809). *La maison rustique* (1810). *De l'Influence des femmes sur la littérature française comme protectrices des Lettres ou comme auteurs* (1811). *Les Bergères de Madian ou la Jeunesse de Moise* (1812). *Mademoiselle de La Fayette, ou le Siècle de Louis XIII* (1813). *Les Hermites des Marais Pontins* (1814). *Histoire de Henri le Grand* (1815). *Jeanne de France, Nouvelle Historique* (1816). *Le Journal de la Jeunesse* (1816). *Les Battuecas* (1816). *Dictionnaire critique et raisonné des étiquettes de la Cour, usages du monde, etc.* (1818). *Les Voyages poétiques d'Eugène et d'Antonine* (1818). *Almanach de la Jeunesse en vers et en prose* (1819). *Les Parvenus ou les Aventures de Julien Delmours* (1819). *Pétrarque et Laure* (1819). *L'Intrépide* (1820). *Le Siècle de Louis XIV* (1820). *Palmyre et Flaminie* (1821). *Six Nouvelles morales et Religieuses* (1821). *Les Jeux champêtres des Enfants* (1821). *Six Nouvelles morales et religieuses* (1821). *Les Veillées de la chaumière* (1823). *Les Dîners du baron d'Holbach* (1822). *Les Prisonniers* (1824). *Mémoires inédits sur le 18e siècle et la Revolution Française* (1825). *Oeuvres Complètes* (1825). *Thérésina ou l'Enfant de la Providence* (1826). *Inès de Castro, nouvelle suivie de la mort de Pline* (1826). *Les Soupers de la Maréchale de Luxembourg* (1828). *Le Dernier Voyage de Nelgis ou*

Mémoires d'un vieillard (1828). *Manuel de la jeune feMme Guide Complet de la maîtresse de maison* (1829). *Athénaïs ou le Château de Coppet en 1807* (posthumous) (1831). *Lettres inédits de Mme de Genlis à son fils adoptif Casimir Baecker* (1902). *Dernieres lettres d'amour. Correspondence inedites de la comtesse de Genlis avec le comte Anatole de Montesquiou* (1954).

Translations: *Theatre of Education* (1781). *Adelaide and Theodore: or Letters on Education* (1783). *The Beauty and the Monster* (1785). *Hagar in the Desert* (1785). *Sacred Dramas*, tr. Thomas Holcroft, in *Three Centuries of Drama: England, 1751–1800* (1785). *Tales of the Castle* , tr. Thomas Holcroft (1785). *Adventures of Alphonso after the Destruction of Lisbon* (1787). *The Beauties of Genlis* (1787). *Lessons of a Governess to her Pupils* (1792). *The Knights of the Swan; or, the Court of Charlemagne* (1796). *Short Account of the Conduct of Mme de Genlis, since the Revolution* (1796). *The History of the Duchess of C—* (1798). *Alphonso and Dalinda: or, The Magic of Art and Nature*, tr. Thomas Holcroft (1799). *Rash Vows: or The Effects of Enthusiasm* (1799). *The Young Exiles; or, Correspondence of Some Juvenile Emigrants* (1799). *La Bruyere the Less: or, Characters and Manners of the Children of the Present Age* (1800). *A New Method of Instruction for Children* (1800). *The Rival Mothers* (1800). *The Depraved Husband and the Philosophic Wife* (1803). *Panrose; or The Palace and the Cottage* (1803). *The Castle of Kolmeras, to Which Is Added Ida Molten* (1804). *The Duchess of la Valliere* (1804). *Alphonsine: or, Maternal Affection* (1806). *Madame de Maintenon* (1806). *The Juvenile Theater* (1807). *The Duke of Lazun; an Historical Romance* (1808). *The Earl of Cork: or, Seduction without Artifice* (1808). *Recollections of Felicia L.* (1808). *The Siege of Rochelle; or, The Christian Heroine* (1808). *The Traveller's Companion* (1809). *Belisarius; a Historical Romance* (1810). *Sainclair, or The Victim to the Arts and Sciences* (1813). *Mademoiselle de La Fayette, an Historical Novel* (1814). *Jane of France, an Historical Novel* (1816). *A Manual Containing the Expressions Most Used in Travelling* (1817). *Placide, A Spanish Tale* (1817). *The Solitary Family: or, The Norman Hut*, in Garret, William, *A Right Pleasant and Famous Book of Histories* (1818). *Petrarch and Laura* (1820). *Six Tales, Moral and Religious* (1822). *Child of Nature*, tr. Elizabeth Inchbald, in *Three Centuries of Drama: English, 1751–1800* (1825). *Memoirs of the Countess de Genlis* (1825). *New Moral Tales* (1825). *Eugene and Lolotte; a Tale for Children* (1828). *Joseph and his Brothers; Fruits of a Good Education*, in *Three Centuries of Drama: American* (1843).

Bibliography

Broglie, Gabriel de, *Madame de Genlis* (1985). Dobson, Austin, *Four Frenchwomen* (1891). Harmand, Jean, *Mme de Genlis* (1912). Jimack, P.D., "The Paradox of Sophie and Julie: Contemporary Response to Rousseau's Ideal Wife and Mother," in Eva Jacobs et al., *Women and Society in Eighteenth-Century France: Essays in Honor of John Stephenson Spink* (1979), pp. 152–165. Krakeur, Lester Gilbert, "Le Théâtre de Mme de Genlis." *Modern Language Review* 35 (1940): 185–192. Krief, Huguette, "Madame de Genlis et le Roman Troubadour." *Licorne* 6 (1982): 313–335. Laborde, Alice M., *L'Oeuvre de Madame de Genlis* (1966). Mittmann, Barbara G., "Women and the Theatre Arts," in Samia I. Spencer, ed., *French Women and the Age of Enlightenment* (1984), pp. 155–169. Naudin, Marie, "Une Avocate des mères célébataires et des enfants naturels: Mme de Genlis." *Kentucky Romance Quarterly* 30 (1983): 349–358. Nikliborc, Ana, "L'Oeuvre de Madame de Genlis." *Acta Universitatis Wratislaviensis* 96, IV (1969). Raaphorst, Madeleine R., "Adele Versus Sophie: The Well Educated Woman of Mme de Genlis." *Rice University Studies* 64 (1978): 41–50. Reish, Joseph G., "Mme de Genlis and the Early American Stage: New Perspectives in the History and Thematics of American Drama." *Proceedings of the Pacific Northwest Conference on Foreign Languages* 28, i (1977): 22–25. Reish, Joseph G., "Myth in the Age of Reason: Mme de Genlis and the Pygmalion Theme." *Papers in Romance* 2 (1980): 172–181. Rowbotham, Arnold H., "Madame de Genlis and Jean-Jacques Rousseau." *Modern Language Quarterly* 3 (1942): 363–377. Saint-Beuve, Charles Augustin, *Nouvelle Galerie de femmes célèbres* (1865), pp. 527–544. Sanders, Jean Butler, "Madame de Genlis and Juvenile Fiction in England." *DAI* 36 (1966): 3936. Spencer, Samia I., "Women and Education," in Samia I. Spencer, *French Women and the Age of Enlightenment* (1984), pp. 83–96. Truchet, Jacques, *Théâtre du XVIIIᵉ Siècle* (1974): 943–969. Viguié, Pierre, "Una drame à Chantilly." *Revue des Deux Mondes* (15 April, 1968): 531–536. Wahba, Magdi, "Madame de Genlis in England." *Comparative Literature* 13 (1961): 221–238. Walker, T.C., "Madame de Genlis and Rousseau." *Romantic Review* 43 (1952): 95–108.

General references: Michaud, Joseph Francois, *Biographie Universelle*, XVI, 156–177. *The New Grove Dictionary of Music and Musicians* (1980): 233–234.

Christy Desmet

Madame du Deffand

Born September 25, 1697, Château de Chamrond, France; died September 23, 1780, Paris
Genre(s): letters
Language(s): French

Daughter of Gaspard and Anne Brulard de Vichy de Chamrond, she married Jean-Baptiste de La Lande, Marquis du Deffand, 1719. Marie Anne de Vichy de Chamrond, whom history knows as Mme du Deffand, was born in her family's chateau in Burgundy in 1696, a daughter of an ancient, though not rich, family. Her mother died when she was a child, and she had two elder brothers and a younger sister. Her father, although a nobleman, was concerned solely with tending his land. At the age of five Marie was sent to a convent in Paris, a well-known establishment for girls of noble families, where she was to spend twelve years. Since the only goal of the girls' education was acquiring the social graces necessary to the courtly society, Mlle de Vichy was taught barely more than how to read and write, a situation that troubled her greatly in her later years. Her teachers in their turn were astonished by her total indifference to religion and her rebellious, independent spirit.

When Marie was twenty-one, her father arranged her marriage to the Marquis du Deffand. Even the first weeks of marriage disappointed the young wife, who found her husband hopelessly dull. Remarkable for her beauty and wit, she tried to find amusement in parties, gambling, and love affairs at the court of the Regent, the Duc d'Orléans. Her behavior was scandalous even for her dissolute society, so that in 1724 she and her husband separated for good. However, the mul-

titude of her love affairs was not the result of a passionate but, on the contrary, of a cold, cynical nature, desperately trying to escape the boredom that was to plague her all her life.

After the death of the Regent in 1723 Mme du Deffand attached herself to the court of the Duchesse du Maine, a royal princess exiled from Paris because of her political intrigues. The Duchesse gathered round herself a court of various people not welcome to the royal court, such intellectuals as Voltaire among them. There the unparalleled wit and intelligence of Mme du Deffand could find full scope.

Mme du Deffand's income was not great for a woman of her class, for her dowry was under the control of her husband. She had only enough to keep a small apartment with a few servants in Paris. Yet it was enough for her to open a salon. Soon her fame was rivalled only by that of Mme Geoffrin, another great salonnière who was not, however, of noble birth. Mme du Deffand was visited on equal terms by the aristocracy and by the foremost intellectuals of that era—Voltaire, Montesquieu, d'Alembert, Diderot. Even foreigners travelling through Paris would beg to be introduced to her.

In 1750 M. du Deffand died. His death left his widow in comfortable financial circumstances, so that she moved into a larger, better set of rooms in the convent of Saint Joseph, henceforth one of the most famous apartments in Europe. Yet, despite her social success, the rest of her life held many misfortunes for her. In 1752 she became blind. She spent a few months in her native place in Burgundy, now owned by her brother. There she met Julie de Lespinasse, her brother's illegitimate daughter by his own mother-in-law, an exceptionally intelligent girl of twenty. Mme du Deffand took a great liking for her young niece. Since the blind marquise needed a companion, two years later she installed Mlle de Lespinasse in Paris in an apartment below her own.

Mlle de Lespinasse was, unfortunately, too talented a companion. Certain guests of Mme du Deffand, mostly the Encyclopaedists led by d'Alembert, liked her conversation so well that little by little they started spending some time in her apartment before visiting her mistress. In 1764, when the egoistic Mme du Deffand found it out, she considered it an act of betrayal and threw her young relative out of her house. Many friends of Mme du Deffand considered her unjust, dissociated themselves from her, and started visiting the salon that Julie now opened, which was to become perhaps the most brilliant of all. One of them was d'Alembert, despite his long friendship with Mme du Deffand, because he was then and ever after in love with Mlle de Lespinasse.

This was a shattering blow for Mme du Deffand's pride. However, she could not really grieve that the Encyclopaedists had left her. Although her spirit was intensely skeptical, her outlook was conservative, and she had always received the progressive thinkers only because of d'Alembert, whom she greatly liked and admired. She continued to keep her salon, but from then on not the intellectuals but the worldly, aristocratic representatives of the old, reactionary views visited her. In consequence Mme du Deffand complained that the conversation had become dull. Even worse was to follow. In her sixty-eighth year the blind old woman fell passionately in love for the first time and with a man twenty years younger than herself, the English writer Horace Walpole, who visited Paris periodically. Naturally, although he liked her and cultivated her friendship, he did not reciprocate her passion.

The old age of Mme du Deffand was extremely unhappy. The carefree society of her youth had given place to the new, serious and progressive spirit, which she did not like, her old friends were dead or not living in Paris, the man she loved did not love her, she suffered from boredom, insomnia, and melancholy. Finally, in 1780 she departed the life she found so intolerable.

After her death the publication of Mme du Deffand's letters to various people—mostly to Voltaire, her intimate friend the Duchesse de Choiseul, and Horace Walpole—established her as one of the greatest writers of the eighteenth century by virtue of the incomparable elegance and precision of her style. But even without her letters she would live in history as the mistress of one of the greatest salons of her age, and a most interesting human being—a supremely intelligent and unhappy woman, who, in spite of the many advantages she possessed, was tormented all her life by pessimism, cynicism, and, most of all, boredom.

Works

Letters of the Marquise du Deffand to Horace Walpole, ed. Mary Berry., 4 vols. (1810). *Correspondance complète de la marquise du Deffand avec ses amis, le Président Hénault, Montesquieu, d'Alembert, Voltaire, Horace Walpole*, ed. M. de Lescure, 2 vols. (1865). *Correspondance de Mme du Deffand avec la duchesse de Choiseul, l'Abbé Barthélémy et M. Craufurt, publiée avec un introduction par M. le Marquis de Sainte-Aulaire*, 3 vols. (1866). *Lettres de la Marquise du Deffand à Horace Walpole*, ed. Mrs. Paget Toynbee, 3 vols. (1912). *Madame du Deffand: Lettres à Voltaire*, ed. Joseph Trabucco (1922). *Letters to and from Madame du Deffand and Julie de Lespinasse*, ed. Warren Hunting Smith (1938). *Horace Walpole's correspondence with Madame du Deffand and Wiart*, ed. W. S. Lewis and Warren Hunting Smith, 6 vols. (1939).

Bibliography

Aimery de Pierrebourg, Marguerite, *Madame du Deffand* (1933). Bellessort, André, "Le Salon de Madame du Deffand." *Les Grands Salons littéraires* (1928). Duisit, Lionel, *Madame du Deffand* (1963). Doscot, Gérard, *Madame du Deffand* (1967). Giraud, Victor, "La sensibilité de Madame du Deffand." *Revue des deux Mondes* VIII, xvi, pp. 688–703. Glotz, M. and M. Maire, *Salons du XVIIIe siècle* (1938). Klerks, Wilhelm, *Madame du Deffand, Essai sur l'ennui* (1961). Koven, Anna de, *Horace Walpole et Madame du Deffand* (1929). Rageot, Gaston, *Madame du Deffand* (1933). Ségur, P. M. M., *Madame du Deffand et sa famille* (1906). Strachey, Giles Lytton, *Books and Characters* (1922), pp. 81–111.

Neda Jeni

Anne Duden

Born 1942, Berlin, West Germany
Genre(s): short story
Language(s): German

Anne Duden was born in Berlin in 1942 and spent her childhood there and in East Germany. She moved to Oldenburg in West Germany with her parents in 1953, where she lived until 1962.

Then she returned to West Berlin again. In 1978 she began to live mostly in London, but she has kept her main domicile in Berlin. She belongs to the younger generation of contemporary German writers and has published two volumes of short stories so far. In 1982 appeared the collection *Übergang* (Transformation) containing *Das Landhaus* (The Country Home), *Herz and Mund* (Heart and Mouth), *Chemische Reaktion* (Chemical Reaction), *Übergang* (Transformation), *Tag and Nacht* (Day and Night), *Der Auftrag, Die Liebe* (The Order and Love), *On Holiday, Die Kunst zu ertrinken* (The Art of Drowning). This was followed by the collection *Das Judasschaf* (The Judas Sheep—the Scapegoat), 1985, containing *E guerra e morte* (Both War and Death), *Panorama Berlin, New York, mit einem Schrei* (New York, with a Scream), and *Der anhaltend letzte Blick* (The Continously Last Look). In 1982 she received the Literary Award of the German Literary Fund. Her short stories deal with the complex interrelationship between the external and internal human self, the intricacies of the human mind trying to cope with subliminal fears and perversion. Death and fear of death and the individual's problem of correlating his self with the external world of the human society are highlighted. Duden is obsessed with images of sickness and decay of the human body. Social and historical aspects are combined with images of concentration camps, mass hysteria, and total negation of the individual by society. In many of her short stories Anne Duden develops a surprising microscopic geography of the human body, on which and in which the main actions take place. Her texts are superb exercises in contemporary German language and impress by their stylistic sophistication.

Works

Übergang [Transformation] (1982). *Das Judasschaf* [The Judas Sheep—the Scapegoat] (1985).
Translation: *Opening of the Mouth*, tr. Della Couling (1985).

Bibliography

Gespräche mit Erich Fried und Anne Duden, ed. Sommeruniversität Toscana/Christoph Klimke/ Jürgen Doppelstein (Berlin, 1985).

Albrecht Classen

Adelaide-Gillette Dufrenoy

Born December 3, 1765, Paris, France; died March 7/8, 1825, Paris
Genre(s): poetry, non-fiction
Language(s): French

Born the daughter of a Parisian jeweler, Mme Dufrenoy received an excellent education early in her life, learning Latin well enough to translate Horace and Virgil, and gaining an appreciation of French verse from a M. Laya, a literary gentleman of some reputation. This gave her an early start and interest in the field of the letters; one that carried through until her death. In 1780 she married an attorney, M. Petit-Dufrenoy, who cultivated her interests in the arts. Her first poem appeared anonymously in the *Almanach des Muses* (Almanac of the Muses) in 1787, "Boulade a un ami." This was followed by a fairly successful play in 1788, *L'Amour chasse* (or *exile*) *des cieux* (Hunted Love of the Heavens).

The Revolution brought an end to her husband's position, however. His health deteriorated, and he died in 1812, sick and almost blind. Mme Dufrenoy lived on, taking care of a son and daughter, while producing the majority of her works, which show a remarkable diversity and power. Two years after the death of her husband, she won a prize from the French Academy for the poem "Dernier moment de Bayard" (Final Moments of Bayard). Her literary work continued until her death in 1825 with much of her latter work focused on childhood and the art of motherhood.

Works

Opuscules poetiques (1806). *Elegies* (1st ed., 1807). *La femme auteur, ou les inconvenients de la celebrite* (1812). *Elegies* (2nd ed., 1813). *La tour de monde* (1814). *Entrennes a ma fille* (1815). *La petite menagere* (1816). *L'Enfance eclaree, ou les vertus et les vices* (1816). *Biographie des jeunes demoiselles* (1816). *Les Francaises nouvelles* (1818). *Les Converstions maternelles* (1818). *Cabinet du petit naturaliste* (1818). *Le livre du premier age* (1822). *Elegies* (3rd ed., 1821). *Les livres des femmes* (1823). *Beautes de l'histoire de la Grece moderne* (1825). *Oeuvres poetiques* (1827). Mme Dufrenoy was also involved in the following projects: *Bibliotheque choisie pour les femmes* (1818–1821),

Hommage aux demoiselles (1818–1827), and *La Minerve litteraire* (1820–1821).

Bibliography

Gerinal, F., *Dernier vers de Mme Dufrenoy* (1825). de Pongerville, M., *Revue encyclopedique* (1825). Jay, M. A., "Observations sur la vie et les oeuvrages de Mme Dufrenoy." *Oeuvres poetiques* (1827).

Stephen Wood

Inez Van Dullemen

Born November 13, 1925, Amsterdam, The Netherlands
Genre(s): novel, travelogue
Language(s): Dutch

Daughter of the Dutch writer Jo de Wit, Van Dullemen was a speech therapist before she started teaching in a theater school and, with her husband Erik Vos, she cooperated on several theater projects.

Van Dullemen leaves her Den Haag home regularly with her family to embark on her many travels, most often to North America. Her travel experiences form the most important recurring theme in her works. Her travel stories (e.g., *Eeuwige Dag, Eeuwige Nacht* [1981; Eternal Day, Eternal Night]) have a documentary quality that combine experience with creative perception.

In her novels, one of Van Dullemen's major interests is the experience of her women characters, even though she rejects the categorization of a separate "women's experience." Van Dullemen engages in such contemporary problems as the nature-civilization conflict (pollution), and the problem of the blacks in the United States. One of her major works, *Vroeger is Dood* (1976; The Past Is Dead) is a response to her mother's experience in a rest home. For this novel she received the much coveted Special Prize of the Jan Campen Foundation.

Her novel *Het Gevorkte Beest* (1986; The Forked Beast) is based on Van Dullemen's theater experiences; the main character, the director Raymond, pushes his actors to self-confrontation although he does not succeed in confronting himself. This book is one of her best, but unfortunately it duplicates the plot and style of Harry Mulisch's *Hoogste Tijd* (1985; Highest Time). A very versatile author with a great variability of styles, Van Dullemen does not allow easy categorization, remaining both elusive and productive.

Works

Novels: *Ontmoeting met de Andere* (1949). *Het Wiel* (1950). *Het Verzuim* (1954). *De schaduw van de Regen* (1960). *Een Hand vol Vonken* (1961, 1969). *Luizenjournaal* (1969, rept. 1979 as De Honger heeft Veel Gezichten). *Vroeger is Dood* (1976). *Oog is Oog* (1977). *Een Ezelsdroom* (1977). *De Vrouw met de Vogelkop* (1979). *Eeuwige Dag, Eeuwige Nacht* (1981). *Na de Orkaan en Andere Verhalen* (1983). *Een Zwarte Hand op Mijn Borst* (1983). *Het Gevorkte Beest* (1986).
Plays: *God op Aarde* (1972).

Bibliography

Bousset, H., in *Woord en Schroom*. Brugge (1977). Veerman, J.W., in *Uitgelezen 6. Reacties op Boeken* ('s-Gravenhage, 1982).

An Lammens

C. Dunca

(see: Constanța Dunca-Şchiau)

C. de Dunca

(see: Constanța Dunca-Şchiau)

Constanța Dunca-Şchiau

(a.k.a. Camille d'Alb, E.D. Albon, C. Dunca, C. de Dunca, Xanta)

Born 1843, Botoşani, Romania; place and date of death unknown
Genre(s): essay, novel, short story, drama, poetry, translation
Language(s): Romanian, French

Constanța Dunca-Şchiau studied in Paris (Collège de France) and Vienna and published a number of articles in French journals. She then returned to Romania and worked as a Professor of Morals and Education at the *Şcoala centrală de fete* (The Central College for Girls) in Bucharest from 1863 to 1872. In 1863 she presented to the Legislative Chamber and to Alexandru Ioan Cuza, who was then reigning over the newly proclaimed Romanian nation, a project for reorganizing girls' education that was taken into account when the Law of Public Instruction was drafted in 1864. This project, published under the title *Fiicele poporului* (1863; The Daughters of the Nation) was also acknowledged by a national prize granted by Al. I. Cuza.

Constanţa Dunca-Şchiau lectured on women's education in several towns of Romania as well as at Vienna and Budapest. In 1904 she published the book *Feminismul în România* (Feminism in Romania). Between 1863–1865 and in 1868 she directed the publication *Amicul familiei* (The Friend of the Family).

In the play *Martira inimei* (1870; A Martyr of Her Heart), Constanţa Dunca-Şchiau criticized the law that interdicted the pursuit of paternity and condemned the state for tolerating and in a sense encouraging the lack of responsibility of father toward child. A young woman, abandoned by the father of her child and chased by her parents goes mad and kills the infant. The comedy *Motiv de despărţenie sau Ce deputat!* (1871; Reason for Separation or What a Deputy!) confronts women's strength with men's weakness.

Under the pseudonym Camille d'Alb, Constanţa Dunca-Şchiau wrote a novel in French—*Eléna* (1862), which was later translated in Romanian under the title *Elena Mănescu*. Other works such as the thriller *Omul negru* (1863; The Black Man) or the historic novel *Radu al III-lea cel Frumos* (1864–1865; Radu the Third the Beautiful) were meant to pave the way for a large cycle called *Sub vălul Bucureştilor* (Under the Veil of Bucharest). A first volume of this cycle was prepared for publication in 1865 under the title *O familie din Bucureşti. Iezuiţii României* (A Family from Bucharest. Romania's Jesuits).

Author of poems and short stories as well, translator into Romanian of the Duchesse de Duras, D. Gastinneau, Rousseau, Malherbe, Ossian, and Pushkin, Constanţa Dunca-Şchiau is mostly acclaimed for her vigorous and fruitful writing on behalf of women's human, social, and cultural rights.

Works

Fiicele poporului [The Daughters of the Nation] (1863). *Femeia femeiei* [Woman's Woman] (1863). "Estella," *Amicul familiei* I (1863): 1–8. "Omul negru" [The Black Man]. *Amicul familiei* I (1863): 9–18. "Radu al III-lea cel Frumos" [Radu the Third the Beautiful]. *Amicul familiei* II (1864): 13–14; II (1865): 18–19. "Fiica zidarului" [The Daughter of the Brick Layer]. *Amicul familiei* II (1865): 20; III (1865): 30–31. "O familie din Bucureşti. Iezuiţii României [A Family from Bucharest. Romania's Jesuits]. *Amicul familiei* III (1865): 30–31. "Fiica adoptată" [The Adopted Daughter]. *Amicul familiei* III (1868): 1–5. *Martira inimei* [The Martyr of Her Heart] (1870). *Motiv de despărţenie sau Ce deputat!* [Reason for Separation or What a Deputy!] (1871). *La Alma. Poveşti noi pentru copii* [At Alma. New Stories for Children] (1881). *Feminismul în România* [Feminism in Romania] (1904).

Bibliography

Chendi, Ilarie, *Portrete literare* (Bucharest): 48. Creţu, Stănuţa, *Dicţionarul literaturii romăne de la origini pînă la 1900* (Bucharest, 1979), pp. 308–309. Vârgolici, Şt. G., "Constanţa Dunca, *Martira inimei*." *Convorbiri literare* V (1871), p. 3. Xenopol, A.D., "Conferinţa domnişoarei Constanţa Dunca asupra *Femeii*." *Convorbiri literare* IV (1870), 13.

Sanda Golopentia

Amandine-Aurore-Lucie Dupin, Baronne Dudevant

(a.k.a. George Sand, Jules Sand)

Born July 1, 1804, Paris, France; died June 8, 1876, Nohant
Genre(s): novel, essay, tale, drama, political articles, letters, autobiography
Language(s): French

Born into the provincial aristocracy, Aurore was raised by her paternal grandmother, an admirer of Rousseau, at the family château de Nohant in Berry and educated at the Couvent des Anglaises in Paris. She returned to Nohant where she was allowed the freedom to develop intellectually and to become acquainted with provincial life. She resumed reading Rousseau, Shakespeare, Byron, Chateaubriand, and other Romantics whose influence on her literary style and romantic point of view was apparent from the beginning of her writing career. In 1822 she married the baron Dudevant, a coarse, narrow-minded retired army officer. After eight years of loveless marriage and two children, she fled to Paris where she took up the bohemian life and tried to earn her living by writing. Dressed like a man ("in order to be free," she said), smoking cigarettes, and engaging in a series of amorous liaisons (usually with younger men), Aurore soon made her reputation as a "free spirit" and a writer. It took courage for her to live an independent life, earning her own living, and openly defying public morality. In 1831 she wrote, "I am embarking on the stormy sea of literature. I need to live. . . . [Social] conventions are rules for people without soul and without virtue. [Public] opinion is a prostitute who gives herself to those who pay her most dearly." Thus, Aurore launched her long and productive career which falls into roughly three phases: the Romantic period when she attacked society and decried the restricted lives of women; her support of the various "isms" that would lead to a better (utopian) society; the idyllic pastoral novels which were set in her native Berry, and also the more prosaic novels of manners.

In 1831 she collaborated with her lover, Jules Sandeau, on a novel, *Rose et blanche, ou la Comédienne et la religieuse* (1831; Rose and White, or the Comedienne and the Nun), using the pseudonym "Jules Sand." Writing alone for the first time under the name George Sand, she published a romantic novel, *Indiana* (1832) [in English, 1935], which was the first of her successful works. As was her writing, this novel was based on personal experience, though she denied it was a self-portrait. However, one can find the author in all her works—the independent individual, sensitive, misunderstood, and suffering from societal restrictions. Themes of romantic passion dominated the first phase of her literary career which included her novels *Indiana* and *Valentine* (1832) [in English, 1902], *Lélia* (1833), *Jacques* (1834) [in English, 1847], and *Mauprat* (1837) [in English, 1847]. Trapped in an unhappy marriage and personally affected by the legal and social inequalities that limited women's choice of lifestyle, she proclaimed their right to pursue free and unshackled lives. Her early novels were considered immoral in the 1830s; she advocated the emancipation of women, justified and even idealized adultery, and described the Romantic idea of passion as

the motive force in life. Her own turbulent liaison with Alfred de Musset was described in *Lettres d'une voyageur* (1834–1836) [1847; Letters of a Traveller]; their disastrous trip to Italy, during which they both engaged in outside sexual ventures, terminated their affair and provided the material for her novel, *Elle et lui* (1859) [1902; She and He]. While suing for a legal separation from Dudevant (c. 1840), Sand was involved in a lengthy, stormy affair with Frederick Chopin; their exasperating visit to the island of Majorca became the subject of her novel, *Un Hiver à Majorque* (1841) [1956; Winter in Majorca]. During this first period her writing always reflected the men and ideas that were most prominent in her life. Her characters struggled against conventional mores imposed on the individual and flaunted their romantic passions in the face of public censure, just as Sand herself did. That she preferred the company of men to women is evident in her love affairs and documented in her novels.

Sand's association with Félicité-Robert de Lamennais, Pierre Leroux, Michel de Bourges, Charles-Augustin Saint-Beuve, and others convinced her that the artist should take an active role in social reform. During the second phase of her literary career, Sand produced a number of novels denouncing the evils of class distinctions, marriage, and property. She also despised revealed religion and social customs that restricted people's lives and interfered with relations between the sexes. Socialism, humanitarianism, and republicanism were enthusiastically embraced; her works such as *Spiridon* (1838), *Le Sept Cordes de la lyre* (1839), *Le compagnon du tour de France* (1840) [1847; The Journeyman Joiner; or The Companion of the Tour de France], *Consuelo* (1842–1843) [in English, 1846], *La comtesse de Rudolstadt* (1843–1845) [1847; The Countess of Rudolstadt], and *Le Meunier d'Angibault* (1845) [1863; The Miller of Angibault], included portraits of her friends and distillations of their theories on the regeneration of society. Her advocacy of democracy and glorification of plebeian virtues dismayed the entrenched bourgeoisie as had Sand's espousal of complete sexual freedom. In her novel, *Spiridon*, Leroux's vague humanitarianism appears as a deistic religion that would supplant Christianity.

This theme is treated in a more philosophical vein in *Sept Cordes de la lyre*, the lyre symbolizing the harmony to which humanity ought to aspire. Harmony through socialism was one of the themes of *Consuelo* and its inferior sequel, *La Comtesse de Rudolstadt*; a melange of discussions on the occult and free-masonry, the transmigration of souls, the brotherhood of man, and of course, the suffering endured by lovers are skillfully blended into a unique pseudo-philosophical utopia. In *Meunier d'Angibault*, Sand attacks inequality due to birth and wealth. The working class hero and the upper-class woman he loves rid themselves of the burden of her fortune and find fulfillment in spreading the gospel of brotherhood. Here socialism is treated in less mystical, more concrete terms.

After 1839 Sand lived a rather bourgeois, though not sedate, existence at her home in Berry. She continued to write, tended to her household, played hostess to her friends, and spent time with her grandchildren. However, the Revolution of 1848 lured her back to Paris. She welcomed the revolution, and she edited and wrote articles for the *Bulletin de la République* under the direction of Ledru-Rollin. A group of republican feminists nominated Sand for the National Assembly in 1848 without her consent; she refused this "honor" for she did not believe a woman's place was in politics. She felt she served the people by her writing on social problems and editing the *Bulletin*, but she was not prepared to expose herself to the rigors of the masculine political arena. Her idealism was soon dashed by the insurrections of June 1848 and the bloody civil war; the coup d'état of Louis Napoleon Bonaparte finished off any hope for a more equitable, free society, and Sand returned to Nohant. Her interest now turned to the pastoral novel, the genre in which Sand made a major contribution to literature.

La Mare au diable (1846) [1890; The Haunted Pool] is the first and perhaps best of her rustic novels that are considered masterpieces of regionalist literature. Sand was no longer bent on reforming the world. In clear, graceful, and quiet language the author depicted the natural beauty of her province, peopled with slightly idealized and sanitized countryfolk. In *La Petite Fadette* (1849; Little Fadette; A Domestic Story), *François*

le Champi (1850) [1889; Francis the Waif], and *Les Maîtres sonneurs* (1852) [1890; The Bagpipers] Sand set the standard for French provincial literature. She changed her attitude toward literature during this period: "In the arts the most simple is the noblest thing to try, but the most difficult to attain." There is a poetic perfection in these works, a successful combination of narrative skill and the characterization of "real" people with human problems. Sand had fashioned the regional novel and given the peasant a prominent place in literature unequalled by earlier writers. After 1860 she turned to the more mannered and less individualistic novel; *Jean de la Roche* (1859), *le Marquis de Villemer* (1861) [1871; The Marquis de Villemer], and *Les Beaux messieurs de Bois-Doré* (1858) [1890; The Gallant Lords of Bois-Doré] are Romantic in style but also more predictable in plot and character development.

Another important literary contribution made by this prolific and creative artist was her correspondence (edited by Georges Lubin, 1964–1985) which comprises 20 volumes. Her *Histoire de ma vie* [Story of my life] in 4 volumes (1854–1855) is also interesting for her frank assessments of her contemporaries; she admired Dumas fils and Flaubert, hated Mérimée and disliked Balzac. For over 40 years Sand produced a torrent of novels, tales, essays, and plays. The latter were enthusiastically received by her contemporaries but are of scant interest today. Her writing style was effortless and lyrically descriptive; she wrote with conviction and an idealism and sensuality that distinguished all of her works. Sand embodied the many facets of the Romantic spirit of the nineteenth century; visionary, passionate, caring, free-spirited, and contemptuous of rigid bourgeois morality, she was called "la harpe éolienne de notre temps," by her contemporary, Ernest Renan. Sand's popularity has waned, but her contributions to the genre of regional literature has secured her reputation in the French literary world.

Works

Adriani (1853). *Les ailes de courage* (1916) [1931; Wings of Courage]. *Les amours de l'age d'or* (1871). *André* (1835) [1947; André]. *Antonia* (1863) [1870; Antonia]. *Autour de la table* (1875). *Le beau Laurence* (1870) [1880; Handsome Lawrence].

Les beaux messieurs de Bois-Doré (1862) [1890; The Gallant Lords of Bois-Doré]. *Césarine Dietrich* (1871) [1871; Césarine Dietrich]. *Les Charmettes*, n.p., n.d. *Le château des désertes* (1851) [1856; The Castle in the Wilderness]. *Le compagnon du tour de France* (1843) [1847; The Journeyman Joiner; or The Companion of the Tour de France]. *La comtesse de Rudolstadt* (1844) [1847; The Countess of Rudolstadt]. *La confession d'une jeune fille* (1865) [1865; Young Girl's Confession]. *Constance Verrier* (1869). *Consuelo* (1842–1843) [1846; Consuelo]. *Contes d'une grand'mère* (1873) [1930; Tales of a Grandmother]. *Les dames vertes* (1863). *La Danielle* (1857). *Le dernier amour* (1867). *La dernière Aldini* (1857) [1871; The Last Aldini: A Love Story]. *Dernières pages* (1877). *Les deux frères* (1875). *Le diable aux champs* (1857). *Elle et lui* (1859) [1902; She and He]. *La famille de Germandre* (1861). *La filleule* (1853). *First and True Love: A Thrilling Novel* (1853) [in English only]. *Flamarande* (1877). *Flavie: les maioliques florentines* (1872). *Francia: une bienfait n'est jamais perdu* (1872). *François le champi* (1850) [1889; Francis the Waif]. *Gabriel* (1840). *Garibaldi* (1860). *Gamiani, ou, Deux nuits d'excès Paris* (1970). *Germaine's Marriage: A Tale of Peasant Life in France* (1892) [in English only]. *Un hiver à Majorque* (1841) [1956; Winter in Majorca; with José Quadrado's Refutation of George Sand also 1902; George Sand and Chopin; a Glimpse of Bohemia]. *Un hiver au midi de l'Europe* (1841). *L'homme de neige* (1856) [1898; The Snowman]. *Horace* (1842). *Impressions et souvenirs* (1873) [1877; Impressions and Reminiscences]. *Indiana* (1832) [1835; Indiana]. *Isidora* (1847). *Jacques* (1834) [1847; Jacques]. *Jean de la Roche* (1860). *Jeanne* (1844). *Journal d'un voyageur pendant la guerre* (1871). *Journal intime* (posthumous) (1926) [1975; The Intimate Journal of George Sand]. *Laura: voyages et impressions* (1865). *Lavinia* (1844). *Légendes rustiques* (1858). *Lélia* (1833). *Leone Leonie* (1837). *Lettres au peuple* (1848). *Lettres d'un voyageur* (1837) [1847; Letters of a Traveller]. *Lucrezia Floriani* (1846). *La mare au diable* (1846) [1847; The Devil's Pool; also 1890; The Haunted Pool]. *Ma soeur Jeanne* (1874) [1874; My Sister Jeanne]. *Mademoiselle La Quintinie* (1860). *Mademoiselle Merquem* (1868) [1868; Mlle Merquem, a Novel]. *Les maîtres mosaïstes* (1838) [1895; The Master Mosaic-Workers]. *Les maîtres sonneurs* (1852) [1890; The Bagpipers]. *Les Majorcains* (1843). *Malgrétout* (1870). *Marianne* (1876). *Le marquis de Villemer* (1861) [1871; The Marquis de Villemer]. *La marquise* (1888). *Mauprat* (1837) [1847; Mauprat]. *Mélanges* (1843). *Melchoir* (1842). *Le meunier d'Angibault* (1845) [1863; The Miller of Angibault]. *Les mississipiens, proverbe* (1840). *Monsieur Sylvestre* (1866) [1871; Monsieur Sylvestre; a Novel]. *Mont-Revêche* (1853). *Mouny-Robin* (1842). *The naiad; a ghost story* (1892). *Nanon* (1872) [1890; Nanon]. *Narcisse* (1859). *Nouvelles lettres d'un voyageur* (1877). *Nouvelles* (1869). *Le nuage rose* (n.d.) [1902; The Rosy Cloud]. *Oeuvres de George Sand* (1860–1892). *Oeuvres choisies* (1851). *Pauline* (1841). *Le péché de Monsieur Antoine* (1846; The Sin of Monsieur Antoine). *La petite Fadette* (1849; Little Fadette; A Domestic Story). *Le Piccinino* (1847) [1900; Piccinino: The Last of the Aldinis, 2 vols.]. *Pierre qui roule* (1870) [1871; A Rolling Stone]. *La politique et le socialisme* (1845). *Pourquoi les femmes à l'Académie?* (1863). *Princess Nourmahal* (1888) [in English only?]. *Procope le Grand* (1844). *Promenades autour d'un village* (1866). *Quelques refléxions sur J.-J. Rousseau* (1854). *Questions d'art et de littérature* (1878). *Questions politiques et sociales* (1879). *Recollections by George Sand in Mérimée, Letters to an Incognita* (1874). *Réponse à diverses objections* (1846). *Le secrétaire intime* (1834) [1843; The Private Secretary]. *Les sept cordes de la lyre* (1839). *Simon* (1836) [18__?; Simon; A Love Story]. *Sketch of Talleyrand*, n.p., n.d. [in English only?]. *Souvenirs de 1848 . . .* (1880). *Souvenirs et impressions littéraires* (1862). *Spiridon* (1848). *Tamaris* (1862). *Teverino* (1845) [1855; Teverino: a Romance; also 1870; Jealousy or Teverino]. *Théâtre de Nohant* (1861). *La tour de Percemont. Marianne* (1876) [1881; The Tower of Percemont and Marianne]. *L'Uscoque* (1838) [18__?; The Uscoque, or, the Corsair]. *Valentine* (1832) [1902; Valentine]. *Valvèdre* (1861). *Une vieille histoire in Heures du soir* (1833). *La ville noire* (1861). *Voyage à Majorque* (18__?). *Voyage d'un moineau de Paris à la recherche du meilleur gouvernement*, in *Vie privée et publique des animaux* (1868).

Plays: *La baronne de Muhldorf* (1853). *Cadio* (1868). *Claudies* (1841). *Cosima: ou, la haine dans l'amour* (1840). *Le démon du foyer* (1852). *Le drac* (1865). *La petite Fadette* (1864). *Flaminio* (1854).

Françoise (1856). *Le lis du Japon* (1866). *Lucie* (1856). *Maître Favilla* (1855). *Marguerite de Saint-Gemme* (1859). *Le mariage de Victorine* (1851). *Mauprat* (1837?). *Molière* (1851). *Le pavé* (1862). *Le pressoir* (1853). *Les vacances de Pandolphe* (1852).

Bibliography

Amic, Henri, ed., *Correspondance entre George Sand et Gustave Flaubert* (n.d.). *The George Sand—Gustave Flaubert Letters,* tr. Aimee L. McKensie (1921). Barry, J., *Infamous Woman: The Life of George Sand* (1977). Beaufort, Raphaël Ledos de, ed., *Letters of George Sand* (1886). Borel, Pierre, ed., *Dix-sept lettres inédites de George Sand* (1959). *Broken Chain; Fragments of Verse from the Correspondence of George Sand and Jules Sandeau,* tr. H.L. White (1959). Buis, L., *Les Théories sociales de George Sand* (1910). Carrère, Casimir, *George Sand amoureuse* (1967). Caro, E.M., *George Sand* (1970). Cate, C., *George Sand: A Biography* (1975). Decori, Félix, ed., *Correspondance de George Sand et d'Alfred de Musset* (1904). Doumic, R., *George Sand* (1909) [1910; *George Sand; Some Aspects of Her Life and Writings*]. Edwards, S., *George Sand: A Biography of the First Modern, Liberated Woman* (1972). Evrard, L., *Correspondance Sand-Musset* (1956). Ferra, B., *Chopin et George Sand à Majorque* (1960) [1963; *Chopin and George Sand in Majorca*, tr. from Spanish by James Webb]. *George Sand's Novels*, 10 vols. (1890–1899). Guillemin, H., *Le Liaison Musset-Sand* (1972). Howe, Marie J., ed., *The Intimate Journal of George Sand* (1975). Hayatt, Alfred H., ed., *Thoughts and Aphorisms from Her [George Sand's] Works* (1911). Ives, G. Burnham, ed., *The Masterpieces of George Sand*, 20 vols. (1900–1902). Karenine, W., *George Sand* (1899–1912). Leblond, M.-A., "George Sand socialiste," in *Revue socialiste* (1904). LeRoy, A., *George Sand et ses amis* (1903). *Lettres à Albert de Musset et à Sainte-Beuve* (1897). "Lettres inédites de George Sand et du prince Napoléon," in *Revue des deux mondes* (1923). Lubin, Georges, ed., *Correspondance de George Sand*, 20 vols. (1964–1985). Lubin, G., *George Sand en Berry* (1967). Lubin, G., *George Sand—Album* (1973). Marieton, P., *George Sand et Alfred de Musset* (1897). Marix-Spire, Thérèse, ed., *Lettres inédites de George Sand et de Pauline Viardot (1839–49)* (1959). Maurois, André, *Lélia: The Life of George Sand* (1977).

Pailleron, M.L., *George Sand, Histoire de sa vie* (1938). Pailleron, M.L., *Les Années glorieuses de George Sand* (1942). Perdeguier, Agricol, ed., *Correspondance inédite avec George Sand et ses amis . . .* (1966). Plauchut, E., *Autour de Nohant* (1897). Salomon, P., *George Sand* (1953). Seyd, Felizia, *Romantic Rebel; The Life and Times of George Sand* (1940). Södergard, Östen, ed., *Les lettres de George Sand à Sainte-Beuve* (1964). *Souvenirs et idées* (1904). *Théâtre complet de George Sand* (Collection Hetzel), 4 vols. (1866–1867). Vincent, L., *George Sand et le Berry.* Vol. I, *Nohant*, Vol. II, *Le Berry dans l'oeuvre de George Sand* (1919).

William T. Ojala

Jeanne A. Ojala

Gabrielle-Anne Du Poilloüe de Saint-Mars

(a.k.a. La Comtesse Dash, Marie Michon, Jacques Reynaud)

Born August 2, 1804, Poitiers, France; died September 11, 1872, Paris
Genre(s): novel, short fiction, biography, memoirs, journalism
Language(s): French

For a third of a century, mostly under the pen name of La Comtesse Dash, Gabrielle-Anne Du Poilloüe de Saint-Mars poured out a stream of novels, short stories, and memoirs chronicling the sentimental and amorous doings of titled French characters, real and fictional, of the *ancien régime*, especially of the seventeenth and eighteenth centuries. Her prolixity, her preoccupation with the "gallantry" and *douceur de vivre* of pre-Revolutionary France, and her mastery of the formulas of the "romantic" literature of consumption suggest a nineteenth-century version of Barbara Cartland.

Born in Poitiers in 1804 of bourgeois stock (and not, as her memoirs would have it, of an ancient noble family), the future Comtesse Dash married a cavalry officer some twenty years older than herself, E.-J. Du Poilloüe de Saint-Mars, in about 1824. Perhaps because of this marriage into the Napoleonic nobility, she entered Parisian social and literary life. She separated from her husband some time before 1835, and, finding herself hard-pressed financially, she promoted herself from viscountess to countess and took the name Dash, supposedly inspired by an affectionate spaniel who happened to be in the salon of her friend the Princess Mestcherski on the evening she chose her *nom de plume*. Sponsored by Alexandre Dumas père and Roger de Beauvoir, she soon became a contributor to the important *Revue de Paris*. Her first novel, *Le Jeu de la reine* (1839; The Queen's Game), appeared at about the same time. She maintained close relations with Dumas and with his son, the dramatist. She wrote "chronicles" for Dumas' *Le Mousquetaire* under the pseudonym Marie Michon in the early 1850s, and may have ghostwritten a dozen or so of Dumas' volumes. For about two years during this decade, under the pseudonym Jacques Reynaud, she produced a series of "contemporary portraits" for the *Figaro* that were later published in book form. A foolish sentimental adventure with a Rumanian who promised to marry her ended badly. Otherwise, she led a life of constant literary activity, producing five or six volumes a year. Ultimately, she produced well over a hundred works. In her later years, she lived modestly in the Batignolles district. Some time after 1860, she wrote the six volumes of her posthumously published *Mémoires des autres* (1896–1897; Memoirs of Others). This collection of anecdotes is, indeed, mostly about others, figures from the *beau monde* of France in the first half of the nineteenth century.

Charming, high-spirited, industrious, the self-styled Comtesse Dash could be said to personify the French woman of letters of her period. She brought a smooth style and a good deal of what passed for psychological insight to her work. This huge body of material was composed of formulaic recreations, either in fiction or popularizing biography, of the love life of highborn men and women who, in her eyes and in those of many of her contemporaries, made *ancien régime* France seem glamourous.

Works

L'Ecran (1840). *La Marquise de Parabère* (1842). *Les Bals masqués* (1842). *La Marquise sanglante*

(1844). *Les Amours de Bussy-Rabutin* (1850). *La Comtesse de Bossut* (1855). *La Duchesse de Lauzun* (1858). *La Duchesse d'Eponnes* (1860). *La Galanterie à la cour de Louis XV* (1861). *Un Amour à la Bastille* (1862). *Mademoiselle Cinquante Millions* (1866). *L'Arbre de la Vierge* (1872). *Mémoires des autres* (1896–1897).

Translations into English: *The Journal of Madame Giovanni*, tr. Marguerite E. Wilbur (London, 1944). [Also attributed to A. Dumas.] *Mademoiselle Fifty Millions, or The Adventures of Hortense Mancini*, tr. Adelaide de V. Chaudron (New York, 1869).

Bibliography

Larousse, Pierre, *Grand Dictionnaire universel du XIXe siècle*, Vol. VI (Paris, 1865–1890). Rochel, Clément, "Préface" to her *Mémoires des autres*, Vol I (Paris, 1896–1897).

General references: d'Amat, Roman, and P. Limouzin-Lamothe, *Dictionnaire de biographie française*, Vol. X (Paris, 1933). Vapereau, G., *Dictionnaire universel des contemporains*. 6th ed. (Paris, 1893).

James S. Patty

Francesca Duranti

Born 1935
Genre(s): novel
Language(s): Italian

Francesca Duranti lives in Milan, writes for the newspaper *Il Giornale*, has a law degree from the University of Pisa, and is herself a translator of novels from French, German and English into Italian.

The House on Moon Lake (published 1986 in the United States) appeared originally in Italy as *La casa sul lago della luna* in 1984. It is, not surprisingly, about a translator who wants to be a writer, and who becomes immersed, even imprisoned, in a fictional world of his own creation and the victim of a character, Maria Lettner, whom he thought he had invented. This is a Duranti-style twist on the older Pirandellian questions: what is truth, who is real, and when is now, and the historically engaging questions about truth and fiction, reality and illusion, ambition and obsession, clarity and obscurity permeate the novel. Fabrizio Garrone, a thirty-eight year old obscure Milanese translator, accidentally discovers that Fritz Oberhofer, a turn-of-the-century obscure Viennese writer, wrote a fourth novel that was privately printed. Through a series of poorly explained premonitions, Garrone decides that *Das Haus am Mondsee* (The House on Moon Lake) is a masterpiece and that both his fortune and reputation will be made by translating it. His publisher, a childhood friend, urges him to write a short biography of Oberhofer to take advantage of the large sale of the novel and the growing and unexpected interest in the author. Garrone invents the last three years of Oberhofer's life, supplies him with both a mistress named Maria Lettner and the fictional details of their love affair; he sets off for Lake Mondsee when he is contacted by the "real" Petra Ebner, the supposed granddaughter of Fritz and Maria. In effect, he becomes Oberhofer, thereby adding to the aforementioned literary themes the element of literary, psychological and "actual" ghosts, and at the novel's end he is, in a sense, a ghost buried alive in a house of ghosts. Up to that point the novel is similar, for example, to Muriel Spark's *Loitering with Intent*, where a female writer ghostwrites the autobiographies of a group of eccentric phonies who then begin to live the lives with which she has provided them.

As Oliver Conant noted in a *New York Times* review, the most engrossing questions here concern Stephen Sartorelli, Duranti's translator, and "the dizziness the translator might have experienced in translating this novel about a translator translating a novel...." *The House on Moon Lake* won the Bagutta Prize, the Martina Franca Prize, and the City of Milan Prize.

Works

The House on Moon Lake (1986).

Bibliography

Conant, Oliver, Review of *The House on Moon Lake*. *New York Times Book Review*, p. 28.
Steinberg, Sybil, *Publishers Weekly* 230 (August 1, 1986): 61.

Mickey Pearlman

Claire (-Louise-Rose-Bonne) Lechat de Kersaint, duchesse de Duras

Born March 22, 1777 or 1778, Brest, France;
died January 1828, Nice
Genre(s): novel
Language(s): French

A French aristocrat caught in the turmoil of the Revolution of 1789, Mme de Duras was forced into exile in America and London with her mother when her father was executed during the Reign of Terror in 1793. Her three main works, novels written after her return to Paris, reflect the romantic theme of the morally and intellectually superior individual, usually a woman, who must suffer and sacrifice himself or herself because of extremely restrictive social pressures. Her works were immediately translated and published in English, Spanish, and German. Mme de Duras' friends and acquaintances are known for their romantic mal-du-siècle reputations. She knew Mme de Staël and Chateaubriand, and her own Parisian salon was frequented by members of the old regime: Talleyrand, Villemain, Barante, Molé, Humboldt, and Chateaubriand.

Mme de Duras' marriage to Amadée in London was apparently a loveless match arranged by relatives. She returned to France in 1800, and M. de Duras returned for a government post in 1807. Her famous liaison with Chateaubriand was considered an emotional one, jealously guarded but innocent. She is said to have sponsored him after the Restoration and was responsible for his being appointed Ambassador to Sweden. Chateaubriand named his three "muses" as Mme de Beaumont, Mme de Récamier, and Mme de Duras.

Mme de Duras' first novel, *Ourika*, published anonymously in 1824, was written in 1821–1822. Mme de Staël had previously written a tale ("Mirza" in *Trois Nouvelles*, 1795) based on the same story. In both works, an extraordinary black woman is raised in white upper-class France and suffers because that society will not allow her to marry because she is not acceptable, and yet she cannot return home because she is too cultured. Interestingly, the tale may have closer origins than Mme de Staël; little more is known about Mme de Duras' mother other than the fact she was a Creole from Martinique.

In *Edouard* (1825), the suffering and superior hero is brutally opposed by a restrictive, mediocre world that controls his ability to find happiness.

In *Olivier* (1826), also anonymous, Mme de Duras symbolically and scandalously links Olivier's sexual impotence to his social restrictions. Paris society was very interested in tracking down the author of this work.

Contemporary interest in Mme de Duras has chiefly been on her first novel, first on the racial theme, and then on the broader theme of repression.

Works

Ourika (1824). *Edouard* (1825). *Olivier* (1826). *Pensées de Louis XIV extraites de ses ouvrages et de ses lettres manuscrites par Mme la duchess de Duras* (1827). *Reflexions et prières inédites* (1839). *Oeuvres de Mme de Duras*, ed. M. Duplessis (1851). Works in English: *Ourika* (1824). *Ourika* (1829). *Madame de Duras' Ourika, Followed by Delphine Gay's poem "Ourika"* (1936).

Bibliography

Ancelot, M., *Les Salons de Paris; Foyers éteints* (Paris, 1858). Bardoux, A., *Etudes sociales et politiques: La Duchess de Duras* (Paris, 1898). Bearne, C., *Four Fascinating French Women* (London, 1910). Biré, E. *L'Année 1817* (Paris, 1895). Chateaubriand, F.-R., *Mémoires d'Outre-Tombe*, new ed. (Paris, 1957). Decreus-Van Liefland, J., *Sainte-Beuve et la critique des auteurs féminins* (Paris, 1949). Heathcote, O., *Three Novels of Mme de Duras* (The Hague, 1975). Pailhès, G., *La Duchess de Duras et Chateaubriand d'après des documents inédits* (Paris, 1910). Sainte-Beuve, C., "Mme de Duras." *Portraits de femmes* (Paris, 1845). Stendhal, G., *Armance ou Quelques scènes d'un salon en 1827*, ed. Martineau (Paris, 1962). Stenger, G., *Grandes dames du XIXᵉ siècle: chronique du temps de la Restauration* (Paris, 1911). General references: *Biographie universelle*, vol. 12 (1880). *Dictionnaire de biographie française*, vol. 12 (1970). *Dictionnaire des lettres françaises*. *Dictionnaire Stendhalienne*. *Oxford Companion to French Literature*.

Other references: *Le Figaro* (25 janv. 1930). *Journal of Negro History* XVIII (July 1933). *Revue de Littérature Comparée* (avril-juin 1962). *Revue de Paris* (mars-avril 1842). *La Revue des Deux Mondes* (1 aout 1968). *Swiss-French Studies* (Nov. 1981).

Marilynn J. Smith

Marguerite Duras

Born 1914, Cochin China
Genre(s): novel, drama, movie director
Language(s): French

Marguerite Duras was born in Cochin China (which was later called South Vietnam), where she spent most of her youth. In 1932, she moved to Paris where she studied law and mathematics (her father was a mathematics teacher, her mother an elementary school teacher), and enrolled in the Faculty of Political Sciences. In 1939 she married Robert Antelme, author of *L'Espèce Humaine* (The Human Species); three years later she met Dyonis Mascolo, author of *Le Communisme* (Communism), with whom she had a son. She became a militant Communist but later left the party. She has long been a prominent figure for feminist readers and critics, her texts focusing on the relation between desire and language, sexuality and gender. She is also considered one of the leading French writers of her time.

For the past forty years, she has been writing novels, plays and numerous essays. She has contributed to many films, starting with the script she wrote for *Hiroshima mon amour* (Hiroshima, My Love), which was directed by Alain Resnais, and created quite a stir at the 1960 Cannes Festival. She has collaborated on movies adapted from her novels (*Un barrage contre le Pacifique* [The Sea Wall], *La Musica, Dix heures et demie du soir en été* [Ten-Thirty PM in the Summertime], *Le Marin de Gibraltar* [The Sailor from Gibraltar], *Moderato Cantabile*), and most recently she has directed them (*Détruire, dit-elle* [Destroy, She Said], *Jaune le Soleil* [Yellow the Sun], *Nathalie Granger*).

Because the same themes and scenes often reappear in her novels, plays, and films, her work resists generic classification and covers several fields at the same time: many of her published scripts can be read as novels (*Hiroshima mon* amour, *India Song*, *Aurélia Steiner*), some of her novels are made of visual figures (*Le Ravissement de Lol V. Stein* [The Ravishing of Lol V. Stein], *L'Homme Atlantique* [The Atlantic Man]; in some of her theater and films the actors actually read their parts, instead of acting them (*Le Camion* [The Truck], *La Maladie de la mort* [The Malady of Death]).

The versatility of her narrative position defies any classification and is reiterated by the elusiveness of her texts, always repeated but never quite the same, which creates both familiarity and defamiliarization. One can define three stages in her work, stages that show a continuation of her themes (childhood, solitude, encounter, love, sexuality, incommunicability, boredom, death, and time), and an evolution in her style.

Her earliest novels (1943–1960) have a simple, coherent plot, a linear and chronological development, and a great thematic unity. Often set during vacations in a hot Mediterranean summer, they tell the story of a crisis in the life of a couple, of love encounters. Many of her characters are passive and drink heavily, but their passivity is often composed of wisdom and silence. They are fascinated by passion and death. Often a peculiar event takes place in their surroundings (fatal accident, crime of passion, suicide). Though these elements are quite ordinary and their repetition rather monotonous, Duras has renewed the art of the novel by her rejection of traditional psychology, her peculiar use of dialogue, her preference for what is suggested rather than explicit and above all by the overwhelming role given to time and duration. The encounter between man and woman leads to a slow, progressive, cautious discovery of love, a love that ignores social barriers and boundaries, and reveals the failure of communication. Time is perceived as both necessary and threatening and creates in Duras' novels an unusual, if sometimes irritating, slow rhythm.

In her later works (1964–1983), the obsession with memory and desire uses repetition even more. The narrative movement is reduced to a minimum; each text is related to the previous ones and can be seen as fragments of a longer narrative. These intertextual repetitions require

from the reader a willingness to reread rather than to consume the text.

Finally, in her most recent novels (1984–1985), Duras reshapes not only her work but her own image in the eyes of the public. With *L'Amant* (The Lover: Prix Goncourt 1984), she has become a popular writer. Part of its success might be due to its advertisement as an "exotic, erotic autobiographical confession," which hides its deep ambivalence: by her narrative use of "I" and "she," Duras pretends to confess but is not committed to truthfulness and plays a seductive game of veiling and unveiling her life.

Works

Les Impudents (1943). La Vie tranquille (1944). Un barrage contre le Pacifique (1950). Le Marin de Gibraltar (1952). Les petits chevaux de Tarquinia (1953). Des journées entières dans les arbres (1954). Le Square (1955). Moderato Cantabile (1958). Les Viaducs de la Seine-et-Oise (1960). Dix heures et demie du soir en été (1960). Hiroshima mon amour (1960). L'Après-midi de Monsieur Andesmas (1962). Le Ravissement de Lol V. Stein (1964). Théâtre I, II (1965). Le Vice-Consul (1966). L'Amante anglaise (1967). Détruire, dit-elle (1969). Abahn, Sabana, David (1970). L'Amour (1972). India song texte-théâtre-film (1973). Nathalie Granger, suivi de La Femme du Gange (1973). With Xavière Gauthier. Les Parleuses (1974). Le Camion, suivi d'Entretien avec Michelle Porte (1977). L'Eden cinéma (1977). [With Michelle Porte], Les Lieux de Marguerite Duras (1977). [With Joël Farges and François Barat], Marguerite Duras (1979). Le Navire Night (suivi de Césarée, Les Mains négatives, Aurélia Steiner, Aurélia Steiner, Aurélia Steiner) (1979). L'Eté 80 (1980). L'Homme assis dans le couloir (1980). Les Yeux verts (1980). Agatha (1981). Outside: papiers d'un jour (1981). L'Homme Atlantique (1982). La Maladie de la mort (1982). Savannah Bay (1982). L'Amant (1984). La Douleur (1985).

Translations: Duras' works have been translated in many languages. The following translations in English: *Hiroshima mon amour* (1961). *Four Novels*, tr. Richard Seaver (1965). *The Ravishing of Lol V. Stein*, tr. Richard Seaver (1966). *The Square*. Three Plays, tr. Barbara Bray and Sonia Orwell (1967). *The Vice-Consul*, tr. Eileen Ellenbogen (1968). *L'Amante anglaise*, tr. Barbara

Bray (1968). *Destroy, She Said*, tr. Barbara Bray (1970). *India Song*, tr. Barbara Bray (1976). *The Little Horses of Tarquinia*, tr. Peter Du Berg (1980). *The Sailor from Gibraltar*, tr. Barbara Bray (1980). *Whole Days in the Trees and Other Stories*, tr. Anita Barrows (1984). *The Lover*, tr. Barbara Bray (1985). *The Malady of Death*. Five Novels (1985). *The Sea Wall*, tr. Herrma Briffault (1985). *The War*, tr. Barbara Bray (1986).

Bibliography

Ames, Sanford, "Mint Madness: Surfeit and Purge in the Novels of Marguerite Duras." *Sub-stance* 20 (1978): 37–44. Andermatt, Verena, "Rodomontages of *Le Ravissement de Lol V. Stein*." *Yale French Studies* 57 (1979): 23–35. Bashoff, Bruce, "Death and Desire in Marguerite Duras' *Moderato Cantabile*." *MLN* 94 (1979): 720–730. Berheim, Nicole Lise, *Marguerite Duras tourne un film* (Paris, 1981). Besnard-Coursodon, Micheline, "Significations du métarécit dans *Le Vice-Consul*." *French Forum* 3, no. 1 (1978): 72–83. Bishop, Louis, "The Banquet Scene in *Moderato Cantabile*." *Romanic Review* 69 (1978): 222–235. Bortin, Mary Ellen, "Une voix, Marguerite Duras." M.A. thesis, Ithaca, NY, 1977. Charpentier, Françoise, "Une appropiation de l'écriture: *Territoires du Féminin avec Marguerite Duras*." *Littérature* 31 (1978): 117–125. Copjec, Joan, "*India Song/Son nom de Venise dans Calcutta désert*. The Compulsion to Repeat." *October*, 17 (1981): 37–52. Eisinger, Erica, "Crime and Detection in the Novels of Marguerite Duras." *Contemporary Literature* 15 (1974): 503–518. Fedkiw, Patricia, "Marguerite Duras: Feminine Field of Hysteria." *Enclitic* 6, no. 2 (1982): 78–86. Foucault, Michel, and Hélène Cixous, "A propos de Marguerite Duras." *Cahiers Renaud-Barrault* 89 (1975): 8–22. Glassman, Debbie, "The Feminine Subject as History Writer in *Hiroshima mon amour*." *Enclitic* 5, 1 (1981): 45–54. Husserl-Kapit, Susan, "An Interview with Marguerite Duras." *Signs* 1 (1975): 423–434. Lamy, Suzanne, and André Roy, eds., *Marguerite Duras à Montréal* (Montreal, 1981). Lydon, Mary, "Translating Duras: 'The Seated Man in the Passage.'" *Contemporary Literature* 24 (1983): 259–275. Lyon, Elisabeth, "The Cinema of Lol V. Stein." *Camera Obscura* 6 (1980): 9–39. Maini, Marcelle, *Territoires du féminin avec Marguerite Duras* (Paris, 1977). Murphy, Carole J., *Exile and Alienation in the Novels of Marguerite Duras* (Lexington, Ky., 1983). Oudart, Jean, "Sur Son Nom de Venise dans Calcutta désert." *Cahiers du Cinéma* 268–269 (1976): 75–77. Ropars-Wuilleumier, Marie-Claire, "The Disembodied Voice: *India Song*." *Yale French Studies* 60 (1980): 241–268. Seylaz, Jean-Luc, *Les romans de Marguerite Duras* (Paris, 1963). Vircondelet, Alain, *Marguerite Duras* (Paris, 1972). Williams, Linda, "*Hiroshima* and *Marienbad*—Metaphor and Metonymy." *Screen* 17, no. 1 (1976): 34–40. Willis, Sharon, *Marguerite Duras: Writing on the Body* (Urbana and Chicago, 1987).

Michèle M. Magill

Nadezhda Durova

(a.k.a. A. Aleksandrov, Kavalerist-devitsa)

Born September 1783, Kherson, Russia; died March 23, 1866, Elabuga
Genre(s): memoirs, fiction
Language(s): Russian

Nadezhda Durova, disguised as a never-maturing boy, served for nine years in the Russian light cavalry during the Napoleonic epoch. Twenty years later, in 1836, she burst on the Russian literary scene with her own edition of the journals of that unique experience, *The Cavalry Maiden* (Kavalerist-devitsa), followed by two other autobiographical works and a series of novels and long tales.

Durova was the archetypal tomboy, torn by her thirst for physical freedom, her memories of early childhood days as a "daughter of the regiment" before her hussar father's retirement, and her mother's cruel insistence that the girl accept the restricted female existence that she herself deplored. After rebelling against an unhappy marriage, in September 1806, Durova ran away from her parents' home in the western foothills of the Urals to join the army. Because she displayed extraordinary bravery as a common soldier in the Prussian campaign of 1807, Tsar Alexander I himself granted her permission to remain in the cavalry and promoted her to officer's rank. He also christened her with his own name, "A. Aleksandrov," which she used as a pseudonym during her literary career.

In *The Cavalry Maiden* Durova describes the mess and muddle of combat and the retreat before the Napoleonic invasion in 1812 with candor and self-deprecating humor, but most of the diary's pages are devoted to sharing more private "adventures" with her family and female contemporaries. Durova found wandering the woods and fields at night, exploring new communities, and meeting new people the fullest expression of the freedom she had won. In later pages a light humor tinged with exasperation underlies her depiction of her fellow officers and the boredom of peacetime duty in backwoods Russia. She introduces her journals with a memoir, "My Childhood Years," in which she analyzes perceptively the psychological roots of her rebellion. *God zhizni v Peterburge* (1838; A Year of Life in Peterburg) is a bitter memoir of Durova's reception in the capital as a performing literary lion, and *Zapiski Aleksandrova* (1839; Notes . . .) are additional, rather scrappy excerpts from her military journals.

Durova's novels and stories, all published in the late 1830s, are part of the last gasp of hyper-Romanticism. Like other semi-educated Russian authors of her time, Durova drew much of her concept of fiction from the Gothic and sentimental literature of late eighteenth century Europe. There is a great contrast between the understatement of her journals and the improbabilities and at times strident lyricism of the tales and novels. Several of the stories are presented as the harvest of Durova's wanderings, vouched for by a frame narrator who is a woman army officer. They range from the harrowing tale of the premature death from syphilis of a woman who was married at thirteen to a dissolute man by foolish but well-meaning parents ("Igra sud'by" ["The Play of Fate"]); the mysterious story of a Polish priest's murder of a ward he loved only too well ("Pavil'on" ["The Summerhouse"]); the historically-based account of a Polish nobleman who deserts a wife of his own class to marry a peasant girl ("Count Mauritius"); and a long novel about the conflict of Christianity and pagan mores in medieval Lithuania (*Gudishki*). The Kama river region, where Durova grew up and to which she returned during her fifty years in retirement, is the setting of several stories in which she depicts sympathetically tragic episodes, either past or contemporary, among the varied native populations. Durova's vigorous command of language did much to overcome the weakness and improbability of her plots, but today her tales read as period pieces.

The pioneering significance of Durova's journals has been overlooked both in the Soviet Union and in the West. Women throughout history have found ways to lead an active life outside the sphere prescribed for their sex; Durova is one of the very few anywhere to leave us a written record of such an exploit. And, just as she personally transcended the social limitations of her sex, the publication of her works broadened the canon of permissible literary *genres* in Russia. She was one of the first women to publish a sizeable body of prose fiction, and her journals of the military years are among the earliest published autobiographies, and the first by a Russian of either sex to find their way into print during the author's lifetime. "My Childhood Years" was an unparalleled evocation of the pains of growing up female. In 1983 the Soviets celebrated the 200th anniversary of their national heroine's birth with the first complete edition of *The Cavalry Maiden* in nearly 150 years.

Works

Izbrannye sochineniia kavalerist-devitsy (1983). *Izbrannoe*, selected works (1984).

Translations: "My Childhood Years," tr. and intro. Mary Zirin. *The Female Autograph* (New York Literary Forum 12–13), Domna C. Stanton, ed. (1984; paperback rpt. University of Chicago, 1987), pp. 119–142. *The Cavalry Maid*, John Mersereau, Jr., tr. (Ann Arbor, Mich., 1987). *The Cavalry Maiden*, Mary Fleming Zirin, tr., intro. and annot (Bloomington, 1988).

Bibliography

Golitsyn, N.N., *Bibliograficheskii slovar' russkikh pisatel'nits* (St. Petersburg, 1889; rpt. Leipzig, 1974), pp. 88–89. Heldt, Barbara, "Nadezhda Durova: Russia's Cavalry Maid." *History Today* (February 1983): 24–27. Heldt, Barbara, *A Terrible Perfection: Women and Russian Literature* (Bloomington, Ind., 1987). *Istoriia russkoi literatury XIX v.: Bibliograficheskii slovar' russkikh pisatel'nits*, K.D. Muratova, ed. (Moscow-Leningrad, 1962), pp. 320–321. *Modern Encyclopedia of Russian and Soviet Literatures*, t. 6, Harry

B. Weber, ed. (Gulf Breeze Florida, 1982), pp. 96–98 (Mary Zirin). Nekrasova, E., "Nadezhda Andreevna Durova." *Istoricheskii vestnik* 9 (1890): 585–612. Saks, A., *Kavalerist-devitsa. Shtabs-rotmistr A.A. Aleksandrov* (Nadezhda Andreevna Durova) (St. Petersburg, 1912).

Mary F. Zirin

Constance-Marie de Théis, princesse de Salm-Reifferscheid-Dyck

(a.k.a. Constance Pipelet, La comtesse de Salm-Dyck, Madame la princesse Constance de Salm)

Born November 7, 1767, Nantes, France; died April 13, 1845, Paris
Genre(s): poetry, memoir, essay, drama
Language(s): French

Called the "Boileau des femmes" (Boileau of women) by her contemporaries, Constance de Salm produced in the course of a long and distinguished literary career of over forty years an extensive and important body of work. Her father provided her with a solid education; her first compositions were short verse. In 1789 she married Jean-Baptiste Pipelet de Leury, a famous physician and surgeon, and settled in Paris. The marriage was unhappy and dissolved in 1799. Her first important literary success came with the drama *Sapho, tragédie mêlée de chants*, first staged on December 14, 1794, shortly after the end of the Terror. This work, whose tone is elevated and noble, won the praise of critics and the public; it ran for over one hundred performances, apparently striking just the right chord in the audience. In 1795 Constance de Salm was received as the only female member of the Lycée des Arts (or the Athénée des Arts, a loose association of former members of the royal academies before the founding of the Institut de France). During the following years she wrote a number of letters on issues directly related to women's participation in the literary canon. Her *Épîtres à Sophie* (Letters to Sophie) detail the rights and duties of women. Her *Épître aux femmes* (1795; Letter to Women) is a spirited defense of women's participation in literature and poetry. Two other letters should also be mentioned to round out the picture of Constance de Salm's role in Parisian literary life during the late 1790s and early 1800s: her *Épître sur les dissensions des gens de lettres* (1798; Letter on the Dissensions among Literary People) argues for the connection between personal integrity and poetic creativity, an argument continued in *Épître à un jeune auteur sur l'indépendance et les devoirs de l'homme de lettres* (1806; Letter to a Young Author on the Independence and Duties of a Man of Letters). In 1803 she married Josef Altgraf (after 1816, Fürst) von Salm-Dyck, who was descended from one of the oldest noble houses in the Rhineland and was a distinguished German botanist in his own right, with ties to Alexander v. Humboldt. The Prince met his future wife during one of his many trips to Paris to secure his rights to his inherited domain, then under French rule. Madame de Salm and her husband spent the winters in Paris and divided the rest of their time between her husband's hereditary family castle (Schloß Dyck bei Neuß) and their nearby city residence in Aachen. She continued her active literary life. Of her works written after this time the following are notable: her novel *Vingt-quatre heures d'une femme sensible* (1824; Twenty-four Hours of a Sensitive Woman), which was frequently reprinted during Constance de Salm's lifetime and was viewed as an accurate portrait of the spirit of the times; *Les Allemands comparés aux Français dans leurs moeurs, leurs usage, leur vie intérieure et sociale* (1826; The Germans Compared to the French in Their Mores, Behavior, Interior and Social Life), which can perhaps be read as a commentary on Madame de Staël's influential work; and her memoirs, *Mes soixante ans, ou mes Souvenirs politiques et littéraries*, (1833; My Sixty Years, of My Political and Literary Memories), an important document of French literary life from 1790 to 1830.

Works

Oeuvres complètes de Madame la princesse Constance de Salm (1841), 4 vols. Vol. 1, *Épîtres et Discours*; Vol. 2, *Sapho, Cantate, Poésies diverses*; Vol. 3, *Vingt-quatre heures d'une femme sensible*; *Pensées*; Vol. 4, *Éloges, Rapports, Notice, Mes soixante ans*. Only one work has been translated into English: *Pensées*, tr. W. Stains (1844), and also into German (1838, 1840). Her novel *Vingt-quatre heures d'une femme sensible* also appeared in German translation in 1825.

Bibliography

Chénier., *Tableau de la littérature française*, . . . "Salm-Dyck, Constance-Marie de Théis, princesse de." *Biographie universelle* [Michaud], Vol. 37, pp. 526–528. Quérard, J.-M., "Salm-Reifferscheid-Dyck, Constance-Marie de Théis." *La France littéraire* 18, Vol. 8 (Paris) pp. 414–418.

Earl Jeffrey Richards

E

Isabelle Eberhardt

Born February 17, 1877, Geneva, Switzerland;
died October 21, 1904, 'Ain Sfra, Algeria
Genre(s): diary, journalism, novel
Language(s): French

Isabelle Eberhardt was the illegitimate daughter of her half-German Jewish mother, Nathalie Eberhardt, and Alexander Trophimovsky, a former priest in the Russian Orthodox Church who had rejected his faith to embrace nihilism. Together with her half-brothers Vladimir and Augustin de Moerder, she had no normal schooling due to her father's disapproval of formal education. She learned Latin, Greek and some Arabic. The children spoke French, German, Italian and Russian; they studied philosophy, geography and history and developed an excellent capacity for voicing their own opinions. She also developed a taste for romantic and exotic literature in addition to reading works by Pierre Loti, D'Annunzio and Dostoyevsky. Isabelle's childhood and adolescence were unhappy ones, however; her father's contempt for her shy and nervous brother Augustin, coupled with her own desperate need to feel independent, made her life intolerable.

Isabelle and her mother escaped the tyrannical life with Trophimovsky and arrived in Algeria in 1897. There she embraced Islam and threw off the Western way of life she had been born into, adopting the Arab dress of the Algerian men, to the shock and resentment of the Europeans. The notion of resignation before the will of God is perhaps the dominant motif of all her writing, in the diaries as well as in her stories. In this respect,

she was a natural mystic. Her new life bestowed a vast amount of freedom upon her and she was known to be quite unconventional, a great carousing drinker and heavy smoker on the one hand, and a rigorous observer of the rules of Islam on the other.

Isabelle's connections with the Qadiriya religious order were the result of her desire to become a female *faqira*. However, her sincerity and knowledge of the Qur'an was so impressive that she was allowed to undergo her initiation as a faqir, a male member of the order.

In January 1901, an attempt on her life was made, which Isabelle regarded as a message from God and as a road opened for her by her potential murderer, whom she quickly forgave. During this period and the subsequent trial, she wrote and published articles for French journals and newspapers. Her roving correspondent's assignments continued to follow the French penetration into Southwestern Algeria. She also worked on her largely autobiographical and unfinished novel, *Trimadeur*. She married a Muslim but continued to live like a vagabond and a recluse, in constant ill health, often malaria-ridden. She died in a flash flood at 'Ain Sfra. Isabelle Eberhardt, in denying herself the privileges of the Western world in which she was born, and embracing the religion and the land she dearly loved, also demonstrated a sense of freedom as awesome as it was unusual.

Bibliography

Mackworth, Cecily, *The Destiny of Isabelle Eberhardt* (London, 1951). Stephan, Raoul, *Isabelle Eberhardt ou la Révélation du Sahara* (Paris, 1930).

Richard J. Pioli

Jeannie Ebner

Born November 17, 1918, Sydney, Australia
Genre(s): translation, poetry, novel
Language(s): German

Jeannie Ebner is a good illustration of the difficulty Austrian writers have in gaining recognition. An accomplished translator, the successful editor of a prestigious literary journal, and the author of several outstanding volumes of poetry and prose fiction, only recently has she come to be widely known and respected outside of Austria.

Ebner is the daughter of Ida Ganaus and Johann Ebner, a native of Wiener Neustadt, near Vienna, who had immigrated to Australia at the age of nineteen. In the 1920s the family returned to Wiener Neustadt, where Jeannie attended school. After study at a commercial college she entered the family business, but an interest in sculpture led her to enroll in the Academy of Fine Arts in Vienna in 1941. The business was destroyed toward the end of the war, and Ebner's life in the early postwar years was difficult. She held a number of jobs, from English tutor to secretary, and somewhat later began to translate English novels. Her own literary works, the first of which was the collection of poetry and short stories *Gesang an das Heute* (1952; Songs for Today), brought her a measure of recognition but little income. In 1964 she married Ernst Allinger and four years later became the editor of *Literatur und Kritik*, a position she held until 1978. Literary works and translations continued to appear regularly.

The novel is the literary form in which Ebner has been most successful, from *Sie warten auf Antwort* (1954; Waiting for an Answer) to *Drei Flötentöne* (1981; Three Sounds of a Flute). The former, as the title implies, has as its principal theme the uncertainties of human life. Although Ebner has denied being influenced by Kafka, similarities do exist, especially in the presence of a self-contained world that seems to bear little resemblance to everyday life and the parable-like essence of the story. It differs from Kafka, however, in one important aspect: in spite of the precarious nature of life, the prospect of improvement through a learning process is held out as a possibility. The novels that followed became more realistic. In *Die Wildnis früher Sommer* (1958; The Jungle of Early Summers) the psychological state of the female protagonist, a dreamer unsuited for life, is examined, and *Figuren in Schwarz und Weiß* (1962; Figures in Black and White) is a thoroughly realistic and to some extent autobiographical portrayal of a woman's life in Vienna from 1925 to 1955. Nineteen years were to pass before the appearance of Ebner's next novel, *Drei Flötentöne*, and the book's style and structure are correspondingly mature and complex. Here Ebner uses a first-person narration for the first time as she explores the interrelated lives of three women. Two of the protagonists come to tragic ends, but the third, a writer, attains a measure of happiness and success; as is typical, the pervasive modern feeling of helplessness is counter-balanced by the presence of hope.

Ebner has achieved prominence in three important areas, as a translator, editor, and author of belletristic works. In her prose fiction the female protagonists are faced with the problems—practical and existential—of modern life. Without minimizing the seriousness of the problems, Ebner consistently, if by no means pervasively, suggests that experience can be a teacher and a measure of equilibrium can be attained.

Works

Gesang an das Heute: Gedichte, Gesichte, Geschichten (1952). *Sie warten auf Antwort: Roman* (1954). *Die Wildnis früher Sommer: Roman* (1958). *Der Königstiger: Erzählung* (1959). *Die Götter reden nicht: Erzählungen* (1961). *Figuren in Schwarz und Weiß: Roman* (1962). *Im Schatten der Göttin* (1963). *Gedichte* (1965). *Prosadichtungen* (1973). *Protokoll aus einem Zwischenreich: Erzählungen* (1975). *Sag ich: Gedichte* (1978). *Gedichte und Meditationen* (1978). *Erfrorene Rosen: Erzählungen* (1979). *Drei Flötentöne: Roman* (1981). *Aktäon: Novelle* (1983).

Bibliography

Johns, J., "Jeannie Ebner: Eine Bibliographie der Werke." *Modern Austrian Literature* 12, Nos. 3/4 (1979): 209–236. Keiber, C., *Jeannie Ebner: Eine Einführung* (Bern, 1985). Obermayer, A., "Jeannie Ebner," in *Major Figures of Contemporary Austrian Literature*, ed. Donald G. Daviau (Bern, 1987), pp. 143–162.

Jerry Glenn

Margarethe Ebner

*Born c. 1291, Donauwörth, Bavaria; died June
20, 1351, the Dominican convent at
Medingen*
Genre(s): letters
Language(s): German

Margarethe took the veil at the age of fifteen.
According to her own accounts, her first twenty
years of life were uneventful. February 6, 1312,
represents a turning point "when God showed
me his paternal love and gave me great sickness
unknown to me before." Her illness lasted three
years, and she never fully recovered. The ensuing
years of suffering were years filled with religious
ecstasies, visions, revelations, and dreams in
which she communicated with deceased family
members. She writes about severe fasting and
self-imposed silence, which are juxtaposed with
orations filled with admonitions to the nuns in
her convent. And she writes of bodily stigmata
and mystic union with Christ.

It was Heinrich von Nördlingen, a priest and
Gottesfreund (God's friend), who encouraged
Margarethe to write her revelations, which she
began in 1344. Her retrospective account begins
in 1312 and spans 36 years of her life. One
additional written document, the only surviving
letter of her correspondence with Heinrich von
Nördlingen (56 letters between 1332–1350), is a
two-page long intercession for Heinrich which
concludes with a brief remark about her illness
and her desire to receive relics from Saint Agnes
(Wilhelm Oehl, *Deutsche Mystikerbriefe des
Mittelalters. 1100–1550* [German letters of mystics from the Middle Ages 1100–1550]).

Margarethe's literary contribution lies in her
astute observations about life inside and outside
the convent walls, her political and social commentaries, all of which represent an important
source for the history of mysticism despite
Margarethe's rather dry and repetitive style. What
impresses more than her writings is her role as a
correspondent with a number of representatives
of what must have been a large intellectual religious community of women and men in twelfth-
and thirteenth-century Germany, Switzerland,
and Alscace, who through their letter exchange
displayed their involvement in a constant exchange of religious ideas.

Works

Buber, Martin, *Ekstatische Konfessionen* (1921),
pp. 98–100. Prestel, Josef, *Die Offenbarungen der
Margaretha Ebner und der Adelheid Langmann*
(1939). Wilms, Hieronymus, *Der seligen
Margarethe Ebners Offenbarungen und Briefe
übertragen und eingeleitet* (1928).

Bibliography

Canisia, M., O.P. Jedelhauser, *Geschichte des
Klosters und der Hofmark Maria Medingen von
den Anfängen im 13. Jahrhundert bis 1606* (Vechta
i.O., 1936), pp. 84–86. Oehl, Wilhelm, *Deutsche
Mystikerbriefe des Mittelalters 1100–1550*
(Darmstadt, 1972) (1931). Pfister, Oskar, "Hysterie
und Mystik bei Margaretha Ebner." *Zentralblatt für
Psychoanalyse* I (1911): 468–485. Pummerer, A.,
"Margareta Ebner, Charakterbild aus der deutschen
Mystik des Mittelalters." *Stimmen aus Maria-Laach*
81 (1911): 1–11; 132–144; 244–257. Strauch,
Philipp, *Margaretha Ebner und Heinrich von
Nördlingen* (Amsterdam, 1966) (1882). Walz,
Angelus, "Gottesfreunde um Margarete Ebner."
Historisches Jahrbuch, 72 (1953): 253–265. Zoepf,
Ludwig, *Die Mystikerin Margaretha Ebner (c. 1291–
1351)* (Leipzig and Berlin, 1914). Zöpfl, Friedrich,
"Margarethe Ebner," *Lebensbilder aus dem
Bayrischen Schwaben*, vol. 2 (1953): 60–70.

Gabriele Strauch

María Ecín

(see: Mercedes Salisachs)

Gabriele Eckart

Born 1954
Genre(s): poetry
Language(s): German

Gabriele Eckart has been writing poetry
since she was seventeen years old, that is, since
1971. She is familiar with Walt Whitman's lyrical
poetry and with the works of the German poet
Hölderlin; both poets served as models for her
poetry. Her poetry reflects life in the German
Democratic Republic; many of her poems are a
"quest for who we are, who we want to be and

who we want to become" as an independent East German nation.

Bibliography

Franke, Konrad, *Die Literatur der Deutschen Demokratischen Republik* (Zürich and München, 1974).

Brigitte Edith Archibald

Ed

(see: Ida Boy-Ed)

Anne Charlotte Edgren

(see: Anne Charlotte Leffler)

Egeria

Flourished c. A.D. 400
Genre(s): pilgrimage memoir
Language(s): Latin

In the late fourth or early fifth century, a Latin-speaking woman from the western part of the Roman Empire made the arduous pilgrimage to the Holy Land, where she traveled extensively and resided for three years in Jerusalem itself. She composed a memoir of her travels that provides one of the most precious records of late antique Christian pilgrimage and worship.

Since the discovery of the sole manuscript of the work, by Gamurrini in 1884, both the identity of the author and the date of her journey have occasioned much discussion. That manuscript is fragmentary and the extant portions are not continuous, so it is unclear how much of Egeria's record has been lost. The clipped and precise descriptions of the work contain few biographical details. Scholarly consensus has attributed the work to "the blessed nun Egeria," a pilgrim mentioned by the seventh-century Spanish monk Valerius. Egeria's work is generally called the *Itinerarium*, or *Travels*, on the basis of a now-lost manuscript which bore that title under Egeria's authorship in the catalogue of a medieval monastic library. Internal evidence suggests that Egeria came from a region on the Atlantic coast, but she could equally have been a Gallo-Roman from the Aquitaine or a Spaniard from Galicia. She was clearly a member of a monastic community and apparently recorded her description largely for the benefit of her sisters. The economic resources required for her journey and the welcome which she was accorded in the Holy Land by such figures as the Bishop of Edessa suggest that she was of high social standing. Although Egeria did not have as firm a command of Latin literary style as such late antique Christian women as Proba, she was well educated and possessed a firm grounding in both Scripture and the Christian literary tradition. She rejoiced when the bishop of Edessa gave her a copy of *The Letter of King Abgar* that she deemed superior to that found in her library at home.

The most vexing question concerning the work is the date of Egeria's journey. This is a matter of some scholarly importance because her description of the liturgy practiced in Jerusalem, a liturgy which served as the basis of various later Eastern rites, is important to the history of the development of those Christian liturgies. The text must have been composed between 363 and 540, but most theories have focused on the years c. 400. Devos, refining arguments first made by Baumstark, has placed Egeria's stay in Jerusalem as lasting from 381 to 384. A persistent set of counter-arguments, begun by Lambert and continued by Gingras, have suggested the years 414–416. Other dates have been put forth by various single commentators. The recent consensus of scholarly opinion has been in agreement with Devos.

The surviving narrative is almost evenly divided between Egeria's journey around the Holy Land and the passages on Jerusalem itself and its liturgy. Egeria desired to bring home specific information to her community about such topics as biblical geography, Christian historical traditions, and liturgical rites. She frequently addressed its members directly, as in her description of the Jerusalem liturgy, "Loving sisters, I am sure it will interest you to know about the daily services they have in the holy places. . . ." Earlier, she had introduced the precious copy of the *Letter of Abgar*, "You yourselves must read it when I come home, dearest ladies, if such is the will of Jesus our God." Like most travelers, she was eager to share her novel experiences with her friends. Like most pilgrims, she was eager for them to share in the spiritual benefits which she had gained. While Egeria's Latin is of a rather plain style, the very descriptive gifts and attention to detail which she placed at the service of her community serve the modern historian extremely well.

Works

The most recent critical editions are O. Prinz, *Itinerarium Egeriae* (1960), and E. Francheschini and R. Weber, *Itinerarium Egeriae*, in *Itineraria et alia geographica* (Corpus Christianorum, Series Latina, vol. 175; 1965). English translations and commentary can be found in G.E. Gingras, *Egeria, Diary of a Pilgrimage* (Ancient Christian Writers, vol. 38; 1970); P. Wilson-Kastner, et al., *A Lost Tradition. Women Writers of the Early Church* (1981); and John Wilkinson, *Egeria's Travels to the Holy Land* (1971, revised 1981). Valuable notes and a French translation can be found in P. Maravel, ed., *Ethérie. Journal de voyage (Itinéraire)* (Sources Chrétiennes, vol. 296; 1982).

Bibliography

Bagatii, B., "Ancora sulla data di Eteria." *Bibbia e Oriente* 10 (1968): 73–75. Baraut, C., "Bibliografia Egeriana." *Hispania Sacra* 7 (1954): 203–215. Bastiaensen, A., *Observations sur le vocabulaire liturgique dans l'Itinéraire d'Egérie* (1962). Davies, J., "The *Peregrinatio Egeriae* and the Ascension." *Vigiliae Christianae* 8 (1954): 93–100. Devos, P., series of articles on the date of Egeria's voyage in *Analecta Bollandiana* 85 (1967): 165–194 and 381–400; 86 (1968): 87–108; 87 (1969): 208–212; and "Une nouvelle Egérie," *Analecta Bollandiana* 101 (1983): 43–74. Ernout, A., "Les mots grecs dans la Pereginatio Aetheriae." *Emerita* 20 (1952): 289–307. Praux, J., "Panis qui delibari non potest." *Vigiliae Christianae* 15 (1961): 105–115. Renoux, A., "Liturgie de Jérusalem et lectionnaires arméniens: Vigiles et année liturgique," in M. Cassien and B. Botte, *La Prière des Heures* (1963), pp. 167–199. Spitzer, L., "The Epic Style of the Pilgrim Aetheria." *Romanische Literaturstudien* (1959), pp. 871–912. Vermeer, G., *Observations sur le vocabulaire du Pèlerinage chez Egérie et chez Antonin de Plaisance* (1965).

General references: *Dictionnaire d'histoire and de géographie eccélsiatiques*, XV, 1–5. *Dictionnaire d'archéologie chrétienne et de liturgie*, V, pp. 552–584. *New Catholic Encyclopedia*, XI, 119.

Thomas Head

Astrid Ehrencron-Kidde

(see: Astrid Margrethe Ehrencron-Kidde)

Astrid Margrethe Ehrencron-Kidde

(a.k.a. Astrid Ehrencron-Müller, Astrid Ehrencron-Kidde)

Born January 4, 1874, Copenhagen, Denmark; died June 30, 1960, Copenhagen
Genre(s): novel, short story, autobiography, children's literature
Language(s): Danish

Unlike women writers such as Karin Michaëlis and Agnes Henningsen, Astrid Ehrencron-Kidde did not participate in the women's rights debates of the early twentieth century. Distancing herself from contemporary issues, she explored universal themes of alienation, frustration and death in psychological-symbolist novels and tales.

Kidde was born into the wealthy Copenhagen bourgeoisie in 1874; at the age of thirty-three, she married the symbolist writer Harald Kidde. The couple traveled extensively in Germany and Sweden, but after the early death of her husband in 1918, Kidde lived a quiet, solitary life devoted to his memory.

The sense of tragedy that permeates Kidde's life and work surfaced in *Aeventyr* (1901; Fairy Tales) and continued into her five novels set in artistic-academic Copenhagen milieus. *Lille Fru Elsebeth* (1904; Little Mrs. Elsebeth) describes the unhappy union between a music-loving wife and her pragmatic-hedonist husband, while *Fru Hildes Hjem* (1907; Mrs. Hilde's Home) portrays a similar marriage in metaphors of resignation and death. *Foraeldrene* (1909; The Parents) is a study of parental egotism disguised as love.

The Swedish phase of Kidde's production, characterized by increased pessimism and gloom, includes the four-volume *Martin Willén's Underlige Haendelser* (1911–1921; The Strange Experiences of Martin Willén) and the *Brødrene Nystad* trilogy (1925–1927; The Nystad Brothers). *Enken paa Hafreljunga* (1923; The Widow of Hafreljunga) and *Historien om Min Moder* (1933; The Story of My Mother) combine typical Kidde themes of disappointed love, loneliness, insanity, and death with another characteristic motif: sexual fear and repression.

With her fantastic plots and realistic settings, Kidde belongs to the Gothic tradition of Ann Radcliffe, Mary Shelley and Isak Dinesen, whose psychological thrillers sought to extend the limitations of the authors' lives—if necessary, into death.

Works

Aeventyr (1901). *Fra Dronningens Taarnrude: Eventyr* (1902). *Livets og Dødens Eventyr* (1903). *Lille Fru Elsebeth* (1904). *Skumringshistorier fra Det Gamle Hus* (1904). *Den Signede Dag: En Historie fra Østerlide Praestegaard* (1905). *De Stille Dage* (1906). *Fru Hildes Hjem* (1907). *Ebbe Hermansens Oplevelser fra Rundetaarn til Frederiksberg Have* (1908). *Foraeldrene* (1909). *Jomfruer i Det Grønne* (1910). *Martin Willéns Underlige Haendelser* (1911). *Alle Sjaeles Nat* (1912). *Kavallererne fra Enghave* (1913). *En Vagabonds Roman* (1915). *Pastor Medin* (1916). *Skriveren fra Filipstad* (1917). *Over Sukkenes Bro* (1919). *Staffan Hellbergs Arv* (1920). *De Sporløse Veje* (1921). *Praestehistorier fra Det Gamle Värmland* (1922). *Enken paa Hafreljunga* (1923). *De Hvide Fugle* (1924). *Brødrene Nystad* (1925). *Brødrehuset* (1926). *Bjaergmandsgaarden* (1927). *Julen paa Brorstrup* (1928). *Den Barmhjertige Samaritan* (1929). *Huset ved Kanalen* (1930). *Under Josefbjaergets Skygge* (1932). *Historien om Min Moder* (1933). *Herskabet Lilja* (1934). *Nu Er Det Vaar* (1935). *Den Lange Aften* (1936). *Den Gode Hyrde* (1937). *Mimi i Storbyen* (1938). *Bronzehaanden* (1939). *Den Slemme Vibeke* (1939). *Karen, Maren og Mette* (1940). *Søskende Jeg Kender Fem* (1941). *Lille Ruth Hermansen* (1943). *Bag Stakittet* (1946). *Hvem Kalder—Fra Mine Erindringers Lønkammer* (1960).
Translations: "Kolaryd Farm," tr. Lida Siboni Hanson. *American-Scandinavian Review* 16 (August and September 1928). "A Tragedy at Herrhult

Station," tr. Henry Commager. *American-Scandinavian Review* 17 (August 1929).

Bibliography

Fabricius, Susanne, "Astrid Ehrencron-Kidde." *Danske Digtere i Det 20. Aarhundrede* I, ed. Torben Brostrøm and Mette Winge (Copenhagen, 1980), pp. 353–360.

Clara Juncker

Astrid Ehrencron-Müller

(see: Astrid Margrethe Ehrencron-Kidde)

Marianne Ehrmann

(a.k.a. Beobachterin [Observing Woman], Verfasserin der Amalia, Verfasserin der Philosophie eines Weibes, Maria Anna Antonia Sternheim)

Born November 25, 1755, Rapperswyl, Switzerland; died August 14, 1795, Stuttgart, Germany
Genre(s): periodical, novel, short essay, short story
Language(s): German

Marianne Ehrmann was important for her journalism and for a novel and several stories that describe milieus seldom represented in eighteenth-century literature, especially that written by and for women. Remarkable pre-feminist ideas characterize much of her later work.

Nothing is known about Ehrmann's early childhood; neither her parents nor her place of birth, beyond the family name Brentano, can be confirmed. She is said to have been raised by an uncle in Frankfurt. Her first marriage, to a man who is routinely identified only as a good-for-nothing, ended in divorce. Thereafter, Ehrmann apparently earned her own living, perhaps with a respectable stint as a governess, definitely for a while as an actress, calling herself Sternheim, after the virtuous heroine of Sophie von La Roche's first novel.

In about 1781 the young woman met and married T.F. Ehrmann, seven years her junior, and soon began writing. After publishing an anti-feminist essay in the tradition of Rousseau, three novels, and one play, and after assisting her husband with several periodicals that he put out, she established a monthly of her own: *Amalia's Leisure Hours, Dedicated to Germany's Daughters*. It survived for three years (fairly typical for periodicals of the time) before a dispute with her publisher forced Ehrmann to give it up. She promptly started another: *The Hermit from the Alps*, which was brought to an end two years later by Ehrmann's ill health. On August 14, 1795, at age 40, she died. Her husband continued to publish more of her works until 1798, including her most important novel, originally published in 1787 as *Amalie, A True Story in Letters*, and republished in 1796 and 1798 as *Antonie von Warnstein, A Story of our Times*.

Ehrmann is important for producing *Amalia's Leisure Hours*, one of the best magazines for women in eighteenth-century Germany. It contains articles on an impressive variety of subjects, poetry by some of the best writers of the day (including Schiller and Hölderlin), and stories and essays by the editor that are frequently remarkable for their freshness and candor. The monthly magazine was a good vehicle in which Ehrmann could develop both her style and her thoughts, which came increasingly into conflict with the dominant confining and complacent view of women. Ehrmann is now recognized as an important representative of pre-feminism. Her novel *Amalie* (later retitled *Antonie von Warnstein*) boldly depicts and justifies the life of an actress and more cautiously discusses the dangerous topic of divorce.

Works

Philosophie eines Weibs [A Woman's Philosophy. Tr. into French] (1784). *Leichtsinn und gutes Herz oder die Folgen der Erziehung. Ein Original-Schauspiel in 5 Aufzügen* [Frivolity and a Good Heart, or the Consequences of Education. An original play in 5 acts] (1786). *Amalie, eine wahre Geschichte in Briefen* [Amalie, a True Story in Letters] (1787); republished as *Antonie von Warnstein. Eine Geschichte aus unserm Zeitalter* [Antonie von Warnstein, a Story of Our Times. 2 vols.] (1796–1798). *Ninas Briefe an ihren Geliebten* [Nina's Letters to Her Beloved] (1788). *Graf Bilding, eine Geschichte aus dem mittlern Zeitalter, dialogisirt* [Count Bilding, a Story of the Middle Ages in Dialogue] (1788). *Kleine Fragmente für Denkerinnen* [Small Fragments for Thinking Women] (1788). *Amaliens Erholsstunden. Teutschlands Töchtern geweiht* [Amalia's Leisure Hours, Dedicated to Germany's Daughters. 3 vols] (1790–1792). *Die Einsiedlerinn aus den Alpen. Eine Monatsschrift zur Unterhaltung und Belehrung für Deutschlands und Helvetiens Töchter* [The Hermit from the Alps, a Monthly for the Entertainment and Instruction of Germany's and Helvetia's Daughters. 2 vols.] (1793–1794). *Erzählungen* [Tales] (1795). *Amaliens Feierstunden. Auswahl der hinterlassenen Schriften* [Amalia's Free Hours, a Selection from the Posthumous Writings. 3 vols.].

Bibliography

Brinker-Gabler, Gisela, ed., *Deutsche Literatur von Frauen: Vom Mittelalter bis zum Ende des 18. Jahrhunderts* (Munich, 1988), pp. 447–448, 459–468. Dawson, Ruth, "'And this shield is called—self-reliance.' Emerging Feminist Consciousness in the Late Eighteenth Century." in *German Women in the Eighteenth and Nineteenth Centuries. A Social and Literary History*, ed. Ruth-Ellen B. Joeres and Mary Jo Maynes (Bloomington, 1986), pp. 157–174. Dawson, Ruth, "Women Communicating: Eighteenth-Century German Journals Edited by Women." *Archives et Bibliotheques de Belgique* 54 (1983): 95–111. Friedrichs, Elisabeth, *Die deutschsprachigen Schriftstellerinnen des 18. und 19. Jahrhunderts. Ein Lexikon* (Stuttgart, 1981), p. 70. Frederiksen, Elke, ed., *Women Writers of Germany, Austria, and Switzerland. An Annotated Bio-Bibliographical Guide* (New York, 1989), pp. 64–65. Geiger, Ruth-Esther, and Sigrid Weigel, eds., *Sind das noch Damen? Vom gelehrten Frauenzimmer-Journal zum feministischen Journalismus* (München, 1981), pp. 13–26. Krull, Edith. *Das Wirken der Frau im frühen deutschen Zeitschriftenwesen* (Charlottenburg, 1939), pp. 236–276. Beiträge zur Erforschung der deutschen Zeitschrift, v. 5.

Ruth P. Dawson

Eikasia

(see: Kassia)

Alice Ekert-Rotholz

Born September 5, 1900, Hamburg, Germany
Genre(s): novel
Language(s): German

Alice Ekert-Rotholz was born in Hamburg on September 5, 1900 to a British father and a German mother. From 1939 to 1952 she lived in Bangkok. Upon her return to Hamburg in 1952, she began to write for the press and radio. Since 1959 she has lived in London.

Her first book *Siam hinter der Bambuswand* (Siam Behind the Bamboo Wall), a travelbook on East Asia, was published in 1953. It was followed in 1954 by her first novel, *Reis aus Silberschalen* (Rice in Silver Dishes). This story of a German family reunited after World War II in Bangkok in 1950 was a great success and is still in print. This novel represents the first exploration of the themes that were to dominate Ekert-Rotholz's subsequent works: the shared humanity of people of all cultures and races, the differences of cultures (especially European and Asian, or European and Caribbean), and the conflicts arising out of these differences. Her second novel, *Wo Tränen verboten sind* (in English translation, *The Time of the Dragons*), addresses these issues directly. Main protagonists of the novel are three half-sisters fathered by the Norwegian Consul in Shanghai; their mothers are respectively French, Norwegian, and Chinese. Their lives are followed through the 1930s to the 1950s in Asia and Europe. *Strafende Sonne, Lockender Mond* (in English translation, *A Net of Gold*) is set among the Dutch colonialists in Indonesia; *Flucht aus den Bambusgärten* (Flight from the Bamboo Gardens), published in 1981, takes place mainly in Southeast Asia and Europe.

Ekert-Rotholz's novels are panoramic in scope: large casts of characters, changing locales, interpolated sections on historical backgrounds, precise geographic descriptions, and social analyses. In her later works, as *Der Juwelenbaum* (The Jewel Tree) or *Nur eine Tasse Tee* (Only a Cup of Tea), she purposefully replaces the narra-tive structure of the novel by episodes related to a central, connecting motif. And in the collections of stories *Elfenbein aus Peking* (Ivory from Peking) and *Füchse in Kamakura: Japanisches Panorama* (Foxes in Kamakura: A Japanese Panorama) she even discards that connecting framework.

The inability of people to communicate with each other, despite their shared humanity, because of the barriers created by different cultures (and their inability to overcome these cultural barriers, much less to become aware of them) is the recurring theme of all her works, regardless of where they take place. Ekert-Rotholz is a very careful observer, recording foreign cultures in telling detail, striving for objectivity and avoiding racial stereotypes. Her special sympathy is for those persons who have parents from two cultures (Dutch and Indonesian, or Norwegian and Malay) and cannot find acceptance in either culture.

The majority of her novels have become best-sellers, and many have remained in print for twenty or thirty years. Over three million copies of her works have been sold. Partly because of her commercial success, partly because of the exotic locales, and partly for their own merit, her works are considered "entertainment." This is probably an intellectual undervaluation; commercial success does not automatically imply lack of artistic quality.

Works

Siam hinter der Bambuswand. Ein ostasiatisches Reisebuch (1953). *Reis aus Silberschalen. Roman einer deutschen Familie im heutigen Ostasien* (1954). *Wo Tränen verboten sind. Roman der Wandlungen* (1956). *Strafende Sonne—Lockender Mond* (1959). *Mohn in den Bergen. Der Roman der Marie Bonnard* (1961). *Die Pilger und die Reisenden. Roman aus Sydney* (1964). *Elfenbein aus Peking. Sechs Geschichten* (1966). *Der Juwelenbaum. Karibisches Panorama* (1968). *Fünf Uhr Nachmittag* (1971). *Limbo oder Besuch aus Berlin* (1972). *Füchse in Kamakura. Japanisches Panorama* (1975). *Die fliessende Welt oder Aus dem Leben einer Geisha* (1978). *Gastspiel am Rialto* (1978). *Grosser Wind, Kleiner Wind. Zwei Karibische Geschichten* (1980). *Flucht aus den Bambusgärten* (1981). *Nur eine Tasse Tee* (1984).

Translations: *The Time of the Dragons* (1958). *A Net of Gold* (1960). *Marie Bonnard* (1962).

Hortense Bates

Eleonore of Austria

(a.k.a. Eleonore of Scotland)

Born 1433, Scotland; died, 1480
Genre(s): prose romance
Language(s): German

One of six daughters of the art-loving James I of the House of Stuart, Eleonore was brought up in Scotland and France. After her marriage to Sigmund of Tyrol, she resided at the court of Innsbruck, which she helped develop into one of the major cultural centers of the German-speaking countries. Her contacts with various Humanist writers of that period made her famous in literary circles. Thus she is praised by Heinrich Stainhöwel in the preface to his German version of Boccaccio's *De claris mulieribus* (1473) as the brightest shining light of womanhood. Any literary activity on her part, however, is not mentioned here.

Her place in literary history is based entirely on her alleged authorship of *Pontus und Sidonia*, the German version of an anonymous French prose romance *Ponthus et la belle Sidoyne* which is derived from the twelfth-century *chanson de geste Horn et Rimenhild*. The plot of this work consists of a skillful blend of knightly motives in the tradition of the *chansons de geste* (warfare against Muslim invaders, exile and reconquest of homeland) and of courtly-sentimental elements (exemplary courtship between prince and princess, betrayal by others, happy reunion). *Pontus and Sidonia* sets the tone for numerous similar works in the sixteenth and seventeenth centuries, becoming one of the most popular German chapbooks (the so-called *Volksbücher*, see also *Elisabeth of Nassau-Saarbrücken*), judging by the number of references to it and the number of its reprintings. While the first edition of *Pontus und Sidonia* came out in 1483, three years after Eleonore's death, the work itself must have been written before 1465, when a manuscript copy was made of it. The opening paragraph of the print states that Eleonore translated the story ("ein schoene Historj") to please her husband the

Archduke. Doubts have lately been voiced regarding the authenticity of Eleonore's authorship in view of the fact that her mastery of the German language (judging by several of her autograph letters) was inadequate at that time for such a task. Hence it is well possible, as Köfler and Maleczek argue, that this translation was done by a cleric at the Innsbruck court, perhaps with Eleonore's help, and later attributed to her by her husband in order to gain fame for her and himself, perhaps also for commercial reasons.

Works

Pontus und Sidonia, ed. H. Kindermann. *Volksbücher vom sterbenden Rittertum* (=Dt. Lit. in Entwicklungsreihen), 1928, pp. 115–236.

Bibliography

Köfler, M., *Eleonore von Schottland.* Diss., Innsbruck, 1968. Köfler, M., and S. Caramelle, *Die beiden Frauen des Erzherzogs Sigmund von Österreich-Tirol* (Schlern-Schriften, 269) (Innsbruck, 1982). Maleczek, W., "Die Sachkultur am Hofe Herzog Sigismunds von Tirol." *Adelige Sachkultur des Spätmittelalters* (=Veröffentlichungen des Instituts für Mittelalterl. Realienkunde Österreichs, 5) (Vienna, 1982), pp. 113–167.
General references: L. Mackensen, "E. v. Österreich," in *Dt. Lit. d. Mittelalters. Verfasserlexikon*, ed. W. Stammler, vol. 1 (1933), pp. 543–547 and H.-H. Steinhoff, "E. v. Ö," in *Dt. Lit. d. Mittelalters. Verfasserlexikon*, ed. K. Ruh, vol. 2 (1980), pp. 470–473.

Karl A. Zaenker

Eleonore of Scotland

(see: Eleonore of Austria)

Elisa, Elise

(see: Elisabeth [Elisa] Charlotte Konstantia von der Recke)

Elisabeth of Nassau-Saarbrücken

Born after 1393 (1397?), Vézélise, France; died 1456, Saarbrücken
Genre(s): prose romance
Language(s): German

Elisabeth of Nassau-Saarbrücken, with whose name the beginnings of a prose fiction tradition in Germany are connected, came from a French-speaking court in Lorraine and was raised by a mother steeped in the tradition of the late medieval *Chansons de geste*. Married to a German count at an early age, Elisabeth combined the tasks of raising her sons and administering her lands (she was widowed in 1429, her oldest son did not succeed to the throne until 1438), as well as translating and introducing French chivalric literature to a German courtly audience. Her family relations extended to the leading cultural centers in Lorraine and Burgundy on the one side and Heidelberg on the other, the home of the younger Countess Palatine Mechthild, the foremost patroness of German literature in southern Germany of the later fifteenth century. Elisabeth's tomb lies in the Collegiate Church of St. Arnual in Saarbrücken (See photo in Burger, p. 87).

The French sources of the four romances attributed to Elisabeth are rhymed *Chansons de geste* connected loosely with the romanticized figures of Charlemagne, his successors, and his enemies. In an ambiguous phrase at the end of *Loher und Maller*, Elisabeth's mother Margarethe of Vaudémont is credited with having written the French version; it is more likely to assume, however, that Margarethe had copies of the *Chansons de geste* produced for herself or her daughter, compilations and adaptations of romances of the thirteenth and fourteenth centuries. Elisabeth must have completed her translations into German prose by 1437, the date found in the *subscriptio* of the second last work, *Loher und Maller*.

The first of Elisabeth's romances is commonly referred to as *Herpin*. Its lengthier title in Simrock's uncritical edition *Der weiße Ritter oder Geschichte von Herzog Herpin von Bourges und seinem Sohne Löw* indicates the three major strands of the narrative that relates the trials of Charlemagne's maligned and exiled retainer Herpin and his son Löw. Various fairy-tale motifs play a major role in the plot, e.g., young Löw (Lion de Bourges) is nurtured by a lioness, four fairies cast their spells over the infant, a grateful ghost (the white knight) comes to his aid in his later heroic fights, a magic horn can only be blown by him, etc. The work was repeatedly printed between 1514 and 1659.

The second romance, *Sibille*, on the other hand, did not achieve this degree of popularity and exists only in the sumptuous set of folio manuscripts of Elisabeth's oeuvre produced after her death by her son Johann. It is the story of the unjustly maligned consort of Charlemagne, Sibille, who while in exile gives birth to Ludwig and is finally reinstated in her honor and reunited with the emperor.

The third romance, *Loher und Maller*, takes the reader a generation further to the struggle for the imperial title between Ludwig and his brother Loher (a fictional conglomerate of the Merovingian Clotaire I of the sixth century and the Carolingian Lothair of the ninth). Loher is banned from the French court and while in exile wins the hand of the East Roman Emperor's daughter. With the aid of his devoted friend Maller he fights the heathens, the Greeks and the Franks, is crowned Roman Emperor by the Pope but loses his beloved wife in childbirth, accidentally kills his friend Maller, and ends in despair as a hermit. This work exists in various manuscript copies of the fifteenth and early prints of the sixteenth centuries and was rediscovered and reprinted in an abridged and modernized form by an outstanding *femme de lettres* of the Romantic movement, Dorothea Schlegel, in 1806, under her husband Friedrich Schlegel's name.

The last and most interesting of Elisabeth's romances is that of *Huge Scheppel* based on the *chanson de geste Hugues Capet*. In an entirely fictional manner it relates the dynastic change from the Carolingians to the Capetians, the ascent of Hugh, the butcher's grandson, to the French throne by winning the deceased Ludwig's daughter through a series of ruthless feats of arms. *Der schneed Gebuwer* ("the loathsome proletarian"), as he is called by his aristocratic enemies, succeeds in blotting out the blemish of his low birth by beating the established caste at their own game: that of warfare, duelling, or murdering (the butcher's grandson excels in that, as the author slyly remarks), and at that of courting and seducing noble ladies. His ten bastard sons who appear at court at an inopportune moment increase his fame rather than his disgrace: "ist wol in Buelschaft groß Thorheit; so ist ouch große Freud und Wollust darin," he justifies his amorous exploits ("while there is great folly in the pursuit of love, there is also great joy and pleasure in it").

Modern critics have pointed out that Elisabeth merely produced a close translation of the French originals without adapting them to the new medium and without shaping the contents herself. The crudity of the source texts whether in the description of brutalities or in the seemingly emotionless erotic encounters is only slightly mitigated. Indeed, the purpose of Elisabeth's literary activity seems to have been to transmit into Germany subject matters popular among the contemporary French aristocracy. In doing so she uses the medium of prose familiar to late medieval French fiction but in Germany hitherto used only for religious or factual texts. Elisabeth thereby stands at the beginnings of a trend in German literature that lasted for over two centuries and produced numerous offshoots (e.g., *Pontus und Sidonia* attributed to *Eleonore Von Österreich*). In its many printed versions this type of literature (the so-called *Volksbücher*) reached the well-to-do bourgeois readers well into the eighteenth century who would marvel at the glorious feats and tribulations of these romantic heroes and heroines but would also be reassured by the message that everybody is bound to the Wheel of Fortune and that submission to God's will is quintessential in everybody's life.

Works

Herpin in K. Simrock. *Die deutschen Volksbücher* 11 (1892; rpt. 1974), pp. 213–445. *Der Roman von der Königin Sibille in drei Prosafassungen d. 14. u. 15. Jahrhunderts*, ed. H. Tiemann (1977), pp. 117–186. *Loher und Maller* (abridged) in Friedrich Schlegel, *Sammlung von Memoiren und Romantischen Dichtungen des Mittelalters aus Altfranzösischen und Deutschen Quellen*, ed. L. Dieckmann (1980), pp. 377–456. *Huge Scheppel*, in H. Kindermann, *Volksbücher vom sterbenden Rittertum* (1928), pp. 23–114.

Bibliography

Frey, W., W. Raitz, and D. Seitz, *Einführung in die dt. Lit. d. 12. bis 16. Jahrhunderts*, vol. 3: *Bürgertum und Fürstenstaat—15/16. Jahrhundert* (Opladen, 1981), pp. 69–91. Liepe, W., *Elisabeth von Nassau-Saarbrücken. Entstehung und Anfänge d. Prosaromans in Deutschland* (Halle, 1920). Liepe. W., "Die Entstehung d. Prosaromans in Dtld," in W. Liepe, *Beiträge zur Literatur—und Geistesgeschichte* (Neumünster, 1963), pp. 9–28. Mackensen, L., *Die deutschen Volksbücher* (Leipzig, 1927). **General references**: Burger, H.O., *Renaissance. Humanismus. Reformation* (Homburg, 1969), pp. 86–91. Steinhoff, H.H., "E. v. N.-S.," in *Dt. Lit. d. Mittelalters. Verfasserlexikon*, ed. K. Ruh, vol. 2 (1980), pp. 482–488. Sudhof, S., "E. v. N.-S." in *Dt. Lit. d. Mittelalters. Verfasserlexikon*, vol. 5, ed. K. Langosch (Berlin, 1955), pp. 194–199.

Karl A. Zaenker

Elisabeth of Schönau

Born 1129; died June 18, 1164, Schönau, Germany
Genre(s): visions
Language(s): Latin

Elisabeth entered the Benedictine monastery of Schönau at twelve years of age and was professed in 1147. Schönau near St. Goarshausen on the Rhine was founded ca. 1130 as a double Benedictine monastery run by an abbot. From 1157 to her death, Elisabeth was the *magistra* of the women's convent. Her literary work was written as guidance for her fellow nuns.

In poor health during all her life, Elisabeth went through a severe crisis in 1152 that led to visionary experiences (a vision of the Trinity among them) that recurred during the remainder of her life. In 1155, Elisabeth urged her brother Ekbert (Eckbert, Egbert) to enter the Schönau monastery. Ekbert of Schönau (d. 1184) became Elisabeth's spiritual advisor, often urging her to find in her visions answers for crucial questions prevalent in the church and state of their time. Upon Elisabeth's dictations in both Latin and

German, Ekbert also composed her visionary works in Latin.

Typical of Elisabeth's visions is the presence of St. John or of an "angel" who interprets to her what she has seen but may not have understood and whose theological concepts at times differ from those of Ekbert (cf. especially Elisabeth's vision of Christ as a woman, *Visiones* III, 4).

Elisabeth of Schönau is a younger contemporary of Hildegard of Bingen (see entry) whom she met and admired and with whom she corresponded. Although a visionary like Hildegard, Elisabeth is unequal to her in scope or originality. Yet, like Hildegard, she exhorts monks and bishops to an inner reform of the church; in fact, at times, she violently attacks the abuses within the church and the offensive behavior of its representatives.

While some of Elisabeth's visions were ridiculed even by her contemporaries, other parts of her work experienced great popularity during the Middle Ages. Over 150 manuscripts are still extant, several among them from the twelfth century, and some spread as far as England and Iceland as early as the twelfth century. There has never been a critical edition nor a complete translation into any vernacular language of Elisabeth's works.

Elisabeth's three most important "visionary cycles" (Köster) are: *Liber viarum Dei* (1156–1157), influenced by Hildegard of Bingen's *Scivias*; *Revelationes de sacro exercitu virginum Coloniensium* (1156–1157), a visionary account of the phantastic legend of St. Ursula and her 11,000 companions (the number presumably a misreading of the name Ximilla). This account was the most widely circulated of Elisabeth's works and exerted an enormous influence on her contemporaries, no doubt accounting for Elisabeth's popularity in her time; and *Visio de resurrectione beatae Mariae virginis* (1156–1159), a response to the great contemporary interest in the details of Mary's life.

Elisabeth's visions were collected, edited, and prefaced by Ekbert of Schönau in three books, *Liber I-III visionum* (1152–1164). About twenty of Elisabeth's letters are also extant.

Elisabeth of Schönau's books have never been acknowledged by the church, nor has she ever been canonized; she is venerated as a local saint only in the Limburg diocese where Schönau is located. Her works were popular throughout the Middle Ages and during the baroque and pietistic periods. A critical edition of *Visiones* is needed for a proper evaluation of her work.

Works

Die Visionen der hl. Elisabeth und die Schriften der Aebte Ekbert und Emecho von Schönau, ed. F.W.E. Roth (Brünn, 1884) (Latin text). *Acta SS.* 1st ed. (June 3, 1701), pp. 604–643 and 3rd ed. (June 4, 1867), pp. 400–532.

Bibliography

Kessel, Johann Hubert, *St. Ursula und ihre Gesellschaft* (Cologne, 1863). Köster, Kurt, *Das visionäre Werk Elisabeths von Schönau* (Speyer, 1952). Köster, Kurt, *Elisabeth von Schönau, Werk und Wirkung* (Speyer, 1951). Petroff, Elizabeth Alvilda, *Medieval Women's Visionary Literature* (New York and Oxford, 1986). Preger, Wilhelm, *Geschichte der deutschen Mystik im Mittelalter*, vol. 1 (München, 1874; rpt. Aalen, 1962). *Schönauer Elisabeth Jubiläum 1965*. Festschrift (Schönau, 1965). Spiess, Emil, *Ein Zeuge mittelalterlicher Mystik* (Rorschach, 1935), pp. 69–116.

General references: Köster, Kurt, *Verfasserlexikon*, 2nd ed., 2 (1980), pp. 488–494, and Krebs, Engelbert, 1st ed., 1 (1933), pp. 554–556. Ochsenbein, Peter, *DLL* (*Deutsches Literatur-Lexikon*) 4 (1972): 154–157. del Re, Niccolo, *BSS* (*Bibliotheca sanctorum*) 11 (1968): 730–732. Laughlin, M.F., *NCE* (*New Catholic Encyclopedia*) 5 (1967): 283. Didier, J.C., *DHGE* (*Dictionnaire d'histoire et de géographie ecclestiastique*) 15 (1963): 221–224. Köster, Kurt, *DSp* (*Dictionnaire de spiritualité*) 4 (1960): 858–888. *Lexikon der Frau* (1953): 915. *Universal-Lexikon* 8 (1734): 841.

Other references: Lewis, Gertrud Jaron, *Jahrbuch für Internationale Germanistik* 15 (1983). Widding, Ole, and Hans Bekker Nielsen, *Mediaeval Studies* 23 (1961). Swartling, Ingrid, *Fornvännen* 40 (1954). Dean, Ruth J., *Modern Philology* 41 (1943/44). Levison, William, *Bonner Jahrbücher* 132 (1927). Whitman, W.F., *Anglican Theological Review* (March 1921). Steele, F.M., *The American Catholic Quarterly Review* 36 (1911).

Gertrud Jaron Lewis

Elisaveta Ivanova Zirkowa

(a.k.a. Elisheva)

Born 1888, Russia; died 1949, Kinneret
Genre(s): poetry, short story, novel
Language(s): Hebrew

Elisheva, Russian by birth, was adopted by the Jewish people. She began her life along the banks of the Volga, and as a schoolgirl was a student in a gymnasium in Moscow. While in Moscow, she developed a friendship with several Jewish families, and this sparked her interest in both Jewish life and literature. She began studying the Hebrew language with the use of a Hebrew grammar given to her by her brother, an Orientalist. As she advanced in her studies she grew more and more attracted to the Zionist ideal, and she finally made her decision to convert to Judaism.

Whether Elisheva's conversion was genuine has been questioned by recent scholarship; however, friends and relatives asserted the reality of her experience at the time, and scholars of her day have written of her devotion to her new people and fatherland, which must have come from her conversion to the beliefs and ways of her new people.

The first volume of poetry published by Elisheva was a small, sixteen-page volume written in Russian, *Tayniya Pyesni* (1919). In this volume she deals with her feelings of maladjustment, of being torn between two peoples, and her desperate need to merge with the new family she has chosen. She prefaces the volume with a quotation from Ruth 1:16, "Your people shall be my people, your God my God." Her passion for the Jewish life emerges in the intimate and somewhat drab verse of this volume.

Two other volumes of poetry, *Kos Ketennah* (A Small Cup) and *Haruzim* (Verses), are thin collections of short poems, mainly consisting of themes of nature and love. Most of Elisheva's poetry is not lyrical, but her short poems of nature certainly come the closest. In these poems she seems to reveal the very dwelling place of her soul, which is lost in the beauty of forests, streams, and the sacredness of the land itself. Elisheva sings of the beauty of the Kinneret and the majesty of the city of Jerusalem. The tone of her poems is not sorrowful or melancholy as with many Hebrew poets, but rather it seems to celebrate her acceptance in the "hallowed land of God" ("Green Pines"). At times she appears wistful for the past, for her native land, but her positive spirit shines through her exquisite Hebrew poetry.

Elisheva's prose deals mainly with two themes, alienation and love. In her first volume of prose, *Sippurim* (Stories), the short story "Nerot Shel Shabbat" (Sabbath Candles) depicts a young Gentile girl who falls in love with a Jew and develops a deep fascination for the rites of the Sabbath. They have a deeper meaning for the young girl as she studies their implications for humanity. In the same volume Elisheva reverses her story in "Malkah la-'Ivrim" (Queen of the Jews). Here a Jewish girl falls in love with a Gentile young man and makes a sad attempt to lose her Jewish identity. In this pathetic process she also loses her lover. She has built a wall between them that can never be destroyed.

Another short story, published separately in 1928, embodies a similar theme. *Mikveh Tafel* (Unimportant Incident) is a story about an assimilated girl who has acquired fluency in Russian and adapted to life in Russia. An old Jew moves to her town, is soon caught with the body of a child in a sack, and immediately imprisoned. The town quickly adopts the cry of "Blood libel" and the growing antisemitism reaches even to the girl's best friend. The girl's relationship with her new people is not broken, but yet it is irreparably damaged.

Alienation was a reality for Elisheva's life, and it was constantly a topic for her writing. This theme is also encountered in her only novel, *Simtoat* (Alleys), about the struggle of a Hebrew writer and a Russian woman poet to retain their love. Even though much of this work came from her own biography (she was married to a Jew), Elisheva's ability to find sustaining imagery and language falls short in such a complex endeavor. Her poems and short stories develop her themes of love and alienation much better.

In 1925 Elisheva was able to capture much of the joy of nature and beauty of her beloved land as she and her Jewish husband, Simon Bichowsky, moved to Israel. It was in this land where she wrote much of her prose and continued to struggle with the alienation and loss of love she experienced. She finally found peace in her resting place on the banks of the Sea of Galilee in 1949.

Works

Tayniya Pyesni (1919). Kos Ketennah [A Small Cup] (1926). Haruzim [Verses] (1927). Sippurim [Stories] (1927). Meshorer ve-adam [Poet and Mankind] (1928–1929). Mikveh Tafel [Unimportant Incident] (1928–1929). Simtoat [Alleys] (1929).

Bibliography

Lubner S.H., and L.V., Snowman, eds. Stories and Poems [by] Elisheva (London, 1933). Silberschlag, Eisig, From Renaissance to Renaissance II: Hebrew Literature in the Land of Israel: 1870–1970 (New York, 1977). Waxman, Meyer, A History of Jewish Literature, Vol. 4 (Cranbury, N.J., 1960).

JoAnne C. Juett

Elisheva

(see: Elisaveta Ivanova Zirkowa)

"rija Elksne

Born 1928
Genre(s): poetry, children's literature, translation
Language(s): Latvian

"rija Elksne (pseudonym of Demidova) has produced several volumes of lyrical poetry, poetry for children, and critical articles on contemporary poetry. She is known also as a translator and editor of literary publications. Her traditional, personally lyrical verse is characterized by precision, clarity and unity, so much so that she has been reproached for her narrow lyrical focus. Although her output is not extensive, she has gained a popular following in Soviet Latvia.

Works

Klusuma Krastā. Majupceļš [The Road Home] (1978). Stari [Rays] (1982).

Warwick J. Rodden

Ellen

(see: Elena Farago)

Gisela Elsner

Born 1937, Nuremberg, Germany
Genre(s): novel, short story
Language(s): German

Gisela Elsner was born into an upper-middle-class educated family as daughter of a scientist turned business executive. After attending a strict Catholic school, she studied German literature and theater in Vienna. She has lived in Rome, London, Paris, Hamburg, and New York and now lives in Munich. She became known when she first read at Group 47 gatherings in 1962 and 1963, immediately after which her novels and story collections started appearing. In 1964, she received the prestigious international Prix Formentor and a grant from the publisher Hoffmann & Campe.

Gisela Elsner must be considered one of the more important West German fiction writers, especially of the satirical genre. Her texts excoriate the monstrous postwar world—children growing up on the twenty-sixth floor, fat old men paying mistresses—and especially the macabre upper-middle class. As her chief literary influences, she has identified Kafka, Beckett, and the Hemingway generation. And to be sure, her oeuvre exhibits parallels with Grass, M. Walser, and Böll, to mention just a few of her German contemporaries. While in her earlier books, the absurd sometimes erupts arbitrarily from outside and above, in her best books it constitutes an integral part of reality, which she observes and describes with relentless precision, choosing often a woman's perspective: in Berührungsverbot, she describes the sexual mores embedded in hypocrisy of bourgeois circles, while Abseits, which has been translated into English, is her contemporary version of Madame Bovary, culminating in the husband's smug good conscience after the wife's suicide.

Works

[With Klaus Roehler], Triboll (1956). Riesenzwerge (1964). Nachwuchs (1968). Berührungsverbot

(1970). *Punktsieg* (1977). *Zerreissprobe* (1980). *Abseits* (1982). *Die Zähmung. Chronik einer Ehe* (1984).

Bibliography

Puknus, Heinz, ed., *Neue Literatur der Frauen* (Munich, 1980). Serke, Jürgen, *Frauen schreiben* (Frankfurt, 1982).

Ute Marie Saine

Anne Karin Elstad

Born January 19, 1938, western Norway
Genre(s): novel
Language(s): Norwegian (bokmål and dialect)

Elstad has made a name for herself first as a historical novelist and later for her contemporary novels, *Senere, Lena* (1982; Later, Lena) and *Sitt eget liv* (1983; One's Own Life). She is one of Norway's most popular writers, and won the Norwegian Booksellers' Prize in 1982 for *Senere, Lena*.

Raised on a traditional farm in western Norway, Elstad learned early to value history. Her grandfather had been one of the founding fathers of modern Norway, and her family was interested in genealogy as well as folk music, literature and art. The second youngest of six children, Elstad lost her mother when she was twelve, and took on a large part of the responsibility for the farm from the age of fourteen.

Though she had wanted to become an actor, she trained as a teacher, and held a full-time teaching position until 1977, combining her writing with caring for her three children.

In her historical novel cycle, *Folket på Innhaug* (1976; The People of Innhaug), *Magret* (1977), *Nytt rotfeste* (1979; Roots Catch Hold Anew), and *Veiene møtes* (1980; The Roads Shall Meet), Elstad shows the solidarity she felt with ordinary people, particularly the women, who had lived before her. She begins in the early 1800s with the story of Oline, the shy, beautiful farm girl, who fell in love with an Englishman and bore him an illegitimate daughter. Elstad then follows the fate of the daughter Magret through her life until she, as an old woman, comes to a deeper understanding of herself and her life.

In her most recent novels, Elstad has moved to the 20th century as she writes about Lena, a product of 1950s values, who is trapped in a conflict-ridden marriage with a man who is unable to understand her. In *Senere, Lena* (1982; Later, Lena), Lena struggles to take responsibility for her own life and to free herself from the "Dollhouse" existence her husband had created for her. The sequel, *Sitt eget liv* (1984; One's Own Life), follows Lena's efforts to make an independent life for herself and her son.

In 1987 Elstad suffered a severe stroke, which impaired her writing for a time. In 1988, however, she published a novel titled *Maria, Maria*, about the experience of dealing with stroke.

Whether she writes about the past or the present day, Anne Karin Elstad is interested in the effects of society and environment on the fate of the individual. She feels that men and women should be equal partners, not adversaries.

Works

Folket på Innhaug [The People of Innhaug] (1976). *Magret* (1977). *Nytt rotfeste* [Roots Catch Hold Anew] (1979). *Veiene møtes* [The Roads Shall Meet] (1980). *Senere, Lena* [Later, Lena] (1982). *Sitt eget liv* [One's Own Life] (1983). *—for dagene er onde* [—for the Days are Evil] (1985). *Maria, Maria* (1988).

Bibliography

Dahl, Willy, *Norges litteratur III: Tid og tekst 1935–1972* (Oslo, 1989), pp. 280, 297ff. Granaas, Rakel Christina, "Anne Karin Elstad: *Senere, Lena. Sitt Eget liv*." *Kjerringråd* 2: 25–26. Review. Halse, Marte, "*Senere, Lena*. Rapport fra et mini-seminar." *Arena* 2: 8–16. Haslund, Ebba, Afterword in *Folket på Innhaug* (Oslo, 1984).

Margaret Hayford O'Leary

Elvire

(see: Julie-Françoise Bouchaud des Hérettes Charles)

Mária Ember

Born April 19, 1931, Abadszalok, Hungary
Genre(s): novel, documentary, short fiction,
    translation, guidebook
Language(s): Hungarian

Mária Ember was educated in the University of Budapest. A journalist by training, she incorporates factual materials in her fiction. Her own experiences in public life inform her novels *I Am Telling a Tale for Myself* (1968) and *Coincidences* (1971). Her major novel, *In the Hairpin Bend* (1974), utilizes personal memories in its portrayal of the deportation of Hungarian Jews to Nazi concentration camps. Ember's mosaic-like insertions of documentary materials increase the credibility of the narrator and raise the level of dramatic tension.

She translated the works of such twentieth-century German authors into Hungarian as Arnold Zweig, Bertolt Brecht and Anna Seghers. Her sketches and short stories were published in 1979 in a volume entitled *Folder Poem and Other Stories*. The novel *Ridiculous* (1979) is a literary parody.

Ember is the author of many guidebooks: *Trips in Bavaria* (1980), *Vienna* (1982), *Berlin, The Capital of the GDR* (1977), *London* (1972), *The Federal Republic of Germany* (1980).

Works

Magamnak mesélek (1968). Véletlenek (1971). Hajtűkanyar (1974). Aktavers és egyéb történetek (1979). Nevetséges (1979).

Bibliography

Pomogáts, Béla, *Az ujabb magyar irodalom története* (Budapest, 1982).

Peter I. Barta

Cornelia Emilian

Born 1840, Zlatna, Romania; died 1910,
    Bucharest
Genre(s): journalism, memoirs, essay, short
    story
Language(s): Romanian

In 1867 and 1894, respectively, Cornelia Emilian created two feminist associations named "Reuniunea femeilor române" (The Reunion of the Romanian Women) and "Liga femeilor" (The Women's League).

A regular contributor to *Revista literară, Fîntîna Blanduziei, Literatorul, Revista poporului, Familia,* Cornelia Emilian is mostly known for her volume *Amintiri* (1886; Memories) in which she discusses feminist issues and presents vivid scenes from the 1848 revolution. Other volumes such as *Fapte ale omului* (1887; Actions of Man) and *Omenirea în stare de pruncie* (1886; Humankind in a State of Childhood) as well as the short story *Un cadavru* (1898; A Corpse) still await a serious literary exegesis.

Works

Amintiri [Memories] (1886). *Omenirea în stare de pruncie* [Humankind in a State of Childhood] (1886). *Fapte ale omului* [Actions of Man] (1887). "Un cadavru" [A Corpse] (1898).

Bibliography

Buzatu, Constanţa, in *Dicţionarul literaturii române de la origini pînă la 1900* (Bucharest, 1979), pp. 311–312. Eminescu, Henriette and Mihail, *Scrisori către Cornelia Emilian şi fiica sa Cornelia* (Iaşi). Predescu, Lucian, *Enciclopedia "Cugetarea"* (Bucharest, 1940). Torouţiu, I.E., *Studii şi documente literare* (Bucharest, 1931–1946), vol. IV, XLVIII-LXIV.

Sanda Golopentia

Emilie

(see: Kathinka [Katharina] Rosa
    Pauline Modesta Zitz-Halein)

Emmeline

(see: Kathinka [Katharina] Rosa
    Pauline Modesta Zitz-Halein)

Anne-Catherine Emmerich (also Emmerick)

Born September 8, Flamske near Coesfeld in Westphalia; died February 9, 1824, Dülmen

Genre(s): spiritual visions

Language(s): German

The daughter of poor peasants, Emmerich felt the longing for religious life since her teens (sixteen) and refused marriage, but, because of her parents' opposition and lack of a dowry, she was accepted among Dülmen Augustinian nuns only in 1802. The convent being suppressed by Napoleonic decrees, Emmerich became a maid for an *émigré* French priest, Jean-Martin Lambert (1812). Lambert was the first one to accept and encourage Emmerich's supernatural gifts: sensitiveness both to holy places and to places where a crime had been committed; encounters with Holy Mary, her guardian angel, and Jesus. When she was eighteen, Jesus offered her two crowns, a rose and a thorny one, and Emmerich chose the thorns. She received stigmata. In 1873 she became very ill and could work no more. Lambert placed her in the care of a poor widow; there Emmerich was bed-ridden until her death, in torments both for her own pains and for the voluntary acceptance of others' diseases and moral worries. Since 1813 there are two major subjects of controversy about her life and what will be her bequest as a dictating author: (1) stigmata; (2) visions. She was examined for stigmata and kept under control by priests and physicians up to a government commission (August 5–29, 1819) which declared Emmerich's effective possibility to feed herself only on water. As for her visions, the Romantic German poet Clemens Brentano (1768–1840), a convert to Catholic practice in 1816, felt that such "visions" were so important that he considered their writing and spreading a providential task to which he devoted himself. He settled in Dülmen from 1818 to until she died in 1824, visiting her almost daily and listening to her dictate in "almost inaudible voice in an almost constant ecstasy." Brentano gives two definitions about such communications: (a) they must be considered as the pious communications of a nun . . . on tales she told out of obedience [so had Emmerich begun after the wish of Overberg, her confessor] and to which she wanted to give a purely human worth"; (b) "not only did she see the Passion of our Savior, but, during three years, she had followed him in all his journeys all over Palestine and beyond that country. The nature of soil, rivers, mountains, woods, the inhabitants and their usages, all that passed by before her in clear and lively images." In fact, the reader is struck by an agreeable and familiar liveliness of details (e.g., Cana's wedding; Lazarus' house, his sisters; the Last Supper . . .). The problem of the genuineness of these *visions* and/or *meditations* remains open. They largely "embroider" on the Gospels' text and plot by additional episodes, dialogues, and attitudes that seem to come from imagination or from apocryphal texts, as well as from rather negligible commentaries or hagiolatry. The part Brentano played in such texts (either consciously or unconsciously) seems important. After the study of sources, Schüddenkopf, the editor of Brentano's *Opera omnia*, presented (1912–1913) the first two books as the personal work of the poet. Not one of these books had been written, even partially, by Emmerich herself, nor submitted to her control; the last one came out fifty-seven years after her death. H. Thurston, S.J. considers these visions as "communications of mediumnic origin or by automatic writing."

Works

Biography: Outline by Brentano as an introduction to the 1st volume of the Visions, Father K.E. Schmöger, *Leben der Gottseligen A.C.E.*, 2 vols., 3rd ed. (1907). Seller, H.J., *Im Banne des Kreuze. Lebensbild des stigmat. August. A.C.E.* (Wurtzburg, 1940; 2nd ed. 1949). Popular presentation: S. Back, *Von der Liebe verwundet, A.C.E.* (1955).

Bibliography

Das bittere Leiden unsers Herrn Jesu Christi. Nach den Betrachtungen der gottseligen A.C.E. . . . (the woeful Passion of our Lord . . .) Brentano (1833). French tr. (Paris, 1835) (*after the meditations*). *Leben der heil. Jungfrau Maria* . . . (Holy Virgin's Life) (1852). Published by Brentano's brother Christian (d. 1851) and by Brentano's sister-in-law. *Das Leben unsers Herrn und Heilendes Jesu Christi. Nach den Gesichten des gottsel.* . . . The Life of our Lord and Savior, 3 vols., 1858–1860, ed. by a Redemptorist, K.E. Schmöger. Recently, ed. in Paris, in several vols.

Mallom, *Brentano-Bibliographie* (Berlin, 1926). Adam, J., *Brentano and Emmerich, Erlebnis, Bindung und Abenteuer* (Freiburg-am-Brisgau, 1956). A fundamental study is Dirheimer, G., *A.C.E., the stigmat. visionary and Brentano, her secretary* (Paris, 1923). An anthology by Isabelle Sandy: *The Magnificent Visions of Emmerich* in French, after the ed. of the *Visions* by Br. J.A. Duley. (Paris, 1864; Tournai-Paris, 1948).

Gabriella Fiori

En Herdinna i Norden (a shepherdess in the Northland)

(see: Hedvig Charlotta Nordenflycht)

August Enders

(see: Kathinka [Katharina] Rosa Pauline Modesta Zitz-Halein)

Engelbirn

Flourished thirteenth to fourteenth centuries, Augsburg, Germany
Genre(s): mystical writings
Language(s): Middle High German

An anchorite at Augsburg's St. Ulrich and Afra Church, Engelbirn stands in the tradition of German women mystics. For a long time Engelbirn was considered a scribe, translator, and poet because her name appears in a medieval manuscript. Recent research suggests that Engelbirn may only have acted as a scribe or perhaps she corrected and augmented mystical texts.

The manuscript in question found in Augsburg, now kept in the Munich Staatsbibliothek (ms cgm 94), contains a mystical prose text and passages from St. Ambrose, Augustine, Bernard, and others, translated into Middle High German. The entire passage, written in a shaky handwriting, ends with this couplet:

bit fur die armen engelbirne
daz si got bekere des is not ir armen sele.
(Pray for poor Engelbirn that God convert her; this is what her poor soul needs.)

Works

"Die Klausnerin Engelbirn," in *Mystische Dichtung aus sieben Jahrhunderten,* ed. Friedrich Schulze-Maizier (Leipzig, 1925), pp. 139–144. *St. Ulrichs Leben*, Johann Andreas Schmeller, ed. (München, 1844), pp. VII–XIII.

Bibliography

Gebele, Eduard, "Engelbirn von Augsburg." *Lebensbilder aus dem Bayrischen Schwaben* 8 (1961): 52–63.

General references: Geth, Karl Ernst, *Die deutsche Literatur des Mittelalters, Verfasserlexikon,* 2nd ed., II (1980), pp. 549f. Stammler, Wolfgang, 1st ed. I (1933), p. 576. Spindler, Max, *Handbuch der bayerischen Geschichte,* 2nd ed., III (1979), p. 1122. *DLL* (*Deutsches Literatur Lexikon*, Kosch ed.), 3rd ed., IV (1972), p. 284 (Rolf Max Kully).

Gertrud Jaron Lewis

Dorothe Engelbretsdatter

Born January 16, 1643, Bergen, Norway; died February 19, 1716, Bergen, Norway
Genre(s): religious poetry (hymn), occasional poetry, rhymed letters
Language(s): Danish (the written language in Norway at this time)

Dorothe Engelbretsdatter is recognized as Norway's first woman writer. Although women wrote before her, she is without doubt the first Norwegian woman to be taken seriously and to gain recognition for her writing.

Born in 1643 in Bergen, Norway's largest and most influential city in the seventeenth century, little is known of her early life. At age eighteen she married Ambrosious Hardenbeck, a pastor, who later took over her father's position as pastor of the cathedral in Bergen. As the daughter and wife of religious leaders, she lived in a very pious milieu. Her social position also afforded her the opportunity to write; it was acceptable for women of her background to read and write.

Dorothe Engelbretsdatter bore nine children and she outlived all of them. Seven of them died in childhood; one disappeared; and one fell in battle. Her husband died in 1683, leaving her to live alone the last thirty years of her life. It is understandable why many critics have emphasized the role sorrow has played in her work and readily point to it as a source of inspiration for her writing.

Her first book, *Siælens Sang-Offer* (Song Offerings of the Soul), published in 1678, was a collection of religious poetry. Many of the poems were set to popular music and became favorite hymns. the book was published after she had buried seven of her children, and in the introduction she comments that "new sorrows have produced new songs."

Two important factors should be mentioned in connection with this book. First, it was written and published in the vernacular. This was significant because much was still being written in Latin. Second, the book was published in Christiania (present-day Oslo). Most books at this time were still being published in Copenhagen. (Copenhagen began printing books in 1482; Norway did not receive its first printing press until 1643). These two factors contributed to making the book accessible to a larger audience.

The book was extremely successful; in fact, it was a best-seller. Twenty-five editions appeared; the last in 1868. There were six editions alone in the period from its publication in 1643 to 1700. Stories are told of people rushing to the bookstore to obtain a copy, only to be turned away. The book was as popular in Denmark as it was in Norway.

Shortly after her husband's death, she published her second book, *Taare-Offer* (Tear Offerings), in 1685. This, however, was not an original work. Rather, it was a paraphrase of a manuscript by the Norwegian pastor Peder Møller, which in turn was a translation of a work by a German writer, Heinrich Müller, published in Germany in 1675.

Following her husband's death, Dorothe Engelbretsdatter was concerned about how she would be able to provide for herself. In 1684 the king granted her life exemption from government taxes. This is regarded as the first artist's stipend in Norway.

It is impossible to view Dorothe Engelbretsdatter's work separate from the religious and political climate of the 1600s. The modern secular mind finds it difficult to grasp this setting. The church (dominated by a strict Lutheran orthodoxy) was the ultimate authority, and there existed a very rigid political order (in the form of an absolute monarchy). Literature had a powerful religious and political function. Poets wrote to entertain and glorify the monarchy as well as to serve the church; the hymn was an integral part of the church service. The genres that Dorothe Engelbretsdatter chose (religious and occasional poetry) fulfilled these two important functions. She also followed very closely the conventions of these two genres.

Her poetry is in some ways very typical of the baroque poetry of the day. Her form was strictly controlled. She was very deft at rhyme, and she employed many of the rhetorical devices of the baroque poet. However, there were some important differences. Her poetry had a very personal, direct tone. It was not intellectualized, but came, as she said "from the heart." One must ask why she was so popular in her time. Her poetry was sincere; she presented a very personal and approachable God. Her imagery was connected to the events of everyday life; people found it very easy to relate to. Filled with emotion, it was different from much of the heavy scholarly literature of the day.

Literary histories have traditionally either overlooked Dorothe Engelbretsdatter or, referring to her as a "tearjerker," dismissed her as a popular, but unimportant writer. However, there has been a renewed interest in her work. In the 1950s her collected works were published in a revised and annotated edition. This made her work more accessible to the Norwegian audience.

Recently, critics have maintained that the image of her as a "tearjerker" is unfair. It seems to be a judgement based on her second book, a much more sentimental piece of writing and one that is not her original work. These critics maintain that emphasis must be placed on her first work, which is her original writing. In addition, one must keep in mind that she was working within the limits of a specific genre. Stronger emphasis has also begun to be placed on her occasional poetry and letters, of which about fifty remain. In doing so, a different picture of her emerges; it is a lighter picture, where humor is also present.

Ludvig Holberg, the famous Danish/Norwegian writer of the eighteenth century lauded Dorothe as "the best poetess the North has known." While one cannot say that she has maintained her popularity through time, there is still interest in her. In 1986, a contemporary Norwegian writer published a novel with Dorothe as a main character. This book (*I Dorotheas hus* by Torill Thorstad Hauger, Oslo: Gyldendal, 1986), attempts to bring the world of Dorothe Engelbretsdatter closer to the modern reader.

Works

Siælens Sang-Offer [Song Offerings of the Soul] (1678). *Taare-Offer* [Tear Offerings] (1685). *Leilighetsbrev/brev* [Occasional poetry and letters]. *Samlede skrifter I-II* [Collected Works] (1955–1956).

Bibliography

Aasen, Elisabeth, "Dorothe Engelbretsdatter." *Fra gamle dage* [From Old Days] (Oslo, 1983), pp. 54–68. Dehlin, Harald Stene, "Dorothe Engelbretsdatter." *Kvinneskjebner og salmevers* [The Destiny of Women in Hymns] (Oslo, 1960), pp. 41–46. Kvalbein, Laila Akslen, *Feminin barokk. Dorothe Engelbretsdatters liv og diktning* [Baroque in Feminine for Dorothe Engelbretsdatter's Life and Work] (Oslo, 1980). Valkner, Kristen, "Forord og opplysninger til D.E" [Introduction and notes to D.E.]. *Samlede Skrifter* [Collected works] (Oslo, 1955–1956).

General references: Bull, Francis, *Norsk Litteraturhistorie* [Norwegian Literary History], Vol. II (Oslo, 1958), pp. 180–183.

Peggy Hager

Magdalene Philippine Engelhard

(a.k.a. Rosalie)

Born October 21, 1756, Altdorf bei Nürnberg, Germany; died September 29, 1831, Blankenburg/Harz
Genre(s): poetry
Language(s): German

With her autobiographical poems, poems for children, and moralizing verse, Philippine Engelhard *nee* Gatterer was the most popular poetess in eighteenth-century Germany.

Born in 1756 outside Nürnberg, Philippine Gatterer was one of fifteen children. Her father, who soon after her birth moved the family to Göttingen, became a famous professor of history there and author of many important historical handbooks. As the daughter of a professor, the girl enjoyed a minimal but nonetheless better-than-usual education, learning French and history but none of the classical languages. She had no training in metrics or other aspects of writing poetry. Yet in her late teens she began secretly composing poems, eventually sharing some of them with a friend, Boie, who revised and published them in his widely read annual poetry anthology. Only then did Gatterer admit her authorship to her parents. Her father responded with encouragement, and in 1778 her first collection was published, with engravings by the respected Berlin artist Chodowiecki. Philippine Gatterer immediately became famous, a highly problematic situation for a woman of her time. In 1780, while her portrait was being painted by Tischbein in Kassel, she met the young war department official, Philipp Engelhard, whom she married that same year. For a while she managed to combine having babies and continuing her literary career. She published her second volume of poetry in 1782, her collection of verse for children five years later. Gradually the contributions to magazines and the single sheet publications became less frequent and then for nine years ceased altogether. Then in 1799, shortly before she became pregnant with her tenth and final child, she began publishing again. In 1821, three years after the death of her husband, her final collection of original verse appeared, followed almost a decade later by a small volume of translations of the poems of Beranger. The next year Philippine Engelhard died. Her eldest daughter, Caroline Engelhard, meanwhile, had become a writer, too.

Engelhard-Gatterer's self-satisfied but spritely poetry uses the various conventions popular in her time. What distinguishes her work are the poems about domestic topics (her fan, her muff) and the numerous autobiographical poems or segments, some of them surprisingly candid for a woman of her time and class (poems expressing her fears about marriage, her impatience while waiting for the birth of her first child, her feelings on the birth of later children).

Works

Gedichte von Philippine Gatterer, poems (1788). *Gedichte von Philippine Engelhard geb. Gatterer*, poems (1782). Neujahrs-*Geschenk für liebe Kinder* [New Year's Present for Dear Children] (1787). *Neujahrswünsche* [New Year's Wishes] (1789). *Neue Gedichte von Philippine Engelhard geborne Gatterer*, poems (1821).

Translation: One poem in *Bitter Healing: Anthology of German Women Authors from Pietism to Romanticism*, ed. Jeannine Blackwell and Susanne Zantop (Lincoln, 1989).

Bibliography

Dawson, Ruth P., "Im Reifrock den Parna besteigen. Die Rezeption von Dichterinnen im 18. Jahrhundert (am Beispiel von Philippine Gatterer-Engelhard)," *Kontroversen, alte und neue*, ed. Albrecht Schöne, v. 6 (Tübingen: Max Niemeyer, 1986), pp. 24–29 (Akten des VII. Internationalen Germanisten-Kongresses, Göttingen 1985). Dawson, Ruth P., "Selbstzähmung und weibliche Misogynie: Verserzählungen von Frauen im 18. Jahrhundert," *Der Widerspenstigen Zähmung*, in Studien zur bezwungenen Weiblichkeit in der Literatur vom Mittelalter bis zur Gegenwart, ed. Sylvia Wallinger and Monika Jonas (Innsbruck, 1986), pp. 133–143. Friedrichs, Elisabeth, *Die deutschsprachigen Schriftstellerinnen des 18. und 19. Jahrhunderts. Ein Lexikon* (Stuttgart: Metzler, 1981), p. 74. Schindel, Carl Wilhelm Otto August von, *Die deutschen Schriftstellerinnen des neunzehnten Jahrhunderts*, vol. 1 (Leipzig: Brockhaus, 1823), pp. 120–124.

Ruth P. Dawson

Marie d'Enntière

(see: Marie Dentière)

José Ensch

Born 1942, Luxembourg
Genre(s): poetry, essay
Language(s): French

José Ensch studied literature and philosophy in Germany and in France, where she conceived a passion for surrealist poetry. As a result she submitted to a Luxembourg board of examiners a thesis on Gisèle Prassinos entitled "De l'enfant prodigy du surréalisme à la romancière d'aujuord'hui; évolutions, correspondances" (1967; From the Infant Prodigy of Surrealism to the Novelist of Today; Evolutions, Correspondences). José Ensch returned to Paris to carry out more intensive research into surrealist poetry, and she presented, under the direction of Michel Decaudin, a second thesis entitled "De l'écriture automatique à la poésie" (Paris-Nanterre 1972–1975) (From Automatic Writing to Poetry). At present she is a teacher at the Lycée Robert-Schuman in Luxembourg, and she organizes poetry readings, lectures, and exhibitions of French artists whom she invites to Luxembourg. She participates in literary radio programs and is the Luxembourg representative at international poetry meetings.

José Ensch has written poetry for some twenty years though she has put off publishing for a long time. She has always wanted her literary creation to mature slowly and deeply. Only since 1982 has she confided her poetry to publishers and editors, rapidly making a name as a "great poet"—as Edmond Dune wrote in a French daily newspaper issued in Luxembourg: "A great poet was born to us!"

José Ensch draws her poetic inspiration from the distressing, even tragic experience of the most personal, the most intimate and yet universal components of daily life. Birth, life, the birth of life, love, creation, the child, nature, beauty, but, also and mainly, sickness, solitude, despair, death—those are the themes she develops in a dramatic language with flaming, sumptuous or black images from whose darkness rise sparks of soothing gentleness and hope. From the long silence José Ensch has willfully kept for years has gushed forth a richness of lyrical expressiveness worthy of a large national and international audience.

José Ensch has also remained an essayist. "A l'écoute de Gisèle Prassinos—une voix grecque" (Listening to Gisèle Prassinos—a Greek voice), a cooperative study of the poetry and prose of Gisèle Prassinos by José Ensch and Rosemarie Kieffer, was published in Canada in 1986.

Works

L'arbre [The Tree] (1984). Ailleurs . . . c'est certain [Elsewhere . . . a certainty] (1985). A l'écoute de Gisèle Prassinos—une voix grecque [Listening to Gisèle Prassinos—a Greek Voice] (1986).

Bibliography

Schneider, Joseph-Paul, "Révélation d'un authentique poète: José Ensch" [Rise of a True Poet: José Ensch], Luxemburger Wort, 10.1 (1985). Dune, Edmond, "Un grand poète nous est né" [A Great Poet Was Born to Use], Le Républicain Lorrain, 23.10 (1985). Kieffer, Rosemarie, "La poésie de José Ensch" [The Poetry of José Ensch], Tageblatt, 11.6 (1985). Kieffer, Rosemarie, "Ces lumières venues de là-bas" [Those Lights from Beyond], Nouvelle Europe, no. 49 (Autumn 1985), pp. 65–67. Verdure, Marie-Claire, "Un Requiem comme un chant d'espoir" [A Requiem like a Song of Hope], Nos Cahiers (Luxembourg, 1987/I,): 85–92.

Rosemarie Kieffer and Liliane Stomp-Erpelding

Louise-Florence-Petronille Tardieu d'Esclavelles d'Epinay

Born March 11, 1726, Valenciennes, France; died April 15, 1783, Paris
Genre(s): letters, memoir
Language(s): French

Louise d'Epinay's father, an officer of Normandic origin, died when she was very young. Her mother, Florence-Angelique Prouveur, a noblewoman from Flanders took the young Louise and went to stay with Mme Bellegarde, the wife of a rich farmer. There, Louise made friends and grew up with Mme Bellegarde's daughter, Elisabeth, who was later to become Mme de Houdetot. Louise married her first cousin Denis de la Live d'Epinay in 1745. It was an unfortunate alliance. Denis d'Epinay was a spendthrift and philanderer and soon abandoned his beautiful young wife for the arms of opera-dancers. Diderot describes Denis as a man who "ate two million without saying a good word or doing a good deed." After his scandalous liaison with one of the Verniere sisters (a dancer at the Comedie Française) Mme d'Epinay detached herself from her husband and tried to seek consolation in a life of endless pleasure and dissipation. She openly took a series of lovers, notable among whom was the very seductive Dupin de Francueil, the son of a rich farmer from Chenonceaux. It was Dupin who introduced her to the liberal society of men of letters where she met and befriended Rousseau who, in turn, introduced her to her life-long and faithful friend, Melchoir Grimm. Among her other intimates at this time were the Baron d'Holbach, Diderot, Saint-Lambert and the poet Desmahis.

Louise d'Epinay is said to have entered into a rather complicated affair with Rousseau soon after they met. Her alliance with Rousseau changed her life irreversibly. During the heyday of their affair, she arranged to have Rousseau settled in a small house on the perimeter of the forest of Mont Morency. There, at L'Ermitage, Rousseau spent two years working on his Le contrat Social (The Social Contract) and meditating on La Nouvelle Héloise (The New Heloise). However, their affair cooled, and Rousseau is said to have developed a strong liking for Mme d'Houdetot, Louise d'Epinay's childhood friend. In Les Confessions (The Confessions), Rousseau describes Mme d'Epinay as being so jealous of his liaison with Mme d'Houdetot that she, along with her friend Grimm, did everything in her power to break up the affair. In December 1757, Rousseau left L'Ermitage and saw Louise as "une perfide collaboratrice de l'oeuvre de tenebres" (A perfidious conspirator in the work of darkness). Thus began a life-long enmity between two friends.

When Rousseau returned to Paris in 1770, he is said to have read fragments of Les Confessions at various salons, emphasizing those sections which were clearly an attack on Mme d'Epinay. Shamed by Rousseau's blatant malice, she called on the lieutenant of Police, M. de Sartines, to stop Rousseau's lectures and, as revenge, rewrote her autobiographical novel, *Histoire de Mme. de Montbrilliant* (The Story of Mme de Mont Brilliant; later published as her *Memoirs*), to include her own attacks on Rousseau. In the re-worked edition, Rousseau (thinly disguised and named René Rousseau) is depicted as a hypocrite, a deceiver, a villain and a blackguard.

Apart from her autobiographical novel, which, according to Saint-Boeuve, is notable for its representation of the spirit of the age and of middle-class corruption, Mme d'Epinay published several other works. She played an indeterminable but active role in Grimm's journal, *La Correspondance Litteraire* (Literary Correspondence). Her publications include a collection of letters to her son, Louis, who made the last years of her life miserable because of his scandalous behavior and *Conversations d'Emilie* (Conversations of Emilie), a volume composed for the education of her granddaughter, Emilie de Belzunce. This volume was accepted by the Academie Française in 1783. The original manuscript of her *Memoires* is divided and preserved in two libraries: the Bibliotheque de L'Arsenal and the Bibliotheque des Archives Nationales.

Mme d'Epinay died on April 15, 1783, in a small house at Chaussée d'Antin in Paris where she lived with Grimm.

Works

Mes Moments Heureux (1758). *Lettres a mon Fils* (1759). *Conversations d'Emilie* (1774). *Memoirs (Histoire de Mme. de Montbrilliant)* (1818; published posthumously).

Bibliography

Fayard, *Dictionnaire des Lettres Francais.* Allingham, E.G., *Memoirs and Correspondence of Mme. d'Epinay* (1930).

Ranee Kaur

Elke Erb

Born 1938, Scherbard, Eifel, Germany
Genre(s): essay, prose, poetry
Language(s): German

Elke Erb spent her early youth without her father, a prisoner of war, but when he returned,

she moved with him to the GDR. She has one child with writer and critic Adolf Endler, to whom she was married. Elke Erb is a respected scholar of Slavic literatures and has translated Gogol, Blok, and Tsvetaeva.

Elke Erb is not concerned with presenting to the public a glamorous, polished text. In the few slim volumes she has written, she traces relentlessly and meticulously the "processes of consciousness (Bernd Allenstein), with special intent to catch and demask those bearing a resemblance to the well-known ones current in the Third Reich. Or their contrary: her story "Einer schreit: Nicht!" (Someone Screams: No) is about four boys hitting each other with sticks supposed to represent guns, while a fifth runs toward them to stop them. All of Erb's texts are intent upon making transparent thought patterns behind the language which is mostly male-dominated: idioms, proverbs, sayings, fairy tale passages—all verbal manifestations are grist for her mill.

She is aware that her approach to writing sometimes borders on the incomprehensible, but with her insistence to produce a literature in which the reader has a crucial place in the process of analysis and creation, she holds an important place in contemporary German letters.

Works

Gutachten (1975). *Einer schreit: Nicht!* (1976). *Der Faden der Geduld* (1978). *Trost* (1980).

Bibliography

Puknus, Heinz, ed., *Neue Literatur der Frauen* (Munich, 1980). Serke, Jürgen, *Frauen schreiben* (Frankfurt, 1982).

Ute Marie Saine

Erinna

Born approximately 370 B.C.(?), possibly on
Telos, a small island in the southeast
Aegean, near Rhodes (according to the
consensus of some modern scholars)
Genre(s): poetry, epigram
Language(s): Greek

Ancient critics deemed Erinna a woman poet second only to Sappho, as supreme in hexameter verse as Sappho was in her lyrics; her fame rested upon a three-hundred-line poem entitled the *Distaff*, whose metrical craftsmanship was rated "equal to Homer's" (*AP* 9.190). References to this work in subsequent literature indicate that it enjoyed a remarkable vogue among poets writing in the first half of the third century B.C. and continued to be cherished, at least by the erudite, down through the Hellenistic period and the early centuries of the Roman empire (Antiphanes, *AP* 11.322). Learned interest in Erinna was stimulated by a sentimental legend that she was an unmarried girl who had written the *Distaff* at the age of nineteen and died, still a virgin, shortly thereafter. In actuality, no biographical data had been handed down, as is evident from the fact that even her birthplace and date are variously given.

Until 1928, Erinna's work was known to us solely through three epigrams preserved in the *Greek Anthology* and a few brief citations in later authors. In that year, however, Italian archaeologists discovered some badly mutilated papyrus fragments of the *Distaff* that have now been pieced together, restored and supplemented to provide about twenty lines of continuous text. These restorations are highly conjectural, and several commentators have expressed grave doubt that much real sense may be made of the whole. It is agreed, though, that Erinna's greatly praised poem was a lament for the speaker's dead friend Baucis, once her girlhood playmate and more recently a bride. This observation in itself signals a clear departure from earlier Greek poetic tradition and a direct influence upon succeeding authors: prior to Erinna, hexameters had not been associated with funerary poetry, but later Hellenistic writers, including Theocritus, readily employed them for that purpose.

If the scholarly conjectures are accurate, the preserved text apparently begins in the middle of the speaker's reminiscences of her childhood life with Baucis. She may have alluded to a girls' tag game in which the "It" player assumed the role of a tortoise who weaves a shroud for her dead son, to playing with dolls, to the household activities of someone's mother, and lastly to the shape-changing nursery monster Mormo; she also apparently spoke of Baucis' forgetfulness of things heard from her mother, this in the context of marriage and Aphrodite. Finally she seems to have turned back to her immediate sorrow, lamenting that she could not leave the house, look upon Baucis dead, or mourn with uncovered head, for which she felt *aidos*, "shame." Further remains of the left-hand side of a column contain possible references to the speaker's present age, nineteen (or, alternatively, to Baucis' age at death); to grey hairs; and to shouts in praise of Hymen, god of marriage, punctuated with cries of grief over Baucis.

The problem of providing a coherent explanation of this fascinating fragment has proven extremely difficult for scholars, not only because the lines themselves are so mutilated but also because ancient and modern critics alike tend to interpret the *Distaff* according to their own preconceptions of its creator. When the work was rediscovered, its use of a first-person speaker prompted autobiographical surface readings that treated it as a young girl's naive and spontaneous expression of sorrow over a friend's death. After the techniques of close literary analysis had disclosed the poem's consummate artistry, one scholar cynically branded it an elaborate literary forgery perpetrated by an unknown male writer, designed to appeal to Alexandrian tastes by passing itself off as the pathetic outcry of a damsel in distress. In contrast, feminist classical scholars have recently argued cases for approaching the *Distaff* as a genuine masterpiece of women's art incorporating a female-ordered perspective upon experience. The focus of that experience is a matter of debate: for Arthur, the poem is a symbolic meditation upon selfhood and personal identity; Pomeroy thinks it concerned itself chiefly with literary creativity; Skinner contends that it examined the fragility of women's bonding and their enforced isolation within a patriarchal society. Because of its important aesthetic and cultural value, it should continue to attract the interest of all students of the female tradition in world literature.

The new concern for the *Distaff* has diverted attention from Erinna's three surviving epigrams. These, however, provide the opportunity to observe how the poet exercises her artistic talents within a smaller compass and may therefore throw light upon the themes of her longer hexameter poem. Two of these pieces are funereal epigrams for Baucis in which the dead girl herself speaks. In the first, the more conventional of the pair (*AP* 7.710), she addresses her own grave-stone, bidding it tell passers-by first, that she had been a bride; second, her name and birthplace; third, that her friend Erinna had had this epitaph inscribed upon it. The markedly original companion piece (*AP* 7.712) makes her accuse the king of the underworld of personal malice, in a phrase that became famous: *baskanos ess', Aida*, "you are jealous, Hades." Elaborately varying the commonplace "bride of death" motif, the last four lines depict Baucis' father-in-law lighting her pyre with the torches kindled for her wedding while the hymeneal song modulates into a threnody. These innovative poetic ideas—which were quickly absorbed into the tradition and soon became cliches—all eroticize the experience of death, or at least forge a subliminal connection between a woman's heterosexual initiation and her death. Remains of verse beginnings and endings suggest that the same emotional association between marriage and death was exploited in the *Distaff*. A third, very different piece (*AP* 6.352) celebrates the verisimilitude of a girl's portrait; its self-conscious preoccupation with the *sophia* of the artist lends weight to Pomeroy's belief that the *Distaff* dealt with the situation of the woman poet. This quatrain, the first known ekphrastic epigram in Greek literature, seems to have directly inspired the work of Nossis (q.v.) and, to a lesser extent, of Anyte (q.v.). Anyte also appears to borrow from Erinna for her own funerary epitaphs on maidens, especially by appropriating and conventionalizing the link between marriage and death as related polarities of female experience. In this way Erinna probably served as the model for an entire later generation of women epigrammatists.

Works

Greek text of the *Distaff* fragments in *Supplementum Hellenisticum*, eds. H. Lloyd-Jones and P. Parsons (Berlin, 1983). Text and English tr. in Select *Papyri III*, ed. D.L. Page, Loeb Classical Library (Cambridge, Mass., 1950). Greek texts and German translations of the epigrams in Homeyer, H., *Dichterinnen des Altertums und des frühen Mittelalters* (Paderborn, 1979). Commentary in *The Greek Anthology: Hellenistic Epigrams*, eds. A.S.F. Gow and D.L. Page, 2 vols. (Cambridge, 1965). English tr. in The *Greek Anthology*, tr. W.R. Paton. Loeb Classical Library, 5 vols. (Cambridge, Mass., 1916).

Bibliography

Bowra, C.M., *Greek Poetry and Life* (Oxford, 1936), pp. 325–342 (rpt. in *Problems in Greek Poetry* [Oxford, 1953], pp. 151–168). Idem, *New Chapters in the History of Greek Literature*, 3rd series, ed. J.U. Powell (Oxford, 1933), pp. 180–185. Lisi, U., *Poetesse greche* (Catania, 1933). Snyder, J.M., *The Woman and the Lyre* (Carbondale, Ill., 1989). Trypanis, C.A., *Greek Poetry from Homer to Seferis* (Chicago, 1981). Wilamowitz-Moellendorff, U. von, *Hellenistische Dichtung in der Zeit des Kallimachos*. I (Berlin, 1924). Idem, *Sappho und Simonides* (Berlin, 1913).

General references: *Oxford Classical Dictionary*, 2nd ed. (Oxford, 1970), p. 406. Pauly-Wissowa, *Real-Encyclopädie der klassischen Altertumswissenschaft* VI.1 (1907), pp. 455–458. Idem, VI (Stuttgart, 1935) pp. 54–56.

Other references: Arthur, M.B., *Classical World* 74 (1980): 53–65. Barnard, S., *Classical Journal* 73 (1978): 204–213. Cameron, A. and A., *Classical Quarterly* 19 (1969): 285–288. Giangrande, G., *Classical Review* 19 (1969): 1–3. Latte, K., *Nachrichten der Akademie der Wissenschaften in Gottingen I: Philologisch-historische Klasse* 3 (1953): 79–94. Levin, D.N., *Harvard Studies in Classical Philology* 66 (1962): 193–204. Luck, G., *Museum Helveticum* 11 (1954): 170–187. Magrini, M.M., *Prometheus* 1 (1975): 225–236. Pomeroy, S.B., *Zeitschrift für Papyrologie und Epigraphik* 32 (1978): 17–22. Scholz, U.W., *Antike und Abendland* 18 (1973): 15–40. Skinner, M.B., *Classical World* 75 (1982): 265–269. West, M.L., *Zeitschrift für Papyrologie und Epigraphik* 25 (1977): 95–119.

Marilyn B. Skinner

Ursula Erler

Born 1946, Cologne, Germany
Genre(s): novel, essay
Language(s): German

Born immediately after World War II, Ursula Erler began writing at the beginning of the 1970s. She is a professor at the University of Cologne.

Ursula Erler's prose, whether fiction or non-fiction, deals with the role of women in modern society. *Die neue Sophie* is a take-off on Rousseau's *Emile*, where women's education is appended in one brief chapter having to do with Emile needing a mate. This is what Erler refutes. Her book about mothers in the Federal Republic deals with women's "destruction and self-destruction," to paraphrase one of her essays. Her novels deal with relationships that might enable women to reconcile a private and professional existence. The titles speak for themselves; *Marriages Are Only Love Stories* or *Games of Trusting*.

Works

Die neue Sophie (1972). *Mütter in der BRD* (1973). *Die lange Reise in die Zärtlichkeit* (1978). *Die Zerstörung und Selbstzerstörung der Frau* (1979). *Auch Ehen sind nur Liebesgeschichten* (1979). *Vertrauensspiele* (1980).

Ute Marie Saine

Ermengarde, Viscountess of Narbonne

Flourished twelfth century; died c. 1197, Rouen, France
Genre(s): patroness of troubadour poets, possibly a poet herself, founder of the Abbey of Fontfroide
Language(s): French

While little is known of Ermengarde's origins and literary activities, published notices on this figure state that she inherited the viscounty of Narbonne in 1142 upon the death of her father Aimeri at the battle of Frage and the subsequent death of her young brother, Aimeri II. Unfortunately, the counts of Narbonne were vassals of the powerful counts of Toulouse. Alphonse-Jourdain, one such count, attempted to seize Ermengarde's property and supplant her rights to rule the viscounty of Narbonne.

Ermengarde was assisted in her long struggle against this count of Toulouse by Roger, Viscount Carcassonn, and by members of the court of Louis VII, especially Raymond Beranger, Count of Barcelona and Provence. Around 1145, Ermengarde married one Bernard d'Anduze of the Nimes family. (This, reportedly, was her second marriage.) He, however, died in 1164, leaving her without issue or heirs. Historians surmise that Ermengarde single-handedly ruled Narbonne in the late twelfth century. Molinier has suggested that the widowed and childless Ermengarde signed over the viscounty of Narbonne in 1192 to Aimeri III, her sister Ermesinde's son, who assumed the rule of Narbonne c. 1194 and created the Narbonne-Lara line.

Ermengarde retired to Rouen toward the close of the twelfth century, and is thought to have died there c. 1197.

Ermengarde's actual existence, contemporary prestige, and love of Troubadour poetry are documented in the verse of Pierre Rogier, a troubadour poet, who dedicated several of his songs to her. His "Aimeri de Narbonne" is especially valuable in documenting some of the life of the elusive Ermengarde and her family background. Evidently, she was a generous patroness of troubadours; and it is entirely plausible that upon her retirement to Rouen she herself began to write verse based on her colorful life. Regrettably, scholars have not as yet been able to shed more light on Ermengarde's literary connections and, possibly, her own writings.

Bibliography

Domergue, J., "Ermengarde." *Dictionnaire de Biographie Française* (Paris, 1968). (N.B. Precious little is available on this much-obscured figure. M. Domergue, in his brief entry on Ermengarde, cites other short notices by Molinier in *History du Languedoc*; J. Girou in *Vies des pers. cel. de l'Aude*; and an article in the *Bul. de la Comm. Archeol. de Narbonne*.)

Maureen E. Mulvihill

Ida Cornelia Ernestine

(see: Ida Boy-Ed)

Dorothea von Erxleben

(see: Dorothea Leporin)

Felipe Escalada

(see: María Gertrudis Gómez de Avellaneda)

L. Escardot

(see: Carme Karr i Alfonsetti)

Natalie von Eschstruth

Born May 16, 1870, Hofgeismar (Hessen),
   Germany; died January 12, 1939,
   Schwerin
Genre(s): novel, drama, short story
Language(s): German

Natalie von Eschstruth's literary career began at a very early age: her first poems were published in the periodical *Deutsche Dichterhalle* before she was twelve years old. Born the youngest daughter of a Prussian officer, she was raised with all the advantages available to a daughter of the higher classes in the second half of the nineteenth century.

In 1875 she was sent to finishing school in Switzerland and wrote there her first novellas "Schweizer Novellen." These were rapidly followed by humorous sketches, tales, stories and plays. Later on she mainly wrote novels and novellas.

She traveled extensively throughout Europe, especially to the fashionable resorts of the era, and maintained an active social life. Encouraged in her writing by ruling princes and literary figures alike, she met most of the major literary figures of her day. Her works reflect this *fin-de-siècle* world dominated by a shallow, glittering aristocracy and maintained by innumerable faithful retainers without faces.

Unfortunately, she never penetrates beyond the glittering surfaces of the *beau monde*. Her novels, although extremely popular when published, are out of favor today and practically forgotten.

Works

Pirmasenz, oder Karl Augusts Brautfahrt (1881). Der kleine Rittmeister (1882). In des Königs Rock (1882). Die Sturmnixe (1883). Der Eisenkopf (1884). Die Ordre des Grafen von Guise (1884). Katz und Maus (1884). Wolfsburg (1885). Gänseliesel: Eine Hofgeschichte (1886). Potpourri (1887). Der Irrgeist des Schloes (1887). Humoresken und andere Erzählungen (1887). Polnisch Blut (1887). Wegekraut (1887). Die Erlkönigin (1887). Zauberwasser (1888). Hazard (1888). Wandelbilder (1888). Sie wird geküt (1888). Verbotene Früchte und andere Erzählungen (1889). Hofluft (1889). Sternschnuppen (1890). Im Schellenhemd (1890). Der Mühlenprinz (1891). In Ungnade (1891). Komödie (1892). Scherben (1893). Die Heidehexe und andere Novellen (1894). Ungleich (1894). Von Gottes Gnaden (1894). Johannisfeuer (1895). Sturmnixe und andere Dramen (1895). Der Stern des Glücks (1896). Jung gefreit (1897). Spuk (1897). Der Majoratsherr (1898). Mondschein-Prinzechen (1898). Der verkannte Puttfarken (1899). Frühlingsstürme (1899). Die Regimentstante (1899). Spukgeschichte und andere Erzählungen (1900). Aus vollem Leben (1900). Nachtschatten (1900). Am Ziel (1901). Regenwetter (1901). Osterglocken (1901). Sonnenfunken (1901). Der verlorene Sohn (1902). Unerklärliches (1902). Die Bären von Hohen-Esp (1902). Am See (1903). Jedem das Seine (1904). Frieden (1905). Am Ende der Welt (1905). Die Ordre des Grafen von Guise. Symone (1910). Die Roggenmuhme (1910). Die Gauklerin (1911). Vae Victis (1911). Das Rodeltantchen (1912). Heckenrosen und andere Erzählungen (1913). Eine unheimliche Torte und andere Erzählungen (1913). Zauberwasser und andere Erzählungen (1913). Sehnsucht (1917). Sein erster Orden (1920). Ewige Jugend (1920). Bräutigam und Braut (1920). Wenn zwei sich nur gut sind (1920). Lebende Blumen (1921). Im Spukschlo Monbijou (1921). Ende gut—alles gut (1921). Ein Stein auf den Straen (1921). Lichtfalter (1922). Junge Liebe und andere Erzählungen (1922). Plappermäulchen und andere Erzählungen (1922). Halali! (1922). Pagenstreiche und andere Erzählungen (1922). Der fliegende Holländer (1925). Erlöst (1926). In goldenen Ketten (1928).

Bibliography

Kürschners Deutscher Literatur-Kalender, Nekrolog 1936–1970 (Berlin, 1973), p. 148. Neue Deutsche Biographie 4 (Berlin, 1959): 651. Sichelschmidt, Gustav, Liebe, Mord und Abenteuer.

Eine Geschichte der deutschen Unterhaltungsliteratur (Berlin, 1969).

Hortense Bates

Mercedes Escolano

Born February 15, 1964, Cádiz, Spain
Genre(s): poetry
Language(s): Spanish

Mercedes Escolano, like many of the writers of her generation, has a M.A. in Spanish literature. At present, she is preparing for her exams in order to become a librarian. Born in the Andalusian city of Cádiz, a region known for its poetic tradition, she is a member of the youngest group of women poets. Despite Escolano's youth, her already sizable production points to a very promising future, as indicated by the variety of literary prizes she has been awarded.

The author describes her first book, *Marejada* (1982), as "a secret diary and initiating volume." Although it does not have an obvious thematic unity, it already evokes the seductive call of love and the sea, motifs which appear in her later works.

The themes of love and the sea are amplified in her second work, *Las bacantes* (1984), by their juxtaposition with death, a constant triad in her poetry. This opposition is clearly treated in more detail in *Antinomia* (1987), a book actually written in 1984: "Las ondas distorsionan el óvalo perfecto/ de sus miembros, desdibujan su rostro/ al chocar contra el flanco de la nave." The presence of these traditional motifs inscribes her work within the current of the most recent Spanish poetry, insofar as larger metaphysical questions supplant the social tendencies of the poetry of the 1950s. As it occurs in contemporary poetry, in *Las bacantes* for example, the transcendental quest is tempered by a Mediterranean classicism—a cultural "byzantinism" that springs from the "novisimos" poets, especially Luis Antonio de Villena and the very influential work of the Greek poet, Konstantino Kavafis. This tradition does not overshadow the personal contributions of the poems, but rather, it illuminates some fundamental stepping stones: poetry as an essential quest following the example of Juan Ramón Jiménez ("si vós me hubieses entonces/

ofrecido la poesía/ habríaosla arrojado/ contra el suelo/ ahora me agacho/ y recojo"); the search for well-rounded and sometimes difficult images reinforced by the lack of punctuation, first used by Mallarmé; the presence of homosexuality as a classical reference (another theme in *Antinomia*); the use of commands that invoke the reader's participation; and the iconicity of symbols that sometimes transforms the poems into a visual experience as in concrete poetry.

In *La almadraba* (1986) and finally in *Felina calma y oleaje* (1986) the opposition between love and death, framed by the symbolic role of the sea (creative uterus/tomb), opens a sexual symphony underwritten in her first book. Eros along with youth and aesthetic delight are presented as protagonists in the Mediterranean classical tradition. In the erotic game, maritime imagery is used to depict courting, conquest, possession, and the disenchantment of romance. The ironic opposition between fishing and love proposes a non-traditional and active feminine character in search of a mate: "Cambiemos de técnica y aparejo aunque el juego sea el mismo/ y, en vez de darme un pez, enséñame a pescarlo." The intertextual references (Homer, Marcel Proust, Luis Cernuda, Peter Weir's *Marat Sade*, Rafael Alberti, Jorge Manrique, Manuel and Antonio Machado, Robert Louis Stevenson, Esther Tusquets, Herman Melville, Carlos Edmundo de Ory, Juan Marsé, medieval ballads, linguistic colloquialisms, etc.) reinforce her generation's predilection for cultural allusions and emphasis upon style. Therefore, within their anecdotal simplicity, the poems present themselves as autonomous entities where language and literature are reordered, reenacted, and rewritten. The recourse to classical rhetorical devices also emphasizes the rhythmic patterns of the verses, linking the "novisimos" formal perfection with the young women poets' innovative erotic discourse.

Works

Poetic prizes: *Marejada* [Undercurrent] (1982; Prize "Poema Joven," Elche, 1981). *Las bacantes* [The Bacchantes] (1984; Prize "Poema Joven," Elche, 1982). *La almadraba* [The Tuna Net] (1986; Prize "Universidad de Cádiz," 1985). *Felina calma y oleaje* [Feline Calm and Surf] (1986; Prize "Luis de

Góngora" Córdoba, 1986). *Antinomia* [Antinomy] (1987). *Paseo por el cementerio inglés* [A Stroll Through the English Cemetery] (1987).

Work in poetic anthologies: Buenaventura, Ramón, ed., *Las Diosas Blancas: Antología de la joven poesía española escrita por mujeres* (1985). Saval, Lorenzo, and García Gallego, J., eds., *Litoral femenino: Literatura escrita por mujeres en la España contemporánea* 169–170 (1986). *Seis nuevos poetas gaditanos* (1987).

Jose María Naharro-Calderón

Florbela de Alma da Conceição Espanca

Born 1894, Vila Vicosa, Alentejo, Portugal; died 1930, Matosinhos
Genre(s): poetry, short story
Language(s): Portuguese

Espanca, cited as "her country's foremost woman poet" in the *Columbia Dictionary of Modern European Literature*, was born illegitimately in the Alto Alentejo province of Portugal. Married at the age of sixteen, she rebelled against the second-class status of Portuguese women. By the time of her divorce at eighteen, she had begun to write lyric poems and short stories in the manner of the symbolist-decadent style then popular. These early works were not published until 1931. Espanca began studying law in Lisbon in her early twenties and soon married for a second time. Her first collection of poems, *Livro das mágoas* (Book of Woes), was published in 1919. This early phase of her work reveals the influence of her mentor, Antonio Nobre. Following her second divorce in 1923, she published the *Livro de Sóror Saudad* (Book of Sister Saudade), the title of which refers to the name given her by Américo Durão, a friend and fellow poet. This collection represents a second phase of her career, and her uninhibited self-disclosure of amorous encounters invites comparison with *The Portuguese Letters* of Sóror Mariana Alcoforado. Espanca's quest for love here reaches cosmic proportions. These two early works went unnoticed by critics of the day, probably due to their unorthodoxy and "impropriety."

Espanca married for a third time and was preparing two collections of poetry when she died, possibly a suicide, on her birthday in 1930. This third phase of her production included the works *Charneca em Flor* (Flowering Heath) and *Reliquiae* (Relics), both published in 1931. The poet here reaches her artistic height, abandoning her barren pursuit of love and experiencing moments of inner peace, which find expression in her sonnets of "sculptural perfection" (*Literatura Portuguesa Moderna*). Her short stories, according to the *Columbia Dictionary of Modern European Literature*, are ". . . dated examples of erotic art nouveau."

Works

Poetry: *Livro das mágoas* (1919; Book of Woes). *Livro de Sóror Saudade* (1923; Book of Sister Saudade). *Charneca em Flor* (1931; Flowering Heath). *Reliquiae* (1931; Relics). *Juvenilia* (1931). **Short Stories:** *As Mascaras do Destino* (1931; The Masks of Destiny). *Domino Negro* (1931; Black Domino).

Bibliography

Bédé, J.-A. and W.B. Edgerton, eds., *Columbia Dictionary of Modern European Literature* (1980). Bessa-Luís, A., *Florbela Espanca, a vida e a obra* (1979). De Sena, J., "Florbela Espanca," in *Da Poesia Portuguesa* (1959). Klein, L., ed., *Encyclopedia of World Literature in the 20th Century* (1981). Moisés, M., ed., *Literatura Portuguesa Moderna* (1973). Régio, J., "Florbela," in *Ensaios de interpretação crítica* (1964).

Paula T. Irvin

Isabella d'Este

Born June 29, 1475, Ferrara, Italy; died February 13, 1539, Mantua
Genre(s): letters
Language(s): Italian

Isabella was born to Eleonora, daughter of Ferrante d'Aragona, King of Naples, and to Ercole I Este, Duke of Ferrara. At the age of six, she was officially engaged to Francesco Gonzaga, a few years her senior, and married him ten years later, in 1490, when he was the Marquis of Mantua. As a child, she was tutored by Jacopo Gallina and Gian Battista Guarino. In her married life, Isabella continued her education with Battista Pio, with Cosmico, then with Francesco Virgilio, preceptor of her son, and with Nicola Panizzato. She is considered to have been the most cultured woman of the Renaissance.

Notwithstanding her young age and her frequent pregnancies—between 1496 and 1509, she gave birth to seven children—Isabella soon emerged as a skillful politician and a good administrator of her estates. Francesco was frequently away from Mantua, as he alternatively led the armies of Venice, the Pope, the king of France and of Emperor Charles V. Thanks to her intelligence, practicality, and tact, the small state of Mantua survived the dangers of the Italian Wars. Beside the interests of the Gonzagas, she kept in mind those of the duchies of Ferrara, Milan, Urbino, as well as of Pesaro and Naples, to whose reigning families she was related. She kept at bay Cesare Borgia, who was threatening her possessions. In 1510, she negotiated the release of her husband, imprisoned by Venice. When France demanded her son as hostage, Isabella paid ransom money to the King and sent to Cardinal Rohan, then stationed in Lombardy, a much-coveted painting by Mantegna. Caught in Rome by the Sack of 1527, Isabella gave shelter to hundreds of people, walled up doors and windows, and waited until she could arrange a safe escape. Back in Mantua, she continued to take part in politics until her death. She was buried in the convent of Santa Paola.

During her times, Mantua became a splendid Renaissance center. She built a court theatre and promoted a season comparable to that of her brothers in Ferrara. Testagrossa, Marchetto Cara, and Tromboncino were among the composers she commissioned to set to music her favorite poems. For the construction and decoration of her famous apartments, the *studiolo*, the *Grotta del Paradiso* and the *Casino bizzarro* of Porto, she hired the best artists of the day. Lorenzo Costa, Mantegna, Dosso Dossi, Gentile and Giovanni Bellini, Giovanni Santi and his son Raphael, Perugino, Francia, Pordenone, Leonardo, Gian Cristoforo Romano, Sebastiano del Piombo, Tiziano, all worked for her. Her collection of paintings, many of which she commissioned, was one of the best in Italy and became the core of the royal collection of En-

gland, after it was sold in 1627. Isabella was also an indefatigable collector of antiques, of rare books, maps, and luxury objects. Jewels and brocades were made after her designs for her and for her ladies-in-waiting. Many artists painted her, but Titian is the one who captured her personality, in a portrait, now in Vienna, showing a young woman richly and jauntily dressed, self-assured and looking straight at the gazer.

As a child, Isabella had been fond of medieval and chivalric epics. At nineteen, when she was in Milan, she entered into disputation about the value of two chivalric characters with Gian Galeazzo of Correggio. Both Boiardo and Ariosto were encouraged in their work by her enthusiasm and her requests for new cantos. Ariosto and Bandello read their stories to her. In her retinue of poets and literati, we find Equicola, Tebaldeo, Aquilano, and Pistoia. Trissino and Giovio were among the contemporaries who wrote about her. Pietro Bembo sent sonnets for her to sing. When her husband was angry at Baldassar Castiglione for moving to Urbino, she maintained with him cordial relations.

The many letters Isabella wrote were private, not written as a literary genre. They are addressed to members of her family, relatives and friends in the various Italian courts, to artists and professionals of all fields. Of each letter, a copy was made and preserved in the Gonzaga Archives. To Elisabetta, Duchess of Urbino, depressed by the turn of historical events, Isabella counsels long rides, pleasant conversation, and concern about her health. To her newly acquired niece, Renée of France, she describes the coronation of Charles V. We read details of theatrical performances, of sets, of dances, actors, and props. As she went on frequent diplomatic missions, she sent to her husband notes on people and events as they were viewed and judged in high places. She gives reports on what she hears among courtiers and soldiers; she advises her husband on how to behave with heads of states, with those she suspects to be secret agents; she anticipates their moves. She discusses Caterina Sforza, Martin Luther, the Pope, Cesare Borgia. Of the capture and suppression of the Signori of Romagna, she gives details and circumstances different from those reported by historians. She gossips: Lucrezia

Borgia takes the longest to wash and dress; her marital relations to Alfonso are coolish. She threatens: when she is told that her rooms will not be ready on her return, she writes the decorator that he will be thrown into the tower, that he ought to try it for comfort. She intervenes in favor of people in distress, such as the poet, Barbara Torelli, abused by her husband. When Gentile Bellini, writes for forgiveness "on his knees" for his long delays, she is appeased and promises her support.

Part of this amazing correspondence are the letters that were sent to her. "To pleasure her" and to satisfy her curiosity, her husband, her brothers, her friends send her books, people, musicians, buffoons, news of the world. One month after Christopher Columbus landed back in Spain, letters arrived at the Mantuan court describing the far-away land, the thick forests, trees giving wool and wax, "men who feed men and eat them, like we do with chicken, and are called cannibals." There is a letter from Bishop Chiericati telling Isabella that one of her former servants "had fallen in love with long voyages." Isabella sent for the man and, after hearing him, prevailed on him to write a description of his journey. The man, who was called Antonio Pigafetta, then wrote the only report we have of Magellan's trip around the world. Above all, the correspondence gives us the portrait of a woman who embodied the ideal portrayed in Renaissance treatises by philosophers and poets: an intelligent and practical woman of wide and unbiased interests, culturally refined, authoritatively demanding, just and gracious, courageous and feminine; a woman who had chosen for herself the motto "neither hope, nor fear."

Works

D'Arco, C., "Notizie d'Isabella Estense moglie a Francesco Gonzaga." *Archivio storico italiano*, Ser. I, App. 2 (1845), pp. 247–326. Braghirolli, W., "Carteggio di Isabella d'Este Gonzaga intorno ad un quadro di Giambellion." *Archivio veneto* 13, I (1877): 370–383. Luzio, A., and Renier, R., *Giornale storico della letteratura italiana* 33–42 (1899–1903), passim.

Bibliography

Bellonci, Maria, "Isabella fra i Gonzaga." *I segreti dei Gonzaga* (Milan, 1947), pp. 33–101.

Bongiovanni, G., *Isabella d'Este, Marchesa di Mantova* (Rome, 1960). Brown, C. Malcolm, "Lo insaciabile desiderio nostro de cose antiche: New Documents on Isabella d'Este's collection of antiquities." *Cultural Aspects of the Italian Renaissance*, ed. C.H. Cough (Manchester, 1976), pp. 324–353. Cartwright, J. (Mrs. Ady), *Isabella d'Este Marchioness of Mantua* (London, 1903). Cian, V., "Isabella d'Este alle dispute domenicane." Giornale storico della letteratura italiana LXVII (1916), 376–386. Luzio, A., ed., L'archivio Gonzaga di Mantova (Ostiglia, 1920–1922). D'Arco, C., Ibid., pp. 203–246. Luzio, A., I precettori d'Isabella. Per nozze *Renier-Compostini* (Ancona, 1887). Luzio, A., "Isabella d'Este e l'Orlando Innamorato." *Studi su M. M. Boiardo*, ed., N. Campanini (Bologna, 1894), pp. 147–154. Luzio, A., *Isabella d'Este e i Borgia* (Milan, 1915). Luzio, A., Isabella d'Este e il sacco di Roma (Milan, 1908). Luzio, A., *Isabella d'Este nei primordi del papato di Leone X e il suo viaggio a Roma nel 1514–1515* (Milan, 1906). Luzio, A., *La galleria dei Gonzaga, venduta all'Inghilterra nei 1627–28* (Milan, 1913). Luzio, A., *La piu illustre collezionista del Rinascimento, Isabella d'Este* (Milan, 1913). Luzio, A., *La reggenza di Isabella d'Este durante la prigionia del marito (1509–1510)* (Milan: Cogliati, 1910). Luzio, A., *Mantova e Urbino. Isabella d'Este ed Elizabetta Gonzaga nelle relazioni famigliari e nelle vicende politiche* (Turin-Rome, 1893). Luzio, A., and R. Renier, *Giornale storico della letteratura italiana* 33–42 (1899–1903). Mazzeo, A., *Donne famose di Romagna* (Bologna, 1973). Meyer, E. Patterson, First Lady of the Renaissance: A Biography of Isabella d'Este (Boston-Toronto, 1970). Solerti, A., *Ferrara e la corte estense* (Ferrara, 1900).

Rinaldina Russell

Nicole Estienne (Madame Liebault)

Born c. 1542, Paris, France; died c. 1584, Paris
Genre(s): treatise, poetry
Language(s): French

Daughter of Charles Estienne, a doctor, writer, and printer belonging to the influential Estienne dynasty, Nicole met in 1559 the poet Jacques Grevin who celebrated her in his 1560 sonnet sequence *Amours d'Olympe*. Their engagement was broken off on account either of Grevin's conversion to Protestantism or of Charles Estienne's bankruptcy—the latter died in a debtors' prison in 1564. Nicole married in 1561 Jean Liebault, dean of the faculty of medicine in Paris and a writer of tracts on health and diseases pertaining to women. Nicole died between 1584, when the bibliographer La Croix du Maine included her in his compendium, and July 1596, the date of her husband's death.

Best known for her posthumously published *Les miseres de la femme mariee*, she is also the author of two lost manuscripts, *Le mepris d'amour* and *Apologie, ou Defense pour les femmes contre ceux qui les meprisent*, as well as the unpublished *Stances pour le mariage* and three sonnets. The *Stances* is a corrective response to Philippe Desportes's 1573 *Stances du mariage*, which drew on the satiric anti-feminist legacy of the medieval *Quinze joies du mariage*. In her subsequent *Miseres*, however, Nicole presented in 35 stanzas a bitter portrait of the abusive impact of contemporary laws of marriage on women. Critics have conjectured that Nicole's change of heart concerning the state of marriage was due to her own presumed deteriorating marital situation. One should recall, however, that Nicole was familiar with the humanist tradition of the paradox in which opposite sides of an issue were argued by the same writer—her father translated Ortensio Lando's famous treatise *Paradossi* (1543) in the 1550s. Moreover, her work belongs to the "Querelle du mariage" that spurred writers at the end of the century to take contrasting positions. The *Miseres* was prefaced with a view favorable to the Counter-Reformation. Its dedicatory epistle to a nun from Rouen praises her choice of the *vita contemplativa* that has spared her "the miseries attendant" to "the care of worldly things."

Works

Stances pour le mariage (c.1578, Bibliothèque Nationale, 500 de Colbert, No. 500, folio 87). Le mepris d'amour; Apologie, ou Defense pour les femmes contre ceux qui les meprisent; Les miseres de la femme mariee (Paris, c. 1587–1595; 2nd ed. (Rouen, 1597; editions by Fournier, Zinguer, and Guillerm, see below). Three sonnets (Bibliothèque Nationale, Fonds Dupuy No. 844, folio 360).

Bibliography

Albistur, M., and Armogathe, D., *Histoire du feminisme* (1977). Bayle, P., *Dictionnaire historique et critique* (1730). Fournier, E., *Variétés historiques et littéraires*, vol. 3 (1855). Guillerm, L., *Le miroir des femmes*, vol. 2 (1984). La croix du Maine, *Bibliothèque* (1584). Zinguer, I., *Miseres et grandeurs de la femme au XVIe siecle* (1982).

General references: *Revue du seizième siècle* 18 (1931). *Annales de la faculte des lettres et sciences humaines de Toulouse*. 1963.

Anne Larsen

Claire Etcherelli

Born 1934, Bordeaux
Genre(s): novel, short story, poetry
Language(s): French

Claire Etcherelli was born in Bordeaux in 1934 into a family of little means. Her father died in the war, and she was educated by the State as far as the *baccalauréat* level. She has earned her living in various trades and came to live and work—for more than two years on a car assembly line—in Paris in 1956. After working in a ball-bearing factory, Claire Etcherelli began, in 1962, while earning her living as a tourist agency receptionist, the work that would lead to the publication of her first novel, *Elise ou la vraie vie* (1967; Elisa or Real Life). This novel, which received the Prix Femina and which eventually became the basis for Michel Drach's film of the same name, was refused by five publishers before being accepted by Denoël. Claire Etcherelli has been editorial secretary of Sartre's *Les Temps Modernes* since 1975. She has two sons.

Elise ou la vraie vie (1967) was described by Simone de Beauvoir as "an admirable tragic story of love between an Algerian and a Frenchwoman." "Above all," she continued, the book gives us "someone: someone who speaks with a voice of unforgettable rightness" of fear and violence, love and delicacy, of all those small, yet grave minutiae of close-knit, stifling human relations, of women in a world that refuses and bruises them despite the enhancement and love they offer us all.

A propos de Clémence (1971; About Clémence), Claire Etcherelli's second novel, is structured upon the device of a shifting, triple narrative voice, a book that tends, like her other novels, less to analyze, to delve into the abstractions of psychology or sociology, than to offer us enactment, involvement, the flow of mental and spiritual engagement, shifting, fragmented and contrapuntal, enigmatic though plainly evidential.

Un arbre voyageur (1978; A Travelling Tree), her third novel, offers us a beautiful, penetrating account of the lives of ordinary, though shrewdly intelligent and inconspicuously sensitive women of France's late sixties and early seventies. It is a novel that, in Etcherelli's characteristically transparent and telescoped style, at once detached and close to consciousness, lucid and compassionate, plunges us into the simple difficulties of many women's existences: the loneliness, the endless responsibility of the children, the economic struggle, the vulnerabilities, the drifting and uncertainty, and so on. Beyond this, however, there is the uplift of both permanent and fleeting human exchange—children, men, women, friends and strangers—; the desire and determination that feed feminine courage; the choosing of one's life within the oppressive constraints imposed. One can see why Claire Etcherelli can say that *Un arbre voyageur* gave her "the most pleasure to write." It is a book of great resistance, of even smiling serenity, despite the bitter struggle it often narrates.

Since this novel, Claire Etcherelli has written *Délirante* (1982; Delirious Woman), a series of poetic texts prepared in the context of an exhibition of Altmann's paintings. She is on the point of completing another novel.

Works

Novels: *Elise ou la vraie vie* (1967). *A propos de Clémence* (1971). *Un arbre voyageur* (1978).
Poetry: *Délirante*, poems for exhibition of Altmann's paintings (1982).

Bibliography

Alliot, Bernard, "La petite musique pour matins blêmes de Claire Etcherelli." *Monde des livres*, 10381 (June 1978): 17. Astruc, Alexandre, "Une femme deux fois traquée." *Paris-Match*, 1126 (Dec. 1970): 96. Autrand, Dominique, "Claire Etcherelli fidèle à elle-même." *Quinzaine Littéraire*, 28 (June 1978): 5–6. Blackburn, Sara, "Book marks," *The Nation*, 209, 3 (July 1959): 89. Boisdeffre, Pierre de, *Histoire de la littérature de langue française des années 1930 aux années 1980* (Paris, 1985), pp. 1059–1062. Bory, Jean-Louis, "Même les héros ne sont pas des surhommes." *Paris-Match*, 1152 (June 1971): 89. Campbell, Danièle, "*Elise ou la vraie vie.*" *Français dans le monde*, 122 (July 1976): 11–16. "Catching up." The *Times Literary Supplement*, no. 3472 (Sept. 12, 1968): 976. Courthay, Claude, "Une femme ordinaire." *Magazine Littéraire*, 141 (Oct. 1978): 35–36. de Beauvoir, Simone, "Portrait d'un exilé." *Nouvel Observateur*, 344 (June 1971): 57–58. de Beauvoir, Simone, *Tout compte fait* (Paris, 1972). Gaugeard, Jean, "Elise ou l'authenticité." *Les Lettres Françaises*, no. 1203 (11–17 Oct. 1967): 12. Gaugeard, Jean, "Enfin Claire Etcherelli." *Les Lettres Françaises*, no. 1210 (29 Nov.–5 Dec. 1967): 9. Gaugeard, Jean, "La jeune fille et le proscrit." *Lettres françaises*, 1392 (July 1971): 5. Guers-Villate, Yvonne, "Claire Etcherelli: *A propos de Clémence.*" *French Review*, 46, 2 (Dec. 1972): 442–444. Guillemin, Henri, "Les braises ardentes de l'espérance." *Nouvel Observateur*, 712 (July 1978): 56. L., G., "Un certain désarroi." *Quinzaine Littéraire*, 121 (July 1971): 5–6. "Les prix littéraires. Femina: Claire Etcherelli; Médicis: Claude Simon." *Le Monde*, no. 7115 (28 Nov. 1967): 28. Melchior-Bonnet, Christian, "Sorti des presses." *A la Page*, no. 44 (Feb. 1968): 318–319. Miller, Judith, "Claire Etcherelli: *Un arbre voyageur.*" *French Review*, S2, 5 (April 1979): 792–793. Ragon, Michel, *Histoire de la littérature prolétarienne en France* (Paris, 1974). Wolfromm, Jean-Didier, "*A propos de Clémence* par Claire Etcherelli." *Magazine Littéraire*, 53 (June 1971): 30.

Michael Bishop

Amarelli Etrusca

(see: Teresa Landucci Bandettini)

Eucheria

Flourished sixth or seventh century
Genre(s): poetry
Language(s): Latin

Eucheria is an unidentified poet from the sixth or seventh century. She is represented only by one poem, although that poem appears in several manuscripts. Dinamius Patricius writes an epitaph for his wife Eucheria, but she is probably a different woman from the poet. Since one line from the poem is quoted by Bishop Julian of Toledo (fl. 680–690), Eucheria may have had some connection to him, although again, the connection cannot be proven.

Eucheria's one extant poem, which begins "Aurea concordi quae fulgent fila metallo," consists of sixteen distichs. The poet begins by comparing base things with noble—golden threads with heaps of hair, or silk coverings with goat skins—then proceeds by amplification, ringing more changes on this theme. Under the circumstances in which the poet finds herself, the hyacinth is equal with fenugreek and rock is said to be as delicate as jasper: "Now indeed let us eat nettles as if they were lilies,/ And press the deadly hemlock as if it were the purple rose." Many of the comparisons involve animals: the lion is joined with the fox, the wise lynx with the ape; the swallow of good fortune "frolics" with the funereal vulture. The point behind this series of apparently unconnected comparisons remains unclear until the poem's conclusion, when the speaker declares: "Then let a peasant slave woo Eucheria." The poet, like the noblest representatives of nature, is undervalued when she is joined with a base companion.

Eucheria's poetry belongs to a period that has earned little praise or attention. But although much secular poetry from this century is dry and academic, Eucheria uses rhetoric to good advantage in this poem; for her simple structure, based on repetitive use of amplification, not only gives the poem a sense of vigorous emotion, it also enhances the irony of the speaker's final revelation.

Works

Buecheler, Franciscus, and Alexander Riese, *Anthologina Latina*, no. 390.

Bibliography

Chevalier, Ulysse, *Repertorium Hymnologicum* 3: 23286. Dekkers, Eligius, *Clavis Patrum Latinorum*, 327–328. Dronke, Peter, *Women Writers of the Middle Ages: A Critical Study of Texts from Perpetua (t203) to Marguerite Porete (t1310)* (1984), pp. 28–29. Teuffel, W.S., *A History of Roman Literature* (1968). Thomas, A., *Archivum Latinatis Medii Aevi* 3 (1927): 49–58. Walther, Hans, *Initia Carminum ac Versum Medii Aevi Posteriorus Latinorum* (1792).

Christy Desmet

Eudokia (Aelia Eudokia)

Born 394, Athens, Greece; died 460, Jerusalem
Genre(s): poetry, translation
Language(s): Greek

Eudokia is of interest today both because of her historical and religious importance as a Byzantine empress and church leader and because of her writings, particularly her legend of Saints Cyprian (the Magician) and Justina, the first known poetic account of a Faust-like story.

The accounts of Eudokia's life give differing details of her birth and death dates and of her parentage, but she is generally thought to have been born in 394 to the pagan rhetorician Leontius. Her father educated her well, and she became famous for her learning and her defense of the pagan faith. On a mission to Constantinople to challenge her father's will, Eudokia so impressed the empress's sister Pulcheria that Pulcheria converted Eudokia to Christianity and arranged for the marriage of Eudokia to the emperor Theodosius in 421. Their daughter, Eudoxia, later married the emperor Valentian III. Eudokia was active in religious missions, making two pilgrimages to Jerusalem. She remained in Jerusalem after her second mission, apparently in banishment, either from an intrigue or from a misunderstanding with Theodosius. Eudokia still remained a devout and influential figure in church decisions. She was buried in St. Stephen in Jerusalem in 460.

Works attributed to Eudokia include a poem commemorating the victory of the Romans over the Persians; a eulogy to the city of Antioch; a paraphrase in Greek hexameters of the Octateuch;

a version of the books of Zachariah and Daniel; a poem in three books on the lives of Saints Cyprian and Justina; and the completion and arrangement of the *Centones Homerici* of Patricius, an account of the life of Christ in Homeric hexameters. Eudokia's works in hexameter are noteworthy for their attempts to render Christian doctrine and spirit in Homeric meter and vocabulary. The legend of Cyprian and Justina appeared in several versions in the Middle Ages and was later adapted by Calderon de la Barca for his drama *El mágico prodigioso*. The basic story tells how the pagan Aglaides asked Cyprian the magician to obtain for him the beautiful Christian convert Justina. Cyprian himself fell in love with her and tried in vain to win Justina through magic spells. In frustration, Cyprian threatened to forsake the devil, whereupon the devil attacked him. Cyprian survived the assault by making the sign of the Cross. The priest Eusebius counseled Cyprian to convert, and Cyprian proved his devotion by burning his magic books. When Diocletian began his persecutions, Cyprian and Justina were arrested, tortured, boiled in pitch, and beheaded. Eudokia's version, of which almost two of the original three books survive, is characterized by its simple yet effective characterization of the two saints and by its vivid, concrete portrayal of the force of evil.

Eudokia's surviving works are of interest as the product of a highly educated and politically important Byzantine woman. It is significant that such a woman should be among the first Christian writers to take up the Faust theme, with its questions about the limits of human knowledge and action.

Works

Editions: *Peri tou agiou Kyrpianou* (On St. Cyprian), in *Patrialogia Graeca*, 85 (1864), 827–864. "In Theodosium Persarum Victorem" [On the Victory of Theodosius over the Persians]; edition contains only a reference by the historian Socrates; "Laudes Antiochiae" (Praise of Antioch—fragments); "Metaphrasis Octateuchi" (Paraphrase of the Octateuch—attribution by Photius); "Metaphrasis Prophetiarum Zachariae et Danielis" (Paraphrase of the Prophets Zacchariah and Daniel—attribution by Photius); "De Martyrio S. Cypriani" (On the Martyrdom of Saint Cyprian); "Homerocentones"

(life of Christ in Homeric hexameters, by Particius, Eudokia, and others) in *Eudocia Augusta, Proclus Lycius, Claudianus: Carmina; Blemyomachia*, ed. A. Ludwich (1897). "De S. Cypriano I" (On St. Cyprian Book 1), in *Dichterinnen des Alterums und des fruhen Mittelalters*, ed. Helene Homeyer (1979).

Bibliography

Gregorovius, Ferdinand. *Athenais/Geschichte einer byzantinischen Kaiserin* (1926). Hunger, Herbert, "On the Imitation (MIMHEIE) of Antiquity in Byzantine Literature." *Dumbarton Oaks Papers 23–24 (1969–1970), 15–38.*

General references: The New Schaff-Herzog Encyclopedia of Religious Knowledge, vol. 3. *Paulys Real-Encyclopädie der classischen Alterumswissenschaft* (new ed.), vol. 11. Smith, William, and Henry Wace, eds., *A Dictionary of Christian Biography*, vol. 3.

Stephen Hale

Euginie

(see: Kathinka [Katharina] Rosa Pauline Modesta Zitz-Halein)

Glacilla Eurotea

(see: Diodata Saluzzo-Roero)

Henriette van Eyk

Born 1897; died 1980
Genre(s): novel, short story
Language(s): Dutch

Her short stories represent a revival of the genre in Dutch literature and have had a significant influence on the work of Dutch story tellers like Godfried Bomans, Belcampo, and Simon Carmiggelt.

No doubt her most successful book is *De kleine parade* (1932; The Little Parade) in which she ridicules the egotism and self-satisfaction of the class-conscious upper tenth for whom wealth, status, and title form the exclusive legitimization of their existence. In the protagonist, Beatrix Wentinck, van Eyk created a woman representative of her milieu and entire class, who is a monster in her callous exploitation of others and merciless progression toward social triumph. Despite its bitter criticism of the upper class, which is a direct expression of the author's indignation, the book is outrageously funny. The humor is both situational and verbal, the style an instrument of comic effect. Unfortunately, Henriette van Eyk's later works are not of the same quality as her earlier ones.

Works

De kleine parade (1932). *Gabriel* (1932). *Aan de loopenden band* (1932, with E. de Neve). *Gabriel; de geschiedenis van een klein mannetje* (1935). *Intieme revue* (1936). *Als de wereld donker is* (1938). *Het eenig echte* (1939). *Truus de nachtmerrie* (1939). *Michiel, de geschiedenis van een mug* (1940). *Sinterklaas blijft een zomer over* (1940). *Sneeuw* (1945). *Bedelarmband* (1948). *Vader Valentijn viert feest* (1948). *Van huis tot huis* (1949). *Avontuur met Titia* (1949). *In vredesnaam* (1950). *Schots en scheef* (1951). *Her verhaal van jonker Flonker* (1951). *Een eindje om* (1951). *De jacht op de spiegel* (1952). *De spookdiligence* (1953). *Klaar . . . over!* (1954). *Het huis aan de gracht* (1956). *Avonturen op de Willem Ruys* (1957). *Vrouw vermoord . . . en zo!* (1957). *Josefine* (1962). *Kasteel Karsesteyn* (1964). *Blauwe Marietje* (1966). *De regels van het spel; een kleine etiquette-gids* (1967). *Het paaspaard en andere verhalen* (1969). *De monsters van Stone Valley* (1970). *Dierbare wereld* (1973). *Het ulevellenlaantje* (1975).

Bibliography

Fonse, Marko, "Henriette van Eyk." In *'Tis vol van schatten hier*, vol. 1, 1750–1940 (Amsterdam, 1986), pp. 320–321. Moerman, Josien. *Lexikon Nederlandstalige auteurs* (1984), p. 72.

Maya Bijvoet

F

Camilla Faa' Gonzaga

Born, 1599, Casale, Italy; died 1662, Ferrara
Genre(s): memoirs
Language(s): Italian

Camilla Faa's life can be read as an example of how unprotected women are in a system in which people in positions of authority can dictate all rules and change all laws. Born into an influential family in the Monferrato region (her father Ardizzino was ambassador to the Gonzagas and her mother Margherita Fassati was a wealthy local heiress), Camilla was educated in a convent before becoming lady-in-waiting at the Gonzaga Court in Mantua. She was fifteen when Duke Ferdinando Gonzaga started to woo her while also trying to convince her father of the seriousness of his intentions. Before long Camilla and Ferdinando were secretly married. Happiness was short lived. Their son was not yet born when the Duke had to bow to political pressures and to petition the Pope to annul his first nuptials in order to marry into a more powerful family. Having become a pawn in a game too difficult for her to understand, Camilla hoped she would be left alone with her child. Instead, he was taken away soon after his birth while she was purposely kept in the dark about events at Court and then repeatedly asked to remarry or to take religious vows. Camilla tried to resist the pressure for five years in the hope that her situation would improve and a way out of her predicament could be found. Finally, she accepted her unwanted destiny of reclusion and became a Clarissa nun. Camilla wrote her memoir in 1622 with the understanding that her Mother Superior would keep it within conventual walls to avoid possible retaliation.

The title "Storia di donna Camilla Faa di Bruno Gonzaga" was most probably not Camilla's own but given to the short memoir by its editor. The manuscript copy is in the Archives of the Convent of the Corpus Domini in Ferrara. The first published edition is that of 1895, prepared by Giuseppe Giorcelli for *Rivista di Storia, Arte, Archeologia della provincia di Alessandria.* Camilla's "Storia" is a short, terse rendering of the events which first led her to marry Ferdinando and then determined her exclusion from the Court, her seclusion from friends, and her reclusion in a faraway convent. The writing is not a plea of innocence nor is its purport to chastise Ferdinando and his counsellors. Camilla seems somehow able to maintain her objectivity and to keep political obligations in mind. This constitutes in many ways the strength of her memoir. She chooses to be proud rather than pathetic; instead of insisting upon her victimization, she decides to inscribe her survival; in place of vituperative sarcasm, she offers articulate questioning. Her dismissal from the Court, the denial of her status, the pressure put on her to become a nonentity as a woman should have doomed and mastered Camilla in the long run. It did not happen. She chose to write in fact exactly when everything seemed lost and when speaking for herself of her self would have made no difference in her status. Camilla spent the rest of her remaining forty years isolated in Ferrara. Today we can read her "Storia" as one of the earliest examples in Italian literature, or possibly the earliest altogether, of female autobiography, and an assertive one at that.

Works

"Storia di donna Camilla Faa di Bruno Gonzaga." *Rivista di Storia, Arte, Archeologia della provincia di Alessandria* 10.4 (1895): 90–99. Rpt. with slight changes as "*Historia della Sig.ra Donna Camilla Faa Gonzaga*," in F. Sorbelli Bonfa, '*Camilla Gonzaga Faa*': *Storia Documentata* (1918).

Bibliography

Costa-Zalessow, Natalia, *Scrittrici italiane dal XIII al XX secolo* (Ravenna, 1982), pp. 14–15. D'Arco, Carlo, "Degli amori sfortunatissimi di Camilla Faa'." *Racconti patrii* (Mantova, 1844). Giacometti, Paolo, *Camilla Faa' da Casale* (Firenze, 1850). Giorcelli, Giuseppe, "Documenti storici del Monferrato." *Rivista di Storia, Arte, Archeologia della provincia di Alessandria* 10.4 (1895): 69–89. Intra, Giambattista, *La bella Ardizzina* (Milan, 1889). Possevino, Antonio, *Historia Belli Monferratensis* (Mantova, 1637). Sorbelli-Bonfa', Fernanda, *Camilla Gonzaga Faa': storia documentata* (Bologna, 1918).

Valeria Finucci

Rina Faccio

(see: Sibilla Aleramo)

João Falco

(see: Irene Lisboa)

Lidia Falcón O'Neill

Born December 13, 1935, Madrid, Spain
Genre(s): essay, journalism, novel, short story, drama
Language(s): Spanish

Lidia Falcón is perhaps the most distinguished feminist writer and theoretician in Spain today. Born in Madrid, she moved to Barcelona in 1941, and all her political and literary activities have centered around that city. A most learned woman, she earned degrees in dramatic arts at the Barcelona Theater Institute; law, peda-

gogy, and journalism at the University. She is a practicing lawyer specializing in domestic law, and is also the founder of the Feminist Party of Spain.

Falcón's literary career started with the publication of numerous short stories in the newspaper *Noticiero Universal* during the years 1959–1961. Her first full-length work was the novel *Substituciones y fideicomisos* (1962), followed by the legal monographs *Los derechos civiles de la mujer* (1963) and *Los derechos laborales de la mujer* (1965). In 1968 Falcón convened more than 600 women for feminist actions, provoking the ire of the Francisco Franco regime. Her essay *Mujer y sociedad* (1969) criticized the position of women in Spanish society and called for reforms. In 1972 Falcón was jailed for six months for antigovernment activities, and in 1973 she published the epistolary essay *Cartas a una idiota española*, in which she exposed the fallacy of women's freedom under patriarchal rule. In 1974 she founded the "Colectivo Feminista," a forerunner of the "Organizacion Feminista Revolucionaria" that would become the Feminist Party of Spain in 1979. In 1975 Falcón published the novel *Es largo esperar callado*, dramatizing life under a dictatorship. The same year she was again jailed, this time for nine months, for suspicion of collaborating on a terrorist attack. The fictionalized chronicle of the suffering of women in jails, entitled *En el infierno*, appeared in 1977, and in 1979 the biographical novel *Los hijos de los vencidos* (1979), centered on the families of the defeated fighters of the Spanish Civil War, portrayed with extraordinary ethos the tribulations of the dissenters under a fascist regime.

In 1981 and 1982 Falcón's most important contribution to feminist theory to date was published. The two volumes of *La razón feminista* provide an exhaustive analysis of woman's place in society and her role as a socioeconomic class and as a reproductive agent. The work was received with exhilaration from the feminists and with caution from the ruling Socialist leaders. Also in these years Falcón published the novel *Viernes 13 y en la calle del Correo* (1981) about the terrorist attack for which she was incarcerated in 1975. This novel, according to Antonio Buero Vallejo, is one of the best of that time. In 1982 her play *Las mujeres caminaron* con el fuego del siglo was presented at the Second International Theater Meet in Athens, Greece. Hers was one of the few plays by Spanish women to be staged. In 1983 Falcón published the novel *El juego de la piel*, and her collection of essays on Spanish life and mores entitled *El alboroto español* came out in 1984. She has published essays and fiction in the newspapers and journals *Madrid*, *Diario Femenino, Triunfo, Cuadernos para el Diálogo, El Periódico*, etc. Besides these professional and literary activities, Lidia Falcón is the editor and director of the journal *Vindicación feminista* and an indefatigable advocate for feminist reforms. Falcón's works have as primary theme the position of women in society, the exploitation suffered by women, and the need for changes in contemporary Spain and the world. Another recurring theme is life under the Franco rule and the fight for freedom in those days. Her work is passionate, prolific, and almost singleminded in its purpose. Hers is a literary production with a mission, and all her works reflect her deep commitment to feminism and freedom.

Works

Essays: *Los derechos civiles de la mujer* [The Civil Rights of Women] (1963). *Los derechos laborales de la mujer* [The Rights of the Working Woman] (1965). *Mujer y sociedad* [Woman and Society] (1969). *Cartas a una idiota española* (1973). *La razón feminista* [The Feminist Reason] (1981) I: El modo de producción doméstico, la mujer como clase social. *La razón feminista*, II: La reproducción humana (1982). *El alboroto español* [The Spanish Uproar] (1984). *El varón español a la búsqueda de su identidad* [Spanish Men in Search of an Identity] (1986).
Novels: *Substituones y fideicomisos* [Substitutions and Trusteeships] (1962). *Lettres a une idiote Espagnole* [Letters to a Spanish Idiot] (1975). *Es largo esperar Callado* (1975). *En el infierno* [In Hell] (1977). *Viernes 13 y en la Calle del Correo* [Friday the 13th in Correo Street] (1981). *El juego de la piel* [Skin Play] (1983). *Rupturas* (1984).
Theater: *Las mujeres caminaron con el fuego del siglo* [Women Walked with the Fire of the Century] (1982).
Biography: *Los hijos de los vencidos* [The Children of the Defeated] (1979).

Bibliography

Galerstein, Carolyn L., ed., *Women Writers of Spain* (Westport, Conn., 1986). Pérez, Janet, *Contemporary Women Writers of Spain* (Boston, 1988). Rague-Arias, María José, "Introducción a la obra de Lidia Falcón." [Introduction to the Work of Lidia Falcón]. *Estreno*, Vol. X, 2(1984): 26–31.

Lina L. Cofresí

Oriana Fallaci

Born June 29, 1930, Florence, Italy
Genre(s): journalism, narrative prose
Language(s): Italian

Oriana Fallaci is one of the most familiar names in contemporary international journalism, renowned for her brilliant and pointed interviewing techniques. Her individual portraits and social studies are celebrated and criticized for their honesty, accuracy, and acute insights if not for their impartiality. Fallaci claims that her journalism is personal, even autobiographical; she is also a subject as interviewer and investigator. As a novelist, the writer blends realistic description with emotional subjectivity. Naturalist scenes unite with meditations, memory, allegorical dreams, musings, and lush imagery in a blend of tones, hues, and narrative techniques joined through the omnipresent psyche of the narrator.

Born of a poor working-class family, Fallaci was drawn to her political and ideological issues at an early age thanks to her father's involvement in the Socialist Party as well as her own experiences in the war. In fact, the adolescent Fallaci acted as a courier for the partisans and Allies, helping save downed fliers and escaped prisoners. During her studies in medicine at the University of Florence, Fallaci began working part-time for an uncle, the founder of the magazine *Epoca*. She soon abandoned her medical books for a career in journalism.

After covering the night police beat for a Florentine daily, Fallaci began a long working rapport with another Italian magazine, *Europeo*, as a special correspondent. Working with a tape recorder and notebook, the journalist traveled worldwide covering such disparate events as wars and weddings. Her books record her interpretation of these experiences: distasteful celebrity interviews became *Gli antipatici* (1963; The Egotist); a world tour on the status of women resulted in *Il sesso inutile* (1961; The Useless Sex); her interest in space produced *Se il sole muore* (1965; If the Sun Dies), an investigation of scientists, NASA, astronauts, and science fiction; her three tours of duty in Viet Nam translated into *Niente e così sia* (1969; Nothing and So Be It), a documentary of the horrors, propaganda, and madness of war.

By the late 1960s, Fallaci was an international celebrity herself and a popular subject for other interviewers. In demand for her inquisitive and somewhat inquisitorial questioning, the journalist began contributing to several American periodicals, including *Look*, *Ms.*, *New Republic*, *The New York Times Magazine*, and the *Washington Post*. Multilingual, she conducts interviews in several languages, which often afford revealing glimpses into the nature and thoughts of her subjects.

Concerned with power and its misuse, injustice, and oppression, her pieces confront these issues by employing journalistic methods to disconcert figures of power, such as statesmen and politicians, and ideologues into unexpected revelations. Her most famous conversations are published in *Intervista con la Storia* (1974; Interview with History). With its fourteen interviews of individuals ranging from the Shah of Iran to Golda Meir, this book is an exemplar of Fallaci's contention that the journalist is a direct witness to the flow of history.

Never married, Fallaci became the companion of Greek freedom fighter Alexandros Panagoulis after an interview, and they remained attached until his suspicious death in 1976. The story of his life and beliefs and their love, blended with political and philosophical meditations on the struggle for human freedom and dignity, are the basis for Fallaci's most famous novel *Un uomo* (1979; A Man).

Another popular and controversial novel is *Lettera a un bambino mai nato* (1975; Letter to a Child Never Born), the tale of a woman's reactions to an unexpected and inconvenient pregnancy as she battles with her own desire for autonomy, the demands and rights of the child, and her conscience and guilt at his loss. Told as a monologue, or confession to the child, this book has been viewed as a strong feminist statement on maternity and social responsibility.

Passionate, involved, and politically engaged, Oriana Fallaci is a model of subjective journalism at its best and most controversial. Rejecting professional remoteness, the writer sees the journalist as a creative artist, a witness to history in process, and a participant in the investigative act. Fallaci's verve, raw energy, and blunt honesty have won her both detractors and admirers. Nevertheless, she has twice won the Saint-Vincent prize for journalism, Italy's equivalent of the Pulitzer, as well as the Viareggio Literary Award for her fiction (1979).

Works

Essay collections: *I sette peccati di Hollywood* (1958). *Il sesso inutile: Viaggio intorno alla donna* (1961). *Gli antipatici* (1963). *Se il sole muore* (1965). *Niente e così sia* (1969). *Quel giorno sulla luna* (1970). *Intervista con la Storia* (1974).

Novels: *Penelope alla guerra* (1962). *Lettera a un bambino mai nato* (1975). *Un uomo: romanzo* (1979).

Translations: *The Useless Sex*, tr. Pamela Swinglehurst (1964). *Penelope at War*, tr. Pamela Swinglehurst (1966). *The Egotists: Sixteen Surprising Interviews*, tr. Pamela Swinglehurst (1968). Also published in England as *Limelighters*. *If the Sun Dies*, tr. Pamela Swinglehurst (1966). *Nothing, and So Be It*, tr. Isabel Quigly (1972). Also published in England as *Nothing and Amen*. *Interview with History*, tr. John Shepley (1976). *Letter to a Child Never Born*, tr. John Shepley (1976). *A Man*, tr. William Weaver (1980).

Bibliography

A.A., "Breaking the Ice with Henry: An In-depth Look at Interview Techniques." *Writers Digest* 53 (June 1973): 22–28. Franks, L., "Behind the Fallaci Image." *Saturday Review* 8 (January 1981): 18–22. Sanford, D., "Lady of the Tapes." *Esquire* 83 (June 1975): 102–105.

General references: A.A., "Fallaci, Oriana." *Contemporary Authors NRS*, Vol. 15 (Detroit, 1985), pp. 120–122. A.A., "Fallaci, Oriana." *Contemporary Literary Criticism*, ed. Dedria Bryfonski, Vol. II (Detroit, 1979), pp. 189–191. A.A., "Fallaci, Oriana." *Current Biography Yearbook 1977*, ed. Charles Moritz (New York, 1977/78), pp. 146–149.

Fiora A. Bassanese

Fanny

(see: Marie Beauharnais [Anne F. Mouchard, Comtesse de,])

Elena Farago

(a.k.a. Ellen, Fatma, Fatma-Constanţa, Elena Farago-Fatma, Elena Fotino, Ileana, Ileana-Fatma, Leana)

Born 1878, Bîrlad, Romania; died 1954, Craiova
Genre(s): poetry, memoirs, children's literature, translation
Language(s): Romanian

Elena Farago (born Elena Praximade) was highly recognized as a poet. She was twice awarded the Academy Prize—in 1907 for her debut volume *Versuri* (1906; Poetry) and in 1920 for the subsequent *Şoaptele amurgului* (1920; Whispers of Dusk). In 1924 she was a recipient of the French Femina Prize. In 1937 she was granted the Romanian National Prize for Poetry.

Farago's poems center upon time, more exactly upon the past. Her first volume is already a nostalgic and muted recalling of lost happiness. The quiet, strong, and discrete celebration of the present, of love fulfilled and of maternity in *Şoapte din umbra* (1908; Whispers from Shadow) is but a brief interlude. Volumes such as *Din taina vechilor răspîntii* (1913; From the Secret of Old Crossroads) and *Şoaptele amurgului* (1920; Whispers of Dusk) will recapture the longing—for lost love and youth—as well as the anxiety and grave meditation in the face of time's relentless flow.

The poet found impressive accents to sing (or to proclaim the possibility of) equal, autonomous love between free and mature partners. In her poems men address their beloved with the invitation to be "neither a slave, nor a master/ neither support, nor burden."

Farago's creation can be divided into three main periods: an initial one in which the influence of Romanian poets such as Eminescu or Coşbuc can still be traced; an intermediary, syncretic period in which symbolism and allegory blend in musical incantation, songs of the soul, evocative of both Maeterlinck and Claudel (Farago appeals to lilies and thorns, speaks about the "blossoming of the blue when," "the leaf of the greenish maybe," "the scythe of autumn," "the hopes' meadow," but also about conventionally symbolic azyme and wine, bowl and scarf); and a last, formally ascetic period, when the poet's voice grows direct and simple in its silent repudiation of all aesthetic strategy. One may connect with the second period Farago's characteristic capitalization of certain adverbs, verbs, pronouns, or even whole phrases which thus acquire in her poems almost the status of characters, mysterious in their vague joys and sorrows, such as: *Încotro* (Whither), *De unde* (Wherefrom), *Ce va să fie* (What Is To Be), *statornicul Este* (the Steadfast Is), *tristul N-a fost* (The Sad Was Not), *blîndul Că n-a fost să fie* (The Mild For It Wasn't Meant To Be), *gingaşul Noi* (the Gentle We), etc.

A regular and vigorous contributor to *Luceafărul, Ramuri, Neamul romănesc literar, Sburătorul, Flamura, Icoane maramureşene, Poezia,* etc., Farago is also acknowledged as a gifted writer for children and as a subtle translator of Maeterlinck, Anatole France, and Villiers de l'Isle Adam into Romanian.

Works

Versuri [Poetry] (1906). *Şoapte din umbră* [Whispers from Shadow] (1908). *Traduceri libere* [Free Translations] (1908). *Din taina vechilor răspîntii* [From the Secret of Old Crossroads] (1913). *Şoaptele amurgului* [Whispers of Dusk] (1920). *Nu mi-am plecat genunchii* [I Didn't Bend My Knees] (1926). *Poezii pentru cei mici* [Poems for Little Ones] (1955, 1957). *Poezii* [Poems] (1957). Edited and with an afterword by Liviu Călin.

Translations: Sadeckij, A., ed., *Antologija rumynskoj poezii* (Moscow, 1958) ("Proxodil celovek po doroge"/"Trecea un om pe drum . . ."; "U kolybeli"/"La leagăn," tr. N. Podgoričani). Sarov, Taško, ed. and tr., *Antologija na romanskata poezija* (Skopje, 1972) ("Imaše eden bunar"/"Era o fîntînă"; "Po patot eden čovek vidov odi"/"Trecea un om pe drum . . ."). Vainer, Nelson, ed. and tr., *Antologia da poesia romena* (Rio de Janeiro, 1966) ("Separação"/"Despărţire").

Bibliography

Călinescu, G., *Istoria literaturii române. Compendiu* (Bucharest, 1968), pp. 268–270. Miller-Verghi, Margareta and Ecaterina Săndulescu, *Evoluția scrisului feminin în România* (Bucharest, 1935), p. 267. Papastate, C.D., *Elena Farago* (Craiova, 1975).

Sanda Golopentia

Elena Farago-Fatma

(see: Elena Farago)

Carmen Farres de Mieza

Born 1931, Barcelona, Spain; died 1976, Barcelona
Genre(s): novel
Language(s): Spanish

Mieza published only two novels, both based on her experience as the daughter of an expatriate. Although she remained in Spain after the Civil War and completed her training as a teacher, in 1954 she joined her father who had fled to Mexico immediately after the war. *La imposible canción* (1962; The Impossible Song) portrays the lives of Catalonian exiles living in Mexico City but dreaming of a return to the homeland, a hope they realize can never be fulfilled. *Una mañana cualquiera* (1965; Any Tomorrow), winner of the Premio Urriza, studies the complex relationships which develop when a late adolescent comes from Spain to Mexico to visit her exiled father and his ignorant lower-class Mexican wife. The father, a doctor, represents the bitterness, desolation and solitude of exile, but the daughter expects to become a citizen of the world. After her return to Spain, Mieza established a publishing firm, Ediciones Marte. She also published several short stories, one of which won the 1960 story contest in "El Correo Catalán" of Barcelona. Her other works are a travel book and a collection of interviews.

Works

La imposible canción (1962). *Una mañana cualquiera* (1965). *Barcelona, Tarragona, Lérida, Gerona* (1966; No. 7 in the *Rutas de España* series). *La mujer española* (1977).

Bibliography

Galerstein, Carolyn, "Spanish Women Novelists and Younger-Generation Writers in Exile and Return: Outsiders or Insiders?" in *European Writers in Exile in Latin America*, ed. H.B. Moeller (Heidelberg: Winter Verlag, 1983), pp. 137–148. Galerstein, Carolyn, "The Second Generation in Exile." *Papers on Language and Literature* 21, No. 2 (spring 1985): 220–228. Valdivieso, Teresa, "El drama de lo tangencial en *Víspera del odio* y *Una mañana cualquiera.*" *Letras Femeninas* XII, Nos. 1–2 (primavera-otono 1986): 24–33.

Carolyn Galerstein

Fatma

(see: Elena Farago)

Fatma-Constanța

(see: Elena Farago)

Ypk van der Fear

(see: L. Post-Beukens)

Cassandra Fedele

Born 1465, Venice, Italy; died 1558
Genre(s): letters, poetry, oration, treatise
Language(s): Latin

Cassandra was born to Angelo Fedele and to Barbara Leoni, both descendants of noble families exiled from Milan at the fall of the house of Visconti. She was first tutored by her father. At the age of twelve, she began to study theology and the sciences with Gasparino Borro but continued to cultivate the classical languages until she was twenty-two. After marrying a doctor from Vicenza, Giovan Maria Mapelli, she travelled to Crete and lived in Retino (Rethimnon) from 1415 to 1520. On the return journey, the ship was caught in a severe storm, and the Mapellis lost most of their property. After her husband's death in 1520, Cassandra dedicated herself to learning. As her fame grew, she received invitations from Louis XII of France, from Leo X and from the Queen of Spain to move to their courts but the Doge forbade her to leave and, in his words, "deprive Venice of its best adornment." Cassandra, however, soon found herself in reduced circumstances. Only when, at the age of 80, in 1547, she appealed for help to Pope Paul III, was she made prioress of the girls' orphanage attached to the church of S. Domenico di Castello in Venice. She held that position until her death, eleven years later.

Only three orations and some letters, of Cassandra's much larger body of writing, have come down to us. She was also known as a poet and, as such, celebrated by Politian, Sansovino, and Panfilo Sasso. A few verses are included in her letter to Pope Paul III. We read of a treatise, *De scientiarum ordine* (On the Order of Sciences), in her letters and in those of her friends, who wrote about it as of a work well known to them. Two more writings are mentioned: *Digressioni morali* (Moral Digressions) and *Elogi degli uomini illustri* (Praises of Illustrious Men).

Cassandra's orations, all of encomiastic nature, were delivered by her at official occasions. When young, she was favored by the doge of Venice, Agostino Barbarigo, and she was invited to state banquets and private gatherings. The speech on the birth of Christ which she addressed to the town dignitaries in San Marco, during the Christmas celebrations, has not come down to us. One of her extant speeches is a praise of literature and was given in the presence of the ambassadors from Brescia. What won Cassandra her fame in Italy and abroad was the oration she delivered at the University of Padua in 1587 on the occasion of the degree conferred on a relative. The speech was given before the President of the University, many professors, and students and was published the same year with the title of *Oration for Bertuccio Lamberti, Receiving the Honors of the Liberal Arts*. According to Cavazzana, in the State Library of Munich, there is a letter dated 1588 addressed to Cassandra by a humanist from Nuremberg, Peter Danhauser, who later became professor of Roman Law in Vienna. After hearing of Cassandra from his friend, Hartman Schadel, who had been present at her speech in Bologna, Danhauser wrote to compliment her most enthusiastically and to ask

for some of her poetry. The third extant oration was the official speech of welcome that Cassandra was asked to deliver upon the arrival in Venice of Bona Sforza, Queen of Poland. Cassandra was then ninety-one years old.

Fedele's correspondence included letters to many dignitaries and men of letters who were prominent in northern Italy, such as Giorgio Sommariva, Lodovico Cendrata, Matteo Bosso, Adriano Cappelli, as well as to Popes Leo X and Paul III, and to Ludovico Sforza, Duke of Milan. From a letter to Girolamo Monopolitano, dated 1514 and not published by Tomasini, we gather that she had been studying philosophy and classical history. Some historians of the University of Padua state, contrary to Tomasini's denial, that Cassandra taught philosophy there in substitution for her relative, Alberto Leonardi.

Among the women who in fifteenth-century Italy achieved a high degree of erudition and literary skill and won fame among their contemporaries, Cassandra is an exception insofar as she was allowed to display her capacities publicly and was appointed as speaker by state authorities. A portrait of her, now lost, was painted by Gentile Bellini. It depicted a young girl in elegant dress with her hair piled high on her head, according to the contemporary Venetian fashion, later severely forbidden by the State. The print shown in Tomasini's edition and a medal in the collection of Papazzo dei Dogi, were drawn from that portrait.

Works

Cassandrae virginis venetae, oratio pro Bertucio Lamberto canonico concordiensi, liberalium artium insignia suscipiente. Habita in Gymnasio patavino (1487). *Clarissinae feminae Cassandrae Fidelis venetae, epistolae et orationes posthumae*, ed. J.F. Tomasini (1636). Petrettini, M., *Vita di Cassandra Fedele* (1814). Simsonsfeld, H., "Zur Geschichte der Cassandra Fedele." *Studien zur Literaturgeschichte, Michael Bernays gewidmet* (1893), pp. 101–108. Cavazzana, C., "Cassandra Fedele erudita veneziana del Rinascimento." *Ateneo veneto* 29 (1906): App. 9, 386–387. "Oration to the Ruler of Venice, Francesco Venerio, on the Arrival of the Queens of Poland," "Oration for Bertuccio Lamberto, receiving the Honors of the Liberal Arts," "Oration in Praise of Letters," "Letter to Alessandra Scala: Whether Marriage Is To Be Preferred to Studies by a Learned Woman, 1492." In M.L. King and A. Rabil Jr., eds., *Her Immaculate Hand. Selected Works by and About the Women Humanists of Quattrocento Italy* (1983), pp. 48–50, 69–73, 74–77, 87–88.

Bibliography

Cappelli, A., "Cassandra Fedele in relazione con Lodovico il Moro." *Archivio storico lombardo* III, 4 (1895): 387–394. Cavazzana, C., "Cassandra Fedele: erudita veneziana del Rinascimento." *Ateneo veneto* 29 (1906): 73–91, 249–275, 361–397. Cosenza, M.E., *Biographical and Bibliographical Dictionary of the Italian Humanists and of the World of Classical Scholarship in Italy, 1300–1800*, 8 Vols., 2nd ed. (Boston, 1962), II, pp. 1415–1416; VI, p. 118. *Enciclopedia Biografica e Bibliografica italiana*, Ser. VI: *Poetesse e scrittrici*, ed. M. Bandini Buti (Rome, 1941), I, pp. 257–259. Gamba, B., *Alcuni ritratti di donne illustri delle provincie veneziane* (Venice, 1826). King, M.L.. "Book-Lined Cells: Women and Humanism in the Early Italian Renaissance," in *Beyond Their Sex: Learned Women of the European Past*, ed. P.H. Labalme (New York, 1980), pp. 66–90. Kristeller, P.O., "Learned Women of Early Modern Italy: Humanists and University Scholars." *Beyond Their Sex*, pp. 91–116. Petrettini, M., *Vita di Cassandra Fedele* (Venice, 1914). Quadrio, F.S., *Della storia e della ragion d'ogni poesia* (Bologna, 1741), II, p. 261. Sansovino, Fr., *Venetia città nobilissima et singulare descritta in XIV libri* (Venice, 1663), XIII, p. 588. Schlam, C.C., "Cassandra Fidelis as a Latin Orator." *Acta Conventus Neo-Latini Sanctanobreani. Proceedings of the Fifth International Congress of Neo-Latin Studies*, ed. I.D. McFarlane (Binghamton, N.Y., 1986), pp. 185–191. Simonsfeld, H., "Zur Geschichte der Cassandra Fedele." *Studien zur Literaturgeschichte, Michael Bernays gewidmet* (Hamburg-Leipzig, 1893), pp. 97–108. Tomasini, J.F., *Gymnasium Patavinum* (Udine, 1654), IV, p. 397.

Rinaldina Russell

Klara Fehér

Born May 21, 1923, Budapest, Hungary
Genre(s): novel, short story, drama, travel
*   literature*
Language(s): Hungarian

A native of the Hungarian capital, Fehér is a quintessential Budapest writer. At the beginning of her career she was a civil servant; later she became a journalist. She started writing fiction in the 1950s. Although she is a prolific author, she has never abandoned journalism. Today, she is the editor of the weekly *Élet és Irodalom* (Life and Literature).

She has a witty, slightly sarcastic sense of humor and her entertaining and readable style makes her a good story-teller. Her characters are mostly middle-class or professional people. Fehér's own experiences supply the material for many of her works. Her first novel, *The Sea*, is about young intellectuals before and after the end of World War II. So, too, is her second novel, *Once and Never More* (1963). Her major novels, *Amidst Lawsuits and Fights* (1966), *Narcosis* (1969), and *Moral Certificate* (1981), deal with the problems and lifestyle of the petit bourgeois in an entertaining yet ironical way. Her comedies, *The Glory of Creation* (1959) and *We Are No Angels* (1960), have strong affinities with the Central-European brand of the well-made play of the fin-de-siècle that was made famous by Arthur von Schnitzler and Ferenc Molnár.

She travelled extensively in the 1960s and 1970s. Her stories and playlets, which incorporate her experiences in various parts of the world, in particular in the English-speaking countries, present the charming yet accurate observations of a bona-fide Central-European tourist.

Very popular are her short sketches which uncover with great sharpness some of the inconsistencies and hypocrisies of contemporary life in Hungary. Many of the short writings in the collection *What Is the Elephant Made Out Of?* (1973) and some of her other works have been televised.

Fehér, as a journalist, maintains an intensive correspondence with her readers, which helps her retain a keen sense of the *hic et nunc*. Although her subject matter is rooted in daily life, her approach—sometimes in Aesopian language—often has a philosophical bent, as her "Ars Poetica" (1973) demonstrates.

Works

A tenger (1956). Egyszer és soha többé (1963). A teremtés koronája(1959). Perben, haragban(1966). Nem vagyunk angyalok (1960). Nem vagyunk ördögök(1968). Narkózis(1969). Miből csinálják az elefántot? (1973). Vakáció Magyarországon (1980). Erkölcsi bizonyitvány (1981).

Bibliography

Pomogáts, Bela, Az ujabb magyar irodalom története (Budapest, 1982) Magyar Irodalmi Lexikon (Budapest, 1976).

Peter I. Barta

Anthonie Feitsma

Born 1928, Brantgum, The Netherlands
Genre(s): essay
Language(s): Fries

An expert in Fries culture, Feitsma writes in De Stiennen Man on questions concerning the Fries movement. She was active in the production of the Woordenboek der Friese Taal. She contributed articles on seventeenth and eighteenth century Fries literature in Estrikken, published by the Fries Institute in Groningen.

Mary Hatch

Judit Fenákel

Born 1936, Budapest, Hungary
Genre(s): journalism, short story, novel
Language(s): Hungarian

Judit Fenákel studied at a teachers' college and worked as an elementary school teacher before she became a journalist. Extensive familiarity with life in the villages, an interest in the fate of "little" people, and a keen awareness of social contradictions characterize her writings.

She launched herself as a writer by publishing several volumes of short stories in the 1960s. She has also written novels: Ten Days in the Country (1967), The Travels of Lili (1973), and The Truly Grand Woman (1976). She published a selection of her shorter works written between 1964 and 1979 in A Certain Hope Street (1979).

The Wife of the Caretaker Called (1985) and Falling Silent (1985) are short novels.

Her voice is ironical and her writings mercilessly uncover unfairness towards women and elderly, poor, and powerless people. In her story "Alone" (1963), she paints a devastating picture of a gynecological ward where the bullying nurse and callous doctors lord over defenseless patients. The first-person narrator in "I Was Late" (1970) is humiliated by vulgar, uneducated apparatchiks. Particularly frightening are her descriptions of old and abandoned women in "Bistro" (1974) and "A Certain Hope Street"(1975).

There is a sense of hopelessness and a strongly depressing quality in her stories. A powerful command of language and sociological and psychological alertness highlight her art.

Works

Két utca lakója(1960). Az élet vidám dolog(1963). Akvárium (1966). Tiz nap vidéken (1967). Vetköztető (1970). Májustól májusig (1974). Dokumentumok U. M.-ról (1975). Az igazi nagy nő(1976). A negyedik segéd monológja(1978). Egy bizonyos Remény utca(1979). Itt járt a hazmesterné (1985), Az elhallgatás (1985).

Bibliography

Pomogáts, Béla. Az ujabb magyar irodalom története (Budapest, 1982).

Peter I. Barta

Margaretha Ferguson-Wigerink

Born 1920, Arnhem, The Netherlands
Genre(s): novel, short story, translation,
    literary criticism
Language(s): Dutch

The author of numerous literary reviews and critical essays as well as short stories, novels, autobiographical narratives, diaries and literary translations from English, German, and Russian (Fay Weldon, Mary McCarthy, Heinrich Böll, Dostoyevsky, Anais Nin, and others), Margaretha Ferguson is also especially known for her travel novels.

The daughter of a melancholy baker and his energetic, rebellious and politically active wife, Margaretha Ferguson was born in the provincial town of Arnhem but moved to the Dutch Indies when she was nine years old. Her best friends in secondary school there were Hella Haasse (1918–) and Aya Zikken (1919–), who both have also become writers. Her interest in literature and writing began early. During her imprisonment in a Japanese concentration camp from 1942 to 1945 she kept a notebook, later published as *Mammie ik ga dood* (1976; Mummie I'm Dying). After the war, she returned to the Netherlands and studied psychology in Utrecht from 1946 to 1948 but did not complete her degree. She has several children, is married, and has been living in The Hague since 1951. In recent years she has traveled extensively in the USSR, the People's Republic of China, and Africa, and used her very personal impressions and views in travel novels about these countries and their cultures.

While frequently autobiographical, Margaretha Ferguson's novels and short stories do not in any direct way reflect her life or person. She sees her writing as primarily motivated by her subconscious, by forces which are not in harmony with her own existence. Writing is not an escape from reality but an entering into reality, a reality which embraces more than one's immediate experiences. Writing is a search for unknown territories, both within herself and in the world.

Her first novel, *Onmogelijke mensen* (1962; Impossible People), revolves around Alex, who in his young adulthood has already finished with life. The story moves toward his suicide. Both Ferguson's male and female characters consider the "inner" world more real than the exterior world. She does not identify especially with her female characters and often uses male protagonists to embody her own views and concerns. In *Onmogelijke mensen*, she describes men and women alternately with sympathy and disapproval. The novel was originally planned as a satirical portrait of a type of man she did not like and yet frequently fell for, the somewhat simplistic he-man macho type, but ended up being a serious, understanding treatment of the charac-

ter after she had crept under his skin and tried to portray him from within, in his own right.

This novel was followed by *Het bloed en de haaien* (1965; Blood and Sharks), re-published under the title *Maanlicht en middagzon* (Moonlight and Afternoon Sun) in 1982. The first part is set mostly in the Netherlands, the second part in the Dutch Indies. Two women, Mirjam and Klara, share a traumatic childhood memory: rape by a "dirty old man" in pre-war Indonesia. A large number of characters are involved with Klara and Mirjam in an array of different relationships. The seemingly chaotic first part exemplifies the awareness that past and present, here and elsewhere, cannot be separated within the human consciousness. The second part, on the other hand, follows a clear chronological order, which in a sense contains the explanation of the previous part. The novel gives expression to a passionate sense of life, in which sexuality, love, degeneration, mysticism and madness all play their part.

In *Elias in Batavia en Jakarta* (1977; Elias in Batavia and Jakarta), she shows how politics can completely change the life of a family and how the decolonization process takes place in the psyche of a number of characters.

Onstuimig Rusland (1972; Tempestuous Russia), written after trips to the Soviet Union in 1966 and 1968, describes her experiences there and her emotional response to those experiences. As with her fictional characters, she tried to see the Russian people in their own right. *Mijn vrienden in Khartoem* (1973; My Friends in Khartum) is an account of her impressions after a month of intense conversations and interaction with people in the Sudan. *Nu wonen daar andere mensen, Terug op Java* (1974; Other People Live There Now, Back in Java), written after her first trip back to Indonesia after twenty three years, records the decolonization process within herself. *Een Haagse dame in China* (1975; A Lady from The Hague in China) contains her personal reactions to stereotyped notions about the People's Republic of China. *China gewoon* (1981; Everyday China) is richer in observations of and contacts with people in China.

In the last few years, Margaretha Ferguson has turned away from journalism and travelogues to re-examine the "inside," her childhood and the time during and after the war. The novel *Chaos* (1983; Chaos), based on diaries and letters, deals with the time when she and her three-year old daughter arrived in Utrecht from Indonesia in a state of complete alienation and disconnectedness from life in the Netherlands. *Brief aan niemand* (1985; Letter to Nobody) is a selection from her diaries. She is currently working on two more novels set in Indonesia.

Works

Anna en haar vader (1979). *Zondag en maandag* (1969, reprinted as *Neurotisch winkelen, Hollands-Indische Verhalen*). *Onmogelijke mensen* (1962). *Het bloed en de haaien* (1965, reprinted as *Maanlicht en middagzon*). *Onstuimig Rusland* (1972). *Mijn vrienden in Khartoem* (1973). *Nu wonen daar andere mensen. Terug op Java* (1974). *Een Haagse dame in China* (1975). *Mammie ik ga dood, aantekeningen uit de Japanse tijd op Java 1942–1945* (1976). *Elias in Batavia en Jakarta* (1977). *Zeven straten en een park* (1977). *Zon en andere doodsverhalen* (1980). *China gewoon* (1981). *Chaos* (1983). *Brief aan niemand* (1985).

Bibliography

Meulenbelt, Anja, ed., *Wie weegt de woorden. De auteur en haar werk* (Amsterdam, 1985), pp. 91–110; 226–227. Moerman, Josien, ed., *Ik ben een God in 't diepst van mijn gedachten. Lexicon Nederlandtalige auteurs* (Utrecht, 1984), p. 75.

Maya Bijvoet

Cristina Fernández Cubas

Born May 1945, Arenys de Mar (Barcelona), Spain
Genre(s): short story, novel
Language(s): Spanish

Among the new women writers to emerge in democratic Spain, Fernández Cubas achieved critical acclaim in 1980 with her first book, *Mi hermana Elba* (My Sister Elba), a collection of four short stories written in the fantastic mode.

Fernández Cubas holds a law degree but has never been a practicing attorney. She has also studied journalism and has worked in this field both in Spain and abroad. She spent two years in Latin America and a year in Cairo, where she studied Arabic and began writing stories set in a mythical Egypt.

The eight tales of *Mi hermana Elba* and *Los altillos de Brumal* (1983; The Attics of Brumal) approach the fantastic from several different perspectives. The stories range from a traditional use of stock elements to parodies of those same conventions. They variously invite psychoanalytical interpretations, explore linguistic codes, and reflect the overlap between the fantastic and metafiction. They also tend to feature female narrators and thus invite a feminist reading.

Fernández Cubas' one novel to date, *El año de Gracia* (1985; The Year of Grace), similarly parodies literary conventions. Inverting the structure of the mythic hero, the protagonist Daniel sets off on a voyage of initiation that takes him from the seminary to the world to an adventure at sea to a desert isle, where he reverts to a primitive state. His travels take him from knowledge to ignorance. In essence defamiliarizing the male quest, the author applies the female quest pattern by presenting an ending in which the protagonist is reintegrated into patriarchal society.

On the basis of these three books, Fernández Cubas has been identified as one of the most promising writers of her generation.

Works

Mi hermana Elba, short stories (1980). *El vendedor de sombras*, children's book (1982). *Los altillos de Brumal* (1983). *El año de Gracia*, novel (1985).

Bibliography

Bellver, Catherine G., "Two New Women Writers from Spain." *Letras Femeninas* 8.2 (1982): 3–7. Suñén, Luis. "La realidad y sus sombras: Rosa Montero y Cristina Fernández Cubas." *Insula* 446 (January 1984): 5. Zatlin, Phyllis, "Tales from Fernández Cubas: Adventure in the Fantastic." *Monographic Review/Revista Monográfica* 3 (1987): 107–118.

General references: *A Dictionary of Literature of the Iberian Peninsula* (New York; Westport, Connecticut; London, forthcoming). *Women Writers of Spain: An Annotated Bio-Bibliographical Guide*, ed. Carolyn L. Galerstein (New York; Westport, Conn.; London, 1986).

Phyllis Zatlin

Anne Bellinzani, Présidente Ferrand

Born 1657, Paris, France; died November 18, 1740, Paris
Genre(s): letters, narrative fiction, memoirs
Language(s): French

François Bellinzani, Ferrand's father, was an officer of the Duke of Mantua, naturalized after residence in France. Under Colbert's patronage he rose to a prominent position in commercial administration and amassed a large fortune. Mme Bellinzani (née Louise Chevreau) displayed their wealth to the extent of becoming a model for the type of the new rich (Arfure) in La Bruyère's *Caractères*. Tutors found their daughter an able and quick student with a taste for reading but impatient and headstrong. To curb these tendencies, a conservative marriage was arranged (1676) with Michel Ferrand, shortly thereafter and until retirement (1721) a sovereign court judge.

After Colbert's death, the Bellinzani fortunes collapsed. Accused of peculation, François was imprisoned and died at Vincennes before coming to trial. The Ferrands' legal separation followed (1686), less a consequence of Anne Ferrand's known liaison with the Baron de Breteuil than of her father's political disgrace. Confined at first to Port-Royal, where her fourth child was born, she was subsequently sent by *lettre de cachet* to a convent near Chartres. During her four years there she composed her autobiographical novel, *Histoire nouvelle des amours de la jeune Bélise et de Cléante* (1689), widely recognized as a fictionalized account of her affair with Breteuil.

In later years Ferrand lived quietly with a circle of friends including her son Antoine (1678–1720), author of *vers galants* praised by Voltaire. Although she published no more, she continued to write. In 1721, she wrote for a mutual friend a lengthy personal account of the recently deceased Mme Dacier. Between 1720 and 1727 she compiled materials and began to write her memoirs. The extant series of papers reveal intentions to defend Colbert (against continuing anti-Colbertian biases in historical writing), her father, and finally her own past. In addition to a keen critical sense, the papers in their excursions into moral philosophy show social thought suggesting Rousseau's (on property, wealth) and a gift for observation of social comedy in the line of La Bruyère's. Prolonged litigation filled her last years and gave Ferrand a place in the legal annals of Besdel's *Causes célèbres* (1786, v. 3). Claiming to be her long-lost daughter (b. 1686), a woman appeared in 1735 demanding her legal part in Ferrand's estate. Although the distinguished Cochin won her case, she was not accepted by Ferrand, who was forced in legal testimony to recount painful years of her past.

Ferrand's novel in its revised 1691 form, with the new title *Histoire des amours de Cléante et Bélise. Avec le Recueil de ses lettres*, is unique for its period in its experimentation with point of view. The narrative of the love story comes first (Pts. I-II) from the heroine, then from Cléante, who makes it a cautionary tale on the disorders of love. The 72 letters, which had circulated in different order before the *Histoire*'s first printing, return to the heroine and offer "evidence" the reader is left to judge. Published until well into the nineteenth century with Heloise's letters and *Les Lettres portugaises*, Ferrand's letters have won a place in the history of epistolary fiction. The directness and intensity of their search for sensual pleasure in love give them a distinctive tone and dramatic quality distinguishing their doubly abandoned woman from Guilleragues' heroine and the vogue of imitated "portugaises" she inspired.

Works

Histoire des amours de Cléante et Bélise. Avec le Recueil de ses lettres (1689, rev. 1691). "Letter on Mme Dacier" (1721), ed. Paul Bonnefon, *Revue d'Histoire Littéraire de la France* 13 (1906): 326–331). *Mémoires* (ca. 1720–1727), ed. Marcel Langlois, *Revue d'Histoire Littéraire de la France* 32 (1925): 497–528.

Bibliography

Asse, Eugène.,*Lettres de la Présidente Ferrand au Baron de Breteuil* (1880). Beugnot, Bernard, *Lettres portugaises . . . et autres romans d'amour par lettres* (1983). Syveton, Gilbert, "Une femme magistrat sous Louis XIV." *La Grande Revue* 9 (1905), pp. 292–324. Williams, Charles G.S., "Doubling and Omission in the Text of Anne Ferrand/Bélise," in David Rubin, ed., *Convergences—Rhetoric and Poetic in Seventeenth-Century France* (1989).

Charles G.S. Williams

Tatiana Fessenko

*Born November 20, 1915, Kiev, The Soviet
    Union*
Genre(s): poetry, essay, literary criticism
Language(s): Russian

Tatiana Fessenko shared the trauma of losing her father at an early age to Soviet government repressions with millions of her countrymen. Notwithstanding this tragedy, she completed all Ph.D. requirements in philology at Kiev University in June 1941 with the collateral appointment of assistant professorship in English. While still a student, Fessenko assumed the position of literary editor at the Ukrainian State Publishing House of Biological and Medical Literature before starting her teaching career in 1939. The odds of World War II terminated Fessenko's academic endeavors and hurled her with husband and mother away from her inhospitable native country to the West. After a brief stay in Germany Fessenko arrived in the United States in 1950 where she first worked as cataloger, then senior cataloger, at the Slavic Division of the Library of Congress (1951–1963), and later as script writer at Radio Liberty Committee, as researcher and bibliographer for the Hoover Institution on War, Peace and Revolution, and as co-editor in the Victor Kamkin Publishing House.

Her writing career began with linguistic studies in collaboration with her husband, Andrew V. Fessenko, also a graduate of Kiev University; two books were produced: *A Manual of English for Ukrainians* in 1947, and *Russkii iazyk pri Sovetakh* (The Russian Language Under the Soviets) in 1955. The latter work is a valuable survey of some of the most striking changes in literary and spoken Russian since the revolution.

The result of Fessenko's enlightened research at the Library of Congress, *Eighteenth Century Russian Publications in the Library of Congress*, 1961, is a lasting contribution to Russian literary scholarship, highly acclaimed by Slavists of many countries (including the USSR) for its erudite accomplishments. Fessenko's memoir *Povest' krivykh let* (The Ragged Years) of 1963, her travelogue *Glazami turista* (As Seen by a Tourist) of 1966, and her collection of verse, *Propusk v byloe* (A Permit into the Past) of 1975,

attest to her remarkable versatility in interest and genre.

Since her arrival in the United States, Fessenko has been a regular contributor to *Novoye Russoye Slovo* (the Russian language newspaper published in New York for which she wrote 181 articles) and to the literary journals *Novyi Zhurnal* (New Review) and *Sovremennik* (Contemporary), writing on cultural, historical, and literary topics. She also compiled, edited, and wrote an introductory essay to the anthology of verse by 75 contemporary Russian émigré poets, *Sodruzhestvo* (Concord), 1966.

Fessenko's prose is marked by magnanimity, optimism, and humor as it introduces the reader to the sufferings and survival under the Soviets and during World War II or entices him or her into exotic journeys through history and culture. Yet her lyric voice is melancholic and elegiac in subtle experimental verses. The writer's distinguished and perceptive testimony to the cruel repercussions of refugee and émigré life is an illuminating addition to Russian literature in exile.

Works

[With Andrew Fessenko], *A Manual of English for Ukrainians* (Munich, 1947; 2d ed., 1950). [With Andrew Fessenko], *Russkii iazyk pri Sovetakh* [The Russian Language Under the Soviets] (New York, 1955). *Eighteenth Century Russian Publications in the Library of Congress*. Catalog (Washington, D.C., 1961). *Povest' krivykh let* [The Ragged Years] (New York, 1963). *Glazami turista* [As Seen by a Tourist] (Washington, D.C., 1966). *Propusk v byloe* [A Permit into the Past], collection of verse (Buenos Aires, 1975). *Sodruzhestvo* [Concord], anthology of verse by contemporary émigré poets (Washington, 1966).

Bibliography

Besterman, Theodore, *A World Bibliography of Bibliographies and of Bibliographical Catalogues, Calendars, Abstracts, Digests, Indexes and the Like*. V. 5, ed. 4. (Lausanne, 1965–June 1966). Chinnov, Igor, "Smotrite Stikhi" [Look at the Poems], *Novyi Zhurnal*, 92 (1968). Goul, Roman, "Dvadtsat' piat' let" [Twenty-Five Years] *Novyi Zhurnal*, 87 (1967). Domogatskii, Boris, "Est' knigi" [There are Books]. *Edinenie* [Unity] (Melbourne, Australia, July 28, 1963). Polivanov, L.,

"Ostanovlennyi mig" [The Halted Instant], *Russkaia Mysl'* (Paris, November 29, 1984). Poltoratzky, Nikolai P., ed., *Russian Émigré Literature. A Collection of Articles in Russian with English Résumés* (Pittsburgh, 1972). Sedykh, Andrei, "Tri emigratsii" [Three Emigrations]. *Novoye Russkoye Slovo* (New York, March 10, 1981). Simmons, J.S.G., *The Book Collector* (London, Winter 1963). Stepanov, V.P., and Iu. V. Stennik, *Istoriia russkoi literatury XVIII veka* [History of Russian Literature of the XVIII Century] (Leningrad, 1968). Tugaev, V., "Tsennyi podarok dlia liubitelei poezii" [A Valuable Gift to Lovers of Poetry]. *Rodnye Dali* [Distant Homeland], no. 158 (Los Angeles, May 1967). Weinbaum, Marc, "Kniga oveiannaia liubov'iu" [A Book Imbued with Love]. *Novoye Russkoye Slovo* (New York, February 20, 1963).

Marina Astman

Renate Feyl

Born July 30, 1944, Prague, Czechoslovakia
Genre(s): novel, essay, literary criticism,
philosophy
Language(s): German

Renate Feyl completed her high school education in Jena. In 1971 she graduated from Humboldt University in East Berlin with a degree in philosophy. She currently resides in East Berlin.

Feyl's novels are ambitious and partisan. Her first two books combine realistic characters and narration with an East German political perspective: *Rauhbein* (1968) recounts the successful rehabilitation of a dissatisfied and misunderstood adolescent who has been caught trying to escape to the West; *Das dritte Auge war aus Glas* (1971) unites a love affair between the students Monika, in East Berlin, and Lars, in West Berlin, with the student unrest and mood of reform of the late 1960s. Less topical, *Bau mir eine Brücke* (1972) describes the tribulations of a newly married couple setting up their first home together.

Since 1972 Feyl has tried her hand, with great success, at literary portraits. *Bilder ohne Rahmen* (1977) examines the lives of twelve German scientists, among them Wilhelm von Humboldt and Albert Einstein, in the context of their social relationships with neighbors, colleagues, and authorities. Following the same principle, *Der lautlose Aufbruch. Frauen in der Wissenschaft* (1981) brings to life the hardships and determination of eleven German women scientists from the late 1700s to the 1940s. Based on extensive archival research, these essays are exemplary contributions to the feminist cause and to the history of science.

Works

Rauhbein, novel (1968; 6th ed. 1981). *Das dritte Auge war aus Glas. Eine Studentengeschichte* [The Third Eye Was Made of Glass. A Student Tale], novel (1971). *Bau mir eine Brücke* [Build Me a Bridge], novel (1972, 5th ed. 1987). *Bilder ohne Rahmen* [Pictures Without Frames], essays (1977, 4th ed. 1985). *Der lautlose Aufbruch. Frauen in der Wissenschaft* [Silent Awakening. Women in the Sciences], essays (1981; 4th ed. 1985 [DDR], 1983 [BRD]). *"Sein ist das Weib, Denken der Mann." Ansichten und Äusserungen für und wider der Intellekt der Frau von Luther bis Weininger* ["Woman Is Being, Man Is Thought." Opinions and Pronouncements from Luther to Weininger for and Against Woman's Intellect], anthology (1984 [DDR and BRD], 2nd ed. 1985 [DDR]). *Idylle mit Professor* [Idyll with Professor], novel (1986).

Bibliography

Albrecht, Günther, and Kurt Böttcher, *Schriftsteller der DDR* (Leipzig, 1974), p. 141. Zacharias, Ernst Ludwig, "Renate Feyl. Romanautorin und Essayistin." *Deutsch als Fremdsprache. Zeitschrift zur Theorie und Praxis des Deutschunterrichts für Ausländer. Sonderheft* 21 (1984), pp. 55–60.

Ann Marie Rasmussen

Mathilde Lucie Fibiger

(a.k.a. Clara Raphael, Sophie A.)

Born December 31, 1830, Copenhagen,
Denmark; died June 17, 1872, Århus
Genre(s): novel, short story, essay, poetry
Language(s): Danish

Mathilde Fibiger was a pioneering feminist whose first novel, *Clara Raphael. Tolv Brev* (1850; Clara Raphael: Twelve Letters), was the first

Danish literary work to specifically call for female emancipation. The book started a heated public controversy over women's education and legal standing, and the name "Clara Raphael" became the battle cry of the feminist movement in mid-nineteenth century Denmark.

The youngest and most gifted of nine children, Fibiger was born in Copenhagen, where her father was head of the Military Academy. Her relatively happy childhood ended with the divorce of her parents in 1843 and the death of her mother the following year. Life with her father and stepmother proved unbearable, and Fibiger studied to become a governess in order to gain her independence as quickly as possible. In 1849 she took a position with the family of a forest superintendent on a lonely estate near Sakskøbing. There she wrote her provocative first novel, *Clara Raphael. Tolv Brev*, a love story that demanded that a women's life be as intellectually free and independent as a man's. Clara, the pseudonymous author and heroine, refuses marriage to a young baron, whom she loves, because she must dedicate her life to the struggle for her ideas. Fibiger sent her manuscript to Johan Ludwig Heiberg, one of the most influential men of letters in Scandinavia and manager of the Royal Theater in Copenhagen. Warmly enthusiastic, Heiberg wrote a foreword to the work and saw to its publication. At first the young author was welcomed as a celebrity in Copenhagen, but the controversy stirred up by her ideas on women's independence soon caused Heiberg to withdraw his support. Fibiger was subjected to much censure and ridicule from both the press and the public for her views. Her family called its "poor, self-liberated daughter" home in shame. The "Clara Raphael feud" went on, however, and her book influenced Parliamentary debate. In 1857 a law was introduced giving unmarried women their majority rights at age twenty-five and making daughters the equal of sons as heirs.

In the year following her scandalous success, Fibiger tried to defend her ideas in two minor prose pieces, "Hvad er Emancipation" (1851; What Is Emancipation) and "Et Besøg" (1851; A Visit). Her next work, the story "En Skizze efter det virkelige Liv" (1851; A Sketch from Real Life), was well received but only because critics mistook it for a recantation of *Clara Raphael*. As she worked on her next novel, *Minona* (1854; Minona), Fibiger sought advice from writer and critic Meir Goldschmidt, who had reviewed *Clara Raphael* in his journal *Nord og Syd*. This led to an ambiguous involvement between the two writers that lasted little more than a year. *Minona*, with its high-strung eroticism, was not greeted favorably by the Danish public.

Fibiger's difficult struggle for economic independence left little time for writing. She supported herself by translating, sewing, painting porcelain, and giving private lessons, living sometimes in the country, sometimes in a small room in Copenhagen. In 1856 the Danish Queen Mother granted her a small pension for life, and in 1866 she accepted a post in Helsingør as the first woman telegraphist in Denmark. Thus she became her country's first female civil servant. By this time her health was already undermined, leading to her early death from tuberculosis.

Fibiger published her last novel, *Den ensommes Hjem* (1869; The Home of the Lonely One), in the same year the influential Danish critic Georg Brandes published his translation of John Stuart Mill's *Subjection of Women*. Two years later the Dansk Kvindesamfund (Danish Women's Society) was organized "to improve the intellectual, moral and economic status of women and make them an active and independent member of the family and the nation." Fibiger, whose short, hard life had led the way, lived just long enough to become a member.

Freedom and independence—personal, economic, and national—were the guiding ideals throughout Mathilde Fibiger's life and work. Though none of her later writings matched the strength and impact of *Clara Raphael*, Fibiger deserves a place of recognition in the literary and social history of women: Clara Raphael's twelve letters ignited the first wide-spread debate in Scandinavia on gender roles and the question of women's rights.

Works

Clara Raphael. Tolv Brev (1850). "Hvad er Emancipation" (1851). "Et Besøg" (1851). "En Skizze efter det virkelige Liv" (1853). *Minona* (1854). *Den ensommes Hjem* (1869). Miscellaneous poems.

Bibliography

Bendix, Eva, "Efterskrift." *Clara Raphael: Tolv Brev* (1976). Dahlsgård, Inga, *Women in Denmark* (1980). *Dansk Biografisk Leksikon*, Povl Engelstoft, ed. (1935). Fibiger, Margrethe, *Clara Raphael* (1891). Pearson, Jean, "Mathilde Fibiger." *Kvindelige forfattere* (1985). Steenstrup, Johannes, *Den danske Kvindes Historie, II* (1917). Welsch, Erwin Kurt, *Feminism in Denmark 1850–1875*. Diss., 1974.

Jean Pearson

Vera Nikolaevna Figner

Born June 15, 1852, Kazanskaia guberniia,
Russia; died June 15, 1942, Moscow
Genre(s): poetry, prose
Language(s): Russian

A true revolutionary of the nineteenth century, Figner began to write only after being put in prison, implicated in the assassination plot of Alexander II. Her poetic work is not nearly as well-known as her autobiographical novel, *V bor'be* (In the Struggle), completed by her cousin in 1966. She continued to write throughout her twenty-two years of incarceration, her central focus being her dreams of freedom. The images she conjures are quite compelling, personal and injured, not nearly the righteous indignation of a political martyr. Her prose also has a liveliness that transcends its "message."

Works

Stikhotvoreniia (1906). *Polnoe sobranie sochineniia* (1932). *Poèty-demokraty 1870–1880–x gg* (1962). *V bor'be* (1966).

Chris Tomei

Margita Figuli

(a.k.a. Morena, Ol'ga Morena)

Born October 2, 1909, Vyšný Kubín, then in
Austria-Hungary, now in Czechoslovakia
Genre(s): novel, short story
Language(s): Slovak

Margita Figuli's work has passed through impressionist short stories and expressionist historical prose based on New and Old Testament themes to unfinished efforts at socialist realism with a complete but disjointed socialist novel in 1974. In the same year she received the title "National Artist."

Born in northern Slovakia, Figuli finished business school and worked in a Bratislava bank. After a few insignificant poems, her first published stories in the 1930s brought critical approval, but her antiwar story *Olovený vták* (The Leaden Bird) in 1940 caused her dismissal from her job. Her next novella was very popular as was her long historical novel; both are basically Christian works. After World War II she published various fragments indicating an effort to change her ideological position, which was apparent in her last novel as well as her various books for children.

Figuli's first impressionist stories were collected as *Pokušenie* (Temptation) in 1937. Contemporary critics related them to the "lyrical prose" that had developed as a form of expressionism, and this relation became explicit with the "naturism" of her next and most important book, *Tri gaštanové kone* (Three Chestnut Horses) in 1940. Immediately a popular success, it was reprinted seven times in the next seven years. Though little more than a hundred pages long, this is an epic treatment of the love of a village tramp and a rich farmer's daughter. Their spiritual growth through tragedy to a happy ending, is mythologized by three horses symbolizing the goodness, beauty, and strength of nature as well as the same three qualities gained by obedience to the Christian moral code. With the rich rhythms and imagery of biblical prose, the work masterfully sustains the atmosphere and tone of fated drama without obscuring the detailed description of Tatra mountain forests or the naive optimism of both villagers. In the same period Figuli published two anti-war stories, *Olovený vták* and *Tri noci a tri sny* (Three Nights and Three Dreams) in 1942. Her longest work was *Babylon* in 1946, a four-volume historical novel about the Babylonian kingdom in sixth century B.C., its capture of the Jews, battles with Persia, etc. Although there were obvious pacifist analogies to the past war, Stalinist critics condemned *Babylon* as escapist and "merely aesthetic." It was republished in 1956 in a changed version as was also *Tri gaštanové kone* in 1958.

Figuli's last novel, *Víchor v nás* (The Whirlwind Within Us) in 1974, begins expressionistically with a magical blacksmith and a troubled girl whose hallucinations are realistically explained through her origin in the rape of her mother by a bestial Nazi soldier. This confusion of mythic and documentary elements persists although midway in the novel the conflict turns into a banal factory problem to illustrate the "building of socialism."

Despite her later failures, Figuli's *Tri gaštanové kone* and *Babylon* remain classics of Slovak literature.

Works

Uzlík tepla [A Tiny Bit of Warmth] (1936). *Pokušenie* [Temptation] (1937). *Tri gaštanové koně* [Three Chestnut Horses] (1940). *Tri noci a tri sny* [Three Nights and Three Dreams] (1942). *Babylon* (1946). *Víchor v nás* [The Whirlwind Within Us] (1974).

Translations: *Tri gaštanové kone*: Czech: *Tři kaštanové kone* (1942, 1971). Magyar: *Három pejló* (1960). *Három gesztenyepej* (1980). Polish: *Trzy kastanki* (1962). English: "Three Chestnut Horses" (1962) (excerpt). Russian: *Trojka gnedych* (1965). Slovenian: *Trije rjavci* (1973). Bulgarian: *Tri doresti konja* (1979). *Babylon*: Russian: *Vavilon* (1968); German: *Babylon* (1968); Czech: *Babylon* (1971).

Bibliography

Čepan, Oskár, *Kontúry naturizmu* (Bratislava, 1977). Chorváth, Michal, *Cestami literatúry* (Bratislava, 1960), I, pp. 134–136, 185–188; II, pp. 207–214. Fischerová-Šebestová, Anna, *Margita Figuli* (Martin, 1970). Matuška, Alexander, *Za a proti* (Bratislava, 1975), pp. 392–399. Miko, František, *Estetika výrazu* (Bratislava, 1969), pp. 133–161. Števček, Ján, *Nezbadaná próza* (Bratislava, 1971), pp. 75–101. Šútovec, Milan, *Romány a mýty* (Bratislava, 1982), pp. 21–93.

General references: *Dejiny slovenskej literatúry*, vol. V (Bratislava, 1984), pp. 641–644 and 724–731. *Encyklopédia slovenských spisovateľov* (Bratislava, 1984), I, pp. 141–144. *Kindlers Literaturlexikon* (Zürich, 1964–1972).

Norma L. Rudinsky

Fimonoï

(see: Fotini Ikonomidou)

Maria Flechtenmacher

Born 1838, Bucharest, Romania; died 1888, Bucharest
Genre(s): poetry, essay, journalism, drama, translation
Language(s): Romanian

Maria Mavrodin was an early orphan and could not attend more than four grades at school because of severe poverty. In 1853 the fifteen-year-old autodidact began her life as an actress in Craiova. She then married composer Al. Flechtenmacher, moved to Bucharest, and played at the Teatrul cel Mare (Grand Theater, later to become the National Theater) for 18 years as a trouper of M. Millo's and M. Pascally's. In 1877 she became one of the four women representatives (the others were Eufrosina Popescu, Maria Vasilescu, and Ana Popescu) who, together with four male counterparts composed the Romanian Drama Society (structured more or less according to the model provided by the Comédie Française). One year later, Maria Flechtenmacher founded her own dramatic company—which she called Teatrul Tineretului (Theatre of Youth) and started publishing articles about theater while at the same time teaching declamation, lecturing about women's civil rights and instruction and directing the feminist periodical *Femeia română* (Romanian Woman, 1878–1881).

Maria Flechtenmacher's poetry is circumstantially patriotic and, at times, written as textual support for her husband's music. She wrote a number of vaudevilles, which were represented in 1875—*Un cap romantic* (Romantic Head), *La sînul mamei* (Mother's Bosom), etc.—as well as some moralizing one-act plays such as *Recunoştinţa orfanei* (The Gratitude of the Orphan Girl), *Gelozia orfanei* (The Jealousy of the Orphan Girl), etc.

Flechtenmacher also translated into Romanian works by Dante, Lamartine, J. Delille, Markel, Scribe, and E. Legouvé.

Works

Poezii şi proză [Poems and Prose] (1871). *Situaţiunea Teatrului Naţional sub direcţiunea domnului Ion Ghica* [Situation of the National Theater under the Direction of Mr. Ion Ghica] (1877). "George Creţeanu," *Femeia română* 1 (1878): 24.

Bibliography

Cardaş, Gh., "Maria Flechtenmacher." *Poeţi munteni pînă la Unire (1787–1859)* (Bucharest, 1937): 497–498. Creţu, Stănuţa, "Maria Flechtenmacher." *Dicţionarul literaturii romăne de la origini pînă la 1900* (Bucharest, 1979): 358. Massoff, I., *Teatrul romănesc*, vol. 2 (Bucharest: EPL, 1961–1974), 27, 329, 348. Miller-Verghi, Margareta and Ecaterina Săndulescu, *Evoluţia scrisului feminin în Romănia* (Bucharest, 1935): 174–177. Nădejde, Lelia, "Maria Flechtenmacher." *Studii şi cercetări de istoria artei* 12 (1965): 1.

Sanda Golopentia

Marieluise Fleisser

Born November 22 or 23, 1901, Ingolstadt, Germany; died February 2, 1974, Ingolstadt
Genre(s): drama, novel, short story
Language(s): German

Marieluise Fleisser was born on November 22 or 23, 1901, the daughter of a hardware store owner in Ingolstadt in Bavaria. She studied *Germanistik* and drama at the University of Munich, during which time she became acquainted with the poet Lion Feuchtwanger (1922). Her first short story "Meine Zwillingsschwester Olga" (My Twin Sister Olga) appeared in *Das Tagebuch*, edited by Stefan Großmann in 1923. At the same time she learned about Bertolt Brecht through Feuchtwanger and watched his plays on the theater. She met Brecht on March 24, 1924, from whence Brecht's long lasting literary influence on her work stemmed. At the end of the same year she broke off her studies in Munich and returned home, to the dismay of her father. On April 25, 1926, her first play, *Die Fußwaschung* (Washing of the Feet), had its premiere in the *Deutsches Theater* in Berlin under the new title *Fegefeuer in Ingolstadt* (Purgatorium in Ingolstadt). In 1929 followed *Pioniere in Ingolstadt* (Pioneers in Ingolstadt), which both depicted the repressions, brutality, and low-class mentality of people in the province. The language used was that of the people in the street, which reflected their psychological deformities. The public reactions were violent and full of hatred and led to many public and personal prosecutions in her home town of Ingolstadt. She moved to Berlin for a short time, but only to return home again. Since she held Brecht partly responsible for the public scandal and since she became engaged to the journalist Draws, who was ideologically the very opposite to Brecht, her contacts with him broke off then. Fleisser and Draws travelled to Sweden in 1929 and to Andorra in 1930, which formed the background for her stories "Ich reise mit Draws nach Schweden" (1929; I Travel with Draws to Sweden) and "Andorranische Reiseberichte" (1930; Andorra Travel Reports). In 1931 her novel *Mehlreisende Frieda Geier* (The Flour Saleswoman Frieda Geier) was published. Its literary quality allowed its reprint in 1972 as *Eine Zierde für den Verein, Roman vom Rauchen, Sporteln, Lieben und Verkaufen* (A Decoration for the Club, a Novel About Smoking, Sports, Love and Selling). In 1932 followed the extended travel account about Andorra in the form of a book.

In 1935 she married Bepp Haindl, a tobacco-shop owner, mainly in order to escape her unstable financial situation and to have support against fascist threats in Ingolstadt. But still the Nazis imposed a total ban on her publications with the exception of six newspaper articles per year. In 1943 Fleisser was called up for public services in the war, but her service only lasted to the end of the year because of her failing health and a nervous breakdown.

In 1950 she met Brecht again, who helped her to get the play *Starker Stamm* (Strong Trunk) performed in the *Kammerspiele* in Munich. Since then until 1963, when her short story "Avantgarde" appeared, she underwent years of personal, financial, and physical crisis, even though she was in contact with Brecht again and temporarily worked for the Bavarian Radio Station in the section of radio plays. Her husband died on January 10, 1958, after many years of financial bickerings with his business partner, and she suffered a heart attack on January 15, 1958. In 1964 she published the story "Der Rauch" (The Smoke), followed by "Die im Dunkeln" (1965; Those Who Stay in the Dark). Since 1966 she reworked her *Pioniere in Ingolstadt*, a collage of which was put on stage by R.W. Fassbinder and published by Suhrkamp in

1968. The premiere was on March 1, 1970, at the *Residenztheater* in Munich. A premiere of *Fegefeuer in Ingolstadt* followed on April 30, 1971, in Wuppertal. In 1969 followed *Abenteuer aus dem Englischen Garten* (Adventure in the English Garden), a collection of short stories. In 1971 she published the short story *Aus der Augustenstraße* (From the Augustenstraße) and an essay on Jean Genet *Findelkind und Rebell* (Foundling and Rebel).

Among other artists and poets, Martin Speer, R.W. Fassbinder, and Franz Xaver Kroetz credited her with being the crucial literary influence on their writing. Although her early works from the period of the Republic of Weimar had been denigrated and scathingly criticized in public, they received new attention and were highly acclaimed since the 1950s, partly because of the Brechtian style and partly for their social criticism. Various literary awards such as the Prize of the Foundation for the Promotion of Literature in 1951, the First Prize in a Literary Competition from the South German Radio Station, the Literature Award from the Bavarian Academy of Liberal Arts in 1953 and the Award for the Promotion of Arts from Ingolstadt in 1961 recognized this fact. In 1956 she even became a full member of the Bavarian Academy of Liberal Arts. She died on February 2, 1974.

Works

Collected works: ed. Günther Rühle (1972).
Novels: *Ich reise mit Draws nach Schweden* [I Travel with Draws to Sweden] (1929). *Andorranische Reiseberichte* [Andorra Travel Reports] (1930). *Mehlreisende Frieda Geier* [The Flour Saleswoman Frieda Geier] (1931), rpt. 1972 as *Eine Ziere für den Verein, Roman vom Rauchen, Sporteln, Lieben und Verkaufen* [A Decoration for the Club, a Novel About Smoking, Sports, Love and Selling]).
Essays: *Sportgeist und Zeitkunst* [Spirit of Sport and Contemporary Art] (1929). *Ein Porträt Buston Keatons* [A Portrait of Buston Keaton] (1930). *Frühe Begegnung* [Early Encounter] (1964).
Drama: *Fegefeuer in Ingolstadt* [Purgatorium in Ingolstadt] (1926). *Pioniere in Ingolstadt* [Pioneers in Ingolstadt] (1929). *Der Tiefseefisch* [The Deep Sea Fish] (1930), with revisions until 1974. *Karl Stuart* (1938–1945, published in 1946).

Short stories: "Die Dreizehnjährige" [The Thirteen Year Old Girl, first published as "Meine Zwillingsschwester Olga" (My Twin Sister Olga)] (1923). "Ein Pfund Orangen" [A Pound of Oranges] (1926). "Moritat vom Institutfräulein" [Ballad of a Boarding School Damsel] (1928). "Die Stunde der Magd" [When the Time Had Come For the Maid Servant] (1928). "Abenteuer aus dem Englischen Garten" [Adventure in the English Garden] (1929). "Die Ziege" [The Goat] (1929). "Des Staates gute Bürgerin" [A Good Citizen] (1929). "Hölderlin in einer Berliner Kneipe" [Hölderlin in a Berlin Pub] (1932). "Frigid" (1934). "Schlagschatten Kleist" [Deep Shadows from Kleist] (1946). "Das Pferd und die Jungfer" [The Horse and the Virgin] (1952). "Ingolstadt" (1963). "Avantgarde" (1963). "Eine ganz gewöhnliche Vorhölle" [A Very Ordinary Purgatorium] (1963). "Er hätte besser alles verschlafen" [He Better Had Overslept Everything] (1963). "Der Rauch" [The Smoke] (1964/65). "Die im Dunkeln" [Those Who Stay in the Dark] (1965/66). "Der Venusberg" [The Venus Mountain] (1969). "Abenteuer aus dem Englischen Garten" [Adventure in the English Garden] (1969).

Bibliography

Dinter, W., "Die ausgestellte Gesellschaft, Zum Volksstück der Fleisser." *Theater und Gesellschaft* (1973). Lethen, H., *Neue Sachlichkeit 1924–1932, Studien zur Literatur des "Weißen Sozialismus."* 2nd ed. (1975). Lutz, G., *Die Stellung Marieluise Fleissers in der bayerischen Literatur des 20. Jahrhunderts* (Frankfurt-Bern-Cirencester, 1979). *Marieluise Fleisser, Anmerkungen, Texte, Dokumente*, Mit Beiträgen von Eva Pfister und Günther Rühle, ed. Friedrich Kraft (Ingolstadt, 1981). *Materialien zum Leben und Schreiben der Marieluise Fleisser*, ed. Günther Rühle (Frankfurt, 1973). Pdewils, C., "In memoriam Marieluise Fleisser" *Jahresring* (1974). Stritzke, Barbara, *Marieluise Fleisser, Pioniere in Ingolstadt* (Frankfurt-Bern, 1982). Tax, Sissi, *Marieluise Fleisser, Schreiben, Überleben, Ein biographischer Versuch* (Basel/Frankfurt, 1984).

Albrecht Classen

Duchess Flemming

(see: Irene Forbes-Mosse)

Alice Marie Céleste Fleury Durand-Gréville (Mme Emile Durand-Gréville, née Fleury)

(see: Henry Gréville)

Alba Florio

Born 1913, Scilla, Calabria, Italy
Genre(s): poetry
Language(s): Italian

Born in 1913, Florio spent her life in the isolation of Scilla, a small seaside town overlooking Sicily named for the monster that, together with Charybdis, terrorized Odysseus and other voyagers in the Straits of Messina. Calabria's mythology had a profound influence on Florio's lyrical, tragic verses. Biographical information about Florio is scarce. Her poems—even if devoid of direct references to her past—accurately portray the loneliness and pain Florio endured.

In her first poems, written when she was only eight years old, Florio already sought an answer to life's riddles in terse, sorrowful language: "un giorno ebbi paura/di dover vivere sempre./La vita mi parve/un grigio deserto/dov'io movevo;" "Andare senza fermarsi/portando il cuore pesante,/la stanchezza senza riposo/fino al riposo eterno" ("One day I was afraid/ of having to live forever./ Life seemed to me/ a grey desert/ through which I moved; Wandering non stop/ a heavy heart in hand,/ weariness without rest/ until eternal rest"). A sense of religious longing and a pessimistic view of human destiny has always characterized her poetry. The major concern of her poetry remains, however, the plight of the South and of its inhabitants, who cannot rebel against the power of ineluctable fate. Harsh landscapes of the Calabrian countryside provide the imagery of her poems, which are also charged with metaphorical significance. A threatening Tyrennian sea dominated by rocky cliffs, volcanoes, dried-up streams, dead trees, houses in ruin, torrid, sun-burnt fields, inclement weather and seasons, and human derelicts serves to visualize Florio's dim view of existence. Her poetry depicts life as a sterile endeavor, a hopeless struggle marked by a sense of loss and despair. Her heroes are the outcasts and the poor, lame, blind, and beggars for whom only the afterlife may bring some relief: "il riposo eterno."

These juvenilia were collected in *Estasi e preghiere* (1929; Ecstasy and Prayers). Like her contemporary, Giovanni Pascoli, Florio shows a predilection for onomatopoeia and synesthesia, literary devices that elicit emotional responses to sounds and colors and are particularly useful in recreating the sense of mystery evoked by contemplation of nature. Echoes of church bells underscore the religious feeling pervading Florio's poetry: "un palpito di trilli, un fremer d'ale," "solinghi campani/rochi lontani/fiochi," "la cima degli alberi sfuma/di rosa nel cielo d'opale" ("a throb of trills," "a flutter of wings," "lonely bells hoarse and faint/ in the distance," "treetops dissolve/ into the pink of an opal sky").

In 1936, with *Oltremorte* (Afterdeath), Florio won a major literary prize, thereby gaining full recognition. This work is important in that it breaks with the prevailing canon dictated by Petrarchism and nineteenth-century models. In doing so, Florio contributes directly, together with other young poets such as Pascoli, Ungaretti, and Quasimodo, to the development of contemporary Italian poetry. The awarding jury cited Florio for her innovative style, her "modernissima," which is "capable of capturing the essence of emotions." The jury also emphasized her sensitive portrayal of nature to depict human suffering, "il mondo elementare" ("the feelings of a troubled life familiar with rocks, sea, and sky").

Oltremorte's poems interpret and further develop her cosmic vision of reality. Nature is transformed in a metaphysical landscape in which the sea is an absolute, eternal, primal force symbolizing the cycle of life: "Serrato è il cerchio/ nessun frutto cade prima del tempo,/tranquilla ogni cosa nasconde/nascite e morti./Così l'acqua dei porti/torbida di rifiuti/esulta di arrivi e partenze/restando ferma ai limiti di pietra:/non c'è infinito che non si riduca/allo spazio più breve" ("Once the circle is closed/ no fruit falls before its time,/ tranquil everything contains/ birth and death./ Likewise, the water of the harbor/ cloudy from the refuse/ exults over arrivals and departures/ even though it is bound by stone:/ there is no infinity that may not be reduced/ to the slightest space").

Unlike such poets as Montale or Neruda, Florio's marine descriptions are devoid of detailed personal reminiscences. Her poetry's mythopoeic classicism can be more closely compared with that of Sicilian Salvatore Quasimodo, master of the Hermetic school. Florio and Quasimodo both reach deeply into the heritage of Greco-Roman antiquity for their inspiration.

Come mare a riva (1956) is Florio's last publication. Previous thematic concerns reappear. The seasonal cycles mirror the immutable course of human destiny; life inevitably produces death: "Tutto si afferma ansioso di durare:/ogni cosa che vive patisce il tempo, con dolore si muta in altre forme./ Dopo breve stagione/ci stacchiamo dall'albero di vita,/ ma nuove foglie s'aprono sui rami/ e colmano di sé le nostre assenze" ("Everything affirms itself with the desire to last:/ every living thing suffers the passage of time, changes, by pain, to other forms,/ After a short season/ we drop from the tree of life,/ but new leaves open upon the limbs/ and fill themselves our absence").

Living in seclusion in her native Calabria, removed from most important cultural and editorial centers, Alba Florio has received inadequate critical attention. Still, her poetry reveals mastery of language and abounds in philosophical insights.

Works

Estasi e preghiere (1929). Oltremorte (1936). *Come mare a riva* (1956).

Bibliography

Piromalli, Antonio, *La letteratura calabrese* (Cosenza, 1965), pp. 215–218. Piromalli, Antonio, "La poesia di Alba Florio." *Indagine e letture* (Ravenna, 1970). Piromalli, Antonio. "Lorenzo Calogero." *Letteratura Italiana. I contemporanei* III (Milano, 1969). Testa, Antonio, *La poesia calabrese del Novecento: Alba Florio, Luigi Calogero* (Cosenza, 1968).

Giacomo Striuli

Emilie Flygare-Carlén

Born August 8, 1807, Strömstad, Sweden; died February 5, 1892, Stockholm
Genre(s): novel, tale, memoirs
Language(s): Swedish

Emilie Flygare-Carlén was Sweden's first regional novelist, writing about the Bohuslän skerries, the rugged coastal life, and the seafaring people she knew intimately from her childhood. Her novels were so popular among middle-class readers in the nineteenth century that she accumulated a small fortune by writing to meet public demand. Because she was able to earn a good living from her literary production, she has been called Sweden's first professional author.

She was born Emilie Smith in Strömstad, a little town on Sweden's west coast. Her father, Rutger Smith, was a successful shopkeeper and shipowner of Scottish descent. The youngest of fourteen children, Emilie received little formal education but gained much practical knowledge of life and people from the freedom of activity she was allowed. As a teenager she accompanied her father on his travels through the skerries, eagerly absorbing impressions from the lives of sailors and fishing folk. She also schooled herself by reading popular novels. Independent and imaginative, Emilie had a strong element of superstition in her nature. But it was her own dramatic and tragic experience of life that turned her into an author.

In 1827 Emilie married the physician Axel Flygare and moved with him to Småland. Their brief life together was a struggle with poverty and illness. Four children were born of whom two died. In 1833 her husband died of tuberculosis. Emilie then returned to Strömstad with her surviving son and daughter only to experience the rapid decline of her family's fortune after the death of her father. In 1834 she became engaged to Reinhold Dalin, a gifted lawyer. She was pregnant when Dalin suddenly died during a cholera epidemic. Curiously, Emilie had refused his request for a death-bed marriage, even though the stigma of illegitimacy would mean social ostracism for both mother and child.

To conceal her pregnancy, Emilie moved to Dalsland where she gave birth to a daughter at the home of a relative of Dalin's. This daughter

415

grew up to become Rosa Carlén (1836–1883), author of numerous novels including *Agnes Tell* (1861) and *Tattarens son, ur svenska folklivet* (1866; The Vagabond's Son; from Swedish Folklife). During the stay in Dalsland, Emilie's daughter by her first marriage died. Regarding this as a punishment from God, Emilie gave up her newborn daughter to be adopted by Dalin's relatives. The later relationship between Emilie and Rosa Carlén was fraught with the psychological complications of abandonment. Each author eventually wrote a novel that features an abandoned child.

In 1837 Emilie returned to Strömstad with her son Edvard. The following year she published her first novel, *Waldemar Klein* (1838), a salon novel modeled after Sophie von Knorring's *Cousinerna* (The Cousins). Although this work was a popular success, it marked the beginning of a lifelong rivalry between the young middle-class author and her aristocratic colleague von Knorring. In 1839 Emilie and her son moved to Stockholm, where she brought out several more salon novels in quick succession. In order to gain acceptance in higher social circles, she concealed that period of her life surrounding Rosa's birth. In 1841 she married the lawyer and writer Johan Carlén and shortly thereafter began to write the novels that established her fame as an author.

In her five "west coast" novels, set in her native region of Bohuslän, Emilie Flygare-Carlén wrote about the people and landscape she knew best. The first of these was the tragic story of murder and retribution *Rosen på Tistelön* (1842; The Rose of Tistelön. A Tale of the Swedish Coast). Held by some critics to be one of the masterpieces of Swedish literature, this novel displays naturalistic tendencies. Its exciting, skillfully developed plot was based on an actual criminal case. *Pål Värning* (1844; Paul Värning), one of her shortest and most well-constructed novels, is a humorous tale of travel and adventure. The author's conscious use of the local dialect of the west coast skerries helps to achieve a humorous, familiar tone, in spite of the dramatic episode in which Nora, Pål's fiancée, tries to conceal the unwanted child she conceived in a brief affair with another man. Her other "west coast" novels from the 1840s include *Enslingen på Johannis-skäret* (1846; The Hermit of St. John's

Islet) and *En Natt vid Buller-sjön* (1847; One Night at Bullar Lake).

In 1852 Emilie's son Edvard died. Grief-stricken, Emilie now insisted that her only remaining child, Rosa, come to live with her. Against her own wishes, Rosa moved to Stockholm in 1853. Three years later she married Rickard Carlén, the brother of her mother's husband. Thus the unique situation arose in which mother and daughter became sisters-in-law by marriage. Their relationship remained strained, however. Rosa refused to read her mother's novels, and Emilie never encouraged her daughter's writing.

For six years after the death of her son, Emilie Flygare-Carlén published nothing. When she again began to write, she published *Ett köpmanshus i skärgården* (1860–1861; A Merchant House in the Archipelago), the "west coast" novel that is generally considered to be her best work. Set in the short-lived boom period of the herring-fishing industry, this work has been called by Victor Svanberg the first novel to sympathize with free enterprise. It contains strong realistic characterizations and many autobiographical elements.

In 1862 Emilie Flygare-Carlén received the gold medal of the Swedish Academy. Her long, often tragic but fascinating life is recounted in her three autobiographical writings: *Skuggspel* (1865; Shadow Play), which tells of her youth, *Tidsmålningar och ungdomsminnen* (1865; Pictures of the Age and Memories from Youth), and *Minnen av svenskt författarliv* (1878; Reminiscences of the Lives of Swedish Authors), in which she writes of her encounters with Sophie von Knorring, C.J.L. Almqvist and other famous contemporaries.

Together with Fredrika Bremer and Sophie von Knorring, Emilie Flygare-Carlén was one of the three major female novelists of prose realism in mid-nineteenth-century Sweden. Of the three she enjoyed the widest popularity among Swedish readers, and nearly twenty of her novels appeared in English translation during her lifetime. Her real literary achievement was her five "west coast" novels. Unlike Fredrika Bremer, Flygare-Carlén was much more interested in telling a story than in advocating reform of social ills. Though she did not take an open stand on the question of women's emancipation, she often portrayed female characters who are or become independent. Especially in her novels of the 1840s one can find women who are rational, practical, and capable of earning their own living. Her novels sometimes suffer from stylistic flaws. Yet Flygare-Carlén drew her characters deeply and vividly, and their passions and actions are psychologically convincing. Next to Fredrika Bremer she was the most widely translated Swedish author before Strindberg.

Works

Waldemar Klein [Waldemar Klein] (1838). *Representanten* [The Representative] (1830). *Gustaf Lindorm* [Gustavus Lindorm] (1839). *Professorn och hans skyddslingar* [The Professor and His Favorites] (1840). *Fosterbröderne* [The Foster Brothers] (1840). *Kyrkoinvigningen i Hammarby* [The Consecration of the Church of Hammarby] (1840–1841). *Skjutsgossen* [The Carriage Boy] (1841). *Kamrer Lassman* [Head Clerk Lassman] (1842). *Rosen på Tistelön* [The Rose of Thistle Island] (1842). *"Ända in i döden"* [Even Unto Death] (1843). *Pål Värning* [Paul Värning] (1844). *Fideikommisset* [The Birthright] (1844). *Vindskuporna* [The Attics] (1845). *Bruden på Omberg* [The Bride of Omberg] (1845). *Ett år* [One Year] (1846). *Enslingen på Johannis-skäret* [The Hermit of St. John's Islet] (1846). *En Natt vid Bullar-sjön* [One Night at Bullar Lake] (1847). *Jungfrutornet* [The Maiden's Tower] (1848). *En nyckfull qvinna* [A Whimsical Woman] (1848–1849). *Romanhjältinnan* [The Heroine of a Novel] (1849). *Familjen i dalen* [The Family in the Valley] (1849). *Ett rykte* [A Rumor] (1850). *Ett lyckligt parti* [A Fortunate Match] (1851). *Förmyndaren* [The Guardian] (1851). *Inom sex veckor* [Within Six Weeks] (1853). *Ett köpmanshus i skärgården* [A Merchant House in the Archipelago] (1860–1861). *Stockholmsscener bakom kulisserna* [Scenes from Stockholm Behind the Stage-Scenes] (1864). *Berättelser från landsorten* [Tales from the Provinces] (1864–1865). *Skuggspel* [Shadow Play] (1865). *Tidsmålningar och ungdomsminnen* [Pictures of the Age and Memories from Youth] (1865). *En hemlighet för världen* [A Secret from the World] (1876). *Minnen av svenskt författarliv 1840–1860* [Reminiscences of the Lives of Swedish Authors from 1840 to 1860] (1878). *Efterskörd*

från en 80–årings författarebana [Gleanings from the Literary Career of an Octogenarian] (1888). *Brev* [Letters, ed. Jan Smith] (1960).

Translations: *The Birthright* (1851). *The Bride of Omberg* (1853). *A Brilliant Marriage* (1852, 1856, 1865). *The Brother's Bet or Within Six Weeks* (1867, 1868). *The Events of a Year* (1855). *The Guardian* (1865). *Gustavus Lindorm or "Lead us Not Into Temptation"* (1853, 1854). *The Hermit* (1853). *The Home in the Valley* (1854). *Ivar or The Skjuts-boy* (1852, 1864). *John; or, Is a Cousin in the Hand, Worth Two Counts in the Bush?* (1853, 1854, 1857). *Julie or Love and Duty* (1854). *A Lover's Strategem or The Two Suitors* (1852, 1865). *The Magic Goblet or The Consecration of the Church of Hammarby* (1845). *The Maiden's Tower. A Tale of the Sea* (1853). *Marie-Louise or The Opposite Neighbors* (1853, 1854). *One Year or Julia and Lavinia. A Tale of Wedlock* (1853). *The Professor and his Favorites* (1843, 1854). *The Rose of Tistelön. A Tale of the Swedish Coast* (1844, 1850). *The Smugglers of the Swedish Coast or The Rose of Thistle Island. A Romance* (1844, 1845). *The Temptation of Wealth or The Heir by Primogeniture* (1846, 1847). *Twelve Months of Matrimony* (1853, 1854, 1862, 1882). *The Whimsical Woman* (1852, many editions). *Woman's Life or The Trials of Caprice* (1852, 1856, 1858).

Bibliography

Afzelius, Nils, *Books in English on Sweden* (1951). Horn, Vivi, *Flickan från Strömstad* (1950). Janzén, Alf, *Emilie Flygare-Carlén: en studie i 1800–talets romandialog* (1946). Kjellén, Alf, *Emilie Flygare-Carlén* (1932). Lyttkens, Alice, *Kvinnan söker sin värld* (1974). Pearson, Jean, "Emilie Flygare-Carlén." *Kvinnliga Författare*, ed. Susanna Roxman (1983). Smith, Ann, "Emilie Flygare-Carlén och Rosa Carlén." *Kvinnornas Litteraturhistoria*, ed. Marie Louise Ramnefalk and Anna Westberg (1981). Svanberg, Victor, "Medelklassrealism, III." *Samlaren*, n.f. XXVII (1946), 102–112.

Jean Pearson

(Fontanges, et al.)

(see: Christiane Benedikte Eugenie Naubert)

Moderata Fonte

(see: Modesta Pozzo)

Irene Forbes-Mosse

(a.k.a. Duchess Flemming)

Born August 5, 1864, Baden-Baden, Germany; died December 26, 1946, Villeneuve/Lake Geneva
Genre(s): poetry, short story, novel translation
Language(s): German

She was the daughter of the Prussian diplomat in Karlsruhe, Albert Duke of Flemming, and Armgard von Arnim. Through her mother she was the great-granddaughter of the famous poetess Bettina von Arnim. She grew up in Karlsruhe, but spent her summer months on her father's estate in Prussia, Bukow. She married her cousin R. Oriola in 1884 but was divorced from him in 1895. Since then she spent most of her time in Rathenow and Brussels. The English Major J. Forbes-Mosse became her second husband (he died in 1904). Until his death she mostly lived in Florence. Afterward she travelled extensively. The Nazis condemned her books. She emigrated from Germany in 1933.

Works

Mezzavoce, poems (1901). *Peregrina's Sommerabende. Lieder für eine Dämmerstunde . . .* [Peregrina's Evenings in the Summer. Songs for a Time at Dusk . . .], poems (1904). *Das Rosenthor* [The Gate of Roses], poems (1905). Berberitzchen und Andere [Barberry and Others], short story (1910). *Der kleine Tod* [The Little Death], short story (1912),. *Die Leuchter der Königin* [The Queen's Candle Lights], short stories (1913). *Laubstreu* [Straw of Leaves], poems (1923). *Gabriele Alweyden oder Geben und Nehmen* [Gabriele Alweyden or Giving and Taking], novel (1924). *Ausgewählte alte und neue Gedichte* [Selected New and Old Poems], poems (1926). *Don Juans Töchter* [Don Juan's Daughters], 3 novels (1928). *Der Schleifstein* [The Grindstone], novel (1928). *Kathinka Plüsch*, novel (1930). *Das werbende Herz* [The Wooing Heart], novel (1934). *Ferne Häuser* [Houses in the Distance], short story (1953).

Translations: H. Drachmann: *Brav-Karl* [Loyal Charles] (1902). *Völung Schmied* [Völund Blacksmith] (1904).

Bibliography

Elschenbroich, A., "Irene Forbes-Mosse." *Neue Deutsche Biographie* (1961). Schaeffer, A., "Die Lyrik der Irene Forbes-Mosse." *Die schöne Literatur* (1932). Seidel, Ina, "Irene Forbes-Mosse als Erzählerin," in Ina Seidel, *Die schöne Literatur* (1927), also in: I.S.: *Dichter, Volkstum und Sprache* (1934). Wittner, D., "Die Enkelinnen der Bettina." *Roland*(1924). Zeggert, I., *Irene Forbes-Mosse, Eine Spätgestalt der deutschen Romantik*, Ph.D. diss., Freiburg/Br. (1955).

Albrecht Classen

Enrichetta Caracciolo Forino

(see: Enrichetta Caracciolo)

Mercedes Fórmica Corsi

Born 1918, Sevilla, Spain
Genre(s): novel
Language(s): Spanish

One of the first women lawyers in Spain, Fórmica has written novels concerning the rights of women and the individual. *A instancia de parte* (1954; On Behalf of the Defendant) presents the situation of a woman whose husband has grown tired of her. Because of the attitudes of Spanish society, and with the connivance of a justice system in which women have no rights, he is able to have her arrested, deprived of her son, held in a convent prison, and deported to her native Philippines. *Monte de Sancha* (1950) depicts the executions carried out simply for revenge by the working class during the Civil War and *La ciudad perdida* (1951; The Lost City) outlines the conflicts in Spanish society ten years after the war. Fórmica has also written memoirs and historical works that display high intellectual standards as well as artistry.

Works

Monte de Sancha (1950). *La ciudad perdida* (1951). *A instancia de parte* (1954). *La hija de don Juan de Austria. Ana de Jesús en el proceso al pastelero de*

Madrigal (1973). *María de Mendoza (Solución a un enigma amoroso)* (1979). *Visto y vivido, 1931–1937. Pequeña historia de ayer* (memoirs; 1982). *Escucho el silencio. Pequeña historia de ayer II* (1984).

Carolyn Galerstein

Luisa Forrellad

Born Sabadell (Catalonia), Spain
Genre(s): novel
Language(s): Spanish

Luisa Forrellad's only novel, *Siempre en capilla* (1954; Always Under Siege), won the prestigious Nadal prize in 1953, but despite its popularity (the book has had at least ten editions) she has not published anything more. Critics like Eugenio G. de Nora (*La novela española contemporánea*, 1979) and José María Martínez Cachero (*Historia de la novela española entre 1936 y 1975*, 1979), make brief mention of the work, but no full length studies on it seem to exist.

Siempre en capilla is markedly different from the sociorealistic novels of Forrellad's contemporaries since it takes place in England, in the late nineteenth century, instead of dealing with the Spanish circumstances during the "posguerra." Narrated by a young English doctor, it tells the story of his and two fellow doctors' efforts to combat a diphtheria epidemic in a poor neighborhood of London. The interest of the reader is maintained through the intricacies of the plot. Some elements of the detective novel and a dry humor reminiscent of English literature are also present. An evident knowledge of medicine brings realism to the narration.

Works

Siempre en capilla (1954).

Concha Alborg

Ol'ga Forsh

(a.k.a. A. Terek)

Born May 16, 1873, Gunib Fortress,
Daghestan, Russian Empire; died July 17,
1961, Leningrad, Soviet Union
Genre(s): novel, short story
Language(s): Russian

Ol'ga Forsh was a Soviet Russian writer, famous for her numerous historical novels. She was the daughter of a high-ranking officer of the Tsar's army. Her education took place in Moscow, Odessa, Kiev and St. Petersburg. She studied painting and taught drawing in the first part of her career before 1917.

Her literary talents developed relatively late in her life; in her mid-30s, she started publishing stories and articles in such journals as *Kievskii vestnik, Dlia vsekh, Zavety, Russkaia mysl'*, and *Skify*. Although she was, to some extent, influenced by several of the major trends of the fin de siècle and the beginning of the century, her major prose was not to be written until the 1920s. The first of her well-known historical novels, *Clad with Stone*, came out in 1925. Written in the form of a diary, the novel treats the revolutionary movement in Russia in the 1870s and 1880s. Her historicism, which is always merged with philosophical and psychological issues, has been compared to Merezhkovsky's. Concern about the role of the artist in society informs the novel *The Contemporaries* (1926). Forsh traces here Gogol's experiences in Rome and his friendship with the painter Alexander Ivanov.

Her three novels, *The Hot Shop* (1926), *The Crazy Ship* (1931) and *The Symbolists* (1933), deal with the history of more recent times which the writer personally witnessed. The first one, *The Hot Shop*, discusses the events and aftermath of the 1905 revolution. The Russian literary world before the 1917 October revolution is the subject of *The Symbolists*, and in *The Crazy Ship*, the same circles are portrayed in the Petrograd of the 1920s.

Forsh's three-volume historical novel, *Radishchev*, came out in three parts between 1932 and 1939. The trilogy evokes with liveliness the epochs of Catherine the Great and

Paul I. The protagonist is the narrator, Alexander Radishchev, whom Catherine exiled to Siberia for his work, *A Journey from St. Petersburg to Moscow*. Forsh's final full-length historical novel, *Pioneers of Liberty* (1953), is about the Decembrist uprising of 1826.

In her short stories, Ol'ga Forsh regularly wrote about contemporary matters. Yet, her reputation depends upon her historical fiction, most of which is devoted to the discussion of the Russian revolutionary tradition. The modernist features of her youthful writings gradually disappear, giving way to the more conventional realism of her later works.

Works

Sobranie sochinenii, 7 vols. (1928–1930). *Sobranie sochinenii*, 8 vols. (1962–1964).

Translations: *Palace and Prison* (1958). *Pioneers of Freedom* (1954).

Bibliography

Lugovtsov, N., *Tvorchestvo Ol'gi Forsh* (Leningrad, 1965). Messer, R.D., *Ol'ga Forsh* (Leningrad, 1965). Skaldina, R.A., *O.D. Forsh. Ocherk tvorchestva 20–30 gg* (Moscow, 1974). Tamarchenko, A.V., *Ol'ga Forsh*, 2d. ed. (Leningrad, 1974).

Peter I. Barta

Margaretha Droogleever Fortuyn-Leenmans

(see: Vasalis)

Elena Fotino

(see: Elena Farago)

Catherine de Fradonnet

(see: dames des Roches)

Anna Frajlich

Born March 10, 1942, Kirghiz, Central Asia
Genre(s): poetry
Language(s): Polish

A graduate of the Warsaw University in Poland, with her master's degree in Polish language and literature, she found her first employment as one of the editors of a magazine for the blind. Having left Poland with her husband and son in 1969, she settled in New York. A Ph.D. candidate in Slavic at New York University, she now teaches Polish at Columbia. Some of her poems in translations appeared in American literary reviews; her Polish work was widely published in the Polish literary press in exile. She is a recipient of the 1981 Koscielski Foundation award; the Foundation, with headquarters in Switzerland, gives its prize to the most outstanding young Polish writer, both in Poland and abroad.

Her poetry was first published in Polish literary magazines in 1958. She received an award at a poetry competition in Poland in 1959.

Compared to Pawlikowska: her lyrical poetry is "woman's stuff," painting-like, in vivid colors and deceptively light, musical and often rhymed, of an almost sing-song quality; preoccupied with emotions, relationships, forever returning to people and places once familiar and loved, yet concrete, succinct, and devoid of sentimentality. Exile is its dominant theme, but the longing for the home where the poet grew up becomes a longing for a place which cannot be found on any map; it represents the longing for one's own youth, for one's self as perceived in the bright world of childhood, the world of order and clearcut values. The real Poland, the lost home, paradise lost, has become a cemetery where "memory is strewn with monuments like the land." It is ruled by raging, vainglorious gangsters, who killed hope with their knives, tear gas, bayonets, and tanks; a country where at Christmas, "even a beast kneels down, but not the gangster"; a country where poets and heroes become recognized only once they are dead. When the monument is raised, "one can kill again." There is actually no native land to return to, and yet "one would love so much to go home, to warm one's hands on the hot tile stove." The tile stove, a symbol of a warm and secure childhood, is a typical image; this poetry finds its expression through the most ordinary and everyday objects and interiors: a table, a bed, a chair, bookshelves, a fireplace, hospital room walls, an underground station. The symbols are concrete, without any pretense at being poetic: like that photograph of the poet's parents' native city on the frame of which her father carved forget-menots with his pocketknife so as "not to forget, not to forget, not to forget Lvov even in America."

The common and banal character of the symbols constitutes both the form and the content of this poetry: its subject, consciously chosen and recognized, is everyday life itself. For common existence itself is our very reality, and a life stripped of concrete objects, of ordinary and everyday experiences, would be no life at all. According to the poet, when we are put "eye to eye/ with naked life/stripped of everyday worries/and passions/ . . . we suddenly realize/that naked life/is nothing but death."

Preoccupation with death, aging, and the passage of time is another important theme of Frajlich's poetry along with exile, the sense of being uprooted, and the need to belong, to become a part of some meaningful entity once more. These are universal themes, and their presence in our experience of everyday reality endows concrete individual objects with the quality of symbols. Here the maple tree "running in" through the poet's window "with rust, ochre, or green" the tree which is her "own, and yet so unfamiliar" takes on the quality of a carrier of what the poet experiences as the sense of self, rooted in the world.

The passage of time is felt intensely and connected with the yearning for the fullness and harmony of experience. Barely in her thirties, the poet reminded herself already that though "it's still summer, [it's] time to think of fall." She does not want to lose even a moment of the precious time and, as often, expresses the intensity of life experience with a painter's brush; while ". . . forests are covered with red, vermillions, and purples/ . . . there's no time for subtle greens/not sprouts/nor leaves/nor buds/just to turn into crimson's scream/before tissues are nipped by frost/and to pass full speed/with bluster/with pigment boiling in blood/overflowing with scarlet juices/at boughs, at branches, at trunks."

The symbols with the help of which the poet phrases her ideas and emotions, originate from the common roots of our culture. These symbols are present in it as natural media to express poetry's eternal and universal themes. Focused on herself, sounding her own intimate feelings, in most of her poems Frajlich appears not only as the voice of her own uprooted generation of Poles and Polish Jews but as a witness and serious student of the past of her country as well as the rest of the world. Her work belies the claim that rhyme has no place in modern poetry. There is nothing artificial in her rhymes: this is simply the way she expresses herself, and her voice sounds authentic. The elusively traditional form of her poetry is in harmony with the traditional character of its universal themes. Next to the already familiar face of an artist who finds her lyrical expression through musical tones and painter's colors, her most recent volume reveals the face of a reader reflecting on the passing of civilizations and the fate of man in history.

Works

Aby wiatr namalowac [To Pain the Wind] (1976). *Tylko ziemia* [Just Earth] (1979). *Indian Summer* (1982). *Ktory las* [Which Forest] (1986).

English translations: appeared in *Introduction to Modern Polish Literature.* (New York, 1982); *Columbus Names the Flowers* (Oregon, 1984); *Terra Poetica, Artful Dodge, The Polish Review, Poet Lore, Wisconsin Review,* and *Mr. Cogito.*

Maya Peretz

Dolores Franco

Born 1916, Madrid, Spain
Genre(s): essay, criticism
Language(s): Spanish

Licenciada en Filología Moderna, Dolores Franco was a disciple of Ortega, A. Castro, Montesinos, and Salinas. Her major contribution to Spanish literature is a precise and penetrating study of the theme of Spain and its problems in the national literature. First published in 1944 as *La preocupación de España en su literatura,* the work was augmented and a new edition published in 1960 under the title *España como preocupación*.

Works

La preocupación de España en su literatura (Madrid, 1944). *España como preocupación*, new ed., augmented (Madrid, 1960).

Bibliography

Bleiberg, G., and J. Marías, *Diccionario de la literatura española* (Madrid, 1953). Torrente Ballester, G., *Panorama de la literatura española contemporánea* (Madrid, 1965).

Carol Stos

Veronica Franco

Born 1546, Venice, Italy; died 1591, Venice
Genre(s): poetry, letters in verse
Language(s): Italian

Born in the Republic of Venice at the height of the Italian Renaissance, Veronica Franco achieved fame in her own lifetime both on account of her poetry and her sexuality. She married a doctor, Paolo Panizza, when very young, but left him soon afterwards and embarked on a series of love affairs, most notably with the poets Marco and Domenico Veniero and briefly with the French king Henri III. Her beauty was renowned in a city full of women surviving as courtesans, and she was painted several times by such artists as Tintoretto. Records of her life are sparse; in 1580 she was accused by the Inquisition of practicing witchcraft in order to make men fall in love with her, but the trial was abandoned for reasons unknown. Her letters indicate that she underwent some form of religious conversion later in life, and in 1580, the same year of her trial, she suggested the idea of opening a refuge for women of the streets. The first such refuge was opened in 1591.

Veronica Franco's poetry is remarkable for its directness as well as for its formal elegance. She writes in a witty, uninhibited manner about the pleasures and pains of love—ungrateful men, overinsistent men, and unfaithful men emerge in fully rounded portraits from her poems. Her poems in terza rima and her sonnets were first collected in an edition of 1575, entitled *Terze Rime*. This collection comprises 25 canti or

sections of which seven are verse letters addressed to Veronica Franco by an unknown lover, probably Marco Veniero. The collection is therefore in the form of an epistolary dialogue. Her letters were published in 1580 and reprinted in 1949 with an introduction by the great Italian critic Benedetto Croce, who comments on her apparent rejection of her life as courtesan. The letters contain accounts of the misery of a prostitute's life, and one addressed to a mother urges her to keep her daughter from following such a path.

There has yet to be a reappraisal of the courtesan poets of the Italian Renaissance, of which Veronica Franco is just one example. Her poetry is powerful because of its directness, and the way in which she introduces strongly personal statements into highly conventionalized verse forms gives her work a truly contemporary quality. Her choice of subject matter and treatment of it are unique.

Works

Terze Rime e Sonnetti, ed. G. Beccari, Lanciano, R. Carabba (1912). *Lettere* with preface by Benedetto Croce (1946). Other items are included in the following: 9 sonnets in Rime di diversi eccellentissimi autori nella morte dell'Illustre sig. Estor Martinengo, Conte di Malpaga (1573). 2 sonnets in Bartolomeo Zacco, *Canzoniere*, unpublished but later printed in E.A. Cicogna, *Inscrizioni Veneziane*, Vol. V, p. 424 (1824–1853). 1 sonnet in collection ed. G. Fratta, Panegirico nel felice dottorato dell'Illustre sig. Giuseppe Spinelli (1575). Reprinted in Bergalli-Gozzi, *Componimenti Poetici Delle Piu Illustri Rimatrici*, p. 26 (1726). 1 sonnet in praise of the tragedy *Semiramis* by Muzio Manfredi, included in the ed. of the play, p. 91 (1593). 1 sonnet in *Codice Miscellaneo Della Biblioteca Dei p.p. Serviti*. Pub. in *Novelle Leteerarie*, p. 320 (1757). Also in Cicogna, op.cit. Vol. VI, p. 884. Maffio Venier and Veronica Franco *Il Libro Chiuso*, ed. Manlio Dazzi (Venice, Neri Pozza: 1956).

Bibliography

Barzaghi, Antonio, *Donne o Cortigiane? La prostituzione a Venezia*. Documenti di costume dal XVI al XVIII secolo (Verona, 1980). Gamba, B., *Lettere di Donne Italiane del Sec. XVI* (Venice, 1832). Magliani, E., *Storia Letteraria delle donne italiane* (Naples, 1885). Masson, Georgina, *Courtesans of the Italian Renaissance* (London, 1975). Tassini, G., *V.F. Celebre Poetessa e Cortigiana del secolo XVI* (Venice, 1888).

Susan Basnett

Marie Louise von Françoise

Born June 27, 1817, Herzberg, Saxony; died
September 25, 1893, Weissenfels, Saxony
Genre(s): novel
Language(s): German

Von Françoise belonged to the school of realism and corresponded with Marie von Ebner-Eschenbach and C.F. Meyer and was herself the author of vigorously realistic novels.

Marie Louise von Françoise was the daughter of a wealthy aristocratic officer whose family derived from an old noble French family. Her mother was of the Saxon nobility. Although wealthy, Marie Louise was not granted an education suitable to her station. She therefore educated herself by reading the works of Adolph Müllner and Fanny Tarnow.

Her father's untimely death, her mother's remarriages, and Marie Louise's removal to her uncle's custody in Potsdam started her on her writing career. Due to her guardian's squandering of her inheritance, Marie Louise's fiancé, Count Alfred of Görtz, broke their engagement, leaving Françoise alone. She moved back to live with her aging mother and ill stepfather to care for them in Weissenfels, where she stayed till the end of her life. She established a friendship with Marie von Ebner-Eschenbach and C.F. Meyer during this time. At the age of fifty-four she was successful in publishing a great novel: *Die letzte Reckenburgerin* (The Last Lady of Reckenburg). Critics agree that this great book is Marie Louise von Françoise's contribution to the permanent fund of literature. In it the poet presents with surprising realism a picture of patriarchal existence at the end of the eighteenth century and the beginning of the nineteenth. Her three great novels, *Die letzte Reckenburgerin* (The Last Lady of Reckenburg), *Frau Ermuthens Zwillingssohne* (Mrs. Ermuthen's Twin Sons), and *Stufenjahre eines Glücklichen* (The Pinnacle Years of a Fortunate One), belong to the historical novels of,

respectively, the Napoleonic Era, the War of Prussian Independence, and the War of 1848. Some critics consider the moral tendencies evident in her works to be a weakness, but these tendencies really show her dependency on eighteenth century literature. Her novels show a strong acerbity, a certain reserve, an earnestness, and a goodness of character. Her conservatism remains free of the decadence of the epigones.

Marie Louise von Françoise holds a high place among German poets. Her works are the products of a penetrating, energetic, yet gentle and forgiving mind.

Works

Ausgewählte Novelle [Selected Short Stories] (1867). *Die letzte Reckenburgerin* [The Last Lady of Reckenburg] (1871). *Erzählungen* [Stories] (1871). *Frau Erdmuthens Zwillingssöhne* [Mrs. Erdmuthen's Twin Sons] (1872). *Geschichte der Preussischen Befreiungskriege 1813–1815. Ein Lesebuch für Schule und Haus* [History of the Prussian War of Independence 1813–1815. A Reader for School and Home] (1873). *Hellstadt und andere Erzählungen* [Hellstadt and Other Stories] (1874). *Natur und Gnade nebst anderen Erzählungen* [Nature and Grace and Other Stories] (1876). *Stufenjahre eines Glücklichen* [The Pinnacle Years of a Fortunate One] (1877). *Der Katzenjunker* [The Squire of Cats] (1879). *Phosphorus Hollunder* (1881). *Zu Füssen des Monarchen* [At the Feet of the Monarchy] (1881). *Der Posten der Frau. Lustspiel* [The Situation of the Woman. A Comedy] (1882). *Judith, die Kluswirthen* [Judith, the Innkeeper's Wife] (1883). *Das Jubiläum und andere Erzählungen* [The Anniversary and Other Stories] (1886). *Briefwechsel mit C.F. Meyer, hrsg. A. Bettelheim* [Correspondence with C.F. Meyer, edited by A. Bettelheim] (1905). *Gesammelte Werke* [Collected Works] (1918).

Bibliography

Allgemeine Deutsche Biographie. Hrsg. von der Historischen Kommission bei der Bayer. Akademie der Wissenschaften, ed. R. von Liliencron and F.X. von Wegele, Vol. 48 (Leipzig, 1904): 628. *Deutsche Schriftsteller im Porträt*, ed. Hiltud Hantzschel. Vol. IV (Munich, 1981). Koenig, Robert, *Deutsche Literaturgeschichte.* Vol. 2 (Leipzig, 1910). *Lexikon Deutscher Frauen der Feder*, ed. Sophie Pataky

(Bern, 1971). *Neue Deutsche Biographie*, ed. The Historical Committee of the Bavarian Academy of Sciences (Berlin, 1960). Stahl, E.L., and W.E, Yuill, *German Literature of the Eighteenth and Nineteenth Centuries* (New York, 1970).

Brigitte Archibald

Anneliese ("Anne") Frank

Born June 12, 1929, Frankfurt-am-Main, Germany; died March 1945, Bergen-Belsen Concentration Camp
Genre(s): diary, essay, fable, short story
Language(s): Dutch

Anne, born in Frankfurt-am-Main on June 12, 1929, was the second daughter of Otto and Edith Frank. As Jews, the family fled Nazi Germany in 1933 and settled in Amsterdam. Anne, a gifted student, hoped to become a writer or a journalist. With the Nazi occupation of Holland in 1940, Jews were soon forbidden to attend public schools. As a result, Anne was enrolled in a Jewish school. Life became increasingly more difficult for Dutch Jews, with deportation to the East beginning in 1942. The Frank family decided to go into hiding on July 9 of that same year. They, along with four others, spent two years in small rooms (the "Secret Annex") behind the offices where Otto Frank had worked. Several Gentile friends brought them provisions and news from the outside. Then, on August 4, 1944, the hiding place was discovered and the occupants were arrested. They were first taken to Westerbork and then to Auschwitz; later, Anne and Margot, her sister, were sent to Bergen-Belsen where Anne died in March of 1945 (two months before the liberation of Holland).

Of the original eight inhabitants of the Secret Annex, only Otto Frank survived. Miep, a friend of the family who had brought them food during the two years, gave him Anne's diary and other writings when she learned that Anne had perished. The writings, which the Nazis had overlooked, were discovered by Miep on the floor of the Secret Annex. The diary, first appearing in published form in 1947 under the title *Het Achterhuis* ("The House Behind"), was soon translated into other languages and became an immediate success. The English edition, *Anne Frank: The Diary of a Young Girl*, came out in 1953 and was followed by dramatic and film versions. Anne's short stories, essays, and fables were published after her father's death in 1980 with the English translation, *Anne Frank's Tales from the Secret Annex*, appearing in 1984. The Anne Frank House, containing the Secret Annex, is now a museum as well as the headquarters for a youth organization dedicated to world peace.

The diary, which Anne addresses as "Dear Kitty," begins on June 12, 1942, and has August 1, 1944, as a final entry. As a preface, Anne wrote: "I hope I shall be able to confide in you completely, as I have never been able to do in anyone before, and I hope that you will be a great support and comfort to me." The diary reveals the thoughts of an inquisitive, observant, and sensitive adolescent over a two-year period. Anne raises questions on a variety of issues, ranging from the personal to those relating to mankind in general. She speculates on such topics as the problems of becoming a woman, attitudes about sex, the war, being a Jew. Anne comments: "Sometime this terrible war will be over. Surely the time will come when we are people again, and not just Jews." A growing self-awareness as well as an optimistic outlook, in spite of the adverse conditions, are evident in the diary. As Anne states: "In spite of everything, I still believe that people are really good at heart."

Works

Anne Frank: The Diary of a Young Girl (1953). *The Diary of Anne Frank*; play (1955). *The Diary of Anne Frank*, film (1959). *Anne Frank's Tales from the Secret Annex* (1984).

Bibliography

Berryman, J., "The Development of Anne Frank." *The Freedom of the Poet* (1976). Bettelheim, B., "The Ignored Lesson of Anne Frank." *Surviving and other Essays* (1979). DeJong, L., *The Netherlands and Resistance* (1968). Ehrenberg, I., *Chekhov, Stendhal, and Other Essays* (1963). Presser, J., *The Destruction of the Dutch Jews* (1965). Schnabel, E., *Footsteps of Anne Frank* (1961). Shapiro, E., "The Reminiscences of Victor Kugler—The 'Mr. Kraler' of Anne Frank's Diary." *Yad Vashem Studies . . .* (1979).
General references: Baudot, M., and H. Bernard, H. Brugmans, M. Foot, H. Jacobsen, eds., *The His-*

torical Encyclopedia of World War II (1980). Keegan, J., ed., Who Was Who in World War II (1978). Reid, A. ,A Concise Encyclopedia of the Second World War (1974). Szonyi, D., ed. The Holocaust: An Annotated Bibliography and Resource Guide (1985). Tunney, C., A Biographical Dictionary of World War II (1972).

Other references: Weils, H., and B. Gough, A Far Cry from Home, Videorecording (1981).

Michael F. Bassman

Magdalena von Freiburg

(a.k.a. Magdalena Beutlerin, Beitlerin, Buttelerin, Büttlerin, Magdalena von Kenzingen)

Born 1407 (or any time until 1412),
    Kenzingen, near Freibrug i. Br., Germany;
    died December 5, 1485
Genre(s): biography, letters, visionary
    literature, prayer book
Language(s): German

In 1407–1412, Magdalena von Freiburg was born the daughter of the merchant Beutler from Kenzingen and his wife Margareta, who herself was a renowned mystic and author of visionary literature. As early as the age of three years, after her father's death, Magdalena experienced visions, perhaps because she was left almost totally alone. Soon after, she was given to the St. Claire convent in Freiburg, where she lived until her death on December 5, 1485. She claimed to have experienced Christ's passion herself and to have been stigmatized. She practiced a strict rule of fasting, but she also suffered from unequivocal signs of hysteria. In 1429 she pretended that her body was raptured, and, while hiding for three days, she threw a letter written with her own blood to the sisters during mass, in which she admonished them to enact the absolute principle of poverty in the convent. Magdalena prophesied the time of her death, 1431, but when a large crowd had gathered in the church to witness the event, nothing happened. She explained it as divine humiliation. Subsequently, her reputation as a saint greatly suffered with the general public but not in the nunnery, where she was said to have experienced several more raptures. It is certain that Magdalena had very serious intentions in her claims and seems to have honestly striven for a saintly life. But, in contrast to many other German women mystics, she demonstrated characteristics of arrogance, righteousness, and extreme harshness against her sisters in the convent. She excelled, however, through her adamant fasting and striving for monastic reform. Her Magdalenen-Buch (Book of Magdalena) contains an unsystematized collection of biographical accounts and letters, visions, and auditions, which deal with traditional topics of women's mysticism, such as Christ's passion, the suffering in Purgatory, the coming of doom's day, appearance of the Christ child, angels, saints, and devils. It is uncertain which parts were dictated or penned by herself even though a redactor is occasionally recognizable, who might well have been her confessor. The Paternoster-Gebetsbuch (Paternoster Prayer-Book) consists of a multiplicity of prayer texts from various sources although they were written under the pretext of being dictated by God. A relatively accurate contemporary account of her life was given by the mystic Johannes Nider, famous as professor, reformer, and diplomat, in his Formicarius, who explained her extreme visions and raptures as a result of her exaggerated fantasies.

Works

Magdalenen-Buch [Book of Magdalena]. Paternoster-Gebetsbuch [Paternoster Prayer-Book].

Bibliography

Dinzelbacher, Peter, and Kurt Ruh, "Magdalena von Freiburg." Die deutsche Literatur des Mittelalters, Verfasserlexikon, vol. 5, ed. K. Ruh (Berlin and New York, 1985), cols. 1117–1121. Oehl, Wilhelm, ed., Deutsche Mystikerbriefe des Mittelalters, 1100–1500 (Munich, 1931; rpt. Darmstadt, 1972): 519–530, 813–815. Schieler, K., Magister Johannes Nider aus dem Ordern der Prediger Brüder (Mainz, 1885): 218–221. Schleussner, W., "Magdalena von Freiburg, Eine pseudomystische Erscheinung des späteren Mittelalters." Der Katholik 87 (1907): 15–32, 109–127, 199–216. Tüchle, H. Kirchengeschichte Schwabens, Die Kirche Gottes im Lebensraum des schwäbisch-alemannischen Stammes, vol. II (Stuttgart, 1954): 161.

Albrecht Classen

Fiammetta Frescobaldi

*Born: January 17, 1523, Florence, Italy; died
    July 6, 1586, Florence*
Genre(s): history, translation
Language(s): Italian

Fiammetta Frescobaldi was born Brigida,
daughter of Lamberto Frescobaldi and Francesca
Morelli on January 17, 1523, one of six children.
She became Sister Fiammetta in the Dominican
convent of San Jacopo di Ripoli in Florence,
entering in 1536 and taking her vows a year and
a half later, in July of 1537. At the age of twenty-
five she was stricken by an illness that made her
lame in one foot and unable to walk.

The convent documents say that Sister
Fiammetta was self-taught, that she had a "wonderful mind and very sharp memory," and that
she used her talents to benefit her convent sisters.
She obtained books for the convent from her
relatives and others, and she translated many of
them—the documents mention 118 saints'
lives—for the edification of nuns who couldn't
read Latin. She also wrote chronicles and descriptions of the entire known world based on
travel journals, letters of missionaries, and important contemporary studies of natural history.
Some of her works are compilations of a wide
variety of things. The *Selva di cose diverse* (Forest
of Diverse Things), for example, contains, among
other subjects, ancient history, geography, customs of various peoples, descriptions of art and
architecture, and a brief Spanish grammar with
phrases for the use of nuns. She scrupulously
cites her sources at the beginning of each work;
they include Columbus, Vespucci, Cortes,
Pizzarro, Oviedo y Valdés, Barros, Sabellico,
Tarcagnotta, Palladio, Vasari, and for the saints'
lives the Dominican Laurentius Surius and many
others. She rewrote Francesco Guicciardini's
History of Italy in abridged form and wrote a
chronicle of the Dominican order (from the birth
of St. Dominic in 1170 to 1579), which deals
primarily with the Dominicans in Florence and
especially in her own convent and during her
lifetime. She also kept a diary from 1575 until a
few days before her death.

None of Fiammetta Frescobaldi's work has
been published, and some manuscripts have
been lost (many of the saints' lives and her

version of Guicciardini). Most of the extant
manuscripts are written in her own beautiful
hand, with title page and colophon in imitation
of printed books. She is mentioned occasionally
in works of erudition, primarily as a translator,
though most of her "translations" are compilations of the works of a number of writers and are
therefore necessarily very different from any one
source.

Works

*Cose prodigiose e calamitose del mondo,
cominciando dal Diluvio infino ai tempi nostri*, 4
vols. in 5 parts, holograph ms., dated 1577–1579,
wanting vol. 3 (pt. 3), Frescobaldi Archives, Poggio
a Remole (Florence); eighteenth-century copy of
part 2, Cod. Moreniano 96, Riccardiana and
Moreniana Library, Florence. *Compendio della
storia di M. Francesco Guicciardini*, 8 books, listed
in 1886 by Ferdinando de' Frescobaldi among the
works of Sister Fiammetta in possession of the
Convent of San Jacopo di Ripoli in Florence.
Cronaca del sacro ordine di San Domenico, holograph ms., dated 1579, Archives of Santa Maria
Novella, Florence. *Diario dall'anno 1575 fino
all'anno 1586 e varie memorie*, holograph ms., diary
1575–1585, Archives of Santa Maria Novella, Florence. *Mutazione della chiesa partiarcale di Venezia*,
holograph ms., 1576, Frescobaldi Archives. *Prato
fiorito*, holograph ms., 1575, Biblioteca Nazionale,
Florence. *Conventi soppressi*, C. 2. 504. *Selva di
cose diverse*, holograph ms., 1562–1585,
Frescobaldi Archives. *La Sfera dell'universo*, 5 vols.,
9 parts, holograph ms., [post 1561]-1580, wanting
vol. 2 (pt. 6), Frescobaldi Archives. *Storia generale
delle Indie Occidentali*, 1 vol., 4 books, holograph
ms., n.d. but after 1556, Frescobaldi Archives.
Storia generale delle Indie Orientali, 1 vol., 4 books,
holograph ms., 1565, Frescobaldi Archives. *La
Storia dei re di Persia*, holograph ms., 1576,
Frescobaldi Archives. *Vite di X beati*, holograph ms.,
1585, Frescobaldi Archives. *Vite di XVII santi
monachi europei*, holograph ms. containing only
nine lives, one or more vols. missing, 1584,
Frescobaldi Archives. *Vite di XXIX santi quasi tutti
vescovi*, holograph ms., 1582, Frescobaldi Archives. A number of other saints' lives mentioned
by Pierattini (below) as belonging to the Frescobaldi
Archives are not there today.

Bibliography

Pierattini, Giovanna, "Sister Fiammetta Frescobaldi cronista del monastero domenicano di Sant'Iacopo a Ripoli in Firenze (1523–1586)." *Memorie domenicane* 56 (1939): 101–116, 233–240, 57; (1940): 106–111, 260–269, 58; (1941): 28–38, 74–84, 226–234, 258–268. Viviani Della Robbia, Enrica, *Nei monasteri fiorentini* (Florence, 1946), p. 196.

Elissa B. Weaver

Rosemarie Fret

Born August 28, 1935, Anklam, Germany
Genre(s): short story, prose, radio play
Language(s): German

Rosemarie Fret studied graphic art in Leipzig, and now makes her living as a freelance photographic commercial artist in Leipzig. Her stories deftly combine satire and fantasy with day-to-day realities. Thus, the fairy-tale mood of "Das Märchen von meiner Erdkugel," vividly evoked by unusual imagery, proves to be an extension of the limited, or at least idiosyncratic, intelligence of the narrator.

Works

Nachsaison [After the Season], short stories (1973). "Der Pantomime," *Neue Erzähler der DDR* (1975). *Das Schattenkreuz* [The Shadowcross], radio talk (1976). *Hoffnung auf Schneewittchen* [Expecting Snow White], short stories (1981). "Das Märchen von meiner Erdkugel." *Im Kreislauf der Windeln. Frauenprosa aus der DDR* [The Fairytale About My Globe], anthology (1982).

Bibliography

General references: *Deutsches Literatur-Lexicon*, Vol. 5, p. 583.

Ann Marie Rasmussen

Margit Friedrich

(see: Margarete Beutler)

Margarete Friedrich-Freksa

(see: Margarete Beutler)

Barbara Frischmuth

Born May 7, 1941, Altaussee, Austria
Genre(s): short story, novel, children's
literature
Language(s): German

Imprinting experiences reflected in Frischmuth's writings are her rural upbringing, her schooling in a nunnery, her Turkish and Hungarian language studies in Graz, Erzerum, and Debrecen, and her Orientalistic studies at the University of Vienna. As a student she was a member of the Graz "Forum Stadtpark," an avant garde literary circle that also produced such well-known writers as Handke and Jonke. In 1967 she gave a successful reading before the "Gruppe 47," which launched her career as an independent writer.

Her first prose piece, *Die Klosterschule* (1968), centers in 14 ironic-defiant chapters around the school life at a Catholic nunnery. She describes its authoritarian atmosphere through the nuns' ritualistic use of language, exposing thus religious–educational structures aimed at female submissiveness. This polemic against a world of questionable values becomes more lighthearted in tone in her next book, a volume of short stories called *Amoralische Kinderklapper* (1969), whose title refers back to J. August Musäus' *Moralische Kinderklapper* (1787), exposing again via rhetoric the discrepancy between children and grown-ups. Language consciousness also permeates her children's stories *Sätze zur Situation: Tage und Jahre* (1971) and *Erzählungen ohne Gewähr: Rückkehr zum vorläufigen Ausgangspunkt* (1973).

Her first real novel, *Das Verschwinden des Schattens in der Sonne* (1973), takes up another issue: should social action be devoted to the past or the present, should it be reflection or participation? Employing her Orientalistic background, Frischmuth situates her narrative into Istanbul, where an Austrian student is doing research for a historical dissertation without understanding the revolutionary mood around her. Only when her Turkish boyfriend is shot by police during a demonstration does she realize that the social necessities of the present forbid irrelevant reflections on the past.

After this novel, all of Frischmuth's writings tend to circle around one particular topic: the emancipatory role of woman, often located in a mixed setting of fantasy and reality modeled after the narrative style of Lewis Carroll, Tolkien, and Irmtraut Morgner. The trilogy novels *Die Mystifikationen der Sophie Silber* (1976), *Amy oder die Metamorphose* (1978), and *Kai und die Liebe zu den Modellen* (1979), all speak of alternative lifestyle possibilities, other forms of communication, counter-worlds, new models of constructive interaction, concepts linked to the feminist discourse. The trilogy itself is flanked by two short story collections; at its beginning there is *Haschen nach Wind* (1974), at its end *Entzug—ein Menetekel der zärtlichsten Art* (1979), both describing the problematic relationship between man and woman.

Frischmuth's writings, which also include many children's books, are highly respected in western and socialist countries alike.

Works

Die Klosterschule (1968). *Der Pluderich*, children's book (1969). *Pilomena Mückenschnabel*, children's book (1969). *Geschichten für Stanek* (1969). *Amoralische Kinderklapper* (1969). *Polsterer*, children's book (1970). *Sätze zur Situation: Tage und Jahre* (1971). *Ida—und Ob*, youth book (1972). *Die Prinzessin in der Zwirnspule und andere Puppenspiele* (1972). *Das Verschwinden des Schattens in der Sonne* (1973). *Erzählungen ohne Gewähr: Rückkehr zum vorläufigen Ausgangspunkt* (1973). *Haschen nach Wind* (1974). *Grizzly Dickbauch und Frau Nuffl* (1975). *Die Mystifikationen der Sophie Silber* (1976). *Amy oder die Metamorphose* (1978). *Kai und die Liebe zu den Modellen* (1979). *Entzug—ein Menetekel der zärtlichsten Art* (1979). *Bindungen* (1980). Radioplays: *Die Mauskoth und die Kuttlerin. Die Unbekannte Hand. Löffelweise Mond. Ich möchte, ich möchte die Welt. Die Mondfrau.*

Bibliography

Daviau, Donald G., "Neuere Entwicklungen in der modernen österreichischen Prosa: Die Werke von Barbara Frischmuth." *Modern Austrian Literature* 13, 1 (1980): 177–216. Johns, Jorun B., "Barbara Frischmuth: Eine Bibliographie der Werke und der Sekundärliteratur bis Herbst 1980." *Modern Austrian Literature* 14, 1 (1981): 101–128.

Interviews: "Die Macht neu verteilen, sodaß sie keine Gefahr mehr für die Welt bedeutet," in Jürgen Serke, *Frauenschreiben* (Hamburg, 1979), pp. 150–163. "Weibliches Bewußtsein in Sprache umsetzen," in Hilde Schmölzer, *Frau Sein und Schreiben. Österreichsiche Schriftstellerinnen Definieren sich selbst* (1982), pp. 63–72.

Margaret Eifler

Frusinica

(see: Smara)

Anna Rupertina Fuchs(in)

(a.k.a. Daphne)

Born December 1, 1657, Pleitner, Elbling/
Prussia; died November 23, 1722,
Sulzbach/Württemberg
Genre(s): drama, lyric poetry
Language(s): German

Anna Rupertina Fuchs lost her mother, a Dutch woman, in 1660 when she was only three years old. Her father, Johann von Pleitner, an officer in the service of Nuremberg, died soon after in a battle against the Turks in 1664. She lived in Nuremberg until she married Georg Christoph Fuchs, a school headmaster in Sulzbach in 1699. She was a skilled poetess and could compose much of her work, particularly her poetry, orally without resorting to writing. For her publications she used the name of Daphne. She died childless in 1722.

Works

Hiob. In einer dramatischen Repräsentation [Hiob, in a Dramatic Enactment] (1714). *Poetischer Gedancken Schatz* [Treasure of Poetic Thoughts] (1720). *Poetische Schriften samt einer Vorrede von dem Leben der Frau Fuchsin* [Poetic Works Together with a Foreword About Ms. Fuchs's Life] (1726), ed. Friedrich Roth-Scholtzen.

Bibliography

Deutsches Literatur-Lexikon, founded by Wilhelm Kosch, 3rd rev. ed. (Bern-Munich, 1978), p. 863. Goedecke, Karl, *Grundriß zur Geschichte der Deutschen Dichtung aus den Quellen*, 2nd. ed., vol. III (Dresden, 1887), p. 328. Jöcher, C.G.,

Allgemeines Gelehrten-Lexicon, 2nd pt. (Leipzig, 1750; rpt. Hildesheim, 1961), col. 793. Zedler, J.H., *Universal-Lexicon* 9 (Halle-Leipzig, 1735): 2200.

Albrecht Classen

María de los Reyes Fuentes Blanco

Born 1927, Sevilla, Spain
Genre(s): poetry
Language(s): Spanish

Fuentes has been active in the cultural life of Sevilla, in addition to serving as Jefe del Negociado de Asistencia Social for the city. She is a member of the International Academy of Poets and the World Literary Academy of Cambridge; Real Academia de Ciencias, Bellas Letras y Nobles Artes de Cordoba; Real Academia Hispanoamerica de Cadiz; Real Academia San Telmo de Malaga; Biblioteca Internazionali di Poesía Contemporanea, de Lecce; and has received the following literary prizes: Premio de Poesía Castellana for "Ciudad de Barcelona," Premio de Literatura for "Ciudad de Sevilla," "Marina," "La Venencia," "Amigos de la Poesía," "Vivienda del Futuro," and special mention for the Premio Nacional de Literatura. Much of her poetry concerns love as a force, sometimes violent and stormy, sometimes nostalgic and melancholy.

Works

Actitudes. *Poetas jóvenes sevillanos* (antología; 1956). *De mí hasta el hombre Sonetos del corazón adelante* (1960). *Elegías del Uad-El Kebir* (1961). *Romances de la miel en los labios* (1962). *Elegías tartessias* (1964). *Oración de la verdad* (1965). *Acrópolis del testimonio* (1966). *Concierto para la Sierra de Ronda* (1966); reedited, with *Fabulilla del diamante salvado*. *Pozo de Jacob* (1967). *Fabulilla del diamante salvado*; reedited, with *Concierto para la Sierra de Ronda*. *Motivos para un anfiteatro*. *Misión de la palabra* (antología). *Apuntes para la composición de un drama*. *Aire de amor* (1977). *Jardín de la revelación*.
Translations: *Elegie andaluse* (Roma: Edizioni Cias-Unesco).

Carolyn Galerstein

Gloria Fuertes

Born 1918, Madrid, Spain
Genre(s): poetry, stories, drama, children's
*   literature*
Language(s): Spanish

Gloria Fuertes was born in a working-class neighborhood of Madrid. Her early studies were at the "Institute of Professional Education for Women" and included sewing, cooking, childcare, and other courses traditionally designed for young women. At the same time Fuertes dedicated herself to less traditional interests such as hockey, basketball and poetry and enrolled in a course in grammar and literature to pursue her interest in poetry. Her youth was indelibly marked by the death of her mother and the impact of the Spanish Civil War, to which she lost her first love.

An officeworker and stenographer as a young woman, in 1939 she transferred from an accounting firm to the editorial office of a magazine. In 1955 she returned to her studies, spending five years earning a diploma in library science and English while working and writing as well. After serving as director of a public library, in 1961 she received a Fulbright Fellowship to teach Spanish poetry at Bucknell University in Pennsylvania. In Spain she has regularly taught and given recitals of her own poetry. Besides her numerous collections of poetry, her work includes several books of stories, verses and plays for children. Much of Fuertes' work has been recorded, both by herself and by others.

Fuertes' poetry has, from the beginning, been difficult to categorize according to such convenient criteria as chronology or literary fashion. Her contemporaries in age include Blas de Otero, Gabriel Celaya, José Hierro, and José Luis Hidalgo. The work of these poets of Spain's first postwar generation is characterized by a sense of existential anguish, a deep social commitment, a rejection of poetry as the expression of an elitist esthetic, and colloquial and at times grotesque language. Gloria Fuertes' poetry shares all of these characteristics. Yet she has also been linked to the poets of the second generation of postwar Spain, poets like Angel González, Claudio Rodríguez, and José Angel Valente, who make up what is often called the "generation of 1956–

1971." Although the majority of Gloria Fuertes' works were published by 1973, she shares with these younger writers a conception of the importance of intertextuality and of poetry as a process of discovering and conveying personal meanings.

At the age of seventeen Fuertes published her first autobiographical poem, "Isla ignorada" ("Ignored Island"), which later provided the title for her first published collection of poetry (1950). The theme of this early work is the solitude that Fuertes perceives as the essential condition of human existence. Thus Fuertes established from the beginning of her literary career the theme of loneliness that underlies all of her work. This loneliness is the result of the failure of love and also of the poet's vision of herself as a bizarre figure, a "tender Amazon" and a "fabulous disaster." Loneliness also takes the form of an overwhelming and omnipresent nothingness (*la nada*), which Fuertes imagines, in her idiosyncratic and endearing way, as an empty refrigerator, a buttonhole, or the hole caused by a pin entering a pincushion. Nothingness is also present in images of drowning, of infinity, and especially of silence.

Gloria Fuertes has a clear vision of what poetry is meant to be, and the title "Poetics" is one which she uses repeatedly. The mission of poetry is manifold: it must thrill and amuse, warn against injustices and be an "immense aspirin" to relieve pain. Most of all, poetry is meant to fill the void that threatens human existence.

In the collection that assured her serious critical attention, *Poet on Guard* (1968), the dominant image is of the poet herself, on the alert for the needy and humble to whom she pledges her primary allegiance and support. Fuertes' work, then, can justifiably be regarded as social poetry in the sense that she is ever aware of the supreme need for communication and love among all peoples. To this end, Fuertes' poetry contains frequent references to stairways, doorbells, and telephones. Further, she turns often to extrapoetic forms to convey her message: letters, radio messages, telegrams, recipes, menus, commercial announcements, even reprimands.

For Gloria Fuertes, poetry is not only the bridge of connection with others, it is also the way she communicates with herself. "Autobio" figures importantly among the titles of her verses,

and *Story of Gloria* (1980) is the name of her most recent collection. Indeed her work is so often self-referential that she is herself her poetry's most frequent subject. She presents herself in a series of bizarre yet charming guises—bullfighter, astronaut, clown, circus master, tango dancer, and athlete among many others. She dons these masks to inspire herself, to dare herself so that, through her poetry, she can challenge, amuse, and tame her loneliness.

In form, Fuertes' poetry takes two directions; one- and two-line verses, almost epigrammatic in character, which compress the message and virtually mask the creative process; and alternately, poems similar to litanies, diatribes, even on occasion an auctioneer's sales pitch. In her very short poems Fuertes confronts her essential solitude by echoing the silence and internalizing it. In the very long verses, marked by repetition, enumeration, or the alliteration of a single sound, Fuertes defies nothingness by externalizing it and by transforming silence into sound.

Gloria Fuertes is an important poet of modern Spain. Her work suggests a generous and loving spirit that refuses to succumb to despair. Rather, her poetry is a constant reaffirmation of her own existence and an exaltation of positive human values.

Works

Isla ignorada [Ignored Island] (1950). *Antología y poemas del suburbio* [Anthology and Poems of the Slum] (1954). *Aconsejo beber hilo* [I Advise You to Drink Thread] (1954). *Todo asusta* [Completely Scared] (1958). *Que estás en la tierra* [Who Art on Earth] (1962). *Ni tiro, ni veneno, ni navaja* [No Shooting, No Poison, No Knife] (1965). *Poeta de guardia* [Poet on Guard] (1968). *Cómo atar los bigotes al tigre* [How to Tie the Tiger's Mustache] (1969). *Antología poética* (1950–1969) [Poetic Anthology (1950–1969)] (1970). *Sola en la sala* [Alone in the Room] (1973). *Cuando amas aprendes geografía* [When You Love You Learn Geography] (1973). *Obras incompletas* [Incomplete Works] (1980). *Historia de Gloria* [Story of Gloria] (1983). **Translations:** Selected passages of Fuertes' poetry are translated in *Recent Poetry of Spain: A Bilingual Anthology,* tr. and ed. Louis Hammer and Sara Schyfter (1983).

Bibliography

Cano, J.L., *Poesía española contemporánea: las generaciones de posguerra* (1974). Debicki, A., *Poetry of Discovery: The Spanish Generation of 1956–1971* (1982). Gonzàlez Muela, J., *La nueva poesía española* (1973). Grande, F., *Apuntes sobre poesía española de posguerra* (1970). Quiñones, F., *Ultimos rumbos de la poesía española* (1966). Other references: *Revista canadiense de estudios hispánicos* (winter 1983). *Mester* (Jan. 1980). *Perspectives on Contemporary Literature* (1981). *Anales de la literatura española contemporánea* 12 (1987). *Siglo XX/20th Century* 5 (1987–1988). *MLN* 104 (March 1989). *Hispania* 72 (May 1989).

Sylvia R. Sherno

Madame de Fumelh

Born ca. 1750, France
Genre(s): feminist polemical essay
Language(s): French

Addressing herself to the nation, Madame de Fumelh presented two speeches during the French Revolution. In both, she asserts her right as a woman to claim her liberties, not only as a citizen but also as a spouse. In this line of thought, her most important contribution, published anonymously but attributed to her by Evelyn Sullerot in the *Histoire de la Presse Féminine des Origines à 1848* (p. 44), is her *Mémoire sur le Divorce* in which she requests an equality little known during the Enlightenment. She argues that, were women given equal rights, they would not try to subjugate men. In this feminist tract, she states that marriage, such as it was in the eighteenth century, is "a state of aching and pain." And she adds: "L'amour de la liberté s'est emparé de tous les esprits; les voeux des peuples, les travaux de l'Assemblée nationale, tout vise à procurer aux Français ce bien inestimable. Liberté, égalité, justice semblent être les devises chéries de la Nation; quand elle fait tout pour atteindre ce but, laissera-t-elle susbsister des loix barbares, qui retiennent dans un esclavage humiliant et ridicule, la moitié de l'espèce humaine? La tyrannie et la force ont présidé à la confection de ces loix; que la raison et la justice les réforment" ("Love of freedom has inflamed every mind; the wishes of the people, the work of the National Assembly, all is intended to bring us this invaluable good. Liberty, Equality, Justice seem to be the cherished slogan of the Nation; when the People are doing all they can to reach this goal, are we going to stand for and accept barbarous laws which maintain in a humiliating and ridiculous slavery over half of the human specie? Tyranny and force were the chief contributors in the making those laws; that reason and justice abolish them").

Madame de Fumelh is also credited with a moral tale, "Miss Anysie, ou le Triomphe des Moeurs et des Vertus."

Works

Discours à la Nation Française. S.1,: n. d., In-8, 21 p. *Second Discours à la Nation Française* (1789), In-8, 35 p. "Miss Anysie, ou le Triomphe des Moeurs et des Vertus." (1788), In-8, vii-177 p.

Bibliography

Michael, Colette, *Sur le Divorce en France* (Geneva, 1989), pp. 36–48. Sullerot, Evelyne, *Histoire de la Presse Féminine des Origines à 1848* (Paris, 1966).

Colette Michael

Gertrud Fussenegger

(a.k.a. Gertrud Dietz, Gertrude Dorn)

Born May 8, 1912, Pilsen (today Czechoslovakia)
Genre(s): novel, short story, drama, poetry, essay, biography, treatise, edition
Language(s): German

Like Maria Janitschek, Gertrud Fussenegger was the daughter of an Austrian officer. She went to high school in Pilsen (today Czechoslovakia) and studied history, art history, German and philosophy in Munich and Innsbruck. She received her Ph.D. in 1934 in which year she also married the sculptor Aloys Dorn. They both moved to Hall in Tyrol, but they lived in Linz since 1961. Her literary concerns focus on historical accounts from the Bohemian past such as in the novels *Die Brüder von Lasawa* (The Brothers of Lasawa), *Das Haus der dunklen Krüge* (The House of the Dark Pitchers) and *Das verschüttete Antlitz* (The Covered Face). Based in traditional narrative techniques, Gertrud

Fussenegger developed new literary forms such as the paralleling and merging of two biographies. In her work she tried to reach answers for general human and historical problems. Individual lives are depicted as expressions of historical movements of epic dimensions. She also included subject matters such as the encounter of Léon Bloy and Madame Curie, research on uranium and radioactivity, religious revivalism. She has been praised for her masterly control of language and her strong imagery.

She received the Adalbert-Stifter Award in 1951 and 1963, the main prize for East German Literature of the Artists's Guild Eßlingen in 1961, the Johann-Peter-Hebel-Award in 1969 and the First Prize for Culture of the Sudeten German People's Federation in 1972.

Works

Novels: *Geschlecht im Advent, Roman aus deutscher Frühzeit* [Family in Advent, Novel of the German Past] (1937). *Mohrenlegende* [Moore Legend] (1937). *Die Brüder von Lasawa* [The Brothers of Lasawa] (1948). *Das Haus der dunklen Krüge* [The House of Dark Pitchers] (1951). *In Deine Hand gegeben* [Given Into Your Hand] (1954). *Das verschüttete Antlitz* [The Covered Face] (1957). *Viktorin* (1957). *Zeit des Raben, Zeit der Taube* [Time of the Raven, Time of the Pigeon] (1960). *Die Pulvermühle* [The Powder Mill] (1968). *Sie waren Zeitgenossen* [They Were Contemporaries] (1983).

Short Stories: *Der Brautraub* [Abduction of the Bride] (1939). *Eines Menschen Sohn. Mit einer autobiographischen Skizze der Verfasserin* [The Son, with an Autobiographical Sketch of the Author] (1939). *Die Leute auf Falbeson* [The People on Falbeson] (1943). *Hochzeitsandenken* [Memories of the Wedding] (1947). ... *wie gleichst du dem Wasser* [How Similar You Are to Water] (1949). *Die Legende von den drei heiligen Frauen* [The Legend of the Three Women Saints] (1952). *Der General* [The General] (1956). *Der Tabaksgarten. Sechs Geschichten und ein Motto* [The Tobacco Garden. Six Stories and One Motto] (1961). *Die Nachtwache am Weiher und andere Erzählungen* [The Night Vigil at the Pond and Other Stories] (1963). *Bibelgeschichten* [Bible Stories, together with J. Grabiansky] (1972). *Kaiser, König, Kellerhals. Heitere Erzählungen* [Emperor, King, and The Covered Entrance To The Cellar, Humorous Short Stories] (1981). *Freue dich, Christkind kommt bald* [Rejoice, The Christ Child Is Coming Soon] (1985). *Jona* (1986).

Plays: *Falkenberg* [Hawk Mountain] (1949). *Verdacht* [Suspicion] (1952). *Eggebrechts Haus* (Eggebrecht's House, appeared in 1957 in Oldenburg under the title *Im Strom—dein Haus* [In the Stream—Your House]). *Die Reise nach Amalfi* (The Trip to Amalfi, radio play, first performance in 1962, published in 1963).

Essays, Treatises, Dissertation, Studies: *Gemeinschaft und Gemeinschaftsbildung im Rosenroman von Jean Clopinel de Meung* [Community and Formation of Community in the *Roman de la Rose* by Jean Clopinel de Meung], dissertation (1934). *Böhmische Verzauberungen* [Enchantment in Bohemia,] travel report (1944). *Südtirol* [Southern Tyrol], text to the Pictorial Travel Book by H. Stursberg-Neizert (1959). *Südtirol in Farben, ein Bildwerk, mit Textbeiträgen von G.F. u.a.* [Southern Tyrol in Colors, A Pictorial Guide, with Text Contributions from G.F. and others] (1961). *Marie von Ebner-Eschenbach oder Der gute Mensch von Zdißlawitz* [Marie von Ebner-Eschenbach or The Good Person from Zdißlawitz], lecture (1967). *Bummel durch Salzburg* [Stroll Through Salzburg], together with R. Löbl (1970). *Sprache* [Language] (1974). *Widerstand gegen die Wetterhähne* [Resistance Against the Weather-Cocks] (1974). *Eines langen Stromes Reise. Die Donau: Linie, Räume, Knotenpunkte* [The Journey of a Long River. The Danube: Lines, Spaces, Crosspoints] (1976). *Der große Obelisk. Gedanken und Erfahrungen . . .* [The Big Obelisk. Thoughts and Experiences] (1977). *Dein Kreuz verkünden wir. Ein Spiegelbild mit Feuersäule. Lebensbericht* [A Mirage with A Column Out Of Fire. An Account of A Life] (1979). *Echolot: Essays, Vorträge, Notizen* [Echo-Sounder: Essays, Lectures, Notes] (1982). *Pilatus—Szenenfolge um den Prozeß Jesu* [Pilate—A Sequence of Scenes of the Trial of Jesus] (1982). *Uns hebt die Welle. Liebe, Sex und Literatur* [The Wave Lifts Us Up. Love, Sex and Literature], essay (1984). *Texte zu einem Kreuzweg von Alois Dorn* [We Are Announcing Your Cross. Texts to a Pictorial Crusade of Alois Dorn] (1985). *Maria Theresia. Biographie* [Maria Theresia. A Biography] (1986).

Poems: *Iris und Muschelmund* [Iris and the Shell Mouth] (1955).

Editions: [With G. Hohenauer and H. Lechner], *Wort im Gebirge. Schrifttum aus Tirol* [Word In The Mountains. Literature from Tyrol], 2 vols. (1956–1959). *J.P. Hebel, Schatzkästlein des Rheinischen Hausfreundes* [J.P. Hebel, Little Treasure Box of the Rhinelandian Friend at Home] (1975). [With others], *Die Rampe. Neue österreichische Literaturzeitschrift* [The Ramp. New Austrian Literary Journal] (1975).
Translation: Newnham, Richard, ed. , *German Short Stories* (Baltimore, 1964) (a few selections).

Bibliography

Gegenwart. Literarische Mittel und Bedingungen ihrer Produktion, ed. P.A. Bloch et al. (1975).
Langer, N., *Dichter aus Österreich*, 2nd ed. (1963).
Schöne, A., "Gertrud Fusseneggers neuer Roman. *Die Pulvermühle*. In *Wirkendes Wort* (1969).
Siegrist, R., *Zeitgenössische Erzähler* (1963).

Albrecht Classen

G

Dora Petrova Gabe

(a.k.a. Bogdan Haritov, Ranina)

Born August 28, 1886, Dŭbovik, Bulgaria;
died February 18, 1983, Sofia
Genre(s): poetry, short story, children's
literature, criticism, memoirs
Language(s): Bulgarian

Gabe is one of Bulgaria's foremost women poets. Her literary creative work is addressed equally to children, youth, and adults. She was the daughter of a Bulgarian journalist whose family returned from Russia and settled in Dobrud'a. She grew up in Dobrud'a, and its plains and fields, its seashore and sunsets had a great influence on her creative work. Gabe attended elementary school in her village and the resort city of Balčik and completed her secondary education in Šumen and Varna. In 1904 she enrolled at the University of Sofia and then in the fall of 1905 travelled to Geneva and in 1907 graduated from the University of Grenoble with a specialization in French language and literature.

Her first poem was published in 1900 and soon after she became a contributor to the journal *Misŭl*. Her first collection of poems *Temenugi* (1908; Violets) was imbued with an ardent yearning for an ideal love. Significantly, the last poem was entitled "Now I Stand Lonely, Hopeless on the Crossroad." The same year she married Bojan Penev, one of Bulgaria's great literary critics and professor of literature at the University of Sofia.

After World War I she actively collaborated in the journal *Zlatorog* and her new collections of poetry appeared as *Zemem pŭt* (1928; Earthly

Way) and *Lunatička* (1932; The Sleepwalker). The heroine of *Lunatička* wanders in a strange city, sympathizing with the unhappiness of the working people but unable to offer any comfort and aid. At the end the heroine exclaimed: "My own helplessness is a burden to me like a guilt." Gabe wrote many poems, short stories, and novels for children and published about thirty volumes in her seventy-five years as a writer. In addition, she edited *Biblioteka za malkite* (Library for the Young) and the journal *Prozorče* (Little Window). According to Gabe a children's writer should always preserve in him/her "the child he/she once was," and be able to see the world from the child's perspective. A few of the titles of her books are characteristic of her writings for children: *Malki pesni* (1923; Little Songs), *Kalinka-malinka* (1924; The Ladybug), *Velikden* (1930; Easter), *Malka Bogorodica* (1937; Little Mother of God), *Naiobicam zalugalki* (1955; I Like Toys the Best) and *Maika Paraškeva* (1971; Mother Paraškeva).

After 1944 there were some changes in her thematic orientation, especially in her writings for children. *Maika Paraškeva* is not only the mother of Georgi Dimitrov, the hero of the Reichstag Fire Trial and leader of Bulgaria, but a hero-mother herself and the embodiment of the primal characteristics of Bulgarian mothers.

In the poem *Vela* (1946), Gabe presents the heroic struggle of a partisan woman. Vela, unlike the Sleepwalker, has a clearly defined goal in life and a determination to fight for a better world. During the past thirty years Gabe wrote some of her best poetry. Many new collections of her writings appeared: *Novi stihove* (1958; New

Poetry), *Počakai slŭnce* (1967; Wait a Little, Sun!), *Nevidimi oči* (1970; Invisible Eyes), *Glŭbini: Razgovori s moreto* (1976; Depths: Conversations With the Sea) and *Svetŭt e taina* (1982; The World Is a Mystery). Her poetry is intimate and optimistic, and the writer shows concern for real people. She treats even the simplest event or idea within a dialectical framework and asks penetrating philosophical questions on life and death. If Gabe had some power over nature she would never permit people to become old. She loved life and beauty and made them the primary subject in her poetry.

Gabe was actively involved in the cultural life of her country. She translated the writings of many Polish, Czech, Russian, and Greek poets into Bulgarian. She was one of the founders and for many years the president of the Bulgarian PEN club. A number of her works have been translated into Czech, Greek, English, French, Polish, Russian, Spanish and other languages. Gabe was awarded many honorary titles and prizes for her writings and public activity.

Works

Nespokoino vreme (1957). *Izbrani tvorbi* (1958). *Lirika: Izbrani stihotvorenija* (1966). *Sgŭstena tisina: stihove* (1973). *Stihotvorenija* (1975). *Izbrani stihove* (1978) in 2 vols. *Poemi* (1982). *Izbrani stihotvorenija* (1982). *Malki pesni* (1923). *Njakoga* (1924, 1971). *Zvŭnčeta* (1925, 1929). *Malkijat dobru'anec* (1927, 1936, 1970). *Mulgalivi geroi* (1931–1940, 1945, 1968, 1980) in 2 vols. *Bjala liulčica* (1933). *Gorskata kustička* (1934, 1954). *Červenoto cvete: Razkazi* (1946). *Za nas malkite* (1967). "Das Tor de Welt." In *Europaische Lyrik der Gegenwart* (1927), p. 217.

Translations: *Depths. Conversation with the Sea*, tr. John Robert Colombo and Nikola Roussanoff (1978).

Bibliography

Dončeva and Sija Atanasova, comp., *Dora Gabe, 1886–1983 Biobibliografski ukazatel* (1985). This is a full bibliography of her works as well as writings on Gabe. Sarandev, Iv., *Kniga za Dora Gabe* (1974).

Philip Shashko

Gabryella

(see: Narcyza Żmichowska)

Madame Gacon-Dufour

Born c. 1762, France
Genre(s): polemical essay, novel
Language(s): French

This very erudite woman, known only as Madame Gacon-Dufour, had many publications to her credit and is among the first women of her time to have taken a frankly feminist stand in her *Mémoire Pour le Sexe Féminin Contre le Sexe Masculin* (1787). In this daring pamphlet, an attack on the chevalier de Feucher who had severely criticized women, Madame Gacon-Dufour asks if the latent and blatant corruption found in eighteenth-century society is not due more to men than to women. In a forceful diatribe, she describes the life of an aristocratic woman, with all the submissiveness involved: "Ce digne Chevalier, qui s'est acharné avec tant de fureur contre nous, qui a eu l'audace de vouloir nous montrer souillées de tous les crimes, qui s'est appliqué de toutes ses forces à justifier toutes ses assertions coupables, par cinq ou six exemples de femmes couvertes de tout le mépris des deux sexes, et qui, afin de faire mieux ressortir ses accusations purement déclamatoires, n'a jamais eu la simple honnêteté de citer une seule de nos vertus, ni même d'en énoncer; ce digne Chevalier penserait-il s'être fait une grande gloire, et avoir bien mérité des hommes eux-mêmes? . . . Tout son sexe ne peut pas être aussi injuste et aussi ridicule que lui" ("This worthy knight, who has spurred so much furor against us, who has had the gall to soil us with all possible crimes and by taking as examples five or six contemptible women scorned by both sexes, has tried in vain to justify his culpable assertions. He never had the decency to cite even one of our virtues, nor did he enumerate any of them. This worthy knight might think perhaps that he covered himself with great glory and that he has thus achieved some dignity among men. . . . [but] all the male gender cannot be as unfair and ridiculous as he is").

Madame Gacon-Dufour was a champion of education for women, publishing in 1807 (Year XIII of the Revolutionary calendar) a volume entitled *De la Nécessité de L'Instruction Pour les Femmes*, on the need of a proper education for women. Also an agronomist, the most famous among her works is her treatise on rural economy. She also wrote several handbooks on the fabrication of assorted soaps and a manual for people living in the country, detailing the chores that had to be handled during the year. These manuals can truly be considered among the first do-it-yourself books, as well as an "encyclopedia" of sciences and arts. Her novel *L'Héroine Moldave* (1818), almost forgotten today, was a lengthy work in three volumes; she also translated from the English a morality novel, entitled *Georgeana*. In collaboration with other women (Mmes de Lavallière, de Montespan, de Fontanges, de Maintenon and other illustrious personalities), she published the *Mémoires, Anecdotes Secrets Galantes, Historiques et Inédites* (1807).

Works

Mémoire Pour le Sexe Féminin Contre le Sexe Masculin (1787, in-12, 50p.). *Recueil Pratique D'Economie Rurale et Domestique* (1804, in-12, 243p.). *De la Nécessité de L'Instruction Pour les Femmes* (1807, in-12, xii-307p.). *Rapport Fait à L'Athénée des Arts Sur les Farines de Pommes de Terre* (s.l., Imp. de C.-F. Patris, s.d., In-8, 8p.). *Manuel de la Mènagére, à la Ville et à la Campagne, et de la Femme de Basse-Cour* (1805, 2 vol. in-12, with portraits and planches). *Manuel complet de la Maitresse de Maison et de la Parfaite Ménagère ou Guide Pratique Pour la Gestion D'Une Maison à la Ville et à la Campagne* (1826, in-12, 262p.). *Manuel du Patissier et de la Patissière, à l'Usage de la Ville et de la Campagne* (1825, in-18, x-288p.). *Manuel Théorique et Pratique du Savonnier, ou l'Art de Faire Toute Sortes de Savons, par une Réunion de Fabricants* (1827, in-18, viii, 272p. with planches).

Bibliography

Michael, Colette, ed., *Les Tracts Féministes en France* (Genève, Paris, Slatkine, 1986). Sullerot, Evelyne, *Histoire de la Presse Féminine des Origines à 1848* (Paris, 1966).

Colette Michael

Emma Gad

Born January 21, 1852, Copenhagen, Denmark; died January 8, 1921, Copenhagen
Genre(s): drama, prose
Language(s): Danish

Although nineteen of Emma Gad's sprightly comedies were published or performed in Denmark between 1886 and 1913, some to resounding success, she has been completely overlooked by the literary and dramatic histories of the period, and remembered only for her rules of etiquette in *Takt og Tone*, a book about everyday life she wrote in her old age.

Emma Gad grew up in a well-to-do home and received what was considered a good education for a woman at the time, including attendance at a girl's school and travel. She married Nicolas Urban Gad in 1872 and had two sons, Henry and Peter. In addition to writing prolifically, Gad was active in numerous literary and women's organizations, and her home played an important role as a meeting place for Copenhagen intellectuals at the turn of the century.

Emma Gad's greatest dramatic success was *Et Sølvbryllup* (A Silver Wedding), which opened at the Dagmar Theater in Copenhagen on July 2, 1890, after having been refused by the Royal Theater as immoral and boring. The public loved it, however, and it continued to be performed throughout Denmark in the years to come: during the year 1900 alone, it was presented 147 times.

This comedy opens on the day of the Selbys' silver wedding anniversary with Mr. Selby telling a fib about a bump he got on his head the night before while on a secret outing with his friend the family doctor. When the truth comes out, his sister-in-law persuades his wife to leave home. A subplot deals with the secret engagement of the Selbys' daughter to the doctor's son, who is reputed to have already ruined a woman. Thus the play contributed to the "double-standard debate" that raged throughout Scandinavia in the late nineteenth century. Gad found this subject an excellent source of humor, using it in a number of other plays, including *En Advarsel* (1890; A Warning), *Den mystiske Arv* (1906; The Mysterious Inheritance) and *Et Forspil* (1894; A

Prelude). Her wit and satire spared no one, male nor female.

Gad's plays appear to have been completely forgotten until Pil Dahlerup unearthed them from archives for her study in *Det moderne gennembruds kvinder* (1983; Women of the Modern Breakthrough). Dahlerup makes a good case for their reevaluation, considering Gad's valorization of self-respect and good humor more significant than the rules of behavior for which Gad has become renowned. Gad's wit provides a welcome contrast to her turn-of-the-century contemporaries, with whom she nevertheless shared a pessimistic view of human nature.

Works

Aabent Visir [Open Visor] (1898). *En Advarsel* [A Warning] (1890). *Et Aftenbesøg* [An Evening Visit] (1886). *Barnets Ret* [The Child's Right] (1911). *Dydens belønning* [The Rewards of Virtue] (1900). *Det forløsende Ord* [The Right Expression] (1900). *Et Forspil* [A Prelude] (1894). *Fruens Politik* [The Wife's Politics] (1909). *Fælles Sag* [Interests in Common] (1889). *Gadens Børn* [Children of the Street] (1903). *Guldfuglen* [The Golden Bird] (1908). *Haandarbejdsbøgen* [Needlework Manual] (1910). *I Rosentiden* [In the Season of Roses] (1895). *I veldædigt Øjemed* [With Charitable Purpose] (1891). *Man skal altid* [One Should Always] (1886). *Den mystiske Arv* [The Mysterious Inheritance] (1906). *Rørt Vande* [Stirred-up Waters] (1895). *Et Stridspunkt* [A Matter in Dispute] (1888). *Et Sølvbryllup* [A Silver Wedding] (1890). *Takt og Tone* [Tact and Tone] (1918). *Tro som Guld* [True as Gold] (1983). *Ægtestand. Med Forspillet De unge Drømme* [Matrimony. With the prelude "The Young Dreams"] (1913).

Bibliography

Dahlerup, Pil, *Det moderne gennembruds kvinder* (Copenhagen, 1983). This book is an important study of 70 women writers who flourished during the 1870s and 1880s in Denmark, a period termed "the modern breakthrough" by the critic Georg Brandes. Dahlerup provides much critical and biographical information previously unavailable or hard to find.

Kristine Anderson

Marie-Louise Gagneur

Born 1832, Domblans (Jura), France; died 1902
Genre(s): novel, essay, polemic
Language(s): French

The novels of Marie-Louise Gagneur were well-known to the mid-nineteenth-century French public, but biographical details (especially concerning her later life) are difficult to locate. In 1856 or 1857 she married Wladimir Gagneur, a veteran of the 1848 Revolution who had helped organize the resistance to Louis Napoleon's 1852 *coup d'état* and had subsequently been deported to Cayenne. After his return to France he established himself as a gentleman farmer in the Jura. The couple had one daughter, Marguerite (1857–1945), who became known as a sculptor under the name "Syamour." With the advent of the Third Republic Wladimir was elected deputy for the Jura, serving from 1871 to 1889.

Marie-Louise Gagneur authored a number of novels, many of which first appeared in serial form in *Le Siècle*. Her writings manifested sharply anticlerical and socialist views as well as strong support for the emancipation of women. Her novel, *La Croisade noire* (1866), inspired by personal recollections of convent life as a schoolgirl, established her literary reputation.

Works (selected)

Le Calvaire des femmes (1863). *La Croisade noire* (1866). *Les Reprouvées; suite et fin du "Calvaire des femmes"* (1867). *Les Forçats du mariage* (1869). *Chair à canon* (1872). *Le Divorce* (1872). *Les Crimes de l'amour* (1874). *La Politique au village* (1874). *Les Droits du mari* (1876). *Les Vierges russes* (1880). *Le Supplice de l'amant* (1888).
Translations: *Qvinnornas Martyrskap. Social roman* (1868). *Poshechnoe miaso* (1873). *A Nihilist Princess* (1881).

Bibliography

Wartelle, Jean-Claude, "Une famille d'intellectuels de gauche au 19ᵉᵐᵉ siècle: Les Gagneur." Thesis, 1981. Typescript at Bibliothèque Marguerite Durand: Paris.

Karen Offen

Erzsébet Galgóczi

Born August 27, 1930, Ménfőcsanák,
   Hungary; died May 20, 1989,
   Ménfőcsanák
Genre(s): novel, short story
Language(s): Hungarian

Galgóczi was educated in Győr and later studied at the Drama Academy. She began her career as a writer for the periodicals *Szabad Ifjúság* and *Művelt Nép*. In 1950 she won a DISZ prize (Young Workers' Association), and in 1957 she became a writer for the Budapest Filmstudio. Since 1959 she has supported herself by writing.

Galgóczi comes from peasant stock, and it is probably this class that she examines most often. In the stories "Egy kosár hazai" (1953; A Basket from Home), "Ott is csak hó van" (1961; There Is Only Snow There Also), and the novel *Félúton* (1961; Halfway) she writes of the great changes that have come about in the life of the peasants since World War II. She has a good feel for her subject and knows the dramatic value in the transitional state she studies. *Öt lépcső felfelé* (1965; Five Steps Up) and *Fiú a kastélyból* (1968; Boy from the Castle) show her literary talents. She is generally regarded as one of the newer writers; she was among those who wrote openly and sincerely even in the mid-1950s, and her works probe human and social problems. Often the conflicts she presents are insoluble, as are the problems and contradictions of society. In her dramas and TV scripts she also examines moral conflicts in society, for example, in *A főügyész felesége* (The Wife of the Attorney General) and *Mérföldkövek* (Milestones).

The greater upward mobility of the Transdanubian peasants in her native region is not without conflicts, and it is these conflicts that provide the theme for her more recent collections of stories. *Kinek a törvénye?* (1971; Whose Law?), *Bizonyíték nincs* (1976; There Is No Proof), and *Közel a kés* (1978; The Knife Is Near) examine moral and ethical problems. In these stories she also moves toward the expression of her own experiences in a universal mode, expanding her view greatly. The problems facing the transformation of the Hungarian village from a simple rural setting to a milieu that is almost urban, one where the values and morals of the city affect all aspects of life, are among her topics. Here she confronts universal problems; only the locale is individualized. *Törvényen kívül és belül* (1980; Outside and Inside the Law) is a masterful blend of a personal and lyrical style with a precise narrative method. This is the hallmark of her art.

Works

Egy kosár hazai (1953). *Ott is csak hó van* (1961). *Félúton* (1961). *Öt lépcső felfelé* (1965). *Fiú a kastélyból* (1968). *Mérföldkövek. Kinek a törvénye* (tales, 1971). *Bizonyíték nincs* (1976). *Közel a kés* (1978). *Pókháló* [Spiderweb], tales (1972). *A Közös bűn* [The Shared Sin] (1976). *A Törvényen kívül és belül* (1980). *Vidravas* [Otter-trap] (1982). **Collected tales:** *Inkább fájjon* [Let it Hurt] (1969). *A Vesztes nem te vagy* (1976). **Novellas:** *Ez a hét még nehéz lesz* [This Week Will be Hard] (1981). *Kegyetlen sugarak* [Merciless Rays] (1966). *Nádtetős socializmus* [Thatched-Roof Socialism] (1970). **Dramatic pieces:** *A főügyész felesége* (1974). *Úszó jégtáblák* [Swimming Icefloes] (1974).

Bibliography

Alexa, Károly, "G.E. *Közel a kés.*" *Kortárs* 12 (1978): 1996–1998. Bór, Amburs, "Galcóczi Erzsébetről." *Film, Szinháa, Muzsika* (1978): 13–15. Galsai, Pongrác, "G.E." *12 a 1 fő.* Budapest, 1978, pp. 55–69. Gárdonyi, Béla, "Nekunk ír, értük ír, beszélgetés G.E.-tel." *Műhely* 1 (1979): 8–16. Kovács, Sándor Iván, "A Jelentől a multig, G.E. pályaképe." *Jelenlévő mult* (Budapest, 1978), pp. 283–300. Széles, Klára, "G.E.-rol." *Kortárs* 4 (1978): 635–643. Vasy, Géza, "Pályatükör egy kisregényben." *Tiszatáj* 3 (1978): 55–61.

Enikő Molnár Basa

Celeste Galilei

Born August 13, 1600, Padua, Italy; died April
   2, 1634, Arcetri
Genre(s): letters
Language(s): Italian

Celeste was born out of wedlock from a relation that Galileo Galilei had with Marina Gamba during his Paduan years. When their parents separated, Celeste and her sister Livia were sent to Florence and there entrusted to the convent of the Nunziatina. Overburdened with the support of his family and often of his pupils, Galileo chose to make nuns of his daughters and applied for special permission to do so before their prescribed age. Celeste took the veil in 1616 and spent the rest of her short life as a sister of the order of Saint Claire in the convent of San Matteo at Arcetri, near Florence.

Celeste's 124 letters to her father were written between May 10, 1623, and December 10, 1633. Some dealt with domestic matters of the Galilei family or with the administration of the convent; many accompanied the exchange of household objects, foodstuffs, and wines. Continuous was the flow of gifts that Galileo sent to his daughters and of supplies he provided to the convent apothecary and pastry shop. In return, Celeste sent special confections prepared by her and other nuns, did sewing or copied manuscripts for him. What is immediately evident from the correspondence is the close and affectionate relationship between father and daughter, their common delight in small pleasures, and their observation of human nature and natural objects. Sister Celeste draws clear and graceful pictures of events occurring in San Matteo and gives straightforward accounts of discomforts, disease, and madness. Most touching are her repeated appeals for money, so that she may pay for a cell of her own and be free of the harassment of a deranged nun. Her amazingly sweet nature allows her to describe situations and people with inner dimension, unbiased by resentment, although she openly refers to the convent as her "narrow prison." Of the relation to her neurotic and self-centered sister she writes: "As Sister Arcangela has a nature very different from mine and rather an extravagant one, it is to my good to surrender in many things in order to live in that peace and union required by the deep affection we feel for each other."

From the correspondence we gather that Galileo informed his daughter of the important events of his life and that she provided him with much needed love and support. It is generally surmised that she was too naive to realize the gravity of Galileo's misfortune or that she did not refer to his condemnation directly out of caution. In one of her letters, however, she councils him to accept his fate—as indeed, she had accepted hers—and she offers to carry out, in his place, the daily penance the Holy Office had imposed on him.

Beside their historical value pertaining to the scientist's family relationships, Celeste's letters are to be admired for their own merits. They give a vivid view of what life was like in a seventeenth-century convent and how people outside, as well as inside, went about their daily occupations. They are also charmingly written in a style that is free of the rhetorical exuberance and obscurity that marred much of contemporary prose. They give the portrait of a writer who—in the words of her bereaved father—was "a woman of exquisite intelligence and of uncommon goodness."

Works
Favaro, A., ed., *Galileo Galilei e Suor Maria Celeste* (1935).

Bibliography
Costa-Zalessow, N., *Scrittrici italiane dal XIII al XX secolo* (Ravenna, 1982), pp. 135–138. D'Ancona, A. and Bacci, O., *Manuale della letteratura italiana*, III (Florence, 1919), pp. 324, 341–342. De Blasi, J., *Antologia delle scrittrici italiane dalle origini al 1800*, I (Florence, 1930), pp. 232–440. Petzonio, G., *Dizionario enciclopedico della letteratura italiana*, III (Palermo, 1966–1970), p. 23.

Rinaldina Russell

Lada Galina

(see: Ganka Slavova Karanfilova)

Beatriz Galindo

(a.k.a. La Latina, M. Francisco Ramírez de Madrid)

Born 1475, Salamanca, Spain; died 1534, Madrid
Genre(s): treatise, poetry
Language(s): Spanish

A Spanish humanist of excellent education, Beatriz Galindo acquired an uncommon knowledge of the Latin language and the classics. Although it was her parents' desire that she enter the cloisters, Beatriz dedicated herself to study rather than follow the religious life. Beatriz served as Latin tutor to Queen Isabel, who rewarded the young woman's virtue and discretion with the distinction of naming her personal advisor and maid of honor. The growing influence of humanism in Spain had inspired Queen Isabel with the desire to learn Latin and to have all her children study it. Beatriz is best known for her teaching, which contributed to the diffusion of the Latin language and the classics among the royalty at the Castilian Court.

After the death of her husband, Francisco Ramírez de Madrid, known as *el Artillero* for his valor in the wars of Granada, Beatriz retired from the court and dedicated herself to a life of charitable work. She funded the construction of the Hospital of the Conception, later renamed La Latina, and founded the Convent of Conception Jerónima where she and her husband were buried.

The culture of this erudite woman bears witness to the pursuit of humanist education in those select families of good formation. The citation and praise of Beatriz by Nicolás Antonio in his *Gynecaeum Hispaniae Minervae* confirms that her preceptorship at the Spanish court left a mark more enduring than either the treatises or poetry attributed to her.

Works

Comentarios a Aristóteles y notas sabios sobre los antiguos. Poesías latinas.

Bibliography

Llanos y Torriglia, F. de, *Una consejera de estado: doña Beatriz Galindo, "la Latina"* (Madrid, 1925). Menéndez Pelayo, M., *Antología de poetas líricos castellanos*, III (Madrid, 1944), pp. 22, 34, 114–116. Ximénez de Sandoval, F., *Varia historia de ilustres mujeres* (Madrid, 1949).

Joan Cammarata

Beatriz Galindo

(see: Isabel de Palencia)

Eulalia Galvarriato

Born 1905, Madrid, Spain
Genre(s): short story, novel, essay, criticism
Language(s): Spanish

Galvarriato, a highly cultured woman, has lived most of her life in Madrid in close contact with literati and scholars due to her marriage to poet-critic Dámaso Alonso (for many years the President of the Royal Spanish Academy, one of the most prestigious positions in Spain's world of letters). During some forty years or more, Galvarriato assisted Alonso in his scholarly investigations, served as his librarian, and helped with editing tasks, which may explain the relative paucity of her literary production.

Galvarriato was a finalist for the 1946 Nadal Prize with her lyrical novel *Cinco sombras* (1947; Five Shadows), much admired by critics of that day. The situation depicted should interest feminist critics: the five "shadows," daughters of a domineering, possessive patriarch, are essentially imprisoned when their despotic father turns recluse following the death of his wife. The only male allowed to visit the house—the son of an old friend—narrates the retrospective evocation of happenings in the late nineteenth and early twentieth centuries as the parent's dictatorial tyranny frustrates the loves and potential marriages of the older daughters one by one. When the older four conspire to facilitate the elopement of the fifth, the father retaliates by incarcerating them for months. Confined to their rooms, not permitted even to speak to each other, they offer not the slightest protest. As the sisters die one by one, only shadows remain in the sitting-room around the sewing box which was the focus of their lives. Galvarriato's portrayal of these five women—once vibrant, beautiful girls reduced to muted shadows by paternalistic dictatorship—comes across as a feminist protest in spite of itself.

Galvarriato has also written a number of highly regarded short stories and recently published a collection including brief fiction, lyric essays, and prose poems, entitled *Raíces bajo el tiempo* (1986; Roots Beneath Time). Many of the short stories are penetrating brief analyses of adolescent psychology, while others focus on children (the youngest narrative consciousness is perhaps three years old). None of the incidents involve unusual or significant happenings; instead, the stories concentrate upon minutiae, the trivia of monotonous everyday existence, elucidating the significance of the seemingly insignificant, the hidden meaning of what appears meaningless, the reasons for the seemingly irrational. Essay-like compositions include tender memories, autobiographical evocations of long-forgotten friends, mystic moments in the inner life of an introverted dreamer.

Works

Cinco sombras (1947). *Raíces bajo el tiempo* (1986).

Janet Perez

María Rosa Gálvez

Born 1768, Málaga, Spain; died October 2, 1806, Madrid
Genre(s): poetry, drama, translation
Language(s): Spanish

Women writers were not a rarity in the "enlightened" days of the eighteenth century in Spain. Adoptive daughter of a distinguished family in Malaga, María Rosa Gálvez showed her literary talents early. After marrying Cpt. José Cabrera y Ramirez, the couple moved to Madrid, where Gálvez joined the social and intellectual circles of that city. She strived to create a national drama within the parameters of French Neoclassicism, and her work was praised by contemporaries, among them the poet Manuel José Quintana. She enjoyed the protection of Manuel Godoy, favorite of King Charles IV, and under his auspices her works were printed with public funds, alleging that they were meritorious of such treatment since they were the first dramatic works published by a woman.

Godoy's protection earned Gálvez many enemies, and when the political climate changed, the praises turned into attacks and even her morals were brought into question. Nineteenth-century Romanticism, repudiating the "Frenchified" style of the Neoclassics, disregarded most of the drama written in that period as worthless. Gálvez's work, which had suffered in her time for being "too violent," was now considered "too formal," and the critics' comments

reflected only the negative opinions they had read after Gálvez' death.

Her work, especially her tragedies, is truly one of the earliest bridges between the Neoclassic and the Romantic periods in Spain. The themes of freedom, individuality, and doomed love prevail throughout her compositions, together with colorful setting and lots of action. One factor that distinguishes Gálvez' work from other pre-Romantic production is that many of her heroes are strong, decisive women. Titles like *Zinda*, *La delirante* (The Delirious), *Blanca de Rossi*, *Florinda*, and *Safo* bear witness to this. She also wrote a comedy, *Un loco hace ciento*, defending the rights of young women in the late eighteenth century.

Of all the women writing at this time, and there were many, not one, including Gálvez, has survived the critics' disdain, an undeserved fate since many less talented and influential male writers are still anthologized or at least mentioned in a positive way in texts and manuals.

Works

Ali-Bek (1801). In *El nuevo teatro español* [New Spanish Theater], vol. 52. *Catalina o la bella labradora* [Catalina or the Beautiful Farmer] (1801). *Un loco hace ciento* [One Madman is Worth a Hundred] (1801) In *El Nuevo teatro español*, Vol. 52. *Obras poéticas* [Poetic Works] (1804).

Bibliography

Blanco García, Padre Francisco, *La literatura española del siglo XIX* [Nineteenth Century Spanish Literature] (Madrid, 1899). Galerstein, Carolyn L., ed., *Women Writers of Spain* (New York, 1986). Jimenez, Pedraza, Felipe y Milagros Rodríguez Cáceres *Manual de literatura española* [Manual of Spanish Literature], Siglo XVIII (Navarra, 1982). Ruiz, Ramon, *Historia del teatro español* [History of the Spanish Theater], I (Madrid, 1967). Serrano y Sanz, Manuel, *Apuntes para una biblioteca de escritoras españolas* [Notes for a Library of Spanish Women Writers from 1401 to 1833]. Biblioteca de autores españoles, Vol. 269 (1903; rpt. Madrid, 1975).

Lina L. Cofresí

Jeanne Galzy

*Born 1883, Montpellier, France; died May 7,
1977, Montpellier*
*Genre(s): novel, biography, poetry, drama,
journalism*
Language(s): French

Jeanne Galzy had an unusually long literary
career, beginning as a poet but devoting herself
primarily to the novel and, to a lesser degree, to
biography. Traditional in style and form, her
novels give a sensitive portrayal of human beings,
usually women, under the stress of solitude,
alienation, or suffering. Many are set in her native
region.

Born in Montpellier in 1883, Jeanne Galzy
was an outstanding student at the Lycée de
Montpellier and, unusual for a girl at that time,
was permitted to audit courses at the Faculty of
Letters in that city's university. Encouraged by a
Professor Gachon, she went to Paris to complete
her studies and to prepare for a teaching career.
After a further *lycée* year in Paris, she won admission to the Ecole Normale Supérieure at
Sèvres, transferred to the Sorbonne for course
work, and ultimately obtained the *agrégation* in
literature. She taught at the Lycée Lamartine in
Paris and then at the Lycée de Montpellier (out of
her teaching experience at a *lycée* for boys was to
come her second novel, *La Femme chez les
garçons* [Women among Boys]; later, in *Jeunes
Filles en serre chaude* [Girls in a Hothouse], she
dealt with education for girls). Her literary career,
however, had begun while she was still in Paris:
from 1910 on, she contributed both poetry—her
first love—and prose to important reviews such
as *Le Mercure de France, La Grande Revue,* and
La Nouvelle Revue Française. Alfred Vallette,
editor of the *Mercure,* soon steered her toward
prose fiction; her first novel, *L'Ensevelie* (The
Buried Woman), appeared in 1912. She began to
attract serious attention with her next novel, the
above-mentioned *La Femme chez les garçons*
(1919) and received the Prix Fémina for her next,
Les Allongés (1923; The Bed-Ridden), inspired
by a long convalescence from Pott's Disease
spent in the hospital at Berck-sur-Mer. Settling in
Montpellier, she produced novels at regular intervals for the rest of her life; after 1927, she
produced a half-dozen biographies, mostly of
women. In 1940 she was elected a member of the
jury for the Prix Fémina. Throughout her literary
career, she contributed to a number of literary
reviews (notably, the *Revue Hebdomadaire, Les
Nouvelles Littéraires,* and *Les Ecrits Nouveaux,*
in addition to those already mentioned), and,
after 1932, to the newspaper *L'Intransigeant.*
When she was well past eighty, she embarked on
a novelistic saga, of which she completed four
volumes under the general title of the first volume
in the series *La Surprise de vivre* (The Surprise of
Being Alive).

Although she never became a literary sensation, Jeanne Galzy produced a large body of
finely-wrought, serious fiction that won respect
from many critics. Influenced by Edouard
Estaunié, combining features inherited from the
French Classical tradition with Romantic and
Realistic elements, she explored the psychology
of souls under pressure, especially those of
women, and sought to reveal "the secret life of
things." Especially in her crowning work, *La
Surprise de vivre* (1969–1976), she depicted the
world of upper-class Protestants in and around
her native Montpellier.

Works

L'Ensevelie (1912). *La Femme chez les garçons*
(1919). *Les Allongés* (1923). *Perséphone,* légende
antique en trois parties avec des danses (1924). *La
Grand'Rue* (1925). *Le Retour dans la vie* (1926).
Sainte Thérèse d'Avila (1927). *L'Initiatrice aux
mains vides* (1929). *Les Démons de la solitude*
(1931). *Jeunes Filles en serre chaude* (1934). *Le
Village rêve* (1935). *Catherine de Médicis* (1936).
Margot, reine sans royaume (1939). *Les Oiseaux
des îles* (1941). *Pays perdu* (1943). *Diane de Ganges*
(1945). *La Cage de fer* (1946). *La Vie intime d'André
Chénier* (1947). *Le Dieu terrible* (1949). *La Femme
étrangère* (1950). *George Sand* (1950). *La Jeunesse
déchirée* (1952). *L'Image* (1953). *Le Parfum de
l'oeillet* (1956). *Celle qui vient d'ailleurs* (1958). *La
Fille* (1961). *Agrippa d'Aubigné* (1965). *La Surprise de vivre* (1969). *Les Sources vives* (1971). *La
Cavalière* (1974). *Le Rossignol aveugle* (1976).

Translations into English: *Burnt Offering*
[*L'Initiatrice aux mains vides.*], tr. Jacques Le Clerc
(1930).

Bibliography

Florenne, Yves, "Membre du jury Fémina, Jeanne Galzy est morte." *Le Monde (des Livres)* (May 10, 1977): 30.

General references: Morelle, Paul, "Jeanne Galzy." *Encyclopaedia Universalis: Universalia: 1977*(Paris, 1978), p. 592. Morembert, T. de, "Galzy, Jeanne." *Dictionnaire de biographie française*, ed. Roman d'Amat and P. Limouzin-Lamothe (Paris, 1982), Vol. XV, pp. 284–285. Pascal, Claire, *Portraits d'écrivains*, première série (Paris, 1979), pp. 35–41.

James S. Patty

Veronica Gambara

Born November 30, 1485, Pratalboino, Italy;
died June 1550, Correggio, Italy
Genre(s): lyric poetry, letters
Language(s): Italian, Latin

Daughter of Count Gianfrancesco da Gambara and Alda Pia, Gambara was a poet and patron of the early sixteenth century. She ruled the small territory of Correggio and presided over a flourishing court where poets, courtiers, and dignitaries gathered. She wrote poetry in the Petrarchist manner of her friend Pietro Bembo, as well as numerous letters. Her friends were prominent political and literary figures of the day.

Gambara was born on November 30, 1485, on her family's estates in Pratalboino, near Brescia. Born into a noble and well-connected family, she received a thorough humanistic education that included studies in Greek and Latin, philosophy, Scripture, and theology. In 1502 she began correspondence with Pietro Bembo, who was the reigning literary figure of the century and the leader of a resurgence of Petrarchism. He became her poetic mentor, and they remained friends until his death in 1547. In 1509 Gambara was married to Count Giberto X, lord of Correggio. Their small court became a fashionable salon for the cultured nobility. Among her guests were Pietro Arentino and Isabella d'Este. As a patron she encouraged the development of the painter Antonio Allegri, known as Corregio. On August 26, 1518, Giberto died, and Gambara was plunged into bitter mourning. She continued to rule Correggio herself and to write poetry. Gambara numbered among her friends the Emperor Charles V, King Francis I of France, Pope Leo X, and numerous cardinals and princes. In 1530, Gambara attended the coronation of the Emperor in Bologna. Both the Emperor and the king of France visited her in Correggio. She died in June of 1550, in Correggio.

Gambara's writings consist of some 50 poems and over 130 letters. The poems are mostly sonnets, but she employs other forms including the madrigal, the ballad, and *stanze* in ottava rima. Her poetry includes several love poems to her husband in the Petrarchan manner, poems on political issues, devotional poems, and Virgilian poems in praise of the countryside of Brescia and Correggio. Many of her poems are addressed to political figures she knew (Emperor Charles V, Francis I, Pope Paul III), exhorting them to stop fighting wars and to make peace. She also addressed poems to other literary figures, such as Pietro Bembo and Vittoria Colonna. Her love poems are generally more interesting. Written to her husband Giberto, they are full of Virgilian and Petrarchan echoes. She employs the Petrarchan terminology formalized by Bembo, and because her poetry adheres closely to Bembo's doctrine of imitation, it often seems overly refined and artificial. Her letters are addressed to her friends, among them Pietro Bembo, the Marchese del Vasto, and Isabella d'Este. Some are familiar and affectionate, others are formal and conventional. Gambara's poetry was circulated privately, and some poems appeared in sixteenth-century anthologies. The first collected edition of her writings (Rizzardi's) appeared in 1759.

Gambara is a good example of the Italian Renaissance woman. She acted as governor, patron, writer, wife and mother. She approached writing casually and probably did not think of herself as a writer by vocation. Her court at Correggio was famous and influential. She is considered to be one of the three foremost women poets of sixteenth century Italy, along with Vittoria Colonna and Gaspara Stampa.

Works

Amadduzzi, Luigi, ed., *Undici Lettere inedite di Veronica Gambara e un'ode latina tradotta in volgare* (Guastalla, 1889). Chiappetti, Pia Mestica, ed.,

Rime e lettere (Florence, 1879). Costa, E., ed., *Sonetti amorosi inediti e rari* (Parma, 1890). Rampini, A.L., ed., *Sonetti inediti* (Padua, 1845). Rizzardi, Felice, ed., *Rime e lettere* (Brescia, 1759). Salza, A., ed., *Rime inedite e rare di Veronica Gambara* (Ciriè, 1915).

Bibliography

de Courten, Clementina, *Veronica Gambara: Una Gentildonna del Cinquecento* (Milan, 1934). Finzi, Riccardo, *Umanità di Veronica Gambara* (Reggio Emilia, 1969). Jerrold, Maud F., *Vittoria Colonna* (New York, 1969). Venturi, Adolfo, *Storia dell'arte italiana: la pittura del cinquecento* Vol. 9 (Milan, 1926), pp. 2, 470.

General references: Cecchi, E., and Sapegno, N., *Storia della Letterature Italiana*, Vol. 4: *Il Cinquecento* (Milan, 1974), pp. 241–258. Tiraboschi, Girolamo, *Storia della Letteratura Italiana*, vol. 7, pt. 3 (Milan, 1824), pp. 1722–1725. *Enciclopedia Italiana di Scienze, Lettere ed Arti,* vol. XVI (Rome, 1950), pp. 352–353.

Richard Poss

Elena Gan (Hahn)

(a.k.a. Zenaida R-va)

Born 1814; died June 2, 1842, Odessa, Russia
Genre(s): short story
Language(s): Russian

Elena Gan ("Zenaida R-va"), Nadezhda Durova and Maria Zhukova all played a role in the last gasp of Russian Romantic fiction in the late 1830s. Gan wrote under the sign of George Sand, publishing a series of stories in which the dramatic fates of her idealistic protagonists are played out against a crude and uncomprehending society.

Gan was the middle link in a family that produced three generations of remarkable women. Her mother, Elena Fadeeva (1788–1860), a person of wide-ranging intellectual interests, was a recognized botanist. Gan's two daughters both had careers in letters: Elena Blavatskaia (1831–1891) is internationally famed as the brilliant and eccentric cofounder of the Theosophist Society, and Vera Zhelikhovskaia (1835–1896) wrote popular fiction, plays, and children's fiction in Russian. Gan's brother,

General Rostislav Fadeev (1824–1883), was a political publicist, historian, and writer on military topics.

Gan's twelve years of marriage to a captain of horse artillery were productive of more than literature. Four children were born, but her elder son died while she moved with her husband from post to post in southern Russia and the Ukraine. An all-too-brief posting to St. Petersburg introduced her into literary circles in 1835, and her last seven years were spent in a fever of writing and, perhaps not coincidentally, in steadily declining health. In "Sud sveta" (1840; Society's Judgment), Gan described bitterly the philistine reactions of her fellow military wives to the strange woman writer in their midst. She spent increasingly long periods of refuge with her parents in Odessa, Astrakhan, and the Caucasus.

Her constant travels furnished Gan with subject matter, characters, and setting. In "Utballa" (1838), the eponymous half-Kalmyk heroine spends a week of bliss with her Russian lover and sends him away, knowing that her savage tribe will condemn her to burial alive for her sin. In "Dzhellaledin" (1838), Gan's one historical tale (set in the reign of Catherine the Great), a Crimean Tatar prince is destroyed by his love for a frivolous Russian woman. Gan and the poet Mikhail Lermontov were both born in 1814, and Lermontov died only one year before his female colleague. In his novel, *A Hero of Our Time*, Lermontov created the figure of the bored, manipulating Pechorin—a character seemingly destined to victimize Gan's heroines like the high-minded provincial lady of "An Ideal" who worships a poet's works from afar but finds the man less than admirable in person. Like Lermontov's late prose, Gan's last stories offer a tantalizing glimpse of a maturing art. While she never outgrew the canons of Romanticism, she began to express a broader range of themes. There is a new element of social pathos in her late works: "Sud sveta," "Teofaniia Abbiadzhio," and "Naprasnyi dar" (A Vain Gift). The first episode of the two tales linked under the last title was loosely based on the actual fate of Elizaveta Kul'man (1808–1825), a Russian girl with great poetic talent who was put through intellectual paces and denied free lyric expression by a rigid

German tutor. Gan's brief life was at least a full and creative expression of her talents and concerns.

Works

Sochineniia, 4 vols. (1843). *Polnoe sobranie sochinenii*, 6 vols. (1905).

Bibliography

Belinsky, Vissarion, "Sochineniia Zeneidy R-voi." *Polnoe sobranie sochinenii*, vol. 7 (Moscow, 1955), pp. 648–678. "M.G." [Gershenzon], "Materialy po istorii russkoi literatury i kul'tury: Russkaia zhenshchina 30kh godov." *Russkaia Mysl'* 12 (1911): 54–73. Golitsyn, N.N., *Bibliograficheskii slovar' russkikh pisatel'nits* (St. Petersburg, 1889; Leipzig, 1974), pp. 61–62. *Istoriia russkoi literatury XIX v.*: Bibliograficheskii ukazatel', K.D. Muratova, ed. (Moscow-Leningrad, 1962), p. 197. Nekrasova, E.S., "Elena Andreevna Gan (Zeneida R-va) 1814–1842: Biograficheskii ocherk" *Russkaia Starina* (1886), 8, pp. 335–354; 9, pp. 553–574. Nielsen, Marit Bjerkung, "The Concept of Love and the Conflict of the Individual vs. Society in Elena A. Gan's *Sud sveta*." *ScandoSlavica* 24 (1978): 125–138. *Russkii biograficheskii slovar'*, vol. 4 (St. Petersburg, 1914), pp. 222–226 (V. Baturinsky). Zhelikhovskaia, V. P., "Elena Andr. Gan: Pisatel'nitsa-romanistka v 1835–42 gg." *Russkaia Starina* 3 (1887): 733–766.

Mary F. Zirin

Hrotsvit of Gandersheim

(name rendered as: Hrotsvit, Hrotsvita, Hrosvita, Hroswitha, Roswitha, Rotsuith)

Born ca. 935, Saxony(?); died after 973, Gandersheim(?), Saxony
Genre(s): drama, narrative poetry (legends of saints, historical epic, verse chronicle)
Language(s): Latin

Hrotsvit, a canoness of the abbey of Gandersheim near Hildesheim in Saxony, composed medieval Latin verse in several genres. She is best known, however, as the author of six Latin plays on Christian themes, written in rhyming prose. Her unusual name, by her own witty testimony, signifies *Clamor Validus Gandeshemensis*: the Great Shout, or Loud Noise, of Gandersheim. She lived in Saxony in the middle of the tenth century, in the convent founded by and for the family of the Holy Roman Emperor Otto the Great; the dates of her birth and death are uncertain and must be inferred from what she herself says in her writings. She was rather older than her friend, teacher, and abbess, the Ottonian princess Gerberga, who was born in 940; she lived at least until the accession of the Emperor Otto II in 973. She was most probably of noble blood and was known personally to the royal family, under whom the culture of Germany and of western Europe in general attained sufficient sophistication to have earned from modern historians the title of "Ottonian Renaissance." Hrotsvit, with her firm grounding in classical Latin learning and literature and her strongly Christian subject matter, stands forth as an important representative of her culture and her time. In the history of drama she is more important still: the first known dramatist of modern times and the first known woman dramatist of any time.

The works of Hrotsvit are contained chiefly in a manuscript, now at Munich, found in 1493 at the monastery of St. Emmeram by the German humanist Conrad Celtes. It consists of two books of verse and prose arranged apparently in order of composition, with a short verse "coda" plus an epic poem. Book I contains seven legends of saints written in Latin hexameters and based on the Bible and the Apocrypha, on the lives of the saints, and on contemporary reports, with a preface in rhyming prose by the author and a dedication to the Abbess Gerberga. Book II begins with a brief comment on the sources of the legends, followed by a second prose preface which sets forth Hrotsvit's purpose in writing her six plays. She writes, she professes, in response to a dismaying tendency among her coreligionists to immerse themselves in the pagan seductions of the Roman playwright, Terence; she undertakes to provide an antidote to Terence's six comedies of lascivious women with six edifying tales of Christian virgins. There follows a letter of dedication to certain unnamed patrons, and then the plays themselves, which, despite their Terentian form and inspiration, are based on hagiographical sources. Both the plays and the legends seem to have been put together according to a single overriding purpose, as a cycle of works on related themes: perpetual and triumphant virginity above all, and with it Christian heroism and the mercy and justice of God. The legends deal for the most part with the exploits of holy men, the plays avowedly with those of holy women. The latter were probably not performed in Hrotsvit's own time, unless perhaps in the form of dramatic readings; there is considerable debate as to whether Hrotsvit was in fact aware of the true nature of Roman drama. Hrotsvit's own plays are, however, highly performable, and have been performed successfully on the modern stage.

At the end of the final play, *Sapientia*, stand thirty-five Latin hexameters on the subject of the Apocalypse of John, followed by a third prose preface and a pair of verse prologues to the 1500-odd lines of the *Gesta Ottonis*, "The Deeds of Otto the Great." This epic poem is, as Hrotsvit attests, the earliest comprehensive account of the first Saxon ruler to claim the throne and the title of Charlemagne.

In addition to the works collected in the St. Emmeram manuscript, Hrotsvit is also known to have composed a verse chronicle of the early years of her own monastery: *Primordia Coenobii Gandeshemensis*, "The Origins of the Convent at Gandersheim." The manuscript of the *Primordia* is no longer extant but must be reconstructed from early printed editions. The text itself is accepted by scholars as Hrotsvit's last known work; it refers to the fire which destroyed the abbey's church in 970 and to the reign of the Emperor Otto II (973–983).

Hrotsvit's position in the history of literature is assured by the simple fact of her having written plays. These plays are not, and are not intended to be, the equal of their Terentian models in style, substance, or literary excellence. They are, however, both witty and erudite, with a genuine gift for dialogue and drama. She is less gifted as a poet. Her *Primordia* is a fairly standard representative of its kind. Her legends are remarkable chiefly for the ways in which she chooses and adapts her sources. Her *Gesta Ottonis* is notable less for the virtuosity of its verse than for the fact that it is, and professes to be, an original composition based on the reports of eyewitnesses, as she had done earlier in composing the legend of St. Pelagius. This is the essence of Hrotsvit's not inconsiderable literary talent. She effectively reinvented classical drama in Christian form and substance at a time when the genre itself had ceased to exist. In the great age of reliance upon one's *auctores*, one's august predecessors, she made use of eyewitness accounts in original compositions. She was, moreover, a woman displaying a broad and conscious erudition in a patriarchal age: a fact of which she was very well aware, and which she expressed in the prefaces to her literary works with great and wicked wit, in the conventional phrases of Christian, and feminine, humility.

Works

Legends (ca. 962): *Historia nativitatis laudabilisque conversationis intactae Dei Genitricis* (Maria) [The History of the Nativity and the Praiseworthy Life of the Virgin Mother of God]. *De ascensione Domini* (Ascensio) [The Ascension of the Lord]. *Passio sancti Gongolfi martiris* (Gongolfus) [The Martyrdom of St. Gongolf]. *Passio sancti Pelagii pretiosissimi martiris qui nostris temporibus in Corduba martirio est coronatus* (Pelagius) [The Martyrdom of the Most Precious Pelagius, who received the crown of martyrdom in Cordoba in our own time]. *Lapsus et conversio Theophili Vicedomini* (Theophilus) [The Fall and Redemption of the Viceroy Theophilus]. *Basilius* [Basil]. *Passio sancti Dionisii egregii Martiris* (Dionysius) [The Martyrdom of the Remarkable Saint Dionysius]. *Passio sanctae Agnetis virginis et martiris* (Agnes) [The Passion of St. Agnes, Virgin and Martyr].

Plays (ca. 967): *Conversio Gallicani principis militiae* (Gallicanus) [The Conversion of General Gallicanus]. *Passio sanctarum virginum Agapis Chioniae et Hirenae* (Dulcitius) [The Martyrdom of the Holy Virgins Agapes, Chionia, and Irene]. *Resuscitatio Drusianae et Calimachi* (Calimachus) [The Resurrection of Drusiana and Calimachus]. *Lapsus et conversio Mariae neptis Habrahae heremicolae* (Abraham) [The Fall and Redemption of Mary, Niece of the Hermit Abraham]. *Conversio Thaidis meretricis* (Pafnutius) [The Conversion of Thais the Courtesan]. *Passio sanctarum virginum Fidei Spei et Karitatis* (Sapientia) [The Martyrdom of the Holy Virgins Faith, Hope, and Charity]. *The Apocalypse of John. Gesta Ottonis* [The Deeds of Otto the Great] (after 968). *Primordia Coenobii*

Gandeshemensis [The Origins of the Convent at Gandersheim] (after 973).

Bibliography

Editions: Celtes, Conrad, ed. *Opera* (Nuremberg, 1501). Homeyer, Helene, ed. *Hrotsvithae Opera.* Munich, 1970. Winterfeld, Paul von. *Hrotsvithae Opera.* Berlin, 1902.

Translations: Bonfante, Larissa, tr. *The Plays of Roswitha.* New York, 1979. St. John, Christopher, tr. *The Plays of Roswitha.* London, 1923. Tillyard, H.J.W., tr. *The Plays of Roswitha.* London, 1923. Wiegand, Mary Gonsalva, tr. *The Non-Dramatic Works of Hrotsvitha.* St. Louis, 1936. Wilson, K. tr. *The Plays of Hrotsvit of Gandersheim.* New York, 1989.

Braet, Herman, Johan Nowé, Gilbert Tournoy, eds. *The Theatre in the Middle Ages.* Louvain, 1985. Butler, Mary Marguerite. *Hrotsvitha: The Theatricality of Her Plays.* New York, 1960. Chamberlain, David. "Musical Learning and Dramatic Action in Hrotsvit's *Pafnutius.*" *Studies in Philology* 77 (1980): 319–343. Coulter, Cornelia C. "The Ý Terentian' Comedies of a Tenth-Century Nun." *Classical Journal* 24 (1929): 515–529. De Luca, Kenneth. "Hrotsvit's Ý Imitation' of Terence." *Classical Folia* 28 (1974): 89–102. Dronke, Peter. "Hrotsvitha." *Women Writers of the Middle Ages.* Cambridge, 1984, pp. 55–83. Fife, Robert Herndon. *Hroswitha of Gandersheim.* New York, 1947. Haight, Anne Lyon. *Hroswitha of Gandersheim: Her Life, Times, and Works, and a Comprehensive Bibliography.* New York, 1965. Homeyer, Helene. "'Imitatio' und 'aemulatio' im Werk der Hrotsvitha von Gandersheim." *Studi Medievali* 9 (1968): 966–979. Köpke, Rudolf. *Die älteste deutsche Dichterin* (Berlin, 1869). Kuhn, Hugo. "Hrotsviths von Gandersheim dichterisches Programm." *Deutsche Vierteljahresschrift für Literaturwissenschaft und Geistesgeschichte* 24 (1950): 181–196. Langosch, Karl. "Hrotsvitha von Gandersheim." *Profil des lateinischen Mittelalters.* Darmstadt, 1967, 187–225. Nagel, Bert. *Hrotsvit von Gandersheim.* Stuttgart, 1965. Newlands, Carole E. "Hrotswitha's Debt to Terence." *Transactions of the American Philological Association* 116 (1986): 369–391. Schütze-Pflugk, Marianne. *Herrscher- und Märtyrerauffassung bei Hrotsvit von Gandersheim.* Wiesbaden, 1972. Sticca, Sandro. "Sacred Drama and Comic Realism in the Plays of Hrotswitha of Gandersheim." *Acta VI: The Early Middle Ages,* ed. William H. Snyder. Binghamton, 1982, pp. 117–143. Sticca, Sandro. "Sin and Salvation: The Dramatic Context of Hroswitha's Women." *The Roles and Images of Women in the Middle Ages and Renaissance* vol. III, ed. Douglas Radcliff-Umstead. Pittsburgh, 1975, pp. 3–22. Wilson, Katharina M., ed. *Hrotsvit of Gandersheim: Rara Avis in Saxonia?* Ann Arbor, 1987. Wilson, Katharina M. "The Saxon Canoness: Hrotsvit of Gandersheim." *Medieval Women Writers,* ed. Katharina M. Wilson. Athens, Georgia, 1984, pp. 30–63. Wilson, Katharina M. *Hrotsvit of Gandersheim: The Ethics of Authorial Stance.* Leyden, 1989. Zeydel, Edwin H. "The Authenticity of Hrotsvitha's Works." *Modern Language Notes* 61 (1946): 50–55. Zeydel, Edwin H. "'Ego Clamor Validus'—Hrotsvitha." *Modern Language Notes* 61 (1946): 281–283. Zeydel, Edwin H. "Knowledge of Hrotsvitha's Works Prior to 1500." *Modern Language Notes* 59 (1944): 382–385. Zeydel, Edwin H. "Were Hrotsvitha's Dramas Performed During Her Lifetime?" *Speculum* 20 (1945): 443–456.

Judith Tarr

Maiia Anatolievna Ganina

Born 1927, Moscow, The Soviet Union
Genre(s): novella, short story, novel,
    travelogue, essay, translation
Language(s): Russian

Of all contemporary women authors published on a steady basis and accorded a measure of recognition in the Soviet Union, perhaps Ganina more than any of her colleagues deserves the label of feminist. Apart from focussing in her own fiction on working women endowed with independence, strong will, and professional skill, Ganina has involved herself in several publishing ventures undertaken specifically to educate the Russian reading public about women's status in the outlying regions of the Soviet state. Certain aspects of her biography indicate that her intense awareness of gender distinctions has roots in the early formative years of her life.

Born in 1927, Ganina was an unwanted child resulting from a misalliance between twenty-year-old Lidiia Ilinskaia and Anatolii Ganin, a Siberian eighteen years her senior. Both parents worked at the Supreme Court until public knowledge of their marital strife and their child's unexpected birth ruined Ganin's legal career. Forced to leave the Supreme Court, Ganin eventually landed a job as an engineer at an autoplant, where he remained until his retirement. He died in 1974 at the age of eighty-five. As Ganina herself acknowledges, he was the single greatest influence on his daughter.

After Ilinskai abandoned both husband and child, Ganina resided with her father in a one-room apartment in the center of Moscow. By any standards her childhood may be judged idiosyncratic. Upon leaving for work, Ganin would lock the girl in the apartment, presumably for safety, and often returned late at night. During the winter Ganina saw hardly anyone for months and relied upon herself for amusement and for her pre-school education. Left to her own devices, from the age of four she began to read insatiably whatever fell into her hands, including Seton Thompson's stories, Galsworthy's *Forsyte Saga*, Russian masterpieces, and foreign classics in translation. Under such circumstances her imagination and need for self-expression developed early. She composed her first poem at six, and thereafter produced both poetry and prose on a regular basis, taking care to hide from everyone but close friends her passion for writing.

In her late teens Ganina enrolled in a Moscow technical school for machine-building and upon graduation worked as a technician at a plant. She simultaneously pursued a training in literature through correspondence courses at the Gorky Literary Institute, which awarded her a diploma in 1954. That same year witnessed the publication in *Novyi mir* (New World) of her novella, *Pervye ispytaniia* (First Trials), a close look at working-class youth. More characteristic of what have become her perennial preoccupations, however, was the story "Nastiny deti" (1957; Nastia's Children), which brought her to the attention of critics and readers alike. This concise, restrained piece sensitively traces the belated psychological maturation of a frivolous, self-centered egotist into a responsible father. Critics deservedly praised the narrative for its simplicity and eloquent understatement and for the assuredness with which Ganina depicted the rural setting. Indeed, her perpetual peregrinations, on which she herself offers extended commentary in "Moi dorogi" (My Roads) (introduction to the collection of her prose entitled *Iabrannoe* [1983; Selections]), have made her intimately familiar with such locales as Siberia and the Northern Urals, which she observes and records with scrupulous fidelity in her fiction and travelogues.

During the late 1950s and early 1960s Ganina continued to bring out a steady flow of stories and also completed a heavily autobiographical novel. *Slovo o zerne gornichnom* (1965; A Word About the Mustard Seed). With the 1970s, she turned to narratives appreciably longer and more complex than the majority of her output, such as *Sozvezdie bliznetsov* (1974; The Gemini) and *Uslysh' svoi chas* (1975; Hear Your Hour Strike). The latter is especially striking for its unvarnished Freud-indebted portrayal of the actress-heroine's ambivalent relationship with her willful, irritating father. As Ganina herself confirms, that relationship is a fictional recreation of her own multifaceted relations with her father, as are other Ganina narratives, including her 1965 novel and the stories "Zapiski neizvestnoi poetessy" (1966; Notes of an Unknown Poetess) and "Put' k nirvane" (1966; Path to Nirvana). Her latest novel, *Poka zhivu—nadeius'* (1986; While There's Life There's Hope), likewise recounts many of her own life experiences in a first-person narrative brimming with rancor and bile.

Ganina's fiction explores subjects that have cropped up fairly frequently in Russian women's prose of the last two decades: the drive for personal and professional fulfillment; the difficulties of sustaining a career while also coping with the role of wife and mother; the emotional hardships attaching to romantic and domestic love in a context of compromise, boredom, and habitual infidelity; the value and resilience of female friendship; the seductiveness of material comfort; the dearth of strong, efficient, ethical men; and the heavy burden of responsibility carried by Soviet children in widowed, divorced, discordant, or illicit families.

In addition to fiction and two volumes of travel notes, Ganina has published a sociological study of the working and domestic life of the women residing in an industrial town on the

Kama River; translations of an epistolary novel and a children's tale from Tatar and Tuvinian respectively; an original children's story; and some musical commentaries. She has also given interviews and made public her opinions about contemporary trends in Russian literature. Much of her work evidences her attraction to Eastern culture and philosophy.

Several critics have justifiably faulted Ganina for the repetitious and almost formulaic nature of some of her stories. Indeed, homogenized, fuzzy, or hackneyed phraseology tends to vitiate Ganina's writing at its weakest, so that her narratives occasionally seem weightless and interchangeable with each other. No reader with perception would call her a brilliant stylist. Her strength as a writer lies in her understanding of human psychology and her ability to portray convincingly, often subtly, forceful characters torn by contradictory drives and allegiances.

Works

Collections of fiction: *Matvei i Shurka. Rasskazy* (1962). *Ia ishchu tebia, chelovek* (1963). *Rasskazy* (1966). *Zachem spilili kashtany?* (1967). *Povest' o zhenshchine. Povesti, rasskazy, ocherki* (1973). *Dal'naia poezdka. Rasskazy* (1975). *Sozvezdie bliznetsov. Povesti i rasskazy* (1980, 1984). *Iabrannoe* (1983). *Sto zhiznei moikh. Roman, povest'* (1983).

Novels: *Slovo o zerne gornichnom* (1965). *Poka shivu—nadeius'* (1986).

Children's literature: *Tiapkin i Lesha. Povest'* (1977).

Travelogues: *K sebe vozvrashchaius' izdaleka* (1971). *Dorogi Rossii* (1981).

Essays: *Kamazonki na rabote i doma [Ocherki o zhenshchinakh Naberezhnykh Chelnov]* (?).

Articles: "'Glokaia kuzdra' protiv 'zhidkoi organiki,'" *Literaturnaia gazeta*, January 9, 1985, p. 6.

Commentary on music: *Russkaia muzykal'naia literatura* (1977, 1982).

Translations: Giliazov, A. *Devich'i pis'ma [Povesti]*, from Tatar (1973). *Povest' o svetlom ma'chike*, from Tuvinian (1977).

Translations by Ganina: "A Stage Actress" (1970), tr. Helena Goscilo. In *HERitage and HEResy: Recent Fiction by Russian Women)*, ed. Helena Goscilo. Bloomington, 1988.

Bibliography

Sheiko, Rena. "Na semi vetrakh." *Literaturnaia gazeta* (December 12, 1984): 5. Starikova, E. "Portrety i razmyshleniia." *Novyi mir* (1963).

Helena Goscilo

Smaranda Garbini[u]

(see: Smara)

Adelaida García Morales

Born 1946, Badajoz, Spain
Genre(s): novel
Language(s): Spanish

In 1985 Adelaida García Morales won the III Premio Herralde de Novela with her novel *El silencio de las sirenas* (1985; The Silence of the Mermaids). Hers is not an isolated case. Today's Spanish literary world is witnessing a notable increase in literary prizes awarded to women writers.

García Morales was born in Badajoz into a family of Andalusian origin. She lived in the south of Spain for most of her youth. In 1970 she graduated from the University of Madrid with a "Licenciatura" in *Filosofía y Letras*. She also studied screenwriting at the Official School of Cinematography. Her life has been marked by diversity and richness: she has taught language, literature, and philosophy in different high schools; she has been a translator for OPEC; worked as a model; and was an acting member of the theater group Esperpento in Seville. She is now married to film director Victor Erice, who adopted her first story, *El Sur*, for the screen.

García Morales' two works of fiction, *El Sur & Bene* (1985; The South & Bene) and *El silencio de las sirenas*, seem to have strong autobiographical elements, both works sharing the locale of Andalusia, where the author spent her youth. *El Sur & Bene* is a grouping of two stories that share thematic and structural traits. Both stories are nostalgic and passionate incursions into childhood memories. With the use of a sustained monologue, the narrator evokes her intense, loving relationship with her father and her painful evolution into adulthood, focusing on the changes that this evolution provoked in their relationship. The second story, *Bene*, is also an incursion into childhood; this time the evoked lost figure is that of a sister, Bene.

The same year, García Morales published her second work, *El silencio de las sirenas*. This is the story of a schoolteacher living in an isolated area in the south of Spain. Through the narrator's voice, the author unveils the true plot of the novel, which is the mysterious love story of the narrator's new acquaintance, Elsa, with an even more mysterious lover who lives in distant Barcelona. The two women build a friendship upon the shared secret of Elsa's relationship, from which arises an almost complete isolation from the outside world. In their isolation, they immerse themselves in a world of magic, dreams, and spiritualism. García Morales' literary language is more evocative than descriptive, yet at the same time it exhibits a style that is precise and rich. Her fiction develops themes that are common to other Spanish women writers, such as isolation, suffering, love, and friendship. Her characters are endowed with imagination and inner strength that contrasts dramatically with their outwardly feeble appearance and makes them truly fascinating to the reader's imagination.

García Morales' fiction has been given a very positive reception by both the critics and the public. She is being considered by some critics as one of the most promising novelists of her generation.

Works

El Sur & Bene [The South & Bene] (1985). El silencio de las sirenas [The Silence of the Mermaids] (1985).

Bibliography

Cambio 16, 735 (December 30, 1985): 23. Sanchez Arnosi, Milagros. "Adelaida García Morales: La soledad gozosa." *Insula* 472 (1986): 4.

Coro Malaxecheverría

Angelina Gatell

Born 1926, Barcelona, Spain
Genre(s): poetry, short story
Language(s): Spanish

Gatell is an outspoken *poeta social*, short story writer, and peace activist. Her dramatic *El poema del soldado* (1954; The Soldier's Poem) is a moving, lyrical, antiwar monologue. In 1963, Gatell braved potentially devastating political and legal consequences with the publication of *Esa oscura palabra* (That Dark Word). Unmistakably critical of the Franco regime, this collection may be considered an urgent cry for justice and liberation within Spain and beyond. *Las claudicaciones* (1969; Capitulations) is perhaps Gatell's most powerful collection of committed poetry. In addition to exposing the many ills of an oppressive culture—frequently from a feminist perspective—the poet looks to a new future molded by a liberated society. *El hombre del acordeón* (1984; The Accordion Man) is a collection of short stories for children.

Works

El poema del soldado (1954). Esa oscura palabra (1963). Las claudicaciones (1969). El hombre del acordeón (1984).

Bibliography

Fagundo, Ana Maria, "Testimonio y poesia en Angelina Gatell." *Cultura* 70 (San Salvador) (July–December 1980): 63–68. Flores, A. and K., *Poesia feminista del mundo hispánico* (1984). Manrique de Lara, J.G., *Poetas sociales españoles* (1974). *Women Writers of Spain*, ed. C. Galerstein (1986).

Barbara Dale May

(Louise-Charlotte-Ernestine) Judith Gautier

(a.k.a. Judith Walther, Judith Walter)

Born August 25, 1845 or 1850, Paris, France;
died December 25, 1917, Saint Enogat
Genre(s): translation, memoirs, monographs,
poetry, tales, music criticism
Language(s): French

Gautier, the first woman elected to membership of the Académie Goncourt in 1910, was a prolific translator and creator of oriental literature. She also helped to popularize the works of Richard Wagner by translating his operas and writing positive reviews.

As the daughter of Théophile Gautier and a ballerina, she was nurtured in the arts by artists. In her youth she learned Chinese from Ting Tun

Lung, who lived with her family while he was compiling a Chinese-French dictionary. As a junior member of Parisian literati, Gautier met a fellow Parnassian Mendès and married him in 1866. Flaubert, who among many others disapproved of the match, witnessed the ceremony. She almost immediately left her new husband. Gautier had studied music with her father, who wrote music reviews. She championed Wagner's work, going to Munich in 1869 to meet the master.

In addition to Gautier's artistic talent, she was a notable beauty. Anatole France included Gautier, referring to her as Judith Mendès, in his "Croquis féminins." He likened her "plastic beauty" to one of her father's lines, saying that "Comme une princesse de légende, les fées sont venues à son baptême" (Like a legendary princess, fairies came to her baptism). Recalling her poetic abilities, France summed up her personality as poetry itself: "Mieux que poétique, elle est la poésie. . . . Elle a la science d'une mandarine et la gaieté d'une Parisienne" (More than poetic, she is poetry. . . . She has the science of a mandarin and the gaiety of a Parisian). Banville, trying to describe her beauty, quoted one of Gautier's lines "délicieuse et savante" (delicious and knowledgeable) which explained it better, he said, than he could: "Derrière les treillages de sa fenêtre, une jeune femme qui brode des fleurs brillantes sur une étoffe de soie, écoute les oiseaux s'appeler joyeusement dans les arbres" (Behind the trellis of her window, a young woman who embroiders some brilliant flowers on a piece of silk, listens to the birds calling joyously in the trees). Nearing her forties, Gautier was still considered beautiful enough to be the subject of six portraits executed by the American painter Sargent.

Gautier's works, the first of which was *Le Livre de jade*, published in 1867, are mainly inspired by Chinese and Japanese poems and tales. Other oriental translations and those works inspired by Eastern culture include: *Le Dragon imperial* (1869), *L'Usurpateur* (1875), *Les Peuples étranges* (1879), *Isoline et la fleur serpent* (1882), *La Femme de Putiphar* (1884), *Poèmes de la Libellule* (1885), *Iskender, histoire persane* (1886), "La Marchande de sourires," (Japanese play, 1888), *Fleurs d'Orient* (1893), *Khou-n-ato-nou; fragments d'un papyrus* (1898).

Gautier also wrote her memoirs, published from 1902 to 1909 in three volumes. In addition, there are the Wagner translations and reviews and the collaborations with composers Benedictus and Pierre Loti. Gautier's published monographs, not even counting the journal articles or several editions, number nearly forty different titles.

In general, the Parisian literary commentators (Anatole France, Banville, the Goncourts) found Gautier to be talented and beautiful. Indeed, comments focused on her poetic talent, and not her life. Unlike the few other women writers in France of her age, her affairs and unhappy marriage were not replayed in her works. It is regrettable that Gautier's works are relatively unavailable.

Works

Le Livre de jade (1867). *Le dragon imperial* (1869). *L'Usurpateur* (1875). *Le Jeu de l'amour et de la mort* (1876). *Lucienne* (1877). *Les Cruautés de l'amour* (1879). *Les Peuples étranges* (1879). *Isoline et la fleur serpent* (1882). *Richard Wagner et son oeuvre poetique depuis Rienzi jusqu'à Parsifal* (1882). *La Femme de Putiphar* (1884). *Poèmes de la Libellule* (1885). *Iskender; histoire persane* (1886). *La Conquête du paradis* (1887). *La Marchande de sourires, pièce japonaise en cinq actes; music by Benedictus* (1888). *Les Musiques bizarres à l'Exposition recueillies et transcrites par Benedictus* (1889). *Les Noces de Fingal, poème en trois parties* (1888). [With A. Tonnery], *La Camargo, ballet pantomime en 2 actes et 3 tableaux* (1893). *Fleurs d'Orient* (1893). Trs., *Parsifal* (1893). *Le Vieux de la montagne* (1893). *Mémoires d'un éléphant blanc* (1894). *La Sonate du clair de lune, opéra en 1 acte, music by Benedictus* (1894). *Les Princesses d'amours, courtisanes japonaises; roman* (1900). *Le Collier des jours: Souvenirs de ma vie* (1902). —*Le second rang du collier* (1903). —*Le troisième rang du collier* (1909). *Le Paravent de soie et d'or* (1904). *Album de poèmes tirés du Livre de jade* (1911). *En Chine; merveilleuses histoires* (1911). *Poésies* (1911). [With P. Loti.], *La Fille du ciel, drame chinois* (1911). *Dupleix* (1912). *Le Japon; merveilleuses histoires* (1912). *Le Roman d'un grand chanteur* (1912). *L'Inde éblouie* (1913). *Un général de cinq ans; images d'Alice Bergerat* (1918). *Les parfums de la pagode* (1919). "Auprès

de Richard Wagner, souvenirs 1861–1882."
Mercure de France (1943).

Works in English: *Chinese Lyrics*, tr. J. Whiteall (1918). "The Magician of Bankok," tr. L. Hearn, in *The Double Dealer* (1921). *Wagner at Home*, tr. E. Massie (1910).

Bibliography

Banville, *Les Camées Parisiens* (1866–1873). Camacho, M.-D., *Judith Gautier, sa vie et son oeuvre* (Geneva, 1939). Crosland, M., *Women of Iron and Velvet* (London, 1976). Flaubert, G., *Correspondence*, vols. 5, 7, 8 (Paris, 1933–1959). France, A., "Croquis feminins." *Portraits littéraires* 32, ed. M. Pakenham (Exeter, 1979). France, A., *La Vie littéraire*, vol. 4 (Paris, 1892). Gourmont, R., *Promenades littéraires* (Paris, 1916). Sabatier, R., *La Conquête du paradis* (Paris, 1980).

General references: *Bibliophile Dictionary* (1904). *Dictionnaire de biographie française*, vol. 15 (1982). *Dictionnaire des lettres françaises; Dictionnaire littéraire du xixᵉ siècle*, vol. 1. *Oxford Companion to French Literature*.

Other references: *Art Quarterly* (Summer 1955). *Bulletin de la Société Théophile Gautier* (1981). *French Review* (April 1985). *Revue des Deux Mondes* (1918).

Marilynn J. Smith

Delphine Gay (Madame Emile de Girardin)

Born January 26, 1804, Aix-la-Chapelle, France; died June 29, 1855, Paris
Genre(s): poetry, essay, novel, short story, drama
Language(s): French

Daughter of the Receiver-General of the Department of the Ruhr, her mother was obliged to rescue the family fortunes when her father lost his post. After the family returned to Paris, Sophie Gay made a success of writing novels and articles for journals, and the family residence became a center for the artistic and literary world of the day. Delphine was thus stimulated to a precocious literary celebrity, reading and reciting her poetry to distinguished guests. Lamartine called her the "tenth Muse" and De Vigny dedicated to her his *Poèmes Antiques et Modernes* (1826; Ancient and Modern Poems). Her own early poems had already been published as *Essais Poétiques* (1824; Poetical Essays). Two years earlier she had won honorable mention in a contest sponsored by the French Academy. Charles X granted her a royal pension.

Théophile Gautier recalled her presence at the celebrated Battle of Hernani, in 1830, when Victor Hugo's romantic tragedy was first presented at the Comédie-Française. The following year she married Emile de Girardin, founder of *La Presse*. For this paper, she wrote a series of weekly letters, the *Lettres Parisiennes* (The Parisian Letters), which came to be both successful and influential, and which she signed Vicomte de Launay. She was also the hostess of a salon as successful as her mother's, and she wrote novels and short stories of charm but little enduring value. After 1839, she turned her attention to the theatre, although her first play, *L'Ecole des Journalistes* (The School for Journalists) was prevented by the Censor from being performed at the Comédie-Française. She had better fortune with two tragedies, *Judith* (1843) and *Cléopatre* (1848) as well as with a comedy, *C'est la Faute du Mari* (It's the Husband's Fault), a proverb in verse of the sort popularized by the theatre of Alfred de Musset.

Although her writings were much admired by her contemporaries and in the period following her death (six volumes of her *Oeuvres Complètes* were published with an enthusiastic preface by Théophile Gautier), they have been largely forgotten. The lively *Lettres Parisiennes*, however, give a vivid and interesting portrait of Paris in the years leading to the crisis of 1848. Modern feminists might well take more notice of both the mother and the daughter who achieved such notable professional success in Parisian society more than a century ago.

Works

Essais Poétiques [Poetical Essays] (1824–1825). *Le Lorgnon* [The Lorgnette] (1831). *La Canne de M. de Balzac* [Monsieur de Balzac's Cane] (1835). *Lettres Parisiennes* [Parisian Letters] (1836–1848). *L'Ecole des Journalistes* [The School for Journalists] (1840). *Judith* (1843). *Cléopatre* (1848). *La Joie Fait Peur* [Joy Is Frightening] (1854). *Le Chapeau de l'Horloger* [The Clockmaker's Hat]

(1854). *Oeuvres Complètes*, 6 vol. (1860–1861; Complete Works).

Bibliography

Malo, Henri, *La Gloire du Vicomte de Launay* (Paris, 1925). Malo, Henri, *Une Muse et sa Mère, Delphine Gay de Girardin* (Paris, 1924). Sainte-Beuve, *Les Causeries de Lundi*, III (Paris, 1858). Séché, Léon, *Le Cénacle de la Muse Française* (Paris, 1909; rpt. Geneva, 1968). Vier, Jacques de, *La Comtesse d'Agoult et son Temps*. 2 vols. (Paris, 1955–1959).

Charity C. Willard

Katharina von Gebersweiler

(a.k.a. Gueberschwiler, Gebilswilr, Guebwiller or Gewerswiler)

Born ca. 1250; died January 22, 1330/45?
Genre(s): prose texts
Language(s): German, Latin

From early childhood on (ca. 1260) Katharina von Gebersweiler was a nun at the Dominican convent of Colmar (Alsace/France), Unterlinden. She can perhaps be identified with a prioress also called Gebersweiler. In her old age (ca. 1310–1320), she wrote a collection of biographical pieces, the so-called *Schwesterbuch* (Sister Book) consisting of a prologue, eight introductory chapters about the life at the Unterlinden convent, founded in 1232, and 42 biographies of members of the convent. The Latin in which she wrote the book has been much admired. She used as a model for her *Sister Book* the works of Gerhard von Fracheto and Dietrich Apolda. In the book she tried to outline an ideal lifestyle as practiced in the nunnery as an example for generations to come. The biographies (*Vitae*) deal only briefly with the sisters' lives before they entered the religious community but emphasize the spiritual, intellectual, and pragmatic aspects such as their prayer practices, studying, chorus singing, music performances, and mystic experiences. Often the appearance of Christ, the Virgin Mother, and of deceased nuns is reported. The *Vitae* offer more than stereotypes of mystics' lives; rather they stress individual characteristics of the members of the convent. It is one of the oldest and most illustrative books of its kind, only partially paralleled by the fragmentary *Book of the Benedictine Nuns of Oostbroek* at Utrecht, the Netherlands.

Works

Thannerius, M., ed., *Venerabilis Catharinne de Geweswilles . . . De vitis primarium sororum monasterii sui liber* (1625), of which no copy seems to be extant. Ancelet-Hustache, J., *Les "Vitae Sororum" d'Unterlinden*, ed. critique du ms. 508 de la Bibliotèque de Colmar *Archives d'histoire doctrinale et littéraire du moyen âge* 5 (1930), pp. 317–509; German tr. L. Clarus, *Lebensbeschreibungen der ersten Schwestern des Klosters der Dominikanerinnen zu Unterlinden* (Reliquien aus dem Mittelalter, 3/4) (1863).

Bibliography

Barth, Médard, *Die Herz-Jesu-Verehrung im Elsaß vom 12. Jahrhundert bis auf die Gegenwart*. Forschungen zur Kirchengeschichte des Elsaß 1 (Freiburg i.Br, 1928), pp. 29–32. Blank, W., *Umsetzung der Mystik in die Frauenklöster, Ausstellungskatalog "Mystik am Oberrhein,"* ed. H.H. Hofstätter (Freiburg i.Br., 1978), pp. 25–36. Dinzelsbacher, Peter, "Katharina von Gebersweiler," in *Die Deutsche Literatur des Mittelalters, Verfasserlexikon*, ed. K. Ruh et al. 2nd ed. (Berlin-New York, 1981), cols. 1073–1075. Görres, Johann Joseph von, *Die christliche Mystik*, vol. 1 (München-Regensburg, 1836), pp. 292–297. Muschg, W. ed., *Mystische Texte aus dem Mittelalter*. Sammlung Klosterberg, Schweizer Reihe (Basel, 1943). Oehl, W., *Deutsche Mystikerbriefe des Mittelalters* (München, 1931). Pieller, M.P., *Deutsche Frauenmystik im 13. Jahrhundert*. Ph.D. diss., Vienna, 1928, pp. 406–411. Wilms, H., *Geschichte der deutschen Dominikanerinnen 1209–1916* (Dülmen, 1920). Zippel, W., *Die Mystiker und die deutsche Gesellschaft des 13. und 14. Jahrhunderts* (Düren, 1935).

Albrecht Classen

Johanka Georgiadesova

(see: Terézia Vansová)

Ágnes Gergely

Born 1933, Hungary
Genre(s): poetry, novel
Language(s): Hungarian

Ágnes Gergely was born in 1933 in a large village on the Hungarian Plain. In 1950, at the age of 17, she entered a factory as apprentice turner. She took a special exam that allowed her to leave factory life by gaining her admission to the University of Budapest, where she studied Hungarian and English literature. She has worked as a secondary school teacher, as a producer for Hungarian Radio, and as a feature editor for the literary weekly *Nagyvilág*. She spent six months in 1973–1974 in the United States as a member of the International Writing Program at the University of Iowa. She is a highly respected translator of English and American poetry.

Gergely's novels and poetry examine the ironies of literary life and the role of the writer in contemporary culture and politics. An exponent of the *nyugat* (Western-influenced) literary movement in Hungary (as opposed to the *népi* movement, which draws inspiration from indigenous Hungarian themes and forms), her experimental lyrics express a fragile humanist world view bolstered by dour humor. Her autobiographical novel *Stációk* (Stations), triangulated among village, factory and university, reflects the disparate focal points of her own life and consciousness. The novel illuminates the conflicts, political and personal, of Hungarians across several social strata—peasants, craftsmen, factory workers, and the intelligentsia.

Gergely is noted for the moral passion and analytical powers she brings to those life experiences, which, through her artistry, become paradigms for contemporary Hungarian life.

Works

Poetry: *Ajtófélfámon jel vagy* (1963). *Johanna* (1968). *Azték pillanat* (1970). *Válogatott szerelmeim*, collection of poems and translations (1973). *Kobaltország* (1978). *Hajóroncs* (1981). Novels: *Glogovácz és a Holdkórosok* (1966). *A Chicagói Változat* (1976). *A Tolmács* (1977). *Stációk*, 1983.

Bibliography

Barnstone, Aliki, and Barnstone, Willis, *A Book of Women Poets from Antiquity to Now* (New York, 1980), p. 360. Pomogats, Béla, *Az újabb magyar irodalom*, 1945–1981 (Budapest, 1981). Vajda, Miklos, ed., *Modern Hungarian Poetry* (New York, 1977), pp. 240–243.

Gyorgyi Voros

Ida G.M. Gerhardt

Born 1905
Genre(s): poetry, translation
Language(s): Dutch

Ida Gerhardt's oeuvre was twice awarded prestigious literary prizes, the *Prijs voor meesterschap der Nederlandse letterkunde* in 1979 and the *P.C. Hooftprijs* in 1980.

She studied classical languages, taught Greek and Latin, and has published in addition to her poetry translations of Lucretius and Virgil.

As a poet, Ida Gerhardt has always felt that she had a task to fulfill. The title of her collection *Kwatrijnen in opdracht* (1949; Quatrains Under Orders) clearly bespeaks this idea. She saw the materialism of the modern world as a degeneration of ancient values rooted in Christianity and classical antiquity. *Het levend monogram* (1955; The Living Monogram) refers to the fish, ancient symbol of Christianity. In the epic didactic poem "Twee uur: de klokken antwoorden elkaar" ("Two O'Clock: The Bells Answer One Another") the poet presents a group of school children who symbolically choose the humanistic values of classical culture. Disappointed with Holland, she escapes to a mythical, Homeric realm, in her case, Ireland, which is evoked in the collections *De slechtvalk* (1966; The Peregrine Falcon), *De ravenveer* (1970; The Raven Feather), and *Vijf vuurstenen* (1974; Five Flints).

She frequently uses water as an archetypal symbol associated with a complex set of images. She writes with great technical skill and poetic feeling, chiseling verses which are classical in every sense of the word. To her the essence of poetry is that which is touched by the divine.

Works

Kosmos (1940). Het veerhuis (1945). Buiten schot (1947). Kwatrijnen in opdracht (1949). Sonnetten voor een leraar (1951). Het levend monogram (1955). De argelozen (1956). De hovenier (1961). De slechtvalk (1966). De ravenveer (1970). Twee uur: de klokken antwoorden elkaar (1971). Vijf vuurstenen (1974). Vroege verzen (1978). Het sterreschip (1979). Nu ik hier iets zeggen mag (1980). Verzamelde gedichten (1980). Dolen en dromen (1980). De zomen van het licht (1983).

Bibliography

Fens, Kees, "Ida G.M. Gerhardt." Ons Erfdeel 14, 1: 107–109. Kuby, Christiane, "Ida Gerhardt: Eine Einführung." Castrum Peregrini (1983): 32(159–160): 30–51. Ross, Haj, "Biografisch I," "Human Linguistics." Georgetown Round Table on Language and Linguistics (1982): 1–30. Spillebeen, Willy, "Het sterreschip van Ida Gerhardt." Dietsche Warande en Belfort, 124: 680–686. Spillebeen, Willy, "Ida Gerhardt doolt en droomt." Dietsche Warande en Belfort 127, 5 (June 1982): 349–354. Vegt, Jan van der, "Ida Gerhardt: Poezie als geweten." Ons Erfdeel 15, iv: 103–106. Vegt, Jan van der, "Krachtens ingeschapen moeten." Ons Erfdeel 23, 1 (Jan.–Feb. 1982): 57–68. Vegt, Jan van der, "Ida G.M. Gerhardt." Tis vol van schatten hier, vol. 2 (Amsterdam, 1986), pp. 40–41.

Maya Bijvoet

Ada Gerlo

(see: Annie Salomons)

Germonde

Flourished c. 1227–1229, Montpellier, France
Genre(s): poetry (sirventes)
Language(s): French

Born in Montpellier sometime in the early thirteenth century, the little-known Germonde distinguished herself among her contemporaries as a learned lady, troubadour poet (*trobairitz*), and devout Christian. When mentioned at all in published notices, she is discussed with reference to her literary and religious antagonist Guillaume Figueiras, a troubadour poet of her day, whose 23–verse unpublished *sirvente* boldly attacked the Pope, clergy, and the organization of the Church. Of what little we know of this paper-war between Germonde and Figueiras, it is reported that the faithful Germonde vehemently responded to Figueiras's heretical charges with an equally-long poem, signed in her own hand, that counterattacked his claims with rational defenses of the Christian faith. Germonde also managed to parody her adversary's poem by mimicking its organization, metre, and rhyme patterns.

Germonde's detractors, Millot and Éméric David, have challenged her authorship of the lengthy *sirvente*. They ascribe the poem to one Izarn, a monk of the thirteenth century and a reputed literary adversary of many heretics.

To date, no MS copy of Germonde's writings exists. Most regrettably, we seldom find her even mentioned in anthologies of troubadour poetry or of early women writers.

Works

A long verse-satire (*sirvente*), untitled and un-published. MS copies of Germonde's poem are non-extant. Reportedly, her poem was signed in her own hand.

Bibliography

Dessalles, L., "Germonde." Nouvelle Biographie Générale (Paris, 1887). Millot's Historie littéraire de la France. 3 vols. (Paris, 1802). Raynourd's Choix de Poesies originale des troubadours. 6 vols. (Paris, 1816–1821). Veran, Jules, Les Poetesses provencales (Paris, 1946). Paden, William, ed., The Voice of the Trobairitz: Perspectives on the Women Troubadors (Philadelphia, 1990).

Maureen E. Mulvihill

Elfriede Gerstl

Born June 16, 1932, Vienna, Austria
Genre(s): poetry, prose, radio drama, essay
Language(s): German

Elfriede Gerstl is known for her parodic and satiric texts on contemporary life in Vienna. With humor and irony she criticizes the cultural establishment and its products while pleading indirectly for tolerance of alternative life styles—be they leftist, feminist, or whatever. Formally her works can be characterized as experimental literature, the specifically Austrian variety of avant-garde art that developed in the 1950s and 1960s in reaction to traditional artistic norms. It is against the stringency of such conventions that Gerstl also protests, and with subtlety and wit she creates "anti-art" as a counter-force to conformity.

Gerstl was born in 1932 of Jewish parents in Vienna. The ambiance of her upper-middle class home was interrupted by her parents' divorce when she was five; that was followed by the horrors of the Nazi regime during which time the family had to remain in hiding to avoid deportation. Although her young years were thus very difficult, such personal, biographical themes do not appear in her literary works, which operate instead on a more abstract, intellectual level. In the 1950s Gerstl studied medicine and psychology at the University of Vienna, and in the 1960s she was married and had a child. A literary breakthrough came in 1964 when she received a scholarship from the Literary Colloquium in Berlin, where she remained for four years. Since then she has lived as a free-lance writer in Vienna, although she also travels a great deal—to Berlin or to other European capitals.

Partly because Gerstl refuses to participate in the competitive marketing industry, she has never gained access to the West German publishing houses. In Austria, however, where she is a member of the Graz Authors' Association, she is well known and highly respected for her linguistic ability and personal integrity.

Gerstl's best-known works to date are *Spielräume* (1977; Room to Play) and *Wiener Mischung* (1982; Viennese Mixture), both of which appeared in the avant-garde series edition. Despite its designation as a novel, *Spielräume* is a loose collection of texts that relates the experiences of a writer, specifically a woman writer, in contemporary society. From cocktail parties in Berlin to coffeehouse conversations in Vienna, Gerstl registers the problems of interpersonal communication—be it between partners, within families, among friends, or in society at large. Human relationships are her specialty, and she writes ironically: "Collecting people is more satisfying than stamps or butterflies . . . [but] collecting entails also being collected." Her works are not representational in the traditional sense

but operate rather with montage, permutation, quotation, serial construction, word plays and puns, and these experimental techniques are developed in ever-new variations throughout her works.

The title *Wiener Mischung* initially suggests a box of assorted candies, but Gerstl's "mixture" is sharp rather than sweet. It consists of aphorisms, notes, dialogues, slogans, poems, and short prose pieces that parody the normative behavior of conventional society. In the section "leiblichesweibliches" (physical-feminine) for example, she feeds back the talk of lovers and gynecologists to disclose its macho ethos. Snippets from Goethe's *Faust* appear beside advertising slogans and both are transformed by the context. A modern Ophelia is created, and there is also a take-off on the genre of nature poetry. Lines of poetry are at times arbitrarily numbered to demonstrate the absurdity of the prevailing quantifying mentality. "Didak-tick" reveals the triteness of conventional certainties and the naiveté of supposing that one can "teach" anyone anything. Gerstl today finds credible only the person who "chooses the unattractiveness of the fragmentary."

Gerstl is keenly aware of the theoretical presuppositions of her work and has written perceptive essays on the role of art in society, as collected in the booklet *Narren und Funktionäre* (1980; Fools and Functionaries). Culture today is seen as compromised by its collusion with the establishment, and the "fools" are the artists who buy into the enterprise. True art is subversive rather than affirmative and is more likely to arise from the subculture of drop-outs than from circles sanctioned by the culture industry. The plight of the radical artist is poignantly presented in Gerstl's account of two colleagues, Buchebner and Laaber, who were driven to suicide. In this case as always Gerstl demonstrates her solidarity with the artist as outsider. She also critically investigates the role of poetry readings and radio plays in an age of mass media and television entertainment. These themes are treated artistically in her radio plays collected in the volume *Berechtigte Fragen* (1973; Legitimate Questions).

Among intellectual influences three are especially prominent: from Freud stems an interest in psychoanalysis and from Wittgenstein a preoccupation with language philosophy. The experimental writing techniques are a heritage of the Vienna Group, particularly of Oswald Wiener. These themes—psychology, language philosophy, and experimental writing—are united in her insightful social portraits. She details the aggressions and neurosis of the individual and also realizes that the tough talk is often a cover-up for weakness and failure. Behind the satire is a sadness at the daily discord and a sense of despair at the structures that so alienate the individual. Although Gerstl is much too sophisticated to postulate any kind of romantic ideal, a utopian vision exists as an implicit backdrop to the insufficiencies of empirical conditions.

Gerstl's works have been recognized as political. Although she declines to portray her childhood experiences in the manner of a latter-day Anne Frank, her experimental writing clearly carries sociopolitical import for our time. Her basic stance is one of skepticism and, realizing the comforts and dangers of ideology, she resists dogma in any form: "Any belief calls for contradiction. I can at best say what I don't believe in." With irony, ambivalence, and a bit of contempt Gerstl caricatures society, but her stance is never bitter, cynical, or militant. She is particularly known for her colorful expressions, idioms, and clever turns of phrase, which are, however, not merely local color but urbane and witty parodies of the social and political forms characteristic of any Western metropolis. Her works present one of the best introductions to contemporary Viennese society and to feminist experimental writing.

Works

Gesellschaftsspiele mit mir. Gedichte (1962). Berechtigte Fragen. Hörspiele (1973). Spielräume. Roman (1977). Narren und Funktionäre. Aufsätze zum Kulturbetrieb (1980). Weiner Mischung. Texte aus vielen Jahren (1982). Ed., eine frau ist eine frau ist eine frau. Autorinnen über Autorinnen (1985). Vor der Ankunft. auf reisen entstandene gedichte (1988).

Beth Bjorklund

Gertrud of Helfta

Born January 6, 1256; died November 17, 1301/02, Helfta, Germany
Genre(s): mysticism
Language(s): Latin

Gertrud of Helfta, also called Gertrud the Great, is of unknown ancestry. She spent her entire life in the convent of Helfta (near Eisleben in today's German Democratic Republic). Her thorough schooling included the seven *artes liberales* as well as comprehensive studies in theology.

Helfta, a Benedictine, Cistercian-oriented convent, was founded in 1229. Under its famous abbess, Gertrud of Hackeborn (in office: 1251–1291), the convent developed into a renowned center of culture and mysticism.

The three Helfta representatives in the literature of medieval mysticism are the abbess' sister, Mechthild of Hackeborn (see entry), the beguine Mechthild of Magdeburg (see entry), and Gertrud the Great; the latter remained the least known. Contemporary reception of Gertrud's work, judging by the few manuscripts extant, remained at most lukewarm. A Middle High German translation, *Der botte der götlichen miltekeit*, of her major Latin work *Legatus divinæ pietatis* appeared about 100 years after her death; it is a shortened version (mainly of Books III to V of the *Legatus*) with moralizing intent.

The Cologne Carthusian Johann Gerecht of Landsberg (Lanspergius) made this mystic known with his first edition of Gertrud's Latin work in 1536. The 1875 first critical edition of Gertrud's work by the Benedictines of Solesmes is now superseded by the Sources Chrétiennes edition.

Gertrud wrote both secular poetry and theological exegetical treatises in Middle High German as well as Latin, but all of this is lost; only an occasional German term or, at most, short passages written in German can be found in her Latin prose. Her Latin work consists of the *Legatus divinæ pietatis* (The Messenger of Loving Kindness) and the *Exercitia spiritualia*, a book of mystical meditations and prayers. Gertrud of Helfta is also one of the writers responsible for Mechthild of Hackeborn's work, *Liber specialis gratiæ*.

Gertrud's *Legatus* is extant in five manuscripts: the best one is clm. 15.332 (1412), Bayerische Staatsbibliothek, Munich; cod. 4224 (1487) österreichische Nationalbibliothek, Vienna; cod. 77/1061 (fifteenth century), partial ms., Stadtbibliothek Trier; cod.13 (fifteenth century) Stadtbibliothek, Mainz; cod.84 (1473), partial ms., Hessische Landesbibliothek, Darmstadt. The *Legatus divinæ pietatis* consists of five books, but only Book II was written by Gertrud herself. Book I represents a *vita* of Gertrud; Books III to V contain an account of Gertrud's spiritual experiences based on Gertrud's dictation, notes, and conversations. There are no manuscripts of the *Exercitia spiritualia* extant. Its authenticity was established through a comparison with Book II of the *Legatus*.

Gertrud of Helfta's writing is influenced by Bernard of Clairvaux' style and diction and, in general, by texts of the daily liturgy and Scriptures, especially the *Song of Songs* and the psalms. A predominant characteristic of Gertrud's work is the intertwining of liturgy with mystical meditations in which bridal imagery (*Brautmystik*) is a major theme. At times Gertrud's use of terms of sweetness—which is quite common for medieval spiritual works in general—may divert today's reader from the fact that her prose is also highly poetic and characterized by startling oxymora and a wealth of almost harsh imagery.

The *raison d'être* for Gertrud's work is Gertrud's mystical experience on January 27, 1281. But she started to compose her memorial, now Book II of the *Legatus*, only in 1289 when she felt a divine call to communicate her inner transformation and mystical experiences. This work is now considered one of the classics of Christian mystical writings. It is characteristic of Gertrud that the experience of *unio mystica* liberates her in such a way that she feels unrestrained by petty rules and regulations. Nonconformist in many ways, she often suggests areas in the church that are in need of reform. She sees herself with authoritative priestly power in the spiritual guidance of fellow nuns and lay people seeking her advice. It is perhaps because of these passages that her work experienced some censorship.

Within the theological context of the thirteenth century, the themes that capture Gertrud's interest most are the eucharist and the veneration of the heart of Jesus. The heart as the intellectual, spiritual, and affective center of the human being in medieval thinking becomes the focus of Gertrud's mystical love of Christ. Her understanding is based on John 7:37f. and 13: 23–25 and is best symbolized in the famous Christ-John-sculpture. The veneration of Jesus' heart is also closely intertwined with and inseparable from the theme of the motherhood of God, as shown in beautiful imagery throughout the *Legatus* and *Exercitia*.

Due to the markedly Benedictine spirituality in her writings, Gertrud has been venerated as a saint within the Benedictine order since the seventeenth century. In 1738, her cult was extended to the entire church. Gertrud is the only German woman ever to receive the title of "the Great."

While in many ways comparable to other mystical works, Gertrud of Helfta's writings are unique in their emphasis on joy, praise, and thanksgiving. Her inner detachment (*libertas cordis*) leads Gertrud not to dwell on the human condition as sinful and suffering, but to burst out at every possible occasion into songs of jubilation. Her beautiful jubilus (*Exercitia*, VI) is a masterpiece of mystical poetry.

Works

Oeuvres spirituelles (Sources Chrétiennes) [Latin-French ed.], 1967 ff. with introductions. *Ein botte der götlichen miltekeit*, ed. Otmar Wieland (1973); *Revelationes Gertrudianae ac Mechtildianae*, ed. Louis Paquelin (1875), *Insinvationvm divinæ pietatis*, ed. Johannes Lansperger (1536).
Translations: *Legatus* (1865), tr. M. Frances Clare Cusak. *Exercitia* (1823), tr. Thomas Alder Pope (1956), tr. Columba Hart; (1989), tr. Gertrud Jaron Lewis and Jack Lewis (CF49); excerpts in *The Soul Afire*, ed. H.A. Reinhold (1944).

Bibliography

Lewis, Gertrud Jaron, *Bibliographie zur deutschen Frauenmystik des Mittelalters. Mid einem Anhang zu Beatrijs van Nazareth und Hadewijch von Frank Willaert und Marie-José Govers* (Bibliographien zur deutschen Literatur des Mittelalters, 10) (Berlin, 1989), 447 pp. and indexes. Lewis, Willaert, Govers, *Bibliographie zur deutschen Frauen mystik des Mittelalters* (Berlin, 1989). Shank, Lillian Thomas,

Medieval Religious Women, vol. 2 (Kalamazoo, Mich., 1987). Petroff, Elizabeth Alvilda, *Medieval Women's Visionary Literature* (New York/Oxford, 1986). Bynum, Caroline Walker, *Jesus as Mother* (Berkeley, 1982). Dinzelbacher, Peter, *Vision und Visionsliteratur im Mittelalter* (Stuttgart, 1981). Ringler, Siegfried, *Viten- und Offenbarungsliteratur in den Frauenklöstern des Mittelalters* (München, 1980). Finnegan, Mary Jeremy. *Scholars and Mystics* (Chicago, 1962; rev. ed. 1990, University of Georgia Press). Vagaggini, Cipriano, *Il senso teologico della liturgica* (Rome, 1957). Lampen, Willibrord, *St. Gertrudis de Grote* (Hilversum, 1939). Volmer, Ansgar, *Die heilige Gertrud die Große von Helfta* (Kevelaer, 1937). Oliver, Michael, *St. Gertrude the Great* (Dublin, 1930). Luddy, Ailbe J., *St. Gertrude the Great* (Dublin, 1930). Luddy, Ailbe J., *St. Gertrude the Great* (Dublin, 1930). Molenaar, Maurits, *Geertruid van Helfta* (Amsterdam, 1925). Hostachy, Victor, *Joie et sainteté* (Paris, 1921). Müller-Reif, Willy, *Zur Psychologie der mystischen Persönlichkeit (Gertrud von Helfta)* (Berlin, 1921). Dolan, Gilbert, *St. Gertrude the Great* (London, 1912). Ledos, Eugène Gabriel, *Ste Gertrude* (Paris, 1901). Hello, Ernest, *Physionomie des saints* (Paris, 1875). Cros, Léonard-Joseph-Marie, *Le coeur de sainte Gertrude* (Toulouse, 1869; English tr. New York, 1888). Cusak, Frances Clare, *The Spirit of St. Gertrude* (London, 1866). Amort, Eusebius, *De revelationibus* (Augsburg, 1744).

General references: Köpf, Ulrich, *TRE(Theologische Realenzyklopädie)* 12 (1984): 538–540. Grubmüller, Klaus, *Verfasserlexikon*, 2nd ed. 3 (1980): 7–10; Krebs, Engelbert, 1st ed., 2 (1936): 43f. Taney, Mary Stallings, *EDR (Encyclopedic Dictionary of Religion)* 2 (1979): 1480. Ruprecht, Robert, *DLL (Deutsches Literatur-Lexikon)* 6 (1978): 286 f. Doyère, Pierre, *NCE (New Catholic Encyclopedia)* 6 (1967): 450 f. Zimmermann, Alfons Maria, *NDB (Neue deutsche Biographie)* 6 (1964): 334. *Lexikon der Frau* 1 (1953): 1212.

Other references: Lewis, Gertrud Jaron, *Cistercian Studies* 24 (1989). Luislampe, Pia, *Collectanea Cisterciensia* 48 (1986). Winter, Gabriele, *Jahrbuch für salesianische Studien* 17 (1981). Doyère, Pierre, *RAM (Revue d'ascétique et de mystique)* 144 (1960). Leclerq, Jean, *Sponsa Regis* 31 (1960). Doyère, Pierre, *Worship* 34 (1960). Finnegan, Mary Jeremy, *MS (Mediaeval Studies)* 19 (1957). Molenaar, Maurits, *OGL (Ons Geestelijk Leven)* 28 (1951). Graef, Hilda, *Orate Fratres* 20 (1945–1946). Couneson, S., *RLM (Revue liturgique et monastique)* 22 (1936–1937) and 20 (1934–1935). Terhünte, P.J.H., *ZAM (Zeitschrift für Aszese und Mystik)* 2 (1927). Campi, T., *Rivista liturgica* 10 (1923). Maritain, Jacques, *Revue des Jeunes* 32 (1922). de Vere, Aubrey, *The Month* 3 (1865).

Gertrud Jaron Lewis

Gertrud von Le Fort

*Born October 11, 1876, Minden, Westphalia;
died November 1, 1971, Oberstdorf,
Allgau*
Genre(s): apology, autobiography
Language(s): German

A Christian apologist presenting her views symbolically and imaginatively, she is considered "the greatest metaphysical writer of the twentieth century" (Carl Zuckmeyer). The themes of kingdom, church, and women figure centrally in her work, which is characterized by its neoclassical language and simplicity of style.

Gertrud von Le Fort's autobiographical sketch, *Mein Elternhaus* (My Parents' Home), provides us with a knowledge of her early life and upbringing. Of Huguenot descent, she was born into an upper-middle class family. Her early years were spent in different garrisons to which her father, a Prussian army officer, had been posted. She was brought up in the Protestant traditions of the family and her father supervised her education for a long time. From him Gertrud inherited her love of history. From her mother, who was a deeply religious Protestant believer, stemmed her interest in religion. It seemed natural that she should carry on to study history and theology at the universities of Heidelberg, Marburg, and Berlin. Following the death of her father, Gertrud had travelled widely with her mother, including a visit to Rome, which undoubtedly had no small effect upon Gertrud's mind in connection with her subsequent conversion to the Roman Catholic faith in 1925. By this time Gertrud was living in south Germany, having moved from Mecklenburg to Baierbrunn near Munich. Gertrud von Le Fort was opposed to the Hitler regime and was forbidden, like so many, to publish after her criticism had become noticeable. The old family estate of Boeck am Mueritzsee was confiscated by the National Socialists and eventually she fled to Switzerland. She returned to Germany soon after the war and lived in Oberstdorf in the Allgäu. Her literary activities, embracing fiction and nonfiction, prose and verse, span some fifty years. In 1948 she was awarded the Droste-Hülshoff prize, four years later she received the Schweizer Gottfried Keller prize and in 1955 the Grosser Literatur Preis of Nordrhein Westfalen. Most of her works are translated into a variety of foreign languages. (In this connection it is noticeable that her work has made an impact in the Orient as well as in the West, judging from the many Japanese translations.)

Fundamental to all her work is her conviction that Christianity is the center of life and must be allowed to pervade all of life, whether that of the Church, the state, or the individual, if the sense of isolation from which the individual of the twentieth century suffers is to be overcome. The conflict between loyalty to the Church and claims of the modern state is presented in her works against the background of the intellectual crisis of the twentieth century.

In most of Gertrud von Le Fort's works the central figure is a woman, and in a small volume, *Die Ewige Frau* (1934), she has presented woman in her theological setting: the woman's greater power for sacrifice and love as the way of redemption for mankind are themes that run through all her work.

Works

Hymnen an die Kirche [Hymns to the Church] (1924). *Der römische Brunnen* [The Roman Fountain] (Das Schweißtuch der Veronika Pt. 1, 1928). *Der Papst aus dem Ghetto* [The Pope from the Ghetto] (1930). *Die Letzte am Schafott* [The Last at the Scaffold] (1931). *Hymnen an Deutschland* [Hymns to Germany] (1932). *Die Ewige Frau* [The Eternal Woman] (1934). *Die Magdeburgische Hochzeit* [A Marriage in Magdeburg] (1938). *Die Abberufung der Jungfrau von Barby* [The Recall of the Virgin of Barby] (1940). *Mein Elternhaus* [My Parents' Home] (1941). *Das Gericht des Meeres* [The Court of the Sea] (1943). *Der Kranz der Engel* (*Das Schweißtuch der Veronika* Pt. 2) [The Wreath of the Angels] (1946). *Die Consolata* [The Consolation] (1947). *Unser Weg durch die Nacht* [Our Path Through the Night] (1947). *Gedichte* [Poems] (1949). *Die Tochter Farinatas* [Farinatas' Daughter] (1950). *Aufzeichnungen und Erinnerungen* [Sketches and Recollections] (1951). *Am Tor des Himmels* [At the Portal of Heaven] (1954). *Der Turm der Beständigkeit* [The Tower of Constancy] (1957). *Das fremde Kind* [The Foreign Child] (1961). *Aphorismen* [Aphorisms] (1962). *Die Tochter Jephthas* [Jephtha's Daughter] (1964). *Die Hälfe des Lebens* [The Half of Life] (1966). *Das Schweigen* [The Silence] (1967). *Erzählende Schriften*, 3 vols. [Narrative Prose] (1956). *Erzählungen* [Stories] (1966).

Bibliography

Focke, A., *Gertrud von Le Fort* (Graz, 1960). Heinen, N., *Gertrud von Le Fort, eine Einführung in Werk und Persönlichkeit* (Luxemburg, 1955). Jappe, H., *Gertrud von Le Fort, das erzählende Werk* (Meran, 1950). Kampmann, T., *Gertrud von Le Fort. Die Welt einer Dichterin* (Warendorff, 1948). Nathan, Alex, *German Men of Letters*, vol. II (Philadelphia, 1964).

Brigitte Archibald

Luisa Giacóni

Born 1870, Florence, Italy; died 1908, Florence
Genre(s): poetry
Language(s): Italian

Luisa Giacóni was born in Florence of a noble but diminished family. She had a melancholy, solitary infancy and childhood, following her father to various Italian cities where he taught mathematics in technical institutes. Her father, Mortole Giacóni, finally settled in Florence, where he studied paintings from the Accademia di Belle Arti and earned his living by copying these famous paintings for foreign tourists.

Luisa wrote a unique volume of poetry called *Tebaide*, published posthumously (1909). This constitutes one of the most significant Italian symbolist poetic works on liberty. Drawing from the rich suggestiveness of French symbolism, from the decadent English style, and from Pascoli and D'Annunzio, Giancóni constructed restless, sharp discourses with reason and emotion. Her poetry scarcely hides the audacity of the symbolist movement, softened only by her taste for music.

Works
Tebaide (Bologna, 1909; rpt. 1912).

Bibliography
Cuchetti, G., *La Poetessa Luisa Giacóni* (Venice, 1928). Spagnoletti, *Antologia della poesia italiana contemporanea*, I (Florence, 1946).

Jean E. Jost

Zuzanna Ginczanka

(a.k.a. Sana Ginzberg, Sana Weinzieher)

Born 1917, Kiev, Russia; died 1944, Cracow, Poland
Genre(s): poetry
Language(s): Polish

Born in Kiev, in the family of Jewish intelligentsia, Ginczanka made her debut in *Kurier literacko-naukowy* (A Literary and Scientific Daily) in 1933. She studied humanities at the Warsaw University. In 1939, she returned to the East, to Rowne in Volhynia, and then left for Lwow (Lemberg) where she was active in literary life. In hiding in 1942, she lived in fear of arrest. She was shot by the Nazis in prison in Cracow in 1944.

Few poems by Ginczanka have been preserved. Among her posthumous works, there are some erotica, delicate and subtle in tone. "By what sign can one recognize love?" the young woman asks in one of her poems and replies: "By the fact that no sign is needed." Her allegory "On Centaurs" has a modern tone: it is a vision of what traditionally has been considered male and female elements, fused together, in art and in life. "I praise passion and wisdom closely united," the poet proclaims. "I have found the noble harmony between passion focused and wise, and wisdom fiery as passion, and forged them together at the waist and in my heart." Murdered at the age of 27, Ginczanka is hardly known in Poland, and there is little material available about her life or work.

Works
O centaurach [On the Centaurs] (1936). *Wiersze wybrane* [Selected Poems] (1953).

Bibliography
Korzeniewska, Ewa, ed., *Slownik wspolczesnych pisarzy polskich* (PWN, 1963), p. 546.

Maya Peretz

Sana Ginzberg

(see: Zuzanna Ginczanka)

Lidiia Ginzburg

Born 1902
Genre(s): history, criticism
Language(s): Russian

Lidiia Ginzburg is a literary historian and author of works on Benediktov, Lermontov, Tolstoy, Viazemskii, Herzen, and Belinskii. She has also contributed to publications on semiotics.

Works
Byloe i Dumy Gertsena [My Past and Thoughts] (1957). *O Psikhologicheskoi Proze* [On Psychological Prose] (1971). *O Literaturnom.Geroe* [On the Literary Hero] (1979). *O Starom i Novom: Stati i Ocherki* [Old and New: Articles and Essays] (1982). *The Semiotics of Russian Cultural History: Essays, in collaboration with Iurii Lotman and Boris Uspenskii* (1985).

Warwick J. Rodden

Natalia Ginzburg

(a.k.a. Alessandra Tornimparte)

Born July 14, 1916, Palermo, Sicily
Genre(s): novel, short story, drama, essay, biography, translation
Language(s): Italian

In her own country, Natalia Ginzburg is recognized as one of Italy's major twentieth-century writers. Best known for her fiction and drama, she is also an essayist, biographer, and translator. She first won the notice of critics after World War II. Since then, she has received numerous literary awards. Ginzburg has also

461

gained an international audience through translations into English, French, Spanish, German, Danish, and Hungarian.

The youngest of five children, Natalia Ginzburg was born in Sicily to Giuseppe and Lydia Levi. Her father's family was Jewish and from Trieste; her mother's family was Catholic and from Milan. After three years, the family moved to Turin, where Natalia grew up. Family interests included science (her father was Professor of Anatomy at Turin University), politics (her father and brothers were involved in socialist and antifascist activities), and literature (the children read extensively, recited poems, and told stories). At the age of seven she wrote her first poem; at seventeen she completed her first story. In 1933, she met Leone Ginzburg, a Russian expatriate writer and political activist. She soon began working at Einaudi, the Turin publishing house, which was to be her publisher for many years. In 1938 she married Leone Ginzburg; he died in 1944 while a political prisoner in Rome. They had three children. In 1950 Natalia Ginzburg married Gabriele Baldini, Director of the Italian Institute in London and later Professor of English Literature at Rome University. The marriage ended with his death in 1969. Since her first childhood poems, through years of personal tragedy and political upheaval, Natalia Ginzburg has continued to write. She is now living in Rome.

Works

La strada che va in citta e altri raconnti (1945; under pseudonym Alessandra Tornimparte, 1942). *Estato cosi* (1947). *Tutti i nostri ieri* (1952). *Valentino* (1957). *Romanzi del 900* (with Giansiro Ferrato; 1958). *Le voci della sera* (1961). *Le piccole virtu* (1962). *Lessico famigliare* (1963). *Cinque romanzi brevi* (1964). *Ti ho sposato per allegria e altre commedie* (1968). *Mai devi domandarmi* (1970). *Caro Michele* (1973; videorecording, 1970). *Paese di mare e altri commedie* (1973). *Vita imaginaria* (1974). *Sagittario* (1975; part of *Valentino*, publ. in 1957). *Famiglia* (1977). *La carta del cielo* (1980; racconti di Mario Soldati; edited by Ginzburg). *Diari, 1927–1961* (1982; di Antonio Delfini edited by Ginzburg and Giovanna Delfino). *La famiglia Manzoni* (1983). *La citta e la casa* (1984).

Translations: *Dear Michael* (1975). *No Way* (1974; 1976). *La route qui m'ene a la ville: quatre romans courts* (1983). *The Advertisement* (1969). *The City and the House* (1986). *The Road to the City/The Dry Heart: Two Novelettes* (1949; rpt. 1990). *Las pequenas virtudes* (1966). *The Little Virtues* (1985, 1986). *Familiealbum* (1968). *Family Sayings* (1967, 1984, 1986). *Voices in the Evening* (1963). *Die Stimmen des Abends* (1970). *Never Must You Ask Me* (1973). *Dead Yesterdays* (1956). *A Light for Fools* (1957). *All Our Yesterdays* (1985; 1986). *Todos nuestros ayeres* (1958). *Alle unsere Jahra* (1967). *Valamennyi tegnapunk* (1979).

Bibliography

Bowne, Clotilde Suave, "The Narrative Strategy of Natalia Ginzburg." *Modern Language Review* 68 (1973): 788–795. Clementelli, Elena, *Invito alla lettura di Natalia Ginzburg* (Milano, 1974). Heiney, Donald, "Natalia Ginzburg: The Fabric of Voices." *The Iowa Review* 1, 4: 87–93. Marchionne Picchione, Luciana, *Natalia Ginzburg* (Firenze, 1978).

General references: *Contemporary Authors*, vols. 85–88 (1980). *Contemporary Literary Criticism*, vol. 5 (1976); vol. 11 (1979).

Lydia A. Panaro

Zinaida Gippius (or Hippius)

Born November 20, 1869, Belev, Tula District, Russia; died September 9, 1945, Paris
Genre(s): poetry, short story, drama, literary journalism
Language(s): Russian, French

One of this century's most remarkable lyric poets writing in Russian, a prolific writer of prose, drama, and criticism and a voluminous correspondent, Gippius was an initiator of Russian symbolism, one of the largest and most influential literary movements in Russia this century. Gippius was not only a leading and well-regarded writer but also wielded considerable institutional power in the avant garde literary establishment of St. Petersburg from the 1890s until her emigration in 1915. With her husband, the writer Dmitrii Sergeevich Merezhkovskii, she was closely involved with the planning and editorial selection of such journals as *New Path*,

World of Art, and *The Scales*; she was also a contributor to the French symbolist journal *Mercure de France*. The famous literary-philosophical gatherings which she organized were attended by most of the leading lights of intellectual Petersburg. She was a central figure in the Religious-Philosophical Society, which sought to reconcile the disaffected Russian intelligentsia with the Orthodox Church; other members included Nicholas Berdyaev and Vasilii Rozanov. After emigration, when she and her husband settled in Paris, she continued organizing philosophical and literary activities, most notably in the form of a discussion society called *The Green Lamp*.

Gippius' institutional prominence, combined with a certain calculated *épatage* of dress and behavior which emerges in the well-known portrait of her by Leon Bakst, made the shocked conventional public regard her as the epitome of decadence. It is doubtful whether any of her contemporaries attracted such violent hostility. Some of this came from writers who were offended by her highhanded treatment of them or wittily acerbic attacks on them, some from observers who found Gippius and her husband's mystical religious beliefs antipathetic or absurd—the poet Innokentii Annenskii, for example, wrote of the Merezhkovskiis: "They have no capacity for abstraction, only instincts and damnable self-love, they haven't a single idea, only a gold ring they wear on their ties." But some of the hatred must undoubtedly be attributed to resentment, in a male-dominated society, that any woman should be so powerful and so flamboyant. The many sexist appellations which she attracted confirm this impression: she was known as "Messalina" and "the white she-devil," and Trotsky wrote of her, "I do not believe in witches in general, not counting the above-mentioned Zinaida Gippius, in whose reality I believe absolutely, though about the length of her tail I can say nothing definite" (*Literature and Revolution*, chapter 1).

Gippius' unorthodox sexuality also led to adverse comment. She rejected stereotyped notions of women's roles, writing in 1928 to the young poet Nina Berberova, "Frankly, I feel no maternal feelings for you; in fact, in general I don't seem to be capable of such feelings." Her marriage to Merezhkovskii was based on affec-tionate companionship, not on sexual interest—Gippius herself encouraged rumors that it had not been consummated. In relationships with other men she herself acted as initiator and hunter, particularly in the case of her long infatuation with Dimitrii Filosofov, whom she treated as a kind of male Muse. Sexual ambivalence was another aspect of Gippius' hostility to convention; this theme emerges especially strongly in her diaries and in some of her short stories, for example "The Mother-of-Pearl Cane."

On the other hand, the complications of Gippius' personality were great, and it is unwise to claim that her ideas can easily be appropriated by modern feminism. She was capable of writing very dismissively of "female psychology," describing it as unstable and unreliable (see her letters to Berberova, pages 36–37). She reacted to other women with suspicion; she was, for example, violently jealous of Marina Tsvetaeva, and seemed happiest in a dominating, patronizing role with a younger woman, such as Berberova. Her attitude to lesbianism was likewise contradictory: her views on sexual freedom had been initiated by an erotic interest in male homosexuality (Karlinsky, 9). She regarded actual sexual contact as secondary to spiritual communication, writing to Filosofov "It was all in God, from God, through Him. A moment of religious feeling (not only for you but for God and for nature) touched my spirit and my soul and *my flesh*" (Zlobin, 88). Her relations with women seem also to have been emotional or sentimental rather than sexual. All in all, she was an advanced case of the so-called Queen Bee complex; that is, a woman who regards freedom as uniquely her prerogative.

Gippius' lyrics present problems for a modern reader. The emotional pain and confusion brought about by the physical state of being a woman, delineated by other women writers such as Shkapskaya and Tsvetaeva, are absent; and the domestic realities of women's lives she ignored as completely as any male writer. Her concern is with the supernatural, the other-worldly; the external world exists only as a collection of deliberately patterned and formulaic attributes, or as props for a metaphysical conflict. The only tradition of women's writing in which she can perhaps be placed is that of the Gothic occult tale or ghost story; her early volume *Mirrors* has some similarity to the writing of Isak Dinesen, for example.

Though hot-house eroticism, often with demonic overtones, is certainly characteristic of Gippius' lyrics, genuine sexual ambivalence is harder to find. She does use masculine pseudonyms and masculine narrators in her lyrics, and female narrators are distanced from the poet's own person (see for example "Annunciation," 1904). But, like all the symbolists, Gippius had a dualistic philosophy, and the contrast between "femininity" and "masculinity" is only one of many polarities in her poetry; at least as important are the contrasts between fear and resolution, and between the moral extremes of God and the Devil. Besides, in keeping with the abstraction of her poetry, it is more satisfactory to read the male and female poems as representations of psychological types, centering round a conventional binary opposition between the female—emotional and fearful—and the male—intellectual and courageous. The term "androgynous" used by some critics is probably the most fitting for her poetry.

Arguably, Gippius' finest achievements as a poet are those to which gender is irrelevant. She has been described as "one of Russia's finest religious poets" (McCormack, 175). Her claim to this rests less on those poems where she expresses pious resignation, in the female voice, or encounters such resignation at second hand, in the male voice; there is usually a note of affectation here. More impressive are the poems in which she starkly, and without hint of gender, portrays metaphysical evil; she writes, for example, with chilling strength in the opening lines of her long poem *The Last Circle*:

The waves of otherworldly nausea foam
up,
Break into spray and scatter in black
mist,
And into darkness, into outermost
darkness,
As they return to subterranean ocean.
We call it pain here, sorrowful and
heartfelt,
But it's not pain, for pain is something
else.
For subterranean and endless nausea

There are no earthly words, for words
are not enough.
(tr. S. Karlinsky)

Gippius' political poetry, which was highly praised by D.S. Mirsky, a critic of outstanding discernment, is equally resolute. The mode is vatic and commanding, as in this attack on the October Revolution:

Will those pure heroes forgive us?
For we have not kept their
commandment.
We have lost all that is sacred;
The shame of our souls, the honour of
the earth.
[. . .]
The nocturnal flock whistles and croaks,
The Neva's ice is bloody and
drunken. . . .
O, Nicholas' noose was cleaner
Than these grey monkeys' fingers!

While the above is in the nineteenth-century publicistic tradition of Pushkin and Tyutchev, it is doubtful whether either could have equalled Gippius' magnificent snub to Blok:

I shall not forgive. Your soul is innocent.
I shall not forgive it. Ever.

The cerebral, rather than emotional, quality of Gippius' verse is suggested also by its construction. She was a poet of considerable technical facility, a pioneer of metrical innovations among the symbolists, such as tonic verse and half-rhyme. Her lyrics are metrically constrained, with formalized word-repetition which in some cases has the quality of a melodious refrain, but in others underlines an ironic *pointe*. The intellectual character of the verse is underlined by perpetual internal debate. Sometimes a single poem expresses conflict or paradox, sometimes alternative versions of one poem complement or contradict each other; or the same title is used for poems of radically different orientation.

Given Gippius' great prolificity, it is not surprising that her output should be uneven and sometimes repetitive. Sometimes she relied too greatly on her very considerable purely lyric talent, turning out poems which are trifling and monotonously musical. But there is no doubt that the intrinsic merits of the best of her work have survived the passage of time; and that, from a literary-historical point of view, her activities laid the foundation for the outstanding tradition of poetry by women in Russia this century.

Works

Stikhotvoreniya, 2 vols. (1972). The various volumes of her *Stories* are most accessible in the facsimile editions, ed. T. Pachmuss, published Munich, beginning 1973.
Correspondence: *Pis'ma Berberovoi i Khodasevichu*, ed. E.F. Sheikholoslami (1978).
Translations: *Selected Works*, tr. and ed. T. Pachmuss (1972). *Women Writers in Russian Modernism, An Anthology*, tr. and ed. T. Pachmuss (1978).

Bibliography

The best short introductions for the English-speaking reader are S. Karlinsky, intro. to V. Zlobin, *A Difficult Soul*, tr. and ed. S. Karlinsky (Berkeley, 1980); and D.S. Mirsky, *A History of Russian Literature*, ed. F. Whitehead (London, 1949), pp. 439–441. Two full-length studies of Gippius in English are T. Pachmuss, *Zinaida Hippius: An Intellectual Profile* (Carbondale, Ill., 1971); and O. Matich, *Paradox in the Religious Poetry of Zinaida Gippius* (Munich, 1972).
For more extensive biographical and bibliographical information, see: McCormack, K., "Z.N. Gippius," *The Modern Encyclopedia of Russian and Soviet Literature*, vol. 8, ed. H.B. Weber (Gulf Breeze, Fla., 1987), pp. 175–183. Pachmuss, T., "Z.N. Hippius." in *Handbook of Russian Literature*, ed. V. Terras (New Haven, 1985), pp. 193–194.

Catriona Kelly

Smara Gîrbea

(see: Smara)

Veronica Giuliani

Born December 27, 1660, Mercatello, near Urbino, Italy; died July 9, 1727, Citta di Castello
Genre(s): mysticism, autobiography
Language(s): Italian

A Capuchin nun, Veronica Giuliani was a mystic in the Franciscan tradition, dedicated to meditation on Christ's Passion. She entered the Capuchin convent in Citta di Castello in 1677. She remained there for the next fifty years. Twenty years after her entry, she received the stigmata. She had already begun her diary in 1695 and would continue it until a few months before her death. Forty-four manuscript volumes remain till this day in the convent at Citta di Castello. Only selections have been published.

Works

Il Diario . . . a cura di Teresa Carboni [The Diary . . . ed. Teresa Carboni] (1954), 2 vols.

Bibliography

Bell, *Holy Anorexia*, pp. 57–83.

Joseph Berrigan

Elena Gjika

(a.k.a. Dora d'Istria)

Born 1828, Bucharest, Romania; died 1882
Genre(s): essay, letters
Language(s): French

Gjika was essentially a publicist, intent on generating popular support for a variety of causes, such as the national aspirations of the Albanian people, the rights of national minorities, equality for women, and popular education.

Being born in an aristocratic family, Gjika was able to travel to the courts of Vienna, Dresden, and Berlin. She was widely admired for her talent and beauty. She lived for periods of time in Russia, Switzerland, and toward the last phase of her life in Italy.

Her best known work on an Albanian theme is the essay, *La nationalité albanaise d'après les chants populaires*, which appeared in the periodical *Revue des deux mondes*, Paris, 1866. It was later translated into Albanian and Italian.

Works

La nationalité albanaise d'après les chants populaires (1866).

Bibliography

Vehbi, Gala, *Jeta e Elena Gjikēs* [The Life of Elena Gjika] (Tiranē, Albania, 1967).

Sanda Golopentia

Jarmila Glazarová

Born 1901, Malá Skála, Czechoslovakia; died
1977, Prague
Genre(s): novel
Language(s): Czech

Glazarová (nee Podivínská) lost both her
parents at the beginning of World War I and
during the war led a difficult life in Prague and
then at a boarding school converted into a military
hospital. After the war she married and led a
quiet life in the countryside. Her literary debut
Roky v kruhu (1936; The Cycle of the Years), a
memoir of her recently deceased husband, incorporates a fond evocation of the seasonal round
of rural life. Glazarová's career as a novelist was
brief. After World War II she concentrated on
propagandistic nonfiction although she also wrote
fiction for children. From 1946 to 1948 she was
cultural attaché for the Czechoslovakian embassy
in Moscow. After the imposition of Communism
in Czechoslovakia, she continued to serve in
official positions. She was awarded the title of
"People's Artist" in 1959.

Glazarová's second work, Vlčí jáma (1938;
The Wolf Pit) is about an orphaned girl and her
stepfather. The most memorable character is the
hypochondriac and thoroughly egotistical Aunt
Klara. Advent (1939) resembles Vlčí jáma in its
harrowing narration of intense psychological
conflict and suppressed emotions. A poor unmarried mother marries a widower in order to
provide for her small son. All her sufferings and
humiliations are brought forward during the
course of one night. The mountain region where
these events take place is described in further
detail in Chudá přadlena (1940; The Poor
Spinner). In a series of loosely connected episodes,
Glazarová depicts the lives of simple country
folk.

Glazarová's novels are part of long tradition
of Czech "village novels," based on first-hand
observations of folk ways. There is an element of
social protest in her novels, but it takes second
place to the psychological drama. Unlike some of
her contemporaries with a similar realist aesthetic
and socialist view (for example, Marie
Pujmanová), she did not essay a socialist realist
novel, instead turning to ideological reportage.
Although Glazarová's novels do have intrinsic
interest, her official reputation today is based
more on her "political correctness" than her
literary achievement.

Works

Glazarová, Jarmila, Dílo [Works] (1953–1960). (For
a complete list of fiction and non-fiction, see
Burianek below.)

Bibliography

Burianek, František, Jarmila Glazarová (Prague,
1979). Součková, Milada, A Literature in Crisis:
Czech Literature 1938–1950 (New York, 1954),
pp. 115–118.

Nancy Cooper

Babette Elisabeth Glück

(a.k.a. Betty Paoli)

Born December 30, 1815, Vienna, Austria;
died July 5, 1894, Baden near Vienna
Genre(s): poetry, short story, novel, essay, epic
Language(s): German

She was the illegitimate daughter of an
Hungarian nobleman and lived with her widowed
mother, a Belgian woman, who took her with her
on many trips and thus gave her the model of an
unstable life with constant moves from place to
place. From 1833 to 1835 she was appointed
governess by a Russian family living close to the
border to Poland, but Paoli's mother could not
cope with the situation and forced her to flee
back across the border to Austria. Her mother
died on the trip due to harsh winter conditions.
From 1843 to 1848 she was the lady companion
of the Duchess Schwarzenberg. After extensive
travels, she finally settled in Vienna, where she
established extensive contacts with the leading
authors and poets including Bauernfeld and Maria
von Ebner-Eschenbach. Her essays and poems,
influenced by Byron, were highly praised by the
public. Grillparzer and Lenau, in particular, were
impressed by her lyric poetry. Her short stories,
however, never gained the same reputation. She
was a friend of Goethe's daughter-in-law Othilie
and thus became the center of the public and
literary life of Vienna.

Works

Gedichte [Poems] (1841). *Nach dem Gewitter* [After the Thunderstorm] (1843). *Die Welt und mein Auge* [The World and my Eye] (1844), 3 vols. *Romancero* (1845). *Neue Gedichte* [New Poems] (1850). *Lyrisches und Episches* [Lyric and Epic Pieces] (1856). *Wiens Gemäldegalerien in ihrer kunsthistorischen Bedeutung* [Vienna's Art Galleries and their Importance for Art History] (1865). *Neueste Gedichte* [Very New Poems] (1869). *Grillparzer und seine Werke* [Grillparzer and His Works] (1875). *Gedichte* [Poems] (1895), posthumous selection, ed. Ebner-Eschenbach. *Gesammelte Aufsätze* [Collected Essays] (1908).

Bibliography

Bettelheim-Gabillon, Helene, "Betty Paoli." *Neue Österreichische Biographie ab 1815*, vol. 5 (Vienna-Munich-Zurich, 1928), pp. 48–65. Bettelheim-Gabillon, Helene, "Zur Charakteristik Betty Paolis." *Grillparzer-Jahrbuch* 10 (1900). Marchand, Alfred, *Les poètes lyriques de l'Autriche nouvelle, études biographiques et littéraires*, 4th ed. (Paris, 1889). Missbach, R., *Betty Paoli als Lyrikerin in ihrer Stellung zu Grillparzer und Lenaus Lyrik*, Ph.D. diss., Munich, 1923. Schmidt, Adalbert, *Dichtung und Dichter Österreichs im 19. und 20. Jahrhundert*, vol. 1 (Salzburg, 1964), pp. 96–98. Schönbach, A., "Betty Paoli." *Historisch-politische Blätter* 142 (1908). Scott, A.A., *Betty Paoli, An Austrian Poetess of the 19th Century* (London, 1926). Werner, R.M., "Betty Paoli." *Östereichisch-Ungarische Revue* 26 (1898). Zinck, K.H., "Betty Paoli und Adalbert Stifter." *Adalbert-Stifter-Institut, Vierteljahresschrift* 22 (1973/74). Zinck, K.H., "Betty Paoli (1814–1894) und Dr. Josef Breuer (1842–1925) in ihrer Zeit." *Adalbert-Stifter-Institut, Vierteljahresschrift* 25 (1976): 143–159.

Albrecht Classen

Glückel of Hameln

Born 1645, Hamburg, Germany; died 1724, Metz
Genre(s): memoirs
Language(s): Yiddish

Glückel was born in Hamburg in 1645 into a wealthy Jewish family. At the age of fourteen, she was married to Hayim of Hameln, a promi-nent businessman. In addition to raising their twelve children, Glückel actively participated in her husband's business. With his death in 1689, she successfully assumed sole responsibility for the business. Two years later, in order to alleviate her continued sorrow, Glückel began to write her memoirs. Her writing was further motivated by a desire to provide her children with a record of their family history as well as to give them guidelines for a life of well-being. In 1700, with her marriage to the banker Cerf Lévy, Glückel moved to Metz and temporarily set aside her memoirs. It was in 1712, upon the death of her second husband, that she resumed her writing. Glückel herself died twelve years later in Metz.

Glückel's memoirs, written in seven books and often considered the first work in "modern" Yiddish literature, were intended for her family and not for publication. In fact, it was not until the end of the nineteenth century that they were published for the first time in the original Yiddish with an introduction in German. Translations into other languages soon followed with the English version appearing in 1932.

The memoirs of Glückel of Hameln provide keen insight into the daily existence of the Jewish communities of the late seventeenth to the early eighteenth centuries in Altona, Hamburg, Hameln, and Metz. In elaborating on her own life, Glückel includes, for example, her thoughts on widowhood, the problems involved in raising children, the responsibilities of the business. She also expresses her concerns about the difficulties confronting the Jews, mostly the constant dangers from the outside world. Glückel is especially interested in the role of the Jewish woman; she therefore explores such different problems as the plight of the abandoned wife. Included also in the writings are moralistic short stories. The art of storytelling, detailed descriptions, and an understanding of human nature are evident in Glückel's memoirs.

Works

Memoirs of Glückel of Hameln (1932).

Bibliography

Minkov, N. *Glikl Hamel* (1952, Yiddish). Winston, M., *Glückel von Hameln: A Dramatization of Her Autobiography* (1941).

Michael F. Bassman

Germaine Goetzinger

Born 1947, Dudelange, Germany
Genre(s): essay
Language(s): German

Germaine Goetzinger pursued her studies of modern literature and history at the University of Tübingen in Germany. At present she is a secondary-school teacher in Diekirch. This young woman is a remarkable essayist who draws her matter from a documentation gathered with minute care of detail and precision and presents the results of her research in a strong, vigorous style with striking lucidity. She is especially interested in the German literature of the nineteenth century as well as in the position, the evolution, and the emancipation of woman. She made her reputation with the publication of an elaborate work dedicated to Louise Aston, German writer and feminist of the nineteenth century.

Germaine Goetzinger also carried out research into the foundation of secondary school education for girls in the Grand-Duchy of Luxembourg. She is an outstanding lecturer and works in the field of the history of Luxembourgish literature—she composed an important study on the literary review "Floréal."

Works

Für die Selbstverwirklichung der Frau: Louise Aston. In Selbstzeugnissen und Dokumenten [For the Self-Realization of Woman: Louise Aston. In Self-Portraits and Documents] (1983). "Floréal': Eine Fallstudie zur literarischen Oeffentlichkeit in Luxemburg ["Floréal': A Case Study towards literary publication in Luxembourg] (1986) in *Clierwer Literaturdeeg 1985.* "Kindermoerderinnen" [Child Murderesses]. Berger, Renate, and Inge Stephan, ed. *Frau und Tod* [Woman and Death] (1987).

Rosemarie Kieffer and Liliane Stomp-Erpelding

Pola Gojawiczynska

Born 1896, Warsaw, Poland; died 1963
Genre(s): novel, short story
Language(s): Polish

Born in Warsaw, in a milieu of blue collar workers and artisans, she was basically self-educated; having completed grade school and a course for kindergarten teachers, she could not afford to continue studies after her father's death. She worked as a kindergarten teacher and librarian; later, when she married and left the capital, she lived in provincial towns and worked at an office. She made her literary debut in 1915 with a short story entitled "Two Fragments" for which she received a prize at a newspaper contest. In 1931, she moved to Silesia, and, thanks to endeavors by the renowned writer Zofia Nalkowska, received a grant to continue her literary career. In 1932, invited by a newspaper to join its board of editors, she returned to Warsaw. She wrote about the life of the Warsaw proletariat and petty bourgeoisie and won much popular acclaim and many literary awards. During the Nazi occupation of Poland, her books were banned and withdrawn from public libraries, and the author herself was arrested and imprisoned. Her life at the Pawiak prison became the subject of one of her post-war novels.

Works

Opowiadania [Short Stories] (1933). *Ziemia Elzbiety* [Elizabeth's Land] (1934). *Dziewczeta z Nowolipek* [The Girls of Nowolipki] (1937). *Rajska Jablon* [The Apple Tree of Paradise] (1937). *Dwoje ludzi* [Two People] (1938). *Slupy ogniste* [Pillars of Fire] (1938). *Stolica* [The Capital] (1946). *Krata* [Behind Bars] (1947). *Milosc Gertrudy* [Gertrude's Love] (1956).

Bibliography

Korzeniewska, Ewa, *Slownik wspolczesnych pisarzy polskich.* Krzyzanowski, Julian, *A History of Polish Literature* (PWN: Warsaw, 1978).

Maya Peretz

Alice Golay

(see: Marthe-Marguerite le Valois de Villette de Mursay, Comtesse de Caylus)

Leah Goldberg

Born 1911, Kovno, Lithuania; died 1970,
Jerusalem
Genre(s): poetry, drama, children's literature
Language(s): Hebrew

Leah Goldberg was born in Kovno, Lithuania in 1911, and was educated there at the Hebrew Gymnasium. She continued her education in philosophy and Semitic languages at the Universities of Bonn and Berlin, and in 1933 was awarded a Ph.D. from the University of Bonn. During this time she adopted Hebrew as her mother tongue. Early in her career, 1935, Goldberg settled in Palestine and joined the experimental literary group Yachdav, along with Natan Alterman and Avraham Shlonsky. She worked closely with Shlonsky as a translator and editor.

Goldberg's career began as a lecturer on the history of the theater for the Habima dramatic school and advisor for its theater. She also joined the newspaper staff of the *Davar* (Word) as a drama and literary critic. She later moved to join the staff of the *Ha-Mishmar* (The Observer). In 1954 she joined the faculty of Hebrew University, Jerusalem as a lecturer in comparative literature. Subsequently, she became Chairman of the Comparative Literature Department and remained in this position until her death in 1970.

Because of her inclusion in the Yachdev group, Goldberg is usually associated with the modernist movement of the thirties, and its Freudian and French symbolist influences. Yet, her works seem to elude any categories or traditionalism.

Part of Leah Goldberg's prolific writing was intended for the delight of children. Her partnership with photographer Anna Rivkin-Brick produced the lively works *Little Queen of Sheba* and *Harpatkah ba-Midbar* (Adventure in the Desert). She also wrote poetry for children, as in *Gan ha-Hayyot* (The Zoo), where she used rhyming verses to describe animals and their matching attitudes.

There are few areas into which Goldberg has not ventured. She was extremely active in the arena of criticism, not only on various newspaper staffs, but also as the author of articles (i.e., "Aspects of Israeli Theatre") and a book on the art of short story (*Omanut ha-Sippur*, or The Art of Narrative). Other publications include a novel, *Ve-Hur ha-Or* (And He Is the Light), and a collection of essays about her native Russia, *Ha-Sifrut ha-Rusit ba-Meah ha-Tesha' 'Esreh* (Russian Literature of the Nineteenth Century). She also did many translations, and even wrote a dramatic play, *Ba'alat ha-Armon* (Lady of the Castle).

As a poet, Goldberg is daring in her imagery. In her collection *Shibboleth Yerokat ha-'Ayin* (Green-Eyed Ear of Corn) she creates a unique evening with such descriptive phrases as "a rug of roofs is spread before my window light", "the antenna clutches like a mast the hem of heaven heaving on the sea", and she wishfully writes, "a star will fall into my cup perchance." There is an edge of intellectual hardness in this use of artistic, sometimes shocking imagery, which serves to bring the reader to a poetic awareness. However, Goldberg felt this philosophical trend lacked a freshness she was seeking, and it was not a path she continued to pursue.

Goldberg later published a volume of poems dealing with nature, *Al ha-Pericha* (Of Bloom), which seems to fulfill her need of giving the reader beautiful imagery while conveying a depth of feeling and love of beauty. This act of moving over that edge of intellectual hardness to a world of feeling and beauty has made Goldberg one of the most beloved of Hebrew poets. Her voice penetrates the internal being of all nature, as she has trees, blades of grass and even the moon sing to the stream, and finally offers the "stream's psalm the world extols." There is a freshness in her imagery as she compares the stone, "the constant, mystery of creation," to the stream, "I am change, its revelation.". The freshness of Goldberg's poetry does not fade as she reflects on the past. She remembers not significant events, but the fleeting images of "a wheat stalk in the greenness of her youth," and "the tree in the middle of her spring." She emphasizes the constant of change in nature and the beauty that one experiences through nature's constant renewal. This is the essence of Leah Goldberg's poetry: each day is a renewal, "every day shall not be like yesterday, and the day before it, and life shall not become trite and habitual." This is the prayer Goldberg offers for not only herself, but her readers as well.

The pinnacle of honors and fame came to Leah Goldberg one year before her death, 1969, when the Institute of Hebrew Studies of New York University awarded her the Irving and Bertha Neuman Literary Prize. Although she died in 1970, her spirit of freshness and boldness is constantly renewed as there is a wealth of wisdom and depth of feeling yet to be discovered in her prolific works.

Works

Jabaot Ashan [Smoke Rings] (1935). *Mihtavim Minsiah Medumah* [Letters from an Imaginary Journey] (1937). *Shibbolet Yerokat ha-Ayim* [Green-eyed Ear of Corn] (1939–1940). *Gan ha-Hayyot* [The Zoo] (1941, 1970). *Mibeti Hayashan* [From My Old House] (1942). *We-hu ha-or* [And He Is the Light] (1946). *Luah ha-ohavim* [The Tablet of Lovers] (195_). *Sifrut yafah olamit be-tirgumaha le-Ivrit* [World Literature in Hebrew Translation] (1951). *Ahavat Shimson* [The Love of Samson] (1951/52). *Pegishah 'Im Meshorer* [Meeting with a Poet] (1952). *Nisim ve-nifla'ot* [Deeds and Wonders] (1954). *Ba 'alat ha-Armon* [Lady of the Castle] (1955). *Barak BaBoker* [Morning Glory] (1955). *Malkat Sheva ha-Ketanah* [The Little Queen of Sheba] (1956). *Ayeh Pluto* [Where Is Pluto?] (1957). *The Chatelaine* (1957). *Ahdut ha-adam vehayekum bi-yetsirato Shel Tolstoi* [The Unity of Man and Survival in the Works of Tolstoy] (1959). *Mukdam ve-Menhar* [Early and Late] (1959). *Tserif Katan* [A Little Cabin] (1959). *Omanut ha-Sippur* [The Art of Narrative] (1963). *Im Halayla Hazeh* [With This Night] (1964). *Ma'aseh be-tsayar* [Work by a Painter] (1965). *Harpatkah ba-Midbar* [Adventure in the Desert] (1966). *Yedidai me-Rehov Arnon* [My Friends from Arnon Street] (1966). *ha-Mefuzar mi-Kefar Azar* [The Scatter-Brain from Kefar Azar] (1967). *Mah osot ha-ayalot* [What Does Do] (1967). *Ha-Sifrut ha-Rusit ba-Meah ha-Tesha' Esreh* [Russian Literature of the Nineteenth Century] (1968). *Sheloshah Sippurim* [Three Stories] (1970). *Yalkut Shirim* [The Back-Pack of Poems] (1970). *Sheerit ha-Hayyim* [Remnants of Life] (1971).

Bibliography

Abramson, Glenda, *Modern Hebrew Drama* (New York, 1979). Alter, Robert, "On Leah Goldberg and S.Y. Agnon." *Commentary* (May 1970). Baumgarten-Kuris, Ora, *Emsta'im Sifruti'im be-*

Shirta Shel Leah Goldberg (Jerusalem, 1979). Glazer, Myra, ed., *Burning Air and a Clear Mind* (Athens, 1981). Kemer, Yaffa, ed., *Leket mi-Shirei Leah Goldberg* (Jerusalem, 1978). Mintz, Ruth F., ed., *Modern Hebrew Poetry* (Berkeley, 1966). Penueli, S.Y., and A. Ukhmani, eds., *Anthology of Modern Hebrew Poetry, Vol. 2* (Jerusalem, 1966). Silberschlag, Eisig, *From Renaissance to Renaissance II: Hebrew Literature in the Land of Israel: 1870–1970* (New York, 1977). Waxman, Meyer, *A History of Jewish Literature, Vol. 5* (Cranbury, N.J.), 1960.

JoAnne C. Juett

Johann Golder

(see: Kathinka [Katharina] Rosa Pauline Modesta Zitz-Halein)

Claire Goll

Born October 29, 1891, Nuremberg, Germany; died March 30, 1977, Paris, France
Genre(s): poetry, prose, letters, autobiography
Language(s): German, French

Claire Goll is mainly known for her expressionistic-surrealistic poetry influenced to a large extent by Rainer Maria Rilke. Conveying enthusiasm and at times pathos, she never distanced herself from the issues described.

Her life was restless and often not very pleasant, but in her letters she created the image of a strong character who could even laugh in and about pain. Her pacifistic background, her own ill health, and general attitude towards humanity permitted her to feel sympathy for the outcasts, the helpless, the suppressed. In general, her poetry expresses this sympathy for and analysis of man in the twentieth century.

Born in Nuremberg, Goll spent her childhood and youth in Munich, where she visited the reform school of the pedagogue Georg Gerschensteiner. In 1911 Claire Goll married the Swiss publisher Dr. Heinrich Studer, in 1912 their daughter Dorothea was born, in 1917 Goll divorced her husband and moved to Switzerland. Living and studying in Geneva, she was actively engaged in the anti-war movement during the first world war. In Switzerland she made the acquaintance of many of the leading literary figures of expressionism, for example Kurt Wolff, the publisher who had left his native Germany, and Franz Werfel. While living in Zurich, she had contacts with Hans Arp, James Joyce, and Stefan Zweig. Her future husband Ivan Goll had published the poem "Requiem für die Gefallenen Europas" (Requiem for the Fallen Soldiers of Europe) in the pacifist paper *Demain*. Through Henri Guilbeaux, the publisher of *Demain* and Romain Rolland, a leading pacifist, she met Ivan Goll after she had congratulated him on his poem. He visited her in Geneva and in 1917 they "married" symbolically. In 1921 a legal ceremony was performed because Ivan pressed her. In 1918 and again in 1921, Claire had spent some time with Rilke, and this very close and intimate relationship probably was the reason for Ivan to take the initiative. The liaison had been celebrated by Rilke in the enthusiastic poem "Liliane," which was Claire's second name. In 1919, Claire had followed Ivan to Paris, where he had joined the surrealist movement. There, Claire made further acquaintances and formed friendships with surrealist painters and poets such as Chaga, Delaunay, Gleizes and Leger. Claire, who had been ill all her life, spent much time away from her husband, and a collection of their letters shows a very deep, emotional and concerned relationship. It is interesting to note that during the years between 1930 and 1939, Hitler and his regime are never directly referred to. The correspondence is full of personal and emotional issues, of detailed descriptions of her illness, of important and very trivial matters. The letters give the idea of how precisely Claire watched the world around her, how concerned she was with the "everyday." In 1937, Ivan had planned a flight to New York; his literary engagement, however, kept him from pursuing the plan. Claire left for London in 1938, and both arrived in New York in 1939, where they stayed until 1947. In New York, Ivan published the literary magazine *Hemisphere* (1943–1947). In 1950, Ivan died of leukemia in Paris. Claire travelled on a lecture tour through the United States between 1952 and 1954. In 1973, the City of Marbach, West Germany, opened the "Ivan and Claire Goll Room" in the German Archive for literature.

The title of the collection of lyrics *Lyrische Films* (1922; Lyrical Films) already showed her extravagance. The first part of the collection are lyrical poems, the second section is called "sentimentalities," and the last part is the *Tagebuch eines Pferdes* (Diary of a Horse). This third part is a prose poem dedicated to "Ivan and all the horses." The first poem of the collection, for example, is a hymn on the twentieth century, the reference, as in all expressionistic works, is to the age of the machine. Nature became automatized: Orpheus does not sing any more, but the "gramophone" becomes the "metallic phoenix." It is a sarcastic, at times perverted, glorification of the machine's domination over man. The style of all these poems is expressionistic-surrealistic, with run-off lines, lack of rhyme, and distorted sentence structure. The first poem in "Sentimentalitäten" is dedicated *To* * (*An* *), and a comparison of body and facial features with non-human objects. The second poem, "Woman," is a critical analysis of woman in her relationship with man. Many poems of this part deal with mankind or especially the woman in modern society, and always, an atmosphere of coldness, criticism, of letting loose is conveyed. The third section of the collection is another sarcastic statement about man and society. The speaker is a horse and describes life in terms of "horse." The poem depicts the life of an active committee member, pulling carts, suffering, enduring, struggling, and Claire develops a picture of the working people in the early twentieth century as she saw it.

The autobiography *Ich verzeihe keinem* (1976; La poursuite du vent) depicts the literary scene of almost fifty years and is also an attempt to order her own past, especially her numerous liaisons with literary celebrities. Despite its historical and poetical importance, the autobiography, therefore, caused considerable scandal.

Works

Prose: *Der Neger Jupiter raubt Europa* (1928). *Eine Deutsche in Paris* (1928). *Ein Mensch ertrinkt* (1931). *Arsenik* (1933). *Der Gestohlene Himmel* (1962). *Memoiren eines Spatzen des Jahrhunderts* (1969). *Traumtänzerin* (1971). *Zirkus des Lebens* (1973).

Lyrics: *Mitwelt* (1918). *Lyrische Films* (1922). *Roter Mond, weißes Wild* (1955). *Das tätowierte Herz* (1957). *Klage um Yvan* (1960). *Les larmes petrifies* (1951). *Le coeur tatoue* (1958). *L'Ignifere* (1969). Collection of poems together with Yvan.

Letters, Autobiography: *Briefe mit Yvan Goll* (1966). *La poursuite du vent* (1976).

Translations: *Ich verzeihe keinem* [*La poursuite du vent*] (1976). *Arsenic* [*Arsenik*].

Jutta Hagedorn

María Gertrudis Gómez de Avellaneda

(a.k.a. La Peregrina, Felipe Escalada)

Born March 23, 1814, Puerto Príncipe, Cuba;
died February 1, 1873, Madrid, Spain
Genre(s): novel, drama, poetry
Language(s): Spanish

The daughter of a Spanish naval lieutenant and a Cuban of Spanish descent, Tula was destined for a passionate and tumultuous life in both personal and literary terms. Through broken engagements, an obsessive, twenty year-long unrequited love, brief affairs and two marriages, her emotions, conflicts, triumphs, and disappointments were chronicled in her works. The best of her writing is that which most clearly was inspired by her personal circumstances.

She was twenty-two when she arrived in Spain and quickly became popular in literary circles, first in Sevilla and then in Madrid where her charm, wit, intelligence, and beauty made her something of a sensation. A prolific writer, producing prose, poetry, and drama, her novels are the least successful of her works. *Sab* (1841) and *Dos mujeres* (1842) are two of the more notable. Her works for theatre brought her her greatest public renown and critical acclaim: *Alfonso Munio* (1844) and *Saúl* (1846) are two of her better-known dramas, and *Baltasar* (1858) was by far her greatest dramatic triumph. It is, however, her lyric poetry for which she is best remembered. Love—profane, sacred and aesthetic—is a major theme developed in her poetry. *Poesías* (1841), re-edited, augmented and published again in 1850, represents the best of her work.

Back in Cuba from 1859 to 1863 she promptly became involved in literary circles on the island and was much feted and honored. Returning to Spain after her husband's death, she turned to religion and mysticism as she had after other traumatic occasions in her life and dedicated herself to the "correction" of her works. Lonely and ill during her final years, she died on February 1, 1873.

Criticism of her works invariably raises the question of national and literary influences and the contrast of "lo varonil" and "lo femenino" in her poetry. The greater portion of Tula's work has lost appeal because its major attraction lay in the brilliance of her style; perceptive and penetrating character development is not consistent in her plays or novels. Her poetry, however, survives because of the depth of personal emotion coupled with the beauty and mastery of expression.

Works

Poetry: *Poesías* (1841). *Poesías* (1850). Theatre: *Leonicia* (1840). *Alfonso Munio* (1844). *Príncipe de Viana* (1844). *Egilona* (1846). *Saúl* (1846). *Flavio Recaredo* (1851). *La hija de las flores* (1852). *La verdad vence apariencias* (1852). *Errores del corazón* (1852). *El donativo del diablo* (1852). *La aventurera* (1853). *Hortensia* (1853). *La sonámbula* (1854). *Simpatía y antipatía* (1855). *La hija del rey René* (1855). *Oráculos del Talia o los duendes del palacio* (1855). *Los tres amores* (1858). *Baltasar* (1858). *Catalina* (1867). *El millonario y la maleta* (1870).

Novels: *Sab* (1841). *Dos mujeres* (1842). *Espatolino* (1844). *Guatimocín* (1846). *La velada del helecho o el donativo del diablo* (1849). *Dolores* (1851). *El artista barquero* (1861). Miscellaneous: *Devocionario* (1846, re-written in 1867). *Autobiografía* (1850). *Obras* (1867–1871). *Obras*, 4 vol, centenary edition (1914–1918). *Epistolario* (1907). *Teatro*, anthology (1965). *Poesías selectas* (1966).

Bibliography

Ballesteros, Mercedes, *Vida de la Avellaneda* (Madrid, 1949). Bravo-Villasante, Carmen, *Una vida romántica: La Avellaneda* (Barcelona, 1967). Chacón y Calvo, J.M., *Gertrudis Gómez de Avellaneda. Las Influencias castellanas: exámen negativo* (Havana, 1914). Cotarelo y Mori, E., *La*

Avellaneda y sus obras. Ensayo biográfico y crítico (Madrid, 1930). Díaz-Plaja, Guillermo, ed., Historia general de las literaturas hispánicas. 5 vols. (Barcelona, 1958). Díez-Echarri, E., and J.M. Roca Franquesa, Historia general de las literaturas españolas e hispánicas (Madrid, 1968). Figarola Caneda, D., Gertrudis Gómez de Avellaneda (Madrid, 1929). Williams, Edwin B., The Life and Dramatic Works of Gertrudis Gómez de Avellaneda (Philadelphia, 1924).

Carol Stos

Carmen Gómez Ojea

Born 1945, Gijón, Spain
Genre(s): novel
Language(s): Spanish

When Gómez Ojea won the Nadal prize of 1981 for her Cantiga de agüero (The Poem of the Omen), she became the first woman in 22 years to be so honored. The award thus attracted considerable national attention.

Gómez Ojea studied at the University of Oviedo and holds a degree in Romance philology. A first short novel, still unpublished, was runner-up for a prize in her native Gijón in 1966. The mother of five children, she continued to write in spite of her family commitments and the nonpublication of her works. By the time she was awarded almost simultaneously the Nadal prize for Cantiga de agüero and the Tigre Juan prize for Otras mujeres y Fabia (Fabia and Other Women), she had authored eight novels, fifty stories, and a book of poems.

Cantiga de agüero is a grotesque and playful work, rich in intertextual references to Galician novelists of the nineteenth and twentieth centuries as well as to Latin American novels, notably One Hundred Years of Solitude by García Márquez. The setting shifts from Galicia (northwestern Spain) to Mexico. Although the action, which traces the story of a particular family over a period of years, includes the Mexican Revolution, the time seems to be distant, more medieval than modern. Partially written in the fantastic mode, the novel debunks mysticism and eroticism as it parodies a variety of literary conventions.

Gómez Ojea's other two published novels, like Cantiga de agüero, are marked by her talent for storytelling. Otras mujeres y Fabia is written in the first person from the perspective of Fabia, who explores her matrilineal roots—the lives of her own female ancestors—and the lives of individual women in her working-class neighborhood in the fictional present. Tarsiana, the protagonist of Los perros de Hécate (Hecate's Dogs), is related to Fabia in her desire to explore other women's lives and, similarly, narrates in the first person anecdotes about other women. In this last novel, the anecdotes involve a series of visits that Tarsiana apparently welcomes solely for their storytelling aspects. There is an occasional use of the fantastic mode in Otras mujeres y Fabia (Fabia's ancestors step down from their portraits to talk to her), but Los perros de Hécate is farther removed from realism in its tendency to relate the various tales to a mythological plane.

Gómez Ojea's published works reflect a talent for creating character and situation, a sense of humor, and a thorough knowledge of literary conventions. She promises to be a major figure within her generation of women writers in Spain.

Works
Cantiga de agüero (1982). Otras mujeres y Fabia (1982). Los perros de Hécate (1985).

Bibliography
Ordoñez, Elizabeth J., "Inscribing Difference: 'L'Ecriture Feminine' and New Narrative by Women." Anales de la Literatura Española Contemporánea 12 (1987): 45–58. Roberts, Gemma, Review of Cantiga de Agüero. Anales de la Literatura Española Contemporánea 7.1 (1982): 144–146. Zatlin, Phyllis, "Women Novelists in Democratic Spain: Freedom to Express the Female Perspective." Anales de la Literatura Española Contemporánea 12 (1987): 29–44.
Reference works: Women Writers of Spain: An Annotated Bio-Bibliographical Guide, ed. Carolyn L. Galerstein (Westport, Conn., 1986).

Phyllis Zatlin

Natal'ya Gorbanevskaya

Born May 26, 1936, Moscow, Russia
Genre(s): poetry, literary journalism,
translation
Language(s): Russian

Natal'ya Gorbanevskaya is best known in the West for her activities in defense of human rights during the 1960s; she is renowned in particular for her part in the Red Square demonstration against the Soviet invasion of Czechoslovakia in 1968. For this and other protests she was incarcerated from December 24, 1969, until February 24, 1972, first in Butyrki prison and then in a psychiatric hospital in the provincial town of Kazan'. Her description of these ordeals has been translated into English (*Red Square at Noon*), and a television documentary based on it was shown in the West some years ago.

In a statement issued from prison in 1970, Gorbanevskaya expressed concern that her poetry should not attract public interest simply because of her status as a political prisoner. She was in fact already an established writer before being imprisoned: her earliest poems date from the mid-1950s, and she had been publishing in *samizdat* since 1961, when some of her lyrics appeared in the volume *Phoenix 1961*; she had even had a few poems accepted for official publication in the Soviet Union (they appeared in the journals *Znamya* [The Banner] and *Zvezda Vostoka* [Eastern Star] in 1966). After her release, Gorbanevskaya continued to write steadily; her emigration in 1975 has not diminished her output. But, unfortunately, her earlier fears about her literary reputation have to some extent proved justified, since the publication of several collections of poetry has not yet gained her the recognition which she deserves amongst a broader public. Much of her work still awaits translation into English, and most of the scanty secondary literature does not go beyond the bare bibliographical facts. Indicative of the neglect is the fact that the major current Anglo-American reference work in the field, *The Modern Encyclopedia of Russian and Soviet Literature*, ignores her altogether.

This situation is deplorable, for Gorbanevskaya is indisputably one of the best poets writing in Russian today. Besides, her work is in no sense hidebound by a "dissident" ideology. Although often inspired by a strong sense of indignation provoked by injustice, Gorbanevskaya does not have blinkered anti-Soviet views. She recognizes inhumanity as a general human condition, and in one poem an urbane acquaintance who mocks a down-and-out schizophrenic in Paris causes her pain:

> I walked away, scattering loose centimes,
> not wiping away my own tear either, the
> tear of no-one,
> flicking the walls with my handkerchief,
> covering my tracks in the side streets.
> (*Peremennaya oblachnost'*, 58)

In the poems written since emigration, the universality of Gorbanevskaya's emotional map is emphasized by blurring of toponyms: Parisian street-names are translated into Russian and mingle with the street-names of Leningrad and Moscow; Western places are given specifically Soviet denominations (a Paris café, for example, can be called a *zabegalovka*, a Soviet term for a sleazy "snack-bar").

Though she neither proselytizes nor hectors the reader, Gorbanevskaya's poems show traces of deep religious belief. Sometimes she appeals in desperation to God and the saints, elsewhere allusions are more indirect; devotional objects, such as statues, may make appearances. As the title of an early cycle, "Lost Paradise," makes clear, unhappiness and injustice are often attributed to the world's falling-off from grace, rather than to any one political ideology.

The tone which predominates in Gorbanevskaya's poetry is melancholic and resigned, and her thematic range is not wide. Her major themes are loneliness, especially in an urban setting, the fragmentation of the individual, the pain of parting, the grief of love, and the frustrations and rewards of the writer. Though her voice has gained in confidence and command, her preoccupations have changed little over the years of writing. This is not to suggest, however, that her poems are monotonous or unvaried. Despite the prevalence of a minor key, Gorbanevskaya is able to puncture abstract or metaphysical discussion by unexpected analogy, down-to-earth detail, or dry irony. In one lyric, for example, she begins in a tone of plangent reflection, "Only pain—that is all love is," but continues briskly, "Right, let's talk about the weather." In another she links poetic creativity and the mundane details of housework, describing Sunday as "the day of washing and writing of verses" (*Poberezh'e*, 66). Though she would probably, like most Russian women writers, be irritated by any suggestion that she is a feminist, these switches in tone often introduce specifically "female" subjects, such as childrearing and domestic duty.

Apart from ironic asides, Gorbanevskaya's most characteristic devices include the use of meteorological conditions for mood evocation (drizzle and sleet figure particularly often), and frequent use of the negative, especially the negative imperative. Sometimes a cliché is wryly reworked:

> All roads do not lead to Rome,
> they lead further and further away.
> (*Poberezh'e*, 47)

Wolfgang Kasack has written that the form of Gorbanevskaya's lyrics is unpretentious, a statement that is true up to a point. Many of her brief, mostly untitled, poems are composed in four-line stanzas of alternate-rhymed iambic verse. But a quantitative study of some of her recent poetry has indicated a readiness to experiment in other meters, too (Smith, 397); and, besides, the artlessness is deceptive. Gorbanevskaya has a strong sense of being heir to the cultural tradition, to which she often takes a more critical or ironic attitude than might a male writer. In "Song about the Unforeseen," she mocks Kant who, in his infinite wisdom, could not predict that his birthplace would be absorbed into the Soviet Union:

> In Kaliningrad long ago
> Immanuil was born,
> But, for Christ's sake, didn't know
> Where he had been spawned.
> He didn't foresee, the wise Herr,
> The flag of the RSFSR.
> (*Peremennaya oblachnost'*, 8)

A favorite cultural reference used "straight" is to the poetry of Anna Akhmatova, whom Gorbanevskaya somewhat resembles, though she is much more self-effacing, posing neither as mother of the people nor as Cassandra. In general, the restraint, limpidity, and overt high-cultural allegiances of Gorbanevskaya's poetry place her, though a native Muscovite, in the tradition of "Petersburg poetry" of which Akhmatova is an outstanding representative. Typically for this tradition, she is an *Augenmensch*; although her love of music is alluded to in many poems, the poems themselves are not musical in the way of much Russian poetry, in which a piano accompaniment seems forever to be rippling somewhere in the background. Though occasionally balladic, they owe little to the folk-song and still less to the drawing-room romance. Their character was best summed up by Gorbanevskaya herself when writing of a contemporary, Dimitrii Bobyshev, "These poems are neither 'singing' nor 'richly orchestrated'; their music is both stricter and more complex."

Since emigrating, Gorbanevskaya has lived in Paris and has worked as editorial secretary, and since 1983 as deputy editor, of the important journal *Kontinent*, which could be described as the mouthpiece of the third wave émigré establishment. She is an influential poetry editor and publishes translations (many from Polish), and reviews.

Works

Poberezh'e: stikhi (1973). *Peremennaya oblachnost'* (1985). Stevanovic, B. and V. Wertsman. *Free Voices in Russian Literature 1950s–1980s: A Bio-Bibliographical Guide* (1987), pp. 147–149; an up-to-date and reasonably complete guide to Gorbanevskaya's works in Russian.

Translations: *Red Square at Noon*, tr. A. Lieven (1972). *Selected Poems*, tr. D. Weissbort (1972). "Three Poems," tr. B. Einzig, B. Heldt and W. Scott. *Russian Literature Triquarterly* 9 (1974): 45–49.

Bibliography

Kasack, W., *Lexikon der russischen Literatur ab 1917* (Stuttgart, 1976). Contains by far the fullest available biographical information on Gorbanevskaya. The brief contribution on her in *Handbook of Russian Literature*, ed. V. Terras (Yale, 1985), is incomplete and inaccurate. A brief critical introduction is G.S. Smith, "Another time, another place," *Times Literary Supplement* 4395 (26.vi.1987): 692–694. On the metrics see idem, "The Metrical Repertoire of Shorter Poems by Russian Emigres 1971–1980," *Canadian Slavonic Papers* 27 (1985): 4, 385–396.

Catriona Kelly

Anna Gorenko

(see: Anna Akhmatova)

Luise Adelgunde Victoria Gottsched

(a.k.a. XYZ der Jüngere, L.A.V.G., Gottschedinn)

Born April 11, 1713, Danzig, Germany; died
    June 26, 1762, Leipzig
Genre(s): drama, journalism, polemic,
    translation
Language(s): German

Luise Gottsched is the most important woman writer of the early Enlightenment in Germany. Her large body of work, frequently with a satirical element, includes plays (originals and translations), polemics, reviews and magazine articles. She was the first German woman journalist of note.

As a young woman, Louise Kulmus received with the help of both her mother and her father an excellent education, studying subjects that ranged from the usual girl's French and music to the very unusual mathematics and philosophy. Along with her education, she absorbed profound conflicts about her female role, for despite having all the tools for independent thought and for creativity, she felt that as a woman she should use them only in subordination to her husband. Under these conditions, her literary development was both enhanced and hurt by her marriage to the domineering Professor Gottsched in 1735. On the one hand the marriage to the most influential literary man of the period gave her the opportunity to be at the center of German literary life in the only way available to a woman at the time. On the other hand, because of the ideology of a wife's subjection to her husband's will, she was unable to object when her husband directed her to stop writing plays, at which she was developing considerable skill, and instead to devote herself completely to translations for him that gave her no chance for further literary creativity. In the face of these contradictions, the gifted woman's self-confidence was crippled and her personal literary achievement restricted in ways that left her embittered and dissatisfied.

She had begun publishing anonymously in 1731 at age eighteen, four years before her marriage but two years after becoming acquainted with Gottsched. After marriage, her life is marked by no clearly identifiable major nonliterary events; she remained childless. For her husband, who was himself a phenomenally productive writer, she did a prodigious amount of translating along with article writing and book reviewing for his periodicals. This activity has earned her the label of being Germany's first important woman journalist. Her plays and translations of plays were very successful, being frequently performed for years after her death. Her polemics reveal her fervent participation in the literary quarrels that marked and then marred her husband's domination of the German literature of his day.

The works which receive the most praise today, three plays, Pietisterei, Das Testament, and Herr Witzling (Pietism in a Whale-bone Skirt, The Will, and Mr. Witty) are comedies that show Louise Gottsched's satirical gift but also reveal undercurrents of ambivalence toward learning and toward women.

Works

Der Frau von Lambert Betrachtungen über das Frauenzimmer, tr. of Anne Thérèse de Marguenat de Courcelles de Lambert, Reflexions sur les femmes (1721); also, poems by Gottsched (1731). Ode: Das glückliche Russland am Geburtstage Ihro Kaiserl. Majestät Anna Iwanowna [Happy Russia on the Birthday of her Royal Highness Anna Iwanowna] (1733). Der Sieg der Beredsamkeit, tr. of Madeleine Angélique Poisson de Gomez, La Triomphe de l'eloquence, 1730 (1735). Kato, tr. of Joseph Addison, Cato, 1713 (1735). Die Pietisterey im Fischbein-Rocke; Oder Die Doctormäßige Frau, Version of Luise Bougeant, La femme docteur ou la théologie janséniste tombée en quenouille (1736). Triumph der Weltweisheit, nach Art des Französischen Sieges der Beredsamkeit der Frau Gomez, nebst einem Anhange dreier Reden [Triumph of World Wisdom. In the manner of the French Triumph of Eloquence by Madam Gomez, with an appendix of Three Speeches] (1739). Der Zuschauer. Neun Theile, tr. of The Spectator, 1711–1714 (1739–1943). Horatii, als eines wohlerfahrnen

Schiffers treumeynender Zuruff an alle Wolfianer [Horatii, the Sincere Call of a Well-meaning Sailor to all Followers of Wolfe] (1740). *Zwo Schriften, welche von der Frau Marquise von Chatelet und dem Herrn von Mairan, das Maaß der lebendigen Kräfte in den Körpern betreffend, sind gewechselt worden,* tr. of *Lettre de M. de Mairan...a Madame* *** [la marquise du Chatelet] *sur la question des forces vives, an reponse aux objections qu'elle lui fait sur ce sujet dans ses Institutions de physique,* 1741 (1741). *Cornelia, Mutter der Grachen,* tr. of Marie Anne Barbier, *Cornélie, mère des Gracques,* 1703. In *Die Deutsche Schaubühne nach den Regeln und Mustern der Alten,* vol. 2, 1741 (1741). *Das Gespenst mit der Trommel,* tr. of Destouches, *Le Tambour nocturne,* 1736. In *Deutsche Schaubühne,* vol. 2, 1741 (1741). *Alzire, oder die Amerikaner,* tr. of Voltaire, *Alzire, ou les Américains,* 1734. In *Deutsche Schaubühne,* vol. 3, 1741 (1741). Der Verschwender, tr. of Destouches, *Le Dissipateur.* In *Deutsche Schaubühne,* vol. 3, 1741 (1741). *Der Poetische Dorfjunker,* tr. of Destouches, *La Fausse Agnes.* In *Deutsche Schaubühne,* vol. 3, 1741 (1741). Tr. of 330 of the 635 articles in *Herrn Peter Gaylens historisches und kritisches Wörterbuch.* 4 vols. (1741–1744). *Der Menschenfeind,* tr. of Moliere, *Le Misanthrope,* 1666. In *Deutsche Schaubühne,* vol. 1, 1742 (1742). *Die Widerwillige,* tr. of Charles Dufresny, *L'Esprit de contradiction,* 1700. In *Deutsche Schaubühne,* vol. 1, 1742 (1742). *Lockenraub, ein scherzhaftes Heldengedicht,* tr. of Alexander Pope, *The Rape of the Lock,* 1714; also tr. of two poems by Antoinette Deshoulières (1744). *Die ungleiche Heirath* [The Unequal Marriage; comedy]. In *Deutsche Schaubühne,* vol. 4, 1744 (1744). *Die Hausfranzösinn, oder Die Mamsell.* In *Deutsche Schaubühne,* vol. 5, 1744 [The French Governess, or Mam'selle; comedy] (1744). Panthea [Panthea], tragedy. In *Deutsche Schaubühne,* vol. 5, 1745 (1744). *Das Testament* [The Will], comedy. In *Deutsche Schaubühne,* vol. 6, 1745 (1745). *Herr Witzling* [Mr. Witty], one-act comedy. In *Deutsche Schaubühne,* vol. 6, 1745 (1745). *Der Aufseher oder Vormund,* tr. of Addison, *The Guardian,* 1713 (1745). *Die gestürzten Freymäurer,* tr. of G.-L. Perau, *Les Franc-maçons écrasés* and *L'Ordre des francs-maçons,* 1747 (1747). *Paisan parvenu, oder der glücklich gewordene Bauer,* tr. of Marivaus, *Paysan parvenu,* 1735 (1748). *Neue Sammlung auserlesener Stücke aus Popens, Newtons, Eachards und anderer Schriften* [New Collection of Selected Pieces from the Writings of Pope, Newton, Eachard, and others] (1749). *Geschichte der königlichen Akademie der Aufschriften und schönen Wissenschaften zu Paris, darin zugleich unzählige Abhandlungen aus allen freien Künsten, gelehrten Sprachen und Alterthümern enthalten sind* [History of the Royal Academy of Letters and Belles Lettres at Paris, Wherein Innumerable Treatises from All the Free Arts, Scholarly Languages, and Antiquities Are Contained] (1749–1757). *Vollständige Sammlung aller Streitschriften über das vorgebliche Gesetz der Natur von der kleinsten Kraft in den Wirkungen der Körper* [Complete Collection of All Pamphlets About the Alleged Law of Nature of the Smallest Effect in the Activities of Bodies] (1752). *Cenie, oder die Großmuth im Unglücke, ein moralisches Stück,* tr. of Mme. de Graffigny, *Cénie,* 1750 (1753). *Der kleine Prophet von Bömischbroda, oder Weissagung des Gabriel Johannes Nepomucenus Franciscus de Paula Waldstörchel* [The Little Prophet from Bömischbroda, or Prediction of Gabriel Johannes Nepomuceus Franciscus de Paul Waldstörchel]. In part a tr. of Friedrich Melchior Grimm, *Le petit Prophète de Boehmischbroda,* 1753 (1753). *Der königlichen Akademie der Aufschriften und schönen Wissenschaften zu Paris ausführliche Schriften, darin unzählige Abhandlungen aus allen freien Künsten, gelehrten Sprachen und Alterthümern enthalten sind* [The Extensive Documents of the Royal Academy of Letters and Belles Lettres at Paris, Wherein Innumerable Treatises from All the Free Arts, Scholarly Languages, and Antiquities Are Contained], 2 vols. (1753–1754). *Der beste Fürst, ein Vorspiel auf das Geburtsfest der verw. Fürstin Johanna Elisabeth von Anhalt-Zerbst* [The Best Prince, a Prologue for the Birthday Celebration of the Widowed Princess Johanna Elisabeth von Anhalt-Zerbst] (1755). *Des Abts Terrason Philosophie nach ihrem allgemeinen Einflusse auf alle Gegenstände des Geistes und der Sitten,* tr. of Jean Terrasson, *La Philosophie applicable a tous les objets de l'esprit et de la raison,* 1754 (1756). *Nachrichten, die zum Leben der Frau von Maintenon und des vorigen Jahrhunderts gehörig sind,* tr. of Laurent Angliviel de La Beaumelle, *Memoires pour servir à l'histoire de Madame de Maintenon et à celle du siècle passé,*

1755–1756 (1757). *Gedanken über die Glückseligkeit, oder philosophische Betrachtungen über das Gute und Böse des menschlichen Lebens*, tr. of Louis de Beausobre, *Essai sur le bonheur*, 1758 (1758). *Briefe, die Einführung des Englischen Geschmacks in Schauspielen betreffend, wo zugleich auf den Siebzehnten der Briefe, die neue Litteratur betreffend, geantwortet wird* [Letters Concerning the Introduction of the English Taste in Plays, Where the Seventeenth Letter About the New Literature Is Answered] (1760). *Des Freyherrn von Bielefeld Lehrbegriff von der Staatskunst*, tr. of Jacob Friedrich von Bielfeld. *Institutions politiques*, 1760 (1761). *Der Frau Luise Adelgunde Victorie Gottschedinn, geb. Kulmus, sämmtliche Kleinere Gedichte* [Collected Shorter Poems, ed. by Her Husband] (1763). *Briefe der Frau Louise Adelgunde Victorie Gottsched* [Letters of Madame Gottsched], ed. Dorothea Henriette von Runckel (1771–1771). Translation: One poem in *Bitter Healing: Anthology of German Women Authors from Pietism to Romanticism*, ed. Jeannine Blackwell and Susanne Zantop (Lincoln, 1989).

Bibliography

Brinker-Gabler, Gisela, ed., *Deutsche Literatur von Frauen: Vom Mittelalter bis zum Ende des 18. Jahrhunderts* (München, 1988), pp. 302–307, 395–397. Friedrichs, Elisabeth, *Die deutschsprachigen Schriftstellerinnen des 18. und 19. Jahrhunderts. Ein Lexikon* (Stuttgart, 1981), pp. 103–104. Frederiksen, Elke, ed., *Women Writers of Germany, Austria, and Switzerland. An Annotated Bio-Bibliographical Guide* (New York, 1989), p. 86. Krull, Edith, *Das Wirken der Frau im frühen deutschen Zeitschriftenwesen* (Charlottenburg, 1939), pp. 25–52. (Beiträge zur Erforschung der deutschen Zeitschrift, v. 5). Richel, Veronica, *Luise Gottsched: A Reconsideration* (Bern, 1973). Sanders, Ruth H., "'Ein kleiner Umweg': Das literarische Schaffen der Luise Gottsched." *Die Frau von der Reformation zur Romantik*, ed. Barbara Becker-Cantorino (Bonn, 1980), pp. 170–194. Schlenther, Paul., *Frau Gottsched und die bürgerliche Komödie. Ein Kulturbild aus der Zopfzeit* (Berlin, 1886).

Ruth P. Dawson

Gottschedinn

(see: Luise Adelgunde Victoria Gottsched)

Marie-Olympe de Gouges

Born May 7, 1745, Montauban, France; died November 4, 1793, Paris
Genre(s): pamphlets, brochures, drama, novel
Language(s): French

Olympe de Gouges was an ardent feminist and an advocate of women's rights during the early years of the French Revolution, 1789–1793. Marie Gouge (or Gouze) was born in Montauban in 1745 (she said 1755) of lower class parents; she married a wealthy, older man, M. Aubry (but never took his name), and had a son. Not much is known of her life before age eighteen, but she had sufficient funds to support herself in Paris, where she pursued a writing career, using her mother's name, Olympe, and assuming the aristocratic "de." In 1785 her first play (a comedy) was performed in the Théâtre Français; none of her verbose, loosely constructed plays was successful. She was poorly educated and never mastered spelling or grammar, a fact of which she was acutely aware.

The Revolution plunged her into the turbulent, male political world and into feminist activities that brought her notoriety, persecution, and finally death. Olympe was the first feminist during this period to call for equal rights for men and women, among the first to try to organize women's groups, and the first to draw up a feminist manifesto (1789). Her program of radical reform did not appeal to many women of any class, and men simply ridiculed and derided her efforts. The Manifesto called for (1) legal equality for men and women, (2) careers open to talent, (3) abolishing the dowry system, (4) equal education for men and women, (5) and a national theatre devoted to producing plays by women. This "high priestess of Feminism" found few supporters for her original and bold ideas. Speaking to a meeting of the Society of Revolutionary Republican Women, she called for an army of 30,000 women to go into battle, to allow women to hold positions in the government, and to put women in charge of educating the young. Her proposals were greeted with laughter and hisses from her female audience who voted to postpone discussion of them. However, nothing deterred her from speaking her mind and pursuing her goals, by violent means if necessary.

Olympe's feminism was constant and consistent, but her political allegiance vacillated between monarchist and republican. In 1789 she welcomed the Revolution, became a royalist when Louis XVI was forced to leave Versailles for Paris (October 1789), turned against the King when he attempted to flee the country (1791), and then offered to defend Louis at his trial (1792); finally, convinced that Louis was a traitor, she supported a republic. Her open opposition to Robespierre and the Terror, and her association with the terrifying female rabble, the Tricoteuses [Knitters], led to her downfall. The Committee of Public Safety saw her as a dangerous and divisive radical, but their attempts to silence her failed. She continued to write political and feminist tracts and to make public speeches that were considered a threat to the aims of the Revolution. Her famous "Les Droits de la Femme de la Citoyenne" (1791) [Declarations of the Rights of Women] boldly set forth her feminist demands: women had the right to participate in politics and to choose a profession, new marriage laws should guarantee equality between partners who would hold all property in common, and the condemnation of unwed mothers must be abolished. She prophetically insisted that if "Woman has the right to mount the scaffold; she must equally have the right to mount the rostrum" (Article X). De Gouges believed women were capable of leadership: "They are the force behind everything," the force that animated man to act. Her political views, rather than her feminism, finally brought about her arrest. In a pamphlet, "Les Trois Urnes" (The Three Urns), she called for a federalist system of government which was a violation of the law.

At her trial she insisted that she had always been a good citizen, a republican, as one could see in her work entitled, "De l'Esclavage des noirs" (1792; The Slavery of Blacks). The Revolutionary Tribunal was unconvinced and found her guilty of several crimes against the government. She was condemned to die. Claiming to be pregnant in order to postpone her execution, de Gouges failed. At 4:00 PM on November 4, 1793, she was guillotined. In her will she "left her heart to her country, her honesty to men (if they needed it), and her soul to women." De Gouges and other feminists did not achieve their program of reform, but they made women aware of their inferior status in society and gave them a set of goals to work toward.

Works

Le Mariage inattendu de Chérubin (1785). *Lucinde et Cardenio* [not published]. *Les Comédiens démasqués, ou Madame de Gouges ruinée par la Comédie-Française pour se faire jouer* (n.d.). *L'Homme généreux* (1786). *Molière chez Ninon, ou le siècle des grands hommes* (1788). *Le Philosophe corrigé, ou le cocu supposé* (n.d.). *Adresses au Roi et à la Reine, au prince de Condé, et Observations à M. Duveyrier sur sa fameuse ambassade* (n.d.). *Zamore et Mirza, ou l'heureux naufrage* (1788). *Lettre au Peuple, ou projet d'une caisse patriotique, par une citoyenne* (1788). *Remarques patriotiques* (1788). *Oeuvres de Mme de Gouges*, 3 vols. (1788). *Mes Voeux sont remplis, ou le don patriotique, dédié aux états généraux* (1789). *Le Bonheur primitif, ou les rêveries patriotiques* (1789). *Discours de l'aveugle aux Français* (1789). *Dialogue Allégorique entre la France et la Verité dediée aux Etats Généraux* (1789). *L'Ordre national, ou le comte d'Artois inspiré par Mentor* (1789). *Séance royale, motion de monseigneur le duc d'Orléans, ou les songes patriotiques* (1789). *Lettre à Mgr. le duc d'Orléans Prince du Sang, par l'amie de amie de tous les citoyens et du repos public* (1789?). *Lettre aux représentants de la nation* (1789). *Départ de M. Necker et de madame de Gouges, ou les Adieux de madame de Gouges à M. Necker et aux Français* (1790). *Action heroique d'une Française ou La France sauvée par les femmes* (1790). *Le Marché des Noirs* (n.d.). *Le Danger du Préjugé ou l'Ecole des Hommes* (n.d.). *Lettre aux littérateurs français* (1790?). *Réponse au champion américain, ou colon très-aisé à connaître* (1790). *Les Droits de la Femme: à la Reine* [Declaration of the Rights of Woman] (1791). *Mirabeau aux Champs-Elysées* (1791). *L'Esclavage des Noirs, ou l'heureux naufrage* (1792). *Réponse à la justification de Max. Robespierre* (1792). *L'Esprit français ou Problème à résoudre sur le labyrinthe des divers complots* (1792). *Lettres à la reine, aux généraux, etc., avec la description de la fête du 3 juin* (1792). *Adresse au Don Quichotte du Nord* (1792). *Grande eclipse du soleil jacobiniste et de la lune feuillantine* (1792?). *Arrêt de Mort que présente Olympe de Gouges contre Louis Capet* (1792?). *Le Bon Sens Français ou l'Apologie de Vrais Nobles, dediée aux Jacobins* (1792?). *La France sauvée, ou le Tyran détrôné* (1792?). *Le Couvent, ou les Voeux forces* (1792). *Le Prince philosophe*, 2 vols. (1792). *Olympe de Gouges, défenseur officieux de Louis Capet, au président de la Convention nationale* (1792). *L'Entrée du Dumouriez à Bruxelles, ou les Vivandières* (1793). *Testament politique d'Olympe de Gouges* (1793). *Complots dévoilés des sociétaires du prétendu théâtre de la Républic* (1793). *Avis pressant à la Convention par une vraie républicaine* (1793?). *Les trois Urnes, ou le salut de la patrie* (1793). *Correspondence de la Cour—Compte Moral rendu et dernier mot à mes chers amis, par Olympe de Gouges à la Convention Nationale et au Peuple . . .* (n.d.). *Le Cri du Sage par une Femme* (n.d.). *Avis pressant ou Réponse à mes calomniateurs* (n.d.). *Pour sauver la patrie il faut respecter les trois ordres* (n.d.). *Observations sur les étrangers* (n.d.). *Dernier Mot à mes chers amis* (1793?). *Mémoires de madame de Valmont* (n.d.).

Bibliography

Bouvier, Jeanne, *Les Femmes pendant la Révolution* (1931). Cerati, M., *Le club des citoyennes républicaines révolutionnaires* (1966). Duhet, Paule-Marie, *Les Femmes et la Révolution, 1789–1794* (1971). Lacour, Leopold, *Les origines du féminisme contemporain. Trois femmes de la Révolution: Olympe de Gouges, Théroigne de Méricourt, Rose Lacombe* (1900). Lairtullier, E., *Les Femmes célébres de 1789 à 1795*, vol. II (1840), pp. 49–142. Latour, Thérèse Louis, *Princesses, Ladies, and Republicans of the Terror* (1930). Michelet, Jules, *Les Femmes de la Révolution* (1854). Sokolnikova, Galina Osipovna, *Nine Women: Drawn from the Epoch of the French Revolution* (1969). Villiers, Baron Marc de, *Histoire des clubs de femmes et des légions d'amazones, 1793, 1848, 1871* (1910). Whale, Winifred Stephens, *Women of the French Revolution* (1922).

Jeanne A. Ojala

Alice Bache Gould

Born January 5, 1868, Quincy, Massachusetts;
died July 23, 1953, Valladolid, Spain
Genre(s): history
Language(s): Spanish

A scholar, philanthropist, and author, Gould is relatively unknown in her native U.S. Gould wrote exclusively in Spanish under the name Alicia B. Gould y Quincy. She graduated from Bryn Mawr and after extensive travel became instructor at Great Lakes Naval Training Center in Chicago. Gould travelled to Spain in 1911 to document a biography of Christopher Columbus but while doing this research, she discovered amazing discrepancies in the many existing biographies. Documents in the Archives of the Indies in Seville simultaneously revealed much of the information heretofore circulating on the crew of Columbus' vessels to be erroneous. She felt that she should some day set the record straight. Returning to Spain in 1921, she began a monumental task which would last until her death in 1953. She reasoned that enough was already written about the great Admiral, but that the fallacious history of his crew should be corrected. She did, however, veer slightly from this self-appointed task to prove definitively that Christopher Columbus was born in Genoa, Italy: an idea which other writers and researchers had postulated through various works without proper documentation.

Her indomitable research led her to all parts of Spain wherever an original document was to be found: from the richest known storehouse of Columbian manuscripts, in the Archives of the Indies in Seville, to the National Archives in Valladolid, to remote villages and baptismal records of old churches in Moguer, reported to be home of many of Columbus' crew. In this village she discovered that the town's records had been sent to the prison to be used as toilet paper by the inmates. Demanding that these documents be salvaged, she was told that she would have to peruse them within the walls of the prison, and thus it was that an elegant old Bostonian entered the prison each day and consequently won the respect and collaboration of its many inmates. On another occasion she retrieved valuable documents from an old cavalry dump where they had been used as horses' bedding during the Napoleonic invasion of Spain.

By dint of such indefatigable research leading to the discovery of many unknown or obscure documents, Gould was able to correct many existing myths and misconceptions about Christopher Columbus and his crew. Gleaning facts from diaries, baptismal and marriage records, ships' logs, viceroy reports and royal statutes, she published a series of articles in the *Boletin de la Real Academia de la Historia* (1924–1943; Bulletin of the Royal Academy of History) in Spain.

Gould discovered the identity of every crew member and wrote a biographical account of each one, modestly entitling the series "Nueva lista documentada de los tripulantes de Colon." The facts presented gave the lie to the popular assumption that they were all convicts. Gould proved that this was applicable to only four cases. She discredited the notion that the crew numbered 60–160, and established that there were 89.

Writing in impeccable Spanish, a language she mastered as a child while visiting her father, Dr. Gould, chief astronomer at the observatory in Cordoba, Argentina, she wrote eleven biographies of crew members in alphabetical order, which were published serially by the Royal Academy of History in Spain (1924–1943). The final article on Vicente Yanez Pinzon, still in manuscript form at the time of her death, was edited and published posthumously by her life-long friend and literary executor, Dr. Jose Maria de la Pena y Camara, in 1973 in the *Boletin de la Real Academia de la Historia, Tomo CLXX*. At this same time Sr. Pena submitted all Gould's notes and manuscripts to the Royal Academy for the inauguration of a new collection entitled "Coleccion de Alicia B. Gould." The series has since been published in book form by the Royal Academy.

The eminent historian Samuel Eliot Morrison, in referring to Gould's works, said, "It was the most important piece of original Columbian scholarship done in the present century (*Admiral of the Ocean Sea* [Boston, 1942], vol. I, p. 197.)

Works

Boletin de la Real Academia de la Historia. Los once articulos de la "Nueva lista documentada de los

Tripulantes de Colon en 1492" publicados en este boletin (1924–1944; 1973).

Bibliography

Advertencia Preliminar, *Boletin de la Real Academia de la Historia.* Tomo CLXX, 173 (May–August): 238–241. Morrison, Samuel Eliot, *Admiral of the Ocean Sea,* vol. 1 (Boston, 1942), p. 197.

Rosita Narcello

La Damoiselle de Gournay

(see: Marie le Jars de Gournay)

Mademoiselle de Gournay

(see: Marie le Jars de Gournay)

Marie le Jars de Gournay

(a.k.a. La Damoiselle de Gournay, Mademoiselle de Gournay, La Fille d'Alliance de Monsieur de Montaigne)

Born 1565, Paris, France; died 1645, Paris
Genre(s): criticism, novel, translation, poetry, polemic
Language(s): French

The editor of Montaigne's *Essays* and a scholar of international reputation, Marie de Gournay was a professional writer and woman of letters who worked to advance the cause of women and who was in France the most scholarly female critic before Mme de Staël.

The daughter of a nobleman with important functions at court, Marie spent most of her childhood at the family estate Gournay-sur-Aronde in Picardie, where she read avidly and taught herself Latin. The discovery, at the age of eighteen or nineteen, of Montaigne's *Essays* marked the beginning of her life-long enthusiasm for the book and its author. A deep friendship—or perhaps even passion—developed between the older man and his "adopted daughter." His death, in 1592, provoked her emotional breakdown and later caused her to start working on her first edition of the *Essays* (1595). After the death of her mother in 1591 she provided generously for her siblings and then moved to Paris to live by herself as a woman of letters, a decision for which her contemporaries criticized her severely. She associated with all important authors and intellectuals of her day and frequently voiced her opinions, which gave rise to controversy and slander. She published steadily throughout her lifetime and in her last years gained Richelieu's favor as well as assistance from the royal exchequer. She died in Paris at the age of eighty.

Marie de Gournay did not only publish eleven different editions of the *Essays*, she also produced one short novel, translations from Virgil, Ovid, Cicero, Tacitus, and Sallust, numerous poems, many essays on the French language, poetry, theory of translation, education, morality and religion, two feminist tracts, and supervised several reprints of her collected works (1624, 1634, 1641).

For many years, Marie de Gournay was accused of opportunism and her editorial integrity questioned. A certain laudatory passage about her in the *Essays* 17:11 was said to have been written by herself. Recent scholarship has established, however, that she edited Montaigne's text with as much care and competence as any good scholar of her day would have done.

Although her work was inspired and influenced by Montaigne's, she did possess originality and creative talent. Her *Le Proumenoir de Monsieur Montaigne* (1594; Walking with Mr. Montaigne) is considered one of the earliest psychological novels in French literature. The plot, borrowed from Claude de Taillemont, centers on an unmarried girl who risks her reputation and accepts hardships to escape a marriage of convenience and follow the man of her choice. The novel is full of digressions in the manner of Montaigne which Marie the moralist uses to show that for women, as for men, the basis of virtue is and must be knowledge.

She was far from a radical feminist but produced very intelligent, highly readable and entertaining contributions to the debate about women's rights and roles. In *L'Egalité des hommes et des femmes* (1622; The Equality of Men and Women), and *Grief des dames* (1626; The Ladies' Grievance), she focuses on theological questions and searches philosophers and churchfathers for "evidence" in favor of Eve's equality. Moreover, to counter the low regard in which women's intelligence was generally held, she insists on the importance of education, arguing that most differences between men and women would disappear if women were given the same education as men. The author's erudition and knowledge of the classics are evident in both essays.

Whereas the effect of *L'Egalité des hommes et des femmes* is muted somewhat by its inner contradictions, the vehement *Grief* is effective moral satire. A supplement to Montaigne's "The Art of Conversation" (3: VIII), it deals with the one aspect of conversation that he ignores, namely the ladies' share in it. With fine psychological insight, Marie shows that the responses of the male participants in this imaginary debate, which appear as so many gestures of politeness, mercy, and tolerance, are in fact evasions motivated by unconscious insecurities and fear.

Though she composed numerous poems on public and private subjects, Marie de Gournay was not much of a poet. She is remembered above all for her critical essays. Her predilection for the poetry of the Pleiade and Ronsard was old-fashioned in the eyes of her contemporaries but must be seen as a vindication of complete poetic liberty, something Malherbe's school and the neo-classicists could not appreciate.

Works

Le Proumenoire de Monsieur Montaigne (1594). *Bien-Venue de Monseigneur le Duc d'Anjou* (1608). *Adieu de l'Ame du Roy de France et de Navarre, Henry le Grand à la Royne* with *La Défense des Pères Iésuites* (1610). *Versions de quelques pièces de Virgile, Tacite et Saluste* with *L'Institution de Monseigneur, frère du Roy* (1619). *Eschantillons de Virgile* (n.d.). *L'Egalité des hommes et des femmes* (1622). *Remerciements au Roy* (1624). *Préface* to the *Essays* of Montaigne (1595, 1599, 1617, 1625, 1635; shortened versions in 1598, 1600, 1694, 1611, 1617). "La Fille d'Alliance de Monsieur de Montaigne," in *Le Tombeau du feu sieur de Sponde* (1595). *L'Ombre de la Damoiselle de Gournay* (1626). *Les Advis ou les Présens de la Demoiselle de Gournay* (1634). *Les Advis ou les Présens de la Demoiselle de Gournay* (expanded, 1641). Letters to Justius Lipsius in *Bulletin du Bibliophile*. (1862): 1296–1311. Letters to Henri

Dupuy, *Nouveaux documents sur Montaigne*, ed. Payen (1850). Letter to Cardinal Richelieu, cited by P. Bonnefon in *Montaigne et ses amis*. Letter to M. Bignon, British Museum, Egerton 21, fol. 63. Letter to Anna Marie van Schuurman, Koninklijke Bibliotheek, The Hague.

Bibliography

Baader, Renate, "Streitbar und unzeitgemäss: Die Moralistik der Marie de Gournay." In *Die Französische Autorin vom Mittelalter bis zur Gegenwart*, pp. 77–89. Bijvoet, Maya, "Marie de Gournay." In *Women Writers of the Seventeenth Century*, ed. Katharina Wilson (Athens, Ga., 1988). Boase, Alan, "Marie de Gournay." In *The Fortunes of Montaigne*. 1970, pp. 48–76. Holmes, Peggy P., "Mlle de Gournay's Defense of Baroque Imagery." *French Studies* 8 (1954): 122–131. Ilsley, Marjorie H., *A Daughter of the Renaissance: Marie le Jars de Gournay, Her Life and Works* (1963). Michel, Pierre, "Une Apôtre du Féminisme au XVIIe siècle: Mademoiselle de Gournay." *Bulletin de la Société des amis de Montaigne* 27 (1971): 45–54. Rowan, Mary M., "Seventeenth Century French Feminism." *International Journal of Women's Studies* 3 (1980–1981): 273–291. Schiff, Mario, *La Fille d'Alliance de Montaigne: Marie de Gournay* (1910). Uildriks, Anne, *Les Idées littéraires de Mlle de Gournay*. Diss., Groningen, 1962.

Maya Bijvoet

Angela Grassi

Born August 2, 1826, Crema, Italy; died September 17, 1883, Madrid, Spain
Genre(s): novel, poetry
Language(s): Spanish

Very little is known of Angela Grassi's life. She was born in Italy and at the age of five went to Barcelona where she was raised. She began her writing career at sixteen with the publication of a play, an historical romance, and a book of poetry. She would later abandon these genres, beginning in the early 1860s to concentrate on novel writing. In the 1840s she collaborated with Carolina Coronado in *El Pensamiento* (Thought) and aligned herself with the protofeminist movement of the day but renounced these ideas in the latter part of the decade. In 1850 she went to Madrid becoming a successful writer and directing the magazine *El Correo de la Moda* (The Fashion Mail) between 1867 and 1883. In it she published essays and many of her own novels in serial form. Grassi often noted that she wrote exclusively for a woman's audience and believed that the purpose of her novels and journal was to elevate the moral and intellectual condition of her readers.

Grassi's novels were widely acclaimed; two of them winning literary prizes—the Royal Academy gave her an honorable mention for *Las riquezas del alma* (1866; The Soul's Riches). Her novels advocate domesticity, Christian values, and virtuous women: friendship, obedience, faith, resignation and real love—nonsexual love—are rewarded by happiness. In her novels she portrays the society of the nineteenth century as having been corrupted by greed, materialism, progress, and vanity. The only solution to this decadent and immoral situation, she suggests, is to return to the values of the past. For Grassi, it is the role of woman to regenerate and, in a sense, redeem society.

Works

El heroismo de la amistad o los Condes de Rocaberti (1842). *Lealtad de un juramento o Crimen y expiación. Drama* (1842). *Un episodio de la Guerra de Siete Años* (1849). *Poesías de la señorita doña Angela Grassi* (1851). *El bálsamo de las penas* (1864). *El lujo* (1865). It was published again in *El Correo de la Moda* (1881). *El hijo* (1865). *Las riquezas del alma. Novela de costumbres* (1866). *El camino de la dicha* (1866). *Los que no siembran, no cogen* (1868). *La dicha de la tierra. Novela histórica* (1868). *La gota de agua* (1875). *El copo de nieve. Novela de costumbres* (1876). *El capital de la virtud. Novela de costumbres* (1877). *Marina. Narración histórica* (1877). *El primer año de matrimonio. Cartas a Julia*, in *Biblioteca Ilustrada de las familias* (1877). *Los juicios del mundo. Novela de costumbres*, in *El Correo de la Moda* (1884–1887). *Palmas y laureles. Lecturas instructivas* (1884). *El favorito de Carlos III. Novela histórica*, in *El Correo de la Moda* (1884–1887). *Cuentos pintorescos* (1886).

Bibliography

Aldaraca, Bridget, "El ángel del hogar: The Cult of Domesticity in Nineteenth-Century Spain," in

Theory and Practice of Feminist Literary Criticism, ed. Gabriela Mora and Karen S. Van Hoofk (Michigan, 1982). Andreu, Alicia G., *Galdós y la literatura popular* (Madrid, 1982). Simón Palmer, María del Carmen, "Escritoras españolas del siglo XIX o el miedo a la marginalización." *Anales de la literatura española* 2 (1983): 477–490.

Alda Blanco

Anne Malet de Graville

Born c. 1490, Château de Marcoussis, France; died after 1543
Genre(s): poetry
Language(s): French

Daughter of the Admiral Malet de Graville, councillor of Louis XII and notable bibliophile, she spent her early years at the family château of Marcoussis not far from Paris. In 1509, she eloped with her cousin, Pierre de Balsac. Later, she was a lady-in-waiting to Queen Claude, the first wife of Francis I, at whose suggestion she wrote, around 1421, a long poem entitled *Palemon et Arcita*, based on Boccaccio's *Teseida*, although it is probable that she made use of a fifteenth century French translation rather than the original. A manuscript of such a translation, copied in the early sixteenth century and bearing the arms and initials of her grandson, Claude d'Urfé, is to be found in Oxford's Bodleian Library (Douce Ms. 329). Her version, exalting feminine dignity, is an interesting reflection of the courtly and aristocratic circle that inspired it. She also rewrote Alain Chartier's fifteenth century poem, *La Belle Dame sans Merci* (The Beautiful Lady Without Mercy) in rondeaux. Like her father, whose library she inherited, she was a collector of books and manuscripts. Some of these qualities seem to have been passed on to her great grandson, the seventeenth-century novelist, Honoré d'Urfé.

Works

La Belle Dame Sans Merci [The Beautiful Lady Without Mercy] (1897). *Palemon et Arcita* (1965).

Bibliography

Bozzolo, C., *Manuscrits des Traductions Françaises d'Oeuvres de Boccace. XVᵉ Siècle* (Padua, 1973). Montmorand, M. de, *Une Femme Poète du XVIᵉ*

Siècle (Paris, 1917). Hauvette, H., *Les Plus Anciennes Traductions de Boccace* (Bordeaux-Paris, 1909).

Charity C. Willard

Marie Eugenie delle Grazie

Born August 14, 1864, Ungarisch-Weißkirchen, Hungary; died February 18, 1931, Vienna
Genre(s): novel, epic, poetry, drama, essay
Language(s): German

Marie Eugenie delle Grazie's career spanned approximately fifty years, during which she produced works in a variety of genres. Her epics and her novels are considered her best work, although she also wrote poetry, plays, prose tales, and essays. Her literary career was at its height during the first decade of this century, when she was regarded as one of the foremost woman writers and thinkers in German. But even before her death her reputation had waned considerably, due in part to her shift from free-thinker to religious writer. In her later years the liberal press lost interest in her, while Catholic publishers held back cautiously and her works did not receive the same exposure as earlier. Yet the contents of her works are typical for turn-of-the-century Austria, and she ranks second only to Ebner-Eschenbach among the important woman authors of that period.

Delle Grazie was born on August 14, 1864 in Weißkirchen, Hungary (now Bela Crkva). Her happy and secure childhood came to an end when her beloved father, a director of a coal mine company, suddenly died in 1872. The family moved to Vienna, where delle Grazie attended a girl's school and for one year a teacher's college. She had to interrupt her studies because of a nervous illness, aggravated by her mother's opposition to her attempts at writing poetry. In 1875 she met the chaplain of St. Leopold in Vienna, Laurenz Müllner (1848–1911), who later became Professor of Christian Philosophy at the University of Vienna. He recognized her talent and furthered her education beyond that of the average woman of the time. He became her mentor and encouraged and criticized her literary productions.

Müllner's death in 1911 left delle Grazie with an enormous sense of loss. During the following summer a mystical experience caused her to convert back to the Catholic faith of her youth, a change prepared by her intellectual disappointment with a number of scientific theories. All of her subsequent works, to her death in 1931, are written from the spirit of her regained faith.

Delle Grazie began composing poetry at an early age, and some of the verses included in her first collection, *Gedichte* (1882; Poems), were written when she was only ten and twelve. These poems already demonstrate her characteristic clarity of language, formal ability, and an atmosphere of pessimism and resignation. The subject matter is often the conflict between spirit and nature, the most prominent theme of all writers at the turn of the century. Her poems often concern love, some describing quiet happiness, but more often renunciation and suffering from unrequited love. Later expanded editions of the poems include discussions of philosophical, scientific, and sociological ideas. Some of the poems in the collection *Italienische Vignetten* (1892; Italian Vignettes) mirror her feelings of hopelessness and disappointment as she compares her youth to the ruins of the historical past. But she finds solace in the sight of the sea, which she perceives as a reflection of her notion of life as a monistic unity of all living things. This pantheism runs through her entire *oeuvre*, although it takes on the guise of mysticism in her later works.

Nature as the force from which everything comes and to which everything returns is evident in the descriptions of the Hungarian landscape in her story *Die Zigeunerin* (1885; The Gypsy), a romantic tale of a gypsy girl, Dora, who, betrayed in love, takes bloody revenge. It also plays a role in her epic *Hermann* (1883), an heroic poem about the Germanic past in which the mystique of the German forest is evoked.

Her blend of talents found its best expression in her next major work, often considered her masterwork, the epic in iambic pentameter, *Robespierre. Ein modernes Epos* (1894; Robespierre. A Modern Epic), on which she worked for ten years. It is in the classical form of twenty-four cantos but is modern in the sense

that it is based on the ideas of the nineteenth-century French philosopher Hyppolite Taine, who regards the beginning of the revolution as a social rather than a political movement, as a struggle for justice which then developed into a political struggle for basic rights. Rousseau's influence is apparent in delle Grazie's contention that in separating nature from spirit and human existence from nature, man became isolated. Modern culture and civilization are no longer in harmony with nature, and the result is nihilism. Despite some reservations about the drastic descriptions of misery, the work was considered epoch-making for modern realism, and Hans Benzmann described it as "one of the most profound and most beautiful works of art of contemporary literature" (*Das literarische Echo* 3).

After the success of *Robespierre*, delle Grazie turned to drama, and the première of *Schlagende Wetter* (Firedamp), a naturalistic play, was held at the Deutsches Volkstheater in Vienna on October 27, 1900. It depicts the exploitation of mine workers by the owner and shows the abyss between the two classes. This social drama in the manner of early Hauptmann was followed by *Der Schatten* (The Shadow), a symbolic play (completed in 1897) dealing with the relationship of art and life, a popular theme at the turn of the century. A poet is suddenly filled with regret for his unfulfilled life, and his envy of his friend drives him to commit crimes. When his conscience helps him overcome the dark shadow that had possessed him, the entire incident turns out to have been a product of his poetic fantasy. Through the shadow the poet was able to free himself from the demonic powers that beset the artist more powerfully and dangerously than other people. The play also shows delle Grazie's interest in the subconscious, including dreams, which she considered an emblematic representation of the unconscious, capable of giving information about art and life. Of herself she says that some of her works were conceived in dreams so vivid that she only had to write them down, like an artist who is able to paint a scene from recollection.

Der Schatten received the Bauernfeldpreis and was performed at the Vienna Burgtheater (Première; September 28, 1901)—evidence of delle Grazie's high esteem at the time. The following four one-act plays, collected under the title *Zu Spät* (1903; Too Late), were also performed at the Burgtheater. They include "Die Sphinx" (The Sphynx), a comedy that was also performed successfully in Berlin, but delle Grazie's next attempt at a comedy, *Narren der Liebe* (1905; Fools of Love), found so little critical approval that she returned to more serious subject matter that was truer to her inclinations in her next play *Ver Sacrum* (1906), which deals with the sexual awakening of a young married woman who experiences true love after having been joined to an older man in an arranged marriage. Although it remained on the stage for only two performances, the drama was awarded the Prize of the Wiener Volkstheater.

Despite the award, delle Grazie recognized that her talent was more in the genre of narrative prose. In 1907 she completed her first novel, *Heilige und Menschen* (Saints and Humans), which was serialized in the *Neue Freie Presse* in 1908 and appeared in book-form in 1909. The plot, set in a girls' convent school in Rome, juxtaposes royal and papal Rome in the political and social spheres, exposes the affected piety and sanctimoniousness professed in the convent, and contrasts dogmatic religion with ethical-liberal attitudes. Delle Grazie shows how a modern scientist who rejects the religion preached in the convent can still believe in a living God in nature and how the feeling of being connected with all living things can create a more genuine ethical feeling of compassion than the pious comedy of altruism.

Ethical feelings motivated delle Grazie's reaction in 1910 to a book denouncing women's emancipation and occasioned two articles in the leading Viennese newspaper, the *Neue Freie Presse* (August 28, and December 11, 1910). Here she expressed her sympathy with the liberation movement although her profession as well as her inclination have kept her removed from the activities of public life. She feels that women who have been repressed for so long under men's laws, who have disguised themselves and humiliated and degraded themselves under the obligation of selling themselves on the marriage market, now have found the courage to tell the truth—about themselves, the marriage market, and men. In addition to her support for the women's cause, she also spoke out against the unjust conditions between subjects and landowners in the novel *Vor dem Sturm* (1910; Before the Storm).

The foreshadowing and beginning of World War I form the background to the novel *O Jugend* (1917; Oh Youth), dealing with four friends who serve as representatives of their generation, whereas the next two novels, *Donaukind* (1918; Child of the Danube) and *Eines Lebens Sterne* (1919; The Stars of a Life), both heavily autobiographical, look back to the childhood and young adulthood of a precocious, imaginative, and proud girl, Nelly. In contrast, modern life—in the trenches, on the road with refugees from Poland, and in the cities—forms the background of *Homo. Der Roman einer Zeit* (1919; Homo. The Novel of an Era), named after an orphaned boy from the war-torn city of Homonna, who becomes the symbol of true Christian love.

After World War I delle Grazie wanted to express her hope for the revival of her lost homeland, and in *Der Liebe and des Ruhmes Kränze* (1920; Wreaths of Love and Glory), set at the time of the Congress of Vienna (1815–1818), she attempts to recreate that unique period of light, brilliance, grace and playful elegance.

Typical for delle Grazie's last works, and often considered the best work of her later period, the novella *Die weißen Schmetterlinge von Clairvaux* (1925; The White Butterflies of Clairvaux), is the tale of a religious conversion. It depicts the inner struggle between Bernard de Clairvaux and a convicted murderer and rapist, the "terror of the woods," who in the end shows true repentance and dies in a state of grace.

In the last major novel, *Unsichtbare Straße* (1927; The Invisible Road), a convent is desecrated by murder, but this action converts the protagonist from class hatred into an advocate of brotherly love, from denying God into believing in Him. He is thus able to overcome his base drives and enter the priesthood out of conviction.

When delle Grazie died on February 18, 1931, she was in the process of putting together a collection of novellas, including "Titanic" and "Matelda." She also left a completed novel, "Die Liebe des Peter Abälard" (1921; The Love of Peter Abelard). Although she considered it one of her best works, she had not submitted it for publication, probably for fear that it could be interpreted as reflecting on her own life.

After her return to the fold of the Catholic church in 1912, the press fell rather silent about delle Grazie. Once hailed as one of the leading personalities on the literary scene, she was almost forgotten by the time of her death. Given the current interest in turn-of-the-century Vienna, this important writer, who anticipated and shared all of the major themes and techniques of the leading Viennese writers, would seem to deserve restoration to a more prominent position in the literary history of her generation.

Works

Gedichte; poems (1882; new edition, 1885, 1902). *Hermann. Deutsches Heldengedicht in 12 Gesängen*, heroic poem (1883, 1885). *Die Zigeunerin. Eine Erzählung aus dem ungarischen Heidelande*, prose tale (1885). *Saul. Tragödie in 5 Acten*, drama (1885). *Italienische Vignetten*, poems (1892). *Der Rebell. Bozi. Zwei Erzählungen*, prose tales (1893). *Robespierre. Ein modernes Epos. 2 Teile*, epic poem (1894). *Moralische Walpurgisnacht. Ein Satyrspiel vor der Tragödie*, play (1896). *Schlagende Wetter. Drama in 4 Akten*, drama (1900). *Liebe*, prose tale (1902). *Der Schatten. Drama in 3 Akten und einem Vorspiel*, drama (1902). *Sämtliche Werke*, 9 vols. (1903). *Zu Spät. Einakterzyklus.*, plays (1903). *Narren der Liebe*, comedy (1905). *Ver Sacrum*, drama (1906). *Schwäne am Land*, drama (1907). *Vom Wege. Geschichten und Märchen*, tales (1907). *Traumwelt*, prose tale (1907). *Heilige und Menschen*, novel (1909). *Vor dem Sturm*, novel (1910, 1924). *Gottesgericht und andere Erzählungen*, prose tales (1912). *Wunder der Seele*, prose tale (1913). *Zwei Witwen*, novella (1914). *Das Buch des Lebens. Erzählungen und Humoresken*, prose tales (1914). *Die blonde Frau Fina und andere Erzählungen*, prose tales (1915). *Das Buch der Liebe*, novel (1916, 1927). *O Jugend!*, novel (1917). *Donaukind*, novel (1918). *Eines Lebens Sterne*, novel (1919). *Die Seele und der Schmetterling*, novella (1919). *Der frühe Lenz*, prose tale (1919). *Homo... Roman einer Zeit*, novel (1919). *Die Blumen der Acazia* (1920, 1932). *Der Liebe und des Ruhmes Kränze. Roman auf der Viola d'Amour*, novel (1920). *Die weißen Schmetterlinge von Clairvaux*, novella (1925).

"Matelda," novella in *Heimlich bluten Herzen. Österreichische Frauennovellen* (1926). *Unsichtbare Straße*, novel (1927). *Titanic. Eine Ozeanphantasie*, novella (1928). *Sommerheide*, novella (1928). *Das Buch der Heimat*, prose tale (1930). *Die Empörung der Seele*, novel (1930). *Die kleine weiße Stadt und andere Kurzgeschichten aus der Banater Heimat*, tales (1977).

Bibliography

Benzmann, Hans, "Marie Eugenie delle Grazie." *Das literarische Echo* 3 (1900/1901): 888–893. Horwath, Peter, "Marie Eugenie delle Grazie. Eine geniale Dichterin aus dem Banat." *Donauschwäbische Lehrerblätter* 21 (June, 1975): 2f, 21–25. Lothar, Rudolph, "Schlangende Wetter. Erste Aufführung am Deutschen Volkstheater." *Die Wage* 45 (1900): 299–301. Mayer-Flaschberger, Maria, *Marie Eugenie delle Grazie (1864–1931): Eine österreichische Dichterin der Jahrhundertwende* (Munich, 1984). Münz, Bernhard, *Marie Eugenie delle Grazie als Dichterin und Denkerin* (Vienna, Leipzig, 1902). Schmid-Bortenschlager, Sigrid, and Hanna Schnedl-Bubenicek, eds., *Österreichische Schriftstellerinnen 1880–1938* (Stuttgart, 1982). [Bibliography] Wengraf, Alice, "Marie Eugenie delle Grazie. Versuch einer zeitgemäßen biographischen Skizze." Diss., Vienna, 1932. Wengraf, Richard, "Der Schatten." *Das literarische Echo* 4 (1901/1902): 204–206. Zenner, Martha, "Marie Eugenie delle Grazie." Diss., Vienna, 1932.

Jorun B. Johns

Trīne Grēciņa

(see: Anna Sakse)

Catharina Regina von Greiffenberg

Born 1633, Seyßenegg, Lower Austria; died 1694, Nürnberg
Genre(s): poetry
Language(s): German

Caught up in the conflicts that occurred during the Reformation and Counter-Reformation, Greiffenberg was one of "die dichtenden

Frauen" ("women who wrote") in the German-language area during that particularly tumultuous time. A Protestant in Catholic Austria who emigrated to Nürnberg because of her evangelical beliefs, as did a number of her fellow Austrians, Greiffenberg was recognized then and subsequently as a talented poet who favored spiritual themes. With the legal dispensation of the marcgrave of Bayreuth, and after considerable contemplation, she married her uncle, Hans Rudolf von Greiffenberg, in 1664; he died in 1677. Her writing career was encouraged by members of the Nürnberg women's writing society of the Ister-Nymphen, in which she was held in high esteem. Moreover, she was mentored by Sigmund von Birken, who helped her in the publication of her poems, as well as by Philip von Zesen. Familiar with Italian poetic forms and, quite late in life, with Greek and Hebrew, Greiffenberg brought to her works usual intensity, considerable poetic technique, and a mystical bent. Her poems combine a strong Christian faith with verbal adeptness.

Works

Geistliche Sonnette (1662). Der Allerheiligst- und Allerheilsamsten Leidens und Sterbens Jesu Christi Zwölf andächtige Betrachtungen (1672). Sämtliche Werke in zehn Bänden, ed. Martin Bircher and Friedhelm Kemp (New York: Kraus Reprints, 1983).

Bibliography

Daly, Peter M., Dichtung und Emblematik bei Catharina Regina von Greiffenberg (Bonn, 1976). Frank, Horst Joachim, Catharina Regina von Greiffenberg: Leben und Welt der barocken Dichterin (Göttingen, 1967). Gersch, H., ed., Catharine Regina von Greiffenberg: Gedichte (Berlin, 1964). Kimmich, Flora, Sonnets of Catharina Regina von Greiffenberg: Methods of Composition (Chapel Hill, N. C., 1973). Mehl, Jane M., "Catharina Regina von Greiffenberg: Modern Traits in a Baroque Poet." South Atlantic Bulletin 45, i (1980): 54–63. Price, Lucy Jean, "The Emblematic and Meditative Poetry of John Donne, George Herbert, Andreas Gryphius, and Catharina Regina von Greiffenberg." DAI (1977) 38: 3470A-71A. Siekhaus, Elisabeth Bartsch, Die lyrischen Sonette der Catharina Regina von Greiffenberg (Bern, 1983).

Susan Clark

I. Grekova

(see: Elena Ventsel)

Marie Grengg

Born Stein an der Donau, Austria; died 1963, Rodau, Austria
Genre(s): novel, youth literature
Language(s): German

Grengg was an artist as well as author. As a young woman she studied art at the Akademie der Angewandten Kunst in Vienna under Karl Moser and Kokoschka. Later in life she concentrated her efforts on writing, but she also illustrated many of her own books.

Her first novel Die Flucht zum grünen Hergott (1930; Flight to the Green God) is the story of a woman, who, unhappy in her marriage, leaves her husband and family and seeks and finds solace in nature. In 1932 she wrote Peterl, a novel set in her native town about a boy who suffers from an unkind stepmother who does not understand the sensitive child. In 1937 she published Der Nusskern (The Kernel of the Nut). This novel, set in the time of Napoleon, concerns a peasant who sacrifices his life for his son and the son's resultant feeling of guilt. Both Peterl and Der Nusskern take place in Wachau, i.e., Stein an der Donau, Grengg's place of birth, and the author describes nature and the landscape in minute detail.

In 1935 Grengg wrote the controversial novel Der Feuermand (The Firebug), the story of a pyromaniac who wants to create a pure race by doing away with all sick and degenerate people. A collection of novels under the title Starke Herzen (1936; Strong Hearts) is a series of portraits of people in crisis. The theme of nature already apparent in Die Flucht zum grünen Herrgott is carried through in all her subsequent work, culminating in Zeit der Erinnerung (1961; Time of Remembrance), where she describes aspects of nature in lyrical prose with a tendency towards the dramatic and baroque.

She has won the following literary awards: Literatur Staatspreis (1937); Martin Johann Schmidt Preis of the city of Krems (1956); and the Niederösterreichischer Kulturpreis (1963).

Works

Novels: *Die Flucht zum grünen Herrgott* (1930). *Peterl* (1932). *Die Liebesinsel* (1935). *Das Feuermandl*(1935). *Der murrende Berg*(1936). *Die Kindlmutter*(1938). *Der Lebensbaum* (1944). *Das Hanswurstenhaus*(1951). *Wie Christkindlein den Kindern half* (1929). *Starke Herzen* (1936). *Der Nusskern* (1937). *Der Tulipan* (1938). *Die Venus* (1947). *Die letzte Liebe des Giacomo Casanova* (1948).

Fiction for adolescents: *Edith ganz im Grünen* (1934). *Nur Mut Brigitt* (1939). *Das Kathrinl* (1950). *Die grosse Begabung* (1954). *Der Wunschgarten; Begegnung im Grünen* (1957).

Miscellaneous: *Niederösterreichisches Wanderbuch* (1936). *Zeit der Besinnung* (1939). *Zeit der Erinnerung* (1961). *Gemalte Blumen* (1962).

Bibliography

Feuchtmuller, Rupert, ed. and intro., *Gemalte Blumen. Das Österreichische Wort*, v. 116 (Graz, Wien, 1962). Spitzenberger, G., *Starke Herzen von Marie Grengg (im Rahmen ihrer ubrigen Werke)*. Diss., Wien, 1939. Thalhammer, Franz J., *Mundartdichter Gedichte* (1933).

General reference: Adalbert, Schmidt, *Dichter und Dichtung Österreichs im 19 und 20 Jahrhundert*, II (Salzburg, 1964), pp. 125f.

M.A. Reiss

Elsa Gress

Born January 17, 1919, Copenhagen, Denmark
Genre(s): non-fiction, novel, autobiography, short story, drama, poetry
Language(s): Danish, English

With the polemical *Det Uopdagede Køn* (1964; The Undiscovered Sex), Elsa Gress triggered the discussions of sexual politics that in the early seventies resulted in the second phase of feminist activism in Denmark. Writing against Simone de Beauvoir and Betty Friedan, Gress dismissed the notion of gender-specific oppression and instead advocated individualism and humanism.

Gress' autobiographical works, *Mine Mange Hjem* (1965; My Many Homes), *Fuglefri og Fremmed* (1971; Birdfree and Foreign), and *Compania* I-II (1976; Compania), partly explain the often puzzling mixture of progressivism and biologism that characterizes her positions. Through a childhood marked by social decline, isolation, and pathology, Gress developed a belief in individuality, fantasy and art as opposed to mass society and vaguely defined "institutions." Her 1977 novel *Salamanderen* (The Salamander) thus attacks Danish cultural committees and institutes, which, in Gress' representation, encourage mediocrity and crush artistic genius.

Despite and because of her polemics against man-hating feminists, left-wing dogmatists and cultural bureaucrats, Gress continues to be a prominent and powerful figure in the intellectual and cultural milieus of contemporary Denmark.

Works

Mellemspil (1947). *Concertino* (1955). *Jorden Er Ingen Stjerne* (1956). *Nye Strejftog* (1957). *Prometheus paa Flugt*(1961). *Det Uopdagede Køn* (1964). *Er Der Nogen Der Hører Efter?* (1964). *Habiba og Andre Noveller* (1964). *Mine Mange Hjem*(1965). *Det Professionelle Menneske: Essays og Artikler 1941–66* (1966). *Om Kløfter* (1967). *Boxigange: Teater som Livsform* (1968). *Lurens Toner* (1968). *Fugle og Frøer: Afsnit og Epistler* (1969). *Philoctetes Wounded and Other Plays* (1969). *Den Saarede Filoktet* (1970). *Fuglefri og Fremmed*(1971). *Apropos Virkeligheden* (1972). *Compania* I-II (1976). *Salamanderen* (1977). *Liv: Menneske Paa Vejen*(1977). *Engagement: Epistler og Essays om Kunst og Liv og Andet Mere* (1977). *Daemoniske Damer og Andre Figurer: Dramatiske Tekster* (1978). *Fanden til Forskel: Essays, Monologer og Dialoger* (1979). *Vist Koster Det Noget* (1980). *Udsigter og Indsigter* (1981). *Det Sker Maaske: Avisvers* (1982). *Kristi Himmelfartsfesten: Et Vulkanstykke* (1983, with Kaspar Rostrup). *Det Gik: Kalenderdigte* (1983). *Blykuglen: Epistler og Essays* (1984).

Translations: *Boxigange: Teater Som Livsform* (1968; Danish and English text). *Philoctetes Wounded and Other Plays*(1969; Written and first published in English). "Revolt," tr. Nadia Christensen. *American-Scandinavian Review* 62.3 (September 1974).

Bibliography

Bruun Andersen, Michael et al., *Dansk Litteraturhistorie*VIII: Velfaerdsstat og Kulturkritik (Copenhagen, 1985), pp. 516–520.

Clara Juncker

Henry Gréville

(a.k.a. Alice Marie Céleste Fleury Durand-Gréville, Mme Emile Durand-Gréville, née Fleury)

Born October 12, 1842, Paris (Seine), France; died May 1902, Boulogne-sur-Mer (Pas-de-Calais)
Genre(s): biography, journal, play, novel, short story, textbook
Language(s): French

Daughter of the liberal Protestant journalist, Jean-Joseph Fleury, Henry Gréville, born Alice Fleury, grew up in a milieu in which literature and the arts were prized. Her father's dissatisfaction with Napoleon III's authoritarian Second Empire prompted him to move to St. Petersburg in 1857 to teach French. There Gréville learned Russian and became familiar with Russian customs, which she began to describe, under the pseudonym of Henry Gréville, in various Russian journals, including the *Journal de St. Petersbourg*. She also married Emile-Alix Durand (1838–1914), an author and professor of French at the St. Petersburg law school. After their return to France in 1872, she wrote about Russian literature and society for such prestigious journals and newspapers as the *Revue des Deux Mondes*, *Le Figaro*, and *Le Temps*. Her Russian experiences were also the basis for many of her seventy novels and volumes of short stories. Among her early successes were *Dosia* (1877), awarded a prize by the Académie Française and published in seventy-three editions by 1890; *Sonia* (1877); and *Les Epreuves de Raissa* (1878). In addition to the novels with young Russian heroines and plots with romantic intrigue, she wrote stories with French settings, such as *Perdue* (1881 and in a thirty-second edition by 1888), *Aurette* (1891), and *Chénerol* (1892).

By the end of the 1870s Henry Gréville enjoyed a substantial international literary reputation. Authors Edmond About and Emile Augier proclaimed her "the heiress of George Sand," and critic Victor Fournel compared her *L'Expiation de Savéli*(1876) favorably to the work of Prosper Mérimée. Her best novels provided amusing accounts of Russian salon life, but others were rambling and boring. More than thirty of her volumes appeared in English translations, and she gave lectures in Belgium, the Netherlands, Switzerland, and the United States.

Theodore Stanton, son of the American feminist Elizabeth Cady Stanton, described Gréville in 1884 as "a broad-minded liberal thinker on all the great reform and progressive questions of the hour" and noted that "Her artistic little house on the heights of Montmartre is an influential centre for the propagation of modern ideas." In T. Stanton's *Woman Question in Europe* (1884) Gréville commented pointedly on changes in nineteenth-century French attitudes toward women authors. Whereas women writers during the first half of the century seemed to the public to be "abnormal, odd, almost reprehensible," they were by the 1880s, she believed, "accepted without exciting any comment" and able to "write on any subject."

Although a champion of women authors, Gréville held many traditional ideas about femininity and women's roles. In *Instruction morale et civique des jeunes filles* (1882), a widely used textbook for primary school girls, she described the ideal woman as sweet, patient, modest, charitable, and reserved. Woman's "place is at home, in the house of her parents or husband . . . ; it is for the foyer that she must reserve all her grace and good humor," Gréville intoned. She also assigned to women the socially conservative role of persuading husbands and sons to respect existing society and to refrain from strikes. She did advise women to learn about politics so that they could discuss a subject of interest to husbands, but, at the same time, she warned that if spouses disagreed about politics, then it was the wife's duty, as a conciliator, to avoid controversial discussions. Women who did not adopt the "joyous resignation" recommended by Gréville were criticized. Indeed, while visiting the United States in 1885–1886, she concluded that many American women suffered from the "defect" of "pretended superiority to the men," a possible result of "the effort to improve the condition of women." That Gréville's textbook was placed on the Index in December 1882, along with three other republican primary school textbooks, was due not to its treatment of women's roles but rather to its lack of material on religion. In 1908 Hugo Thieme described her as a "prominent" writer who was "a domestic woman, keeping aloof from all feminist movements." She did participate, however, in the International Congress on Women's Charities and Institutions, held in Paris in 1900, where some participants espoused moderate feminist positions.

Works

Biography: *Maurice Sand* (1889).

Journal: *Un peu de ma vie* [A Little of My Life] (1897).

Novels: *L'Expiation de Savéli* [Saveli's Expiation] (1876). *A travers champs, Autour d'un phare* [Across Fields, Around a Beacon] (1877). *Dosia* (1877). *Les Koumiassine* [The Koumiassins] (1877). *La Maison de Maurèze* [The House of Maurèze] (1877). *La Princesse Oghérof* [The Princess Ogherof] (1877). *Sonia* (1877). *Suzanne Normis* (1877). *L'Amie* [A Friend] (1878). *Ariadne* (1878). *Les Epreuves de Raissa* [The Trials of Raissa] (1878). *Marier sa fille* [Marrying Off a Daughter] (1878). *La Niania* (1878). *Bonne-Marie* (1879). *Les Mariages de Philomène* [Philomène's Marriages] (1879). *Un violon russe* [A Russian Violin] (1879). *Cité Ménard* (1880). *L'Héritage de Xénie* [Xenia's Inheritance] (1880). *Lucie Rodey* (1880). *Les Degrés de l'échelle* [The Steps of the Ladder] (1881). *Madame de Dreux* (1881). *Le Moulin Frappier* [Frappier's Mill] (1881). *Perdue* [Lost] (1881). *Le Fiancé de Sylvie* [Sylvia's Betrothed] (1882). *Rose Rozier* (1882). *Angèle* (1883). *L'Ingénue* [The Ingénue] (1883). *Louis Breuil, histoire d'un pantouflard* [Louis Breuil, The Story of a Stay-at-Home] (1883). *Une trahison* [A Treason] (1883). *Le Voeu de Nadia* [The Vow of Nadia] (1883). *Folle avoine* [Wild Oats] (1884). *Les Ormes* [The Elms] (1884). *Un crime* [A Crime] (1884). *Clairefontaine* (1885). *Le Mors aux dents* [The Bit Between the Teeth] (1885). *Cléopâtre* [Cleopatra] (1886). *Le Comte Xavier* [Count Xavier] (1886). *La Fille de Dosia* [Dosia's Daughter] (1887). *Frankley* (1887). *Nikanor* (1887). *La Seconde mère* [The Second Mother] (1888). *L'Avenir d'Aline* [The Future of Aline] (1889). *Chant de noces* [Wedding Song] (1889). *Louk Loukitch* (1889). *Le Passé* [The Past] (1890). *Un mystère* [A Mystery] (1890). *Aurette* (1891). *L'Héritière* [The Heiress] (1891). *Péril* [Peril] (1891). *Chénerol* (1892). *Le Mari d'Aurette* [Aurette's Husband] (1892). *Jolie propriété à vendre* [Attractive Property to Sell] (1893). *Un vieux ménage* [An Old Couple] (1893). *L'Aveu* [The Confession] (1894). *Fidelka* (1894). *Le Fil d'or* [The Thread of Gold] (1895). *Céphise* (1896). *Vie d'hotel, impressions de Céphise* [Hotel Life, Impressions of Céphise] (1898). *Villoré, snobs de province* [Villoré, Provincial Snobs] (1898). *Petite princesse* [Little Princess] (1899). *Zoby* (1900). *Le Coeur de Louise* [The Heart of Louise] (1901). *La Mamselka* [Mam'zelle] (1901). *La Demoiselle de Puygarrou* [The Young Lady of Puygarrou] (1902). *Le Roi des milliards* [The King of Billions] (1907). *Mon chien Bop et ses amis* [My Dog Bop and His Friends] (1911).

Plays: *Denise* (1877). *Pierrot ermite* [Pierrot Hermit] (1877). *Comédies de paravent* [Comedies of the Folding Screen] (1888).

Short Stories: *Nouvelles russes: Stéphane Makarief, Véra, L'Examinateur, Le Meunier, Anton Malissof* [Russian Short Stories] (1878). *Croquis* [Sketches] (1880). *Idylles* [Idylls] (1885). *Récits et nouvelles* [Accounts and Short Stories] (1892).

Textbook: *Instruction morale et civique des jeunes filles* [Moral and Civic Instruction for Girls] (1882).

Bibliography

Clark, Linda L., *Schooling the Daughters of Marianne: Textbooks and the Socialization of Girls in Modern French Primary Schools* (Albany, 1984), pp. 30–34. "Henry Gréville." *La Fronde* (Paris, May 27, 1902). Stanton, Theodore, "Literary Notes from Paris." *The Critic* 41 (August 1902): 174–175. Stanton, Theodore, ed., *The Woman Question in Europe* (New York, 1884), pp. 280–289. Thieme, Hugo Paul, *Woman in All Ages and Countries* (Philadelphia, 1908), p. 414.

General references: Lanthenay, M., "Durand-Gréville, Alice-Marie-Céleste-Henry, Mme Emile." *Dictionnaire de biographie française*, vol. 12 (Paris, 1970).

Linda L. Clark

Tatiana Gritsē-Milliex

(see: Tatiana Gritsi-Milliex)

Tatiana Gritsi-Milliex

(a.k.a. Tatiana Gritsē-Milliex, Tatiana Gritsi Milliex)

Born 1920
Genre(s): novel, short story
Language(s): Greek

Tatiana Gritsi-Milliex (also, Gritsē Milliex, Gritsi, Ghritsi) started writing in the 1940s as one who identified with the resistance movement. Even in this early "political" writing one can detect elements developed in her later work: great sensitivity, concern for her fellow man, interest in social issues, acuteness in observation. Her marriage to Roger Milliex was not only a turning point in her life but also in her writing. She was greatly influenced by contemporary French prose, especially by the *nouveau roman*, and in *Idou ippos chlōros* (1963) she makes a bold break with past forms and writes in a style that can stand up next to that of her French contemporaries.

Sparagmata (1981; Lacerations) is a short volume of narrations that appear to be disconnected. The fragmentary nature of the work, however, is suitable to a book dealing with human cruelty and injustice that drive individuals to hopelessness and despair.

Anadromes (1982; Going Back) is a collection of eighteen short stories dealing with such recurring motifs as loneliness, rootlessness, insecurity, and the inability to communicate. Although in writing these stories Gritsē-Milliex is "going back" over her life and experience, the stories themselves are not simply chronicles of the past but artistic renditions of individual situations.

Gritsē-Milliex's work has been translated into Swedish, Russian, German, French, and Romanian.

Works

Plateia Thēseiou [Theseion Square] (1947). *Dromos tōn angelōn* [The Way of the Angels] (1950). *Kopiōntes kai pephortismenoi* [Laboring and Burdened] (1951). *Ēmerologio* [Journal] (1953). *Se prōto prosōpo* [In the First Person] (1953). *Allazoume?* [Shall We Change?] (1961). *Kai idou ippos chloros* [And Behold a Green Horse] (1982). *Sparagmata* [Lacerations] (1973, 1981). *Vythoskopēseis* [Depth Watchings] (1978). *Anadromes* [Going Back] (1982).

Bibliography

Mirasgezē, Maria, *Neoellēnikē Logotechnia*, vol. 2 (Athens, 1982). Politis, Linos, *A History of Modern Greek Literature* (Oxford, 1973). Politis, Linos, *Historia tes Neollēnikes Logotechnias* (Athens, 1980). Proussis, C.M., Review, *Books Abroad*, vol. 49, no. 3, p. 593. Robinson, Christopher, review. *World Literature Today* 57, No. 4 (Autumn, 1983): 670.

General references: *Macmillan Guide to Modern World Literature* (London, 1985).

Helen Dendrinou Kolias

Anne-Lise Grobéty

Born December 21, 1949, La Chaux-de-Fonds, Switzerland
Genre(s): novel, short story, poetry, journalism, radio plays
Language(s): French

Anne-Lise Grobéty has told an interviewer that she began working towards the goal of becoming a writer at the age of fourteen. Her determination was crowned with success: the novel *Pour mourir en février* (1970), written while Grobéty was still a pupil at the "Gymnase cantonal" [high school] in La Chaux-de-Fonds, won the coveted Prix Georges Nicole, was a bestseller, and was brought out in German by the prestigious publishing house Kindler. In this quietly melancholy work eighteen-year-old Aude recalls her friendship with an older, freer woman, its strengths and its ultimate failure. *Pour mourir en février* was followed by *Zéro positif* (the title refers to the narrator's blood type), the introspective monologue of a woman nearing thirty undergoing a crisis of female identity: Does she desire the child that the society she moves in expects her to produce? The conflict between the desire to conform and the need to rebel leads to a state of paralysis punctuated by the cycle of the narrator's menstrual flow.

After discontinuing her studies of literature at the University of Neuchâtel, Grobéty worked as a journalist, married, and for a time held a seat in the legislative council of the Canton of Neuchâtel. Today, the mother of three young daughters finds little time for creative writing.

Works

"Eveil" [Awakening] *Textes 68. La Chaux-de-Fonds* [Gymnase cantonal], short story (1968). *Pour mourir en février* [To Die in February], novel (1970). *Zéro positif* [Zero Positive], novel (1975). *Maternances. 6 poems* [Maternities] (1979). *Les Ramoneurs* [The Chimneysweeps], poems (1980). "Du côté de l'écriture féminine. . . ." *Littérature féminine ou féministe?* ["L'écriture féminine" Today; Feminine or Feminist Writing?] (1983). *La Fiancée d'hiver* [The Winter Fiancée], short stories (1984).

Translations into German: *Um in Februar zu sterben* (1971), tr. of *Pour mourir en février.* *Fluchtbewegungen* (1977; 1980), tr. of *Zéro positif.* *Ricos Zaubergarten*, children's book (1972).

Bibliography

Cardinaux, Patrick, "*Zéro positif,* roman de la négativité." Mémoire de licence (University of Lausanne, 1981). Carrard, Philippe, "Variations sur le 'je.' Quelques aspects du récit homodiégétique dans la littérature contemporaine de Suisse romande." *Présence francophone* 20 (Québec, 1980), pp. 163–178. Chaignat, Christine, "Des cercles et des spirales: essai de lecture du roman d'Anne-Lise Grobéty *Zéro positif.*" Mémoire de licence (University of Geneva, 1982). Erhardt, Eva, "*Pour mourir en février* et *Zéro positif,* deux romans d'Anne-Lise Grobéty. Essai de caractérisation des deux principaux personnages féminins." Travail de séminaire, littérature française (University of Bern, 1982). Huber, Margrit, "'Etwas tun, das mich herausfordert'—Anne-Lise Grobéty." *Schritte ins Offene* 14.1 (1984): 23–24. Nicca-Baumgartner, Judith, "*Zéro positif* d'Anne-Lise Grobéty." Mémoire de licence (University of Zürich, 1984).

Ann Marie Rasmussen

Paula Grogger

Born July 12, 1892, Öblarn, Styria, Austria; died January 1, 1984, Öblarn
Genre(s): novel, legend, poetry, drama, autobiography
Language(s): German

Paula Grogger's *oeuvre* has been labeled trivial, and she has been accused of displaying a reactionary, chauvinistic spirit in her fiction. At the same time, she is considered one of the finest representatives of Austrian regional literature. Her novel *Das Grimmingtor* (The Door in the Grimming) is, according to some critics, no less than a part of world literature.

However contradictory critics may see Grogger, she has been extremely popular with readers, particularly in her native state of Styria, where she spent her entire life. Born in the small town of Öblarn, she attended a Catholic teachers' college in Salzburg where the foundations of the profound Catholicism that is characteristic of her entire work were laid.

Das Grimmingtor is Grogger's first book. It was an instant success. Written as a family chronicle, it is set in the region surrounding the Grimming, a mountain in Northern Styria, during the Napoleonic wars. The novel is an amalgam of history, myths, and legends narrated in a unique blend of High German, local dialect and the peculiar idiom of a seventeenth century chronicle. *Das Grimmingtor*, with its emphasis on the region, its customs and the values of family, nature, and religion puts Grogger in the tradition of many Austrian writers of the pre-World War II era who successfully attracted readers traditionally indifferent to literature. Following its success in Austria and Germany, *Das Grimmingtor* was translated into many languages. Its American edition in 1936, however, fell victim to the political development in Europe. Grogger was placed into that category of "popular tellers of sentimental folktales who made contributions to the nationalism in Germany and were happy with Hitler." Indeed, Grogger's attitude to the Nazi regime that took over her native Austria in 1938 was no different from that of many of her contemporaries. She, too, paid homage to the new masters, but, for the rest, she stayed out of politics and remained aloof, even hostile to the Nazi authorities.

Grogger could never repeat the success of *Das Grimmingtor* (which as early as 1930 appeared in thirty editions and still sells well). Among other works, her collections of legends (*Die Sternsinger, Die Räuberlegende*) and her later autobiographical books (*Späte Matura oder Pegasus im Joch, Der Paradeisgarten, Die Reise nach Brixen*) must be considered the strongest components of her *oeuvre*.

In 1984 Grogger died in Öblarn and was buried there. While she has received much of the recognition a writer can expect in Austria, her role as a major figure of Austrian literature of the twentieth century has not yet been adequately researched and determined.

Works

Das Grimmingtor (1926). Die Sternsinger (1927). Die Räuberlegende (1929). Das Gleichnis von der Weberin (1929). Vom Röcklein des Jesukindes (1932). Das Spiel von Sonne, Mond und Sternen (1933). Die Auferstehungsglocke (1933). Der Lobenstock (1935). Die Hochzeit: Ein Spiel vom Prinzen Johann (1937). Bauernjahr (1947). Der Antichrist und Unsere Liebe Frau (1949). Gedichte (1954). Die Reise nach Salzburg (1958). Aus meinem Paradeisgarten (1962). Späte Matura oder Pegasus im Joch (1975). Der himmlische Geburtstag (1977). Sieben Legenden (1977). Die Räuberlegende: Roman (1977). Der Paradeisgarten: Geschichte einer Kindheit (1980). Die Legende von der Mutter (1985). Die Reise nach Brixen (1987). Selige Jugendzeit (1989).
Translations: *The Door in the Grimming*, tr. Caroline Cunningham (1936).

Bibliography

Binder, Christoph Heinrich, *Paula Grogger: Ein biographischer Abriß* (Trautenfels, 1985). Holzinger, Alfred, "Einleitung." Paula Grogger, *Aus meinem Paradeisgarten*, ed. Alfred Holzinger (Graz, Vienna, 1962), pp. 5–27. Umfer, Peter, "Paula Groggers 'Grimmingtor': Sprache und Stilmittel." Diss., Innsbruck, 1979.

Jürgen Koppensteiner

Rose Gronon

(see: Marthe Bellefroid)

Maria de Groot

Born 1937, Amsterdam, The Netherlands
Genre(s): poetry
Language(s): Dutch

Maria de Groot is a major modern poet working outside the mainstream of post-war Dutch poetry in which religious themes play a negligible role.

As a child in Amsterdam, during the second world war, Maria de Groot witnessed the deportations of the Jews, which left an indelible impression. She studied Dutch literature and theology at the university and in 1961 saw her first poem "Beatrijs" receive the first prize in a poetry contest organized by the University of Amsterdam.

The titles of her collections point to the religious nature of her work in which the old link between religion and poetry is constantly reaffirmed. The poet experiences earthly reality as being perpetually in contact with the sacred and the divine and feels that she herself stands in the tension of that contact. Refusing the rigid mold of institutionalized religion or a particular faith, she uses Jewish, Catholic, and Protestant themes and symbols.

Her point of departure is the need to write poetry, to master language and through rhythm and rhyme infuse it with spirit in order to make the text the tangent plane of the real and the sacred. Since her experience of the contact between the two gives meaning to her life and can be expressed only through poetry, writing poetry is for Maria de Groot an existential necessity.

The poet's relation with Christ, a major theme, is presented as a relationship between a man and a woman. In this respect there is an affinity with the great Dutch mystic Hadewijch, although Maria de Groot is not a mystic herself. Earthly objects and relations stand for themselves and are not symbolic of spiritual ones.

In *Amsterdams getijdenboekje* (1966; Amsterdam Breviary, completely reprinted in her collection *Gedichten* or Poems of 1971) the poet gives expression to her awareness of death, her search for meaning, and her experience of contact with the divine. In *Brevier van een Romaanse reis* (Breviary of a Journey to Rome), she attempts to establish a connection between her own emotions and old Roman statues of human figures seen in the South of France. The cycle deals with a journey and emphasizes throughout the poet's bond with the earth. *Het Florentijns circus* (1967; The Florentine Circus), a lyrical epic of 752 lines, is one of her best poems, although it went almost unnoticed by the critics when it came out. The narrator, a woman, tries to choose between Christ and Dionysus, but her dilemma remains unresolved, for both have their risks as well as their rights and to make a choice is impossible. The divine must touch human existence through the earthly and physical.

Maria de Groot has a good sense of rhythm, language, and style. Accused of being too academic and intellectual and of assuming too much knowledge on the part of her reader, she writes the kind of poetry that becomes more accessible with each reading. It is intelligent, carefully written, serious, yet alive with concrete details and decors.

Though little known, Maria de Groot is one of the most important poetic talents of the post-war period in the Netherlands.

Works

Amsterdams getijdenboekje (1966). *Rabboeni* (1966). *Het Florentijnse circus* (1967). *Liedboek van Kevin* (1968). *Gedichten* (1971). *Brevier van een Romaanse reis. Het huis van de danser* (1975). *Carmel* (1977). *Album van licht* (1979). *De bronnen van Jaweh* (1981). *Vlierbessen* (1982).

Bibliography

Interview. *NCRV-Literama* (Oct. 25, 1971). Moerman, Josien, ed., *Ik ben een God in het diepst van mijn gedachten: Lexicon Nederlandstalige auteurs* (1984), p. 89. Vegt, Jan van der, "Maria de Groot: een belangrijke dichteres." *Ons Erfdeel* 15, ii (1971–1972): 88–91.

Maya Bijvoet

Sophie de Grouchy de Condorcet

Born 1766, near Meulan, France; died September 8, 1822, Paris
Genre(s): edition, translation
Language(s): French

Sophie de Grouchy knew how to read and write at age six. She also enjoyed the lessons given by the Abbey de Puisié to her younger brother Emmanuel and was very greatly influenced by the writings of Jean-Jacques Rousseau. In 1784, she was admitted as a canoness at Neuville-en-Bresse, an institution which accepted only personalities able to prove their peerage (nine generations on the paternal side and three on the maternal side). It is at Neuville that she began translating Tasso. She read not only Latin but several other languages as well. Her marriage to the Marquis Caritat de Condorcet was celebrated on December 26, 1786. It became known as one of the rare love matches of the century. The Marquis de Lafayette was best man. The Marquis and Marquise de Condorcet established themselves in Paris at the Hotel des Monnaies, which soon became a very fashionable meeting place for philosophers, writers, and scientists. Among her many famous guests, one can count Christian VIII, King of Denmark, as well as Adam Smith and Thomas Paine. Sophie de Condorcet acquired a reputation of beauty—she was called the pretty nymph with black eyes—and wit. It is told that when she was introduced to the Emperor Napoleon, he complained to her that women were meddling too much in politics; she made this wry answer: "In a country which cuts off their heads, the least they can do is ask why!" The Marquis de Condorcet died in prison March 25, 1793. From 1801 to 1804, Sophie de Condorcet published with the help of Cabanis and Garat, the complete works of her husband. She is also credited with the translation of Adam Smith's *Theory of Moral Sentiments*, accompanied with several letters on sympathy. She died September 8, 1822 and is buried not far from Chopin's tomb.

Works

Editions of her husband's work: *Oeuvres Complètes du Marquis de Condorcet* (1804). *Eloges des*

Académiciens de l'Académie Royale des Sciences Morts depuis l'an 1766 jusqu'en 1790 (1799). *Esquisse d'un tableau historique des progres de l'esprit humain* (1795). *Moyens d'Apprendre à Compter* (1799).

Translations: *The Theory of Moral Sentiments* (1759).

Bibliography

Goncourt, Edmond and Jules, *La Femme au XVIIIe Siècle* (1862). Guillois, Antoine, *La Marquise de Condorcet* (Paris, 1897). Valentino, Henri, *Madame de Condorcet, ses amis et ses amours, 1764–1822* (1750).

Colette Michael

Benoîte Groult

Born January 31, 1920, Paris, France
Genre(s): novel, journalism
Language(s): French

Benoîte Groult was born of well-to-do parents in Paris in 1920; her sister Flora, with whom she was to write some of her more entertaining books, was born four years later. Education at the Cours Sainte-Clotilde, the Lycée Victor Duruy and at the Faculté des Lettres in Paris led to qualifications in literature and English, and during the early years of World War II, Benoîte Groult was a teacher in a secondary school in Paris. From 1944 to 1953 she worked as a journalist with RTF, the French broadcasting service. She has married three times. Benoîte Groult's first major literary endeavors were translations of works by Dorothy Parker, and then she collaborated with her sister Flora on *Journal à quatre mains*. In the form of diary entries by two sisters, the novel is both an engaging narrative of two young people growing up at different rates and a moving account of the stresses and strains of France during the difficult years of the Occupation and Liberation. Humor and emotion are mingled no less expertly than private matters and public issues, and the double focus is developed with great acumen. *Le féminin pluriel*, which some critics rate even higher, uses similar techniques to explore the eternal triangle from some new directions, and *Il était deux fois…* continues to exploit the rich vein with wit and sophistica-

tion. Somewhat less convincing is *Les Trois Quarts du temps* which, without any particular originality of style, takes up and recycles some of the material which had already served so well in the *Journal à quatre mains*, and the rather routine artificiality of *La Part des choses* is not enough to put life into some commonplace problems.

Ainsi soit-elle, with an irresistible play on words in its title, an essay on the feminine condition which, in attitudes no less than in its use of source material, looks back to Simone de Beauvoir's *Le Deuxième Sexe* of 1949. The theme that society's treatment of women is pernicious and is in need of radical reform is also the basis of much of Benoîte Groult's journalistic work.

Works

Journal à quatre mains [Diary in Duo] (1962), tr. Humphrey Hare (1965). *Le féminin pluriel* (1965), tr. Walter B. Michaels and June Wilson (1968). *Il était deux fois* [Twice upon a Time] (1968). *Histoire de Fidèle* (1976). *Ainsi soit-elle* [So Be She] (1975). *Le Féminin au masculin* (1977) *La Part des choses* [The Portion] (1972). *La Moitié de la terre* (1981). *Les Trois Quarts du temps* [Three Quarters of My Time] (1972). [With Flora Groult, Paul Guimard, Blandine de Caunes, Lison de Caunes, and Bernard Ledwije], *Des nouvelles de la famille* (1980).

Translations by Groult: Parker, Dorothy, *Comme ils sont* (1960). Parker, Dorothy, *La Vie à deux* (1983).

Bibliography

Gontier, Fernande, "Benoîte Groult." *Femmes en littérature: Nos contemporaines* (Paris, 1978).

Christopher Smith

Flora Groult

Born 1924, Paris, France
Genre(s): novel
Language(s): French

Flora Groult and her sister Benoîte were brought up in Paris in an artistic milieu. Their parents' friends included famous painters and writers Marie Laurencin, Van Dongen, Max Jacob, Cocteau, Pierre Benoit. Their mother always insisted that a modern woman should work and not depend on a man. While Benoîte was brilliant in school, Flora was just an average student.

They started writing novels together, which immediately became best-sellers. In their co-authored works, each sister assumed the point of view of a female character. After four books written in common, Benoîte and Flora decided to write on their own.

Flora relies often on her own diary and personal life to create contemporary female characters and realistic situations. *Maxime ou la déchirure* (Maxime Breaks Away), for example, describes the decision of a woman to escape her married life: in spite of her hesitations, guilt and fear, Maxime rediscovers the joys of belonging to herself.

In all of Flora's books, the themes of love, motherhood and friendship not only appear in modern situations, but also reach universal dimensions of hope, illusions, and solidarity between women. Though Benoîte is considered to be more active in feminism, Flora's characters reveal the problems women still have to face in our time. In their works both sisters reflect the positions of the feminist movement in the 1960s and 1970s, but cannot always escape the conformism and stereotypes of a bourgeois novel.

Works

Maxime ou la déchirure (1972). Mémoires de moi (1975). Un seul ennui, les jours raccourcissent (1977). Ni tout à fait la même, ni tout à fait une autre (1979). Une vie n'est pas assez (1981). Le paysage intérieur (1982).
In collaboration with Benoîte Groult: Journal à quatre mains (1962). Le féminin pluriel (1965). Il était deux fois (1968). Histoire de Fidèle (1976). [With Benoîte Groult, Paul Guimard, Blandine Lison de Caunes, and Bernard Ladwije], Des Nouvelles de la famille, Editions Mazarine.

Michèle M. Magill

Argula von Grumbach

Born ca. 1492, Seefeld, southern Bavaria; died 1554(?), Zeilitzheim (Schweinfurt)
Genre(s): pamphlets, letters, poetry
Language(s): German

Argula Freiin von Stauf was an unusually well educated woman for her time; she had an impressive knowledge of the Bible. She became one of the first women in Germany to follow Martin Luther in his Reformation. Her father, Bernhadin von Stauff, was constantly involved in fights against his lord, Duke Albrecht von Bayern. Argula lost her parents in 1510 and lived with her uncle, the Marshall of the Court Hieronymus von Stauff, until he lost his position and was sentenced to death by decapitation in 1516. Argula then moved to the Bavarian court, where she became maid of honor for the Duchess Kunigunde. There she met Friedrich von Grumbach. She married him in the same year and moved to Dietfurth in Franconia, where he held the position of governor. The Würzburg priest, Paul Speratus, convinced Argula to support the Reformation. Soon she began to correspond with the leaders of this movement, Andrian Osiander, Georg Spalatin, and Martin Luther. Spalatin provided her with Luther's work, which she studied thoroughly. In 1523 she heard of a young scholar, Arsacius Seehofer, at the University of Ingolstadt, who was sentenced to abjure his evangelical belief which he had expressed in 17 heretical articles, and he was imprisoned in the Ettal monastery. Since no one else defended him, she sent, after consultations with Osiander, a public letter to the university and the city of Ingolstadt and to the Duke of Bavaria on behalf of Seehofer. This caused a political scandal and gave her much notoriety, since no woman before her had come forth to argue about religious matters. She also sent some public letters and pamphlets to Duke Electorate Friedrich von Sachsen and Count Palatinate Johann at the Imperial Assembly at Nuremberg, in which she urged them to defend the Lutheran belief. This attracted more attention to her. Count Palatinate Johann von Simmern, also a member of the imperial government, gave her an audience in Nuremberg. But all her efforts were to no avail, because she could not move these high ranking figures to join the Reformation. She also resisted pressure from her family to give up her religious fervor. Her husband even lost his position as a governor because of her activities. Argula strongly believed that Christ would come soon and thus thought it necessary to preach God's word. She wrote a letter to the city of Regensburg on June 29, 1524, to protest against measures to suppress evangelical sermons in church. Only a few letters exist after 1524, since she withdrew from society. In one of them she urged Martin Luther to get married. She visited him at the Castle Coburg in 1530 and sent some letters of consolation to Augsburg. Unfortunately, all her letters to Spalatin, Luther, and Osiander seem to be lost. She never wanted to be labelled a Lutheran, claiming to be nothing else than a pure Christian. After her first husband's death in 1529 she married Count Schlick in 1533 but became a widow again very soon afterward. The rest of her life she dedicated to the education of her children. Of her three sons only Gottfried and Hans Georg outlived her, but perhaps her life lasted longer than we think, since she might be identified with the "old Staufferin," Frau von Köferin, who was arrested in 1563 on charges of trying to convert the people in and around Köfering to the Lutheran belief. This could, however, also have been her daughter, about whom nothing is known.

Works

Her letters were first printed by Ph. Ulhart in Augsburg, then by Hergot in Nuremburg; a first collection appeared in 1524. Some of her works also were included in Ludwig Rabus, *Märtyrerhistorie* (1556). Modern editions are H.A. Pistorius, *Frau Argula von Grumbach und ihr Kampf mit der Universität zu Ingolstadt* (1854) and Felix Joseph Lipowsky, *Argula von Grumbach*, with historical documents (1801). One letter is published in Georg R. Spohn, "Widmungsexemplare Ulrichs von Hutten und ein Sendschreiben Argulas von Grumbach an Pfalzgraf Johann II. von Pfalz-Simmern," *Archiv für mittelrheinische Kirchengeschichte* 23 (1971): 141–146.

Bibliography

Classen, A., "Woman Poet and Reformer: The 16th-Century Feminist Argula von Grumbach." *Daphnis* (1980). Deubner, K.A., "Das Leben der Argula von Grumbach." *Die Wartburg* 29 (1930): 73–81. Engelhardt, Eduard, *Argula von Grumbach, Die bayerische Tabea, Ein Lebensbild der Reformationszeit für christliche Leser* (Nuremberg, 1860). Hensius, Maria, *Das Bekenntnis der Frau Argula von Grumbach*. Christliche Wehrkraft 34 (Munich, 1936). Hensius, Maria, *Das unüberwindliche Wort, Frauen der Reformationszeit* (Munich, 1951), pp. 134ff. Kolde, Th., "Arsacius Seehofer und Argula von Grumbach." *Beiträge zur Bayrischen Kirchengeschichte* 11 (1905): 49–77, 97–124, 149–188; 28 (1922): 162–164. Rieger, G.C., *Das Leben Argulae von Grumbach* (Stuttgart, 1737). Stupperich, Robert, "Eine Frau kämpft für die Reformation, Das Leben von Argula von Grumbach." *Zeitwende* 27 (1956): 676–681. Saalfeld, H., "Argula von Grumbach, die Schloßherrin von Lenting." *Sammelblätter des historischen Vereins Ingolstadt* 69 (1960): 42–53. Stupperich, Robert, "Argula, geb. Freiin von Stauff." *Neue Deutsche Biographie*, vol. 7 (Berlin, 1966), p. 212. Stupperich, Robert, "Die Frau in der Publizistik der Reformationszeit." *Archiv für Kulturgeschichte* 37 (1955): 204–233, especially 218–224.

Albrecht Classen

Aniela Gruszecka

(a.k.a. Jan Powalski)

Born May 18, 1884, Warsaw, Poland; died April 18, 1976, Cracow, Poland
Genre(s): novel, short story, criticism
Language(s): Polish

Despite her education in exact sciences, Gruszecka devoted her life to literary pursuits. In her historical novels for young readers, she demonstrated a deep insight into and a feeling for life in the past, especially in the Middle Ages. *Król* (1913; The King), for example, deals with the reign of the medieval Polish king Przemysław Pogrobowiec. Similarly, *Nad jeziorem* (1921; By the Lake), an idyll set in the thirteenth century, even demonstrates a skillful use of archaic language that adds authenticity to the narrative. However, Gruszecka displayed her versatility by using an innovative style in the psychological novel *Przygoda w nieznanym kraju* (1933; Adventure in an Unknown Country), where she explored the environment in the artistic and intellectual circle of Cracow, of which she was a part. In contrast, in the six-volume cycle *Powieść o kronice Galla* (1960–1970; A Novel About the Gallus Chronicle), she examined the origins of this early chronicle and its influence upon the study of history and other sciences by subsequent generations. She also published literary studies and a handbook. Finally, in her last work published the year of her death, *Całe życie w przyrodzie mowy ojczystej* (1976; A Lifetime Spent Immersed in My Mother Tongue), she offered a testimonial to her abiding interest in and devotion to language and literature.

Works

Novels: *W słońcu* [In the Sun] (1912). *Król* [The King] (1913). *W grodzie żaków* [In the Town of Schoolboys] (1913). *Sztandary Ksiecia Józefa* [Duke Josef's Banners] (1914). *Nad jeziorem* [By the Lake] (1921). *Przygoda w nieznanym kraju* [Adventure in an Unknown Country] (1933). *Powieść o kronice Galla* [A Novel About the Gallus Chronicle], 6 vols. (1960–1970).

Short stories: *W zaklętym zamku* [In the Enchanted Castle] (1913). *Od Karpat na Bałtyk* [From the Carpatians to the Baltic] (1946).

Scholarship: *O powieści* [About the Short Story] (1927). *Stare i nowe w powieści współczesnej* [The Old and the New in the Contemporary Novel] (1933). *Klasyfikacja a życie na terenie powieści* [Classification and Life in the Realm of the Novel] (1934). *Całe życie w przyrodzie mowy ojczystej* [A Lifetime Spent Immersed in My Mother Tongue], in the style of popular science (1976). Lesser works, articles, debates, and critical reviews in periodicals.

Bibliography

Eustachiewicz, Leslaw, "Saga o Kronice Galla." *Życie Literackie* (July 4, 1971): 10. Korzeniewska, Ewa, ed., *Słownik współczesnych pisarzy polskich*, vol. 1 (Warsaw, 1963). Rzymowski, Jerzy, "Gruszecka, Aniela." *Literatura polska; Przewodnik encyklopedyczny*, ed. Julian Krzyzanowski, vol. 1 (Warsaw, 1984).

Irene Suboczewski

Mme Adrien Guebhard

(see: Séverine)

Eugénie-Henriette-Augustine de Guérin

Born January 29, 1805, Le Cayla, Tarn, France; died May 31, 1848, Le Cayla
Genre(s): diary, letters
Language(s): French

Eugénie de Guérin's life was uneventful; what makes it exceptional is the intensity with which she experienced and recorded it. The daughter of parents belonging to the rural gentry, she was born at the family manor of Le Cayla in the department of Tarn, not far from Albi, and she received her education, which was pious and literary in orientation, at home. Her brother, Maurice, was born in 1810, and after the premature death of her mother, Eugénie became devoted to his well-being. Much of her writing can be seen as a direct response to his absences from home, for she wrote to him continually and her diary was conceived primarily as a record of her existence while he was away in Paris studying at the Collège Stanislas and, after abandoning thoughts of a career in the law, seeking fame as a writer. She visited the capital only twice, for her brother's marriage and, after his death from tuberculosis, to settle his affairs, and she rarely left Le Cayla. There she died, also a victim of tuberculosis, in 1848. She never married.

Deeply and emotionally Catholic, Eugénie de Guérin records in her *Journal* the thoughts and sentiments of a sympathetic heart. Her gift was to respond to stimuli and to record delicately all that she felt. In a life virtually without action though not sheltered from tragedy, for illness was an ever-present danger and death a threat that could not long be held at bay, she unconsciously developed a remarkable sensitivity and a no less considerable capacity to express it clearly but without exaggeration. Like Michel de Montaigne, she became consubstantial with her book as her personality developed as she sought to express it. Her *Journal* may well be called "intimate," not because it reveals secret anecdotes and facts that are concealed from the public gaze but because it reveals the most private truths about her. Her letters reveal the same caring nature, and they are also of interest because they cast some light on the no less fascinating personality of Maurice de Guérin, author of *Le Centaure.*

Though she was eager that her brother's works should be published, she took no steps to have anything of her own printed, and it was not until the middle of the nineteenth century that editions of her letters and diary were brought out.

Works

Lettres, ed. G.S. Trebutien (1865). *Journal et fragments*, ed. G.S. Trebutien (1862; tr. William Lightbody, 1886). *Journal*, ed. Emile Barthès (1929).

Bibliography

Barthès, Emile, *Eugénie de Guérin*, 2 vols. (Paris, 1929). Smith, Naomi Ruth, *The Idol and the Shrine* (London, 1949).

Christopher Smith

Amalia Guglielminetti

Born 1885, Turin, Italy; died 1941, Turin
Genre(s): poetry, novel, short story,
*   journalism, children's literature*
Language(s): Italian

Born into a well-to-do family, Guglielminetti rebelled against the strictures of conventional life to forge for herself a position in the literary circles of Turin. She gained notoriety both for her work and for her liaisons with two men of letters: the frail poet Guido Gozzano, of the decadent group of "crepuscolari," and the more fashionable, but less vulnerable novelist, Pitigrilli. Besides authoring poems, novels and short stories, she actively contributed to *La stampa* and *La donna*. She founded and directed her own periodical, *Seduzioni*. Guglielminetti lived her last years in deep depression and died from the consequences of a fall suffered during an air-raid alarm.

In *Le vergini folli* (1907; Mad Virgins) and *Le seduzioni* (1909; Seductions), her most representative collections of poetry, Guglielminetti depicted a mundane, turn-of-the-century society, where women of aesthetic propensities and unescapable seductiveness move in perfumed, Art Nouveau interiors. Her evocative style conveying a morbid sensitivity and a good measure of self-indulgent eroticism is not indicative of her own personality but rather suggests the vein of Swinburne or D'Annunzio. Guglielminetti recreated in her own life the myths and the stereotypes of literature and recited, in both, the part of the modern, restless woman, inconsiderate of the emotional needs of men and dangerous in her pursuit of sensual pleasures.

The same mundane and aesthetic atmosphere prevails in her novels, of which *Gli occhi cerchiati d'azzurro* (1920; Eyes Circled with Blue) was the most successful. Here we find a gallery of upper-class women, voluptuously cruel and morbidly vulnerable. There is an almost palpable delight in beautiful objects, expensive bibelots, and fashionable clothes. But behind the elegant mask, there lurks an undefinable agitation that becomes the sign of the heroine's tragic destiny. Lighter in tone are some of her short stories. In "When I Had a Lover," "The Key of the Mystery," and "The Brilliant Writer," the author pokes fun at male complacency and smiles with sardonic gaiety at life's strange coincidences and ironic twists.

On the whole, Guglielminetti's work is to be appreciated for her capacity to describe the lifestyle of her social milieu, and for the beguiling feminine sensibility with which she expresses the self-eroding restlessness of the newly liberated woman.

Works

Voci di giovinezza (1903). *Le vergini folli* (1907). *Le seduzioni* (1908). *L'amante ignoto* (1911). *L'insonne* (1913). *I volti dell'amore* (1913). *Le ore inutili* (1919). *Gli occhi cerchiati d'azzurro* (1920). *La porta della gioia* (1920). *Il regno incantato* (1922). *La rivincita del maschio* (1923). *Anime allo specchio* (1925). *Nei e cicisbei* (1926). *Tipi bizzarri* (1931). *Quando avevo un amante* (1933). With G. Gozzano, *Lettere d'amore* (1951).

Bibliography

Borgese, G.A., *La vita e il libro*. I (Bologna, 1923), pp. 171–178. Cecchi, E., *Letteratura italiana del Novecento* (Milan, 1972), pp. 489–497. Gastaldi, M., *Amalia Guglielminetti* (Milan, 1957). Pellizzi, C., *Le lettere italiane del nostro secolo* (Milan, 1929), pp. 77–78. Pitigrilli, *Amalia Guglielminetti* (Milan, 1919). Russo, L., *I narratori, 1850–1950)* (Milan-Messina, 1951), pp. 200–201. Serra, R., *Le lettere* (Rome, 1920), pp. 96–69, 107–117, 223. Vincenti, F., *J Contemporanei*, IV (Milan, 1972), pp. 151–168.

Rinaldina Russell

Élisabeth Guibert

Born March 31, 1725, Versailles, France; died
  ca. 1787/88
Genre(s): drama, occasional verse
Language(s): French

Very little is known about the life of Élisabeth Guibert except that she is referred to in published sources, such as L'Almanach des Muses (The Muses' Almanac), as "pensionnaire du roi" (pensioner of the King). Most of her works are accessible only in rare eighteenth-century editions. She wrote plays for the court of Louis XV whose titles betray their stock quality, such as La coquette corrigée (1764; The Corrected Flirt) or Les filles à marier (1768; The Girls to Marry). Her occasional verse, published in part in one volume in 1764 but also including pieces that appeared in L'Almanach des Muses from 1766 to 1769, is highly conventional. It suffers from the faults shared by many works that appeared in L'Almanach des Muses: outdated rhetorical artifices, symptomatic according to one twentieth-century critic, Edmond Estève, of the general exhaustion of French verse prior to Romanticism. While this characterization is certainly true to some extent, it should be noted that Élisabeth Guibert's works are frequently printed next to verses by Voltaire and that despite even contemporary criticisms of her diction (printed as footnotes by L'Almanach's editors), she was able to achieve a certain delicacy in her poetry, as the dedication of her Poésies from 1764 clearly shows:

Heureux talent des vers, agréable manie,
   vous remplissez le vuide de ma vie
je ne tiens rien, ni ne veux rien de vous.
Les dieux, en vous bornant, ont su me
   satisfaire,
vous me servez à plaire
et ne suffisez pas pour faire des jaloux.
(Oh happy talent for verse, a pleasant
   enough madness,
you fill the void of my life
I hold nothing, want nothing from you.
The gods, in limiting you, knew how to
   satisfy me,
you help me to please,
but are too weak to make others
   jealous.)

It is to be hoped that further archival research may turn up more on this literary figure of the court of Louis XV. Several of her works reveal a profound knowledge of the classics, such as her piece Les philéniens ou le patriotisme, which recounts the story related by Sallust and Valerius Maximus of the Philaeni, two Carthaginian brothers who allowed themselves to be buried alive out of love for their country. Many of her verses are madrigals, attesting to her sensitivity to the interrelationship between music and verse. Clearly, a reassessment is long overdue.

Works

Les filles à marier [The Girls to Marry] (1768). Pièces détachées [Separate Works] (1770). Les philéniens ou le patriotisme (1775; The Philaeni or Patriotism). Poésies et oeuvres diverses [Poetry and Divers Works]; contains the text of La coquette corrigée (1764). Le sommeil d'Amythe [The Sleep of Amythaon] (1768). Occasional verses published in L'Almanach des Muses (1766–1769).

Bibliography

Quérard, J.-M., "Guibert, Mme." La France littéraire, vol. 3 (Paris, 1829), p. 517.

Earl Jeffrey Richards

Margherita Guidacci

Born April 25, 1921
Genre(s): poetry
Language(s): Italian

Guidacci is a poet and university lecturer in English and American literature at the University of Macerata. She lives in Rome. She has won the following awards: Carducci Prize, 1957; Ceppo Prize, 1971; Lerici Prize, 1972; Gabbici Prize, 1974; Seanno Prize, 1976.

Works

La Sabbia e l'angelo (1946). Morte del Ricco (1955). Giorni dei santi (1957). Paglia e polvere (1961). Poesie (1965). Un Cammino incerto (1970). Neursuite (1970). Terra senza orologi (1973). Taccuino slavo (1975). Il Vuoto e le forme (1977).

Robert Harrison

Jacquette Guillaume

Flourished c. 1665, Paris, France
Genre(s): prose discourse, prose fiction
Language(s): French

Jacquette Guillaume is the author of two recorded works: (1) a very rare 443-page book, *Les Dames illustres, ou, par bonnes et fortes raisons, il se prouve que le sexe feminin surpasse en toutes sortes de genres le sexe masculin*, published in Paris in 1665, and dedicated to Mlle D'Alencon (NUC lists only two institutional copies, at the Library of Congress and Duke University); and (2) a short piece of prose-fiction, no longer extant, *La Femme Genereuse*.

In *Les Dames*, the only work of Guillaume's thus far uncovered by French scholars, Guillaume enters the popular *querelle des femmes* debate in seventeenth-century French belles-lettres with a radical book which argues for women's moral and intellectual superiority over men. Guillaume's ambitious discourse is well researched, and its overall orientation and rhetoric reflects the Rationalism of Descartes (particularly his publications of the 1630s and 1640s) which attracted many feminist apologists, both on the Continent and in England. Guillaume also allies herself with the tradition of learned ladies (cf. the late medieval feminist, Christine de Pisan) when methodologically she assembles impressive, erudite evidence for her occasionally extreme claims. Guillaume finds models of female excellence throughout human history as well as in the animal kingdom. While obviously knowledgeable and confident, Guillaume's feminist *brio* is sometimes stridently assertive and her conclusions could have been significantly strengthened with more reliance on biblical history, which offers persuasive models of female leadership and governance.

Guillaume's lengthy work consists of two principal sections. The first part sets out the superiority of woman's moral character and humanity. Guillaume catalogues historical examples of male cruelty, vice, and infidelity, and then contrasts them with models of female generosity and high principles (the biblical Judith, the French national heroine Jeanne d'Arc). The second part of Guillaume's *Dames* identifies and celebrates French *femmes savantes*. The book objectively concludes with a list of unfortunate women throughout history and, in its organization and thematic concerns, it owes a large debt to Pisan's feminist writings. Significantly Guillaume's survey of accomplished women was comprehensive enough to attract the serious attention of the celebrated English Anglo-Saxon scholar Elizabeth Elstob, who proudly acknowledged Guillaume as one of four sources used in her workbook of sketches of learned women; Elstob's workbook provided the foundation of George Ballard's important feminist survey *Memoirs of Several Ladies of Great Britain Who Have Been Celebrated for Their Writings . . .* (London, 1752).

A long-neglected, obscured contribution to the history of early French feminism, Guillaume's *Dames* is best appreciated within contemporary feminist contexts, such as the distinguished work of Poulain de la Barre and Du Bosc in France; Anna Maria van Schurman in the Netherlands; and Bathsua Makin in England. All of these figures were prominent seventeenth-century feminist pioneers whose theoretical essays pointed the way for the florescence of feminism in the eighteenth century.

Marie-Anne Guillaume, a close relation of Jacquette's, was also an explicit feminist writer. Her prose discourse *Que le sexe feminin vaut mieux que le masculin* (1668) is obviously modeled on Jacquette's book. Regrettably, none of Marie-Anne's writings is extant.

The Guillaume women, especially Jacquette, offer themselves as attractive Enlightenment case-studies in the roots of feminist apologetics. It is to be hoped that they will be investigated by present-day French scholars as potential sources for de La Barre and other early feminist thinkers.

Works

Les Dames illustres, ou, par bonnes et fortes raisons, il se prouve que le sexe feminin surpasse en toutes sortes de genres le sexe masculin (1665). *La Femme Genereuse* (n.d.).

Bibliography

Hale, Sarah Josepha, *The Woman's Record* (New York, 1855). Weiss, "Guillaume, Jacquette et Marie-Anne." *Michaud's Biographie universelle, ancienne et moderne*, 45 vols. (Graz, Austria, 1966–1970).

Maureen E. Mulvihill

Guillelma de Rosers

Flourished mid-thirteenth century
Genre(s): poetry
Language(s): Provençal

As with so many of the *trobairitz*, the information we have on Guillelma de Rosers comes in part from her name, in part from her poetry, and in part from the *vida* of the male with whom she debated in her poem. Guillelma's name suggests, to Bogin at least, three possible provenances: Rougiers (near Italy, in Provence proper), Rosieres (Ardeche), or Roziers (Lozere). Given that her poetry consists of one *tenso*, "Na Guillelma, man cavalier arratge," in which the male is a certain Lanfrancs Cigala, and given that Cigala can be securely identified as a Genoese, Rougiers seems the most likely choice. We are lucky in the case of Guillelma to also have an anonymous *canso* in her honor, "Quan Proensa ac perduda proeza" that laments her absence from Provence in Genoa.

The *tenso* with Cigala consists of six *coblas unissonans* of eight lines each with two *tornadas* of four lines. The rhyme scheme is *ababcccb*. More than most other *trobairitz' tensos*, this one reads as a true debate in that it sets a problem in the first stanza, which is then pursued through the rest of the poem. The problem is this: two barons, on their way to visiting their ladies, overhear some traveling knights lamenting their distance from home. One baron turns to aid the knights; the other continues to his lady. Which of the two acted more appropriately? The *tenso* then continues by debating the relative values of love and courtesy and the degree to which the two are, or should be, related.

The anonymous poem in Guillelma's honor, "Quan Proensa ac perduda proeza," is edited by Schultz (p. 31) and mentions a Guillelma in line 10 and again in line 37 where she is referred to as "belha de Rogier." It is her stay in Genoa that is being lamented, apparently by Cigala's rival in Provence.

Works

Ed., Schultz, p. 27; Bogin, pp. 134–137; Perkal-Balinsky, pp. 96–104; Mahn III, 127; Véran, pp. 144–146; Branciforti, pp. 173–176.

Bibliography

Bec, P., "*Trobairitz* et chansons de femme: Contribution à la connaissance du lyrisme féminin au moyen âge." *CCM* 22 (1979): 235–262. Bogin, M., *The Women Troubadours* (New York, 1980). Boutiére, J., and A.-H. Schutz, *Biographies des troubadours*, 2d ed. (Paris, 1964). Branciforti, F., *Il canzoniere di Lanfrancesco Cigala* (Florence, 1954). Bruckner, M., "Na Castelloza, *Trobairitz*, and Troubadour Lyric." *Romance Notes* 25 (1985): 1–15. Chabaneau, C., "Les biographies des troubadours en langue provençale." *Histoire générale de Languedoc*, X (Toulouse, 1885). Dronke, P., *Women Writers of the Middle Ages* (Cambridge, 1984). Mahn, C.A.F., *Die Werke der Troubadours in provenzalischer Sprache* (Berlin, 1846). Perkal-Balinsky, D., *The Minor Trobairitz*. Diss., Evanston, Ill., 1986. Raynouard, M., *Choix des poésies originales des troubadours*. 6 vols. (Osnabruck, 1966). Riquer, M., de. *Los trovadores*, 3 vols. (Barcelona, 1975). Schultz, O., *Die Provenzalischen Dichterinnen* (Leipzig, 1888). Shapiro, M., "The Provençal *Trobairitz* and the Limits of Courtly Love." *Signs* 3 (1978): 560–571. Tavera, A., "A la recherche des troubadours maudits." *Sénéfiance* 5 (1978): 135–161. Véran, J., *Les poétesses provençales* (Paris, 1946).

Sarah Spence

Pernette du Guillet

Born ca. 1520, Lyons, France; died July 7,
1545, Lyons
Genre(s): lyric poetry
Language(s): French

In 1536, Pernette met the learned poet Maurice Scève, who was beginning to compose the Petrarchist poems that would later assure his fame. Frequenting the literary salons of Lyons, which were also frequented by Scève, Pernette, like many of her contemporaries, began to write Petrarchist verse. In 1538, she married du Guillet. Seven years later, at age twenty-five, she died. Wishing to honor her memory, her husband asked the eminent scholar Antoine du Moulin to prepare an edition of her poems. The volume of about eighty pages was published six weeks later under the title of *Rymes*.

Consisting of sixty epigrams (mostly eight or ten lines long, but occasionally only four), ten songs, five elegies, and two *épîtres*, Pernette's corpus is slender. Some of the pieces are clearly little more than exercises. In her best poems, however, she pitches her voice in a register that is distinctly hers. Calling the beloved the source of knowledge and joy, Pernette gives a Platonic cast to the Petrarchist conventions she adopted. In language that is limpid, fluid, and deliberately "colorless," she expresses the purity of her love, resorting often to images of light and water.

Unlike most Petrarchist verse, which recounts the pain of the lover and the indifference of the beloved, Pernette's poems celebrate a love that is shared. Her small body of work contains two or three lyrics that are among the most exquisitely fashioned love poems of the French Renaissance.

Works

Rymes, ed. Victor E. Graham (1968).

Bibliography

Ardouin, Paul, *Maurice Scève, Pernette du Guillet, Louise Labé: l'amour à Lyon au temps de la Renaissance* (Paris, 1981). Cottrell, Robert D., "Pernette du Guillet's *Rymes*: An Adventure in Ideal Love." *Bibliothèque d'Humanisme et Renaissance* 31 (1969): 553–571. Griffin, Robert, "Pernette du Guillet's Response to Scève: A Case for Abstract Love." *L'Esprit Créateur* 5 (1965): 110–116. Perry, T. A., "Pernette du Guillet's Poetry of Love and Desire." *BHR* 35 (1973): 259–271. Saulniter, V. L., "Etude sur Pernette du Guillet." *BHR* 4 (1944).

Robert D. Cottrell

Irén Gulácsy

Born September 9, 1894, Lázárföldpuszta, near Szeged, Hungary; died January 1945, Budapest
Genre(s): short story, novel
Language(s): Hungarian

Gulácsy married at sixteen and lived in the Hánság and near Szeged for a while but later moved to Nagyvárad (now Oradea, Romania). Her husband became an invalid relatively early, so she supported the family by writing for the journal *Nagyvárad*. Her short stories soon attracted attention, and the critics felt there was the promise of a good writer: both her imagination and vocabulary showed great originality, although the influence of Zsigmond Móricz and Dezső Szabo was also noticeable. Her first novel, *Hamueső* (1925; Rain of Ashes) did not receive unqualified praise, but it was felt she would become an important writer. *Zord Idők*, a journal in Marosvásárhely (now Targu Mures, Romania) published her *Förgeteg* (1925; Storm), and her ties to Transylvania remained strong. Her themes were patriotic, and she dealt with some of the problems of the times. In this work she examined the question of land reform. About the same time, she also won a prize for her drama, *Napáldozat* (Sun Sacrifice, performed at the Magyar Színház in Kolozsvár (now Cluj-Napoca, Romania). The promise of her writings was never really fulfilled, but she had a very successful novel, *Fekete vőlegények* (1927; Black Bridegrooms) that was a critical success as well. She died during the siege of Budapest.

Gulácsy's style unites Naturalism and Romanticism, but her theme is the necessity for cooperation and unity to achieve national goals. Like many of her contemporaries who sought to come to grips with the national tragedy of Trianon, she examines, through history and fiction, the causes that led to the decline of national strength and unity. While touching on social problems, she emphasizes the need for sacrifice and dedication. The two heroes of *Fekete vőlegények*, set in the late fifteenth and early sixteenth centuries, the time between the death of King Matthias and the defeat of the Hungarian forces at Mohács, are two such martyrs of national ideals. The story is well-crafted, though full of incidents; the protagonists emerge as full-fledged human figures and not merely symbols. While some of the supporting characters are less well drawn, and certain prejudices color their presentations, the novel succeeds both as a historical recreation of a critical time in Hungarian history and as a literary warning against selfish motives that can destroy a country in any age.

Works

Hamueső (1925). *Förgeteg* (1925). *Fekete vőlegények* (1927). *Pax vobis* (1930). *A Kálloi kapitány* [The Captain from Kálló] (1933). *Nagy Lajos* [Louis the Great] (1936). *Jezabel* (1941–1944).

Bibliography

Bánhegyi, Jób, "P.G.I. regényei." *Pannonhalmi Szemle* (1937): 180–187, and *Magyar nőírók* (Budapest, 1939), pp. 159–189. Bodor, Aladár, "A Mai erdélyi nőírók." *Protestáns Szemle* 5 (1925): 291–299. Harsányi, Kálmán, "G.I. *Hamueső.*" *Fekete vőlegények. Emberek, irások, problémák* (Budapest, 1929), pp. 285–302. Illés, Endre, "*Pax vobis.*" *Nyugat* I (1931): 408–411. Németh, László, "Az Erdelyi irodalom." *Készülődés* (Budapest, 1941), p. 79. Schöpflin, Aladar, "A *Hamueso.*" *Nyugat* I (1925): 407–409. Thurzó, Gábor, "Gulácsy Irén vagy a siker útjai." *Magyar Csillag* I (1942): 147–150.

Enikő Molnár Basa

Karoline von Günderrode

(a.k.a. Tian, Jon)

Born February 11, 1780, Karlsruhe, Germany;
*   died July 26, 1806, Winkel am Rhein*
Genre(s): poetry, drama
Language(s): German

Considered a member of the German Romantic Movement, Günderrode's poems and dramas also show classical influences. She is most remembered for her suicide and from Bettine von Arnim's novel about her.

Karoline von Günderrode's life and work are defined by irreconcilable conflicts; caught between her desire to be loved and her need to write, trapped by her financial situation, Karoline was never able to escape her circumstances. She was born in Karlsruhe on February 11, 1780, the eldest of six children. Her father, a court advisor and writer, died in 1786, and the family moved to Hanau. Karoline was educated at home by her mother, Louise, a learned woman who had studied Fichte's philosophy and had anonymously published short essays and poems. In May 1797 Karoline entered the *Cronstetten-Hynspergisches Damenstift* in Frankfurt am Main, a Lutheran cloister for widows and spinsters from certain families.

In Frankfurt she pursued her private studies in history and spent long hours reading, despite her frequent severe headaches and vision problems. In 1801 Günderrode met Bettine Brentano (later von Arnim) at the home of Sophie LaRoche, Bettine's grandmother. LaRoche published one of Günderrode's earliest works in her journal *Herbsttage* (1805; Autumn Days). In 1799 Günderrode fell in love with Karl von Savigny, but soon his interest was limited to her intellect, and he became engaged to Gunda Brentano in 1803. This same scenario repeated itself with Clemens Brentano, whom she met in 1801, but he married the writer Sophie Mereau in November 1803. And yet again, in August of 1804, Karoline became tragically involved with Friedrich Creuzer, a professor in Heidelberg, who finally rejected her love and returned to his wife. Her search for a place in the world and for a family led her to deny her erotic impulses as the price of acceptance and continued friendship with these couples. To accomplish this reversal of erotic energy, she sometimes refers to herself in letters as a male friend or in the third person masculine. Karoline was obsessed with death, and her failed relationship with Creuzer served as a catalyst for her long-discussed suicide. After vacillating for two years between his wife and Karoline, Creuzer decided to terminate their affair. Karoline received the news third hand on July 26, 1806. That evening she stabbed herself on the banks of the Rhine.

The tensions in her life are also reflected in her works. Her poems are written with both male and female speakers, but the most personal have female voices. Her dramas, which are her least successful works, include scenes of violent death and suicide, exile, and revenge. The settings, at first primarily Germanic, become more exotic. Thematically emphasized is the power of men to shape their fate while women cannot. Both her poems and her dramas have one pervading theme: death. It is not seen as a negative force but as a place of hope, union, and of escape from pain and solitude. Death is the invisible reverse side of life. In her poem, "Die Malabrischen Witwen" (The Malabrian Widows), Günderrode writes of the women who throw themselves on the funeral pyre as a celebration of love that unifies divided elements, so that the end of life becomes the culmination of existence. Her earliest poetry reveals the influence of the medieval Celtic myths. With her *Apokalyptisches Fragment* (Apocalyptic Fragment) the presence of the German Romantic Movement is felt, advocating a view of the world where there is a unity of spirit with nature, an individuation of this spirit in creation, and a belief in the infinite drive for fulfillment in all the elements of the world.

Christoph von Nees published two volumes of her writings under the pseudonym "Tian": *Gedichte und Phantasien* (Poems and Fantasies) in 1804 and *Poetische Fragmente* (Poetic Fragments) in 1805. A third volume, *Melete*, was prepared for publication but was never issued. One drama appeared in a yearbook. Friedrich Creuzer and Carl Daub published two plays in 1805 in their journal, *Studien*. These were: *Udohla*, which takes place in Delhi and has Moslems as characters and *Magie und Schicksal* (Magic and Fate), which takes place in Greece. Her work was widely commented upon and she was recognized as a promising new writer. Her letters and some poetry entered the literary canon with the publication of Bettine von Arnim's *Die Günderode* (The Günderode) in 1840. German literary history has preoccupied itself much more with her suicide than with her literary production. Yet the American philosopher Margaret Fuller decided to translate into English Bettine's book on their friendship. Some of Günderrode's best poems are: "Don Juan," "Der Ku im Traume" (The Dream Kiss), "Des Wanderers Niederfahrt" (The Wanderer's Descent), "Wandel und Treue" (Change and Fidelity), and "Liebst du das Dunkel" (Do You Love the Darkness?).

Works

Gesammelte Werke, 3 vols. (1970).
Collections: [With Doris Hopp], Preitz, Max, ed., *Karoline von Günderrode in ihrer Umwelt. Jahrbuch des freien deutschen Hochstifts* (1962, 1964, 1975). Wolf, Christa, "Der Schatten eines Traumes. Karoline von Günderrode—ein Entwurf." *Der Schatten eines Traumes*, by Karoline von Günderrode, ed. Christa Wolf (Darmstadt and Neuwied, 1979), pp. 5–65.

Bibliography

Arnim, Bettine von, *Goethes Briefwechsel mit einem Kinde* (1835). Burwick, Roswitha, "Liebe und Tod im Leben der Günderode." *German Studies Review* 3 (1980): 207–223. Fuller, Margaret, "Bettine Brentano and Her Friend Günderode." *The Dial* 2 (January 1842): 313–357. Geiger, Ludwig, *Karoline von Günderode und ihre Freunde* (Stuttgart, 1895). Kohlschmidt, Werner, "Ästhetischer Existenz und Leidenschaftlicher Mythos von Wirklichkeit der Karoline von Günderode." *Zeitwende* 51 (1980): 205–216. Lazarowicz, Margarete, *Karoline von Günderrode. Portrait einer Fremden* (Frankfurt am Main, 1986). Preisendanz, Karl, *Die Liebe der Günderode. Friedrich Creuzers Briefe an Caroline von Günderode*, rpt. 1912 (Bern, 1975). Riley, Helene M. Kastinger, "Zwischen den Welten. Ambivalenz und Existentialproblematik im Werk Caroline von Günderrodes." *Die Weibliche Muse. Sechs Essays über Künstlerisch schaffende Frauen der Goethezeit* (Columbia, S.C., 1986), pp. 91–119. Schwartz, Karl, "Karoline von Günderrode." *Allgemeine Enzyklopädie der Wissenschaften und Künste*, ed. J.S. Ersch and J.G. Gruber, vol. 97, rpt. 1878 (Graz, 1977), pp. 167–231. Susman, Margarete, "Karoline von Günderode." *Frauen der Romantik* (Köln, 1960), pp. 134–160. Wilhelm, Richard, *Die Günderrode. Dichtung und Schicksal* (Frankfurt am Main, 1938). Wolf, Christa, *Kein Ort. Nirgends* (Darmstadt and Newied, 1979). Wolf, Christa, *No Place on Earth*, novel about Günderrode and Heinrich von Kleist, tr. Jan van Heurck (New York, 1982).

Marjanne E. Goozé

Agnes Günther

Born June 21, 1863, Stuttgart, Germany; died February 16, 1911, Marburg an der Lahn
Genre(s): novel, drama
Language(s): German

Considering the contrast between the volume of her work and its popularity, Agnes Günther (née Breuning) was a mysterious writer. She died of a lung disease before she could finish her only novel, *Die Heilige und ihr Narr* (The Saint and Her Fool), begun only when she was bedridden. Her husband Rudolf Günther, a professor of divinity in Marburg, completed the fragment, which then became one of this century's bestsellers with more than one hundred editions. It deals with a Württembergian legend of the seventeenth century, in which an alleged witch is freed from prison and torture and marries the count of Brauneck. Her death by gunshot at the hand of her mother-in-law turns her atheistic husband into a believer in God. A stage version of the story was performed in Langenburg (Hohenlohe) in 1906.

Works

Von der Hexe, die eine Heilige war [About the Witch Who Was a Saint] (1913). *Die Heilige und ihr Narr* [The Saint and Her Fool] (1913).

Bibliography

Bayer, D., *Der triviale Familien-und Liebesroman im 20. Jahrhundert* (Tübingen, 1963). Günther, G., "Ich denke der alten Zeiten, der vorigen Jahre." *Agnes Günther in Briefen, Erinnerungen und Berichte* (1972). *Die Heilige und ihr Narr.* In *Kindlers Literatur Lexikon* III (Zurich, 1964), p. 1571. Killy, W., *Deutscher Kitsch. Ein Versuch mit Beispielen* (Göttingen, 1961). Riess, C., *Bestseller, Bücher die Millionen lesen* (Hamburg, 1960).

Albrecht Classen

Elena Guro

(see: Genrikhovna von Notenberg)

Concepción Gutiérrez Torrero

(see: Concha Lagos)

Marie Guyart

(a.k.a. Marie de l'Incarnation, O.S.U.)

Born October 28, 1599, Tours, France; died
    April 30, 1672, Quebec, Canada
Genre(s): religious and historical tracts
Language(s): French

Called by Bossuet the "Teresa (of Avila) of our times and of New France," Marie was the daughter of Florent Guyart, master baker of Tours, and of Jeanne Michelet. She attended a local country school. Her family arranged her marriage to Claude Martin, master silk-worker,

in 1617; he died in 1619, leaving her with a six-month old son, Claude. Marie put her husband's business in order and then helped in the household of her brother-in-law, Paul Buisson, in Tours. By 1625, she was confided with the administration of his enterprises in that city (this involved transporting merchandise). We know from her spiritual autobiography—the *Relation of 1633* and then the *Relation of 1654*, written at the urging of her spiritual directors—that her earlier aspirations for religious life had reawakened after her husband's death, and that beginning in 1620, she began to have continual experiences of mystical prayer. With spiritual direction, in 1631 she entered the Ursuline nuns, newly established at Tours. In the Ursuline Convent, where she took the name Marie de l'Incarnation, she read the Jesuit *Relations* concerning the Canadian Mission and told her Jesuit spiritual director of her missionary aspirations. Then in 1638, when Mme Marie-Madeleine de la Peltrie, widow of Alençon, presented to the Jesuits her idea of founding a school for the Indians in Canada, she was directed to Marie. By 1639, Marie had arrived at Cap Diamant, Quebec, with Mme de la Peltrie and two Ursuline companions to found a school; three French Hospitalière Sisters from Dieppe were also with them to establish a hospital. She was never to return to France.

Marie's collected letters tell us of her three-month sea journey with its perils of icebergs, storms, and fog. When she arrived, Quebec was a fort and a Jesuit mission, with few homes; she was to see it develop into a city. Her letters recount the group's joy in seeing the Indians' eagerness to give them their daughters to be taught Christian doctrine—the teaching was extended to the adult Indian chiefs, sorcerers, warriors, and their wives as well. They relate in detail the conversions of hundreds of Indians, especially of the Algonquin and Huron tribes; the trials and joys of establishing both the school and the monastery, where Indian and French girls were taught hygiene, reading, and music as well as Christian doctrine; their assistance to poor and starving Indians, especially in winter; the ravages of smallpox; then the fierce Iroquois attacks, their cannibalism, and the brutal martyrdom of some of her now-famous canonized

Jesuit associates, among whom were Isaac Jogues and Jean de Brébeuf—for New France at that time included what is now northern New York State, the New England border, and the Great Lakes Region. Marie narrates the ways and customs of her "chers sauvages," giving graphic, individualized descriptions of the affection of the Indians and of the girls in the school. When she died in 1672, it was said all Quebec attended her funeral.

Marie's *Relations* of 1633 and of 1654 were included in her *Vie*, published in Paris (1677) by her son Claude Martin, who had become a Benedictine of St.-Maur in France. Her collected *Lettres* were also published by Dom Claude in Paris (1681), along with her *Méditations*, *Retraites*, and *Ecole Sainte* (Catechism for the Indians). We know that she wrote works on Indian languages, but these have been lost. Both of Marie's *Relations*, as well as her letters, are filled with her experiences of mystical prayer: mystical union with God in the Divine Espousals; visions of the Trinity and of the Word Incarnate. She also wrote an exposition on the *Canticle of Canticles*. Her work is recognized as parallel with the works of St. John of the Cross and of Teresa of Avila (whom she mentions) on the unitive way of prayer and mystical marriage in the ecstasy of Divine Love. Her ascetical practices, however, should be recognized as having been written in an era that knew neither health sciences nor modern psychology with its concept of a healthy self-esteem and the place of the emotions, an era that saw the rise of Jansenism.

Today the tomb of Marie de l'Incarnation lies in the Ursuline Monastery, Quebec, where the archives on her life are also kept, as well as a Church-and-government-sponsored display of her foundation of the first schoolroom of Canada, including the children's playthings and notebooks. On June 22, 1980, Marie was declared "Blessed" by the Roman Catholic Church, the last step before canonization as a Saint.

Works

Jamet, Dom Albert, ed., *Marie de l'Incarnation, Ursuline de Tours, Fondatrice des Ursulines de la Nouvelle-France: Ecrits Spirituels et Historiques, publiés par Dom Claude Martin*, 4 vols. (1929–1939). Martin, Dom Claude, ed., *La Vie de la Vénérable Mère Marie de l'Incarnation, Première Supérieure des Ursulines de la Nouvelle-France, tirées de ses lettres et de ses écrits* (1677). Martin, Dom Claude, ed., *Lettres de la Vénérable Mère Marie de l'Incarnation, Première Supérieure des Ursulines de la Nouvelle France, divisées en 2 parties* (1681). Oury, Dom Guy, *Correspondance de Marie de l'Incarnation* (1971).

Bibliography

Bremond, Henri de, *Histoire Littéraire du Sentiment Religieux en France*, vol. VI (Paris, 1922; rpt. 1967). Latz, Dorothy L., "Marie de l'Incarnation, O.S.U.," in *17th Century Women Writers*, vol. II, ed. K. Wilson (Athens, Ga.: 1988). Marshall, Joyce, tr. and ed., The *Selected Letters of Marie de l'Incarnation* (Toronto, 1967). Oury, Dom Guy, *Ce Croyait Marie de l'Incarnation* (Paris, 1972). **Translations:** Sullivan, John J., S.J., ed. and tr., *The Autobiography of Venerable Marie of the Incarnation, Mystic and Missionary* (Chicago, 1964). (The *Relation of 1654* only).

Dorothy Latz

Jeanne-Marie Bouvier de la Motte, Mme Guyon

Born April 13, 1648, Montargis, France; died June 9, 1717, Blois
Genre(s): essay, poetry, pamphlet, letters, memoirs
Language(s): French

Born into a prominent noble family in Montargis, Mlle de la Motte was a delicate child. At an early age she exhibited symptoms of hysteria; visions, hallucinations, morbid fears of damnation, and tendencies toward self-sacrifice caused her constant mental anguish. Educated at convents in Montargis, she returned home at age twelve, determined to enter religious life. She found spiritual comfort in the writings of St. Francis de Sales and Jeanne de Chantal (foundress of the Order of the Visitation) who had a profound impact on the rejuvenation of religion in France at this time.

The young girl's desire to enter a convent was opposed by her parents who arranged her marriage, at age sixteen, to Jacques Guyon, a solid, wealthy, thirty-eight-year-old counsellor of the Parlement of Paris. Five children were born (three survived) during their 12-year marriage. After she was widowed, Mme Guyon left her children in the hands of a guardian, abandoned her wealth, and immersed herself in the mystical teachings of the Spanish priest, Miguel de Molinos (c. 1640–1697). In 1680 she arrived at the pinnacle of mystical Quietism, called the "Peace of God" and travelled to Paris where she met d'Aranthon, Bishop of Geneva, who convinced her that she had a sincere religious calling. Through her brother, Père La Motte, she became acquainted with Père Lacombe, also a Barnabite priest, who confirmed that she was destined for an extraordinary religious mission. Lacombe became her spiritual director, and in 1681 they began preaching, first at the Ursuline convent in Thonon, and then at Turin, Grenoble, and Verceil. For five years they travelled and spread their mystical beliefs; the Bishop of Geneva grew alarmed at their success and withdrew his support.

Mme Guyon's Quietism was a form of religious mysticism based on the writings of Père Molinos; he was imprisoned by the Inquisition in 1685 and his writings condemned in 1687. These beliefs centered on passive contemplation, renunciation of self, complete submission to the will of God, spiritual quietude, and total indifference to life, death, and salvation. Only the mind had value; one's soul communed directly with God, eliminating the need for the Sacraments. As long as the communion with God remained unbroken, the body could indulge in sinful acts without affecting the spiritual purity of the soul. Mme Guyon's increasingly bizarre behavior led to condemnation and persecution. She called herself the "pregnant woman of the Apocalypse," the "foundress of a New Church," prophesied that "all hell would band together against her," and claimed that she was a saint and a bride of Jesus. In her raptures, Mme Guyon said that "woman would be pregnant from an internal spirit" and in fact her own body which was at times abnormally swollen seemed to give credibility to her claim.

In July 1686 Guyon returned to Paris; in 1688 she was living at the Visitation convent on the rue Saint-Antoine and frequenting the Court at Versailles and the girls' school of St-Cyr.

Lacombe and Guyon were arrested in 1687 on suspicion of heresy and immorality, but Mme de Maintenon had her released. Maintenon, morganatic wife of Louis XIV and foundress of St-Cyr, supported Guyon's Quietist doctrines and had introduced her to high-placed ladies who enthusiastically embraced her beliefs. Guyon's eloquence and warmth, and her genuine piety convinced many that she was a saint, and she served as spiritual director to some of these devout women, replacing their priestly confessors. The King disapproved of ostentatious religious display but chose not to interfere because Mme de Maintenon encouraged and protected Guyon's activities both at Court and among the noble girls at St-Cyr. Her two early works, *Le Moyen court et tres facile pour faire l'oraison* (The Short and Easy Method of Prayer) and *Les torrents spirituels* (Spiritual Torrents), won for Guyon the devotion and friendship of François de Salignac de la Motte-Fénelon, tutor of the royal children, later Archbishop of Cambrai and member of the French Academy.

But critics of Guyon's mystical doctrines were extremely vocal; to defend her beliefs and her virtue she asked that a commission be appointed to examine charges against her. Her morals were not an issue, only the orthodoxy of her writings were in question. Mme de Maintenon never doubted that her friend's writings would be exonerated. The Conference of Issy that lasted for several months found 34 "errors" in her works, *Le Moyen court* and *Explication de Cantique des Cantiques* (Explanation of the Song of Songs), which were eventually condemned by the French church hierarchy. Guyon reluctantly accepted its judgment, and was allowed to retire wherever she chose; she returned to Paris and the controversy surrounding her soon led to her arrest and imprisonment at Vincennes and then the Bastille.

Fénelon, who had been a member of the Issy Commission, had agreed to the suppression of her erroneous beliefs but would not condemn her personally. He and the conservative Bishop Bossuet disagreed on Guyon's methods of prayer. Due to Fénelon's support, Guyon was allowed to move to a convent in Paris. However, the King was determined to end this religious controversy and ordered Guyon back to the Bastille and

Fénelon to return to his diocese. The Holy See in 1699 condemned Fénelon's work, *L'Explication des Maximes des Saints sur la vie intérieure* (Explanation of the Maxims of the Saints on the Inner Life), a defense of Quietism.

The influence of Quietism quickly subsided as its adherents bowed to the Pope's decision. Guyon was released from the Bastille in 1702 and went into exile in Blois where she engaged in charitable works for the last fifteen years of her life. In her final testament she deplored the false accusations made against her writings, especially blaming the enmity of her brother and his influence on the Archbishop of Paris for her troubles. Her works continued to be published in many languages through the eighteenth century. *Opuscules spirituels* (Spiritual Pamphlets) was her first major work in which she described men's souls as naturally longing to return to and merge with God. The soul must die before it can live again. The book culminated in a description of "spiritual purity" which most mystics never attained. In *Les livres de l'Ancien et du Nouveau Testament . . .* (The Books of the Old and New Testament . . .), Guyon attempted to explain the Apocalypse; she played the prophet, claiming to be a vehicle for transmitting thoughts received directly from the Lord, and recounting visions. She left a manuscript (*Justifications*) and some mystical verses which were published after her death. *La vie de Mme Guyon* [The Life of Mme Guyon], published in Cologne in 1720, was probably not a single work but a collection of memoirs she had furnished to officials for the Conference of Issy. This account of her life is incomplete and inaccurate at times. Its importance lay in her claims to be able to fathom the depths of the soul and "that God had chosen her to destroy human reason and re-establish divine reason."

Mme Guyon was the greatest French mystic of the seventeenth century. Her beliefs were condemned, but her morals were never impugned. Seemingly identifying herself with an apostolic mission she stated "That which I bind will be bound; that which I unbind will be unbound." Believing that she had attained perfection, she could no longer pray to the saints or the Virgin Mary. To the end of her life she adhered to her religious mysticism, which had had a tremendous influence in France.

Works

Cantiques spirituels, ou emblèmes sur l'amour divin, 5 vols. (n.d.). *Le Cantique des cantiques de Salomon, interpreté selon le sens mystique & vraie représentation des états intérieurs . . .* (1688) [*The Song of Songs of Solomon with Explanations and Reflections Having Reference to the Interior Life*], tr. James W. Metcalf (1865). *Le Moyen court et très facile pour faire l'oraison* (1688). *Recueil de Poésies spirituelles*, 5 vols. (1689). *Advice by Madame Guyon to a Young Ecclesiastik, Who Was About to Commence Preach[ing]* (170_). *Opuscules spirituels*, 2 vols. (1704). *Les torrents spirituels* (1704) [*Spiritual Torrents*], tr by A. E. Ford (1853)]. *La Vie de Mme Guyon, écrite par elle-même*, 3 vols. (1704). *Les livres de l'Ancien et du Nouveau Testament, traduits en français avec des explications et des réflexions qui regardent la vie intérieure*, 20 vols. (1713–1715) [*The Mystical Sense of the Sacred Scriptures. or, The Books of the Old and New Testaments (Including the Apocrypha), with Explications and Reflections Regarding the Interior Life*], 2 vols., tr. Thomas W. Duncan (1872). *L'Ame amante de son Dieu représentée dans les emblemes de Hermanus Hugo sur ses pieux désirs, et dans ceux d'Othon Vaenius sur l'amour divin* (1716). *Discours chrétiennes et spirituels [sic] sur divers sujets qui regardent la vie intérieure*, 2 vols. (1716). *Lettres chrétiennes et spirituelles sur divers sujets qui regardent la vie intérieure ou l'esprit du Christianisme*, 4 vols. (1717–1718). *Poésies et cantiques spirituels sur diverse sujets qui regardent la vie intérieure, ou l'esprit du vrai Christianisme*, 4 vols. (1722). *Regel der Kindheit Jesu-Genossen* (1752). *A Short and Easy Method of Prayer*, tr. Thomas Digby Brooke (1775). *The worship of God in spirit and in truth. or, a short and easy method of prayer . . . to which is added, Two letters concerning a life truly Christian . . .* (1775). *La Sainte-Bible* (1790). *Spiritual Progress. or, Instructions in the Divine Life of the Soul* [with Fénelon] (1853).

Bibliography

Autobiography of Madame Guyon (1880). Bédoyère, M. de la, *The Archbishop and the Lady* (1956). Bossuet, Jacques-Bénigne, *Relation sur le Quietisme* (1698). *Choice excerpts from Madame Guyon's mystic sense of the scriptures* (1891).

Cognet, Louis, "La spiritualité de Madame Guyon." *XVIIe siècle* 12–14 (1951–1952): 269–275. Dutoit-Mambrini, P., ed., *Oeuvres spirituelles de Madame Guyon*, 40 vols. (1790–1791). *The Exemplary Life of the Pious Lady Guion, Translated from her Own Account in the Original French. To Which Is Added a New Translation of Her Short and Easy Method of Prayer* (1775). Guerrier, Louis, *Madame Guyon, sa vie, ses doctrines et son influence* (1881). *A Guide to True Peace; or, The Excellency of Inward and Spiritual Prayer* [by Fénelon; includes writings of Mme Guyon] (1946). *Das innere Leben* (1901). *Justifications de la doctrine de Mme de la Motte-Guion . . .*, 3 vols. (1790). *The Life and Religious Experience of the Celebrated Lady Guion . . . Exhibiting her Eminent Piety, Travels, and Sufferings. To Which Are Annexed Her Poems*, tr. William Cowper, esq. *And a Short Account of the Lives of Several of Her Most Eminent Friends* [Fénelon, Molinos, and St Teresa] (1820). Lowery, D. D. ed., *Selections from the Devotional Writings of Madame de La Mothe-Guyon* (1904). Morrow, Abbie C. ed., *Sweet Smelling Myrrh: the Autobiography of Madame Guyon* (1898). *Poems; Selected and Tr. William Cowper* (1782). Reiff, Anna C., *Madame Guyon; An Autobiography* (1911). Ribadeau-Dumas, F., *Fénelon et les saintes folies de Madame Guyon* (1968). Scillière, E., *Madame Guyon et Fénelon* (1918). *Spiritual Letters* (1895). Upham, P. L., *Letters of Madame Guyon* (1858). Upham, T. C., *Madame Guyon* (1858). Ziegler, Gilette, *The Court of Versailles*, ch. XVIII (1966), pp. 281–297.

Jeanne A. Ojala

William T. Ojala

María Isidra Quintina de (Marquesa de Guadalcázar) Guzmán y de la Cerda (y De Sousa)

Born 1768, Madrid, Spain; died 1803, Madrid
Genre(s): poetry, philosophical treatise
Language(s): Spanish

Perhaps the first woman to earn a doctorate (in Philosophy and Letters) at the University of Alcalá (1785), Guzmán was, without a doubt, the first woman elected to the Real Academia Española in 1784 and the first woman admitted to the Real Sociedad Matritense (and Vascongada) de los Amigos del País two years later. She continued her intellectual pursuits even after her marriage to Rafael Alonso de Souse, Marquis de Guadalcázar, in 1789, and the births of their three children. In addition to her other awards, she was named honorary professor of modern philosophy by the University of Alcalá de Henares. A child prodigy, her historic accomplishments were sanctioned and nurtured by Carlos III. One source described Guzmán's poetry as having a "strong neo-classical influence." But "la doctora de Alcalá" died of a life-long tubercular condition at the early age of thirty-five, before her unique talents and position in early nineteenth-century Spanish academia could be felt. It is feared that all of her non-poetic works, including her papers on the Aristotelian system, have been lost.

Works

Oración de ingreso (1785). *Oración del género eucarístico que hizo a la Real Academia Española* (1785; according to one source, this was published in the *Memorial Literario* [de la Sociedad Económica], v. 5.) *Oración eucarística* (1786). *Oración del género eucarístico que hizo a la Real Sociedad de Amigos del País de esta corte la Excelentísima Señora Doña. Doctora en Filosofía y Letras humanas, Consiliaria perpetua, Examinadora de cursantes en Filosofía, y Cathedrática honoraria de Filosofía moderna en la Real Universidad de Alcalá, Socia de la Real Academia Española, y Honoraria y Literarata, de la Real Sociedad Bascongada de los Amigos del País. En el día 25 de febrero del año de 1786* (1786; an extract appeared in the *Memorial Literario* [de la Sociedad Económica], March 1786, pp. 357–361).

Bibliography

Galerstein, Carolyn L., ed., *Women Writers of Spain* (Westport, Conn., 1986). Serrano y Sanz, Manuel, *Apuntes para una biblioteca de escritoras españolas*. Biblioteca de Autores Españoles, vol. 269 (1903; rpt. Madrid, 1975).

Rosetta Radtke

Thomasine Gyllembourg

(a.k.a. Author of "An Everyday Tale")

Born November 9, 1773, Copenhagen,
Denmark; died July 1, 1856, Copenhagen
Genre(s): tale, novel, drama, letters
Language(s): Danish

Mother of the famous dramatist and critic Johan Ludvig Heiberg, Thomasine Gyllembourg pioneered realistic prose fiction in Denmark in the 1820s. Her highly popular "Everyday Tales" and the salon she led helped to create the "Heiberg school," whose influence dominated literary taste in Denmark for several decades.

Thomasine Christine Buntzen Heiberg Gyllembourg, more commonly known as Fru Gyllembourg, was the eldest daughter of city assessor Johan Buntzen and his second wife, Anna Bolette Sandgaard. Her mother died when she was eight. Her father encouraged his favorite daughter's literary inclinations, providing her with excellent tutors. One of these was the dramatist P.A. Heiberg, whom Thomasine married at age seventeen. The match was ill-suited temperamentally. Heiberg was a brilliant but quarrelsome rationalist, whereas Thomasine adhered to the cult of the heart à la Rousseau. The couple's only child, Johan Ludvig Heiberg, was born in 1791. Shortly before her husband was exiled from Denmark for his political views, Thomasine had fallen in love with a gallant Swedish nobleman, Baron Carl Frederik Gyllembourg. Gyllembourg was himself living in exile because of his involvement in the assassination of the Swedish King Gustav III.

The dissolution of Thomasine's first marriage, by royal decree, in 1801 and her immediate remarriage to Baron Gyllembourg was one of the most celebrated scandals in the history of Scandinavian literature. This stormy and traumatic period of her life provided Thomasine Gyllembourg with the subject matter for much of her later writing. Her love letters to Gyllembourg before their marriage are worthy rivals to those in Rousseau's novel *La nouvelle Héloïse*, while her "lettre remarquable" to Heiberg, asking for the divorce, became a standard text in Danish high-school readers.

From her anonymous literary debut in 1827 to her collected works in 1851, Thomasine Gyllembourg's writings were edited and published by her son, J.L. Heiberg. He even brought out a few of her more controversial works under his own name. In 1828 Fru Gyllembourg's story "En Hverdagshistorie" (An Everyday Tale) appeared in Heiberg's influential journal *Den flyvende Post* (The Flying Post). This story marked a clear break in Danish literature with romanticism and earlier forms of fiction. Portraying the contemporary life and problems of the Copenhagen bourgeoisie, Fru Gyllembourg here provided the psychological realism the public was seeking. "En Hverdagshistorie" was the first of a long and immensely popular series of modern prose tales and novels, all referred to as "Everyday Tales."

Her next major work, *Slaegtskab og Djaevelskab* (1830; Genealogy and Demonology), was a family chronicle inspired by Greek tragedy. It became for a time the most famous novel in Scandinavia. Though it contains some overwritten scenes of Gothic horror, it reveals Gyllembourg's psychoanalytic skill in the portrayal of compulsive neurosis and hysteria. In her four plays, published together in 1834, she tried to establish a modern realistic drama based on the psychological probing of erotic conflicts. Her plays include *Sproglaereren* (1834; The Language Teacher), on the theme of happy marriage despite age differences, and *Fregatskibet Svanen* (1834; H.M.S. Swan), a tolerant treatment of the problem of bigamy. Among her most penetrating psychological studies are two confessional novels in the style of Rousseau: *Maria* (1839) and *Een i Alle* (1840; One in All). Here Gyllembourg perceptively analyzes childhood traumas of an erotic nature and their lasting effects on character. *Een i Alle*, the more vital work, sympathetically portrays the adventures of gallant Trolle, a Don Juan figure. Fru Gyllembourg's last work, *To Tidsaldre* (1845; Two Ages), is her literary testament in the form of a novel. Here she compares the world of her youth to the world of her old age, weighing contemporary bourgeois values against the aristocratic and revolutionary ideals of the eighteenth century. This work inspired Kierkegaard to write *The Literary Review*, a little book devoted to her novel.

After the death of her second husband, Fru Gyllembourg lived with her son and his wife, the gifted Fru Heiberg, who became nineteenth-century Scandinavia's most celebrated actress. The three of them worked together in literary and theatrical collaboration and created an exclusive and extremely influential salon. By the 1840s the "Heiberg school" was regarded as the literary establishment in Denmark.

In her "Everyday Tales" Thomasine Gyllembourg portrayed Danish middle-class life with exact attention to detail and realistic dialogue. The didactic purpose of her fiction led her to criticize the middle classes for their lack of genuine culture and to urge higher standards of education. The refinement of the heart remained her ideal. In many ways an heir of the eighteenth century, she was an unconventional, humane, and passionately intelligent artist whose work led the way to realism in Danish literature.

Works

Familien Polonius [The Polonius Family] (1827, 1834). "Den magiske Nögle" [The Magic Key] (1828). "En Hverdagshistorie" [An Everyday Tale] (1828). "Kong Hjort" [King Stag] (1830). "Den lille Karen" [Little Karen] (1830). *Slaegtskab og Djaevelskab* [Genealogy and Demonology] (1830). *Noveller, gamle og nye af Forf. til "En Hverdagshistorie"* [Stories, Old and New by the Author of "An Everyday Tale"] (1833). *Magt og List* [Force and Cunning] (1834). *Sproglaereren* [The Language Teacher] (1834). *De Forlovede* [The Engaged] (1834). *Fregatskibet Svanen* [H.M.S. Swan] (1834). *Findelön* [The Reward] (1834). *Nye Fortaellinger af Forf. til "En Hverdagshistorie"* [New Stories by the Author of "An Everyday Tale"] (1835–1836). *To Noveller af Forf. til "En Hverdagshistorie"* [Two Novelettes by the Author of "An Everyday Tale"] (1837). *Maria* (1839). *Een i Alle* [One in All] (1840). *Naer og Fjern* [Near and Far] (1841). *En Brevveksling* [A Correspondence] (1843). *Castor og Pollux* [Castor and Pollux] (1844). *Korsveien* [The Crossroad] (1844). *To Tidsaldre* [Two Ages] (1845).

Collected Works: *Skrifter af Forf. til "En Hverdagshistorie,"* ed. J.L. Heiberg, 12 vols. (1849–1851).

Letters in: *Heibergske Familiebreve*, ed. Morten Borup (1943).

Bibliography

Heiberg, Johanne Luise, *Peter Andreas Heiberg og Thomasine Gyllembourg* (1882). Fenger, Henning, and Frederick J. Marker, *The Heibergs* (1971). Hude, Elisabeth, *Thomasine Gyllembourg og Hverdagshistorierne* (1951). Pearson, Jean, "Thomasine Gyllembourg." *Kvindelige Forfattere*, ed. Susanna Roxman (1985).

Jean Pearson

Gyp

(see: Sibylle-Gabrielle-Antoinette de Riquetti de Mirabeau, duchess of Martel de Janville)

H

H., H.A.N.

(see: Helena Augusta Nyblom)

H.D.S. (Hija del Sol)

(see: María Gertrudis de Hore y Ley
[de Fleming])

Carolina Lea de Haan

(a.k.a. Carry van Bruggen and,
  occasionally, Justine Abbing)

*Born January 1, 1881, Smilde, The
  Netherlands; died November 16, 1932,
  Laren, The Netherlands*
*Genre(s): novel, novella, short story,
  philosophical study*
Language(s): Dutch

One of the many children in the family of a
poor Jewish *hazan*, Carry van Bruggen was trained
as a teacher. Her debut as a writer consisted of
contributions—a lady's column spiced with
unconventional opinions on matters like idealism, sex education, or Christian intolerance—to
the *Deli Courant*, a paper she co-edited with her
first husband, the writer and journalist Kees van
Bruggen, during a brief period in the Dutch East
Indies. Throughout her life, she continued to
vent her radical ideas in passionately argued
articles and lectures.

Van Bruggen's early fiction was set in the
Indies. Her first novels of importance were *De
verlatene* (1910; The Abandoned), the tragic
story of an orthodox Jew whose children (like the
author herself) abandon the old faith and values,
and *Heleen* (1913), a perfect example of van
Bruggen's autobiographical inspiration, her
psychological realism, and typical probing style.
Lacking dialogue and a substantial plot, *Heleen*
is a scientifically minute and slow study of the
main character's spiritual and sentimental development. *Een coquette vrouw* (1915; A Coquette), inspired by the author's own failed
marriage, and *Eva* (1927), her last and major
work of fiction and a candid piece of self-revelation, are written in the same analyzing vein. In
nervously fragmented prose, Eva comes to terms
with herself, the world, and sexuality. Like almost
all of van Bruggen's women protagonists, Eva is
confronted with a basic dilemma: full submission
to the man she loves (though he may be her
inferior) or preservation of self-respect. When
van Bruggen's women choose the first, like Ina in
Een coquette vrouw, they invariably lose their
sense of self-esteem; when they choose the latter,
like Marianne in *Uit het leven van een denkende
vrouw* (1920; From the Life of a Thinking
Woman), they forsake the possibility of total and
passionate surrender. Eva, however, eventually
finds peace in a spiritually as well as physically
fulfilling relationship.

Drawing on her childhood memories, Carry
van Bruggen was also one of the first in Dutch
literature to address the social misery of Jewish
children. In *Het huisje aan de sloot* (1921; The
Small House by the Creek)—her most popular
work—*Avontuurtjes* (1922; Adventures), and
Vier jaargetijden (1924; Four Seasons), she wrote
with compassion and humor about growing up

514

in the secure yet repressive intimacy of a provincial Jewish community and the sense of isolation and inferiority experienced when confronted with the outside world.

The emphasis on the individual's identity that characterizes so much of Carry van Bruggen's fiction was also the main drive for her ambitious philosophical studies, which, in spite of their longwindedness and digressions, still appeal to the modern reader. *Prometheus* (1919) deals with the fundamental conflict between man's desire to be a distinct individual and his desire to belong to a collectivity. The book greatly influenced the development of the writer Menno ter Braak, but, since it was written by a woman, a teacher, and a nonacademic, it was frowned upon by a large part of the Dutch intellectual community. In *Hedendaags Fetischisme* (1925; Contemporary Fetishism), Carry van Bruggen further pursued her fear and aversion for dogma and traditional beliefs, this time attacking nationalism and excessive adulation of the mother tongue. Both, she contended, are products or fetishes of the "impersonal genius of the herd." (Unlike her brother, the poet Jacob Israel de Haan, Carry van Bruggen never warmed to the ideals of Zionism.)

Her second marriage in 1918 to the art historian Dr. Aart Pit was apparently a very happy union. From 1928, however, she suffered severe depressions and was in and out of mental hospitals. She died in 1932, having taken an overdose of sleeping pills.

Carry van Bruggen's penchant for rigorous self-revelation and detailed psychological analysis, her nonconformism, and her attention to the conflicting emotions of modern intellectual woman make her stand out among the many—now forgotten—"lady" novelists of the beginning of the century. Though she spoke out in favor of feminist issues such as education for women and financial independence (she characteristically refused alimony), she remained too much of an individualist and too suspicious of idealism to be attracted by any organized form of Women's Liberation. Never a feminist in the present sense of the word, she described the plight of modern woman not so much as a sociocultural problem, but as a painstaking, psychological and, above all, very personal conflict. It gave her prose a remarkably intense quality.

Works

In de schaduw (1907). Een badreisje in de tropen (1909). Goenong-Djatti (1909). Breischooltje (1910). De verlatene (1910). Heleen. Een vroege winter (1913). Het Joodje (1914). Een coquette vrouw (1915). Vaderlandsliefde, menschenliefde en opvoeding (1916). Van een kind (1918). Om de kinderen (1918). Prometheus. Bijdrage tot het begrip der ontwikkeling van het individualisme in de litteratuur (2 vols., 1919). Enkele bladen uit Helene's dagboek (1919). [Justine Abbing, pseud.], Uit het leven van een denkende vrouw (1920). De zelfvermomming des absoluten (1920). Het huisje aan de sloot (1921). Een Indisch huwelijk (1921). [Justine Abbing, pseud.], Een kunstenaar (1921). Avontuurtjes (1922). [Justine Abbing, pseud.], Het verspeelde leven (1922). Maneschijn met koek en Al om een suikerballetje (1923). [Justine Abbing, pseud.], De vergelding (1923). Vier jaargetijden (1924). De grondgedachten van "Prometheus" (1924). Hedendaagsch fetischisme (1925). Een leerstoel voor "zuivere rede"? (1925). De klas van twaalf (1926). Tirol (1926). Eva (1927). Seideravond (1934). Vijf brieven aan Frans Coenen, ed. J.M.J. Sicking (1970). Vijf romans (1979). Tegen de dwang (1981).

Bibliography

Coenen, F., "Carry van Bruggen's *Heleen*." Introduction to the second printing of *Heleen* (1934). De Haan, M., *Carry van Bruggen, mijn zuster* (1960). Fontijn, J., "Prometheus en de allumeuse. Carry van Bruggen als grensfiguur." *De Revisor* 4 (1977). Fontijn, J. and D. Schouten, *Carry van Bruggen. De Engelbewaarder* 3, No. 13 (1978, rpt. 1985). Gomperts, H.A., *Jagen om te leven* (1949). Holtrop, A., ed., *Vrouwen rond de eeuwwisseling* (1980). Jacobs, M.-A., *Carry van Bruggen, haar leven en literair werk* (1962). Meijer, J., *Waar wij ballingen zijn* (1968). Nieuwenhuys, R., *Oostindische Spiegel* (1972). Otterspeer, W., "Carry van Bruggen, het denken als deernis." *Maatstaf* 29 (1981). Postma, H., "Een verkenning van *Eva*." *De Nieuwe Taalgids* 69 (1976). Romein-Verschoor, A., *Vrouwenspiegel* (1936). Salomons, A., *Herinneringen* 1 (1957). Sicking, J.M.J., "Prometheus, een poging tot bewustwording." *De Revisor* 2 (1975). Sicking, J.M.J., *Menno ter Braak*

(1978). Ter Braak, M., *Verzameld werk* 1 & 6 (1949–1951). Stamperius, H., *Vrouwen en literatuur* (1980). Wolf, R., *Van alles het middelpunt. Over leven en werk van Carry van Bruggen* (1980).

General references: *Cassell's Encyclopaedia of World Literature. De Nederlandse en Vlaamse auteurs van Middeleeuwen tot heden* (1985). Knuvelder, G.P., *Handboek tot de geschiedenis der Nederlandse letterkunde* 4 (1971). *Moderne encyclopedie van de wereldliteratuur*(1980–1984). *Winkler Prins Lexicon der Nederlandse letterkunde* (1986).

Other references: Fontijn, J. and D. Schouten, "Een gesprek met Kees van Bruggen over zijn moeder Carry van Bruggen." *Vrij Nederland* (December 15, 1979). Van Amerongen, M., "*Prometheus*. Het uitzichtloze individualisme van Carry van Bruggen." *Vrij Nederland* (August 12, 1978).

Ria Vanderauwera

Hella Haasse (Helene Serafia Haasse)

Born February 2, 1918, Batavia, Dutch Indies
Genre(s): novel, essay, poetry, drama,
    translation, short story, autobiography
Language(s): Netherlandic

Hella S. Haasse is commonly acknowledged as the Netherlands' major living female author. Although she is best known for her prose work and essays, Haasse made her debut as a poet. She also delivered meritorious work as a playwright and translator.

Born as the daughter of Katharina Diehm Winzenhohlen, an esteemed concert pianist, and W.H. Haasse, a government functionary, the author spent part of her youth in the Dutch Indies. Due to her mother's illness, which demanded a stay in Switzerland, Haasse was separated from her parents for three years, during which time she attended Dutch boarding school. Afterwards, she returned to Batavia where she started high school. Here, her interest in Dutch literature was stimulated. In 1938, Haasse left for the Netherlands to study Scandinavian languages at the University of Amsterdam. The following year, she met her future husband J. van Lelyveld who encouraged her to contribute to *Propria Cures*, a student magazine.

In time, Haasse's interest in Scandinavian languages waned, leading her to join the drama department in 1940. Three years later, she closed a contract with a company, *Centraal Toneel*, directed by Cees Laseur.

Haasse made her literary debut with poems in the literary journal *Werk*. She only gained her reputation, however, with the publication of "Oeroeg" (1948). This short narrative describes the friendship between an Indian boy, Oeroeg, and a Dutch boy, the son of an administrator from whose point of view the story is told. Both children are raised together, but they start growing apart as they approach manhood. When the Dutch boy returns to India after finishing his studies in the Netherlands, the close friendship with Oeroeg no longer exists. Oeroeg has become a fervent nationalist who despises the Dutch, including his former friend. The narrator realizes that an unbridgeable abyss separates them; Oeroeg has become a stranger whom he has never understood and never will. The author stated that she wrote "Oeroeg" as a memory to the country where she was born and from a secret feeling of guilt with respect to the population she never really had learned to know. With "Oeroeg," Haasse cut the umbilical cord that still connected her to her country of birth.

In *Het Woud der verwachting* (1949), Haasse's first novel, the author relates with historical accuracy the life of Charles d'Orléans. She depicts him as a sensitive man who, against his will, got involved in intrigues of the 100-Year War. D'Orléans was captured by Henry V of England and only twenty-five years later was he released from prison. He returned to France where he spent the rest of his life doing the only thing that gave him consolation: writing poetry. *Het woud der verwachting* is often called a historical novel, a term that should be used with some reservation. Haasse has done extensive research on the political and historical background of fifteenth-century France, but her work is more than a chronicle. She has stated that she has always felt akin to d'Orléans, a dreamer who fails because he lacks practical sense. Only when he explores his literary talents does he find the satisfaction and self-confidence a political career could never offer him. Haasse says this novel mirrors her world from 1935 to 1945—"a transitional period of self-contained reveries towards a more conscious concern for people and society." She recognizes herself in the increasing loneliness the medieval poet experienced. Haasse's historical novels are not romanticized histories. Her primary aim is to discover patterns between the realities of the past and the present. Haasse says she looks at our present reality from the perspective of the past, because it renders human reality visible.

De scharlaken stad (1952) takes us back to fifteenth-century Rome. The author wrote this novel out of fascination for the enigmatic figure of Giovanni Borgia. In opposition to the previous novel, *De scharlaken stad* has a more complicated composition.

De Ingewijden (1957) refers to the "Euleusinia" or the secret rituals in honor of the goddesses Demeter and Persephone. According to Greek mythology, he who wanted to be initiated in the mysteries of life and death and experience the oneness with the primordial being had to find his way through a treacherous subterranean labyrinth. Haasse gives this ancient ritual a modern setting by introducing six protagonists who meet each other by coincidence on the island of Crete shortly after World War II. Haasse contrasts ancient Greece, which evokes the Eulesian mysteries, with the cold modern period, which is controlled by war and fascism.

Een nieuwer testament (1966) is based on an imaginary trial between the last poet of the Roman Empire, the pagan Claudius Claudianus. His antagonist, the prefect Hadrianus, who represents Christianity, the official Roman religion, banned Claudius for being involved in pagan rituals. When Claudius has the audacity to return to the city, Hadrianus has him arrested. While in prison, Claudius writes a "new-er" testament, an improved version of the New Testament that emphasizes man's independent creative personality thereby rejecting the vision that the son (man) should follow the father (Christ). When Hadrianus is finally confronted with Claudianus the day of the trial, he becomes aware that he has been defending a false religion. As a manifestation of his rebellion, he sets Claudius free and commits suicide.

In *Een gevaarlijke verhouding of Daal en Bergse brieven* (1976), Haasse introduces Mme de Merteuil, Choderlos de Laclos' evil female of *Les Liaisons Dangereuses* (1782). Haasse picks up the thread where Laclos left off. Mme de Merteuil is dwelling in The Hague in the Daal (val-) en Bergse (Mont) Lane. The marchioness defends and justifies her past way of life, which gives her the opportunity to take up a number of topics such as love in a male-oriented society and the relationship between man and wife. Although Haasse's style remains traditional throughout her career, her fictional work seems to become more and more essayistic. Large parts of this novel approach the essay form.

Mevrouw Bentinck of onverenigbaarheid van karakter (1978) and *De groten der aarde, of Bentinck tegen Bentinck* may also be considered among Haasse's historical novels. Willem Bentinck, Sr., friend and confidant of the Dutch King Willem II, was one of the most remarkable figures in the Netherlands of the eighteenth century. When Haasse got access to the Bentinck archives, she became fascinated by Willem Bentinck, Jr., and his wife Charlotte Sophie von Aldenburg. Haasse composed a book in collage form, the greater part consisting of authentic texts about the doomed-to-fail marriage between Bentinck and his wife, which has not been treated extensively by Bentinck biographers. Haasse wanted to throw a different and more truthful light on the Bentinck figure, and she intended to use Charlotte Sophie's escapades as an example of female emancipation in the Age of Enlightenment.

De groten der aarde, of Bentinck tegen Bentinck (1982) deals with the period 1730–1750 after Bentinck, Jr., and his wife have broken up their marriage. More so than in the previous Bentinck novel, the author narrates more in her own voice. She still uses the collage technique—although to a lesser extent—to give the impression of presenting an epic report, as she calls it. In all of her historical novels, Haasse is concerned with the same thematics, that is, the search for one's identity and the purpose of man's existence.

Haasse wrote two autobiographical novels. *Zelfportret als Legkaart* (1954) combines alternatively descriptions of the author's youth in India, the wartime in Amsterdam, her studies, and her marriage. *Persoonsbewijs* (1967) may be considered as a sequel. Except for the first chapter which is biographical, the novel is dedicated to the problematics of being an author and to Haasse's own literary works. Here, Haasse argues that through the process of writing, she analyzes and renders conscious that which is usually buried deep within her. As in previous novels, Haasse expresses her conviction in the interconnectedness of happenings we are not even conscious of.

Works

Prose: *Kleren maken de vrouw* (1947). "Oeroeg" (1948). *Het woud der verwachting* (1949). *Het leven van Charles D'Orleans* (1949). *De verborgen bron* (1950). *De scharlaken stad* (1952). *Zelfportret als legkaart* (1954). *De ingewijden* (1957). *De vijfde trede* (1957). *Cider voor arme mensen* (1960). *De meermin* (1962). *Een nieuwer testament* (1966). *Persoonsbewijs* (1967). *De tuinen van Bomarzo* (1968). *Huurders en onderhuurders* (1971). *De meester van de neerdaling, De duivel en zijn moer* (1973). *Een gevaarlijke verhouding of Daal-en Bergse brieven* (1976). *Mevrouw Bentinck of Onverenigbaarheid van karakter* (1978). *De groten der aarde of Bentinck tegen Bentinck* (1981). *De wegen der verbeelding* (1983).

Major essays: *Het versterkte huis, Kastelen in Nederland* (1951). *Klein Reismozaiek, Italiaanse Impressies* (1953). *Eem kom water, een test vuur* (1959). *Anna Blaman* (1961). *Leestekens* (1965). *De tuinen van Bomarro* (1968). *Tweemaal Vestdijk* (1970). *Krassen op een rots* (1970). *Zelfstandig bijvoeglijk* (1972). *Het licht der schitterende dagen, het leven van P, C. Hooft* (1981). *Ogenblikken in Valois* (1982).

Plays: *Een Amsterdamse jongen redt de beurs* (1951). *Het treurig spel van Jan Klaassen en Katrijn Ongeschikt voor de Houwelijcke Staat* (1951). *Hoe de Scout zichzelf aan de schandpaal bracht* (1951). *Liefdadigheid naar vermogen of Graag of niet* (1957). *De vrijheid is een assepoes* (1955). *Een draad in Block. Geen Bacchanalen* (1971).

Translations: *Oeroeg* and *De Verborgen Bron* are translated in Welsh, *Het Woud der Verwachting* and *De Ingewijden* in German and *De Scharlaken Stad* in German, English, Swedish and Serbo-Croatian.

Bibliography

Ceulaer (De), J., *Te Gast bij Nederlandse Auteurs* ('s-Gravenhage, Rotterdam, 1966). Diepstraten, J., *Hella S. Haasse. Een Interview* ('s-Gravenhage, 1984). Popelier, Ed., *Grote Ontmoetingen Hella S. Haasse* (Brugge, 1977). Wispelaere (De) P. *Facettenoog* (Brussels, 1968).

Dianne Van Hoof

Mechtild von Hackeborn

Born 1241 in or near Magdeburg, Germany;
    died November 19, 1299, Helfta
Genre(s): mystical vision, letters
Language(s): German

Mechthild von Hackeborn was one of the most influential women mystics of the thirteenth century. Her visions, prayers, and songs, like those of Saint Gertrud the Great, had a crucial impact on Catholic piety for centuries. When seven years old, Mechthild, along with her parents, visited her sister Gertrud in the Cistercian nunnery Rodersdorf (Bishopry of Halberstadt), founded in 1229 by Elisabeth, Countess of Mansfeld. At that time the monastery was run by the abbess Kunigunde of Halberstadt. Despite her parents' resistance, Mechthild finally got their permission to enter the order. Her sister became abbess in 1251 (died in 1292) and moved the convent to Helfta (or Helpede) to the territory of the Lords Albrecht and Ludolf von Hackeborn. In 1343 it was destroyed in a feud between Brunswick and Mansfeld and founded again in Eisleben. The Dominicans controlled the women's convent during the reign of Gertrud, who promoted the study of liberal arts, liturgy and exegesis. Thus the outstanding Dominican philosophers Albert the Great (died in 1280) and Thomas Aquinas (died in 1274) were well known to Mechthild (*Liber Specialis Gratiae* V. 9). Mechthild excelled in liturgical chorals and mass singing, which both deeply influenced her early mystical visions. But only at the age of 50, after a prolonged period of sickness, did the intensity of her visions increase, and she began to talk about them. A student of hers, Gertrud, who had entered the convent as a five-year-old child and who later was to become the Sainte Gertrude the Great (died in 1301), and some other anonymous nuns wrote down her accounts and arranged them into the *Liber Specialis Gratiae*, as the acting abbess Sophie of Querfurt had ordered them. The original text was in German, but that manuscript is lost, and only the later Latin version survives. The most important manuscript can be found in the library of Wolfenbüttel, written in 1370 by the priest Albert from St. Paul in Erfurt. There are three manuscript traditions: A, B, and C.

Mechthild's spiritual sisters did not show her the book until much later, and she then hesitantly agreed to it. Only a few letters to a matron were actually written by Mechthild herself (IV, ch. 59).

The book includes: 1. Mechthild's visions in close parallel to the liturgy, 2. her familiar contacts with Jesus, 3. the right way of praising God and 4. of mystical dedication, 5. her visions of the beyond, 6. virtue and blessedness of her sister Gertrud, and 7. her blessed transfiguration at her death on November 19, 1292. Both Gertrud the Great's *Legatus Diviniae Pietatis* and Mechthild's visions were often copied and printed together. Mechthild has been seen as the model for Dante's (Purg. XXVIII, 40f.) or Boccaccio's Matilda (Dec. VII, 1), but this theory is still heavily disputed and the controversy continues. Various schools of thought have considered Mechthild's insistence on justification of divine grace and on the notion of predestination as an anticipation of the Reformation.

Works

Revelationes Gertrudianae et Mechtildianae, Vol. 2 (Poitier, 1877). *Leben und Offenbarungen der heiligen Mechthild von Hackeborn*, German, ed. J. Müller (1880).
Translations: *The boke of gotlye grace of Mechthild of Hackeborn*, tr. Theresa A. Halligan (1979). *Mechthild von Hackeborn: Das Buch vom strömenden Lob*, German tr., ed. H.U. von Balthasar (Einsiedeln, 1955).

Bibliography

Howard, John, "The German Mystic: Mechthild of Magdeburg," in *Medieval Women Writers*, ed. K.N. Wilson (Athens, Ga., 1984), pp. 153–185. Laughlin, M.F., "Mechthild of Hackeborn." *New Catholic Encyclopedia* IX (New York, 1967), cols. 545–546. Lubin, A., *La Matelda di Dante* (Graz, 1860). Preger, J.W., *Dantes Matelda* (München, 1873). Schmidt, Margot, "Elemente der Schau bei Mechthild von Magdeburg und Mechthild von Hackeborn. Zur Bedeutung der geistlichen Sinne," in *Frauenmystik im Mittelalter*, ed. P. Dinzelbacher and D.R. Bauer (Ostfilden, 1985), pp. 123–151. Schmidt, Margot, "Mechthild de Hackeborn." *Dictionnaire de Spiritualité* X (Paris, 1980), cols. 873–877. Walz, Angelo, "Matilde di Hackeborn." *Bibliotheca Sanctorum* IX (Rome, 1967), cols. 96–101.

Albrecht Classen

Hadewijch

Date and place of birth and death unknown; probably lived in the beginning or middle of the thirteenth century in the Brussels area
Genre(s): poetry, letters, visionary literature
Language(s): Dutch (Brabant dialect)

A thirteenth-century mystic, Hadewijch is considered one of the early representatives of the so-called *minnemystiek*. Her work contains letters, visions, stanzaic poems, and a small set of poems mostly in rhyming couplets. Her stanzaic poetry belongs to the very few extant Middle Dutch love songs in the troubadour tradition and her prose, together with that of the Cistercian mystic Beatrijs of Nazareth (ca. 1200–1268), is the earliest extant prose in the vernacular.

Besides her name and work, we know very little, if anything, of Hadewijch. The erudition emerging from her writing almost certainly indicates a noble or aristocratic descent. Her letters—the only source of biographical information—suggest that though she was not a nun, she lived for some time in one or two small communities of religious women. She may also have lived part of her life as a *reclusa*. Like many other women of her time, the so-called *mulieres religiosae*, she took part in the great spiritual revival that marked the twelfth and thirteenth centuries. She must have read or, at least, known about the great mystic writers. Most probably she knew Latin: passages in her letters have been identified as translations of William of Saint Thierry and Richard of Saint Victor, though she may have borrowed from existing translations.

The basic shift of focus in religious life and thought from *knowledge* of God to *experience* of God, which had been initiated by Saint Bernard, undoubtedly inspired Hadewijch's *minnemystiek*. The central concept in her thinking was *minne*—love. A full understanding of all the connotations of Hadewijch's *minne*, often personified, has yet to be established, but it is easiest to see *minne* not so much as God or Christ but rather as the personification of an abstract quality or, better, an experience (of God). Three basic moments can further be distinguished: the awareness of a distance between *minne* and Hadewijch—*een ghebreken*, "a lack"; the complete surrendering to *minne*—*een ghebruken*, "using and enjoying"; and, finally, balance restored. The tension between *ghebreken* and *ghebruken*, i.e., the mystic's craving for *minne*, runs through most of Hadewijch's work. The motifs of courtly love—unattainable lover, the submissive service to love, the complaints, the hope and despair, the all-pervading power of love—all acquire a spiritual dimension in Hadewijch's writing. She reinterprets the unattainability of *minne*, as an ontological given, which time and again she attempts to transcend by striving for and reaching a state of union with *minne*.

Developing the theme of *minne*, Hadewijch wrote her stanzaic poems in much the same way as the troubadours had done before her, elaborating the imagery and vocabulary of courtly love and the techniques of *Natureingang*, tripartition, tornada, concatenation, rhyme scheme and rhyme. Instead of using *coblas unisonas* (the same rhyme and rhyme scheme), which are hard to achieve in a Germanic language, she used *coblas singulars* (the same rhyme scheme but not the same rhyme). But her repertory of rhymes and rhyming words remains small with respect to the actual possibilities of Middle Dutch. Rather than being Romance syllabic, Hadewijch's rhythm is the Germanic stress rhythm highlighted by profuse alliteration, assonance, and repetition. Though written with great technical skill, the stanzaic poems are not entirely free of easy verse filling. Sometimes the reader is given the impression of thoughts and emotions forced into a rigid stanzaic format.

In the letters Hadewijch emerges as an accomplished, articulate, and sensitive writer. They were probably addressed to a woman (or women) who belonged to a religious community of which Hadewijch herself had once been a member. Some of the longer letters are real treatises on religious and spiritual problems and illustrate very well Hadewijch's powerful and passionate thinking about *minne* as well as her superior skill as a writer of prose. Others are more intimate communications in which Hadewijch gives practical advice on living a life of charity and devotion to *minne*. She developed similar themes in her nonstanzaic poetry, the so-called *mengeldichten*. Her advisory tone suggests that she must have enjoyed the high regard of whomever she wrote to; perhaps she had been the leader of the community. There are also indications that she might have been the victim of enmity and jealousy.

Hadewijch's visions are increasingly regarded as one of the greatest achievements in Dutch artistic prose of the Middle Ages, by far excelling her stanzaic poems in literary importance and aesthetic value. They were apparently written at someone's request and served as descriptions of actual ecstatic experiences. For the modern reader, unacquainted with the conventions or the psychology of mystic experiences in Hadewijch's age, the visions might, however, be difficult to appreciate, larded as they are with the allegories, symbols, angels, and seraphim typical of the genre in that period.

Hadewijch's work was known, copied, excerpted, paraphrased, and occasionally translated (into German and Latin) up to at least the late fifteenth and, particularly, in the fourteenth century. She was especially known in Brabant where the tradition of speculative mysticism was continued by Jan van Ruusbroec (1293–1381) among others. Ruusbroec built his systematic doctrine on thoughts similar to those developed by Hadewijch. At that time she was also known in Germany by the name of Saint Adelwip from Brabant.

In the seventeenth and eighteenth centuries, however, Hadewijch's work was virtually lost. She only claimed her definitive place in the Dutch literary canon with the "discovery" of the manuscripts of her work in 1838. She then came to be regarded as one of the most gifted literary women of her period and found a place in every school anthology treating Dutch literature from its very beginnings.

Works

(Three complete manuscripts of her work contain 45 stanzaic poems, 31 letters, 14 visions, 29 poems mostly in rhyming couplets [one ms. has only 16 of them], 13 of which were probably not by her.) *Brieven,* ed. J. van Mierlo. 2 vols. (1947; with modern Dutch tr., 1954, eds. F. van Bladel and B. Spaapen). *Mengeldichten,* ed. J. van Mierlo (1952). *Strophische gedichten* (1942; 2 vols., ed. J. van Mierlo; With modern Dutch translations, 1961; eds. E. Rombauts and N. de Paepe. With modern Dutch translations, 1982; ed. M. Ortmans). *Visioenen* (1924–1925; 2 vols., ed. J. van Mierlo. With modern Dutch translations, 1979; 2 vols., ed. P. Mommaers. With modern Dutch translations, 1980; ed. H.W.J. Vekeman).
Translations: *The Complete Works,* ed. and tr. C. Hart (1980). Selected letters, in *Mediaeval Netherlands Religious Literature,* tr. and intro. E. Colledge (1965). Selected letters and poems, tr. R. Vanderauwera, in *Medieval Women Writers,* ed. K.M. Wilson (1984). Of the stanzaic poems, *Hadewijch d'Anvers. Amour est tout: poèmes strophiques,* tr. R. van de Plas, intro. A. Simonet (1984).

Bibliography

Axters, S., *Geschiedenis van de vroomheid in de Nederlanden* 1 (1950). Boeren, P.C., *Hadewijch en Heer Hendrik van Breda* (1962). Breuer, W., "Mystik als alternative Lebensform: Das 37. Stophische Gedicht der Sister Hadewijch." *Zeitschrift für Deutsche Philologie* 103 (1984). Colledge, E., tr. and intro., *Mediaeval Netherlands Religious Literature* (1965). De Paepe, N., *Hadewijch. Strofische gedichten. Een studie van de minne in het kader der 12e- en 13e-eeuwse mystiek en profane minnelyriek* (1967). Gooday, F.A., "Mechtild von Magdeburg and Hadewijch of Antwerp: A Comparison." *Ons Geestelijk Erf* 48 (1974). Guest, T.M., *Some Aspects of Hadewijch's Poetic Form in the "Strofische gedichten"* (1975). Hart, Sister M.C., "Hadewijch of Brabant." *American Benedictine Review* 13 (1962). Janssen, J.D., *Hoofsheid en devotie in de middeleeuwse maatschappij* (1982). Janssens, J., "Hadewijch en de riddercultuur van haar tijd." *Ons Geestelijk Leven* 54 (1977). Mens, A., *Oorsprong en betekenis van de Nederlandse begijnen–en begardenbeweging* (1947). Porion, J.-B., *Hadewijch d'Anvers* (with French translations, 1954). Porion, J.-B., *Hadewijch. Lettres spirituelles. Béatrice de Nazareth. Sept degrés d'amour* (1972). Reynaert, J., *De beeldspraak van Hadewijch* (1981). Ruh, K., "Beginenmystik: Hadewijch, Mechtild von Magdeburg, Marguerite Porete." *Zeitschrift für deutsches Altertum und deutsche Literatur* 106 (1976). Schottmann, H., "Autor und Hörer in den 'Strophischen Gedichten' Hadewijchs." *Zeitschrift für deutsches Altertum und deutsche Literatur* 102 (1973). Vanderauwera, R., "The Brabant Mystic: Hadewijch," in *Medieval Women Writers,* ed. K.M. Wilson (1984). Van der Kallen, M., *Een grammaticaal en rhythmisch onderzoek van Hadewijchs poëzie* (1938). Vekeman, H., "Begeerte en religie in de Middelnederlandse en Middelhoogduitse vrouwenmystiek." *Klasgids* 19 (1984). Weevers, Th., *Poetry of the Netherlands in Its European Context: 1170–1930* (1960). Willaert, F., *De poëtica van Hadewijch in de "Strofische gedichten"* (1984).
General references: *Cassell's Encyclopaedia of World Literature. De Nederlandse en Vlaamse auteurs van middeleeuwen tot heden* (1985). Knuvelder, G.P., *Handboek tot de geschiedenis der Nederlandse letterkunde,* 1 (1970). *Moderne encyclopedie van de wereldliteratuur* (1980–1984). *Winkler Prins Lexicon der Nederlandse letterkunde* (1986).

Ria Vanderauwera

Clara Haesaert

Born March 9, 1924, Kraainen, Belgium
Genre(s): poetry, novel
Language(s): Dutch

Clara Haesaert was a civil servant in the Ministry of Dutch Culture in Brussels. She has translated French literature into Dutch, and she has contributed poems to the literary magazines *De Meridiaan, Podium,* and *Komma.*

Works

De Overkant [The Opposite] (1953). *Omgekeerde Volgorde* [Inverted Order] (1961). *Onwaarschijnlijk Recht* [Unlikely Justice] (1967).

Spel van Vraag en Aanbod [Play of Question and Offer] (1970).

Adolf von Württemberg

Inger Hagerup

Born 1905, Bergen, Norway; died 1985, Norway
Genre(s): poetry, radio drama, short story, essay, memoirs, translation
Language(s): Norwegian

During a long and productive writing career extending over four decades, Inger Hagerup published more than ten volumes of poetry, as well as radio plays, memoirs, translations and essays. Her poems for children are widely used in school texts and many of her lyrics have been set to music.

Inger Hagerup was born Inger Halsør in Bergen, Norway. After her father's death, her mother took the five-year-old Inger and her younger brother to live with relatives, first in Nordfjord and then in Volda. Here she completed her secondary education in 1924. In 1931 Inger Halsør married Anders Hagerup. She began the study of philology, German and history at the University of Oslo, but her studies were broken off by the onset of World War II.

Hagerup made her literary debut in 1939, with her first volume of poetry, *Jeg gikk meg will i skogene. Flukten fra Amerika* followed in 1942. These first two volumes of poetry represent Hagerup as a poet solidly in the tradition of Olaf Bull and Arnulf Overland, but with her own distinctive voice.

The influence of Modernism was not felt to any great extent in Norwegian literature until the end of the 1940s, ten years after Hagerup's debut, and had little impact on her work. Hagerup was not so much interested in experimenting with new forms as in mastering completely the traditional ones.

Hagerup's reputation as one of Norway's foremost lyric poets was secured with the publication of her third volume of poetry, *Videre*, in Sweden in 1944, and in Norway in 1945. Her first volume of children's verse, *Så Rart*, was published in 1950, followed by *Lille Persille* in 1961. Memories of Hagerup's childhood and

youth appear in three volumes of prose, *Det kommer en pike gående, Hva skal du her nede?*, and *Ut og søke tjeneste*, published between 1965 and 1968.

Although Inger Hagerup's stature as a poet is based primarily on her ability to create poems that are intensely personal, political and social commentary are also found throughout her authorship. "Aust-Vågøy," a poem circulated anonymously in Norway during the Second World War, was the best-known poem of the Norwegian resistance.

Inger Hagerup is one of Norway's finest lyric poets. Although she remained a traditionalist as new influences were felt in Norwegian literature, Hagerup's poetry is still among the most popular and widely-anthologized poetry in Norway.

Works

Jeg gikk meg vill i skogene [I Lost My Way in the Woods] (1939). *Flukten fra Amerika* [Flight from America] (1942). *Videre* [Wider] (1944 in Sweden, 1945 in Norway). *Den syvende natt* [The Seventh Night] (1947). *Sånn vil du ha meg* [You Would Have Me Thus] (1949). *Så rart* [So Strange] (1950). *Mitt skip seiler* [My Ship Is Sailing] (1951). *Hilsen fra Katerina* [Greetings from Katerina] (1953). *Drømmeboken* [The Book of Dreams] (1955). *Den tredje utvei* [The Third Way Out] (1956). *Strofe med vinden* [Stanza in the Wind] (1958). *Lille Persille* [Little Parsley] (1961). *Fra hjertets krater* [From the Heart's Crater] (1964). *Dikt i utvalg* [Selected Poems] (1965). *Det kommer en pike gående* [A Girl Comes Walking] (1965). *Hva skal du her nede?* [What Are You Doing Down Here?] (1966). *Trekkfuglene og skjaera* [The Birds of Passage and the Magpie] (1967). *Ut og søke tjeneste* [Out Looking for Work] (1968). *Den sommeren* [That Summer] (1971). *Samlede dikt* [Collected Poems] (1976). *Hulter til Bulter* [Helter-Skelter] (1979).

Translations: "The Woman at Klepp," tr. Torild Homstad., in *An Everyday Story*, Katherine Hanson, ed. (Seattle, 1984), pp. 139–142. "My Love," "I Am the Poem," tr. Thord Fredenholm. "Dies Irae," "Love Itself Must Also Die," "I Trust—," tr. Martin Allwood. "The Crazy Boy," tr. Harold P. Hanson. "We Hold Our Life," tr. Carl Nesjar and Martin Allwood. "Emily Dickinson," tr. Martin Allwood and Robert Lyng, in *Modern Scandinavian Poetry*

1900–1975, Martin Allwood, ed. (New York, 1982). "I Am the Poem," "I Believe—," "Emily Dickinson," tr. David McDuff, in *20 Contemporary Norwegian Poets: A Bilingual Anthology*, Terje Johanssen, ed. (New York, 1984).

Bibliography

Hagerup, Klaus, *Alt er sa nær meg* (Oslo, 1988). Heiberg, Hans, *Peilinger, artikler on nitten norske skribenter* (Oslo, 1950), pp. 128–132. Vold, Karin Beate, "Til kvinner er vi født . . .: Synspunkter på Inger Hagerups lyriske forfatterskap—med særlig vekt på kjærlighetstematikken." (Oslo, 1976). Vold, Karin Beate, "Sånn vil du ha meg. Feminist synspunkt på Inger Hagerups lyrikk," in *Et annet språk*, Janneken Øverland, ed. (Oslo, 1977), pp. 153–175.

Torild Homstad

Ida, Countess von Hahn-Hahn

Born June 22, 1805, Tressow, Mecklenburg, Germany; died January 12, 1880, Mainz
Genre(s): novel, poetry
Language(s): German

Ida, Countess von Hahn-Hahn was the daughter of a well known theater supporter, Karl Friedrich von Hahn, who, because of his great love and passion for the theater died in poverty and impoverished his daughter also. Ida married her wealthy cousin, Count Friedrich Hahn, in 1826 but divorced him in 1829. After her divorce she travelled extensively and converted to Roman Catholicism, entered a convent in 1850, and held a brief novitiate. She was an indefatigable campaigner for the emancipation of women and later for the Church. Her flamboyant personality caused a sensation in her time. Her novels, which clearly reflect her abrupt change in outlook, retain interest as social documentation.

In her works, Hahn-Hahn elected German high life as a congenial field and easily attained popularity early in her career. When reading her works, one feels a sense of the *misera plebs*. Her characters appear well-groomed and polite, but they oscillate between ballroom and boudoir as the natural poles of mundane existence. Into this world of the painted and perfumed formalities,

Ida von Hahn-Hahn makes the most startlingly unconventional things occur. The Countess revels in tragedies of the soul. The characters fidget with their glaring paradoxes; one feels a certain fascination when a morbid subjectivity is astoundingly revealed amidst all the gorgeous trappings. By virtue of this frankness Ida von Hahn-Hahn is decidedly modern. The countess is said to have drawn her poetry and novels from life and went to the mirror in quest of models. Her heroes and heroines are gushing enthusiasts, doting but capricious lovers, fanatical devotees. They are drowned in a sea of emotional conflicts. Hahn-Hahn, by the strongly individualistic tendency, foreshadows the *Herrenmoral* or gentleman's morality of a later period. She is the prophet of "emancipation" for which the Young Germans, notably Gutzkow and Laube, were striving. The enlarged freedom, however, is not offered to the men or women of ordinary caliber. It is exclusively the prerogative of the exceptional person—the great personality who happens usually to be an aristocrat. For Ida von Hahn-Hahn the only characters worth writing about were aristocrats: the aristocrat alone was capable of true salvation, true love, true honor, true intellectual comprehension. She was greatly influenced by the French poet George Sand. In her work *Gräfin Faustine* (Countess Faustine) the heroine is a female Don Juan, and adultery is glorified. The Countess Faustine travels to the Orient and finally ends up in a cloister to expiate her sins.

Ida von Hahn-Hahn's later works were of a more serious nature: the purpose of the later works was to show to the lost souls the way to the Church in Rome.

Works

Gedichte [Poems] (1835). *Lieder und Gedichte* [Songs and Poems] (1837). *Ilda Schönholm* [Ilda Schönholm] (1838). *Gräfin Faustine* [Countess Faustine] (1841). *Ulrich* [Ulrich] (1841). *Gräfin Cecil* [Countess Cecil] (1844). *Aus der Gesellschaft* [From the Realm of Society] (1845). *Sybille* [Sybille] (1846). *Von Babylon nach Jerusalem* [From Babylon to Jerusalem] (1851). *Die Liebhaber des Kreuzes* [The Lovers of the Cross] (1852). *Maria Regina* [Maria Regina] (1860). *Peregrin* [Peregrin] (1864). *Die Glocknerstochter* [The Bell-ringer's Daughter]

(1871). *Vergib uns unsere Schuld* [Forgive Us Our Trespasses] (1871). *Wahl und Führung* [Choice and Leading] (1878). *Gesamtausgabe* [Complete Works: Protestant Works] (1851), 21 vols. *Gesammelte Werke* [Collected Works: Catholic Works] (1930), 45 vols.

Bibliography

Deutsches Literatur-Lexikon 7, ed. Heinz Rupp and Ludwig Lang (Bern, 1979). *German Literature of the Eighteenth and Nineteenth Centuries*, ed. E.L. Stahl and W.E. Yuill (New York, 1970). Heller, Otto, *Studies in Modern German Literature* (Massachusetts, 1905). Koenig, Robert, *Deutsche Literaturgeschichte*, Vol. 2 (Leipzig, 1910). Kruger, Anders Hermann, *Deutsches Literatur-Lexikon* (München, 1914).

Brigitte Archibald

Ursula Haider

Born 1413, Leutkirch, Swabia; died January 20, 1498, Valduna, Vorarlberg
Genre(s): chronicle, letters, prose texts
Language(s): German

Ursula Haider was born in 1413 as the only daughter of a citizen in Leutkirch, Swabia. Since her parents died very early, she was taken care of by her uncle, the priest Johannes Ber ("Bör"), her mother's brother, and by her grandmother. At the age of nine she was sent to the small Franciscan convent of the Tertiary Order in Reute near Waldsee, where she was strongly influenced by Elsbeth Achler von Reute (died in 1420), who was also known as the "good Beda." In 1430 she returned to her home town, but she refused to get married, as her relatives urged her to do. Instead she joined the order of St. Claire in Valdung, Vorarlberg on July 29, 1431, where she was to become, after 36 years, the abbess in 1467. On April 18, 1480, she and seven other sisters were called to Villingen (Baden-Württemberg) to reform the Bickenkloster through the introduction of seclusion by the request of the city and the Franciscan provincial, Heinrich Karrer from Straßburg. She was successful in her efforts and established a form of a *New Jerusalem*. In 1489 she had to resign because of illness, but she kept her spiritual leadership until her death. She

ordered symbolic imitations of holy places in Rome and Jerusalem to be built at her nunnery, which were all granted the same right of absolution as the real places by Pope Innocent VIII in 1491. During her lifetime she was considered a blessed person, and worship still takes place there, although the convent was transformed into the Institute of St. Ursula in 1782. Her remains are entombed in Villingen.

Her literary work has been handed down to us only through a secondary source, the *Chronicle of the Bickenkloster at Villingen*, which was composed in 1637/38 by the prioress and later abbess Juliana Ernestin (1589–1665). She used at least seven written documents and many oral reports of older sisters. The *Chronicle* consists of an outline of the foundation of the nunnery and of a historical biography of Ursula Haider. Also included are several texts of Ursula herself, such as a letter to Pope Innocent VIII asking for the right to dispense absolution at the holy sites at her monastery, two speeches at the New Year's celebrations of 1495 and 1496, a short letter detailing the right way of life, and notes of her thoughts and revelations. The last part was probably based on Ursula's own manuscript, kept at the hospital of the convent, which seems to have been forgotten and lost since 1636. Her mystical experiences and all her oral reports, however, were never copied down and thus have not been transmitted to us.

Ursula Haider emphasized the imitation of Christ's passion and the observation of repeated meditations on it. The human will is to be suppressed in favor of God's will, whereby a union with God might be possible. Often she claims to have heard an answer to some pressing questions expressed in her prayers. Apparently she was a more intellectual and rational person and did not experience visions as such. She copied many texts of fourteenth century German mystics in her *büechlin*, the lost manuscript. Influences from Tauler and Heinrich Seuse can be detected in her extant works.

Works

Glatz, K.J., ed., *Chronik des Bickenklosters zu Villingen 1238 bis 1614* (1881). Excerpts also in New High German in W. Oehl, *Die Deutschen Mystikerbriefe des Mittelalters 1100–1500,*

Mystiker des Abendlandes 1 (1931), pp. 650–656, 832f.

Bibliography

Breder, K., "Der seligen Ursula Haider Lebenszeit und Lebensalter." *Schwäbisches Archiv* 29 (1911): 22–25. Frank, H. "Der 'Besuch der sieben Kirchen' als religiöse Übung der ultramontanen Observanz." *Franziskanische Studien* 37 (1955): 268. Kunze, G., *Studien zu den Nonnenvisiten des deutschen Mittelalters, Ein Beitrag zur religiösen Literatur im Mittelalter.* Ph.D. diss., Hamburg, 1953, pp. 97–99. Loes, G., "Villingen-Klarissen." *Alemania Franciscana Antiqua* 3 (1957): 45–75. Rech, H., *Äbtissin Ursula Haider 1413–1498, Ein Beitrag zur Heimatgeschichte von Villingen, nach einer alten Handschrift* (Villingen, 1937). Richstätter, K., *Die Herz-Jesu-Verehrung des deutschen Mittelalters,* 2nd. ed. (Munich, 1924), p. 190f. Ringler, Siegfried, "Ursula Haider," in *Die deutsche Literatur des Mittelalters, Verfasserlexikon,* 2nd ed. by Kurt Ruh et al. (Berlin-New York, 1981), cols. 399–403. Ringles, S., *Viten- und Offenbarungsliteratur in Frauenklöstern des Mittelalters, Quellen und Studien.* MTU 72 (Munich, 1980): 59f. Roder, Ch. and K. Kiefer, *Die selige Äbtissin Ursula Haider zu St. Clara in Villingen* (1908). Tuechle, Hermann, *Kirchgeschichte Schwabens, Die Kirche Gottes im Lebensraum des schwäbisch-allemannischen Stammes,* Vol. II (Stuttgart, 1954), p. 162f.

Albrecht Classen

Maša Hal'amová

Born August 28, 1908, Blatnica, then in Austria-Hungary and now in Czechoslovakia

Genre(s): lyric poetry

Language(s): Slovak

With the title of "National Artist" given her in 1983, Maša Hal'amová is doubtless the leading lyric woman poet in Slovakia today. She follows in the Slovak symbolist tradition of Ivan Krasko and was thus influenced by the Czech and French symbolists.

Born in a small town in central Slovakia, she attended school there, but her mother's death sent her to live in Yugoslavia until Czechoslovakia was established in 1918. She graduated from a Bratislava business school, published her first book of verse in 1928, then spent a year studying in Paris. She married physician Dr. Ján Pullman and lived in the Tatra Mountains until his death in 1956. After 1959 she began to write children's stories and has also translated children's literature from Russian, Czech, and Lusatian-Sorbian.

Her first collection of poems, *Dar* (Gift) in 1928, expressed intensely her relation to the simple facts of her small world, but it also emphasized the polarity of hope and disappointment, of good fortune and suffering. Her second collection of poems, *Červený mak* (Scarlet Poppy) in 1932, still carried this theme but with a wider social content that enlarged the framework of her poems about love and the beauty of the mountains. In some works she used the ballad form. She published nothing more until 1955, when several new poems were added to the re-edition of her earlier poems. Hal'amová's last collection appeared in 1966, occasioned by the death of her husband in 1956. Called *Smrt' tvoju 'ijem* (I'm Living Out Your Death), it was addressed to her own loneliness and to a circle of similarly suffering people.

Hal'amová is a poet "of the heart," of intimate, private experiences generalized only through their clarity and intensity. She has achieved her status with a tiny body of less than one hundred published verses and without any political attachment in a highly politicized world.

Works

Dar [Gift] (1928). *Červený mak* [Scarlet Poppy] (1932). *Básne* [Poems] (1955). *Smrt' tvoju 'ijem* [I Am Living Out Your Death] (1966).

Translations: Czech: *Dar* (1979). English: "Legend" and "Elegia" (1947). "Legenda/Legend" (1976).

Bibliography

Bartko, Michal. *Poézia prostoty: Esej o diele Maše Hal'amovej* (Bratislava, 1983). Pišút, Milan, "Lyrický triptych Maše Hal'amovej." *Slovenské pohl'ady* 94 (1978): 4–9. Rúfus, Milan, Afterword in *Básne* (Bratislava, 1972), pp. 127–131. Sabo, Gerald J., "The Poetry of Maša Hal'amová." Annual Convention of the American Association for the Advancement of Slavic Studies (AAASS), October, 1984. Šmatlák, Stanislav, "Poézia ako dar srdca, ktoré bolo (kedysi) l'udom nepotrebné." *Romboid*

13 (1978): 2–9. Tomčík, Miloš. Afterword to *Básne* (Bratislava, 1955), pp. 88–91. Tomčík, Milos, *Básnické retrospectivy* (Bratislava, 1974), pp. 215–220.

General references: *Dejiny slovenskej literatúry*, Vol (V. Bratislava, 1984), pp. 177–180. *Encyklopédia slovenských spisovateľov* (Bratislava, 1984), I, 180.

Norma L. Rudinsky

Marie Robert Halt

(a.k.a. Marie Malézieux, Mme Louis-Charles Vieu)

Born May 30, 1849, Saint Quentin (Aisne), France; died February 21, 1908, Paris
Genre(s): novel, short story, textbook
Language(s): French

Marie Robert Halt wrote fiction for adults and children and achieved noticeable success as the author of textbooks for primary schools. The daughter of a painter, she married Louis-Charles Vieu, a former secondary school professor who turned to writing after being embroiled in controversy with educational authorities during the Bonapartist Second Empire. Mme Vieu adopted her husband's pseudonym, Robert Halt, and the two collaborated on the stories "Ladies et gentlemen," "Battu par des demoiselles," and "Les Suites d'un Cook's tour," published in a single volume in 1885. Her *Histoire d'un petit homme* (1883) received recognition from the Académie Française.

The Robert Halts were well connected with the middle-class republican leadership that made the secularization of public schools a major priority in educational reform; the issue grew in importance after republicans wrested political power from monarchist and Catholic opponents at the end of the 1870s, the first decade of the Third Republic. Mme Halt belonged to the Women's Committee (Comité des Dames) of the influential Ligue de l'Enseignement, an important pressure group organized by supporters of republican educational reform. The Women's Committee, founded in 1901, consisted of fifty members, most of whom were the wives of important politicians and educational leaders; some members were leading women educators.

Mme Halt purchased a field in the Seine-et-Oise commune of Condé-sur-Vègre so that school children could learn gardening and farming.

The three volumes of Halt's *Suzette* series, published between 1889 and 1905, were the most successful girls' textbooks of the Third Republic. They remained in use after World War I, and by 1932, 865,000 copies of *L'Enfance de Suzette* and more than 1,535,000 copies of *Suzette* had been sold. The main character, little Suzette, was the daughter of a modestly successful farmer. At age seven, she learned in school that girls' education should prepare them primarily to be good wives and mothers. At ten, when her mother died, her ability to run the household helped motivate her father and brothers to overcome despair and save the farm from ruin. In *Le Ménage de Mme Sylvain* Suzette functioned as a model farmer's wife and mother of three. This volume combined a story line with many detailed lessons on home economics. Although Halt did not challenge the predominant domestic ideology for women that the schools presented, she depicted women's personal strengths and indicated that unmarried women might very well need to work to earn a living. In the textbook *Le Droit Chemin* (1902) she presented circumstances under which a woman could justifiably leave an abusive husband and also celebrated women's capacity for friendship with other women.

Works

Novels: *Histoire d'un petit homme* [Story of a Small Man] (1883). *La Petite Lazare* (1884). *Monsieur Maurice* (1887). *Jacques la Chance et Jean la Guigne, suivi de l'Oncle Hubert* (1890). *Le Jeune Théodore* [The Young Theodore] (1891).

Short Stories [With Robert Halt] *Ladies et gentlemen, Battu par des démoiselles, Les Suites d'un Cook's tour* [Ladies and Gentlemen, Beaten by Young Women, The Results of a Cook's Tour] (1885).

Textbooks: *Suzette, livre de lecture courante à l'usage de jeunes filles* [Suzette, Reader for the Use of Girls] (1889). *L'Enfance de Suzette, livre de lecture courante à l'usage des jeunes filles (degré élémentaire)* [The Childhood of Suzette, Reader for the Use of Girls (Elementary Class)] (1892). *Le Ménage de Mme Sylvain, livre de lecture courante à l'usage des jeunes filles* [The Household of Mme

Sylvain, Reader for the Use of Girls] (1895). *Premières lectures, Leçons de morale et leçons de choses, éducation du sentiment, instruction usuelle, proverbes et maximes en action* [First Readings, Moral Lessons and Lessons about Objects, Education of Sensibility, Practical Instruction, Proverbs and Maxims in Action] (1897). *Deuxièmes lectures, leçons de morale et leçons de choses, éducation du sentiment, instruction usuelle, proverbes et maximes en action* [Second Readings . . .] (1897). *Le Droit chemin, livre de lecture courante, à l'usage des jeunes filles (degrés moyen et supérieur), éducation de la volonté, éducation du sens moral, devoirs sociaux, antialcoolisme* [The Straight Path Reader for the Use of Girls (Middle and Upper Primary Classes), Education of the Will, Education of the Moral Sense, Social Duties, Antialcoholism] (1902).

Bibliography

Clark, Linda L., *Schooling the Daughters of Marianne: Textbooks and the Socialization of Girls in Modern French Primary Schools* (Albany, 1984), pp. 45–47, 54. *Dictionnaire de biographie française* [Dictionary of French Biography], vol. 17 (Paris, 1986). *Polybiblion*, v. 112 (1908). Vapereau, Gustave. *Dictionnaire universel des contemporains*, 6th ed (Paris, 1893).

Linda L. Clark

Helvi Hämäläinen

Born June 16, 1907, Hamina, Finland
Genre(s): poetry, novel, verse drama
Language(s): Finnish

Helvi Hämäläinen left high school due to financial difficulties and took temporary jobs as a proof reader and clean copy typist, until 1931 when she became a free-lance writer. Her breakthrough came with a novel *Katuojan vettä* (1935; Gutter Water), partly based on her own experience. In it she takes a stand on abortion, emphasizing the value of biological life and motherhood. Several of her works deal with women's problems, but in her later writing erotic emphases displace the social angle.

Hämäläinen became a believer in D.H. Lawrence's sexual mysticism in the 1930s and a supporter of Freud's teaching. Lawrence's influence is seen most clearly in her novels *Lumous* (1934; Enchantment) and *Tyhjä syli* (1937; Empty Arms). Her so-called village series, *Kylä palaa* (1938; The Village Burns), *Kylä vaeltaa* (1944; The Village Roams), *Pouta* (1946; Fair Weather) and *Tuhopolttaja* (1949; The Arsonist) also emphasize strongly the fruitfulness of woman and nature as a protest to war and death.

Besides the worship of life's vitality, Hämäläinen's work is characterized by her picturesque, artistic style, reflecting the writer's strongly aesthetic view of life. These features are at their best in her principal work, *Säädyllinen murhenäytelmä* (1941; A Respectable Tragedy), portraying a marriage crisis in a cultural family. The book deals with the problem of the conflict between culture and nature. The writer sets the trials of the individual against the background of a period of political and cultural crisis. As a description of the educated classes, this novel explored new territory in Finnish literature, whose tradition had tended towards description of the common people.

Many of the themes in Hämäläinen's prose works are repeated in her poetry, which she has published since the 1930s. But it was not until the forties that she aroused attention with her colorful, ecstatic poetic language and powerful visions. In her finest collections, *Voikukkapyhimykset* (1947; Dandelion Saints), *Surmayöt* (1957; Nights of Death), *Punainen surupuku* (1958; Red Mourning Dress), and *Sukupolveni unta* (1987; Dreams of My Generation) as well as in her prose works one of the central themes has been the individual's close relationship with nature.

Works

Novels: *Hyväntekijä* [The Benefactor] (1930). *Lumous* [Enchantment] (1934). *Katuojan vettä* [Gutter Water] (1935). *Tyhjä syli* [Empty Arms] (1937). *Kylä palaa* [The Village Burns] (1938). *Säädyllinen murhenäytelmä* [A Respectable Tragedy] (1941). *Velvoitus* [Obligation] (1942). *Hansikas* [The Glove] (1943). *Kylä vaeltaa* [The Village Roams] (1944). *Pouta* [Fair Weather] (1946). *Sarvelaiset* [The Sarvelainens] (1947). *Ketunkivi* [The Fox's Stone] (1948). *Tuhopolttaja* [The Arsonist] (1949). *Kasperin jalokivet* [Kasper's Jewels] (1953). *Kolme eloonherätettyä* [Three

Resurrected] (1953) . *Karkuri* [Deserter] (1961). *Suden kunnia* [Wolf's Honor] (1962).

Poetry: *Lapsellinen maa* [Childish Land] (1943). *Voikukkapyhimukset* [Dandelion Saints] (1947). *Pilvipuku* [Cloud Dress] (1950). *Surmayöt* [Nights of Death] (1957). *Punainen surupuku* [Red Mourning Dress] (1958). *Pilveen sidottu* [Bound to a Cloud] (1961). *Poltetut enkelit* [Burnt Angels] (1965). *Sokeat lähteet* [Blind Springs] (1967). *Valikoima runoja* [Selection of Poems] (1958). *Valitut runot* [Selected Poems] (1973). *Sukupolveni unta* [Dreams of My Generation] (1987).

Poetic Drama: *Aaverakastaja* [Ghost Lover] (1936). Also poems. *Kuunsokea* [Moonblind] (1937). *Viheriä poika* [Green Boy] (1946). *Pilvi* [Cloud] (1946).

Other: *Miss Eurooppa* (1934; Miss Europe).

Translations into English of Hämäläinen's poems in anthologies: Tompuri, Elli, ed., *Voices from Finland* (1947). Vuosalo, Leo, and Steve Stone, eds., *The Stone God and Other Poems* (1948; 4th ed., 1960).

Bibliography

Helvi Hämäläisen selostus [Hämäläinen's Report], Ritva Haavikko, ed., in *Miten kirjani ovat syntyneet 2* [How My Books Have Originated 2] (Porvoo, 1980). Laurila, Aarne, "Helvi Hämäläinen." *Suomen kirjallisuus* V [Finnish Literature V], in Annamari Sarajas, ed. (Kevruu, 1965), pp. 542–551. Vaittinen, Pirjo, "*Säädyllinen murhenäytelmä*: romaani muutosten kourissa" [*A Respectable Tragedy*: The Novel in the Grip of Change]. With English summary. *Sananjalka 21* (Turku, 1979), pp. 145–160.

Ulla-Maija Juutila

(Anne) Marie (Andersen) Hamsun

Born November 19, 1881, Elverum, Norway; died August 5, 1969, Nørholm, Norway
Genre(s): autobiography, poetry
Language(s): Norwegian

In her touching, unforgettable accounts of life with the literary titan Knut Hamsun, Marie (Andersen) Hamsun has won an acknowledged, merited place in Norwegian letters. Marie Hamsun's two autobiographical works, *Regnbuen* (1955; The Rainbow) and, especially, *Under Gullregnen* (1959; Under Laburnum) depict the author's love for and life with Knut Hamsun, an artist of lyrical and verbal mastery (*Aschehoug og Gyldendal*, 5, 468). Marie Hamsun's works also offer a self-portrait of a woman of special courage, endurance, dedication, and intelligence. In peaceful times at home with the family in Nørholm; in times of conflict, war, and post-war imprisonment; and, in the more tranquil, ebbing years of Knut Hamsun's life, Marie Hamsun stood by, and then went on to create a remarkable memoir of a literary giant and a portrait of his life companion, Marie Hamsun herself.

As a young girl, Anne Marie Andersen dedicated herself to an academic career; she received her first student degree in 1901, and began a teaching career. Andersen taught for three years before turning to the theater and the life of an actress. She remained with the theater, until she married Knut Hamsun in 1909. At the time of their marriage, she was 28 and Knut Hamsun was approaching 50; he had already had a wealth of life experiences, literary success, and fame.

Marie and Knut Hamsun became the parents of four children: two sons, Tore and Arild, and two daughters, Ellinor and Cecilia. Marie Hamsun made her own literary début with a collection of short, engaging, poems, *Smaadikte*, in 1922. She then directed her talents to children, writing a series of short stories about childhood in rural Norway, *Bygdebarn* (1924, 1926, 1928, 1932; Village Child) as well as an individual work of poetry, *Barnebilleder* (1925; Pictures of Childhood). A collection of verses for children, *Tripp og Trapp og Trulle* (1933; Tripp and Trapp and Trulle), and another collection of poems, *Vintergrønt* (1934; Wintergreen) followed. Marie Hamsun returned to her *Bygdebarn* series with *Bygdebarn: folk og fe på Langerud* (1957; Village Child: People and Creatures at Langerud), and she also completed an additional book for young people, *Tina Toppen* (1955), and *Reisen til Sørlandet* (1956; The Journey South).

Of special note are Marie Hamsun's two autobiographical works, *Regnbuen* and *Under Gullregnen*. *Under Gullregnen* is a remarkable portrait of not only Knut Hamsun, the author of *Pan, Sult* (1890; Hunger), *Under Høststjærnen* (1906; Under the Autumn Star), *Markens Grøde*

(1917; The Growth of the Soil), *Landstrykere* (1927; Wanderers), *August* (1930), *Ringen sluttet* (1936; The Ring Closed), and of the incredibly beautiful *Paa gjengrodde Stier* (1949; On Overgrown Paths). The work is also a rare portrayal of the author, Marie Hamsun. The Hamsuns, particularly Knut but also Marie, had expressed rather naive sympathies and support for the Germans before and during World War II, and Marie was a former member of the National Socialists. Their involvement led to interrogation, examination, and imprisonment for both Hamsuns after the war. In *Under Gullregnen* Marie Hamsun has described her imprisonment, and separation from her family and from Knut, a man in his eighties at the time.

After a period of separation, illness and, for Knut Hamsun, psychiatric examination by the authorities, the Hamsuns were finally reunited at their homestead, Nørholm. Knut Hamsun wrote his final, remarkable work, *Paa gjengrodde Stier* (1949), expecting new recognition after a very long international career. Marie Hamsun remained by his side until his peaceful death in 1952, at age 93. In *Under Gullregnen*, Marie Hamsun recalls family life, sorrows, separations, and many joys, as well as Knut Hamsun's extraordinary talents, gift, and genius, and she offers a final, very personal and poignant tribute to the man "who broke into my life when I was 26" (*Under Gullregnen*, p. 13).

Marie Hamsun's literary career reached its high point with her descriptions of life with Knut Hamsun, *Regnbuen* and *Under Gullregnen*. Marie Hamsun presents a multifaceted portrait of Knut Hamsun as well as a touching depiction of herself as an artist's life companion. Marie Hamsun was also a gifted reader-interpreter of Knut Hamsun's and her own works. A series of letters from Knut to Marie Hamsun was published by Tore Hamsun as *Brev til Marie* in 1970. Marie Hamsun was a gifted poet; a sensitive, fine writer for young people; and the supremely dedicated companion, interpreter, and reader of the Norwegian master of style, poetry, and modern prose, Knut Hamsun.

Works

Smaadikte [Small Poems] (1922). *Bygdebarn. Hjemme og paa Sæteren* [Village Children. At Home and on the Mountain Pasture] (1924). *Barnebilleder* [Pictures of Childhood] (1925). *Bygdebarn om Vinteren* [Village Child in Winter] (1926). *Bygdebarn: Ola i byen* [Village Child: Ola in Town] (1928). *Bygdebarn: Ola og hans Søsken* [Village Child: Ola and his Brothers and Sisters] (1932). *Tripp og Trapp og Trulle* [Tripp and Trapp and Trulle] (1932). *Vintergrønt* [Wintergreen] (1934). *Regnbuen* [The Rainbow] (1953). *Tina Toppen* (1955). *Reisen til Sørlandet* [The Journey South] (1956). *Bygdebarn: folk og fe på Langerud* [Village Child: People and Creatures at Langerud] (1957). *Under Gullregnen* [Under Laburnum] (1959).

Bibliography

Aschehoug og Gyldendals Store Norske Leksikon: Bind 5, G-Hom (1983), p. 468. Dahl, Willy, *Norges Litteratur II: Tid og Tekst 1884–1935* (Oslo, 1984), pp. 231–238. *Dette skrev kvinner: Bibliografi over norske kvinnelige forfattere med debut før 1931* (Oslo, 1984), pp. 94–95.

Lanae Hjortsvang Isaacson

Françoise Hàn

Born 1928, Paris, France
Genre(s): poetry, translation
Language(s): French

Françoise Hàn was born in Paris of French and Vietnamese parents. She studied at the Faculté de Lettres, Paris, and has worked in various capacities ever since—industrial secretary initially and presently copyright executive with a major publisher—while at the same time writing and collaborating with certain literary reviews (*Avant-Quart* and *Europe*, especially).

Her first publication, *Cité des hommes* (1956; City of Men), was followed by a long quasi-silence of fourteen years. It is a powerful collection of socially conscious poems, speaking of the horrors of past and present history, and of the need to resist, to dare—not for the self but for others. Hàn stresses life's residual, essential "splendor," courage, hope, self-sacrifice, the all-conquering power of love so central to the poetry of so many contemporary women poets. Françoise Hàn, here as in the volumes to come in the seventies and eighties, is a solemn writer, considered, largely unelliptical, deep, subtly direct.

Par toutes les bouches de l'éphémère (1976; Through the Mouths of the Ephemeral) demonstrates something of a shift in expressive mode: free verse and prose persist yet the style is at once more telescoped and more entropic, more "kaleidoscopic," as she herself might say, reflecting a greater sense of disruption and chaos. The same preoccupations largely remain. The perspectives are chilling and yet poetic persistence is sure.

The most recent book of poetry of Françoise Hàn—she has edited, however, a special number of *Poésie I: Poésie Combat* (1986), with contributions from many modern poets—is *Dépasser le solstice?* (1984; Beyond the Solstice?). The volume shows Françoise Hàn's greater cosmic and evolutionary sense without modifying the telluric rooting of her work. Poetry's destiny is one of resurgent resistance despite vulnerability. It is a "wood fire, that stings the eyes a bit, and crackles." Beyond all heroism—perhaps "heroinism" is what is needed—poetry is a "treading of presence," an interspace between self and others, what is and what can be.

Works

Cité des hommes (1956). L'Espace ouvert (1970). Saison vive, poème-sérigraphie, ill. de Rodolphe Perret (1973). Par toutes les bouches de l'éphémère (1976). Le Temps et la toile (1977). Est-ce une praire (cernée) (1979). Le Réel le plus proche (1981). Le Désir, l'inachevé (1982). Malgré l'échange impossible (1983). Dépasser le solstice (1984). Palissades, poème manuscrit, ill. de Rodolphe Perrer (1985).

Bibliography

L'Année poétique (Paris, 1977). Boisdeffre, Pierre de, Histoire de la littérature française (Paris, 1985), p. 213. Breton, Jean, Chroniques sur le vif (Paris, 1982). Brindeau, Serge, "Françoise Hàn." La Poésie contemporaine de langue française depuis 1945 (Paris, 1973), pp. 360–361.

Michael Bishop

Enrica von Handel-Mazzetti

Born January 10, 1871, Vienna, Austria; died
    April 8, 1955, Linz, Austria
Genre(s): drama, novella, tale, short story,
    letters, poetry
Language(s): German

Enrica von Handel-Mazzetti was the daughter of a captain in Austria's imperial army who died before she was born. She received her early education from her mother, attended an Institute for English girls in St. Pölten, Austria, from 1886–1887, then studied languages and literature in Vienna. From 1905 to 1917 she lived in Steyr, then moved to Linz. 1914 she received the Ebner-Eschenbach prize for literature; in 1936 she was made an honorary citizen of Linz. The boycott of her (strongly religious) work during the Hitler era resulted in a growing isolation from society during her latter years. In 1951 the Handel-Mazzetti prize was established for the annual recognition of an Austrian writer. The Handel-Mazzetti-Archives are located in the "Bundesstaatliche Studienbibliothek" in Linz, Austria.

Works

Plays (incl. nativity and Paschal plays): *Nicht umsonst* (1892). *Pegasus im Joch* (comedy 1895). *Talitha* (1895). *In terra pax, hominibus bonae voluntatis!* (1899). *Die wiedergeöffnete Himmelstür* (1900). *Weihnachts- und Krippenspiele* (1912). *Ich kauf ein Mohrenkind* (1922).

Novellas, Tales, Short Stories: *Meinrad Helmperges denkwürdiges Jahr* (1900). *Der Verräter. Fahrlässig getötet* (1902). *Erzählungen*, 2 vols. (1903). *Ich mag ihn nicht* (1903). *Als die Franzosen in St. Pölten waren* (1904). *Der letzte Wille des Herrn Egler* (1904). *Novellen* (1907). *Historische Novellen* (1908). *Erzählungen und Skizzen* (1910). *Bunte Geschichten* (1912). *Ritas Briefe*, 5 vols. (1915–1921). *Caritas. Die schönsten Erzählungen* (1922). *Seine Tochter* (1926). *Christiana Kotzebue* (1934). *Das heilige Licht* (1938).

Novels: *Jesse und Maria* (1906). *Die arme Margaret* (1910). *Stephana Schwertner*, 3 vols. (1912–1914). *Brüderlein und Schwesterlein* (1913). *Ilko Smutniak, der Ulan* (1917). *Der deutsche Held* (1920). *Ritas Vermächtnis* (1922). Karl-Sand-Trilogy, vol. 1: *Das Rosenwunder*, 2: *Deutsche Passion*, 3: *Das Blutzeugnis* (1924–1926). *Johann Christian Günther* (1927). *Frau Maria*, 3 vols. (1929–1931). *Die Waxenbergerin* (1934). *Graf Reichard*, 2 vols. (1939–1940).

Poems and "Lieder": *Deutsches Recht und andere Gedichte* (1908). *Acht geistliche Lieder* (1909). *Imperatori. Fünf Kaiserlieder* (1910).

Other works: *Skizzen aus Österreich* (1904). *Sophie Barat. Gedenkblatt* (1910). *Geistige Werdejahre*, 2 vols. (1911–1912). *Napoleon und andere Dichtungen* (1912). *Friedensgebet* (1915). *Der Blumenteufel. Bilder aus dem Reservespital Staatsgymnasium in Linz* (1916). *Die Heimat meiner Kunst* (1934). *Renate von Natzmer. Eine Paralleldichtung zu Schillers "Kindsmörderin"* (1951).

Letters: *Der Dichterin stiller Garten. Briefwechsel mit Marie v. Ebner-Eschenbach* (1918).

Bibliography (existing lexica give varying data)

Berger, F., et al., *Festschrift zum 75. Geburtstag H.-M.s* (1945). Bourgeois, J.E., *Ecclesiastical Characters in the Novels of E. v. H.-M.* Ph.D. diss., U. of Cincinnati, 1956. Brecka, H. *Die E.v. H.-M.* (1923). Doppler, B., "Möglichkeiten eines H.-M.-Archivs." *Adalbert Stifter Institut des Landes Oberösterreich: Vierteljahrsschrift* 26 (1977): 41–62. "E.v. H.-M. Gedächtnisschrift zu ihrem 100. Geburtstag." *Adalbert Stifter Institut des Landes Oberösterreich: Vierteljahrsschrift* 20 (1971), pp. 9–55. Enzinger, M., "Schriften von und über E.v. H.-M." *Adalbert Stifter Institut des Landes Oberösterreich: Vierteljahrsschrift* 20 (1971). Fischer, J.M., *E.v. H.-M.* (1912). Freylinger, M., *E.v. H.-M.: Biographie und Werke* (1971). *Katholische Literatur und Literaturpolitik E.v. H.-M. Eine Fallstudie* (1980). Korrodi, E., *E.H.-M.* (1909). Kröckel, J., *Das Kompositionsgesetz in den Romanen von E.v. H.-M.* Diss., Frankfurt, 1926. Langer, N., "E.v. H.-M." *Dichter aus Österreich* 2 (1957). Mumbauer, J., *Der Dichterin stiller Garten. M.v. Ebner-Eschenbach und E.v. H.-M.* (1918). Münckel, T., *Die archaisierenden Stilmittel der Erzählkunst der E.v. H.-M.* Diss., Frankfurt, 1931. Muth, K., "Jesse und Maria." *Hochland* (1905–1906). Rodenberg, J., *Briefe über einen deutschen Roman* (1911). Schnee, H., *E.v. H.-M.*, 1934. Siebertz, P., ed., *E.v. H.-M.s Persönlichkeit, Werk und Bedeutung* (1931). Speekmann, B.W., *Quellen und Komposition der Trilogie Stephana Schwertner.* Diss., Groningen, 1924. "Tribute to Schiller." *Monatshefte* 51 (1959). Vancsa, K., "Nur ein Zettel. Aus dem H.-M.-Archiv." *Jahrbuch für Landeskunde von Niederösterreich*, N.F. 34 (1958–1960). Vancsa, K., *In Memoriam E.v. H.-M.* (1955). "Vom *Waisenkind* bis zur *Deutschen Rundschau*: Publikationsorgane katholischer Schriftsteller zwischen 1890 und 1918." *Österreich in Geschichte und Literatur* 21 (1977): 304–320.

Helene M. Kastinger Riley

Margarete Hannsmann

Born February 2, 1921, Heidenheim
   (Württemberg), Germany
Genre(s): poetry, prose fiction, radio drama
Language(s): German

Margarete Hannsmann enjoys a reputation as a master of short and long lyrical forms. A socially and politically conscious author, she explores the Nazi past as well as a variety of contemporary issues in her works.

Hannsmann is the daughter of Gotthold Wurster, a teacher who was seriously wounded in World War I. Wurster was an ardent supporter of Hitler, and Hannsmann at first shared her father's enthusiasm, becoming a leader of a Nazi youth group. In the late 1950s she met her future husband, the anti-Nazi journalist Heinrich Hannsmann, and began to lose her admiration of Hitler. Soon after the war her husband suffered a nervous breakdown, and to Hannsmann fell the responsibility for supporting the couple's two children. Only in the late 1950s, after her husband had died and her children were approaching adulthood, did she begin to write. For seven years she lived with the poet Johannes Poethen, with whom she made frequent trips to Greece, and then established a relationship with the graphic artist HAP Grieshaber that was to last until his death in 1981. The poem *Abschied von HAP Grieshaber* (1981; Farewell to HAP Grieshaber) is a poignant poetic tribute to the artist, whose woodcuts appear in many of Hannsmann's books, and *Pfauenschrei: Die Jahre mit HAP Grieshaber* (1986; Peacock's Cry: The Years with HAP Grieshaber) contains a detailed narrative account of the relationship.

Until the late 1960s Hannsmann's verses tended to be short and personal. Nature—landscapes—was a prominent theme, and in many poems an instant, the essence of a scene, was captured in short snapshots. Her first major collection, *Zwischen Urne und Stier* (1971; Between Urn and Bull), is a product of her travels to Greece. Mythology and landscape are important, but another dimension is added: a strong social and political consciousness. Nature and politics continue to be significant in the numerous later collections of verse. Ecology is one of her favored topics: the destruction of the environment by encroaching civilization and by war. The form as well as the theme changes in Hannsmann's later verse, as many poems extend over several pages. *Lebenslauf in Deutschland* (A Life in Germany), some twenty pages in length, represents the poet's thoughts on events in Germany during her lifetime.

In many poems Hannsmann examines the present in light of the past, with an eye to the future. The same is true of her autobiographical novels, *Drei Tage in C.* (1965; Three Days in C.), written from the perspective of a mature woman visiting her past, and *Der helle Tag bricht an: Ein Kind wird Nazi* (1982; The Bright Day Dawns: A Child Becomes a Nazi), in which the development of her infatuation with the Nazis is portrayed and the beginning of her disillusionment described.

Works

Tauch in den Stein (1964). *Drei Tage in C.: Roman* (1965). *Maquis in Nirgendwo* (1967). *Zerbrich die Sonnenschaufel* (1966). *Grob, fein und Göttlich* (1970). *Zwischen Urne und Stier: Gedichte* (1971). *Das andere Ufer vor Augen* (1972). *Ins Gedächtnis der Erde geprägt* (1973). *Fernsehabsage: Gedichte* (1974). *Blei im Gefieder/ Du plomb dans le plumage: Ein Paris Gedicht*, dual language, tr. Henry Fagne (1980). *Kreta* (1975). *Santorin* (1977). *Aufzeichnungen über Buchenwald* (1978). *Schaumkraut: Gedichte* (1975). *Landkarten* (1980). *Spuren: Ausgewählte Gedichte 1960–1980* (1981). *Abschied von HAP Grieshaber* (1981). *Der helle Tag bricht an: Ein Kind wird Nazi* (1982). *Du bist in allem: Elegie auf Lesbos* (1983). *Drachmentage: Gedichte* (1986). *Pfauenschrei: Die Jahre mit HAP Grieshaber* (1986).

Bibliography

Jäschke, B., "Margarete Hannsmann," in *Neue Literatur der Frauen*, ed. H. Punkus (Munich, 1980), pp. 65–69. Serke, J., *Frauen schreiben* (Frankfurt, 1982), pp. 353–355. Wallmann, J., *Argumente* (Mulacker, 1968), pp. 101–104.

Jerry Glenn

Aase Hansen

Born March 11, 1893, Frederiksværk, Denmark; died 1981, Copenhagen, Denmark
Genre(s): novel, essay, translation, scholarship
Language(s): Danish

The many significant novels of Aase Hansen deal with intelligent, intellectual women caught at cross-purposes with society; with traditional expectations, mores, and roles; and, most importantly, with the ambivalent desires, purposes, and achievements of such women and their hopes for—and fears of—independence. For all the female protagonists in Aase Hansen's novels, the promise of freedom, the merits of meaningful work and a new equal place in society, as subjects of the story, inevitably involve scary choices, genuine fears of freedom and of an independent life. The choice for independence, "the burden of freedom" (Dalager, p. 72), leads to "tears, isolation, loneliness, resignation, and no personal life to speak of" (*Dansk Litteraturhistorie* 7, 506). Aase Hansen's characters are torn between a longing for all important self-realization and their own *angst* in choosing and then living a life of freedom. Hansen answered the quintessential dilemma for herself with her own authorship: "Her solution becomes [her own] writing. By remembering and retelling, [Aase Hansen] can achieve a little of that pivotal status which neither love nor a career can really bring women" (*DLH* 7, 508). Hansen's writing gave impetus to current, constant discussions concerning the difficult choices which women must make—and the negative aspects of such choices.

Aase Hansen was born on March 11, 1893, in Frederiksværk, Denmark. She was the daughter of Frederik Carl Hansen (1853–1915), the town merchant, and of Mette Kirstine Pedersen (1852–1928). In 1913, Hansen passed her entrance examinations for the university, graduating from Frederiksborg State School. She continued her education at the University of Copenhagen, finishing her Cand. Mag. University Degree in the fields of Danish, German, and English, in 1921 (*Dansk biografisk Leksikon* 5, 699). Hansen's first position was as a visiting teacher at Ålborg Cathedral School; she later obtained a permanent appointment as Adjunct to Vejle School, but she did not secure tenure for that position, for, as she recognized, she wasn't the born pedagogue. Hansen had long nourished a childhood dream of becoming a writer, but she postponed her literary *début* by working for a year in Copenhagen's Office of the National Registry and by teaching seven additional years at Ullerslev Secondary School on *Fyn* (Fünen). (Hansen wrote her first two books, *Ebba Berings Studentertid* [1929; The Academic Career of Ebba Bering] and *Et Par Huse om en Station* [1930; A Few Houses by a Station], while still at Ullerslev.) In 1932, Hansen resigned her post at the secondary school, returning to Copenhagen as a full-time writer and translator. Hansen's academic career set its mark on her subdued, tranquil style, and she sketched her characters with careful human and humane insight and with her own experiences and challenges as an independent intellectual in mind. Never married, Hansen died in Copenhagen in 1981, after a literary career spanning virtually 50 years, from her 1929 *début* to her final work, *I Forvitringens Aar* (1977; In Years of Decline).

The major theme of Aase Hansen's novels is the personal conflict caused by intellectual promise on the one hand and the desire for a meaningful, traditional love relationship on the other. Hansen's characters desire importance, freedom, and self-reliance, but they also fear "women's [inevitable] lot: loneliness, unfulfilled dreams, and self-deception" (*DBL*, 5, 700). Hansen drew on her own life experiences, her training as a scholar, to sketch portraits of women facing the inherent burdens and drawbacks of their own life decisions and of their intense longing for recognition and self-acceptance. Hansen succeeded in portraying women at every stage, from "earliest childhood [to] the uncertainty of puberty, [from] the searching student years [to] the mature woman's life and loves, [and, finally, to] the sharp, bittersweet realization and clarity of age" (*DBL* 5, 700).

Hansen's debut novel, *Ebba Berings Studentertid*, deals with the protagonist Ebba's transition from naive provincial girl to university student; Ebba and her friends share a desire to break free of a close, confining provincial background "into new experiences in the capital and at the University" (Dalager, p. 70). Ebba's friends

all find satisfaction in language and literature studies, while Ebba remains discontent, disillusioned, and uninvolved in her own political science studies. Ebba's path through academia is a rocky one because of her own lack of commitment, her disinterest and disappointment in her studies; in addition, she lacks necessary "concrete experience in the male-dominated world [of] abstract, theoretical political science" (Dalager, p. 71), and she regrets her own choice of study. Ebba's sexual awakening with an older, married man clearly reveals her bitterness and loneliness, her disappointment, and her own admitted failure to take her studies seriously. Ebba finishes her studies unprepared for "a share in life" and cut off from "the traditional secure marriage, the role of wife and mother of which she [very belatedly] dreams" (Dalager, p. 72). Aase Hansen reveals Ebba's conflicts and lack of commitment all too clearly; her unresolved yearnings for independence and for love and security lead Ebba to a problematic, lonely existence. In *Ebba Berings Studentertid*, Aase Hansen sketches the hard decisions which educated women still face; she also discloses the essential conflict within her protagonist, Ebba's lack of dedication to science and statescraft.

In *Et Par Huse om en Station*, Aase Hansen further demonstrated her keen insights into local milieu and her ability to use her own experiences in sketching characters and setting. Hansen's novels, *Vraggods* (1933; Wreckage) and, particularly, *Stine* (1933; Stine) deal with self-conflict and self-reflection; in the latter novel, the student Rigmor loses her lover to the more earthy, direct, uncomplicated Stine. With *Stine*, "Aase Hansen's stories begin to focus on the psychology and history of self-discord as a theme . . . and [they take] modern women's fate as a point of departure (*DLH* 7, 505). Hansen's mature work, *En Kvinde kommer hjem* (1937; A Woman Comes Home), deals with a modern mature woman's return home to her dying mother, without work or lovers. Hansen's novel reveals the modern protagonist-narrator's conflicting desire and fear of freedom "as an inner dialogue between those powers which continually and unresolvedly dwell within [all of] Aase Hansen's characters" (*DLH* 7, 506). Hansen followed *En Kvinde kommer hjem* with *Drømmen* om i Gaar (1939; The Dream of Yesterday), a portrayal of the chance reunion of two school friends during a summer trip. The two women have followed entirely different life-paths, and neither way has proven happy or carefree; one has chosen "traditional marriage, a demonic lover, many suicide attempts, and perpetual turmoil" (DLH 7, 506), while the narrator has resisted involvements and passions in favor of loneliness, isolation, and a position on the sidelines. Both of Hansen's characters in Drømmen om i Gaar reflect self-dissension which the lonely, detached narrator might have weathered only a little bit better and at a very high price. Aase Hansen's later novels, Den lyse Maj (1948; Light May) and Skygger i et Spejl (1951; Shadows in a Mirror) continue to sketch the life experiences of women, the love conflicts, and the modern problematics of work, career, hopes, and dreams. In Skygger i et Spejl, two women travel home together; and they present two sides of essentially the same story of "passion . . . difficult and painful love affairs" (DLH 7, 508). The narrator's story develops through dream and reverie in contrast to her companion's more vivid and actual accounts.

Aase Hansen's oeuvre focuses on the essential transitions, conflicts, and changes confronting and challenging every woman. Hansen drew on her own experiences as an intellectual, as a provincial woman who excelled academically, and, then, confronted self-conflicts, fears, hopes, loneliness, and several hard personal decisions, and she found meaning and a niche in her writing. Aase Hansen's many novels, her essays and memoirs, raise still relevant questions about goals, hopes, and purposes.

Works

Ebba Berings Studentertid (1929). Et Par Huse om en Station (1930). Stine (1933). Vraggods (1933). En Kvinde kommer hjem (1937). Drømmen om i Gaar (1939). De røde Baand [The Red Bands] (1943). Madammen i Sundgaarden, hørespil [The Lady of Sundgaard] radio play (1933, 1942). Tordenluft [Thunder Air] (1945) . Den lyse Maj (1948). Skygger i et Spejl (1951). Fra den grønne Provins [From the Green Province], memoirs in essay form (1952). Ursula og hendes Mor [Ursula and her Mother] (1956). Klip af et Billedark [Clippings from a Picture Sheet], memoirs (1973). I Forvitringens Aar (1977).

Bibliography

Dalager, Stig, and Anne-Marie Mai, Danske kvindelige forgattere. Bind II (København, 1982). Dansk biografisk Leksikon. Bind 5 (København, 1979), pp. 699–700. Dansk Litteraturhistorie, Bind 7 (København, 1983), pp. 505–510. Nielsen, Drude, Rejse i Tid. Aase Hansens Forgatterskab (København, 1975). Nielson, Fr., Danske digtere i det 20. Aarhundrede. Ny udgave II (København), pp. 301–314. Plesner, K.F. "Aase Hansen." Nordiska tidskrift för vetenskap, konst, och industri (1941), pp. 595–602. Woel, Cai M., Tyvernes og tredvernes digtere I (1941), pp. 175–188.

Lanae Hjortsvang Isaacson

Françoise d'Issembourg d'Happoncourt (de Graffigny)

Born February 13, 1695, Nancy, France; died December 12, 1758, Paris
Genre(s): novella, novel, drama
Language(s): French

Mme de Graffigny, whose Lettres d'une Péruvienne (Letters of a Peruvian Woman) took Paris intelligencia by storm in 1747, was convinced by the circumstances of her life that bad luck would follow her to paradise—if she went there. She decided, therefore, never to complain about anything but the trivial (letter ā26, Cirey, Monday 12 January 1739.)

Daughter of an officer of the Duke of Lorraine—a fortune-hunter who was granted nobility by the king in 1695—and grand-niece of the engraver Jacques Callot, Françoise's bad luck started when she married, at a very young age, the Chamberlain of the Duke of Lorraine, a man called Hughes de Graffigny. Hughes, a violent and brutal man, made her life a living hell until he was imprisoned and ended his days in captivity.

Her luck seemed to turn when, at age forty-three, she was befriended by Voltaire, who gained her admittance to the estate of his friend Mme du Chatelet. There, at Cirey, Mme de Graffigny finally had some peace and could recuperate from the cruelties of her husband. But all too soon, even that chapter of her life was to end in disaster. Within a couple of months her new-found friends accused her (rightly, it would seem) of sending to her friend Devaux an unauthorized copy of a canto of Voltaire's "La Pucelle," a manuscript that Mme du Chatelet is supposed to have guarded jealously under lock and key. With this indiscretion came the end of her stay at Cirey and Mme de Graffigny went on to Paris where, financially destitute, she was given refuge by the Duchess of Richelieu at her residence. In Paris, she opened a salon which soon gained fame.

At the urging of friends, Mme de Graffigny began writing and her first work was published in 1745 when she was fifty years of age. It was a novella entitled *Le mauvais exemple produit autant de virtus que de vices* (The Bad Example Produces as Much Virtue as Vice) and was published in a book called *Recueil de ces Messieurs* (Collections of These Gentlemen). Her novella was severely criticized, but she probably owed her writing career to that criticism because it was in replying to her critics that she found her enthusiasm to write her second novel, *Lettres d'une Péruvienne* (Letters of a Peruvian Woman). First published anonymously in 1747, that work became an instant success. The novel narrates, in the form of letters, the painful story of Zilia, a young Peruvian woman who is kidnapped on her wedding day by European conquerors. Zilia's yearning for her fiance, Aza, and her homeland is portrayed with great emotion and sincerity and is probably the reason why the novel became so popular.

Lettres d'une Péruvienne (Letters of a Peruvian Woman) has a very interesting publishing history that deserves mention. Mme de Graffigny signed her name to the second edition (1752) in which she added several more letters that are said to present an ideal of love that presages Rousseau's in *La Nouvelle Héloise* (The New Heloise). After her death came another edition, in 1798, that added to the text the "*lettres d'Aza*" (letters of Aza). Several reprints followed in 1812, 1822, 1826, and 1858 testifying to the continued popularity of the novel. The novel was translated into several languages—Italian in 1760 and 1811; English in 1818; Spanish in 1823. A number of these editions were illustrated.

To return to Mme de Graffigny, however, after completing her second novel she turned her imagination to drama. *Cénie*, a sentimental comedy in five acts and prose, was first performed on June 25, 1750 and enjoyed twenty-five very successful stagings. *Cénie's* success consolidated the reputation that *Lettres . . .* had gained for Mme de Graffigny, but true to her bad luck, success did not stay with her for too long. Her second attempt at drama, *La fille d'Aristide* (Aristide's Daughter), premiered on April 27, 1757 and was a major flop. L'abbe de Voisenon, Mme de Graffigny's spiritual friend to whom she is said to have read her play, said about it: "She read it to me and I found it bad and she found me bad. It was played; the public died of boredom and she died of chagrin."

Mme de Graffigny is also credited with writing two plays, *Phasa* and *Ziman et Zenise* (Ziman and Zenise), for the court of the Emperor of Vienna. He supposedly promised her an award of 1500 livres per year for the rest of her life on the condition that she would never publish the plays or have them performed.

After a lifetime of struggling for financial comfort Mme de Graffigny died, penniless, on December 12, 1758.

Works

Le mauvais exemple produit autant de virtus que de vices (1745). Lettres d'une Péruvienne (1747). Cenie (1751). La fille d'Aristide (1757).
Posthumous collections: Oeuvres choisies (1783). Oeuvres Completes (1788). Vie privee do Voltaire et de Mme. du Chatelet, ou Six mois a Cirey (1820).

Bibliography

Fayard, *Dictionnaire de Lettres Francais*. Asse, Eugene, *Lettres: Madame de Graffigny* (1972).

Ranee Kaur

Bogdan Haritov

(see: Dora Petrova Gabe)

Genoveva Hartlaub

Born June 7, 1915, Mannheim, Germany
Genre(s): short story, novel, travel literature,
*   radio drama*
Language(s): German

Genoveva Hartlaub belongs to a group of lesser-known German writers, who have tried to cope with unsolved experiences and impressions from WW II. She was born on June 7, 1915, in Mannheim, Germany, the daughter of the art historian and director of the Kunsthalle in Mannheim, Gustav Hartlaub. Since her father lost his position in 1933 because of his political opposition to the Nazis, Genoveva was not allowed to enter the university. Instead she began an apprenticeship as a merchant and became a foreign correspondent in a machinery company. In 1938 she spent a year in Italy and was conscripted to the army in 1939. During the war she was taken prisoner in Norway. After the war she worked as a lector for the journal *Die Wandlung*, edited by Dolf Sternberger; afterward she became a free lector. In 1957 she was appointed editor of the Hamburg weekly *Sonntagsblatt*. Her works deal with the situation of Germany during WW II and how people were able to cope with such events and problems. She also investigated contemporary marriage problems, generational conflicts and ethical and moral issues.

Works

Novels: Die Kindsräuberin [The Child Abductress] (1947). Anselm, der Lehrling [The Apprentice Anselm] (1947). Die Tauben von San Marco [The Pigeons from San Marco] (1953). Noch im Traum [Still in Dreams] (1943). Windstille vor Concador [Lull of Wind at Concador] (1958). Gefangene der Nacht [Prisoners of the Night] (1961). Nicht jeder ist Odysseus [Not Everybody is Ulysses] (1967). Lokaltermin Feenteich [A Courtroom View at Fairy Lake] (1972). Die Schafe der Königin [The Queen's Sheep]. Wer die Erde küßt, Orte, Menschen, Jahre [He Who Kisses the Earth: Places, People and Years] (1975). Das Gör [The Nasty Girl] (1980). Freue dich, du bist eine Frau, Briefe der Priscilla [Rejoice, You Are a Woman, Letters by Priscilla] (1983). Muriel (1985).

Short stories: Die Enführung [The Abduction] (1941). Der Mond hat Durst [The Moon is Thirsty] (1963). Die gläserne Krippe, Moderne Weihnachtsgeschichten [The Manger of Glass, Modern Christmas Stories] (1968). Rot heißt auch schön [Red Is Also Called Beautiful] (1969).

Travel literature: Unterwegs nach Samarkand, Eine Reise durch die Sowjetunion [A Trip to Samarkand, A Journey Through the Soviet Union] (1965).

Radio plays: Die Stütze des Chefs [The Support for the Boss] (1953). Das verhexte ABC [The Bewitched ABC] (1959). Melanie und die gute Fee [Melanie and the Good Fairy] (1959). Eine Frau allein in Paris [A Woman Alone in Paris] (1970). Leben mit dem Sex [Live with Sex] (1970). She translated a number of Italian and French novels into German and edited the literary works of her brother Felix Hartlaub in 1955. She also wrote many children's radio plays and edited *Mutterdarstellung in der bildenden Kunst* [Depictions of the Mother in Visual Arts] (1962).

Bibliography

Balka, M., "Die Tauben von St. Marko," in *Der Romanführer*, vol. 13, ed. J. Beer (Stuttgart, 1964), pp. 134f. Balka, M., "Gefangene der Nacht," in *Der Romanführer*, vol. 13, ed. J. Beer (Stuttgart, 1964), pp. 135f. Best, O.F., "Windstille vor Concador." *Neue Deutsche Hefte* 6, 57 (1959): 77–78. "Genoveva Hartlaub," *Autorenlexikon deutschsprachiger Literatur des 20. Jahrhunderts*, ed. M. Brauneck (Hamburg, 1984), pp. 232–233. "Genoveva Hartlaub." *Deutsches Literatur Lexikon*, vol. 7, 3rd ed., H. Rupp and G.L. Lang (Bern-Munich, 1979), p. 387. Gresky, W., "Die Schafe der Königin." in *Der Romanführer*, vol. 16, Ed. A.C. Baumgärtner (Stuttgart, 1979), pp. 112–113. Gresky, W., "Nicht jeder ist Odysseus," *Der Romanführer*, vol. 16, ed. A.C. Baumgärtner (Stuttgart, 1979), pp. 113–114. Zehetmeier, W., "Genoveva Hartlaub," *Lexikon der deutschsprachigen Gegenwartsliteratur* (Munich, 1981), p. 193.

Albrecht Classen

Iulia Hasdeu

(a.k.a. Camille Armand)

Born 1869, Bucharest, Romania; died 1888, Bucharest
Genre(s): poetry, short story, essay, drama
Language(s): French, Romanian

Iulia Hasdeu learned to read at three, spoke French, German and English at eight, finished high school at eleven and went to Paris in 1880, accompanied by her mother, to attend the courses of the Sévigné College. In 1886 she studied at the Sorbonne Faculté de lettres and at the Ecole des

Hautes Etudes while at the same time writing poems in French, preparing a thesis about "the unwritten philosophy of the Romanian people" and lecturing on "The Logic of Hypothesis" or "The Second Book of Herodotus." In 1887 tuberculosis was diagnosed and, after a short period of treatment in Switzerland, she returned to Romania to die before reaching nineteen.

When she died, Iulia Hasdeu had published only four poems. It was her father, Bogdan Petriceicu Hasdeu, an acclaimed Romanian writer, philologist, linguist and historian who took upon himself the publication of Iulia Hasdeu's posthumous work (poems, fiction, plays, essays, maxims) and translated part of it into Romanian.

Iulia Hasdeu's poems, for which she had chosen the title *Bourgeons d'Avril* (1889; April Burgeons) have been compared to a journal in which the evocation of medieval love and heroism and the pantheistic notes are superimposed upon the strong presentiment of early death. She had conceived and partially developed over fifty play-projects inspired from classic mythology or Romanian history—among which *L'ami de Trajan* (The Friend of Trajan) and *Les Heïduques* (The Outlaws) were in the most advanced state—as well as several novels. She wrote for children a "conte bleu," *La princesse Papillon* (1972; Princess Butterfly), as well as a miniature novel, *Mademoiselle Maussade* (1970; Miss Gloomy). Her correspondence with her father has been recognized as a most interesting example of the epistolary genre at that time.

Works

Oeuvres posthumes [Posthumous Works], ed. and intro. B.P. Hasdeu (1889–1890); vol. I. Bourgeons d'Avril. Fantaisies et Rêves [April Burgeons. Fantasies and Dreams]; vol. II. *Chevalerie, Confidences et Canevas* [Knighthood, Confidences and Canvas]; vol. III. *Théâtre, Légendes et Contes* [Theatre, Legends and Stories]. *Sanda* (1904) [originally written in Romanian]. [Poems published in] Miller-Verghi, Margareta and Ecaterina Săndulescu, *Evoluția scrisului feminin în România* (1935), pp. 71–76 and Doicescu, Ciprian, *Iulia Hasdeu. Cu tălmăciri din poeziile sale* (1941). *Mademoiselle Maussade. Domnișoara Ursuza* [Miss Gloomy]. tr. by B.P. Hasdeu (1970). *Prințesa Fluture* [Princess Butterfly], ed. Crina Decusară (1972).

"Frumusețea" [Beauty] (1973). "Correspondența B.P. Hasdeu-Iulia Hasdeu" [The Correspondence between B.P. Hasdeu and Iulia Hasdeu], in Cornea, Paul, Elena Piru, Roxana Sorescu, eds., *Documente și manuscrise literare* III. *Versuri. Proză. Corespondență* [Poems. Prose. Correspondence], ed. and intro. Crina Decusară-Bocșan (1976).

Bibliography

Apostolescu, Nicolae, L'*influence des romantiques français sur la poésie roumaine* (Paris, 1909), pp. 358–397. Apostolescu, N.I., *Studii literare, estetice, filologice.* (Bucharest, 1904), pp. 85–97. Balan, Th., *Copii minune* (Bucharest, 1970), pp. 122–152. Barral, L., "Iulia Hasdeu, poète français." *Convorbiri literare* LXVI (1933): 2. Decusară-Bocșan, Crina, *Camille Armand—pseudonimul Iuliei Hasdeu* (Bucharest, 1974). Doicescu, Ciprian, *Iulia Hasdeu. Cu tălmăciri din poeziile sale* (Bucharest, 1941). Drăgoi, Gabriela, in *Dicționarul literaturii române de la origini pînă la 1900* (Bucharest, 1979), pp. 431–432. Gubernatis, A. de, "Julie Hasdeu, femme-poète de la Roumanie," In Julie B.P. Hasdeu, *Oeuvres posthumes* I (Bucharest, 1889), pp. XV-XLVIII. Hașeganu, I., *La France dans l'oeuvre des écrivains roumains contemporains de langue française* (Paris, 1940), pp. 16–42. Ionnescu-Gion, G.I., *Portrete istorice* (Bucharest, 1894), pp. 159–189. Iorga, Nicolae, *Oameni care au fost* IV (Bucharest, 1939), pp. 275–276. Léger, Louis, "Un poète français en Roumanie," in Julie B.P. Hasdeu, *Oeuvres posthumes* II (1889) pp. XVII-XVIII. Manolache, Constantin, *Scînteietoarea viață a Iuliei Hasdeu* (Bucharest, 1939). Manolescu, Ion Aurel, *Iulia Hasdeu* (Bucharest, 1939). Miller-Verghi, Margareta and Ecaterina Săndulescu, *Evoluția scrisului feminin în România* (Bucharest, 1935), pp. 67–70. Negreanu, Aristița, "Aspecte inedite în opera Iuliei Hasdeu." *Analele Universității București. Limbi romanice* XIX (1970). Odobescu, A.I., "Poeziile domnișoarei Iulia B.P. Hasdeu." *Convorbiri literare* XXIII (1889), p. 1., *Revista nouă* I, nr. 11 (1888) (dedicated to Iulia Hasdeu).

Sanda Golopentia

Eveline Hasler

Born Glarus, Switzerland
Genre(s): prose, poetry
Language(s): German

After studying psychology and history in Freiburg and Paris, Eveline Hasler spent a brief period as a teacher. She wrote a number of children's books, for which she was repeatedly acclaimed internationally and also worked for television.

She was awarded a prize of the Schiller Foundation for her first novel *Novemberinsel* (November Island), which was published in 1980. 1982 marked the appearance of a volume of lyric poetry entitled *Freiräume* (Free Spaces) and the novel *Anna Göldin, Letzte Hexe* (Anna Göldin, The Last Witch), published in Stuttgart and Zürich, respectively. In her novel Hasler investigates the story of a woman who, as the last known witch in Europe, was sentenced by an official court and consequently executed. This occurred on June 18, 1782, at the time of the German *Aufklärung*, when the expression "judicial death" was coined to describe the case.

In her carefully researched novel the author presents the picture of an unusual woman, independent, who radiates a sensual power; she raises herself from poor beginnings only to become the victim in a power struggle of the then ruling families. Described as impressive, thrilling, vivid and sensitive, the novel has won much praise from contemporary critics who claim that it " . . . draws on artistic intuition as much as on its expert subject knowledge."

Eveline Hasler is now married with three children and lives and writes in St. Gallen.

Works

Novemberinsel [November Island] (1980). *Freiräume* [Free Spaces] (1982). *Anna Göldin, letzte Hexe* [Anna Göldin, Last Witch] (1982).

Warwick J. Rodden

Ebba Haslund

Born 1917, Seattle, Washington
Genre(s): novel, short story, essay
Language(s): Norwegian

Ebba Haslund made her literary debut in 1945 with a collection of short stories, *Også Vi*. Since that time she has published almost a dozen novels, short stories, essays and articles, radio plays and children's books.

Det hendte ingenting, first published in 1948, explores the friendship and love between three young women at the University of Oslo just prior to the Second World War. Ignored by the critics at the time, it was rediscovered as one of a very few Norwegian novels to deal with women's love for each other and republished in 1981. In 1988 it was published in English translation as *Nothing Happened.*

Drøømmen om Nadja (1956) shows the damage that can be caused by a childhood lacking in love and stability, and how expectations and dreams can kill the reality.

In *Bare et lite sammenbrudd* (1975) Haslund is concerned, as she is in many of her other works, with society's expectations of women's roles, and especially with the expectations of motherhood as it is often used to keep women in their place. Many of her children's books also explore gender roles in our society, viewed from a feminist perspective. Haslund writes with understanding and irony about marital and family relationships in a contemporary middle-class Oslo milieu.

Politically active, Haslund was the first woman to chair the Norwegian Writers' Union, holding that position from 1971–1975. Ebba Haslund is one of Norway's most popular and best-selling writers, both in adult and children's literature. She is also one of Norway's leading feminist writers and takes an active role in Norwegian cultural life.

Works

Også Vi [We Too] (1945). *Siste halvår* [The Last Half Year] (1946). *Det hendte ingenting* [Nothing Happened] (1948). *Middag hos Molla* [Dinner at Molla's] (1951). *Frøken Askeladd* [Miss Ashlad] (1953). *Krise i august* [Crisis in August] (1954). *Drømmen om Nadja* [The Dream About Nadja]

(1956). *Tøff kar, Petter* [Cool Guy, Petter] (1958). *Barskinger på Brånåsen* [Tough Guys on Branasen] (1960). *Hvor går du Vanda?* [Where Are You Going, Vanda?] (1960). *Miss Eriksen oppdager Amerika* [Miss Eriksen Discovers America] (1964). *Det trange hjerte* [The Constricted Heart] (1965). *Syndebukkens krets* [The Scapegoat's Circle] (1968). *Aldri en grå hverdag* [Never a Gray Day] (1970). *Midlertidig stoppested* [Temporary Stop] (1972). *Bare et lite sammenbrudd* [Just a Little Breakdown] (1972). *Hver i sin verden* [Each in Their Own World] (1976). *Født til klovn* [Born a Clown] (1977). *Opprør i nr. 7* [Revolt in No. 7] (1977). *Behag og bedrag* [Pleasure and Deceit] (1978). *Kvinner, fins de?* [Do Women Exist?] (1980). *Mor streiker* [Mother Goes on Strike] (1981). *Skritt i mørke* [Footsteps in the Dark] (1982). *Hønesvar til hanefar* [The Hen's Answer to the Rooster] (1983). *Døgnfluens lengsel* [The Mayfly's Longing] (1984). *Spurv i hanedans* [Sparrow in the Rooster Dance] (1986). *Som plommen i egget* [The Life of Riley] (1984). *Men Benny, da* [But Benny, Then] (1988). *Med vingehest i manesjan* [With Pegasus in the Circus Ring] (1989).

Translations: *Nothing Happened*, tr. Barbara Wilson (Seattle, 1987). "Santa Simplicitas," tr. Katherine Hanson, in *An Everyday Story*, Katherine Hanson, ed. (Seattle, 1984), pp. 166–180.

Torild Homstad

Kristina Hasselgren

Born 1920, Stockholm, Sweden
Genre(s): novel
Language(s): Swedish

Kristina Svanfelt finished her schooling after the required eight years, then worked at a variety of jobs. Later she received stipends and traveled variously to England, France, Germany, Italy, the United States and Japan. She was married to Stig Hasselgren between 1942–1944 and to Vilgot Sjöman from 1955 to 1960. As a writer she retained the name of her first husband. Relatively late in life, in 1968 she continued her education at Stockholm's University where she studied literature, Nordic languages, aesthetics and religion. She stopped in 1971 with her phil. cand.

A fashion consultant for 21 years (1942–1963), Kristina Hasselgren began her writing career with the publication of her "prose lyric" *Sandmålning* (Sand Painting) in 1956. A novel about the world of fashion, *Nöjet är en ros* (Pleasure is a Rose), followed in 1959. Her second novel, *Vinterberättelse* (A Winter Story), deals with the famine in early nineteenth century Sweden. However, Kristina Hasselgren is best known for her trilogy *Anna Carolina* (1967), *Stora flickan* (1975; The Big Girl) and *Känslokapitalisterna* (1979; The Emotion Capitalists). It is the story of the foster child Anna Carolina, her growing up in a loveless, uncaring world and the scars her experiences leave on the sensitive girl's psyche. Largely autobiographical, the story of Anna Carolina is, at the same time, an indictment against the mores and social conditions of Swedish society in the twenties. Her stories helped to obtain more humane legislation for foster children.

The story itself may not be new. But Hasselgren, influenced by the unconventional writing of Alexander Kluge, Gabriele Wohmann and Monique Wittig, "dared to leave the conventional, traditional form of storytelling" for something that to her feels truer and more in character with what she has to say, as Hasselgren explains. Her remarkable experimental form gives her books an artistic, very personal perspective.

In 1986 Hasselgren published a translation from English of *The Tale of Genji*, an eleventh century tale by the Japanese noblewoman Murasaki Shikibue. Hasselgren is very active in the Swedish movement against atomic weapons and the International P.E.N.

Works

Sandmålning (1956). *Nöjet är en ros* (1959). *Vinterberättelse* (1965). *Anna Carolina* (1967). *Stora Flickan* (1975). *Känslokapitalisterna* (1979). Essays: "Det manipulerande språket" [The Manipulating Language], *Vårt arbete för freden* [Our Work for Peace] (1985). "Mod att vara skrivande," *Tryckpunkter* (1967): 103–111.

Bibliography

Algulin, Ingemar, *Contemporary Swedish Prose* (Stockholm, 1983), pp. 52–53, 87. Lundqvist, Åke, "Vi måste värna om rätten att misslyckas." *Dagens Nyheter* (May 19, 1973), n.p. (Interview).

Hanna Kalter Weiss

Klara Hätzlerin

Born sometime before 1450, Augsburg,
Germany; died sometime after 1476,
Augsburg
Genre(s): transcription
Language(s): German

Klara Hätzlerin was one of the first tran-scriptionists of medieval books in Germany. She was registered as a taxpayer in the *Augsburg Register* for the years 1452–1476. Many critics believed she was a nun, but Ruth Westermann in *The German Literature of the Middle Ages* finds this untenable because of Hätzlerin's entry as a taxpayer in Augsburg. Karl Bartsch in his article in the *Allgemeine Deutsche Biographie* indicates that she was a nun in Augsburg and that her transcriptions are all contained in the Heidelburg Manuscripts of the fifteenth century.

Not much is known about her life either as a private citizen or as a nun. Her exact date of birth and exact date of death are also unrecorded.

Hätzlerin is best known for the *Liederbuch* (Songbook), which is located in Prague because it served as the transition from the Minnelied to the folksong. The *Songbook* has only a few songs; it contains mostly poems, narrative and didactic literature. The book is divided into two parts: Part I has 85 narrative poems, and Part II has 134 lyrical poems. In addition, there are 119 am-bivalent proverbs.

Hätzlerin lists some of the poets from whom she has compiled the songs: Heinrich Teichner, Suchenwitt, Suchensinn, Hermann von Sachsenheim, Oswald von Wolkenstein, der Mönch von Salzburg, Jörg Schiller, Rosenplut, Freidank, Neithart. There are also anonymous poems.

Works

Transcriptions: *Die Bekrönung Kaiser Fridricks* [The Crowning of Emperor Frederick] (1467). *Doctor Johann Hartliebs buch aller verbotenen kunst, unglaubens und zauberei* [Doctor Johann Hartliebs' Book Against All Forbidden Necromancy, Unbelief and Sorcery] (n.d.). *Das erst buch vahet also an und lert praissen* [The First Book Begins and Teaches Praise] (1468). *Heinrich Mynsinger, Von den Valcken, habichen, sperbern, pfariden und hunden* [Heinrich Mynsinger: Of Falconry, Hawks, Sparrow Hawks, Peacocks and Dogs] (1471). *Hie hebent sich an die Ehaften und alle recht, die diese statt von ir Herschafft Her hatt pracht* [Now Commence the Honorable and Just Ones Who Have Been Removed from His Majesty by the State] (n.d.). *Liederbuch.* [Songbook] (1471; new ed. Quedlingburg, 1840).

Bibliography

Allgemeine Deutsche Biographie, Hrsg. von der Historischen Kommission bei der Bayer. Akademie der Wissenschaften, ed.: R. von Liliencron and F. X. von Wegele. vol. 11 (Leipzig, 1904). *Die Deutsche Literatur des Mittelalters: Verfasserlexikon*, ed. Wolfgang Stammler, vol. 2 (Berlin, 1936). Gauther, Karl, *Studien zur Liederbuch der Klara Hätzlerin* (Halle, 1899). Krüger, Hermann Anders, *Deutsches Literaturlexikon* (Munich, 1914). *Lexikon deutscher Frauen der Feder*, ed. Sophie Pataky (Bern, 1971).

Brigitte Edith Zapp Archibald

Frederikke (Rinna/Renna) Elisabeth Brun Juul Hauch

Born June 13, 1811, Helsingør (Elsinore),
Denmark; died March 24, 1896,
Frederiksberg, Copenhagen
Genre(s): novel
Language(s): Danish

Together with her husband, the poet Carsten Hauch, Renna Elisabeth Hauch presided over the literary and artistic milieu of Sorø, site of the Sorø Academy on the island of Sjælland (Den-mark). Renna Hauch was well acquainted with the leading literary and intellectual figures of her day, and she maintained a "life-long friendship with [the very important literary critic and scholar] Georg Brandes, who much admired her strong and tolerant nature" (*Dansk Litteraturhistorie*, 475). Renna Hauch was very concerned with modern principles of child-rearing, in the spirit of Rousseau. A member of *Dansk Kvindesamfund* (The Danish Society of Women) in the 1870s and an elderly but still active, engaged participant in the fledgling Social Democratic Movement, Renna Hauch managed to raise a large family, preside over Sorø intellectual society, and establish her own independent intellectual connections. The author of several smaller narratives and two novels, *Tyrolerfamilien* (1840; The Tyrol Family, with an introduction by Carsten Hauch) and *Frue Werner*(1844; Mrs. Werner), Renna Hauch caused no end of consternation in Sorø "with her nude bathing, her abandonment of the corsette mode [or craze], and with the freedom she accorded her daughters in connection with young men" (*DLH*, 475). Although she never thought of rejecting motherhood as a part of woman's nature, as the natural course for women, Renna Hauch did argue for a free upbringing for young women, for an "educational model of freedom for the individual . . . [who grows up] undeterred by society's norms and conventions" (Stig Dalager and Anne-Marie Mai, *Danske kvindelige forfattere*, 1, p. 180), in an open, free loving home.

Frederikke Renna Elisabeth Brun Juul was born on June 13, 1811, in Helsingør (Elsinore), Denmark. Her parents, who both died while still quite young, were Svend Brun Juul, the city magistrate in Helsingør (1774–1813), and Helene Elisabeth von Munthe af Morgenstierne (1781–1820) (*Dansk biografisk Lekiskon*, "Carsten Hauch," 1979, 86). Renna Juul grew up in the cultured home of her uncle Wullf; he was a military commander and a renowned translator of all the works of William Shakespeare. At the age of seventeen, Renna Juul was married to the 40-year-old poet, Carsten Hauch, and thereby firmly established in the artistic and literary milieu of Sorø. Renna Hauch wrote her first novel, *Tyrolerfamilien*, in 1840; her husband Carsten Hauch offered a foreword to the story of Marie who flees both her family and the patriarchal Copenhagen society to become the wife of a peasant in the Tyrol. Renna Hauch's other novel, *Frue Werner*, was published in 1844, when her own daughters were nearly grown and she was thirty-three; Hauch's second novel deals with the widow Mrs. Werner's attempts to raise her daughter Marie "far from the multifaceted society of the city" (*DLH*, 475), in a free, natural, open milieu, and, with the dual processes of sexual maturation and *løsrivelse*, letting go. Renna Hauch lived a "long life of engagement in the new radical trends of the time" (*DLH*, 477); many of her ideas won a ready, receptive, tolerant audience among the poets, writers, and artists of

Sorø. Hauch won the recognition of her many friends and intellectual associates for her practical endeavor, her social engagement, and for her role as "the poetic muse, 'sagakvinden' (the saga woman), as the poets admiringly called her" (*DLH*, 477). Renna Hauch died in Frederiksberg, Copenhagen, on March 24, 1896, at the age of eighty-five, after a life of intellectual and social commitment.

Renna Hauch's first novel, *Tyrolerfamilien*, depicts a young, motherless protagonist, Marie; Marie has family roots in the cultured civil servant class, but she flees a vindictive step-mother, who forbids Marie's piano-playing, her music; a punitive upbringing at the hands of her uncle; and a constrictive, authoritarian Copenhagen milieu, to travel to the Tyrol and an alternative to the urban, civil life of Copenhagen women. Marie is "robust, engaged, strong, a courageous young girl" (Dalager, 1, p. 190), who undertakes the trip from Copenhagen to the Tyrol completely alone and frequently employs her strength, intelligence, and pluck to save herself from dangerous, threatening situations. Marie becomes the passionate, loving wife of a peasant, Franz; as Hauch suggests, Marie's passion for Franz is a dangerous feeling which burdens their mutual relationship. In *Tyrolerfamilien*, Hauch describes a marriage based solely on love; her second novel, *Frue Werner*, proposes an alternative to all-encompassing marital passion—the marriage based on nurturing, sheltering, and protection. Frue Werner has given her young daughter Marie a careful, protective upbringing, a good home. Marie falls in love with a young man, Erhard Selmer; as an informed and free-thinking widow, Frue Werner "does not oppose [her] daughter's love but helps with [the transition, the inevitable] letting go" (*DLH*, 475). Frue Werner even negotiates the rough waters of passion with her daughter, also instructing Erhard in the need for young men to "go slowly," to "win the love of their young wives before they win their bodies" (*DLH*, 476). Erhard becomes a protective, sheltering substitute for Frue Werner; when Marie's mother suddenly falls ill, Erhard is summoned to the dying woman's bed, to marry, to step in as Marie's protector and as Frue Werner's "surviving alter ego" (*DLH*, 476). Sexual passion between marriage partners, between Marie and

Erhard as intellectual and psychological equals, is suppressed or hidden in fleeting dream episodes, in visions or symbols, and Erhard assumes the watchful role once played by the caring and careful Frue Werner.

Renna Hauch was at the center of a lively, stimulating, intellectual circle of poets, writers, playwrights, composers, and artists at Sorø. Together with Carsten Hauch, she came in close contact with the leading literary and cultural figures of the day, and she won no small measure of their admiration and esteem. Hauch never questioned the naturalness of her role as mother or wife, and she did not dispute the given sexual division of work; Hauch did, however, support a free, positive, liberal education that would enable young women to use their talents and give their natural curiosity free rein. Renna Hauch committed herself to the causes of educational reform and social justice, and she played an active role in the Danish literary circles and society of her day.

Works

Tyrolerfamilien (1840). Frue Werner (1844).

Bibliography

Dalager, Stig, and Anne-Marie Mai, Danske kvindelige forfattere 1: Fra Sophie Brahe til Mathilde Fibiger. Udvikling or perspektiv. 2 vols. (København, 1983). "Carsten Hauch." Dansk biografisk Leksikon (1979). Dansk Litteraturhistorie (København, 1985).

Lanae Hjortsvang Isaacson

Marlen Haushofer

Born 1920, Frauenstein, Upper Austria; died 1970, Vienna
Genre(s): novel, novella, children's literature
Language(s): German

Marlen Haushofer, née Frauendorfer, studied German literature in Vienna and Graz after having had to do one year of social service in East Prussia under the Nazis in 1939. She married a dentist, whom she assisted, and raised two boys, living in Steyr. She tried to convince her husband that "being a writer is not a hobby like crocheting," but finally divorced him in 1956. When she remarried him two years later, it was not because problems were resolved, but because she was made to accept her guilt feelings. Since that time, her writing, in which males play a less-than-heroic role, became an attempt to come to terms. She has received the Schnitzler Prize in 1963, year of her best novel, Die Wand, and twice the Vienna children's book prize, in 1965 and 1967.

Marlen Haushofer's works have women characters who are forced to cope with strange painful events for which they have never been prepared. In Die Wand (The Wall), after a nuclear-like event that obliterates the rest of the world, a woman survives in an unknown dense forest with only a dog and a cow. Forcing herself to be cheerful and industrious, she slides into bouts of depression and chronic sleep, while one catastrophe after another turns against her, until she dies, spent like a burned-down candle. Representing a powerful reaction to the nuclear obsessions of the 1950s, this book nevertheless stands out in that it presents no social or family situation, but rather one woman alone. Similarly, her last novel, Die Mansarde, deals with isolated and depressed human beings lost in a melancholy haze of pain, anguish, and meaninglessness.

Works

Das fünfte Jahr (1951). Eine Handvoll Leben (1955). Die Vergissmeinnichtquelle (1956). Die Tapetentür (1957). Wir töten Stella (1958). Die Wand (1963). Himmel der nirgendwo endet (1966). Die Mansarde (1968).

Bibliography

Lorenz, Dagmar C.G., "Marlen Haushofer—eine Feministin aus Österreich." Modern Austrian Literature 12, 3/4 (1979).

Ute Marie Saine

Hedyle

Born 4th c. B.C.
Genre(s): elegiac poetry
Language(s): Greek

Hedyle came from a literary family, most probably in Athens. Her mother, Moschine, was a composer of iambic verses and her son, Hedylus, was well known c. 270 B.C. as a writer of epigrams. She may well have been one of the Athenian settlers sent out to the island of Samos in the first half of the 3rd century B.C.

In the course of discussions of the mythological figure Glaukos, Athenaeus (7.297A) quotes the only surviving piece of Hedyle's work: a five-line fragment from her poem entitled *Skylla*. The poem was written in elegiacs and appears to have been one of the several Hellenistic treatments of the story of Skylla which lie behind the Ovidian version (*Metamorphoses* 13.730 ff.) The pseudo-Virgilian *Ciris* represents another tradition. The five lines describe how Glaukos shyly brought gifts of seashells and kingfisher nestlings to his beloved, but unresponsive, Skylla and how even the virginal Siren felt sorry for him as he wept.

Little or no assessment of Hedyle's talents can be made from these few lines, but she seems to have shared the general Alexandrian interest in small picturesque details, displays of learning, and unhappy or unusual love affairs.

Bibliography

A text and translation are to be found in Athenaeus, *The Deipnosophists*, translated by C.B. Gulick, *Loeb Classical Library*, vol. 3 (London, 1929), pp. 330–333. For other Hellenistic treatments of the story, see G. Knaack's "Hellenistische Studien," *Rheinisches Museum für Philologie* 57 (1902), 205–230. On Skylla and Glaukos in general, see W.H. Roscher, *Ausführliches Lexikon der griechischen und römischen Mythologie* (Leipzig, 1884–), sub vv.

David H.J. Larmour

Johanne Luise Heiberg

Born November 22, 1812, Copenhagen, Denmark; died December 21, 1890, Copenhagen
Genre(s): autobiography, biography, drama, letters, poetry
Language(s): Danish

From her debut in 1826 until her retirement from the Royal Theater in 1864, Johanne Luise Heiberg was the most celebrated Danish actress of her time. As the wife of Johan Ludvig Heiberg, whom she married in 1831, Heiberg occupied a position at the center of the intellectual bourgeoisie that gathered in the Heibergs' *salon* in the 1830s and 1840s.

Heiberg's literary career began with the vaudevilles *En Søndag paa Amager* (1848; A Sunday on Amager) and *Abekatten* (1849; The Monkey), written at the height of her stage popularity. In a series of anonymous articles published in the 1850s, Heiberg saw contemporary attempts at "ladies' emancipation" as unnatural and advocated a return to domesticity and traditionalism.

After her husband's death, Heiberg edited the correspondence between his parents in *Peter Andreas Heiberg og Thomasine Christine Gyllembourg I-II* (1882), but her most important literary contribution remains *Et Liv, Gjenoplevet i Erindringen I-IV* (A Life, Relived in Memory), which she began in 1855. Conceived as a polemical defense of Johan Ludvig Heiberg's disputed theatrical politics, *Et Liv* also analyzes and discusses Heiberg's many dramatic roles and the literary personalities who created them.

Heiberg's correspondence, however, more authentically reveals the woman behind the mask. Her letters to her husband are studies in sublimation and self-discipline, qualities essential to Heiberg's domestic role as the perfect, cultivated wife and hostess.

Johanne Luise Heiberg has traditionally entered literary history as the muse of romantic and romantist playwrights such as Oehlenschläger, Herz and Heiberg. Heiberg's own writings are modeled on the period's idealized femininity, which she epitomized, but they also represent a budding female *öffentlichkeit* emerging from respectable bourgeois drawingrooms.

Works

En Søndag paa Amager (1848). *Abekatten* (1849). "Quinde-Emancipation" (1851). "Ogsaa et Ord on Quindens Huuslige Dyder" (1857). "Om Huusvaesenet og Pigebørns Opdragelse" (1859). *Et Liv, Gjenoplevet i Erindringen* I-IV (1855–1885). *Peter Andreas Heiberg og Thomasine Christine Gyllembourg: En Beretning Støttet paa Efterladte Breve* I-II (1882). *Johanne Luise Heiberg og Andreas Frederik Krieger: En Samling Breve 1860–1889* I-II, ed. Aage Friis and P. Munch (1914–1915). *Fra Det Heibergske Hjem: Johan Ludvig og Johanne*

Luise Heibergs Indbyrdes Brevveksling, ed. Aage Friis (1940). *Breve fra og til Johanne Luise Heiberg*, ed. Just Rahbek (1955).

Bibliography

Aschengreen, Erik, *Fra Trine Rar til Maria Stuart: En Studie i fru Heibergs Kunst* (Copenhagen, 1961). Fenger, Henning and Frederick J. Marker, *The Heibergs* (New York, 1971). Forssberger, Anna, *Johanne Luise Heiberg: Ekko og Spejling*, tr. Inger Holm-Jacobsen (Copenhagen, 1973). Hude, Elisabeth, *Johanne Luise Heiberg som Brevskriver* (Copenhagen, 1964). Kierkegaard, Søren Aa., *Crisis in the Life of an Actress and Other Essays on Drama*, tr. and ed. Stephen Crites (New York, 1967). Larsen, Hanna Astrup, "Johanne Luise Heiberg." *American-Scandinavian Review* 34 (June 1946): 103–112. Levy, Jette Lundbo, "Johanne Luise Heiberg: Et Kvindeligt Redskab i Borgerskabets Klassekamp." *Teaterarbejde* 4 (1979): 62–72. Marker, Lise-Lone and Frederick J., "Fru Heiberg: A Study of the Art of the Romantic Actor." *Theatre Research* 13 (1973): 22–37. Rahbek, Just, *Omkring Johanne Luise Heiberg* (Copenhagen, 1948).

Clara Juncker

Claudine Helft

Born June 5, 1937, Paris, France
Genre(s): poetry, essay
Language(s): French

Born in Paris, just prior to the Second World War, into an old French family of "Israelite confession," Claudine Helft (née Wallier) studied journalism before working with the newspaper *Combat* and the "Association Méditerranéenne." In 1960 she married the art expert Léon Helft. She has only one son. She has undertaken graphological studies, founded a youth group within the Aid to Israel organism, and published literary reviews and commentaries. Her first volume of poetry appeared in 1975: *L'Entre-deux* (Interspace). Upon the death of her husband in 1983, she took up the literary management of the Editions du Hameau and in 1985, began a regular broadcast on Radio Cosmopolitique.

Parhélies (1979; Parhelions) is the third volume of poetry by Claudine Helft and reveals her rapid maturation as a poet. Her poetry does not retire into self-esteem or aestheticism nor into impotence and idle fury. It recognizes the anguish of loss and suffering, the fragility of speech and writing, yet it opts for love. Poetic language, for Claudine Helft, becomes a channel for possibility, giving, extension, reconciliation, prayer, divinity: "a perfect equation of other to self, self to universe."

Métamorphosis de l'ombre (1984; Metamorphosis of the Shadow) also illustrates this well. It is Claudine Helft's most recent collection although she has since published with Louise Le Roux a book of writings on writing, by other contemporary authors, along with graphological analyses. *Métamorphosis de l'ombre* is a book of grieving and pain; yet it manages to opt for a faith in being, in what still remains possible.

Works

Poetry: *L'Entre-deux* (1975). *Un risque d'absolu* (1976). *Parhélies* (1979). *Métamorphosis de l'ombre* (1984).

Essay: *Visages de l'écriture* (1985).

Bibliography

Bosquet, Alain, "Claudine Helft." *Figaro* (oct. 1984). "Labarrière—Helft." *Luxemburger Wort* (juill. 1985). Sedir, Georges, "Poésie vivante." *Républicain Lorrain* (sept. 1986).

Michael Bishop

Monika Helmecke

Born October 16, 1943, Berlin, West Germany
Genre(s): short story, radio play
Language(s): German

After training as a stenographer, Monika Helmecke received degrees in financial management and computer science. She lives in Berlin (DDR) with her three children and is at present a housewife and freelance writer.

Helmecke's themes are taken from everyday life. While the stories collected in *Klopfzeichen* transport their ordinary subjects into the realm of fantasy or insanity (the title story describes a young woman's nervous breakdown following an abortion), her newest stories remain entirely in the realm of realistic observations. They inquire into the moments of transition faced by her unexceptional protagonists: a sullen teenage boy confronted with the routines of an old people's home ("Der Neuerervorschlag," 1983); a confused young woman just beginning to understand the complexities of reality ("Prüfungsangst," 1986); a widower coming to terms with the loss of his wife ("Im Spiegel," 1983). The choice of moment and the pedestrian quality of her diction predisposes Helmecke's latest work to an open-endedness that mimics a lack of aesthetic shaping. Yet her quiet, earnest stories about quiet, ordinary people have a plain and straightforward candor about them, and their effect is unusually stimulating.

Works

Klopfzeichen [Pulse Signals], short stories and novellas (1979, 4th ed. 1986);. The story "Die Republik der Tauben," included in this volume, is reprinted in two West German anthologies, *Gespräche hinterm Haus. Neue Prosa aus der DDR* (1981) and *Auskunft 2* (1978). The versions differ slightly. The title story "Klopfzeichen" is reprinted in *Im Kreislauf der Windeln. Frauenprosa aus der DDR* (1982). *Nerz und Masch* [Mink and Mesh], radio play. *Aus der Schule geplaudert* [School Gossip], radio play. *Rose bleibt Rose* [Always Rose], radio play for children. *Hedwig und ihre Enkel* [Hedwig and Her Grandchildren], radio play for children. Numerous publications in literary journals, including: "Der Neuerervorschlag." *Sinn und Form* 35.4 (1983). "Im Spiegel." *NDL* 31.10 (1983). "Missglückter Versuch." *NDL* 32.12 (1984). "Prüfungsangst." *NDL* 34.1 (1986). "Die Steuerhaus-Werkstatt-Schuppen-Werkstatt." *NDL* 34.4 (1986).

Bibliography

Hildebrandt, Christel, *Zwölf schreibende Frauen in der DDR. Zu den Schreibbedingungen von Schriftstellerinnen in der DDR in den 70er Jahren* (Hamburg, 1984), pp. 167–269. Rosenberg, Dorothy, "Another Perspective: Young Women Writers in the GDR." *Studies in GDR Culture and Society, 4. Selected Papers from the Ninth New Hampshire Symposium on the German Democratic Republic,* ed. Margy Gerber (Lanham, Md., 1984), pp. 187–198. Schmitz, Dorothee, *Weibliche Selbstentwürfe und männliche Bilder. Zur Darstellung der Frau in DDR-Romanen der siebziger Jahre* (Frankfurt a.M., 1983). Schmitz-Köster, Dorothee, "DDR-Frauenliteratur der siebziger und achtziger Jahre. Sammelbesprechung." *Feministische Studien* 5.1 (1986); 159–165.

Ann Marie Rasmussen

Heloise

Born c. 1098; died May 15, 1164
Genre(s): letters
Language(s): Latin

Heloise has become one of the most celebrated women of the Middle Ages, largely because of her tragic love affair with the noted philosopher Peter Abelard. She was also well known to her contemporaries as an example of feminine learning.

Born to a wealthy Parisian family, Heloise was noted for her devotion to classical studies early in life. Her family engaged Abelard as her tutor. Their subsequent affair led to the birth of a child, named Astralabe, Abelard's castration by Heloise's enraged uncle, and Heloise's eventual entrance into the convent of Argenteuil. On the close of that convent, the community took refuge at the Paraclete, an abbey founded by Abelard, who had by then left for Britanny. Heloise became the new convent's first abbess and presided over its flourishing growth. She was buried beside her former lover in the cemetery of the Paraclete, but in 1817 both their remains were moved to Père-Lachaise cemetery in Paris.

Heloise's most famous works are three letters to Abelard that survive as collected with Abelard's lengthy replies and other of Abelard's letters, including the famous *Story of My Misfortunes*. Heloise's letters indicate an abiding love for Abelard. She stressed her service to him, which continued even in her religious vocation: "I have kept nothing back for myself, unless to become yours now even more." Heloise reproached her absent lover for his refusal to aid her. When Abelard replied, he advised her to redirect her love from him to God. This correspondence created the famous legend of their love affair, which inspired such varied writers as Jean de Meun, Dante, and Petrarch. The authenticity of this corpus is, however, problematic. Some have suggested that Abelard himself, or perhaps some third party, wrote the entire correspondence as a comprehensive treatise on love. Others have maintained the authenticity of Heloise's authorship of the letters attributed to her in the manuscripts. While the question remains unanswered, the problems surrounding the authenticity of these letters are sufficient to require the historian to use them with care. In any case, the letters are valuable evidence for the development of ideas about love and the human personality in the twelfth century.

Apart from these letters, Heloise sent a series of theological questions, chiefly concerning scriptural passages, to Abelard. They survive, together with Heloise's covering letter and Abelard's replies, in a text known as the *Problemata*. A brief letter from Heloise to Peter the Venerable, the powerful abbot of Cluny who protected Abelard in his last years, also survives. No one has seriously questioned Heloise's authorship of these works.

Works

Letters to Peter Abelard in J.T. Muckle, "The Personal Letters Between Abelard and Heloise." *Medieval Studies* 15 (1953): 47–94; in J.T. Muckle, "The Letter of Heloise on Religious Life and Abelard's First Reply." *Medieval Studies* 17 (1955): 240–281; and Peter Abélard, *Historia Calamitatum*, J. Monfrin, ed. (1967). "Letter to Peter the Venerable," in G. Constable, ed., *The Letters of Peter the Venerable*, 2 vols. (1967), I, pp. 400–401. *Problemata* in J.P. Migne, ed., *Patrologia Latina*, vol. 178, cols. 677–730.

Bibliography

Bourgain, P., "Héloise," in *Abélard en son temps* (1981), pp. 211–237. Dronke, P., *Abelard and Heloise in Medieval Testimonies* (1976). Gilson, E., *Héloïse et Abelard* (1964). Thomas, R., et al., eds., *Petrus Abaelardus (1079–1142). Person, Werk und Wirkung* (1980) (articles by Luscombe, Benton, and Dronke). van den Eynde, D., "Chronologie des écrits d'Abélard pour Héloïse," *Antonianum* 37 (1962): 337–349.

General references: *Lexicon für Theologie und Kirche* I, 5–6. *New Catholic Encyclopedia* VI, 1014.

Thomas Head

Amalie von Helvig

*Born August 16, 1776, Weimar, Germany;
    died December 17, 1831, Berlin*
*Genre(s): short verse drama, tale, poetry,
    translation*
Language(s): German

Von Helvig was recognized early by leading figures of Weimar Classicism. After her marriage, while living in Heidelberg and later in Berlin, she associated with members of the Heidelberg Romantic movement.

Shortly after her birth, her family moved to Nürnberg where she was educated by her father who taught her English and French. Amalie also spent some time at a *Pension* in Erlangen. Her father died when she was twelve; she and her mother then returned to Weimar. As the niece of Frau von Stein, Amalie and her mother socialized with Goethe in Weimar and Schiller in Jena. Amalie was inspired by them to learn Greek in order to read Homer in the original. She also studied painting and drawing with some success. Goethe and Schiller admired her early poetic efforts although Schiller felt that she had no vocation as a writer. Goethe admired her poetry as well as her painting. About 1800 she became a lady-in-waiting to Duchess Luise of Weimar. Many of her short dramatic works and poems were written for the ladies of the court. In 1802 she met the Swedish officer Carl von Helvig and was married the following year. In late 1804 she reluctantly moved to Stockholm, realizing that her marriage would bring her brief writing career to an end. She believed that women had less opportunity for study and self-expression in Sweden than in Germany. Suffering from extreme homesickness, Amalie von Helvig returned to Germany with her three children in 1810. While living in Heidelberg she met Achim von Arnim and Clemens Brentano who stimulated her interest in Germanic folklore. Following the deaths of two children in 1811, she devoted herself to her writing. Germanic and Catholic influences are strongly evident in her book of folktales, written with Friedrich la Motte Fouqué. Her husband visited her in 1812, but Napoleon had him arrested and sent to Mainz; Amalie was able to arrange his release through her contacts with the Weimar court. In 1814 she returned to

Sweden for a visit and while staying in Uppsala met contemporary Swedish writers. Returning to Germany in 1815 she settled in Berlin with her husband, who had joined the Prussian army. She reassumed her connection with Romantic writers and became friends with Bettine von Arnim and Gneisenau. She wrote art criticism for several journals, published reports of her travels, and worked for Greek independence. She died in Berlin on December 17, 1831.

Von Helvig never challenged traditional women's roles, viewing the possibilities for women as limited. She felt she had moderately crossed the boundaries set for women by becoming a writer, and yet she defended women as writers since they could offer their feminine perspective. Amalie believed that bright independent women were usually unhappy.

Working within the feminine realm, she wrote occasional poetry and two "dramatic idyls" for the court and her family: *Die Schwestern auf Corcyra* (The Sisters of Corfu), written in 1806 and published in 1812; and *Die Tageszeiten. Ein Cyklus griechischer Zeit und Sitte, in 4 Idyllen* (The Hours: A Cycle of Greek Times and Morals in 4 Idyls), which also appeared in 1812. Schiller published her works in his journals *Die Horen* (The Hours) and the *Musenalmanach* (Muses' Almanach). The first is a poem in six cantos, *Abdallah und Balsora* (1797; Abdallah and Balsora). Her most significant work is *Die Schwestern von Lesbos* (The Sisters of Lesbos), a poem in six songs written in hexameters and edited by Goethe who taught her to write in this form. First published in Schiller's *Musenalmanach für 1800* (Muses' Almanach for 1800) and then independently, it was a popular success, reprinted three times. It is set in ancient Greece, depicting the tale of two "sisters," one noble and one a foundling, who loved the same man. At the wedding of the noble couple, Likoris stabs herself in despair. Recognizing her sister's true love, the noble sister gives her betrothed to Likoris. Other works in verse are: "Das Fest der Hertha" (The Festival of Hertha), *An Deutschlands Frauen. Von einer ihrer Schwestern* (1816; To Germany's Women: From One of Her Sisters), and *Sammlung von Gedichten zum Besten der unglücklichen Witwen und Waisen in Griechenland* (1826; Collection of Poems for the Unhappy Widows

and Orphans in Greece). The latter was published to raise money for Greek relief efforts. Her interest in folklore is revealed in: *Taschenbuch der Sagen und Legenden* (1812, 1817; Pocketbook of Sagas and Legends), which she edited with Fouqué and *Die Sage vom Wolfsbrunnen, dem Nekarthal entsprungen, mit Hineinverwebung nordischer Überlieferungen* (1821; The Saga of the Wolf's Well from the Nekar Valley, Interwoven with Nordic Motivs). In 1824 she also published a novel, *Helene von Tournon*. In addition to her fictional writings, von Helvig wrote *Die Rheinreise im Oktober 1811 und der Sommertag im Norden. Fragmente aus dem Tagebuche von A.v. Helvig* (The Rhine Journey in October 1811 and the Summer's Day in the North. Fragments from the Diary of A.v. Hellvig). Also of note are her reviews of art exhibitions for Friedrich Schlegel's journal, *Deutsches Museum* (1812, 1813; German Museum). Amalie von Helvig's experiences in Sweden led to translations of works by contemporary Swedish writers and the widely circulated *Tegner's Frithofs-Sage* (1826; Tegner's Saga of Frithof).

Bibliography

Bissing, Henriette von, *Das Leben der Dichterin Amalie von Helvig, geb. Freiin von Imhoff* (Berlin, 1889). Düntzer, Heinrich, "Die Dichterin Amalie von Imhoff zu Weimar." *Westermanns Monatshefte* 61 (1886/7): 368–383, 526–541.

General references: Elschenbroich, Adalbert, "Amalie von Helvig." *Neue Deutsche Biographie*, pp. 568–569. von Liliencron, "Amalie von Helwig." *Allgemeine Deutsche Biographie* 11, pp. 714–715.

Marjanne E. Goozé

Marie Hennerová

(see: Marie Pujmanová)

Emmy Hennings

Born 1885, Flensburg, Germany; died 1948, Sorengo-Lugano
Genre(s): novel, poetry, biography
Language(s): German

The daughter of a ship rigger in a seaport, Emmy married a printer (Hennings) when she was seventeen, and both went into the theater. Abandoned by Hennings, she became a well-known performer in satirical cabarets. In 1913, Franz Werfel published her first collection of poems, *Die letzte Freude,* in his prestigious expressionist series *Der Jüngste Tag.* In 1913–1914, she met Hugo Ball, initiator of the dadaist Cafe Voltaire in Zurich, whom she married in 1920. Emmy Hennings offered her considerable charisma as a performer to the dadaists and significantly contributed to their success among the public. Nevertheless, she is an interesting writer in her own right.

Her most revealing text is the novel *Gefängnis,* in which a young female shoplifter undergoes the agonies of incarceration, reduced to a rock-bottom existence of self-doubt and hope. This haunting text, avoiding both expressionist pathos and dadaist stance—except for certain satirical descriptions of people—is written in the laconic staccato of *reportage.* The novel was republished in 1980—a hopeful sign that it will emerge from undeserved obscurity.

After 1920, the couple lived an increasingly withdrawn and religious, but also poverty-stricken, life. Hennings maintained a moving correspondence with Hermann Hesse, who often helped the Balls financially. After Ball's death in 1927, she was reduced to working in factories, devoting her free time to books about her mate and her childhood.

Quite as much as her fiction, her poetry deserves to be reread. It blends Romantic and folkloric motifs with an almost Rilkean voice, creating at times strikingly abstract images reminiscent of orphist or cubist painting.

Works

Die letzte Freude(1913). Das Gefängnis(1918). Das Brandmal (1920). Helle Nacht (1922). Das ewige Lied(1923). Der Gang zur Liebe(1926). Hugo Ball. Sein Leben in Briefen und Gedichten(1929). Hugo Balls Weg zu Gott (1931). Blume und Flamme (1938). Der Kranz (1939). Das flüchtige Spiel (1940). Ruf und Echo. Mein Leben mit Hugo Ball (1953). Briefe an Hermann Hesse (1956).

Bibliography

Brinker-Gabler, Gisela, *Deutsche Dichterinnen* (Frankfurt, 1986).

Ute Marie Saine

Agnes Kathinka Malling Henningsen

Born November 18, 1868, Ullerslev, Denmark; died April 21, 1962, Copenhagen
Genre(s): novel, autobiography, drama
Language(s): Danish

A twentieth-century naturalist who began her career as a protégée of the Brandes brothers and Herman Bang, Agnes Henningsen focused her writings—and her life—on the liberation of love and sexuality from social conventions.

An open marriage to Mads Henningsen, who in 1895 immigrated to the United States after an erotic scandal, left the twenty-seven-year-old Agnes Henningsen with four children by two men, with an undiminished insistence on sexual and social autonomy, and, ultimately, with a body of work devoted to the exploration of female desire.

Henningsen's debut novels, *Glansbilledet* (1899; Glitter) and *Strømmen* (1899; The Stream), both describe stifling feminine enclosures—one a ladies' pension in which the unmarried inmates passively await a knight who might rescue them from marginality; the other, a petit bourgeois provinciality that equates female sexuality with immorality.

While Henningsen in *Polens Døtre* (1901; Daughters of Poland) depicts sexuality as destructive and promotes a platonic man-woman relationship, another early novel, *De Spedalske* (1903; The Lepers) places sexual desire at the center of all emotional, social, and economical relationships. In her trilogy *Kaerlighedens Aarstider* (1927–1930; Seasons of Love), Henningsen explores the dependence and eventual victimization of the sexually awakened woman, who cannot reconcile a conventional existence with her sexual instincts.

The titles of Henningsen's seven volumes of *Erindringer* (1941–1955; Memoirs), which begin with *Let Gang paa Jorden* (1941; Light Walk on Earth), *Letsindighedens Gave* (1943; The Gift of Recklessness) and *Byen Erobret* (1945; Conquered City), suggest the celebration of pleasure and *joie de vivre* that permeates Henningsen's work. In the impressionistic vignettes which make up *Erindringer,* provocative self-revelations blend with descriptions of characters and milieus of her period's Copenhagen.

Henningsen's confessional mode of fiction, her celebration of the erotic female, and her insistence on sexual and social equality make her a precursor of the more politicized generation of women writers who in the 1970s and 1980s continue the quest for female identity and autonomy.

Works

Glansbilledet (1899). *Strømmen* (1899). *Polens Døtre* (1901). *De Spedalske* (1903). *Den Uovervindelige* (1904). *Lykken* (1905). *Elskerinden* (1906). *Ungdommens Fyrste* (1909). *Den Elskede Eva* (1911). *Den Store Kaerlighed* (1917). *Den Guderne Elsker* (1921). *Barnets Magt* (1923). *Den Fuldendte Kvinde* (1925). *Kaerlighedens Aarstider* (1927). *Det Rige Efteraar* (1928). *Den Sidste Aften* (1930). *Le Kun* (1935). *Det Rigtige Menneske* (1938). *Let Gang paa Jorden* (1941). *Letsindighedens Gave* (1943). *Byen Erobret* (1945). *Kaerlighedssynder* (1947). *Dødsfjende-Hjertenskaer* (1949). *Jeg Er Levemand* (1951). *Den Rige Fugl* (1953). *Skygger Over Vejen* (1955). *Druer paa en Digters Bord* (1948). *Vi Ses i Arizona* (1956). *Den Lidenskabelige Pige* (1958). *Bølgeslag* (1959).

Translations: "Spring," tr. Ann and Peter Thornton in *Contemporary Danish Prose: An Anthology*, ed. Elias Bredsdorff (1958).

Bibliography

Dalager, Stig and Anne-Marie Mai, *Danske Kvindelige Forfattere* II. (Copenhagen, 1982), pp. 56–63. Rasmussen, Mary, "Agnes Henningsen: Kaerlighedens Aarstider, 1927." *Litteratur og Samfund* 31 (1980): 140–167. Wamberg, Bodil, "Agnes Henningsen," in *Danske Digtere i Det 20. Aarhundrede* I, ed. Torben Brostrøm and Mette Winge. (Copenhagen, 1980), pp. 315–329. Wamberg, Bodil, *Letsindighedens Pris: En Bog om Agnes Henningsen* (Copenhagen, 1983).

Clara Juncker

Luise Maria Hensel

(a.k.a. Ludwiga, Louise, Luise, Minna)

Born March 30, 1798, Linum, Brandenburg, Germany; died December 18, 1876, Paderborn
Genre(s): religious lyric poetry
Language(s): German

Luise Hensel was born in Linum, Brandenburg in 1798 and wrote her first poems as a child of eight years old. Her father, a Protestant pastor, died when Luise was twelve, and the family moved to Berlin. During the years from 1809 to 1819 when Hensel lived in Berlin, she wrote more than half of her approximately 220 poems. Together with her brother Wilhelm (1794–1861), who later became well-known as a painter and the husband of Fanny Mendelssohn-Bartholdy, she was introduced into artistic and noble circles. Hensel wrote much of her poetry for the artistic gatherings at the home of her friend Hedwig von Stagemann, where she met Wilhelm Muller, Ludwig von Gerlach, and the composer Ludwig Berger. Her "Gärtnerlieder" (Garden Songs) were written for the 1816 production of *Die schöne Müllerin* (The Pretty Miller's Daughter). The same year at the von Stagemann home, Luise Hensel met Clemens Brentano, upon whose life she had a significant impact. Brentano was deeply moved by her religious poetry and sent twenty of Hensel's lyrics in a letter to his brother Christian in 1817. These poems are characterized by their abstract religious subject matter, sentimental tone, and regular rhyme scheme. As with the vast majority of her lyrics, many are comprised of four-line iambic pentameter stanzas with alternating feminine and masculine rhymes. Hensel responded to Brentano's passionate declarations of love with sisterly affection and encouraged him to return to his Catholic faith.

In 1818 Luise Hensel herself converted to Catholicism and spent the rest of her life in service to others. She had a strong desire to become a nun, a wish she never realized because of family obligations, especially the upbringing of the son of her dead sister, Karoline Roch. She left Berlin to work as a companion to the elderly in Munster and Düsseldorf, where she continued to write religious poems. Her literary activity gradually decreased as she worked in various positions—as a nurse to the sick in Koblenz, as a teacher in Boppard and Aachen, as a governess, in Cologne and Wiedenbruck—before finally retiring to a convent in 1874.

Because Hensel did not consider herself a poet, she took little interest in the publication of her works. Clemens Brentano freely altered and edited a number of her poems for Diepenbroch's collection, *Geistliche Blumenstrauß* (1829; Spiritual Bouquet). In 1857 Kletke published *Gedichte von Luise und Wilhelmine Hensel* (Poems of Luise and Wilhelmine Hensel), making changes without Hensel's approval. In 1861, Christoph Schluter in Munster undertook to gather Hensel's poems, working with her to distinguish her own work from Brentano's. Included are "Krippenlieder" (Cradle Songs), poems to Mary and the saints, and occasional poems to friends and relatives. The *Sämtliche Lieder* (Collected Songs) were published in 1869, attained immediate success, and numerous editions followed.

Though not a first-rate poet, Luise Hensel exerted a profound influence on Clemens Brentano, and her religious lyrics evidence a depth of feeling and nobility of conviction.

Works

Geistliche Blumenstrauß, ed. Diepenbroch (1829). *Gedichte von Luise und Wilhelmine Hensel*, ed. Kletke (1857). *Lieder*, ed. Schluter (1869; later eds. 1870, 1877, 1879, 1882, 1898, 1904, 1907, 1909, 1911, 1917, 1922). *Aufzeichnungen und Briefe*, ed. Hermann Cardauns (1916). *Aus Luise Hensel's Jugendzeit: Neue Briefe und Gedichte*, ed. Cardauns (1918). *Lieder: Vollständige Ausgabe*, ed. Cardauns (1923).

Bibliography

Bartscher, F., *Die innere Lebensgang der Dichterin Luise Hensel* (1882). Binder, F., *Luise Hensel* (1885). Flaskamp, F., "Luise Hensel in Groß-Barthen." *Heimatblätter der Gloke* 3.4 (1972). Mathes, J., "Ein Tagebuch Clemens Brentanos für Luise Hensel." *JbFDtHochst* (1971). Reinkens, J.H., *Luise Hensel und ihre Lieder* (1877). Rupprich, H., *Brentano, Luise Hensel, und Ludwig von Gerlach* (1927). Spieker, F., "Brentano und Luise Hensel." *JEGP* 34 (1935). Spieker, F., *Luise Hensel als Dichterin* (1936). Spieker, "Luise Hensel and Wilhelm Muller." *GR* 8 (1933).

Ann Willison

Herchenefreda

Born late sixth century, southwestern France, possibly in the area of Obregue; died early seventh century
Genre(s): letters
Language(s): Latin

Herchenefreda married into a great Gallo-Roman family, the Syagrii. She gave birth to three sons, whom she encouraged to receive a literary education. Desiderius started a career as a courtier and served as a treasurer of the court of King Flothar II of Neustria, where he met St. Arnulf of Metz and St. Eligius. He also served as treasurer of Flothar's son and successor, King Dagobert I, and later for the count of Albi. Another son, Syagrius, became governor of Marseille, and the other, Rusticus, became bishop of Cahors. In 630, Syagrius was killed as governor and Rusticus was murdered in his cathedral. King Dagobert savagely tried to avenge Bishop Rusticus' murder by mutilating some of the murderers, putting some to death, and exiling others. At the pleas of the people, King Dagobert appointed Desiderius bishop to succeed his brother. As bishop, Desiderius worked most zealously for the spiritual and temporal betterment of his diocese. He founded monasteries, fortified the city, and built an aqueduct. He gave his considerable fortune to the diocese in 649.

Three letters that Herchenefreda wrote to her son Desiderius survive. Two of them are filled with moral and spiritual advice. In the first, she admonishes him to know God assiduously, to think about God perpetually, to be faithful to God—always loving and fearing Him. In the second, she tells him to act properly in the name of God, to strive hard for the perfection of his soul, to guard his chastity above all things, and to be cautious in his speech and work. And she tells him to repent quickly if he should do anything evil. In her third letter, Herchenefreda has a desolate and tragic tone, since she writes after the assassination of Syagrius and Rusticus. She mentions that with his father dead and his two brothers murdered, he is her "pious security," and she warns him to protect himself continually in the way of God so that he would not walk into destruction. She encourages him to be strong so that he may bring some good out of his brothers.

Bibliography

Herchenefreda, "Letters to Her Son, Desiderius" ed. Br. Krusch. *Vita Sancti Desiderii Episcopi Cadurcensis. Corpus Christianorum, Series Latina.* Vol. 117 (Turnholt, 1957). Dronke, Peter, *Women Writers of the Middle Ages* (Cambridge, 1984).

Bruce W. Hozeski

Johannes Herdan

(see: Alma Johanna Freifrau von Koenig)

Jenny P. d'Héricourt

(a.k.a. Jeanne-Marie-Fabienne Poinsard, Mme. Marie, Félix Lamb)

Born 1809, Besançon, France; died 1875, Paris
Genre(s): essay, novel
Language(s): French

The civil identity of the French woman who published under the name of Jenny P. d'Héricourt has long been shrouded in mystery. It is now established that she was born to French Protestant parents in Besançon in 1809. Her father died when she was eight, and she moved with her mother and younger sister to Paris. There she was educated and became a teacher. At the time of her marriage in August 1832 to Michel-Gabriel-Joseph Marie, she was the proprietor of a girls' school. The marriage was evidently unhappy and after several years she left her husband. They had no children. During the 1840s Poinsard became a follower of Etienne Cabet, the theorist of French communism, and wrote serialized novels on the misery of the working classes in Cabet's periodical, *Le Populaire*. She has been credited, under the pseudonym of Félix Lamb, with authorship of the novel *Le Fils du reprouvé* (Son of the Outcast), and with several Icarian movement songs.

During the revolution of 1848, Poinsard was an active participant in women's clubs and the revolutionary women's press. Under her pseudonym, "d'Héricourt," derived from her father's birthplace in the Franche-Comte, she signed the published manifesto of the Society for Women's Emancipation. She was probably a contributor to the *Voix des femmes* (Women's Voice), under the name of Jeanne Marie, and was active in Cabet's revolutionary club, the Société fraternelle centrale. She studied medicine privately with a homoeopathic practitioner and apparently became a certified midwife as well.

In the mid-1850s she began to publish extensively in the *Revue philosophique et religieuse* (Philosophical and Religious Review), and in *La Ragione* (Reason, published in Turin). A celebrated polemic with P.-J. Proudhon led in 1860 to the publication of *La Femme affranchie: réponse à MM. Michelet, Proudhon, E. de Girardin, A. Comte et aux autres novateurs modernes* (which appeared in an 1864 English translation as *A Woman's Philosophy of Woman, or Woman Affranchised*). Through her contacts with M.L. Mikhailov and the Shelgunovs, her influence was felt among Russian intellectuals as well.

By the mid-1860s she was living in the United States. Settling in Chicago, she aspired to establish a medical practice for women. During this stay she established ties with American women's rights activists, published a number of articles in the feminist press of the late 1860s, and facilitated contacts between American and French women. She spoke at the 1869 congress of the American Equal Rights Association, advocating the formation of an international association of women. But in articles published in France by her friend Charles Fauvety during this period, she spoke wistfully of her yearning to return to France. By 1873 she was again in Paris, where she became active in the circle centered around *L'Avenir des femmes* (Women's Future), published by Léon Richer. She died suddenly in 1875 and was buried in a common grave in St. Ouen, on the outskirts of Paris.

Works

Le Fils du reprouvé [Son of the Outcast, attributed] (1844). *La femme affranchie; réponse à MM. Michelet, Proudhon, E. de Girardin, A. Comte et aux autres novateurs modernes* [A Woman's Philosophy of Woman, or Woman Affranchised] (1860; rpt 1987). Essays in La *Revue philosophique et religieuse;* La *Ragione;* Le *Droit des femmes;* The *Agitator,* The *Women's Journal;* Solidarité, and other periodicals.

Translations: *A Woman's Philosophy of Woman, or Woman Affranchised: An Answer to Michelet, Proudhon, Girardin, Legouvé, Comte, and Other Modern Innovators* (1864, 1981).

Bibliography

Anteghini, Alessandra, *Socialismo e femminismo nella Francia del XIX, secolo: Jenny d'Héricourt* (Genoa, 1988). Offen, Karen, "A Nineteenth-Century French Feminist Rediscovered: Jenny P. Héricourt." *Signs* 13 (Autumn 1987). Offen, Karen, "Qui est Jenny P. d'Héricourt?: Une Identité rétrouvée." *1848, Révolutions et Mutations au XIXe siècle: Bulletin de la Société d'Histoire de la Révolution de 1848 et des Révolutions du XIXe siècle,* no. 3 (1987).

Karen Offen

Herrad of Hohenberg

Born c. 1130, Alsace; died July 25, 1195, Hohenberg
Genre(s): poetry (encyclopedia)
Language(s): Latin

Herrad served as abbess in the last third of the twelfth century at the convent of Hohenberg where she was active in the reforming effort begun by her predecessor, Relinda. Herrad was once known as Herrad of Landsberg but her connection with the noble family of Landsberg has been seriously questioned.

Herrad is chiefly remembered for *Garden of Delights (Hortus deliciarum),* an encyclopedic collection of texts made c. 1170 for the spiritual and educational benefit of the canonesses. Her contribution was primarily in the form of explanatory verses. The texts provided information on a wide range of biblical, theological, spiritual, and historical topics compiled from sources ranging from the Church fathers to her contemporaries. The collection indicates both the breadth of Herrad's learning and the strength of the library at Hohenberg. *Garden* may have

provided educational lessons that were read aloud to the community.

The unique codex of the work was lavishly illustrated; the final miniatures pictured Herrad and forty-six canonesses gazing upon their predecessors in the community making offerings to its heavenly patrons. This codex was destroyed by fire in 1870, and the work is now known only through the notes and sketches of nineteenth-century scholars; a team of scholars has reconstructed both the texts and the miniatures insofar as is possible. Despite these problems, Herrad's magnificent compilation of words and images stands as a monument of both manuscript illumination and encyclopedic scholarship.

Works

Hortus deliciarum, ed. A. Straub and G. Keller (1879–1899), folio edition with plates; ed. J. Walter (1952), text only with introduction and notes; ed. R. Green, et al., 2 vols. (1979), folio edition with plates, extensive notes, and commentary.

Bibliography

Autenrieth, J., "Einige Bemerkungen zu den Gedichten im Hortus deliciarum Herrads von Landsberg," in *Festschrift Bernhard Bishchoff* (1971), pp. 307–321. Büttner, H., "Studien zur Geschichte des Stiftes Hohenberg im Elsass während des Hochmittelalters," *Zeitschrift für die Geschichte des Oberrheins* 52 (1939): 103–138. Engelhardt, C.M., *Herrad von Landsberg* (1818). Schmidt, C., *Herrade de Landsberg* (1897).

General references: *Dictionaire de Spiritualité,* VII, pp. 366–369. *Lexicon für Theologie und Kirche,* V, pp. 269–270. Manitius, *Geschichte der lateinischen Literatur des Mittelalters,* III, pp. 1010–1014. *New Catholic Encyclopedia,* VI, p. 1082.

Thomas Head

Jeanne Hersch

Born July 13, 1910, Geneva, Switzerland
Genre(s): prose, philosophy
Language(s): French

After attending primary and secondary school in Geneva, Jeanne Hersch went on to study literary history and philosophy at the Paris Sorbonne, in Heidelberg, and Freiburg as well as in Geneva, completing her first university degree there in literary history in 1931. From 1933 to 1955 she taught at the Ecole Internationale in Geneva, interrupting her work with trips to Chile in 1935–1936 and to Thailand in 1938–1939. In 1946 she presented her doctoral dissertation "Etre et la Forme." On receiving her postdoctoral lecturing qualification in 1947, she became private lecturer and from 1956 to 1977 she was Professor of Philosophy at the University of Geneva. Jeanne Hersch was a visiting lecturer at other universities, including Pennsylvania State University (1959) and Hunter College, New York City University during 1961–1962. From 1966 through 1968 she was the Director of the Department of Philosophy at UNESCO in Paris, and in the fall of 1968 she resumed her teaching duties at the University of Geneva. As a representative for Switzerland she was a member of the Executive Council of UNESCO from 1970–1972.

In her distinguished career Hersch has given countless lectures on philosophy and culture at cultural events held by the German Trade Union Congress in Recklinghausen as well as at the Academy of Evangelism in Loccum and the universities of Zürich, Basel, Fribourg and Paris. She has also participated as a group leader in international courses for adult education and for many years was a member of the Swiss Commission at UNESCO. In her work *Die Hoffunug, Mensch zu Sein* (The Hope of Being Human), the author presents speeches and essays in which she takes a stance on the basic questions and concrete problems of our times.

Das Philosophische Staunen (Philosophical Amazement) is qualified as an insight into the history of thinking, portraying the amazement of great philosophers at our world and its multitude of manifestations, along with their conclusions. This has been aptly described as a masterly work by Hersch, a philosopher of international repute. *Schwierige Freiheit: Gespräche mit Jeanne Hersch* (Difficult Freedom: Conversations with Jeanne Hersch) makes it abundantly clear that the author lives for the freedom of the individual in society. The book is strongly autobiographical and gives details on the personal background of Hersch's thinking. We read, "A little nostalgia, much bitterness, to affect the reader: these conversations . . . are impressive, informative, concise and captivate the truth because of Jeanne Hersch's declaration of belief." In these conversations the author fascinates the reader with her inimitable ability to present even the most complex of concepts comprehensibly and interestingly.

Jeanne Hersch currently lives and writes in Geneva.

Works

Entretiens Sur le Temps: sous la direction de Jeanne Hersch et René Poirier [Conversations on Time: Under the Direction of Jeanne Hersch and René Poirier] (1967). *Le Droit d'Etre un Homme* [Birthright of Man] (1968). *Problèmes Actuels de la Liberté* [Contemporary Problems of Freedom] (1973). *Temps Alternés* [Alternate Times] (1976). *L'Individu, est-il Condamné?: Réflexions sur l'Idéologie de la "Mort de l'Homme"* [Is the Individual Condemned?: Reflections on the Ideology of the "Death of Man"] (1978). *Karl Jaspers* (1979). *Antithesen zu den "Thesen zu den Jugendunruhen 1980" der Eidgenössischen Kommission für Jugendfragen: der Feind Heisst Nihilismus* [Antitheses to the "Theses to Youth Unrest 1980" of the Confederate Commission for Youth Problems: the Enemy Is Nihilism], German translation of French original (1982). *Die Voraussetzungen der Freiheit in den Medien: Analysen und Vorschläge* [Prerequisites for Freedom of the Press: Analysis and Suggestions] (1982). *Die Hoffnung, Mensch zu Sein* [The Hope of Being Human]. *Das Philosophische Staunen* [Philosophical Amazement]. *Schwierige Freiheit: Gespräche mit Jeanne Hersch* [Difficult Freedom: Conversations with Jeanne Hersch].

Translation: *Birthright of Man: A Selection of Texts Prepared Under the Direction of Jeanne Hersch* (1969).

Bibliography

Aron, Raymond et al., *Penser dans le Temps: Mélanges Offerts à Jeanne Hersch* [Thinking in Time: a Miscellany of Essays for Jeanne Hersch] (1977). Larese, Dino, *Jeanne Hersch: eine Lebensskizze* [Jeanne Hersch: A Life Sketch] (1976).

Warwick J. Rodden

Henriette Herz

Born September 5, 1764, Berlin, Germany;
died October 22, 1847, Berlin
Genre(s): letters, memoir, travelogue, novel
Language(s): German

Most renowned as a Jewish salonière in the Berlin of the Enlightenment and Classical eras, Henriette Herz' letters and memoirs illuminate that brief period of social tolerance among classes and religions.

The daughter of a Portuguese Jewish family, Henriette de Lemos was born on September 5, 1764 in Berlin. Her father was a physician, and her family socialized with other enlightened Jews in Berlin, particularly with the family of Moses Mendelssohn. His daughter, Dorothea, and Henriette were close friends. Known for her extraordinary beauty and talents, Henriette, even as a young girl, played a prominent role in the Jewish community. At the age of twelve and one-half she was engaged to Marcus Herz, a physician and student of Kant, whom she had never met and who was fifteen years older than she. On December 1, 1799, she was married at the age of fifteen. During her engagement to Herz she was introduced to the reading group which met weekly at Moses Mendelssohn's. While only Jews participated in Mendelssohn's group, a second reading circle, organized by Marcus in the mid-1780s, included all the prominent men and women of Berlin. After her marriage Henriette organized the *Tugendbund* (Society of Virtue), an adolescent group which indulged in games as well as more serious pursuits. The group's organization reflected the influence of the freemasons and the pietists.

These groups, Marcus' lectures in their home, and Henriette's beauty led to her salon of the 1790s. Her home became a center of cultural life in Berlin, a place where Jews, aristocrats, and intellectuals gathered and mixed. Among the visitors were: Alexander and Wilhelm von Humboldt, Jean Paul Richter, Schiller, Mirabeau, Madame de Genlis, and Princess Luise von Radziwill. Many young Jewish women, including Dorothea Mendelssohn-Veit, met their future gentile husbands there. After Herz's death in 1803, she remained alone, and although her close friendship with Friedrich Schleiermacher was the subject of gossip and ridicule, it was platonic. Her friendship with Schleiermacher also led to her conversion to Christianity. Henriette was baptized in a quiet ceremony outside of Berlin in 1817. She then traveled to Italy and did not return to Germany until 1819. Henriette was renowned for her charity work, teaching and assisting impoverished girls and young women. After Marcus' death her financial situation worsened; she became a governess in 1808. Following the Napoleonic Wars her situation improved, but by 1845 she was very poor and Alexander v. Humboldt persuaded King Friedrich Wilhelm IV to give her a grant and a pension on the basis of her charitable activities. She died on October 22, 1847.

Henriette Herz's greatest talents were conversation and languages. She knew Hebrew, Greek, and some Latin; spoke English, French, and Italian with fluency and some Swedish, Danish, and Portuguese; and later in life even studied Turkish and Sanskrit. The two works published during her lifetime were translations of two English travel books. She also wrote two novels which she later destroyed. She did not destroy the fragmentary memoirs begun in 1823 and taken up again in 1829. Henriette burned most of her correspondence shortly before her death but was soon persuaded that this was a mistake. To compensate for its loss she narrated her experiences to Julius Fürst, who wrote them down.

Works

Mungo Parks Reise in das Innere von Afrika in den Jahren 1795–1797. In 12. Bd. *Geschichte der See- und Landreisen* (1799). *Welds des Jüngeren Reise in die vereinigten Staaten von Nordamerika.* In *Magazin von merkwürdigen neuen Reisebeschreibungen* by J.R. Forster (1800). *Henriette Herz. Ihr Leben und ihre Erinnerungen,* ed. J. Fürst (1850). *Schleiermacher und seine Lieben, nach Originalbriefen* (1910). *Henriette Herz. Ihr Leben und ihre Zeit,* ed. Hans Landsberg (1913). *Henriette Herz in Erinnerungen, Briefen und Zeugnissen,* ed. Rainer Schmitz (1984). *Letters to Immanuel Bekker from Henriette Herz, S. Pobeheim and Anna Horkel,* ed. Max Putzel. German Studies in America 6 (1972). German texts with English commentary. *Henriette Herz in*

Erinnerungen, Briefen und Zeugnissen, ed. Rainer Schmitz (1984). Berliner Salon, Erinnerungen und Portraits, ed. Ulrich Jantzki (1985).

Bibliography

Drewitz, Ingeborg, Berliner Salons. Gesellschaft und Literatur zwischen Aufklärung und Industriezeitalter (Berlin, 1965). Geiger, Ludwig, Briefwechsel des jungen Börne und der Henriette Herz (Oldenburg and Leipzig, 1905). Hargrave, Mary, Some German Women and their Salons (New York, 1912). "Henriette Herz," The Jewish Encyclopedia (New York, 1901), Vol. 6, pp. 366–367. Hertz, Deborah, Jewish High Society in Old Regime Berlin (New Haven, 1988). Kühne, Ferdinand Gustav, ed, Deutsche Männer und Frauen. Eine Galerie von Charakteren (1851), pp. 214–244. Meyer, Bertha, Salon Sketches: Biographical Studies of Berliner Salons of the Emancipation (New York, 1938).

Marjanne E. Goozé

Judith Herzberg

Born November 4, 1934, Amsterdam, The
Netherlands
Genre(s): poetry, drama, screenplay
Language(s): Dutch

Judith Herzberg, the daughter of the Zionist lawyer and writer Abel Herzberg, is the author of very accessible poetry that is among the most original in present-day Dutch letters. After her debut in 1961 in the Dutch weekly Vrij Nederland (she enjoyed earning the 25 guilders a poem the paper paid), her talent was quickly recognized. Since then her poems have appeared in various journals, and several collections have been published. Her recent work also includes theater plays and scripts for films and television. Since 1983 she has lived alternately in Ramat-Gan, Israel, and Amsterdam.

Herzberg's poetry is based on a combination of observation and reflection set in simple everyday and often domestic surroundings. The prevailing motifs are the transitoriness of life, the temporariness of relationships, man/woman's futility, fear of illness and old age. Though most of her poems do not have a "happy" outcome, Herzberg stops short of bitterness and cynicism, while her tone remains gentle. She seems to record, ponder, and smile. There is some resemblance to the English poetess Stevie Smith, some of whose poems Herzberg translated, adapted, and included in Strijklicht (1971; Floodlight).

Herzberg's language is close to that of natural speech. She shuns clichés, elaborate and speltout metaphors, and artificial rhetoric. The seemingly "normal" speech is, however, interrupted by (discreet) wordplay, unusual collocations, and unexpected ellipses. Occasionally, English words and lines are interspersed in the Dutch. Herzberg's talent for simple yet poetic phrasing is well illustrated by the beautiful love songs in 27 liefdesliedjes (1971), adaptations of the biblical Song of Songs commissioned by the makers of a children's television program.

Poetry, Herzberg concedes, should have some degree of humor. Communications that seem confidential at first sight make surprising turns, such as in the poem where war "heroes" invited for tea in 1945 seem to have little use for peace, or in the poem of the woman who wants to desperately become an invalid because her husband would then constantly pamper her. Het maken van gedichten en het praten daarover (1977; The Making of Poems and the Talking About Them), a slim volume relating Herzberg's experiences with a poetry workshop she conducted, offers interesting insights into her own poetics.

Precisely because of the "spoken" quality of her poetry, Judith Herzberg was asked to participate in a special project in which Dutch authors were invited to write for the theater. She adapted, translated, and wrote various plays for the Amsterdam group Baal.

Leedvermaak (1982; Gloating), a combination of theatrical and musical performance, received the 1982 prize of theater criticism. At a wedding reception fourteen people are trying to probe into each other's past lives and experiences during World War II. The question of man's responsibility towards one's fellow human beings and the problem of how to survive despite the memory of Auschwitz underlies the play. En/of (1985; And/Or) pictures the fake tolerance and emotions of a seemingly perfect triangle—a takeoff on the permissive sixties. The chamber opera *Marg* (1986; Marrow) renders the pain and emotions of two brothers, one of whom needs a transplant from the other.

Judith Herzberg collaborated on or wrote the script of various Dutch and international films. *Charlotte*, on the life of the Jewish painter Charlotte Salomon who died in Auschwitz, was favorably received at the Venice Film Festival.

In her theater work as well as in her poetry, Herzberg has proved to be a fine observer of people's behavior and emotions. She does not take sides or fight for a cause. Her only commitment seems to be to the daily life of modern men and women. Her novel and original voice has gained wide critical acclaim. *Botshol* (1980) received the 1981 Jan Campert Prize, and she was awarded the Joost van den Vondel Prize for her entire oeuvre in 1984. Herzberg's collections are regularly reprinted, and several of her poems as well as the play *Leedvermaak* have been translated into English and German.

Works

Poetry: *Zeepost* (1963). *Beemdgras* (1968). *Vliegen* (1970). *Strijklicht* (1971). *27 liefdesliedjes* (1971). *Botshol* (1980). *Dagrest* (1984). *Twintig gedichten* (1984).

Plays: *Dat het 's ochtends ochtend wordt. De deur stond open. Twee toneelstukken* (1974). *Leedvermaak* (1982). *De val van Icarus* (1983). *En/of* (1985). *Marg* (1986). *De kleine zeemeermin* (1986).

Essays: *Het maken van gedichten en het praten daarover* (1977). *Charlotte. Dagboek bij een film* (1981).

Translations: (of *Dat het 's ochtends ochtend wordt*) *That Day May Dawn*, tr. M. Schoorel-Wagenaar (1977). Poetry, in *The Shape of Houses. Women's Voices from Holland and Flanders*, ed. and tr. M. Wolf (1974). Poetry, tr. P. Nijmeijer and S. Rollins, in *Quartet; an Anthology of Dutch and Flemish Poetry*, eds. K. Hopkins and R. van Boekel (1978). Poetry, in *Nine Dutch Poets*, eds. S. Rollins and L. Ferlinghetti (1982). Poetry, in *Dutch Interiors: Postwar Poetry of The Netherlands and Flanders*, eds. J.S. Holmes and W.J. Smith (1984).

Bibliography

Balk-Smit Duyzentkunst, F., "Getransformeerde directe rede en toch geen indirecte rede. Over de grammatica en poëtica van Judith Herzberg." *Fo-*

rum der Letteren 24 (1983). De Coninck. H., *Over de troost van pessimisme* (1983). Guépin, J.P., *In een moeilijke houding geschreven opstellen* (1969). Poll, K.L., *De eigen vorm* (1967).

General references: *De Nederlandse en Vlaamse auteurs van middeleeuwen tot heden* (1985). Article on Herzberg, R.L.K. Fokkema, in *Kritisch Lexicon van de Nederlandstalige Literatuur na 1945* (1986). *Moderne encyclopedie van de wereldliteratuur* (1980–1984). *Winkler Prins Lexicon der Nederlandse letterkunde* (1986).

Other references: Kunkeler, J., "Judith Herzberg. Het blijft gaan om het weefsel van de taal" (interview), *De Tijd* (September 29, 1979). T' Sas, R. "Een gedicht moet iets grappigs hebben" (interview), *HN Magazine* (January 25, 1986).

Ria Vanderauwera

Marie Herzfeld

(a.k.a. H.M. Lyhne, Marianne Niederweelen)

Born 1855, Guns, Hungary; died 1940, Mining, Austria
Genre(s): essay, criticism, translation
Language(s): German

In the 1880s, Herzfeld studied Scandinavian languages and literature in Vienna. An excellent translator, she was instrumental in the dissemination of Scandinavian literature in the German language. She translated authors such as Arne Gaborg, Jonas Lie, Knut Hamsun, J.P. Jacobsen, S. Michaelis, Bjornson, and Ola Hansson.

Herzfeld's first publications were pseudonymous. She published articles under her own name in journals such as *Wiener Zeit, Moderne Rundschau, Wiener Literatur Zeitung*, and *Allgemeine Theater Revue fur Bühne und Welt*.

Works

Menschen und Bücher, Literarische Studie (1883). *Die Skandinavische Literatur und ihre Tendenze* (1909). *Leonardi da Vinci, der Denker, Forscher und Poet*, tr. and intro. Marie Herzfeld, 4 editions (1911).

Bibliography

Von Hofmannsthal, Hugo, *Briefe an Marie Herzfeld* (Heidelberg, 1967). Wunbert, Gotthart, ed., *Die*

Wiener Moderne, Literatur Kunst und Musik zwischen 1890–1910 (Stuttgart, 1981), pp. 319, 313, 701.

M.A. Reiss

Magdalena Heymair (or Heymairin)

Born between 1530 and 1540, probably in Regensburg; died after 1586, probably in Kaschau (Kosiçe, presently Czechoslovakia)
Genre(s): rhymed adaptations of the Bible
Language(s): German

"This must be the end of time, when also women are publishing books." Thus exclaims an admiring Josua Opitz in his preface to Magdalena Heymair's second work, *Jesus Sirach* (1571). Heymair's entry into this hitherto male domain was, to be sure, dictated by economic necessity. Married to the Straubing school teacher Wilhelm Heymair, she was forced by "lack of money and food" (Foreword to the *Epistles*) to supplement the meager school master's income by teaching, first as a home tutor, then as a schoolteacher in Straubing, Cham, and Regensburg. In 1586 we find her in Kaschau (presently Kosiçe in Czechoslovakia) as the Hofmeisterin (governess) in the household of the widow Judith Reuber, née von Fridensheim. After 1586, nothing further is heard of Magdalena Heymair.

Heymair's works are an outgrowth of her teaching endeavors, and, as stated in titles and forewords, they are expressly intended for youth. All were adaptations of the Bible: *The Epistles* (first printed 1568), *Jesus Sirach* (1571), the *Apostelgeschichten* ("The Acts," 1573), *Tobias and Ruth* (1580), selections tailor-made for the traditional curriculum in the "German schools" as those institutions were called that taught German reading and sometimes writing and arithmetic. *The Epistles* (with the Gospels) was recommended as reading material in many of the school ordinances; so was *The Acts*, designed to replace the legends of the Saints in the Lutheran schools. Tobias and Ruth were biblical role models of children obedient to their parents. As she explains in the foreword to the *Episteln*, Heymair

chose to rewrite each Epistle in the form of a song in imitation of Niklaus Herman's popular *Sontagsevangelia*. According to Heymair, Herman had gotten the idea of his gospel songs from a schoolteacher, who wanted to use them as reading and memorization material in her schools. In deviation from Herman, Heymair used not only religious melodies but also secular ones and expresses the hope that her texts will replace the ones of the popular ditties sung in the streets. A valiant attempt has been made to make the biblical material comprehensible to a child. Difficult theological concepts are glossed over, with the emphasis instead on Christian ethics. Like Herman's, her doggerel is often forced, her rhyme not very pure, the word order strained to facilitate rhyme. The naiveté and simplicity, however, make these songs very appealing and they do lend themselves well to singing.

Measured by the standards of her time, Heymair's success as an author was immediate. Her *Epistles* saw three editions, *Jesus Sirach* no less than eight, the *Apostelgeschichten* one and *Tobias* and *Ruth* two. That Heymair was able to break into the publishing field at all is in itself remarkable. Although schoolbooks proved to be a consistent and lucrative income for many a printer, to take the work of a newcomer, a woman, must have posed a risk. It is likely that Heymair's reputation as a schoolteacher was a factor. The well-to-do mother of two of her pupils, Catharina von Degenwerg, appeared to have used her influence and also introduced Heymair to other acquaintances, to whom Heymair then dedicated her works and who receive favorable mention in the forewords. These women read her works and used them with their children. The immediate success of her first work must also have made further publishing easier. This reputation as a teacher and an author also accounts for the fact that Magdalena Heymair published these school texts under her own name rather than that of her husband. She was the only woman teacher to contribute in this way before the eighteenth century.

Works

Die Sontegliche Epistel vber das gantze Jar in gesangweis gestelt. durch Magdalenam Heymairin Teütsche Schul maisterin zue Chamb. Mit einer

Vorrede Magistri Bilibaldi Ramsbecken Stadt predigers zu Chamb [The Epistles] (1566). Das Büchlein Jesu Syrach in Gesange verfasset vnd der lieben Jugendt zu gutem in Truck gegeben durch Magdalena Heymairin, Teutsche Schulmeisterin zu Regenspurg. Mit einer schönen Vorred . . . [Jesus Sirach (Ecclesiastes)] (1571; Staatsbibl. Munich, Harvard, 1573, 1574, 1578) [Wolfenbüttel Herzog August Bibliothek]. Die Apostel Geschicht Nach der Historien Gesangs weiß gestelt Durch Magtalena Heymairin, diser. Zeytt Teutsche Schuelhalterin zu Regenspurg [The Acts] (1573). Das Buch Tobiae samt etlichen vnd 50 geistlichen Liedern vnd Kindergesprächen, wozu noch viele Weynacht-Oster-vnd Pfingstgesänge zu rechnen . . . [The Book of Tobias] (1580). Das Buch Tobiae Jnn Christliche Reimen Vnnd Gesangweiße gefast und gestellet Gott dem lieben Ehestand allen frommen Christleibenden Eheleuten und Jungfrewlichen Kinderschulen zu ehren erinnerung vnd Trost Durch Frauen Magdalenen Heymairin Jetz aber durch einen gut Hertzigen Christen gebessert vnnd gemehret vnd von newem mit anderen ein verleibten Gesänglen in Truck verfertiget. Anno, 1586. . . . Volget das Büchlein Ruth auch Gesangsweiß als ein zugab Durch obgemelten Auctorem vnd correctorem. M.D. LXXVI [The Books of Tobias and Ruth] (1586).

Bibliography

Cless, Johann, Univs seculi. . . . II: Catalogi librorum germanicorum alphabetici (Frankfurt, 1602). Eberti, Johann Caspar. Eröffnetes Cabinet deß Gelehrten Frauenzimmers/ . . . (Frankfurt und Leipzig, 1706), p. 178. Finauer, Peter Paul, Allgemeines Historisches Verzeichniss gelehrter Frauenzimmer (München, 1761), p. 114. Frawenlob, Johann, Die lobwürdige Gesellschaft der Gelehrten Weiber (1633), p. 22. Hollweck, Joh. Nep, Geschichte des Volksschulwesens in der Oberpfalz (Regensburg, 1895), p. 58. Lehms, Georg Christian, Deutschland Galante Poetinnen . . . Franckfurt am Mayn: In Verlegung des Autoris, Und zu bekommen bey Anton Heinscheidt/Buchdr. An. 1715, p. 74. Mayr, Maximiliane, "Magdalena Heymair, Eine Kirchenlied-Dichterin aus dem Jahrhundert der Reformation." Jahrbuch für Liturgik und Hymnologie 14 (1969), pp. 134–140. Mettenleitner, D., Musikgeschichte der Oberpfalz (Amberg, 1867), pp. 134–139. Moore, Cornelia N., "Biblische Weisheiten für die Jugend; die Schulmeisterin Magdalena Heymair." Schriebende Frauen, Eine Sozial-und Kulturgeschichte, ed. Gisela Brinker-Gabler (Stuttgart, 1988), pp. 172–184. Moore, Cornelia N., The Maiden's Mirror. Reading Material for German Girls in the Sixteenth and Seventeenth Centuries (Wiesbaden, 1986), pp. 88–92. Robinson, Therese A.L. (pseud. Talvj), "Deutschlands Schriftstellerinnen bis for hundert Jahren." Historisches Taschenbuch (Leipzig, 1861), pp. 1–141, esp. pp. 66f. Traeger, Lotte, "Das Frauenschrifttum in Deutschland von 1500–1650." Diss. Prague, 1943, pp. 44–51 and app. p. 5. Wackernagel, Philipp, Bibliographie zur Geschichte des deutschen Kirchenliedes im XVI. Jahrhunderts (Frankfurt a. Main, 1855), p. 413 Nr. 994, p. 373 Nr. 928, p. 395 Nr. 956. Wallner, Bertha Antonia, Musikalische Denkmäler der Steinätzkunst des 16. und 17. Jahrhunderts (München, 1912), p. 271. Wetzel, Johann Caspar, Analectica Hymnica, das ist Merckwürdige nachlese der liederhistorie . . . (Gotha, 1751–1756), VI, pp. 63–65. Wilken, Friedrich. Geschichte der Bildung, Beraubung, und Vernichtung der alten Heidelbergischen Büchersammlungen . . . (Heidelberg, 1817). Winkler, Karl, Literaturgeschichte des oberpfälzisch-egerländischen Stammes (Kallmünz, 1940), I, pp. 182–183.

Cornelia Niekus Moore

Margarita Hickey-Pellizzoni

(a.k.a. Antonia Hernanda de la Oliva, M.H.)

Born 1753, Barcelona, Spain; died c. 1791, Madrid, Spain
Genre(s): poetry
Language(s): Spanish

Margarita Hickey-Pellizzoni's poetry is essentially autobiographical. In her verses she laments the disappointments in her life and emphasizes the injustices to which the women of her time were subjected. But the fact that the men in her poetry generally appear in an unfavorable light did not stop her from also writing beautiful love sonnets. Hickey believed that women could better men in the arts and in science, a belief that garnered her a reputation as an eccentric. Because of the personal nature of her poetry, she published it under a pseudonym. She was one of the first to translate classical French theater into Spanish, and she was also an early writer in the field of geography.

She was born in 1753 in Barcelona to an Irish-Italian family. Her father, born in Dublin, was an Irish army officer and her mother was an opera singer, born in Milan. During her childhood, her family moved to Madrid, where she would live the rest of her life. She was married at an early age to Juan Antonio de Aguirre, an elderly nobleman from Navarre. She became a widow at the age of twenty-six. Although her beauty and talent attracted many suitors, Margarita Hickey-Pellizzoni never remarried. Her productive years began in 1779, shortly after she became a widow, when she was finally able to dedicate most of her days to her literary pursuits and her research in geography.

In 1789 the Royal Press of Madrid published her poetry in *Poesías varias sagradas, morales y profanas o amorosas* (Selected Sacred, Moral and Profane or Amorous Poetry). In these poetic pages of *endechas*, sonnets and romances, she describes her feelings about love, its contradictions, and men's lack of understanding about women. Notable is Hickey-Pellizzoni's poem "Afectos del alma al amor divino, y desengaño y reconocimiento de la fealdad del amor profano" (Longings of the Soul for Divine Love, and Disillusion and Recognition of the Ugliness of Profane Love) religious *endechas*, in which Hickey professes that the love of Jesus purifies, while the love of a man leads to decadence. This same book includes epic poems in praise of Captain General Pedro Cevallos and Captain Velasco's heroic defense of Havana against the British in 1762. The book *Poesías varias...* also contains some of Hickey's translations such as Racine's "Andromache" and Voltaire's "Zaïre." Hickey's work *Descripción geográfica e histórica de todo el orbe conocido hasta ahora* (Geographic and Historical Description of the Whole Known World to the Present) was rejected by the Spanish Academy of History and never published.

Hickey's confessional poetry is more of thematic than aesthetic interest. Although her style has been criticized for its naivete, her heartfelt expressions of the feminine condition are of interest to contemporary readers. Today she is remembered more as a translator of French drama than as a poet or an intellectual.

Works

> *Poesías varias sagradas, morales y profanas o amorosas* (1789).

Bibliography

> *Antología de poetisas líricas*, Vol. II (Madrid, 1915), pp. 227–255. *Panorama antológico de poetisas españolas* (Madrid, 1987), pp. 57–58. *The Defiant Muse, Hispanic Feminist Poems from the Middle Ages to the Present* (New York, 1986), p. 139.

Carlota Caulfield

Hildegard von Bingen

Born ca. 1098, Bermersheim in Rheinhessen,
Germany; died September 17, 1179,
Rupertsberg near Bingen
Genre(s): poetry; musical lyric; drama;
medical, political and religious treatises
Language(s): Latin

Hildegard von Bingen is the first major German mystic. She wrote profusely as a prophet, a poet, a dramatist, a physician, and a political moralist, communicating often with popes and princes, influential persons and common folk. Exerting a tremendous influence on the Western Europe of her time, she was an extraordinary woman who stood out from the corruption, misery, and ruin—both temporal and spiritual— of the twelfth century.

Hildegard's father was Hildebert, a knight in the service of Meginhard, the count of Spanheim. At the age of six, the child began to have the visions that continued the rest of her life and which she later recorded. At the age of eight, she was entrusted to the care of Jutta, who was the sister of Count Meginhard of Spanheim. She continued her education under Jutta, learning to read and sing in Latin. At the age of fifteen, she was clothed in the habit of a nun in the hermitage of Jutta, following the Rule of Saint Benedict. When Jutta died in 1136, Hildegard, at the age of thirty-eight, became the abbess of the community. Between 1147 and 1150, Hildegard moved her community to a dilapidated church and unfinished buildings at Rupertsberg, near Bingen. Hildegard saw to the building of a large and convenient convent that continued to attract increasing numbers. She lived here, except during her extensive travels in Western Europe, did most of her writing here, and continued as abbess until her death. She was buried in her convent church where her relics remained until the convent was destroyed by the Swedes in 1632; her relics were then moved to Eibingen.

Being a woman of extraordinarily energetic and independent mind, Hildegard wrote voluminously. She recorded her visions in three books: *Scivias* (May You Know, or Know the Ways) written between 1141 and 1151, *Liber Vitae Meritorum* (The Book of the Life of Meritorious Works) written between 1158 and 1163, and *Liber Divinorum Operum Simplicis Hominis* (The Book of the Divine Works of a Simple Man) written between 1163 and 1173. The illuminated manuscript of Hildegard's *Scivias*, the "Riesenkodex," Hessische Landesbibliothek, Wiesbaden, cod. 2 (Rupertsberg, c. 1180–1190), is an excellent preservation and is of the highest value to scholars of mysticism, history, and medieval art. The visions of *Scivias* develop Hildegard's views on the universe, on the theory of macrocosm and microcosm, the structure of man, birth, death, and the nature of the soul. They also treat the relationship between God and humans in creation, the Redemption, and the Church. *Scivias* also discusses the importance of the virtues by explaining the idea of "viriditas." "Viriditas" literally means greenness; symbolically, growth or the principle of life. According to Hildegard and other thinkers of her time, life from God was transmitted into the plants, animals, and precious gems. People, in turn, ate the plants and animals and acquired some of the gems, thereby obtaining "viriditas." People then gave out "viriditas" through the virtues, hence their importance in the chain of being. The last vision of *Scivias* contains *Ordo Virtutum*. Written between the years 1141 and 1151, the play is extremely important, since it appears to be the earliest liturgical-morality play yet to be discovered.

Liber Vitae Meritorum describes the vision of a very large circle in which the Virtues and Vices are grouped. Hildegard gives us a description of all these Virtues and Vices, but the book is less mystical and more moral and practical than *Scivias*. *Liber Divinorum Operum Simplicis Hominis* is found in an important illuminated manuscript in the municipal library at Lucca. This book contains many of the same dogmatic and ascetic thoughts that are found in *Scivias*, but it is arranged differently. The fundamental idea of the book is the unity of creation. Hildegard herself does not use the terms macrocosm and microcosm, but she succeeds in synthesizing into one great whole her theological beliefs along with her knowledge of the elements of the universe and the structures within the human body. This work is often considered as the epitome of the science of her time.

Besides these three books recording her visions, Hildegard also wrote a long physical treatise entitled *Physica: Subtilitatum Diversarum Naturarum Creaturarum* (Physical Things: Subtitled of Various Natural Creatures) and her book of medicine entitled *Causae et Curae* (Causes and Cures). Although her theoretical knowledge of medicine as found in these works may seem crude today, she must have been successful because large numbers of sick and suffering persons were brought to her for cures. In addition, Hildegard wrote *Vita Sancti Disibodi* (The Life of Saint Disibod) and *Vita Sancti Ruperti* (The Life of Saint Rupert). Her *Solutiones Triginta Octo Quaestionum* (Answers to Thirty-eight Questions) comments on various theological and scriptural subjects. Her *Explanatio Symboli Sancti Athanasii* (Explanation of the Symbol of Saint Anthanasius) is self-explanatory, as is her *Explanatio Regulae Sancti Benedicti* (Explanation of the Rule of Saint Benedict), which she wrote at the request of the Benedictine monastery of Huy in Belgium. For the nuns of her own convent, Hildegard wrote hymns and canticles—both words and music—and between 1151 and 1158 collected them into a cycle entitled *Symphonia Armonie Celestium Revelationum* (The Harmonious Symphony of Heavenly Revelations). Approximately seventy sequences of hymns, antiphons and responsories are found in the cycle and were written for a wide range of liturgical celebrations, from important Church feasts to feasts of lesser-known saints. Finally, Hildegard wrote letters to popes, cardinals, bishops, abbots, kings and emperors, monks and nuns, men and women of various levels of society both in Germany and abroad. Her letters helped Hildegard become known throughout Europe, and they unfold important political and ecclesiastical information concerning the history of her time. Migne prints one hundred and forty-five of her letters in *Patroligiae Cursus Completus, Series Latina.*

In spite of all her writings and correspondence, Hildegard was not confined to her convent. She traveled considerably for her time and circumstances. Very little is known about her means of travel, but she visited many places along the Nahe River, the Main, the Moselle, and the Rhine—the highway of Western Germany—most likely traveling by boat. The exact dates of her various travels are difficult to ascertain, but her various letters make many references to her travels. Sometimes she founded convents, as she did at Eibingen, on the opposite side of the Rhine near Rudesheim and only a mile from her own convent. Sometimes she visited courts and palaces. In 1155, Frederick Barbarossa invited Hildegard to visit him at the old royal palace that he had restored at Ingelheim (traditionally held as the birthplace of Charlemagne). Frederick Barbarossa was king at the time, but he was hoping to receive the Imperial Crown. In a letter to Hildegard that Frederick wrote several years after the visit, he comments that some of the prophecies she made to him at Ingelheim had come true.

In a letter to the people of Cologne, Hildegard comments on her earlier visits to Treves or Cologne and also comments that she was exceedingly tired, having been traveling for the last two years and preaching to various masters, doctors, and other learned men. Sometime in her life she also visited Trier, Metz, Wurzburg, Ulm, Werden, Bamberg, and other places as distant as Belgium and Switzerland. Near the end of her life, she visited France. In the Acts of Inquisition concerning Hildegard's life and miracles, it is stated that she made a pilgrimage to the shrine of St. Martin of Tours, and then went on to Paris. It is also stated that she took three or four of her books, including *Scivias*, with her on this journey. Finally, her correspondence indicates that she preached and prophesied during her various travels, exerting a tremendous influence.

It is no surprise that Hildegard is considered significant and is sometimes compared to writers like Dante and Blake. She is the first major German mystic; the illuminated manuscripts recording her visions and their commentary—*Scivias* in particular—are important to historians and those studying mysticism as well. Her *Ordo Virtutum* at the end of *Scivias* is the earliest morality play yet discovered, and her various other writings are significant advances in the understanding of the relationship of the individual person to his or her universe and in the understanding of medieval medicine. Her collection of her hymns and songs is a significant one that is only now being thoroughly studied. She corresponded actively with the religious and political leaders of her day who were molding the future of Europe in particular and the whole world in general. In her travels, preaching and prophesying, Hildegard has influenced numerous geographical areas and their peoples.

Bibliography

Barth, Pudentiana, M. Immaculata Ritscher, and Joseph Schmidt-Gorg, eds., *Lieder: Nach den Handschriften herasugegeben* (Salzburg, 1969). Fuhrkotter, Adelgundis, ed. and tr., *Griefwechsel: Nach den altesten Handschriften ubersetzt und nach den Quellen erlautert* (Salzburg, 1965). Fuhrkotter, Adelgundis and Angela Carlevaris, eds., *Scivias.* Corpus Christianorum, Continuatio Medievalis 43. 2 vols. (Turnhout, 1978). *Heilkunde: Das Buch von dem Grund und Wesen und der Heilung der Krankheiten; nach den Quellen ubersetzt und erlautert* tr. Heinrich Schipperges (Salzburg, 1957). Kaiser, Paul, ed., *Hildegardis Causae et curae* (Leipzig, 1903). *Der Mensch in der Verantwortung: Das Buch der Lebensverdienste (Liber vitae meritorum); nach den Quellen ubersetzt und erlautert,* tr. Heinrich Schipperges (Salzburg, 1972). Migne, J.P., ed., *S. Hildegardis abbatissae Opera omnia.* Patrologiae cursus completus, Ser. Lat. 197 (Paris, 1882). *Naturkunde: Dash Buch von dem inneren Wesen der verschiedenen Naturen in der Schopfung; nach den Quellen ubersetzt und erlautert* tr. Peter Riethe (Salzburg, 1959). Pitra, Joannes Baptista, ed., *Analecta Sanctae Hildegarids opera spicilegio Solesmensi parata.* Analecta Sacra

8 (1882, rpt. Farnborough, England, 1966). *Welt und Mensch: Das Buch "De operatione Dei"; aus dem Genter Kodex ubersetzt unde erlautert* tr. Heinrich Schipperges (Salzburg, 1965). *Wisse die Wege: Nach dem Originaltext des illuminierten Rupertsberger Kodex der Wiesbaden Landesbibliothek in Deutsche ubertragen und bearbeitet* tr. Maura Bockeler (Salzburg, 1954).

Printed Bibliographies: Lauter, Werner, *Hildegard-Bibliographie: Wegweiser, zur Hildegard-Literatur* (Alzey, 1970). Lauter, Werner, *Hildegard-Bibliographie: Wegweiser zur Hildegard-Literatur. Band II 1970–1982* (Alzey, 1984).

Other References: Dronke, Peter, *Women Writers of the Middle Ages* (Cambridge, 1984). Grant, Barbara L., "A Feather on the Breath of God." *Parabola* 9.2 (April 1984): 94–96. Hozeski, Bruce, tr., *Scivias by Hildegard of Bingen* (Santa Fe, 1986). Kraft, Kent, "The German Visionary: Hildegard of Bingen," in *Medieval Women Writers*, Katharina Wilson, ed. (Athens, Georgia, 1984). Newman, Barbra, "Hildegard of Bingen: Visions and Validation." *Church History* 54 (1985): 163–175. Petroff, Elizabeth, Alvilda. *Medieval Women's Visionary Literature* (New York, 1986). Potter, Robert, "The *Ordo Virtutum*: Ancestor of the English Moralities?" *Comparative Drama* 20.3 (Fall, 1986): 201–209. Sacks, Oliver, "The Visions of Hildegard," in *The Man Who Mistook His Wife for a Hat* (Berkeley, 1986).

Bruce Hozeski

Ella Hillbäck

Born 1915, Mölndal (Gothenburg), Sweden;
*   died 1979, Mariefred (Sörmland province)*
Genre(s): lyric poetry
Language(s): Swedish

The daughter of textile worker Johannes Johansson and his wife Hilda Holmgren, Ella Hillbäck spent a quiet and rather uneventful childhood and youth in her native Mölndal, outside of Gothenburg. Already in school she showed her interest in literature and became eventually a literary critic for the newspaper *Ny Tid*. By the time she met and married the poet and writer Östen Sjöstrand in 1949 she had already published several collections of poetry and two novels. Making at first their home in

Stockholm, the hub and center of intellectual activity in Sweden, they moved eventually to Mariefred, an old, picturesque little place on the shore of Lake Mälaren in the province of Sörmland, full of Swedish tradition. They found a quaint, old house right on top of the hill "Båtmansberget," from where they had a grand view over Lake Mälaren on one side. On the other side was the city and beyond that Gripsholm Castle with its beautiful old gardens where once King Gustaf III used to promenade. Here Ella lived a quiet life with her husband, unassuming and rather reticent about her personal life, though in close contact with the townspeople, while watching the eternal flow of seasons of the beautiful Sörmland countryside go by, until her death in 1979.

Despite her retiring way of life, Ella Hillbäck could not avoid the social issues of her time as Sweden changed from an agrarian economy of primarily tenant farmers working for the wealthy landowners in often wretched circumstances to a more industrialized state run by a socialist government that promoted the social equalization of its people. Explaining that she did not live in an ivory tower, she could not get away from the political and social issues of her generation, its rootless existence and search for a secure center point, she expressed these concerns in her poetry and prose.

However, Ella Hillbäck admitted readily that her images and figures came about through an inner force which was strongly colored by a deeply Christian view. Her early, rather simplistic "psalmbook religiosity" under the influence of Tolstoy and Dostoyevsky, Master Eckehart, Pascal, and Ruysbroek, changed to an all encompassing Christian mysticism which she experienced out in Nature as a mystical "all-presence . . . the way Linné used to describe." Ethics alone were too moralistic for her. God exists in every human being, she maintained.

In her strongly emotional, naive mystical poetry Ella Hillbäck fuses the outer and inner world, the visible and invisible, of the human being in connection with his relationship to his natural surroundings in order to reach a deeper knowledge about man's existence, his condition and possibilities. Her goal was to do with her poetry that which she wished others to do: "give each others courage, the courage to live."

Works

Poetry: *Hos en poet i kjol* (1939). *En gång i maj* (1941). *Världsbild* (1947). *Poesie* (1949). *I denna skog* (1953). *Det älskvärda* (1956). *Vägar, rastställen* (1960). *Lovsångens fält* (1962). *Skapelsesånger: Poems 1947–1962*, the new lyrics (selected collection) (1964). *Förgäves-men ej förgäves* (1966). *En mörkblå redovisning* (1969). *Dikter i mitt ljus* (1980).

Novels: *Albatross* (1943). *Klämtande sommar* (1948). *Gullhöna, flyg!* (1955). *Cirkusvagnen* (1959). *Det tvåfaldiga livet* (1964). *12 Blickar på verkligheten. Åren 1968–1972* (1972). *Swedenborgsvisionen. En prosasvit i sju avsnitt* (1973).

Translations: Weiss, Hanna K., "Four Poems by Ella Hillbäck." *Vox Benedictina* 2 (1986): 63–65. (Includes bibliography).

Bibliography

Anderberg, Bengt, "Sångerska, lyssnerska." *Röster i Radio/tz* 23 (1953): (n.p.). Florén, Uno, Östen Sjöstrand och Ella Hillbäck." *Idun* 30 (1962): (n.p.). Göransson, Lars, "Sann och vibrerande." Röster i *Radio/tz* 34 (1956): 15. Mannberg, Gustaf Adolf, "Ett dikterpar i en liten stad vid Mälaren." *Böckernas Värld* 3 (1971): 25. Mannberg, Gustaf Adolf, "Ella Hillbäck, ljuv och galen." *Böckernas Värld* 1 (1971): 33–35. Mårtensson, Jan, "För oss är detta mognadens ort," interview, *Bogens Verden* 1 (Copenhagen: (1970): n.p. Rying, Matts, "Ella Hillbäck-Östen Sjöstrand: Att befria själva materien, den frusna anden," interview, *Diktare idag* (Stockholm, 1971), pp. 87–110.

Hanna Kalter Weiss

Esther ("Etty") Hillesum

Born January 15, 1914, Middelburg, Holland; died November 30, 1943, Auschwitz Concentration Camp
Genre(s): diary, letters
Language(s): Dutch

Esther Hillesum, a Dutch Jew, was born on January 15, 1914, in Middelburg, Holland. Her father, a teacher and a scholar, taught at schools in various cities until he was appointed head-master of a gymnasium in Deventer. Esther's mother had come to Holland in order to escape persecution in her native Russia. A student of law, Esther received her degree from the University of Amsterdam. She later returned to the university to pursue interests in Slavic languages and in psychology. Her passion was reading, especially Russian literature, the Bible, and Rilke.

In the early months of 1941, Esther met Julius Spier, who was twenty-eight years her senior and the founder of psychochirology. They became involved physically, emotionally, and intellectually. The following year, 1942, was crucial to the Jews of Holland as the Nazis, who had been occupying the country for two years, began deportation to the East. It was during that year, when Anne Frank and her family went into hiding, that Esther was offered a position as a typist with the Jewish Council. She found the work very monotonous; she was even more disturbed, however, by the fact that the position protected her from deportation. Esther believed that she should be with her people in the camps in order to share their destiny as well as to help them: "But I don't think I would feel happy if I were exempted from what so many others have to suffer." Accordingly, Esther volunteered to go to Westerbork where she remained for a year. During that time, with the assistance of the Jewish Council, she was occasionally permitted to return to Amsterdam. In 1943, Esther and her family were sent to Auschwitz where she died on November 30. Esther had previously given her diaries and "letters from Westerbork" to a gentile friend with instructions that they be published after the war. It was not, however, until 1981 that the diaries/letters appeared in print; the English version came out two years later.

Esther's diaries and letters begin on March 9, 1941, and end on August 24, 1943. They disclose the life and thoughts of an intelligent, perceptive, and sensitive woman. It is difficult for Esther to come to terms with personal issues as she witnesses the destruction of her people and her country ("I mustn't let myself be ground down by the misery outside"). Nevertheless, she manages to resolve many of her conflicts and is truly able to grow and become her own person. In the diaries/letters, Esther elaborates on her sexuality and her relationship with men, especially with her lover Spier. She discusses at length the problems raised in trying to maintain her own identity while involved with a man. Esther goes so far as to explore the status of women: ". . . the essential emancipation of women still has to come. We are not yet full human beings; we are the 'weaker sex.' We are still tied down and enmeshed in centuries-old traditions. We still have to be born as human beings, that is the great task that lies before us." Esther also struggles with other issues, such as her relationship with God ("It is difficult to be on equally good terms with God and your body").

The diaries and letters of Esther reveal, on an intense level, the engrossing thoughts of a woman who is evolving into a self-confident and independent person. What also emerges, in spite of the circumstances of the time, is an underlying optimism and faith in mankind (similar ideas were expressed by Anne Frank). As Esther says: "If there were only one human being worthy of the name of 'man,' then we should be justified in believing in men and in humanity."

Works

The Diaries (1981). Letters from Westerbork (1981).

Bibliography

Pomerans, A. tr., An Interrupted Life—The Diaries of Etty Hillesum, 1941–1943, intro. J.G. Gaarlandt.

Michael F. Bassman

Zinaida Hippius

(see: Zinaida Gippius)

Anovo Hirejo zu Hortowey

(see: Anna Ovena Hoyers)

Valeria Konstantinovna Hoecke (née Gubanova)

Born August 12, 1904, Kiev, Russia; died
   March 28, 1986, Shirley, New York
Genre(s): poetry
Language(s): Russian, Church Slavonic

Born into a cultured family of the intellectual élite, Valeria Gubanova was a child prodigy. Her remarkable literary and musical talents were early fostered by equally extraordinary teachers (among others the famous pianists L. Pyshnov and A. Borovsky). While concentrating on her musical virtuosity Gubanova also began writing lyric poetry at an early age. A brilliant musical and literary career seemed warranted. All these hopes were cruelly twisted by the 1917 revolution as the family had to flee Russia and settle as emigres in Belgrade, Yugoslavia. Yet, Gubanova managed to graduate from the Belgrade Conservatory and the Faculty of Eastern Orthodox Theology at the Belgrade University. Her musical training and impeccable mastery of several languages became her major source of income in the trying years during and after World War II. In 1936, Gubanova married a young German theologian, a convert to Russian Orthodoxy, Paul Hoecke, who subsequently was ordained as a priest. Valeria Hoecke followed him to his parish in Potsdam, Germany, where Father Paul became a victim of Stalin's terror during the Soviet occupation of East Germany; he was deported to one of Siberia's gulags where he perished for his faith. Valeria Hoecke was forced to seek safety for her three little children and aged mother in more hospitable places. She accepted an invitation to teach music and foreign languages first in Jerusalem and later in Beirut. In 1958, the family made a final move to the United States.

As Hoecke was using her musical and linguistic accomplishments for economic survival, she simultaneously devoted her poetic talent to the unusual art genre of liturgical poetry in Church Slavonic.

Since the 1930s Hoecke has written liturgical texts for twenty-five entire services (which include all texts required to conduct a full service: troparia, kontakia, hermoi, stikheria, ypakoi, etc.); her texts are services for special icons, new Saints, or

Saints and particular occasions (e.g. blessings of motor vehicles, airplane travels) for whom or which divine services have not previously been composed. She also composed liturgical music and continued to write secular lyric poetry in Russian, which, although strictly adhering to classical versification, is unusual for its transcendent quality. Her lyrics address a responsive cord in the reader dealing mainly with the theme of how man, the perennial *homo viator*, encounters joys and sorrows in his ephemeral existence and finds solace in Divine Providence. Hoecke's poetry awaits posthumous publication.

By the general consensus of Church authorities, Valeria Hoecke has by far surpassed her ninth century predecessor—the nun Kassia—whose work was influential in shaping early medieval church liturgy and hymns and who is always favorably compared to the greatest liturgical poets and hymnologists St. John Damascene and St. Romanos Melodos. Hoecke's skill in combining concise elegance with theological depth in her liturgical poetry makes her unique in her contribution to Eastern Orthodox Christianity in particular and to world culture at large.

The following works have been published by church printing houses under the auspices of the Synod of Bishops of the Russian Orthodox Church in Exile, in Yugoslavia in the 1930s, and, after WW II, in Munich and the United States. All listed services have been reprinted by the Printing Press, St. Job of Pochaev, Holy Trinity Monastery, Jordanville, N.Y. 13361–0036.

Works

The Icon of Our Lady of Kursk. Saint Blessed Empress Theophania. Saints Martyrs Kiriakia, Valeria, Maria. The Venerable Humble Paul. Saints John, Iraklemon, Andrei, and Theophilos. Saints Spiridon and Nikodim. Saint Philareth the Merciful. Saint Taisia. Saint Ireneus of Srem. Saint Anastasios of Sinai. Saint Isidora of Tavenna. The Holy Icon of Our Lady of Kozelshchans. Canon for the Holy Martyr Sebastian. Martyrs Zinaida and Philonilla. Saint Empress Tamara. The Holy Icon of Our Lady Of Lesninsk. Saint Juvenal, Patriarch of Jerusalem. Saint Martyr Agnia. Saint Blessed Ksenia of Petersburg. Saint Blessed Brigita of Kildar. Saint King Edward. Saint Patrick, Apostle of Ireland. Akathistos for the Holy Icon of Our Lady of Kursk. Blessing for Travellers by Air. Blessing of Motor Vehicles and Airplanes.

Bibliography

N., N., "Iubilei V.K. Kheke" [Anniversary of V.K. Hoecke]. *Tserkovnai Zhizn'* [Church Life] 9–10 (New York, 1984). Schatiloff, A. "Kassia dvadtsago veka" [Kassia of the Twentieth Century]. *Novoe Russkoe Slovo* (April 8, 1986). Schatiloff, A., "Novaia Kassia dvadtsago veka" [New Kassia of the Twentieth Century], a somewhat expanded version of the above article, *Russkaia Zhizn'* [Russian Life] (San Francisco, April 4, 1986).

Marina Astman

Franziska Gräfin von Hohenheim, Duchess of Württemberg

Born January 10, 1748, Adelsmannsfelden, Germany; died January 1, 1811, Kirchheim unter Teck
Genre(s): diary, catalogue
Language(s): German, French

Due to her family's poverty Franziska never received a proper education and never learned to write well. When she was sixteen she was married to the deformed Freiherr von Leutrum, not because of love but for his money. He apparently realized her dislike of him and kept her almost a prisoner in his castle in Pforzheim. After moving to the court, she met the Duke Carl Eugen in Wildbad in 1769, who, having fallen in love with her, brought her to his court and divorced her from her husband in 1712. She became his mistress and began to exert a considerable influence on him, which changed his previously wild, boisterous, and luxurious lifestyle. She also convinced him to move to a more bucolic environment at Hohenheim. Although she was not allowed to play a role in politics, she could subtly influence his form of absolutist government, which threatened to ruin his country and had already alarmed the Emperor and the other Imperial estates. She was able to convince him to apply a form of enlightened absolutism. For this she earned the sympathy of the whole country. Duke Carl Eugen tried from then on to promote the economy and the arts, founded the university, and offered much aid to the poor. Franziska was deeply religious and leaned towards Pietism. In her extensive correspondence she discussed these religious matters with people like Klopstock, Lavater, or Niemeyer. At the same time she devoted much attention to botanical and other scientific experiments. This resulted in her *Catalogue systematique des arbres et arbustes étrangers* (1780; The Catalogue of Exotic Trees and Bushes).

The Duke, who had married her in 1785 after his first wife's death, made every effort to establish her position in the country with namesday and birthday celebrations to which even the famous poet Friedrich Schiller contributed. He also elevated her to an Imperial Countess. Franziska accompanied the Duke on his many trips, always studying and reading to compensate for her poor education. Her diary from 1771 to 1795 is a vivid description of all her efforts to improve the country and of her idyllic life in Hohenheim. After the Duke's death in 1793 she had to move to Kirchheim unter Teck, because the successor, the later King Friedrich von Württemberg, did not want to have her in his dominion. In Sindlingen she also had a little estate, where she hosted the pietist Michael Hahn. In her old age she resorted more intensively to religion, particularly to pietism. In 1796 she fled from the French revolutionary troops to Vienna. Later she spent some time in Karlsbad (today Czechoslovakia) at the famous spas for her illnesses.

Works

Tagbuch der Gräfin Franziska von Hohenheim, späteren Herzogin von Württemberg [Diary of the Countess Franziska von Hohenheim, the Later Duchess of Württemberg], ed. A. Osterberg (1913). *Catalogue systematique des arbres et arbustes étrangers, la plupart de l'Amerique-Septentrionale . . . dans le jardin dit Americain de la terre de Madame la Contesse de Hohenheim* [Systematic Catalogue of the Exotic Trees and Bushes Coming in Particular from Northern America . . . in the Gardens Called American Gardens of the Countess of Hohenheim] (1780).

Bibliography

Keppler, U., "Franziska von Hohenheim." *Lebensbilder aus Schwaben und Franken* 10 (1966): 157–183. Stälin, Paul, "Die beiden Ehen des Herzogs: Franziska von Hohenheim." *Herzog Karl Eugen von Württemberg und seine Zeit*, vol. I (Esslingen, 1907), pp. 79–102. *Tagebücher seiner Rayßen . . . von Herzog Carl Eugen selbsten geschrieben und Franziska von Hohenheim gewidmet*, ed. Robert Uhland (1968). Uhland, Robert, "Franziska von Hohenheim, Porträt einer liebenswürdigen Frau." *Baden-Württemberg* 4/5 (1964). Uhland, Robert, "Hohenheim, Franziska Gräfin von." *Neue Deutsche Bibliographie*, vol. 9 (Berlin, 1972), p. 483f. Vely, E., *Herzog Karl von Württemberg und Franziska von Hohenheim*, 1st and 2nd ed. (Stuttgart, 1876).

Albrecht Classen

Gro Holm

Born October 5, 1878, Odda, Hardanger, Norway; died August 25, 1949, Odda, Norway
Genre(s): novel, editor of regional newspapers for young people in Hardanger
Language(s): Norwegian

The Norwegian novelist Gro Holm began her literary career with the 1932 novel *Sut* (Grief); she was fifty-four years old at the time of her début. Holm's life spanned an entire era in Norwegian cultural, political, and social history, for she witnessed and experienced the often difficult transformation of the traditional Hardanger *bygda* (rural village) into a modern industrial community. Holm's tranquil home village—and countless similar villages—inevitably confronted modern technological society; as the literary critic Otlu Alsvik has remarked, "Gro Holm did not preserve the rural culture she loved; but she has given us such a fine picture of it that it remains with our fondest memories, becoming living history for us" (Alsvik, "Gro Holms hovedverk," 1951, 621). Such is Gro Holm's literary gift to us: a series of seven novels dealing with the lives and traditions of rural people—and particularly farm women—of the Hardanger region of Norway.

Gro Holm was born on October 5, 1878, in the town of Odda, Hardanger; her father was in charge of the parsonage lands, and the family took its last name, Prestegård or Prestegaren, from its connection to the local parsonage. Gro Prestegaren was an *odelsjente* (heiress), having title to an ancestral farm owned by her aunt, and, as a young girl, she shared actively in the farm chores. Prestegaren's schooling was limited to public school; yet she was an avid reader and put the resources of the local library to constant, thorough use.

In 1893, *Odda Ungdomslag* (Odda Youth Society) was founded, and Gro Prestegaren participated actively as contributor and editor of the organization's newspapers and bulletins; as she later said, "It was there (at *Odda Ungdomslag*) I learned to write" (Breivik, p. 82). Her work with the newspaper was a modest beginning to her literary career. In 1908, Gro Prestegaren married the Bergen engineer Olav Holm; she accompanied Holm on several foreign trips and study tours, notably to Sweden, Berlin, and Paris; she also lived in Oslo for a short time. For all her travels, Holm's novels center on the local, "often hard in their realism, calling for change, so that the farm wife had a better life, the servant girl was not exploited, and industry did not destroy the best of the old culture" (Dale, 28). Gro Holm inherited the family farm Berjaflot (Odda) in 1920 and operated the farm until her death.

It was as a faithful, realistic portrayer of Hardanger farm women and their lives that Gro Holm made her mark and has retained her place in Norwegian regional literature. Her first novel, *Sut*, with its central narrator, the farm wife Brita Løstøl, realistically depicted the hardships, trials, and conditions of farm families, particularly of farm wives who often worked in poor health, with tattered hopes, plans, and, then, dreams, and went to an early grave. *Sut*, the first volume of Gro Holm's trilogy *Løstølsfolket* (1951; The Løstøl Family), was followed by *Odelsjord* (1933; The Farm Inheritance) and *Kår* (1934; Subsistence); in the trilogy, we follow the lives of Brita Løstøl, her husband Lars, and her family through early poverty, care and hardship, to possibilities of prosperity or at least relief from constant adversity and worry, and in *Kår*, to Brita's remove to her children in America and to new problems and difficulties as the old Hardanger confronts a new, materialistic Norway. In *Løstølsfolket*, Brita reveals her life in the old, rural community, its hardships and harmonies, its flaws and merits;

the final volume of the trilogy points to a new way of life and new possibilities for failure as well as promise, for conflict as well as peace for Hardanger villagers. Brita remains the central character of *Løstølsfolket*, "the one who defends the best traditions, the strong, wise, and mild farm wife" (Dale, 23).

With the conclusion of *Løstølsfolket*, Gro Holm focused on the confrontation between the rural village—and its older, traditional values and lifestyle—and the new industrial, competitive, materialistic society. Her next work, *De hvite kull* (1936; The White Peaks) depicts a rural family (and indeed a rural society) and its inevitable meeting with industry and tourism, with a changing world. In *De hvite kull*, a farm family loses its land through its naiveté and the trickery and deception of others; the young farmer's son, Johan Rokkejuv, joins an industrial community not without its share of social conflict. Holm's next work, *Takk, så var det ikke mer* (1937; Thanks, and So Nothing More) sketches the hard, demanding, demeaning life of two servant girls, Ruth and Jenny. Exhausted by hard work, Ruth eventually returns home, broken in spirit, mind, and health, while Jenny manages to find a better post and protest against unfair treatment. Holm's novel raises an effective protest against such treatment. In the novel, *Hjelpelaus* (1946; Helpless) Holm returns to a rural setting and a couple who struggle, prosper, and fall prey to "a new milieu and people with another lifestyle. They were helpless because they did not hold on to each other and their own ways" (Alsvik, 1949, 39). In Holm's final novel, *Monsens Hotell* (1948; Monsen's Hotel), the hotel owner Monsen and his wife Selma fail in their enterprise, due to their own personal weaknesses (Monsen's drinking and Selma's whims) and their lack of traditional values and standards; only the neighbors and the housemaid Astrid reflect and hold to the "solid qualities of the rural milieu" (Alsvik, 1949, 41), and they manage to prosper in the new society. Odda provides the setting for *Monsens Hotell*, as it does for the other Holm novels.

Gro Holm used her local community and its rural village society as a continual source of inspiration for her work. Holm modelled her characters, settings, and situations on her own experiences, memories, and personal acquaintances in Odda; Brita Løstøl represents many of Holm's actual neighbors and friends. Holm depicted life in Hardanger simply, realistically, and effectively; she also protested against the hardships and deprivations of rural society. Holm did not view all of traditional Hardanger culture as an idyll. In her novels, Gro Holm endeavored to defend the best of the traditional rural community and its values and beliefs while speaking eloquently on behalf of the hard-pressed, overworked rural women of Hardanger.

Works

Sut (1932). Odelsjord (1933). Kår (1934). Løstølsfolket, trilogy (1951). De hvite kull (1936). Takk, så var det ikke mer (1937). Hjelpelaus (1946). Monsens Hotell (1948).

Bibliography

Alsvik, Otlu, "Gro Holm og hennes siste bøker." Vinduet (1949): 37–42. Alsvik, Otlu. "Gro Holms hovedverk." Vinduet (1951): 615–621. Beyer, Harald, A History of Norwegian Literature, tr. and ed. Einar Haugen (New York, 1956), pp. 285, 327. Breivik, Inger Lise, Kvinner i nynorsk prosa. Red. av. Inger Lise Breivik (Oslo, 1908), pp. 82–89. Dale, Johannes A., "Gro Holm." Syn og Segn (1949): 19–28. Dannemark, Nils I.S., "Gro Holm—ei av dei glømte kvinnene i den nynorske litteraturen." Syn og Segn (1978). Øverland, Janneken, "Kjerringråd og kjerringdåd, etterord." Gro Holm, Løstølsfolket (Oslo, 1978).

Lanae Hjortsvang Isaacson

Honolulu

(see: Fotini Ikonomidou)

María Gertrudis de Hore y Ley (de Fleming)

(a.k.a. H.D.S. [Hija del Sol])

Born 1742, Cádiz, Spain; died 1801, Cádiz
Genre(s): poetry
Language(s): Spanish

Called "la hija del Sol" for her beauty and intelligence, María Gertrudis de Hore y Ley was born of Irish parents. After her marriage to Esteban Fleming in 1762, she spent a good deal of time in Madrid high society. Her life and writing career changed drastically when, according to Fernán Caballero, the secret affair she was having was discovered, and unknown assailants murdered her lover in the garden of her home. Following this abrupt turn of events, she asked and received permission from her husband to enter the convent. In 1779, Hore became a nun at the Convent of Santa María in Cádiz.

Hore was already well known when the eighteenth century luminaries, D. Nicolás Fernández de Moratín and D. José Cadalso, were just beginning to write. In fact, in Eustaquio Fernández de Navarrete's opinion, even Meléndez "could have taken lessons from" Hore. Her poems, written in the eighteenth-century anacreontic modality, were tinted with sentimentality and regard for nature. She displayed special compassion for animals and concern for human cruelty. Typical of the pre-Romantic tonality of her poetry is the following line from the eleven syllable romance, "Los dulcísimos metros de tu pluma. . . ." "I gather myself inside my happy melancholy." Young's Nights, which Hore quoted in this work, was the obvious inspiration for the poem which is a blend of stoicism and attraction for ruins, nocturnal landscapes, cemeteries, and what lies beyond the grave. The essence of melancholy pervaded and shaped not only this poem but Hore's work in general.

A few of Hore's sonnets, "endechas," "endecasílabas," and "anacreónticas," were published in "Poesías," in Poesía lírica del siglo XVIII, v. 67 in 1875, by Leopoldo Augusto de Cueto, who wrote, "We publish only a small portion, as an example of the writer's style." In 1903–1905, Manuel Serrano y Sanz brought out "Poesías," in Apuntes para una biblioteca de escritoras españolas desde el año 1401 al 1833 in which he reproduced portions of Hore's poems, many of which were originally published in El Diario de Madrid or copied from Cueto's earlier collection. He also included documents of Hore's baptism, marriage, religious profession, and death.

Although most of Hore's poetry was written in the twenty-year period prior to her religious life, 1760–1780, it is thanks to her bishop, who saved many of the poems she attempted to burn, that her manuscripts are now safely located at the Biblioteca Nacional.

Works

"Poesías," *Poesía lírica del siglo XVIII*, v. 67, ed. by Leopoldo Augusto de Cueto (1875), pp. 555–559. "Poesías," *Apuntes para una biblioteca de escritoras españolas desde el año 1401 al 1833*, by Manuel Serrano y Sanz (1903–1905), v. 1:2, pp. 523–532.

Bibliography

Galerstein, Carolyn L., ed., *Women Writers of Spain* (New York, 1986). Pedraza Jiménez, Felipe B., and Milagros Rodríguez Cáceres, *Manual de literatura española*, vol. V, Siglo XIII (Navarra, 1982). Serrano y Sanz, Manuel, *Apuntes para una biblioteca de escritoras españolas*. Biblioteca de Autores Españoles 269 (1903; rpt. Madrid, 1975).

Rosetta Radtke

Eliška Horelová

Born 1925, Cerhenice, Czechoslovakia
Genre(s): poetry, prose, drama, children's
literature
Language(s): Czech

Eliška Horelová graduated from the philosophical faculty of Charles University. After teaching at a number of schools, she entered the Pedagogical Research Institute in Prague. She is currently a senior lecturer in the philosophical faculty of Charles University. Horelová made her literary début with the poetry collection *Stojím Na Červenou* (Standing at the Red Light), published in 1963, after which she became better known as a writer of novels for children. She is also a writer of radio plays and television scenarios.

Works

Stojím Na Červenou [Standing at the Red Light] (1963). *ZdivoČela Voda* [Raging Water] (1973). *Stěhovaví Ptáci* [Migratory Birds] (1974). *Čas Onhě. Čas šeřiku* [Time of Fire, Time of Lilac] (1976). *Stěstí Má Jméno Jonáš* [Happiness, Your Name Is Jonas] (1977). *Strhané Hráze* [Burst Dams] (1978).

Warwick J. Rodden

Agneta Horn

Born August 18, 1629, Riga, Latvia; died
March 18, 1672, Stockholm, Sweden
Genre(s): autobiography
Language(s): Swedish

The author of one of the most intensely personal literary documents from the Age of the Swedish Empire, Horn has frequently been the object of both historical and literary scrutiny since the manuscript of her autobiography was discovered in 1885. The intrinsic aesthetic value of the text has been heightened among scholars by Horn's impressive family connections: her maternal grandfather, Axel Oxenstierna, was the Swedish Chancellor (1612–1654) and her father, Gustav Horn, a Field Marshal in the Swedish Army. In contrast to the memoir and diary formats of most Swedish life-writings of the period, Horn's autobiography is a fascinating and ruminative document, partly secular, partly spiritual. Born and reared in the various arenas of conflict of the Thirty Years' War, Horn uses the tragic plagues and calamitous battles of that war as a backdrop for her personal disasters: the loss of her mother, the bitter feuds with her family, her protracted resistance against a proposed spouse promoted for the sake of political advantage, the death of her husband and so on. Her life's drama, richly narrated with an unprecedented reliance on dialogue, unfolds largely among the aristocratic circles of the Lake Mälare region and concludes with her spouse's death in the Polish campaign of 1656.

The 550 lines of quotations from *The Psalms* and *Job* which follow the narrative in the manuscript have been widely dismissed as little more than the jottings of a devout widow. It has been pointed out in a recent edition of these citations, however, that a binding error earlier in this century led to a misreading of Horn's intentions. The careful ordering and systematic personalization of the verses leave little doubt but that Horn regarded this portion of the autobiography as the spiritual counterpart to the narrative section; in it, she sought to give expression to her theodical misgivings and to equate her suffering with that of Job, David, and the Israelites. Horn also wrote a short poem treating the major themes of her autobiography. Although neither a prolific nor well-known writer, it has nevertheless been suggested that she be regarded as the author of "the first Swedish novel." Certainly she stands out as one of the most compelling and introspective narrators of the Swedish Baroque.

Works

Agneta Horn. Beskrivning över min vandringstid, ed. Gösta Holm (1959). Agneta Horns lefverne efter Ellen Fries efterlämnade manuskript, ed. Sigrid Leijonhufvud (1908). Fries, Ellen, "En sjelfbiografi från sextonhundratalet." Dagny (February 1886), pp. 33–44; (March 1886), pp. 70–80; (May 1886), pp. 129–147.

Bibliography

Mitchell, Stephen A., Job in Female Garb: Studies on the Autobiography of Agneta Horn. Skrifter utgivna av Litteraturvetenskapliga Institutionenen vid Göteborgs universitet, 14 (Göteborg, 1985). Mitchell, Stephen A., "Reflections on the Seventeenth-Century Autobiography of Agneta Horn." Scandinavian Review (Spring 1987): 87–92. von Platen, Magnus, "Så tuktar en argbigga." Biktare och bidragare: Litterära essäer. (Stockholm, 1959), pp. 16–38. Strandberg, Kerstin, "Ingen skall tvinga mig—varken himmel eller jord," in Kvinnornas litteraturhistoria, ed. Marie Louise Ramnefalk and Anne Westberg (1981), pp. 36–51.

Stephen A. Mitchell

Maria Teresa Horta

Born 1937, Lisbon, Portugal
Genre(s): essay, journalism, novel, poetry, short story
Language(s): Portuguese

Maria Teresa Horta is one of the most innovative and daring writers of her generation. Born and educated in Lisbon, Horta has been connected to literature and arts since early in her life, working as a journalist, a movie and literary critic, and a magazine editor. She directed and contributed to the literary pages and supplements of such newspapers and periodicals as A Capital, Eva, O Expresso, Flama, and is now chief editor of the feminist magazine Mulheres. Horta participated in the movement to renew and preserve Portuguese music and is an important figure in the cinematic world, co-directing in 1963 with Antonio de Macedo the production of a short film entitled Verao Coincidente, based on her poem by the same name.

Horta's first book of poetry, Espelho Inicial (1960) won critical praise, and her second, Tatuagem (1961), established her as an important member of the movement "Poesia 61," which tried to instill new life in contemporary Portuguese poetry. Horta's emphasis on the erotic feelings of women has made some of her books controversial and hotly debated. In 1970, her first novel, Ambas as Mãos Sobre o Corpo, caused a critical uproar, and in 1971, so did the collection of poetry Minha Senhora de Mim, which calls women to exercise their rights to sensual pleasure. This book was censored.

In 1972 Maria Teresa Horta collaborated with Maria Isabel Barreno and Maria Velho de Costa in Novas Cartas Portuguesas. The work, an exploration of the feelings of women about love, war, the mores of society, and the erotic nature of life, was declared "offensive to public morals" under the dictatorship of Marcello Caetano, and the three writers were arrested and tried, provoking an international reaction to the dictatorship and gathering support for the nascent feminist movement in Portugal.

In 1974 Horta published her second novel, Ana, and in 1975 her essay, Aborto: Dereito a Nosso Corpo, written with Celia Metrass, established her as the speaker for the Portuguese feminist movement. In the same year she published the collection of poetry entitled Educação Sentimental, which continued to probe the links between the erotic and the psychological. The volume Mulheres de Abril (1977) denounces the annihilating everyday life of Portuguese women and announces hope for a new order. In 1983 the book Os Anjos undertakes the exploration of androgyny and sensuality. In 1985 Horta published her third novel, Ema. Her latest work, Minha Mae, Minha Amor (1986) deals with the relationships of mothers and daughters.

Works

Poetry: Espelho Inicial [Initial Mirror] (1960). Tatuagem [Tatoo] (Poesia 61) (1961). Cidades Submersas [Submerged Cities] (1961). Verão Coincidente [Coincident Summer] (1962). Amor Habitado [Inhabited Love] (1963). Candelabro [Candelabra] (1964). Jardim de Inverno [Winter's Garden] (1966). Cronista não é Recado [The

Chronicler Is not the Message] (1967). *Minha Senhora de Mim* [My Lady of Mim] (1971). *Educação Sentimental* [Sentimental Education] (1975). *Mulheres de Abril* [April's Women] (1977). *Os Anjos* [The Angels] (1983). *Poesia completa, 1: 1960–1966* [Complete Poetry, 1: 1960–1966] (1983). *Poesia completa, 2: 1967–1982* [Complete Poetry, 2: 1967–1982] (1983).

Essays: [With Celia Metrass], *Aborto: direito a nosso corpo* [Abortion: The Right to Our Bodies] (1975). Novels/Short Stories: *Ambas as Mãos Sobre o Corpo* [Both Hands on the Body] (1970). [With Maria Isabel Barreno and Maria Belho da Costa], *Ana* (1974). *Ema* (1985). *Minha Mae, Minha Amor* (1986). *Novas Cartas Portuguesas* [New Portuguese Letters] (1972)

Bibliography

Coelho, Nelly Novaes, "Novas *Cartas Portuguesas* e o Processo de Conscientização da Mulher: Seculo XX" [*New Portuguese Letters* and the Process of Consciousness Raising in Women: 20th Century]. *Letras* (Curitiba) 23 (1975): 165–171. Lobo, Luiza, "O Medo e o Grito: Uma Analise Estrutural de *Ambas as Mãos Sobre o Corpo*, de Maria Teres Horta" [Fear and Screams: A Structural Analysis of *Both Hands on the Body* by Maria Teresa Horta] *Revista Brasileira de Lingua e Literatura* 3(7) (1981): 23–29. Sousa, Joao Rui de, "Maria Teresa Horta: Gesto de Amor, Gestos da Voragem" [Maria Teresa Horta: Gestures of Love, Gestures of Chaos]. *Journal de Letras, Artes & Ideas* 3(85) (Lisbon, Feb. 21–27, 1984):14. Souto, Jose Correia do, *Dicionario da Literatura Portuguesa* [Dictionary of Portuguese Literature] (Porto, 1984).

Lina L. Cofresí

Nicole Houssa

Born 1930, Liège, Belgium; died 1959, Liège, Belgium
Genre(s): critical studies, poetry
Language(s): French

In the course of her tragically brief life, Nicole Houssa accomplished four significant studies of the writing of Colette; she was particularly concerned with style and choice of language. Nicole Houssa was perhaps attracted to the French writer's openness, sensuality, affirmation of life and appetite as a complement to her own inner world, which was dominated by the imagery of darkness, drowning, and closure. Houssa's poetry, collected in the volume *Comme un collier brisé* (1970; Like a Broken Necklace), is clearly inspired by fin-de-siècle Belgian verse. Her neo-Symbolist imagery includes grey cities of non-being, submerged Atlantises, the enclosed life of convents, and figurative substitution of nun and Ophelia for the poet. Moods of floating disincarnation and of weighted lassitude are evident throughout the young poet's oeuvre; the pessimistic severance from hope and active engagement in life are less a poetic stance than a revelation of the interior landscape of a promising writer who died before her thirtieth birthday.

Works

Poetry: *Comme un collier brisé* (1970).
Criticism: "Analyse d'un extrait du Fanal bleu de Colette." *Revue des langues vivantes* (1960). "Au pays de Colette." *Marginales* (1959). "Balzac et Colette." *Revue d'histoire littéraire de la France* (1960). *Le souci de l'expression chez Colette*. Palais des Académies (1958).

Donald Friedman

Anna Ovena Hoyers

(a.k.a. Anovo Hirejo zu Hortowey, Hans Owens Tochter Anna)

Born 1584, Koldenbüttel, Holstein, Germany; died 1655, Westerwick, Sweden
Genre(s): poetry, devotional literature for children, religio-political tract, letters
Language(s): German

Daughter of Hans Owen or Oven (1560–1584), landowner and astronomer, and Wenneke Hunnens (1567–1587). Married Herman Hoyer or Hoyers von Hoyersworth, an executive officer of the Duke of Holstein, April 15, 1599.

Anna, daughter of Hans Owen, was born in 1584 in Koldenbüttel (Holstein) as a member of that class of influential wealthy landowners/farmers known as *Bauernadel*. Her father, who died when she was very young, also had a reputation as an astronomer. Her later penname Anna Ovena Hoyers is unusual for her time as most women did not have an official maiden name. In her decision to include a Latinized version of her father's name (Ovena), she pays allegiance to her membership in the Holstein *Bauernadel*. At age fifteen, Anna married Herman Hoyers, the *Staller* or executive officer of the Duke of Holstein in Eiderstedt, bringing with her the considerable dowry of 100,000 Lübeck Thaler. She bore nine children, three of whom died young. When her husband died in 1622, she found herself the sole guardian of her younger children and the executor of an estate that was heavily encumbered with debts. In those troubled times, she turned to devotional literature for consolation, especially to the works of Caspar Schwenckfeld, David Joris, and Valentin Weigel, that is, to those authors outside of the prevalent Lutheran orthodoxy whose followers were persecuted for heresy. Earlier she had tried her hand at poetry and written a German versification of the story of Eurali and Lucretia. She now took up the pen to provide her children with appropriate reading material, based on her favorite authors, from which they would not only learn the true relationship to God but also the appropriate way of life and thus provide an outer sign for inner holiness. Although she was aware that she was one of the few women to provide devotional literature for her children in this way, she based her authority to do so on her motherhood, and expected her children to follow her dictates. Her first publication "Gespräch eines Kindes mit seiner Mutter. . . ." (Dialogue of a Child with Its Mother About the True Road to Piety) with its emphasis on Christian living and God's willingness to aid and protect those that try, was well received and underwent several editions, including an anonymous prose adaptation published by Philipp Jakob Spener in 1698. Several of her later works are likewise written for her children ("Christi Gülden Cron," 1643, and "Posaunenschall," 1643). They address personal shortcomings and virtues and stress the individuals' preparation to receive Christ in their hearts. This same theme is carried in other works like "Bedencken von Schwenckfelds Buch vom Wort Gottes" (1642) and "Deutsche Warheit" (1644).

Far more controversial than her motherly advice were her attempts to aid the followers of Schwenckfeld, Joris, and Weigel. In a low German farce ("De Denische Dörp-Pape") and vari-

ous open letters, she attacked and ridiculed the persecutors of these followers, the orthodox Lutheran clergy, by comparing the lifestyles of prosecutors and prosecuted and invariably finding the former wanting. The Lutheran clergy, so maligned, was not pleased and in 1632, beleaguered by financial difficulties and political adversaries, Anna Hoyers left for Sweden, armed with a letter of recommendation for Queen Eleonora from the Duchess of Holstein, her protectress over the years. The first years in Sweden were difficult. Gustav Adolf died in battle shortly after Hoyers arrived, the situation of his widow was ambivalent at the court of the new Queen-to-be, her own daughter Christina. But by 1642, Anna had been given a small piece of land named Westerwick near Stockholm and had achieved a certain degree of financial and political independence that allowed her to continue to participate in political and religious affairs of her homeland and elsewhere. Again the recipients of her open letters were seldom pleased. But as Hoyers stated: "Who loves giving old women strife, will be a fool all his life." Her collected works were published by the renowned house of Elzevier in Amsterdam in 1650. The edition was probably arranged by Queen Christina's London correspondent, a Dutchman named Michel le Blon, who might also have instigated Hoyers to write a furious tract upon the decapitation of Charles I of England. Her works were publicly burned with other Weigelian literature, but several copies have survived. So has a manuscript of her poetry collected and written by her sons Caspar and Friedrich Hermann.

Her doggerel shows no familiarity with the new literary movements of her time. Still the stinging attacks in defense of her brethren-in-the-faith place her among the best and most effective authors of religio-political works; especially her farce "De Denische Dorp Pape" ranks high among similar works in that genre. Her exhortations to her children contain the best poetic qualities when Hans Owens Tochter Anna, as she calls herself in one poem, extols her faith and trust in God and sings in expectation of entering the new Jerusalem to be found either in heaven or here on earth when peace will reign again among the warring factions in her native country.

Works

Manuscripts: "Lieder verfaßt oder gesammelt von Anna Ovena Höyer 1624–1655" ("Songs Made or Collected by Anna Ovena Hoyers"). *Süßbittere Freude, oder Eine Wahrhafftige Historie von zwey liebhabenden Personen unter verdeckten Namen Euryali und Lucretiae* [Sweetbitter Joy or the True Story of Two Lovers Euryalus and Lucretia] (1617). *Gespräch Eines Kindes mit seiner Mutter Von dem Wege zur wahrer Gottseligkeit* [Conversation of a Child with His Mother] (1628). *Christliches Gespräch eines Kindes mit seiner lieben Mutter...* [Christian Conversation of a Child with His Dear Mother] (1698) anonymous prose version of *Gespräch* of 1634. *Das Buch Ruth In Teutsche Reimen gestellet* [The Book of Ruth] (1634). *Ein Schreiben über Meer gesand...* [A Letter Sent Across the Sea] (1649). *Anna Ovenae Hoijers Geistliche und Weltliche Poemata* [Religious and Secular Poemata] (1650). *Anna Ovena Hoyers Geistliche und Weltliche Poemata*, ed. Barbara Becker-Cantorino (1986, with introduction, biography, and bibliography). "Auff/ Auff/ Zion/" and "Liedlein von den Geld-liebenden Welt-Freunden." *Deutsche Dichterinnen vom 16. Jahrhundert bis zur Gegenwart*, ed. Gisela Brinker-Gabler (1978), pp. 75–82). "An den Christlichen Leser; For the Christian Reader." *The Defiant Muse; German Feminist Poems from the Middle Ages to the Present, a Bilingual Anthology*, ed. Susan L. Cocalis (1986), pp. 8–9.

Bibliography

Becker-Cantarino, Barbara. "Die Stockholmer Liederhandschrift der Anna Ovena Hoyers," in *Barocker Lust-Spiegel. Festschrift für Blake Lee Spahr*, ed. Martin Bircher (Amsterdam, 1984), pp. 329–344. Lohmeier, Dieter, "Anna Ovena Hoyers." *Schleswig-Holsteinisches-Biographisches Lexikon* Vol. III (Neumünster, 1974) pp. 156–159. Moore, Cornelia Niekus, "'Mein Kindt, Nimm diß in acht,' Anna Hoyers' 'Gespräch eines Kindes mit seiner Mutter von dem Wege zur wahren Gottseligkeit' als Beispiel der Erbauungsliteratur für die Jugend im 17. Jahrhundert." *Pietismus und Neuzeit* 6 (1980): 164–185. Moore, Cornelia Niekus, "Anna Hoyers' Posaunenschall: Hymns of an Empire at War and a Kingdom Come." *Daphnis* 13 (1984): 343–362. Roe, Ada Blanche, *Anna Owena Hoyers. A Poetess of the Seventeenth Century*. Diss., Bryn Mawr, 1915. Schütze, Paul, "Anna Ovena Hoyers, eine holsteinische Dichterin des 17. Jahrhunderts." *Zeitschrift für allgemeine Kultur-, Literatur-und Kunstgeschichte*, 2 (1885): 539–550. Schütze, Paul, "Anna Ovena Hoyers und die niederdeutsche Satire 'De Denische Dörp-Pape'." *Zeitschrift der Gesellschaft für die Geschichte der Herzogtümer Schleswig, Holstein und Lauenburg* 15 (1885): 243–299.

Cornelia Niekus Moore

Sofia Hrisoscoleu

(see: Sofia Cocea)

Hroswitha

(see: Hrotsvit of Gandersheim)

Hrotsvit

(see: Hrotsvit of Gandersheim)

Hrotsvita

(see: Hrotsvit of Gandersheim)

Hrotsvitha

(see: Hrotsvit of Gandersheim)

Ludwig Ferdinand Huber

(see: Therese Huber)

Therese Huber

(a.k.a. Ludwig Ferdinand Huber)

Born May 7, 1764, Göttingen, Germany; died June 15, 1829, Augsburg, Germany
Genre(s): short story, journalism, translation
Language(s): German

Therese Huber was the daughter of the classicist C.G. Heyne, professor of philology at the University of Göttingen since 1763. In 1784 she married J.G. Forster, whose political troubles added to the couple's domestic sorrows. After Forster's death in Paris in 1794, Therese married L.F. Huber. At this point she began an extensive career in writing, translating, and editing. In 1795–1797 her edition of French plays appeared (*Neueres französisches Theater*, 3 vols.). In 1807 she became affiliated with the journal *Morgenblatt* in Stuttgart and from 1816 to 1824 Huber was managing editor of the paper. Her literary bequest remains in the Stadt- und Universitätsbibliothek Göttingen and in the Deutsches Literaturarchiv und Schiller-Nationalmuseum, Marbach.

Works

Emilie von Varmont. Eine Geschichte in Briefen (1794). Der Trostlose, comedy (1794). Drei Weiber (1795). Adele von Senange (1795). Die Familie Seeldorf (1795). Erzählungen, 3 vols. (1801–1802). Bemerkungen über Holland (1811). Hannah, der Herrenhuterin Deborah Findling (1821). Jugendmuth (1824). Ellen Percy, oder Erziehung durch Schicksale (1827). Die Ehelosen (1829). Erzählungen, 6 vols. (1830–1833). Die Weihe der Jungfrau bei dem Eintritt in die größere Welt (1831). Die Geschichte des Cevennen-Kriegs (1834).

Bibliography

Ernst, F., "T.H.," in F.E., *Essais II* (1946). Geiger, L., *T.H.* (Berlin, 1901). Müller, E., *T.H. in ihrer Stellung zu Staat und Gesellschaft.* Diss., Jena, 1937.

Helene M. Kastinger Riley

Cornelia Hubertina

(see: Neel Doff)

Ricarda (Octavia) Huch

(a.k.a. Richard Hugo, R.I. Carda)

Born July 18, 1864, Braunschweig, Germany; died November 17, 1947, Kronberg (Taunus), Germany
Genre(s): novel, history, essay, criticism, short story, novella, drama, biography, poetry
Language(s): German

Ricarda Huch was born into a patrician Hanseatic family with notable artistic incursions (her brother Rudolf and her cousins Felix and Friedrich were all writers). As a girl her scholarly aptitude and literary skill were obvious, but as German universities at the time did not admit female students, she was compelled to go to Switzerland for her education. She took a doctorate in history at Zurich in 1892 and worked for several years as an archivist and teacher in Zurich and Bremen before marrying an Italian dentist and living with him for a decade in Trieste and Munich. An amicable divorce was followed soon by a second, utterly disastrous marriage with her childhood sweetheart, her cousin Richard Huch. After their separation she lived for the most part with her daughter's family in Berlin, Heidelberg, Freiburg, and Jena. She died near Frankfurt shortly after leaving the East Zone.

Generally acknowledged to be Germany's most significant woman writer of the early twentieth century, she won fame first for her neoromantic novels, later for her historical romances and her studies of Germanic history and literature. She received the Goethe Prize of the city of Frankfurt in 1931 and was the first woman to be elected to the Prussian Academy of the Arts, an honor she relinquished in 1933 in protest of the Nazi regime's expulsion of such writers as Heinrich Mann and Alfred Döblin.

Her literary career lends itself to a division into three overlapping periods. The earliest, in which the influence of Nietzsche is most apparent, is marked by the emergence of a recurrent theme: the inability of the human will to cope with those overmastering irrational forces by which Fate manipulates—and frequently destroys—its chosen victims. Her first novel, *Erinnerungen von Ludolf Ursleu dem Jüngeren*, which bears a passing resemblance to Thomas Mann's *Buddenbrooks*, chronicles the fall of a great Hanseatic family. Her second, *Aus der Triumphgasse*, takes its name from an alley in Trieste where amid the squalid houses struggling up the mountainside there stands a small Roman arch. Straddling the alley, overgrown with grass, and built into the wall of a tenement, no one recalls today what ancient victory the arch once celebrated.

Despite the obvious symbolism, this is not merely another tale of present squalor contrasted with the splendor of the past. The desperately poor people who inhabit the street have a glory of their own, and beyond the brutal, tawdry reality of their everyday lives the perceptive eye can discover heroism, romance, even beauty.

Her next two novels, *Vita somnium breve* and *Von den Königen und der Krone*, move to a more mystic-romantic plane, in a manner reminiscent of D.H. Lawrence, but the main theme remains unaltered. Contemporary with these romantic novels was Huch's first major work of historical scholarship, *Die Romantik*, in which she sought, through an examination of spiritual and esthetic values and by means of exemplary biographies, to define the essence of Romanticism.

Her second period was devoted principally to an exploration of heroic ideals of the past, both in novels and essays. Her research into the *Risorgimento* culminated in two panoramic novels on Garibaldi and his times that combine history, biography and fictional narrative. Here her talent found perhaps its perfect expression in her ability to embellish bare historical fact in a natural, lucid style that is precise yet never ponderous. Her trilogy *Der grosse Krieg in Deutschland* again united history and fiction in a chronicle of the Thirty Years' War. Less weighty but equally interesting is *Der Fall Deruga*, a crisply-written short novel that employs the framework of the *roman policier* to make a compelling argument for euthanasia.

In her later career Ricarda Huch devoted herself to historical, critical, and philosophical studies. Her study of Martin Luther reflects her commitment to Lutheran Protestantism, her biography of Michael Bakunin interprets the revolutionary as an early rebel against the bourgeois mentality. Her adamant opposition to the Third Reich may be seen in the fact that the third and final volume of her monumental *Deutsche Geschichte* had to await the end of World War II for publication. She had been associated with some of those involved in the plot to assassinate Hitler in July 1944, and her last project—left unfinished at her death—was a series of biographical sketches of German resistance fighters of the era.

Works

[Richard Hugo, pseud.] *Gedichte*, poems (1891). *Erinnerungen von Ludolf Ursleu dem Jüngeren*, novel (1893). *Der Mondreigen von Schlaraffis*, novella (1896). *Teufeleien*, novellas (1897). *Der arme Heinrich*, novella (1899). *Fra Celeste und andere Erzählungen*, short stories (1899). *Aus der Triumphgasse: Lebensskizzen*, novel (1902). *Vita somnium breve*, novel (1903; also published under the title *Michael Unger*, 1909). *Von der Königen und der Krone*, novel (1904). *Das Judengrab*, novel (1905). *Die Geschichten von Garibaldi*, novels (1906–1907). *Die Romantik*, 1908). *Der letzte Sommer*, novella (1910). *Der grosse Krieg in Deutschland*, novels (1912–1914). *Luthers Glaube: Briefe an einem Freund*, essays and criticism (1916). *Der Fall Deruga*, novel (1917). *Entpersönlichung*, essays (1921). *Alte und neue Götter: Die Revolution des neun-zehnten Jahrhunderts in Deutschland*, history (1930). *Frühling in der Schweiz*, memoirs (1938). *Herbstfeuer*, poetry (1944). *Der lautlose Aufstand*, biographies (completed posthumously by Günther Weisenborn (1953). *Gesammelte Schriften*, essays, speeches, and autobiography (1965). *Gesammelte Werke*, novels, short stories, novellas, histories, poetry, speeches, essays, and autobiography, 11 vols. (1966–1974).

Bibliography

Baumgarten, Helene, *R.H.* (Cologne, Graz, 1968). Baum Marie, *Leuchtende Spur: Das Leben Ricarda Huchs* (Tübingen, 1960). Hoppe, Else, *R.H.* 2nd ed. (Stuttgart, 1951).

Robert Harrison

Hugeburc of Heidenheim

Born England; died Saxony; fl. second half of
*   the eighth century*
Genre(s): hagiography
Language(s): Latin

Hugeburc was an Anglo-Saxon nun who moved shortly after 761 to Germany as part of the missionary movement. Her only extant work is a life of two Anglo-Saxon brothers, who were also missionaries in Germany: Willibald, bishop of Eischstätt, and Wynnebald, abbot of Heidenheim.

The prologue is marked by a tension between conventional expressions of the author's "womanly foolishness" and a vital sense of her strong compunction to compose the text. The reader senses an attitude called by Dronke "half-fearful, half-defiant." That tension is mirrored in the fact that Hugeburc concealed her name in an ingenious cryptogram, solved for modern scholarship by Bischoff. The work is more a collection of incidents known to the author about the two men than an attempt to recount their careers in full. The most remarkable feature is the narrative of Willibald's pilgrimage to the Holy Land, which the bishop himself had dictated to her in 776. She says that the knowledge of such important facts about the two holy men compelled her to write.

Hugeburc's Latin style, which betrays her Anglo-Saxon upbringing and education, is ambitious in the extreme, filled with classical allusion, alliteration, rare words, and complexity. Unfortunately her mastery of Latin was not always equal to the task, and the end result included a plethora of bizarre word forms and agreements. Despite these peculiarities, Hugeburc's work remains an important record of the Anglo-Saxon missionary venture in Germany and a personal testimony to a woman who overcame the acutely felt bounds of cultural convention.

Works

Vita s. Willibaldi episcopi Eichstetensis et s. Wynnebaldi abbatis Heidenheimensis, in Monumenta Germaniae historica, Scriptores in folio, O. Holder-Egger, ed., XV, part 1, pp. 86–117. For a full list of editions, see Bibliotheca hagiographica latina, no. 8931 and no. 8996.

Bibliography

Bischoff, B., "Wer ist die Nonne von Heidenheim?" Studien und Mitteilungen zur Geschichte des Benediktinerordens 49 (1931): 387–388. Dronke, P., Women Writers of the Middle Ages (1984), pp. 33–34. Gottschaller, E., Hugeburc von Heidenheim. Philologische Untersuchungen zu den Heiligenbiographien einer Nonne des achten Jahrhunderts (1973).

Thomas Head

Richard Hugo

(see: Ricarda [Octavia] Huch)

Rahel Hutmacher

Born 1944, Lausanne, Switzerland
Genre(s): short story
Language(s): German

Rahel Hutmacher studied in Zurich, where she became a librarian. From 1971–1975, she studied again to become a psychotherapist and lectured at the university. Since 1977, she has lived and practiced also in Düsseldorf. In her short prose texts that resemble prose poems told by a fairy-tale persona and are sometimes assembled to form larger narrative units, she explores archaic forgotten relationships between humans and nature, the former consisting mainly of women and the latter of a large primeval forest in which survival becomes an emotional reminiscence rather than an unpleasant chore.

Socialization is presented as feminine and matriarchal rather than in feminist terms. Indeed, her books can be conceived as a kind of speech therapy that promises healing through free association. Of special note is Tochter, a book consisting of a mother's lyrical perceptions of a daughter, and vice versa. Rahel Hutmacher has received several prizes: the Förderpreis der Stadt Zurich, the Rauriser Förderungspreis, and the Förderungspreis Nordrhein-Westfalen.

Works

Wettergarten (1980). Dona (1982). Tochter (1983).

Ute Marie Saine

I

I.B.M.

(see: Ivana Brlić-Ma'uranić)

Dolores Ibárruri

(a.k.a. Pasionaria)

Born December 9, 1895, Gallarta, Spain
Genre(s): autobiography, political essay
Language(s): Spanish

Known primarily as a political figure, Dolores Ibárruri has written two autobiographies, a history of the Spanish Civil War and, from her youth to the present, has contributed numerous articles and essays to the press. She has used her pseudonym "Pasionaria" since the publication of her first article in *El Minero Vizcaíno* (The Biscayan Miner) in 1918.

Ibárruri has devoted her life and her writing to the freedom of the Spanish people. Born into a family of miners and married to a miner, she never accepted the poverty and exploitation to which these workers were submitted. She participated in and organized many strikes. Because she was literate, she also put her pen to the service of the working class movement. She was a founding member of the Communist Party of Spain and in the 1936 Parliamentary elections was elected to the Cortes. By the beginning of the Civil War (1936–1939) she was known not only as an activist but also as a charismatic speaker. During the war it was her voice that was heard over the airwaves encouraging the Loyalists to continue their fight against the Franco forces. She became, for many, the symbol of Loyalist Spain. In 1939 she went to the Soviet Union where she was exiled until her return to Spain in 1977. That same year she was again elected to the Spanish Cortes.

Ibárruri's autobiography, *They Shall Not Pass* (1963), is a moving text that chronicles her life until the end of the war. Spain has never been known for its autobiographical literature and less so for its working-class autobiographies. Because of this Ibárruri's is a rarity. Perhaps the most impressive part of this life story is the narration of her childhood and youth in the mining area of the Basque country. She focuses much of the narrative on the role of women within the mining community. The story of her life as a political activist, again, concentrates on the difficulties and problems facing women who have to juggle a family life and a life in the public sphere of politics. It is the story of courage, loneliness, and sadness.

In her second autobiography, *Memorias de Pasionaria* (1984; Memoirs of Pasionaria) she portrays herself as an elder stateswoman, a position she had won through years of struggle and impressive leadership. Because the text spans her years in exile, it evokes the nostalgia, frustration, and hope felt by the community of Spaniards exiled in the Soviet Union. These two autobiographies are important texts for the student of Spanish women.

Works

El único camino (1963). *Guerra y revolución en España 1936–1939.* 2 vols. (1966). *Memorias de Pasionaria 1936–1977* (1984).

English Translations: *They Shall Not Pass: The Autobiography of La Pasionaria* (1966).

Bibliography

Pámies, Teresa, *Una española llamada Dolores Ibárruri* (Barcelona, 1976). *Pasionaria: Memoria Gráfica* (Madrid, 1985).

Alda Blanco

Carmen de Icaza

Born 1899, Madrid, Spain
Genre(s): novel
Language(s): Spanish

Daughter of a Mexican diplomat, Icaza has traveled widely, and her works are known for their cosmopolitanism.

Works

La boda del Duque Kurt (1935). *Talia; la boda del Duque Kurt* (1951). *Cristina de Guzmán, profesora de idiomas* (1936). *¿Quien sabe!* (1939). *Soñar la vida* (1941). *Vestida de tul* (1942). *El tiempo vuelve* (1945). *La fuente enterrada* (1947). *Yo, la reina* (1950). *Las horas contadas* (1953). *Obras selectas* (1957; Contents: *Cristina Guzmán, Vestida de tul, La fuente enterrado, Yo, la reina, Las horas contadas*). *Talia* (1960). *Obras selectas* (1971; Contents: *Cristina Guzmán, La fuente enterrada, Las horas contadas*).

Translations: *Cristina, professora moderna* (Lisboa: Portugalia Editora, 1952). *La fuerte enterrada* [Irene] (Berlin: Deutsche Buchgemeinschaft, 1953).

Carolyn Galerstein

Rózsa Ignácz

Born 1910, Transylvania; died 1979
Genre(s): novel, short story, autobiography, travel sketches
Language(s): Hungarian

Rózsa Ignácz completed her education in Transylvania; later, she moved to Budapest, where she worked as an actress in the National Theater. Her early novels depict the cultural history of Transylvanian Hungarians, an ethnic minority in what is now Romania. Following the Soviet "liberation" of Hungary during World War II, she published two more novels; then she remained silent for ten years. Her work began to appear again in 1957. She returned to her early concern for the vicissitudes of the daily lives of Transylvanian Hungarians. *Prospero Szigetén* (On Prospero's Island) is a collection of profiles on actors. She published her autobiography, *Ikerpályáimon* in 1975. In addition to her fiction, Ignácz was noted for her travel sketches.

Works

Fiction: *Anyanyelve magyar* (1937). *Rézpénz* (1938). *Született Moldovában* (1940). *Róza Leányasszony* (1942). *Titánia Ébredése* (1946). *Mámoros Malom* (1947). *Márványkikötő* (1947). *Tegnapelőtt* (1957). *Mindenki Levele* (1958). *Tóparti Ismerősök* (1961). *Szavannatűz* (1970). *Névben Él Csak* (1977).
Nonfiction: *Prospero Szigetén* (1960)
Autobiography: *Ikerpályáimon* (1975)

Bibliography

Pomogats, Béla, ed. *Az ujabb magyar irodalom, 1945–1981* (Budapest, 1981).

Gyorgyi Voros

Ikasia

(see: Kassia)

Fotini Ikonomidou

(a.k.a. Fimonoï, Honolulu)

Born 1856, Athens, Greece; died 1883, Athens
Genre(s): poetry
Language(s): Greek

Fotini Ikonomidou was born in 1856, in a well-to-do family of Athenian merchants and intellectuals. She received the modest education accorded to the middle-class young girls of her time—a few years in a ladies' seminar. She had the opportunity, though, to complete her education by herself, reading books from her father's imposing library and listening, behind the doors, to the everyday literary and political debates that were taking place in the salon of her uncle, a university professor. She secretly started to write poetry at the age of thirteen and stuck to it, in spite of the severe objections raised by her family. Before she was twenty years old, her parents lost their fortune and died a little later; she therefore had to live in the dependent and humiliating condition of an unmarried relative in her guardian's house, facing the scorn of a society that abhorred female celibacy as much as "blue stockings."

As we learn from her writings, poetry was her only consolation, her entire *raison d'être*. Ikonomidou grew up during a period in which romanticism dominated the Greek literary production and shaped the poetic vision of her generation. She was deeply marked by its atmosphere of extreme pessimism, morbidity, and desperate desire for escape, which fitted only too well her own perception of life as a woman. Her poetry is haunted by metaphors of slavery and confinement, by images of "cages," "prisons," and "chains" in which is caught the subjectivity of what she calls the "female being." Despite the rigidity of her verse and her rhetoric style, Ikonomidou is one of the most important representatives of the first generation of Greek women poets who, writing in the first person, expressed the impossibility of making their lives and feelings conform to the dominant models of femininity. Her writings suggest a desperate quest for an autonomous female identity, through the exploration of her own "unsatisfied longings" and "impudent aspirations."

Although Ikonomidou did not have the opportunity to publish a book, she was a permanent contributor to some of the most influential literary publications of her time as *Parnassos* (Parnassus), *Attikon Imerologuion* (Attic Almanac), *Vyron* (Byron) and *Pikili Stoa* (Miscellaneous Porticum). She was respected by many of her contemporary poets and critics as Kostis Palamas who considered her verse "original, of high artistic quality and powerful expression" and who wrote a moving obituary on her death, in 1886.

Works

"Sfallo?" [Am I to Blame?]. *Vyron* II (1876). "Is tin eftyhian" [To Happiness]. *Vyron*, II (1876). "Matin" [In Vain]. *Pikili Stoa*, third year (1883). "Thiati?" [Why?]. *Pikili Stoa*, fourth year (1884).

Bibliography

Eleni . . ., "How she became a poet," in *Attikon Imerologuion of 1885* (Athens, 1884). Palamas, Kostis. (under the pen name "Honolulu"), "Fotini Ikonomidou," in *Mi hanesse* [Don't Get Lost] (April 2, 1883). Tarsouli, Athina, *Ellinides piitries* [Greek Women Poets] (Athens, 1951).

Eleni Varikas

Nataliya Iosifovna Il'ina

Born May 6, 1914, St. Petersburg, Russia
Genre(s): article, parody, satirical review,
    novel, autobiography
Language(s): Russian

Both of Il'ina's parents were people of the pre-Revolutionary intelligentsia who emigrated with their two daughters in 1920. The family lived first in Harbin, then Shanghai. In the meanwhile the father, an indolent and impractical man, left his family. Hence, the two daughters were to suffer economic privations while under the care of their intelligent and forceful, yet equally impractical, mother. Nataliya Iosifovna worked for the Shanghai branch of TASS during WWII and for a Russian newspaper of a pro-Soviet orientation, *New Life*. In 1946 she published her first book of satirical articles *Through Other Eyes: Essays on Shanghai Life*. She returned to the Soviet Union in 1947 with other repatriates. Il'ina graduated from the Gorky Institute of Literature in 1953. Her writings have been appearing in newspapers and magazines since 1950, and from time to time they have been published as collections.

Il'ina's *feuilletons* deal primarily with problems of everyday Soviet life: rude clerks, shoddy products, and obfuscating bureaucracy. The satire is not particularly witty, yet her prose is written in a wonderfully easy, conversational style. Her novel *Vozvrashchenie* (books 1–2, 1957–1965) centers on the fate of "second-generation" Russians in China. Most interesting are her later works of autobiographical prose. The first of these is the book *Sud'by* (1980), which contains descriptions of some famous acquaintances, including Anna Akhmatova and Kornei Chukovsky. *Dorogi* (1983) describes Il'ina's renewed interest in her own past. Scenes of her impoverished childhood in China lend the reader interesting insights into the plight of Russian emigrants possessed of no marketable skills. However, the author is not much given to introspection in this memoir, and the reader must infer for himself those mental processes that induced Il'ina to return to her "Motherland." The work throughout is skillfully interspersed with extracts from letters and diaries. In all it makes for interesting, if not riveting, reading.

Works

Vnimanie: opasnost'! (1960). *Ne nado ovatsii!* (1964). *Chto-to tut ne kleitsya* (1968). *Vozvrashchenie,* books 1–2 (1969). *Tut vse napisano...*(1971). *Svetiashchiesya tablo*(1974). *Sud'by* (1980). *Dorogi* (1983)

Bibliography

Lipelis, A., "Vnimanie: opasnost'!", review. *Literaturnaya gazeta* (December 15, 1960). Roshchin, M. "Dolgie dni vozvrashcheniya." *Novyi mir 6* (1966).

Laura Jo Turner McCullough

Ileana

(see: Elena Farago)

Ileana-Fatma

(see: Elena Farago)

Kazimiera Illakowiczowna

Born 1892, Vilnius, Poland; died 1970
Genre(s): poetry
Language(s): Polish

Born in Vilnius, Illakowiczowna was orphaned early. She was educated first at home, then at a boarding school for girls from noble homes in Warsaw. Between 1906 and 1909, she visited Switzerland and England, where she studied in Oxford and later in London. In 1909, she matriculated in St. Petersburg, passing exams in Greek and Latin. Between 1910 and 1914, she studied humanities at the Jagiellonian University in Cracow and, upon graduation, joined a Polish unit in the Russian army as a nurse. Her health damaged, she returned to Poland in 1918 and until the beginning of the World War II worked as a secretary for government ministries. When Hitler attacked Poland, she was evacuated to

Romania along with other employees of the Foreign Ministry; she remained there until 1947 and made her living by teaching foreign languages. In 1947, she returned to Poland and settled in the western city of Poznan (Posen).

A very prolific but—according to some critics—uneven poet, Illakowiczowna is not linked closely to any particular poetic group: in spite of the fact that she did join the "Skamander" in 1922, she remained stylistically and thematically separate. The author of some seventeen collections of poems, she is recognized for "exuberance and power of imagination, as well as ... tendency toward fantastic ..., particularly in her eerie treatment of characters and objects" [Kridl]. It was said that her language "transforms physical phenomena into pure lyrical states," which is probably another way of saying that the intensity of feeling shapes her perception of natural phenomena.

It is the intensity of faith, coupled with the poet's intellectual integrity, independence, and moral courage that constitute the strength and appeal of her poetry. Illakowiczowna was elected a member of Polish Academy of Literature in 1932, yet refused the honor. A devout Catholic, she published religious poetry in the years of the worst Communist terror. In the situation when men of letters could either become the regime's official court poets, or write for "the drawer alone," Illakowiczowna published poems and tales for children as well as numerous translations from German, Russian, Hungarian, and English (Emily Dickinson among others). She was clearly aware that dealing with the "pure poetics of Nature" offered no escape from harsh reality. Her verse is far from traditional; length of lines varies; remote assonances abound in rhymes, or there are no rhymes at all; the poet frequently introduces words of her own coinage.

Illakowiczowna is an original and important poet, and it is difficult to understand why her name was not mentioned by Milosz in his *The History of Polish Literature.*

Works

Collections of poems: *Ikarowe loty* [Flights of Icarus] (1911). *Wici. cienio roku 1914 poswiecone* [A Call to Arms. To the Memory of the Shadows of 1914] (1914). *Rymy dzieciece* [Childlike Verses]

(1923). *Polow* [Catch] (1926). *Placzacy ptak* [The Weeping Bird] (1927). *Zwierciadlo nocy* [Mirror of the Night] (1927). *Z glebi serca* [From the Depth of the Heart] (1928) *Popiol i perly* [Ashes and Pearl] (1930). *Ballady bohaterskie* [Heroic Ballads] (1934). *Slowik litewski* [The Lithuanian Nightingale] (1936). *Wiersze o Marszalku Pilsudskim. 1912–1935* [Poems about Marshal Pilsudski] (1936). *Wiersze bezlistne* [Leafless Poems] (1942). *Wiersze 1940–1954* [Poems 1940–1954] (1954). *Lekkomyslne serce* [A Happy-go-lucky Heart] (1959). *Wiersze 1912–1959* [Poems 1912–1959] (1980).

Bibliography

Illakowiczowna, Kazimiera, *Wiersze 1912–1959* (1980). Korzeniewska, Ewa, ed., *Slownik wspolczesnych pisarzy polskich* (1963). Kridl, Manfred, *An Anthology of Polish Literature* (New York, 1957). Bartelski, Leslaw M., *Polscy pisarze wspolczesni. Informator 1944–1970* (Warsaw, 1972).

Maya Peretz

Vera Inber

Born July 10, 1890, Odessa, Russia; died November 11, 1972, Moscow
Genre(s): poetry, journalism, fiction
Language(s): Russian

Vera Inber's programmatic poem, "In a Low Voice" (1932; Vpolgolosa) both apologizes for her slowness to develop civic spirit and defends her quiet way of dealing with social imperatives (in distinction to Vladimir Maiakovsky's "At the Top of One's Voice") (1930; Vo ves' golos). Elsewhere she said, "I simply take refuge in humor whenever I am moved to tears." This quiet voice and light touch unite her work in prose and poetry over a long and productive career in Soviet literature.

Vera Inber was born into a middle-class family and had a sheltered childhood in Odessa. She spent the years from 1910 through 1914 in Switzerland (under treatment for pulmonary weakness) and in Paris. Inber later wrote that the titles of her first books of collected poetry— *Pechal'noe vino* (1914; Sad Wine), *Gor'kaia uslada* (1917; Bitter Pleasure), and *Brennye slova*

(1922; Fleeting Words)—serve as adequate description of their contents. Her early verse was self-absorbed; the upheavals of the war and revolution are almost totally absent from her pages. The best of these poems catch the mood of a day or a season, the worst are dated bits of exoticism typical of the time. They already show the love of farfetched simile that characterizes Inber's writing lifelong.

Inber left Odessa for Moscow and a career in theater and journalism in the early 1920s. There is controversy over the degree to which she can be considered a part of the Constructivist movement of those turbulent years, but she had no doubt that their emphasis on concrete detail and topical plot (*siuzhetnost'*) left their mark on her style, reinforcing her light, but not trivializing, ability to pick out salient characteristics and incidents. She honed this talent in the humorous sketches and short stories of the early Moscow years. Inber's reminiscences of childhood, "O moem ottse" (1938; My Father) and "Kak ia byla malen'kaia" (1953; How I Was Little), a tale told from the child's viewpoint and intended for children's reading, along with her low-key, objective memoir of life in Odessa during the civil war (1918–1921), "Mesto pod solntsem" (1928; A Place in the Sun) are among her best prose works.

In the 1930s, when the norms of socialist realism were enforced and writers sent on journalistic field trips, Inber developed a distinctive way of working over the same experiences in prose and poetry simultaneously and began producing that peculiar Soviet *genre*, the verse travel diary. When her husband was named director of a large medical institution in Leningrad in August 1941, Inber chose to join him as a working journalist. She recorded her experiences of the siege—killing cold, starvation, repeated bombardments—and the gradual recovery in a terse and compelling diary, *Pochti tri goda* (Almost Three Years), and synthesized those same years in an effective poem, *Pulkovo Meridian*. In both works, composed on the scene, the energy of the language is itself a defiance of the German invaders. On the other hand, the postwar verse travelogues in which she compares Iran to Soviet Azerbaidjan and a cycle on new water projects in arid Central Asia, *Put' vody* (1956; The Path of Water), are dry and uninspired.

The image of the lamp which lights the author's working space appears in *Pulkovo Meridian* and recurs several times in Inber's poetry. In *Mastery and Inspiration* (Masterstvo i vdokhnovenie), Inber returns in prose to the themes of her pre-war poem, *Ovid*. Both works are meditations on the creative process and its power to overcome the most difficult physical circumstances.

Works

Sobranie sochinenii, 4 vols. (1965–1966).

Bibliography

Grinberg, I., *Vera Inber* (Moscow, 1961). *Handbook of Russian Literature*, Victor Terras, ed. (New Haven, 1985), pp. 200–201 (John E. Bowlt). *Kratkaia literaturnaia entsiklopediia*, vol. 3 (Moscow, 1966), cols. 115–116 (I. V. Rodnianskaia). Sorokina, M.N., "U istokov tvorchestva Very Inber." *Voprosy russkoi literatury 1* (1981), 43–48. Tarasenkov, An., *Russkie poety XX veka: 1900–1955* (Moscow, 1966), pp. 159–160 [bibliography].

General reference: *Pisateli: Avtobiografii i portrety sovremennykh russkikh prozaikov*, Vl. Lidin, ed. (Moscow, 1928), pp. 148–155. *Sovetskie pisateli: Avtobiografii*, B. Ia. Brainina i E. F. Nikitina, comp. (Moscow, 1959), vol. 1, pp. 472–549.

Mary F. Zirin

Carolina Invernizio

Born 1858, Voghera, Italy; died 1916, Cuneo, Italy
Genre(s): short story, novel
Language(s): Italian

One of the most successful and prolific writers of popular fiction in the nineteenth century, Carolina Invernizio achieved fame and fortune selling her tales of sentimental love, maidens in distress, ghosts, violence, and gothic atrocities. Her pulp novels are an entertaining mixture of emotional titillation and naturalist description and offered her predominantly lower middle-class and working class audience an amusing reading experience with moral overtones.

Having begun her career by writing serial stories for the Turin *Gazetta*, Invernizio moved on to Florence and celebrity with the exciting, if artificial, plots of her fiction. Although she never attained artistic renown, Invernizio was widely read and her intriguing stories are still in demand as plots for Grade-B Italian movies. The titles are indicative of the author's contents and tone: *Satanella, or the Hand of Death* (1888), *The Kiss of a Dead Woman* (1889), *Dora, the Daughter of the Assassin* (1895), and *The Black Fairy* (1910).

Carolina Invernizio is currently undergoing critical reappraisal as a cultural prototype: a writer dedicated to producing recreational literature for mass consumption. Her novels are considered instruments for exploring the popular culture of *fin-de-siècle* Italy.

Works

Rina o l'angelo delle Alpi (1877). *La vita domestica* (1885). *La contessa Miranda* (1887). *Satanella, ovvero la mano della morte* (1888). *Anime di fango* (1888). *La trovatella di Milano* (1889). *Le figlie della duchessa* (1889). *Il bacio d'una morta* (1889). *La gobba di Porta Palazzo* (1892). *La bastarda* (1892). *Pia de' Tolomei* (1892). *L'orfanello di Collegno* (1893). *Paradiso e inferno* (1894). *Cuor di donna* (1894). *L'ultimo bacio* (1894). *La vendetta d'una pazza* (1894). *Dora, la figlia dell'assassino* (1895). *L'orfana del Ghetto* (1895). *Bacio infame* (1895). *Amori maledetti* (1896). *Birichina* (1896). *La sepolta viva* (1896). *Cuor di madre* (1897). *La peccatrice* (1897). *Mariti birbanti* (1897). *Catena eterna* (1898). *I drammi dell'adulterio* (1898). *I ladri dell'onore* (1898). *Il delitto della contessa* (1898). *Il segreto d'un bandito* (1898). *La figlia della portinaia* (1900). *Il figlio dell'anarchico* (1901). *I misteri delle cantine* (1902). *La regina del mercato* (1903). *Le avvelenatrici* (1904). *Amore che uccide* (1904). *I disperati* (1904). *Il treno della morte* (1905). *L'albero del delitto* (1905). *Un assassino in automobile* (1905). *La risurrezione di un angelo* (1905). *La fata nera* (1910). *La figlia del mendicante* (1910). *I drammi degli emigranti* (1910).

Bibliography

Arslan Veronese, Antonia et al., *Dame, droga e galline: Romanzo popolare e romanzo di consumo fra '800 e '900* (Padua, 1977). Bartolomei, Giangaetano, "Pscicoanalisi di Carolina Invernizio." *Belfagor*, 28 (1976): 109–115. Davico Bonino,

Guido and Giovanni Ioli, *Carolina Invernizio* (Torino, 1983). Eco, Umberto, Marina Federzoni, Isabella Pezzini, and Maria Pia Pozzato, *Carolina Invernizio, Matilde Serao, Liala* (Florence, 1979).

Fiora A. Bassanese

Maria Iordanidou

Born 1897, Constantinople
Genre(s): novel
Language(s): Greek

Maria Iordanidou was born and spent her early childhood in Constantinople (present-day Istanbul). Afterwards she lived in Piraeus and later in Russia. She attended a Russian high school in Stavropol. Eventually she settled in Athens.

She is best-known for her best-seller, *Lōxandra*, which has gone through twenty-one printings since it first appeared on the Greek literary scene in the 1960s.

Iordanidou's works trace the course of her life, although they are not strictly autobiographical. *Lōxandra* takes place in Constantinople. *Diakopes ston Kaukaso* (Vacation in Caucasus) deals with Lōxandra's granddaughter, Anna, and her trip to the Caucasus, which, in Odyssean fashion, lasts five years. In *San ta trella poulia* (Like Crazy Birds) Anna returns from Russia and continues her life in Alexandria and then in Athens. *Stou kyklou ta gyrismata* (In the Circle's Turnings) deals with the German occupation of Athens and beyond.

Iordanidou's, and especially *Lōxandra's*, phenomenal success is explained in part by the fact that her works filled a need for many Greeks: the need for a chronicle of life in Constantinople, which many of them were forced to abandon with the exchange of populations between modern-day Greece and Turkey. Beyond this explanation, however, is the character of Lōxandra herself, a vibrant representation of the Greeks of Constantinople, a down-to-earth, comic, and lovable individual who attains legendary proportions as she embodies a way of life long gone. Although Iordanidou's work has flaws in organization and style, her contribution to the recording of the modern Greek experience is significant.

Works

Lōxandra (1963, 1983, etc.). *Diakopes ston Kaukaso* [Vacation in Caucasus] (1965, 1978). *San ta trella poulia* [Like Crazy Birds] (1978, 1982). *Stou kyklou ta gyrismata* [In the Circle's Turnings] (1982).

Bibliography

Mirasgezē, Maria, *Neoellēnikē Logotechnia* (Athens, 1982). Review, M. Byron Raizis. *World Literature Today* 54, No. 2 (1980): 318.

Helen Dendrinou Kolias

Luce Irigaray

Born ?
Genre(s): nonfiction, feminist theory
Language(s): French

Luce Irigaray is a contemporary psychoanalyst and philosopher. She was a member of the Freudian school of Paris, founded by Jacques Lacan. She taught at Vincennes, Department of Psychoanalysis, from its founding after the student riots in Paris in 1968, to 1974, when her seminar was cancelled shortly after the publication of her doctoral thesis in philosophy, *Speculum de l'autre femme* (Speculum of the Other Woman). The circumstances surrounding Irigaray's dismissal from Vincennes remain obscure.

The central concern of Irigaray's work is woman's desire and woman's language. Her first book, *Le langage des déments*, discusses the relationship of demented people to language, which, according of Irigaray, is similar to that of women. Both women and the demented are most frequently passive objects of discourse, spoken about rather than speakers in their own right. In *Speculum de l'autre femme* Irigaray states that female sexuality has remained the "dark continent" of psychoanalysis. Through a rereading of texts from Plato to Freud, she concludes that patriarchal discourse has castrated women, excluded them from language and history, and turned them into victims of incredible distortion. Her chief argument is against Freud, whose statements on femininity reveal the misogynist bias of the father of psychoanalysis.

In *Ce sexe qui n'en est pas un* (This Sex Which Is Not One), Irigaray compares herself to Alice in Lewis Carroll's novel, looking at the world from the other side of the mirror. The reverse side of the mirror is analogous to female desire, which according to Irigaray, is absent from the traditional scene of representation. How do we speak about that other side? How do we invent a language to express female sexuality in a way that escapes the old phallic distortions? The title of the book has a double meaning. First of all, it is a statement that female desire does not exist within patriarchal culture; second, it expresses Irigaray's hypothesis that female desire is not centered, but multiple. Female pleasure is, according to Irigaray, spread out to various parts of the body unlike male pleasure, which is centered in the phallus. This multiple sexuality is analogous to women's language, which lacks the focusing logic of male discourse. Instead, women express themselves in a fluid, tentative manner that escapes exact definition and closure.

In *Parler n'est jamais neutre*, Irigaray once again returns to the language of schizophrenics, hysterics, and other marginal persons in an attempt to determine the unconscious or preconscious schemas of an individual's discourse. She concludes that language is never neutral or universal. It is always influenced by gender, history, social situation, etc., and meaning is created on the basis of these differences. To deny differences would annul meaning. Irigaray's feminism is utopian, based on a faith in female bonding. The brief, poetic text, *Et l'une ne bouge pas sans l'autre* evokes the relationship between mother and daughter, and at the conclusion of each of her major works (*Speculum de l'autre femme*, *Ce sexe qui n'en est pas un*, and *Parler n'est jamais neutre*), Irigaray reiterates her regret for the rupture between mother and child, which feminists frequently see as the basis for the triumph of patriarchy and the exclusion of women from culture. For the balance to be restored, women must reconnect with each other to reject the sexless roles they have been assigned by the fathers, defend their own desire, and finally claim a place for it on the stage of representation.

Works

Le langage des déments (1981). *Speculum de l'autre femme* [Speculum of the Other Woman] (1974). *Ce sexe qui n'en est pas un* [This Sex Which Is Not One] (1977). *Et l'une ne bouge pas sans l'autre* (1979). *Amante Marine. De Friedrich Nietzsche* (1980). *Le corps-à-corps avec la mère* (1981). *Passions élémentaires* (1982). *L'oubli de l'air. Chez Martin Heidegger* (1983). *La croyance même* (1983). *L'éthique de la différence sexuelle* (1984). *Parler n'est jamais neutre* (1985).

Translations: Speculum of the Other Woman, tr. Gillian C. Gill (1985). This Sex Which Is Not One, tr. Catherine Porter and Carolyn Burke (1985).

Bibliography

Burke, Carolyn, "Irigaray Through the Looking Glass." *Feminist Studies* VII, 2 (Summer 1981): 288–306. Burke, Carolyn, "Introduction to Luce Irigaray's 'When Our Lips Speak Together.'" *Signs* VI, 1 (Autumn 1980): 66–68. Moi, Toril, *Sexual/Textual Politics. Feminist Literary Theory* (London and New York, 1985), pp. 127–149. Wenzel, Hélène, "Introduction to Luce Irigaray's 'And the One Doesn't Stir Without the Other.'" *Signs* VII, 1 (Autumn 1981): 56–59.

Randi Birn

Isabella

Born c. 1180, Thessaly
Genre(s): poetry
Language(s): Italian

What we know of Isabella comes from the fact that her one extant work ("N'Elias Cairel, de l'amor") is a *tenso* with En Elias Carel, whose *vida* informs us that he came from near Périgord, traveled to Romania, was in Salonika in 1207, then went to Italy in 1215–1225. From this Bogin surmises that Isabella was one of three women: the daughter of Boniface of Montferrat, the daughter of Marchesopulo Pelavicini or the daughter of Guido Marchesopulo, lord of Bodonitza in Thessaly. All had daughters named Isabella. Boutiére mentions that the first (born c. 1160) was a patron of troubadours; Bogin assumes it is his daughter who is the *trobairitz*.

Further confusion is elicited by mention of a patriarch in line 40. The base manuscript (O) reads Vian. Schultz and Bogin take this as Ivan and assume it refers to a figure in the Eastern church, though, as Perkal-Balinsky points out, Ivan could also refer to Chretien's hero, Yvain. Evidently there does exist a *vita* attesting to a St. Vincentian or Viance who reputedly lived in France in the seventh century; the *vita* is now considered an (unreliable) eleventh-century work, suggesting that Saint Vian might still have had some currency in the time of this poem.

Works

Ed., Schultz, pp. 22–23; Bogin, pp. 110–113; Raynouard, V, p. 142; Véran, p. 152; Perkal-Balinsky, pp. 72–79.

Bibliography

Bec, P., "*Trobairitz* et chansons de femme: Contribution à la connaissance du lyrisme féminin au moyen âge." *CCM* 22 (1979): 235–262. Bogin, M., *The Women Troubadours* (New York, 1980). Boutiére, J., and A.-H. Schutz, *Biographies des troubadours*. 2d. ed. (Paris, 1964). Branciforti, F., *Il canzoniere di Lanfrancesco Cigala* (Florence, 1954). Bruckner, M., "Na Castelloza, *Trobairitz*, and Troubadour Lyric." *Romance Notes* 25 (1985): 1–15. Chabaneau, C., "Les biographies des troubadours en langue provençale." *Histoire générale de Languedoc*, X (Toulouse, 1885). Dronke, P., *Women Writers of the Middle Ages* (Cambridge, 1984). Mahn, C.A.F., *Die Werke der Troubadours in provenzalischer Sprache* (Berlin, 1846). Perkal-Balinsky, D., *The Minor Trobairitz*. Ph.D. diss., Northwestern University, 1986. Raynouard, M., *Choix des poésies originales des troubadours*, 6 vols. (Osnabruck, 1966). Riquer, M. de, *Los trovadores*, 3 vols. (Barcelona, 1975). Schultz, O., *Die Provenzalischen Dichterinnen* (Leipzig, 1888). Shapiro, M., "The Provençal *Trobairitz* and the Limits of Courtly Love." *Signs* 3 (1978), 560–571. Tavera, A., "A la recherche des troubadours maudits." *Sénéfiance* 5 (1978): 135–161. Véran, J., *Les poétesses provençales* (Paris, 1946).

Sarah Spence

Nana Isaia

Born 1934, Athens, Greece
Genre(s): poetry, diary, translation
Language(s): Greek

Nana Isaia (or *Issaia* or *Ēsaia*) was an artist before she started writing poetry. She studied painting at the School of Fine Arts in Athens and has taken part in many art exhibitions. Her first book of poems (*Poiēmata*) came out in 1969. In 1980 she received the Second National Prize for Poetry. Her poetry has been translated into English, Russian, and Italian.

Poiēmata (Poems) depicts a nihilistic world in which the "I" is trapped with no possibility or hope of escape. Poem after poem reveals feelings of loneliness and disillusionment and encounters with nothingness. The persona in the various poems fails to make any leaps beyond the stifling atmosphere of the room that is the usual setting of these poems. Others, people or places, are seldom brought in, and, when they are, they become not links to the outside, but parts of the fantastic, nightmarish world of "the room." The only way out of this entrapment appears to be death.

Ena vlemma (A Glance) came out in 1974, the same year as her translation of Sylvia Plath's poetry. This fact is significant, not simply for the sake of attributing influences but for the purpose of understanding the consciousness that formed Isaia's early poems and set the stage for her later poetry. *Ena vlemma* is marked by the same pessimism that we find in Isaia's earlier poetry and in much of Greek poetry written since the 1950s. In this work, however, the "I" is not simply the solipsistic individual of her earlier poems but also the poet-persona, reflecting on the role of the poet and questioning the value and purpose of writing. In a world of Nothingness, what is the use of poetry, she appears to be asking. In fact, there are many actual questions left unanswered in this collection.

Her awareness of herself as a poet writing a poem is also seen in her 1982 edition, *Synaisthēsē lēthēs* (Consciousness of Oblivion). "I'm writing . . . a poem about silence," we read ("*Siōpē*," p. 97). In this collection that deals with an unhappy love affair, and in which the poet explores the aftermath, beginning with the suicidal feeling of despair and leading to an eventual state of voluntary silence, the influence of Sylvia Plath and Susan Sontag, whose *Aesthetics of Silence* Isaia translated in 1979, is obvious. Although Isaia toys with death and oblivion, she in fact does not die but writes poems, very pessimistic poems to be sure. In fact, she gets caught up in her own negativity and never quite reaches the stage of forgetfulness that is the gift of *Lethe*.

Stēn taktikē tōn pathōn (In the Tactics of Passion), also published in 1982, deals with probably the same unhappy love affair in a different manner. Part I is in prose—diary entries, letters, meditative essays. Part II includes many short poems that bring to mind Plath's candid, confessional mode. In both parts the poet attempts to analyze, objectively, and understand an emotionally traumatic personal experience.

Isaia is admittedly a poet with a great deal of depth. Her importance in the long run will rest on such poems as "The Magician" (*Modern Poetry in Translation*, No. 34), which indicates that she can be inventive and playful despite her basic pessimism. This poem not only affirms the positive function of poetry as play but serves as a negation of the confining, solipsistic world of the majority of her poems.

Works

Poiēmata 1969 [Poems] (1969). *Persona* (1972). *Ena Vlemma* [A Glance] (1974). *Meres kai nychtes chōris sēmasia* [Days and Nights Without Significance] (1977). *ē Alikē stē chōra tōn thavmatōn* [Alice in Wonderland] (1977). *Morphē* [Form] (1980). *Synaisthēsē lēthēs* [Consciousness of Oblivion] (1982).
Prose and Poetry: *Stēn taktikē tōn pathōn* [In the Tactics of Passion] (1982).
Prose: *Allē—ēmerologio 1981-1983* [Journal 1981-1983] (1983).
Translations: *Book of Women Poets from Antiquity to Now*, ed. Aliki Barnstone and Willis Barnstone (1980). *Contemporary Greek Poetry*, tr. Kimon Friar (1985). *Modern Poetry in Translation 34* (Summer, 1978).

Bibliography

Anghelaki Rooke, Katerina, "A Note on Greek Poetry in the 1970s." *Modern Poetry in Translation* 34 (Summer, 1978). Decavalles, Andonis, Review. *Books Abroad.* 46 (1972): 339. Spanos, William, Review. *Books Abroad* 45, 2 (1971): 357-58. Stavrou, Theofanis G., Review. *Books Abroad* 50, 3: 699. Decavalles, Andonis, "Modernity: The Third Stage, the New Poets." *The Charioteer* 20 (New York, 1978). Beaton, Roderick, Review. *World Literature Today* 57, 4 (1983): 672. Raizis, M. Byron, Review. *World Literature Today* 55, 4 (1981): 711-712. Raizis, M. Byron, Review. *World Literature Today* 57, 1 (Winter, 1983): 145.

Helen Dendrinou Kolias

Ulla Margareta Isaksson

Born 1916, Stockholm, Sweden
Genre(s): novel, short story, biography, film, television drama
Language(s): Swedish

Ulla Lundberg grew up in a middle class and extremely religious home and she remained in this milieu when she married civil engineer David Isaksson in 1938. Divorced in 1961, she married professor of literature and writer Erik Hjalmar Linder in 1963.

Already at the age of 12 Ulla Isaksson wanted to write, and she has never done anything else. It comes as no surprise to find her strict, religious upbringing the focus in all her literary efforts. She returns to the problems of her Christian faith in story after story. Good and evil, God and his adversary, earned or unearned grace, total and unquestioning submission to the laws of God are among the major issues Isaksson's characters must face.

Her first three novels written during the forties, *Trädet* (1940; The Tree), *I denna natt* (1942; During This Night), *Av Krukmakarens Hand* (1945; By the Potter's Hand), are rather stereotype. However, influenced by the Swedish writer Lars Ahlin, she came into her own with her next novel *Ytterst i havet* (Far Out in the Sea) in 1950, which shows a more artistic approach free from moral convention. Isaksson considers this novel about a preacher who has lost his belief her real debut as a writer. In her many novels since then Ulla Isaksson has continually improved her craft with regard to plot, theme and character portrayals. Her presentation of religious issues has become more complex and truer to life. Most of her protagonists are women, whom she portrays with psychological insight and warmth.

Together with her husband she has published a biography in two volumes of Swedish writer and feminist Elin Wägner *Amazon med två bröst* (1977; Amazon with Two Breasts) and *Dotter av Moder Jord* (1980; Daughter of Mother Earth).

Even though the novel has always been Ulla Isaksson's main interest, she has written plays for television and the movies. Ingmar Bergman made two of her novels, *Nära livet* (1958; Brink of Life) and *Jungfrukällan* (Virgin Spring), into movies during the fifties. In 1986 Bergman produced Isaksson's novel *De två saliga* (1962; The Blessed Ones) for television. During the seventies the movie based on Isaksson's novel *Paradistorg* (1973; Market of Paradise) created a public stir and initiated heated public debate for its presentation of modern youth, the "Aniara-man"—the borderline-human—whom Isaksson considers the creation and product of modern society.

Ulla Isaksson has received many literary awards, among these the esteemed award from the Swedish Academy. She has been a member of the distinguished Swedish literary society De Nio since 1976. Many of her books have been translated into Danish, Finnish, Norwegian, German, Dutch and two of her novels, *Virgin Spring* and *The Blessed Ones*, were published in the United States (dates not available).

Works

Trädet (1940). I denna natt (1942). Av krukmakarens hand (1945). Ytterst i havet (1950). Kvinnohuset (1952). Dödens faster (1954). Dit du inte vill (1956). Klänningen (1959). De två saliga (1962). Våra torsdagar 91964). Klockan (1966). Amanda (1969). Paradistorg (1973).
With Erik Linder: Amazon med två bröst (1977). Dotter av Moder Jord (1980).

Bibliography

Kussak, Å., "Insikt och försoning." *Bonniers Litterära Magasin* (1959): n.p. Paulin, Hillewi, "Den krossade skålen." *Ord och bild* (1960), n.p.

Hanna Kalter Weiss

Magda Isanos

Born 1916, Iasi, Romania; died 1944,
*   Bucharest*
Genre(s): poetry, drama, translation
Language(s): Romanian

Although only one of her volumes of poetry was published during her life, Magda Isanos is recognized as a uniquely vibrant voice in Romanian literature. Her writing blends the transfiguring knowledge of proximate death with a mature and loving expression of life's intimate grain.

Her poems might remind one of Rilke's decanted violence, with flowers through which the dead open windows toward the world, oak forests that are ready to grow from the hands obediently joined over the dead poet's breast, girls carrying their thin stems under a sky that doesn't understand their dreams, sun rotting into apples, fruit through the beauty of which one can see the lustre and dreaded smile of death, autumns in which the earth renders the light that was given to it during rich summers, thoughts that fall slowly and patiently inside ourselves as do the overripe fruit, and trees so full still of the poet's love that they would blossom even during winters.

The posthumous volumes *Cintarea munţilor* (1945; The Song of the Mountains) and *Tara luminii* (1946; Land of Light) attest to other facets of Magda Isanos' poetry. There is, on the one hand, the reflexive meditation upon a poet's art and, on the other, a strong and deep communion with the country oppressed by war and poverty.

The poet is viewed as a new Robinson on an island which happens to be more and more frequently not her solitary room but the hospital in which people dream of life and die muted but intense deaths. The symbiosis between poet and song is total. One couldn't answer the question whether it is the poet who absorbs the song or the song that absorbs the poet. For Magda Isanos the song of the poet is the equivalent of full silence in other human beings. Issued from solitude, the imminence of death, the blind depth of being, poems are built upon the ground of dead love.

The presentation of the Romanian plight during the Second World War, with peasant soldiers whose dead bodies feed wheat and rye in Russia, the evocation of the perennial oppression of the peasant women, the Catrinas, Marias, and Savetas who flower one single time, one single day, when they wed, and then know nothing but poverty and solitude indicates the visionary, prophetic vein in Magda Isanos' poetry. She alternately calls to throw the spear into another, different century and to invent much-needed hymns for better balanced skies.

Works

Poezii [Poems] (1943). *Cintarea munţilor. Poeme* [The Song of the Mountains. Poems] (1945). [With Eusebiu Camilar], *Focurile* [The Fires], drama in four acts (1945). *Ţara luminii. Versuri* [Land of Light]. Poems (1946). *Versuri.* [Poetry], ed. and pref. by Marin Bucur (1964).

English Translations: Dorian, Marguerite and Elliott Urdang, trs., "The Angels." *2 Plus.* A Collection of International Writing (1985), p. 359.

Bibliography

Baltazar, Camil, *Contemporan cu ei* (Bucharest, 1962), pp. 29–40. Bucur, Marin, "Prefaţă." *Versuri* (1964), pp. 3–28. Ciopraga, Constantin, "Magda Isanos." *Iaşul literar* 1 (1956): 88–92. Constantinescu, Pompiliu, *Scrieri alese* (Bucharest, 1957).

Sanda Golopentia

Louise d'Isole

(see: Adine Riom)

Lyudmila Issaeva

Born 1926, Shoumen, Bulgaria
Genre(s): poetry, children's literature
Language(s): Bulgarian

After graduating in pedagogics, Lyudmila Issaeva now works as editor for the Bulgarski Pissatel Publishing House. Her poems have been translated into English, French, German, Russian, Romanian, Hungarian, Polish, Serbo-Croatian, Turkish and Arabic.

Works

The Heart Speaks. A Lyrical Biography (1963). Truth (1967). Do Not Let the World Grow Old

(1970). Essence (1975). A Confession (1976). Poems (1978). Fate (1979). Letters from the White Home (1983).

Warwick J. Rodden

Sofija Pšibiliauskienė-Ivanauskaitė

(a.k.a. Lazdynų Pelėda)

Born September 16, 1867, Pareigiai, Lithuania;
died March 15, 1926, Pareigiai
Genre(s): short story, sketch, short novel
Language(s): Lithuanian

Sofija Pšibiliauskienė belongs to the first group of writers—several of them women—of the national Lithuanian renaissance. Coming from a Polish-speaking background, she soon awakens to her commitment to her country and uses her work to create consciousness in others. Her works fall within the limits of realism, although with strong undercurrents of romanticism and inclination for melodrama.

The penname Lazdynų Pelėda was used concurrently by her sister, Marija Lastauskienė, with whom she produced several works in collaboration. The authorship is generally attributed to Sofija for works written before 1920 (until then, Marija wrote only in Polish, and Sofija translated and edited her stories). Having received no formal education, Sofija married an impoverished, alcoholic aristocrat and had to assume the management of the estate. She left her husband in 1903, after an unsuccessful attempt at suicide, and had then to earn her living however she could in order to support her children. This brought her into contact with working-class people and furnished material for her stories. She lived in extreme poverty and died from tuberculosis.

Her work reflects her life experience. A pessimistic outlook, a stifling atmosphere, and somber colors prevail. The characters are usually divided in black and white; her sympathy rests with illiterate farm hands or small artisans and clerks in the city. She tends to present two forces in opposition: country/city, aristocracy/country folk, Lithuanian national consciousness/Polish servility. Her great topic is the degeneration of nobility on the country estate and the ensuing injustice, with moral and social focus. At first ideologically oriented toward the left, she gradually loses faith in the socialist revolution and reaches almost cynical resignation.

Three of her early works exemplify her themes and procedures. "Stebuklingoji tošelė" (1907; The Wondrous Reed-pipe) deals with a country girl who is seduced by a nobleman. As a reaction to it, her secret adorer, a poor orphan, hangs himself below her windows, and she dies of sorrow. Unusual is the creation of an almost supernatural atmosphere: the orphan concentrated all his feelings in a simple melody played on a reed-pipe. This melody survives the death of both lovers and is heard constantly in the woods where the lad is buried. It becomes a legendary reminder of the exploitation by the rich and an exhortation to fight their power.

"Ir pra'uvo kaip sapnas" (1908; And All Disappeared Like a Dream) shows the destruction of the peaceful existence of small tenants by a rich landlord who has "forgotten his roots," has married a foreigner, and decides to enlarge his property by demolishing the huts of all the settlers. The story presents the resistance and total annihilation of these. Outstanding is the character of an old man who communicates directly with nature and develops great lyrical power in his interior monologues, affirming his moral superiority.

Klaida (1908; A Mistake) depicts the gradual degeneration of a young lad from the country who goes to St. Petersburg to study, marries a Polish aristocrat, becomes rich, and forgets all moral precepts and his link with the homestead. He later gets involved in the revolution and perishes at the end. Every important step in his life has been a mistake. This short novel is significant because of a truthful recreation of the background and because it raises the important issues related to slowly emerging Lithuanian civil consciousness.

Lazdynų Pelėda is at her best when presenting sketches from country life, with artful use of colloquial speech and some folklore elements, which include magic and superstition. Her dialogues are lively; she achieves dynamic effects by incorporating local color. There is seldom exact temporal setting in her stories, as if suggesting that the same conditions are perpetrated. Men are usually assigned a more important role (this reflects the social structure), but seldom does she endow her characters with psychological depth. The message prevails over form.

Works

Našlaitė [The Orphan] (1898). *Kas priešas* [Who Is the Foe?] (1900). *Proklamacijos* [Proclamations] (1900). *Vienas iš daugelio* [One Among Many] (1900). *Sugriautas gyvenimas* [Ruined Life] (1901). *Judošius* [Judas] (1902). *Klajūnas* [The Wanderer] (1902) *Davatka* [A Bigot] (1905). *Pavasario rytmetį* [On a Spring Morning] (1905). *Stebuklingoji tošelė* (1907). *Motulė paviliojo* [Mother Called Her Back] (1908). *Klaida* (1909). *Kaliniai* [Prisoners] (1909). *Vienas u' visus* [One for All] (1911). *Dzidė* (1912). *Iš senelio Juozo pasakojimų* [From Uncle Juozas: Tales] (1912). *Nesitikėjau. Ištverk, motute* [Bear with It, Mother] (1912). *Ponas Dramblevičius* (1921). *Raštai*, 4 vols. [Works] (1921–1922).

Bibliography

Brazaitis, Juozas, "Rašytojo palū'imas: Lazdynų Pelėdos melodramai," (1938) and "Sofija Pšibiliauskienė." *Raštai* II (Chicago, 1981), pp. 222–256. Kelertienė, Violeta, "Moteris moterų prozoje: II." *Metmenys* 50 (1981): 68–93.

Birutė Ciplijauskaitė

Iraida Gustavovna Ivanoff (nee Heinecke)

(a.k.a. Irina Vladimirovna Odoevtseva)

Born 1909, Riga, Latvia, Russia
Genre(s): poetry, novel, memoirs
Language(s): Russian

Iraida Gustavovna Ivanoff, although she began writing while still living in her native Russia, lived mostly abroad and rightly belongs in the category of émigré writers. While still in Russia, she was a participant of the literary salon "The Living Word" (Zhivoe slovo) where she met Gumilev and was noticed favorably. Others who admired her writing include K. Chukovsky, M. Gorky, E. Zamiatin, and A. Bunin. She moved to Paris in the early 1920s where she continued to write with some popularity. Of her poetic oeuvre, the later cycles, *Kontrapunkt* (1951; Counterpoint) and *Stikhi napisannye vo vremia bolezni* (1952; Verses Written During Illness), are her best known. Her novels, particularly *Izol'da* and *Ostav' nadezhdu navsegda* (Abandon Hope Forever), are most remarkable for the psychological portraits of the characters, painted realistically and very engagingly, and with great fluidity.

Works

Poems: *Dvor chudes* (1922). *Kontrapunkt* (1951). *Stikhi napisannye vo vremia bolezni* (1952). *Desiat' let* (1961). *Odinochestvo* (1965). *Zlataia tsep'* (1975). *Portret v rifmovanoi rame* (1976).

Novels: *Angel smerti* (1928). *Izol'da* (1929). *Zerkalo* (1939). *Ostav' nadezhdu navsegda* (1954).

Plays: *Est' li zhizn' na Marse? P'esa v trekh aktakh* (1961).

Memoirs: *Na beregakh Nevy* (1967). *Na beregakh Seny* (1983).

Translations: *Out of Childhood*, tr. D. Nachshen (1930). *Ljuka der Backfisch*, tr. W.E. Groeger (1930). *Laisse toute esperance* (Paris: Editions Self, 1948).

Christine Tomei

Astride Ivaska

Born 1926, Latvia, The Soviet Union
Genre(s): poetry
Language(s): Latvian

Astride Ivaska emigrated from Latvia in 1944 (as did Baiba Bičole) and studied classical, Ro-mance, and Slavic languages at the University of Marburg. In 1949 she immigrated to the United States to settle permanently, first in Minnesota, then in Oklahoma since 1967. Apart from four volumes of poetry and a collection of prose sketches, she has also published a children's book.

For *Ziemas Tiesa* (1968; Winter's Judgment) she received the Zinaida Lazda Prize (as did Bičole) and the Culture Foundation of Latvians Prize for Literature for *Solis Silos* (A Step into the Forest), published in 1973. Ivaska's verse is concerned with lyric elements, new sounds and meanings for words, internal rhymes and alliteration, and explores the harmony of people and nature.

Works

Ezera Kristibas [The Lake's Christening] (1966). *Ziemas Tiesa* [Winter's Judgment] (1968). *Solis Silos* [A Step into the Forest] (1973). *Līču Loki* [Curving Bays] (1981). *Gaisma Levainoja* [The Light Wounded] (1982).

Translation: *At the Fallow's Edge* (1981).

Warwick J. Rodden

M. Īve

(see: Mirdza Ķempe)

J

Berta Jacobsohn-Lask

(see: Berta Lask)

Denise D. Jallais, Denise Jallais

(see: Denise Dubois-Jallais)

Clara Janés

Born 1940, Barcelona, Spain
Genre(s): poetry, novel, essay, biography,
*   translation*
Language(s): Spanish, Catalan

Janés was reared in a moderately enlightened family of the Catalan bourgeoisie (wealthy upper-middle and upper class) during the Franco regime. A university student during some of the disturbances of the 1960s, she was especially influenced by existentialist currents, suffered with Spain's collapse of religious ideals, and experienced a period of idealized political activity. She obtained a degree in history from the University of Barcelona, and subsequently studied comparative literature at the Sorbonne, receiving the equivalent of a Master's degree. Janés learned several languages on her own (including Czech and Romanian) and also works as a translator. She has traveled extensively, especially in South Central Europe (Czechoslovakia, Rumania, Italy). *Las estrellas vencidas* (1964; Conquered Stars), her first collection of poems, suffused with existential themes, was followed by a novel,

La noche de Abel Micheli (1964; Abel Micheli's Night), after which several years passed without publication of other collections of poetry. A second novel, *Desintegración* (1969; Disintegration) expands upon the sense of existential crisis, together with the theme of love, one of the major thematic nuclei of Janés. She has been identified as one of the Spanish language's great feminine love poets by Rosa Chacel, presently Spain's senior woman novelist. Several other poetry collections have since appeared: *Límite humano* (1973; Human Limit), *En busca de Cordelia y poemas rumanos* (1975; In Search of Cordelia and Rumanian Poems), *Antología personal (1959–1979)* (1979; Personal Anthology), *Libro de alienaciones* (1980; Book of Alienations), *Eros,* (1981), *Vivir* (1983; Living), *Kampa* (1986), *Fósiles* (1987; Fossils), and *Lapidario* (1988; Lapidary). From her poetry of the 1970s onward, there is a definite stylistic evolution as the poet becomes more concerned with language per se and with a finely chiseled form, moving away from the predominantly free-verse style of initial collections. Similarly, her initial existential sentiment, concern for time, and rebellious rejection of a rapidly changing world have given way to more complex thematics which include affirmation of life, love, friendship, and nature (including animals, objects, and landscapes). In her most recent collection, *Lapidario*, her focus is upon stones and light—elements present in her poetry from very early on, but which become poetic protagonists, with all the characteristic virtues traditionally attributed to stones. Her later works have a visionary quality, full of intuitions and epiphanies. Janés has also written a

591

number of prose works, including an award-winning biography, *La vida callada de Federico Mompou* (1975; The Quiet Life of Frederic Mompou), a travel book entitled *Sendas de Rumania* (1981; Paths and Byways of Romania), several short stories, and a third novel, *Los caballos del sueño* (1989; Horses of Sleep/Dreams), hailed as the history of her generation. Although part of the novel is an adolescent love story, it also offers a mosaic of characters and motifs set into the overall fabric of Spain's evolution from the 1960s to the present, portraying a progressive loss of ideals and undermining of values. A novel almost two decades in the writing, it is a complex work which incorporates various genres: epistle, drama, philosophical essay, diary, poetry, and narrative. An autobiographical section includes the author's first published writing in Catalan.

Works

Antología Personal 1959–1979 (1979). *Los caballos del sueño* (1989). *Desintegración* (1969). *En busca de Cordelia y poemas rumanos* (1975). *Eros* (1981). *Las estrellas vencidas* (1964). *Fósiles* (1987). *Kampa* (1986). *Lapidario* (1988). *Libro de alienaciones* (1980). *Límite humano* (1973). *La noche de Abel Micheli* (1964). *Sendas de Rumania* (1981). *La vida callada de Federico Mompou* (1975).

Janet Perez

Maria Janitschek

(a.k.a. Marius Stein)

Born July 23, 1859, Mödling near Vienna, Austria; died May 4, 1927, Munich
Genre(s): lyric poetry, novel, short story, novella
Language(s): German

Like many other female writers of her time, Maria Janitschek (née Tölk) was mainly concerned with the women's movement of her time. Her father was an officer in the Austrian army. She spent her childhood in Hungary. In 1878 she moved to Graz, the capital of the Austrian state of Steiermark. There she started to work as a journalist. In 1882 she married the art historian Hubert Janitschek, with whom she lived in Straßburg and in Leipzig. After her husband's death she moved to Berlin and later to Munich,

where she died in 1927. Her work deals with the discrepancy between people's idealistic demands on their environment and neighbors on the one hand, the sober reality on the other. Her *balladesk* poems utilize motives and subject matters from the Old Testament.

Works

Lyrics: *Legenden und Geschichten* [Legends and Stories] (1885). *Im Kampf um die Zukunft* [Fight for the Future] (1887). *Verzaubert* [Enchanted] (1888). *Irdische und unirdische Träume* [Real and Unreal Dreams] (1889). *Gesammelte Gedichte* [Collected Poems] (1892). *Im Sommerwind* [In the Summer Wind] (1895). *Aus alten Zeiten* [From Old Times] (1900). *Gesammelte Gedichte* [Collected Poems] (1911). *Gesammelte Gedichte* [Collected Poems] (1917). *Ausgewählte Gedichte* [Selected Poems] (1925).

Novels, Short Stories: *Aus der Schmiede des Lebens* [From the Blacksmith's Workshop of Life] (1890). *Gott hat es gewollt* [It Was God's Wish] (1895). *Charakterzeichnungen* [Depictions of Characters] (1896). *Der Schleifstein* [The Grindstone] (1896). *Gelandet* [Landed] (1896). *Vom Weibe* [About Woman] (1896). *Ninive* (1896). *Raoul und Irene* [Raoul and Irene] (1897). *Ins Leben verirrt* [Lost in Life] (1898). *Stückwerk* [Patchwork] (1901). *Kinder der Sehnsucht* [Children Full of Longing] (1901). *Harter Sieg* [Pyrrhos Victory] (1902). *Die neue Eva* [The New Eve] (1902). *Aus Aphroditens Garden* [From the Garden of Aphrodite] (1902). *Esclarmonde* (1903). *Mimikry* (1903). *Das Haus in den Rosen* [The House in the Roses] (1905). *Wo die Adler horsten* [Where the Eagles Have Their Nests] (1906). *Eine Liebesnacht* [A Night Full of Love] (1907). *Irrende Liebe* [Erring Love] (1908). *Heimweh* [Longing Home] (1909). *Im Finstern* [In the Darkness] (1910). *Lustige Ehen* [Funny Marriages] (1911). *Liebe, die siegt* [Love Which Overcomes] (1914). *Die Sterne des Herrn Ezelin* [Mr. Ezelin's Stars] (1915). *Der rote Teufel* [The Red Devil] (1916).

Novellas: *Lichthungrige Leute* [People Starving For Light] (1892). *Atlas* (1893). *Pfadsucher* [Path Finder] (1894). *Lilienzaube* [Magic of Lilies] *r* (1895). *Die Amazonenschlacht* [Battle of the Amazons] (1897). *Kreuzfahrer* [Crusader] (1897). *Überm Thal* [Above the Valley] (1898). *Im Sonnenbrand* [In the Fire of the Sun] (1898). *Nicht vergebens* [Not In Vain] (1898). *Der Bauernbub* [The Peasant Boy] (1898). *Ein Irrtum* [An Error] (1898). *Herr Laubenstock* (1898). *Gerichtet* [Judged] (1898). *Leopold* (1898). *Eine Harzreise* [Journey to the Harz] (1898). *Frauenkraft* [Woman's Strength] (1900). *Olympier* [Olympic Man] (1901). *Auf weiten Flügeln* [On Wide Wings] (1902). *Pfingstsonne* [The Sun of Pentecost] (1903). *Stille Gäste* [Quiet Guests] (1912). *Ausgewählte Novellen* [Selected Novellas] (1925).

Bibliography

Amlong, Dietlind, Article on *"Die Amazonenschlacht,"* *Kindlers Literatur Lexikon* I (Zurich, 1964), col. 526. Volsansky, Margarete, *Die Lyrik Maria Janitscheks.* Ph.D. diss., Vienna, 1951. Wernbach, Isolde, *Maria Janitschek. Persönlichkeit und dichterisches Werk.* Ph.D. diss., Vienna, 1950.

Albrecht Classen

Tove Marika Jansson

Born August 9, 1914, Helsinki, Finland
Genre(s): children's literature, novel
Language(s): Swedish

Tove Jansson was born in Helsinki and spent her childhood partly in that city, in a flat dominated by the studio shared by her father and her mother, both of them prominent artists; partly on the summer island off the south coast of Finland, an island that inspired some of the landscapes of the Moomin-stories.

Tove Jansson does not fit into any specific literary genre and does not conform to given literary or stylistic patterns. She creates a Moomin-world all her own, and the protagonist of this fairytale sequence for children and adults was developed from three sources. The name dates back to her Stockholm years when she studied arts and stayed with relatives. She used to sit up reading till very late, then get hungry and raid the kitchen cupboard. Once her uncle warned her not to do this, as the cupboard was the abode of the "moomintrolls" who would come out and blow at you. In an argument over some philosophical issue with her brother, she got annoyed and decided to draw the nastiest creature she could: the result was the prototype of the Moomin-

troll, a figure she then used as a signature for drawings in the dailies of the 1940s. Her narrative sphere in the Moomin-books was the safety of the family circle, and much of the material is drawn from her own background and family folklore. The Moomin-series began in 1945, but in *Trollvinter* (1957; Troll Winter), the method of writing changes and appeals more directly to adults. From then on the Moomin-stories become more decidedly serious literature, not primarily intended for children, with acute psychological observations in fictive worlds, parallel to our own but deviant at crucial points to bring out keen points of view. The Moomin-troll, too, has to grow up, to leave the safety of the family, and the maturing process with all its new encounters enfolds in the following books of the series. The autobiographical element is given full play in *Bildhuggarens dotter* (1968; The Sculptor's Daughter), but we also witness the maturing process coming to an end in *Sent i november* (1970; Late in November). In *Sommarboken* (1972; The Summer Book) she approaches the problem of aging, a preoccupation that stayed in *Solstaden* (1974; The Sun Town). Her collection of short stories called *Dockskåpet* (1978; The Doll's House) is considered her finest work. It looks at the dilemma an artist has to face: the necessity to utilize one's own life, everybody else's life as material in the creative process, and the tensions this breeds.

Tove Jansson's works have been translated into as many as 27 languages, and her Moomin-series are published daily in newspapers around the world with an estimated readership of roughly 20 million people per day. She drew all the Moomin illustrations herself between 1952 and 1959; since then her brother Lars (both artist and writer) has drawn the series.

Tove Jansson has been awarded a great many literary prizes, among them The Svenska Dagbladet Prize for Literature in 1952, the Nils Holgersson plaquette in 1953, the Elsa Beskow plaquette for her illustrations in *Trollvinter* in 1958, the State Literature Prize in Finland in 1963, the H.C. Andersen Medal in 1966, the Prize of the Swedish Academy in 1972, the Great Literature Prize of the Society for Promotion of Literature in 1977, the Topelius-prize in 1978, the Austrian State Prize in 1978.

Works

Småtrollen och den stora översvämningen [The Small Trolls and the Big Floord] (1945). *Kometjakten* [The Comet Hunt] (1946; rpt. 1956, 1968 with slightly changed titles). *Trollkarlens hatt* [The Wizard's Hat] (1949). *Muminpappans bravader* [The Moomin-Dad's Feats] (1950). *Hur gick det sen* [What Happened Next?] (1952). *Farlig midsommar* [Dangerous Midsummer] (1954). *Trollvinter* [Troll Winter] (1957). *Vem skall trösta knyttet?* [Why Shall Comfort the Little 'un?] (1960) *Det osynliga barnet och andra berättelser* [The Invisible Child and Other Stories] (1962). *Pappan och havet* [Dad and the Sea] (1965). *Bildhuggarens dotter* [The Sculptor's Daughter] (1968). *Mumintrollen,* the TV-series (1969). *Sent i november* [Late in November] (1970). *Lyssnerskan* [The Listener] (1971). *Sommarboken* [The Summer Book] (1972). *Solstaden* [The Sun Town] (1974). *Den farliga resan* [The Dangerous Journey] (1977). *Dockskåpet* [The Doll's House] (1978). *Den ärliga bedragaren* [The Honest Betrayer] (1982). *Stenåkern* [The Stone Field] (1984).

Bibliography

Holmquist, Ingrid, and Ebba Witt-Brattström, eds., *Kvinnornas Litteratur-Historia* (Delz, Malmö; 1983). Örjasaeter, Tordis, *Möte med . . . Tove Jansson* (Stockholm; 1985). Warburton, Thomas, *Åttio år finlandssvensk litteratur* (Helsingtors; 1984). Willner, Sven, "I mumindalen." *På flykt från världsåskådningar* (Tammerfors; 1964). Zweigbergk, Eva von, *Barnboken i Sverige 1750–1950* (Stockholm; 1965).

Many articles in magazines and newspapers.

Gunnel Cleve

Sibylle-Gabrielle-Antoinette de Riquetti de Mirabeau, duchess of Martel de Janville

(a.k.a. Gyp)

Born August 15, 1849, Koëtsal/Morbihan, France; died June 29, 1932, Neuilly
Genre(s): novel, short story
Language(s): French

She was the great-granddaughter of Mirabeau and, like him, became actively involved in the politics of her time. Thus her literary work contains strong political statements about society in the Second Empire and about women's roles. She wrote more than 100 novels and short stories, most of which are forgotten today. She attacked society's hypocrisy, racism, and antisemitism, the dominance of capitalism, the rule of the aristocracy, and the military. Her female heroines represent the novel type of a woman aggressively asserting her role as an equal partner of man. Gyp often illustrated her own works. She also contributed to a large number of journals and magazines, for instance *La Vie Parisienne* (The Life in Paris), *Revue de Paris* (Paris-Review), or *Revue des Deux Mondes* (Review of Two Worlds).

Works

Petit Bob [Little Bob], novel (1882). *Autour du mariage* [About Marriage], novel (1883). *Un Homme Délicat* [A Man of Delicate Manners], novel (1884). *Joies Conjugales* [Marital Joys], novel (1887). *Pauvre P'tite Femme* [Poor Little Woman], novel (1888). *Les Chasseurs* [The Hunters], novel (1888). *Bijou* [Jewelry], novel (1896). *Le Baron Sinaï* [The Baron Sinaï], novel (1897). *Le Mariage de Chiffon* [The Marriage of Chiffon], novel (1894). *Le Bonheur de Ginette* [Ginette's Good Fortune], novel (1896). *Israël et Lune de Miel* [Israel and the Honeymoon], novel (1898). *Autour du Divorce* [About Divorce], novel (1901). *L'Age du Mufle* [The Age of the Muzzle], novel (1902). *L'Amour de Line* (Line's Love), novel. *Les Profitards* [The Profiteers], novel (1918). *Mon Ami Pierrot* [My Friend Pierrot], novel (1921). *Napoléonette*, novel (1925). *Mme Guérand*, novel (1927). *Le Coup de Lapin* [The Rabbit Strikes], novel (1929). *Celui Qu'on Aime* [The Beloved], novel (1931).

Bibliography

de Beaumarchais, M.-A., "Gyp." *Dictionnaire des Littératures de Lange Française*, vol. 2 (Paris, 1984), p. 1006. de Morembert, T., "Gyp." *Dictionnaire de Biographie Française*, vol. 17 (Paris, 1986), pp. 442f. Moreau, Pierre, "Gyp." *Dictionnaire des Lettres Françaises*, XIX Siècle, ed. P.M. (Paris, 1971), p. 469.

Albrecht Classen

Vidmantė Jasukaitytė

Born 1948, Lithuania
Genre(s): poetry, novel
Language(s): Lithuanian

Vidmentė Jasukaitytė reaches far beyond customary socialist realism long imposed by the Soviet regime. Her first novel is a unique phenomenon in Lithuanian letters, somewhat akin to Juozas Baltušis' *Sakmé apie Juzą*; it shows affinities with Latin-American novels of magic realism but surpasses them in lyrical intensity.

She made her debut as poet but achieved fame principally with her extraordinary novel. From the very first book of verse she creates half real/half mythical worlds that later give a touch of magic to her novel. There are also allusions to the unbreakable chain of women of various generations who, like the ancient vestals, guard the eternal fire (here, the fire of femininity endowed with a sacral power). She prefers loose rhythms, abandonment, or innovative variations of rhyme, almost prosaic sequences with hardly any melody. The poetry arises from unusual imagery, superposition of temporal levels, and a deep, all-encompassing emotional note. Her poems are fragmented; there is no subject, just a series of instantaneous reactions from within combining heterogeneous elements.

Stebuklinga patvorių 'olė (1981; The Miraculous Grass Along the Fences), has a tight overall structure that enhances the effects of each part. Many lyrical passages combine with a fantastic note while portraying the history of six generations of Lithuanian women. This gives the book a certain epic quality: the action of the three parts is set in periods of the fight for Lithuania's independence. At the same time, it represents the emerging consciousness and independence of Lithuanian woman by reaffirming her inner strength.

The novel consists of three "ballads" (this points to the musical quality and to its reliance on folklore). Each "ballad" tells the life story of a woman: the first goes back to 1863; the last reaches contemporary times. The three are united by their experience of twofold love: one elected by the heart, the other one imposed by circumstances. It is the first one which gives almost magic power to the woman. Externally, each woman succumbs to her destiny. Internally, each develops a power of resistance that allows her to strike an affirmative note and sing a song of praise. While the details of married life are referred to in matter-of-fact prose and related to history, the secret love inspires intensely lyrical passages and leads to visions. The last part adds yet another dimension: metafiction. Thus the experience of loving in the three women becomes the experience of writing: recording the legendary message carried through a century.

In *Stebuklinga patvorių 'olė*, Jasukaitytė does not adopt a militant feminist stance. On the contrary: she shows that it is possible to retain traditional feminine qualities without feeling defenseless or submissive. Woman's task is seen here as one of taming words and endowing them with the power of incantation in order to create new myths and legends. These, in turn, affirm woman's magic gifts: she is able to communicate with the dead souls of her ancestors, see in the dead of night, hear words spoken miles away. Jasukaitytė's style shows many characteristic traits of feminine writing: cyclical time, litany-like repetitions, great fluidity, symbols of water and birds, lyrical introspective passages going back to the childhood of each protagonist, the oral aspect of discourse. With this novel Jasukaitytė has created one of the most original novels written in the last decade in Europe.

Works

Ugnis, kurią reika pereiti [Fire That Must Be Crossed] (1976). *Taip toli esu* [I Am So Far] (1979). *Stebuklinga patvorių 'olė* (1981). *Mano broli 'mogau* [Man, My Brother] (1982). "Balandė, kuri lauks." *Nemunas* 12 (1989).

Bibliography

Ciplijauskaitė, Birutė, "Vidmantės Jasukaitytės 'Stebuklinga patvorių 'ole.'" *Draugas* (February 25, 1984): 1–2. Iešmantaitė, Rasa, "Knyga apie nuostabų sesrijos pasaulį." *Aidai* 5 (1985): 234–239. Klišytė, Anelė, "Po am'inosios vasaros dagum." *Pergalė* 5 (1983): 166–168.

Birutė Ciplijauskaitė

Elfriede Jelinek

Born October 20, 1946, Mürzzuschlag,
Steiermark, Austria
Genre(s): novel, drama, lyric poetry, radio
drama, film
Language(s): German

Elfriede Jelinek grew up in the post-war Vienna, Austria, where she also began her studies of drama, art history and music. In 1972 she lived in Berlin, in 1973 in Rome. Today she lives in Vienna, Munich, and Paris and works as a freelance writer. Very early she published short lyric and prose texts in anthologies and literary journals, in which she depicted alienated individuals manipulated by an anonymous mass society through *Kitsch* images of happiness. In her first novel *Wir sind Lockvögel, Baby* (We Are Decoys, Baby), she analyzed the parallels of language and conscience patterns in our society. The unity of the traditional novel is broken up through the combination of traditional linguistic and ideological structures of the sentimental patriotic novel with pornographic, comic and horror elements. Her second work *Michael, Ein Jugenduch für die Infantilgesellschaft* (1972; Michael, Book for a Teenager of the Infantile Society) reveals the stereotypes and ideological deformations of TV stars by contrasting their ideals with reality. The novel *Die Liebhaberinnen* (1975; The Mistresses) satirizes the mentality and milieu of two women of the lower class. All her novels reveal her political concern as a Marxist feminist. Jelinek's drama *Was geschah, nachdem Nora ihren Mann verlassen hatte* (1979; What Happened After Nora Had Left Her Husband) is a continuation of an Ibsen play reflecting upon a woman's submission by a male society. The play *Clara S.* (1982) presents the problems of the artist Clara Schumann, whose husband forces her to give up her creativity. Jelinek also wrote many radio plays dealing with woman's emancipation. Most of her characters belong to the sociological category *type moyen* or *type collectif* (Emile Durkheim), whereas most of her work, negative and depressing in its character, represents an experimental approach to literature.

She received the Award for Lyric Poetry of the Austrian University Faculties in 1969, the Austrian National Stipend for Literature in 1973, the Roswitha-Memorial Medal of the City of Bad Gandersheim in 1978 and the Award for the best Film Script of the Secretary of the Interior of West Germany in 1979.

Works

Novels: *Wir sind Lockvögel, Baby* [We Are Decoys, Baby] (1970). *Michael, Ein Jugendbuch für die Infantilgesellschaft* [Michael, A Book for Teenagers of the Infantile Society] (1972). *Die Liebhaberinnen* [The Mistresses] (1975). *Bukolit—ein Hörroman* [Bukolit—a Novel for Listening] (1979). *Die Klavierspielerin* [The Pianist] (1983). *Oh Wildnis, oh Schutz vor ihr* [Oh Wilderness, Oh, Protect Us From It] (1985).

Plays: *Was geschah, nachdem Nora ihren Mann verlassen hatte* [What Happened After Nora Had Left Her Husband] (1979). *Clara S.* (1982). *Theaterstücke*, collected plays (1984).

Lyric Poetry: *Lisas Schatten* [Lisa's Shadow] (1967). *Ende* [The End] (1980).

Collected Works: *Die endlose Unschuldigkeit. Prosa. Hörspiel. Essay* [The Infinite Innocence. Prose. Radio Play. Essay] (1980).

Radio Plays: *Wien-West* [Vienna-West] (1972). *Wenn die Sonne sinkt, ist für manche schon Büroschluß* [When the Sun Sets, Some Take It As the End of Their Office Hours] (1972). *Untergang eines Tauchers* [Drowning of a Diver] (1973). *Kasperl und die dicke Prinzessin oder Kasperl und die dünnen Bauern* [Kasperl and the Fat Princess or Kasperl and the Thin Peasants] (1974). *Die Bienenkönigin* [The Queen of the Bee Stock] (1976). *Porträt einer verfilmten Landschaft* [Portrait of a Landscape], taped on film (1977). *Jelka* (1977). *Die Jubelarin* [The Woman Who Celebrated Her Anniversary] (1978). *Die Ausgesperrten* [Those Who Are Locked Out] (1978).

Film: *Die Ramsau im Dachstein* [The Ram Pig on the Roof] (1976).

Bibliography

Beth, Hanno, "Elfriede Jelinek." In *Neue Literatur der Frauen*, H. Puknau, ed. (Munich, 1980), pp. 133–137. Engerth, Rüdiger, "Modelle und Mechanismen der Trivialliteratur." *Die Furche* (7/25/1970). Kosler, Hans Christian, "Elfriede Jelinek." *Kritisches Lexikon zur deutschsprachigen Gegenwartsliteratur*, ed. H.L. Arnold (edition text a kritik) 3 (1981). N.N., "The Pop Parade" *The Times Literary Supplement* (7/2/1970). Serke, Jürgen,

"Wenn der Mensch im Irrgarten verschwindet," in J.S., *Frauen schreiben* (Hamburg, 1979), pp. 295–297. Vormweg, Heinrich, "Das Porträt Elfriede Jelinek." *Stimme der Frau* (3/3/1978).

Albrecht Classen

Grete Stenbaek Jensen

Born 1925, Skjern, Denmark
Genre(s): novel, short story
Language(s): Danish

Grete Stenbaek Jensen is one of many working-class writers to have emerged in the seventies. She grew up in a rural area and had only seven years of school but was politically active on the left wing as a member of a socialist party for many years before publishing her first book, *Konen og aeggene* (1973), which was very favorably received by the critics, sold well, and in time became one of the most analyzed working-class books by the academic community.

This book is Stenbaek Jensen's major work, pioneering a detailed, realistic, unsentimental, personal description of the kind of hard, demeaning, underpaid jobs unskilled women are forced to take, viewing the problems from a socialist perspective, showing how only a change of politics and committed political action on the part of women as well as men will change women's conditions.

Stenbaek Jensen's next book, *Waterloo retur* (1978), tries sympathetically but not very successfully to demonstrate solutions to the problems presented in her first book, whereas *Marta! Marta!* (1979) deals with her childhood in a small, religious rural community. Stenbaek Jensen's strength lies in her ability to describe women's conditions based on personal experience and relate them to the political system that caused them, thus making the reader politically aware and able to draw constructive conclusions.

Works

Konen og aeggene (1973). *Waterloo retur* (1978). *Marta! Marta!* (1979). *Thea* (1984). *Dagen lang* (1985).

Bibliography

Brostrøm, Torben, *Danske digtere i det 20 århundrede* (1982). Gaul, Bente, *Undertrykkelse,* *oplevelse og modstand i den nye kvinderoman* (1978). Holmgaard, Alice og Anne Aagaard, *Kvindebevidsthed omkring den seksuelle frigørelse* (1976). Juncker, Beth, *Documentarismens proces mod samfundet.* HUG! 3–4 (1975). Karlsen, Hugo, Udbrud. *Afsøgning i litteratur og samfund 1968–1972* (1977). Kyndrup, Morten, *Dansk socialistisk litterature i 70'erne* (1980). Lundbo, Levy Jette, *De knuste spejle* (1976).

Merite von Eyben

Luzmaría Jiménez-Faro

Born 1937, Madrid, Spain
Genre(s): poetry, criticism
Language(s): Spanish

Jiménez-Faro and her husband, the poet Antonio Porpetta, are instances of singular and intense devotion to poetry, not only the production of their own poems but assisting other poets in finding outlets for their works and, through critical and editorial endeavors, preserving some poetic texts of the past from oblivion. She is the founder and director of Ediciones Torremozas in Madrid, a publishing house specializing in the works of women poets. Jiménez-Faro began publishing her own poems in 1978 with the collection *Por un cálido sendero* (Along a Warm Path), followed by *Cuarto de estar* (1980; Sitting Room) and *Sé que vivo* (1984; I Know that I Live). The first of several books of criticism, in collaboration with Antonio Porpetta, was *Carolina Coronado: Apunte biográfico y antología* (1983; Carolina Coronado: Biographical Notes and Anthology), a contribution to the scholarly reevaluation of the nineteenth-century woman poet. In the same year, she published *Poemas*, a selection of works by new women poets, and in 1984, *Veinte poetisas* (Twenty Women Poets), a second anthological selection of new or relatively little-known women lyricists. Several similar anthologies have been published, more or less annually, as well as a number of specialized anthologies, including her *Panorama Antológico de Poetisas Españolas (Siglos XV al XX)* (1987; Panoramic Anthology of Spanish Women Poets from the 15th to the 20th Centuries), *Ernestina de Champourcín: Antología poética* (1988; Anthology of Poems of Ernestina de Champourcin), and *Breviario del deseo (Poesía erótica escrita por mujeres)* (1989; Prayer-book of Desire: Erotic Poetry by Women). *Letanía doméstica para mujeres enamoradas* (1986; Domestic Litany for Women in Love) is her most recent collection of original poems and is typical of her intimate, passionate dialogue with a beloved interlocutor; it is poetry of communication whose persona is unfailingly feminine but whose images frequently evoke the biblical Song of Songs and recall the erotic metaphors of the mystics.

Works

Breviario del deseo (Poesía erótica escrita por mujeres) (1989). *Carolina Coronado: Apunte biográfico y antología* (1983). *Cuarto de estar* (1980). *Ernestina de Champourcín: Antología Poética* (1988). *Letanía doméstica para mujeres enamoradas* (1986). *Panorama autológico de Poetisas Españolas (Siglos XV al XX)* (1987). *Poemas* (1983). *Por un cálido sendero* (1978). *Sé que vivo* (1984). *Veinte poetisas* (1984).

Janet Pérez

Eeva Joenpelto

Born June 17, 1921, Sammatti, Finland
Genre(s): novel, drama
Language(s): Finnish

As a student, Eeva Joenpelto's subject was sociology. She is a freelance writer and has been a member of the Council of Finnish International PEN. She is Vice-Chairman of the Finnish Society of Authors. She has been awarded several literary prizes, was appointed Professor of Arts in 1980, and in 1982 received an honorary doctorate at Helsinki University.

Broad epic narrative has always been one of the most characteristic features of the Finnish novel. Beginning with Aleksis Kivi, the founder of the Finnish novel and still a living classic today, this line has since continued in the work of a great many writers.

Eeva Joenpelto was a well-known and successful writer long before her most famous work, the *Lohja Trilogy*, was published. She made her breakthrough in 1955 with the novel *Neito kulkee vetten päällä* (The Maiden Walks on the Waters), in which an impractical, weak-willed man meets

his opposite, as so often in Joenpelto's books, a purposeful, energetic and strong woman, who is both individualistic and sure of her aims in life. The book is full of disappointments in life, but a love affair rises above the ordinariness of everyday. This longing for beauty and happiness is a theme constantly reiterated throughout Joenpelto's work. It also runs through the novel *Missä lintuset laulaa* (1957; Where Birds Sing). Over the next ten years, Joenpelto's writing branched off into a variety of directions, including both historical events and the problems of contemporary human beings.

Joenpelto's home district of Lohja is about sixty miles southwest of Helsinki, an area with a long history going back to medieval times. It is a prosperous agricultural area as well as an industrial district of modern limestone and cement plants, pulp-mills, and saw-mills. The characters in this series of novels reflect the social changes that have occurred, but social circumstances provide only the background. The focal point lies in the main characters, among them strong women and their fickle men. It is the women who keep the wheels of life turning.

The great strength of Joenpelto's writing lies in her natural and powerful portrayal of people, her plots, which show no lack of dramatic peaks, and the exact historical picture of the times. Below this realistic narrative runs a more philosophical theme: life goes on regardless of human will. "The future cannot be predicted" is one of Joenpelto's favorite themes. Life does not flow along on a logical and consistent level. One can fulfill one's hopes and desires through hard work, but fulfillment often comes too late.

Although her work is firmly anchored in a historical background, the dominant ideas in Joenpelto's novels are universal and so are of interest to a very wide readership. Her trilogy has consequently been translated into several other languages.

The three novels published since the Lohja trilogy, in a way typical of Joenpelto, all have a woman as their central character, a self-sufficient, enterprising, and active person who manages to get through the most difficult stages in life. Her latest novel, *Jottei varjos haalistu* (1986; So Your Shadow Shall Not Fade) is set in the late 1940s, with a family tragedy as its focal point. On the level of ideas, it portrays the collision between humanistic idealism and cold rational thinking. The moral of the story is that tragedy is the savior of mankind, a tragic life elevating the central character above the others. The novel is particularly absorbing for its sound narrative and psychological clarity of vision.

Works

Seitsemän päivää [Seven Days] (1946). Kaakerholman kaupunki [The Town of Kaakerholma] (1950). Tulee sittenkin päivä [The Day Comes After All] (1950). Veljen varjo [Shadow of a Brother] (1951). Johannes vain [Just Johannes] (1952). Kivi palaa [The Stone Burns] (1953). Neito kulkee vetten päällä [The Maiden Walks on the Waters] (1955). Missä lintuset laulaa [Where Birds Sing] (1957). Ralli [Ralli] (1959). Syyskesä [Late Summer] (1960). Kipinöivät vuodet [The Sparkling Years] (1955). Naisten kesken [Between Women] (1962). Viisaat istuvat varjossa [The Wise Sit in the Shadow] (1964). Ritari metsien pimennosta [The Knight from the Darkness of the Forests] (1966). Liian suuria asioita [Too Great Things] (1968). Halusit tai et [Whether You Wanted It or Not] (1969). Vessissä toinen silmä [On the Verge of Tears] (1971). Vetää kaikista ovista [Draughts from All Doors] (1974). Kuin kekäle kädessä [A Firebrand in the Hand](1976). Sataa suolaista vettä [It's Raining Salt Water] (1978). Eteisiin ja kynnyksille [To the Hallways and Thresholds] (1980). Elämän rouva, rouva Glad [Life's Mistress, Mistress Glad] (1982). Rikas ja kunniallinen [Rich and Virtuous] (1984). Jottei varjos haalistu [So Your Shadow Shall Not Fade] (1986).

Bibliography

Koskimies, Rafael, "Eeva Joenpelto. A Time of Reckoning." Books from Finland 3 (1977). Laitinen, Kai, "Eeva Joenpelto and Her Lohja Trilogy." World Literature Today 1 (1980). Laitinen, Kai, "Elämän saumakohdassa. Eeva Joenpellon Lohja-sarja." Metsästä kaupunkiin (Helsinki, 1984). Niiniluoto, Marja, "A Literary Portrait: Eeva Joenpelto." Books from Finland 2 (1969).

Marianne Bargum, translated by Joan Tate

Inger Johanne

(see: Dikken Zwilgmeyer)

Friederike Christiane Henriette John

(see: Eugenie Marlitt)

Anna Jókai

Born 1932, Hungary
Genre(s): novel, short story
Language(s): Hungarian

Jókai has worked most of her life as a teacher. Her 1968 novel *4447* criticizes the world of the petty bourgeois; her forte, however, is not social criticism but the evocation of human character. Her setting is Budapest; her heroes are broken, bewildered people seeking mates and happiness. According to Béla Pomogats, her portraits of lone women longing for love are particularly rich.

Jókai's short stories have been collected in *A Reimsi Angyal* (1975; The Rheims Angel). Several of her works have been successfully rendered on the stage: for example, "Fejünk felől a tetőt, (1969; The Roof from Over Our Heads); *Tartozik és Követel* (1970; Indebted and Demanding). Jókai is a popular writer, whose novels and short stories are distinguished by her direct, colloquial voice.

Works

4447 (1968). Tartozik és Követel (1970). Napok (1972). Mindhalálig (1977). Kötél Nélkül (1969). A Labda (1971). Szeretteink, Szerelmeink (1973). A Reimsi Angyal (1975). A Panasz Leírása (1980).

Bibliography

Pomogats, Béla, Az Újabb Magyar Irodalom: 1945–1981 (Budapest, 1982), pp. 523–524.

Gyorgyi Voros

Ragnhild Jølsen

Born 1875, Enebakk, Norway; died 1908, Oslo
Genre(s): novel
Language(s): Norwegian

The period from 1890 up to 1910 represents a transition from new romanticism and symbolism to new realism in Norwegian literature. To this period Ragnhild Jølsen contributes a distinct but troubled voice. Her use of legends, tales, archaic linguistic forms combined with brilliant in-depth studies of female sexuality, in particular, stand unparalleled in Norwegian literary history.

Jølsen was born into an old, wealthy land-owner family in an isolated, densely forested farm district southeast of Christiania (later Oslo). The youngest of five children she received what at the time must have been a highly unconventional female upbringing, one free of the socially expected female passivity, obedience, and demand for self-obliteration and self-sacrifice. The close proximity to nature, with its large, deep woods, its solitude and "endlessness," gave her a sense of freedom that contrasted sharply with the petit-bourgeois way of life she came to know upon the family's move to the capital. The move came as the result of financial mismanagement, which some years later led to the bankruptcy of the entire estate.

In Christiania Jølsen entered high school. It soon became evident that she did not care for school-learning, rather, she pursued other far more fascinating aspects of life in the city. Especially, the bohemian late-night life in the many city cafés attracted her. There she made acquaintances among the intellectual and artist "rebels," and in a few instances, she became sexually involved. Her behavior, which involved drugs and drinking, scandalized her family and ruined her "good name." In spite of the stir she created Jølsen insisted on living life her way. A great beauty, she never married. At the age of thirty-three, she died from an overdose of veronal.

While in Christiania Jølsen worked short periods as a telegraph operator and a governess. When her family returned to the estate, in a futile attempt to save what was left, she went with them. She was twenty-one.

At home, in Enebakk, Jølsen began to collect oral stories, folktales, proverbs, and songs. She had always been interested in history, especially, the Middle Ages. History subsequently became an important source of inspiration for her writing. She started to write in earnest, and with the approval of her parents she made her debut with the novel *Ve's mor* (1903). It was favorably reviewed in the daily press. Her talent was recognized and encouraged by other writers. Her description of female sexuality and female/male relationships and desire, however, surprised and shocked critics as well as readers. In her later writing Jølsen, again and again, returned to the exploring of female psychological development, to women's conflict-filled visions of love, and to their ill-fated experiences in "real life." These are the major themes in *Rikka Gan* (1905), and *Fernanda Mona* (1905).

Her works can perhaps be seen as thematically centered around a strong protest against the conventions that shaped and circumscribed women's lives. She wrote critically of the role religion and church exerted on women's attempts at self-development. She also wrote fiercely against the pervasive fear of sex. In Enebakk, far from her life in Christiania and the illusion of freedom she had experienced there, she had come to view the Norwegian society as an inhibitively patriarchal one.

The individual characters in her works are first and foremost seen in terms of their relationship to the family, past and present. The fate of the individual woman and man is inextricably woven together with that of the family. The attempt to separate oneself, in order to create a life on one's own, always fails and eventually leads to death. In her portraits of women and men, Jølsen is guided by a firm belief in nineteenth century notions of determinism and the powerful role of the sexual instincts. It is especially the women, who represent the ancestral heritage in her writing, and they are always solitary figures, hypersensitively connected to nature, never able to cross over to the larger human collective. Openly sensual, dreaming, and erotic, they fall for men who are capable of satisfying their sexual needs. But their love-ideal collides not only with the norms, but also with itself; the men they love (physically) are not the men they can respect.

Jølsen's female figures exist in the border areas between dream and reality. Their lives are marked by broken illusions. They are torn between responsible, loyal husbands, and attractive, somewhat demonic, but in the end weak, lovers.

Jølsen constructs her narratives in strong images and scenes, built around tension-filled and climactic moments, which is part of the aesthetics of the period. In Jølsen's case one may speak of a literary *Jugendstil*. Her language is apostrophic, stylized, archaic (fairy tales, ballads, legends). Motifs and milieux may resemble those of Selma Lagerlöf, as in the case of *Hollases Krønike* (1906). Imagery, in general, is characterized by an extensive use of animal and fire symbolism. In *Brugshistorier* (1907), her last work, each of the short stories are characterized by a clear, realist style, full of humor, with none of the melancholy, the grotesque, and the mysticism, which are present in the other works.

Works

Samlede skrifter, B. 1–3. (1909). *Efterladte arbeider*, ed. Antonie Tiberg (1980).

Translations: "Fiddlemusic in the Meadow," "Twelfth Man in the Cabin," in An *Everyday Story: Norwegian Women's Fiction*, ed. Katherine Hanson (Seattle, 1984).

Bibliography

Bjørneboe, Jens, *Drømmen og hjulet* (Oslo, 1964). Bukdahl, Jørgen, "Den røde høst," in *Norsk national kunst*, J. Bukdahl, ed. (Oslo, 1924), pp. 169–221. Christensen, Kari, "Det kvinnelige livsmønster i Ragnhild Jølsens *Rikka Gan*." *NLÅ* (1983), pp. 35–46. Dahl, Willy,. foreword to *Hollases krønike* (Oslo, 1975). Hvistendahl, Rita, "Ragnhild Jølsens *Hollases krønike* som mytologiserende fortelling." *Edda* 3 (1972):157–167. Nilsen, Louise Bohr, "Drømmen og virkeligheten og døden." *Vinduet* 4 (1949):251–262. Tiberg, Antonie, *Ragnhild Jølsen i liv og digtning* (Christiania, 1909).

Pål Bjørby

Jon

(see: Karoline von Günderrode)

Zhuljana G. Jorganxhi

Born 1946, Korçë, southeastern Albania
Genre(s): poetry, reportage
Language(s): Albanian

Jorganxhi has had an active career in the media. Following studies in literature and journalism at the University of Tiranë, she worked for the magazine *Shqiptarja e re* (The New Albanian Woman), as a reporter. In 1975 she took a post as literary editor with the Albanian Radio and Television network in Tiranë.

Works

Net provimesh [Exam Nights] (1969). *Rritje* [Growth] (1974). *Lule në pemën e lirisë* [Flowers on the Tree of Freedom] (1982). *Fëmijët e teto Nastës* [Aunt Nasta's Children] (1975).

Philip Shashko

Maria Jotuni

Born 1880; died 1943
Genre(s): short story, drama
Language(s): Finnish

Maria Jotuni's reputation as a writer rests on her daring and highly individual portrayals of women and on her gifts as a dramatist. Her works concentrate on analyses of the human condition, the contradictions, the frustrations, the fantasies. As the creative "observer" she is both deeply sympathetic and ruthlessly revealing.

Maria Jotuni grew up in the Eastern Finnish province of Savo, and her early work draws richly on that background for subject matter and local color. Her style owes something to the lilting rhythms of the Savo dialect—and something to the lyricism of the Finnish Bible, with which she was familiar from her earliest years. She describes with charm her early ventures and the thrill of manipulating words. "I had drafted in block capitals on a scrap of paper a poem: 'A brook bubbles up in a grove.' I thought this was an astonishing achievement; the invention thrilled me enormously. 'Grove' was not a word a child would naturally use. These were magic words, because I saw the brook and the whole wood. And it made me exceedingly happy."

The year 1905 was an important one for Finnish literature. In this year Maria Jotuni published her first work, *Suhteita* (Relationships). The work is a collection of short stories, full of insight into human behavior. It was well received. Her career as a writer looked full of promise. The next collection of stories called *Rakkautta* (Love) evoked the reactions that later came to be associated with Jotuni's work. She was attacked for her outrageous view of life, the open sensuality of her female characters, her alleged disrespect for the deeper human values. For a generation accustomed to idealized pictures of women it was obviously difficult to approach her characters.

In 1909 the publication of a story entitled "Arkielämää" (Everyday Life) was an artistic breakthrough for Jotuni. In this story she takes us through a sunny summer's day in a rural community in Savo, as seen through the eyes of the main character, a tramp called "the Priest." The Priest is skillful both as a tinker and a mender of shattered human relationships.

People and human relationships particularly intrigued Jotuni. She was content to leave descriptions of the environment to visual artists. For her, the human voice could reveal the inner soul of the speaker even when the words themselves could not be distinguished.

Detailed observation of the individual has a natural affinity with dramatic expression, and it was as a dramatist that Maria Jotuni achieved her greatest artistic successes. Her plays are still performed successfully in the theatre and have stood up to many new interpretations.

The years before the First World War were active ones for Maria Jotuni in both her private and her professional life. She married in 1911 and in 1912 she gave birth to two sons. The establishment of a family seemed to give her even more energy for her writing. In 1913 she published a collection of short stories *Kun on tunteet* (When You Have Feelings). The National Theatre produced *Miehen Kylkiluu* (The Rip of Man) in 1914 and *Savu-uhri* (Burnt Offering) in 1915.

Jotuni had an effective weapon in her sense of humor. It had enriched her early short stories, and its significance as an internal source of inspiration and as an explanation of life grew stronger with time. The side effects of the First World War, speculation, financial insecurity, man's sense of moral futility, all provided subjects out of which grew the comedy *Kultainen vasikka* (1917; The Golden Calf).

The events that caused the greatest stir in Finnish cultural life during the 1920s were the preparation and presentation of Jotuni's comedy *Tohvelisankarin rouva* (The Wife of the Henpecked Hero). While writing this comedy, Jotuni was much oppressed by thoughts of death and loneliness. The play appears to have opened up for her a new understanding of her own ability as a writer as well as a productive connection with the most modern trends in art and theatre. The play glows with the colors of an Expressionist painting and glitters with the dramatic and farcical techniques of, say, a Pirandello.

Maria Jotuni herself did not think the play would be understood by her contemporaries— and she was right. Outraged discussion of the play even went as far as Parliament, where it was proposed that the National Theatre's state subsidy should be withdrawn as a punishment for presenting plays that could corrupt morals.

By the late 1920s Jotuni was moving towards a new phase in her writing. *Tyttö ruusutarhassa* (Girl in a Rose-garden) is a more classical collection of short stories in which the juxtaposition of tragedy and comedy becomes more markedly individual. In the early 1930s she published two collections of aphorisms: *Avonainen lipas* (The Open Casket) and *Vaeltaja* (The Wanderer). A third collection *Jäähyväiset* (Farewells) appeared posthumously.

Fantasy and reality, the aims of art and literature, the lives of women: Jotuni's reflections extended keenly and fearlessly into many different areas. "Marriage can be a dreadful shackle; fortunately, we are unaware of the seriousness of the fetters when we are young, haven't time to suffer over the cruelty of it when we are middle-aged and don't even feel sickened by its scars when we are old."

Towards the end of her career, Jotuni turned her attention to the analysis of the uncouth underbelly of civilized society. In 1930 she won first prize in a major Scandinavian short story competition. She also took part in a novel competition with her work *Huojuva talo* (The Shifting House). The enormous scope of the book did not match the expectations of the panel of judges, and *Huojuva talo* was not published until 1963, twenty years after Jotuni's death. It brought about a profound reappraisal of her writings. The novel itself was exceptional both in quantity and quality. It is a massive six-hundred-page family epic in which middle-class life and the institution of marriage are depicted as a plague or curse on the human race.

Huojuva talo has much in common with Jotuni's last play *Klaus, Louhikon herra* (Klaus, Master of Louhikko). The historical play is heavy with the atmosphere of war and rich with Shakespearean imagery. It also stresses, as demanded by Jotuni's deepest vision, a belief in the triumph of a moral and ethical world system.

Works

Short stories: *Suhteita* [Relationships] (1905). *Rakkautta* [Love] (1907). *Kun on tunteet* [When You Have Feelings] (1913). *Martinin rikos* [Martin's Crime] (1914). *Tyttö ruusutarhassa* [Girl in a Rose-garden] (1927).
Novels: *Arkielämää* [Everyday Life] (1909). *Huojuva talo* [The Shifting House] (1963).
Plays: *Vanha koti* [The Old Home]. *Miehen kylkiluu* [The Rib of Man] (1914). *Savu-uhri* [Burnt Offering] (1915). *Kultainen vasikka* [The Golden Calf] (1917). *Tohvelisankarin rouva* [The Wife of the Hen-pecked Hero] (1924). *Olen syyllinen* [I Am Guilty] (1929). *Klaus, Louhikon herra* [Klaus, the Master of Louhikko] (1946).
Children's Books: *Musta härkä* [The Black Bull] (1915). *Jussi ja Lassi* [Jussi and Lassi] (1921).
Aphorisms: *Avonainen lipas* [The Open Casket] (1929). *Vaeltaja* [The Wanderer] (1933). *Jäähyväiset* [Good-bye] (1949). *Äiti ja lapsi* [Mother and Child] (1965).

Bibliography

Kupiainen, Unto, *Huumorin sukupolvi* [The Humor Generation] (1954). Niemi, Irmeli, *Maria Jotuni näytelmät* [Maria Jotuni's Plays] (1964). Niemi, Irmeli, "Maria Jotuni. Money, Morals and Love." Tr. of the short story "Hilda Husso, a Phone Call Between Hotels," by Herbert Lomas. *Books from Finland* 1(1980).

Irmeli Niemi

Julia

(see: Balbilla)

Jeanne de Jussie

Born c. 1500, Geneva, Switzerland; died after 1557, Annency, France
Genre(s): memoirs
Language(s): French

A member of a cloistered convent of Clarissas in Geneva, Jeanne wrote a lengthy memoir, entitled *The Seeds of Calvinism, or The Beginning of the Heresy in Geneva*, about the turbulent years of the reform of Geneva, 1526–1535. The work ends in August 1535 with her community being forced to abandon their convent and move to new quarters in Annency. Jeanne eventually became its abbess.

Jeanne composed most of the work shortly after her arrival in Annency but did not complete it until 1557. It was not published until 1611 as part of a propaganda effort on the part of Duke Charles-Emmanuel of Savoy who wished to reassert a claim of authority over Geneva. In it, she described the reformation in Geneva through a series of detailed vignettes, many focused on the women of the city and the religious choices they made. She was convinced that women remained Catholic more steadfastly than did men, pointing out that many of the Franciscan friars of the city had left the church and married, whereas only one member of her convent had converted to the evangelical cause.

Largely because of its length and detail, the work provides a precious record of women's involvement in the reform movement and of the reaction of Catholic women to the revolutionary changes in their social and religious world.

Works

Le Levain du Calvinisme, ou Commencement de l'heresie de Geneve (1611).

Bibliography

Douglass, J., "Women and the Continental Reformation," in R. Ruether, ed., *Religion and Sexism. Images of Woman in the Jewish and Christian Traditions* (1974). Kingdon, R., "Was the Protestant Reformation a Revolution? The Case of Geneva," in *Transition and Revolution. Problems and Issues of European Renaissance and Reformation History* (1974). Rilliet, A., *Notice sur Jeanne de Jussie et sur le livre intitulé Le levain du Calvinisme* (1866). General references: Hauser, *Sources de l'histoire de France*, II, p. 113.

Thomas Head

Helvi Juvonen

Born 1919, Iisalmi, Finland; died 1959, Helsinki
Genre(s): poetry
Language(s): Finnish

After graduating from high school, Juvonen worked as a bank clerk; she became a free-lance writer in 1948. Her works include six collections of poetry appearing over a decade and one book of animal fables. In Finnish poetry, Juvonen belongs to the turning point between metrical and free verse. In the former her models are Otto Manninen and Uuno Kailas, masters of polished and laconic expression in traditional Finnish poetry; in the latter she is among the first Finnish masters. This duality is not only stylistic but is also reflected in her thought: in her traditional poems the ego strives toward communication, whereas in her modernist poems the self dissolves in the experience expressed by perceptual images. Thematically, Juvonen's poetry deals with questions of the self, suffering, truth, and belief. In the last-mentioned area, her thinking moves somewhere between Christianity, mysticism, and pantheism. Its intellectual clarity, severe imagery, fervent striving, and polished asceticism of expression have kept Juvonen's poetry in high esteem. In the eyes of posterity she is one of the first masters of poetic modernism in Finland.

Works

Kootut runot [Collected Poems] (1960). *Pikku Karhun talviunet* [Little Bear's Winter Sleep] (1947).

Bibliography

Anhava, Tuomas, "Helvi Juvonen." *Sanantuoja* (1959). Polkunen, Mirjam, "Rose und Bär." *Mitteilungen aus der deutschen Bibliotek* 10 (1976).

Markku Envall

K

Elena Kadare

Born 1943, Fier, Albania
Genre(s): novel, short story
Language(s): Albanian

Kadare was the first woman in post-war Albania to publish a novel. She attended school in Elbasan, central Albania, and the University of Tiranë. Since the completion of her studies, she has worked as a journalist and editor. Kadare made her reputation as a writer initially by dealing with problems of women's emancipation.

Works

Një lindje e vështirë [A Difficult Birth] (1970). *Bashkëshortët* [The Spouses] (1981). *Shuaje dritën, Vera!* [Turn Off the Light, Vera!] (1965). *Nusja dhe shtetrre-thimi* [The Bride and the State of Siege] (1978).

Philip Shashko

Margit Kaffka

Born June 1, 1880, Nagykároly, Hungary; died
December 1, 1918, Budapest
Genre(s): poetry, novel
Language(s): Hungarian

Kaffka studied at Nagykároly, and later Budapest, gaining both an elementary school teacher's certificate and later, a secondary school teacher's diploma. She taught most of her life, and her publications include texts for the use of secondary girls' schools. She married Bruno Fröhlich, an engineer, in 1905 but they were divorced a few years later. In 1910 she was married again, this time to Ervin Bauer, a physician and the brother of the writer and sociologist Béla Balázs, a member of the *Nyugat* circle. During World War I her husband was stationed at Temesvár (now Timoşoara, Romania), where she also spent some time. She died during the influenza epidemic of 1918–1919 with her son.

A poet and a novelist, Kaffka is one of the important writers of the early twentieth century and one of the first recognized women writers in Hungary. Her stories and novels present the world in which she grew up and study the fate of women faced with limited choices. Her two major themes are the decline of the gentry, that is, of the lesser nobility represented by her mother's family, and the fate of women at the turn of the century. The gentry, becoming slowly impoverished, clung to their old ways, stifling themselves and passing up opportunities as a result.

Three periods can be identified in her work: from 1905 to 1908 when the periodical *Nyugat* was started, from then until the out outbreak of World War I, and the war years until her death. She began as a poet, and her first pieces appeared in *Magyar Géniusz* and other progressive journals (*A Hét, Figyelő, Szerda*). She belonged to the new generation, both in her choice of everyday themes and language and in her searching for the meaning of life. She was associated with *Nyugat*, and this proved to be salutary for her development. Endre Ady, the leading figure of the group and foremost poet of turn-of-the-century Hungary, encouraged her to move towards a more critical, even a revolutionary view of society and to experiment with forms that would eventually lead her to free verse.

Still, her prose is more important than her poetry. Kaffka's first important novel, *Színek és évek* (Colors and Years) shows the decline of the gentry through the life of a woman, thus uniting her two favorite themes. In 1917 she published *Hangyaboly* (Anthill), a harsh critique of convent schools based on her own experiences. Her two other novels, *Mária évei* (Maria's Years) and *Állomasok* (Stations) continued the theme of the first novel, probing the possibilities and pitfalls of the women of her generation. While in *Mária évei* the heroine has some options—she has at least received an education—her life is unfulfilled. *Állomások* is too close to her own time, to immediate problems, and lacks the perspective needed for a satisfactory literary examination of these problems. Two collections of short stories, *A Révnél* (At the Haven) and *Az Élet utján* (On the Path of Life) are more successful.

In the poems she exhibits a fine feeling for a woman's and a mother's point of view. Her early poems were more narrative than lyrical, but she exhibited even then a sensitivity and a facility for describing details that reflect psychological states—a trait seen also in her novels.

Works

K.M. *Válogatott művei*, ed. and intro. György Bodnár (1956). *Lázadó asszonyok*, 2 vols., ed. Sándor Kozocsa (1958). *Hullámzó élet, cikkek, tanúlmányok*, ed. and intro. György Bodnár (1959). K.M. *összes versei*, 2 vols., ed. and intro. Sándor Kozocsa (1961). K.M. *regényei*, ed. György Bodnár (1968). *Csendes válságok, elbeszélések*, ed. Sándor Kozocsa (1969).

Bibliography

Bölöni, György, *Magyarság, emberség* (Budapest, 1959). Brunauer, Dalma, "A Woman's Self-Liberation; the Story of Margit Kaffka, 1888–1919." *Canadian-American Review of Hungarian Studies* 2 (1978): 297–325. Denes, Tibor, *Kaffka Margit* (Pécs, 1932). Galóczy, Claire, "Marquerite Kaffka." *New Hungarian Review* II (1934): 401–407. Győri, János, "Az Édenvesztéstöl a remekmüig K.M. világában." *Uj Irás* 3 and 8 (1976): 91–99; 103–106. Herczeg, Gyula, "Impressionizmus és realizmus K.M. prózájában." *Magyar nyelv* 1 and 2 (1982): 19–29; 136–145. Hatvany, Lajos, *Irodalmi tanúlmányok* (Budapest, 1960). Király, István, "K.M." *Irodalom és társadalom* (Budapest, 1976), pp. 124–133. Radnóti, Miklos, *Kaffka Margit müvészi fejlődése* (Szeged, 1943). Raisz, Rózsa, "K.M. prózája és stilusa." *Hevesi Szemle* 3 (1978): 13–14. Rónay, György, *A Regény és az élet* (Budapest, 1947). Török, Sophie, "K.M." *Költőnők antológiája* (Budapest, 1943).

Enikő Molnár Basa

Maria Kahle

*Born 1891, Wesel, Lower Rhine, Germany;
died 1975, Olsberg, Westphalia*
Genre(s): essay, poetry, short story, fairy tale
Language(s): German

After private lessons and secondary school, Maria Kahle (née Kessler) worked as a foreign correspondent in Rio and São Paulo, Brazil. She returned to Germany in order to edit the daily *Der Jungdeutsche* (The Young German) in Cassel, a title that would suggest a "volkisch" or nationalist bias, like many of Maria Kahle's publications. Based on her familiarity with emigrated Germans in Brazil, Maria Kahle became an expert on issues of the "Auslandsdeutschen" (German ethnic groups abroad) already in her publications before the national socialist takeover of 1933, an expertise that recommended her to the regime, which consistently exploited that issue. In due time, Maria Kahle became the founder of the "Ostmarkhilfe." Titles such as "The German Woman and Her Volk" and "Germans Beyond the Borders" illustrate her contributions. After 1945, Maria Kahle returned to poetry and fairy tale.

Works

Liebe und Heimat (1916). *Urwaldblumen* (1921). *Ruhrland* (1923). *Deutsches Volk in der Fremde* (1933). *Deutsche jenseits der Grenze* (1934). *Die Frau und ihr Volk* (1934). *Deutsches Herz zwischen Heimat und Fremde* (1937). *Deutsche Frauen im Ausland und in den Kolonien* (1937). *Umweg über Brasilien* (1942). *Westfälische Bauern im Ostland* (1940). *Was die Schildkröte erzählte* (1950). *Herz der Frau* (1959).

Bibliography

von Wilpert, Gero, *Deutsches Literatur-Lexikon*. 2nd edition (Stuttgart, 1975).

Ute Marie Saine

Lisa Kahn

Born July 15, 1927, Berlin, Germany
Genre(s): poetry, prose fiction, literary
*   criticism*
Language(s): German

Lisa Kahn is perhaps still best known as a tireless champion of the cause of women who live in America and write in German. With the anthology *Reisegepäck Sprache* (1979), the expanded dual-language edition (1983; In Her Mother's Tongue), and several essays in scholarly and literary journals, she has effectively called attention to a significant but largely neglected group of writers. Recently, however, her verse has received critical acclaim, and she is now recognized as a poet of stature.

Kahn is the daughter of Ludwig and Margarete Kupfer. After attending school in Leipzig she enrolled at the University of Heidelberg, where she earned her doctorate in German in 1953. In 1950–1951 she attended the University of Washington as a Fulbright scholar; while in America she met her future husband, Robert Kahn, who was to become a poet and prominent literary scholar. In 1953 her son Peter was born, now an artist and the illustrator of some of Kahn's books. A daughter, Beatrice, was born in 1959. In 1962 the Kahns moved to Houston, where Robert was Professor of German at Rice University until his death in 1970. Lisa has been on the faculty of Texas Southern University since 1968. She has been married to Herbert Finkelstein since 1973.

Kahn turned to creative writing relatively late in life, and her first works are correspondingly mature. A distinctive style—a contemporary poetic idiom written in a controlled free verse—is evident from the beginning, as is a wide thematic range. In *Feuersteine* (1978; Fire Stones), nature is significant, both the seasons and specific European and American scenes. Personal poems are also present, as are five concrete poems. In her next books, as some of the titles reflect, America assumes greater importance, as does Kahn's position as a German in America: *Denver im Frühling* (1980; Denver in the Spring), *Utahs Geheimnisse* (1981; Utah's Secrets), and the dual-language collection *From My Texan Log Cabin/Aus meiner texanischen*

Blockhütte (1984). The majority of these poems explore some aspect of a Western landscape, and in *Utahs Geheimnisse*, eleven allude directly to a color photograph reproduced on the facing page. The landscape is one of silence and solitude.

As the poems of *Denver im Frühling* most clearly illustrate, Kahn's position as a German-speaking author living in America is variously manifested in her work: a respect for her adopted home, a fascination with the awe-inspiring vastness of the American West, and an awareness of the difference between her poetic language and that spoken around her on a daily basis are constantly in evidence.

Some of Kahn's later works continue the patterns already established. The relationship between picture and poem is of central importance to *Bäume* (1983; Trees) and *Tor und Tür* (1986; Gate and Door). Each contains a sequence of poems on the theme suggested by the title, many of them directly related to a photograph. New developments, however, are also present, as in *David am Komputer und andere Gedichte* (1982; David at the Computer and Other Poems). In the title cycle, King David has traded his harp for a computer, and his psalms of praise and repentance have given way to the questions— some serious, some silly—of contemporary society. The execution is no less striking than the concept, as David is seen to become more and more familiar with computer programming as the cycle progresses.

Lisa Kahn's contributions as a scholar and critic, most notably in the areas of the contemporary lyric, German-American literature, and the relationship between poetry and the visual arts, are significant. Her poetry reflects similar themes: the German-American experience and a concern with the relationship between visual image and poetic word.

Works

Klopfet an so wird euch nicht aufgetan: Gedichte (1975). Feuersteine: Gedichte (1978). Denver im Frühling (1980). Utahs Geheimnisse: Gedichte (1981). David am Komputer und andere Gedichte (1982). From My Texan Log Cabin/ Aus meiner texanischen Blockhütte(1984). Baüme(1984). Wer mehr liebt: Kurzgeschichten und Märchen(1984).

Tor und Tür (1986). Kinderwinter: Gedichte (1986).

Jerry Glenn

Anu Kaipainen

Born March 14, 1933, Muolaa, Finland
Genre(s): novel, poetry, drama
Language(s): Finnish

Anu Kaipainen has dealt with topical matters in her novels through history and myth and has thus established her own territory in the newer Finnish prose writing. In her works, a woman generally acts as a social conscience and dissents from her indifferent environment. Her works often contain powerful feelings about society and the world, but illustrate the author's humor and irony.

Her early works at the beginning of the 1960s were rather bloodless descriptions of the everyday life of a doctor's wife and teacher, of which the author had personal experience. Her first real achievement was a fantastic historical novel Arkkienkeli Oulussa (1967; An Archangel in Oulu) in which the present is projected into history, the war between Finland and Russia 1808–1809. The novel Magdaleena ja maailman lapset (1969; Magdaleena and the Children of the World) is one of the best works written in Finland during the socially active sixties. Topical material, with abundant pamphlet and collage content, is combined with a folk tale about a woman who kills her child and the Bible stories of the sinful Mary Magdalene and Martha and Mary. The myth technique is used both to objectivize contemporary material and to show how little the position of woman, for example, has changed. In the seventies this technique became stereotyped in Kaipainen's novels. She was most successful when she abandoned it: Poimisin heliät hiekat (1979; I Would Pluck the Bright Sands) is a poetic, archaically stylized biographical novel of Larin Pareske, a famous Karelian woman rune singer who lived in the nineteenth century. Kaipainen has also rendered an account of her marriage and her husband's death in Kun on rakastanut paljon (1986; When One Has Greatly Loved).

Works

Utuiset neulat [Hazy Needles] (1960). Kädet helmassa [Hands in One's Lap] (1961). Puolikovat [The Half-boiled] (1962). Kaksi lukukautta [Two Terms] (1965). Ruusubaletti [Rose Ballet] (1966). Arkkienkeli Oulussa [An Archangel in Oulu] (1967). Magdaleena ja maailman lapset [Magdaleena and the Children of the World] (1969). Surupukuinen nainen [Woman in Mourning] (1971). On neidolla punapaula [The Maid with the Red Ribbon] (1973). Naistentanssit [Ladies' Evening] (1975). Kellomorsian [Mystic Bride] (1977). Poimisin heliät hiekat [I Plucked the Bright Sands] (1979). Kuninkaan paikka [The King's Place] (1981). Kaihoja kukkuvat käet [Yearning the Cuckoos Call] (1983). Kun on rakastanut paljon [When One Has Greatly Loved] (1986). Virulinnut [Shivering Birds] (1987).

Bibliography

Polkunen, Mirjam, An Interpretation of "Magdaleena ja maailman lapset." Romaani ja tulkinta [The Novel and the Interpretation], ed. Mirjam Polkunen (1973), pp. 180–188. Tarkka, Pekka, "Anu Kaipainen." Suomalaisia nykykirjailijoita [Finnish Modern Writers] (1980), pp. 75–78.

Liia Huhtala

Isabelle Kaiser

Born October 2, 1866, Beckenried,
    Switzerland; died February 17, 1925,
    Beckenried
Genre(s): novel, short story, poetry
Language(s): French, German

Isabelle Kaiser, now almost forgotten, was a much-read and honored author of novels, short stories, and poetry. She did not belong to any special literary group or movement. Her earlier works, such as Sorcière (1896; Witch) and Notre Père (1900; Our Father) are strongly influenced by French romantic authors, but gradually she became more realistic and even naturalistic, as exemplified in Der wandernde See (1910; The Moving Lake). She also showed interest in social problems and the situation of the indigent, as in Rahels Liebe (1920; Rachel's Love) and the women's rights movement, as can be seen in Die

Friedensucherin (1908; The Woman Who Searched for Peace).

Isabelle was born in the German-speaking part of Switzerland, but when she was three years old the family moved to Geneva, where only French was spoken. Ten years later her father found other employment in the little town of Zug, and Isabelle had to switch from speaking French to German. This early experience enabled her to write prose as well as poetry in both languages, in all, thirteen books in French and twelve in German. When she was nineteen she fell in love with a young man who inspired her to write a diary, that afterwards became the source of *Die Friedensucherin*. After three years her lover ended their relationship. This sad love story is reflected in many of Kaiser's poems, short stories, and novels; it is most clearly reflected in *Rahels Liebe*, and a German revision of the French *Coeur de femme* (1891; Woman's Heart). She won a literary prize for the German version.

More objective are Kaiser's regional works, in which she describes the daily life of the simple inhabitants of the mountainous region around her village, Beckenried. To the village itself she devoted several poems. However, the description of the people in these works shows an unrealistic idealism; no matter how poor, they are always happy and satisfied with their life's circumstances. The growing socialistic movement did not influence Isabelle Kaiser.

Although she lived in isolation in her chalet, she was not immune to world events. In her *Novellen und Skizzen* (1914; Short Stories and Sketches) she pleads for peace, strongly asserting the poetic and social mission of the literary artist.

In spite of her weak constitution, Isabelle Kaiser travelled in Switzerland and throughout Europe (Italy, Germany, Belgium, and France). In these countries she became a popular elocutionist, reading fragments of her novels and reciting her poems in German as well as in French; she was admired in Parisian literary circles. She considered herself a priestess of literary art. She was awarded the Swiss Schiller prize (1911) and the prize of the French Academy for her work *Juteau Davigneux* (1910) as the best Catholic novel of the year.

Works

Ici bas (1888). *Sous les étoiles* (1890). *Coeur de femme* (1891). *Fatimé, chants de deuil* (1893). *Sorcière* (1896). *Des ailes* (1897). *Héro* (1898). *Notre Père* (1900). *Wenn die Somne untergeht* (1901). *Vive le roi!* (1903). *Der Roman der Marquise* (1904). *Seine Majestät* (1905). *Vater Unser* (1906). *L'éclair dans la voile* (1907). *Mein Herz* (1908). *Die Friedensucherin* (1908). *Marcienne de Flue* (1909). *Der wandernde See* (1910). *Le jardin clos* (1912). *Mein Leben* (1913). *La vierge du lac* (1914). *Von ewiger Liebe* (1914). *Le vent des cimes* (1916). *Unsere deutschen Kriegsgefangenen am Vierwaldstättersee* (1916). *Rahels Liebe* (1920). *Die Nächte der Königin*, Schweizer Erähler Vol. 13 (1923). *Letzte Garbe* (1929).

Bibliography

Carnot, P. Maurus, "Erinnerungen." *Frauenland* (Juni, 1934). Federer, Heinrich, "Isabelle Kaiser." *Neue Zürcher Nachrichten* 19, II (Abendblatt, 1925). Marbach, Felix, *Isabelle Kaiser* (Rapperswil, 1940). Odermatt, Herm, "Isabelle Kaiser." *Neue Zürcher Nachrichten*, No. 60–63 (1935). Spitteler, Carl, *Gesammelte Werke* 9 (Zürich, 1950), pp. 356–358. Sprenger Viol, Inge, *Merk-würdige Frauen* (Almona, 1986), pp. 93–101. Steiner, Adolf A., *Isabelle Kaiser und zug* (Zug, 1967).

Judy Mendels

Mascha Kaléko

Born June 7, 1907, Schidlow, Poland; died January 21, 1975, Zurich
Genre(s): novel, poetry
Language(s): German

Mascha Kaléko, the daughter of a Russian father and Austrian mother, shared the fate of many of the more fortunate German-speaking Jews of eastern Europe. During the First World War the family was evacuated to Marburg. The father was interned on account of his Russian nationality, and after the war, when he proved unable to establish himself in Germany, Mascha and her mother moved to Berlin without him. For a few years Mascha's fortunes improved. She married, her whimsical poems found favor with Berlin's literary elite, and her first book, *Das lyrische Stenogrammheft* (1933; The Lyrical Stenographer's Notebook), was a phenomenal success. Her situation deteriorated after Hitler's assumption of power, and in rapid succession in 1938 her marriage of ten years ended in divorce, she married the musician and composer Cemjo Vinaver, a son, Steven, was born, and the family fled to America. They soon settled in New York, which was to remain their home until Kaléko and her husband immigrated to Israel in 1966. The last years of her life were lonely and bitter. Steven died suddenly in 1968, and Cemjo died after an extended illness in 1973. Kaléko failed to adapt to her new environment and wrote little after leaving New York.

In attempting to characterize Kaléko's early works, critics found such comparisons as Morgenstern, Ringelnatz, Kästner, and Tucholsky, four of the most important authors of satirical verse in German. The style of these poems is disarmingly simple, as are the themes. In the first poem of *Das lyrische Stenogrammheft*, "Interview mit mir selbst" (Interview with Myself), Kaléko sets the tone of her early work, as she ironically examines her life: "My teacher spoke . . ./ of ethical *niveau*./ He said we would now embark upon life's journey./ . . . But I, alas, embarked only upon a job in an office." The language is thoroughly colloquial and totally untranslatable; rhyme is used with great effectiveness, as, for example, the rhyme words "niveau" and "Büro" (office) in the passage quoted above.

Although Kaléko's basic style never changed, her experiences in exile made her verse more bitter and the satire more biting. Comparisons came to be made with another German-Jewish exile, Heinrich Heine. Kaléko herself comments ironically on the comparison between Heine and herself in the expanded second edition of *Verse für Zeitgenossen* (1958; Verses for Contemporaries), the first postwar collection published in Germany. In the poem "Deutschland, ein Kindermärchen" (Germany: A Children's Fairy Tale)—a direct allusion to Heine's "Germany: A Winter's Fairy Tale"—Kaléko, with her typical irony, records her impressions of Germany during a visit in 1956, commenting on the alleged disappearance of all traces of Nazism by means of such images as vegetarian wolves.

Mascha Kaléko's highly promising literary career, like that of many other German writers of her generation, was shattered by Hitler. She continued to write in her New York exile but never regained her earlier prominence. As she ironically comments in a poem from *Verse für Zeitgenossen*, "And if [in Germany] the names of poets of the second-rank are listed, mine is named too." Only since her death has her work again come to receive attention.

Works

Das lyrische Stenogrammheft (1933). *Kleines Lesebuch für Große: Gereimtes und ungereimtes* (1935). *Verse für Zeitgenossen* (1946). Expanded rpt. (1958). *Der Papagei, die Mamagai und andere komische Tiere* (1961). *Verse in Dur und Moll* (1967). *Das himmelgraue Poesie-Album der Mascha Kaléko* (1968). *Hat alles seine zwei Schattenseiten* (1973). *In meinen Träumen läutet es Sturm: Gedichte und Epigramme aus dem Nachlaß* (1977). *Feine Pflänzchen: Rosen, Tulpen, Nelken & Nahrhaftere Gewächse* (1977). *Der Gott der kleinen Webefehler* (1977). *Heute ist morgen schon gestern: Gedichte aus dem Nachlaß*, ed. Gisela Zoch-Westphal (1980). *Tag und Nacht Notizen*, ed. Gisela Zoch-Westphal (1981). *Hat alles seine zwei Schattenseiten: Sinn—und Unsinngedichte und der Kasseler Vortrag*, ed. Hilda Arnold (1983). *Ich bin von anno dazumal: Chansons, Lieder, Gedichte*, ed. Gisela Zoch-Westphal (1984).

Bibliography

Frankenstein, A, "Mascha Kaléko." *Emuna* 10 (1975): Supplement, pp. 40–44.

Jerry Glenn

Aino Kallas

Born 1878; died 1956
Genre(s): novel, short story, diary
Language(s): Finnish

Aino Kallas was the daughter of a distinguished Finnish family. Her father, Julius Krohn, was one of the prime movers of the mid-century national movement, the man who set in motion the scholarly collection and study of Finnish oral tradition. At the age of twenty-two, she married Oskar Kallas, one of Estonia's leading folklorists.

With her marriage to Oskar Kallas she shifted from the center of the Finnish national movement to the center of the emerging Estonian national movement. Although Aino Kallas had already begun to write before her marriage, she only became fully aware of her literary calling after she had settled in Estonia. In her choice of themes and style and almost certainly in her purpose, however, she differed markedly from her own generation of Finnish writers. Her themes sprang largely from her commitment to the Estonian national movement. Although she wrote in Finnish for Finns, her writings were translated immediately into Estonian by Friedebert Tuglas, himself an outstanding author. Works such as *Meren takaa* (1904, 1905; From Beyond the Sea) and *Lähtevien laivojen kaupunki* (1913; The Town of the Departing Ships) have been characterized by one critic as "indignation realism," an attempt to evoke the centuries of suffering endured by the Estonians at the hands of the Baltic-German overlords. A selection of short stories from this period appeared in English in 1924 under the title *The White Ship* and won considerable critical acclaim.

In 1922 Oskar Kallas was entrusted with the diplomatic representation in London and the Hague. Aino Kallas described her move to London as a "leap into the ocean." Despite her close connections with literary circles in London, it is, however, difficult to detect any direct influence on her writings from this period. The seeds of inspiration continued to come from the Estonian past. During this period Aino Kallas wrote four of her most profound works, a series of novellas: *Barbara von Tisenhusen*, *Reigin pappi* (The Rector of Reigi), *Sudenmorsian* (The Wolf's Bride), and *Pyhän joen kosto* (The Revenge of the Holy River). Like her earlier stories, these are set in historical Estonia and are rich in detail; the sense of history is also heightened by the deliberate use of archaic language and often by a chronicle style. If her earlier works were historical narratives, these are historical ballads, into which the author projects her own often difficult and strained inner life, both real and imagined.

The most personal and symbolic of these stories is *The Wolf's Bride*. In this and other stories Kallas' characters wander dreamlike through life until they experience, suddenly and by accident, almost as if bewitched, a strange event. It brings the character a moment of great bliss but at the same time destroys. In the 1920s and the 1930s these works were received with enthusiastic acclaim in Finland, Estonia, and Great Britain.

Aino Kallas is one of the best-known Finnish writers outside her own country. Her books were enjoyed as masterly historical accounts of forbidden love, and they retain their attraction at this level: the very timelessness of her theme explains their continuing popularity both in Finnish and in translation. It was the appearance of the first edition of her diaries, however, that prepared the way for the appraisal of her work that is still in hand.

Works

Lauluja ja balladeja [Song and Ballads] (1897). *Kuloa ja kevättä* [Forest Fire and Spring] (1899). *Kirsti* (1902). *Meren takaa I* [From Beyond the Sea, I] (1904). *Ants Raudjalg* (1907). *Virolaisia kansansatuja* [Estonian Folk Tales] (1910). *Merentakaisia lauluja* [Songs from Beyond the Sea] (1911). *Lähtevien laivojen kaupunki* [The Town of the Departing Ships] (1913). *Seitsemän* [Seven] (1914). *Suljettu puutarha* [The Closed Garden] (1915). *Tähdenlento* [Falling Star] (1915). *Nuori Viro* [Young Estonia] (1918). *Musta raita* [Black Stripe] (1919). *Katinka Rabe* (1920). *Vieras veri* [Strange Blood] (1921). *Barbara von Tisenhusen* (1923). *Reigin pappi* [The Rector of Reigi] (1926). *Langatonta sähkö* [Wireless Electricity] (1928). *Sudenmorsian* [The Wolf's Bride] (1928). *Novelleja* [Choice of Novellas] (1928). *Pyhän Joen kosto* [The Revenge of the Holy River] (1930). *Marokon lumoissa* [Enchanted by Morocco] (1931). *Batseba Saarenmaalla* [Bath-Sheba of Saarenmaa] (1932). *Mare ja hänen poikansa* [Mare and Her Sons] (1935). *Talonpojan kunnia* [The Honor of the Peasant] (1936). *Valitut teokset I-III* [Selected Works I-III] (1938). *Kuoleman joutsen* [Swan of Death] (1942). *Kuun silta* [The Moon Bridge] (1943). *Löytöretkillä Lontoossa* [Exploring in London] (1944). *Polttoroviolla* [At the Funeral Pile] (1945). *Mallen tunnustukset* [Malle's Confession] (1945). *Kanssavaeltajia ja ohikulkijoita* [Fellow Travellers and Passers-by] (1946). *Uusia kanssavaeltajia ja ohikulkijoita* [New Fellow Travellers and Passers-by] (1946). *Kolmas saattue*

[The Third Procession] (1947). *Seitsemän neitsyttä* [Seven Virgins] (1948). *Virvatulia* [Ignis Fatuus] (1949). *Rakkauden vangit* [Prisoners of Love] (1951). *Päiväkirja vuosilta 1897–1906* [Diary from the Years 1897–1906] (1952). *Päiväkirja vuosilta 1907–1915* (1953). *Päiväkirja vuosilta 1916–1921* (1954). *Päiväkirja vuosilta 1922–1926* (1955). *Päiväkirja vuosilta 1927–1931* (1956). *Vaeltava vieraskirja* [Wandering Guest Book from the Years 1946–1956] (1957). *Elämäntoveri* [Life's Companion] (1959). *Aino Kallaksen kauneimmat runot* [Aino Kallas' Most Beautiful Poems] (1959). English translations: *Barbara von Tisenhusen. A Livland tale* (1925). *Bath-Sheba of Saarenmaa* (1924). *Eros the Slayer. Two Estonian Tales* (1927). *The White Ship. Estonian Tales* (1924). *The Wolf's bride. A Tale from Estonia* (1930). *Three Novels* (*Barbara von Tisenhusen, Reigin pappi, Sudenmorsian*) (1975).

Bibliography

Laitinen, Kai, *Aino Kallas 1897–1921* (1973). Laitinen, Kai, *Aino Kallaksen maailmaa* [The World of Aino Kallas] (1978). Laitinen, Kai, "Aino Kallas 1878–1956. Ambassador Extraordinary." *Books from Finland* 4 (1978). Nirk, Endel, *Estonian Literature* (Tallinn, 1970).

Kai Laitinen

Vera Kamenko

Born July 7, 1947, Sombor, Yugoslavia
Genre(s): autobiography
Language(s): German

Vera Kamenko's *Unter uns war Krieg. Autobiographie einer jugoslawischen Arbeiterin* (1978; War Between Us. Autobiography of a Yugoslavian Woman Worker) was the first contribution by a woman to the growing body of literature by immigrant workers in post-World War II West Germany. Although immigrant workers (first euphemistically known as *"Gast"* arbeiter ("guest" workers) had been a virtual staple of the booming West German economy since the mid-1950s, it was not until their presence as (more or less) permanent residents had been established a generation later that they began to produce a literature of their own. Kamenko's autobiography is important, not only

as one of the very first literary expressions of German *"Gast" arbeiter* in their own voice but because she is writing as a woman about a life shaped by the intersection of gender, class, and race oppression.

Unter uns war Krieg is the story of Kamenko's life. Born in a small town in rural Yugoslavia in 1947, her childhood marked by poverty, family closeness, sexual repression and assault, she leaves her country, her husband, her mother, and her son for work in West German factories and the promise of a better life. While her early years are telescoped into the first four chapters of the autobiography, the body of the text focuses on her time in Germany from 1969 to 1976: four years of factory work in Munich and Berlin, three years in prison for manslaughter after the beating death of her child. Two appended chapters, written by her German editor and collaborator, Marianne Herzog, describe Kamenko's life after her deportation back to Yugoslavia and record her reflections on her German experience.

Of particular interest in this autobiography is the way in which its production—what it meant for her to write it, what it took to get it published—is made conscious and problematized. The issue of language is foregrounded. For Kamenko writes *in* German, but not *as* a German. Her broken German, "corrected" in most of the text by Herzog, illustrates the ways in which language is both a source of empowerment for those who master its rules and a means of discrimination against those who do not master it properly. The final chapter ("Return Home") also illustrates the particular dilemma of non-native writers, who are at home neither in the foreign language nor in their mother tongue. *Unter uns war Krieg* broke ground on which the work of immigrant women in Germany writing after her (Aysel, Özakin, Saliha Scheinhardt) have been building ever since.

Works

Unter uns war Krieg. Autobiographie einer jugoslawischen Arbeiterin [War Between Us. Autobiography of a Yugoslavian Woman Worker] (1978).

Bibliography

Clausen, Jeanette, "Broken But Not Silent: Language as Experience in Vera Kamenko's *Unter uns war*

Krieg," in *Women in German Yearbook 1: Feminist Studies and German Culture*, Marianne Burkhard and Edith Waldstein, eds. (Lanham, Md., 1984), pp. 115–134.

Angelika Bammer

Anna Kamienska

Born April 12, 1920
Genre(s): poetry
Language(s): Polish

Anna Kamienska was the wife of the late poet Jan Spiewak, to whom she devoted her 1970 volume *White Manuscript*, which was awarded the 1971 prize by the Minister of Culture and Art. She made her debut in 1945 with the October/December issue of the weekly *Odrodzenie* (Renaissance), with the poems "Wiosna" (Spring) 1942 and "Listopad" (November) 1942.

A poet of intellect and sensitivity, Kamienska's vast culture and knowledge of philosophical roots and traditions are combined with an easy familiarity with the world of physical nature. Puzzled by the paradoxes of human existence, the sense of indivisibility from the world of nature, compounded with separateness and loneliness, and constant striving for the union with something larger than herself, her poetry reflects her all-embracing compassion for life. Her lavish use of language and prevailing natural imagery are rich in cultural allusions to the Bible, both Christian and Jewish, as well as the memory of mythical visions.

Works

Wychowanie [Upbringing]. *Wiersze* [Poems] (1940–1948). *O szczesciu* [On Happiness] (1949–1951). Poezje (1952). *Bicie serca* [Heartbeat] (1954). *Pod chmurami* [Under the Clouds] (1957). *Poezje wybrane* [Selected Poems] (1959). *O oku ptaka* [In Bird's Eye] (1960). *Zrodla* [Sources] (1962). *Rzeczy nietrwale* [Things Transitory] (1963). *Odwolanie mitu* [Myth Recalled] (1967). *Wygnanie* [Expulsion] (1970). *Bialy rekopis* (1970). *Poezje wybrane* (selected and introduced by the author) (1971). *Herody* (1972). *Poezje wybrane* (1973). *Drugie szczescie Hioba* [Job's Other Happiness] (1974). *Rekopis znaleziony we snie* [A

Manuscript Found in a Dream]: *wiersze z lat 1973–1975* [Poems from the Years . . .] (1978–1979). *Milczenia* [Silences] (1979). *Wiersze jednej nocy* [Poems of One Night] (1981).

Maya Peretz and Sergiusz Piasecki

Elsa Sophia, baroness von Kamphoevener

Born 1878, Hamelin, Germany; died 1963, Traunstein
Genre(s): fairy tale, legend
Language(s): German

Elsa Sophia von Kamphoevener spent more than the first 40 years of her life in Turkey, where her father was called to reorganize the Turkish army. When she returned to Germany in 1921, she was able to find employment in the UFA film studios in Berlin because of having already published some fiction. She worked there till 1931, devoting the rest of her life to the task she loved of making accessible to a German public the legends of Turkey and the Islamic countries in general. Her collection of fairy tales *An Nachtfeuren der Karawan-Serail* became a best-seller in postwar Germany. In her *oeuvre*, Kamphoevener carried on the fascination of German poets, such as Brentano, Heine, and Hauff, with the Orient and, in the caravansary tales told in series, she has presented an Oriental antecedent of a form that has been important in European letters ever since Boccaccio's *Decameron*.

Works

Der Smaragd des Scheich (1916). *Die Pharaonin* (1926). *Flammen über Bagdad* (1934). *An Nachtfeuern der Karawan-Serail* (1956). *Am alten Brunnen der Bedesten* (1958). *Anatolische Hirtenerzählungen* (1960). *Der Zedernbaum* (1960). *Islamische Christuslegenden* (1963).

Bibliography

von Wilpert, Gero, *Deutsches Literatur-Lexikon*. 2nd edition (Stuttgart, 1975).

Ute Marie Saine

Olympia Karagiōrga

Born 1934
Genre(s): poetry, translation, essay
Language(s): Greek

Olympia Karagiōrga is known for her translations and studies of other writers, such as F.G. Lorca, D.H. Lawrence, A. Camus, Oscar Wilde, and Virginia Woolf, as much as for her own poetry.

Her poems are perceptive and thought-provoking, her language is economical and to the point, and her choice of words is excellent. She is not an image-maker but an observer and analyst of human behavior. Her psychological insights are remarkably accurate.

Poios (Who) is a study in four parts. The point of view is that of the female "I" addressing and responding to the male lover or contemplating the physical and mental sensations of the affair in unusually candid fashion. Parts I, II, and III trace the progress of the relationship from youthful eagerness to mature letting go when the speaker realizes that the emotional response is no longer there. Part IV consists of two poems dated almost seven years apart that apparently mark the beginning and the end of an actual relationship. The first one communicates an intoxication with and a seemingly endless thirst for love and life. In the second poem the lover is gone, and the speaker recognizes the fact that there may be no more lovers. The one constant is Poetry. "It" not only serves as replacement for the lover who is not there anymore but becomes the loved one: "I want again/ To rest my head on your shoulder, Poetry. . . . Stay, Poetry,/ Endure my Kiss." This poem answers the question posed in the title: Who? The "Who" is an activity capitalized and raised to a level worthy of a human. Poetry is the lover who will always be there.

Works

Chiliades prosōpa tēs tychēs [Thousands of Faces of Chance] (1961). *Ta megaphōna* [The Loudspeakers] (1966). *To megalo kyma* [The Big Wave] (1974). *Poios* [Who] (1985).

Helen Dendrinou Kolias

Ganka Slavova Karanfilova

(a.k.a. Lada Galina)

Born February 6, 1934, Burgas, Bulgaria
Genre(s): short story, novel, drama, poetry, children's literature
Language(s): Bulgarian

Lada Galina completed her primary schooling in her native city and her secondary education in the new city of Dimitrovgrad. Ganka displayed her literary interests early in life when she started working for a local newspaper and founded, together with the poet Penyo Penev, a literary society. Her first works appeared in *Narodna mlade'* (The People's Youth) and *Literaturen front* (Literary Front). Ganka studied at the University of Sofia and graduated in 1958 in Bulgarian literature. She married the prolific literary critic and essayist Efrem S. Karanfilov. In 1975–1976 Ganka specialized in Spanish language and literature, worked for the Committee for Friendship and Cultural Relations with Foreign Countries, and for many years served as an editor of the monthly *Plamŭk* (Flame), the weekly *Literaturen front*, and the children's journal *Spetemvriiče* section of Radio Sofia, as chief dramatist of the theatre of satire, and as a member of the Union of Writers is active in PEN. Ganka is currently editor of the Trade Union Publishing House. Ganka is the author of more than thirty books. Almost all of her works deal with aspects of contemporary city life. For example, in *Drugijat brjag na zaliva* (1963; The Other Short of the Bay), *Aerogara* (1965; Airport), *Cvetŭt na izvorite* (1966; The Colors of Springs), Ganka presents sketches of individuals and situations that depict the feelings, spiritual world, and daily behavior of simple people, especially women, striving to better themselves. Harmony of character and even circumstances pervades most of her work. Although there are conflicts in the inner life of the heroes and conditions, no insurmountable social or spiritual encounters are depicted. Her characters are mostly professionals, young and optimistic, with a positive view of life. They are spiritually rich and sensitive to social and human problems with a strong sense of justice and truth.

From the start of her career as a writer Ganka has been interested in assisting children develop their curiosity, and she still continues to publish books for children. A tireless traveler, Ganka has shared her impressions with the public in such works as *Mečtata ne e prostreljana: čiliiski dnevnik-73* (1974; Hope Is Not Shot: Chilean Diary-73), *Visokite zvezdi na Kirgizija* (1978; The Lofty Stars of Kirghizia) and *Ot Balkana do Siera Nevada* (From the Balkan Mountains to the Sierra Nevada). Her *Toplite kamŭni* (1969; The Warm Stones) and other plays have been put on stage. Ganka is an energetic writer whose later volumes have a greater elaboration in character and setting. A number of her works have been translated into English, French, Russian, Spanish, and other languages.

Works

Malki prikazki (1957). Nai-hubavijat mig (1957). Momčeto porasnalo (1958). Liastovičkata. Povest (1960: Samoletŭt islŭnceto. Noveli (1964). Maiska sesija. Razkazi (1968). Malka povest (1969). Šošeto ne e kosmos (1971). Esen v dŭbovete (1979). Koi po-skoro šte porasne (1985). Maisko zeleno (1987).

Bibliography

Sestrimski, I, "Tri noveli." *Plamŭk* 1 (1964): 103–104. Šikov, H., "Konflikti i harakter." *Narodna malde'* 220 (1965). Andonova, N., "Stremez kum vglŭbjavane." *Narodna kultura*, 3 (January 21, 1967). Bojad'ieva M., "V tvorcesko tŭrsene." *Plamŭk* 3 (1967): 76–77.

Philip Shashko

Margarita Karapanou

Born 1946, Athens, Greece
Genre(s): novel
Language(s): Greek

Margarita Karapanou was born in Athens in 1946, but she spent most of her childhood in Greece and France. She studied cinema and philosophy in Paris and later worked as a nursery school and kindergarten teacher. She is the daughter of well-known Greek fiction writer Margarita Liberaki, whose works have been translated in French and English. Karapanou's first short novel, published in 1976, was *Kassandra and the Wolf*, translated into English by N.C. Germanacos. Her second novel, *O Ipnovatēs* (The Sleepwalker), was published in 1986 and Karapanou herself translated it into French. She was recently given the Goncourt Award (best foreign fiction) for *Ipnovatēs* (1988).

Her first novel discusses a young girl's (of pre-school age) experiences of morality, love, sexuality, and class differences. As Kimon Friar says in his review of the novel's translation, "[the adult world] is seen through the eyes of a child who is neither moral nor immoral but simply amoral as a kitten."

Karapanou's second novel takes place in Hydra, a Greek island known for its intellectual and cosmopolitan non-Greek citizens. In this work, Karapanou satirizes an adult world of perverse sexuality, emotional instability, and unhappiness. Murders, death, and sexual corruption is the framework within which the characters move; Karapanou's solution to this world seems to be the appearance of an attractive yet murderous Greek policeman, who is the new God-sent Messiah, the world's second chance.

Karapanou's work ridicules contemporary upper-class Greek society and cosmopolitan "intellectuals," yet, at the same time, her writing expresses a profound concern for the state of affairs that she parodies. Even though Karapanou, like Zateli, has published only two books, she can be considered among the most important Greek women writers.

Works

Ē Kassandra ke o Lykos (1976). O Ipnovatēs [The Sleepwalker] (1986).
Translations: *Kassandra and the Wolf*, tr. N.C. Germanacos (1976). *Cassandre et le loup* (1976). *Kassandra och Vargen* (1979).
Critical Work: "Ē Metaphrasē: Enas Viasmos." ["Translation: A Rape."] *Ē Leksē* 56 (July-August 1986): 776–777.

Bibliography

Friar, Kimon, Review. *Kassandra and the Wolf*, tr. N.C. Germanacos, *World Literature Today* 51 (Spring 1977).

Aliki P. Dragona

Anna Aleksandrovna Karavaeva

Born 1893, Perm', Russia
Genre(s): short story, novel, propaganda,
    correspondence, editions
Language(s): Russian

Anna Karavaeva has claimed it was her privilege to begin her literary career "when the greatest genius of the revolution was governing, Vladimir I. Lenin." She is a most dedicated proponent of the new order as her career clearly demonstrates.

Coming from a not very auspicious background in the Ural town of Perm', as an eighteen-year-old, Karavaeva saved her resources, despite the adversity caused by the death of the male members of her family, and went to school for one year, the extent that her savings allowed her. While at the university, she won a scholarship to the history-philology department and eventually finished the Higher Women's (Bestuzhevsky) course in Kizel. She began writing in 1921 and became a party member five years later in 1926. She became the editor of the Young Communist League journal, *Molodaia gvardiia* (The Young Guard), in 1931 and remained in this position until 1938. During World War II, she became a correspondent for *Pravda* (Truth). In 1951 she won the Stalin Prize for literature for her novel trilogy, *The Motherland* (Rodina).

Karavaeva's literary achievements do not relate much to the Western world as mutely testified by the rarity of translations of her works. She is very much a product of a dedicated and sincere social realism, trained in that utilitarian school where "art" must teach. Inasmuch as this is the program into which she was cultivated, it should not be overlooked that Karavaeva has earned herself a respectable position in the social realist tradition.

Works

Baian i iabloko (1933). Izbrannye proizvedeniia (1933). Krutaia stupen'; zapiski kontrol'nika (1933). Svoi dom (p'esa v chetyrekh aktakh) (1934). Pervoe pokolenie, rasskazy (1951). Sobranie sochinenia, 5 volumes (1957). Lesozavod (1961). Grani zhizni (1963). Vechnozelenye list'ia; dnevnik pisatelia (1963). Svet vcherashnii, vospominaniia (1964).

Translations: Das sägewerk (Berlin: Bücherkreis, c. 1929). Fabrik im Walde, A. Ramm, tr. (1930).

Bibliography

Zhenshchiny—slavnye mastera (Ogiz-Sverdlgiz, 1942).

Christine Tomei

Kåre P.

(see: Nini Roll Anker)

Zoe Karelli

(a.k.a. Chryssoula Argyriadou)

Born 1901, Thessaloniki, Greece
Genre(s): short story, poetry, drama, essay
Language(s): Greek

The sister of the prominent writer N.G. Pentzikis, Argyriadou studied foreign languages and music. She started her literary career with the short story "Diatheseis" (Moods) in 1935, and in 1940, she published her first poetic anthology, the *Poreia* (Course), which was followed by various other poetic collections, such as *Epochi tou Thanatou* (1948; The Season of Death), *I Fantasia tou Chronou* (1949; The Imagination of Time), *Tis Monaxias kai tis Eparsis* (1951; Of the Solitude and Pride), *Chalcographies kai Eikonismata* (1952; Chalcographies and Icons), *To Ploio* (1955; The Ship), *Cassandra kai alla Poiemata* (1955; Cassandra and Other Poems), *Antitheseis* (1957; Oppositions), *O Kathreptis tou Mesonychtiou* (1958; The Mirror of Midnight) and others.

She also deployed her literary skills in writing plays and essays; her plays *O Diavolos kai i evdomi entoli* (1955; The Devil and the Seventh Commandment) and the *Suppliants* (1962), as well as her essays "About Doubt," "The Absolute in the Work of Claudel," "Waiting for Godot or the Passion of Inertness," among others gained her a very high reputation in the Greek literary elite.

Argyriadou, from the beginning of her literary career, revealed a highly personal style, that marked her entire work thereafter. Her surrealistic style, her metaphysical religious feeling, and her existentialist anxieties about death, solitude, and decay dominate her writings. Refusing to use the traditional forms of poetry, she very early began to experiment with new forms of expression. Her paratactic speech and abstract, somewhat convoluted way of expressing herself have made her writing rather inaccessible to the public.

Her collection *Oppositions* reveals a change in her attitude vis-à-vis her existentialist quests and a strained search for new, inconceivable realities. K. Friar remarks that Argyriadou's "vigilant consciousness keeps watch on the ambiguous borderland between the material and the immaterial, between the time world of Heraclitean flux and the space world of eternal silence, trying to spy out a realm where space and time are coequal and codeterminate." Argyriadou strives to relate the realm of eternal silence to the material world of speech. Her themes, as K. Friar points out, are almost exclusively concerned with the split in the person of sensibility tormented by the attempt to find integrity and create ties of continuity in a world of spiritual disintegration.

A poem, as described in "Worker in the Workshops of Time" and in "Adolescent from Antikythera," becomes for Argyriadou "erotic shapes for whatever exists/ within time." She treats poetry not only as an aesthetic receptacle of time but also as the best spiritual medium of modern times with which to understand contemporary man's struggle to give meaning to his existence in a time of deteriorating values.

Her plays, in which the poetic element is very strong, are "poems" in a dialogue form. The central idea of *The Devil and the Seventh Commandment* is the strength of voluptuousness, the negation of conventional family bonds, and the omnipotence of the demonic. Argyriadou, herself liberated from social "conventions," openly challenges her readers for further quests.

Her verse technique is a mixture of "Byzantinism" (the language of Byzantine hymnology) and free verse; she shifts the order of words, thus also producing semantic shifts, and plays with syntax. These techniques refresh her expression and incorporate rhetorical figures and abstract concepts. Her language mixes "demotic" with "archaic" (*katharevousa*) elements. Her poetry is almost devoid of imagery

and usually depends for its effects on the passionate expression of thought. Her words are bare of sentimentality and are mainly those of philosophical speculation.

In 1956, she was awarded the second State Prize of Poetry for her collection *Cassandra and other Poems*; in 1974, she obtained the first State Prize for her poems of the period 1940–1973. For her outstanding literary contribution she was awarded the "Palmes Académiques" by the French government. She is the only Greek poetess who has fully realized her role as a European poetess; her ideas, concepts, and personal anxieties reflect the anxieties of our times. Her poems have been translated in several European languages, including Polish and Hungarian.

Works

Poems: "Course" (1940). "Season of Death" (1948). "Imagination of Time" (1949). "Of Solitude and Pride" (1951). "Chalcographies and Icons" (1952). "The Ship" (1953). "Cassandra and Other Poems" (1955). "Garden Tales" (1955). "Oppositions" (1957). "The Mirror of Midnight" (1958). Two collective volumes of her poems appeared in 1973. Vol. 1 covers the period 1940–1955 and Vol. 2 the period 1955–1973, including her recent collections *The Crossroads* (1973) and the *Diary* (1955–1973). Plays: *The Devil and the Seventh Commandment* (1955). *Suppliants* (1962). *Simonis, the Royal Child of Byzantium* (1965).

Essays: "About Doubt" (1958). "The Absolute in the Work of Claudel" (1959). "Waiting for Godot or the Passion of Alertness" (1967). "Essays on C.P. Kavafi, T.S. Eliot, J. Joyce, F. Kafka, F. Dostoyevski, L. Pirandello, N. Gogol, and A. Camus."

Translations: In Greek, T.S. Eliot's "The Family Reunion" and "The Cocktail Party."

Bibliography

Argyriou, A., "Criticism on Some of Z. Karelli's Poems." *Greek-English Review* 8 (1955). Argyriou, A., *The Greek Poetry* (Athens, 1979), pp. 318–333. Christianopoulos, D., *Essays* (Thessaloniki, 1961), pp. 36–41. Chryssanthis, K., "Z. Karelli's Poetry." *Pneumatiki Kypros* 173 (1975). Dictaeos, A., "Z. Karelli's Poetry." *Kainourgia Epochi* (1956). Friar, K., *Modern Greek Poetry, from Kavafis to Elytis* (New York, 1973), pp. 103–106. Gianos, M., *Introduction to Modern Greek Literature* (New York, 1969). Karantonis, A., *About the Contem-*

porary Greek Poetry (Athens, 1961). Lavagnini, B., *La Letteratura Neohellenica Academia* (Milano, 1969). Melissanthi, "Reflexions about Z. Karelli's Poetry." *Kainourgia Epochi* (1968). Meraklis, G., "About Z. Karelli." *Literary Critique* (Thessaloniki, 1976), pp. 102–110. Meraklis, G., "Z. Karelli." *Kritika Fylla* 21 (1975). Mourelos, G., "The Poems." *Nea Poreia* 231 (1974). Paraschos, Kl., "Z. Karelli: Cassandra and Other Poems." *Kathimerini* (5/25/55). Patsis, Ch., *Great Encyclopaedia of Neohellenic Literature*, vol. 8 (Athens, 1968), pp. 289–294. Peranthis, M., *Anthology of Neohellenic Poetry*, 5 (Athens: n.d.), pp. 252–256. Politis, L., *A History of Modern Greek Literature* (Oxford, 1973), p. 270. Sinopoulos, T., "Zoe Karelli." *Simerina Grammata* 8 (1955). Spandonidis, P., *Contemporary Literary Thessaloniki* (Thessaloniki, 1960). Spandonidis, P., *Modern Poetry in Greece* (Athens, 1955). Tarsouli, A., *Greek Poetesses* (Athens, 1951), pp. 347–361. Terzakis, A., "Z. Karelli." *Vema* (12/14/68). Themelis, G., *Our Modern Poetry* (Athens, 1963), pp. 114–124. Vitti, M., *Poesia Greca dell 1900* (Pazma, 1966).

Other references: Additional translations of poems in English appear in the *Literary Review* 3 (1973) *Charioteer* 10 (1968) and 14 (1972) in *Folder* 1 (1954).

Aristoula Georgiadou

Marianna Karousou

(see: Marianna Koutouzi)

Carme Karr i Alfonsetti

(a.k.a. L. Escardot)

Born 1865, Barcelona, Spain; died 1943, Barcelona
Genre(s): short story, drama, novella, children's literature
Language(s): Catalan, Spanish

Carme Karr, the niece of the French novelist Alphonse Karr, was active in the turn-of-the-century *Modernisme* (Catalan Modernism) movement. She collaborated in a number of literary magazines, as well as editing *Feminal*, a women's monthly. After publishing songs in Catalan, she turned to short fiction, plays, and essays on social literary and feminist issues. As one of the leaders of early Catalan feminism, Karr founded and directed La Llar (a residential college for women teachers and students).

Bolves, quadrets (1906; Shapes and Blocks), a collection of seven pieces of brief fiction, contains two geographically unified sections, one a group of country vignettes, stressing descriptions of nature and neglected children, the other with an urban setting, contrasting upper and lower class existence in Barcelona. In *Clixies, estudis en prosa* (1906; Snapshots: Studies in Prose), a second collection of short narratives, Karr employs the unifying metaphor of photography, titling many stories as landscapes, interiors, etc. Most of these "snapshots" portray women who are immobilized by entrapment—whether by marriage, social class, or socioeconomic limitations.

Karr's short novel, *La vida d'en Joan Franch* (1912; The Life of John Franch) received a silver cup in Barcelona competition the year of its publication. Other brief fiction includes *Cuentos a mis nietos* (1932; Stories for my Grandchildren), nine myths and exemplary tales simply retold; *Garba de Contes* (1935; Bouquet of Stories); and *El libro de Puli* (1958; Pauline's Book), more cautionary tales for children. Karr is also the author of a play entitled *Els idols* (1911; The Idols), a one-act comedy in which a mother and daughter confront the problem of marital infidelity, and the daughter encounters the double standard of morality. Men are "the idols," perpetual adolescents.

This writer's early interest in furthering education for women, her initial writing on women's problems and social issues, gave way in the postwar period to works for children, a redirecting of her didacticism into a politically acceptable channel. Simultaneously, the modernism and concern for style of her early years were replaced by a simpler, unadorned language, and irony, one of Karr's most characteristic traits, was attenuated as she wrote progressively more for a younger audience. Hers is a case of a potentially significant feminist voice silenced by historical circumstance.

Works

Bolves, quadrets (1906). Caritat (1918). Clixles, estudis en prosa (1906). Cuentos a mis nietos (1932). Garba de Contes (1935). Els idols, comedia en un acte i en prosa (1917). El libro de Puli (1942). Raiq de sol (undated play). La vida d'en Joan Franch. L'esquitx (1912).

Bibliography

General references Women Writers of Spain, ed. C.L. Galerstein (Westport, CT, 1986).

Janet Perez

Anna Luise Karsch(in)

Born December 1, 1722, near Schwiebus, Brandenburg, Germany; died October 12, 1791, Berlin
Genre(s): poetry, letters
Language(s): German

Anna Luise Karsch is best known because of the unusual combination that she represented, a village woman adept at composing poetry extemporaneously who became the first German woman to earn her living as a writer.

She was born in 1722 on a dairy farm, "Auf dem Hammer," in a part of easternmost Germany that was populated by both Poles and Germans, where her father, a beer brewer, and her mother kept an inn. Neglected at home, she was fortunate to be taken away at about age six by a great uncle, who taught her to read and write in German and was considering teaching her as much Latin as he knew too when her mother came to fetch her back. Her father had died. Her new stepfather moved the family to the village of Tirschtiegel, where the girl worked variously as a cradle rocker, cowherd, and house maid to a middle-class woman. In 1738 she married a weaver named Hiersekorn and had two children. In 1745, with two living children and a third on the way, she reluctantly acquiesced in a divorce, the first to be granted in Prussia, which had recently revised its marriage law. Penniless, she married, at her mother's behest she said, a tailor named Karsch, who took his new wife into central Poland, to Fraustadt. (Twenty-one years later the poet would force a similar unwanted and unsuccessful marriage on her daughter.) The tailor was an alcoholic and seldom worked. Driven onto her own resources to feed herself and the children, Karsch began seeking opportunities to use a skill she had been practicing at home for years, composing poems extemporaneously. When she celebrated in verse various occasions in the lives of the more prosperous citizens around her, her efforts were rewarded with gifts and money. In 1755 she was finally able to move back westward, as she had long wished, to Glogau, again on the German side of the border with Poland. Meanwhile some of her occasional poems were published, in single-sheet format. In January 1760 Karsch apparently arranged to have her husband pressed into the Prussian Army, thus relieving herself of his unwanted presence by an act her daughter still found unforgivably callous decades later. Yet it freed Karsch to make the most momentous move of her life. At the invitation of an aristocratic mentor, the poet went with her children to Berlin.

She was passed around there from one aristocratic salon to another, becoming acquainted along the way with Prussia's literary elite, most of them academic poets and theorists to whom Karsch's experience and improvisational manner of composing were alien. Nevertheless, they became her models and mentors whose advice she eagerly sought, signing her name as they dubbed her, "the German Sappho." With one of them, Gleim, three years her elder, and the author of flirtatious and witty anacreontic verse, Karsch fell deeply in love. Incapable of responding with equal emotion, he did however help her with her publications, which began to appear in book form in 1764. Despite her widely discussed first volumes, it was another eight years before she published her next collection although she continued writing profusely and published often in magazines and single sheets. Evidently she found that she could survive on honoraria despite always being short of money. After an extraordinary interview with her hero, King Friedrich the Great, which Karsch recorded in detail, she hoped to be granted a house for herself, but this wish was not fulfilled until two years before her death, when the next Prussian king came to the throne. Her last collection appeared posthumously, edited and introduced by her daughter,

Caroline von Klencke, who was a poet and dramatist in her own right, as was her daughter, Karsch's granddaughter, Helmine von Chezy.

When Karsch taught herself to compose verse extemporaneously, she followed as much as she could the poetic conventions of her day, which especially included liberal sprinklings of classical allusions. Her work still conveys the often jarring but also unique manner of its composition. Also notable for their freshness and candor are her letters, especially a series containing her autobiography.

Works

Auserlesene Gedichte [Selected Poems] (1764). Einige Oden über verschiedene hohe Gegenstände [Some Odes About Various High Subjects] (1764). Poetische Einfälle, erste Sammlung [Poetic Ideas, First Collection] (1764). Kleinigkeiten [Trivialities] (1765). Neue Gedichte [New Poems] (1772). Gedichte [Poems] (1792) [with biographical sketch by her daughter].

Translations: One poem in: Cocalis, Susan L., ed., The Defiant Muse. German Feminist Poems from the Middle Ages to the Present (1986).

Bibliography

Beuys, Barbara, ed., Herzgedanken. Das Leben der "deutschen Sappho" von ihr selbst erzählt (Frankfurt, 1981). Bovenschen, Silvia, Die imaginierte Weiblichkeit. Exemplarische Untersuchungen zu kulturgeschichtlichen und literarischen Präsentationsformen des Weiblichen (Frankfurt, 1979). Brinker-Gabler, Gisela, ed., Deutsche Dichterinnen vom 16. Jahrhundert bis zur Gegenwart. Gedichte und Lebensläufe (Frankfurt, 1978), pp. 135–142. Brinker-Gabler, Gisela, ed., Deutsche Literatur von Frauen. Vom Mittelalter bis zum Ende des 18. Jahrhunderts (München, 1988), pp. 313–324. Dawson, Ruth P., "Selbstzähmung und weibliche Misogynie: Verserzählungen von Frauen in 18. Jahrhundert," in Der Widerspenstigen Zähmung. Studien zur bezqungenen Weiblichkeit in der Literatur vom Mittelalter bis zur Gegenwart, ed. Sylvia Wallinger and Monika-Jones (Innsbruck, 1986), pp. 133–143. Friedrichs, Elisabeth, Die deutschsprachigen Schriftstellerinnen des 18. und 19. Jahrhunderts. Ein Lexikon (Stuttgart, 1981), p. 153. Hausmann, E., Die Karschin. Friedrich des Großen Volksdichterin. Ein Leben in Briefen. (Frankfurt/Main, 1933). Krull, Edith, Das Wirken der Frau im frühen deutschen Zeitschriftenwesen (Charlottenburg, 1939), pp. 79–89. Beiträge zur Erforschung der deutschen Zeitschrift, v. 5. Singer, Heidi Maria, Leben und Zeit der Dichterin A.L. Karschin. Diss., City University of New York, 1983. Wolf, Gerhard, ed., O, mir entwischt nicht, was die Menschen fühlen. Anna Louisa Karschin. Gedichte und Briefe, Stimmen von Zeitgenossen (Berlin, 1981).

Ruth P. Dawson

Josiane Kartheiser

Born 1950, Differdange, Luxembourg
Genre(s): poetry, drama, short story
Language(s): German, English, Luxembourgish

Josiane Kartheiser completed her secondary-school studies in Luxembourg and pursued her academic career at the University of Kent, Canterbury, where she specialized in English and American literature. Not wanting to be "like everybody else," i.e., go into teaching, she chose to become a journalist. She is highly committed to public life and topical problems—the problems of woman in society, the dangers of drug-taking, the freedom of thought—not only does she deal with these questions as a journalist but also as a poet, dramatist, and writer of narratives. Josiane Kartheiser is vividly interested in the art of cabaret and takes an active part in the programs of Luxembourg artists to which she contributes both as a comedian and as a producer.

Her poetry, marked by her strong personality and written in free verse, is powerfully imbued with the rhythm of contemporary music. She is a woman who accuses, and her narratives and plays boldly blame all those who seem to banter thought and thus favor the development of hypocrisy.

Works

Flirt mit Fesseln [Flirting with Fetters], travel reports, short prose, poetry (1978). Wenn Schreie in mir wachsen [When Screams Rise Within Me], short stories, poetry, a rock opera. (1980) Linda , short stories. (1981) Co-author of Tom, report on the drug-situation in Luxembourg. (1981) De

Kontrakt [The Contract] (1985). *Hárgottskanner* [Children of God] (1985).

Rosemarie Kieffer and Liliane Stomp-Erpelding

Marie Luise Kaschnitz

Born 1901, Karlsruhe, Germany; died 1974, Frankfurt
Genre(s): poetry, novel, essay, short story
Language(s): German

Born into a noble family of Baden, Marie Luise Kaschnitz grew up in Potsdam and Berlin. After her studies, she worked as a bookdealer in several cities, lastly in Rome, until marrying professor of archeology Guido von Kaschnitz-Weinberg in 1925. After seven years in Rome, she lived in Marburg and, after 1941, in Frankfurt. From 1955–1958, she again lived in Rome.

Marie Luise Kaschnitz was one of the important writers of the post-war era. Having published only two slim books in 1933 and 1937, one autobiographical and one on mythology, and withheld her poetry of 20 years, which was not published till 1947, her vast classical erudition, immaculate nonfascist background, and general versatility made her ideally suited, in the 1950s and 1960s, to figure as a fitting "praeceptora Germaniae" concerning life and letters. She has received most major prizes and was appointed visiting professor of poetics at the University of Frankfurt in 1960. In her early *oeuvre*, a classical, Humboltian orientation dominates. After 1945, war and the Holocaust or, more abstractly, human failure, guilt, and the abuse of power become important themes. Having been considered a poet before, she now turns to the short story, no longer as a reformulation of classical mythology, but rather in the style of Poe or Blixen with life's enigmas looming unresolved and inexplicable. However, rather than exploring twentieth-century answers, she has always remained committed to tradition. Of interest is her preoccupation with French realist painter Courbet, on whom she published an epic in 1949, later reworked as biography (1967). Kaschnitz views Courbet as a figure who exposes himself unflinchingly to reality—"the truth, not the dream"—but still transfigures it in his art. Of particular importance within her *oeuvre* are two volumes dedicated to the theme of death: the *Totentanz* of 1947 concerning World War II, continuation of an old medieval and Renaissance theme, and *Dein Schweigen—Meine Stimme* (Your Silence—My Voice) of 1962, her coming to terms with the death of her husband in 1958.

Works

Liebe beginnt (1933). *Elissa* (1937). *Gedichte* (1947). *Totentanz und Gedichte zur Zeit* (1947). *Gustave Courbet* (1949). *Zukunftsmusic* (1950). *Das Haus der Kindheit* (1956). *Lange Schatten* (1960). *Dein Schweigen—Meine Stimme* (1962). *Wohin denn ich* (1962). *Uberallnie Ausgewählte Gedichte 1928–1965* (1965). *Beschreibung eines Dorfes* (1966). *Vogel Rock. Erzählungen* (1969). *Steht noch dahin* (1970). *Zwischen immer und nie. Gestalten und Themen der Dichtung* (1971). *Orte* (1973).

Bibliography

Borchers, Elisabeth, and Hans-Ulrich Müller-Schwefe, *Im Jahrhundert der Frau* (Frankfurt, 1984). Brinker-Gabler, Gisela, *Deutsche Dichterinnen* (Frankfurt, 1978). Puknus, Heinz, ed, *Neue Literatur der Frauen* (Munich, 1980).

Ute Marie Saine

Lina Kasdaglē

(a.k.a. Lina Kasdagli)

Born 1921, Corinth, Greece
Genre(s): poetry, translation
Language(s): Greek

Lina Kasdaglē (or Kasdagli) was raised in Athens where she resides. She has published two collections of poetry and numerous articles in such periodicals as *Nea Estia*, *Tachydromos*, *Epoches*, and *Ios*. She has translated Steinbeck's *The Red Pony*, Mauriac's *Les anges noirs* and Gide's *Symphonie pastorale* into modern Greek. She also writes literature for children.

She became known in the United States because of her free-verse poem entitled "Traffic Lights" that was included in *Eighteen Texts*, a collection of writings by various writers that came out in Athens in 1970 and in the United States in 1972. Greece was under a military dictatorship at that time, and *Eighteen Texts* questioned the practices of the established regime. "Traffic Lights" is a simple poem about a man attempting to cross the street and go on his way; however, he is stopped by the traffic lights and is stuck in the middle of an intersection. The regimentation of the system robs him of his ability to go on.

Works

Hēliotropia [Heliotropes] (1952). Oi dromoi tou mesēmeriou [Noon Streets] (1962). "Traffic Lights," tr. Edmund and Mary Keeley, in Eighteen Texts, ed. Willis Barnstone (1972).

Helen Dendriou Kolias

Lina Kasdagli

(see: Lina Kasdaglē)

Kasia

(see: Kassia)

Kassia

(a.k.a. Kasia, Kassiane, Eikasia, Ikasia)

Born c. 805, probably Constantinople; died c. 865, in the convent she founded in Constantinople
Genre(s): Christian hymns, nonreligious gnomic poetry
Language(s): Greek

The most distinguished female poet of the Byzantine period, Kassia composed both secular and religious verse under the reigns of Theophilos (829–842) and Michael (842–867). She came from a noble family: her father was a kandidatos at the Imperial Court. As a young woman, she was determined to become a nun and was active in the campaign against the iconoclasts. When Theodoros Studites, the great champion of the icons, was exiled, Kassia sent him gifts and letters. The story that Kassia took part in a beauty contest at which the emperor Theophilos was to choose a wife and lost the throne with a witty riposte to one of his questions is old but apparently untrue. Later, possibly in 843, the year marking the end of the iconoclast controversy, she founded a convent bearing her name in Constantinople. There she spent the rest of her life and wrote the greater part of her poetry. The exact date of her death is unknown, but the evidence suggests she did not live beyond the reign of Michael.

After the restoration of the icons, there was an increase in the writing of hymns, and Kassia's are among the more interesting pieces. The problems concerning the authenticity of works attributed to Kassia are highly involved, but the following are probably genuine: the kanon On The Dead, the tetraodion for Easter Sunday, and 21 other hymns for different days in the religious calendar. There are another 25 pieces whose authorship is disputed and 10 more falsely ascribed to Kassia. Her most famous hymn is On Mary Magdalene (Wednesday in Holy Week), which is still sung in the Orthodox church. Also noteworthy are On St. Peter and St. Paul (June 28th), On St. Eustratios and his Fellow-martyrs (December 13th), and For Christmas Day. While there is no direct evidence, it is likely that Kassia also composed music to accompany her hymns.

In general, Kassia eschews the expression of deep spiritual thought and concentrates on the historical side of religion. Her language is ornamental and relies heavily on the use of rhetorical devices, especially antithesis, which are often, but not always, deftly employed. There are several vivid images littered throughout the corpus. The lack of any significant originality is mitigated by a trusting sincerity and a preference for expressing the more joyous aspects of the Christian faith.

Apart from the religious works, about 300 lines of Kassia's gnomic verses survive. Among these, there are a collection of epigrammatic pieces on such subjects as stupidity, woman, fortune, beauty, wealth, and the faults of Armenians, 32 verses on the theme of friendship, and a group of statements on the sublimity of the monastic life. The best of the secular verses are the 27 trimeters which all begin with "I hate" and which scrutinize human social habits with a perceptive eye. Again, there is no great originality of conception or expression, but the traditional themes are handled with a pleasing artistry.

Kassia's religious poetry stands far above that of her contemporaries. She remained a figure of influence and interest after her death and since the middle of the nineteenth century has been featured in several novels and plays by Greek and other writers.

Bibliography

The texts of Kassia's works are most easily located through the footnotes in I. Rochow, *Studien zu der Person, den Werken und dem Nachleben der Dichterin Kassia (Berliner Byzantinistische Arbeiten 38)*. This also contains a comprehensive bibliography. Several of the hymns are printed and translated in H.J.W. Tillyard, "A Musical Study of the Hymns of Casia," *Byzantinische Zeitschrift* 20 (1911): 420–485. The secular verses are edited by K. Krumbacher, *Kasia, Sitzungsberichte der philosophisch-philologischen und der historischen Classe der k.b. Akademie der Wissenschaften* (1897), pp. 305–370. Argyropolous, J., *Kassia, Her Life and Poetry* (in Greek) (Athens, 1924). Trypanis, C.A., *Greek Poetry from Homer to Seferis* (London, 1981), pp. 435f., 445–447.

David H.J. Larmour

Kassiane

(see: Kassia)

Nina Katerli

Born 1940s, Leningrad, The Soviet Union
Genre(s): short story, novella
Language(s): Russian

A native and resident of Leningrad, Katerli graduated from the Lensoviet technical school with a degree in engineering. Since her literary debut in 1973, she has published comparatively little, most of it contained in her two prose collections of 1981 and 1986. Her stories range from five to forty pages in length and vary in style and quality. At her most experimental Katerli gives free rein to her imagination and incorporates pure fantasy, inexplicable shifts in locale and point of view, radical temporal jumps, unexpected juxtapositions, and modified stream of consciousness into her narrative. Katerli's forays

into fantasy represent only one side of her fictional manner, and the risks she takes in that mode sometimes yield uneven returns.

In a less venturesome but more consistent vein, Katerli also recreates in concrete detail modern urban settings against the background of which she explores romantic ties, family problems, communal living, and the inconsistencies and irrational, destructive involutions of the human psyche. Her cast of characters covers the full spectrum of old, middle-aged, young and adolescent of both sexes. She favors an elliptical style, complicated by rapid geographical and temporal shifts, full of animal imagery, literary allusions, colloquialisms, and jagged sentence fragments.

Works

Collections: *Okno* (1981). "Treugol'nik Barsukova" (1981), tr. David Lapeza, and "The Barsukov Triangle," eds. Carl and Ellendea Proffer, In *The Barsukov Triangle, The Two-Toned Blond, and Other Stories* [1984]. *Tsvetnye otkrytki* (1986).
Stories: "Kurzap" (1986).
Translations: "The Farewell Light," tr. Helena Goscilo and Valeria Sajez; "Between Spring and Summer," tr. John Fred Beebe, both in *HERitage and HEResy: Recent Fiction by Russian Women*, ed. H. Goscilo (1988).

Helena Goscilo

Kavalerist-devitsa

(see: Nadezhda Durova)

Galatea Kazantzaki

(a.k.a. Lalo di Castro, Petroula Psiloreiti)

Born 1886, Herakleion, Crete; died 1962, Athens, Greece
Genre(s): novel, drama, poetry, short story
Language(s): Greek

She was the daughter of the publisher S. Alexiou. Her sister, Elli Alexiou, is a well-known writer. In 1911, she married the world-famous writer N. Kazantzakis, whom she divorced thirteen years later. In 1933 she married the critic and poet M. Augeris but continued using her name from her first marriage.

G. Kazantzaki started her literary activity in 1906 with various contributions to the periodicals *Pinakothiki*, *Nea Zoe*, *Alexandria*, and *Noumas*. At that time, Greek women were not encouraged to pursue a literary career. Consequently, she wrote under the pseudonyms "Lalo di Castro" and "Petroula Psiloreiti." Her first novel, *Ridi Pagliaccio*, which established her reputation as a writer, appeared in four parts in the periodical *Noumas*, in 1909. This novel was warmly received and praised by the leading literary figures of her time. It reflects her realistic attitude and her crystal clear intellect. Her future husband, N. Kazantzakis, revolted at the toughness of her realism, characterizing it as a "red, rebellious dissonance."

Her literary talents were not limited to novel writing. She also wrote plays, some of which became great theatrical successes, such as *Pasi Thysia* (1911; At All Costs), *Mia Nychta* (One Night), *Omorphos Kosmos* (The Beautiful World), and *Eno To Ploio Taxideuei* (The Ship Sails On) in 1931; in the latter especially, Kazantzaki uses various symbolical figures and images: the boat is the symbol of life, of reality, the passengers of the ship symbolize the social classes and their aspirations. She also wrote school books, such as *I Megali Hellas* (The Great Hellas), *Oi Treis Filoi* (The Three Friends) and *Ta Dyo Vassilopoula* (The Two Princes). Her poems have not been published yet in a complete collection, but are to be found in various periodicals. Poems such as "To Amartolo" (The Sinful), "Mnistires" (Pretenders), "Sti Manna mas" (To Our Mother), "Ston Erota" (To Eros), and others, confirm her great reputation as a writer. The romantic element in her poems gave way, gradually, to prosaic realism.

Kazantzaki's short story collection, *Oi Krisimes Stigmes* (The Crucial Moments), published in 1952, focuses mainly upon women, and is, above all, a substantial, early contribution to women's literature. The "woman" is no longer perceived as the symbol of tenderness, love, and pain, as was so often the case in the traditional literature of her times although, in some cases, the sentimental touch is not entirely absent. Through the "woman," Galatea attacks social injustice with humor and irony. Her novel *Anthropoi kai Hyperanthropoi* (Men and Supermen), which she published in 1957, is mainly autobiographical, and in it she reveals, under fictitious names, her life and relations with her first husband. Its intense subjectivity diminishes its value as a piece of literature.

Kazantzaki also wrote books for children, such as *I Mikri Heroida* (The Little Heroine) and an autobiographical novel *Ligo Prin Dysei O Elios* (Just Before the Sun Sets). Except for her short stories, which were collectively published in three volumes, most of her work remains unpublished. Her profound psychological insight, the clarity of her expression, and her perceptive depiction of life place her in a prominent position among Greek women writers.

Works

Novels: *Ridi Pagliaccio* (1909). *Foteini tou Anegnosti*(1910). *Me, All You* (1910). *The Red Life* (1911). *The Sick City*(1914). *Women*(1933). *Men* (1935). *Men and Supermen* (1957). *Villa Victoria* (1957). *Just Before the Sun Sets* (c. 1957/8).

Plays: *At All Costs* (1911). *The Wounded Birds* (1925). *As the Ship Sails On* (1931). *Master Mavrianos and his Sister. On Saint John's Night. The Beautiful World. One Night. Yesterday Today and Tomorrow.* All her theatrical plays, nine long plays and eight one-act plays, have been published under the title *Aulaea* in 1959.

Poems: "The Sinful"; "Don Quixote"; "Pretenders"; "Sirens"; "Columbus"; "To Our Mothers"; "Prayer"; "Unknown Mistress"; "To Eros"; "The Prostitute"; and others.

Short Story Collections: *11 am–1 pm* (1927). *The Crucial Moments* (1952). *The Dying World and the Coming World* (1963).

Bibliography

Augeris, M., M.M. Papaioannou, V. Rotas, Th. Stavrou, *An Anthology of Greek Poetry*, vol. 4 (Athens, 1959) p. 2. Charis, P., *Hellenica Grammata*, vol. 1 (1927), p. 342. Chourmouzios, A., *Kathimerini* (10–21–1935). Daralexis, C., *Panathenaea*(1911), p. 223. Kaliyiani, T., *Paratiritis* (12–2–1962). Kazantzakis, N. (Karmi Nirvami), *Noumas* 357 (1909). Kazantzakis, N., *Letters to Galatea*(Athens, 1959). Kokkinis, S., *Anthology of Neohellenic Poetry 1708–1971* (Athens, 1971). Mavroeidi-Papadaki, S., *Hellenis* 5 (1932).

Mirambel, A., *Anthologie de la Prose Neo-hellenique 1880–1948* (Paris, 1950). Nirvanas, P., *Pinacothiki* (1910–1911), pp. 40–41, 167–168, 196–197. Papas, K.N., *Nea Zoe* (Alexandria 1915), pp. 214–226. Patsis, Ch., *Great Encyclopaedia of Neohellenic Literature* (Athens, 1968). Peranthis, M., *Anthology of Neohellenic Poetry* (Athens, n.d.). Peridis, M., *Grammata* (Alexandria, 1915–1916), pp. 132–134. Porphyris, K., *Poetic Anthology 1650–1984* (Athens, 1964). Rodas, M., *Noumas* (1914), p. 299. Rosenthal-Kamarinea, I., *Neugriechische Erzaehler* (Olten und Freiburg im Breisgau, 1953). Sachinis, A., *The Prose Writers of Our Times* (Athens, 1967). Tarsouli, A., *Greek Poetesses* (Athens, 1941). Thrylos, A., *Philologiki Protochronia* (1953), p. 315.

Aristoula Georgiadou

Nadya Kehlibareva

Born 1933, Sofia, Bulgaria
Genre(s): poetry, children's literature
Language(s): Bulgarian

Nadya Kehlibareva graduated in French linguistics from the Kliment Ohridski University in Sofia, then worked as a schoolteacher. Since 1969 she has held the post of editor with the Bulgarski Pissatel publishing house. Some of her thirty-plus books have been written for children, and her poems have been translated into English, French, German, Russian, Armenian and Romanian. Her poetry shows a strong affinity for the sea and is characterized by indirect imagery, symbolism, pantheism, and a political and social reality.

Works

My Sea (1960). Mountain of the Strong (1965). Winds over the Bay (1970). Round Year (1974). Peacock Gates (1975). Coast of Waiting (1979). *Krasota Vuri Prez Delnika* (1980). *Povest za Bulgarkata* (1981). Women's Worlds (1982). Sailors' Land (1984). With Your Smile (1985). *Cvetlianata na Migovete* [The Light of Instants] (1985).

Warwick J. Rodden

Judit Kemenczky

Born 1948, Budapest, Hungary
Genre(s): poetry
Language(s): Hungarian

Judit Kemenczky attended university at the Eötvös Loránd Tudományegyetem in Budapest, where she studied Japanese language and literature. An editor by profession, she resides alternately in Budapest and Boston. Her work appears regularly in Hungarian literary journals and is included in several recent anthologies, including *Tengerláto* (1977), *Szép Versek* (1980, 1985), *Hulámlovaglás*, and *Ne Mondj Le Semmiröl*. Kemenczky is currently working on a study of medieval Japanese drama, forthcoming from Europa Könyvkiado. She has a strong interest in the visual arts as well as in poetry, and she has exhibited her drawings and aquarelles during her poetry readings.

Kemenczky is considered a representative of the avant garde. Her formal experiments entail manipulating both the visual and linguistic components of poems. She adopts the techniques of concrete poetry in using colored inks, typography arranged in floral or geometric shapes, and words patterned to create borders around poems.

Linguistically and thematically, Kemenczky's poetry integrates Western modernist influences with classical Japanese and Chinese philosophies. Her sensibility is metaphysical; her language vernacular. Her poems are verbal collages juxtaposing high and popular culture and esoteric scholarship. In her volume *Sorsminta*, Paracelsus appears within lines of Wrigley's Chewing Gum; one poem contains references to Rousseau, Kirkegaard, Jacob Bohme, Max Ernst, and Cortez in quick succession. In Kemenczky's poetry, East overlaps West, and the ancient overlies the modern, supplying ironic commentary: in one poem, the flute of an ancient Japanese warrior issues from a transistor radio.

Kemenczky's disjunctions and discontinuities do not so much reflect psychological fragmentation as they do an encyclopaedic mind resounding with the myriad (not to say excessive) cultural stimuli—both sacred and profane—of the twentieth century. Kemenczky seeks spiritual authenticity through a rapid-fire poetic speech adequate to the milieu of cultural overload.

Works

A Vesztő (1979). Sorsminta (1982). Gyémant Evő (forthcoming). Géniusz Skalp (forthcoming).

Gyorgyi Voros

Mirdza Ķempe

(a.k.a. M. Īve)

Born February 9, 1907, Liepāja, Latvia; died
    April 12, 1974, Rīga, Latvia
Genre(s): lyric poetry, criticism
Language(s): Latvian

Mirdza Ķempe, a gifted poet of broad interests and sympathies, is largely ignored in the West but admired in the USSR and other Eastern European countries. She is one of a number of writers who adjusted their personal inclinations to fall in line with the official ideology of Soviet Latvia at the price of much of their freedom and individuality.

At a very early age Ķempe lost her father, a business agent. While she was a child, her mother and brother joined the illegal Communist movement. (Her brother Emils, whom Ķempe idolized, went to Spain in 1938 and was killed there fighting on the Republican side.) In 1927 Ķempe entered the University of Riga to study law and agriculture. Because of financial difficulties she discontinued her studies and began working for the radio, first as announcer then as writer and translator, activities that continued under the Soviet occupation. In 1931 she married the Latvian writer Eriks "damsons (d. 1946). At the approach of the German army during World War II, she fled to Russia, where she helped organize and direct a Latvian puppet theater. After the war she continued this venture in Latvia.

In 1946, along with many other Latvian writers, Ķempe was harshly criticized by the Soviet government for being insufficiently political. She thereupon turned her attention to topics and approaches more acceptable to her critics: instead of writing predominantly personal lyrics, she turned to celebration of and sympathy with victims of oppression, mainly in the Third World. She acquired many prizes and honors, among them the title of People's Poet of the

Latvian SSR (1967) and an honorary doctorate from the University of Vishabharati, India (1972). In addition to her own poetry, much of which has been translated into Russian, Ķempe translated numerous works into Latvian from Russian, English, French, and German prose and verse.

Works

Rīta vējš (1946). Drauga vārdi (1950). Mieram un dzīvībai (1951). Dzejas (1955). Mīlestība (1957/58). Es nevaru klusēt (1959). Skaudrā liesma (1961). Mirkļu mūžība (1964). Gaisma akmenī (1967). Dzintara spogulis (1968). Cilvēka ceļš (1969). ērkšķuroze (1973). Numerous critical articles and brochures.

Bibliography

Bērsons, Ilgonis, Padomju Latvijas rakstnieki (Riga, 1976). Ekmanis, Rolfs, Latvian Literature Under the Soviets: 1940–1975 (Belmont, Mass., 1978).

Zoja Pavlovskis

Diana Kempff

Born 1945, Thurnau, Oberfranken, Germany
Genre(s): novel, experimental prose miniature,
    fantastic allegory, poetry
Language(s): German

Daughter of the famous pianist Wilhelm Kempff, Kempff decided she would become a writer when she was thirteen. By the age of seventeen she was writing but hesitated to publish for a long time. One of her characteristic traits, she says, is slowness. After finishing secondary education (she failed in German for "not mastering the language well enough"), she has worked as editor in several publishing houses. Presently she dedicates full time to writing. In 1983 she was awarded the Münchener Förderungspreis, and in 1983, the Heinrich-von-Kleist Preis. Some of her work has been translated into Swedish.

Kempff's turn to poetry as the first means of expression indicates her overall orientation: to move away from reality and create imaginary spaces filled with dreams and visions. Her books of poetry show preference for short units: the first consists of haiku-like miniatures pervaded by a melancholy mood, full of unusual images. Already in it she starts questioning the finality of life. The second presents dense vignettes whose meaning goes beyond enunciation, delving into dreams, raising uncertainties, perceiving/intuiting different truths. There is no rhyme and little rhythm: the verses surge as movements of the psyche.

Her great breakthrough came with *Fettfleck* (A Blotch of Fat), her only prose work that conforms to the parameters of a novel. Construed with autobiographic elements, it can be considered as a *Bildungsroman* that relates the growing up of a solitary, very fat girl who soon finds out that life is not all roses and fairy tales. Other children shy away from her, and she is obliged to create for herself an imaginary world. The extraordinary quality of this novel rests on its artful handling of language: a mixture of dialect and child's talk, slowly evolving to a "normal" discourse. Within contemporary women's writing, such effect of immediacy is approached only in *Mandei-lhe uma boca* (1983) of Olga Gonçalves. In the choice of subject—although not in its treatment—*Fettfleck* reminds one of Marie-Louise Kaschnitz's "Das dicke Kind." The little girl's reactions transmitted in a monologue show some characteristics of feminine writing: introspective flow of thoughts, paratactic sentences; short, fragmented paragraphs, subjective perception of time. One is struck by the psychological veracity of a child's secret world, her acute perception of what is going on, her urgent need to communicate, which finally leads her to determine that she will be a writer. It is a cruel world that Kempff presents, and the closing paragraph confirms the cruelty. Yet, there is a kind of stoic acceptance on the part of the child who, through it, is able to convert some of her experiences into poetry and introduce lyric quality into the narrative.

Hinter der Grenze (Beyond the Limit) oscillates between fairy tale and science fiction, between *Alice in Wonderland* and Orwell's *Animal Farm*. It presents the transformation of a little girl who goes to the zoo and suddenly steps "beyond," into "no man's land," peopled with talking and even verse-writing animals. The book is full of literary and allegorical allusions; plays on words abound: it is a literary piece. In *Der Wanderer* the fantastic note becomes even stronger, the mood more somber, although an exhortation is given to "speak of light which arises

out of darkness." It shows subterranean labyrinths of the unconscious in a state of pre-formation rendered in long, unending paragraphs. At the very beginning a warning is issued: "I am not I, not only I, not I alone, I, the Dreamer," pinpointing further: "there is nothing real in this game, I hide behind my 'why'." One critic sees in it "dreamscapes of fright" filled with "postapocalyptic imagery." Others speak of nightmarish visions. Again, it is the wrestling for adequate expression which adds an affirmative note even to this nihilistic world. Between the two fantasies Kempff releases *Der vorsichtige Zusammenbruch* (The Careful Breakdown), which consists of fifty short prose fragments-meditations on life and death but also on writing. It is permeated by existential *angst*, yet the experience of creating new language rings a positive note.

Kempff pays particular attention to dreams, fantasy, and experimentation with language. She is interested in inner worlds and excels in transmitting the psychological processes of a child. Often, the image of a door or a wall is used as a symbol of the necessity to go beyond reality perceived by the senses. She has a particularly fine ear for music and rhythm. Her sense of language cannot be matched easily. Working with language appears as the only solution in a depressing world, but then even its ultimate validity is put to doubt. Recurring themes in her work are solitude, selfishness, cruelty, death. Long monologues function as self-analysis. Hinted at as "a mixture of elegant sarcasm and fierce despondency," Kempff's writing stands out among her contemporaries through its mastery in combining the real with the fantastic, her ability to infuse lyricism without veering toward sentimentalism, her extraordinary gift for language, and the poetic quality born out of the struggle in her best pages, as in *Fettfleck*.

Works

Vor allem das Unnützliche [The Useless Above All] (1975). *Fettfleck* [A Blotch of Fat] (1979). *Hinter der Grenze* [Beyond the Limit] (1980). *Der vorsichtige Zusammenbruch* [The Careful Breakdown] (1981). *Herzzeit* [Time for the Heart] (1983). *Der Wanderer* (1985).

Bibliography

Kaiser, Joachim, "Bewunderung, Bestürzung, Ratlosigkeit." *Süddeutsche Zeitung* (March 27/28, 1982). Kaiser, Joachim, "Träumende und Geträumte." *Süddeutsche Zeitung* (May 11, 1985). Katherein, Karin, "Die Schrecken des Kindseins." *Die Presse* (August 1, 1979).

Birutė Ciplijauskaitė

Friederike Kempner

Born 1836, Opatow, province Posen; died
    1904, Friederikenhof near Breslau
    [Wroclaw], Poland
Genre(s): poetry, essay, drama, novel
Language(s): German

Friederike Kempner was the daughter of a wealthy landowning *junker* of Jewish extraction. Her dramas and novellas, most of historical content, preach ideas of social harmony typical of subliterary genres of the so-called *Grunderzeit* era. Her poems, for the most part, are sheer *larmoyant* sentimentality. About to be blissfully forgotten, a fact that her embarrassed family had contributed to by making disappear each successive edition of her poems, she was "discovered" by critic Max Lindau in 1879 as the "genius of the involuntarily comical," i.e., a writer who made her readers shed tears of laughter by being solemn and pompous. This literary parlor game was continued by editors Hermann Mostar in 1953 and Percy Eichbaum in 1961, hurting only the famous Berlin critic Alfred Kerr (1867–1946), nephew of Friederike. Last but not least, her obsession of being buried alive, expressed in the 1856 treatise on the need for mortuaries to observe the dead for three days, has been endlessly made fun of. However, a more serious approach to her writing as an expression of the aspirations and nightmares of the Kaiserreich, and a comparison with other pulp authors such as Karl May, Marlitt, or Courths-Mahler, could be fruitful.

Works

Berenice (1860). *Eine Frage Friedrichs des Grossen. Roger Bacon* (1961). *Rudolf II oder Der Majestätsbrief* (1967). *Gedichte* (1873; 7 editions till 1903). *Ein Wort in harter Zeit* (1899). *Gedichte*, ed. by Georg Witkowski (1931; Bibliophile edi-

tion). *Ausgewählte Gedichte*, ed. and intro. by Hermann Mostar (1953).

Bibliography

von Wilpert, Gero, *Deutsches Literatur-Lexikon*, 2nd edition (Stuttgart, 1975).

Ute Marie Saine

Magdalena von Kenzingen

(see: Magdalena von Freiburg)

Susanne Kerkhoff

Born 1918, Berlin, Germany; died 1950, Berlin
Genre(s): poetry, essay, novel
Language(s): German

Susanne Kerkhoff was the daughter of renowned literary historian and professor Walther Harich and Eta Harich-Schneider, well-known musicologist. After brilliant studies, she became a journalist for the *Berliner Zeitung* in 1948. Under the Nazi regime, she very courageously tried to save those persecuted for racial and political reasons. Her novels are autobiographical, and the title of one of them, *Daughter of a Good Family*, recalls almost verbatim one of Simone de Beauvoir's. Her impeccable antifascist past and her exciting, if melancholy works, which she continuously published throughout the 1940s, seemed to predestine her to play an important role in postwar German literature when she committed suicide in 1950.

Works

Tochter aus gutem Hause (1940). *Das zaubervolle Jahr* (1941). *In der goldenen Kugel* (1944). *Das innere Antlitz* (1946). *Die verlorenen Stürme* (1947). *Menschliches Brevier* (1948). *Berliner Briefe* (1948).

Bibliography

von Wilpert, Gero, *Deutsches Literatur-Lexikon*. 2nd edition (Stuttgart, 1975).

Ute Marie Saine

Marie-Thérèse Kerschbaumer

Born August 31, 1936, Garches near Paris,
France
Genre(s): prose, poetry, radio and television
drama, essay, translation
Language(s): German

Marie-Thérèse Kerschbaumer has emerged in recent years as one of the leading women prose writers in German. Perhaps it was her own difficult childhood (of which she is reluctant to speak) that subsequently led her to sympathize with the disenfranchised people of the world. Repression and exploitation of minorities and the underprivileged is her central theme in individual and highly successful artistic forms. She is also active in the European peace movement and takes a public stance on many sociopolitical issues.

Fleeing the Spanish Civil War, Kerschbaumer's Austrian mother and Spanish father went to France, where Marie-Thérèse Raymonde Angèle was born near Paris in 1936. Her childhood years were spent in part in Costa Rica but primarily with her grandparents in the Austrian province of Tyrol. To escape the unhappy family situation she went to England to work for a year when she was seventeen and subsequently to Italy. Back in Austria in 1957 she attended night school to earn her high school diploma, but her plans to study the visual arts were frustrated. In 1963 she began her studies at the University of Vienna with a concentration in Romance languages and literatures. After spending two years in Romania, where her first volume of poetry was published, she received her doctorate from the University of Vienna in 1973 with a dissertation on structural linguistics in Romanian. In 1971 she married the painter Helmut Kurz-Goldenstein, and they have one son. Kerschbaumer lives today as a free-lance writer in Vienna, where she manages to find time for both family and career as well as for political activities.

Kerschbaumer's best-known work to date is *Der weibliche Name des Widerstands* (1980; The Feminine Name of Resistance). It won wide recognition for the author when it was produced as a television film in 1981, and the following year it was reprinted in a prominent paperback series. Noteworthy is the fact that the book was written years before the topic of anti-fascism became fashionable, which is indicative of Kerschbaumer's individualistic and pioneering stance. The book consists of seven "reports" about women killed in Nazi concentration camps. Although based on historical accounts, the reports are themselves fictional, representing a unique amalgam of documentary and imaginative literature. The seven portraits present women of various types and backgrounds: writer, professor, nun, gypsy, seamstress, teacher, and working-class woman. The seven stand as representative of those who were persecuted because of their race or religion or opposition to the Hitler regime. The author describes the courageous resistance—ultimately futile—of these women to the sufferings, humiliation, and horrors of fascism. Part of the power of the work derives from the fusion of temporal categories, whereby past and present are inextricably intertwined, just as are the personal pronouns "I," "you," and "she," creating a fusion of identities. The work thus succeeds in making a general statement by focusing on particular individuals, with the language and style adapted in each case to the personality of the figure. Interspersed are reflections on the writing process itself that reveal the ethical and aesthetic commitment of the author to be one and the same.

The theme of oppressor versus victim in modern European history appeared already in Kerschbaumer's first major work, *Der Schwimmer* (1976; The Swimmer), cast against a backdrop of the Franco regime in Spain. It describes the attempt of inmates to escape from an institution and flee on a ship that is to aid the refugees. The plot line, however, remains in the background, and foregrounded are the thoughts and feelings, memories, and associations of the first-person narrator, expressed in a highly rhythmical and metaphorical language. Such experimental techniques were perfected in *Der weibliche Name des Widerstands*, which was followed by an ambitious lengthy novel, *Schwestern* (1982; Sisters). It presents the fictional account of several Austrian families against a background of twentieth-century history: collapse of the monarchy, inflation and economic crisis, political instability, and catastrophe. The red thread, consisting of the story of sisters who vie for the affection of patriarchal fathers, recurs through several generations, places, and social classes. The careers and ruinations of the fathers are reflected in the lives of the female family members, most of whom fail, although one develops into a political activist. The motif of the sisters in the novel is representative of Austrian sociopolitical structures, which are depicted as bogged down in ultra-conservative entanglements. Kerschbaumer also writes radio plays, which, although not available in published form, have been highly successful on Austrian radio. One example is "Kinderkriegen" (1979; Having Kids), which deals with the deplorable situation in hospital maternity wards.

Kerschbaumer is one of the few writers successfully to unite ethical and aesthetic issues. Although the summaries may sound black and white, the author depicts the characters and situations with great subtlety and consummate skill, and her moral commitment thus requires no sacrifice of artistic quality. The protagonists in her works are women, and she is particularly interested in portraying a female perspective. She rejects, however, the concept of a specifically feminine aesthetic, and women's issues are seen rather in connection with the general struggle of oppressed individuals and classes to resist domination and repression. "Sensitivity is probably not linked with gender but rather a matter of attitude, conscience, and knowledge," stated Kerschbaumer in an interview. In contrast to autobiographical women's writing Kerschbaumer chooses historical settings, and she unites historical events and literary-philosophical reflections with sensitive character portrayals (which occasionally contain autobiographical elements). She regards literature as a means for the reflective individual to combat the misuse of power, and she sees her specific task as speaking for the underprivileged who have no audible voice of their own. As a member of the Artists for Peace organization as well as the Graz Authors' Association she works to realize the slogan "Nie Wieder Krieg" (No More Wars).

Works

Gedichte (1970). *Der Schwimmer. Roman* (1976). *Der weibliche Name des Widerstands. Sieben Berichte* (1980; rpt. 1982). *Schwestern. Roman* (1982).

Bibliography

Höller, Hans, "'Wer spricht hier eigentlich, das Opfer, eine Leidensgenossin oder ein weiblicher Autor?' Marie-Thérèse Kerschbaumers Roman *Der weibliche Name des Widerstands.*" *Frauenliteratur. Autorinnen, Perspektiven, Konzepte*, ed. Manfred Jurgensen (Munich, 1983), pp. 141–152. Schmid-Bortenschlager, Sigrid, "Die Vermittlung zwischen gestern und heute, der Heldin und uns. Zu Marie-Thérèse Kerschbaumers *Der weibliche Name des Widerstands.*" *Frauenliteratur. Autorinnen, Perspektiven, Konzepte*, ed. Manfred Jurgensen (Munich, 1983), pp. 153–157.

Beth Bjorklund

Mensje van Keulen

Born June 10, 1946, 's-Gravenhage, The Netherlands
Genre(s): novel, short story
Language(s): Dutch

Mensje van Keulen (née Mensje Francina van der Steen) belongs to a group of writers who set a (minor) trend in Dutch literature of the early seventies: the return to "readability." After a Roman Catholic education, she went to England. There she worked as a domestic and as a salesgirl in an antique shop, in the meantime taking a painting course at the East End Art School of London. She returned to Holland in 1966 and settled in Amsterdam, where she still lives with her son Aldo. Van Keulen is the name of her former husband Lon van Keulen, a photographer from whom she is divorced.

In 1969, the author made her debut with drawings, stories, and poems in different leading literary magazines. She was an editor of one of these, *Maatstaf* (Criterion), between 1973 and 1981. She has also done occasional work as a journalist. Her prose has been associated with the naturalist tradition around the turn of the century, but it absolutely lacks the bathetic bitterness or moralization of her "Dutch uncles." *Ironic realism* could be an adequate definition. Van Keulen's characters—especially the women figures—are often weighed down with a very physical sense of dissatisfaction: unattractive, solitary, marked by boredom and (petty) bourgeois routine, they are unable to break out and find a lasting happiness. All this is recognizably rendered through a plain but at times soapy style, in which dialogues prevail. Van Keulen's poetry of more recent date, *De avonturen van Anna Molino* (1980; The Adventures of A.M.), is even explicitly burlesque. The novel *Overspel* (1982; Adultery), the short story *Bleekers zomer* (1972; Bleeker's Summer), and the story collection *De ketting* (1983; The Chain) have repeatedly been reprinted.

Works

Allemaal tranen [All Tears] (1972). *Van lieverlede* [Bit by Bit] (1975).

Bibliography

Peene, B., *Kritisch lexicon van de Nederlandstalige literatuur na 1945* (1985).

Frank Joostens

Irmgard Keun

Born February 6, 1905, Berlin, Germany; died May 5, 1982, Köln
Genre(s): novel, short story, poetry
Language(s): German

Keun was born in 1910 in Berlin and grew up in an upper-class liberal atmosphere. She owed her free and independent thinking partly to the influence of her cultivated father. At age sixteen she worked for a short while as an actress but quickly realized the limits of her talent. The writer Alfred Döblin encouraged her to write, and in 1931 she published her first novel, *Gilgi, eine von uns*. Its huge success, however, was surpassed by her second novel, *Das kunstseidene Mädchen*. The National Socialists meanwhile had risen to power and confiscated Keun's books in 1933. When Keun sued them for damages, she was arrested by the secret police, the "Gestapo." A huge ransom paid by her father got her released, and she sought exile in Ostende, Belgium, where many other emigrants lived. Her husband, the author Johannes Tralow, whom she had married in 1932, sympathized with the National Socialists and remained in Germany. In her Belgian exile Keun met the Austrian writer Josef Roth.

For the next two and a half years Keun lived and travelled with Roth and continued to write novels and short stories. In 1937 she divorced her husband and in 1938 also left Roth, whose jealousy had ruined the relationship. In 1940 she was captured in Amsterdam by the invading German troops but managed to return to Germany with false documents. Her underground existence in Germany was partly helped by the fact that official sources had declared her dead in 1940. After the war she worked for newspapers and radio stations. Her last novel, *Ferdinand, der Mann mit dem freundlichen Herzen* was, however, mainly ignored. In 1953 she gave birth to a daughter, whom she raised on her own. Unknown, lonely, and with insufficient financial means, Keun spent the last years until her death in 1982 in the area around Bonn. She did witness the renaissance of her books in the late seventies.

The publications of Keun, which include seven novels and a collection of short stories and poems, reflect her experiences in the Weimar Republic, in exile, and in post-war Germany. Her fiction gives a detailed, vivid and witty portrait of the German society of this period. Keun focuses on the individual destinies of unpretentious people, thereby revealing the overall social and political atmosphere in Germany. This becomes particularly evident in her major novels, *Gilgi, eine von uns* (1931), *Das kunstseidene Mädchen* (1932), and *Nach Mitternacht* (1937), which are narrated from the first-person perspective of young women from the lower classes. Keun shows the gender and class specific obstacles that hinder these heroines in establishing independent, self-determined lives. In *Das kunstseidene Mädchen*, which is regarded as Keun's best novel, the young, unemployed Doris tries "to become glamorous." She reports in her diary her unsuccessful attempts at this goal "like a film." Keun employs in this novel narrative structures that reflect the techniques of the new media film, thus creating an innovative combination of film and literature. All three works, especially *Nach Mitternacht* depict the rise of National Socialism. Keun exposes its absurd logic and brutality, unmasking at the same time the over-eagerness with which a huge number of people followed the fascist ideology. Keun's works manifest a critical awareness of the injustice, hypocrisy, and hierarchical power structures that become particularly apparent in society's treatment of women and members of the lower classes. Her portraits of these individuals combine a penetrating power of observation with an extraordinary gift for humorous description.

Works

Gilgi, eine von uns (1931). Das kunstseidene Mädchen(1932). Das Mädchen mit dem die Kinder nicht verkehren durften(1936). Nach Mitternacht (1937). D-Zug dritter Klasse (1938). Kind aller Länder (1938). Ferdinand, der Mann mit dem freundlichen Herzen (1950). Wenn wir alle gut wären: Kleine Begebenheiten, Erinnerungen und Geschichten (1954). Blühende Neurosen: Flimmerkisten-Blüten (1962).

Bibliography

General references: Dialog: Festgabe für Josef Kunz, ed. R. Schönhaar (1973). Serke, J., Die verbrannten Dichter(1983). Zur deutschen Exilliteratur in den Niederlanden, ed. H. Wurzner (1977).

Other references: The Germanic Review 4 (1985). Jahrbuch für Internationale Germanistik 2 (1982). Literaturmagazin 10 (1979).

Monica Shafu

Nadezhda Khvoshchinskaia

(a.k.a. V. Krestovsky [fiction]; V. Porechnikov and N. Vozdvizhensky [criticism])

Born May 20, 1824, Riazan' province, Russia; died June 8, 1889, St. Petersburg
Genre(s): fiction, poetry, criticism
Language(s): Russian

Literature was primarily an avocation for the women of mid-nineteenth century Russia who were well educated enough to practice it. Nadezhda Khvoshchinskaia is the rare example of a woman who made writing her profession. For over forty years she struggled to support herself and various dependents—her mother, a sister, her brother's orphaned children and, briefly and quixotically, a much younger husband dying of tuberculosis—by writing for major journals and reprinting earlier works in separate and collected editions. Her total production comprises nearly 100 poems, mainly on civic themes, published between 1842 and 1858, including one long tale in verse "Derevenskii sluchai" (1853; A Country Case); ten novels, over forty shorter works of fiction and a few dramatic sketches; literary criticism for the magazine Otechestvennye zapiski (Notes of the Fatherland) from 1861–1864 and the newspaper Russkie vedomosti (Russian Gazette) from 1876–1881; and translations, primarily from French and Italian, throughout her career. It is remarkable that she managed this complex career from the provincial fastness of Riazan', 100 miles southeast of Moscow. For many years, although the fact that "V. Krestovsky" was a woman was widely publicized, the identity behind her masculine pseudonyms remained known only to her editors and colleagues. Writing came naturally to the family. Her sister Sofia was a talented author (see separate article), and her youngest sister, Praskovia Khvoshchinskaia (1832–1916), published one volume of undistinguished stories under the pseudonym "S. Zimarova": V gorode i v derevne: Ocherki i rasskazy (1881; In the City and In the Country: Sketches and Stories).

Khvoshchinskaia perceived herself as an honest craftswoman: ". . . nobody sees better than I my blunders and ignorance—in a word, all that is justifiably ridiculed. I would have stopped writing long ago, if it were not for the necessity of working; that's why I write so much. But, once I decided on that form of day labor, I told myself that I would never utter a dishonorable word, I would not betray that truth, faith in which unites the best of people; in that faith I am the equal of those people. . . ." (Letter to N.V. Shelgunov, December 10, 1874 [Russkaia Mysl', 1891, 2, pp. 182–183]). As this quotation suggests, there was a reforming impulse behind her writing from the first civic poems to her last story, "V'iuga" (1889; The Snowstorm), that depicts the fate of an exiled revolutionary. Khvoshchinskaia was an intelligent observer who portrayed the cycles of succeeding generations with a pessimism which bothered radical critics much more than her artistic lapses.

Today much of Khoshchinskaia's prose is best read as social history, but there are works which stand out above the overall competent but monotone level. Her best novel, V ozhidanii *luchshego* (1860; In Hope of Something Better) depicts a grotesque family of provincial nobles who flee abroad in fear of the impending emancipation of the serfs. "Bratets" (1858; Brother) has a bleak, satiric tone and a jaundiced view of family life that resembles the late 1870s *Gospoda Golovlevy* (The Golovlevs) by her friend and editor Mikhail Saltykov-Shchedrin. Some of her late "sketches" (*ocherki*), particularly those published in *Album: Groups and portraits*, 1879, create effective montages of a variety of contrasting characters without confining them to a tight plot. "Ridneva" (1875) is a chilling depiction of the humiliations suffered by a feckless, poverty-stricken actress. Among Khvoshchinskaia's more striking repeated types are the careerist who is not averse even to robbing his family to further his goals ("Brother"; "Pervaia bor'ba" [1869; Early Struggles]); the aspiring girl mired in a self-satisfied provincial milieu ("V doroge" [1854; On the Road]; *Bol'shaia medveditsa* [1870–1871; Ursa Major]), and the reformer or revolutionary who remains true to the ideals of his generation after his comrades and family have sold out ("Schastlivye liudi" [1874; Happy People]; *Obiazannosti* [1885; Obligations]).

In April 1883 Khovshchinskaia's literary "jubilee" was celebrated with the presentation of a watch and a commendation signed by 731 people, including some of the leading artistic and scientific figures of the day. After the death of her mother, she moved to Petersburg in 1884. When Khvoshchinskaia died in 1889, she did not leave enough money to pay for the funeral.

Works

Polnoe sobranie sochinenii, 6 vols. (1912–1913). *Povesti i rasskazy*, ed. and intro. M.S. Goriachkina (1963). *Poety 1840–1850kh gg*(Leningrad, 1972), pp. 259–270.
Translations: *La signora Ridneff*, tr., S. de Gubernatis-Besobrasoff (1876). *Veriaguine*, tr., Victor Derely (1888).

Bibliography

Arsen'ev, K.K., "Sovremennyi russkii roman v ego glavnykh predstaviteliakh. [Krestovskii, pseud.]," *Kriticheskie etiudy po russkoi literature*, vol. 1 (St. Petersburg: 1888), pp. 255–350. Golovin, K., *Russkii roman i russkoe obshchestvo* (St. Petersburg: 1897), pp. 239–249. *Istoriia russkoi literatury XIX v.: Bibliograficheskii slovar' russkikh pisatel'nits*, K.D. Muratova, ed. (Moscow-Leningrad, 1962), pp. 381–383. *Kratkaia literaturnaia entsiklopediia*, vol. 3 (Moscow, 1966), cols. 819–820 (M.S. Goriachkina). Mogilianskii, "N.D. i S.D. Khvoshchinskie." *Istoriia russkoi literatury*, vol. 9.2 (Moscow-Leningrad, 1953), pp. 228–237. Ponomarev, S.I., *Nashi pisatel'nitsy* (St. Petersburg: 1891; rpt. Leipzig, 1974), pp. 60–71 [bibliography]. Semevsky, V.I., "N.D. Khvoshchinskaia-Zaionchkovskaia." *Russkaia Mysl'* (1890), 10, sec. 2, pp. 49–89; 11, sec. 2, pp. 83–110; 12, sec. 2, pp. 124–148. *M. Stasiulevich i ego sovremenniki v ikh perepiske*, M.K. Lemke, ed., vol. 5 (St. Petersburg, 1913), pp. 92–130. Tsebrikova, M., "Ocherk zhizni N.D. Khvoshchinskoi-Zaionchkovskoi." *Mir bozhii* 12 (1897), pp. 1–40. Tsebrikova, M., "Khudozhnik-psikholog (Romany i povesti V. Krestovskogo-psevdonim)." *Obrazovanie* 1 (1900), pp. 7–34; 2, pp. 37–54.

Mary F. Zirin

Sofia Khvoshchinskaia

(a.k.a. Iv. Vesen'ev)

Born May 20, 1828, Riazan' province, Russia; died August 5, 1865, Riazan'
Genre(s): fiction, essay
Language(s): Russian

Sofia was the most talented writer of the three Khvoshchinsky sisters. Unlike her sisters, who were chiefly tutored at home, she was educated at the Ekaterinsky Institute in Moscow. She studied painting and is known for her portrait of the artist Aleksandr Ivanov (1806–1858).

In her late twenties Khvoshchinskaia turned to writing and, from the start, displayed a strong voice, a light, sure touch with detail, a sly humor, and an ability to sum up the temper of her times in sketches of varied characters and scenes. "Kak liudi liubuiutsia prirodoi (1860; How People Admire Nature) is both a humorous look at Russians abroad and an essay on esthetic values. Like her elder sister Nadezhda, she often used the first-person voice that went with her male pseudonym. "Plach provintsiala" (1861; A Provincial's Lament) sums up the dislocations of the early years of Alexander II's reformist reign on a conservative provincial community. In the philosophical essay "Koe-chto iz nashikh nravov" (1862; Something About Our *Mores*), the narrator comments on the discrepancy between the smooth public faces Russians wear and their private expressions of a liberty that confines itself to gratifying whims and crotchets at the expense of servants and family; he finds their capricious behavior a poor omen for the new era created by the abolition of serfdom.

Twice Khvoshchinskaia described and deplored the conditions of the contemporary girls' boarding schools. In her 1858 story "Nasledvsto tetushki" (Aunty's Legacy), a young man is horrified by the "moral murder" of the atmosphere of the so-called "closed" institute in Peterburg where his deceased aunt taught. Under the pseudonym "N.," Khvoshchinskaia sketched in a long article the years wasted by the girls of her own school, cut off from normal development and the "genuine" life of the family (1861; Reminiscences of Institute Life).

Sofia Khvoshchinskaia fiercely guarded the privacy that permitted her to speak frankly, and after her early death her sister Nadezhda fought to respect Sofia's wish to remain known only as "Iv. Vesen'ev." The elder Khvoshchinskaia was only too successful. Sofia's legacy—three short novels, *Mudrenyi chelovek* (1861; A Tricky Man), *Gorodskie i derevenskie* (1863; City Folk and Country Folk), *Domashniaia idilliia negavnego vremeni* (1863; A Domestic Idyll of Recent Times), fourteen stories or sketches, and a few articles—has never been collected or reprinted.

Works

Mudrenyi chelovek [A Tricky Man] (1861). *Gorodskie i derevenskie* [City Folk and Country Folk] (1863). *Domashniaia idilliia negavnego vremeni* [A Domestic Idyll of Recent Times] (1863). Fourteen stories or sketches and a few articles.

Bibliography

Demidov, N., "Khvoshchinskaia, S. (Vesen'ev Iv.): Literaturnaia spravka." *Russkoe bogatstvo* 2 (1899). Golitsyn, N.N., *Bibliograficheskii slovar' russkikh pisatel'nits* (St. Petersburg, 1889; rpt. Leipzig, 1974), p. 265. *Kratkaia literaturnaia entsiklopediia*, vol. 8 (Moscow, 1975), cols. 243–244 (G.M. Mironov). Mogiliansky, A.P., "N.D. i S.D. Khvoshchinskie." *Istoriia russkoi literatury*, t. 9 (Moscow-Leningrad, 1956), pp. 228–237.

Mary F. Zirin

Rosemarie Kieffer

Born 1932, Luxembourg
Genre(s): tale, short story, essay
Language(s): French

After studying literature and philosophy at the Sorbonne and at the Ecole des Langues Orientales in Paris, Rosemarie Kieffer started teaching Latin, French, and philosophy at the Lycée Robert-Schuman in Luxembourg. She takes an active part in the public and cultural life of her country. Not only is she committed to French studies and writings, she is also highly interested in world literature. She has studied Russian and Arabic and published numerous articles on both Luxembourgish and foreign literatures, above all Baltic, Slavonic, and Georgian. For the last thirty years she has written and published stories, both humorous and grave which, in the course of years, have evolved into short lyrical prose.

In her narrative, descriptive, and evocative writings Rosemarie Kieffer attacks social injustice, exposes the destruction of nature, and claims for all the right to harmonious, intellectual, and moral expansion. Her prose, however, is open to a world of dreams and fancies giving free play to her poetic imagination.

Rosemarie Kieffer's sensitive compassion reminded the Belgian Hellenist Claire Préaux of certain Federico Fellini films and of the Giulietta Massima in *Gelsomina* and *Les nuits de Cabiria*. The French scenario-writer Jean-Paul Le Chanois saw points of similarity between the expression of feelings in Rosemarie Kieffer's prose and the sensuality of Anatole France. According to the Soviet novelist Veniamine Kaverine, the Russian translation of her prose sounds like the voice of Turgenev. She has made regular contributions to the local press, publications abroad (both in Western and Eastern countries), lectures, and radio talks.

Works

Alchimie et toute-puissance, essai sur l'esthétique littéraire de Léon Bopp [Alchemy and Omnipotence,

Essay on the Literary Aesthetics of Léon Bopp] (1959). *Amphithéâtre D 53*, nouvelles [A Black Cat in Galway], short stories (1962). *Les Forêts de Perm, Villes mortelles au coeur de l'homme*, deux contes [The Forests of Perm, Mortal Cities in the Heart of Man, two tales] (1972). *La Nuit d'avril sereine*, contes et nouvelles [The Serene April Night, tales and short stories] (1974). *Pluie d'argent*, vingt et un contes [Silver Rain, twenty-one tales] (1977). *Fantaisie sur un moineau mort*, contes et images [Fantasy on a Dead sparrow, tales and images] (1979). *Littérature luxembourgeoise de langue français* [Luxembourgish Literature in the French Language] (1979) (Collective work published by Rosemarie Kieffer]. *Le petit Cochon qui savait voler* [The Piglet That Could Fly] (1982) *Les Canard sauvages étaient partis*, contes, scènes et images (The Wild Ducks Had Left, tales, scenes, images), *Un chateau dans les arbres*, contes, scènes et images [A Castle in the Trees, tales, scenes, images] (1987). [With José Ensch], *A l'écoute de Gisèle Prassinos—une voix grecque* [Listening to Gisèle Prassinos—a Greek Voice] (1986).

Bibliography

Astalos, Georges, "Rosemarie Kieffer." *Nouvelle Europe* 3 (1973): 32–33. Kraemer, Jean-Pierre, *La nouvelle et le conte* [The Short Story and the Tale], in *Littérature luxembourgeoise de langue française* (Sherbrooke, 1980), pp. 44–46. Livansky, Karel, "Rosemarie Kiefferova." *Littérature mondiale* 4 (1976): 108–109. Timoféieva, O., "La prose lyrique de Rosemarie Kieffer" [The Lyrical Prose of Rosemarie Kieffer]. *Littérature internationale* 9 (1975), pp. 268–269. Tournava, Sergo, "Rosemarie Kieffer et la littérature géorgienne" [Rosemarie Kieffer and Georgian Literature]. *Almanach de l'Union des Ecrivains géorgiens* 2 (1985): pp. 307–315. Zografakis, Georges, "O livres. . . ." *Pariana* (May, 1984): 61.

Liliane Stomp-Erpelding

Johanna Kinkel

Born July 8, 1810, Bonn, Germany; died November 15, 1858, London
Genre(s): poetry, essay, short story, novel, musical composition
Language(s): German

As a young woman growing up in Bonn, Johanna Kinkel was a gifted pianist and singer. Her father, Peter Joseph Mockel, provided lessons for her with Franz Anton Ries, Beethoven's first teacher. A singing society that she directed met weekly in the houses of Bonn families. This group, in which Annette von Droste-Hülshof also participated, was the first musical organization initiated by a woman. Kinkel began composing songs, cantatas, and musical stage works for the society.

At age twenty-two she married Johann Paul Mathieux, a bookseller from Cologne. Their marriage was unhappy, and lasted only five months. A legal separation, which Johanna desired, came much later in 1840.

Kinkel's years in Berlin, beginning in 1836, were very influential to her artistic growth. Here she came in contact with Felix Mendelssohn, Dorothea Schlegel, and Bettine von Arnim and her circle. Kinkel took voice and piano lessons, conducted choral groups, composed, and supported herself by giving piano lessons. She adopted a leftist philosophy and supported the ideas of the revolutionary literary movement in Germany advocated by Varnhagen, Gutzkow, Boerne, and Heine.

Returning to Bonn, she met Gottfried Kinkel, who was then a lecturer in church history at the university and religion teacher in a high school. The two worked together to form the "Maikäferbund" (Junebug Society) and published the newspaper the *Maikäfer*. Johanna converted to Protestantism and married Gottfried in 1843. Gottfried Kinkel became increasingly active politically, and eventually broke with his theological training to accept a position as a professor of art and cultural history at the University of Bonn. In the German Revolution of 1848, he organized the democratic party of Bonn and became deputy to the National Assembly in Berlin. In 1848 he was captured and sentenced to life imprisonment, but two years later, freed by Karl Schurz, the

Kinkels escaped to London, where they lived in exile. Their home became a center for immigrants in London. During this time, Gottfried Kinkel became a professor of German at the University of London, and Johanna was occupied with musical and literary activities.

The collection of *Erzählungen* (Short Stories) published with her husband in 1849 was later revised (1883). Johanna Kinkel's contributions to this work deal frequently with musical topics, as titles such as "Aus dem Tagebuch eines Componsisten" (From the Diary of a Composer), and the strongly autobiographical "Musikalische Orthodoxie" (Musical Orthodoxy) suggest. *Acht Brief an eine Freundin über Klavier-Unterricht* (1852, Eight Letters to a Friend on Piano Playing) is primarily addressed to women living in rural areas who instruct their own children in piano. The letters emphasize musicality as opposed to virtuosity of technique in performance. They stress the necessity for historical study and attention to musical form as well as the integration of music into other fields. Kinkel saw Beethoven sonatas as the ultimate goal of the piano student, which shows her musical insight. Her autobiographical, two-volume novel, *Hans Ibeles in London* (1860), portrays the lives of 1840 immigrants exiled in London.

In November of 1858 Johanna Kinkel fell or threw herself from her bedroom window to her death. She was eulogized in a poem by Ferdinand Freiligrath. Her musical contributions as pianist, singer pedagogue, and composer are substantial but must be viewed as secondary to her literary contributions.

Works

Acht Briefe an eine Freundin über Klavier-Unterricht (1852). *Hans Ibeles in London: Eine Familienbild aus dem Flüchtlingsleben.* 2 vols. (1860). *Der letzte Salzbock* (political drama in 5 acts). "Chopin." *Deutsche Revue* (January 1902). [With Gottfried], *Erzählungen* (1849, 1883).
Translations: *Piano Playing: Letters to a Friend*, tr. and ed. Winifred Glass and Hans Rosenwald (1943).

Bibliography

Asten, Adelheid von, "Johanna Kinkel in London." *Deutsche Revue* (1901). Böttger, Fritz, ed., *Frauen in Aufbruch: Frauenbriefe aus dem Vormärz und der Revolution von 1848* (Berlin, 1977). Rosenwald, Hans, ed., "Introduction." *Piano Playing: Letters to a Friend* (Chicago: Chicago Publishers Development Co., 1943), pp. 4–16. Schultz, J.F., *Johanna Kinkel* (1908). Weissweiler, Eva, *Komponistinnen aus 500 Jahren: Eine Kultur und Wirkungsgeschichte inBiographien und Werkbeispielen* (Frankfurt am Main, 1981) pp. 217–234.

Ann Willison

Elisabeth von Kirchberg

Born first half of the fourteenth century
Genre(s): biography
Language(s): German, Latin

Except for her works almost nothing is known of Elisabeth von Kirchberg, who mentions herself only once in her *Irmegard-Vita* (B, 230v). At four and a half years old she entered the Dominican nunnery in Kirchberg (Württemberg) and seems to have died there as well. Elisabeth had a very close contact with the mystic Irmegard, a member of the same convent. Initially, she copied down Irmegard's visions and revelations on a black board, then on parchment. Irmegard noticed these activities only later, and, since she could not prevent Elisabeth from continuing it, she herself became involved in the process of editing the text in a third version of the *Vita*. The *Kirchberger Schwesternbuch* (The Sister Book of Kirchberg) can also be attributed to Elisabeth on the basis of stylistic and editorial criteria. It highlights, among many other biographies of the convent's sisters, the life of Mechthild von Waldeck. A report about the convent's priest Walther is also included. Similar to the *Irmegard-Vita*, various redactions are extant.

Elisabeth's authorship of the *Ulmer Schwesternbuch* (Sister Book of Ulm) is uncertain. Elisabeth excels as a very individual author and thus clearly differs from the many other authors of Sister Books.

Works

Irmegard-Vita; Kirchberger Schwesternbuch (Sister Book of Kirchberg) and the *Ulmer Schwesternbuch* (Sister Book of Ulm) (?).

Bibliography

Krauss, R., "Geschichte des Dominikaner-Frauenklosters Kirchberg." *Württembergisches Vierteljahresheft für Landesgeschichte* NF 3 (1894): 291–332. Ringler, Siegfried, "Elisabeth von Kirchberg," *Die deutsche Literatur des Mittelalters, Verfasserlexikon*, ed. by Kurt Ruh et al., vol. 2 (Berlin and New York, 1980), cols. 479–482.

Albrecht Classen

Sarah Kirsch

Born 1935, Limlingerode, Harz, Germany
Genre(s): poetry, journalism
Language(s): German

Born Ingrid Bernstein to a middle-class family of Jewish roots, which the father disavowed and Sarah reaffirmed, she had an exemplary communist youth. After working in a sugar factory, she studied biology in Halle, followed by literary studies at the Johannes R. Becher Institute in Leipzig. Sarah Kirsch's musings about nature and ecology, e.g., in *Gesprach mit dem Saurier* or *Katzenleben*, have always profited from the concrete, sometimes anxiously or playfully inverted, look through the microscope. After marrying the poet Rainer Kirsch, with whom she also collaborated, she moved from Halle to Berlin, where her volume *Landaufenthalt* (1967), republished with revisions as *Gedichte* in West Germany in 1969, established her as an interesting major new voice. At one point or another, Sarah Kirsch has befriended most of today's important East German writers, a tightly knit and highly talented generation. After separating from Kirsch, whose name she kept, she had a relationship with poet Karl Mickel, whom she bore a son. Her love poems in *Rückenwind* are dedicated to Christoph Meckel. After signing a statement in 1976 protesting the forced expatriation of poet and singer Wolf Biermann, she was expelled from the SED and the GDR writers' association and became, in 1977, one of many prominent East German writers and intellectuals immigrating to the Federal Republic. Sarah Kirsch accomplished this difficult change more successfully than most, but she more joyfully took in life in Italy after having been awarded a prestigious grant involving life at the villa Massima in Rome.

This phase has enriched Sarah Kirsch's range of expression.

Without a doubt, Sarah Kirsch is the most important German poet today, respected by fellow writers and popular among lay readers as well, with the possible exception of Ernst Jandl, whose range is, however, limited to concrete poetry. Although she has once jokingly remarked that she wished "there were witches who could use her poetry as a handbook," she avoids the deliberate archaism of other women poets with her unique ability of turning everyday events into encantatory, rhythmically sophisticated riddles, without, however, having them lose their sting as predicaments. She borrows freely from past epochs, especially from the Romantics and their interest in fairy tale and other exotic realms, while resolutely keeping her feet on twentieth-century ground. Similarly, while doing highly experimental things with language, both on the sound and image level, her poetry is never incomprehensible or even excessively complex, like that of some, but remains almost deceptively, and therefore intriguingly, simple. By coining the half envious and half pejorative term "the Sarah sound," East German playwright Peter Hacks has perhaps hinted at a certain surfeit of facility in Kirsch's recent production. Moreover, since her poetry is republished furiously in East and West in ever-new constellations, volumes, anthologies, and journals, it has become difficult at times to discern how much of it is new. Yet these objections are mere quibbles in comparison with the admiration Sarah Kirsch commands and deserves for her output. She has also shown an interest in the feminine condition: donning the journalist's cap, she has interviewed five women from all walks of life in *Die Pantherfrau*, nonchalantly subtitled "five unkempt narrations from the cassette recorder." Nevertheless, she shuns the women-only stance. Since her chief subject avowedly is "that thing [called] soul, that bourgeois piece," as she ironically puts it, her poetry boldly, but not cruelly, scrutinizes love and its entanglements, which, in her case, definitely includes men.

Works

Gespräche mit dem Saurier (1965). *Landaufenthalt* (1967). *Die Pantherfrau* (1973). *Die ungeheuren berghohen Wellen auf See* (1973). *Zaubersprüche* (1973). *Es war dieser merkwürdige Sommer* (1974). *Rückenwind* (1976). *Musik auf dem Wasser* (1977). *Katzenkopfpflaster* (1978). *Erklärung einiger Dinge* (1979). *Drachensteigen* (1979). *Sieben Häute* (1979). [With Irmtraud Morgner and Christa Wolf], *Geschlechtertausch* (1980).

Bibliography

Brinker-Gabler, Gisela, *Deutsche Dichterinnen* (Frankfurt, 1986). Puknus, Heinz, ed., *Neue Literatur der Frauen* (Munich, 1980). Serke, Jürgen, *Frauen schreiben* (Frankfurt, 1982).

Ute Marie Sache

Anna Kiss

Born 1939, Hungary
Genre(s): poetry
Language(s): Hungarian

Anna Kiss is a teacher in Budapest. Her long poems describe a self-contained world peopled by mythical figures and marked by themes and motifs derived from Hungarian folklore—superstitions, ghost stories, and folk beliefs. Her work is dramatic in structure and technique.

Works

Fabábu (1971). *Feketegyűrű* (1974). *Kísértenek* (1976). *Világok* (1978).

Bibliography

Pomogats, Béla, *Az Újabb Magyar Irodalom: 1945–1981* (Budapest, 1982).

Gyorgyi Voros

Eila Kivikkaho

Born February 8, 1921, Sortavala, Finland
Genre(s): lyrical poetry, translation
Language(s): Finnish

Eila Kivikkaho is a classic writer of modern Finnish poetry on the borderline between traditional and modern style. Her range is wide: she has written concise tanka poems, straightforward rhymed poetry, and free verse rich in imagery.

Her real name is Eila Sylvia Sammalkorpi (maiden name Lamberg). She was born in Sortavala (today part of the Karelia ceded to the Soviet Union). After graduating from high school in 1940, she worked in an office and a library. Since 1947 she has been a freelance writer; she has translated a considerable volume of children's literature into Finnish, and lately poetry (including Soviet verse).

Kivikkaho has published five collections: *Sinikallio* (1942; Blue Cliff), *Viuhkalaulu* (1945; Fan Song), *Niityltä pois* (1951; Away from the Meadow), *Venelaulu* (1952; Barcarole), and *Parvi* (1961; The Flock). Her *Kootut runot* (1975; Collected Poems) contain in addition the equivalent of a volume of new poems from 1961–1975. This long-awaited collection confirmed her status in modernist Finnish poetry. Her song-like first collections represented a last flowering of traditional poetry. But they disclosed an individual voice, a born singer, especially in such little poems of memory and yearning as "Nocturne." Kivikkaho's technical skill as a poet is concealed; her voice is exceptionally powerful.

Along with *Parvi*, *Niityltä pois* is Kivikkaho's most significant collection. It contains many topical poems, even of a protest nature, but also qualities of modernism and image that were not understood when they appeared (the "Otsa" [Forehead] sequence). Throughout her works one can feel the experience of the war and the loss of her native district, and the sympathy of the speaker in the poems is on the side of the insignificant people of the country. *Parvi* is a memorable work in the new Finnish poetry. It appears as the poem of a whole generation—the generation that grew up in the forties and in whose name her poem speaks: "How could you conquer one/who suffered defeat?" The work included extensive monumental poems ("Ararat"), and at the same time 17-syllable haiku, of which "Soitin" (Instrument) is the most distinguished as an image perception: "Reed that is severed./A transverse flute./ In its hollows/ an intact voice.

Works

Sinikallio [Blue Cliff] (1942). *Viuhkalaulu* [Fan Song] (1945). *Niityltä pois* [Away from the Meadow] (1951). *Venelaulu* [Barcarole] (1952). *Parvi* [The Flock] (1961). *Kootut runot* [Collected Poems] (1975).

Bibliography

Laitinen, Kai, Monogrammi [Monogram]. *Parnasso* 3 (1962). Launonen, Hannu, Hiljaisuuden lohkareesta [From a Block of Silence], *Parnasso* 5 (1977). Saarenheimo, Kerttu, Eila Kivikk'aho *Suomen kirjallisuus*—Finnish Literature VI (1967). Tarkka, Pekka, Eila Kivikkaho, *Suomalaisia nykykirjailijoita*. Modern Finnish Writers (1980). Viikari, Auli, Kutsumaton haltijatar [Uninvited Fairy Godmother] *Parnasso* 1 (1978).

Marianne Bargum

Karin Kiwus

Born November 9, 1942, Berlin, Germany
Genre(s): lyric poetry
Language(s): German

Karin Kiwus is one of the leading modern German poets of the post student-revolution years. Her contributions to poetry, among others, initiated the renaissance of lyrics in Germany in the 1970s, the so-called "New Subjectivity." She grew up in West Berlin, where she studied journalism, *Germanistik* and political science, and graduated with her masters degree in 1970. From 1973 to 1975 she was lector at the Suhrkamp Publishing House in Frankfurt, West Germany. Since 1975 she has held the position of secretary of the literature section at the Academy of Arts, Berlin. In 1978 she was a visiting professor at the University of Texas at Austin. She received the Prize for the Promotion of Literature from Bremen, West Germany, and the Visiting Stipend from Graz, Austria, both in 1977.

Her work includes *Von beiden Seiten der Gegenwart* (1976; From Both Sides of Reality), and *Angenommen später* (1979; Supposedly Later), both collections of poetry. In 1978 she edited, together with Henning Grunwald, *Vom Essen und Trinken* (About Drinking and Eating), a collection of various types of texts about men's habits of eating and drinking throughout world history. In her poetry, which immediately met very positive criticism (Helmut Heißenbüttel), she undertakes to perceive life from a new individualized point of view, which represents a crossing between collective experiences and the feelings of a sensitive individual. Past and future are interchangeable perspectives, reflecting the loss of general truths and the poet's oscillation between hope and desperation to achieve a new understanding of life. Both the process of writing and the *condition de femme* are submitted to the soul-searching effort by the poet. A nostalgic view colors the memories of the revolutionary 1960s, filled with a sense of futility and helplessness.

The feeling of disillusionment dominates most of her poems, in which she tries to experiment with a plethora of new forms and styles. Her poetic language recalls the jargon of the intellectual movements in the 1960s and 1970s and reveals its double standards and shallowness through surprising oppositions and isolations. Thus the reality of everyday life is subjectively documented and also dismissed for its illusionary character.

Works

Von beiden Seiten der Gegenwart [From Both Sides of Reality] (1976). *Vom Essen und Trinken* [About Drinking and Eating] (1978). *Angenommen Später* [Supposedly Later] (1979).

Bibliography

Hamburger, M., "Seizing the moment." *The Times Literary Supplement* (Nov. 17, 1976). Jäger, M., "Highway oder Kesselhaus?" *Neue Deutsche Rundschau* 4 (1979): 621–625. Siering, J., "Karin Kiwus Angenommen Später." *Neue Deutsche Hefte* 26 2 (1977): 358f. Wischenbart, R., "Karin Kiwus." *Kritisches Lexikon zur deutschsprachigen Gegenwartsliteratur*, ed. H.L. Arnold, Vol. 4 (München: edition text a kritik, 1978ff.).

Albrecht Classen

Stella Kleve

(see: Mathilda Malling)

Charlotte von Klipstein

Born January 22, 1837, Lotheißen,
    Pfifflingheim near Worms, Germany; died
    September 25, 1898, Darmstadt
Genre(s): short story, poetry
Language(s): German

She was the oldest daughter of the minister Georg Lotheißen in Pfifflingheim near Worms, who was later transferred to Wersau in the Odenwald. After his death, the mother moved with the whole family to Darmstadt. There Charlotte married the superior forest ranger Emil von Klipstein in 1866. She lived with him in Auerbach first, then they moved back to Darmstadt. He died in 1875. From that time on Charlotte dedicated all her energy to raising her children and to her literary works. She wrote mainly lyric poems but also authored several short stories. Her children posthumously edited her works.

Works

Erlebtes und Geschautes [Experiences and Visions] (1900).

Bibliography

"Klipstein, Charlotte." Lexikon der deutschen Dichter und Prosaisten vom Beginn des 19. Jahrhunderts bis zur Gegenwart, ed. Franz Brümmer. 6th rev. ed., vol. 3 (Rpt. Nendeln/Liechtenstein, 1975), p. 19.

Albrecht Classen

Editha Klipstein

Born November 13, 1880, Blaß, Kiel,
    Germany; died May 27, 1953, Laubach in
    Upper Hesse
Genre(s): novel, essay, memoirs, short story
Language(s): German

Her father was an archaeologist. She herself received an education as a painter and travelled extensively afterwards. In Spain she married the painter and graphic designer Felix Klipstein.

Works

Anna Linde (1935). "Sturm am Abend" [Storm in the Evening] (1938). Der Zuschauer [The Spectator] (1942). Erinnerungen an eine Gelehrten-Republik [Memories of a Republic of Scholars] (1947). Die Bekanntschaft mit dem Tode [Acquaintance with Death] (1947). Geestern und Heute [Yesterday and Today] (1948). "Das Hotel in Kastilien" [The Hotel in Castilie] (1951). Erfülltes Wunschbild, Mein Leben im Waldhaus [Fulfilled Dream Picture, My Life in the Wood Cabin] (1952).

Bibliography

Delbruck, M., "Editha Klipstein." Die Tat 112 (1948). Petzet, W., "Editha Klipstein: Anna Linde." Deutsche Zeitschrift 49 (1936). Schlamp, H.J., "Editha Klipstein: Der Zuschauer." Europäische Literatur 2 (1943). Wehrli, Max, "Gesellschaftsroman." Neue Schweizer Rundschau 10 (1942/43).

Albrecht Classen

Simke Kloosterman

Born November 25, 1876, Twijzel,
    Netherlands; died December 5, 1938,
    Leeuwarden, Netherlands
Genre(s): novella, novel
Language(s): Fries

The daughter of the Fries poet Jan Ritskes Kloosterman (1849–1914) and descendant of the eighteenth-century poet Eelke Meinerts, Kloosterman was imbued with love of the Fries language and literature. Beginning with her early works in 1898, she wrote exclusively in the Fries language. Her works are characterized by intense emotion, individualism, and aristocratic pride. Her love lyrics, nature lyrics, and her lyrical prose are distinguished by variety of metaphor and originality of description. The majority of her novellen describe the life of Fries landowners in her native country.

De Hoara's fen Hastings (1921) is the first significant novel about the Fries community written in a neoromantic style. This work reflects the author's intimate knowledge of the tradition and everyday life of the Fries farm community. The historical novel of the French period It jubdjier (1927) has a strongly political and patriotic intent. The historical novel Hengist en Horsa (1933) retells romantic legend. Many of the sayings of Kloosterman have become Fries proverbs.

Works

De Hoara's Fen Hastings (1921). It jubdjier (1927). Hengist en Horsa (1933). Swanneblommen. Frisia. Us Striid. Verzamelde verhalen (1936–1940). Verzamelde poezie (1952–1960).

Bibliography

Folkertsma, E.B., Toer en tsjerke (1934). Piebinga, J., Koarte skiednis fan de Fries skriftekennisse (1957). Wumkes, A.D., S. Kloosterman (1964).

Mary Hatch

Margareta (Meta) Moller Klopstock

Born March 16, 1728, Hamburg, Germany;
*   died November 28, 1758, Hamburg*
Genre(s): letters, drama, hymn, dialogue
Language(s): German

Well known in literary and social circles of her time (though mainly as the wife of Friedrich Gottlieb Klopstock, the celebrated author of *Der Messias* [The Messiah]), Meta Klopstock has only begun to be given full recognition as a writer in this century. It was not until 1958 that the University of Hamburg acquired an important portion of her work, which had previously been tied up in private estate. A supplement to the collection published by Tiemann in 1956 was presented by H.T. Betteridge, who wrote in his review of the former edition, "In my experience, only Goethe's mother and perhaps Bismarck can equal her (Meta) in making themselves and their surroundings come to life for us."

The correspondence between Meta and her family and friends documents the major phases of her adult life, including her courtship with Friedrich (set off by "love at first reading" of *The Messiah*), the waiting period until her family accepted him as her fiancé, and the happy marriage years (1754–1758) in Copenhagen, ending with her death in childbirth at the age of thirty.

Gifted and well-educated, Meta Klopstock read Latin, French, Italian, and English and admired Lessing, Edward Young, and Edward Moore. She corresponded in English with the British novelist Samuel Richardson. Friedrich submitted and dictated some parts of *The Messiah* to her and asked her about a particular

author because she was able to read the original language. Encouraged by her sister and husband to write, during the last years of her life she began to try her hand at fiction, having already taken on the role of fictional letter writers in some of her "sent" letters.

Her only drama, *Der Tod Abels* (The Death of Abel) can be read in connection with Friedrich's play *Der Tod Adams* (1757). As with all of her works, it must be considered within the context of *Empfindsamkeit* (a literary movement approximating British "sentimentality"), which stressed excited feeling rather than enlightened reason and which, joined with pietistic tendencies, concentrated on the inner experience of the love of God and the intense movements of the soul. This emotional coloration, combined with direct moral instruction, admonishment, and encouragement, is once again present in the ten *Briefe von Verstorbenen an Lebendige* (Letters from the Dead to the Living).

Her work also includes two hymns, "Das Vergangne Jahr" (The Year Gone By) and "Die Liebe Gottes" (The Love of God), the first of which begins by lamenting the swift passing of life but then changes to eager expectation of the next, the second of which encourages the reader to pray to God, a merciful and loving father. The last work contained in the collection of posthumous writings is the *Fragment eines Gesprächs* (Fragment of a Dialogue) in which Friedrich and Meta discuss motives for writing (i.e., friendship with living readers rather than greed for glory). In recording the conversation, Friedrich wished to memorialize his wife's keen perception and understanding.

The works mentioned above were first published in the 1759 edition of Meta Klopstock's works. But Meta also wrote a witty and humorous essay entitled "Ein Brief über die Moden" ("A Letter about Fashions"), published for the first time in the 1816 edition.

Although her career was short, Meta Klopstock's writings clearly merit attention as models of participation in the literary and religious movements of pietistic *Empfindsamkeit* and as independent and original art.

Works

Hinterlassene Schriften von Margareta Klopstock, ed. Friedrich Klopstock (1759). See also the 1816 edition for "Ein Brief über die Moden."

For "sent letters" (non-fictional): The new *Hamburger Klopstock-Ausgabe* of Meta's correspondence appeared in December 1987 (*Klopstock, Friedrich Gottlieb: Werke und Briefe*, begr. von Adolf Beck et al., hrsg. von Horst Gronemeyer et al. [1975]). Betteridge, H.T., "Additions and Corrections to the Correspondence of Meta Klopstock." *MLR* 54 (1959): 518–532. Tiemann, Hermann, hrsg., *Meta Klopstock geb. Moller, Briefwechsel mit Klopstock, ihren Verwandten und Freunden* (1956). Tiemann, Hermann und Franziska, hrsg., *Geschichte der Meta Klopstock in Briefen* (1962) (See also 1980 edition: *Es sind wunderliche Dinger, meine Briefe*).

Translations: Smith, Elizabeth, tr., *Memoirs of Frederick and Margaret Klopstock* (1809, 1910). Preface.

Bibliography

Betteridge, H.T., Rev. of *Meta Klopstock. Briefwechsel* by Hermann Tiemann. *MLR* 53.1 (1958): 129–131. Bogaert, André, *Klopstock: La religion dans la Messiade* (Paris, 1965). Brunier, Ludwig, *Klopstock und Meta* (Hamburg, 1860). Hanstein, Adalbert v., *Die Frauen in der Geschichte des deutschen Geisteslebens des 18. und 19. Jahrhunderts*, 2 vols. (Leipzig, 1899), Jansen, Hans Helmut, hrsg, "Der Tod der Meta Klopstock. Ein Versuch über des Dichters Auffassungen von Tode" by Elisabeth Höpker-Herberg. *Der Tod in Dichtung, Philosophie und Kunst* (Darmstadt, 1978). Horvath, Eva, "Die Frau im gesellschaftlichen Leben Hamburgs. Meta Klopstock, Eva König, Elise Reimarus." *Wölfenbütteler Studien zur Aufklärung* 3 (1976): 175–194. Kind, John Louis, *Edward Young in Germany* (London, 1906). Madigan, Kathleen, "Forever Yours: The Subgenre of the Letter from the Dead to the Living with Thematic Analyses of the Works of Elizabeth Singer Rowe and Meta Klopstock." Diss., U. of North Carolina at Chapel Hill, 1988. Muncker, Franz, *Friedrich Gottlieb Klopstock: Geschichte seines Lebens und seiner Schriften* (Stuttgart, 1888). Murat, Jean, *Klopstock; les thèmes principaux de son oeuvre* (Paris, 1959). Rohn, Adeline Elisabeth, "Meta Klopstock, geb. Moller." *Die Garbe* 13 (1929/30): 244–249. Schmitt, Wolfgang, "Die pietistische Kritik der Künste: über die Entstehung einer neuen Kunstauffassung im 18. Jahrhundert." Inaug. Diss., Köln, 1958. Sperber, Hans, "Der Einfluss des Pietismus auf die Sprache des 18. Jahrhunderts." *DVjS 88* (1930): 497–515. Stecher, Henry F., *Elizabeth Singer Rowe, the Poetess of Frome* (Bern, 1973). Thayer, Terence K., "Klopstock and the Literary Afterlife." *Literaturwissenschaftliches Jahrbuch.* Neue Folge 14 (1973): 183–208. Trunz, Erich. "Meta Moller und das 18. Jahrhunders." (Tiemann, 1956). See also introduction by editor (under Works). Wolf, Louise, "Elizabeth Rowe in Deutschland: Ein Beitrag zur Literaturgeschichte des 18. Jahrhunders." Diss., Heidelberg, 1910. Wohlenberg, Gustav. "Zur Erinnerung an Meta Klopstock." *Der Alte Glaube* 4 (1902/03): 759–764.

Kathleen M. Madigan

Sophie von Knorring

Born September 29, 1797, Gräfsnäs Castle, Västergötland, Sweden; died February 13, 1848, Skälltorp
Genre(s): novel, sketches
Language(s): Swedish

Sophie Margareta Zelow von Knorring was born in the castle Gräfsnäs in Västergötland. Her father, Major Christer Göran Zelow, was descended from the Polish aristocracy and had been a member of the court of Gustav III. Sophie was raised in the conservative traditions of the landed aristocracy and received a careful education from tutors and governesses. She wrote about the class she lived among. Her novels of contemporary Swedish life are a mixture of romanticism and realism, frequently colored by a skillful touch of satire. Her sense of life was formed by the ideals and sentiments of the Enlightenment. Her writing was influenced by the works of Rousseau, Madame de Staël, and Anna Maria Lenngrenn. Like Fredrika Bremer, she was a moralist in her fiction.

As a young woman, her gifted conversation and lively wit and beauty made her an attractive and popular figure at provincial salons. In 1820 she married the much older Baron von Knorring, her father's second cousin, and settled down to a rather monotonous existence in the country, varied by occasional travels. Her health was gradually undermined by tuberculosis. Although she wrote her first novel, *Cousinerna* (The Cousins), in 1829, it was not published until 1834, when it appeared anonymously. Here, as in her later novels, the central theme is a young woman's conflict between her duty to her husband, family, and tradition and her erotic attraction to another man. The young heroine, Amalie, trapped in a marriage of convenience, finally dies of her unfulfilled passion for the dark, Byronic lover, Axel. Von Knorring was especially successful at portraying the emotional turmoil of adolescent girls. Manor houses, balls, and parties form the usual settings for the author's keen observations on the social life of the Swedish aristocracy. Other novels were published in quick succession, all under the anonymous designation of "The Author of *The Cousins*": *Vännerna* (1835; The Friends), *Qvinnorna* (1836; Women), *Axel* (1836; Axel), *Illusionerna* (1836; The Illusions), and *Stånds-Paralleler* (1838; Class Parallels). The semi-autobiographical novel *Illusionerna* is among her best works and contains von Knorring's amusing recollections of Madame de Staël at the Swedish Royal Court during the winter of 1812–1813, where the great Frenchwoman's first public appearance in Stockholm coincides with the young narrator's "coming out" into society at a royal ball.

In a departure from her earlier novels, von Knorring also wrote one of the first "peasant novels" in Sweden: *Torparen och hans Omgivning* (1843; The Peasant and His Landlord). In this tale of forced marriage and murder, her concern focuses on the problems of poor country people though with a somewhat condescending sympathy. This novel, regarded by many critics as her best work, contains authentic and beautiful descriptions of nature and folk life. Von Knorring was apparently inspired to write this novel as a rebuttal to Carl Johan Love Almqvist's controversial novel on the marriage problem, *Det går an* (1839; Sara Videbeck). Her portrayal of love and marriage was diametrically opposed to Almqvist's radical view that the institution of marriage was immoral. Von Knorring championed the inviolability of the marriage vow, always placing duty and law above desire. She was not in sympathy with the forces of the time that supported female emancipation.

In spite of her conservative and conventional moralism, Sophie von Knorring was a gifted observer of the life around her. Though the limitations of her class and its problems hindered her from becoming widely popular in Sweden, she was, together with Fredrika Bremer and Emilie Flygare-Carlén, among her country's most famous realist novelists during the first half of the nineteenth century.

Works

Cousinerna (1834). Vännerna (1835). Qvinnorna (1836). Axel (1836). Illusionerna (1836). Tante Lisbeths 19: de testamente (1838). Stånds-Paralleler (1838). Skizzer I (1841). Förhoppningar (1843). Torparen och hans omgivning (1843). Skizzer II (1845). Två fruar [Two Women. Tr. of Ida Hahn-Hahn's novel Zwei Frauen] (1846). Bref till hemmet, under en sommarresa 1846 [Letters Home, During a Summer Trip in 1846] (1847). En kunglig sekter [A Court Clerk] (1861). Novel published posthumously in serialized form in the newspaper Aftonbladet.

Translations: The Peasant and His Landlord (1848).

Bibliography

Böök, Fredrik, Fem porträtt (1929). Nelson, Barbro, Sophie von Knorring. En svensk roman-författarinnas liv och dikt (1927). Pearson, Jean, "Sophie von Knorring." Kvinnliga Författare, ed. Susanna Roxman (1983). Wallen, Nils Erik, Sophie von Knorring och samhället. Diss., 1962 (includes a comprehensive list of unpublished letters and manuscripts).

Jean Pearson

Natalija Kobryns'ka

Born 1855, Beleluji, Ukraine, The Soviet Union; died 1920, Bolexol
Genre(s): novel, short story, essay
Language(s): Ukrainian

The question of Ukrainian feminism first absorbed Kobryns'ka following her meeting with M. Drahomanov in 1882 who promoted the idea of Ukrainian literature within the frame of European influence and also encouraged the entry of women into intellectual life. As a result, she worked at organizing women's consciousness-raising groups in Western Ukraine. At the same time she began to write short stories of a traditional, realistic character dealing with women. Then in the 1890s, she turned to stories of "fairy tales," whose psychological and symbolic content attested to a relationship with Ukrainian modernism.

Educated at home in the village of Beleluji in Galicia where her father was a priest, as well as a delegate to the Austrian Parliament, Kobryns'ka avidly read Turgenjev, Gogol, and Mickiewicz. At twenty, she married the theologist Teofil' Kobryns'kyj who futhered her intellectual development. When he died prematurely six years later, Kobryns'ka returned to her father's home, and, to help relieve her grief, her father took her to Vienna. There she became acquainted with members of the Ukrainian student association "Sic," and stimulated by the experience wrote her first work "Pani Sumins'ka" and began work on "Pan Sudja." That same year, upon meeting Drahomanov in Switzerland, she began to think about women's rights and the question of self-determination.

In her first work, "Pani Sumins'ka," Kobryns'ka describes the conflict of a woman from a traditional value system when she is confronted with the radical outlook of the younger generation of women. In her story "Zadlja Kusnyka Xliba" ("For the Sake of a Piece of Bread") she describes the fate of an orphan, who not having an adequate education to enable her to make her own living, marries a man whom she doesn't love "for the sake of a piece of bread." Kobryns'ka's novel *Jadzja i Katrusja* presents the parallel stories of two young women from the same village: Jadzja, an aristocrat, and Katrusja, a peasant whose mother had worked in Jadzja's household. In this novel she contrasts the selfish, passive, empty life of the aristocrat and the active, painful, and joyful experiences of the peasant woman. While continuing to write short stories and novels, Kobryns'ka also wrote editorials on the role of education for women and their need for economic self-sufficiency.

Although Kobryns'ka continued to work in the women's movement as well as to publish women's literary almanacs, the lack of support from the women in Galicia disheartened her, and

she returned to her native village where she died in isolation. Nevertheless, her contributions to the history of Ukrainian feminism assures Kobryns'ka a place in Ukrainian literary history.

Works

Vybran'i tvory (1958). [With Olena Pchilka], *Pershvi Vinok* (1984).

Bibliography

Knysh, Irena, *Smoloskypy u temrjavi: Natalija Kobryns'ka i ukrajinski zinochi rux* (Winnipeg, 1957). Romanenchuk, Bohdan, *Z Zyttja i tvorcosty Natalii Kobryns'koji* (Philadelphia, 1951).

Christine Kiebuzinska

Ol'ha Kobyljans'ka

Born November 25, 1863, Hurahomor,
    Ukraine, The Soviet Union; died March
    28, 1942, Cernivci
Genre(s): short story, novel, drama
Language(s): Ukrainian, German

Kobyljans'ka came from a Ukrainian family pervaded by Germanism. She studied German literature, particularly German Romanticism and the philosophy of Nietzsche. Under the influence of these ideas she submitted her first stories in German to journals in Berlin and Vienna. Upon being exposed to the work of the Ukrainian feminist Natalja Kobryns'ka, Kobyljans'ka began to write in Ukrainian, initially reflecting the influence of Ukrainian literary realism although some of her later works clearly reflect her modernism.

Kobyljans'ka's most significant works portray women of universal ideas who strive for greater enlightenment and desire to become independent members of society. In *Tsarivna* (1895; The Princess), written in the form of a diary, Kobyljans'ka presents a psychological portrait of a young woman, Natalka, with a poetic sensibility who must struggle to survive amidst life's harsh realities. Natalka adheres to high ideals for which she is willing to suffer although her extremely sensitive temperament renders her incapable of doing positive work among the people she scorns. The novel *Zemlja* (1910; The Soil) depicts the emotional attachment of peasants to the soil. The conflict of the brothers, Myxajlo and Sava, is played out against the background of the elemental passion of Ukrainian peasants for their village and the experiences of one of the brothers, Myxajlo, who having been inducted into the army, yearns to return to his home. The novel *V Nedilju rano zillaja kopala* (1909; She Gathered Herbs on Sunday Morning) reflects Kobyljans'ka's sensitivity to the smell, color, and the sound of the beautiful, haunting natural world of her native region Bukovina. Based on the plot of a folk song about betrayal in love, the main character, Mavra, a free-spirited Gypsy woman, bears a son, Hryc, whom she is forced to give away. Cast out by the Gypsies, she goes into service and helps rear her master's daughter Tetjana. Once Tetjana grows up, Marva retreats into the forest and supports herself by gathering herbs. Tetjana meets Hryc, falls passionately in love with him, and when she's rejected by him for another, she seeks Mavra out in the forest to give her a magic potion to reclaim Hryc. Upon drinking this potion, Hryc dies, Tetjana goes mad, and Mavra finds out that she had unwittingly killed her son.

Kobljans'ka's contributions to Ukrainian literature reflect a lyrical talent as well as a great gift for observation. The characterization of her heroines reveals the need to admit women into professions that would give them a goal in life and provide a liberation from the bondage of primitive, traditional laws. In *V nedilju rano zillja kopala*, Kobyljans'ka breaks with realism by projecting the plot through romantically symbolic descriptions of the deep undercurrents of the magical world played out against the background of Gypsy passion and the mystery of nature.

Works

Liudyna. Tsarivna. povisti(1958). Liudyna. Zemlja. V nedilju rano zilja kopala. povisti (1955). Meliankholijny valets. Novelia z zhyttia na Bukovyni (1957). Vybranji tvory (1977).

Bibliography

Babyshki, Oleh Kindratovich, *Olha Kobyljans'ka* (Kyjiv, 1963). Biletskyj, Leonid, *Try Sylvetky: Marko Vovcok, Olha Kobyljans'ka, Lesja Ukrajinka* (Winnipeg, 1951). Kopach, Oleksandra, *Movostyl' Olhy Kobyljans'kojia* (Toronto, 1972). Luciw, Luke, *Olha Kobyljans'ka v 100-ricja jiji narodyn* (New York, 1958).

Christine Kiebuzinska

Alma Johanna Freifrau von Koenig

(a.k.a. Johannes Herdan)

Born August 18, 1887, Prague,
*   Czechoslovakia; died ca. 1942, Minsk*
Genre(s): novel, lyric poetry
Language(s): German

Honored with the "Prize of the City of Vienna" in 1925 for her novel *Die Geschichte vom Half dem Weibe* (The Story of Half Woman) and celebrated as both lyricist and novelist in Vienna following the First World War, Alma Johanna Koenig incorporated into her works many of the currents of early twentieth-century German literature, particularly an interest in classical antiquity and in medieval Nordic lore. Her lyrics reflect the influence of Rilke, who corresponded with her and even dedicated a poem to her. She was born on August 18, 1887, in Prague of well-to-do, assimilated Jewish parents who moved to Vienna with her shortly after her birth. Although she did not receive a religious upbringing, she returned later in her life to her Jewish heritage. Her poetry and narrative fiction are marked by a profound sensuality and eroticism.

In 1921, she married Bernhard Freiherr von Ehrenfels, an athletic, blond, and blue-eyed man eleven years her junior and clearly her intellectual inferior. Her husband epitomized a Nordic ideal of beauty toward which she felt powerfully attracted. The couple spent an extended period of time in the late twenties in Algiers, where Ehrenfels served for a time as honorary Austrian consul, a position from which he was removed in 1930 for malfeasance. They separated in 1930 and divorced in 1936. Her experiences in this marriage formed the basis for her novel *Leidenschaft in Algier* (Passion in Algiers), which portrays the loves of a cultivated and aesthetic Austrian woman living in Algeria who is drawn to a handsome but unscrupulous man. The novel was well received and widely reviewed. In 1934 she met Oskar Jan Tauschinski, then twenty years old, to whom she remained attached for the rest of her life. After the Nazi seizure of power in 1933, Austrian publishers ceased printing or selling her works, and she was reduced to holding lectures on literary topics in order to eke out a living. After Austria's incorporation in the Third Reich in 1938, she was evicted from her apartment. Several half-hearted efforts at emigration failed, and the outbreak of the Second World War sealed her fate. She was forced from one apartment to the next some ten times between 1938 and 1942, always keeping the manuscript of her last novel, *Der jugendliche Gott* (The Youthful God), with her. This novel, which treats Nero's relationship to his mother Agrippina, that is, the question how a son could come to murder his mother, was conceived and written under the worst conditions imaginable. On May 27, 1942, she was deported from Vienna, supposedly to Minsk. Nothing more was ever again heard from her.

Her novels are, generally speaking, historical romances. *Die Geschichte vom Halfe dem Weibe* (1924) is set in tenth-century Iceland and relates the story of a young Viking who was declared to be a girl at birth in order to escape baptism. Half grows into a Nordic hero straight out of the sagas. Koenig's interest in Germanic lore is also apparent in her modern German rendition of *Gudrun* (1928). Her lyrics, though, have a special force, as seen in the following excerpt from a sonnet written during the dark and troubled times just before her deportation:

> Denn wie der Sperrling, ohne Unterla
> Im Abfall pickend, seine Nahrung findet,
> So such auch ich in einer Welt voll Ha
> nach Liebe, die uns tiefgeheim verbindet.
> Und davon lebe ich, mich erhält nur das:
> Ich liebe.—Und wer liebt, der überwindet.
> (For as the sparrow, without shelter,
> Picking in the trash finds its food,
> So I also search in a hate-filled world
> For love, which ties us together in secret.
> And I live from one thing and only that sustains me:
> I love. And whoever loves, triumphs.)

Works

Hanna, Westermanns Monatshefte 62 (1917/18). *Die Windsbraut* [The Bride of the Wind] (1918). *Schibes, Hundenovelle* (1920; 1928, with concluding remarks by Eugen Antoine). *Die Lieder der*

Fausta [Fausta's Songs] (1922). *Der heilige Palast* [The Holy Palace] (1922). *Die Geschichte vom Half dem Weibe* [The Story of Half the Woman] (1924). *Gudrun, Stolz und Treue* [Gudrun, Pride and Fidelity] (1928, rpt. 1951, 1964, 1973). *Liebesgedichte* [Love Poems] (1930, 1955). *Leidenschaft in Algier* [Passion in Algiers] (1932). *Sonette für Jan* [Sonnets for Jan] (1946). *Der jugendliche Gott* (1947, 1958). *Sahara, Nordafrikanische Novellen und Essays* [Sahara, North African Novellas and Essays] (1951). *Gute Liebe—böse Liebe* [Good Love—Evil Love] (1960). *Vor dem Spiegel, Lyrische Autobiographien* [In Front of the Mirror, Lyrical Autobiography] (1978).

Bibliography

Raynaud, Franziska M.E., "Alma Johanna Koenig (1887–1942?), Leben und Dichten einer Wienerin." *Leo Baeck Institut-Bulletin* 64 (1983): 29–54. Tauschinski, Oskar Jan, "Die lyrische Autobiographie der Alma Johanna Koenig," *Literatur und Kritik* 72 (March 1973): 65–77.

Earl Jeffrey Richards

Musine Kokalari

Born 1920, Gjirokastër, southern Albania
Genre(s): short story
Language(s): Albanian

Kokalari became widely known immediately upon the publication of her folkloric narrative, *Sic më thotë nëna plakë* (1941; As My Old Mother Tells Me). The book is a collection of short stories, of much value for their lively dialogue in the dialect of Gjirokastër and depiction of the prevailing mores in the region.

Works

Sic më thotë nëna plakë [As My Old Mother Tells Me] (1941).

Philip Shashko

Kokhanovskaia

(see: Nadezhda Sokhanskaia)

Jaromíra Kolárová

Born 1919, Prague, Czechoslovakia
Genre(s): prose, drama, children's literature
Language(s): Czech

After finishing grammar school, Jaromíra Kolárová studied Czech and French in the philosophical faculty of Charles University, Prague. For many years then she worked in film and television as a writer, although the majority of her output is novels, novellas, and writing for children. She made her literary début in 1946.

Works

Psala Jsem Pro Tebe [I Wrote for You] (1946). Jen o Rodinných Zále'itostech [Of Family Affairs Only] (1965). Domy Na Zelené Louce [Houses on a Green Meadow] (1967). Dobrou Noc, Rozume! [Good Night Reason] (1972). Můj Chlapec a Já [My Boy and Me] (1974). Záhadný Host [The Mysterious Visitor] (1975). Cizí Děti [Other People's Children] (1975). Náš Malý, Docela Maličký Svět [Our Little Quite Tiny World] (1977). Voda! [Water!] (1980). Holky z Porcelánu [Porcelain Girls], film script. Léto s Kovbojem [Summer with a Cowboy], film script.

Warwick J. Rodden

Annette Kolb

Born February 2, 1870, Munich, Germany;
    died December 3, 1967, Munich
Genre(s): novel, short story, essay, article,
    diary, translation
Language(s): German

Annette Kolb was born on February 2, 1870 in Munich. Her father was a German garden architect and her mother a French pianist. This cosmopolitan couple often appears in Annette Kolb's novels without many changes. Likewise her childhood, which she mostly spent in Munich, is repeatedly reflected in her works. Very early she began to publish articles and essays, for which she received the Fontane Award in 1913. During WW I she was actively involved in the pacifist movement in Switzerland. From 1920–1933 she lived in Badenweiler and fled Germany as one of the first emigrants through Switzerland to Paris when Hitler rose to power. In 1940 she successfully escaped to New York and only returned to Paris in 1945. Until her death on December 3, 1967, she lived in Badenweiler, Paris and Munich. She received, in addition to the Fontane Award, the Gerhard Hauptmann Prize in 1932, the Literature Award from Munich in 1951, the Goethe Prize in 1955, the Cologne Literature Award in 1962, and, above all, the prestigious Order Pour le Mérit.

Her first novels Der neue Schlag (1912; The New Beat Drum), Das Exemplar (1913; The Example), reprinted in 1982, and Die Last (1918; The Burden) were enthusiastically greeted by Rainer Maria Rilke, who sent glowing letters to her praising her for these books, and were also highly acclaimed by the critics. The next novels included strong autobiographical elements in them and depict the life of a young girl in Munich before the First World War. Later works portray the aristocratic society in Europe of that period and promote pacifism and the idea of a united Europe. The essay, the letter, and the diary offered her the proper medium to express these ideals. Since she belonged to the leading literary circles of Munich in the 1920s, she became a model for Thomas Mann's Munich chapter in his novel Doktor Faustus. Her contribution to the arts and literature were highly recognized even after WW II. In the later autobiographical essays, however, Kolb shifted her focus from pacifism to a strong Catholicism.

Works

Der neue Schlag [The New Beat Drum] (1912). Das Exemplar [The Example] (1913). Die Last [The Burden] (1918). Westliche Tage [Days in the West] (1922, 1973). Daphne Herbst [Autumn of Daphnis] (1928, 1982). Die Schaukel [The Seesaw] (1934, 1982). König Ludwig II. von Bayern und Richard Wagner [The Bavarian King Ludwig II and Richard Wagner] (1947). Mozart (1937). Franz Schubert, sein Leben [Franz Schubert, His Life] (1941). Glückliche Reise, Tagebuch einer Amerikafahrt [Happy Journey, Diary of a Journey to America] (1940). Festspieltage in Salzburg [Music Festival Days in Salzburg] (1937). Festspieltage in Salzburg und Abschied von Österreich [Music Festival Days in Salzburg and Good Bye from Austria] (1938).

Collected short works: *Spitzbögen* [Pointed Arches] (1925). *Wera Njedin* (1925). *Kleine Fanfare* [Little Fanfare] (1930).

Essayistic works: *Blätter in dem Wind* [Leaves in the Wind] [With J. Gould](1954). *Farbenfrohe Vogelwelt* [Colorful World of Birds] (1956). *Memento* (1960). *1907–1964, Zeitbilder* [1907–1964 Historical Documentation] (1964). *Alle Männer Europas haben versagt. Ein paar Ausrufezeichen von A.K.* [All European Men Have Failed. A Few Exclamation Marks from A.K.] (1933).

Diary notes: *Sieben Studien—L'âme aux deux patries* [Seven Studies—My Soul in Two Different Home Countries] (1906). *Wege und Umwege* [Directions and Detours] (1914). *Briefe einer Deutsch-Französin* [Letters by a German-French] (1916). *Zarastra, westliche Tage* [Zarastra, Days in the West] (1921).

Political works: *Das Beschwerdebuch* [Book of Complaints] (1932). *Versuch über Briand* [Essay on Briand] (1929).

In addition she translated a large number of English and French novels, edited various letter collections such as *Die Briefe der heiligen Catarina von Siena* (1906) [The Letters of the Saint Catarina da Siena), *Markgräfin Wilhelmine von Bayreuth: Memoiren* (1920) [Marquesa Wilhelmine of Bayreuth: Memoirs].

Translations: *Mozart*, tr. R.P. and T. Blewitt (1939). *Mozart*, tr. Jean Giraudoux (1956).

Bibliography

Benyoetz, E., *Annette Kolb und Israel* (Heidelberg, 1970). Buchmann, H., "Die Frau im deutschen Roman." *Bücherwelt* 26 (1929): 85–89. Burckhardt, R., "Drei Romane der Annette Kolb." *Gate* 2/3 (1948): 22–25. Lemp, R., *Annette Kolb. Leben und Werk einer Europäerin* (Mainz, 1970). Rauenhorst, D., *Annette Kolb. Ihr Leben und Werk* (Fribourg, Switzerland, 1969; also as a dissertation, 1969). Rinser, L., *Der Schwerpunkt* (Frankfurt am Main, 1960). Rychner, M., "Annette Kolb" *Merkur* 18 (1964): 814–826. Walter, F., "Daphne Herbst." *Kindlers Literatur Lexikon* II (Munich, 1964), cols. 558–559. Zivsa, I., "Die Schaukel." *Kindlers Literatur Lexikon* VI (Munich, 1971), cols. 890–892.

Albrecht Classen

Alexandra Kollontai

Born 1872, St. Petersburg, Russia; died 1952
Genre(s): political tract, novella
Language(s): Russian

Although born into the Russian aristocracy, Kollontai spent her life fighting for working-class women. Several years before the Revolution, Kollontai left her husband and young son to study in Zurich, Switzerland. Later, despite the fact that Lenin did not fully agree with her radical feminist views, she became the highest-ranking female in Lenin's government and the Soviet ambassador to several countries.

Kollontai's writing reflects her belief that women's roles as wives, mothers, and workers needed to be totally redefined. The considerable bulk of her writing is comprised mostly of political speeches and pamphlets, but she also wrote some fiction. Her fiery political works deal with feminism and communism and seem calculated to encourage the social change she advocated through revolution.

Kollontai's fiction, written after the revolution, consists of novella-length works concerning love relationships between young communist workers. The stories are written from the viewpoints of the young women who seem to suffer in the relationships more than the young men. The themes in Kollontai's fictional works reflect clearly her belief that family life and accepted roles needed much more far-reaching change than was brought about by the revolution. Like sentimental romances, Kollontai's stories are aimed at young working-class women. Her chief female characters' zeal for their lovers is second only to their belief in communism. But unlike love in romances, love in Kollontai's relationships is filled with pain as well as passion. While seemingly fulfilling at first, the relationship between Vasilisa and Volodya in *Liubov pchel trudovykh* quickly deteriorates as the young woman's work and identity begin to suffer. When Vasilisa is finally able to extricate herself from the situation, she can continue her work productively and resume her identity, but Kollontai leaves her readers with the nagging question as to whether or how a woman can have her own identity and also the love of a man.

In "Trú pokolencya" Kollontai explores the possibilities of "free love"—love without commitment to sexual fidelity. When a daughter seeks her mother's husband as a lover, great pain is inflicted upon all three. Kollontai seems to suggest that non-erotic love is more binding and powerful than sexual love.

For Alexandra Kollontai, equality and traditional marriage are incompatible. She worked diligently throughout her life through politics and writing to bring about a new morality, one in which a woman would be free to pursue an identity beyond her roles as wife and mother.

Works

Bol'shaia liubov' (1927). Liubov' pchel trudovykh (1923).

Translations: A Great Love, tr. Cathy Porter (New York, 1981). Love of the Worker Bees, tr. Cathy Porter (London, 1977). Alexandra Kollontai: Selected Articles and Speeches, tr. Cynthia Carlile (New York, 1984). Autobiography of a Sexually Emancipated Woman, tr. Salvator Attanasio, ed. Irving R. Fletcher (New York, 1971).

Bibliography

Clements, Barbara Evans, Bolshevik Feminist: The Life of Alexandra Kollontai (Bloomington: Indiana University Press, 1979).

Nanette Jaynes

Käthe Kollwitz

Born 1867, Königsberg, Germany; died 1945,
    Moritzburg/Dresden
Genre(s): journal, letters
Language(s): German

Käthe Kollwitz is known primarily as a graphic artist, who in her drawings, etchings, woodcuts, lithographs and sculptures gave a deeply sympathetic portrait of the pain, rage, tenderness, and joy in the lives of working-class men, women, and children. Her insistence on a politically engaged "art for use," an operative, functional art that at the same time upholds the highest standards of artistic integrity, makes hers a political aesthetic of particular importance in twentieth-century culture. Kollwitz' view of the potential of art and the responsibility of the artist marks her literary work as well. In both her diaries and her letters she explores the relationship between art, politics, and everyday life from her position as a woman artist deeply involved in the struggles of her time.

Born 1867 in Königsberg to a free-thinking, socially conscious, and politically active family, Käthe Kollwitz was encouraged early on to think independently and take responsibility for her choices. Choosing to become an artist, she studied at the Women's School of Art, first in Berlin, and then in Munich. After her marriage to Karl Kollwitz, they settled in a working-class neighborhood in Berlin; his medical practice was on the first floor, their apartment on the second, and her studio on the third. Refusing to make a choice between family and career, Kollwitz structured a life in which family life, work, and political engagement were not only inseparable, but mutually sustaining and interdependent components. By the time of her death in 1945, Kollwitz had become internationally recognized as one of the primary artists of her time, the recipient of numerous prestigious awards (including the Villa Romana Prize in 1907), and the first woman elected to the Prussian Academy of the Arts. Above all, she had become known as an artist who never compromised her vision of an art that could be of service toward the construction of a more just and humane world.

Despite (or perhaps because of) her fame and broad popularity as an artist, a woman whose work is appreciated both by the art establishment and by the common people whose lives she depicted, Kollwitz' written work—her diaries and letters—has never in its totality been made available in published form. Only selections and excerpts have been published; the eleven volumes of her diary, an invaluable record of her life and times in Germany between 1909 and 1943, as yet exist only in manuscript form in the archives of the Berlin Academy of Arts. The published work includes two autobiographical sketches—"Erinnerungen" (1923; Recollections) and "Rückblick auf frühere Jahre" (1941; Looking Back at Earlier Years)—both written for and at the request of her son Hans, excerpts from her diaries, and letters to her husband, sons, friends, colleagues, and comrades.

Reluctant to focus on herself (what ultimately counts, she insisted, was not what a person *is* but what she or he *produces*), she positions herself as one of the players in the unfolding drama of history at a given moment. Like the figures depicted in her art, she emerges in her writing as an individual who is always representative of her time. Thus, the seemingly unemotional surface, the almost documentary tone of her writing, in her letters as well as in her autobiographical texts, merely reveal her passionate refusal to give in to sentimentality. Grieving the death of her youngest son Peter, killed at age eighteen in Flanders within the first months of World War I, she writes in her diary: "This morning, January 1, there is a bright, clear sky. On Peter's bed a strip of sun. Move on and get through. Take your hands, hold yourself together and look ahead" (January 1, 1919).

Whether she is writing about the death of a beloved child, the murder of Karl Liebknecht, difficult moments in her marriage, or times of depression in which she is unable to be productive in her work, the axiom Kollwitz lived by was always firm and clear: not to weep, but to act. Thus, her work as an artist—whether her tool is a chisel, charcoal, or a pen—is characterized by the stark simplicity of a line that focuses in on the essential: "Strength: that means, taking life as it is and, without allowing it to break you—without complaining and much crying—to go about your work with energy. To not deny yourself— the person you happen to be, but to focus in on the essential (Diary entry, February 1917).

Works

Tagebuchblätter, 1909–1943 [Diaries]. Manuscript, 11 vols. *Tagebuchblätter und Briefe,* ed. Hans Kollwitz (1948, rpt. 1985) [Selection tr. Richard and Clara Winston (1955; The Diary and Letters of Käthe Kollwitz)]. *"Ich will wirken in dieser Zeit." Auswahl aus den Tagebüchern und Briefen aus Graphik, Zeichnungen und Plastik* ["I Want to be Effective in These Times": Selections from Diaries and Letters, Graphic Art, Drawings and Sculpture], ed. Hans Kollwitz (1952, rpt. Ullstein, 1981) *Aus meinem Leben* [From My Life] (1958). *Briefe der Freundschaft und Begegnungen* [Letters of Friendship and Encounters], ed. Hans Kollwitz (1966). *Bekenntnisse* [Confessions], ed. Volker Frank (1981).

Bibliography

Kearns, Martha M., *Käthe Kollwitz: Woman and Artist* (Old Westbury, N.Y., 1976). Klein, Mina C., and H. Arthur, *Käthe Kollwitz, Life in Art* (New York, 1972). Rukeyser, Muriel, "Käthe Kollwitz," in *No More Masks! An Anthology of Poems by Women*, Florence Howe and Ellen Bass, eds. (Garden City, N.Y., 1973), pp. 100–104. Smedley, Agnes, "Käthe Kollwitz: Germany's Artist of the Masses." *Industrial Pioneers* 2 (September 1925): 8–13.

Angelika Bammer

Anise Koltz

Born 1928, Luxembourg
Genre(s): lyric poetry, children's literature
Language(s): French, German, Luxembourgish

Anise Koltz-Blanpain writes in the three literary languages of the country—French, German and Luxembourgish. Her first steps in literature—outstanding from the start—were taken in German, and she has written stories for children in the Luxembourgish language. Though her exceptional talent for the German language has surprised German critics for a long time, Anise Koltz eventually turned to French as her favorite means of literary expression. However, she still translates French literary works into German—such as, for example, her translation of Léopold Senghor for a German editor.

Anise Koltz has carried off several book-prizes and has been awarded various decorations. As a member of literary and poetic academies she founded in 1962 the "Journées Poétiques de Mondorf," meetings of German and French poets that took place every two years until 1974. In 1969 Anise Koltz organized a meeting of German and French writers at Pont d'Oye in Belgium, thus assuring literary and cultural co-operation and exchange in Europe.

Since its first publication the poetry of Anise Koltz has struck the note of perfect lyricism, remarkable in its concision and its concentration of thought and feeling. Her images are daring, audacious; her language is harsh at times, crudely unveiling life in its sullied and evil nakedness. Brief visions will comfort the troubled mind, visions, simple and beautiful, denoting the poet's grand mastery of language.

In the literary world of Luxembourg and beyond its borders the work of Anise Koltz bears witness of the vigor of contemporary poetry and turns the poet herself into an authentic witness of the human condition.

Works

Maerchen [Fairy-tales] (1957). *Gedichte* [Poems] (1959). *Spuren nach innen* [Inward Tracks] (1960). *Steine und Vögel* [Stones and Birds]. *Le Cirque du Soleil* [The Circus of the Sun] (1966), tr. Andrée Sodenkamp. *D'Kreschtkennche kennt* [The Christ-Child Is Coming] (1968). *Den Tage vergraben* [Burying the Day] (1969). *Nachahmung des Tages* [Imitation of the Day] (1969). *Vienne quelqu'un* [If Only Somebody Came] (1970). *Fragmente aus Babylon* [Fragments from Babylon] (1973). *Fragments de Babylone* [Fragments from Babylon] (1973). *De Clown* [The Clown] (1975). *Le Jour inventé* [The Imagined Day] (1975). *La Terre monte* [The Earth Is Rising] (1980). *Sich der Stille hingeben* [Dedication to Silence] (1983) *Vigilance* [Vigilance] (1980). *Naissances accélérées* [Accelerated Births] (1980).

Translations: *Poèmes d'Andrée Sodenkamp* [Poetry of Andrée Sodenkamp], German tr. Anise Koltz (1967). *Bis an die Tore der Nacht* [To the Gates of Night], a selection of poems by Léopold Sédar Senghor (1985).

Rosemarie Kieffer and Liliane Stomp-Erpelding

Liv Køltzow

Born January 14, 1945, Oslo, Norway
Genre(s): novel, short story, drama
Language(s): Norwegian

Liv Køltzow emerged as a writer in the early 1970s. She has always focused strongly on women's issues. Born in Oslo, Norway in 1945, she studied history and literature at the University of Oslo. She has worked as a teacher in northern Norway and has been active in several Norwegian literary magazines.

In the late sixties Køltzow worked closely with *Profilgruppa*. This influential group, composed mostly of university students and taking its name from the journal which became the organ for the group, reacted strongly against the literary, social, and political climate in Norway. In the beginning phases the group experimented with form and style, rejecting the psychological realism of the prevailing generation of Norwegian writers. However, the group, strongly influenced by Marxism, soon rejected modernism and began to advocate a clear social program, demanding that literature help achieve their political goals.

Køltzow's early development as a writer closely parallels that of *Profilgruppa*. In her first book, *Øyet i treet* (The Eye in the Tree), published in 1970, Køltzow experiments with form and style. She examines the difficulty young girls and women have in making decisions and acting on them. This inability to act and the resulting passivity are central themes in Køltzow's work.

Hvem bestemmer over Bjørg og Unni? (Who's in Charge of Bjørg and Unni?), published in 1972, is stylistically a clear departure from her first book. Experimentalism is replaced by a direct, almost documentary approach. This book also addresses specific women's issues. In the novel, two women from quite different social backgrounds are politicized and drawn together to fight an unwanted road that will destroy their children's play area. The book is tendentious, and it fits the social realist's call for debate and action. The protagonists find meaning in their act of joining together and fighting the system. However, already in this novel Køltzow begins to question the Left and its inability or unwillingness to deal with many of the issues that affect women.

Historien om Eli (The Story of Eli), published in 1975, represents another change in Køltzow's style. The book is a realistic psychological *Bildungsroman*. The style is more subjective and impressionistic than her previous book. The author follows Eli, the protagonist, through childhood, adolescence, and marriage to the eventual break with her parents and husband. Køltzow is interested in the effects of the socialization process on young girls; Eli has been raised to seek security and to avoid confrontation. Hiding behind a smile, she never develops any real sense of identity. She never acquires the skills she needs to deal with reality, and she isolates herself in a world of dreams.

While the book is a relentless criticism of the traditional patriarchal family and the socioeconomic system which supports it, Køltzow does not spare the Left. Although Eli becomes politicized by marrying a "good" socialist, she does not find the freedom she is looking for. Eli is not saved through her involvement in politics.

Løp, mann (Run, Man), published in 1980, is a strong critique of our capitalistic male-dominated society and the traditional family's role in preventing women from realizing their full potential. At the same time, it is a harsh commentary on the Leftish-socialist movement and its simplistic, ideological approach to women's issues.

In this novel Køltzow explores the relationship between Jon and Rita. Jon is a politically correct socialist employed as a teacher. Rita is trapped in her role as wife and mother, struggling to complete her education. Jon believes in the liberation of women for everyone but his wife. He is unable to put his ideas into practice; Jon is not merely blind to his partner's situation, but he deliberately pits himself against her in a power struggle that he is determined to win.

Køltzow's latest book, *April/November* (1984), consists of two long short stories. The female protaganist in each story is out of the 1980s; both are divorced women confronted with the overwhelming task of coping with everyday reality—children, job, housework—on their own. Once again, Køltzow examines the powerlessness of her characters. Life seems an endless round of meaningless events; repetition and routine have sapped these women's energy. She picks up where her other books have ended. Both women have left a relationship that did not satisfy them. However, this is not viewed as a final solution but as one step in the struggle for identity and liberation.

Køltzow never places her characters in a social vacuum. However, she also stresses the importance of the individual's own role in the struggle for liberation.

Liv Køltzow remains unknown to the American audience, but she has gained some attention in West Germany, where two of her books have been translated.

Works

Øyet i treet [The Eye in the Tree] (1970). *Hvem bestemmer over Bjørg og Unni?* [Who's in charge of Bjørg og Unni?] (1972). *Jenteloven* [The Law for Girls], script (1983). *Historien om Eli* [The Story of Eli] (1975). *Løp, mann* [Run, Man] (1980). *April/November* (1984).

Bibliography

Engelstad, Irene, "Hverdagen slår sprekker: Liv Køtzow: Løp, mann." [Day to Day Life Cracks: Liv Køtzow: *Run, Man*], *Vinduet* 34, No. IV (1980): 9–13. Engelstad, Irene, "Kvinnespråk og kvinnelig bevissthet" [Women's Language and Consciousness], in *Artikler om kvinnelitteratur: fra Amalie Skram til Cecilie Løvid*, ed. Irene Engelstad and Janneken øverland (Oslo, 1981), pp. 217–235. Rottem, Øystein, "Kontroll, Kappløp, Kamuflasje: Om Live Køltzows Løp, mann." [Control, Race, and Camouflage: About Live Køltzow's *Run, Man*]. *Norsk Litterær Årbok* (1984), pp. 98–114.

Peggy Hager

Maria Komornicka

(a.k.a. Nałęcz, Włast, P.W.O.)

Born July 25, 1876, Grabów, Poland; died February 8, 1949, Izabelin, Poland
Genre(s): poetry, drama, essay, criticism
Language(s): Polish

In a departure from more common experiences of contemporary Polish girls, Komornicka studied at Cambridge University for a time and described her impressions in a series of articles titled *Raj młodzieży* (1896; Young People's Paradise). She published the first collection of short stories at the age of eighteen, and followed these with a second collection two years later. In these and subsequent works, the recurrent theme that obviously deeply preoccupied the author is the role of the individual, especially a talented one, in society. Her characters tend to be introverted, high-strung, even neurotic or slightly decadent, and consequently at odds with their environment. Yet she denounced the alienation and isolation from society of such "artistic" temperaments and advocated their acceptance and involvement in worldly concerns. In her contribution to a collaborative volume, *Forpoczty*

(1895; Outposts) she attacked those she considered Philistines, people satisfied with prevailing social and economic conditions and the inferior status of women. In a collection of poetry and prose, *Biesy* (1903; Demons), she analyzed the psychological stress of a sensitive person who is conscious of being unique and different yet craves unquestioning acceptance by others.

While rejecting the optimism of the "positivists," she embraced the "vitalism" as propounded by Nietzsche, with its sometimes apocalyptic world view. As a result, her poetry displays seeds of early expressionism and her personal philosophy reflects a foreshadowing of existentialism. Like Nietzsche, she passionately defended almost unlimited freedom for "superior" individuals, including women, especially in her poetry. In an ironic twist of fate, she, like her idol, succumbed to bouts of mental illness and was forced to withdraw from social contacts at the age of thirty-one.

Works

Z życia nędzarza, Staszka [From the Life of the Beggar Stan] (1892). *Szkice* [Sketches] (1894). "Powrót ideałów" [The Return of Ideals], "Przejściowi" [Transients], "Dlaczego" [Why], and "Liryka prozą i wierszem" [Lyrics in Prose and Verse] in *Forpoczty* [Outposts] (1895). *Raj młodzieży* [Young People's Paradise] (1896). *Skrzywdzeni* [The Wronged Ones] (1898). *Baśnie, Psalmodie* [Fables, Psalmodies] (1900). *Biesy* [Demons] (1903). Critical reviews and minor works in various periodicals.

Bibliography

Dernałowicz, Maria, "Piotr Odmieniec Włast." *Twórczość* 33.3 (1977): 79–95. Grela, Katarzyna, "Podobny księciu na obłoku." *Poezja* 10.5 (1974): 67–72. "Komornicka, Maria," in *Literatura polska; Przewodnik encyklopedyczny*, ed. Julian Krzyżanowski, Vol. 1 (Warsaw, 1984). Podraza-Kwiatkowska, Maria, "Komornicka." *Polski Słownik Biograficzny*, Vol. 13 (Wrocław, 1967–1968).

Irene Suboczewski

Helga Königsdorf

Born 1938, Gera, German Democratic Republic
Genre(s): novel, short story
Language(s): German

Helga Königsdorf is a well-known mathematician by profession. She began to write only in the late seventies, beginning with *Meine ungehörigen Träume* (1978) and *Der Lauf der Dinge* (1982), collections of short stories, a selection of which appeared under the title *Mit Klischmann im Regen* (1983) in West Germany. Many of these stories deal with the emancipated woman having to face some weakness in her life. In 1986 Königsdorf published her first novel: *Respektloser Umgang*. It is the story of a woman mathematician, suffering from a terminal illness, which is kept under control by medical drugs. Under this threat of death she experiences chemically induced hallucinations in which she confronts Lise Meitner, atomic physicist and colleague of Otto Hahn. She asks her existential questions, which are actual questions to her own self: questions concerning the ambition to be respected in the world of male-dominated science, questions concerning scientific responsibility under such circumstances, questions of values, of life, of resistance in view of personal death and global destruction. In a direct but precise narrative style, Königsdorf crafted an intellectually poignant and emotionally gripping literary piece, which qualitatively enriches women's literature with another step forward.

Works

Meine ungehörigen Träume, short stories (1978). *Der Lauf der Dinge*, short stories (1982). *Mit Klischmann im Regen*, short stories (1983). *Respektloser Umgang*, novel (1986).

Margaret Eifler

Maria Konopnicka

Born 1842, Suwalki, Poland; died 1910
Genre(s): poetry, short story, fairy tale
Language(s): Polish

Born in a small town, Suwalki, in northeastern Poland, daughter of a lawyer, Jozef

Wasilowski, Konopnicka was brought up in a country manor and then sent to a boarding school run by nuns in Warsaw, where her lifelong friendship with another future writer, Eliza Pawlowska (later Orzeszkowa) started. Like her friend, she was married to a man much older than herself. She lived with him on his estate long enough to bear him six children. Yet eventually she rebelled against all accepted conventions of her time and left her husband, taking her children with her to Warsaw, where she managed to maintain her family by writing. A person of unusual courage and energy, she collected much of her material in court rooms and became one of the first women reporters and editors. Radical in making the predicament of the poverty-stricken urban and rural population the subject of her writing and denouncing the callousness and indifference of the clergy, she was charged with impiety and accused of inciting peasants to rebellion while the strongly nationalistic tone of her poetry drew the special attention of Russian censors.

Straightforward and preoccupied mainly with social and patriotic themes, Konopnicka's poems were extremely popular during her lifetime; there was probably no other poet as loved as she. Her work still constitutes standard reading in Polish schools. Now, however, she is paying for her popularity, as critics dismiss her work for lacking personal elements. Yet generations were brought up on her poetry and for decades she remained the only model available for Polish women poets.

The appeal of her work was due to its subject, form, character, and tone as well as to the fact that it fulfilled the readers' expectations. Traditionally in Poland, men of letters were looked upon as leaders in the struggle for national liberation, for a "just cause." Konopnicka was very much aware of that atmosphere, and in this respect, differed little from her male predecessors; her opus is both a product of that traditional attitude and its contributing factor. She never forgot for whom she wrote. Personal lyrics are rare in her poetry; the pronoun "I" is hardly ever heard; the author's voice is almost never a direct expression of her feelings. Most often, Konopnicka voices someone else's concerns, and usually speaks in the collective voice of a community, social class, or the nation. The characters in her realistic tableaux of poverty stricken urban or rural families are very often children, which accounts for much of their appeal. The form of her poems followed the pattern of folk songs, and enchanted the unsophisticated reader with its directness and musicality.

The volume of Konopnicka's work is huge but its quality uneven. Her short stories, hardly noticed in her lifetime, are among the best Polish literature possesses. Her literary studies are highly original and profound. Although some critics consider her more interesting as an emancipated woman than as a poet, none denies her breadth of intellectual interests nor her daring. She passionately wrestles with God, whom she accuses of merciless silence, indifference to people, and lack of knowledge of the world he created. Her tone is that of sacrilegious irony. Some critics point to the shallowness of her social ideas and their "metaphysical chime" as she places all responsibility for the shortcomings of public life on the shoulders of God. Yet others call for reevaluation of her work as a poet whose words are direct extensions of her courage in choosing a definite philosophical stand.

Works

Poetry: *Poezje*, 3 vols. (1881, 1883, 1887). *Italia* (1901). *Pan Balcer w Brazylii* (1910).
Short stories: *Cztery nowele* (1888). *Nowele* (1889). *Ludzie i rzeczy* [People and Things] (1898).
Fairy tales for children: *O krasnoludkach i sierotce Marysi* [About Gnomes and the Little Orphan Mary].

Bibliography

Konopnicka, Maria, *Wiersze wybrane* [Selected Poems] with an introduction by Anna Kamienska (PIW, 1974). Kridl, Manfred, *An Anthology of Polish Literature* (New York, 1957). Kryzanowski, Julian, *A History of Polish Literature* (Warsaw, 1978). Milosz, Czeslaw, *The History of Polish Literature* (California, 1969).

Maya Peretz

Antonina Koptiaeva

Born 1904, Siberia, The Soviet Union
Genre(s): novel
Language(s): Russian

Born in far eastern Siberia into an upper-middle-class family, Antonina Koptiaeva combines journalism with socialist realist writing. Koptiaeva's heroines display a strength of purpose and resilience that she herself developed in her harsh native climate. She writes, however, with a great deal of sensitivity on women's issues, as in *Ivan Ivanovich* published in 1949. This is the first of a trilogy of novels tracing the relationship of a highly respected surgeon and an admiring paramedic who eventually marry after wartime experiences on the battlefront. Koptiaeva was awarded the Stalin Prize for Literature for the first novel of this trilogy.

Works

Comrade Anna (1946). *Ivan Ivanovich. Roman v. Dvukh Chastiakh* [Ivan Ivanovich. Novel in Two Parts] (1949). *Friendship* (1954). *Daring* (1958). *The Gift of Earth* (1963). *On the Ural River* (1971). Translation: *Ivan Ivanovich. A Novel in Two Parts*, tr. Margaret Wettlin (1952).

Warwick J. Rodden

Ljarissa Kosac

(a.k.a. Lesja Ukrajinka)

Born February 25, 1871, Zvjahel, Ukraine, The Soviet Union; died August 1, 1913, Saram
Genre(s): lyric poetry, dramatic poetry, drama
Language(s): Ukrainian

Lesja Ukrajinka was the first Ukrainian poet whose creativity transcended the process of national revival. Daughter of Olena Pcilka and niece of M. Drahomanov, Ukrajinka adopted their ideas on the necessity of cultural expansion and the elevation of the Ukrainian literary language. The cultural atmosphere in the Kosac home attracted visitors such as the playwright Staryckyj and the composer Lysenko and stimulated Ukrajinka's creativity as well as exposed her to discussions of the function of the arts in society. In particular, she was indebted to Drahomanov for expanding her acquaintance with world literature, and this influence is reflected in her first efforts in lyric verse, a translation of Heine.

The first period of Ukrajinka's creativity as a lyric poet projects the optimism of a young girl who is gravely ill with a desperate tubercular condition and compelled to travel around the world in search of a better climate to alleviate that condition. Ultimately, despite painful operations, long sojourns in Egypt, the Caucasus, Crimea, and Georgia, Ukrajinka died in Saram and was buried in Kiev.

Lesja Ukrajinka wrote her first poems at the age of twelve. Her lyric poetry is not generally considered to be her crowning achievement although the poems display both courage and strength as well as a moving quality in the description of her intimate moods and feelings. The first anthology of her lyric poetry *Na Krylach Pisen'* (On the Wings of Song) appeared in 1892, and in 1899 was followed by the collection *Dumy i Mriji* (Thoughts and Dreams), and in 1902 by *Vidhuky* (Echoes).

It was in the writing of the second period of her creativity, particularly in such long dramatic poems as *Samson, Robert Bruce, Kassandra*, and *Davnja Kazka* (An Old Tale) that the prototypes of her future dramatic concerns emerged. The dramatic poem, then, serves as a transitory stage between the lyric and drama, and these poems provide a lyrical element and a well-developed plot as well as dramatic conflict. In these poems, Ukrajinka not only creates a mood; she provides an epic view that relates to her concerns with Ukrainian culture. The poem *Robert Bruce* gives an indication of these concerns; the hero, Bruce, the only Scottish lord who remained faithful to his people in their struggle against the invading Englishmen, leads the Scots to a victory and saves the independence of Scotland. In this poem Ukrajinka's interests in the struggle for Scottish independence reflect her engagement in the struggle of Ukrainians for their own national autonomy.

As a dramatist, Ukrajinka moved in the opposite direction from the currents in the modern theater of Ibsen, Hauptmann, or Maeterlinck to the ancient theater of Aeschylus, Sophocles, and Euripedes. Her dramas are not only classic in structure but contain elevated themes, high style, and a clearly defined structure. It is in her dramas that Lesja Ukrajinka steps beyond the confines of the current tradition of realism. Representative settings for her plays are classical antiquity, the Middle Ages, the world of Mohammed, as well as early Ukrainian history in the play *Bojarynja* (1910; The Noblewoman) and the context of early Christianity, in such plays as *V Katakombax* (1906; In the Catacombs), *Advokat Martijan* (1913; The Advocate Martianus), and *Na rujinax* (1904; In the Ruins). The main theme of the plays is the historical process and human aspirations that are extended symbolically to Ukrainian contemporary history.

In one of her most memorable works, *Lisova Pisnja* (1911; The Forest Song), Ukrajinka uses symbolism to extend her fascination and love for nature into a conflict between the natural world and the material world. In this work, fantastic wood nymphs, fairies, and mermaids, and in particular the wood nymph Mavka, represent not only the beauty of nature but the spirit of poetry. When the poetic spirit of Mavka meets Lukash, who does not understand the spirit of the forest world, tragedy ensues. As exemplified by this work, ultimately the significance of Lesja Ukrajinka in Ukrainian literature lies in her concern for both the expansion of language and the search for new forms, thereby extending the Ukrainian realist tradition into the stream of world literature.

Works

Tvory Lesi Ukrainky (1953). *Tvory v desiaty tomakh* (1963–1965). *In the Catacombs*, tr. John Weir (1971). *Spirit of Flame. A collection of the Works of Lesya Ukrainka*, tr. Percival Cundy. *The Babylonian Captivity. Five Russian Plays*, ed. C.E. Roberts (1946).

Bibliography

Bida, Konstantyn, *Lesya Ukrainka: Life and Work*, tr. Vera Rich (Toronto, 1968). Biletskyj, Leonid, *Try Sylvetky: Marko Vovcok, Olha Kobyljans'ka, Lesja Ukrajinka* (Winnipeg, 1951). Kasprak, Arsen, *Lesji Ukrajinky literaturnyj portret* (Kyjiv, 1958). Kostenko, Anatolii Illich, *Lesja Ukrajinka* (Kyjiv, 1971). Stavytskyj, Oleksij, *Lesja Ukrajinka: Etapy tvorcoho slaxu* (Kyjiv, 1970).

Christine Kiebuzinska

Ol'ha Petrivna Kosaceva

(a.k.a. Olena Pcilka)

Born April 17, 1849, Hadjac, Ukraine, The Soviet Union; died 1930, Kijev
Genre(s): short story, drama, translations, editor
Language(s): Ukrainian

Olena Pcilka was among the first Ukrainian writers to support the expansion of the Ukrainian language in literature. She pointed out that the supporters of an exclusively popular language were restricting the use of Ukrainian to private life and domestic usage, thereby causing linguistic stagnation. She contributed to Ukrainian ethnography by collecting folktales and songs, which she published in 1876 under the title of *Ukrainian Ornament*. At the same time, as an anti-Russian activist, she promulgated a Ukrainian literature that would reflect purely national values. She frequently published in women's journals, among them those of Natalja Kobryns'ka's *Persyj Vinok* (1887; The First Garland), which she co-edited. She also edited the newspaper *Ridnyj Kraj* (Native Land) until 1914, in the face of Russian censorship.

Olena Pcilka and her brother M. Drahomanov grew up in the environment of the Eastern Ukrainian intelligentsia, which was much given over to Ukrainian folklore and poetry. Her brother exerted great influence on her creative consciousness, particularly when she moved in with Drahomanov and his wife and, as a result, had the opportunity to meet other Ukrainian intellectuals. In 1868 she married Kosac, and while rearing her children, she continued to be active in establishing Ukrainian language libraries, collecting folk tales, and promulgating native crafts. These interests were later to be reflected in the work of her daughter, the famous poet Lesja Ukrajinka. Pcilka's stories, which appeared in separate collections from 1907 to 1911, were not especially well received. Similarly, her theatrical pieces were either unsuccessful or denied stage presentation. The stories and plays reflect village life; however, a few tales, among them "Tovarysky" (1887; Girlfriends) and "Pigmalion" (1884), explored cultural and political questions. Her tradition of realistic writing is associated with the depiction of broad scenes, the detailed portrayal of characters, as well as the exploration of their interior lives. Later she wrote stories dealing with the life of people in the city, with the intelligentsia, and with Ukrainian youth. Her significance in the history of Ukrainian literature lies more in the realm of the development of Ukrainian culture and the extension of a Ukrainian literary language than in her own literary contributions.

Works

Tvory (1971). Zbentezhena vecheria (1970). "Tovaryshky." Suchasnist 25 (1): 108–110.

Bibliography

Odarchenko, Petro, "Iak suchasna radianska tzenzura pokalichyla opovidannia Oleny Pchilky 'Tovaryshky.'" Suchasnist 25 (1).

Christine Kiebuzinska

Zofia Kossak-Szatkowska (Szczucka)

Born August 8, 1890, Kosmin, Poland; died
    1968, Silesia
Genre(s): historical novel
Language(s): Polish

One of the granddaughters of the famous painter Juliusz Kossak, Zofia Kossak was born to landowning gentry in eastern Poland (Kosmin, Lublin region) on August 8, 1890. She studied fine arts in Warsaw and Geneva, making her literary debut in 1922 with a book of war recollections. A prolific writer, Kossak was very popular during the short two decades of Polish independence. The publication of her Golden Freedom was hailed by her enthusiastic admirers as a literary event of great importance, and the author was proclaimed a successor to the worshipped Nobel prize winner Henryk Sienkiewicz. In 1932, she received a literary award of the region of Silesia for her book Nieznany Kraj. Present-day critics dismiss her writing as characteristic of the Polish Catholic milieu: superficial, intellectually inferior, and lacking a thorough acquaintance with history.

During the Nazi occupation of Poland, Kossak was active in the underground resistance movement, a member of the patriotic "Front of Reborn Poland," and the Council to Aid the Jews (Zegota); for these causes, she edited illegal publications. She was an inmate of Auschwitz concentration camp between 1943–1944, and, after being released, she took part in the armed anti-German Warsaw uprising of August 1944. Between 1945 and 1956, Kossak lived in Great Britain. Upon her return at the time of the short-lived "thaw," she was awarded a national literary award. She lived her last years in a provincial town in Silesia, near the border of Czechoslovakia, away from the centers of intellectual and political activity, where she wrote several books of historical tales for young readers.

Works

Pozoga [Conflagration] (1922). Szalency Bozy [Divine Fanatics, short stories] (1929). Krzyzowcy [Crusaders; Krzyzanowski quotes the English title as Angels in the Dust] (1935). Krol tredowatv [The Leper King] (1937). Bez oreza [Blessed Are the Meek] (1937). Suknia Dejaniry [Gift of Nessus] (1939).

Bibliography

Bartelski, Leslaw M., ed., Polscy pisarze wspolczesni [A Dictionary of Contemporary Polish Writers] (Warsaw, 1972). Krzyzanowski, Julian, A History of Polish Literature (Warsaw, 1978).

Maja Perez

Helene Kottanner

Born ca. 1400, Ödenburg (now Sopron in
    Western Hungary); died after 1470,
    possibly in or around Vienna
Genre(s): memoir
Language(s): German

Helene Kottanner's account of her role in contemporary political events anticipates the historical novel and represents a unique phenomenon in German literature, in which the memoir form did not develop and flourish until many centuries later.

Married first to a patrician of Ödenburg, Peter Gelush, then to the chamberlain of the provost of the Viennese cathedral Hans Kottanner, Helene became in 1436 chambermaid at the court of Duke Albrecht V of Austria and his wife Elizabeth in Vienna. She followed them to

Hungary after their coronation as sovereigns of that country in 1437. When Albrecht died in October 1439, Hungary's leading nobleman urged Elizabeth, thirty-one years old and five months pregnant, to marry the sixteen year-old Wladislaus III of Poland, which she did not want to do. To secure the legitimate rights of her unborn child—her physicians had predicted that it would be a boy—she sent her confidante Helene Kottanner on a secret mission to fetch the heavily guarded Holy Crown of St. Stephen with which all Hungarian monarchs were crowned. The secret abduction took place in February 1440, and the little Ladislaus Posthumous was crowned king at the age of three months, in May 1440. After the queen's death in 1442, Helene Kottanner and her husband probably returned to Vienna. As late as 1470, she appealed to the Hungarian King Matthias Corvinus for a greater reward for her service to the royal family.

She must have written down or dictated her *Denkwürdigkeiten* shortly after 1442 with the intention both to inform the little Ladislaus of the singular circumstances of his birth and coronation and to induce the boy's guardians to grant her the recompense that she claims Queen Elizabeth promised her. Unlike most chronicles of the period, Kottanner's narration has literary merit. It is of particular importance because of its feminine focus and because it provides highly accurate information on that period in Hungarian history. Besides describing in chronological order the key events, from Albrecht's coronation and death until after the little boy's baptism and coronation and Elizabeth's decision to send the child to another town for security reasons, the narrator imparts a sense of the historical process at work and impresses upon the reader the tremendous importance that the crown and royal insignia held in her late-Medieval world, feudal yet wont to challenge the divine sanctions of hereditary kingship. That this is the work of a simple lay woman is particularly significant.

Works

Die Denkwürdigkeiten der Helene Kottanner (1439-1440) (ca. 1450; new edition 1972).

Bibliography

Bijvoet, Maya C., "The Literary Chambermaid, Helene Kottanner," in Katharina Wilson, ed. *Women Writers of the Renaissance and Reformation* (1987). Doderer, Heimito von, "Helene Kottanner: Denkwürdigkeiten einer Wienerin von 1440." *Die Wiederkehr der Drachen* (München, 1970), pp. 221–226. Freytag, Gustav. *Bilder aus der deutschen vergangenheit*, Vol. II (Leipzig, 1924), pp. 370–382. *Geschichte der deutschen Literatur von den Anfängen bis zur Gegenwart*, eds. H. de Boor, R. Newald. Vol. 4, Part I (1970), pp. 145–146. Gross, L., "Zur Biographie der Helene Kottannerin." *Monatsblatt des Vereins für Geschichte der Stadt Wien* 7 (1925): 65–67. Rupprich, Hans, "Das Wiener Schrifttum des ausgehenden Mittelalters." *Österreichische Akademie der Wissenschaften* 228:5 (1954). *Verfasserlexikon: Die deutsche Literatur des Mittelalters*, ed. Kurt Ruh, Vol. 5 (Berlin, 1985), pp. 326–327. Wengraf, Alice, "Aus den Denkwürdigkeiten der Helene Kottannerin." *Ungarische Rundschau* III (1914): 434–441. Zeman, Herbert, "Österreichische Literatur: Zwei Studien." *Jahrbuch der Grillparzer-Gesellschaft* 3/8 (1970): 11–65.

Maya Bijvoet

Emily Aenou Kourteli

(a.k.a. Emily Daphne)

Born 1887, Marseille, France; died 1941, Athens, Greece
Genre(s): poetry, novel, drama
Language(s): Greek

The daughter of the well-known journalist Y. Kourtelis, Emily Kourteli was exposed to many figures of the Athenian literary world from an early age. Her beauty inspired S. Skipis' poem "Ta Mallia tès Berenikès" (The Hair of Berenice). In 1911, she married Th. Zoiopoulos, a minor poet who wrote under the name of Stephanos Daphnes. She wrote verse, novels, and plays, most of them published in the periodical *Nea Estia*, but she is remembered most for her lyric poems.

Above all other modern Greek women poets, she marks the start of spontaneous lyricism mixed with strong naturalistic and symbolistic elements; the latter reflect her immersion in French symbolism. These features are seen especially in "Hē Gynaika" (The Woman), "Hē Litaneia ton Skiōn" (The Litany of the Shadows), "Proseudē stē Dyname" (A Prayer to the Power), and "Flōga sto skotadi" (Flame in the Darkness). Several of her poems bear witness to her thorough knowledge of ancient Greek lyric poetry and mythology, best seen in "Ellēnikes Nychtes" (The Greek Nights) and "Klōthō" (Clotho); others are infused with biblical references together with symbolic figures of speech and images. "O Sporeas" (The Sower), for instance, is considered one of the best poems in Neo-Hellenic literature. Kourteli's work marks the end of the decaying romanticism that had characterized much of the work of women poets of the previous generation. Her first poems, those included in the "Chrysanthema" (Chrysanthemums) collection, exhibit the first signs of mysticism and metaphysical inspiration, that later crystallized in her anthology *Ta Chrysa Kypella* (The Golden Cups) and took their final shape in her final, uncollected poems. Her strong passion, reverie, and elegiac tone take on a meditative character. Deep sadness and anxiety predominate in her poems, that betray her constant chasing of the inaccessible and her attempt to answer the questions within her soul. Her poems reveal not even a slight indication of her identity as a woman.

Her two novels, *He Xenē Gē* (The Foreign Land) and *To Talanto tēs Smarōs* (The Talent of Smaro), are an almost complete departure from her poetic style. One may even see in Kourteli a "character dichotomy." They are realistic, down to earth, "romans des moeurs" with lower-class and poor Athenian characters whose lives and aspirations are usually limited by the narrow bounds of their Athenian neighborhood.

Her one-act play, *Gloria Victis* was awarded a prize. The *Istories Louloudiōn* (Flower Stories), a collection of short stories that Kourteli wrote in collaboration with her husband, were published only in part. She translated into Greek poems from the *Yugoslavian Anthology*, which were published in the periodical *Nea Estia*.

Although poetry had been composed by a number of educated women in the Phanariot Circle, in the Ionian islands, and in Athens after the liberation of Greece, only Emily Kourteli and Myrtiotissa, another leading figure of her age among women poets, can make true claims to art. Unfortunately, so far no complete edition of Kourteli's literary work has been attempted.

Works

Verse: *Chrysanthemums* (1902). *The Golden Cups* (1923).

Novels: *Smaro's Talent* (1923). *The Foreign Land* (1937).

Plays: *Gloria Victis; The Old Men; Liberation; The Blind; The Poor People; At the Seaside*, all published in an occasional series in *Nea Estia* in Athens. *The House with the Wild Dog*, in *Nea Estia*, nos. 433–435 (1945).

Short stories: [With St. Daphnes], "The Jasmin," from the *Flower Stories. Nea Estia* 166 (1933): 1209.

Translations: Greek translations of various French and Yugoslavian poems by G. Le Roy, E. Verhaeren, G. de Bouhelier, J. Laforgue, E. Harancourt, P. Chabeneix, J. Dusic, J. Pogacnik, A. Grandnik, and others, all published in various issues of *Nea Estia*.

Bibliography

Greek: Agras, T., "The Poetess." *Nea Estia* 30 (Athens, 1941), pp. 631–632. Agras, T., "The Prose Writer." *Nea Estia* 31 (Athens, 1941), pp. 692–693. Drandakis, P., *Great Greek Encyclopaedia*, vol. 8 (Athens), p. 922. Gryparis, Y., "A Letter to Emily Daphne about 'The Golden Cups'." *Noumas* (Athens, 1923), p. 649. Lampikis, D., *Greek Poetesses* (Athens, 1936), p. 24. Palamas, K., "On Emily Daphne." *Philologike Protochronia* (Athens, 1952), p. 46. Patsis, Ch., *Great Encyclopaedia of Neo-Hellenic Literature*, vol. 6 (Athens, 1968), pp. 142–145. Pattichis, M., "Emily Daphne." *Philological Cyprus* (Nicosia, 1963). Peranthis, M., *The Neo-Hellenic Greek Poetry 1900–1920* (10th ed. Athens, 1979), pp. 325–335. Sikelianos, A., "A Poetess." *Nea Estia* 52 (Athens, 1952), pp. 59–60. Tarsouli, A., *Greek Poetesses (1857–1940)* (Athens, 1951), pp. 67–81. Yiakos, D. and A. Fouriotis, "On Emily Daphne." *Aetos* 21 (Athens, 1953), pp. 45–47, 351–362.

English: Dimaras, C.T., *A History of Modern Greek Literature* (New York, 1922). Trypanis, C.A., *Greek Poetry from Homer to Seferis* (London, 1981), pp. 681–682.

Aristoule Georgiadou

Marianna Koutouzi

(a.k.a. Marianna Aenou-Koutouzi, Marianna Karousou)

Born 1922(?), Cephallonia, Greece
Genre(s): novel, short story, poetry, children's literature
Language(s): Greek

Marianna Aenou-Koutouzi was born in a small village in the island of Cephallonia. She was the youngest child of a large family, and while she was growing up her father was working in the United States. In her teens, Koutouzi went to Athens. She finished high school in Athens and then attended the School of Drama of the National Theater (Ethniko) as well as Rondērēs' School of Drama. She married Neoclēs Koutouzis, and has worked for a number of years for the bibliographic services of the library at the French Institute of Athens.

Koutouzi started writing long before she published her first work, *Sugarcane*, around 1979(?). She illustrates her own work, and in 1982, she exhibited her paintings and drawings at the French Institute of Athens. She has often been invited to lecture on her writing and exhibit her paintings. In 1985, the Academy of Athens gave Koutouzi the First Award for her novel *Sugarcane*, which is the first volume of her two-volume autobiography. Translations of this novel are being prepared in French, Spanish, and English. Koutouzi has also written two poetry collections, six children's books, and three short novels. She is mostly known for her children's books and fiction.

Her fiction writing is poetic, the chapters of her novels are loosely connected and there are usually many events taking place at the same time. Often minor stories interrupt the flow of the major story and take control of the chapter—and, of course, of the reader. Koutouzi's stories may then be concluded in the following chapter or even many chapters later. Like that of many Greek women writers, Koutouzi's writing is unstructured, does not follow any specific literary movements, and is highly autobiographical—yet her charm lies there. She usually writes in the first person narrative mode, often addressing the reader, and one has the illusion that the stories

are being told orally—Koutouzi's strength as a writer is her superb storytelling. Childhood memories, women's issues (contemporary problems as well as problems Greek village women faced between the two world wars), and a profound concern for older people's problems are some of the basic themes in her fiction.

Marianna Aenou-Koutouzi has been acknowledged as one of the leading figures in contemporary Greek literature, and her work deserves serious critical attention.

Works

Poetry collections: *Rizes* [Roots]. *Sirēnes ke Dakrigona* [Sirens and Tear Gas]. *Diplē Aphtoktonia ston idio Anthropo* [Double Suicide of the Same Person]. *Stē Zoē tou Telous* [At the End's Life]. *Zacharokalama* [Sugarcane] (1979). *To Avgo tēs Agapēs* [The Egg of Love] (1986). *Mia Fasolia ston Ourano* [A Beanstalk in the Sky]. *Piso ap'ton Kero* [Beyond Time] (1979). *Krinio ē Gorgo ke to Athanato Nero* [The Swift Krinio and the Immortal Water]. *Vrēkan Mia Dictatoria* [They Found A Dictatorship] (1983). *Perfoutēs ke to Chorio tēs Philias* [Perphoutis and the Village of Friendship].

Aliki P. Dragona

Kalina Kovacheva

Born 1943, Bozhouritsa, Bulgaria
Genre(s): poetry
Language(s): Bulgarian

Kalina Kovacheva was born in the Pleven district of Bulgaria and attended university at the Cyril and Methodius University in Veliko Turnovo, where she graduated in Bulgarian philology. She has worked for the newspaper *Narodna Mladezh* as head of arts and aesthetical education and is currently Deputy Editor-in-Chief of the journal *Lada*. Her poetry has been translated into English, French, German, Greek, Hungarian, and Russian.

Works

You Have to Be (1970). Weather Report (1977). Personal Poems (1981).

Warwick J. Rodden

Sofia Kovalevskaia

Born January 3, 1850, Korvin-Krukovskaia,
*   Moscow, Russia; died, January 19, 1891,*
*   Stockholm*
Genre(s): mathematics, drama, poetry,
*   journalism, memoirs*
Language(s): Russian

With the abolition of serfdom in 1861, a generation of young Russian noblewomen began to hope that some of the restrictions governing their lives could be lifted also. Their hopes for higher education were dashed: after the student unrest of 1862, girls lost even the grudgingly awarded privilege of attending university lectures. By the late 1860s these frustrated Russians began streaming into West Europe to study at institutions of higher learning. Sofia Kovalevskaia (née Korvin-Krukovskaia) is exemplary among these vital women. At her tragically early death (from pneumonia or pleurisy), she was at once a source of inspiration to talented girls throughout the world and anathema to those who feared women's aspirations outside the domestic sphere. Kovalevskaia's scientific legacy is still being explored by modern mathematicians (see Koblitz, pp. 239–255). Her second career, as a writer whose dashing style reflects her notable gifts as conversationalist and storyteller, has given us a first-hand account of her childhood and lifelong advocacy of political reform and social justice.

Kovalevskaia's life, covered effectively in Ann Koblitz's recent biography in English, is the stuff of legend. Her great-grandfather on the maternal side was the Russianized German astronomer-mathematician Friedrich Shubert. She proved her own exceptional talent as a child by teaching herself the elements of higher mathematics from pages of a textbook used to paper the walls of her room at the family estate of Palibino, Vitebsk province (*A Russian Childhood*, 122–123). Her father, a retired major-general, was persuaded somewhat reluctantly to let Sofia be tutored during the winters the family spent at the Shubert home in St. Petersburg. Since it was unlikely that he would agree to higher education abroad for his daughter, at eighteen Sofia contracted a "fictitious marriage" with the young paleontologist and publisher of scientific books, Vladimir Kovalevsky. (Such marriages were part of the romantic radical *mores* propagated in Chernyshevsky's famous novel, *What's To Be Done*, 1863.) With Kovalevsky as their "guardian," both Sofia and her elder sister, Anna, escaped to West Europe. Sofia pursued her studies in Berlin, persuading the famous German mathematician Karl Weierstrass to tutor her and sponsor her for a doctorate *in absentia* from Gottingen University; Anna went to Paris and married a French Socialist, Victor Jaclard (see Anna Korvin-Krukovskaia).

By 1874 Kovalevsky's devotion to his "wife" won her over to a real marital relationship. The young couple returned to seek academic positions in Russia, but their radical connections and Kovalevskaia's sex worked against them. They worked for a progressive new newspaper and undertook an unsuccessful project to construct rationally designed apartments in St. Petersburg. In 1878 their daughter, also Sofia, was born. Prodded by Weierstrass to return to mathematics, Sofia separated from her husband in 1881 and moved to Paris. The following year she took a teaching post at Stockholm University. Vladimir finally received a position at Moscow University, but it came too late; implicated in the crash of a speculative oil venture in the Russian Near East, he committed suicide in 1883.

The first woman professor in modern Europe, Kovalevskaia was internationally famous in the 1880s. Her Swedish sponsor, the mathematician Gustav Mittag-Leffler, and his sister, the writer Carlotta Leffler, became her close friends. The two women collaborated on a set of plays, one showing an unsuccessful life and the other the same life transformed by rational conditions, under the blanket title *A Struggle for Happiness*. When Leffler married a handsome young Italian nobleman, Kovalevskaia remarked wistfully that Carlotta was "happiness," while she herself was destined to remain "struggle."

Kovalevskaia's last years continued to be marked by deep contradictions. In a vote of confidence by her colleagues in West Europe, she was awarded the prestigious French *Prix Bordin* for her work on the revolution of a solid body about a fixed point ("Kovalevsky's top"). She never ceased hoping for a post in her native land, where she was named adjunct member of the Russian Academy of Science—and denied admission to meetings of its mathematical division. A stormy romance with the exiled Russian political scientist and historian Maxim Kovalevsky intensified the problems of combining a career and personal happiness.

All her life Kovalevskaia wrote verse. In the 1870s she produced articles on scientific and theatrical topics and in the late 1880s described visits to French hospitals and a Swedish school for leading Petersburg newspapers. She began to write prose seriously during the years in Sweden and in 1890 published her charming reminiscences of childhood, in which she depicts not only the varied influences on her own life, but also her sister's search for an outlet for her literary talents. Kovalevskaia's memoir of the Polish rebellion of 1863 has only recently been printed in the Soviet Union. Six years after George Eliot's death, Kovalevskaia published a sympathetic reminiscence of two visits with the English author, one during her years with G.H. Lewes and the other during her late marriage to the much younger J.W. Cross. Kovalevskaia's unfinished novel, *Vera Barantzova* (A Nihilist Girl) the heroine of which is a self-sacrificing radical of the 1870s, was printed in Russia only in 1906.

Works

Vospominaniia i pis'ma, S. Ia. Shtraikh, ed. (2nd. rev. ed., 1961). *Vospominaniia. Povesti*, P. Ia. Polubarinova-Kochina, ed. (1974). *Izbrannye proizvedeniia* (1982).
Translations: *Vera Barantzova*, tr. Sergius Stepniak and William Westall (1895). *A Russian Childhood*, tr., ed., and intro. Beatrice Stillman, with an *Analysis of Kovalevskaya's Mathematics* by P.Y. Kochina, USSR Academy of Sciences, New York (1979).

Bibliography

Koblitz, Ann Hibner, *A Convergence of Lives, Sofia Kovalevskaia: Scientist, Writer, Revolutionary* (Boston, 1983) [bibliography].

Mary F. Zirin

Anka Kowalska

Born February 22, 1932
Genre(s): poetry
Language(s): Polish

First published poetry in 1953. A devout Catholic, she nevertheless bitterly argued against the conciliatory position of the Church during the "Solidarity" period. Interned after the military coup in 1981, she wrote and smuggled poems out of camp. She has been banned since 1981.

Works

Credo najmniejsze [The Smallest Credo] (1960). *Psalm z doliny* [A Psalm from the Valley] (1969). *Spojrzenie* [A Look] (1974).

Maya Peretz

Anna Kowalska

Born 1903, Lwow (Lemberg), Poland; died 1969
Genre(s): novel, short story
Language(s): Polish

Born in Lwow (Lemberg) in the east, which was then as it is now, under the Russian rule, she studied and was married there to a well-known classical scholar. Together with her husband, she wrote novels and short stories, many of which took place in antiquity and the Middle Ages. Widowed in 1948, she settled in the formerly German western city of Wroclaw, which became the subject of her short stories.

Works

Opowiadania greckie, a travelogue (1948). *Safona*, a tale about Sappho (1959) *Uliczka klasztorna*, a novel (1949). *Opowiesci wroclawskie*, short stories (1955). *Wojt wolborski* (1954) and *Astrea* (1956) fictionalized biography of the eminent sixteenth-century humanist Andrzej Frycz Modrzewski.

Bibliography

Alexander M. Schenker, ed., *Fifteen Modern Polish Short Stories* (New Haven, CT, 1970).

Maya Peretz

Nadezhda Kozhevnikova

Born Moscow, The Soviet Union
Genre(s): short story, novella
Language(s): Russian

A graduate of the Gorky Literature Institute, Kozhevnikova is a native and resident of Moscow and a member of the Writers' Union. From her literary debut in the early 1970s, Kozhevnikova's fiction has explored the romantic and domestic lives of the urban intelligentsia. Time and again Kozhevnikova returns to the themes of love, familial ties and pressures, generational differences, the obligations and complexities of parenthood, the uncertainties and misunderstandings, as well as lack of communication, that undermine marital relations, and the erosion of romantic illusion. Although several of her works have also analyzed betrayal (in "Vera Perova"), loss ("Magazin igrushek" [A Toy Shop]), and the impossibility of complete mutual understanding ("Evridiki" [Eurydice]), the mere title of one of her novellas, "O liubvi materinskoi, dochernei, vozvyshennoi i zemnoi" (About Maternal, Daughterly, Elevated, and Earthly Love), accurately points to her chief concern as a writer. Her entire output, in fact, may be seen as a modern gloss of sorts on Tolstoi's "Family Happiness" and *Anna Karenina*, with a touch of Trifonov.

A firm believer in gender distinctions, Kozhevnikova is fascinated by the contrasting roles carved out for men and women by biology, society, and historical precedent and circumstance. Accordingly, she equates professionalism with male values and "domestic" worries with female psychology. Her narratives often present women caught between these two spheres or attempting to make the transition from one to the other. Whatever their situations, Kozhevnikova's women are acutely aware of just how significantly their psychology and conduct contrast with the cultural male paradigm. Like most women writing in Russia today, Kozhevnikova presents the world of her fiction through the eyes of her female protagonists, whose voice invariably merges with the omniscient narrator's. That conflation creates a distance between the reader and Kozhevnikova's male characters that often makes the latter objects of dispassionate assessment rather than full-fledged humans on a par with their female counterparts. With a few exceptions (e.g., "Domoi" [Home]), Kozhevnikova depicts male characters externally, while leaving the field wide open for her women to reveal their inner world in minute detail.

Unlike such experimental writers as Tolstaia and Katerli, Kozhevnikova adheres faithfully to a conventional, low-key, realistic narrative. Retrospection accounts for the modified time shifts in her fiction, which follows a linear plot, avoids mystification and ambiguity, and favors a language almost wholly devoid of colorful imagery and anything redolent of modernism.

Works

Collections: *Chelovek, raka i most: povesti i rasskazy* (1976). *Vremia molodosti (ocherki)* (1978). *Doma i liudi* (1979). *O liubvi materinskoi, dochernei, vozvyshennoi i zemnoi; povesti, rasskazy, ocherki* (1979). *Elena prekrasnaia* (1982). *Postoronnie v dome: povesti* (1983). *Vnutrennii dvor* (1986).
Collections for children: *Okna na dvor: rasskazy i ocherki* (1976). *Vorota i novyi gorod: ocherki* (1978).
Translations: "Home," tr. Marina Astman, in *HERitage and HEResy: Recent Fiction by Russian Women*, ed. Helena Goscilo (Bloomington, 1988).

Helena Goscilo

Urszula Koziol

Born June 20, 1931, Rakowka, Poland
Genre(s): poetry, prose
Language(s): Polish

Born in Rakowka, a village in central Poland, Koziol is a teacher by profession with a degree in Polish literature from the University of Wroclaw. Her first poems were published in literary journals. Her long poem "Sun Beat" (or "In the Rhythm of Sun"), published in No. 12, 1968 issue of the *Literary Magazine* was staged at the Wroclaw Student Theater. "Kalambur" by Boguslaw Litwiniec was a great success. She made her debut with the poem "Juz jesien" (Autumn Already) in the No. 46 issue of *Sprawy i ludzie* (Problems and People), a supplement to the Wroclaw *Gazeta robotnicza* (Workers' Gazette) in 1953.

Dubbed "a classically oriented and yet an untraditionalist poet," she now lives and works in Silesia.

Works

Gumowe klocki [Rubber Bricks] (1957). *W rytmie korzeni* [Root Beat] (1963). *Smuga i promien* [A Trail and a Sunray] (1965). *Lista obecnosci* [A Roll Call] (1967). *Poezje wybrane* [Selected Poetry, compiled and introduced by the author] (1969). *W rytmie slonca* (1974). *Wybor wierszy* [Selected Poems] (1976). Also: In the English and French language versions of the magazine *Poland*, 1968. Anthologies: *Neue polnische Lyrik* (1965). *Polish Writing Today* (1967). *Postwar Polish Poetry* (1965). *The New Polish Poetry, A Bilingual Collection* (1978).

Maya Peretz

Hertha Kräftner

Born April 26, 1928, Vienna, Austria; died
November 13, 1951, Vienna
Genre(s): poetry, prose sketches
Language(s): German

Hertha Kräftner's life remains a mystery. A young woman of great promise, she committed suicide at the age of twenty-three. Her work, consisting mainly of poetry and prose sketches, initially fell into oblivion, but it was rediscovered in the 1970s and has since undergone a remarkable revival.

Although born in Vienna, Kräftner grew up and attended school in Mattersburg in the province of Burgenland. In 1946 she returned to Vienna to begin her studies at the university with a major in German literature and minors in English, philosophy, and psychology. At the time of her death she had already begun her dissertation on surrealism in the works of Kafka. She began writing creatively at the age of seventeen while still in high school. Her poetry was published in magazines and newspapers, and in Vienna she was associated with the prominent circle of postwar poets that gathered around Hans Weigel and the journal *Neue Wege*. Her extraordinary literary talent was recognized and later likened to that of Ingeborg Bachmann. Kräftner traveled to Scandinavia and Paris, and

particularly her trip in 1950 resulted in intense literary production. Her death the following year from an overdose of sleeping pills remains inscrutable.

Kräftner's work stems from a six-year period between the ages of seventeen and twenty-three. As such it is fragmentary, yet it demonstrates phenomenal perfection. She is primarily known for her poetry, which shows a development from youthful imitation to mature invention. After a period of dependence chiefly on Rilke but also on Hofmannsthal and Trakl, she emerged with an original, individual voice. Her poetry is highly imaginative, even visionary, and is characterized by a strong visual element that manifests itself in new and striking images. Her work bears witness to the heights and depths of a hypersensitive individual who took her own dreams and anxieties, ideals and disillusionments as the object of art. The viewpoint is subjective and emotional but at the same time controlled and objectified. A fantastic, magical element, reminiscent of fantastic realism in the visual arts, easily flips over into a macabre, grotesque strain of surrealism. The infernal moments of which life is ostensibly composed are highly suggestive in their lucidity. Beneath it all is an undercurrent of death, which runs as a central theme throughout her works. One of her best-known poems reads as follows in translation: "Who still believes that coral reefs await us there and birds who sing the secret and dip their frail beaks in rose-colored water and that we will be met by the aroma of slivered almonds and the white root of rare plants? Oh, death will smell like pepper and marjoram because he has been with the fish dealer who choked on the silver tail of a pickled herring."

Her prose works are less mature, more personal, for the author was clearly still working toward an individual style. Nevertheless they have received renewed attention in recent years by critics attempting to unravel the riddle of her life and her death. Most notable is her "Pariser Tagebuch" (Paris Diary), which precisely and uniquely captures the atmosphere of her visit in the city. External experiences are immediately internalized and transformed into intuitive vision. Her falling in love and the ensuing joys and sorrows are recorded with all the radiance and despair of youth. The self-forgetting abandonment to the immediacy of experience is accompanied by and stands in contrast to a constant awareness of death in the background. The prose sketches also contain notes for a first-person novel giving evidence of the labyrinths of the soul. It is astonishing to read the clarity with which she foresaw the end, for already months before her suicide she wrote an analysis of the motives and possibilities of death. She remained true to herself throughout, and perhaps it was the uncompromising nature of her idealism, together with a heightened consciousness of futility, that precluded continued life.

Although single poems by Kräftner appeared in newspapers and magazines during her lifetime, after her death her work was soon forgotten. The first book appeared in 1963, collected and edited by her friends and fellow-poets, Otto Breicha and Andreas Okopenko, and entitled *Warum Hier? Warum Heute?* (Why Here? Why Now?). It provisionally rescued her writing from oblivion, but it was soon out of print. In 1977 the PEN Club of Burgenland re-issued the Breicha/ Okopenko edition as *Das Werk* (Works), thereby paving the way for her rediscovery. In 1981 the prominent Luchterhand firm published a new edition entitled *Das blaue Licht* (The Blue Light), also edited by Breicha and Okopenko with a postscript by Peter Härtling. Her poems were increasingly included in anthologies, a stereo record was made of her poetry in 1986, and in the same year a film was made reconstructing her life. It is undoubtedly the puzzle of her early death that in part stimulated public interest. Why would a vibrant young person, intelligent, attractive, and seemingly on the road to success choose to end her life? We will never know. Perhaps it is best to disregard the pathos of the personal fate and to focus instead on her actual accomplishments. They include, besides immature attempts, works of astonishing brilliance and consummate mastery. Kräftner is sure to find a place in literary history as a poet of intense poetic vision.

Works

Warum Hier? Warum Heute? Gedichte, Skizzen, Tagebücher, ed. Otto Breicha and Andreas Okopenko (1963; rpt. as *Das Werk. Gedichte,*

Skizzen, Tagebücher, 1977). *Das blaue Licht*, ed. Otto Breicha and Andreas Okopenko (1981).

Beth Bjorklund

Eliška Krásnohorská

(a.k.a. Al'běta Pechová)

Born November 18, 1847, Prague, Czechoslovakia; died November 26, 1926, Prague
Genres: lyric poetry, social and literary criticism, children's literature, opera libretto, and translation
Language(s): Czech

Krásnohorská, whose real name was Al'běta Pechová, was born into an artisan's family and lived most of her life in Prague. From youth, she suffered from a rheumatic disease which grew progressively worse and restricted her literary work in her later years. The writer Karolina Světlá introduced Krásnohorská to both literature and the movement for women's rights. Among other activities in the movement, Krásnohorská edited a feminist journal for a time and helped to found the first girls' *gymnasium* in Prague.

As a serious writer, Krásnohorská concentrated on lyric poetry. Her first published collection was *Z máje 'iti* (1871; From the Maytime of Life). Probably her best known collection of verse, however, is *Ze šumavy* (From the Sumava Mountains), with its poem "Chodská," which was inspired by the struggle for freedom among the Southern Slavs. Later in her career she satirized current abuses in society in *Bajky velkých* (1889; Big Fables).

Today Krásnohorská's poetry as a whole is commonly criticized as formally correct but lacking life and originality. She was also a literary critic of some influence in her day but is remembered now chiefly for her failure to appreciate Jaroslav Vrchlický and other rising poets of the 1890s.

Aside from her influence as a feminist, however, she left her mark on Czech culture in other ways: as a writer of numerous children's books, the author of several opera librettos (including some for the Czech composer Smetana), and the translator of important foreign literature (including works by Pushkin and Byron).

Works

Z máje 'ití (1871). Ze šumavy (1873). K slovanskému jihu (1880). Vlny v proudu (1885). Tři pohádky (1885). Svéhlavička (1887). Letorosty (1887). šumavský Robinson (1887). Bajky velkých (1889). Na 'ivě struně (1895). Svéhlavička nevěstou (1900). Svéhlavička 'enuškou (1900). Pohádky zimního večera (1901). Svéhlavička babičkou (1907). Zvěsti a báje (1916).

Bibliography

Nejedly, Z., O literatuře (1953). Strejček, F., Eliška Krásnohorská (1922). Pra'ák, A., Míza stromu (1940).

Reference works: Čeští spisovatelé deseti století, ed. R. Šťastný (1974), and čeští spisovatelé 19. a počátku 20. století, eds. K. Homolová, M. Otruba, and Z. Pešat (1982).

Clinton Machann

Aina Kraujiete

Born 1923
Genre(s): poetry
Language(s): Latvian

Before immigrating to the United States in 1949, Aina Kraujiete had trained as a medical researcher in Frankfurt and at the Sloan-Kettering Institute and continued in this profession until 1976. She began publishing her verse as early as 1963 with Es Esmu Vasara (I Am Summer) and has released at least five volumes of poetry described variously as intellectual, emotional, philosophical, romantic, and rich in fantasy. Her work has been translated into both English and Lithuanian. She is currently occupied as a creative writer and editor of Jaun Gaita, a journal devoted to Latvian literature.

Works

Es Esmu Vasara [I Am Summer] (1963). No Aizpirktās Paradīzes [From a Bartered Paradise] (1966). Ne Bungas Ne Trompetes [Not Drums Nor Trumpets] (1974). Kristalls Un Māls [Crystal and Clay] (1976).

Warwick J. Rodden

Ursula Krechel

Born April 12, 1947, Trier, West Germany
Genre(s): drama, novel, poetry, editions, journalism
Language(s): German

Ursula Krechel's talents are many-faceted. She is a playwright, poet, novelist, editor, and journalist. Once an activist in the student movement of the sixties, she has also been identified as a feminist.

Born in 1947, Krechel started out as a journalist while still a student. Later, she joined the WDR and worked for the Kölner Stadtanzeiger. She had her university education between 1966 and 1971 in Köln, studying theater, art history, and German Studies. She graduated with a dissertation on the film critic Herbert Ihering. In 1969–1970 and 1971–1972, she was the dramaturge at the Städtischen Bühnen Dortmund, and a theater worker for juveniles under custody. She has travelled widely and at present lives in Frankfurt.

Krechel's feminist inclinations can be found early in her career. "I write about women because of the fact that there is a contradiction between what they are and what society thinks of them. . . . I am motivated to dramatize contradictions I find in society, whatever they might be"—with these words Krechel introduced her play, Erika, in Theater heute (August 1974; Theater Today). This piece for seven women characters deals with Erika's emancipatory revolt against the suppressive mechanism of marriage and work. In the play, Erika leaves her husband, but gets pregnant with a stranger. In the "happy ending," she returns ironically to her marriage and work with a baby and the realization that things could have been much more catastrophic than they are. Erika muses upon the situation: "I always thought I am dumb as a woman. . . . But a man is dumb too." The play is not merely a piece of mental propositions; drawing upon social reality, it attempts, hesitantly and painfully, to reveal contradictions in the everyday action and prattle of the petite bourgeoisie as if they were scars.

The problematization of woman's identity has been a persistent theme in Krechel's writing ever since Erika. Her position as a feminist can be summarized in terms of an astute remark about the "New Women's Movement." "One should not," she wrote, "grasp feminism as a theory and as a mental construct (*Denkgebäude*), but rather as a ground-structure (*Grundstruktur*) for consciousness."

In her book of factual report, *Selbsterfahrung und Fremdbestimmung* (1975; Self's Experience, Other's Destiny, 2nd edition in 1978 with the afterword "Fortsetzung des Nahkampfes mit weitsichtigeren Mitteln," or "Continuation of the Combats: The Long-Term Strategy"; new edition in 1983), Krechel further concretizes the contradictions of female existence by integrating theoretical exposition with the method of storytelling. In doing so, she attempts to force open the internal aspects of feminism itself. These "reports of the New Women's Movement" represent a collection of the positions, experiences, and struggles in the wide area of conflict in female emancipation, which she unravels and analyzes. The book is also enhanced by an aesthetic quality which some critics characterize as the production of an objective reality through an overt subjectivity. As the title of the book suggests, in the narratives one could find the authorial Self's Experience merging into, while still distinct from the Other's Destiny.

This paradoxical but apparent unity of subjective self-experience and objective observation of contemporary life accounts for Krechel's poetic style in *Nach Mainz!* (1977; To Mainz!) and *Verwundbar wie in den besten Zeiten* (1979; Vulnerable as in the Best of Times), both concerned about problems of self-identity in a world of male-gendered realities. Resisting the lighthearted sing-song jingle of the new lyrical subjectivism, poems in these volumes exhibit an angular hardness and biting harshness. *Nach Mainz!*, which opens with an eloquent story of the persona's mother, is a collection of narrative poems, condensed and distilled from embittered day-to-day activities, and from dreams and disjointed utopias. More complex but also evoking an inner world of illusions and delusions, *Verwundbar wie in den besten Zeiten* is a many-layered series of poems weaving vulnerability, sufferings, wounds, complaints, and some kind of unresigned sorrow into a thematic matrix. While mapping, through reflective thought, the causalities of these elements, Krechel experiments with complex forms of expression. In particular, the painful sense of foreignness and cold motivates her to violate the conventional use of language: "But the particulars could/ not have had any names"; "Speeches have lost their words." The result of this approach is a startling wealth of colorfully differentiated pictures and names. Her language is melodious and rhythmic but goes against syntactical and paratactical conventions.

Krechel's inclinations drew her attention not only to the flaws of society, sufferings, love, and politics, but also to the New Women's Movement and its literature. She was attracted to the writings of Irmgard Keun, whom one can now read again since Krechel's rediscovery, and to Elisabeth Langgässer's *Unauslöschliches Siegel* (Unerasable Seal), which she edited with a new afterword in 1979.

In 1981, Krechel published her first great prose, *Zweite Natur* (Second Nature). Incorporating dreams and calculated chance elements, this work adopts in part a method of organization akin to surrealism. It has a loosely structured, episodic, and serendipitous form with little if any epical integration and psychological portrayal. There is scarcely any hint at where the climactic moments are. All of these characteristics seem to suggest a rejection of bourgeois codes of narration. Despite the fact that the story is about how four young people go about trying out the "new form of life (*die neue Lebensform*) in the community (*Wohngemeinschaft*)" of Frankfurt and "fall out of the nest of biographies," this novel is no Bildungsroman or adolescent fiction either. It is situated at the border between reality and fiction, where the claims of both areas are constantly at odds with one another. That "heartless people deserve this state" is an experience which the young people of the novel and Krechel's writings defend against with vigor. The melancholic knowledge that it is insufficient to create these characters, and much less suitable if at another time, weighs heavily on the narrative, and determines the end of the novel, which remains rather ambivalent: three women and a pair of doves leave the community with the boys.

Rohschnitt. Gedicht in sechzig Sequenzen (Raw Cuts: Poetry In Seventy Sequences), a book-length lyric published in 1983 and composed according to the principle of film-cutting, also deals with the kind of "right dreams in the wrong reality" depicted in *Zweite Natur*. Stringed together throughout by means of narrative moments, this great cycle of poems demands understanding and double readings. As a point of departure, Krechel chooses to discourse at length on the self or "*I*," who remains astonished by and disapproving of her attributes and labels of identification: "the *I* I have been is to be/ in the grass, that have I dreamed/ that the *I* I have been is to be." The departure from the *I* means a departure from the roles, the establishments, and the realities with which we are surrounded. The *I* can be plural, as in "die Schöne die Kluge die Mutter" (The Beautiful the Intelligent the Mother)—the three travel, together with a child, into an indistinct future: "charts, folded plans, departure is invention/ is a raft made of cork, a hole from Wanting-no-more/ an idea of more." Krechel has no particular aversion to greatness of form such as that achieved in Rilke's *Duino Elegies*, but the nature of her playful narratives, which resist thematic conscription, is not conducive to it. There seems to be a number of moves associated with deconstruction, the critique of the Enlightenment, and the transvaluation of values. Perhaps the poems are just what they are: "raw cuts" which, according to film terminology, are only initial montage clippings belonging together. At any rate, the technique of ordering used already constitutes a subversion of the classical concept of the lyrical subject.

In her more recent poems, *Vom Feuer lernen* (1985; Learn from Fire), Krechel has turned to lyrical suggestiveness. As "The Common Language Sealed" ("versiegelt die geläufige Sprache," the title of the first poem in the volume) suggests, she has rejected the direct pragmatic applications of her poetry. Her language is constantly both literal and symbolic, and even intentionally oblique. In line with the shift of interest to the "New Subjectivity" in the German writing of the eighties, this latest development indicates that Krechel is also moving beyond the precepts of the student movement in which she came of age.

Krechel has worked with many genres. A recent work deserving attention is her theatrical piece *Aus der Sonne* (stage manuscript 1985; From the Sun). Introducing the play, she asks: "Why cope with the changes of life by creating out of sheer invention a world which the firm reality will outdo anyway?" In the play, Edith's first line goes: "Unplayable. I will not laugh at that. That is my life. It will be played." The idea of life as play is presented not only in terms of the blurring of the distinctive borders between life and play, but also gotten across by means of a stylish grasp of life in the forties and fifties. This idea is also the preoccupation in another novel written in 1985, *Die Papsttochter* (The Pope's Daughter), in which fiction and reality illuminate one another, and truth and fiction cross over.

Works

Creative Writings: *Erika*, play (premiered 1974, pub. 1975). *Zwei Tode* (1975). *Nach Mainz!*, poems (1977). *Verwundbar wie in den besten Zeiten*, poems (1979). *Zweite Natur*, novel (1981). *Rohschnitt. Gedicht in sechzig Sequenzen*, poems (1983). *Vom Feuer lernen*, poems (1985). *Aus der Sonne*, play (manuscript, 1985). *Die Papsttochter*, novel (manuscript, 1985).

Other Works: *Information und Wertung*, dissertation on the theater and the film criticism of Herbert Ihering (1972). *Selbsterfahrung und Fremdbestimmung* (reportage, 1975, 1978 m. Nachw. "Fortsetzung des Nahkampfes mit weitsichtigeren Mitteln," erw. neuausg. 1983). *Die Entfernung der Wünsche am belien Tag* (1977). *Women's Liberation. Frauen gemeinsam sind stark!*, texts and materials about the Women's Liberation Movement in the United States (1977). *Das Parkett ein spiegelnder See* (1979). *Lesarten*, texts about poetry (1982). *Glückselig feindselig vogelfrei* (1984). *Der Keksgigant* (1986). *Leuk und Lachen oder die Grammatick des Austausches* (1987).

Miscellaneous: Contribution to "Theater heute" (August 1974). Editor of Elisabeth Langgässer's *Unauslöschliches Siegel* (1979). "Ich bin eine erstklasige Schriftstellerin zweiter Güte." In *die Karriere der Vicki Baum*, television play by Ursula Krechel and Herbert Wiesner (1985). Afterword to Irene Brin's *Morbidezza*, short poems of snobbishness between the two World Wars (1986).

Bibliography

Brinker-Gabler, Gisela, ed., *Deutsche Literatur von Frauen*. 2 Vols., Vol. II (München, 1988). Wiesner, Herbert, and Alexander von Bormann, "Krechel." In *Lexikon der deutschsprachigen* (München, 1981).

The following works contain brief references to Krechel: Bangerter, Lowell A., *German Writing Since 1945: A Critical Survey* (New York, 1988). Demetz, Peter, *After the Fires: Recent Writing in the Germanies, Austria, and Switzerland* (New York, 1986). Durzak, Manfred, *Deutsche Gegenwartsliteratur. Ausgangspositionen und aktuelle Entwicklungen* (Stuttgart, 1981). Hamburger, Michael, *After the Second Flood: Essays in Modern German Literature* (New York, 1986). Schnell, Ralf, *Die Literatur der Bundesrepublik: Autoren, Geschichte, Literaturbetrieb* (Stuttgart, 1986).

Balance Chow

V. Krestovsky

(see: Nadezhda Khvoshchinskaia)

Vesna Krmpotić

Born June 17, 1932, Dubrovnik, Yugoslavia
Genre(s): poetry, essay
Language(s): Croatian

Vesna Krmpotić is an important figure in the diverse postwar generation of Croatian writers. The salient characteristics of her writing are its careful, precise diction and its eclectic blend of Eastern mysticism with Western reflectiveness.

Krmpotić was born in Dubrovnik and graduated from the University of Zagreb with a B.A. in psychology and English language and literature. She has also lived and studied in India and Egypt and received a diploma from the University of New Delhi. Krmpotić has worked for Radio Television Zagreb and as a literary editor, and currently lives in Belgrade. A wife and mother, poet and scholar, Krmpotić often combines the personal and particular with the cosmic; in her "spiritual autobiography," *Eyes of Eternity*, she describes how marriage and a family have led her to see the "spray of the fountain rather than the crystal jet."

A poet, essayist, translator, and anthologist of Eastern literature, Krmpotic has also written critical essays, including the preface to an edition of the poetry of fellow Croatian poet Vesna Parun. Krmpotić's poetry and poetic prose tend to fall into two categories—love poetry and philosophical or religious poetry influenced by Eastern religions—but this division is not absolute, for much of her love poetry deals with death, identity, and the quest for self-knowledge. Her earliest book *Poezija* (*Poems*), as well as the poems that follow, treat the speaker's often painful meditations with a diction and tone that are restrained and concise but often startling as well. The poems emphasizing love are typically trenchant and elliptical, while the more philosophical poems are more stately, relying at times on parallelism and repetition to create an atmosphere of reflective calm. In the autobiographical essays of *Eyes of Eternity*, the author seeks to undermine the rationalist stance of the typical prose essay and to use the poet's devices of imagery, association, and free syntax to evoke for the reader the narrator's experience of an inward journey. Combining the dreamlike and the everyday, the erudite and the personal, the essays range from Zagreb and Dubrovnik to Cairo and Alexandria, quoting or referring to Swedenborg, the Vedas, the Tao Te Ching, and Sufi proverbs. Christianity, for Krmpotić, acts as an intermediary between the individual and God, and thereby blocks the individual's inward quest for the divine; *Eyes of Eternity* seeks to re-establish for the reader the mystical apprehension of the spiritual world. Krmpotic's recent poems, *Ljevanica za Igora*, written after the death of the poet's son Igor, describe her quest to understand the meaning of her son's death; eventually the speaker comes to realize the futility of grief and continuity of all life:

> I am that part of You
> that doesn't know where you are now.
> You are that part of me
> that knows where you always are.
> I am that part of You
> which awaits a dead child.
> You are that part of me
> which knows that there's no death. ("I
> Am, You Are")

Krmpotić's creation of a quietly intense personal style and her assimilation of Eastern thought establish the poet as a distinctively important figure in contemporary literature. Her philosophical eclecticism and her subtle innovations in prose and verse serve to universalize the powerful emotions underlying such an art.

Works

Poezija [Poems] (1956). Pijesak koji govori [Sand that Speaks] (1958). Plamen i svijeća [Fire and Candle] (1962). Jama bića [Essence of Being] (1965). Raskorak [Discrepancy] (1965). Pisma iz Indije [Letters from India] (1965). Krasna nesuglasja [Beautiful Discords] (1969). Hiljada lotosa [A Thousand Lotuses] (1971). Dijamantni faraon: Antologia srednisnjega glasa [The Diamond Pharaoh: Anthology of the Middle Voice] (1975). Čas je ozirise: Antiantologija stare egipatske knjiizevnosti [The Time of Osiris: Anti-anthology of Ancient Egyptian Literature] (1965). Ljevanica za Igora: Pesme [Casting for Igor: Poems] (1981). Dvogovor: Izbrane pjesme [Dialogue: Selected Poems] (1981). Jednina i dvojina [Single and Double] (1981).

Translations: Eyes of Eternity: A Spiritual Autobiography [translation of Diamantni faraon] (1979). Selected poems translated by Vasa D. Mihailovich and Ronald Moran in The Bridge 19–29 (1970): 67–69. Anita Lekić-Trjojević, Stevan Raickovic, Branko Miljković, and Vesna Krmpotić: An Introduction to and Translation of Poems by Three Yugoslav Poets. M.A. thesis, University of Maryland, 1983. Selected poems translated by Vasa D. Mihailovich: "A December Forest," in Women Poets of the World, ed. Joanna Bankier and Deidre Lashgari (1983). "A Manifold Life," "An Interlude," "Father's Grave." Most 1–2 (1985): 118–119.

Bibliography

Eekman, Thomas, Thirty Years of Yugoslav Literature (1945–1975) (1978). Gluščevic, Zoran, "Posle smrti: Vesna Krmpotić, Ljevanica za Igora." Knji'evnost (1979), pp. 972–987. Vaupotic, Miroslav, Contemporary Croatian Literature (1966).

General References: Contemporary Authors 102 (198-), p. 314. Who's Who in the Socialist Countries (1978).

Stephen Hale

P. Kronikar

(see: Terézia Vansová)

Mina (Wilhelmina Jakoba Paulina Rudolphine) Kruseman

Born September 25, 1839, Velp, Netherlands; died August 2, 1922, Boulogne-sur-Seine, France
Genre(s): novel, novella, drama
Language(s): Dutch, French

Mina Kruseman seems to have been opposed to every form of organized feminist action even though she clamorously condemned female subservience and dependence.

As a classical singer she made under the name Stella Oristorio di Frama a successful tour through the southern United States in 1872. Back in the Netherlands, she drew enthusiastic crowds acting out her own novellas in which she denounced the limitations imposed upon women in her society. She later married and settled in France, where she kept writing novellas, novels, and numerous letters which she referred to as her "parting-gift to the narrow-minded Netherlands." In 1916, she published a pacifist plea to all women of the world to resist and oppose war.

De moderne Judith (1873; The Modern Judith) contains the short stories she acted out on stage and the critical response they received in the press. The author shows how prejudiced and contradictory the criticism leveled against her feminist ideas was. This caused her to be forever hated by the press. Her novel Huwelijk in Indie (1873; Marriage in India) is composed of a curious mixture of traditional romanticism and emphatically sincere feminist realism.

Her letters give insight among other things into her relationship with one of Holland's greatest and most controversial authors, Multatuli (Eduard Douwes Dekker), whose play Vorstenschool (School for Sovereigns) was eventually performed as a result of her efforts with herself in the main role. After her marriage and her move to France she began writing in French. With the exception of the pacifist appeal of 1916, her later works are of little significance.

Mina Kruseman's rebellious and quarrelsome character made her an epoch-making pioneer. She lacked the literary talent to have an enduring influence on Dutch letters, but as a proponent of women's independence she has made an important contribution.

Works

De moderne Judith (1873). Een huwelijk in Indie (1873). Willen en handelen (1874). Mijn leven, 3 vols. (1877). Cendrillon (1880). Hélène Richard (1880). Two letters to Urbain Gohier, the first in response to his article "Les Femmes" in L'Aurore of March 27, 1899. "Appel à toutes les femmes du monde entier" (1916).

Bibliography

Ammers-Küller, J. van, Een Pionierster. M. Krüseman en haar verhouding tot Multatuli (1921). Moerman, Josien, ed., Ik ben een God in het diepst van mijn gedachten. Lexicon Nederlandstalige auteurs (1984), p. 137. Romein-Verschoor, Annie H.M., Vrouwenspiegel: Een literair-sociologische studie over de nederlandse romanschrijfster na 1880 (1935), pp. 24, 65–66. Waal, Margot de and Suzanne Piet. "Woman of Letters." Insight Holland 15 (March 1980): 2.

Maya Bijvoet

Agnes Julie Frederika von Krusenstjerna

Born: 1894, Växjö, Sweden; died 1940, Stockholm
Genre(s): novel, short story, poetry
Language(s): Swedish

A daughter of an upper-class family, Agnes von Krusenstjerna was educated in girls' schools. Her first novels were regarded as traditional girls' books along the lines of those of Louisa May Alcott, but neither her life nor her art was to remain within conventional bounds. In 1918 she was hospitalized for the first time for the severe mental illness that for the rest of her life was to alternate with, and occasionally overlap, periods of extraordinary productivity.

Von Krusenstjerna achieved critical recognition with the semi-autobiographical "Tony" books, a three-volume depiction of the physical and emotional stages of a young girl's development into womanhood and gradual slide into mental illness. Though the Tony books raised eyebrows with their frank discussions of feminine sexuality, they were generally well-received.

The next novel cycle, the seven-volume Fröknarna von Pahlen (The Misses von Pahlen), raised a storm of controversy. In highly uneven prose bordering at times on pornography, von Krusenstjerna portrays a degenerate upper-class milieu in which healthy erotic passion is threatened by sexual frustration and perversion of every kind. The influence of David Sprengel, a caustic critic and unsuccessful writer with an ax to grind, whom von Krusenstjerna married in 1921, is decisive for better and for worse in this work.

The author regained a more balanced style in the incomplete novel cycle Fattigadel (Poor Nobility), in which she focused mercilessly on the stultifying atmosphere of the upper-class life into which she had been born.

Despite its uneven quality, Agnes von Krusenstjerna's work broke new ground in Swedish literature in its frank, intense depiction of mental illness and feminine erotic experience.

Works

Samlade Skrifter [Collected Works], 19 vols., ed. and foreword by Johannes Edfelt (1946). Ninas dagbok. Helenas första kärlek (1917; 1918). Tony växer upp. Scener ur ett barndomsliv (1922). Tonys läroår. Resa till Kejsarenshotell (1926). En Dagdriverskas anteckningar. Händelser på vägen (1923; 1935). Fru Esters pensionat (1927). Fröknarna von Pahlen (1930–1935): Den blå rullgardinen, Kvinnogatan, Höstens skuggor, Porten vid Johannes, Älskande par, Bröllop på Ekered, Av samma blod. En Ung dam far till Djurgårdsbrunn. Delat rum på Kammakaregatan (1933; 1933). Vivi, flicka med melodi. Dikter. Ur bästa noveller. Fattigadel. Viveka von Lagercronas historia (1935–1938): Fattigadel, Dunklet mellan träden, Dessa lyckliga år, I livets vår.

To date there are no translations of Von Krusenstjerna's work into English.

Bibliography

Ahlberg, Alf et al., Dikten, diktaren och samhället (Stockholm, 1935). Ahlgren, Stig Johan Axel, Krusenstjerna-studier (Stockholm, 1940). Ahlgren, Stig Johan Axel, Obehagliga stycken; kritik och polemik 1933–1944 (Stockholm, 1944), pp. 63–73. Åkerhielm, H., "Drömmen om kvinnoriket." Tiden 34 (1942): 493–501. Blomberg, Erik, "Kvinnospegel." Mosaik (1940): 106–116. Brøgger,

Niels Christian, "En stø roman," *Det moderne menneske og andre essays* (Oslo, 1937). Edfelt, Johannes, "Agnes von Krusenstjernas ungdomsdiktning." *BLM* 12 (1943): 459–457. Green, Allan, "Om Agnes von Krusenstjernas novel *Originellupplagan*." *Bokvännen* 20: 171–176. Gustaffson, Alrik, *A History of Swedish Literature* (Minneapolis, 1961), pp. 488–492, 638. Jaensson, Knut, "Agnes von Krusenstjerna." *Nio moderna svenska prosaförfattare* (Stockholm, 1941), pp. 5–12. Lagercrantz, Olof, *Agnes von Krusenstjerna* (Stockholm, 1951; 1963; 1980). Olsson, Hagar, "Agnes von Krusenstjerna." *BLM* 6 (1937), pp. 515–526. Örnkloo, Ulf, *Preludier till Krusenstjernafejden: Om presskritiken av Agnes von Krusenstjernas böcker fram till 1930* (Uppsala, 1968). Sprengel, David, *Förläggarna, föfattarna, kritikerna om Agnes von Krusenstjerna och hennes senaste arbeten etc.* (Stockholm, 1935). Teiler, Börge, *Agnes von Krusenstjerna och David Sprengel* (Hallstahammar, 1977).

Jeanette Atkinson

Maria Krysińska

Born 1857, Warsaw, Poland; died 1908, Paris
Genre(s): poetry, short story, novel
Language(s): French

Maria Krysińska belongs to the Symbolism-Decadence movement. Her father was a lawyer in Warsaw, and Polish was presumably her home language. However, even though she did not go to Paris until she was sixteen, she was thoroughly at home in French; there is no trace of bilingual interference and little internal evidence that she was not a lifelong French resident. She went to Paris apparently to continue her piano instruction, but she soon dropped out of the Paris Conservatory. To judge from her account, traditional music discipline exasperated her. Starting in 1878, she was associated with one wild group of French and expatriate writers after another, Hydropathes, Zutistes, Je-m'en-foutists. She made her living as a cabaret accompanist and *chanteuse* "Marylka la Polonaise" first at the Chat noir and later at the Café Procope. She was also reading widely to educate herself. By 1882–1883, she had achieved some reputation for setting poems of Verlaine and Cros to music. As early as 1881, she was placing poems and short stories in the little magazines that were radical in politics and iconoclastic in literature, e.g., *Le Chat noir, La Plume, La Revue Indépendante, La Libre Revue, La Revue blanche*. She found literary revolt particularly appealing and began experimenting with verse forms. By 1886 when her one-time crony Gustave Kahn claimed *vers libre* (slight deviations from traditional French forms, not "free verse" in the Anglo-American sense) as his invention, she countered that she had been writing poetry with such innovations as early as 1882. Critical consensus has been inclined to give her the credit for using *vers libre* first but to deny her credit for writing good poetry and hence letting the kudos go to Kahn. What is probably true is that the time had come to make French verse more flexible and less rule-bound, and it was inevitable that poets would happen upon some of the techniques nearly simultaneously. In her introduction to *Intermèdes nouveaux* (1904) she states that *vers libre* should have a worthwhile message, a form which a competent listener or reader will recognize as poetic and a musicality as evident to the ear as that of traditional French poetry. She herself recommends rhyme or assonance and *rime riche* and Alexandrines for effect. She concludes with a wry comment: "Une initiative émanant d'une femme-avait sans doute décrèté le groupe-peut être considérée comme ne venant de nulle part, et tombée de droit dans le domaine public" (p. xxi). She married Impressionist painter Georges Bellenger and accompanied him to the United States in 1885–1886. The reader can only wonder about the "Ballade" on infidelity which she dedicated to him. She published steadily up to *La Force du désir*, a *roman à clef* in 1905. In any event, when she died impoverished in 1908, she had no family either in Poland where her father had died in 1882 and her mother in 1890, or in France. She was placed in a common grave at Saint-Ouen since there was no one to pay for her tombstone.

Her serious poetry is not impressive. She tends either to space poems like traditional lyrics omitting rhymes or to use self-consciously "poetic" short paragraphs of equal length. However, she can use traditional metrics. What is impressive here is her identification with strong women in cultural history like Eve, Ariadne, Helen of Troy,

Mary Magdalene. She is also very responsive to nature and sincerely devout. Her rare pieces of satiric verse deflate male complacency and use rhyme with the piquancy of a good night club comedian. More accessible to contemporary readers is her fiction, which has a spare narrative style and plots based on actuality. All of her work has been out of print for over eighty years, and much of it is now easier to locate in periodicals.

Only research libraries have held on to her work, for that common grave symbolizes her reputation. In her lifetime, she was ridiculed as a fat pianist, a barmaid, a "Saint-Jeane Baptistine du vers libre." (This last epithet is particularly nasty when the Decadents' love-hate idolatry of Salomé is recalled.) As late as 1947, a literary historian dismissed her as flotsam and jetsam. Indeed, while it may be possible to rehabilitate some of her work, the facts of her life have been washed away.

Works

L'Amour chemine (1894). Folle de son corps (1895) (unable to verify). *La Force du désir* (1905). *Intermèdes* (1904). *Joies errantes. Nouveaux Rhythmes pittoresques* (1894). *Rhythmes pittoresques* (1890).

Poems and short stories in *Arts et Critiques* (1890), *Le Capitan* (1883, unable to verify), *Le Chat Noir* (1882, 1883, 1889, 1890, 1891, 1893, the best immersion in her milieu), *La Cravache Parisienne* (1889, unable to verify), *La Libre Revue* (1883), *Le Messager Français* (1891), *La Plume* (1890), *La Revue blanche* (1893), *La Revue Indépendante* (1889, 1898, 1899), *La Revue universelle* (1883, 1901).

Bibliography

A fair selection of her poetry is available in Bernard Devaille, *La Poésie symboliste* (Paris, 1971). The only attempt at rehabilitating documentation is in Maria Szarama-Swolkieniowa, *Maria Krysińska Poetka Francuskiego Symbolizmu* (Krakow, 1972).

Marilyn Gaddis Rose

Marja Kubašec (Kubasch)

Born July 3, 1890, Quoos (Kreis Bautzen),
Germany; died 1976, Bautzen, Germany
Genre(s): novel, drama
Language(s): Upper Lusatian-Sorbian used by
the enclave of western Slavs in East
Germany

Marja Kubašec was the first woman prose writer in Upper Lusatian-Sorbian history. This enclave of west Slavs isolated in Germany from their kinsmen among the Poles, Czechs, and Slovaks had to develop a literary language in the eighteenth to nineteenth centuries because it had almost disappeared after a promising beginning in the sixteenth century. Kubašec's novels carry themes of Sorbian history from its beginnings to the mistreatment of this Slavic minority in Nazi Germany.

The daughter of a farmer, Kubašec studied at the teachers' academy in Erfurt, then taught school and became active in the Sorbian national movement. From 1911 to 1925 she edited the children's magazines *Raj* (Paradise) and *Serbski Student*, as well as wrote, directed, and staged plays for the Sorbian amateur theater. She spent the war years as a schoolteacher. From 1952 until her retirement in 1956, she was a professor of Sorbian and German literature at the Sorbian Pedagogical Institute in Kleinwelka. Kubašec also translated Pushkin, Turgenev, Tolstoy, Gorky, and Alois Jirásek into Lusatian-Sorbian. In 1929 she was given the Preis des Borsenvereins der Deutschen Buchhandler. In 1962 she received the ćišinski-Preis, and also the Domowina prize, and in 1975 the J.R. Becher Medal.

Kubašec's literary debut was the allegorical novella *Wusadny* (1922; Leprous), in which she castigated renegades of her nation. Her next major works, after World War II, realistically described the tragic fate of people caught by war and also the problems remaining after the defeat of Nazism. These works included *Row v serbskej holi* (1949; A Grave in the Serbian Virgin Forest) and *Koło časow* (1959; Circle of Time). This theme continued in her important biography of the Sorbian anti-fascist Christian-socialist Dr. Maria Grólmusec in *Hwězdy nad bjezdnom* (1960; Stars over the Chasm) which was based on Grólmusec's letters from Ravensbruck concentration camp where she died. Kubašec's trilogy *Bosćij Serbin* (1963–1965) treated the life of an illegal schoolteacher in the eighteenth century. Her cycle of novels *Lĕto wulkich wohenjow* (1970; The Summer of the Great Fire) and *Nalĕtnje wĕtry* (1978; Spring Winds) continued her theme of national education. Related to Kubašec's historical novels were her biographies of important Sorbian figures.

Kubašec's significance as the first woman novelist in Upper Lusatian-Sorbian is clear, and her historical fiction is also important for its authentic cultural detail over a period of two centuries.

Works

Novels and novellas: *Wusadny* (1922; in the Journal *Luzica*). *Row v serbskej holi* (1949). *Koło časow* (1959). *Wanda* (1962). *Bosćij Serbin* (1963–1965). *Lĕto wulkich wohenjow* (1970). *Nalĕtnje wĕtry* (1978).

Plays: *Tĕi hodowne hry za d'ĕči* (1923). *Chodojta* [Sorceress] (1926).

Bibliography

Frinta, Antonín, *Lu'ičtí Srbové a jejich Písemnictvi* (Prague, 1955).

General references: *Lexikon deutschsprachiger Schriftsteller von den Anfängen bis zur Gegenwart*, Vol. I (Leipzig, 1972), p. 504. Lorenc, Kito, ed., *Serbska čitanka: Sorbisches Lesebuch* (Leipzig, 1981), pp. 496–497. *Mały słownik pisarzy zachodnio-słowiańskich i południowo-słowiańskich* (Warsaw, 1973), p. 255.

Norma Leigh Rudinsky and Milan Žitny

Žofia Kubini

(a.k.a. Žsofia Kubinyi, Žofia Kubiniová)

Born early to mid-seventeenth century, Vlachy (Liptov) in Austria-Hungary, now Czechoslovakia; died Smrečany (Liptov)
Genre(s): religious hymn
Language(s): Slovakized Czech

Kubini's work belongs to both Czech literature (for its language) and Slovak literature (for its origin and content). Since the old Czech language of the sixteenth century translation of the Bible was used in Slovakia for the liturgy by Slovak Protestants, it became the language of religious (and later secular) literature. Baroque poetry was still close to church hymns and was usually written for a particular melody. The pietist tradition encouraged personal religious expression.

Žofia Kubini is believed to have lived in the mid- and late seventeenth century although her exact dates are unknown. A member of the aristocratic Kubini family, she married Peter Szmrecsany, son of a similar family who was an official on the estates of the powerful Illésházy counts. Both families were prominently associated with the Protestant nobility then rebelling against the Catholic dynasty of the Hapsburgs in Vienna. It is probably also important that Žofia was a close cousin of the poet Kata-Sidónia Petróczy (Countess Pekry of Košece near Trenčin), who wrote Magyar language political poems against Vienna as well as her religious poetry, sometimes based on Slovak melodies. Since Petróczy is regarded as the best baroque woman poet in Hungary, presumably such an acquaintance was supportive for the relatively unknown Žofia.

Only one poem attributed to Žofia Kubini has survived but its polish shows a practiced hand. In the Old Testament tradition of the Song of Songs, *Ženíchu můj spanilý* (O, Comely Bridegroom) mixes the language and imagery of secular poetry (e.g. the lover as beautiful as a lily) with the mystical tradition of marriage to Christ. Yet it remains fresh and intimate with the impatience of a wife expecting her husband. Reflecting contemporary pietism in its warm, personal tone, the song was first published in the standard Lutheran hymnal in 1741. Since public Protestant liturgy was very restricted by the Hapsburg policy of re-Catholization, private ceremonies became a common part of domestic life, and this song was soon a popular part of wedding celebrations, spreading also to Bohemia and Yugoslavia among Slovak emigrants.

Much of the early Slovak literature was circulated only in handwritten anthologies, remaining unpublished for political, religious, and cultural reasons. Much also was lost in the two-centuries-long Turkish battle and the repeated rebellions against Vienna. Therefore, the few known women poets at least demonstrate the existence of women interested in self-expression. Žofia Kubini's authorship has been disputed, mainly as an improbability, but similar evidence based on acrostics is accepted for male poets. Several other attributions of religious hymns to women in this period (especially Anna Czobor, Anna Kubini, and the women active in several printers' families) indicate a fertile field for study.

Works

"Ženíchu můj spanilý." *Cithara sanctorum*, ed. Samuel Hruškovič (1741) and all subsequent editions.
Translations: Modern Slovak: *Tranovského Kancionale* (1984).

Bibliography

∂ urovič, Ján, *Evanjelická literatúra do tolerancie* (Martin 1940), pp. 346–347. Haan, L'udevít, *Cithara sanctorum, jeji historie, jeji původce a tohoto spolupracovníci* (Pest 1873), pp. 65–65. Kubinyi, Ferenc, *A Felső-kubini Kubinyi csalad* (Budapest, 1906). Minárik, Jozef, *Baroková literatúra* (Bratislava 1984), pp. 155, 160. Mišianik, Ján, *Pohl'ady do staršej literatúry* (Bratislava 1974), p. 207. Nagy, Iván, *Magyarország családai* (Pest, 1858). Slavkovská, Gizela, *Já miluji, nesmím povídati* (Bratislava 1977), pp. 145–146, 453.

Norma L. Rudinsky

Žofia Kubiniová

(see: Žofia Kubini)

Žsofia Kubinyi

(see: Žofia Kubini)

Matilda Kugler-Poni

(see: Matilda Cugler-Poni)

Oleksandra Myxajlivna Kuliseva

(a.k.a. Hanna Barvinok)

*Born May 5, 1828, Motrnivci, The Ukraine,
    The Soviet Union; died July 23, 1911*
Genre(s): short story
Language(s): Ukrainian

Hanna Barvinok has been called the writer of women's sorrows. Her first story "Lyxo ne bez dobra" (1960; "Misfortune Not Without Good") first appeared in an anthology published by her husband, the writer Pantelejmon Kulis. In her stories, Barvinok drew on folk motifs intermingling them with elements from folk songs. Representative of Ukrainian late Romanticism, her writing reflects the influence of Marko Vovcok, her husband Kulis, and Taras Sevcenko. The main focus of her stories is the fate of women in love and marriage.

Born on the estate of her father Motronivci near Brozno, Barvinok met her husband through her brother Vasyl' Bilozers'kyj, the editor of *Osnova*. Despite her mother's objections, she married Kulis in 1847, and present among the wedding guests was the poet Taras Sevcenko, who so enraptured Barvinok that she was determined to give away her dowry to enable the poet to travel abroad in order to further his education. This generosity in spirit is also reflected in her determination to follow her husband into exile, where she tried to make his life as comfortable as possible. Notwithstanding her husband's frequent unfaithfulness, Kuliseva remained devoted to him, and after his death she carefully collected his works.

While some of her stories have the character of ethnographic observations, the central focus of the stories is the lot peasant women have to endure. The language of these stories is direct expressing the unhappiness of women married to drunkards or those who have chosen the handsome, but poor suitor. In one such story, "Pijak" ("The Drunkard"), Barvinok describes the determination of the main character to survive and rear her children in face of public criticism. In other stories, as for example "Rusalka" ("The Water Nymph") love is presented as a saving grace in the face of poverty, trials and hopelessness. In 1902 the collection of her stories, *Opovidanj'a z narodnyx Ust* (Tales from the People) appeared, and in 1909 a collection of stories. She published in many anthologies including *Xata*, *Osnova*, and *Pravda*.

Hanna Barvinok's contributions to Ukrainian literature lie in her moving portraits of peasant life, and the women's lot. Despite the romantic orientation of her early works, her later stories anticipate a more realistic presentation of characters and a concern with native Ukrainian themes.

Works
Virna Para.

Christine Kiebuzinska

Margarethe Susanna von Kuntsch

Born September 7, 1651, Allstedt Castle
(Saxony); died March 27, 1717, Eisenach
(or Altenburg)
Genre(s): autobiography, poetry
Language(s): German

In 1720 appeared posthumously the collected works of Margarethe Susanna von Kuntsch, entitled: *Sämmtliche GeistĆ und Weltliche Gedichte. . . .* Arranged as a loving tribute by her grandson Christoph Gottlieb Stockmann, the book contains a foreword by the then-noted C.F. Hunold (pseud. Menantes), an autobiography written by Margarethe three years before she died, and the collected poetry arranged in four sections, called "Eichenwald," "Cypressenwald," "RosenĆ und Myrthengebüsche" and "FeldĆBlumen und Kräutlein."

From Menantes' foreword and Margarethe's autobiography, the following biographical composite can be drawn. Born in the castle of Allstedt, where her father was the official in charge, Margarethe married the Councillor to the duke of Mansfeldt and moved with him to Altenburg when he became Councillor to the Duke of Saxony-Gotha. She bore him in rapid succession ten children, of whom only one reached the age of maturity, ruled over a household befitting to a councillor's wife and tried her hand at poetry. Whereas the two ac-

counts lend themselves well for such a composite, they are markedly different as to what aspects they stress in the life of von Kuntsch. The collection of poetry reflects this dichotomy.

Menantes praised Susanna's virtues, her knowledge of religious as well as secular matters, her mastery of Latin, her "handsome" library, well equipped with moral and political works, her well-run household. He was less satisfied with her poetic endeavors and appeared somewhat embarrassed at having been asked to write the introduction. He faulted the editor for not having made a more careful selection and the poetry for not always following the established (that is Opitzian) rules. He did find her choice of topics appropriate for a woman and admitted that her poetry shows "spirit." "The wise Creator," he wrote, "has planted into the sensible female gender so many excellent qualities of the soul that one should attribute the frequent lack of knowledge and intellectual thought to a lack of education and careful attention, better devoted to divinely ordained woman's work."

Margarethe Susanna's autobiography shows a slightly different picture. As she summed up: "I got accustomed to being unhappy." Although belonging to the upper strata of society, Margarethe shared the fate of many parents of her time of seeing their children die in childbirth or infancy. Of ten children, only the second one, a daughter, lived to maturity. Margarethe mentions them all. If not stillborn, they were graced with a name. They put in their short attendance and then succumbed. But they did take center stage in the life of von Kuntsch. Their faithfully recorded births, deaths, and burials form a litany in the account of the sixty-three-year-old woman who remembered them all vividly twenty years after the last infant son had died. Little mention is made of the well-run household, of the husband, who is invariably described as loving. Even her erudition, so praised by Menantes, is played down here. In her youth, she had wanted to study languages and science, she writes, but her parents "judged sensibly that such was more an exercise for noblewomen than for women of the middle class, and they had me discontinue my studies after a short while." Her library and Menantes' comments show that she did pursue these interests as an adult, but the autobiography makes no mention of this.

Although her autobiography is equally silent about her poetic efforts, they do reflect both the representational life of the councillor's wife and the love and sorrows of motherhood stressed in the autobiography. In the grandson's arrangement, the first section, called "Gott-Geweihtes Eichenwald," contains poems written as a reaction to various works read by Margarethe. The poems themselves are less interesting than the fact that they provide an excellent overview of the reading list of an educated woman at the turn of the eighteenth century, with an emphasis on works that provide consolation and treatises on the relativity of life on earth. All of the works are devotional and all are well-known classics in that genre like Johann Arndt's *Wahres Christenthum*, Joachim Lütkemann's *Vorschmack Göttlicher Güte*, Heinrich Müller's *Himmlischer Liebesküß*, and others; Erasmus Francisci is represented with two works; his *Letzte Rechenschafft* was read repeatedly, with poems composed after each reading.

The second section, entitled "Düsterer Cypressenwald," contains poems written as a reaction to the deaths of various children. They are touching *Erlebnispoesie* and quite accomplished poetically. They also belie the modern notion that parents in previous ages did not love their children and were resigned to the fact that many died in infancy. Especially revealing in this respect is a poem called "Dialogue of the Soul Between the Natural Motherly Love and the Christian Acceptance of Providence After the Death of Two Most Beloved Children."

The third section "Das blühende und grünende Rosen-und Myrthen Gebüsche" contains occasional poetry for the weddings and birthdays in Margarethe's extensive circle of family and friends. Section four, "Feldblumen," contains miscellaneous poetry, a poem for a *Stammbuch* (poetry album), a poem "upon seeing her picture as a young girl," a treatise about the supposedly fickle nature of women, and the like.

Menantes is right, the quality is uneven. The poems about the deaths of her children and some of the poetry in the last section stand out, and these are the poems that appear in various later anthologies. On the whole, however, we can only applaud Stockmann's decision to include all of his grandmother's poetry. It provides an excellent insight into the literary activities of the educated woman both as an author and a reader and gives us a rare glimpse of the personal life of a woman at that time.

Works

Sämmtliche GeistĆ und Weltliche Gedichte [Collected Religious and Secular Poems] (1720).
Translation: "An einem guten Freund welcher mit der Königin Anna Exempel der Weiber Unbeständigkeit beweisen wolte; To a Good Friend Who Would Prove the Fickleness of Women with the Example of Queen Anna," in *The Defiant Muse; German Feminist Poems From the Middle Ages to the Present, a Bilingual Anthology*, ed. Susan L. Cocalis (1986), pp. 10–11.

Bibliography

Brinker-Gabler, Gisela, *Deutsche Dichterinnen vom 16. Jahrhundert bis zur Gegenwart* (Frankfurt a.M., 1978), pp. 101–106. Corvinus, Gottlieb L., *Nutzbares/ galantes und curiöses Frauenzimmer-Lexicon...* (Leipzig: 1715), pp. 917–918. Hanstein, Adalbert von, *Die Frauen in der Geschichte des deutschen Geisteslebens des 18. und 19. Jahrhunderts* (Leipzig, 1900), p. 100. Jöcher, Christian Gottlieb, *Allgemeines Gelehrten-Lexikon* (Leipzig, 1750. Rpt. Hildesheim, 1961), II, p. 2187. Klemm, Gustav, *Die Frauen, Culturgeschichtliche Schilderungen* VI (Dresden: 1859), pp. 291–296. Rauschenbach, Johann Tobias, *Die Freundin des Lammes*, eulogy (Altenburg: 1717). Traeger, Lotte, "Das Frauenschrifttum in Deutschland von 1500–1650." Diss., Prague, 1943, Anhang p. 23. Woods, Jean Muir, and Maria Anna Fürstenwald, *Women of the German-speaking Lands* (Stuttgart, 1984), p. 61. Zedler, Johann Heinrich, *Grosses Vollständiges Universal-Lexikon* XV (Leipzig und Halle, 1735; rpt. Graz, Austria, 1961), p. 1248.

Cornelia Niekus Moore

Carmen Kurtz

(see: Carmen de Rafael Marés de Kurz)

Isolde Kurz

Born December 21, 1853, Stuttgart, Germany;
died April 5, 1944, Tübingen
Genre(s): poetry, novella, novel, biography,
fairy tale, aphorism, essay, autobiography
Language(s): German

Isolde Kurz came of age in a politically liberal family during Bismarck's rise to power and the founding period of the German Empire. She led an exceptionally long and productive literary life, publishing during the course of fifty years in almost every genre but the drama.

Isolde Clara Marie Kurz was the daughter of the Swabian novelist and editor Hermann Kurz and of Marie von Brunnow Kurz, a freethinking aristocrat who had participated in the Revolution of 1848. Kurz's childhood in the town of Tübingen was intellectually free and physically active but often lonely and at odds with bourgeois society. With her four brothers she did not attend school but was taught at home by her mother. She documented her childhood and youth in great detail in the works *Aus meinem Jugendland* (1918; From the Land of My Youth), *Hermann Kurz* (1906), and *Meine Mutter* (1926; My Mother). Well read in socialist writings as well as classical literature and several foreign languages, Kurz began her literary career as a translator after the death of her father in 1873. In 1877, glad to escape the stifling political and cultural climate in Germany under the Iron Chancellor Bismarck, she moved to Italy with her mother and seriously ill youngest brother. The family settled in Florence where Kurz remained until 1913. Here she associated with a circle of German artists and for decades looked after her mother, with whom she lived. At the outbreak of World War I she returned to Germany and resided in Munich until the year before her death. Though she never married, she cultivated friendships with leading intellectuals and artists of her age, including her father's friend, the author Paul Heyse, and the artists Arnold Böcklin and Adolph Hildebrand.

Like other nineteenth-century women writers, Kurz found in the city of Florence a more liberal and stimulating atmosphere than in her native country. Here she translated Italian literature and immersed herself in the study of Renaissance history. Her first volume of poems, *Gedichte* (1889), was soon followed by the *Florentiner Novellen* (1890; Tales of Florence, translated 1919), a collection of passionate love stories set in the Italian Renaissance. This early work contains some of her masterpieces, including "Die Vermählung der Toten" ("The Marriage of the Dead"—a Romeo and Juliet love story with a happy ending), "Die Humanisten" ("The Humanists"), "Der heilige Sebastian" ("St. Sebastian"), and the grim tale of betrayal and revenge through love "Anno Pestis" ("The Plague Year"). These novellas reveal Kurz's great skill in suspenseful story-telling, as well as her psychological insight into the nature of desire and her deep familiarity with death. Though her classical sense of form and her fascination with the personalities of the Italian Renaissance have led to frequent comparison of her work with the novellas of the poetic realist Conrad Ferdinand Meyer, Kurz claimed Boccaccio, de Maupassant, and her own father as the formative influences on her style. The *Florentiner Novellen* and her subsequent volume of *Italienische Erzählungen* (1895; Italian Tales) firmly established Kurz's literary reputation. In her depiction of female characters as well as in her aphorisms (*Im Zeichen des Steinbocks* [The Sign of Capricorn] (1905) Kurz expresses a strong sense of the innate power of the female and the oppression of her potential under patriarchy.

In her poetry, Kurz fuses romantic and realistic elements in a highly original manner. A second volume of poems, *Neue Gedichte* (New Poems), appeared in 1905. Her lyric verse is delicate yet free-spirited, revealing a thoughtful woman who has encountered the demonic depths of existence and who responds to the human and the natural world with a unique mixture of humor and melancholy. In 1908 Kurz published her epic poem *Die Kinder der Lilith* (The Children of Lilith). Other volumes of poetry are *Schwert aus der Scheide* (1916; Drawn Sword), *Aus dem Reigen des Lebens* (1923; From the Dance of Life), and *Leuke* (1925).

The problem of life versus art is central to a number of Kurz's prose works and is treated most extensively in the novel *Der Despot* (1925; The Despot). The human tragedy of a life fanatically possessed by art is here exposed in the figure of Gustav Bork, a poet of Faustian striving who sacrifices his own and others' lives for the sake of intensifying his productivity as an artist.

At the age of seventy-seven, Kurz finished her great tragic novel *Vanadis* (1931). Subtitled "The Fateful Way of a Woman," this novel of development has been hailed by some critics as the female counterpart to Goethe's *Wilhelm Meister. Vanadis* (the name of the heroine and of a Germanic goddess) is characterized by an abundance of narrative invention yet is autobiographical in many details. Here, the heroic ideal of the old Germanic worldview confronts a benevolent Christian aestheticism. After a long life of sorrows and suffering, Vanadis reaffirms her mystical sense of existence by refusing the sacraments of the church. Her happiness, she realizes, is a great renunciation. Kurz's autobiography *Die Pilgerfahrt nach dem Unerreichlichen* (1938; The Pilgrimage to the Unattainable), is alive with the same productive spirit of paradox.

A poet and storyteller of classical form and human pathos and beauty, Isolde Kurz is a gifted, highly regarded, but curiously neglected poetic realist. Her eminently readable poems, stories, and novels deserve far more critical attention than they have so far received.

Works

Gedichte [Poems] (1889). *Florentiner Novellen* [Tales of Florence] (1890). *Phantasien und Märchen* [Phantasies and Fairy Tales] (1890). *Italienische Erzählungen* [Italian Tales] (1895). *Von dazumal* [From Those Days] (1900). *Die Stadt des Lebens* [The City of Life] (1902). *Im Zeichen des Steinbocks* [The Sign of Capricorn] (1905). *Neue Gedichte* [New Poems] (1905). *Hermann Kurz* (1906). *Lebensfluten* [Floods of Life] (1907). *Die Kinder der Lilith* [The Children of Lilith] (1908). *Florentinische Erinnerungen* [Florentine Memories] (1909). *Genesung* [Recovery] (1912). *Wandertage in Hellas* [Days of Travel in Hellas] (1913). *Schwert aus der Scheide* [Drawn Sword]

(1916). *Aus meinem Jugendland* [From the Land of my Youth] (1918). *Traumland* [Dreamland] (1920). *Legenden* [Legends] (1920). *Nächte von Fondi* [Nights of Fondi] (1922). *Aus dem Reigen des Lebens* [From the Dance of Life] (1923). *Leuke* (1925). *Die Liebenden und der Narr* [The Lovers and the Fool] (1924). *Vom Strande* [From the Shore] (1924). *Der Despot* [The Despot] (1925). *Der Caliban* [Caliban] (1925). *Meine Mutter* [My Mother] (1926). *Die Stunde des Unsichtbaren* [The Hour of the Invisible] (1927). *Der Ruf des Pan* [The Call of Pan] (1928). *Ein Genie der Liebe* [A Genius of Love] (1929). *Vanadis, Der Schicksalsweg einer Frau* [Vanadis. The Fateful Way of a Woman] (1931). *Der Meister von San Francesco* [The Master of San Francisco] (1931). *Werthers Grab* [Werther's Grave] (1932). *Die Nacht im Teppichsaal* [The Night in the Hall of Tapestries] (1933). *Die Pilgerfahrt nach dem Unerreichlichen* [The Pilgrimage to the Unattainable] (1938). *Das Haus des Atreus* [The House of Atreus] (1939). *Gesammelte Werke* [Collected Works] (1925).

Translations: *Tales of Florence* (1919). Poems in: *Poems from the German*, ed. James T. Hatfield (1901). *Twentieth Century German Verse*, ed. Herman Salinger (1953).

Bibliography

Bäumer, Gertrud, "Isolde Kurz." *Gestalt und Wandel. Frauenbildnisse* (1939). Brinker-Gabler, Gisela, "Isolde Kurz." *Deutsche Dichterinnen vom 16. Jahrhundert bis zur Gegenwart* (1978). Heinrich, G., *Lebenswerk der Dichterin Isolde Kurz* (1933). Hesse, Otto Ernst, *Isolde Kurz* (1931). Klein, Johannes, "Isolde Kurz." *Geschichte der deutschen Novelle* (1954). Nennecke, Charlotte, *Die Frage nach dem Ich im Werk von Isolde Kurz.* Diss., 1958 (Contains bibliography of secondary literature). Pearson, Jean, "Isolde Kurz." *Kvinnliga Författare*, ed. Susanna Roxman (1983). Wenke, A., *Die italienische Renaissance in den Werken der Isolde Kurz.* Diss., 1950.

Jean Pearson